October 19–21, 2014
Toronto, ON, Canada

Association for
Computing Machinery

Advancing Computing as a Science & Profession

CHI PLAY 2014

Proceedings of the 2014 Annual Symposium on
Computer-Human Interaction in Play

Sponsored by:

ACM SIGCHI

Supported by:

GRAND Network of Centres of Excellence,
Gaming & Entrepreneurship Lab,
University of Ontario Institute of Technology,
& Unity Technologies

Association for
Computing Machinery

Advancing Computing as a Science & Profession

The Association for Computing Machinery
2 Penn Plaza, Suite 701
New York, New York 10121-0701

Notice to Past Authors of ACM-Published Articles
ACM intends to create a complete electronic archive of all articles and/or other material previously published by ACM. If you have written a work that has been previously published by ACM in any journal or conference proceedings prior to 1978, or any SIG Newsletter at any time, and you do NOT want this work to appear in the ACM Digital Library, please inform permissions@acm.org, stating the title of the work, the author(s), and where and when published.

ISBN: 978-1-4503-3014-5 (Digital)

ISBN: 978-1-4503-3379-5 (Print)

Additional copies may be ordered prepaid from:

ACM Order Department
PO Box 30777
New York, NY 10087-0777, USA

Phone: 1-800-342-6626 (USA and Canada)
+1-212-626-0500 (Global)
Fax: +1-212-944-1318
E-mail: acmhelp@acm.org
Hours of Operation: 8:30 am – 4:30 pm ET

Printed in the USA

Foreword and Welcome to CHI PLAY

It is our great pleasure to welcome you to the first *ACM SIGCHI Annual Symposium on Computer-Human Interaction in Play – CHI PLAY'14.* CHI PLAY is a new international and interdisciplinary conference series for researchers and professionals across all areas of play, games and human-computer interaction (HCI), we call it: "player-computer interaction." This conference is the first of its kind and we see CHI PLAY as a great opportunity to highlight and foster discussion of current high quality research in games and HCI as foundations for the future of digital play. This year is the inaugural year of this symposium and is bound to set future traditions of being the premier forum for presentation of research results and experience reports on leading edge issues of novel game interaction, player experience evaluations, neurogaming, gamification, exertion games, games user research, player psychology, social game systems, serious games, game developer applications, interaction design and theory. The mission of the symposium is to share insights into game interaction design and analysis that fulfill the needs of developers, researchers and designers and identify new directions for future research and development in HCI and games. CHI PLAY gives researchers and practitioners a unique opportunity to share their perspectives with others interested in the various aspects of HCI in games. The conference provides a meeting place of practitioners and academics for presenting and discussing peer-reviewed academic papers and the latest breaking results and approaches from industry.

The call for papers attracted submissions from Asia, Canada, Australia, Europe, and the United States. We selected a program committee of experts in human-computer interaction and game research to lead the scientific review process. All full papers were blind reviewed by peer reviewers as well as a committee member. Accepted papers are published in the ACM Digital Library. The program committee reviewed and accepted the following:

Venue or Track	*Reviewed*	*Accepted*	
Full Technical Papers	104	30	29%
Works-In-Progress	45	29	64%

Putting together *CHI PLAY'14* was a team effort. We are extremely thankful to the contributors of this conference: our staff of this event, our partners, our volunteers, the authors who submitted their high quality work to our conference and provided the content of the program, the program committee, who managed the reviews on a short timeline, our reviewers who ensured a high-quality conference, and our local organizing committee. Finally, we thank the University of Ontario Institute of Technology, our sponsor, ACM SIGCHI, and our generous corporate supporters, Graphics, Animation, and New Media Network of Centres of Excellence, the Gaming and Entrepreneurship Lab in Port Hope and Unity Technologies.

We hope that you will find this program interesting and thought-provoking and that the symposium will provide you with a valuable opportunity to share ideas with other researchers and practitioners from institutions around the world.

Lennart E. Nacke
CHI PLAY'14 General Chair
University of Ontario Institute of Technology, Canada

T. C. Nicholas Graham
CHI PLAY'14 Program Chair
Queen's University, Canada

Message from the Papers Chairs

We are very happy to present the papers track for the inaugural CHI PLAY conference. As the games industry has grown over the last few decades, research in games and play within HCI has been growing too. The number of high-quality submissions that we received is a testament to the strength of the researchers in the field of player-computer interaction.

We put together a Program Committee of 25 individuals from Canada, the United States, Europe, Asia, and Australia. Each paper submitted to CHI PLAY was assigned to two members of the program committee (PC); one as the primary associate chair (1AC) and one as the secondary PC associate chair (2AC). These PC members together solicited three external reviewers for each paper. In addition, the 2AC was available to provide an additional review in cases where the reviewers were split on their opinion or the paper was rated as borderline for acceptance. The 1AC synthesized the reviewer opinions and wrote a meta-review to give feedback to authors. The papers chairs made the final decisions in consultation with the Program Committee. Because we received so many high-quality submissions, accepted papers had to be comprised of excellent research, on par with the quality expected of a venue sponsored by SIGCHI.

Thanks very much to the authors who submitted their work for consideration, to the external reviewers whose efforts are fundamental to the peer review process, and to the members of the Program Committee, who made this conference possible.

Regan L. Mandryk
CHI PLAY'14 Papers Co-Chair
University of Saskatchewan, Canada

Florian "Floyd" Mueller
CHI PLAY'14 Papers Co-Chair
RMIT University, Australia

Table of Contents

Doctoral Consortiums

Student Games Competitions

Works-in-Progress

Workshop Summaries

Keynote Address I

Course Descriptions

Keynote Address II

CHI PLAY 2014 Symposium Organization

General Chair: Lennart E. Nacke *(University of Ontario Institute of Technology, Canada)*

Program Chair: T. C. Nicholas Graham *(Queen's University, Canada)*

Papers Chairs: Regan L. Mandryk *(University of Saskatchewan, Canada)*
Florian "Floyd" Mueller *(RMIT University, Australia)*

Works-In-Progress Chairs: Peta Wyeth *(Queensland University of Technology, Australia)*
Paul Cairns *(York University, UK)*

Student Game Design Competition Chairs: Vero vanden Abeele *(University of Leuven, Belgium)*
Bieke Zaman *(University of Leuven, Belgium)*

Workshops Chairs: Zach Toups *(New Mexico State University, USA)*
Georgios Christou *(European University Cyprus, Cyprus)*

Courses and Tutorials Chairs: Regina Bernhaupt *(IRIT, University Paul Sabatier, Tolouse III, France)*
Michael Lankes *(University of Applied Sciences Upper Austria, Austria)*

Industry Chairs: Anders Drachen *(Game Analytics, Denmark)*
Ben Medler *(Electronic Arts, USA)*

Doctoral Consortium Chairs: Anna Cox *(University College London, UK)*
Drew Davidson *(Carnegie Mellon University, USA)*

Local Committee: Pejman Mirza-Babaei *(University of Ontario Institute of Technology, Canada)*
Jessica Clarke *(University of Ontario Institute of Technology, Canada)*

Publicity Chairs: Kathrin Gerling *(University of Lincoln, UK)*
Ben Kirman *(University of Lincoln, UK)*
Zac Fitz-Walter *(Queensland University of Technology, Australia)*

Student Volunteer Chair: Victoria McArthur *(University of Toronto, Canada)*

Proceedings Chair: Louise Barkhuus *(University of Stockholm, Sweden)*

Steering Committee Chair: Lennart E. Nacke *(University of Ontario Institute of Technology, Canada)*

Steering Committee: T. C. Nicholas Graham *(Queen's University, Canada)*
Regan L. Mandryk *(University of Saskatchewan, Canada)*
Florian "Floyd" Mueller *(RMIT University, Australia)*
Peta Wyeth *(Queensland University of Technology, Australia)*
Regina Bernhaupt *(IRIT, University Paul Sabatier, Tolouse III, France)*

Program Committee: Kevin Stanley *(University of Saskatchewan, Canada)*
Paul Cairns *(York University, UK)*
Joe Marshall *(University of Nottingham, UK)*
Ben Schouten *(Eindhoven University of Technology, The Netherlands)*
Daniel Johnson *(Queensland University of Technology, Australia)*
Stefan Greuter *(RMIT University, Australia)*
Kathrin Gerling *(University of Lincoln, UK)*
Janet Read *(University of Central Lancashire, UK)*
Elizabeth Lawley *(Rochester Institute of Technology, USA)*
James Wallace *(University of Waterloo, Canada)*
Jussi Holopainen (*RMIT University, Australia*)
Conor Linehan *(University of Lincoln, UK)*
Mark Hancock (*University of Waterloo, Canada)*
Christiane Moser *(University of Salzburg, Austria)*
Katherine Isbister *(Polytechnic Institute of New York University, USA)*
Anna Cox *(University College London, UK)*
Rilla Khaled *(University of Malta, Malta)*
Anton Nijholt *(University of Twente, The Netherlands)*
Louise Barkhuus *(Stockholm University, Sweden)*
Pejman Mirza-Babaei *(University of Ontario Institute of Technology, Canada)*
Scott Bateman *(University of Prince Edward Island, Canada)*
Nadia Bianchi-Berthouze *(University College London, UK)*
Perttu Hämäläinen *(Aalto University, Finland)*
Staffan Björk *(University of Gothenburg, Sweden)*
Jonna Koivisto *(University of Tampere, Finland)*

CHI PLAY 2014 Sponsor & Supporters

Sponsor: SIGCHI

Supporters: GRAND (Graphisme, animation et nouveaux médias / Graphics, Animation and New Media)

GEL (Gaming + Entrepreneurship)

University of Ontario Institute of Technology

Unity

Evaluation of Recording Methods for User Test Sessions on Mobile Devices

Andrea Abney, Brooke White*, Jeremy Glick*, Andre Bermudez, Paul Breckow, Jason Yow*, Rayna Tillinghast-Trickett, Paul Heath
Disney Interactive
1200 Grand Central Ave, Glendale, CA 91201
andrea.abney@disney.com, andre.bermudez@disney.com, paul.breckow@disney.com, rayna.tillinghast-trickett@disney.com, paul.c.heath@disney.com

ABSTRACT
Disney Interactive produces mobile games, applications, and websites. The user research group is responsible for evaluating games and apps through user testing. We have been working on refining our video capture and streaming solutions for user tests on mobile devices.

We designed this experiment to see if any of the recording methods we used were changing player behavior and impacting their gameplay performance. We assessed changes in absolute score for two different games to determine impact to player efficacy. We analyzed observational data and player self-ratings on performance, comfort, awareness, and focus. We evaluated children, young adults, and older adults.

The results across all of the data were consistent and this paper explains the experiment and provides recommendations for mobile recording of user test sessions.

Author Keywords
Mobile user testing; usability testing; mobile recording methods; games user research; usability lab design.

ACM Classification Keywords
H.5.2. User Interfaces: Evaluation/methodology.

INTRODUCTION
In recent years, the user research group at Disney Interactive has been asked with growing frequency to conduct studies on mobile games in addition to our console and PC-based testing. Studies run on mobile games now account for a significant portion of all user research at Disney Interactive. The user research group at Disney Interactive has adapted over the past few years to address the evolving needs of the company. This shifted focus to the mobile experience inspired further research into updated recording solutions for mobile research.

Mobile games are increasingly using gestural user interfaces that require careful evaluation. The screen's small size and touch-based interface can introduce unique usability challenges, including illegible user interface elements, small or overlapping hit boxes, and instances where players' fingers or hands obscure part of the screen. To be able to evaluate the unique usability challenges on mobile devices, it is important to evaluate interactions with the device hardware in addition to interactions with the game software. The form factor of mobile devices can cause players to hold them in their hands near their bodies. This makes observation challenging, especially for the development teams, who need to be able to observe from outside the test lab.

The Disney Interactive user research group has experimented with variations of three different solutions, all of which have their respective strengths and weaknesses:

1. **Direct "over the shoulder" observation with no recording device:** This method allows the researcher to observe the player directly interacting with the device as naturally as possible in a test facility with an observer. However, it is ineffective for game development teams, who are unable to observe the gameplay outside of the test facility and video recordings are not an option.

2. **Overhead camera observation and recording:** Using this method, a camera is suspended over players' hands by either utilizing a document camera or a webcam attached to a stand. The camera simultaneously streams and records images of the players' hands and the gameplay on the screen. Players do not have to hold an additional object, allowing for a potentially more natural play experience. However, the user is still required to keep the mobile device under the camera, resulting in frequent observation challenges resulting from player posture obscuring the camera and players' tilting the mobile screen away from the camera.

CHI PLAY '14, Oct 19-22 2014, Toronto, ON, Canada
ACM 978-1-4503-3014-5/14/10.
http://dx.doi.org/10.1145/2658537.2658704

3. **Camera sled observation and recording:** In this configuration, the mobile device and camera are both attached to a device called a sled, which players hold in their hands. This keeps the camera at a fixed distance between players' hands and the device, but allows players to hold and move the device without interfering with the camera's line of sight.

   We used two different mobile recording sleds.

   The white plastic sled [6] comes as a flat piece of pre-cut plastic. We had to bend the sled and attach our own webcam. In contrast, the clear plastic sled [7] came as a finished product with an attached document camera. It did not require additional finishing. The clear sled is smaller and lighter than the white sled. It has a smaller camera, making the top portion less intrusive in the players' field of view. We had concerns about the weight, balance, and intrusiveness of the white sled.

Our researchers hypothesized that our recording methods might be negatively impacting player behavior and performance. The teams and our researchers were concerned that these solutions for mobile testing might be impacting participant behavior.

These factors led us to study this issue in an attempt to find the potentially least intrusive observation and streaming method for mobile user testing.

RELATED WORKS

A 2005 study [2] examined the differences between using an overhead document camera and a wireless mobile recording sled for recording user tests. To test each device, the researchers used the same script and asked participants to complete the same tasks. They conducted the document camera tests in a lab and the mobile sled tests in the field. In the document camera condition, the phone was attached to a tripod placed under the camera, which kept participants from moving the phone around. Though the results showed that there were mainly similarities between the two, there were a few important differences. Participants using the document camera took more time to complete the tasks and gave up more frequently. They were also less satisfied with their experience. The researchers found the greatest number of usability problems in the document camera condition, but this could be due to environmental differences caused by testing the document camera in the lab and the wireless sled in the field.

In 2007, researchers from PayPal [4] recorded usability tests with a mobile device taped to a table to limit its movement and also conducted cognitive walkthrough sessions where participants were allowed to hold the device naturally. They did not find any differences in task completion between the two methods. It's important to note that all results from this study are purely observational. The researchers did not look at any quantitative measures.

Also in 2007, Google researchers [9] outlined the criteria for a mobile observation setup, including infrastructure issues, mobile device-specific issues, and usability study context issues. They pointed out that one of the most important factors is allowing participants to hold the device naturally in order to capture accurate interaction information. The bulk of the paper outlines their iterations on their mobile recording setup. They found the sled's weight and the user's comfort were important to running a successful mobile study with natural interaction. After a few iterations, they developed a lightweight wooden sled.

In a related paper, Carolyn Wei of Google [10] discussed multiple methods for capturing mobile phone usage,

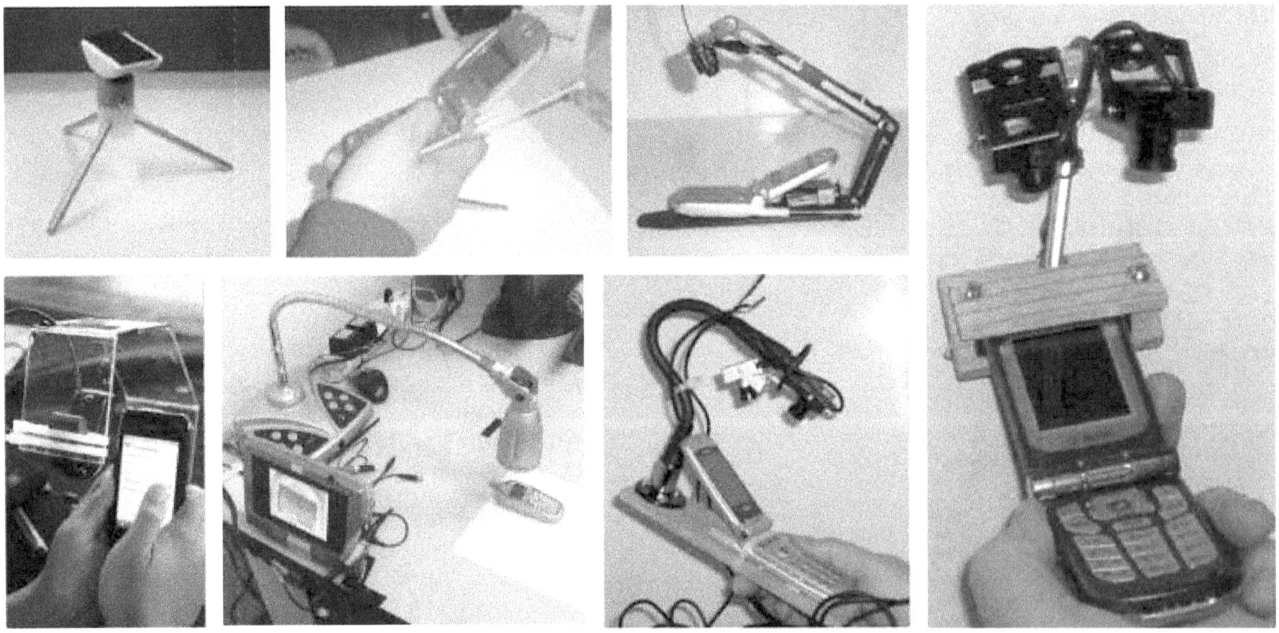

Figure 1. Previous mobile recording devices (clockwise from top left): Tripod [2], phone attached to tripod [2], wireless mobile sled [2], wooden clamp sled [10], wooden base sled [10], document camera over phone [10], clear mobile sled [8]

including interviews, surveys, diaries, and video recordings of behavior. She observed that video recording behavior with cameras mounted to mobile devices might result in the most accurate data collection. There are some drawbacks, such as wires and obtrusive equipment, which make this method more suited to lab studies rather than field studies.

A more recent study [8] detailed the creation of a mobile sled that is similar to the sleds used in our study. Unlike the previous sleds, this sled was designed to be used with a touchscreen smartphone. When building the sled, the researchers had several requirements: participants had to be able to hold the phone naturally while a webcam recorded the screen, the solution had to use existing equipment as much as possible, and the device had to look professional.

Some researchers have developed more novel approaches to mobile recording, including cameras and equipment built into clothing and accessories [3, 5]. We have discussed experimenting with wearable recording equipment in our labs, but we have chosen to focus on refining the sled devices. We may revisit wearable recording devices in the future. Further research in this area could compare wearable devices to handheld sleds.

There is still work to be done in developing solutions for recording on mobile devices. Many other researchers have gone through the process of iterating on recording solutions and no current solution is without its drawbacks. Mobile gaming presents some new challenges and nothing in the literature directly addresses them, creating the need for us to develop our own test of solutions for recording mobile games user research sessions.

METHODS

To determine whether or not our recording methods were impacting participant behavior and understand the magnitude of any discovered changes, we designed a counterbalanced, within-subjects experiment. We started with a null hypothesis stating that player performance should not be affected by data capture method.

Participants

Thirty participants residing in and around the Glendale, California area participated in the study. They ranged in age from 8 to 60. Ten participants were 8 to 12 years old, ten were 18 to 35 years old, and ten were 40 to 60 years old. None of these participants had participated in any prior usability research studies, so none of them had experience with the recording devices used in the study. Participants' gaming experience ranged from casual to hardcore, but all had experience playing games on iOS devices. They were each compensated $100.

Materials

Mobile Devices

The mobile device used in the study was the iPhone 4S, which weighs 140 grams.

Headphones

The headphones used were generic, full size headphones with a 90 degree bent headphone jack.

Games

Participants played two mobile games, *Ridiculous Fishing: A Tale of Redemption* and *Fruit Ninja*. We selected these games because they are action-oriented titles with game rounds that are short in length. *Ridiculous Fishing* was played in portrait orientation while *Fruit Ninja* was played in landscape orientation. *Ridiculous Fishing* relies on the use of the iPhone's accelerometer. *Fruit Ninja* does not use the accelerometer but requires rapid gestural interaction.

For *Ridiculous Fishing*, the game parameters were 200m line, shotgun equipped, basic lure, and "Home Waters" map with no tech equipped. For the *Fruit Ninja* trials, participants played in the 60-second arcade mode.

Recording Devices

- **Overhead Camera:** A webcam is attached to a plastic stand 40 cm tall. The webcam is pointed down at the table.
- **White Sled:** The sled is made of white plastic and is 20 cm tall. The camera is attached to the top of the sled with a binder clip and rubber bands, which allow the camera to be adjusted forward or backward as needed. The sled and camera weigh 161.59 grams. The phone was attached to this sled with adhesive dots.
- **Clear Sled:** This sled is made of clear plastic and is 18 cm tall. The camera is adhered to the top of sled with double-sided tape. The sled features an additional piece that slides on the bottom to support the phone while in landscape orientation. Without the additional piece, the sled and camera weigh 110.56 grams. With the additional piece, they weigh 172.93 grams. Adhesive dots were also used with this sled.

Design

There were four conditions and players played both games in each condition:

A. No recording device (control)

B. Overhead camera

C. White sled

D. Clear sled

This study used a counterbalanced, within-subjects design. Each participant went through the conditions in a different order to reduce sequencing and order effects.

Procedure

We set up four stations and ran participants in groups. Three of the stations contained one mobile recording device

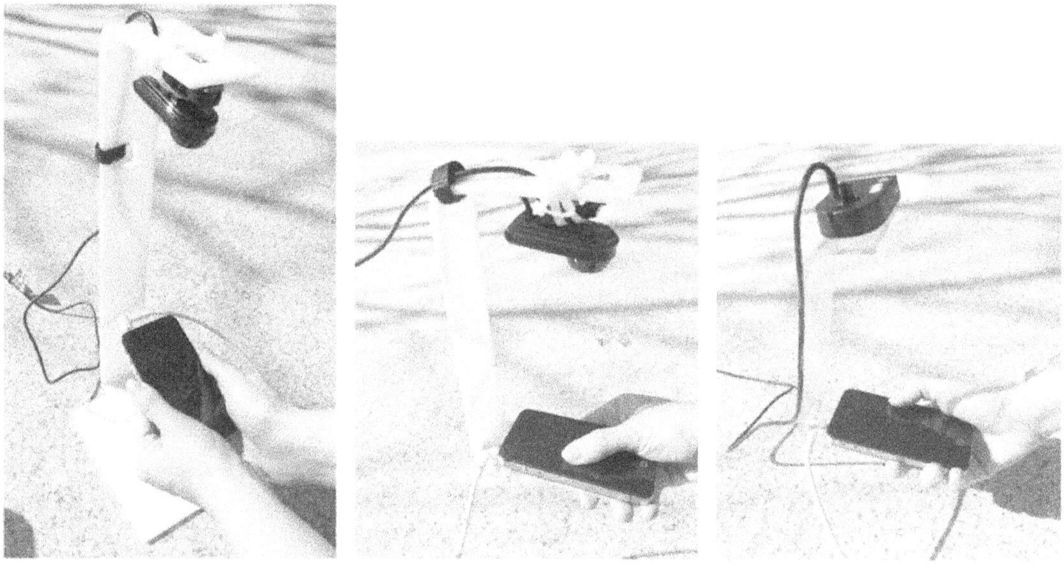

Figure 2. Our recording devices, from left: Overhead camera, white sled, clear sled

and a smartphone with attached headphones. The fourth station was the control station, which had a smartphone with headphones but no recording device.

Each participant sat at one of the four stations with an assigned researcher. The researcher moved his or her participant between stations according to a predetermined order.

Before playing either game, participants filled out a short survey asking how familiar they were with the two games, *Ridiculous Fishing* and *Fruit Ninja*. After the survey, the moderator described how to play each game and then allowed participants to play through each game twice in order to familiarize themselves with the games' rules and objectives. During this time, the mobile devices were not attached to the recording devices and researchers recorded the participants' baseline posture, handgrip, and body language. The smartphones had headphones attached for the entire session.

After participants tried each game, we attached the smartphones to the sled recording devices. For the stationary overhead camera, we told participants to hold the smartphone under the camera and reminded them to keep their heads out of view of the recording device, as well as keep the smartphone as flat as possible in relation to the camera. For the sleds, we handed the sled to each participant and encouraged them to hold the devices as naturally as possible. We did not force participants to hold the sleds if they set the sled down on the table while playing.

Participants played five trials of *Ridiculous Fishing* followed by five trials of *Fruit Ninja* at each station. After each trial, we recorded our assigned participants' scores. While the participants were playing, we noted qualitative observations with a focus on posture, handgrip, head position, and body language.

Every time the players completed all trials at a station, they completed a survey regarding their perceived performance with the recording device, how comfortable they felt with it, their ability to focus on gameplay at the station, and how aware of the recording device they were while playing the game. They rated each of these on a 5-point Likert scale. Researchers then moved with participants to the next station in their counterbalanced sequence and repeated this procedure for each of the remaining three stations.

When all participants had completed all four conditions, they completed one last survey question, which showed photos of each mobile recording device and asked participants to rank the devices in order of preference.

During each session, we stationed two to three researchers in the observation room who watched camera feeds of each station, noting any observation errors that occurred during the sessions. This included obstructed camera views and other obstacles to observation that resulted from the recording capture method.

RESULTS

To evaluate the results of the study, we used quantitative analysis of scores, player self-reported data, researcher notes, and notes from the observation room.

Quantitative Analysis of Findings

Player Score

To analyze the quantitative score results of this study, we used a series of mixed regression analyses with crossed and nested random effects. All models were run in R using the "lmer" function from the lme4 library [1]. The primary dependent measure of interest was the game score.

In the first model, we examined the overall effect of the recording devices across games. The scores for each game were Z-transformed separately across all users and all sessions so that the games had scores with equal mean and variance. The model included a fixed effects term for the station, dummy-coded with the control group as the reference group. Random effects were included for the session, for the individual participant within the session, for the order of the station within each participant (i.e., first station through four station, without reference to the device present at that station), and for the repetition of the game within each station (i.e., first through fifth replay of the game at that station). Finally, a random effect of the game was included, which was crossed with all other random effects because each participant completed the above structure for each of the two games.

In this model, there was a statistically significant omnibus effect of the station (Chisq(4) = 11.2, $p = 0.025$), indicating that the different types of recording device did impact the scores of the players. Examining the individual stations, only the white sled showed a significant difference from the no-recording control station, with an estimated score decrease of -0.16 standard deviations versus control ($t = -2.2$, $p < 0.05$). The results are shown in Table 1.

In order to determine what was driving this effect, we performed several additional regression analyses. First, we repeated the above analysis separately for each game. Since there was no need to make the scores from each game commensurate, the dependent measure for each model was the untransformed game score. The random effect of game was removed from each model.

For *Ridiculous Fishing*, the results appeared similar to the overall results described above. The omnibus station effect was again significant (Chisq(4) = 12.8, $p = 0.012$). The individual dummy-coded station effects were all negative in sign, indicating an overall decrease in score due to any kind of setup. However, the only station effect that appeared statistically significant was again the white sled, which penalized players by -22 points (from a baseline score of 86 points) ($t = -3.4$, $p < .01$). Results are shown in Table 1.

For *Fruit Ninja*, the results were quite different. First, the omnibus effect of the station, while present, was only marginally significant (Chisq(4) = 7.85, $p = .097$). Second, the pattern of results was different. The stations with overhead camera and white sled had effectively 0 impact relative to the no-recording control, while the effect of the clear sled was directionally positive. Results are shown in Table 1.

It seems the overall effects from the original analysis are primarily driven by the consistent effect on *Ridiculous Fishing*, but the impact on *Fruit Ninja* was more variable.

Overall player score			
Device	**Estimate**	**Std. error**	**t value**
(Intercept)	0.032456	0.143560	0.226
Overhead Cam	-0.069208	0.074315	-0.931
White Sled	-0.162632	0.074315	-2.188
Clear Sled	-0.000493	0.074315	-0.007
***Ridiculous Fishing* player score**			
Device	**Estimate**	**Std. error**	**t value**
(Intercept)	86.373	13.041	6.623
Overhead Cam	-7.493	6.573	-1.140
White Sled	-22.220	6.573	-3.380
Clear Sled	-10.267	6.573	-1.562
***Fruit Ninja* player score**			
Device	**Estimate**	**Std. error**	**t value**
(Intercept)	269.83333	12.90359	20.911
Overhead Cam	-3.00667	11.38769	-0.264
White Sled	0.09333	11.38769	0.008
Clear Sled	15.83333	11.38769	1.390

Table 1. Player score analysis results

If we enter the game as a fixed instead of a random effect into our model, and allow it to interact with the station effect, then the omnibus Game*Station interaction term is marginally significant (Chisq(4) = 7.9, $p = .095$).

Player Characteristics

Having understood something about the overall impact of different types of recording devices, we were interested to know whether these results differ for different player demographics. User research is performed with a variety of groups of players including children, younger adults, and older adults. In this study, each of these groups was represented by separate sessions, with two sessions of five players for each type of player (children 8 to 12, adults 18 to 35, and adults 40 to 60).

In order to evaluate the effect of station on each of these player types, we created planned orthogonal contrasts from the session identifier. The first component compared children to adults, taking the value -2 for children and the value 1 for both groups of adults. The second component compared younger adults to older adults, taking the value -1 for younger adults, 1 for older adults, and 0 for children. These predictors were then included as fixed effect terms in the across-game model and were allowed to interact with the station terms.

Ranking	1st	2nd	3rd	4th
Control	**24**	3	1	2
Overhead Cam	1	**13**	9	7
White Sled	2	1	10	**17**
Clear Sled	2	**13**	11	4

Table 2. Number of participants who selected each rank for each recording devices

The results revealed no systematic impact of player type on recording device impact. The omnibus effect of the Station*Age interaction was not statistically significant (Chisq(8) = 6.0, n.s.), and no individual Station*Age term rose to the level of statistical significance (all ts < 1.1, n.s.). It appears that the effect of different recording device, while possibly different for different types of games, does not differ systematically for users of different ages.

Questionnaire Ratings

The most objective measure of recording device impact on player performance is the final game score, as analyzed above. We can also measure the impact of the recording devices on players' perceptions of gameplay and ease of use, which may or may not correspond perfectly to any objective measure. Player ratings may be of particular interest when there are concerns about ergonomics or user comfort.

Players were asked to rank the stations in order of how well they felt they performed in each (rank 1 = best, rank 4 = worst). The results are shown in Table 2. Although we do not present a statistical significance test, the differences between the stations is clear. The majority of players chose the station with no recording device as leading to the best performance. The most frequent responses put the overhead camera or the clear sled in the second rank and the white sled in the lowest rank.

Players also answered a set of four questions about each of the four stations. Ranking questionnaires are useful for breaking ties between alternatives while ratings are useful for evaluating how players felt about each station individually. The four questions were:

1. **Performance:** "How do you feel you performed using this device?"
2. **Comfort:** "How comfortable or uncomfortable were you using this device?"
3. **Focus:** "How would you describe your ability to focus on the gameplay while using this device?"
4. **Awareness:** "How aware or unaware of this recording device were you while playing the game?"

The first three questions were asked of all four stations. The fourth question was asked about all stations other than the station with no recording device.

Among the results, the mean ratings (see Figure 3) again show the station with no recording device as the clear winner, and seem to favor the overhead camera and the clear sled over the white sled.

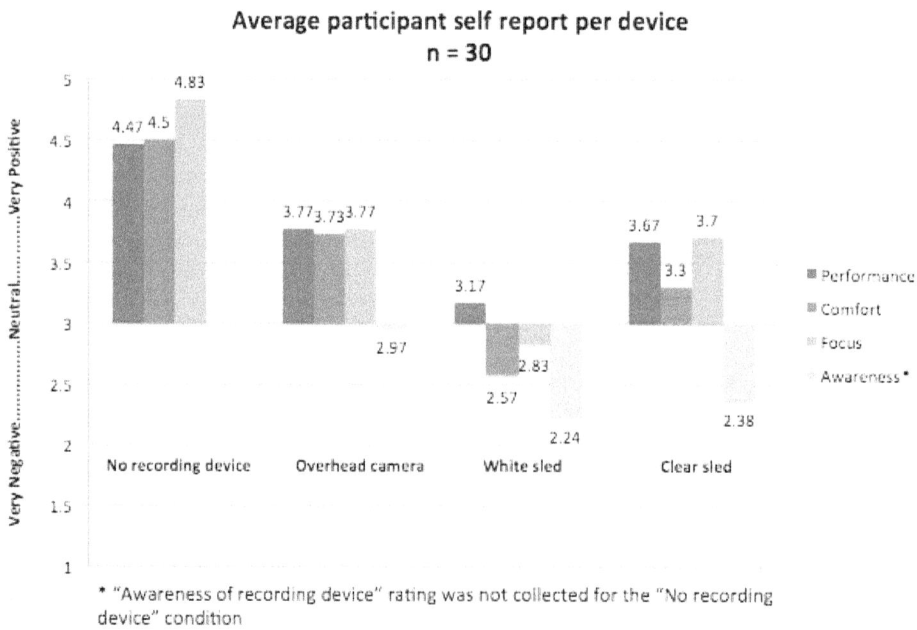

Figure 3. Participants rated each device in terms of performance, comfort, focus, and awareness

The white sled was at the bottom of every measure. The average ratings are the simplest way to interpret these results since only the station with no recording device has an unambiguous distribution of responses.

The overall ranking preferences do not seem to be driven solely by any one aspect reflected in these questions. The station with no recording device is clearly preferred in all cases and the white sled always received the lowest average rating.

We wondered whether any of these questions help predict an individual's ranking of each station. Taking the ranking data and all ratings as numerical values on a continuous scale, we ran several more mixed regression models. Each question individually can help predict the overall rankings, with performance being the weakest predictor (Chisq(1)=13.9, $p<.0005$) and the others all somewhat stronger (Chisq(1)>20, $p<.0001$). Since all four questions are highly correlated with each other on an individual basis ($r>0.5$ in all cases), no question adds significant value in the presence of the other three ($t(1) < 1.6$, n.s.).

It seems that we can take any one or two of these questions as a valid gauge of a player's perception of their overall performance with a piece of user-testing equipment. Of the four questions, the focus rating appears to provide the most direct reflection of the overall rankings, but even the performance rating does a reasonable job. We believe the question of ability to focus could be a decent indicator of recording device impact.

Participant Behavior and Observation Side Errors

Qualitative comparison of adults and children during the study revealed that adults displayed more visible symptoms of fatigue and loss of enthusiasm when playing mobile games for 40+ minutes. Adults were able to use the different recording devices more easily than the children, though this may be related to the physical limitations of the players. Children had difficulty adjusting their chairs to table height and their feet often did not touch the ground.

While players frequently cited the overhead camera as their preferred condition due to added freedom, this condition was suboptimal for observation. Observers were often unable to view the device based on the orientation of the iPhone, as players tilted the phone to view it better or pulled their hands/device out from under the camera. Added vertical freedom also required constant autofocusing of the camera, resulting in more observation errors. With this camera setup, children tended to lean in beneath the camera and put their heads in between the lens and the phone screen. This did not happen with adults except in a few cases where they were wearing hats that extended under the camera. Researchers frequently had to stop participants' gameplay in order to correct these observation issues.

While the two sleds had the best overall observer experience, including the ability to consistently see the gameplay and players' hands, several issues were common to both. The sleds' added weight changed the way players held and manipulated the mobile devices. Some players held the necks of the sleds as if they were handles.

The white sled caused unique player behavior errors. Players frequently complained that the sled was top heavy. Children dropped or lost control of the device due to its uneven weight distribution. These issues were more evident during *Ridiculous Fishing* because the use of the accelerometer required tilting the device back and forth. The plastic neck of the sled and the camera were in the way, which caused players to look at the mobile device from the side. Playing *Fruit Ninja* in landscape mode was difficult due to a lack of surface area between the iPhone and the sled base, which often resulted in the iPhone falling off the sled.

While many players stated a preference for the clear sled, observation errors still occurred in this condition. When players chose to play with the sled flat on the desk, they sometimes found that the device would slip away or fall over during play. Adding the crossbar to this sled for landscape play added weight to the device, which may have made participants more likely to put it down.

CONCLUSION

Performing usability research on mobile applications is important in helping development teams make successful products. Teams that can observe users interacting with their applications come away with an understanding of issues and behavior that assists them with making informed decisions. The scope of possible issues with mobile applications encompasses visual, gestural, and interaction challenges, so it is important for development teams to be able to observe both software and hardware interactions. In order for researchers and teams to observe all types of usability errors, it's crucial for the user to behave as naturally as possible, holding the device and interacting with the application as they normally would.

We set up this experiment to evaluate a variety of mobile recording devices and determine our current best solution for recording and streaming mobile user tests. All methods of recording caused some type of effect to player behavior, observed qualitative changes and, in the case of the white sled, significant changes in score. In addition, two of the four conditions provided poor or no observation of the tests: no recording and limited observation for the control and consistent problems with observing from the overhead camera. The two sleds provided good to great observation of players' screens and hands, but they caused some unnatural player behavior.

After analyzing the results of this study, we were able to determine which device offered the best observational data (hands and screen) while impacting players' natural behavior the least. While the overhead camera seems to cause fewer changes to player behavior than the sleds, the

Figure 4. Based on the results of this study, the clear sled is our current best solution [7]

observational issues it causes means that the moderator must frequently intervene to correct the issue. With the two sleds offering the best observational data, it came down to a choice between the white sled and the clear sled. The white sled was consistently ranked the lowest in all metrics by players and was the only device that had a statistically significant negative effect on the player score. The white sled is larger and has poorer balance than the clear sled. These factors led to more severe and more frequent behavioral changes than we saw with the clear sled.

The clear sled has multiple positive attributes and its physical characteristics helped it perform best. It didn't cause statistical score change. It provided the best observational experience with clearly recorded hand position, fingers, and screen. The sled is clear, making it less noticeable to players and observers. The camera is small, light and flat, which allows it to be attached firmly. Without the landscape attachment, it's lighter than the white sled. With the attachment, it's only slightly heavier while adding physical support for a landscape-oriented device that is lacking from the white sled. It is compact, so the camera doesn't get in the way of the player's vision. Most importantly, the weight is well balanced. This makes it easier for players to hold for an extended period and assists when engaging with gesture heavy applications and applications using the accelerometer.

We have decided that the clear sled is our current best solution for our mobile research needs, both providing good viewing for the observers and not causing significant behavioral changes in players. However, we will continue to evaluate and iterate on our mobile recording methods.

ACKNOWLEDGMENTS

We would like to thank Liz Heron, Nathan Cook, Derek Speir, and Joseph Quevedo for their contributions in data collection, review, and moral support.

*Brooke White, Jeremy Glick, and Jason Yow are no longer employed by The Walt Disney Company.

REFERENCES

1. Bates, D., Maechler, M., Bolker, B., and Walker, S. lme4: Linear mixed-effects models using Eigen and s4. R package version 0.999375-42. http://cran.r-project.org/web/packages/lme4/index.html.
2. Betiol, A.H. and de Abreu Cybis, W. Usability testing of mobile devices: A comparison of three approaches. Human-Computer Interaction-INTERACT, Springer Berlin Heidelberg (2005). 470-481.
3. Burghardt, D. and Wirth, K. Comparison of Evaluation Methods for Field-Based Usability Studies of Mobile Map Applications. International Cartographic Conference 2011 (2011).
4. Griffin, K., Kim, J., and Vakhariya, P. Overcoming Mobile Usability Testing Hurdles: A Mobile Payments Case Study. Proc. UPA 2007 (2007), 1-8.
5. Oulasvirta, A., and Nyyssönen, T. (2009). Flexible hardware configurations for studying mobile usability. Journal of Usability Studies 4,2 (2009), 93-105.
6. Ponoko iPhone usability testing sled. http://www.ponoko.com/design-your-own/products/iphone-usablilty-testing-sleds-6854
7. Poole, D. Smart Sled. http://smartsled.com.
8. Racadio, R., Rose, E., and Boyd, S. Designing and evaluating the mobile experience through iterative field studies. Proc. SIGDOC 2012, ACM Press (2012), 191-196.
9. Schusteritsch, R., Wei, C. Y., and LaRosa, M. Towards the perfect infrastructure for usability testing on mobile devices. Ext. Abstracts CHI 2007, ACM Press (2007), 1839-1844.
10. Wei, C. Y. Capturing mobile phone usage: Research methods for mobile studies. Proc. IPCC 2007, IEEE (2007), 1-6.

TF-CBT Triangle of Life: A Game to Help with Cognitive Behavioral Therapy

Etaba Assigana, Eric Chang, Seungsuk Cho, Vivek Kotecha, Bing Liu, Hannah Turner, Yan Zhang, Michael G. Christel, Scott M. Stevens
Entertainment Technology Center, Carnegie Mellon University
Pittsburgh, PA USA
{eassigan, erchang, seungsuc, vkotecha, bingl, hrt, yanzhan1}@andrew.cmu.edu,
{christel, sms}@cs.cmu.edu

ABSTRACT
Under direction of medical professionals associated with the National Child Traumatic Stress Network, a mobile game was developed for children ages 10-12 to teach the Cognitive Triangle concept of feelings, thoughts, and behaviors. This triangle is an essential component of Trauma-Focused Cognitive Behavioral Therapy (TF-CBT). A storybook experience with minigames was quickly prototyped, but first playtests showed a lack of engagement with children. The game was revised to emphasize side-scroller platform advancement where success in a level was tied intrinsically to cognitive triangle classification. Children rated the game highly across a series of playtests. The game has potential to be used by clinicians delivering TF-CBT as an appealing exercise for children.

Author Keywords
Games for health; playtesting; iterative game development.

ACM Classification Keywords
H.5.m. Information interfaces and presentation (e.g., HCI): Miscellaneous; K.3.1. Computer Uses in Education: Computer-assisted instruction (CAI).

INTRODUCTION
There are numerous sources for childhood trauma, including sexual and physical abuse, witness to domestic violence, victim or witness to school violence, bullying, weather-related events, terrorism, and travel-related accidents. The National Child Traumatic Stress Network (NCTSN) was launched by the U.S. Congress in 2000 to raise the standard of care and improve access to services for traumatized children, their families, and communities [11]. The NCTSN web site notes that more than 25 percent of American youth experience a serious traumatic event by the age of 16, and many children suffer multiple and repeated traumas. Not all children exposed to traumatic events develop a traumatic stress reaction. For those children that do suffer traumatic stress reactions, the consequences can be an inability to concentrate, depression, substance abuse, and future employment problems. It can change how children view the world and their own futures, and it can change their behavior, interests, and relationships with family and friends [9].

CHI PLAY'14, October 19–21, 2014, Toronto, ON, Canada.

http://dx.doi.org/10.1145/2658537.2658684

Trauma-Focused Cognitive Behavioral Therapy (TF-CBT) is a treatment approach for traumatized children using a flexible components-based model with individual child and parent treatment sessions, as well as joint child-parent sessions [2]. TF-CBT has been tested in 13 completed randomized clinical trials across a number of countries and situations for children ages 3 to 17. It has proven to be effective treatment for the serious issue of child traumatic stress.

TF-CBT has components which are identified by "PRACTICE" [2]:

- Psychoeducation and Parenting Skills
- Relaxation
- Affective Modulation
- Cognitive Processing
- Trauma Narrative
- In Vivo Desensitization
- Conjoint parent-child sessions
- Enhancing safety and social skills

Within "Cognitive Processing", therapists are assisting children and parents in gaining cognitive coping skills, i.e., recognizing the connections among thoughts, feelings, and behaviors as they relate to everyday situations. The medical professionals working with TF-CBT identified a need to help both therapists and children with this particular objective. Children should have more practice in working with the triangle of thoughts, feelings, and behaviors. Therapists need opportunities for children to get additional practice in generating alternate thoughts.

Tools on mobile devices have been used for anxiety therapy with children, explicitly tools to support children in their reporting of symptoms and feelings. In one study, children were found to be very receptive to mobile devices prompting for information in ways formerly performed through paper questionnaires [4]. With TF-CBT, the hope is for an engaging exercise delivering practice with thoughts, feelings, and behaviors, beyond just reporting through a tool. Others have found that video games can benefit children with therapeutic needs, e.g., with autism spectrum disorders [5]. This paper focuses on the creation of a mobile game to help children through TF-CBT.

Specifically, the "Cognitive Processing" TF-CBT step has therapists encouraging children and parents to identify thoughts related to upsetting events. Then, children and parents are to determine the feelings and behaviors they had associated with those thoughts, and to evaluate whether these thoughts are accurate and helpful. Children and parents can be encouraged to generate alternate thoughts for each situation, and then explore what feelings and behaviors would be associated with these thoughts and whether these would be more soothing [2]. Success in this step shows the children that they have control over their own thoughts and, via the triangle, consequently over their feelings and behaviors, allowing for self-soothing of negative trauma reminders [2].

This paper discusses the development of a game for mobile devices (Android and iOS tablets and phones) that can be played by children to help with this cognitive processing step. The emphasis is on the first stage of development: producing an experience that children in the target demographic are happy to play and where success in the game indicates success in obtaining skills sought from the TF-CBT "Cognitive Processing" step. Medical validation through randomized clinical trials are planned for the future, to prepare for the game to be included in TF-CBT "train the therapist" packets and other resources, but that formal step will take significant time and is not part of this report. Here, the emphasis is on game design focused on certain objectives, and the iterative process through which the game was built with frequent playtest iterations.

DEVELOPMENT CONTEXT: TEAM, TIMEFRAME, TOOLS

A graduate student team of seven students produced the game, with two faculty instructors advising the project-based course during its 15-week semester. Weekly meetings to review decisions and progress were held with the medical professionals, experts in TF-CBT, who served as client points of contact for the project. The seven students took on the roles of producer, creative director, game designer, programmers, composer/sound designer, background artist and character artist. The goals for the game included the following:

- Target children ages 8-12, both boys and girls, with age range subject to narrowing based on formative playtests
- Produce a game that works on Android and iOS tablets and phones
- Give children experience in classifying thoughts, feelings, and behaviors
- Give children experience in swapping out negative thoughts for new, positive ones
- Produce an experience that children are eager to play
- Produce an experience which does not trigger undue stress (given that this is planned for use with TF-CBT therapy)

Note that these goals, while framed to provide a game that can be used in the Cognitive Processing step of TF-CBT, have broader applicability in that they address the general area of cognitive behavioral therapy. Hence, other CBT counselors might find value in the work in the future, in addition to the TF-CBT context.

We chose the Unity game engine for development, as that supported exporting to different mobile platforms. We initially produced a number of theme ideas, which were reviewed with faculty and clients and reduced to the two with the most promise: a pirate/ship theme and an African savannah theme. The latter was chosen as having greater potential appeal to both girls and boys, and more opportunities for soothing, non-aggressive situations.

DESIGN

The game had to center around the cognitive triangle, shown in Figure 1. A review of children's activities that promoted these three categories of thoughts, feelings, and behaviors led to strong stories, such as folk tales like those in [1] and [13]. Folk tales involving animals presented a template into which a game with a series of characters could progress through mishaps grounded in misunderstood behaviors and incorrect thoughts. Setting our story in the animal kingdom sidestepped human biases, preconceptions, and expectations. We could focus on generating simple conflicts between the animals and avoiding extra human complexity.

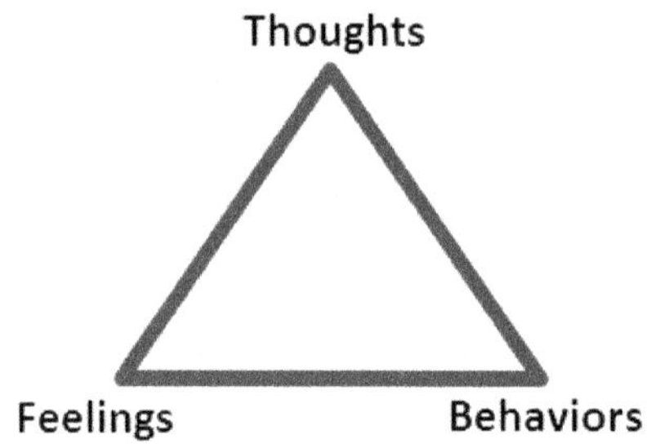

Figure 1. Cognitive triangle used in TF-CBT (and other forms of cognitive behavioral therapy as well).

We did not want to stress the child player, but did wish to offer entertaining, comfortable game mechanics. We wanted the child player to fill an advisory role in the game because traumatized children often belittle themselves and their own problems. Having them help others with their problems would teach children the triangle in a better way. If they had multiple examples to work with in an appealing format, then the child would get experience in working with the triangle.

Jesse Schell offers 100 lenses through which a game design can be viewed and improved [12]. A number of lenses deal with story, such as: does the game need a story, does the story have a good obstacle worth overcoming, and is there weirdness in the story to make it interesting? These game design lenses were used to prepare and refine the story.

In addition, educational game developers have wrestled with concepts of ideal flow for the learner [3], intrinsic motivation within instructional setting [7], and a framework for motivation [6]. These are brought together well by Paras and Bizzocchi [10] who note that games foster "play" and produce a state of flow, which in turn increases motivation and causes learners to stay engaged and gain more skill. Paras and Bizzocchi continue, "though someone may be pushing their skills to the limit they may not be reflecting on the experience and are therefore limiting what they can learn from it" [10]. So, an opportunity to reflect within the game, to relax the pacing, may serve to both increase the educational benefit and position the game as a low-stress tool in a TF-CBT setting that focuses on stress.

The initial design was for a 20-minute experience in which you play the role of Lioness, advisor to Lion who is king of the jungle. The goal was to speak to the various animals around the Savannah and help them solve their cognitive issues. The world is created in the manner of a storybook with radically different mini-games dispersed between text conversations with each animal. (One popular mobile game nesting multiple mechanics together in a suite of mini-games is McCann's *Dumb Ways to Die* for train safety [8].)

In designing the story, one important client constraint was to avoid content that could potentially cause negative memories to resurface in the children who will be playing our game. Therefore, while writing the story and dialogue for the game, we made sure to obtain medical client approval to be certain of appropriate story themes, locations, and vocabulary level. As with [1], we produced a story structure in which a seemingly small interaction between two characters has a reverberating impact on the other characters in the world around them.

The aesthetics of our game were likewise influenced by [1], in that we were struck by the African Batik art style of the book. Our character designs incorporate bold white outlines that accentuate the various animals and give them visual flair.

FIRST PLAYTEST ON THE INITIAL DIRECTION

Early design decisions were reviewed with game design faculty who suggested three modifications: (1) provide a clear sense of progress through the experience, (2) make text displays more readable on mobile devices, and (3) break up the text screens requiring player reading with play interaction. For the latter, we introduced minigames such as "look for Wolf in his various hiding places" and "tickle Panther to wake her up" (shown in Figure 2).

Eight children ages 7 through 12 (7 male, 1 female) tested the first game with Android tablets. The children were watched and video-recorded as they played, then given surveys afterward. The focus for the playtest was on the information in the game, vocabulary comprehension, ease of navigation through the app, whether the game was enjoyable, and some of the aesthetic choices.

From the observation and survey data, it was clear that the most favored moment by the users was the Monkey chase minigame, a side-scroller platform experience. The reading was too linear and too frequent for children within the storybook component: several testers skipped through the reading. As the reading is a precursor to more activities with the cognitive triangle, this was a major concern. Also, the children did not find the experience enjoyable. We initially looked to see how to make the storybook elements more appealing, as do other interactive storybooks with clickable objects, animated backgrounds, and interactive "hot" areas. We almost took out the Monkey chase mini-game, and then we realized that we were taking the wrong approach. That mini-game of the Monkey chase was the time when the children were most visibly enjoying the game. Rather than dismiss it, we decided to emphasize it: we "followed the fun" [14].

Figure 2. Interface for "Tickle Panther" minigame.

The other mini-games (like Figure 2) were removed from the experience. The storybook was removed. Instead, the story would play out through thoughts, feelings, and behaviors that would be integrally tied into the side-scrolling platformer game, i.e., the Monkey chase minigame would evolve into the primary game. By seeing children's reactions in the first playtest, we changed the flow (as shown in Figure 3). Instead of our game having 3 distinct components of education, extensive reading, and arbitrary mini-games, we reduced the reading and integrated it along with the education into the gameplay itself.

The player now helps animals by diving into their memories, identifying their thoughts, feelings, and behaviors, and offering solutions to resolve their negative cognitions. The target demographic was also narrowed to ages 10-12 for the remainder of development.

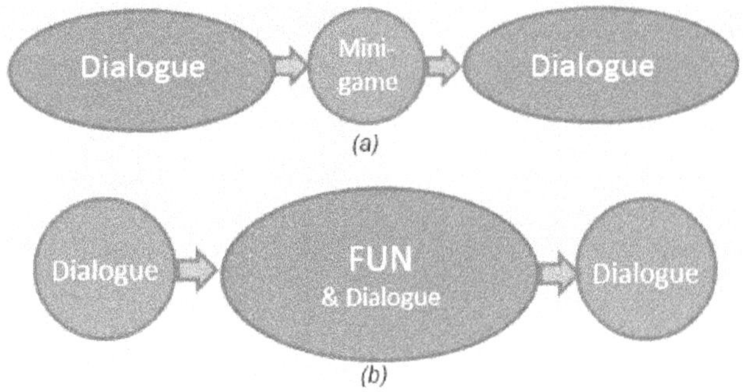

Figure 3. Original design (a), and new design (b) where dialogue was integrated with the "fun" side-scroller.

SECOND PLAYTEST ON SIDE SCROLLER WITH INTEGRATED THOUGHTS AND EXPERIENCES

The next iteration of the game brought together the thoughts, feelings, and behaviors into the side-scroller design. A player who does well with classifying text into these three categories earns additional platform elements that make progressing through levels easier. Successful use of the cognitive triangle unlocks new animal levels, i.e., new game levels with different background art and elements, opening up the path to successful completion of the story. Earlier work confirmed that both boys and girls preferred to direct the male lion through levels, as it had more visual flair than the lioness, and so Lion was chosen as the avatar to be controlled during the side-scrolling action. The Lion progresses through the savannah, conversing with the other animals and piecing together the chain of events that have led to Wolf no longer howling, as well as the consequences of that.

Figure 4 shows a screen shot of Lion as he moves through a level collecting all of the alternate thought gems and experience swirls. The gems and swirls are both collectibles in each level and serve as the elements for working through alternate thoughts in the cognitive triangle.

Figure 4. Early version of side-scroller interface, with player moving and jumping the lion to proceed through levels collecting needed memories (pink swirls) and alternate thoughts (diamond gems) that drive later dialogues.

In order to beat each level, players must collect all of the memories of the event that are troubling an animal friend. These memories take the form of pink circles in the tested version. When you reach the exit door, you must correctly associate the memories with their respective points on the cognitive triangle (using a drag-and-drop interface as shown in Figure 5). Also scattered throughout the level are gems that represent alternate thoughts that the animal could have used in their situation. These must also be collected, and players must choose the best alternate thought to help solve the animal's dilemma. We then show the animal's positively changed feelings and behaviors to match the new thought, and exit into a dialogue scene. The animal will summarize what it learned, thank you, and allow you to go help the next animal. This gameplay lets players learn the correlation of thoughts, feelings, and behaviors, and learn that changing how you think can have positive effects.

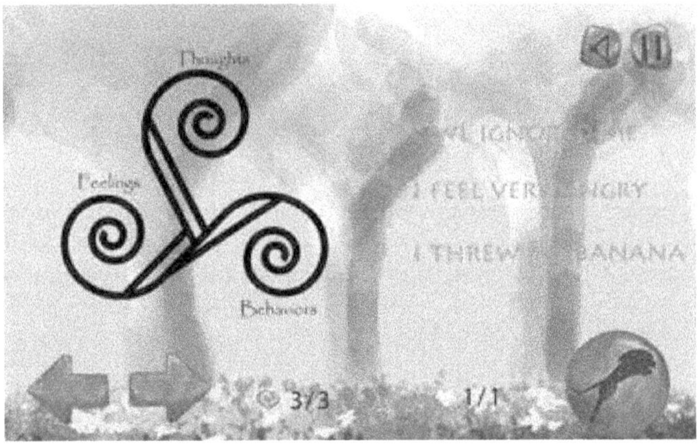

Figure 5. Early version of cognitive triangle: user classifies text into thoughts, feelings, and behaviors.

The second playtest was conducted with Android tablets at a middle school. Twenty-one classmates across two grades (ages 11-13; 11 male and 10 female) tested the game, using player observation and post-game surveys to capture the sessions. The primary question for this round of playtesting was confirming whether we "followed the fun": do players enjoy the platform game shown in part in Figure 4? Did we pollute the fun by introducing too much of the cognitive triangle into it? The survey responses indicated that we were on a good development path. Here are four representative child-provided answers to "What was your favorite part of this game":

- "Jumping onto the different places to get to where you need to go"
- "Putting the feelings, behaviors, and thoughts in the right place"
- "Helping different animals"
- "When you had to collect the items"

It was very encouraging to see the children eager to play through the provided first 3 levels of the game. We were delighted to find that the educational elements were called out as favorite parts of the game. We had changed the side-scroller to make the educational parts internal obstacles to overcome and achievements that help players progress, rather than just external problems to solve. The reduction of reading along with "following the fun" and emphasizing the side-scrolling platform game provided an experience that the children rated as enjoyable. The children also wanted more levels, and an increasing difficulty in levels, and so we continued development on this path.

SUBSEQUENT PLAYTESTS: MORE LEVELS, MORE POLISH TO INTERFACES

After additional levels and an integrated tutorial were added to the game, a third playtest session was conducted with eleven children ages 9-12 (5 male, 6 female) using Android tablets and phones. They enjoyed navigating through the levels, were all able to figure out how to classify the three components of the cognitive triangle in our game system, and all understood the concept of collecting major experiences that tell the story. They identified several areas for work, some obvious (better text readability; not the all red upper case text you see in Figure 5 for example), and others, more subtle, such as using "Thought Stone" instead of gem as a collectible in the platformer to communicate alternate thoughts.

The visual and aural feedback to let the player know whether a choice was correct or incorrect was still weak or missing. An improved beginning and end were also needed. The story had to be introduced quickly so as not to bore the audience, but strong enough to communicate animal mishaps due to misunderstandings. A wrap-up was needed to provide a grand sense of finality so players feel that they have made a difference in the game world. These elements were added, and a fourth and fifth playtest conducted to confirm that player satisfaction with the game remains high, and that interest in playing to the end remains strong. The goal of the playtests was to confirm that children stay with the game because it is fun rather than because it is an assignment.

The fourth playtest was conducted with Android tablets at a middle school. Ten classmates across two grades (ages 11-13; 4 male and 6 female) tested the game, using player observation and post-game surveys to capture the sessions. The same instruments were used in a fifth playtest at the developer studio with six girls ages 12-14 using Android tablets and phones. These 16 users were visibly engaged with the game, and rated it as enjoyable. The full set of levels was available for the fifth playtest, and all six testers finished the game on their own initiative within 20 minutes.

Insights from the fourth and fifth playtests underscored the need for additional points of polish in the interface (color choices, layouts, more puzzles and variety in platforms). For example, to help provide the player with a sense of progress and an indicator as to what is to come, the animals in the story represent levels, and those levels not yet unlocked are shown as such in the navigation menu of Figure 6. The footprints animate to show the path that you as the player traverse, starting conversations with Fish and proceeding to Monkey, Owl, Rhino, Elephant, Panther, and Wolf.

Figure 6. Navigation menu showing progress through game.

These last three playtests differed from the first two in that with the interface updates, the children now actually read the text sequences. Dialogues were shortened significantly from the start of the project, and many text elements are now within the platform gameplay rather than left in separate dialogue interfaces.

There was still the need to stitch the story together of animals' confusion due to negative thoughts, requiring interfaces like that of Figure 7. However, the background art keeps the player situated in the nature context and clicks on the shown animal speaker's head play that animal's sounds for extra amusement. The reading interfaces were no longer called out as a negative for the game.

Figure 7. Example of dialogue interface communicating the story web, which connects the animals through thoughts, feelings, and behaviors.

The platformer needed to have some variety, in order to retain an interest curve in the game. We wished to have players pleasantly frustrated, in a flow zone of not-too-easy, not-too-hard challenges as recommended by Schell with the Lens of Flow [12] and detailed in [3]. The first levels provide in-game help where you play tutorial steps to advance. Later levels offer platforms on which to jump (Figure 4 is early version). Still later levels make use of giraffes whose necks rise and fall as additional platforms. Subsequent levels introduce birds on which to fly (moving platforms) and hippos on which to jump (trampolines to reach high platforms). See Figure 8 for an example. Note the swirls are now gray-shaded rather than pink as in Figure 4, and collectibles have Thought Stones (1 of 3 found so far) rather than diamond gems.

Figure 8. Lion riding a stork to get to a high swirl.

To bring more of the cognitive triangle task into the side-scroller, glowing object outlines are introduced. At first glows are only for missing platforms, as shown in Figure 9, but then later they represent giraffes, birds, and hippos (Figure 10), with shape cues. These glows help players collect the Experience swirls and Thought Stones.

Figure 9. Yellow glowing objects (one is at upper right, shaped like a grass platform), when tapped, ask the player to classify a bit of text as thought, feeling or behavior.

When a glow area is tapped, the player is shown the cognitive triangle interface and asked to classify a bit of text from the animal featured in the level. Classifying it correctly, as is done in Figure 11, shows more story text from the featured animal and fills in the glow object, e.g., a grass platform in Figure 9 or a hippo trampoline for Figure 10. Sorting it incorrectly triggers help text from the Lion and leaves the glow in place.

Figure 10. Another example of a yellow glowing object, here shaped like a sleeping hippo directly in front of Lion. Clicking glowing objects lets player get through level more easily with correct classifications (in this case, putting a hippo in place).

Figure 11. Dragging the experience swirl for "I jumped up and down" text to Behaviors, a correct classification which triggers more feedback in platformer screen (plus filling in the glow object).

After all swirls and Thought Stones are collected for an animal level, the sorting interface is presented with three items to sort, as shown in Figure 12. Successful sorting leads to an interface for plugging in an alternate thought, e.g., for Monkey instead of "Owl ignored me" the thought "Maybe Owl didn't notice Monkey because he was busy" can be substituted, leading to a new feeling of calming down and a new behavior of apologizing to Fish. Success with the alternate thoughts unlocks new animal levels.

These interfaces of Figure 11 and 12 directly address the cognitive triangle of Figure 1. They address the educational goals of the TF-CBT therapists to give children practice in classifying thoughts, feelings and behaviors and support replacement of negative thoughts with positive ones in order to see changes in subsequent feelings and behaviors. These activities are integral to advancing through the puzzle platformer game, rather than in a separated interactive storybook divorced from its minigames. The child players flowed easily from the interfaces of side-scroller (Figures 9 and 10), single-item classification (Figure 11), and three-item classification (Figure 12). The appearance of animal character art and nature backgrounds connected the activity. Improved tutorials, text cues from animals, text rendering, feedback on touch tapping, dragging, and touch target areas (including menu of Figure 6) all made for an experience that children rated as easy to use in these latter playtests.

Figure 12. Sorting to triangle by dragging swirls (here, the act of dragging "I was angry" to Feelings is just about finished).

SUMMATIVE PLAYTEST AND DISCUSSION

With the final interface changes in place, we wished to test our game with sixth and seventh graders in a local school to see whether we produced an engaging game that would not induce stress, i.e., would trend toward easy on an easy-difficult rating scale. We tested with 20 children ages 11-14 at the school. One had a reading disability and did not fill out the questionnaire afterward. Data from the remaining 19 students are summarized in Figures 13 and 14 to the question "I thought the game was..." with 5-point Likert scale responses.

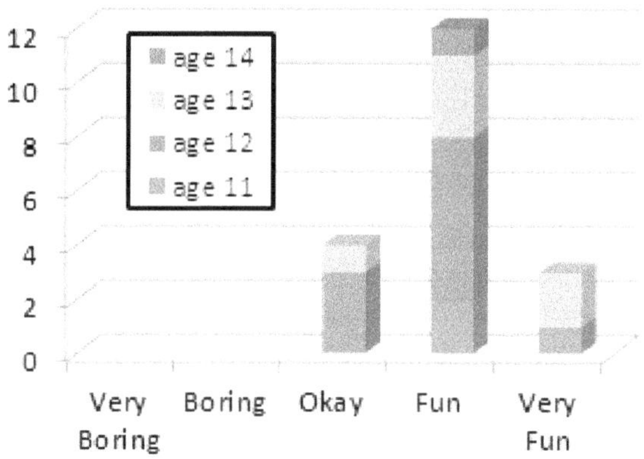

Figure 13. Final playtest showed children rating game as fun.

These testers rated the game as fun or very fun. The choices on polish for text and characters were all received well and met with enjoyment by child players. *TF-CBT Triangle of Life* was designed to be a fun game that gives children experience with the cognitive triangle. That objective has been met. The subsequent objective, whether the game will educate children well enough for effective trauma-focused cognitive behavioral therapy, will be addressed in clinical trials that will take time to schedule and approve.

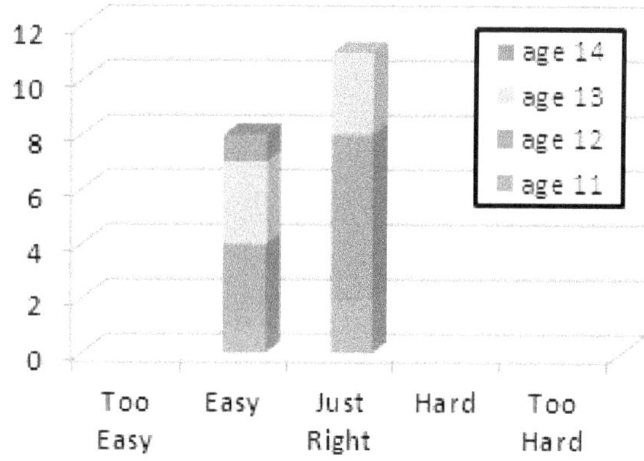

Figure 14. Final playtest showing the game was considered as a bit on the easy side, as planned given its initial requirements.

Our later playtests skewed a bit older (to 14) and the game was still playable and enjoyable, although older teens ages 13 and 14 rated it as easy. We do not want to make the puzzles too difficult in order to advance through a level, in that we wish the game to still be playable by younger children. We also wish to remain true to an initial design parameter of not inducing too much stress in the child. Faced with the choice of putting the player into a good flow zone with some challenge, and having no challenge at all for no stress but also no enjoyment, we opted to produce an easy puzzler. The levels can be solved within a minute or two, and the whole game within twenty minutes. We realize this may make the game more suited to younger, more novice players, and hence claim a younger demographic of 10-12, rather than 10-14. After discussion with our medical expert clients, we chose this child age range because such children have the reading skills needed to understand thoughts, feelings, and behaviors in our story, and are a significant percentage of the target demographic for TF-CBT. As we did significantly reduce the length of text blocks to be read in the game as it evolved through iterations, the game may be suitable once more to even younger players, a point that will be investigated in follow-up testing with eight and nine year olds.

CONCLUSION

We created an educational mobile game that gives children opportunities to explore thoughts, feelings, and behaviors. As an integral part of gameplay, child players advance through puzzle platform levels collecting experiences to use with the cognitive triangle. By generating alternate thoughts to encourage more positive feelings and behaviors, players help the animals solve personal crises. The hope is that this game will serve as a useful tool within TF-CBT for traumatized children working through cognitive processing training.

As discussed in [10] and detailed in [6], the ARCS model identifies four essential strategy components for motivating instruction:

- Attention strategies for arousing and sustaining curiosity

- Relevance strategies that link to learners' needs, interests, and motives
- Confidence strategies that help students develop a positive expectation for successful achievement
- Satisfaction strategies that provide extrinsic and intrinsic reinforcement for effort

TF-CBT Triangle of Life, the game discussed here, covers these A-R-C-S points. It addresses attention by having a folk tale, a string of mishaps between animals and the ability to move a Lion through the environs to unravel the issues. Playtesting confirmed relevance: the child learners were interested in the animals and their problems: they were eager to solve the posed crisis. The means of helping was through the cognitive triangle, and so the learning goals of classification and alternate thoughts were aligned well with the game. Players' confidence was boosted with in-game dialogue from the animals, seeing a progression of animals unlock (Figure 6), and having level difficulty increase over time to keep the player motivated. Satisfaction was promoted in the process of each animal resolving its unease with positive alternate thoughts, and a closing win scene (shown with all animals celebrating together as in Figure 15). A series of five playtests with 56 children (29 female) informed the iterative development of *TF-CBT: Triangle of Life* with an emphasis on player motivation and enjoyment.

Figure 15. Win scene with Wolf howling in happiness and all animals celebrating together.

This paper stepped through the development of the game, informed by frequent playtests with children. After our initial plans of creating an interactive storybook, our playtests directed us towards following the fun, producing the puzzle platformer that pulls together education, interaction, and player interest.

ACKNOWLEDGMENTS

This work is made possible through careful mentoring and review by our medical professionals Judith Cohen and Anthony Mannarino at Allegheny General Hospital, Pittsburgh, PA. Based on the positive reception from children during the series of playtests, the professionals may now pursue IRB approval to conduct clinical trials within medical care settings to determine the effectiveness of the game within a formal TF-CBT environment.

REFERENCES

1. Aardema, V. *Why Mosquitoes Buzz in People's Ears: A West African Tale*. Dial Press, New York, 1975.
2. Cohen, J.A., and Mannarino, A.P. Trauma-Focused Cognitive Behavioural Therapy for Children and Parents. *Child and Adolescent Mental Health 13*, 4 (2008), 158-162.
3. Csikszentmihalyi, M. *Flow: The Psychology of Optimal Experience*. Harper and Row, New York, 1990.
4. de Sa, M., and Carriço, L. Fear Therapy for Children - A Mobile Approach. In *Proc. Engineering Interactive Computing Systems 2012*, 237-246.
5. Hiniker, A., Daniels, J.W., and Williamson, H. Go Go Games: Therapeutic Video Games for Children with Autism Spectrum Disorders. In *Proc. Int'l Conf. Interaction Design and Children 2013*, pp. 463-466.
6. Keller, J.M. Development and use of the ARCS model of motivational design. *Journal of Instructional Development 10*, 3 (1987), 2-10.
7. Malone, T.W. and Lepper, M.R. Making learning fun: A taxonomy of intrinsic motivation for learning. In *Aptitude, Learning and Instruction, Vol. 3: Conative and Affective Process Analyses*, 223-253. Erlbaum, Hillsdale, NJ, 1987.
8. McCann Australia. *Dumb Ways to Die*. http://www.gamesforchange.org/play/dumb-ways-to-die/
9. National Child Traumatic Stress Network, Child Trauma Facts, http://www.nctsn.org/resources/audiences/for-the-media/online-press-kit
10. Paras, B. and Bizzocchi, J. Game, Motivation, and Effective Learning: An Integrated Model for Educational Game Design. In *Proc. DIGRA 2005*, http://www.digra.org/wp-content/uploads/digital-library/06276.18065.pdf
11. Pynoos, R.S., et al. The National Child Traumatic Stress Network: Collaborating to improve the standard of care. *Professional Psychology: Research and Practice 39*, 4 (2008), 389-395.
12. Schell, J. *The Art of Game Design: A Book of Lenses*. Morgan Kaufmann, Burlington, MA, 2008.
13. Tresselt, A. *The Old Man and the Tiger*. Wonder Books, New York, 1965.
14. Vandenberghe, J. The Four Fs of Game Design. *Game Developer Magazine 19*, 12 (Dec. 2012), 44-46.

Relating Gaming Habits with Student Performance in a Gamified Learning Experience

Gabriel Barata **Sandra Gama** **Joaquim Jorge** **Daniel Gonçalves**
INESC-ID / Instituto Superior Técnico, Universidade de Lisboa
Rua Alves Redol 9, 1000-029 Lisbon, Portugal
{gabriel.barata, sandra.gama}@ist.utl.pt, {joaquim.jorge, daniel.goncalves}@inesc-id.pt

ABSTRACT
Gamified education is a novel concept, and early trials show its potential to engage students and improve their performance. However, little is known about how different students learn with gamification, and how their gaming habits influence their experience. In this paper we present a study where data regarding student performance and gaming preferences, from a gamified engineering course, was collected and analyzed. We performed cluster analysis to understand what different kinds of students could be observed in our gamified experience, and how their behavior could be correlated to their gaming characteristics. We identified four main student types: the Achievers, the Regular students, the Halfhearted students, and the Underachievers, all representing different strategies towards the course and with different gaming preferences. Here we will thoroughly describe each student type and address how different gaming preferences might have impacted the students' learning experience.

Author Keywords
Gamification; Education; Cluster Analysis; Student Performance; Gamer Profiles; BrainHex

ACM Classification Keywords
H.5.2. User Interfaces: Evaluation/methodology

INTRODUCTION
Gamification is a recent process that consists of using game design elements in non-game processes [9, 10], as a means to make them more fun and engaging [20, 24] and thus, encourage users to adopt specific behaviors. Gamification has been used for many different purposes, such as engaging users with marketing programs [25], helping in driving instruction [13], promoting fitness and health awareness [7], improving one's productivity [23], and encouraging eco-friendly driving [15].

CHI PLAY '14, October 19 - 22 2014, Toronto, ON, Canada

ACM 978-1-4503-3014-5/14/10...$15.00.
http://dx.doi.org/10.1145/2658537.2658692

Introducing and training new skills has been one of the major uses of gamification. For example, Jigsaw [12] teaches Photoshop by using a jigsaw puzzle to challenge players to match a target image, and users stated they were able to explore the application and discover new techniques with this gamified approach. GamiCAD [16] is a tutorial system for AutoCAD that encourages users to perform line and trimming operations, to help NASA build a spacecraft. Users reported to have completed tasks faster and found the experience to be both more engaging and enjoyable with the gamified version of the tutorial. Prominent services that have adopted a similar approach are Microsoft Ribbon Hero[1] and Adobe Level Up[2], which rely on game elements like points, challenges and badges to get users to explore Microsoft Office and Adobe Photoshop respectively.

Given the great pedagogical possibilities games potentiate [14], gamification has been explored as a means to improve learning. In his book, Lee Sheldon [22] explains how a conventional course can be turned into a game, without using technology, where students start with an F grade and go all the way up to an A+, by completing challenges and gaining experience points. On another study, Domínguez et al. [11] compare two methods of taking optional exercises on an ICT course, where one consisted of consulting PDF files and the other of using a gamified system. In the latter, students were awarded with badges and medals on completion. Results show that students that used the gamified approach had better exam grades and reported deeper engagement with the course. Well-known online learning services like Khan Academy[3] and Codeacademy[4] teach students by providing them with video lessons and exercises to complete, while student progress is tracked using visual elements like points and badges.

Previously we have presented a long-term experiment in which we gamified a college course named Multimedia Content Production (MCP) [2]. Here, course activities were encapsulated into achievements and meaningful challenges, and game design elements like experience points, levels, badges and a leaderboard were added. We thoroughly compared data regarding student performance and online

---

[1] http://www.ribbonhero.com/ (visited April 5th 2014)
[2] http://adobe.ly/19dBNh1 (visited April 5th 2014)
[3] www.khanacademy.org (visited April 5th 2014)
[4] www.codecademy.com (visited April 5th 2014)

participation, between gamified years and also between gamified and non-gamified years. Results show that students were more proactive and participative in the gamified version of the course, and that they found our course to be more motivating and interesting than other non-regular courses. However, we still know very little about how different types of students experience the course, and previous research work in this matter is scarce.

In this paper we present a new study where we analyzed how students performed over the term, and used clustering algorithms to identify what different types of strategies were adopted by students. Four types of students were identified, the Achievers, the Regular students, the Halfhearted students and the Underachievers, each representing different approaches towards our gamified course. In order to understand how their gaming preferences influenced the whole experience, we have also collected quantitative and qualitative data regarding their gaming habits, as well as their player profile according to the BrainHex model [18], which is based on neurological research related to gameplay. Here we will present a detailed description of each student type and correlate them with the students' gaming profiles.

GAMER PROFILING

A lot of groundwork has been established regarding player profiling, because the better we understand what different types of players like, the better we can tailor gaming experiences directed to them. One of the earliest and most well-known works is that of Richard Bartle [3, 4], were he identified what different types of MUD (multi-user dungeon) users enjoyed the most. Players could be classified according to their gaming preferences within a two axes system, each of which with two mutually exclusive forms: Acting – Interacting and Players – World. Four player types were thus considered: Socializers, who prefer to interact with other players (Interacting, Players); Killers, players that enjoy imposing and causing distress upon others (Acting, Players); Achievers, who assign themselves game goals and set out to achieve them (Acting, World); and Explorers, players that try to explore and find out as much about the world as possible (Interacting, World). A quiz consisting of a series of 30 questions was later created, which produces a score that classifies players into categories, based on their preferences. One of the main limitations of this model was that players could only have a single type at the same time.

Other classification models were later developed, such as the Demographic Game Design 1 (DGD1), proposed by Chris Bateman [5], which was primarily based on the Myers-Biggs personality model [17]. This model had the advantage of allowing players to be classified with combined playing styles, in opposition to the Bartle types. A subsequent model was developed, named BrainHex [18], which was based upon neurobiological responses inherent to playing games [6]. This model comprises seven player archetypes, each characterizing a specific playing style:

1. Seeker: typically "curious about the game world and enjoys moments of wonder". They usually prefer games where they can explore and find "strange and wonderful things".
2. Survivor: enjoys experiencing terror, which has normally a negative appraisal. They like to escape from "hideous and scary threads", and take "pulse-pounding risks".
3. Daredevil: this play style is all about the rush, taking risks and playing on the edge. They enjoy "dizzying platforms" and "rushing around at high speed".
4. Mastermind: these players "enjoy solving puzzles and devising strategies, as well as focusing on making the most efficient decisions."
5. Conqueror: these players are very challenge-oriented and they "enjoy defeating impossibly difficult foes, struggling until they achieve victory, and beating others."
6. Socializer: players fitting this archetype usually enjoy talking to other players, helping them and hanging around with people they trust.
7. Achiever: these players are more goal-oriented, and are motivated by long-term game achievements, like collecting special objects and amassing currency.

This model allows players to have both a main and a secondary class, and it comprises a list of oppositions to each style of play. We chose the BrainHex model to classify our students regarding their gameplay style because it is one of the most complete works in the field and it draws on the results of previous works, like the DGD1 and DGD2. Furthermore, an online questionnaire for this model is available, which makes it of easy access and easy administration.

THE MCP GAME

Multimedia Content Production is an MSc engineering gamified course in Information Systems and Computer Engineering, at Instituto Superior Técnico, University of Lisbon. The course follows a blended learning program, where students attend theoretical lectures and lab classes, but also get involved in discussions and complete assignments online using the Moodle[5] platform. Theoretical lectures cover multimedia concepts such as capture, editing and production techniques, multimedia standards, copyright and Digital Rights Management. In lab classes, varied concepts and tools are taught on image, audio and video manipulation, and there are regular assignments.

[5] www.moodle.org (visited April 5th 2014)

Figure 1. AvatarWorld.

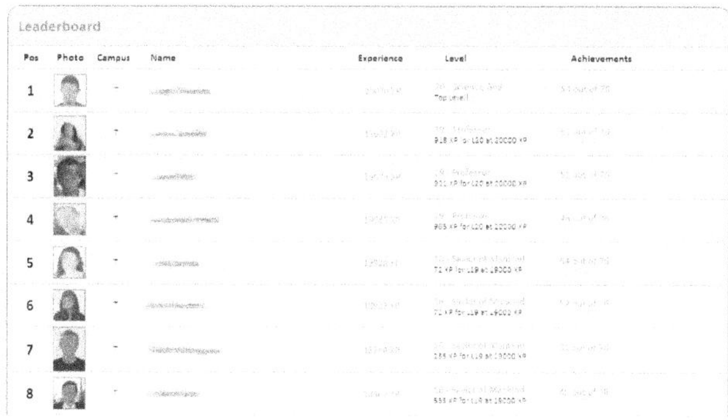

Figure 2. The MCP leaderboard.

Instead of receiving traditional grades, students participate in a game-like experience, where they had to accumulate experience points (XP) by completing course activities, which included a multimedia presentation (20% of total course XP), lab classes (15%), a final exam (30%), Skill Tree participation (10%), and a set of collectible achievements (30% plus a 5% extra). These required students to perform specific tasks, which would earn them XP and badges. Examples of these are attending lectures, finding resources related to class subjects, finding bugs in class materials, or completing challenges. Five percent of extra grade were distributed by several achievements so that students could achieve the 100% through different paths.

Achievements could either be single-level or multi-level, depending on how many iterations they required. Each iteration earned students XP and a badge. Although most achievements did not have a time limit to be accomplished, some involved the completion of time limited tasks. For example, Theoretical and the Lab Challenges required students to do creative works related to subjects taught on theoretical lectures and lab classes within periods of one to two weeks. There was also the MCP Quest, which was an online-riddle (similar to of Notpron[6]) where students started from a webpage with some sort of multimedia content, which they had to edit and manipulate to find the URL for the next clue of the riddle (or next level). The amount of awarded XP was proportional to the level of quest. In order to encourage every student to participate, they were required to contribute once in order to be awarded the XP, but a student could not post twice in a row. The MCP Quest and the Challenges were posted to course fora by faculty, and students had to post their responses accordingly. In order to allow students to do more of what they like, they were allowed to post up to three times in the same challenge, to make up for lack of participation in other less appealing challenges. Posts were evaluated by the faculty staff with a rating from 0 to 4, which was then translated to a specific amount of XP.

We also had an innovative game element, called AvatarWorld [1]. It was a 2.5D virtual world that evolves and grows as students are awarded with XP, with new buildings and characters being added. Students are represented by an avatar that can be used to explore the world. Its equipment can be customized with clothing and handheld objects, which students can unlock by acquiring certain course badges. Students can also create custom content for the game, like buildings and equipment, using tools and techniques taught in class. These were very specific tasks, which usually required more effort than most of the challenges and the quest. Submissions were also made via posts and were then graded by faculty, based on their creativity and technical correctness, and 600XP could be earned from it. In previous editions of the course, students requested more opportunities to be creative and autonomous in the course. Thus, AvatarWorld was introduced in this year, in an effort to improve both learning and gaming experience.

The Skill Tree is a game element that consists of a precedence tree where each node represented a thematic task, which would earn students XP upon completion. There were 6 base nodes that were already unlocked at the beginning of the course, and subsequent nodes could be unlocked when two preceding ones were completed. Students could gain a fair amount of XP from the Skill Tree, and this could be achieved by different paths. Each branch of the tree represented a theme, and students could either go all the way up to a top level node or just complete more base ones, according to their liking. Just like AvatarWorld, Skill Tree tasks were very specific and more demanding than most of the challenges or the MCP quest.

Students began the game with 0 XP and were awarded with more XP for undertaking course activities, which provided students with instant gratification. This was previously shown to be successful in motivating college students [19]. For each 1000 XP students increased in experience levels, and each level was labeled with a unique honorary title. Students had to reach level 10 in order to pass the course, and Levels max out at 20 (20000 XP), to match the traditional 20-point grading system used in our university.

[6] http://notpron.org/notpron/ (last visited: April 18th, 2014)

The leaderboard was the main entry point to the gamified experience, allowing students to perform comparisons with others (see Figure 2). It was publically accessible from the forums, displaying students' scores sorted in descending order by level and XP. Each row showed the player's rank, photo and name, campus, XP, level and achievements completed. The leaderboard allowed students to assess both their progress and their peers'. By clicking on a student's row, the achievements and achievement history for that player were displayed. This turned game progression into a transparent process, by showing what had already been accomplished and what was yet to complete. Furthermore, it also transmitted valuable feedback that allowed students to learn by watching others.

STUDENT PROFILE ANALYSIS

Our previous study shows that students consider our course to be more motivating and interesting than other "regular" courses. Moreover, a comparison of several performance measures between gamified and non-gamified years shows that students are more proactive and participative on the gamified version of the course [2]. However, we do not yet fully understand how different types of students might experience our course, and neither do we know how they feel about games and what their gaming habits are. To better understand the nature of our students, we performed a new study where data regarding their performance and gaming preferences were collected and analyzed using cluster analysis.

In order to categorize students into different types, we had to identify a single measure of progress in the gamified experience, adequate to plot over time and use with a clustering algorithm. We initially considered both accumulated XP and rank over time as viable measures, but rejected the latter because students with equal performance could never be at the same rank. By plotting accumulated XP over time for every student, a few patterns became apparent, which seem to support the existence of different student categories. We then proceeded to cluster analysis, by using accumulated XP per day as attributes, to group students by similarities of XP acquisition. Expectation-Maximization (EM) [8] was the selected clustering algorithm, given that our sample was small and the number of clusters was not known beforehand [21]. The course lasted for 156 days and we had 54 enrolled students.

Usually, during the first days, most students have zero XP, either because they are not fully enrolled in the course or because there was still no significant activity. This makes all students' activity to look alike, which might mislead the clustering algorithm to group all students into the same cluster. To avoid this, we excluded from the analysis the first days that satisfied one of the following criteria: 1) there were still students whose enrollment process was not completed and were not playing the game yet, and 2) students were tied up at zero score due to lack of initial activity. As a result of this filtering process, 17 days were

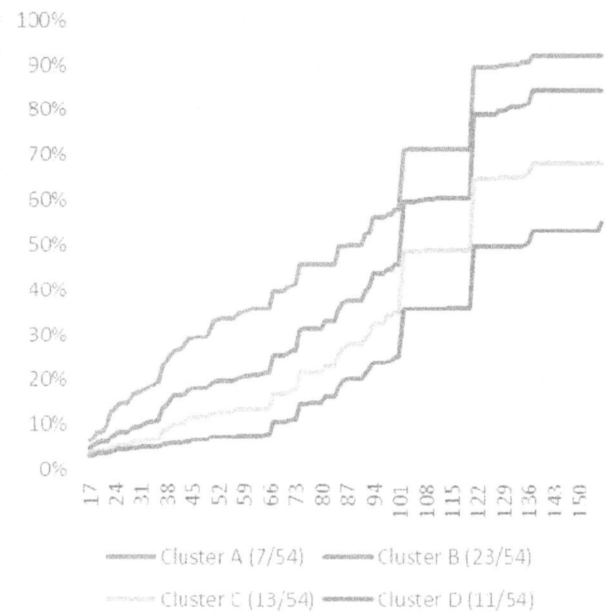

Figure 3. Average accumulated XP per day.

excluded from the study. This large number resulted mainly from significant lack of activity during the first two weeks, given that the professors were attending a conference during the first week, and not all students were enrolled yet in the second week. This limited student participation during the first days.

Four clusters were identified (from A to D), each portraying different XP acquisition patterns. In this section we will describe each one of them, taking into account student performance and participation measures. We also asked students to answer the BrainHex questionnaire and self-report the resulting classes in a questionnaire of our own, which also included additional questions regarding videogame playing habits. These will also be here addressed. Given that normality could not be assumed due the clusters' small size, we checked for differences between them using a Kruskal-Wallis test, with post hoc Mann-Whitney's U tests and Bonferroni correction. Questionnaire data was compared based on the responses' mode and respective percentage of students.

Cluster A

The first identified cluster was composed by 7 students, and it was characterized by a steep XP accumulation curve, which suggests these students were most of the time ahead of the others, as see in Figure 3. Here, every slope represents a significant XP acquisition, and these students appear to have grabbed every XP they could. This had a direct manifestation over their average ranking over the semester, with the top positions being mostly occupied by these students (see Figure 4). These students usually had the highest lab and final grade, made the most posts (both initial posts and replies), made the most rated posts and had

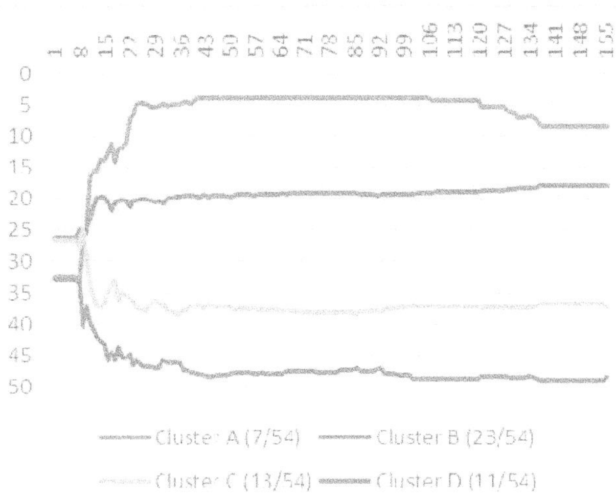

Figure 4. Average ranking per day.

the highest mean average rating per post, and earned the most XP from every game component (i.e. Challenges, MCP Quest, Skill Tree, AvatarWorld, and the Achievements) (see Figure 5).

All students from cluster A replied to the player characterization questionnaire, where 71% of the students were male. A majority of them (57%) affirmed they played videogames every day, and 43% of them considered they were something between a hardcore and a casual gamer. All of cluster A students stated they preferred multiplayer games over single player games, and 86% stated that computer is the device they usually play the most with. All students from this cluster considered they usually played in a personal computer, 71% in videogame consoles, and 86% said that they did not usually play with portable videogame consoles, tablets or smartphones. The most played type of videogame by this cluster was Role Playing Game (RPG), and the most common BrainHex classes were Mastermind and Socializer (29% of the students, each) for the main class, and Conqueror (71%) for the secondary class.

Cluster B

Cluster B, the largest one with 23 students, was characterized by a less steep XP accumulation curve than that of cluster A. These students had slightly above average XP accumulation levels, which put them right below cluster A students in the leaderboard. They had the highest mean multimedia presentation grade and exam grade, made the second most posts, and had the second highest mean average rating per rated post. These students performed close to cluster A students on most game components, with the exception of the Skill Tree and AvatarWorld, where they fell behind.

All cluster B students replied to the player characterization questionnaire, but one claimed to never play games. Consequently, this student's data was excluded. A large portion of them (61%) was male, and 39% stated they

Property	A	B	C	D	All	Significant Differences ($p < 0.05$)
Labs Grade (%)	96.24	94.28	89.23	73.36	89.06	(B, D)
Presentation Grade (%)	78.50	83.33	82.23	64.18	78.54	None
Exam Grade (%)	63.67	65.50	56.02	55.67	60.98	(B, C)
Final Grade (%)	91.79	84.28	68.09	54.94	75.38	(A, C), (A, D), (B, C), (B, D), (C, D)
Attendance (%)	82.31	87.78	50.55	33.77	67.11	(A, D), (B, C), (B, D)
Posts (#)	76.71	48.09	21.77	10.55	37.81	(A, B),(A, C), (A, D), (B, C), (B, D)
First Posts (#)	3.86	2.39	0.46	0.55	1.74	(A, C), (A, D), (B, C)
Reply Posts (#)	72.86	45.70	21.31	10.00	36.07	(A, B),(A, C), (A, D), (B, C), (B, D)
Rated Posts (#)	44.57	28.22	14.08	7.55	22.72	(A, B),(A, C), (A, D), (B, C), (B, D)
Mean Rate	3.46	3.35	3.33	3.01	3.29	None
Challenge Posts (#)	16.86	16.26	9.69	5.27	12.52	(A, C), (A, D), (B, C), (B, D)
XP from Challenges (%)	100.00	95.65	71.79	40.26	79.19	(A, C), (A, D), (B, C), (B, D)
Theoretical Challenge Posts (#)	8.71	8.65	5.54	2.82	6.72	(A, D), (B, C), (B, D)
XP from Theoretical Challenges (%)	100.00	95.65	71.79	36.36	78.40	(A, D), (B, C), (B, D)
Lab Challenge Posts (#)	8.14	7.61	4.15	2.45	5.80	(A, C), (A, D), (B, C), (B, D)
XP from Lab Challenges (%)	100.00	95.65	71.79	45.45	80.25	(A, D), (B, C), (B, D)
Skill Tree Posts (#)	20.86	12.43	4.62	3.18	9.76	(A, B),(A, C), (A, D), (B, C), (B, D)
XP from Skill Tree (%)	100.00	64.57	20.77	17.95	49.12	(A, B),(A, C), (A, D), (B, C), (B, D)
Explored Skill Tree Nodes (#)	11.71	7.91	2.69	2.27	6.00	(A, B),(A, C), (A, D), (B, C), (B, D)
MCP Quest Posts (#)	2.29	2.30	1.31	0.18	1.63	(A, D), (B, D)
XP from MCP Quest (%)	100.00	95.65	69.23	18.18	74.07	(A, D), (B, D)
AvatarWorld Posts (#)	17.57	5.17	3.62	0.09	5.37	(A, B),(A, C), (A, D), (B, D)
XP from AvatarWorld (%)	97.62	25.36	10.26	1.52	26.23	(A, B),(A, C), (A, D)
AW Submissions (#)	21.86	6.261	2.462	0.182	1.593	(A, B),(A, C), (A, D)
Badges (#)	50.43	40.70	28.77	20.09	34.89	All
XP from Achievements (%)	100.00	93.88	69.97	44.36	78.83	(A, C), (A, D), (B, C), (B, D), (C, D)
Completed Achievements (#)	14.57	11.52	6.92	4.55	9.39	All
Explored Achievements (#)	22.71	18.91	15.69	11.09	17.04	All

Figure 5. Student performance metrics per cluster.

played videogames every week. Furthermore, 52% of them considered they were casual gamers, 57% showed preference for multiplayer games over single player ones, and 70% said the personal computer was the device they played the most with. All cluster B students confirmed they usually played in a personal computer, whereas videogame consoles and smartphones were also usually played by 57% of them. However, 83% and 78% considered they did not usually play with portable video game consoles and tablets respectively. The most played type of game by cluster B was Real-time Strategy (RTS), and the most common BrainHex classes were Achiever and Mastermind (26% of the students, each) for the main class, and Conqueror (39%) for the secondary class.

Cluster C

Cluster C was composed by 13 students, and they typically presented a sub average XP accumulation curve and an average ranking lower than that of Cluster B. These students typically had grades below those of clusters A and

B, with the exception of the multimedia presentation and the exam grades, which were the second highest. Cluster C students made the third most posts but had the lowest number of first posts, even though this difference was not significant in comparison to any of the other clusters. They also made the third most rated posts and had the third highest mean average rating per post. These students contributed poorly to the Skill Tree and AvatarWorld, and had below average participation in the other game components.

Regarding the player characterization questionnaire, we had responses from all but one student on this cluster. Of these students, 92% were male, and 58% stated that they play videogames every day. Also, 42% considered themselves something between a hardcore and a casual gamer, 83% preferred multiplayer games over single player, and 67% affirmed that the personal computer was the device they played the most with. All students from this cluster affirmed they usually played videogames on a personal computer, 58% on videogame consoles and 50% on smartphones, but 83% considered that they usually did not play on a tablets and 75% on portable videogame consoles. The most played game type by these students was Shooter, but RPGs were also predominant. A majority of the students (67%) had the Conqueror as their main BrainHex class, and 42% had Mastermind as the secondary one.

Cluster D

The fourth cluster was composed by 11 students, and it was characterized by a rather low and less steep XP accumulation curve, as compared to any other cluster, which pushed them to the bottom positions of the leaderboard. Students from this cluster had the lowest grades on all evaluation components, posted the least, and had the lowest average rating per rated post. They ignored the Skill Tree, AvatarWorld, and the MCP Quest, and performed below average on the Challenges.

All students from this cluster replied to the player characterization questionnaire, where all were male, and 55% affirmed they played games every day. Furthermore, 45% considered to be something between hardcore and casual gamers, 64% preferred single player games over multiplayer, and all of them confirmed that the personal computer where the device they played the most with. All students stated they usually played with the computer and 55% also with videogame consoles. Yet, 91% considered they usually did not play with portable videogame consoles, 82% with tablets, 73% with smartphones. The most played type of game played by these students were RPGs. The most common BrainHex classes were the Conqueror for the main class (36%) and the Conqueror, the Daredevil and the Mastermind (27% each) for the secondary class.

DISCUSSION

By analyzing student data from our experiment we identified different student profiles, each with different gaming habits and different approaches towards our course. In order to improve the knowledge about our students, and be able to better shape our learning experience according to their needs, we will answer two research questions: 1) what characterizes the four clusters and how do they compare to each other, and 2) how do their gaming habits relate to their performance and preferences in the course.

Student Characterization

Cluster A was the smallest, and it was composed by students that did all they could to get XP – they wanted to collect every single achievement in the game. This was the only cluster acquiring 100% of all grade reserved for challenges, the Skill Tree, the MCP Quest, and all achievements. They also scored almost the maximum grade on AvatarWorld, had the best lab grade, and were the most proactive and participative in terms of posts. They made the most rated posts in an effort to get as much XP as they could get, which is reflected by their rating/#posts ratio, which is the lowest (0.078). As a result, these students had the highest mean final grade. Because these students went after every achievement and XP they could get, we named them the *Achievers*. These students seem to have benefited the most from the gamified components of the course.

Cluster B was the largest cluster, which included almost 43% of the students. These students' lab grade was almost as high as that of the Achievers, and they had the highest multimedia presentation grade and exam grade. Their performance on game components like the challenges, the MCP Quest, and achievements, was really close to that of the Achievers, but they worked significantly less for AvatarWorld and the Skill Tree. While they still managed to grab almost 65% of the total grade allocated to the Skill Tree, they only got 25% of that reserved for AvatarWorld. They were also significantly less participative than the Achievers, but yet managed to perform the second highest number of rated posts, in order to squeeze some additional XP. Thus, their rating/#posts ratio was the second lowest (0.119). Cluster B students represented the largest number of students in our course, which were characterized by high participation levels on almost every component, with the exception of AvatarWorld and the Skill Tree, and also high performance levels, slightly lower than those of cluster A. These students often ended the course with above average final grade (with the average being 75.38%). Because of these features, we named these the *Regular students*.

Cluster C was the second largest cluster, and it consisted of students that had poorer performance than the aforementioned two clusters, in every aspect except for the multimedia presentation, where they scored the second highest grade. These students still managed to grab around 70% of the grade allocated to challenges and to the MCP Quest, but their participation on the Skill Tree and AvatarWorld was rather low, which earned them respectively around 20% and 10% of the allocated grade. Cluster C students had the lowest number of first posts and the second lowest number of reply posts, which rendered them the cluster with the lowest proactivity levels. However, they still performed slightly more rated posts than cluster D and managed to get a mean post rating almost as high as that of the Regular students, which granted them with the second highest rating/#posts ratio (0.237). These students typically ended the course in a slightly below average final grade. Even though these students went after the XP available on challenges and the MCP Quest, they seemed generally uninterested by most of the other components. Because of this, we named them the *Halfhearted students*.

Cluster D was composed by the students with the poorest performance. They had the lowest grades on the exam, the lab classes, the multimedia presentation, and also on the challenges, the MCP Quest, the Skill Tree and the AvatarWorld. These students seem to have ignored most of the game components of the game, having scored only 44% of the XP allocated for the achievements. They had the lowest mean final grade (55.67%), slightly above the minimum required to pass the course (50%). These students also had the lowest participation values, even though they were similar to cluster C in terms of first posts. They also performed the fewest rated posts, but really made them count, with an average rating of 3. Thus, they presented the highest rating/#posts ratio (0.397). Given their low performance we named these students the *Underachievers*.

Our data suggests that our students are structured into four tiers, each representing four distinct levels of performance. Halfhearted students and Underachievers seem to be easily identifiable in comparison with each other and with the Achievers and the Regular students, as they present very distinct levels of final grade and grade earned from achievements. This is easily observable by taking a look at their final ranking at the end of the course (see Figure 6), where they seem to occupy distinct areas of the bottom half of the leaderboard. However, it is harder to tell the Achievers and the Regular students apart, as they equally shared the top 1/3 of the leaderboard. The differences in terms of final grade and grade earned from achievements are not significant; what changes is how they achieved those grades.

Achievers put a lot of effort in every game component of the course, acquiring 100% of the XP allocated to them, but they were also the best on the lab classes. On the other hand, Regular students performed close to the Achievers on most achievements and game components, with the exception of the Skill Tree and AvatarWorld, but were still able to make up for it by having the best scores on the multimedia presentation and the exam. This allowed both student types to share the same position of the leaderboard, because they accumulated similar levels of XP through different paths.

Distinguishing the Halfhearted students and the Underachievers is easier, as both presented a gradual loss of

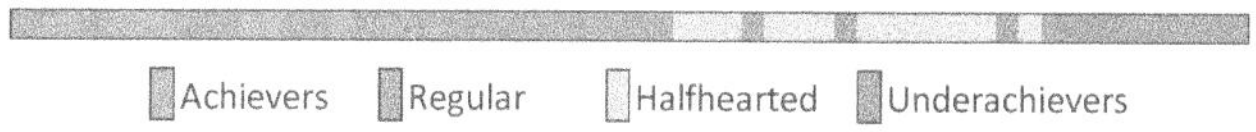

Figure 6. Final student ranking, with the first position on the far left.

performance in almost all evaluation components. However, the Halfhearted students tried to grab XP from both the challenges and the MCP Quest, which were usually easier to attain than participating on the Skill Tree and AvatarWorld. Consequently, these two components were mostly ignored. On the other hand, Underachievers seem to have ignored most of the game aspect of the course and focused solely on getting just enough XP to pass.

Student Gamer Profiling

Most student types preferred multiplayer over single player games. The exception were the Underachievers, whose majority preferred single player games. Coincidently, these students also had the worst performance, but further statistical analysis must be carried out to understand any effect of this factor over student performance.

Most students considered themselves to be something between a hardcore and a casual gamer, which we considered normal was it was a middle ground between both. Still, Regular students had the largest incidence of students considering themselves as casual gamers, and they also affirmed that they played weekly rather than daily, as compared to the other student types. Coincidently, this was also the cluster with the largest female population, which suggests that the greater incidence of female students might have rendered this cluster as playing less frequently. We found a weak correlation between gender and being an hardcore gamer or not (Cramer's V coefficient, $\varphi_c = 0.324$), and between gender and frequency of play ($\varphi_c = 0.288$), which weakly suggests that female students might have considered themselves as being more casual gamers than male students and as playing less too. Interestingly, we also found significant differences in terms of grades between genders (Mann Whitney's U test, $p < 0.02$), with girls having an average grade of 85.03% as compared to the boys' 72.72%.

Most students played the most with the computer, but video game consoles were also very predominant. The Achievers typically preferred to play RPGs the most and their predominant main class were the Socializer and the Mastermind. While Socializers usually prefer multiplayer experiences where they can hangout and collaborate with people, Mastermind players typically enjoy strategic play. We deem our experience has being potentially more appealing for these two types of BrainHex players, given that the inherent experience is collective and that different strategies can be employed to achieve the top grade, by exploring different paths and thr rule system.

Regular students typically preferred RTS games and their main BrainHex classes were the Achiever and the

Mastermind. Again, Mastermind players like to use strategy to overcome obstacles, and Achievers like to complete tasks and collections. We believe that our experience might also have been very appealing to this type of students, given the wide variety of achievements, Skill Tree nodes and challenges to explore and complete.

Both the Halfhearted students and the Underachievers presented a similar configuration regarding their BrainHex classification, with the main class being the Conqueror. Conqueror players usually enjoy defeating difficulty foes and beating other players. We believe that our gamified experience was not appealing to this type of player, given that there was never a concrete opponent to defeat and to struggle against. This might have been an additional factor contributing to the reduced engagement of these two student types, which might have contributed to their reduced performance.

Study Limitations

This study has a few limitations, mostly related to the small size of our sample, which caused one of the clusters to have as few as 7 students. This makes it hard to drawn any major conclusions from this study. However, it is still an important and valuable contribution to help us better understanding how different students experience gamified learning and how their gaming habits may potentially influence their behavior.

CONCLUSIONS AND FUTURE WORK

In a previous experiment we had gamified an engineering MSc course, where course tasks were encapsulated into meaningful challenges and game elements like experience points, levels, badges, and a leaderboard were added. A thorough study showed that students participated more and could perform better with our course, and that they also considered it more motivating and interesting than other non-gamified courses.

In this paper we presented a new study where we collected and analyzed data regarding the students' performance in the course and also regarding their gaming habits and preferences, in order to find how different types of students experienced our new learning method. We performed cluster analysis in our data and four types of students became apparent: the Achievers, who strived to collect every achievement in the game; the Regular students, who had good overall performance but avoided some of the more demanding game components; the Halfhearted students, whose interest by the course was limited and usually performed below average on most aspects; and the Underachievers, who performed the worst and did just enough to pass the course. These students were also characterized by distinct gaming habits. For instance, Regular students seem to play less often than other student types, and also seem to be predominantly classified as Mastermind and Achievers, according to the BrainHex types. Our Achievers, on the other hand, were classified as the BrainHex's Socializer and Mastermind classes, while the Halfhearted students and the Underachievers were labeled as the Conqueror.

Not only did this study enrich our understanding about how different students might address gamified learning, and how their gaming preferences might relate to how they experience it, but it also laid valuable groundwork for future research. We would like to further explore more possible correlations between the BrainHex classes and what students enjoy doing in the course, and study how this could be used to make the system adapt to them. Furthermore, we would like to perform a more thorough statistical analysis to unveil potential correlations between student performance and their gaming preferences.

ACKNOWLEDGEMENTS

This work was supported by FCT (INESC-ID multiannual funding) under project PEst-OE/EEI/LA0021/2013 and the project PAELife, reference AAL/0014/2009. Gabriel Barata was supported by FCT, grant SFRH/BD/72735/2010.

REFERENCES

1. Gabriel Barata, Sandra Gama, Manuel J. Fonseca, and Daniel Gonçalves. Improving student creativity with gamification and virtual worlds. In *Proc. Gamification 2013*, 95–98, 2013.
2. Gabriel Barata, Sandra Gama, Joaquim Jorge, and Daniel Gonçalves. Improving participation and learning with gamification. In *Proc. of Gamification 2013*, 9–16, 2013.
3. Richard Bartle. Hearts, clubs, diamonds, spades: Players who suit muds. *Journal of MUD research*, 1(1):19, 1996.
4. Richard A Bartle. *Designing virtual worlds*. New Riders, 2004.
5. Chris Bateman and Richard Boon. *21st Century Game Design (Game Development Series)*. Charles River Media, Inc., Rockland, MA, USA, 2005.
6. Chris Bateman and Lennart E. Nacke. The neurobiology of play. In *Proc. of Futureplay '10*, 1–8, ACM, 2010.
7. Philipp Brauner, André Calero Valdez, Ulrik Schroeder, and Martina Ziefle. Increase physical fitness and create health awareness through exergames and gamification. In Andreas Holzinger, Martina Ziefle, Martin Hitz, and Matjaž Debevc, editors, *Human Factors in Computing and Informatics*, volume 7946 of *Lecture Notes in Computer Science*, pages 349–362. Springer Berlin Heidelberg, 2013.
8. Arthur P Dempster, Nan M Laird, and Donald B Rubin. Maximum likelihood from incomplete data via the em algorithm. *Journal of the Royal Statistical Society. Series B (Methodological)*, 1–38, 1977.
9. Sebastian Deterding, Dan Dixon, Rilla Khaled, and Lennart Nacke. From game design elements to

gamefulness: defining "gamification". In *Proc. of MindTrek '11*, volume Tampere, F, 9–15. ACM, 2011.

10. Sebastian Deterding, Miguel Sicart, Lennart Nacke, Kenton O'Hara, and Dan Dixon. Gamification. using game-design elements in non-gaming contexts. In *Proc. CHI EA '11*, 2425–2428, ACM, 2011.

11. Adrián Domínguez, Joseba Saenz-de Navarrete, Luis de Marcos, Luis Fernández-Sanz, Carmen Pagés, and José-Javier Martínez-Herráiz. Gamifying learning experiences: Practical implications and outcomes. *Computers & Education*, 63(0):380 – 392, 2013.

12. Tao Dong, Mira Dontcheva, Diana Joseph, Karrie Karahalios, Mark Newman, and Mark Ackerman. Discovery-based games for learning software. In *Proc. of CHI '12*, 2083–2086, ACM, 2012.

13. Zachary Fitz-Walter, Peta Wyeth, Dian Tjondronegoro, and Bridie Scott-Parker. Driven to drive: Designing gamification for a learner logbook smartphone application. In *Proc. of Gamification 2013*, 42–49, 2013.

14. James Paul Gee. What video games have to teach us about learning and literacy. *Comput. Entertain.*, 1(1):20–20, October 2003.

15. O. Inbar, N. Tractinsky, O. Tsimhoni, and T. Seder. Driving the scoreboard: Motivating eco-driving through in-car gaming. In *Proc. of the CHI 2011 Workshop Gamification: Using Game Design Elements in Non-Game Contexts*. ACM, 2011.

16. Wei Li, Tovi Grossman, and George Fitzmaurice. Gamicad: a gamified tutorial system for first time autocad users. In *Proc. of UIST '12*, 103–112, ACM, 2012.

17. Isabel Briggs Myers and Mary H McCaulley. *Myers-Briggs Type Indicator: MBTI.* Consulting Psychologists Press, 1988.

18. Lennart E. Nacke, Chris Bateman, and Regan L. Mandryk. Brainhex: Preliminary results from a neurobiological gamer typology survey. In *Proc. of ICEC '11*, 288-293, 2011.

19. L. Natvig, S. Line, and A. Djupdal. "age of computers"; an innovative combination of history and computer game elements for teaching computer fundamentals. In *In proc. of FIE 2004*, volume 3, S2F – 1–6, 2004.

20. B. Reeves and J.L. Read. *Total Engagement: How Games and Virtual Worlds Are Changing the Way People Work and Businesses Compete*. Harvard Business Press, 2009.

21. Narendra Sharma, Aman Bajpai, and Mr Ratnesh Litoriya. Comparison the various clustering algorithms of weka tools. *facilities*, 4:7, 2012.

22. L. Sheldon. *The Multiplayer Classroom: Designing Coursework as a Game*. Course Technology PTR, 2011.

23. S. Sheth, J. Bell, and G. Kaiser. Halo (highly addictive, socially optimized) software engineering. In *Proc. of GAS '11*, volume 11, 29–32, 2011.

24. B. Shneiderman. Designing for fun: how can we design user interfaces to be more fun? *interactions*, 11(5):48–50, 2004.

25. G. Zichermann and C. Cunningham. *Gamification by Design: Implementing Game Mechanics in Web and Mobile Apps*. O'Reilly Media, Inc., 2011.

Paradigms of Games Research in HCI: A Review of 10 Years of Research at CHI

Marcus Carter, John Downs, Bjorn Nansen, Mitchell Harrop and Martin Gibbs
Interaction Design Lab and Microsoft Centre for Social NUI
Computing and Information Systems
The University of Melbourne
marcusc | jpdowns | nansenb | mharrop | martin.gibbs | @unimelb.edu.au

ABSTRACT
In this paper we argue that games and play research in the field of Human-Computer Interaction can usefully be understood as existing within 4 distinct research paradigms. We provide our rationale for developing these paradigms and discuss their significance in the context of the inaugural CHI Play conference.

Author Keywords
Human-computer interaction; Game Studies; paradigms.

ACM Classification Keywords
K.8.0 [**Personal Computing**]: General – *Games*.

INTRODUCTION
The study of games, gaming and play is now an established domain of research within the field of human-computer interaction (HCI). However, this sub-domain, which has been referred to as 'Player-Computer Interaction' (PCI), remains marginalized; authors of PCI studies are frequently challenged to justify their work as HCI or situate it within the context of, or articulate its contribution to, non-game/play HCI work. This is in contrast to games research in many other disciplines which staunchly defend games as artifacts worthy of study in their own right.

With the founding of the CHI Play conference, such justifications look to become unnecessary. After all, a study of HCI in a business context does not need to justify its contributions to the study of HCI in a gaming context. Alternatively, the separation of PCI from 'mainstream' HCI conferences may work to further marginalize games-related work to the periphery of HCI. We argue studies of PCI are legitimate works of human-computer interaction inquiry. The purpose of this paper is to chart what games and play HCI research *is* in the context of other HCI work, in order to better understand what constitutes PCI – and how this differs from games research conducted elsewhere.

CHI PLAY'14, October 19–21, 2014, Toronto, ON, Canada.

http://dx.doi.org/10.1145/2658537.2658708

In order to accomplish this, we identified all research on the topic of games, gaming and play that has been published at the SIGCHI Conference on Human Factors in Computing Systems (CHI) between 2003 and 2013 (178 papers). Using a process of open and axial coding, we identified a number of discrete research domains of PCI, which we argue can be usefully conceptualized into four paradigms of research. These paradigms are:

Operative games research that leverages knowledge gained from the study of games or play to exert control upon the world, such as encouraging exercise or learning.

Epistemological games research that uses games as a vehicle for understanding the use of *all* technologies, rather than only in the context of the unique modes of interactions or affordances of games and play, such as virtual embodiment or interfaces.

Ontological games research that is concerned with the design and understanding of the ontology of games; rules, aesthetic, interfaces, fiction and game design patterns.

Practice games research that is concerned with the emergent practices and experiences that occur as a result of interaction with games or toys, or when interacting with technology with a lusory attitude [44].

We argue these paradigms are useful for understanding what is happening in contemporary HCI as research on play, games and gaming expands as a legitimate and popular domain of research. We note how each of these paradigms places games and play in a different conceptual arena, consequently leading to differences in typical research questions, fields of research and methods employed. These paradigms are not independent, but an awareness of these differences will serve to better help HCI scholars contextualize their research, understand what it means to do HCI research on games, gaming and play, and to understand some informal conflicts directed at and internal to the HCI field.

Our paper begins with a review of literature that has engaged with the perilous task of defining or describing the broader field of HCI, a foundation that we later draw on to indicate the relationship between PCI and HCI as it has previously been understood. Following an explanation and justification of the methods we used in this review of the CHI literature, we describe the different PCI research domains presented at CHI and highlight their methodological and conceptual approaches to the phenomena studied. On this foundation we describe and provide examples of the four research paradigms, and then discuss the manner in which awareness of these paradigms is constructive for future scholarship.

As well as discussing the results of this systematic review of CHI play literature, we will discuss the broader transdisciplinary field of Game Studies and its intersections with HCI in the context of our review. The purpose of this discussion is to assist HCI scholars involved with research on games and play in contextualizing their research within principally humanities-based games research. Each of these contributions serves to coalesce existing scholarship at the foundation of our own independent conference; CHI Play.

RELATED WORK

The Interdiscipline of Human Computer Interaction

The aims of this paper are threefold. First, we wish to understand what constitutes HCI research on games and play. Second, we want to understand PCI is integrated with other HCI research. Finally, we want to understand what distinguishes PCI from other work in the broad field of Game Studies. Through accomplishing these aims, we hope to better articulate the contributions of PCI work to both HCI and Game Studies, as well as encouraging reflection on how these distinctions influence ongoing work.

Consequently, in order to do this, we must establish some form of understanding regarding what 'HCI' is. Reflecting the transdisciplinary, eclectic and fluctuating history of the field, such an endeavor is complicated. In order to acknowledge this, we purposefully avoid specific, encompassing definitions in this paper.

Largely, HCI as a discipline emerged in the late 1970's, a period of which has since been referred to by John Carroll [7] as HCI's *golden age*, because "*there was a wide tacit agreement as to the overarching research paradigm*" [7, p.3]. This '*vision*' was "*to bring cognitive science methods and theories to bear on software development*" [7, p. 3]. Indeed, HCI was formed out of the traditions of cognitive and experimental psychology, and historically was primarily concerned with notions of task efficiency, work performance, ease of use, and utility [19].

In recent years, however, HCI researchers have begun to broaden the application areas that are considered to be worthy of research attention [21, 4]. At the same time, the methods and approaches used in HCI have expanded beyond those used in experimental psychology and now include a range of social science methods and techniques such as ethnography, ethnomethodology, and a number of other qualitative research tools [3, 14].

HCI is now concerned as much with experiential qualities such as pleasure, human values, and supporting sociality as it is with utility and ease of use. Technologies to support playfulness are explicitly within the boundaries of this redefined HCI, and research frequently considers the design and evaluation of games and other technologies for play.

The Polyphonic Discipline of Game Studies

While research on games fits within this more experientially-oriented HCI, the design-driven approach to games within HCI maintains a distinction to the broader field of Game Studies. Research in Game Studies draws on a wide range of social science and humanities methods and traditions including literary, film and media studies, communication studies, sociology, anthropology and psychology. It is, then, a field composed of many voices, or as Frans Mäyrä has recently articulated, a polyphonic discipline [33].

Based on these diverse histories, the relatively nascent field of Game Studies does not limit its focus to the structure, functionality or design of games, but instead pays serious attention to games as cultural artifacts and ludic activities worthy of study in their own right. Consequently, Game Studies have emphasized the importance of games titles, player experiences, game cultures and the contexts of game play [32]. This focus has helped to produce accounts and debates around the aesthetics, cultural meanings and economic value of digital games.

Today, the commercial success and social popularity of digital games has helped to legitimize their independent study. As an increasingly formalized and distinct discipline, Games Studies continues to draw on its diverse traditions as well as evolve through ongoing theoretical discussions and methodological approaches to games. For example, and of increasing relevance to PCI research, what has been described as a material turn within Games Studies is highlighting the significance of the embodied experiences, political economies, and technical platforms that constitute game play [1].

METHOD

In order to identify the relevant papers for this literature review, we used the following Boolean search string in the ACM Digital Library:

((Title:game*) or (Title:gaming*) or (Title:play*) or (Abstract:game*) or (Abstract:gaming*) or (Abstract:play*)) and (PublicationTitle:SIGCHI Conference on Human Factors in Computing Systems) and PublishedAs:proceeding)

This search identifies all articles published in CHI proceedings that have either 'game*' (games, gamer etc), 'gaming*' or 'play*' (playing, player etc) in the title or abstract of the paper. We note that this automated method may have overlooked a small number of papers (for example, on virtual worlds), but we feel that not mentioning any of these terms in either the title or abstract is indicative of research unintegrated with literature relevant to CHI Play, therefore not diminishing our review.

This search resulted in 316 papers from the CHI proceedings between 2003 and 2013. In performing the first step of analysis, we identified 138 papers that were not relevant to this literature review but that had been identified by the search string that we used. A large component of these were HCI studies in the field of music technologies (*playing* music), while others were flagged for phrases such as '*the role that X plays in…*' These papers were discarded as being not relevant to our aims. Any discards were verified by a second researcher.

In accordance with a grounded theory-inspired methodology, we performed iterative open coding on the remaining 178 papers to identify different categories of research, followed by axial coding of these categories for underlying themes. The research paradigms presented emerged out of this coding. Practically this took the form of three workshops involving the authors of this paper. Open coding during the first workshop involved tangible copies of the papers being distributed, discussed, and placed in piles with similar papers. Descriptions for these groups were constructed and noted. These categories were then clustered into the "genres" detailed in the next section. At a second workshop, these categories were axially coded for qualities such as methodology, instrumentalisation of games or play, aims, justifications as HCI, CHI conference sessions, integration with literature and so forth. The third workshop then focused on analyzing these axial themes and reconciling them into coherent and useful clusters based on discernible patterns in the approach to research taken in each paper. These discernible patterns formed the basis for the identification and development of our paradigms. It should be noted that in the process papers remained with the categories initially assigned to them, but the categories were shuffled to reflect different affinities between categories as they became apparent through the process of analysis.

RESULTS

Before reporting the results of our analysis, we note that the volume of game- or play-related work at the CHI conference has grown over the past decade, in tandem with the corresponding growth of CHI. As a percentage (see Figure 1), PCI work typically reflects between 5-10% of the overall proceedings. Of note is 2006, which had a peak not being matched again until 2012. We suspect these percentages do not reflect the actual quantity of games research being conducted by HCI academics.

Open Coding: Categories of HCI Games Research

Our first workshop involved open coding and categorization of the literature, a collaborative and sometimes heated process. This process resulted in 21 separate categories of research emerging, each thematically similar in its treatment or approach to the game, gaming or playing phenomena. At the conclusion, these were grouped into similar genres. We will present each of these with a brief overview. Later in the paper we will examine and discuss these categories in more detail, and reflect on what they imply for games research in HCI.

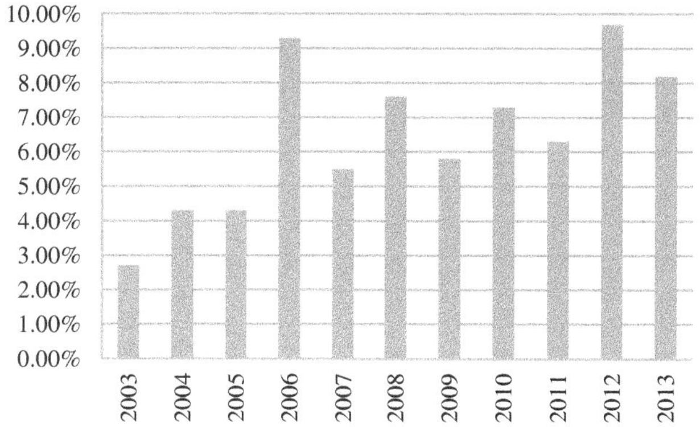

Figure 1. Percentage of CHI proceedings concerning games or play, 2003-2013.

***Games for a Purpose* (n=60)**

By far the largest of our clusters (33.7%), games for a purpose included papers that focused on the study or design of games for normative benefit beyond the ostensive benefits from games as normally played; such as health, exercise, volunteerism, education and data collection.

As can be seen in Figure 2 below, the absolute numbers of 'games for a purpose' papers have increased dramatically in recent years. As a percentage of the number of games related work in the CHI proceedings, it has also increased; games for a purpose has become the dominant form of HCI research on games since 2010.

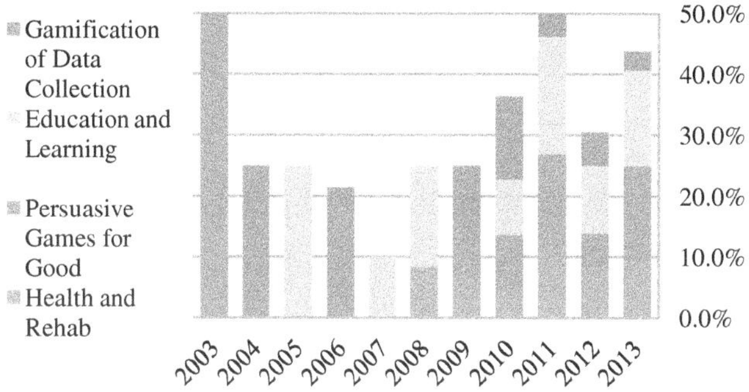

Figure 2. PCI papers in the CHI Proceedings categorized into the 'Games for a Purpose' genre, 2003-2013. There were only 2 papers in 2003.

Health & Rehabilitation (12): Research pertaining to the application of games for broader health concerns. These studies were design- and evaluation-oriented, and were typically presented as leveraging the entertainment appeal of digital games for interventionist health benefit, such as rehabilitation [6].

Persuasive Games for Good (15): Research concerned with the positive, persuasive potential for games. While health was a dominant focus, it was passive rather than interventionist. This category was dominated by 'exergame' research [35] but also included topics around behavior change, such as volunteerism [24]

Education & Learning (20): Research concerned with educational games, again leveraging the interest in [13] or entertainment appeal of games for learning and education. Distinct from persuasive games, these were typically interventionist rather than passive. Research focused on the design and evaluation of the learning or education benefit to participants. In contrast, only one study [23] was interested in how players learnt the game, as opposed to an external learning benefit.

Gamification of Data Collection (13): As opposed to the other three categories in this genre, concerned with designing games for the benefit of the player, this category leveraged the appeal of digital games for the benefit of someone other than the player, such as social networking systems metadata [e.g., 27] or web accessibility [e.g., 45].

***Games for Play* (n=33)**

Research in this second genre concerned the study and design of games with regards to their distinguishing mode of interaction: play. This included research reflecting game development, play studies, as well as game design methods and evaluations. Figure 3 suggests a growth and decline of this genre over the past 10 years as a percentage of our identified PCI work at CHI.

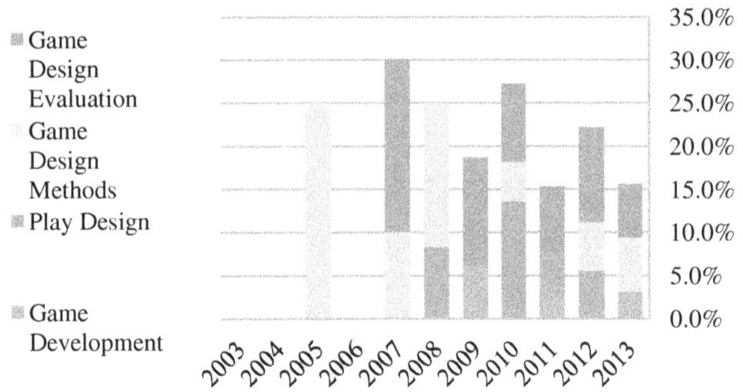

Figure 3. PCI papers in the CHI Proceedings categorized into the 'Games for Play' genre.

Game Development (3): Research in which the focus of the paper was the design and subsequent evaluation of a game. These were distinct from other categories as the evaluation was in the context of in-game experience, rather than health benefit or learning.

Play Design (7): Research where the focus of the paper was on designing for 'free' play, as opposed to game-based play. This included studies like Lindley *et al.* [29] that reported incidental play from a platform design, and studies that explicitly sought to design free-play [e.g., 47].

Game Design Methods (9): Research which, rather than reporting the design and evaluation of a game, presented design methodologies (such as ethnography, [50]), techniques [48] or games-user research [34] *for* the broader design of digital games for gameplay experience (ostensibly fun rather than, say, learning or health outcomes).

Game Design Evaluation (14): This research was concerned with the evaluation of granular aspects of game design and experience. These studies were significantly more experimental, concerning controlled studies (e.g., comparing 3D and 2D displays [30]) or evaluating the impact of very specific facets of games (such as narrative [9] or challenge [10].

***Domain Specific Games Research* (n=34)**

As consequence of our iterative, grounded methodology, many of the categories that emerged were placed into their research domains such as location based games, tangible and tabletop games, public screens and play, game spectatorship and digital storytelling. In making these judgments, we drew upon our awareness of prominent research in these domains in other conferences (such as CSCW) and HCI journals. Many of these studies could have been categorized as *Game Design Methods* [e.g. 46] or *Education and Learning* [e.g. 22], but were not in accordance with the way the core contribution of the paper was articulated. This will be further justified and explored later in the paper. Figure 4 depicts the early dominance of domain specific games research in PCI work as a percentage of our sample.

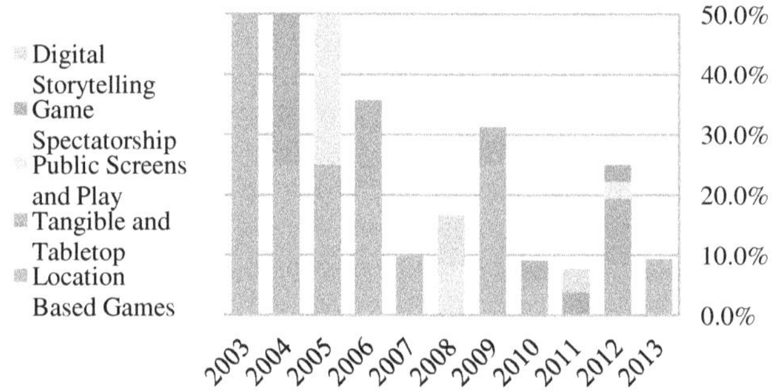

Figure 4. PCI papers in the CHI Proceedings categorized into the 'Domain Specific' genre.

Location Based Games (18): Research on location based (typically mobile) games, including augmented reality games. This research reflected 10% of our sample. They included game development studies, design methods and evaluations – underrepresented research in the 'games for purpose' genre.

Tangible & Tabletop Games (9): Whereas the majority of other research that we have described has pertained to virtual games, research in this category involved the design and evaluation of tangible hybrid digital games. This encompassed games for learning (e.g., interactive tabletop exhibits in museums, [22]) and early work was heavily integrated with the HCI domain of tangible computing.

Public Screens & Play (3): Research on games and play on public screens. Like tangible and tabletop games research, this work was prominently contextualized within HCI research on public computing. These were concerned with the context of gaming [e.g. 39], motivated by behavior change [*à la* persuasive games, 2] and control systems [20].

Games Spectatorship (2): This research was distinct in that its concern was with the spectatorship of, rather than interaction with, games.

Digital Storytelling (2): Research concerned with the role of narrative and potential for digital storytelling in the context of games and play.

***Interaction Design* (n=33)**
Distinguished from 'Games for Play' above, this genre of PCI research involved work approaching games or play in-line with the HCI sub-discipline of Interaction Design, into which we categorized both interface design and interaction studies. The prominence of this work at CHI has varied over the past 10 years, as reflected in Chart 5.

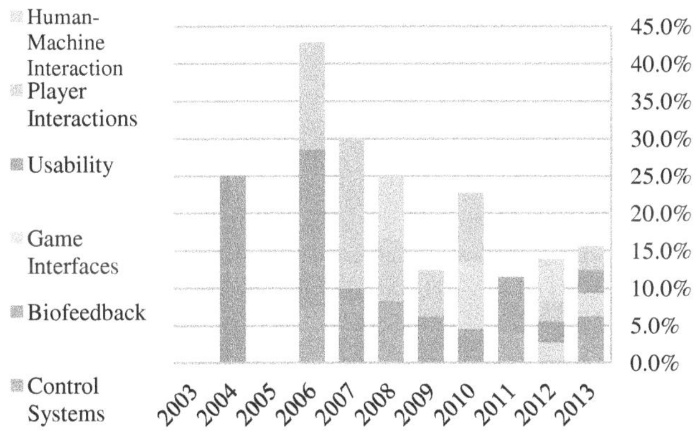

Figure 5. PCI papers in the CHI Proceedings categorized into the 'Interaction Design' genre.

Control Systems (4): Research on game control systems, such as controllers and motion-based input devices.

Biofeedback (9): Control systems research in the HCI domain of biosignal and biofeedback research (e.g., heart rate as an input device [36]). Unlike games for purpose research, all of this work was presented in the context of digital game design, ostensibly for 'fun', or normatively positive experiences within the bounds of gameplay.

Game Interfaces (4): Research on game interfaces and displays, such as the IllumiRoom [25]. This work is typically presented in the context of games for enjoyment.

Usability (3): Research on usability issues facing digital games. There are, however, no studies in the context of disabilities, which is prominent in the field of HCI usability and accessibility studies (although somewhat related was Pinelle et. al. [40]).

Player Interactions (10): Research concerning both the study of and design for player interactions during the play of digital games (encompassing both collocated and distributed players). These studies encompassed novel game development [e.g., 18] as well as the evaluation of existing games [e.g., 16], and interactions such as cooperation, commitment and intimacy.

Human-Machine Interaction (3): Human-Agent/Human-Robot interaction research (such as artificial team-mate research) in the context of game-play.

***Experience* (n=14)**
This smaller genre of PCI research represents an important perspective on virtual embodiment and the emotional, personal experiences of playing games. The prominence of this work over time is harder to gauge due to the smaller numbers involved and hence we have omitted a graph for this genre. However, there does appear to have been a decline, from a high of 20% in 2007, to only 6% in 2013.

Embodiment (6): Research on embodiment, both in the context of Natural User Interface (NUI) technologies and avatar design and personalization and the impact of embodiment on experience. Some [e.g., 17] contextualized within games for learning (impact of embodiment on learning) while most drew lessons for future designs of games and virtual environments.

Gamer Behaviour (8): Studies of player-behavior within online games, again pertaining to normatively positive experiences within the bounds of gameplay (rather than for health or learning). Overwhelmingly research categorized here was quantitative, including both in-game data analysis as well as 'big data' surveys.

Miscellaneous (4)

Further to these, we found four papers that we did not feel could be suitably categorized with any of the aforementioned 21 sub-categories. These outliers fit the scope of a conference like CHI Play, but were unique; Pace et al's [38] study of *World of Warcraft* machinima, Cassidy et al's [8] study on game genres, Lomas et al's [31] study on the use of outdated computers, which encompassed co-located game play on 8bit computers, and Wang et al's [49] study of virtual currency in game worlds. We note that three of these four outliers were published in the 2013 CHI proceedings, potentially indicating a growing acceptance of broader, non-operational research in games-HCI work, and that none of these papers would have been out of place in a games specific journal or conference.

REFLECTION

Before we move on to the analysis and discussion of our literature review, we wish to reflect on some cursory insights that have affected our subsequent theory development, and discuss some of the limitations of our methods and how this has affected the way the 178 PCI papers from CHI have been categorized.

In the previous section we have presented the 21 categorizations and 4 genres that emerged out of three workshops, where physical copies of each paper were briefly read, discussed and categorized by the authors of this paper. As noted, and in accordance with our methodology, this process was iterative, and this process was unavoidably subjective, but the use of multiple independent categorizations by different researchers and discussion of categories gives us confidence that our categorizations are reliable and repeatable. Rather than establishing specific criteria for each category, we independently placed similar papers together and allowed themes to define these categories to emerge through discussion and debate. Several papers could also have legitimately been placed into several categories, but we decided to categorize each paper once, and placed each paper according to how the paper articulated its core contribution.

Consequently, the quantitative data presented so far is only included in the context of this iterative, subjective process; we do not mean to suggest our analysis has uncovered objectively definable categories of PCI research. Rather, we consider them useful indicators of volumes of research in comparison to one another, revealing interesting longitudinal changes that encourage particular points of discussion in the subsequent sections. Further, we do not present these categorizations as the limit of genres, but to indicate the methodology of our literature review and how this contributed to the development of our paradigms.

We also note that some distinct domains were largely populated by specific researchers (and their colleagues). While this does not demonstrate large communities of HCI researchers working in this area, or established traditions of PCI work beyond individual labs or researchers, it is a reflection of these researchers' prominence in the broader games research community, and the strength of their work *as HCI* in the eyes of the CHI reviewers.

PARADIGMS OF GAMES AND PLAY RESEARCH IN HCI

Drawing on the insights from these categories and genres, we then reexamined to the literature in order to develop useful theory to better understand the various forms and strategies of HCI work involving games, game technologies and play. Echoing Harrison et al. [21], we consequently present four paradigms that assist us in understanding differences between PCI work, as well as the relationships between HCI, PCI and broader work in the transdisciplinary field of Game Studies. These are not intended to map one-to-one to our previous categorizations.

We adopt Rogers et al.'s [41 p. 55] definition of a paradigm as "*a general approach that has been adopted by a community of researchers and designers for carrying out their work, in terms of shared assumptions, concepts, values, and practices*". They also suggest that to follow a paradigm means "*adopting a set of practices that a community has agreed upon*", including what research questions get asked, how those research questions are framed, what is chosen to be studied, and how findings are analyzed and interpreted [41, p.55]. Our use of paradigm is meant to suggest discernable patterns in research approaches and is not meant to suggest that the identified approaches to games research are radical departures from one another and "*incommensurable*" in the Kuhnian sense of the term. Despite the short history of HCI, we feel our paradigms reflect emergent consensus on approaches, foci, and justifications.

The First Paradigm – Operative

The first and most clearly distinguished paradigm that we identified in the course of this literature review is HCI research that uses games, play, or games research as an operative instrument for achieving extrinsic goals or objectives that are peripheral to what is normally within the bounds of game playing (e.g., leisure, fun or social interaction). All examples of games research within this paradigm that we identified (contained within the 'games for purpose' genre) instrumentalize games for a normative benefit: improved health or rehabilitation; increased learning; engagement with fitness; or for collecting data.

By operative, we refer to the way in which research in this paradigm is framed as using games, or facets or insights from games, as an instrument or tool for achieving external (i.e. non play or non-fun) goals. The shared values of researchers in this paradigm are consequently not focused on the study of games, per say, or for the inherent value of simply understanding them better. Rather, this research is focused on questions concerned with how to use the appeal of games for more 'worthy' or valuable endeavors.

One curious distinction we noted within this paradigm is found in the work that operationalizes games for data collection [e.g., 27, 45], which is distinct from other HCI research in this paradigm. Whereas games for health, exercise or education focus on improving the health, fitness or knowledge of the *player*, games for the collection of data operationalize the appeal of game playing for the benefit of an external third party. Though this can be symbiotic, this is an interesting ethical distinction.

Within this paradigm is the popular field of gamification research, defined by Deterding et al. [12] as "*the use of game design elements in non-game contexts*". Despite the overwhelmingly positive intent of most gamification research, this type of work receives significant amount of criticism from non-HCI games researchers, particularly those in the humanities and the supposedly polyphonic Game Studies discipline [e.g., see 5]. These critiques often describe 'gamification' as a marketing gimmick, as obscuringly reductive, concerningly evangelistic, or as fundamentally flawed [26].

Without dismissing the content of these critiques, we consider the negative reputation of gamification work a consequence of the way in which games and play are situated within these studies. The research questions asked, how those research questions are framed, and what is studied in this first paradigm emerge out of (or at least imply) a suggestion that the typical normative benefit of gameplay (fun or leisure) is not sufficiently 'good', and additional benefits must be incorporated in order to justify study. The negative reputation that this type of research has outside of HCI could be construed as a result of implying that non-instrumentalized play is of significantly reduced, or even insufficient, value or worth.

Despite this, the operative paradigm is a dominant form of PCI research. Based on the numbers of papers assigned to these categories during coding, operative PCI comprises over 40% of contemporary games research at CHI.

The Second Paradigm – Epistemological

The second paradigm that we feel is strongly distinguished from other PCI research is studies where games or play is used to generate insights into other areas and topics of study. This includes research identified as domain specific research, such as the work studying tabletop games for insight into tangible computing as well as public screen usage. This paradigm also contained research using games to investigate the embodiment, gamer behavior, control systems and biofeedback categories.

We reflected earlier in this paper on the fact that domain specific research has declined as a percentage of the overall games and play related papers in the CHI proceedings. While this also reflects the implication seen in *operative* games research that game play itself is not sufficient for study alone, and must be contextualized with some form of broader, non-game benefit, an alternative explanation can be suggested. Research on embodiment, for example, has perhaps been inevitably drawn towards games due to the fact that games offer the most technically advanced examples of widely engaged with virtual worlds. Thus, it is not so much that games are themselves insufficient for study and must make some external contribution to another domain of knowledge in order to be valuable research, but that games themselves have offered excellent opportunities for researchers interested in developing knowledge about non-game contexts. This could explain its early adoption.

Reflecting on the way we have presented this paradigm reveals our own prejudice. We consider games as an artifact that exists independently from other HCI artifacts. Both the process of engaging with games, and consequent demands for design, distinguish it from other contexts for research. If games and play are not fundamentally dissimilar to non-game, or non-playful interaction, explicating this as a distinct paradigm could obscure insights relevant for a wide variety of HCI research programs.

The Third Paradigm – Ontological

Distinct from these first two paradigms is ontological research, which draws on traditions in various HCI disciplines such as User Experience (UX) studies, interaction design and software engineering. This is research concerned with the design and evaluation of the ontology of games as objects, encompassing categories identified earlier in this paper such as game design, play design, as well as that research concerned with the design and evaluation of various categories in the interaction design genre, such as game interfaces or control systems.

As opposed to the first two paradigms that instrumentalize games within their research frameworks for peripheral purpose or benefit, research in this paradigm has the shared value of being concerned with the constituent parts of 'games' such as rules, fiction, interfaces, aesthetics and various game design patterns; missions, levels, rewards, modes and so forth, in the context of their lusory interaction and capacity to generate play.

The Fourth Paradigm – Practice

Similar to the third paradigm, and in contrast to the first two, research in this paradigm also studies games and play as objects worthy of study within the discipline of HCI, without instrumentalizing the research for insight beyond deepening our understanding of games and play as a unique site of study. However, rather than focusing on the game and its ontology (design, rules, control systems, embodiment and so forth), studies within this paradigm focus on the experience and consequent interactions between users that occur as a result of interaction with the game, or as a result of entering a lusory attitude.

This paradigm predominantly included studies of the behavior, experience, player interactions, and spectatorship categorizations summarized earlier in the paper. We note that papers within this paradigm were much more likely to engage with non-HCI, Game Studies literature and similarly much more likely to have been cited, or gained traction, in these fields. Thus we consider this paradigm to be the one with the closest alignment to Game Studies, represented at conferences like *DiGRA* and journals such as *Game Studies* and *Games and Culture*.

However, much of the HCI work we consider to be within this paradigm reflected a wider variety of methodologies than are common in Game Studies, in particular drawing on quantitative data such as big-data surveys or in-game data. Further, we noted that studies in this paradigm are not strictly devoid of design recommendations, and are more closely integrated with reconciling observations about play or gameplay with the affordances of the technology involved. Frequently, the discussion or later analysis within these studies will consider the relationship between emergent practices identified or studies and their implications for the design of games (or toys). This is a phenomenon previously identified and criticized in HCI [see 14] which we will discuss in the subsequent section.

DISCUSSION

In observation of the inaugural 2014 CHI Play conference, the purpose of this paper has been to understand the various forms and strategies of HCI research involving games, game technologies and play. This is an important contribution to the increasingly independent PCI sub-discipline as it allows researchers to look back and understand the types of games research accomplished in HCI, while also allowing researchers to look forward by suggesting important, yet neglected, topics for future research. In order to accomplish this, we collected and reviewed all games papers that have been accepted into the proceedings of the premier international HCI conference, CHI, in the past decade. In accordance with grounded theory, we employed open and axial coding to categorize this research in order to better understand how PCI work is contextualized *as* HCI work, and what divisions, if any, exist within the sub-field of PCI. This iterative coding process resulted in 21 categorizations placed into 4 genres of PCI research. These have been included in detail in this paper as we believe these (and the corresponding numerical values of published papers) are themselves insightful, but also in an effort to ensure our methodology is transparent.

Drawing on this analysis, we have suggested the existence of 4 paradigms of games research within the field of human computer interaction. We believe that the distinctions drawn between these paradigms are useful for understanding what is currently 'going on' in HCI and PCI games research, and for understanding various internal and external conflicts of relevance to researchers presenting at the inaugural 2014 CHI Play conference.

The first two of these paradigms, *Operative* and *Epistemological*, each instrumentalize games or play, or the study of games or play, for purposes peripheral to what is normally considered to be within the bounds or purposes of games or play. They are distinguished by purpose and focus. Whereas *epistemological* games research seeks to leverage the interest in or success of games for broader knowledge relevant to other systems of design or interaction (such as embodiment, or interfaces), *operative* games research seeks to understand how the interest in or success of games can be leveraged for the (ostensibly positive) exertion of influence, change or for control.

In contrast to these paradigms, games research in the *ontological* and *practice* paradigms are interested in games, play and games technology in the context of what makes them distinct from other forms of human computer interaction. *Ontological* research focuses on the ontology of games; rules, interfaces, fiction, aesthetics, game design patterns and so forth for the purposes of creating play experiences within the bounds of what is normally expected with games; fun or leisurely experiences. Similar to this were studies of *practice*; research concerned with the emergent interactions and experiences as a result of engagement with these ontologies. This is, perhaps, our narrowest distinction, but the difference between these two paradigms is most pronounced when considering their methodologies and engagement with (and popularity outside of) HCI work.

These paradigms are useful for understanding the emerging field of PCI for a number of reasons. Firstly, we have argued that both *operative* and *epistemological* paradigms implicitly devalue games as being unworthy of study in their own right, a suggestion of some consequence to *ontological* or *practice* games research. These distinctions, offer some explanation towards the hostility some game researchers (within and external to HCI) feel towards the first two paradigms.

We have noted that *operative* and *epistemological* games research is the most represented form of games research in the CHI proceedings, but that *ontological* and *practice* games research has risen rapidly over the past 6 years, being largely under-represented in the early half of our data set. We believe that this is reflective of the growing legitimacy of games as objects of independent value for study, the growing games industry, and the ascension of younger CHI reviewers who have grown up with (or themselves study) games or play. This is of note, as these changes are internal within games papers at CHI.

We believe this reiterates earlier observations by (non HCI) games researchers such as Greg Lastowka who notes that, in contemporary culture, play and games are "*defined in large part by their divergence from a superior form of action: productive labour*" [28]. He argues that academic discussions of games and play are haunted by the cause of this divergence – "*protestant capitalism*" [28] - that sees academic discussion of games devalued if lacking relevance to the pursuit of productive labor. For example, see Dabish et al.'s [11] justification of a *World of Warcraft* study in the context of business. We are not aware of any business-based HCI research that justifies their 'HCI-ness' in the context of their contribution to the study or understanding of games or play.

This has some similarity to Paul Dourish's [14] suggestion that ethnography in HCI was often seen as a requirements gathering task for the purposes of some larger software engineering endeavor. This has led to ethnographic studies in HCI being judged on or evaluated by their ability to generate 'implications for design' rather than on their own merits as pieces of ethnographic research regarding the use or influences of technology. We can argue this problem has persisted with games papers at CHI (while disappearing largely in other domains), with authors needing to include sections on implications for business practices or other fields despite their fieldwork being primarily concerned with games.

There is also a further influence upon the success or prominence of some PCI paradigms over others; research funding. It is worth speculating about whether the prominence and recent growth of *operative* research is due to how research funding is allocated, again attributable to the "*specter of Protestant capitalism*" [28]. Research grants suggesting we understand games better in order to make the broader world a better place is quite likely to be positively reviewed by national funding bodies and to fit national research priorities in comparison to research grants less tied to claims about extrinsic goals. We hope that with the growing interest of the games industry in PCI research, this influence becomes less pronounced.

Finally, these paradigms are useful for understanding the way in which our research's existence within these paradigms influences the sites of our study, the research questions asked, and the way this research is conducted. *Operative* games research is, by virtue of its shared values, research that performs action; contributions report the design and successful (or sometimes, unsuccessful) change to the world, be it through increasing learning, awareness, volunteerism, health or fitness. Similar to much 'hard-science' work, papers reporting the lack of success, or no results, were rare. Perhaps this is because of a perception that *operative* research 'fails' if control is not exerted upon the world. This research also raises ethical questions (which are reflected in some criticisms of 'games for change' [see 26]) in that studies investigate and reflect the potential for games to enact 'good', but not 'bad' upon the world.

The articulation of these paradigms prompts a further discussion of relevance to CHI Play in its inaugural year. The CFP for CHI Play reflects the majority of the topics of work we had identified, but there are notably some topics mentioned that we did not find in our review; studies of developers, casual game design studies, and tools for game creation. Is CHI, as its name suggests, a 'parent' conference for CHI Play? And if so, what kind of parent is it? Is CHI Play for research marginalized from mainstream HCI that does not sufficiently reflect the 'values' of HCI (or at least, CHI reviewers)? Is the purpose of CHI Play to legitimate the discipline of PCI as a subset of HCI, or as an independent field of work in a similar fashion to CSCW? Without reflecting on the types of research submitted and accepted to CHI and CHI Play, we risk marginalizing *ontological* and *practice* oriented games research to HCI's periphery just as it has begun growing in representation at CHI. For reasons we have discussed, such marginalization may only serve to cause institutional hostility and further malign the reputation of HCI research within the broader discipline of Game Studies.

CONCLUSION

This review has been specifically timed to catalyze discussions at the inaugural CHI Play conference about where and what we are as a field of research in order to prompt further critical awareness about what distinguishes our work within our field, and how our history influences our ongoing work. We strongly believe that research on games and play within the field of 'player-computer interaction' has strong contributions to the broader field of 'human-computer interaction' and vice versa, and concentrating on what distinguishes our work as well as what unites our work will only make these contributions more transparent. We believe that continuing this type of analysis in other HCI conferences, as well as various HCI journals, will provide further insight into what constitutes games and play research in the field of HCI and how this influences our ongoing work.

ACKNOWLEDGMENTS

This research was funded by the Australian Research Council (ARC) Discovery Project (DP130101519), a Discovery Early Career Researcher Award (DE130100735), the Institute for a Broadband Enabled Society (IBES) and the Microsoft Research Centre for Social NUI.

REFERENCES

1. Apperley, T. & Jayemanne, D. Game studies' material turn. *Westminster Papers 9*, 1 (2012), 5-25.
2. Arroyo, E. et al. Embedded Interaction in a Water Foundatin for Motivating Behavior Change in Public Space. In *Proc. CHI'12*, ACM Press (2012), 685-688.
3. Bannon, L.J. A pilgrim's progress: From cognitive science to cooperative design. *AI & Society 4*, 4 (1989), 259–275.
4. Bargas-Avila, J.A. and Hornbæk, K. Old wine in new bottles or novel challenges? A critical analysis of empirical studies of user experience. *Proc. CHI 2011*, ACM Press (2011), 2689–2698.
5. Bogost, I. Persuasive Games: Exploitationware. http://goo.gl/QDOIKG. (2013).
6. Boulanger, C. et al. Stroke Rehabilitation with a Sensing Surface. In *Proc. CHI'13*, ACM Press (2013), 1243-1246.
7. Carroll, J. *HCI Models, Theories and Frameworks: Toward a Multidisciplinary Science*. Morgan Kaufman, San Francisco, CA, 2003.
8. Cassidy, B. et al. Using an Open Card Sort with Children to Categorize Games in a Mobile Phone Application Store. In *Proc. CHI'13*, ACM Press (2013), 2287-2290.
9. Chu Yew Yee, S. L. et al. Investigating Narrative in Mobile Games for Seniors. In *Proc. CHI'10*, ACM Press (2010), 669-672.
10. Cox, A. et al. Not Doing but Thinking: the Role of Challenge in the Gaming Experience. In *Proc. CHI'12*, ACM Press (2012), 79-88.
11. Dabbish, L., Kraut, R. & Patton, J. Communication and Commitment in an Online Game Team. In *Proc. CHI'12*, ACM Press (2012), 879-todo.
12. Deterding, S. et al. From Game Design Elements to Gamefulness: Defining "Gamification". In *Proc. MINDTREK'11*, ACM Press (2011).
13. DiSalvo, B. et al. African American Males Constructing Computing Identity. In *Proc. CHI'11*, ACM Press (2011), 2967- 2970.
14. Dourish, P. Implications for Design. In *Proc. CHI 2006*, ACM Press (2006), 22-27.
15. Ducheneat, N. et al. The Life and Death of Online Gaming Communities: A Look at Guilds in World of

Warcraft. In *Proc. CHI'07*, ACM Press (2007), 839-848.

16. Ducheneaut, N. Body and Mind: A Study of Avatar Personalization in Three Virtual Worlds. In *Proc. CHI'09*, ACM Press (2009), 1151-1160.

17. Edge, D. et al. Learning Language through Body Motion. In *Proc. CHI'13*, ACM Press (2013), 469-472.

18. Graham, T. C. N. et al. Villains, Architects and Micro-Managers: What Tabula Rasa Teaches us about Game Orchestration. In *Proc. CHI'13*, ACM Press (2013), 705-714.

19. Grudin, J. A moving target: The evolution of human-computer interaction. In J.A. Jacko, ed., *Human–Computer Interaction Handbook*. Taylor & Francis, 2012.

20. Hämäläinen, P. et al. Martial Arts in Artificial Reality. In *Proc. CHI'05*, ACM Press (2005), 781-790.

21. Harrison, S. et al. The three paradigms of HCI. In *Proc. alt.CHI'07*, ACM Press (2007).

22. Horn, M. et al. Of BATs and APEs: An Interactive Tabletop Game for Natural History Museums. In *Proc. CHI'12*, ACM Press (2012), 2059-2068.

23. Huang, J. et al. Mastering the Art of War: How Patterns of Gameplay Influence Skill in Halo. In *Proc. CHI'13*, ACM Press (2013), 695-704.

24. Jianqiang, D. S. et al. Farmer's Tale: A Facebook Game to Promote Volunteerism. In *Proc. CHI'11*, ACM Press (2011), 581-584.

25. Jones, B. R. et al. IllumiRoom: Peripheral Projected Illusions for Interactive Experiences. In *Proc. CHI'13*, ACM Press (2013), 869-878.

26. Keogh, B. Games Evangelists and Naysayers. *The Conversation*, 2014.

27. Kirman, B. et al. Improving Social Game Engagement on Facebook through Enhanced Socio-Contextual Information. In *Proc. CHI'10*, ACM Press (2010), 1753-1756.

28. Lastowka, G. Rules of Play. *Games and Culture 4*, 4 (2009), 379-395.

29. Lindley, S. E., Harper, R. & Sellen, A. Designing a Technological Playground: A Field Study of the Emergence of Play in Household Messaging. In *Proc. CHI'10*, ACM Press (2010), 2351-2360.

30. Litwiller, T., LaViola, J. L. Evaluating the Benefits of 3D Stereo in Modern Video Games. In *Proc. CHI'11*, ACM Press (2011), 2345-2354.

31. Lomas, D. et al. The Power of Play: Design Lessons for Increasing the Lifespan of Outdated Computers. In *Proc. CHI'13*, ACM Press (2013), 2735-2744.

32. Mäyrä, F. *An Introduction to Game Studies*. SAGE Publications, 2008.

33. Mäyrä, F. Game Studies: a Polyphonic Discipline?. http://goo.gl/Edv6fr, 2014.

34. Mirza-Babaei, P. et al. How does it Play Better? Exploring User Testing and Biometric Storyboards in Games User Research. In *Proc. CHI'13*, ACM Press (2013), 1499-1508.

35. Mueller, F. et al. Designing Sports: A Framework for Exertion Games. In *Proc. CHI'11*, ACM Press (2011), 2651-2660.

36. Nenonen, V. et al. Using Heart Rate to Control an Interactive Game. In *Proc. CHI'07*, ACM Press (2007), 853-856.

37. Pace, T., Bardzell, S., Bardzell, J. The Rogue in the Lovely Black Dress: Intimacy in World of Warcraft. In *Proc. CHI 2010*, ACM Press (2010), 223-242.

38. Pace, T. et al. A tribute to Mad skill: expert amateur visuality and World of Warcraft Machinima. In *Proc. CHI 2013*, ACM Press (2013), 2019-2028.

39. Peltonen, P. et al. "It's Mine, Don't Touch!": Interactions at a Large Multi-Touch Display in a City Centre. In *Proc. CHI'08*, ACM Press (2008), 1285-1294.

40. Pinelle, D. et al. Heuristic Evaluation for Games: Usability Principles for Video Game Design. In *Proc. CHI'08*, ACM Press (2008), 1453-1452.

41. Rogers, Y. et al. *Interaction Design: Beyond Human Computer Interaction*. John Wiley & Sons: UK, 2011.

42. Seif El-Nasr, M. et al. Understanding and Evaluating Cooperative Games. In *Proc. CHI'10*, ACM Press (2010), 253-262.

43. Seay, A. F., Kraut, R. E. Project Massive: Self-Regulation and Problematic Use of Online Gaming. In *Proc. CHI 2007*, ACM Press (2007), 829-todo.

44. Suits, B. *The Grasshopper: Games, Life and Utopia*. Broadview Press: Toronto, 1978.

45. von Ahn, L. Liu, R. & Blum, M. Peekaboom: A Game for Locating Objects in Images. In *Proc. CHI'06*, ACM Press (2006), 55-64.

46. Waern, A., Montola, M., Stenros, J. The Three-Sixty Illusion: Designing for Immersion in Pervasive Games. In *Proc. CHI'09*, ACM Press (2009), 1549-1558.

47. Waern, A. et al. Athletes and Street Acrobats: Designing for Play as a Community Value in Parkour. In *Proc. CHI'12*, ACM Press (2012), 869-878.

48. Walsh, G. et al. Layered Elaboration: A New Technique for Co-Design with Children. In *Proc. CHI'10*, ACM Press (2010), 1237-1240.

49. Wang, Y. & Mainwaring, S. "Human-Currency Interaction": Learning from Virtual Currency Use in China. In *Proc. CHI'08*, ACM Press (2008), 25-28.

50. Wyeth, P. Ethnography in the Kindergarten: Examining Children's Play Experiences. In *Proc. CHI'06*, ACM Press (2006), 1225-1228.

Screen Ecologies, Multi-Gaming and Designing for Different Registers of Engagement

Marcus Carter Bjorn Nansen Martin Gibbs
Interaction Design Lab and Microsoft Centre for Social NIU
Computing and Information Systems
The University of Melbourne
marcusc@unimelb.edu.au nansenb@ unimelb.edu.au martin.gibbs@ unimelb.edu.au

ABSTRACT
In this paper, we propose the notion of screen ecologies and argue for its importance in the study of contemporary digital game play. We draw on findings from a range of studies to highlight the interplay between screen ecologies, game design, and registers of engagement. We discuss how game play is increasingly mediated by multiple screen configurations, and in turn, how the design of different games are suited to or appropriated within these different screen ecologies. From this analysis we propose a number of modalities of game-engagement that we argue will assist further HCI research into game design and player experience research.

Author Keywords
Screen ecology; games; play; engagement; EVE Online; World of Warcraft; Candy Crush; DayZ; multi-gaming

ACM Classification Keywords
K.8.0 [**Personal Computing**]: General - *Games*.

General Terms
Design, Human Factors, Theory.

INTRODUCTION
As computing technologies have grown increasingly ubiquitous, a proliferation of screens has occurred. In addition to the widespread preference amongst gamers (and non-gamers) for multiple monitors; televisions, laptops, tablets and smart phones have all invaded the domestic personal computing space. Rather than a single screen sitting on a table capturing the full attention of the user, the modern computing experience is commonly much more complex and distributed across multiple devices. Users' engagement with any or all of these screens varies depending upon context or activity. This characterizes the contemporary screen ecology.

In 2008 Daniel Pargman and Peter Jakobsson noted that games increasingly involved the simultaneous consumption of media, such as watching television in the background, while playing [26]. The intensification of domestic screen ecologies has also led to a rise in multi-gaming; the simultaneous play of digital games. In this paper, we discuss the variety of ways in which this practice supplements, supports and augments the player experience of individual games, and in turn the ways that contemporary screen ecologies are influencing how players experience digital gameplay. Based on our findings, we make a number of recommendations for the design of digital games in the context of the contemporary screen ecology, and articulate a taxonomy of engagement modalities for digital games suitable for this purpose.

Studies of domestic technology use have been a core concern in Human Computer Interaction (HCI) for decades, but rarely has the focus of these studies been on their implications for the play and design of digital gaming experiences. Consequently, we contribute to earlier work by acknowledging the interplay between game design and technology. This paper also integrates with recent work in HCI that has begun considering how multiple frames of activity across screens and non-screens are being consumed by users, and the possibility of this as a resource for design [14, 18]. As screens become more and more ubiquitous in the home, and the capacity for these devices to communicate is increased, the domestic screen ecology only looks to become more complex. While some futurist perspectives may emphasize the likelihood of immersionist, virtual reality digital gaming (*á la* the *Occulus Rift* headset, or [13]), the appeal of multi-gaming and simultaneous consumptions of media suggests an alternate, though perhaps only interim, future which aught be considered in studies of domestic gaming and in game design. Such considerations place the experience of digital games within frames of activity that encompass screens and play, as well as their relation to the material and social frames of everyday life [1, 20].

THE DOMESTIC SCREEN ECOLOGY
This study is situated within the broader trend of multiplying screens and multiple screen activities within domestic environments. Australia, like many developed countries around the world, is undergoing a transformation in the number and variety of computing devices and digital screens populating the home, and an associated transformation in the way people use and interact with media technologies. This trend is being driven by the

CHI PLAY'14, October 19–21, 2014, Toronto, ON, Canada.

http://dx.doi.org/10.1145/2658537.2658686

intersection of a number of factors, including: the penetration of newer and cheaper consumer electronic products such as tablets, smart phones and consoles; the growth in wireless networks and mobile technologies within the home; and the bandwidth to support the simultaneous operation of multiple internet-connected devices enabled through faster broadband, such as the rollout of a National Broadband Network of fibre-optic infrastructure cabling in Australia [2, 3, 22]

Rather than substituting for older media, however, the addition of newer devices are being used to complement traditional activities such as television viewing with other so-called 'second screen' activities such as simultaneous internet browsing and social networking [25]. Whilst multi-tasking may not necessarily be new, certainly the increasing speed of the internet alongside the mobility of devices is contributing to a situation that affords new configurations, patterns and intensities of screen activities, which we address in this paper in relation to the interplay between gaming, screens and registers of engagement.

MULTIPLE SCREENS AND CONTEMPORARY GAMING

The use of multiple screens during computer use has been long-noted in HCI [e.g., 24], both in the contexts of professional work [11] and non-gaming leisure, such as television viewing [4, 12]. However, Brown et al. [4] note that "*there has been very little research systematically investigating how attention is split during dual-screen human-computer interaction*" [p. 666], with studies focusing on task performance in lab settings or on the usability of dual screen systems [19]. Both Brown et al. [4] and Holmes et al. [12] investigate use in the context of companion applications (TV 'apps' that augment viewing).

In the context of gaming, researchers like Kauko & Häkkilä [15] have explored using multiple smartphone devices to create larger shared displays for social gaming experiences. While Tran et al. [28] have studied multiplayer games that have dual-monitor configurations (where a secondary screen can be used to display information like in-game maps or chat, leaving the central screen less cluttered), finding that secondary screens supported communication and coordination. However, we are not aware of any studies that have investigated the use of multiple screens for distinct, simultaneous frames of leisure activities.

RESEARCH DESIGN

Our interest in the impact of multiple screens on the consumption and engagement with contemporary digital games arose out of a number of separate studies into multiple game titles, including *DayZ*, *EVE Online*, *Candy Crush Saga* and *World of Warcraft*, along with a series of ongoing studies exploring the changing domestic technology environment [22, 29], including children's use of touch screen devices [21], and broadband adoption in the context of Australia's National Broadband Network (NBN). These studies involve qualitative methods such as household technology tours and interviews aimed at understanding the adoption and use of media and communications technology in the home. In each of these studies, the shift to more complex screen ecologies and interactions emerged as a relevant finding. Consequently, we extended our analysis beyond Australia-specific household screen practices by purposefully collecting further online data on gaming screen configurations and uses relevant to this paper. In particular, we archived and analyzed posts on the reddit gaming forums which featured discussions around the use of multiple screens while playing games. These typically took the form of images of people playing multiple games at once (example Figure 5). The majority of comments on these pages self-reported similar multi-gaming experiences, from which we collected 97 game-combinations and further insight into the role that the screen ecology plays in affecting contemporary game play. These combinations formed the theoretical framework for developing the taxonomy presented later in the paper.

RESULTS

As noted in the introduction, the purpose of this paper is to draw attention to how the proliferation of computing technologies has created a screen ecology in domestic environments which is reshaping the way in which contemporary digital games are engaged with and consequently, experienced. By 'screen ecology', we refer to both powerful computers with multiple screens, but also the parallel use of separate computing devices; tablets, smart phones, laptops and televisions.

In this paper we pull together relevant results from our separate studies into domestic computer-gaming in order to consider and discuss the interplay between screen ecologies, game design, game play and registers of engagement. We begin by documenting different configurations of multiple screens in domestic settings, then discuss various 'combinations' of different games and screen-based activities through the practice of 'multi-gaming'; the simultaneous play of multiple digital games. We then shift into detailed analyses of individual case studies for the specific games we have studied, some of which featured prominently in online discussions around multi-gaming. We discuss how the play of these games is affected by the contemporary screen ecology and in turn, how different game designs are suited to different screen configurations and registers of engagement. Following this close analysis, we propose a taxonomy of game-engagement modalities that we argue will assist further HCI research into game design and player experience research in the context of the contemporary domestic screen ecology.

Screen Configurations

In this section we document typical domestic spatial and technical set-ups in which multiple screens are available for appropriation in game play. This includes configurations of multiple screen ecologies for the purpose of simultaneously playing digital games alongside other screen-based media, such as web-browsing and television, but also for simultaneously playing multiple digital games. The images provided are intended as a representative sample of the scope of domestic multiple screen use as an introduction to the contemporary screen ecology.

Figure 1: Parallel screen set up posted to /r/battlestations forum on reddit.com by user Phaym.

Figure 1 represents a typical configuration of multiple screens and monitors. Dual monitors, connected to a single desktop computer, are nearly always placed parallel to one another. This is likely due to how the Windows OS handles multiple screens, allowing the user to have applications, images and cursor movements move between one edge of the screen onto another, as if they were one long rectangular screen. In this set up, we also see how laptop computers are often used to extend the length of these screens, and tablet computers (and often smart phones) are placed in the foreground for easy interaction without obscuring the desktop computer screens. Seen in action in Figure 5, the physical affordances of these objects make them easily maneuverable, augmenting their easy integration with other, more fixed screens and screen-based play.

Figure 2: Multi-user post on /r/battlestations titled, 'Husband-wife minecraft battlestation. The TV screen is displaying a top-down map of their Minecraft world, augmenting their play. By user '2cats1dog'.

Larger screens, such as television screens, were often wall-mounted and placed above desk-based computer screens, as in Figure 2. As well as working to increase the distance from the user to the screen (necessary for viewing comfort), this example shows how this peripheral screen is being appropriated to augment their play experience by displaying a top-down map of a Minecraft server being played on one of the desktop screens.

Of note in Figure 3 and 4 are the affordances of the traditional desk chair. Unlike the majority of other chairs, desk chairs feature a swivel feature allowing the user to easily re-orientate their body towards a different area. This affordance encourages wrap-around screen configurations as seen in Figure 3. So, in addition to the physical affordances of laptop and tablet computers allowing for easy switches of engagement, the rarely acknowledged but ubiquitous computer chair does have impact on how screen ecologies are set up and consequently, the effect they have on domestic computer use. The affordances and affects of non-digital objects like furniture, and their relationships with the use of digital objects, demand further study in HCI.

Figure 3: 7 screen configuration, involving laptop, PC and console based play. Via reddit.

Similarly depicting the raised, wall-mounted larger television screen, Figure 4 shows the interplay between TV screen based console play, passive television watching (the screen in the lower left), the swivel desk chair, and desktop computer and tablet use. This set up allows for quick reorientation between passive and active games, as well as other broader screen based frames of engagement.

Figure 4: 5 screen perpendicular configuration, including a passive television screen. Via reddit.

Multi-Gaming Combinations

To gain insight into the breadth of multiple-screen use during play we also archived and analyzed posts on the 'Gaming' page on *reddit* which featured discussions around the use of multiple screens while playing games. While this is a practice possible on a single screen (by 'alt tabbing' between active games or having split windows), multiple screens has enhanced ability of players to rapidly and seamlessly switch engagement between simultaneously active games without hiding them or reducing their size. Comments on these posts provided self-reported combinations of simultaneous game-playing, which we drew on to develop our taxonomy of engagement modalities.

Overwhelmingly, comments reflected that the purpose of

multiple screen ecologies was to fill in momentary lapses in activity during gameplay on the primary screen. Figure 5, from a popular reddit post, depicts someone playing *Rome II Total War* (a mostly passive turn based game that can take over 10 hours to play) in between *Battlefield 4* deaths, a first-person shooter game that requires a player's active attention when alive, and no attention when they are deceased or between the 2-5 minute matches. Comments on this post similarly described combining passive games that do not demand the player's attention during the play of first-person shooter games;

I like to do this when playing civilization and halo. Keeps my mind fresh and active.

Used to do this with CS [Counter Strike] and Civ 4 (desktop and laptop), so indulgent.

Other comments and replies suggested similarly browsing sites like reddit (unsurprising, as this was where the data was sourced from) and social networking sites like Facebook.

Figure 5: Photo posted to reddit titled, 'Ladies and Gentlemen. My brother. Playing Rome II total war in between Battlefield 4 deaths' by user 'Coleey'. Image received 680,000+ views.

Recent installments in the *Civilization* series were a prominent game that featured in these discussions. Like in *Total War* games, the player controls a civilization maneuvering whole armies and developing technology and infrastructure within their borders. These 'grand strategy' games are turn based; *Civilization* does not make time-sensitive demands on the player. In addition to this passiveness, the complexity of these games on less powerful machines means they can take over 2 minutes to calculate non-player moves before it is the user's turn. The top voted comment on the Figure 5 post was consequently '*More like playing Battlefield 4 in between Rome 2 load times.*'

In addition to FPS games, 'MOBA' games (Multiplayer Online Battle Arena) such as *League of Legends* (LoL) were frequently mentioned. Like FPS games, MOBA games demand the player's attention but feature regular downtime due to player-death. The player has to wait a set amount of time before they can respawn and re-enter the game.

This makes me incredibly happy. Just that I do LoL and Civ V nowadays.

This is too familiar....in longer LoL games, between deaths I'll play CoD zombies. nice stress reliever after getting fucked by fucking Jinx's ult

This latter comment reveals not just the contribution of secondary-games to sustaining engagement, but as a complementary form of leisure; working to de-stress the user following stressful play of other games.

While not all comments revealed the composition of these multi-playing situations, many reflected on the use of multiple devices (as in Figure 1) or the combination of desktop and console based gaming. For example, one comment stated; "*I play Infamous second son* [a PS4 exclusive] *in between League of legends* [deaths]". Another, replying to the same thread:

I do that all the time, but i'm more of a Civ 5 (PC) / Skyrim (PS3) kinda guy.

This perhaps reflects limitations in computing power (running modern games simultaneously is beyond all but the most powerful machines) but also potential contributions of control-change; switching between a console controller and keyboard/mouse controls works to distinguish play and limit possible interruptions. Reflecting on these combinations in the context of the screen configurations we discussed earlier in this paper, it is evident how configurations like in Figures 3 and 4 afford (or respond to) the appeal of this kind of multi-gaming.

Revealing the imaginative potential for integrating multi-gaming, one commenter revealed how they imagined the two discreet activities were somehow interlinked, playing two fantasy based games simultaneously;

I like to play Pixel Dungeon on my phone and Banished on PC at the same time. I imagine my warrior is fighting for the village.

Similarly, one player reported playing both the PS3 and smart phone versions of *Madden* (an American Football simulator) while watching American Football on TV. So while in the majority of cases the contemporary screen ecology is affording the simultaneous play of discreet games, these two examples highlight a potential rich space for future design where multi-gaming becomes an integrated experience.

Other games that were prominent were games in the RPG genre, both single-player and MMOG equivalents (such as *Runescape*). The types of RPG/MMOG play these revealed were passive, time-based or the types of play colloquially referred to as 'grinding' (defined as repetitive tasks to gain experience points and progress by Ducheneaut et. al. [10]).

I used to time it perfectly where I could play a round of CoD and it ended just in time for me to harvest and replant all my crops in Runescape.

I do my wow auctioning while playing battlefield 4.

I played probably 1000 games of Halo 3 while playing Runescape. I got three 99's doing it.

MMOG games like *EVE Online* and *World of Warcraft*, while criticised for their 'play-labour' styles of play, can be seen here to instead be integrating themselves with the player's gaming interests by offering a variety of ways to play with different registers of engagement. This facet of this genre should be considered further in analyses of their play and appeal.

The variety of these examples reflects a complex network of gaming practices. The contemporary screen ecology (be it through multiple monitors or multiple devices) affords different styles of play depending upon the affordances and constraints of games, the appropriation of multiple devices/hardware and screens, and the interests and creativity of players. We now turn to the relationship between different screen ecologies, gaming configurations and combinations, and registers of engagement.

Registers of Engagement

In this section we focus on four specific games as case studies to explore in greater detail the ways registers of engagement are produced through the interplay between game design and screen ecologies. In particular, we note that the designs of different games lend themselves to being accommodated within different screen configurations and gaming combinations.

Boring play and EVE Online

First released in 2003, *EVE Online* is a science-fiction themed MMOG with a number of interesting design configurations of relevance to bodies of literature in HCI. Unlike other MMOGs, which have been studied for their use of humanoid, personalized avatars [see 30, 5], interactions between players in *EVE Online* occur in-space between uncustomizable spaceships. These interactions do not necessarily demand consent; at any time in *EVE*'s vast universe, you are vulnerable to attack. Unlike (most) other MMOGs, this carries enormous consequence; when destroyed, the value of your ship is lost permanently. EVE also demands players trust each other in interactions and in tandem, allows treachery and betrayal [see 8], but despite this (and of potential interest to CSCW research) players form enormous communities of players (+10,000) which demand considerable logistical and work-like play.

Many of the participants in our *EVE Online* study referred (in jest) to their chosen MMOG as a 'boring' game. This was not to imply boring as a pejorative with any negative connotations (being tedious; irksome; tiresome) but as a state of engagement (or lack thereof). This is because a number of *EVE Online* play 'styles' do not require the player's full attention and consequently encourage the use of multiple screens.

For example, one participant used two desktop monitors (21.5" and 23") sometimes engaged in 'cloaky camping', which is where an *EVE* player waits hidden in a solar system hoping to find an unsuspecting victim acting carelessly. When they were playing this way, they used the second monitor to "*play whatever game I want, this is commonly either tf2* [Team Fortress 2] *or CSGO* [Counter Strike: Global Offensive] *simply because those are my current addictions.*" During large fleet battles, where hundreds of *EVE* players fight in coordinated battles, this same player used their second screen to " *play something that can I drop quickly or pause, games like FTL* [Faster Than Light] *are great for this because action is divided into short sections and its easy to pick up where I left off.*" This allowed them to stay engaged while waiting for commands to be issued to the fleet (often players have to wait several minutes at a time for instructions), but still able to quickly respond should an enemy fleet attack.

Another *EVE* play style that was often mentioned when discussing multiple monitors was mining. Mining involves orbiting asteroids, 'shooting' them with mining lasers, and then waiting until the player's ship is filled with minerals. When done in 'high security' space, the player will rarely come under attack, and consequently this is a very passive style of *EVE Online* play. One player mentioned how this integrated with their work, as "*it is easy to mine in one window on the computer screen, while writing in another.*" This is thus similar to 'cloaky camping', but more cyclical; a mining barge will be full at regular intervals, whereas a player might go hours camping a system without having opportunity to engage.

Another miner instead used their other screen to display a second instance of the *EVE* client, so that they could pilot two ships simultaneously. In the course of this study, we have encountered players who run over 6 instances of the *EVE* client simultaneously, and have seen posts online depicting over a dozen. *EVE's* low demand on the computer likely contributes to the occurrence of this play style.

In addition to these examples of multi-gaming and using multiple screens to do two discreet activities, we also encountered multiple screens augmenting the *EVE Online* experience. One player would use their second screen to display a third-party program which allowed them to compare ship-fits easier than the game client, while several use their second screen for IRC chat windows, TeamSpeak and game forums.

Each of these examples demonstrates the way in which *EVE Online*'s 'boring' play styles - in that it often has low registers of engagement - allow and encourage the simultaneous engagement with other, sometimes non-*EVE* media during *EVE* play. These included web browsing sites like reddit, video media like TV shows and game streaming, and the play of other games. This simultaneous media engagement is made possible due to the contemporary screen ecology; multiple screens and the ability to place the *EVE Online* client in windowed mode afford simultaneous engagement on a single computer. The ubiquity of other devices in the domestic environment, such as laptops, smartphones and televisions, further transform the way *EVE Online* is played.

The above vignettes provided around styles of *EVE Online* play exemplify how players play *EVE* differently depending on the type of engagement they want to have; *EVE* as a passive game, during the play of another, or *EVE* as a demanding game, wholly consuming the player's attention. Thus it is not just that the contemporary screen ecology transforms the way *EVE Online* is played and experienced, but we suggest that the design of *EVE Online* affords and is therefore inclusive of a multi screen ecology, which lends itself to a more attractive play experience.

Group play and Progression Raiding in World of Warcraft

World of Warcraft is a popular fantasy themed MMORPG familiar to games research in HCI [10, 17, 23, 30]. In this study we examined the culture and practices of players of *World of Warcraft* who identified themselves as 'raiders' and engaged in 'progression raiding' (see below). In 2009 and 2010 (during the *Wrath of the Lich King* expansion) fourteen players were interviewed. Where possible, interviews were conducted in participants' homes and then a session of raiding was observed and video recorded. Follow-up questions and interviews were also conducted.

At the time of the study, raiding involved groups of 10 or 25-players, and was a particularly challenging form of play. It required strong group coordination and the individual prowess of group members to achieve success. Many players engage in a form of raiding known as 'progression raiding' that was the focus of this study. Progression raiding typically occurs in stable player guilds because of the difficulty of the encounters, the need for good coordination and for the group to have well-equipped individual players. Most 'boss encounters' (very powerful monsters) have complicated and unique game mechanics that need to be understood by players and are telegraphed through various sights, sounds other information in the game interface and often announced through the use of game modfications. During the 5-10 minutes of a boss fight players must concentrate intensely on what is occurring and make split-second decisions on how to act and respond.

Progression raiders in our study predominately made significant use of single screens, with other screens present in the domestic screen ecology turned off or silenced during raids. Raiding has a rhythm, particularly when guilds are working on a boss fight they have not yet mastered; periods of intense, demanding activity while the fight is going on, alternating with the low key, undemanding activity of preparing for the next attempt. However these periods are cyclical and predictable, and do not resume until the raid leader instructs the group to re-enter the fray. Consequently, like one player who had his computer in the corner of the lounge room, players could turn their attention elsewhere, to his wife were she sat at the dining room table knitting, or glance over at the television show his daughter was watching and engage in snippets of conversation. He had his computer in this room so he could be with his family in these cyclical periods of 'downtime'.

Per the demanding reliance on group coordination, raiding groups were typically required to be logged-on and ready to start 15 minutes before the raid's scheduled beginning. While waiting, some players watched television or interacted with mobile phones, while others alt-tabbed out of the game and did email, chatted on line, browsed YouTube, and so forth, and the distinctive sound of an raid invitation pulled their attention back to the *WoW* client.

Those players with multiple screens attached all had a designated 'central' screen, with a secondary screen peripheral to their set up. This second screen was used similarly, but also encouraged the inclusion of more simultaneous activities. One player used his second screen to review video and text strategy guides during the low-demand preparation for the next fight (such as running back to the group after dying). During the high-intensity fights, he displayed his VoIP client as well as a 3rd party text chat application. One player had *WoW* spread across horizontally adjacent screens allowing a wider view of the game world and cited the importance of "*peripheral vision*", especially in his role as a healer. Two neighbors, who raided together, and were also the raider leaders and fulfilled the important and complementary roles of 'main tank' and 'tank healer', had desktop computers, each with a single screen, in the living room of the same house. The desks were arranged side-by-side, allowing them to see each other's screens if they craned their necks.

While there are many ways to engage with *World of Warcraft*, and some of these lend themselves to engaging in other activities while playing, the intense experience of raiding in *World of Warcraft* meant that players were predominately focused on the game's single screen. Interestingly, the rhythm of raiding with alternating periods of attention demand did not result in a proliferation of screens as seen in the *EVE Online* cases. Rather, we observed players literally leaning forward intensely during fights and leaning back with a sigh or a curse after another failed attempt at a boss, and went from playing with two hands on mouse and keyboard, to playing with one hand. This switch to relatively relaxed play seemed to be an opportunity to recover and unwind, rather than an opportunity to quickly engage with another screen-based activity.

Intense play and DayZ

DayZ is a zombie-themed survival FPS with configurations of character and virtual world persistence common in the MMOG genre, and is consequently referred to as a MMOFPS. Like games in the blockbuster *Call of Duty* series, the player controls an armed humanoid avatar, navigating a virtual environment where they are able to shoot other avatars controlled by players. However, pertinent to prior research in HCI on the affect of voice configuration on the social experiences of virtual worlds [6], *DayZ* has a uniquely configured proximity-voice system that allows collocated, but ostensibly opposed, players to communicate and negotiate.

Unlike *EVE Online*, *DayZ* does not have a 'windowed'

mode, and thus does not easily allow players to use two monitors on the same machine (various third party programs and scripts do exist to overcome this issue). It is also a significantly more demanding game; at any moment while playing, another user could encounter the player and kill them. This has permanent consequence in *DayZ*, as dying removes all in-game advantage [see 7].

Thus, *DayZ* presents as a game unlikely to encourage the use of multiple monitors; it is an excellent example of a game that commands the player's attention at all times, and with a design that discourages distraction. However, in our study we saw several examples of player's integrating *DayZ* within other frames of their domestic screen ecology.

One case involved watching television, YouTube videos or 'live-streams' while playing *DayZ*. These were justified as ways to supplement 'boring' *DayZ* play; such as long walks players had to do to get their character between locations in *DayZ's* vast virtual world, or a player who would lie hidden along commonly traversed paths with a powerful sniper rifle waiting for unsuspecting players to pass by. Often these YouTube videos would be 'Lets Play!' style videos of *DayZ* play, or live-streams of *DayZ*, allowing the player to be entertained by *DayZ* when the actual *DayZ* was being passive or 'boring'. Players also used the ubiquity of multiple devices to circumvent the restrictions of *DayZ's* lack of 'windowed' mode:

because I couldn't run it [DayZ] *in windowed mode, I would use my laptop to show the map and I ended up running team speak off it as well*

Another participant cited their use of an iPad for this purpose, displaying a third-party map program that allowed users to share their in-game locations with friends, and orientate themselves within the virtual world. This practice also circumvents how *DayZ* demands significant computing power; running other applications (such as a web browser or teamspeak client) on the desktop while *DayZ* is running may negatively affect play.

The above exemplifies the manner in which, when examining the relationships between the contemporary screen ecology and the play of digital games, we have to look beyond just screens on single computers to the multiple devices that constitute the complex screen ecology. The restrictions and affordances of these different devices work to allow players creative reappropriations to ensure their gaming experiences meet their gaming needs. While *DayZ* demands intense and focused engagement, and is ostensibly enjoyed as an immersive experience, we found that it still lent itself to multiple screen configurations. These were not as distractions, *per se*, but instead supported and augmented *DayZ* as the focus of their engagement.

Casual play and Candy Crush Saga

In contrast to *EVE Online* and *DayZ* which are commonly referred to as some of the most 'hardcore' games [27], *Candy Crush Saga* is a prominent 'casual' tile-matching puzzle game which can be played on mobile devices and on the social networking website, Facebook.com. First released in 2012, *Candy Crush Saga* is currently the most popular game on Facebook and quotes over 100 million unique players per day, suggesting it is the most popular individual game of all time. Like *EVE*, *Candy Crush* was a game commonly cited in online discussions as a multi-play game.

As a mobile game, *Candy Crush* is played in a variety of locations and times and interacts with a player's daily life in a different way to games like *EVE Online* that are restricted to play on powerful computers. This is of course relevant to HCI research on mobile gaming, which has however typically focused on the mobile context of play rather than the way mobile play is accommodated within a domestic environment [20]. Participants in this study – which involved semi-structured interviews with 13 participants, aged 18-64 [see also 9] – reported a number of different, salient ways in which the flexibility of mobile-screen gaming integrated with the consumption of media on other screens.

Several participants reported playing *Candy Crush* while watching television, both on desktop computers and laptops and traditional television screens. Our oldest participant described where they played;

I play it on an iPad. In the back room of my house, the lounge room kind of thing. And generally whilst watching TV that isn't particularly engaging.

Of note with this simultaneous frame of engagement was the type of TV typically watched; low demand (not 'particularly engaging') TV, or TV the participants had already seen. So unlike many of the multi-gaming situations already discussed, this example presents the integration of two low demand practices; *Candy Crush* rarely commands the player's full attention.

Those of our participants who were students, including several PhD students, reported playing *Candy Crush* while doing screen-based work, such as writing essays or marking assignments. In these cases, *Candy Crush* was played "*as more of a break between studying*"; the ease with which players could pick up their smartphone or tablet and play a single game of *Candy Crush* meant that they could quickly switch between play and work. Rather than suggesting this was a negative distraction, several participants felt this integrated well with their work tasks;

When I was doing something and I feel very tired with the work/research I like to take some breaks or change my mind to something else, to change my concentration to something else, then maybe I would play

One of the benefits of *Candy Crush* for this type of engagement is its implementation of limited lives. Players have a maximum of 5 lives in *Candy Crush*, and each time they fail an attempt, they lose a life. When no lives remain, the player can either wait 25 minutes for a life to regenerate or pay $0.99. This is thus one of the developer's primary sources of income, but the artificial limitation also served to help integrate *Candy Crush* play with the use of other screens and devices. This is best exemplified by one participant who used it as a *"reward system"* in between spouts of work. Thus we see how *Candy Crush*'s timer, similar to the cyclical play of *EVE* mining, allows player attention at certain times while restricting it at others. Though an annoying restriction when the player wants control over their play, it means play can occur at regular intervals as breaks from, or in between, other types of screen engagement such as work or play.

GAMING MODALITIES

Having now discussed common physical arrangements of multiple screens in the domestic environment, overviewed various types of multi-gaming made possible by this screen ecology, and discussed how four games integrate with player engagement and appeal in this context, we will now propose a taxonomy of engagement modalities. The purpose of defining these modalities is to capture the different ways that modern games register player engagement in order to inform both the design and study of domestic gaming. This is not intended to be comprehensive taxonomy, but rather reflect the different genres of attention that we identified in this research and encourage deeper consideration about additional ways games can integrate with other games, as well as other domestic activities.

Cyclical Intermittent Games; games with regular, predictable cycles of 'downtime' - where the player does not need to interact of provide attention - and 'uptime', where the player must commit the majority of their attention. These include games in the FPS genre (such as *Call of Duty*, *Halo*, *Battlefield*) and MOBA genre (such as *League of Legends*) which have intense periods of play interspersed with waiting periods in excess of one minute (typically in the 'lobby' between player-versus-player games). As multiplayer games, the player has no ability to pause play to divert their attention.

Non-Cyclical Intermittent Games; games with irregular, unpredictable cycles of 'downtime' - where the player does not need to interact and only needs to provide little attention - and 'uptime' where the player must be committing the majority of their attention. The most prominent example in this genre was styles of *EVE Online* play, such as system-camping (whereby you wait, cloaked, for an unsuspecting victim to pass by) or some nullsec PvE (demanding little attention except when attacked).

Pausable Games; games which demanded the majority of a user's attention but could be paused when their attention is demanded elsewhere. These were typically single player RPG games, such as *Fable* or *Assassins Creed* or the campaign modes in FPS games like *Halo* or *Call of Duty*. Unlike cyclical intermittent games, the player has the ability to control when they need to give their full attention.

Slow Games; games which have regular periods of *active* waiting and rarely command the user's full attention for times in excess of one minute. The typical games in this genre are city building games such as *Sim City*, *Banished* or *Dwarf Fortress* where regular intervals of non-interactivity are demanded because of the manner in which certain aspects of the game require time to have passed (resources having been moved and a building having been built in *Banished*, for example). During this time, however, a small amount of attention must be paid unless something goes wrong (e.g., a goblin raid in *Dwarf Fortress*). Worth noting, the games in this genre that we observed players multi-playing all featured the ability to pause the game; if the game was at a situation where it was commanding the player's attention at an inconvenient time, the player could simply pause it.

Timed Games; those games which had regular intervals of *passive* waiting during which there is no ability for the player to interact. These were typically mobile games, such as *Candy Crush* or *Clash of Kings*, which use the freemium monetization pattern of playing by appointment [31], but also timed play in other games (like farming in *Runscape*). Players have to wait intervals of 10 or 25 minutes between performing in-game actions, after which the game would not demand attention but simply be accessible to play.

Passive Games; games which were entirely passive, never demanding the user provide their attention at any given moment. The most prominent example of these was *Civilization 5*, a turn based grand strategy game without simulated combat. The user is never *required* to attend to *Civilization 5*. Along with the similar *Total War* series, these were the most popular 'secondary' games.

DISCUSSION

In this paper, we have argued that the proliferation of screens in the domestic environment – referred to as the contemporary screen ecology – have transformed the way in which digital games are played and consequently, experienced. This has allowed the simultaneous play of digital games along with other screen-based media, such as web-browsing and television, but has also given rise to the phenomena of multi-gaming; the simultaneous play of multiple digital games.

We've explored this phenomenon through different screen configurations and multi-gaming combinations observed in our research of gaming in domestic environments. We also analyzed online discussions around multi-gaming on the site 'www.reddit.com'. These studies revealed a broad and complex network of practices that have emerged as a consequence of the contemporary screen ecology. These include the simultaneous play of multiple games, creative and imaginative practices, as well as the use of secondary games to overcome the arduousness of certain facets of modern games, such as grinding. In this analysis, it is clear that not all screens are equivalent or equal. Instead, different kinds of screens – TC, PC, laptop, tablet, mobile phone – lend themselves to different frames of activity and engagement.

We then analyzed four distinct case studies, drawing from separate research projects on the very-different *EVE Online*, *World of Warcraft*, *DayZ* and *Candy Crush Saga*. From these focused analyses, we identified the ways in which the contemporary screen ecology can not only transform the play of games, but the ways in which games can (or don't) respond to and indeed thrive as part of this ecology. We highlighted aspects of the design of these games that encouraged their attraction for 'multi-gaming', such as having timed-features, windowed mode, and so forth. In the case of *DayZ* and *World of Warcraft*, which were not used to multi-game, we saw how they were still affected by the contemporary screen ecology even during the most demanding examples of play.

The consequences of these insights are threefold. Firstly, we wish to argue for a de-emphasis of what occurs 'within' the game for understanding the experience of digital games. It would be erroneous to analyze the play of *EVE Online* or *Candy Crush* if limited to the events within that individual game; the broader social, cultural and gaming contexts affect its play and consequently experience [1, 16]. As noted by Brendan Keogh [16], video game play is a *"messy assemblage"* that functions *"across worlds and across bodies"*. We thus join Keogh in challenging the dominance of immersion in conceptualizations of game experience; how immersed can a player be reasonably considered being if they're playing *Pokemon* in between *Morrowind* load times? Or *Peggle* during *World of Warcraft* raids?

Our second insight is thus into the prominent role that the contemporary screen ecology is playing in how modern games are played and experienced. Whereas the 'gamer' is typically conceptualized as a nose-to-the-screen fully attentive, wholly engaged user, our results indicate a much more nuanced and varied practices of distributed interaction and engagement, that presents future research questions regarding how it is affecting gamer's attentiveness and capacity to multi-task. Such research should consider the different modes of sensation and interaction demanded by different screens, especially as touch, gesture and motion controlled screens continue to proliferate. Further, the embodied and material dimensions of such frames suggests a need for research that also considers the affordances and implications of physical spaces, peripheral's and furniture.

This latter note is interesting in the context of futurist perspectives that emphasize the likelihood of immersionist, virtual reality digital gaming (*á la* the *Occulus Rift* headset), as an inevitable step. This study complicates notions of immersion that emphasise the visual, and its sensory realism or capture, reflected in a game development paradigm that idolises *The Matrix*-esque virtual reality as the 'end-game' for game development. Rather, in this study we see how domestic technologies are being appropriated in ways that distribute immersion across multiple screens and modalities of input, or sometimes dilute game immersion through integration with the real world, suggesting a more complex conceptualization of immersion is needed.

Finally, we believe our insights highlight a number of rich areas of potential for future design. As far as we are aware, there do not exist any games where the simultaneous play of two games occurs in a symbiotic fashion, where one game affects the other and vice versa. Many games (such as the *Total War* genre) feature dramatic changes in game-play and engagement over the course of play (switching from passive, turn-based grand strategy to active, real-time strategy battles where the player controls the squads in his armies on the battlefield). However these occur in sequence; events outside of the battlefield do not progress until the battle is concluded. Simultaneous play, such as with one commenter's imagined link between their *Pixel Dungeon* play (where they control a *Dungeons and Dragons*-esque warrior raiding dungeons) and *Banished* (a medieval town builder-sim), reflects a way game design could incorporate the contemporary screen ecology.

Conversely, our insights could inspire the design of games which are designed to be consumed simultaneously with any number of other games which complement the way they demand the player's engagement. Rather than designing games meant to consume a player's entire attention, games could be designed to be slow, tedious or even *boring* and remain attractive to players because they engagingly mesh with their play of other games (or engagement with other media) on other screens.

In order to bolster this contribution of the paper, we have articulated the various combinations of games we identified in our analysis of multi-gaming examples sourced from our interviews and online discussions into genres. The purpose of articulating these genres is to encourage the consideration of how games are co-consumed with other media and activities, and the impact that new technologies can have on the play and experience of games and other computer-products. By expressing this as a taxonomy, we contribute to future HCI work that may consider the different ways games demand player attention and how this can be leveraged in the design of positive experiences or for other purposes (such as health or learning).

FUTURE WORK

In our next steps, we propose to extend Holmes et al.'s [12] earlier study on simultaneous TV & tablet use using eye-tracking data to examine levels of attention and engagement with game play on multiple screens. Though this will not reveal further insight into the broader screen ecology (e.g., mobile games, TV) (thus the strength of this qualitative, exploratory approach) this will allow us to create a taxonomy in accordance with game design patterns.

We also aim to explore screen configurations in domestic gaming through the 'battle stations' phenomena in more depth. In our examinations of screen configurations, we saw a complex interplay between gaming culture, capital, history and devices that prompt consideration for the design of both software and hardware, with implications for the play and enjoyment of digital games.

In this paper we have emphasised simultaneous computer use as our focus was on the changing contemporary screen ecology. However, the engagement modalities we have presented in this paper could just as easily be integrated with other non-computer activities, such as cooking, cleaning, studying and professional work. We therefore recommend future work consider more broadly how gameplay is integrated with other frames and activities, and the relationships between them, to better understand player experience as a potential rich site for design.

ACKNOWLEDGMENTS

This research was funded by an Australian Research Council (ARC) Discovery Project (DP130101519), a Discovery Early Career Researcher Award (DE130100735), and the Institute for a Broadband Enabled Society. We would like to acknowledge the thoughtful feedback from the anonymous reviewers, and our participants who shared their homes and experiences.

REFERENCES

[1] Apperley, T. & Jayemanne, D. Game studies' material turn. *Westminster Papers in Communication and Culture, 9,* 1 (2012), 5-25.

[2] Australian Centre for Broadband Innovation. Broadband Connected Homes: Opportunities for Developing Broadband Applications and Services. (2012)

[3] Australian Communications and Media Authority. Digital Australians: Expectations about Media Content in a Converging Media Environment (2011).

[4] Brown, A. et al. HCI over multiple screens. In *Proc. CHI EA'14*, ACM Press (2014), 665-675.

[5] Carter, M., Gibbs, M. & Arnold, M. Avatars, Characters, Users and Players: Multiple Identities at/in Play. In *Proc. ozCHI'12*, ACM Press (2012), 68-71.

[6] Carter, M., Wadley, G. & Gibbs, M. "Friendly! Don't Shoot!: How Communication Design can Create Novel Social Interactions. In *Proc. ozCHI'12*, ACM Press (2012), 72-75.

[7] Carter, M., Gibbs, M. & Wadley, G. Death and Dying in DayZ. In *Proc. IE'13*, ACM Press, (2013).

[8] Carter, M. Massively Multiplayer Dark Play: Treacherous Play in EVE Online. In T. Mortensen & J. Linderoth (Eds.), *The Dark Side of Game Play*, (2014) London: Routledge. [forthcoming]

[9] Carter, M. & Björk, S. Cheating in Candy Crush Saga. [under review].

[10] Ducheneaut, N. et al. Alone Together?" Exploring the Social Dynamics of Massively Multiplayer Online Games. In *Proc. CHI'06*, ACM Press (2006), 407-416.

[11] Grudin, J. Partitioning Digital Worlds: Focal and Peripheral Awareness in Multiple Monitor Use. In *Proc. CHI'01*, ACM Press (2001), 485-465.

[12] Holmes, M., Josephson, S. & Carnet, R. Visual attention to television programs with a second-screen application. In *Proc. Eye Tracking Research and Applications*, ACM Press (2012), 397-400.

[13] Jones, B. et. al. IllumiRoom: Peripheral Projected Illusions for Interactive Experiences. In *Proc. CHI 2013*. ACM Press (2013).

[14] Judge, T. & Neustaedter, C. Sharing Conversation and Sharing Life: Video Conferencing in the Home. In *Proc. CHI'10*, ACM Press (2010), 655-658.

[15] Kauko, J. & Häkkilä, J. Shared-Screen Social Gaming with Portable Devices. In *Proc. MobileHCI'10*, ACM Press (2010), 317-325.

[16] Keogh, B. Across Worlds and Bodies: Criticism in the Age of Video Games. *Journal of Games Criticism 1*, 1 (2014).

[17] Livingston, I.J. et al. How players value their characters in World of Warcraft. In *Proc. CSCW'14*, ACM Press (2014), 1333-1343.

[18] Macaranas, A. et al. Sharing Experiences over Video: watching video programs together at a distance. *Human Computer Interaction – INTERACT 2013*, Springer (2013), 73-90.

[19] Mackinlay, J. & Heer, J. Wideband Displays: Mitigating Multiple Monitor Seams. In *Proc.CHI EA'04*, ACM Press (2004), 1521-1524.

[20] Nansen, B. Exertion Gaming as Kinaesthetic Technicity. *Second Nature: International Journal of Creative Media* 1,2 (2009), 64-91.

[21] Nansen, B. Parental intermediation on YouTube: From moderating to modulating children's digital culture. *Proceedings of Childhood conference*. Inter-disciplinary Press, (2014, forthcoming).

[22] Nansen, B., Arnold, M., Wilken, R. & Gibbs, M. Broadbanding Brunswick: High-speed Broadband and Household Media Ecologies. (2013), Sydney: ACCAN.

[23] Nardi, B, & Harris, J. Strangers and Friends: Collaborative Play in World of Warcraft. In *Proc. CSCW'06*, ACM Press (2006), 149-158.

[24] Norman, K. et. al. Cognitive Layours of Windows and Multiple Screens for User Interfaces. *Int. Journal of Man-Machine Studies 25*, 2 (1986), 229-248.

[25] Oztam. Australian Multi-Screen Report, quarter 1 (2013).

[26] Pargman, D. and Jakobsson, P. Do you believe in magic? Computer games in everyday life. *European Journal of Cultural Studies 11*, 2 (2008), 225-246.

[27] Paul, C. *Wordplay and the Discourse of Videogames*. London: Routledge, (2012).

[28] Tran, M. H., Craick, J., Yang, Y. & Raikundalia, G.Dual Monitors Support Group Awareness in Multiplayer Computer Games. In *Proc. ozCHI'04*, ACM Press (2004), 231-235.

[29] Wilken, R, Arnold, M, Nansen, B, and Gibbs, M. National, Local and Household Media Ecologies: The Case of Australia's National Broadband Network. *Communication, Politics & Culture 46*, 2 (2014)

[30] Yee, N., Ducheneaut, N. & Nelson, L. Introverted Elves & Concientious Gnomes: the expression of personality in World of Warcraft. In *Proc. CHI'11*, ACM Press (2011), 753-762.

[31] Zagal, Z, Björk, S. & Lewis, C. Dark Patterns in the Design of Games. In *Proc. FDG'13*, SASDG (2013), 39-46.

Improving Player Balancing in Racing Games

Jared Cechanowicz[1], Carl Gutwin[1], Scott Bateman[2], Regan L. Mandryk[1], and Ian Stavness[1]
[1]University of Saskatchewan
Saskatoon, Canada, S7N 5C9
firstname.lastname@usask.ca
[2]University of Prince Edward Island
Charlottetown, Canada, C1A 4P3
sbateman@upei.ca

ABSTRACT
In competitive games where players' skill levels are mismatched, the play experience can be unsatisfying for both stronger and weaker players. *Player balancing* provides assistance for less-skilled players in order to make games more competitive and engaging. Although player balancing can be seen in many real-world games, there is little work on the design and effectiveness of these techniques outside of shooting games. In this paper we provide new knowledge about player balancing in the popular and competitive racing genre. We studied issues of noticeability and balancing effectiveness in a prototype racing game, and tested the effects of several balancing techniques on performance and play experience. The techniques significantly improved the balance of player performance, were preferred by both experts and novices, increased novices' feelings of competitiveness, and did not detract from experts' experience. Our results provide new understanding of the design and use of player balancing for racing games, and provide novel techniques that can also be applied to other genres.

Author Keywords
Player balancing; driving games; dynamic balancing.

INTRODUCTION
There are many gameplay situations in which players' skill levels are mismatched. For example, when parents play with their children, or when friends play socially, one person can be considerably better at the game than others. In a competitive game, the mismatch means that play experience can be much less satisfying – for both the stronger and the weaker player. For skilled players, the game is uninteresting because there is little challenge; for weaker players, the game is frustrating because there is little chance of winning.

Player balancing seeks to address this problem by adjusting game parameters to boost performance of weaker players. Player balancing is different from typical game balancing in that it does not attempt to equalize the opportunities provided to each player (e.g., by giving players capabilities of equal strength); rather, the motivation behind player balancing is to provide a more engaging and fun experience for all players. In fact, player balancing works by *un*balancing the game in the traditional sense, in that it gives weaker players greater capabilities or resources.

Forms of player balancing have been seen in real-world games (e.g., handicaps in golf or "head starts" in running games) and in some video games (e.g., the "Bullet Bill" powerup in MarioKart, which allows players at the back of the race to catch up, or the "Fatboy" mod in Unreal Tournament, which makes successful players wider and easier to hit). These balancing techniques are effective, but are also often highly obvious – which may cause all players to feel that the game is unfair, reducing players' engagement.

Previous research has also examined player balancing, but only in a limited number of situations (e.g., [5,11,16,20]). For example, recent studies have shown that player balancing can be effectively applied in 2D and 3D shooting games [5,20]. However, this previous work also showed that applying these techniques in games can be difficult because there are many factors that can reduce the effectiveness of a balancing technique in a particular game or game genre. For example, applying balancing techniques in a more complex 3D game [20] proved to be more difficult than in a simple 2D game [5], because of game elements such as choice of weapons or targets that shoot back. In addition, player awareness of the assistance can reduce its efficacy [3].

Although this previous work shows the potential for player balancing, there is still relatively little known about how player-balancing techniques can be applied in real games. In particular, there are no studies that look at player balancing in game domains that do not involve targeting – and other genres introduce many factors that may change the way that player balancing should be designed.

In this research, we add to understanding about player balancing by investigating the design and application of balancing techniques in an untested genre – racing games. Driving and racing games are a popular genre that is highly competitive but very unlike the shooting games in which player balancing has previously been studied. Some current racing games already contain balancing techniques (such as Mario Kart's "Bullet Bill" powerup), suggesting that there is a real-world interest in player balancing for racing games. In designing balancing techniques for racing games, we focused on three goals: first, to *reduce noticeability*, since the obviousness of current balancing techniques for racing games can detract from the play experience; second, to *cover a large*

CHI PLAY'14, October 19–21, 2014, Toronto, ON, Canada.

ACM 978-1-4503-3014-5/14/10...$15.00.
http://dx.doi.org/10.1145/2658537.2658701

range, to be able to balance players with substantially different skill levels; and third, to *identify effects on other gameplay elements*, since there could be elements that are important to the play experience other than the main game outcome (wins and losses).

To explore these goals in the context of the racing genre, we carried out a series of studies with a custom-built realistic driving game (based on the Racing Game code provided with the XNA environment [18]). We also built a driver simulation system that allowed us to carry out many initial comparisons of different factors, and to have human participants race against opponents with consistent skill levels. Within our prototype, we developed several *player-balancing techniques* – which are composed of a set of balancing mechanism and an adaptation algorithm. We introduced four innovations in order to meet the design goals:

- *Using multiple mechanisms for balance.* We tested the value of balancing more than one game mechanism simultaneously (steering, speed, and acceleration), both to increase the adaptive capability of the system and to reduce the obviousness of any one manipulation.
- *Using assistance and hindrance.* We examined whether additional balancing power (and reduced noticeability) could be obtained by making the skilled player's game mechanics more difficult, rather than just making the weaker player's mechanics easier. For example, the system can push experts' cars away from the center of the road, at the same time as it attracts novices' cars.
- *Using different techniques for dynamic adaptation.* We developed four dynamic-adaptation techniques that use different approaches for calculating when to re-balance the game (two continuous distance thresholds, one fixed distance threshold, and one time-based sliding window).
- *Using a simulated driver.* We built a feedback-control based simulated opponent to perform automated tests of our adaptation algorithms and to provide consistent opponents in our studies with human participants.

We tested the effects of our balancing techniques both on several performance variables (e.g., wins, lead changes, distance and time between players), and also on game-experience variables that provide a richer view of a player's subjective experience (e.g., feelings of competence and autonomy, and subjective assessment of enjoyment, engagement, fun, and fairness).

Our studies provide six main findings:

- Using multiple balancing mechanisms simultaneously worked best both for increasing the balancing range, and for decreasing the noticeability-to-effect ratio;
- Using hindrance for experts substantially increased balancing range – and in addition, negative adaptations were less noticeable to expert players;
- Our techniques were able to balance several gameplay metrics. Gameplay metrics include measures other than game outcome (i.e., wins or losses) – e.g., distance between players or number of lead changes;
- Different adaptation algorithms led to different kinds of balance in the game (some techniques led to more lead changes, others to smaller distances), but also had different degrees of noticeability and perceived fairness;
- The balancing techniques significantly improved the subjective play experience for novices (e.g., they felt that they had a better chance of winning), and did not detract from the subjective play experience for experts;
- The technique that led to more lead reversals was ranked first by both novices and experts, suggesting that there is particular value in manipulations that lead to balance in gameplay metrics (such as the number of lead changes).

Our studies are the first broad examination of the design and effectiveness of player balancing techniques in racing games. We provide four main contributions. First, we show that player balancing techniques can work well in this genre. Second, we show that balancing multiple mechanisms simultaneously (including both assistance and hindrance) shows promise for increasing the range of the system and reducing noticeability on the player's own performance. Third, we show that different approaches to dynamic balancing have different effects on game results and perceived gameplay. Fourth, we show that there are several gameplay metrics that capture important elements of the overall play experience, over and above typical win/loss outcomes. Our work broadens the understanding of player balancing and suggests new ways to improve games' ability to support shared play.

RELATED WORK

Game Balancing

Flow is a concept that describes optimal experience, and it occurs when people are engaged and interested in their tasks without feeling overly anxious [8]. Game designers and developers try to *balance* games to provide players with the right mix of challenge and achievement [10], which can promote the experience of flow. Designing games to be balanced is extremely important – if a player finds part of a game too easy or too difficult, they may become disengaged or frustrated [17]. Balancing is an essential part of games because part of people's willingness to play games is based on whether or not they find a game enjoyable [17,21].

In order for people to have fun together in multiplayer games, each player should have an equal chance to win [1], and it is people's ability to compete that often motivates them to participate [21]. However, an important challenge for multiplayer games is that performance is often based upon previous experience, complex in-game skills (e.g., producing button combinations) and physical abilities (e.g., reaction time). These differences in abilities and experience can lead to substantial differences in performance between two players, which can reduce competition and fun [17]. Therefore, game designers are also interested in how balancing competition (i.e., player balancing) can be achieved. This has been recognized in the game industry, where play testing and simulations help uncover such game elements.

Player Balancing

We identified four main ways that player balancing can be achieved in video games.

1. Matchmaking: Grouping players by ability is one way in which multiplayer online games balance player competition. Some games make use of complex systems that work to identify groups of players with similar skill levels [17]. These systems work in a manner similar to ladders for squash, and are important parts of Halo [12] and StarCraft 2. Two problems with matchmaking are that it requires an accurate idea of player skill, which may not be available [22], and that it requires a pool of available players of different skill levels.

2. Asymmetric Roles: Many games allow players to perform different tasks or roles that suit their level of skill or their abilities. For example, in sports, players can have very different responsibilities (e.g., offence or defence). In games like World of Warcraft, a successful raid party is composed of several different roles (e.g., tanks and healers).

3. Difficulty Adjustment: Difficulty adjustment is a common way to match a game's level of challenge to a player's ability. For example, many games have explicit difficulty levels that can be selected before the game starts. Adaptive difficulty adjustment is a less explicit approach that changes game elements or controls based on player performance [14]. While this can provide appropriate levels of challenge, adaptive difficulty adjustments must be designed carefully. For example, obvious techniques such as the "rubber-band" effect used to speed up trailing players in Mario Kart can lead to a sense of frustration for experienced players who can feel cheated [17]. Further, scaling game difficulty based on player performance or progress can lead to a player feeling that their achievements are meaningless [6].

4. Assists: Assists adjust a player's ability to perform basic in-game actions by simplifying the input required to correctly perform an action. For example, aim assistance helps a player aim to a target. Recent studies have shown that aim assistance can improve player performance in both 2D [5] and 3D games [20]. One study showed that players with less skill were able to improve and better compete with more skilled partners, and players reported having more fun with the game when the competition was tighter [5]. Further, these studies have shown that assists balance games, and yet players have difficulty noticing them, or may not notice them at all. These studies also show, however, that as games become more complex, other game elements can overshadow the effectiveness of aim assistance – e.g., one FPS study suggested that player movement, weapon choice, presence of friendlies, and enemy aggressiveness can change aim assistance [20].

Video Racing Game Balancing and Assists

A wide range of research has been carried out with racing games. For example, studies have examined the effects of input device [1,15], view [1] and track width [1] on player satisfaction and performance; or the extent to which players modify cars or tracks, or use game mode options [13].

Some modern racing games provide user-controlled assists. In Forza 4, a player can selectively activate assists for stability control, traction control, braking, steering, shifting, damage, and optimal path guidance. Recently, Debeauvais et al. [9] analysed the use of these assists, showing that certain assists were used by most players and never turned off (e.g., limiting the amount of damage from collisions), and some players actively try enabling and disabling assists as their performance improves; however, they did not investigate the use of assists for balancing in racing games.

Other racing games provide player balancing techniques, such as the Mario Kart examples discussed above. Mario Kart is primarily a social game, however, and few examples of player balancing are available in more "serious" titles.

PLAYER BALANCING FOR RACING GAMES

Racing games are competitive multi-player games that involve different play mechanisms than 2D or 3D shooters. Racing games typically involve two or more players racing on a specified track – each player controls a car, and the system provides a realistic simulation of accelerating, braking, and cornering. Racing games often use standard game controllers, with a joystick for steering and buttons for controlling accelerator and brake pedals. The view for these games provides a third-person view of the car (sometimes a first-person view is used or is an alternative) and the track, with feedback about car state (e.g., a speedometer and gear indicator) and the race state (e.g., indicators of the player's current position). Figure 1 shows our example racing game that follows these conventions – in this game, the two players' views are shown in a split-screen format.

Figure 1. Two-player racing game used in the study. Local participant at right; simulated opponent at left.

Factors affecting play experience in racing

We analysed existing racing games to determine gameplay metrics that could be used in player balancing techniques.

- *Wins and losses.* The most obvious result of a race is who wins – this is the traditional outcome that is a natural target for balancing; however, winning a race is made up of a driver's performance on several factors, and it may be difficult to balance wins without introducing obvious and artificial assists that detract from the play experience.

- *Distance between cars.* Regardless of the final outcome, players have a sense of being "in the race" and of competing by being close during the contest – if a player is too far back, they feel that there is no chance of winning.
- *Other car within sight.* For both the leader and the follower, being able to see the other car can increase the sense of competitiveness and the chance of challenging for the lead. Conversely, if the leader is out of sight, a race devolves to a single-player game for both players.
- *Lead changes.* Passing the current race leader can increase excitement and feelings of competition for both players – again, regardless of the eventual outcome of the race.

We designed balancing techniques to target these important game elements. Our techniques are made up of three parts: 1) *a set of balancing mechanisms* (i.e., the parts of the game that are manipulated to change player performance), 2) a set of *levels* that determine the strength of the mechanisms, and 3) a set of *adaptation algorithms* that determine when, and by how much, to apply the mechanisms during the race.

Assist-based Balancing Mechanisms

We implemented three assist balancing mechanisms that affect different aspects of a driving game: the car's speed, the car's acceleration, and the player's steering accuracy. Each mechanism can be manipulated in either direction to provide assistance to novices, or hindrance to experts.

Speed. Speed is adjusted by adding or subtracting a fixed amount from the player's current speed, based on the level of assistance or hindrance (from -5 to +5), and scaled proportionally to the top speed of the car. For example, when moving at the top (unassisted) speed, a level of +5 adds 5 m.p.h. to the car's speed, and a level of -5 subtracts 5 m.p.h.

Acceleration. Acceleration is adjusted by manipulating the airFriction parameter of the car, using an empirically-determined constant multiplied by the assistance level (from -5 to +5). A level of -5 meant that the car took about 1.5x the baseline time to reach top speed, and with +5, about 0.75x.

Steering. To adjust steering, the system compares the car's current heading to the direction of the road, and calculates the steering error – a number from 0 (no error) to 1 (90 degrees off course). The player's current steering amount is then adjusted by an amount proportional to the error and to the level (-5 to +5), either towards the optimal path (assistance) or away from it (hindrance). This means that the system does not steer for the player, it only adjusts the player's own steering actions (pilot testing showed that this feature was important for reducing noticeability).

We combined the three balancing mechanisms into a single approach that contained ten levels of possible adjustment to players' performance: five of assistance, and five of hindrance (i.e., from +5 to -5).

Adaptation Algorithms

We developed four schemes for applying the balancing mechanisms, plus a control condition with no balancing.

Realtime100. This algorithm sets the level of the balancing based on the distance between the players. Every 100 meters represents a level of assistance or hindrance – for example, if the player is 1-100 meters behind, they receive level +1 assistance; if they are 101-200 meters behind, they receive level +2 assistance. Similarly, if the player is 1-100 meters ahead, they receive level -1 hindrance.

Realtime40. Uses the same principle as Realtime100, but changes the balancing level with every 40-meter difference in distance (rather than 100 meters), thus it is more aggressive in adapting performance – players reach the maximum level of assistance or hindrance when there is 200 meters between players (rather than 500).

Rolling. Averages the level of assistance or hindrance from the Realtime100 scheme, using a rolling window of 50 seconds. The time window means that balancing takes longer to have an effect, but any advantage or disadvantage also lasts longer; e.g., a player who is behind will not receive assistance immediately, but after 50 seconds, their assistance level will remain, even if they pass the other player.

MaxDistance. A player's level of assistance is that used for the maximum distance that they were ever behind or ahead (using Realtime100), but all balancing is turned off when the gap between players is less than 50 meters. This scheme therefore balances the play to bring weaker players up to stronger players, but does not interfere once they are close.

Driving Game Apparatus

We implemented our algorithms in C# in a realistic two-person driving simulation based on the *Racing Game* prototype included with Microsoft's XNA environment [18] (Figure 1).

Simulating Opponents

To test our adaptation algorithms and to provide consistent opponents in our main study, we simulated the opponent in the game by building an automatic driving controller. Simulated opponents can provide a more reliable level of performance across different races and different participants, and also reduced the overall number of participants needed for the study, allowing us to gather data about more conditions.

Car speed and steering were automatically controlled in order for the simulated driver to follow a target path around the track. The controller used a proportional-derivative feedback control law [2] so that the simulated driver would automatically respond to disturbances, such as collisions, and continue racing. The performance of the simulated driver could be hindered by adding noise to the feedback so that the controller's actions were not perfect, and consequently the simulated driver's lap time increased.

Past work has used a predetermined script of driving actions or behaviors [7]. Our controller-based simulated driver uses feedback of in-game events to respond appropriately in the context of a specific race. Importantly, balancing mechanisms can be directly incorporated into the controlled driver, which is not possible with a pre-scripted driver.

Simulated drivers were used in a pilot study to tune the parameters in the balancing mechanisms. Races between two simulated drivers with different levels of performance were conducted over a wide range of balancing mechanism parameters in order to estimate a range of parameters that resulted in the best-balanced races. This simulation-based tuning approach allows for large numbers of simulated races to be performed in a fraction of the time that would be required if done with human participants. The study showed that multiple mechanisms are more effective in adjusting performance than single mechanisms, and that the combination of all three performed best of all. We therefore used all three mechanisms in the main study.

Simulated drivers were also used in the main study to act as the opponent for our human participants. The target path around the racetrack for the simulated drivers was determined empirically by recording the path taken by expert and novice human drivers prior to conducting our experiment. Four different paths (source traces) were used for each of the expert and novice simulated drivers, which allowed for minor lap-to-lap variation, making the simulated drivers seem more realistic to the human players.

Pilot Test of Noticeability on Players' Own Performance

We carried out a pilot study to assess the noticeability of the three balancing mechanisms on a player's own performance, at different global levels of assistance or hindrance. Four participants from our lab carried out solo races with the different levels of assistance and hindrance, and then guessed at the level. The system applied either one mechanism or all three.

Results of the pilot showed that although all mechanisms had a roughly linear effect on performance (both with negative and positive modifications), noticeability was greater when individual techniques were used. The idea of "spreading around" the assist/hindrance appeared to reduce the noticeability in any one area. In addition, hindrances were consistently less noticeable than assists. We further discuss the issue of noticeability later in the paper.

STUDY: TESTING AND COMPARING THE TECHNIQUES

Our final study compared the effects of the four adaptation algorithms (which determined when and how the balancing mechanisms were applied) plus a control condition.

Experimental Conditions

Each condition combined the three balancing mechanisms (speed, acceleration, and steering) with one of the five adaptation algorithms (Control, Realtime100, Realtime40, Rolling, and MaxDist) in our racing game. Each adaptive algorithm (other than Control) used the mechanisms in the same way; therefore there were five experiment conditions, comprised of the four adaptation algorithms and the control.

Procedure

Participants completed a consent form and demographics questionnaire, and were introduced to the controls for the driving simulator. Participants self-identified as a novice or expert in racing games, and the experimenter subjectively confirmed these self-assessments (no participants were found to have over- or under-estimated their skill level). Participants were introduced to the two-player version of the game (see Figure 1), and told to complete the course as quickly as possible. Participants then completed 10 two-person races, two for each adaptation condition (order was rotated using a Latin Square, blocked by condition and data from the two races were aggregated for central tendency).

To provide opponents whose skill remained consistent across participants and conditions, all opponents were simulated drivers: we simulated a novice driver if the participant was an expert, and an expert driver if the participant was a novice. The simulated opponent was implemented as previously described, and one of the four described source traces was used for each condition (source trace order was counterbalanced). Participants were told that their opponents for the races were other humans – either novices or experts – who would be playing across the network from another location. We also stated that each set of races could involve a set of (unspecified) manipulations to the cars.

After each race, participants completed an experience survey. The questionnaire included subjective questions about enjoyment, competitiveness, and perception of fairness, and also included PENS questions [19] that examine the concepts of competence, autonomy, and relatedness from self-determination theory. After the session, participants ranked all conditions in terms of overall preference.

Participants and Apparatus

Thirty participants were recruited from a local university (7 female; mean age 24 years); 15 were experts, and 15 were novices (based on self-assessment as described above).

The study was conducted on a Windows 7 PC with a 1920x1080 screen. The software recorded all experimental data including race times and player positions.

Design and Research Questions

The study used a 5×2 mixed-factorial repeated-measures design, with between-participants factor *Expertise* (Expert or Novice) and within-participants factor *Adaptation* (Control, Realtime100, Realtime40, Rolling, MaxDist). We examined dependent measures relating to performance (wins, time differences, distance between cars, number of lead changes), and measures relating to experience (perception of enjoyment, competitiveness, and fairness; and measures of competence, autonomy, and relatedness).

We explored five questions in the study:

Q1. *Does balancing work?* Will the gap between expert and novice performance be reduced in the balancing conditions compared to the control condition?

Q2. *Does balancing improve novice experience?* Are novices' ratings of subjective experience higher in balancing conditions than in the control condition?

Q3. *Does balancing detract from expert experience?* Are experts' ratings of subjective experience worse in the balancing conditions?

Q4. *Is balancing preferred overall?* Do players prefer the balanced conditions over the control condition?

Q5. *How do the adaptation schemes differ?* What are the differences in the adaptation conditions' effects on performance and experience measures?

Results

Our results are organized below by analysis of performance measures and experience measures; we return to the research questions after the presentation of results.

Performance Measures

The subsections below consider win/loss rate, race time, mean distance between players over the course of the race, lead changes, and the amount of time that players were close enough to see one another (within 80 meters). Recall that experts and novices both played against simulated opponents (of the opposite skill level), and thus all novice-expert comparisons are comprised of independent race data.

In all of the performance analyses where experts and novices could be compared, experts were significantly better (all $p < 0.05$). This was expected, so we do not report these results, in order to focus on the effects of the balancing techniques. In all charts, error bars show +/- one standard error.

Wins and Losses

As expected, experts won the large majority of races: human experts won 94.6% of their races; human novices, only 7.3%. The win-loss results are shown in Figure 2; only two balancing techniques led to any wins for human novices, and three techniques led to losses for human experts.

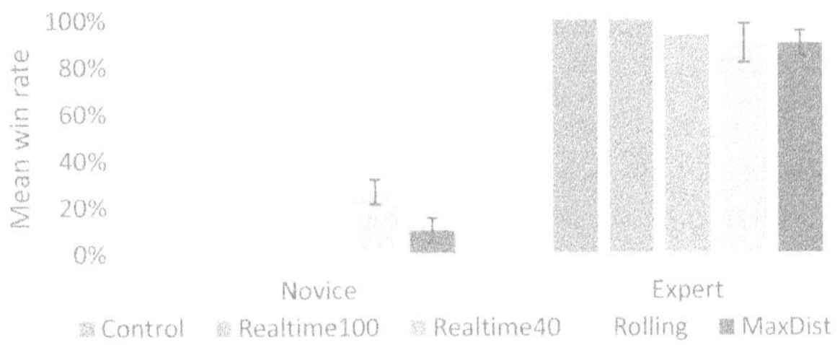

Figure 2. Mean win percentage by expertise and adaptation.

RM-ANOVA showed no overall main effect of Adaptation ($F_{4,112}$=2.24, p=.069) on wins, but did show an interaction between Adaptation and Expertise ($F_{4,112}$=7.31, p<.0001). For experts, there was no effect ($F_{4,56}$=1.59, p=.189), but for novices, the effect of Adaptation was significant ($F_{4,56}$=7.66, p<.0001).

A follow-up Tukey HSD test on the novice results showed that *Rolling* and *MaxDist* had significantly more wins than the other three balancing techniques, and also that *Rolling* was significantly higher than *MaxDist* (all p<0.01).

Difference in Race Time

Overall, human experts finished their races 6.6 seconds ahead of their simulated opponents, and human novices finished 11.2 seconds behind. The results for the different adaptation conditions are shown in Figure 3.

Repeated-measures ANOVA showed an overall main effect of Adaptation ($F_{4,112}$=148.3, p<.0001), and an interaction between Adaptation and Expertise ($F_{4,112}$=15.33, p<.0001). A follow-up Tukey HSD test on the main effect showed that all of the balancing conditions had smaller time differences than the control condition (all p<0.01) and that *MaxDist* had a smaller time difference than *Realtime100* (p<0.05). The interaction is illustrated in Figure 3: there was less of a time difference between human experts and their simulated opponents than for human novices and their opponents.

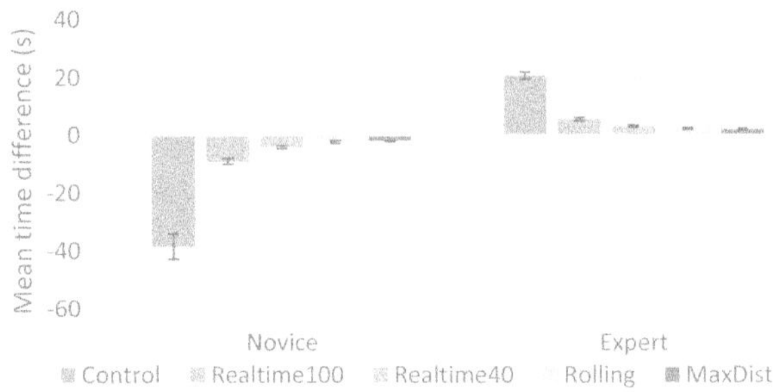

Figure 3. Mean time difference between players.

Mean Distance Between Players Over Entire Race

We recorded the distance between the players throughout the race. On average, human experts were 92 meters ahead of their simulated opponents, and human novices were 112 meters behind their simulated opponents (see Figure 4).

Figure 4. Mean distance between players over the race.

RM-ANOVA showed an overall main effect of Adaptation ($F_{4,112}$=155.9, p<.0001), and an interaction between Adaptation and Expertise ($F_{4,112}$=18.66, p<.0001). As before, human experts were not as far ahead of their simulated opponents as the human novices were behind their opponents. A follow-up Tukey HSD test on the main effect showed that all of the balancing conditions had smaller distance differences than the control condition (all p<0.01) and that *MaxDist* and *Rolling* had smaller differences than *Realtime100* (p<0.05).

Lead Changes

The number of times the lead changed during the race is shown in Figure 5. Overall, the races with human novices had 4.6 changes, and the races with human experts had 3.1.

RM-ANOVA showed an overall main effect of Adaptation ($F_{4,112}$=45.84, p<.0001), but no interaction between Adaptation and Expertise ($F_{4,112}$=1.19, p<.318). Tukey HSD showed that *Rolling* and *MaxDist* had significantly more lead changes than the other three conditions, and that *Rolling* also had more than *MaxDist* (all p<0.01).

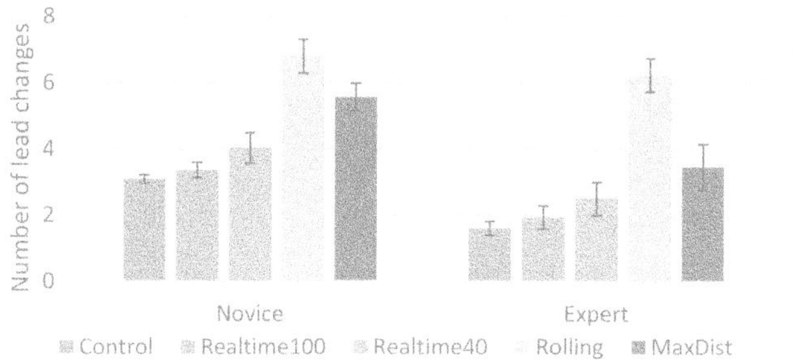

Figure 5. Mean number of lead changes.

Time that Players were Within 80m

To analyse how the different conditions kept players within sight of one another, we recorded the number of seconds that the distance between the two cars was 80m or less (an estimate of the distance at which the front car could be seen, based on informal tests). Results are shown in Figure 6.

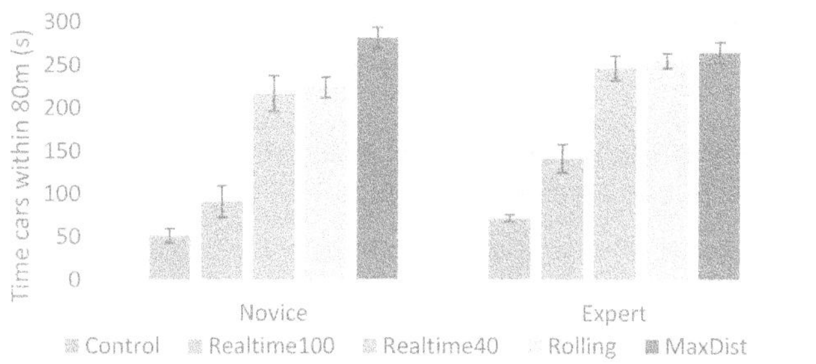

Figure 6. Mean time players were within 80m.

Repeated-measures ANOVA showed an overall main effect of Adaptation ($F_{4,112}$=162.1, p<.0001), and an interaction between Adaptation and Expertise ($F_{4,112}$=3.01, p<.05). Tukey HSD on the main effect showed that all the balancing conditions led to significantly longer times where players were within 80m (all p<0.01), that *Realtime100* led to less within-sight time than the other balancing conditions (p<0.01), and that *MaxDist* had a longer time than *Realtime40* (p<0.05). The interaction can be seen in Figure 6; there was no difference between *MaxDist* and *Rolling* or *RealTime40* for Experts, but there was for Novices.

Experience Measures

Subjective Questions

Participants completed a questionnaire after each adaptation condition. A summary of responses to the subjective experience questions on this survey is shown in Figure 7. (Means are shown in the charts, but all analyses discussed below used non-parametric tests on the rank data).

We used Friedman ranks tests to look for effects of Adaptation on the four experience measures. We analysed experts and novices separately; Table 1 shows the results.

Figure 7. Mean subjective experience responses (5-point Likert scale: 1 = "strongly disagree", 5 = "strongly agree").

We used Friedman ranks tests to look for effects of Adaptation on the four experience measures. We analysed experts and novices separately; Table 1 shows the results.

	Experts		Novices	
	χ^2_r	p	χ^2_r	p
I enjoyed the competition	1.69	.79	2.60	0.63
I had a chance of winning	0.53	0.97	25.2	**<0.01**
My opponent had an unfair advantage	18.4	**<0.01**	8.04	0.09
I had fun	1.20	0.88	6.64	0.16

Table 1. Friedman rank tests of subjective responses.

For the two measures that showed significant effects of Adaptation, we carried out follow-up pairwise Wilcoxon tests. For the novices' responses to "I had a chance of winning", followup showed that *Realtime40, Rolling*, and *MaxDist* had significantly higher ratings than *Control* (p<0.05). For experts' responses to "My opponent had an unfair advantage", followup showed that *Rolling* had higher ratings than *Control* and *Realtime100* (p<0.05).

PENS Measures

We gathered perceived competence, autonomy, and relatedness using a validated scale after each condition. RM-ANOVA revealed a main effect of Adaptation on competence ($F_{4,112}$=3.9, p<.005) and relatedness ($F_{4,112}$=4.6, p<.002). Players rated their competence as lower after *Control* than after *Realtime40, Rolling*, or *MaxDist* (all p<0.02); however, a significant interaction with Expertise ($F_{4,112}$=4.3, p<.003) shows that these results held true for Novices, but that there were no differences for Experts. A significant interaction of Adaptation and Expertise on Autonomy ($F_{4,112}$=2.7, p<.004) revealed that Novices rated their autonomy lower after *Control* than after *Rolling* or *MaxDist* (all p<0.03), whereas there was no difference for Experts. Both experts and novice players rated their relatedness after *Control* lower than after *Realtime40, Rolling*, or *MaxDist* (all p<0.05) with no interaction with Expertise (p>0.06).

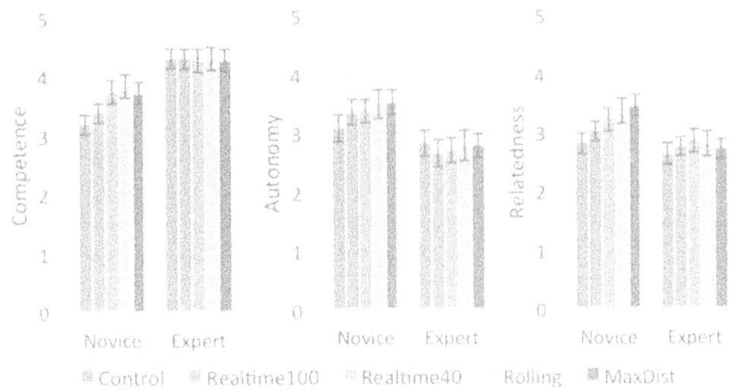

Figure 8. Mean perceived competence, autonomy, and relatedness by expertise and adaptation (1-5, higher is better).

Overall Preferences

At the end of the session, participants ranked the five conditions in order of overall preference (5 = least preferred, 1 = most preferred). Mean rankings are shown in Figure 9. As shown in the figure, there were some differences between novices' and experts' preferences (e.g., experts ranked *Control* higher than novices), but both groups ranked *Rolling* as the best condition overall, both in terms of average rank and number of first-rank votes (10 of 15 novices and 6 of 15 experts ranked *Rolling* in first place).

We looked for effects of Adaptation on preference with a Friedman rank test. There was a significant effect for novices (χ^2_r=19.36, p<0.001) but not for experts (χ^2_r=6.03, p=0.20).

Follow-up pairwise Wilcoxon tests for novices' data showed that *Rolling* was preferred over *Control* and *Realtime40*, and that *MaxDist* was preferred over *Control* (all p<0.05).

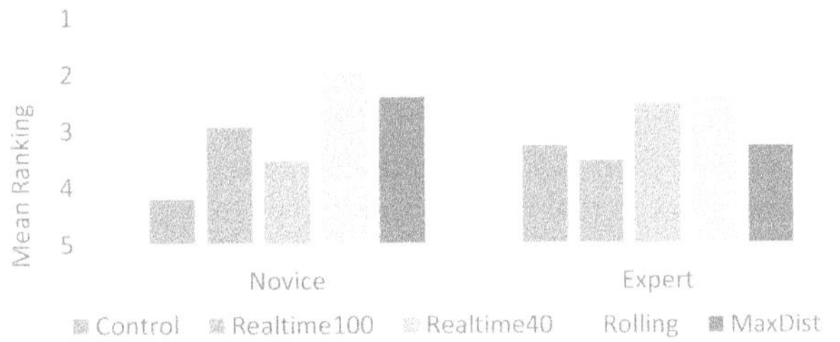

Figure 9. Mean rankings by expertise and adaptation

Summary of Results by Research Question

Q0: Does balancing multiple mechanisms simultaneously increase range and reduce noticeability?

- Pilot studies showed that combining all three mechanisms was best at increasing range (using simulated drivers) and reducing noticeability (using human participants).

Q1. Does balancing work?

- All of the adaptive algorithms had positive effects on at least some of the race performance variables, although experts still won the large majority of races.
- Various adaptations improved all of the elements of performance that we tested (win/loss rates, time differential, distance between cars, and lead changes).
- The *Rolling* and *MaxDist* adaptations were best at reducing performance differences between experts and novices.

Q2. Does balancing improve novice experience?

- Three adaptations (*Rolling*, *MaxDist*, and *Realtime40*) changed novices' experience of the game's competitiveness, and improved experienced competence and relatedness to the opponent. *Rolling* and *MaxDist* also raised the experience of autonomy.
- No effects were found for subjective enjoyment or fun.

Q3. Does balancing detract from expert experience?

- One adaptation (*Rolling*) changed experts' perception of fairness; this technique led to increased feelings that the other player had an unfair advantage.
- No effects were found for questions about enjoyment, fun, or competitiveness, and experts did not rate their competence lower for adaptions that hindered them.
- Three adaptations (*Rolling*, *MaxDist*, and *Realtime40*) improved experts' feelings of relatedness to the opponent.

Q4. Is balancing preferred overall?

- The *Rolling* technique was the top-ranked technique by both novices and experts.
- Novices ranked all of the adaptations higher than the control condition.
- Novices significantly preferred the *Rolling* and *MaxDist* conditions over the other conditions.

Q5. How do the adaptation schemes differ?

- The more aggressive adaptations (*Rolling* and *MaxDist*) had greater effects on performance variables – and were the only techniques that led to wins for human novices.
- The more aggressive techniques also led to an increase in experts' feelings that the opponent had an unfair advantage; but also represented the most preferred technique overall by novices and experts (*Rolling*).

DISCUSSION

In the following sections we discuss explanations for our results and underlying ideas that are applicable in other settings and for other games.

Explanations for Results

Why did the balancing techniques succeed?

Player balancing techniques work by artificially assisting the weaker player (or by hindering the stronger player), but the presence of a balancing technique does not guarantee that the outcome of play will be balanced, since there are many aspects of a game that can complicate the application of balancing [19]. In our study, there are three main reasons why the player balancing techniques worked well.

Continuous balancing. Our techniques involved game activities that happen continuously (e.g., steering and speed) rather than discrete events such as the shooting events studied in previous studies [4,19]. This is valuable for player balancing because it provides more opportunity to assist (or hinder) the player – as a result, the manipulation can be smaller and potentially less noticeable.

Increasing the adaptation range. Player balancing schemes can fail to work effectively if they cannot provide enough assistance (i.e., experts are too good). Our techniques substantially increased the range of abilities that could be balanced through two innovations: manipulating three game mechanisms instead of one, and using both positive and negative manipulation. These innovations made a major difference in the range of differences that could be balanced, and did not increase noticeability.

Effects on important in-game events. Two of our techniques (*Rolling* and *MaxDist*) led to larger changes in the game state, which meant that there were more changes to elements of the race that are important to players. For example, lead changes or keeping the players within sight of one another appears to add more excitement and competitiveness to the game than other manipulations.

Why were Rolling and MaxDist preferred over Realtime?

The *Rolling* and *MaxDist* techniques led to the largest changes in game variables, were preferred by participants, and led to increased feelings of relatedness. The main differences between these techniques and the two *Realtime* techniques were the aggressiveness and duration of the balancing manipulations, and these differences indicate that these qualities may be important for improving play experience. The *Realtime* techniques can be considered as "asymptotic" methods, in that the level of assistance or hindrance is proportional to the distance between the players. This means that as the novice player catches up to the expert, assistance is gradually reduced – resulting in Sisyphean situations where the novice can get close to the expert but never reach them.

In contrast, *Rolling* and *MaxDist* do not follow an asymptote, but rather use a "pendulum" approach that maintains a stronger manipulation for a time period (*Rolling*) or until a distance threshold is reached (*MaxDist*). Although this approach makes it more obvious that players are being helped (reducing feelings of autonomy for novices), the effects on game events (e.g., lead reversals, occasional wins by novices) made for a more competitive experiences for all.

This result may underlie the design of existing techniques like the Bullet Bill powerup – that is, it is more fun (for all players) if the last-place driver occasionally moves into the lead than for them to remain in last place but by a smaller margin. Techniques like *Rolling* represent an important advance over the obviousness of Bullet-Bill-style assists, however, since *Rolling* is applied dynamically and invisibly (rather than as an explicit powerup) and only affects the player's driving actions, rather than taking over control of the car.

Generalization and Application of the Results

Application to other game genres

Several of the successful ideas used here can be applied to player balancing in other games. First, there are many genres that use the basic idea of racing as one element in the larger game (e.g., military simulations often involve travel by vehicle, and many games involve attempts to reach an objective before others). In these situations, the balancing techniques used here could be directly applied (although they will only balance the race-based parts of the game).

Second, balancing through simultaneous manipulation of multiple mechanisms could be used in several game types. For example, balancing in a first-person shooter game could involve factors such as health, hitbox size, movement speed, or visibility to other players; in an RTS game, balancing could affect factors such as the appearance rate of resources, or a unit's speed, power, or build time.

Third, the idea of continuous balancing could be applied even in genres where many of the important game elements are discrete events (e.g., shots in FPS games). In these situations, continuous balancing could be used on game variables such as avatar movement, the control-to-display ratio of aiming actions, or healing speed.

Fourth, assistance and hindrance can also be applied to other genres. Pairing hindrance with continuous game activities may be more effective than with discrete events, because whereas experienced players may notice even small degradations in the discrete behaviour of the system (e.g., shooting accuracy), it may be more difficult for them to predict the exact behaviour of a continuous variable.

Noticeability and Fairness

Our assessment of noticeability was limited to people's perception of how different techniques affected their own performance (in the pilot), and their perception of whether the other person had been given an advantage (main study). There are several other aspects of both of these issues that can be explored, and our investigation is only a starting point. Nevertheless, our findings suggest several issues that designers should consider regarding the obviousness of balancing techniques in real-world racing games.

Noticeability of effects on other players may have been higher in our study than in the real world. We stated that balancing techniques could be in use; it is possible that experts over-estimated the help that their opponent received – experts felt like their opponent had a small advantage even in the control (i.e., no balancing) condition (Figure 7).

It may be that noticeability has more to do with the players' previous knowledge of each others' abilities than with in-game changes caused by the techniques. Players in our study likely built up this kind of knowledge over the five races (even though the opponent was simulated, it had similar base ability throughout), and so the adaptations may have been more obvious than they would be in the real world. Suggesting experimentally that the participants are racing unique players each race could tease out the differential effects of algorithm and familiarity. The possible relationship between player familiarity and technique noticeability suggests that in situations where players do not know their opponent's abilities, it will be more difficult for them to notice balancing.

Future Work

We will extend this research in several ways. First, we will further test our techniques by examining their use in real-world social play situations – e.g., a race tournament to determine whether pairs of players with skill differences react like the expert-novice pairings studied here. Second, we will further explore effects of our techniques on different types of noticeability. Third, we will test the underlying ideas of multiple-variable balancing and positive-and-negative effects in a different genre such as FPS or RTS. Fourth, we will further examine the relationship between balancing and in-game play experiences that are not part of ultimate game outcomes.

CONCLUSION

Player balancing is a solution to the problem of competitive play situations in which players have different skill levels. Although player balancing can be seen in many games, few studies look at the design and effectiveness of these techniques – particularly outside of shooting games – and the research that has been done suggests that real games introduce many elements that can complicate balancing. In this paper, we provide initial knowledge about player balancing in the popular and competitive racing genre.

We carried out investigations to explore noticeability and balancing effectiveness, and tested the effects of several balancing techniques on measures of game performance and play experience. A comparative study found that balancing techniques can be very successful in a realistic racing game – our techniques significantly reduced differences in several aspects of race performance, were preferred by both experts and novices, increased novices' feelings of competitiveness, and did not detract from the play experience for experts. Our results provide initial understanding of how player balancing techniques can be designed and used in multi-player racing games, and suggest ways that the principles underlying our techniques can be applied to other genres.

REFERENCES

1. Adams, E. *Fundamentals of Game Design*. New Riders, 2010.
2. Araki, M. PID control. *Control systems, robotics and automation, 2*. 2002.
3. Baldwin, A., Johnson, D., & Wyeth, P.A. The effect of multiplayer dynamic difficulty adjustment on the player experience of video games. In *Proc. CHI EA*, 2014, 1489-1494.
4. Bateman, S., Doucette, A., Xiao, R.B., Gutwin, C., Mandryk, R.L., & Cockburn, A. Effects of View, Input Device, and Track Width on Video Game Driving. In *Proc. GI, 2011*, 207-214.
5. Bateman, S., Mandryk, R.L., Stach, T. and Gutwin, C. Target assistance for subtly balancing competitive play. In *Proc. CHI 2011*, ACM Press (2011), 2355-2364.
6. Bostan, B., and Öğüt, S. Game challenges and difficulty levels: lessons learned From RPGs. In *International Simulation and Gaming Association Conference*, 2009.
7. Chan, H. *Vehicular racing simulation: a MEL scripting approach* (Phd dissertation, Texas A&M Univ.), 2014.
8. Csíkszentmihályi, M. Flow: *The Psychology of Optimal Experience*. Harper and Row, 1990.
9. Debeauvais, T., Zimmermann, T., Nagappan, N., Carter, K., Cooper, R., Greenawalt, D., & Solberg, T. Off With Their Assists: An Empirical Study of Driving Skill in Forza Motorsports 4. In *Proc. FDG 2014*.
10. Falstein, N. Understanding fun – the Theory of Natural Funativity. In *Introduction to Game Development*, Rabin, S. (ed.), Charles River Media, 2005, 71-98.
11. Gerling, K., Miller, M., Mandryk, R., Birk, M., Smeddinck, J. Effects of Balancing for Physical Abilities on Player Performance, Experience and Self-Esteem in Exergames In *Proc. CHI 2014*, 2201-2210.
12. Herbrich, R., Minka, T., and Graepel, T. TrueSkill(TM): A Bayesian skill rating system. In *Advances in Neural Information Processing Systems*, 20, 569-576, 2007.
13. Hullett, K., Nagappan, N., Schuh, E., and and Hopson, J. Empirical analysis of user data in game software development. In *Proc. ESEM 2012*, 89-98.
14. Hunicke, R. The case for dynamic difficulty adjustment in games. In *Proceedings of Advances in Computer Entertainment Technology*, vol. 265, 429-433, 2005.
15. Kavakli, M., Thorne, J.R. A Usability Study of Input Devices on Measuring User Performance in Computer Games. In *Proc. of ICITA* 2002.
16. Mueller, F., Vetere, F., Gibbs, M.R., Edge, D., Agamanolis, S., Sheridan, J.G., and Heer, J. Balancing Exertion Experiences. In *Proc. of CHI 2012*, 1853-1862.
17. Newheiser, Mark. Playing Fair: A Look at Competition in Gaming. *Strange Horizons*. Published March 9 2009, www.strangehorizons.com/2009/20090309/newheiser-a.shtml. Accessed May 6, 2014.
18. Nitschke, B. *XNA Racing Game*. www.exdream.com/XnaRacingGame, accessed May 6, 2014.
19. Ryan, R., Rigby, C., & Przybylski, A., Motivational pull of video games: A self-determination theory approach. Motivation and Emotion, 2006, 30, 347-365.
20. Vicencio-Moreira, R., Mandryk, R.L., Gutwin, C., and Bateman, S. The effectiveness (or lack thereof) of aim-assist techniques in first-person shooter games. In *Proc. CHI 2014*. ACM Press (2014), 937-946.
21. Vorderer, P., Hartmann, T., and Klimmt, C. Explaining the enjoyment of playing video games: the role of competition. *Proc. Entertainment Computing 2003*, 1-9.
22. Youssef, A. and Cossell, S. Thoughts on adjusting perceived difficulty in games. In *Proc. Australasian Conference on Interactive Entertainment*, 1-4, 2009.

The First Hour Experience: How the Initial Play can Engage (or Lose) New Players

Gifford Cheung
The Information School
University of Washington
giffordc@uw.edu

Thomas Zimmermann
Microsoft Research
Redmond, WA
tzimmer@microsoft.com

Nachiappan Nagappan
Microsoft Research
Redmond, WA
nachin@microsoft.com

ABSTRACT
The first time a player sits down with a game is critical for their engagement. Games are a voluntary activity and easy to abandon. If the game cannot hold player attention, it will not matter how much fun the game is later on if the player quits early. Worse, if the initial experience was odious enough, the player will dissuade others from playing. Industry advice is to make the game fun from the start to hook the player. In our analysis of over 200 game reviews and interviews with industry professionals, we advance an alternative, complementary solution. New design terminology is introduced such as "holdouts" (what keeps players playing despite poor game design) and the contrast between momentary fun vs. intriguing experiences. Instead of prioritizing fun, we assert that *intrigue* and *information* should be seen as equally valuable for helping players determine if they want to continue playing. The first sustained play session (coined "first hour"), when inspected closely, offers lessons for game development and our understanding of how players evaluate games as consumable products.

Author Keywords
Game design; first hour; approachability; first impression

ACM Classification Keywords
H.5.m. Information interfaces and presentation (e.g., HCI): Miscellaneous; K.8.0 [Personal Computing]: Games

INTRODUCTION
Retail computer and video game sales from 2009 to 2012 ranged from 188 to 298 million units per year[1]. Combined with the statistic that 58% of Americans play games, naïvely speaking, this averages to 1 to 2 new games purchased per gamer, every year. Thus, unlike productivity software that is adopted once and used for years or decades, video gamers consume new game products on a repeated, regular basis: encountering and learning new games frequently.

CHI PLAY '14, October 19 - 22 2014, Toronto, ON, Canada

ACM 978-1-4503-3014-5/14/10...$15.00.
http://dx.doi.org/10.1145/2658537.2658540

Consumable games are designed to be experienced for a set period of time (i.e. a promised amount of gameplay that rarely exceeds 100 hours). On a repeated basis, gamers commit a number of hours to learn how to play and, then, to experience these games until they have completed the storyline, all of the game content, or, as Raph Koster asserts [13], when the player has mastered the game.

In this paper, we focus on the initial segment of this timeline: the first hour. By "first hour", we mean the initial play session where players encounter the gameplay and familiarize themselves with it. In reality, this ranges from a few minutes to 4 or 5 hours, depending on the specific game. In fact, our interviews reveal a variety of names for this period: the "initial experience", the "first time user experience", "tutorial time", the "5-5-5" (five seconds, minutes, hours), "the first 10 seconds, the first minute, the first ten minutes, the first hour", and "setting the hook". We retain the shorthand, "first hour", due to its use in industry [5] and in the media (e.g. firsthour.net). Also, we prefer this name because it is clear that players have played the game and have done so for a sustained period of time.

We focus on the first hour because it is the gateway into the main experience of the game. This is a probationary period. In this time, players reconcile their expectations with their initial experience, setting the tone for the rest of the game or, perhaps, giving up on playing the rest of the game entirely. Secondly, the first hour is a learning experience. Players may lack the knowledge or skills to enjoy the game. Even experienced gamers need to figure out how this game is meant to be played. Also, there is synergy with gamification [8]. One goal of gamification is to draw users into a non-game activity. Similarly, the design of the first hour is to drawn in users to the full experience of the game. We believe that the design concepts in this paper can be transferred with minimal adaptation to the gamification domain. Furthermore, the first hour generalizes beyond the typical publishing model for retail games. Alternate models of releasing game content include trial periods (e.g. in the "free-to-try" option for the game streaming service Ouya), game

[1] Essential Facts about the Computer and Video Game Industry: Sales, Demographic and Usage Data 2013, http://www.theesa.com/facts/pdfs/esa_ef_2013.pdf

demos, free to play models (e.g. **League of Legends** by Riot Games or **Clash of Clans** by Supercell) where the first experience is critical, not only for future enjoyment of a game, but in convincing trial players to become regular ones.

In summary, this paper offers a thick description of the first hour that applies to many domains such as software-as-a-service, free to play models, and gamification. Now, we turn to the related work in which we surface the tacit knowledge of game designers regarding the first hour.

RELATED WORK

Expert Game Designers

Game designers consider the first hour to be very important. User researchers have specifically mentioned the "first hour" as critical and influential on continuing play [5].

Game designers are well aware that players abandon games. Phillips [16] reports that popular games only have about 70% of players play to the end. For those who quit out of frustration, Phillips recommends better feedback and appropriate goals for players who are still learning to play.

Game designer Bruce Shelley writes, "A player must be actively engaged by a new game within 15 minutes of starting or we risk losing the player forever." He writes that designers need an interesting start situation, minimal barriers to entry, and to design a good progression from a few decisions that increase in number [17]. If the game is complicated due to special controls, character introductions, or back story, Shelley's advice is to include tutorials or to find clever ways to educate the player while providing entertainment. He warns that uninteresting manuals, introductions, or tutorials (what he calls 'pre-play work') and frustrating interfaces are likely to stop new players.

In Sid Meier's keynote, "The Psychology of Game Design", for GDC'10, he explains that the first fifteen minutes need to offer rewards that are "really compelling, really fun, almost a foreshadowing of all the cool stuff that's going to happen later in the game". Meier advises designers to make players feel comfortable in the game world and on the right track. During this initial time period, he believes that the game almost cannot reward the player enough to get them invested, committed, and part of the game world. One example is in his game, **Civilization IV**. This game offers nine difficulty levels to give players a way to progress and advance while feeling mastery and challenge.

Henry Jenkins also reports that game designers craft a solid emotional payoff and an early moment of mastery or movement to spark the player's appetite [11].

These assertions are based on game designer's rich experience in the industry. They make it plain that game designers wrestle with the first hour, wanting it to be approachable and, above all, fun. We now turn to related literature in the field of game studies.

Game Studies

There is a great deal of work that is relevant to the first hour, but research with a specific focus on the first play session is relatively under-explored.

Desurvive and Wiberg [7] address the initial experience of gamers in their heuristics for game approachability, coined GAP (Game Approachability Principles). These heuristics include recommendations for allowing practice of new skills/tools, good demonstrations of how to play, feedback, offering self-efficacy, scaffolding, clarity, and information. In the process of validating their heuristics, they show that approachability is a distinct area from usability. Their work establishes how important it is to treat the first hour differently than the rest of the game play experience and offers key themes for understanding the first hour. Our contribution will build on this work by taking a naturalistic approach, examining data from a large set of games, reviewed by people who have actually purchased the game. This will provide additional context and describe causal links that flesh out Desurvive and Wiberg's work.

One study by Wu et al. [20] examines how online games retain users. It claims to study the initial trial experience. Wu et al. hypothesize that "player's initial gratification (trial) experiences in playing an online game will positively affect their continuance motivation". These gratifications have three categories. They are achievement, enjoyment, and social interaction. Although their survey results are statistically significant, Wu et al.'s survey instrument does not contain questions that specify the initial experiences of gameplay. Instead, the survey focuses on the continued use of the game alone, leading to a possible conflation of the first hour and later hours of play.

Livingston et al. [15] study the time *before* the players touch a controller. They measure players' first 15 minutes of gameplay after they read a positive or negative review of the game itself. Among their results, they find that reading reviews does not directly affect play experience as measured through physiological sensors.

Other related works only cover some facets of the first hour such as game tutorials. Anderson et al. [1] conduct a multivariate experiment on the effectiveness of game tutorials for three games. They conclude that investment in tutorials may not be justified for games that can be learned through experimentation. They find tutorials are effective depending on the complexity of the game. Only their most complex game, **Foldit**, benefited from a tutorial. The other two games were simpler, casual web games that were easier to learn through experimentation. Also, they found no evidence that players learn better in a restricted training mode.

Player engagement is another topic that intersects with the first hour. Here, the sign of a good first hour is when the players become so engaged in the experience that they keep playing into the future. A related theory is flow [4], the psychological theory of how a person can become deeply absorbed in a challenging and enjoyable activity. It is relevant to games [19] as well as the first hour experience. Csíkszentmihályi [4] describes flow as a careful balance between skills and challenge. An overly easy game is boring. An overly difficult game creates anxiety about failure. This could apply to the first hour. A game starts with simple challenges to deeper ones and requires players to become increasingly skillful. The first hour must provide the right balance of challenge and skill to put players on the right track to enter a flow state.

Similarly, Brown and Cairn conducted a grounded investigation of immersion in games [3]. They characterize immersion as a series of deepening degrees that are divided by barriers. For example, the minimal stage of immersion is engagement which occurs early in time. Brown and Cairn identify barriers at each stage. For the engagement stage, do the gamer's preferences (e.g. genre or theme) prevent them from getting involved? Do the controls offer enough feedback to allow them to learn to play? Also, players think about investment of time, effort and attention. Naturally, they look forward to a reward for these investments. Like most of the related work here, Brown and Cairn are not precise about the timing of immersion which is understandable due to the idiosyncrasies of each game. Their two latter stages of engrossment and total immersion both contain efforts and features that could apply to the first hour. They report about how players prepare the physical environment by turning off the lights before playing to prepare to be engrossed. For total immersion, they identify features such as graphics and sound to be important for atmosphere, however, it is not clear that these features are necessarily preceded by the lighter forms of immersion.

In summary, the industry consensus is that games must start by grabbing the player's attention, feeding their interest for the future. Frustrations must be minimized. The player needs to be taught how to play, rewarded emotionally and with a sense of control.

Meanwhile, the research directly focused on the first hour is introductory. Preliminary heuristics exist as well as a clear delineation of game approachability as its own topic of game design. Individual aspects of the first hour have been widely studied, but findings need some care to be transferred to the first hour. The work on tutorials offers some understanding to the learning portion of the first hour. Also, much has been written about immersion and continued play. Although this is useful in discussing facets for increasing the depth of engagement, our understanding of the first hour requires a more comprehensive picture, attention to what makes the first hour distinct, and greater detail about features of games and how they are encountered for the first time. We aim to provide this in our naturalistic study. Last, our study contributes a time-based view of software that is shared by other studies of technology [12].

GOAL

Our goal is to explain the first play experience of gamers. We contribute a thick description of the progression of the first hour and insights about designing a compelling one. We frame a game as a product with a natural lifespan and ask what is best in this lifespan's first hour?

METHODOLOGY

Approach

Since our current understanding of the first hour lacks a diverse perspective on the breadth of games, we sought a larger contextual picture. Thus, we collected data that crosses over many games. We sought to create a thick description for situating the prior literature on approachability, tutorials, and immersion. Another approach we could have taken would have been a finer-grained, telemetric accompaniment to Desurvive and Wiberg's think-aloud procedure. However, this was an impractical approach for the number of games we wanted to study. Certainly, such in-depth analysis will be useful for a narrower set of games (e.g. targeting one game genre).

Data Collection

We collected reviews from gaming websites (35 reviews) and Amazon (212 reviews in 30 different genres; see Table 2). We scoped our study to Xbox 360 games because of the popularity of the console and because of similarities across all first hour experiences such as a common hardware specification. Amazon reviews have proven to be a useful source of usability and user experience data [10]. We chose them because they offered self-reports from contexts that are more naturalistic rather than a lab and because the large numbers of reviews per game would increase the likelihood for finding data about the first experience. On the Amazon website, the first author navigated to the review page for Xbox games and used the site's search box. He searched for game reviews that contained keywords such as "first" or "hour(s)". As data collection progressed, he added terms that also appeared frequently in the reviews such as "start", "minute(s)". He also included reviews without a search

Amazon reviews	212 reviews **Search terms**	
	first	67
	first, hour	50
	hour	40
	start	31
	first, minutes	11
	minute	4
	hours	3
	first, hours	1
	minutes	1
	none (found while reading other reviews for the same game)	4
Game reviewers	35 "first hour" reviews	
Professionals	Interviews: 3 Game Designers, 2 Test leads, 1 UX Researcher	

Table 1. Data sources

term that were displayed in the reviews page and fit the criteria of a first hour review. His inclusion criteria was that the review explicitly identified part or all of the review as a first time experience by mentioning an initial time period. Table 1 includes a break-down of the search terms used. Despite the name "first hour" in this paper, we reemphasize that our collection was not restricted to exactly 60 minute reviews. Our data range from initial seconds to initial hours.

Because they offered greater detail than the Amazon reviews, 35 long-form reviews were collected from game review sites (firsthour.net, gamesforlunch.blogspot.com, videogameimpressions.blogspot.com, shakkirules.com, and GameSpot). These reviews specifically report on the first hour. Many describe the gameplay in a minute-by-minute format (e.g., see Figure 1). The reviews were written by 13 different authors. As sources by domain experts, game reviews are a genre of games journalism [21] that has value in informing game design [2].

We decided to analyze the Amazon reviews together with these 35 reviews because the reviews were written from the perspective of a first-time player. Together, the Amazon and first hour reviews comprised our sample of the first hour experience for gamers. Although we do not distinguish strongly between the two datasets, when we refer to our dataset, we will use "Amazon reviews" to refer to the set of 212 reviews and "first hour reviews" to refer to the set of 35.

To situate our findings in the game development context, we also conducted 6 interviews with professionals in the game industry. (Hereafter, Designer A, B, C, Test A, B, and User Researcher A.) There were three game designers, each with about 20 years of experience in the industry working on AAA-class games and each having worked for 3 or more major game studios. The two interviewees from game testing worked in the area with 15 years and 8 years of experience each. The game user researcher had 10 years of experience at a major studio.

Genre	Reviews
Action	28
Modern First-Person Shooter	32
Sci-Fi First-Person Shooter	21
Modern Action Adventure	17
Role-Playing	16
Sci-Fi Shooter	16
Fantasy Action Adventure	10
Puzzle	9
Adventure	9
Rhythm / Music	7
Sports	6
Racing	5
2D Platformer	4
Shoot-'Em-Up	3
Strategy	3
Beat-'Em-Up	3
Driving	3
GT / Street Racing	3
Action Role-Playing	2
3D Platformer	2
Wrestling	2
Football	2
Snowboarding	2
2D Fighting	1
Sci-Fi Action Adventure	1
Modern Shooter	1
Historic First-Person Shooter	1
Rhythm / Dancing	1
Fantasy Online Role-Playing	1
Olympic Sports	1

Table 2. Genres of Collected Amazon Game Reviews. The genre categories for each game are based on the online games publication, GameSpot.

00 - I click New Game and the first hour of Call of Duty 4 begins. We're looking at a view of Eastern Europe. A voice over is introducing the situation and explaining everything that is going on in the area. The game zooms in to a U.K. training ground. I have control now, a man tells me to take a rifle from the table. He points me to a shooting range and I take aim.

01 - We conduct various aiming exercises. Looks like there's some auto aim built in when you look down the sight.

02 - I knife a watermelon. "Your fruit killing skills are remarkable!"

03 - I follow my objective pointer and meet Captain Price. I have to run an obstacle course now.

05 - I had to complete the obstacle course in less than 60 seconds, which is easy enough. Basically just have to shoot targets and toss flash grenades. My recommended difficulty is Recruit, the easiest difficulty level. Hmm... I'll go with Regular.

07 - Quick loading screen and then the globe whips around to the Bering Strait. We're looking at a cargo tanker, looks like it's our first mission. I'm told the crew is expendable, sweet.

08 - We blast the crew members on the bridge catching them off guard. Whoops! Just shot a friendly, as in someone on my own team. Ouch. have to start the level over now.

Figure 1. Minute-by-minute style of a first hour review

Analysis

We analyzed the data with Dedoose [6]. The coding process was conducted by the first author from a phenomenological lens and using grounded theory [18] which is well-suited for the underexplored nature of the first hour. In this method, there are three steps: open, axial, and selective coding.

For this study, open coding involved the discovery of codes through sentence-by-sentence analysis. The Amazon reviews and the first hour reviews were both subjected to open coding. Bond and Beale's grounded analysis of game reviews [2] was used as sensitizing theory, meaning that their findings and categories informed the coding process but did not strictly dictate the analysis. Bond and Beale's categorization served as a generic categorization of game review topics (e.g. narrative, gameplay, etc...) that allowed the first author to start coding for first hour-related categories inside generic game review categories. The open codes were closely associated with the data in that, often, the names for these initial codes were direct quotes, such as "Stuck". Next was axial coding [18], the goal of which was

Figure 2. Photo of the analytic process with excerpts from the Amazon and first hour reviews organized by code.

to draw out larger themes. This involved grouping sets of codes together by affinity and reviewing these sets for cross-cutting themes. Using the software, the existing codes were re-organized into sets of similar codes. The sets of excerpts were printed out for closer scrutiny (see Figure 2). The description of the codes and the discovery of larger themes were informed by analysis of these aggregated excerpts. Last was selective coding where, by logical inference, the first author revised and refined the categories.

In addition, during the axial phase of analysis, we solicited interviews from domain experts: industry professionals with years of experience. We used the developing codes as an interview guide. This was a single iterative loop in the analysis where the interviews allowed us to supplement our ongoing analysis and to better situate our findings.

Because we only had the first author analyze the data, we improved the trustworthiness of our findings by following the guidelines by Lincoln & Guba [14] for auditing our findings. An outside auditor was invited to review the study methodology and the developing categories. The auditor reviewed samples of the raw data, the coding process, and the developing categories. He was instructed to confirm that the initial codes were driven by the data and that the inferences from the data were logical. Under his advice, we recognize that some user experiences are not easy to verbalize as a written review and may not have been captured by our method. Also, small adjustments to the category structure were implemented according to his recommendation.

Our findings are presented next. First, we set the stage with a description of the relationship of the first hour to the professional game development process.

THE INFLUENCE OF THE GAME DEVELOPMENT PROCESS ON THE FIRST HOUR

Our interviewees were familiar with the common topics about the first hour of gaming: capturing the player's attention, easing them into a complex game, abandonment, and setting the tone for the rest of the play experience.

For example, the designers expressed that they had thought a lot about what to offer new players early in a game (coded as "Locked elements" in our analysis) such as a weapon too expensive to purchase. They report that there are two schools of thought about locked elements. The first is to make the players earn progressively powerful items as they play. The second is to offer a glimpse, a "taste of power", in the first few minutes, then strip it all away so that a new player will have enjoyed the core gameplay, but still be challenged (and incentivized) as they pursue those powers.

Additionally, designers were current on the ongoing discussion in industry about the pros and cons of offering free demos, the developing free-to-play business model, and the fact that many players never finish a game.

In the remainder of this paper, we show that our analysis complements this industry knowledge with more contextual details and surfaces new, useful design rationales. But before moving on, we would like to discuss a cross-cutting theme that emerged from the interviews as a whole.

There is an influence of the game development process on the game's design (and software quality) especially on the first hour of gaming. Because our interviews cut across design, UX research, and quality assurance, we collected observations from different corners of the game development process. We found that because of the structure of the game development process, the first hour of gaming receives a higher proportion of development attention than other parts of the game experience.

As developers for AAA commercial games, game designers understand that their choices have implications on a large scale, affecting the enjoyment of a large user base. Because they are aware that not everyone plays a game to the end and that everyone will at least encounter the first hour, their design attention gravitates towards it. In the quality assurance (QA) department, attention is weighted to the first hour for three reasons. First, QA receives much of its direction from the game designers, so, naturally, their priorities follow the designer's priorities for the first hour. Secondly, because games are often designed and programmed sequentially (create the 1st level, then the 2nd level, etc...), the QA department spends more time testing starting levels. Third, due to constantly changing builds and limited testing tools, in some games, QA testers cannot always jump to a chosen section in a game to test mid-game or end-game stages. Instead, they must play a game from the beginning every time they test a feature. Thus, the first hour is the path most traveled (and most tested). In the user-experience department, the researchers own research process favors the first hour. Conducting a usability study means that all participants will be first-time players and follow-up studies with the same users are too expensive. The result is that from the design department to QA and to usability, the most polished aspects of a game can be expected to be the first hour, due in part to how important the first hour is, but also heavily due to the structure of the game development process.

This attention is a reasonable fit for the games as a consumable product. In the interviews, designers regard their game as a success as long as the player had an entertaining experience for a set period of time, no matter if they didn't finish the game. A positive first hour translates to a positive recommendation to friends and a likelihood of offering players a sufficient return in enjoyment for their purchase.

Extending this thought beyond the scope of the first hour, we recognize that there are other models for releasing games. For example, some games are expected to have a lifespan not of hours, but of years. Consider the area of games as electronic sports: One might see the attention on the first hour to be less relevant for the successful design and development of a game like **League of Legends**. After an electronic sport has gained traction among a user-base, design attention is better spent on fine-tuning game balance to improve the sport experience. Thus, the development process outlined above is a poor fit for maintaining a successful competitive franchise. Also, alternate development processes exist such as independent games created by individual programmers. Suffice to say, our understanding of the relationship between the development process and the end-product promises to be interesting future work for game studies as new models of games emerge (e.g. software-as-service or free-to-play) and as game development processes evolve.

FINDINGS ON THE FIRST HOUR

Our qualitative analysis produced a comprehensive description of the first hour. Three major categories emerged. In the first category, we describe the experiences of the players. The second describes how the player learns to play. The third is a shift in perspective. It describes the how players approach the experience proactively.

THE FIRST EXPERIENCE ARC

Expectation → Experience → Outcome

The experience of the first hour maps to a simple arc: Players have expectations; they play the first hour; and, based on new expectations, they choose to continue playing or to stop. Broadly speaking, this progression aligns with the concepts of flow and immersion: greater flow and immersion leads to greater motivation to keep playing. While this may seem no different than the advice for general game design, our analysis uncovers nuances that are specific to the first hour. In the next section, we briefly describe each category for completeness sake and then highlight characteristics that are particular to the first hour.

Expectations

Unsurprisingly, players enter gameplay with expectations. Early expectations stem from personal experience with an earlier game in a franchise and similar games or genres. The surrounding gaming community will also influence expectations. This includes a vague sense of what others think of a game, influential reviews, industry buzz, and recommendations from friends. Last, players experience snippets of the game: they see trailers of gameplay, rent the game, or play demos.

Here, a key first hour subcategory is what we have identified as anticipated elements. These are expectations that are concrete and specific – as exemplified in this quote:

"Can't wait to actually tackle this first main mission--the intro level doesn't count as that was clearly more of a tutorial and lacked fun augmentations and options--and see how Jensen does sneaking past terrorists and saving hostages" Amazon review of **Deus Ex: Human Revolution**

An anticipated element may not actually appear within the first hour of play. The advice given in a review of **The Elder Scrolls V: Skyrim** is to look forward to meeting your first dragon, a creature that isn't encountered until a few hours in. Thus, there are times when players have an unfulfilled anticipation throughout the entire first hour experience – sometimes because it is simply infeasible to get to that point in the game in a typical initial play session.

Experiences

Like any evaluation of a game, experiences can be distinguished as positive or negative, but a further distinction can be made between those that satisfy a player versus those that intrigue her. These intrigued players express interest in playing beyond the first hour. We have labeled these experiences as memorable versus engaging. Memorable experiences are positive, but can be momentary. Players express awe at a detailed, well-crafted environment, weapon, or enemy unit. Key descriptors include, "cool", "awesome", "wow", "exciting", "fun", "impressed", and "neat". The reviewers mention these highlights in a positive light, but really do not have more to say.

In contrast, engaging aspects are those are accompanied by a reviewer's enthusiasm for more. These are experiences where they express being "hooked", "engaged", "interested", "addicted", "immersed", and emotionally invested. Features that elicit this engagement are compelling narratives, novel game mechanics and conceptual themes. For example, a first hour reviewer of **Condemned: Criminal Origins** is intrigued when he discovers that his ammunition is designed to be limited.

"I hit Y to reload my gun, only to realize that it doesn't actually get reloaded. Instead, my character checks the amount of rounds in the gun. According to the game, I'm limited to the ammunition that is found in weapons. Hmmm...I'm going to have to be a little bit more conservative with my ammo and quit hosing down these perps with a steady stream of lead. Very interesting game concept..."

This same distinction can be applied to negative experiences. Disengaging experiences are ones that reduce the confidence that first time players have in the rest of the game. In our analysis, the emergent categories for negative experiences fall into three buckets: annoyances, frustrations, and tedium. Each risks disengagement in its own way. Annoyances are small negative experiences for gamers such as annoying music, sound effects, or glitches in the camera view of a game. Alone, they can be dismissed, but when they accumulate, players begin to disengage. Frustrations are acute, immediately causing players to consider quitting: being unable to play a game because of hours of patching are required, an unbeatable first level, and terrible controls. Tedium builds when a game is boring or repetitive, lacking variety. It is a signal to players that they may have already exhausted the value of the time spent playing.

On souring impressions and winning over skeptics

Building on this categorization, we evaluated changes of sentiment in which an initial positive experience can sour or where a skeptic is won over. In the reviews where there was such a change, the following pattern was observed.

When there is a change in sentiment, both positive and negative initial experiences are accompanied by momentary adjectives that are replaced by engaging or disengaging elements. A common descriptor in the Amazon reviews is "at first" which allowed us to identify reviews that changed directions. Here are two examples:

"each section gave you the declassify option which would just give you various ways to make each section harder. At first it was cool, but it quickly became very gimmicky." **Gears of War: Judgment**

"At first I felt that [slow motion-style combat] didn't go well with heck&slash gameplay, but in half and hour I began to love it and I especially enjoyed the creative use of it during enemies and boss fight. [sic]" **Metal Gear Rising: Revengeance**

This simple relationship implies that we must reprioritize our design choices for the first hour. The typical advice from industry is to polish the "wow"-factor to grab the player's attention. Ian Milham, art director for **Dead Space 2**, in a GDC 2011 lecture, describes a strategy where the first encounter with an alien is constructed as an "epic moment", carefully directed to be cinematic and memorable, using extra detail in the character modelling to impress the user. Later, these models are swapped out with lower polygon models for performance reasons. He reasons that the first impression has done its job, positively influencing the player's perception from that point on. While this "epic moment" may impress the player, we argue that it does not compel players to continue playing. In fact, this is the dilemma of offering game demos, free trials, and the free-to-play model. If the player is satisfied by the first taste of the game, why play more?

Our answer is because there is more to see and explore. Thus, our recommendation is to polish the engaging aspects (as mentioned above: the narrative, the depth of the game mechanics and conceptual themes) and if it is impossible to truly experience it in the first hour, to give players the informational cues about the depth of story and depth of gameplay so that they choose to further invest themselves.

Outcomes

The close of the first hour is an outcome; the reviews that we analyzed were a mix of eagerness to play again, giving up and returning a purchase, and everything in between.

Abandonment

Players quit, or "eject" (Designer A), or "shelve the game" (Designer B). Not only might they quit, but on a smaller scale they also abandon parts of the game experience. Reviewers reported that they turned off the music, muted the voices, and gave up on certain levels.

Sometimes, abandonment is gradual. In the reviews, low quality (e.g., bugs or bad controls) or boring games simply "ground to a halt". (Amazon review of **Dead Island: Riptide**).

Sometimes, the abandonment is abrupt. Disappointed reviewers would complain about deal-breakers. As expected, deal-breakers are frustrations in the game experience that supersede all positive experiences. According to one Amazon reviewer, **Blitz: The League** interrupted the simulated football game with too many unskippable cut-scenes. He exclaimed, "Reselling this ASAP!" Even though he expressed that the gameplay was pretty good, his frustration was too great.

The category of deal-breakers inspired us to ask a follow-up question. If something can supersede good experiences, how about the reverse? Can something (or the promise of something) supersede the bad?

Holdouts

Clearly, positive experiences lead to continued play, but some players also promised to continue even when the game experience was mediocre. Also, even those who quit express regret. They would have liked to continue, they say. These players are being pulled back towards the game. In surfacing these reasons, we have identified what influences players to continue playing a game that they don't want to play. We have named these reasons holdouts.

A holdout is something that keeps players playing even when annoyance, frustration, or boredom accumulates. It does not mean that the player is excited about a game. Instead, holdouts buy the game a second chance. Ideally, players who hang on past the first hour will find a reason to enjoy the game.

Observed holdouts include anticipated elements as defined above. Players will stick with a game at least until they get to an anticipated element. As mentioned before, there is the **Skyrim** player who was advised to keep playing until he fought his first dragon. In the first hour review of **Crysis 2**, the reviewer expresses some disappointments, but exclaims, "I can't stop before meeting some aliens, right?".

A holdout can be a single enjoyable game mechanic. In **Captain America: Super Soldier**, it is the combat system that keeps this gamer playing for the moment:

"Would I keep playing? I guess so. I really do like the combat system, which captures Captain America's acrobatic grace and power quite well, but the limited enemy variety is allowing that repetitious feeling to sink in. ... I'll soldier on for a bit, but I don't expect to finish this fight." First hour review of **Captain America: Super Soldier**

A good narrative can act as a holdout. This first hour reviewer of **Army of Two: the 40th Day** laments the lack of story as motivation to continue. *"So far seems an extremely linear, hard-to-control, ugly third-person shooter slog with no interesting story or even motivation to pull me along."*

Aside from game features, some players are self-described completionists. They want to be able to say they beat a game. Others, like the **Skyrim** example, were encouraged by their friends to keep playing. A first hour review of **LEGO**

Harry Potter: Years 5-7 continues to play for social reasons despite repetitive game content: *"only because my wife and I have a blast figuring these out together. If I was going at this alone, I might actually be worried that I had bought the first game for a second time. From what I've seen so far, all of Hogwarts has been copy/pasted over into the new game..."*

In summary, we have mapped a progression from expectation to experience, then outcome for the first hour. Specific to the first hour, we have introduced subcategories such as anticipated elements, momentary vs. engaging experiences, and holdout features. Together these imply that modeling the ideal first hour as a simple progression in immersion is an incomplete picture. Instead, in addition to enjoying the first moments of the game, players are assessing how they will enjoy gameplay elements into the future. Having described this arc, we now discuss an accompanying trial period in the first hour.

FIGURING OUT THE GAME

A new game must be learned. Games each have their own distinct control schemes, game mechanics, and user interfaces that impose a learning curve on their players. Plus, designers have their own agenda for gameplay:

The way it's supposed to be played

In our interviewees consistently described game designers as people with a clear vision of how they want players to play their game. They feel responsible for bringing the player into contact with that experience as soon as they can.

Players are aware of the ideal play experience. They want to "get the hang of the game", to "figure it out", and look forward to when the game "opens up". There is a consistent connection in the Amazon reviews from (a) figuring it out to (b) attachment: *"once you get the hang of it you won't be able to pull yourself away."* (**Far Cry 3**, Amazon Review) Naturally, the negative case occurs where the core gameplay disappoints: *"once the patterns were figured out, the enthusiasm died down quickly."* **Kung Fu Panda 2 (Kinect)**

We now note two challenges: pitfalls and a tricky tradeoff.

Pitfalls: Simple, Costly Mistakes in Understanding

If a player misses a key detail in learning about the game and it is a deal-breaker, he will abandon the game. This is a pitfall of the first hour that is primarily an information problem rather than a game-play issue. For example, it turns out that the player who hated **Blitz: The League** did not know that he could skip the annoying cut-scenes. Had he known this, he would not have abandoned the game. One Amazon review of **Defiance** chronicles a dramatic reversal after being misinformed. What is now a glowing review (*"First impressions - not withstanding - the worst game ever is now a Favorite!"*) was once a list of complaints. The reviewer was blaming the game for a poor experience when the culprit may have been his internet connection instead. The comment section for this review has several people explaining this. The frustrated player fixed this and came to enjoy the game so much that he revised his review.

Tradeoffs: Discovery vs direction, emotional ups and downs

The data shows both a demand for clear directions and, yet, for the freedom to discover the game on the player's own. This echoes the challenges that designers have in locking elements early and that Anderson et al. investigate for game tutorials [1].

As confessed in the reviews, players get lost. They run into impasses. They make incorrect assessments about the difficulty of an enemy unit. They get confused with the crafting system, where to go next, how they died, inventory management, mini-games, game controls, and even the interface ("I think it's a loading screen in disguise" first hour review of **Assassin's Creed**). They want directions that tell them: where to go in an open-world game (**LEGO Harry Potter: Years 1-4**), which missions are the main narrative path and which are optional (**Borderlands 2**), the meaning of the jargon in the game (**Stoked**), or simply how to get out of a tutorial section (**Bionic Commando**).

In the absence of explicit directions, players struggle to make sense of the game world. They die often. They look for clues. Subcategories of clues include visual clues (e.g., glowing items), narrative clues, and artifacts in the environment (e.g., what might look like a spawning point for an enemy unit). These clues are grasped by players with varying success. Often, a game has poor cohesion between its story and the game mechanics. **Overlord** places the protagonist in the role of an evil overlord. This moral reversal put one player at a loss when the he encountered a farmer asking for help. Is he supposed to help him or murder him?

We observe an emotional facet in all of this. When directions are missing, players feel frustrated. *"Finally after running everywhere, I see there's a hallway up above the room with no access to it for anyone who can't fly. ... Not seeing it made me feel stupid. I don't like it when games make me feel stupid."* (First hour review of **Iron Man 2**) In contrast, when players discovered things on their own, they were enthusiastic. In **Forza Horizon**, a player discovered a golf course big enough for him to drift his car, later exclaiming *"Man that was fun!"* (Amazon review). Thus, on one hand, self-discovery is rewarded by enthusiasm and on the other hand, the lack of direction is met with frustration.

In summary, we want to emphasize that the learning portion of the game requires more than just a low-level acquisition of gameplay skills, but also a high-level grasp of the ideal game experience as conceptualized by the game designer. The challenges that we outlined are, in many ways, information challenges laced with a risk of emotional letdown. Before we enter a closing discussion, we want to make some brief remarks about player agency.

PLAYER AGENCY

So far, our focus is on how the game designer can entice the gamer. This is a passive view of the end-user that does not account for the player's own initiative. To accompany our experience arc and the learning curve, in this section we offer observations about player agency.

Doing your homework

Some gather information before playing and urge others to. *"If you read all of the in-game instructions and you aren't afraid to dig around in the menus, you'll work through the learning curve quickly."* (**Create**, Amazon review)

"At first it was hard to play and I got my butt handed to me, but that was because I just went straight into the match and tried it right away. Then i studied the controls and figured it out." (**WWE '13**, Amazon Review)

Players may take a practicing stance. Death comes quickly and often, but they expect it. They expect to fail if they do not yet know the controls or if they didn't get the hang of it. Players do not complain about dying but about the precision of the controls and slow loading times between deaths. This echoes Phillips' [16] recommendation for good feedback.

Skipping ahead

Players take a direct route to the action, skipping tutorials, levels, and other decision branches. This is sometimes premature, as shown in the **WWE '13** quote above, but this is what the players are eager to do. They want to have the full experience of the game, not a tutorial level, not character tweaking, nor exploring upgrades. In our data, players wait for cut-scenes to end, skip tutorials, skip crafting systems; reviewers count the minutes to action; they wonder when the game will "open up" or when they'll finally meet the alien, kill the dragon. They search for the direct path, shortcuts, and experiences that allow them to get figure out the game and to do this quickly.

Adjusting to the game

However, players also take time to prepare themselves to enjoy a game. To improve their experience of the game, players tinker with the difficulty level of a game. After finishing three levels of **Captain America: Super Soldier**, one player restarted it on a higher difficulty setting to transform his experience from an overly easy game experience to an enjoyable challenge. Despite a rocky start, his adaptation to the game proved positive, leading to a rating of four out of five stars. In a similar example to the prior work on immersion [3], one Amazon review describes a husband and wife preparing to enjoy the first mission of **Aliens: Colonial Marines** at its best by dimming the lights, tweaking the volume settings, and adjusting the difficulty level. They also assert that they've read the negative reviews and have tailored their expectations accordingly.

SUMMARY

Our investigation paints a picture of a first hour that is playful, but tentative. The predominant perspective from the related work is that there is a simple progression from low immersiveness to greater that should be exciting and enjoyable. Our findings reflect this, but we have found a collection of outliers to this model which short-circuit it (such as deal-breakers and pitfalls) or contradict it (e.g., holdouts).

What leads players to retain their interest in the game? It appears to be the depth of the narrative and the gameplay, both of which cannot be fully absorbed in the first hour of play. Thus, as players struggle to figure out the game, it is imperative for them to glimpse the designer's vision. As a result, they are not only playing the first hour, but are evaluating it, skipping around, and adjusting to it.

IMPLICATION: INTRIGUE TRUMPS ENJOYMENT

As a concrete design implication, consider how one might design the first element in a game: the first weapon or enemy unit. We assert that intrigue and engagement trump enjoyment. Momentary pleasures are not valuable for leading into further play except by promising the player that he will see more of the same. Even this can be a false promise. For example, the high quality model in **Dead Space 2**, as mentioned before, will never resurface in the remaining hours of play. One might even argue that if beautiful graphics are desired and after encountering the most intricate unit model in the game, there is no reason to keep playing.

Thus, we although agree that the memorability of a first game element is important, we would emphasize intrigue over memorability. For example, acquiring a weapon can engender confidence about the way the rest of the game will play out. *"...as soon as i whipped out two crimson blades i knew i would like the game, and spent the next two hours fighting stormies."* (**Star Wars: The Force Unleashed II**, Amazon Review #2) For inspiring greater engagement, designers should ask how a new weapon, enemy, or element might spark the interest of a new player.

Furthermore, we can apply this prioritization to explain what is important about existing design strategies such as showing players unaffordable items in a store or offering an initial taste of power. The goal is to fix an anticipated element in the player's mind and to show them the possible depth of gameplay. We further advise that the balance that designers must strike with the early taste of power is to use it to communicate the strengths of the game-to-come and not just to be a momentary enjoyable experience.

Game evaluation doesn't have to be 'fun'

It should not escape the reader that we are deemphasizing fun in the first hour. We argue that this can be done because players are looking for the central purpose of the game and that information seeking behavior should be evaluated by efficiency rather than entertainment value. This explains why players skip levels or are willing to do their homework. As an illustration, consider how online websites such as GameFAQs.com are highly valued for learning how to play a game. Users would not be much better served if these sites were redesigned to be more flashy or entertaining.

Taking this utilitarian approach to the first hour, we weigh in on the dilemma between direction and discovery (our aforementioned tradeoff). We assert that players who are in 'practice mode' or 'learning mode' may enjoy spontaneous moments early on, but are more interested in acquiring information about the game. Thus, while skills are being learned, the less emotional route (direction) is preferable. Design the first hour to emphasize direction in a way that both instructs and hints at the depth of the game into the future and save room for discovery after the first hour.

IMPLICATIONS FOR DEVELOPMENT

Our findings show that the first hour receives a lot of game development attention as a consequence of the structure of the game development process. However, we are not convinced that this attention translates to improving the way the first hour can inspire players or solve their information seeking problems. Arguably, the process favors the creation of memorable first hours rather than intriguing ones. We encourage game development teams to continue to explore how process impacts the game as an end-product.

LIMITATIONS, FUTURE WORK, & THANKS

Our analysis, conducted from a phenomenological lens, is limited to what could be verbalized by players and what they chose to post online. Also, the genres in Table 2 ought to be taken into consideration when transferring our findings to domains such as children's and casual games.

A natural next step will be to explore other "hours" of these games-as-consumables. What, for example, makes an ideal "last hour" of play, ending a game well? Also, we have found a utilitarian activity in information-seeking for games. This mundane aspect in a playful activity ought to be further examined. Furthermore, we observe that these solutions are embedded in the design of the game. For example, story-gameplay cohesion is not a usability solution, but rather, an aspect of game design. Understanding how game design is a source of information would have wider implications; and, of course, would improve the first hour, leading to many memorable hours of future play.

Thanks to MS Game Studios for sharing their vast experience, to Emerson Murphy-Hill for auditing, to the team at the ESE Group at Microsoft for their guidance, and to the reviewers for their excellent comments.

REFERENCES

1. Andersen, E. et al. The impact of tutorials on games of varying complexity. In *Proc. of CHI* (2012), ACM, 59--68.
2. Bond, M. and Beale, R. What makes a good game?: using reviews to inform design. In *Proc. of HCI* (2009), British Computer Society, 418--422.
3. Brown, E. and Cairns, P. A., grounded investigation of game immersion. In *CHI '04 Extended Abstracts* (2004), ACM, 1297--1300.
4. Csikszentmihalyi, M. *Flow: The Psychology of Optimal Experience*. Harper Perennial, 1991.
5. Davis, J. et al. A survey method for assessing perceptions of a game: The consumer playtest in game design. *Game Studies*, 5, 1 (October 2005).
6. *Dedoose Version 4.5.96*. SocioCultural Research Consultants, LLC, Los Angeles, 2013.
7. Desurvire, H. and Wiberg, C. User Experience Design for Inexperienced Gamers: GAP -- Game Approachability Principles. In Bernhaupt, R., ed. *Evaluating User Experience in Games*. Springer-Verlag London Ltd., 2010.
8. Deterding, S. et al. From Game Design Elements to Gamefulness: Defining "Gamification". In *Proc. of MindTrek'11* (Tampere, Finland 2011), ACM, 9--15.
9. Hamari, J. and Eranti, V. Framework for designing and evaluating game achievements. *Proc. DiGRA 2011: Think Design Play*, 115 (2011), 122--134.
10. Hedegaard, S. and Simonsen, J. G. Extracting usability and user experience information from online user reviews. In *Proc. of CHI* (2013), ACM, 2089--2098.
11. Jenkins, H. Games, the new lively art. In *Handbook of computer game studies*. MIT Press, Cambridge, 2005.
12. Karapanos, E., et al. User experience over time: an initial framework. In *Proc. of CHI* (2009), ACM, 729--738.
13. Koster, R. *A Theory of Fun for Game Design*. O'Reilly Media, 2013.
14. Lincoln, Y.S. and Guba, E.G. *Naturalistic Inquiry*. SAGE Publications, 1985.
15. Livingston, I. J. et al. Influencing experience: the effects of reading game reviews on player experience. In *Proc. of ICEC* (2011), Springer-Verlag, 89--100.
16. Phillips, B. Staying power: Rethinking feedback to keep players in the game. *Game Developer*, 16, 6 (2009).
17. Shelley, B. Guidelines for developing successful games. *Gamasutra* (August 2001).
18. Strauss, A. and Corbin, J.M. *Basics of Qualitative Research: Techniques and Procedures for Developing Grounded Theory*. SAGE Publications, 1998.
19. Sweetser, P and Wyeth, P. GameFlow: a model for evaluating player enjoyment in games. *Comput. Entertain.*, 3 (July 2005), 3--3.
20. Wu, J. et al. Falling in love with online games: The uses and gratifications perspective. *Computers in Human Behavior*, 26 (2010), 1862--1871.
21. Zagal, J.P. et al. Characterizing and understanding game reviews. In *Proc. of FDG* (2009), ACM, 215--222.

What's in a Name? Naming Practices in Online Video Games

Nicole Crenshaw
University of California, Irvine
Irvine, CA 92697 USA
crenshan@uci.edu

Bonnie Nardi
University of California, Irvine
Irvine, CA 92697 USA
nardi@uci.edu

ABSTRACT
Recent research suggests that participation in online video games allows players to create an "idealized self" through their characters, that is, a character perceived to be more attractive or interesting than the player. However, our research indicates that players use carefully created character names to develop a persistent, pragmatic identity to maintain social relationships across games and related sites, and to express their personalities by incorporating elements of popular culture, literary references, and aspects of their own personal histories. Identity in gaming is thus more complex than identification with the physical representation of the character.

Author Keywords
Identity; Handles; Names; Player-Character Relationship; Online Video Games

ACM Classification Keywords
K.8.0 PERSONAL COMPUTING; Games

INTRODUCTION
In previous exploratory interviews with video gamers, we found that players considered their character names a critical aspect of their identity. We decided to systematically study naming practices to understand why players felt that character names were so important. This paper reports the results of that research. We define *identity* as a representation of the self comprised of personal experiences and interactions that players construct for functional, pragmatic purposes.

Previous research suggests that the player-character relationship provides an opportunity to create a better version of the player through the character [5, 8]. For example, Bessière et al. [5] reported that players used their characters to construct an idealized self, i.e., "[a] physical or psychological self that the player wishes to be." The authors emphasized that the fantasy elements of online video games "free players from the yoke of their real-life history and social situation, allowing them to be more like the person they wish they were" [5]. Ducheneaut et al. [8] analyzed the relationship between online and offline identities, and determined that players perceived their video game characters to be more attractive and socially adjusted than the players perceived they themselves were. In contrast, our results suggest that players used their character names as *sincere* representations of their identities, that is, expressive of who they felt they actually were as revealed by character names that embedded bits of a player's experiences, interests, and preferences. Our findings do not suggest that arguments about the character as an idealized self are wrong, but that they are not the entire story. Players expressed their identity through character names for various pragmatic reasons that we will discuss.

Digital embodiment, or the physical representation of a person in a virtual space, has been a research concern since early studies of online social interaction [4, 18, 24, 25; see also 3, 26]. These studies pushed research on player identity towards a focus on the character's graphical representation, but have not yet addressed naming. Our research begins to fill this gap by examining practices surrounding the creation and use of character names in online video games.

In addition to the undeniable importance of names in all of our interactions with others [16, 28], we note that in video games, many social interactions take place when the physical representation of the character is absent. For example, in global chat, private messages, and in-game mail, a player is identified by their character name, not by their embodied character. As one of our study participants said, *"And like, you're always in general chat or a chat, so your [character] name's pretty important."* The importance of a character name frequently extends beyond the game-world into related contexts. For example, in many online games players identify each other in game, on the official game forums, and on private guild forums by their character names.

A few studies have begun to consider the functions of character names [7, 10, 11, 27]. Guitton [10] examined naming patterns for characters of different genders and races in World of Warcraft, and found that female characters had a higher concentration of vowels in their names. Building on Guitton's work, Thurau and Drachen [27] recorded the names of over eight million World of Warcraft characters and 3,000 first-person shooter

CHI PLAY '14, October 19 - 22 2014, Toronto, ON, Canada
Copyright 2014 ACM 978-1-4503-3014-5/14/10 $15.00.
http://dx.doi.org/10.1145/2658537.2658685

gamertags. With big-data methodologies, they discovered where character names originated, and which names players used more frequently for certain races or classes. Drachen et al. [7] reported that character names had rich semiotic meaning influenced by the aesthetics and lore of a game world.

Hagström [11] examined character names and their relation to player identity in World of Warcraft. She found that players had clear understandings of what constituted a game-appropriate character name, and outlined many aspects of character naming that players considered important. For example players argued that character names that included race- or class-specific components showed a player was uncreative and had an inappropriate name [11].

Building on previous research [7, 10, 11, 27], we sought to contribute to the current understanding of the functions of names in the player-character relationship. In our interviews we examined *why* players chose particular character names and *how* character names contributed to a player's identity. To address these questions, we used Gottlob Frege's theory of reference and sense. Frege defines *reference* as the object or subject to which a word points, and *sense* as the meanings, connotations, and associations of a word [9; see 16, 19]. As we will discuss, maintaining a character name as a referent allows a player to establish a persistent identity across games and related contexts, and embedding sense in a character name allows a player to represent aspects of himself to other players.

METHODS

We conducted semi-structured, audio-taped interviews with 20 gamers. Interviews took place in-person (9 participants) or remotely via Skype (11 participants). Players who participated in interviews in-person met with the interviewer at public locations such as coffee shops and restaurants.

Interviews

Players discussed their video game naming practices, where their character names originated, and reported their opinions about different name types and stylistic choices within a name, such as use of accented letters, punctuation, numbers, and misspellings. We asked players about any game that required them to create a unique character name. Players discussed naming practices in Massively Multiplayer Online games, i.e., World of Warcraft, EVE Online, Guild Wars 1, Guild Wars 2, Final Fantasy XIV: A Realm Reborn, Star Wars the Old Republic, Star Wars Galaxies, Path of Exile, Asheron's Call, Secret World, Dragon Court, Day Z Elder Scrolls Online, Holy Beast Online, Aura Kingdom, Dragon Nest, Spirit Tales, Planetside 2, Dark Ages of Camelot, Everquest, Aion, and City of Heroes; and online arena or strategy games, i.e., Dota2, Hearthstone, League of Legends, Civilization 5, Team Fortress 2, Starcraft, and Starcraft 2.

While offline gaming was not the focus of the study, many players discussed their naming practices in offline role-playing games as well, i.e., Mass Effect (1, 2, and 3), Diablo (2 and 3), Borderlands, Borderlands 2, Elder Scrolls: Fire Emblem: Awakening, Skyrim, Monster Hunter, Pathfinder, Shadowrun, and Dungeons and Dragons.

Participants

We recruited participants via email, Facebook, and snowball sampling. Participants contacted via email were involved in one of the first author's previous studies, and had requested to participate in future research. Participants contacted through Facebook were members of gaming-related interest groups. Our sample included 6 females and 14 males aged 19-62 ($\bar{X}$=29.2; M = 27.5). Eligible participants were required to currently play at least one online video game and/or self-identify as someone with a history of online gaming. We did not recruit participants based on information about their naming practices. All participants consented to the use of their actual character names for this paper. We anonymized any other names mentioned in the interviews during transcription.

RESULTS

We examined why players maintained a persistent referent through their character names, and how they embedded meaning into character names to represent and distinguish themselves within and across social contexts.

Reference

Frege observed that, "The reference of a proper name is the object itself which we designate by its means" [19]. We discuss how names functioned as identity objects and as persistent referents of identity online and offline.

Names as identity objects

Just as we quickly become accustomed to nicknames in offline life, players found it natural for others to refer to them by their character names in-game. One participant explained: *"I think it's almost become like, my online identity where it like, just becomes natural. When like, I introduce myself in real life I say, 'My name's [my real name].' When I introduce myself online I say Venusa."*

Many participants considered their character name as important to their identity as their real name: *"It's as much a name for me as my name in real life...It's part of my name, part of my identity."* Players often maintained their character names in other online contexts as well: *"All forums or anything I sign up for it'll be Skrunk, and if that's taken, just some variation of it."* Many players reported feeling happy when they were able to reuse a name in a new context: *"If I can get just 'Drain', like without any modifier on it, then I am super happy."*

What happens if a favorite name is unavailable when a player joins a new game? Some players reported agitation after discovering that "their" name was taken: *"I would be really frustrated and then I would have to go back and think about it for an hour. Like, the naming is so important, if it's not right...I'll delete the character."* Players invested time in name creation because they knew it would become the means by which others identified and referred to them. They were aware of the risks of losing a well-used name, and sometimes devised solutions to the problem. For example, some players used phonetically similar letters across names e.g., Zythan and Xythen. Some doubled the name e.g., Skrunk and Skrunkskrunk, or added additional letters e.g., Treasure and Treasurez. Others embedded the name in a longer name e.g., Venusa and VampireVenusa. Some players took more extreme measures to secure a character name: *"I'm usually pretty careful to make sure that when I play a game to get in as early as possible to make sure I get that name."*

Sometimes players were misidentified by a character name that shared similarities with another name. One player was confused with someone else who shared his naming motif. He had to explain this coincident to others to prevent identity confusion:

> *...When I first joined up with my Ragebarf character on World of Warcraft I was mistaken for a very prominent member of the server who had recently left. And people were messaging me like, "Oh are you this guy?" Whose name was Rage...something. And I was like "No I have no idea what you're talking about. Sorry." That happened a few times...people just thought I was [his] alt.*

Some players were critical of others who did not, in their opinion, choose their names carefully enough. One player criticized the use of common names from fantasy literature such as Legolas or Gimli: *"Why call yourself something that you could get mixed up with somebody else? You can do it if you want, but...you [might] get mistaken for a person...they [might] get mistaken for you."* Common fantasy names defeated the purpose of using names to accurately identify others in-game.

Fear of identity confusion sometimes arose when accounts were hacked. One player explained:

> *It feels almost as if there's somebody else running around in your own skin. Because when I play a character I'm scared about when, like, if somebody were to hack my account...And just [be] in my body running around. Our reputations could get mixed, our personalities could get mixed, just, the whole identification. It's not so much the items that I care about, but more like, if somebody else got into my account and starting saying things to my friends and my guild mates. It would just feel weird that somebody else could do that and basically take on that persona.*

Anxieties about names included identity confusion, identity theft, and having a favorite name taken by another player. Players worked hard to make sure their names did not misidentify them to others.

Names as persistent referents of identity in online gaming

Cultivating a persistent identity helped players recognize each other in-game and provided the opportunity for players to sustain relationships across contexts. Maintaining reference allowed players to establish continuity between characters and across games:

> *Errant Venture is the main character I have in every game as long as it's available...It was a good way to like, carry some continuity through to different games. Like, I'd build a community of friends in one game and when some of them moved to another and I moved to the same game, then it was nice to keep that continuity.*

Another player explained:

> *I have had people recognize me across games. So like, I've been in one game, like I was in a big guild when I played Dark Ages of Camelot for a long time. And in both World of Warcraft and in, when I played Warhammer Online I had, I ran across other payers who saw my name and were like, "Oakbeard, did you play Dark Ages of Camelot? Were you in this guild?" who like recognized me and then I fell in with them, you know?*

This player was able to reconnect with other players when he joined a new game by maintaining a name from a previous game.

Many players believed once they chose a name it stuck with them, sometimes even after the player deleted or stopped using the character with that name. One player described how a name could stick with a player long after a character no longer existed:

> *There were lots of people who [had character names]...we knew each other by, that we called each other by even though we no longer had any characters named that anymore...So someone new would join the guild or something, or was new to the scene, and you'd know, "Okay, this guy is Menos, even though he doesn't have any characters named that" because that's what everyone was calling him.*

In this sense, the name, unlike the physical representation of the character, had a life of its own. The name carried a player's history across contexts, and became associated with the player himself in a way that the physical representation did not. Players emphasized the importance of choosing the "right" name initially: *"Because, you know, the name is something you're stuck with for a long time. You can cover yourself with armor if you're hideous."* Players could change the character's physical appearance ("cover yourself with armor"), but a name persisted. Though character name changes are now a common feature in online games, they frequently require a player to pay in offline currency. We address character name changes more in-depth in the Discussion.

How did players approach naming multiple characters? Many games allow players to create several characters for different purposes or roles. For example, a player may have one character for healing and another for maximizing damage. Often players have one "main," or most frequently used character, and several "alts," or alternative characters. While main character names were generally those players identified with the most, they also used alt character names to represent aspects of their identity to other players. One player discussed a problem that arose when he named an alt that subsequently became his main:

> *My main character was actually going to be...It was going to be my alt. So I kind of just gave it a random, stupid name that I didn't think was going to stick and now I'm stuck with it and I hate it. It's uh, Stinkypeen... I hate it. It's kind of embarrassing, I don't want to be, I don't want that to be associated with my name.*

This player created a name that reflected his somewhat lewd sense of humor. He assumed his character would be an alt he only played in certain contexts, such as player versus player combat where vulgar names are more acceptable. Once he started using the character as his main, he became concerned that it reflected poorly on him as a player.

Names as persistent referents of identity in non-gaming contexts

Reference established through a character name sometimes extended to offline and social media interactions. Many players reported that when online relationships moved to non-gaming contexts, the player's character name, not their real name, prevailed as the form of identification. One player explained how her character name in World of Warcraft, a game she had not played for several years at the time of the interview, had become a referent for her in offline conversations, in social media, and on the phone:

> *Kotomi, my main character in World of Warcraft, people still like, a lot of people still refer to me as Kotomi or Koto or variations of that name. Real life friends, and you know people I text often and etcetera. I know I'm in people's phones as Kotomi still. Even after like the advent of Facebook.*

Some players bridged the gap between online and offline referents by referring to themselves as their character names in offline contexts:

> *I actually use my online moniker in real life a lot. There's people who know me as Clockwork in real life, like I see on a weekly basis. When I introduce myself to people I say, you know "I'm [real name], but all my friends call me Clockwork, and whichever's easier for you to remember."*

Summary

In the same way a person develops an attachment to their real name [12], players frequently developed strong emotional attachments to their character names. The importance of character names was apparent in several ways: the care with which players created identity objects which they expected to be persistent, their sense of ownership of particular names, their anxieties about what could happen to their names, and even taking character names offline and to social media.

Sense

Reflecting on the nature of sense, Frege said, "It is natural...to think of there being [meaning] connected with a sign (name, combination of words, letter), besides that to which the sign refers...what I should like to call the *sense* of the sign" (emphasis in original) [19].

We discovered that players developed rich meanings through their character names by embedding connotations and associations with a specific word, concept, media reference, or style into the name itself. Players considered a name the most customizable part of a character, and thus the appropriate vehicle with which to express meanings. As one player said:

> *[Your name] gives an impression in people's minds about who you are beyond like, when you're playing World of Warcraft or something there's a finite number of characters you can play and items to wear, and so the whole idea of customization, really honing your character, is somewhat limited. So you know, when you have a character name, it's like one of the first things you see and you see it all the time and it's one of the few things that you can completely customize, barring offensive language. It's of larger importance than other aspects of customization.*

We identified two key practices for creating sense in names: alluding to other media and creating a name that "fit" a game or character. Allusions to other media showed others how the player identified herself with respect to common shared media so that other players would immediately know something about her. Players deepened identification with their characters by carefully "fitting" their names to lore or other aesthetic aspects of a game.

Allusions to other media

Players sometimes drew inspiration for their names from sources external to a game, such as foreign languages, literature, and pop-culture references. One player who used Japanese names for all her characters had "Hikario," a Japanese phrase that the player translated as "For the light!" Another player named his characters after Shakespearean figures, taking "Lafeu" from *All's Well That Ends Well*. Many players used fantasy literature such as Tolkien's *The Lord of the Rings* or Rowling's *Harry Potter* to find character names. One player named her character "Cercie," an edited spelling of a character from the *Game of Thrones* television show.

Books, comics, TV shows, music, and other popular media were frequently source materials for creating names.

Players found that allusions to popular media could be useful for social interactions:

> *If I think someone within WoW will understand or know the fandom, like it'll be close enough to the actual name that they'll get it...Just like hoping that they'll maybe chat about it if we happen to be in a party together or if you're just walking around in the main city maybe someone will like bring up the topic. Or sometimes it's to show that I'm a fan.*

This player embedded meaning in her character names to start conversations with others and to find players who shared her interests.

Creating sense was not always easy to accomplish. Unintentional allusions were a concern for many players. One player explained why he stopped using a name that contained an unintended allusion to other games:

> *I don't tend to use Morrigan online because it's become a little bit clichéd...I know there was a character in Dragon Age that used that name...I think because a lot of people have played Dragon Age they'll see that name and...they'll think that's where I got the name from. But also, it sends a slightly different signal...perhaps it would evoke understandings of characters from the game rather than from the goddess.*

"Morrigan" evoked a different sense than he originally intended. Since the allusions to more recent characters overshadowed his allusion to the goddess, the player felt this name ended up sounding clichéd.

Players believed that others formulated impressions about them based on their character name even before any social interactions:

> *[A name] is what you're projecting to the rest of the world. By definition with MMOs you're playing amongst a bunch of other people ...If you call yourself "Ieatpuppies" that sets a different impression than like, "reallycoolguy97" or whatever. People see that and they think certain things before you even get a chance to direct them in any other way.*

Some players used allusions to reflect personal interests: *"Stormwitch was my mage...Stormwitch is the name of a song by The Sword and it's really, really good and I really like it. But I figured it was relevant because she's a mage, and it just sounded cool."* This player was able to incorporate a song he liked into his character name to reveal his musical preferences to other players.

Creating a name that "fit"

Players often took game aesthetics into account when creating a name. They worked to create character names that "fit" with the contextual aesthetics of a game world; a name that did not break immersion and could plausibly occur somewhere within the game world. Some players made their names fit the lore: *"I think the priority for me is that it sounds exotic but realistic and that it fits the lore."* Other players created names that fit their character's attributes such as race and class: *"I try to make [the name] fit...like based on what they look like, and what their class is."* One participant reflected on how he created a name in Guild Wars 2 for a character whose class relied on illusions and mind-manipulation for combat:

> *I try to figure out what the class is or what I'm going to do with that character and then try to think of words that are associated with that. So like, for my Mesmer there's a lot of illusions and clones so I figured "Geist" because a geist, like a ghost and something that's illusive and isn't exactly tangible... [Those are some game] lore and class specifications I tend to go with.*

Players frequently used descriptors in a name to establish a good fit based on the character's function: *"[I create names based on] whatever the class or race brings to mind. Just make it have thematic integrity."* Players took into account a character's race, class, or crafting profession to create a sense of that character's purpose through the name. The popularity of names with race- or class-specific identifiers contradicts what players in Hagström's study considered to fit with game aesthetics [11]. Many players in our study argued that using race- or class-specific material in a name provided information to other players who could see the name but not the embodied character. For example, Table 1 shows a list of names one participant emailed us showing his characters' names, races, and classes in Guild Wars 2.

Name	Race; Class
Penelope Soulbinder	Human; Necromancer
Penelope Soulshield	Human; Guardian
Penelope Twoblades	Human; Thief
Pennie Chancer	Norn; Mesmer
Penumbra Ghostclaw	Charr; Ranger
Tinkah Pendix	Asura; Engineer
Penelope Thorn	Sylvari; Elementalist

Table 1. Character names and corresponding races and classes.

When asked about his naming process, he said, *"It's finding a way that I can still include [Penelope] or Pen, and come up with a name that fits the lore."* The player continually used the name "Penelope" to identify himself, differentiating his characters by a surname that reflected the character's race or class. The sense of these names fit each character's attributes. For example, the surname Twoblades is an obvious allusion to a rogue-like character who would use knives.

Another player mentioned the importance of game genre and character class for creating a name that fit:

I won't name a super robot something high-fantasy sounding unless it's also a high-fantasy setting, and then, by reverse, I won't name a high fantasy character something robotic sounding or, you know, use terminology that wouldn't be used for that setting. So lore is a big part. The style of character is important [too]. So, if I'm playing a sneaky character I try to find a sneaky name. If I'm playing a big, strong character I do something that sounds like a big, strong character.

Creating a name that fit displayed a player's seriousness about immersive game play, and gave the impression to others that the player was familiar with, and knowledgeable about, the game.

Sometimes previous experiences with similar games influenced whether or not players deemed certain names to fit:

I feel like a lot of the games I play are similar when it comes to the fantasy setting, and then names that I come up with in World of Warcraft might also fit into the fantasy of, you know, like, say I'm going to create a character in World of Warcraft, it will fit into the Skyrim universe or the Diablo universe, or something like that.

Players also assessed fit with regard to a name's subjective appeal, that is, the pleasing look, sound, and "feel" of a name: *"I want it to sound good to me...It has to sound right. Which is obviously a purely subjective thing."* Another player said:

Like when I named Pewdew I was like, "Oh I want to think of a silly name that looks like it would fit a fat little panda bear." You know? Or I had a rogue named BoneyJones and I thought it fit an undead rogue perfectly...I don't RP [role play] or anything, but I still like to have an aspect of realism when I name my characters for something that would fit into the universe that I'm playing in.

Players frequently mentioned names that broke game immersion as detracting from the gaming experience: *"[I don't like] names that don't, like aren't immersive. So they have to have, they have to make sense to the character that the name is associated to...[Or] it breaks the immersion of the game that I'm playing."*

Sometimes players did not know enough about a particular game world or element of the game prior to creating a name. In this case, they set aside time to do some research during the naming process: *"I had to sit there for like an hour trying to figure out [how to make the name appropriate for my character's race]."* One player reflected on her experiences engaging with unfamiliar aesthetics when creating a character name for a Pandaren, a race from World of Warcraft with distinctively Chinese cultural elements:

I spent, for example, on the Pandaren, I spent probably two nights working on those names...I wanted the names to fit them, and I'm not very familiar with Chinese, and then I wanted to make sure the Chinese names that I looked up were accurate and not, you know, something else entirely. Because, you know, you never want to offend somebody by picking something that means something awful...or look like an idiot.

After realizing she was unable to create a name with a good fit for her character, she took time to research Chinese words to find a name that would appropriately represent her and her character. She was preemptively anticipating impressions players might develop if her character name was not well-chosen. Creating a name with a good fit was a way for her to display competence and creativity.

Why were players so concerned with having a name that fit? Fit allowed players to maintain a degree of immersion in-game for themselves and others: *"So, I think that's part of the immersion not just for me, but for other players. So, yeah I don't want to see a character with, with a name that doesn't fit the setting of the game."*

Summary

Naming allows a character to become more than an assortment of pixels that result from customization sliders and pre-set facial options. By giving a character a name, players have creative control over the creation and customization of the sense a name evokes for others. Players incorporated elements in character names that represented information about themselves. They tailored this information in a way that fit the aesthetics and lore of the game world.

DISCUSSION

Previous research has demonstrated that physical character creation and customization are important aspects of the video gaming experience [5, 8, 25, 26]. But these studies concern only one aspect of the player-character relationship, and there has perhaps been a tendency to equate player identity with the physical representation of the character. We found that players used character names to develop a sincere, rather than idealized, identity in order to create a consistent, representative identity useful in interacting with others. Taylor [25, 26] discussed how characters' virtual bodies facilitated social engagement, and we found that naming was also critical to building and sustaining social relationships.

Character names function in ways digital embodiment cannot. Names allowed players to develop a unique identity that persisted over time. A persistent identity made sustaining social relationships across games easier, as players were able to identify other players. Names allowed players to make visible aspects of their identity such as their creativity, their favored media, and their personal interests. Character names sometimes even became part of players' offline and social media lives. Character names afforded players the ability to cultivate an identity that consistently referenced them, sincerely represented them, and persistently identified them, regardless of context.

Other contexts such as forums, voice over IP applications, and some third-party sites require players to use a name for identification. For example, sites such as Arena Junkies, draw information about player versus player (PvP) ratings, team compositions, and win/loss ratios from the World of Warcraft Armory, a database of World of Warcraft characters that is accessible to anyone. It is beneficial for a player wishing to participate in the Arena Junkie forums to use her World of Warcraft character name to identify herself to other players. These contexts encourage players to identify themselves by their character names to establish credibility associated with their posts, provide continuity between games and related sites, and build a community of identifiable individuals. As a player travels between different game-related contexts, his character name becomes a central piece of his identity and links information about him to a single identifier.

Character name creation has its own set of norms and appropriate behaviors. Game developers create some norms, such as whether or not the game allows for surnames, numbers, and profane language in a character name, while the player community creates others, such as what names are considered appropriate or creative. There is, however, some overlap. Name generators, for example, are tools provided by game developers or third-party sites to help players who are unfamiliar with a game create a name that fits within the game world. While this seems like a beneficial feature, many of our participants believed that using a name generator indicated a lack of creativity: *"I'm creative enough to come up with my own names. I'm not super lame."* Some players mentioned using name generators as a source of inspiration, but rarely used an unaltered, generated name: *"I've just never felt the need to use [name generators]. If there's like, 'click here to randomly generate a name' I might click it a couple of times to get an idea of what the developers thought an in-lore name should sound like."* Current name generators may not be useful to players with longer histories in the gaming community. Instead, they may be oriented towards newer players who are looking to create their first name in an online game.

Conversely, character name changes, a feature rapidly gaining popularity, appear to benefit long-time players looking to alter their character names. Games have monetized the name-change process, allowing players to rename a character they may have significant play time on for a small fee. Stinkypeen, one participant's unlikely main character, was already maximum level, but had a name the player resented: *"I've got a lot of whispers, like people that think it's humorous...but I still don't like it, and I'm probably going to [purchase a] name change."* As several of our participants explained, a name alone was often justification to delete a character: *"Like, whenever I chat...I see my name pop-up, and if I don't like that name then I will go back and delete [that character]."* Name generators and name changes are two features of character name creation and cultivation that provide a unique angle to online identity development oriented towards new players and veteran players, respectively.

Our research shows that players of social video games often went through a lot of trouble to maintain names across games and related sites. They sometimes even became quite upset when their names were taken or they could not use them for some other reason. However, in some contexts, such as reddit, the opposite is true. Reddit participants deliberately create multiple names to hide personal information from others [22]. Shelton et al. [22] found that participants preferred to keep social spheres such as work, family, and friends separate through the use of multiple account names. Sometimes participants created "throwaway" accounts used for a small number of posts before discarding the account, or they created work-safe-accounts for posting conservatively [22].

What causes naming practices to differ between video games and sites such as reddit? Participation in online video games encourages collaborative practices and interpersonal interactions because players enjoy playing with others [20, 21, 23, 29]. Players facilitated social relations by maintaining a consistent character name. Reddit participants did not build relationships on the site itself because they often wanted anonymity to post things they did not want to be held accountable for, such as revelations of an extremely personal nature, off-color jokes, or material others might consider inappropriate [22]. Participants viewed reddit as a place to write without restraint, and thus did not want their identity associated with a recognizable name.

Our research suggests that proposals insisting that users use their real names online miss such nuances of online life. Requiring users to identify themselves by their real names would squelch important affordances of online communication. Given the ways gamers manage character names and reddit participants use a series of pseudonyms to enhance online experiences, proposals such as those of Mark Zuckerberg seem dubious. He argues that maintaining a single persistent identity online is important for developing transparency in self-representation. He has said, "You have one identity…having two identities for yourself is an example of a lack of integrity" [14]. Similarly, Jonathan Zittrain argued for the use of real names online:

> When we participate in other walks of life—school, work, PTA meetings, and so on—we do so as ourselves, not wearing Groucho mustaches, and even if people do not know exactly who we are, they can recognize us from one meeting to the next. The same should be possible for our online selves [30].

But these arguments misconstrue the complexities of identity and politics in everyday life, and the difficulties that may accompany the use of real names. For example, one of our study participants elaborated on how he explored his gender identity online and offline. His found the process fraught with enormous difficulty offline, but easier in online gaming contexts because he could choose how to identify himself through his character names. He reflected on the affordances the use of character names provided that were impossible offline:

> *After thinking about how I felt about my gender for a long time I realized that I wanted to be, or felt, male and soon identified as transgender. Being around the community in th[e] game offered me the opportunities I could [use to] express myself [that] real life couldn't.*

His character name did not restrict and misgender him the way his real name did offline. He chose names that reflected his identity as he perceived it: *"I always try to either keep [my character names] gender neutral or male."* Online, this player could not only present to others as his chosen gender, he could switch between gender-neutral and male choices that made him comfortable, and allowed for "opportunities to express himself."

Such identity concerns are common for different kinds of people. One of the redeeming qualities of the internet is that it affords the possibility to carefully manage identity. For example, some countries monitor and regulate people with certain sexual orientations, religious affiliations, political opinions, racial backgrounds, or gender expressions. Individuals with the "wrong" characteristics may be subject to legal action if their identity is revealed. Online, pseudonyms allow a person to protect himself, and to express aspects of his identity, such as our transgender player did. Nardi [21] found that Chinese World of Warcraft players sometimes used character names to express dissatisfaction with the Chinese government, a form of free expression that would be near impossible using real names. Our own society may criticize people who identify, or are identified, as gamers. During state Senator Colleen Lachowicz's campaign in 2012 in Maine, her opponents used her participation in World of Warcraft to attack her qualifications for office [13]. Opponents posted Lachowicz's character name and excerpts of her online chats on a website with a header that read: "In Colleen's online fantasy world, she gets away with crude, vicious and violent comments like the ones below. Maine needs a State Senator that lives in the real world, not in Colleen's fantasy world." [31] While Lachowicz won the election, her case shows why people may prefer to manage their identity through pseudonyms to avoid senseless trouble such as that created by Lachowicz's opponents. It is unclear who revealed her real name, but proposals to enforce real name use online make situations like the one Lachowicz experienced more probable and more acceptable.

Real names may put female users at risk for harassment in gaming communities and elsewhere [2, 15, 17]. For example, Kuznekoff and Rose [15] used pre-recorded voices in online game matches to measure player reaction to gendered voices. They found that female voices received more hostile, negative, and sexist comments [15]. Female players should be able to choose whether or not to reveal their gender identity, not have it revealed de facto, without their consent, through a real name.

In 2010, Blizzard Entertainment introduced a Real-ID system that would identify players in-game by their real names, not their character name or another pseudonym. Albrechtslund [1] analyzed player quotes from the official thread where Blizzard proposed the change and found that players were outraged. The thread had almost 50,000 posts from players protesting the implementation of the Real-ID system [1]. Players' concerns ranged from identity theft to harassment to backlash from employers. A 21-year-old player communicated her concerns with the prospect of players being able to identify her gender without her consent:

> *By revealing my name, you can now find out everything about me. What does that do to a 21–year–old disabled woman? It makes me a target. Now, obviously not everyone is going to go insane and start going on WoW murdering sprees, but I have already had some pretty unkind things said about me when people do find out. I'm not going to stand for this. I will not yet again be taunted and harassed by ignorant, uncaring jerks, just because they're able to see who I am.* [1]

The nuanced ways in which our study participants managed their online identities argues that we should allow users to choose whatever names they choose online, and to craft their identities according to the specific venue they are in (whether games, reddit, or anywhere else). An appropriate naming convention in one context is not necessarily appropriate in another. Gamers are aware of the power of names, and our study has shown how much work a carefully chosen name does for a player in terms of social relationships and personal expression. We advocate that internet policy take a page from gaming and give users free rein to call themselves whatever they prefer, within the bounds of acceptability in the particular communities in which they participate.

We found that players used their character names as a means to sincerely represent aspects of their identity, such as personal interests and individual creativity. Such practices would not even be possible were users required to use their real names. Donath [6] argued that the use of pseudonyms can be beneficial for both the individual and the community: "A persistent pseudonym establishes a local identity: you always use it on a certain site or sites, and you build up a history and reputation under that name…" Our study indicates that players had many legitimate reasons for maintaining and using freely chosen character names for their online identity, and we agree with Donath that the use of pseudonyms is a positive aspect of online culture.

CONCLUSION

In this paper, we analyzed players' practices for creating character names in online video games using Frege's semantic theory of reference and sense. We examined the pragmatic and personal functions names served for players. Players viewed character names as a means of representing a unique identity for themselves, developing persistent relationships with other players, and starting conversations about common interests with others. The care with which players created and managed their character names indicates their value to the gaming experience, and suggests a broader importance of naming practices online.

This exploratory study of naming practices and identification in online gaming opens new research venues for online identity. Several of our older participants mentioned a dramatic shift in their naming practices at some point during their adolescent years. Many players mentioned it was possible to identify younger players based on names or naming styles. How do players identify which names and naming patterns younger players use? Are the stereotypes associated with the names of younger players accurate? What factors contribute to better understandings of acceptable naming practices in online games? A cohort or longitudinal study of online names could provide insights into the temporal differences in naming practices based on a player's age.

While the current study focuses on naming practices in online games, several participants mentioned extending these practices into offline games. Why do players choose to use their online names in offline games? Are there instances where this pattern is broken, such as when a character has a canonical name in a game world (e.g., Link from Legend of Zelda, Lightning from Final Fantasy, etc.)? What purpose does using an online name in an offline game serve for players? Examining player behaviors in offline games may provide better insights about how character names contribute to players' concept of themselves and their identity beyond online interactions.

Finally, a more inclusive examination of identity in online contexts ranging from online gaming to social media to online dating could provide a better understanding of how a user connects or separates his identity across contexts. In what spaces do users reuse a name? When do users create a new name? Determining the factors that encourage users to reuse a name in a new context could provide important information about overlapping online social spheres and spaces users wish to keep separated.

The current study extends existing research on player identity by examining the practices and behaviors surrounding creating character names in online games. We have demonstrated that character naming is frequently a time-consuming and intensive process and functions as a way for players to convey information about their identities to others.

ACKNOWLEDGMENTS

The authors would like to thank study participants for their time and dedication during interviews, the TechDec lab at the University of California, Irvine for their astute feedback during the paper's inception, Nathan Fulton for his insightful comments on earlier drafts, and our anonymous reviews for their helpful suggestions on the final version of the paper.

REFERENCES

1. Albrechtslund, A. M. (2011). Online identity crisis: Real ID on the World of Warcraft forums. *First Monday*, *16*(7).
2. Ballard, M. E., & Lineberger, R. (1999). Video game violence and confederate gender: Effects on reward and punishment given by college males. *Sex Roles*, *41*(7-8), 541-558.
3. Bardzell, J. and Bardzell, S. (2008). Intimate interactions: Online representation and software of the self. *Interactions – We must Redesign Professional Design Education for the 21st Century*, 15(5), 11-15.
4. Benford, S., Bowers, J., Fahlén, L. E., Greenhalgh, C., & Snowdon, D. (1995, May). User embodiment in collaborative virtual environments. In *Proceedings of the SIGCHI conference on Human factors in computing systems* (pp. 242-249). ACM Press/Addison-Wesley Publishing Co..
5. Bessière, K. Seay, A.F., and Kiesler, S. (2007). The ideal Elf: Identity exploration in World of Warcraft. *CyberPsychology & Behavior*, 10(*4*), 530-535.
6. Donath, J. S. (2014). We need online alter egos now more than ever. Retrieved from http://www.wired.com/
7. Drachen, A.; Sifa, R. & Thurau, C. (2014) The Name in the Game: Patterns and Inspirations for Character Names and Gamer Tags. Invited Paper. Accepted for *Entertainment Computing* (Elsevier Publishers).
8. Ducheneaut, N., Wen, M. H., Yee, N., Wadley, G. (2009). Body and mind: A study of avatar personalization in three virtual worlds. *Proceedings of the 27th international conference on human factors in computing systems*, 1151-1160.
9. Frege, G. (1892). On sinn and bedeutung.
10. Guitton, M. J. (2010). Cross-modal compensation between name and visual aspect in socially active avatars. *Computers in Human Behavior*, *26*(6), 1772-1776.
11. Hagström, C. (2008). Playing with names: Gaming and naming in World of Warcraft. *Digital Culture, Play, and Identity a World of Warcraft Reader*, 265-286.
12. Hoorens, V., & Todorova, E. (1988). The name letter effect: Attachment to self or primacy of own name writing?. *European Journal of Social Psychology*, *18*(4), 365-368.

13. Kilkenny, K. (2012). GOP goes after World of Warcraft-loving candidate. Retrieved from http://www.slate.com/
14. Kirkpatrick, D. (2011). *The Facebook effect: The inside story of the company that is connecting the world*. Simon and Schuster.
15. Kuznekoff, J. H., & Rose, L. M. (2013). Communication in multiplayer gaming: Examining player responses to gender cues. *New Media & Society*, *15*(4), 541-556.
16. Lyons, J. (1977). Semantics. 2 vols.
17. McDermott, I. E. (2012). Trolls, cyberbullies, and other offenders. *Searcher: the Magazine for Database Professionals*, *20*(10), 7-11.
18. McDonough, J. P. (1999). Designer selves: Construction of technologically mediated identity within graphical, multiuser virtual environments. *Journal of the American Society for Information Science*, *50*(10), 855-869.
19. Moore, A. W. (1993). Meaning and reference.
20. Nardi, B., & Harris, J. (2006, November). Strangers and friends: Collaborative play in World of Warcraft. In *Proceedings of the 2006 20th anniversary conference on Computer supported cooperative work* (pp. 149-158). ACM.
21. Nardi, B. (2010). My life as a night elf priest. *Ann Arbor: University of Michigan Press*.
22. Shelton, Martin 2014. Examining the Influence of Online Forums on Conversational Practice in "Spaces Beyond." In preparation.
23. Steinkuehler, C. A., & Williams, D. (2006). Where everybody knows your (screen) name: Online games as "third places". *Journal of Computer-Mediated Communication*, *11*(4), 885-909.
24. Stone, A. R. (1991). Will the real body please stand up. *Cyberspace: first steps*, 81-118.
25. Taylor, T. L. (1999). Life in Virtual Worlds Plural Existence, Multimodalities, and other Online Research Challenges. *American Behavioral Scientist*, *43*(3), 436-449.
26. Taylor, T. L. (2002). Living digitally: Embodiment in virtual worlds. In *The social life of avatars* (pp. 40-62). Springer London.
27. Thurau, C., & Drachen, A. (2011). Naming virtual identities: patterns and inspirations for character names in world of warcraft. In *Entertainment Computing–ICEC 2011* (pp. 270-281). Springer Berlin Heidelberg.
28. Valentine, T., Brennen, T., & Brédart, S. (1996). *The cognitive psychology of proper names: On the importance of being Ernest*. Taylor & Frances/Routledge.
29. Yee, N. (2006). Motivations for play in online games. *CyberPsychology & behavior*, *9*(6), 772-775.
30. Zittrain, J. (2008). The future of the Internet. *London: Allen Lane*.
31. Maine Republican Party (2014). Colleen's World. Retrieved from http://www.colleensworld.com/

Towards Tangible Gamified Co-Design at School

Two Studies in Primary Schools

Gabriella Dodero, Rosella Gennari, Alessandra Melonio, Santina Torello
Free University of Bozen-Bolzano
Piazza Domenicani 3
39100 Bolzano, Italy
name.surname@unibz.it

ABSTRACT

Co-design is an ideal approach to design with users. It allows designers to create products, such as games, with their intended users and in their natural environment, e.g., children and their teachers in their school. Nowadays school contexts, however, pose their own requirements to co-design, which can affect its success. For instance, school contexts tend to be associated to boring rote by learners, who are used to interactive digital games. Gamification can then help in creating a positive engaging experience for school classes that co-design, as games do. This paper takes up such a view: it gamifies co-design contexts in order to positively engage school classes. To this end it presents two studies with gamified co-design in primary schools: heterogeneous teams co-designed prototypes by resolving missions as in a game, in the first short-term study; they did it in an even more gamified context, in the second long-term study. Results of both studies are encouraging for the approach. The paper also advances basic guidelines for tangibly gamifying co-design at school, grounded in the studies and literature.

Author Keywords

Game design; co-design; gamification; empirical studies; performance; engagement; children; schools

ACM Classification Keywords

H.4 Human-centred computing: Interaction design Interaction design process and methods

INTRODUCTION

Co-design, in the sense of [24], is a general approach to design that extends several others and can be used in any stage of the design process by designers and non-designers for "collectively creating". When designing products for children such as games, co-design with children becomes the ideal companion to *user experience* (UX) design [22]: with co-design methods and techniques, children and teachers become members of design teams in their own environment, that is, in their school. Nowadays schools pose their own challenges, listed in [6]. At school, educators face heterogeneous classes, having children with diverse learning styles and social skills. Moreover children are exposed to interactive products and environments [4, 29], in particular games. As Prensky states, "unlike previous generations of students, who grew up without games, [these generations] know what real engagement feels like" and, at school, "they know exactly what is missing" [20]. Positively engaging all children at school is thus becoming increasingly difficult, and can be determinant for the success of (co-)design in such a setting. Given that, we propose to gamify co-design contexts for positively engaging children at school as in a game.

For studying the viability of the approach, the authors of this paper ran several pilot studies, and then three main studies with gamified co-design at school. This paper reports two out of these three studies, run in two primary schools: one at the start of 2013; the other at the start of 2014. The main goal of this paper is to outline results from the first study, and how they affected the design of the second study. The latter study shows a more tangible gamification of the co-design context, namely, of both the environment and tasks for co-designing.

The paper starts presenting the strictly necessary background on co-design with children; a comprehensive survey of methods and techniques for co-designing with children is [9]. The essentials of gamification are also presented. Then the paper speculates on how one can gamify co-design with children at school, leveraging on the literature and the authors' first-hand experience. The authors' two main studies in primary schools are then presented, and general results of the studies are highlighted in the conclusions.

BACKGROUND

Co-design with Children in a Nutshell

Sanders and Stappers characterised co-design as an approach that extends several others, such as participatory design and co-creation, and aims at involving stakeholders as collaborative designers [24]. When stakeholders are children, specific methods are used. *Cooperative inquiry* is among the best known co-design methods with techniques for children, and that collaborative teams of adults and children can use throughout the design process [7, 8, 12, 32]. Examples are sticky noting, for offering design suggestions on existing artifacts, and layered elaboration, for expanding on others' ideas

CHI PLAY '14, October 19–22, 2014, Toronto, ON, Canada.

http://dx.doi.org/10.1145/2658537.2658688

by layering transparent sheets over others, without affecting the original sheets and ideas.

In this view of co-design, team members are involved in the design process on equal footing, albeit they have diverse roles: users become co-designers as "experts of their experience"; researchers become facilitators to ease users' expression of creativity; designers, expert of the product under design, will bring in their professional experience. When co-design studies take place at school, the latter two roles are often merged, and teachers can also be members of the co-design team, mainly as experts of education and of school context. See [24, 28].

Co-design at school, albeit not new, has received increasing attention in recent years [11, 31]. However, co-design in current formal learning contexts, such as schools, presents several challenges [6]. In particular, the work of Garzotto and others stresses that co-design tasks at school should be engaging, possibly fun, for children [10]. However, *how to design tasks and environments that positively engage* wide and diverse groups of nowadays' learners, who are used to engaging interactive products, and often equate school with boring rote? We unveil our proposal in the following section.

Gamification in a Nutshell

Designers can create games moving from game mechanics to game aesthetics [14]. At the core of the mechanics is the view of a game as a transition system [1]: a game needs a *goal*, an *initial state* and *terminal* states, intermediate states with *challenges* to overcome, and a set of *actions* of players that allow them to move from state to state, according to the game rules. Other game elements are [16]: *competition* or *cooperation* elements; *reward* structures with juicy *feedback*; game *missions* whereby players progress from one mission to the next one(s) as they move toward the termination of the game; *story lines*, providing context to the game. All such game elements are experienced by the player by means of the game aesthetics, that is, how the game "looks, sounds, smells, tastes and feels" [26].

Game design, from mechanics to aesthetics, is behind the broad area of gamification. In its most common acceptation, gamification means properly using game-based elements, such as those listed above, for a non-game goal and in a non-game context in order to positively engage people, e.g., see [16]. Participants are then regarded as players.

Diverse motivation theories are invoked to explain why gamification can positively engage players [16]. In particular, this paper follows researchers that base their work on *self determination theory* (SDT) [5]: in brief, a gamification that nourishes a sense of competence, control and autonomy, as well as social relatedness can lead to a positive engaging experience, e.g., an experience of enjoyment and deep concentration. The literature reviews of Hamari et al. and Kapp show that, depending on the context and types of players, gamification provides players with positive experiences for engagement, at least in the short term, and possible negative effects such as increased competition [13, 16].

GAMIFICATION OF CO-DESIGN AT SCHOOL

If one wishes to apply gamification to co-design contexts, firstly one should design and present co-design tasks as missions of a game, one building upon the other, with a goal valuable for all co-designers. The relevance of the adult designer that is expert of the co-designed product should fade though missions.

The design of each mission for schools also requires to think of learners as players. According to Lazzaro classification, there are four main player profiles: hard-fun players who go for challenges and strategy-based play, easy-fun ones who love intrigue and curiosity, altered-state ones who play for escaping from their world, and people-factor ones who use games for social experiences [17]. However school classes tend to be highly heterogeneous, which means designing missions for all player profiles, or for teams that group children with different player profiles.

By referring to SDT, independently of their profile, all children should experience a sense of progression through missions, so as to feel more and more competent. To this end, according to their complexity, missions can be chunked into small progressive challenges, disclosed when needed with clear rules, of which the first challenge should be easy to take up by all learners. Growing avatars, progression maps or completion rewards, which are contingent to co-design, help in conveying the idea of growth through missions and challenges. Rewards can be tangible or not. For instance, tangible rewards are (fake) coins that are earned on completion of co-design challenges or missions. An example non-tangible reward is positive oral feedback in case of errors.

Positive failure feedback is also important for enhancing a sense of control; to the point that game designers invest considerable time in creating failure feedback that is immediate, fun, spectacular so as to make players "more optimistic about [their] odds of success" [19]. To this end, the adult designer should congratulate learners every time they try out hard and fail a difficult challenge, and help them with rapid constructive feedback on demand. His or her role can be made clear and visible, for instance, via expert-cards, which children can spend whenever they feel in need of the adult designer's help.

A co-design context that invites children's free exploration and choice, like an unexplored game world, can even more tangibly promote a sense of autonomy and control over their co-design work, as prescribed by SDT. A simple example is a context that allows children to choose different co-design challenges from a map. An even simpler example is as follows: on completion of a mission or challenge, children are invited to choose one among different completion rewards, which they may also customize or seek in the environment, and to use the reward for their next co-design challenge or mission. In this manner they gain the feeling that their actions have a tangible effect on their co-design work, and that they are in control of choosing parts of this.

Relatedness needs are also important components of games according to SDT. Gamification of co-design contexts, however, should be done fostering cooperation, so as to be faithful to the co-design partnership principle, e.g., rewards should not increase competition within groups. Such a constraint can be met by providing rewards that mildly favor only inter-group competition so as to promote "intra-group positive interdependence" and cooperation [23], and still satisfy relatedness needs.

Progression maps can also be used to connect with others and satisfy relatedness needs. Shared maps can show other learners that a group or an individual could overcome a co-design challenge, and are available for sharing their co-design experience and acquired expertise.

THE FIRST STUDY

Goals

Our 2013 study was run in primary schools. Classes read aloud and discussed a story with their teacher. Then they were asked to develop a game for applying what they had read about in the story[1], e.g., story setting or characters. This study aimed at using gamified co-design for producing low-fidelity prototypes of such games.

The study inspected several UX goals. Hereby we focus on the following two: (g1) children's performances with co-design missions; (g2) children's engagement in relation to gamified co-design. As typical in measuring UX, performance as in (g1) can be used to estimate children's behaviour with gamified co-design—if it allows them to produce prototypes. Instead, engagement as in (g2) can be used to estimate children's perception of gamified co-design. See [2].

Participants and Roles

The study was conducted with four primary-school classes: two of younger learners, 8–9 year old; two of older learners, 10–11 year old. In total, we involved 56 learners, 4 teachers, and 4 designers.

Roles of participants were as follows. Children were the main game prototype designers. Their work was organised for either small groups of 4 or for individuals, or for the entire class. Designers were experts of the product under design: among them, one was more experienced in child development studies, whereas the others were more experienced in digital game development. They were one per group of learners in this study. Each designer took care of illustrating the organisation of work, coaching and scaffolding proper development in their group (e.g., to resolve possible doubts, assist learners in case of serious risks of failure) by providing rapid but non-intrusive feedback. Teachers took care of composing small groups and reporting group composition by using a pre-defined group form, conducting the story reading and their comprehension interventions in class, and stimulating conversation in class when required by designers.

Study Design and Execution

The study was organised as an empirical one along 3 main activities: pre-activity, main activity, post-activity.

[1]The term "application" is used in the sense of Bloom taxonomy [3].

Pre-activity: Training

During the pre-activity, designers organised a meeting with the school dean and interested teachers in each school. Therein, the study design was explained and discussed. A week before the main activity, a training session for all teachers was organised, specifying the role of each co-design team member. During the latter meeting, teachers were asked to choose a child story for creating games, and to fill in the group form. This mainly served to create balanced and heterogeneous groups of learners in terms of their learning and social styles.

Main Activity: Prototyping

Missions. The main activity took four sessions, one per school class, with always 4 designers and a teacher per class. Each session was split in 3 missions with predefined timings, lasting c. 2 hours and a half also due to school constraints. In the first mission teacher and learners read and discussed the chosen story in class, under teacher guidance. The second and third missions required to work in groups, that were organised with cooperative learning methods [15]. In the second mission, groups of 4 children worked for co-designing a game prototype. See Figure 1. Each group prototype was discussed with the class in the third and final mission, and then displayed as in a gallery tour, see [15] and Figure 3. Figure 2 shows two game prototypes, one by a group of younger children and the other by a group of older ones.

Rapid feedback. Rapid feedback was mainly verbal across missions. In the first mission, it was the teacher feedback for their class. In the second, it was the designer feedback for their group and peer feedback within the group. In the third mission, feedback was of the class for each group.

Rules and challenges. Each mission came with its own rules and progressive challenges. Challenges were linearly organised, each building on the previous one, so that each had to be completed before moving to the subsequent one. The second mission challenges required diverse skills. For instance, its first challenge required groups of children to discuss and negotiate the so-called game idea [1] in relation to the assigned goal. Verbal skills were then those mainly elicited. When realising the game scenario on paper in the second challenge, visual-motor skills were those mainly activated.

Cooperation, competition and rewards. At the end of the first mission and before children were divided into small groups for the second mission, teachers made it clear that groups would be competing against each other in creating game prototypes: the group best collaborating according to designers and teachers, and realising the best game according to other learners would see a valuable reward: their prototype implemented as a 'real' game for tablets, to play with. However children were also told that the work of each group would receive a reward: their presentation of how to play with their game prototype was video-recorded in the third mission, and made available online to all school participants.

Post-activity: Debriefing

In the post-activity, debriefing interviews were run by teachers with the help of designers. Moreover, children were sub-

Figure 1. Work in groups of 4 children for prototyping

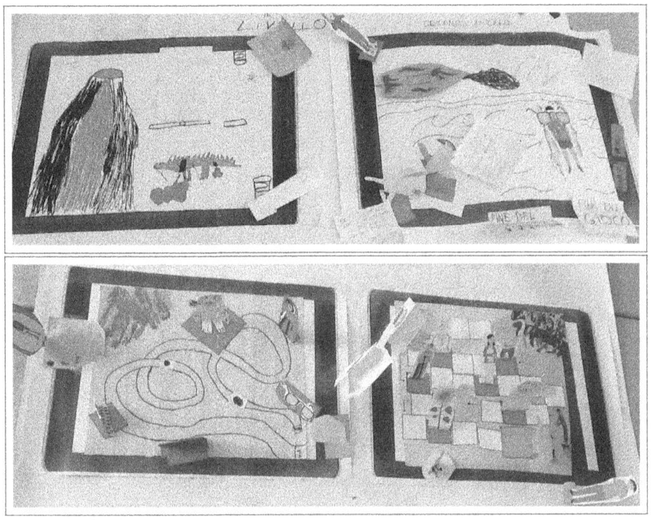

Figure 2. Game prototypes: the top by younger children, the bottom by older children

sequently questioned in class by their teachers to report their interest and enjoyment for the study experience.

Figure 3. Gallery tour during the third mission

Material and Environment

The study material included: a TERENCE [30] child story; envelopes; paper bins; A2, A3, A4 paper sheets; post-it paper sheets; pencils and markers; story characters and elements; scissors and glue. Co-design was in classroom which was big and full of light. Tables were arranged in groups of 4 for the study, with sufficient distance between groups and allowing every member of the group to easily grab the study material from a central table. The organisation of tables was thought so as to promote face-to-face work and avoid distractions.

Data Collection and Results

A mixed-method approach was used for gathering data: data were collected with quantitative and qualitative methods. For the main activity (prototyping), we employed triangulation as much as possible for quality reasons [18]. During it, data were collected by designers using a pre-defined common protocol and form. Each group of children was video-recorded. Transcribed data and videos were jointly revised by designers in meetings, then discussed and revised with teachers. In brief, the main activity had multiple data sources, investigators and collection methods.

This section presents the main data analysis results, relevant for this paper, and related to the study goals—performance and engagement—besides issues with our gamified co-design.

Performance

We assessed groups' performances by tracking their success in establishing game elements. We distinguished game elements that children were explicitly required from those that children spontaneously produced. Required game elements are those necessary in every game, e.g., in order to distinguish games from drawings: rules with player moves and challenges; termination conditions; feedback; scenario, that is, where the gameplay takes place.

For each group, success per required element is equal to: 1 if the group established the element in time, under the guidance of their designer, who did not produce the element on behalf of the group; 0 otherwise. For each group, success for an emerged element is equal to: 1 if the group by themselves established the element; 0 otherwise.

For each element, we computed the proportions of groups producing it and related 90% *confidence intervals*[2] (CI's) with the Adjusted Wald method [25].

All groups managed to produce all required elements, with $CI[0.88, 1]$. Additional game elements spontaneously emerged. In particular, .81 of groups layered their game into levels, with $SD = 0.4$ and $CI[0.6, 0.92]$; .12 of groups created a storyline, with $SD = 0.34$ and $CI[0.03, 0.32]$. Results are rather homogeneous across age groups.

From such results, it seems that children would tend to create diverse levels for games; the majority of levels were of progressive difficulty whereas some levels were totally independent from one other. The absence of a storyline could be due to the fact that game prototypes were designed starting from a given story.

Engagement

Engagement was mainly assessed through observations of designers during the main activity (prototyping) and interviews to children during the post-activity (debriefing). In line with [27], engagement is the culmination of: concentration;

[2]A CI for a sample statistics gives an estimated range of values which is likely to include the unknown population parameter. Were this procedure to be repeated with future groups of learners, the calculated CI would encompass the true population parameter 90% of times.

interest; enjoyment. In this sense, results of our study were generally positive, e.g., all classes showed to have enjoyed co-designing: except one, all asked designers to do the experience again and again,"every week".

Other Issues

Several issues emerged with the 2013 gamified co-design. Post-activity (debriefing) interviews highlighted that the majority of children felt highly constrained in expressing their ideas by timings in mission challenges, which children perceived as too short. The most difficult challenge to start for children was the drafting of the so-called game idea [1].

Such findings are also confirmed by designers' notes taken during the main activity (prototyping), according to whom: children required no more designers' help for starting the subsequent challenges, still designers were necessary for maintaining consistency of group choices across mission challenges; children felt too often in a hurry to complete their missions and complained about it.

Discussion

The reported study assessed that the gamified study was generally effective in terms of: (1) performances of groups of children in designing their prototype elements, by tracing which elements children successfully designed within the given timings; (2) children's engagement, by reporting their concentration, interest and enjoyment.

Specifically, performance results show that gamified co-design can be effectively used at school by working groups of 4 children coached by a designer. Engagement results are mainly due to observations. Therefore, even if we tried minimising biases as best as possible, caution should be used with these results. That said, they are mostly positive.

Moreover several issues emerged that gave indications for future editions of gamified co-design. For instance, the role of designers required refinement. Designers were necessary for their groups of children mainly for maintaining the consistency of their product design choices across missions and for starting the drafting of the "game idea".

Most importantly, the majority of children perceived mission challenges as too short, and so did teachers. In other words, even if the co-design study was generally effective for producing game prototypes and children felt engaged, the quality experience of children could be be improved so as to allow them to fully express their ideas, as independently as possible from designers.

THE SECOND STUDY

According to the 2013 study results, the co-design of game prototypes should take longer to allow children to better express their ideas. Therefore the new study protocol had to be planned for running on different days with other children, and be even more integrated within school activities, thereby bringing benefits related to learning as well as experiential school objectives. Maintaining participants' engagement became even more important and difficult.

In order to engage children, we moved the yardstick of gamification of co-design contexts a step further. We gamified the co-design protocol even more, with more missions and challenges, each with its own game-like material for co-designing. We also added something totally new: the gamification of classrooms, enriched with low-cost game-like tangible material, which classes could easily pick up, imitate or adapt for their future needs. Explaining how we did is the focus of this section.

Goals

The second study was run in 2014 in primary schools. Also the 2014 study aimed at using gamified co-design for producing low-fidelity game prototypes, starting from another story for children. See Figure 4. However, the 2014 study tried to make gamification more tangible so as to engage children in a long-term co-design activity, spread across different days. One of the goals of the second study, which we focus on in this paper, became to study the behaviour and engagement of children with the gamified material. More precisely, the goal became to assess whether (g) children grabbed the intended usage of the gamified material for co-designing (behaviour), and they were interested in it or enjoyed it (engagement). In the remainder, we give the essential information about study participants, material and environment, in relation to the reported UX goal.

Participants and Roles

The study was conducted with two primary-school classes: one of younger learners, 8–9 year old, and one of older learners, 9–10 year old. In total, the study involved 36 learners, 2 teachers and 2 support teachers, and 2 expert designers.

Roles of participants were as follows. As in the 2013 study, children were the main game prototype designers, mainly working in groups of 3–5 members, for a total of 9 groups. Within groups, roles in co-design were assigned by teachers and for each mission, e.g., of secretary or silence-keeper. Such roles rotated among group members so as to ensure that all children had a chance to play different roles and, hence, to use diverse cognitive and social kills.

In contrast to the previous study, teachers had a more prominent role: assisted by expert designers, teachers took care of illustrating the organisation of missions and related challenges, of supervising that children could progress in time through challenges, of coaching and scaffolding group work by using specific cooperative learning techniques.

Designers were two, with two different roles: one of game designer, who followed each group providing non-intrusive feedback and assisting each groups, when required, on their prototype development; the other, more experienced of child development studies, acted as passive observer, referred to as observer below.

Study Design and Execution

The study was organised as an empirical one along 3 main activities, like the 2013 study. Pre-activity training was different than in 2013. A workshop for teachers, lasting circa 6 hours, was organised and a more focussed training was thus

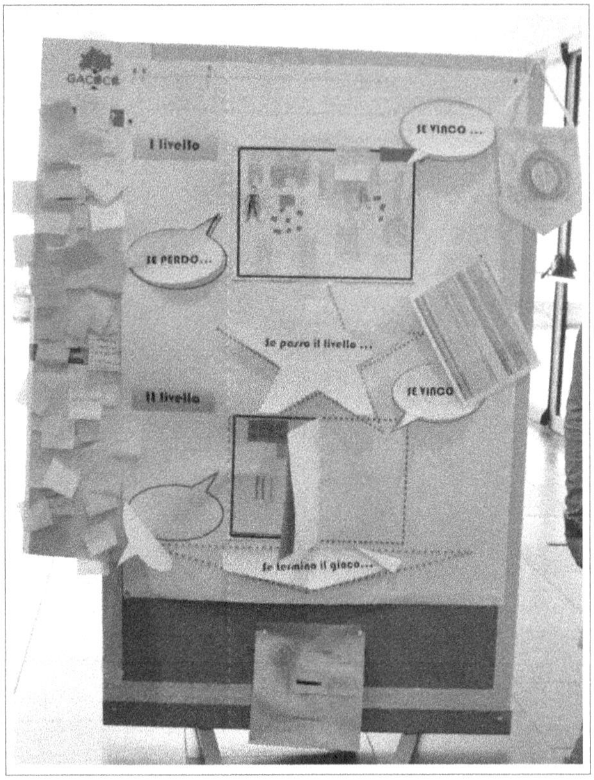

Figure 4. A game prototype developed in the second study

performed. For instance, during the workshop, the protocol of each mission was explained by expert designers, and so were the main ideas of gamification and game design. Teachers worked in group and experimented the protocol for children by co-designing games themselves. Also children were trained to game design principles. This training lasted circa 20 minutes.

The main difference between 2013 and 2014 was anyhow in the main activity for prototyping. This was by far longer, more structured, and in a tangibly gamified context (see the below subsection). The main activity consisted of 6 missions, of which the last was run in the university premises, whereas all the others were run in classroom.

Each mission lasted circa 2 hours and a half. Missions were organised linearly with progressive challenges. Challenges followed a recurring pattern, albeit each had different surprise rewards, its own objective, its specific co-design material, rules and feedback.

As in 2013, the last activity mainly consisted of a conclusive debriefing, with feedback from teachers and children.

Material and Environment

This part is concerned with the main activity for prototyping. During all missions except the last one, children worked in their classrooms. At the start of a mission, each group arranged classroom tables in groups of 4 as in the 2013 study. Each group had jute baskets for storing the different objects of each mission on their tables. Other gamified material for co-designing was arranged in classroom. See Figure 5.

Figure 5. Gamified objects in a classroom

In particular, three A0 posters were used in the gamified co-design at school. One was a paper-version of a progression bar, on display in classroom during all missions. Another showed a country land, with spots for trees growing in relation to the growth of the groups' game prototypes. This is referred to as the tree map, and was on display in classroom across all missions as well. The third was a frame, one per group, for assembling parts of game prototypes. This was used only in the last mission at school, the fifth one. From the second mission onwards, a wood shop with objects to buy, resembling an automated one, was positioned in a specific location of the classroom, referred to as shopping point. Across all missions at school, children had also a signalling disk for expressing their opinions. Details of such material are described in the following.

Progression bar (Figure 6). Each group had their place card, with their group logo printed on, to move across challenges of the progression bar, hung on the classroom wall. Each challenge in the bar had a tangible reward in the form of a removable coin, made of wood. When a group grabbed their coin, on completion of a challenge, they found a positive feedback behind it. Those coins work as completion-contingent rewards, that is, a group could earn a coin only after completing a challenge.

Tree map (Figure 7). In the progression bar, the end of each mission was represented with a door hiding special rewards, that is, parts of a tree in the form of stickers. Children had to use these in the tree map for assembling their tree, showing that they progressed in the completion of their game prototype. Each group had their dedicated portion of land on which to stick their portion of tree. Firstly each group had to plant the seed into the soil, secondly to water the seed and then to grow their tree, piece by piece across missions.

Shop (Figure 8). At the end of each mission, groups could use their coins, found in the progression bar. Coins served to buy objects for the prototypes they were co-designing. Groups had to move to the shopping point, where they found the wood fabric shop with 20 jute pockets, containing objects for

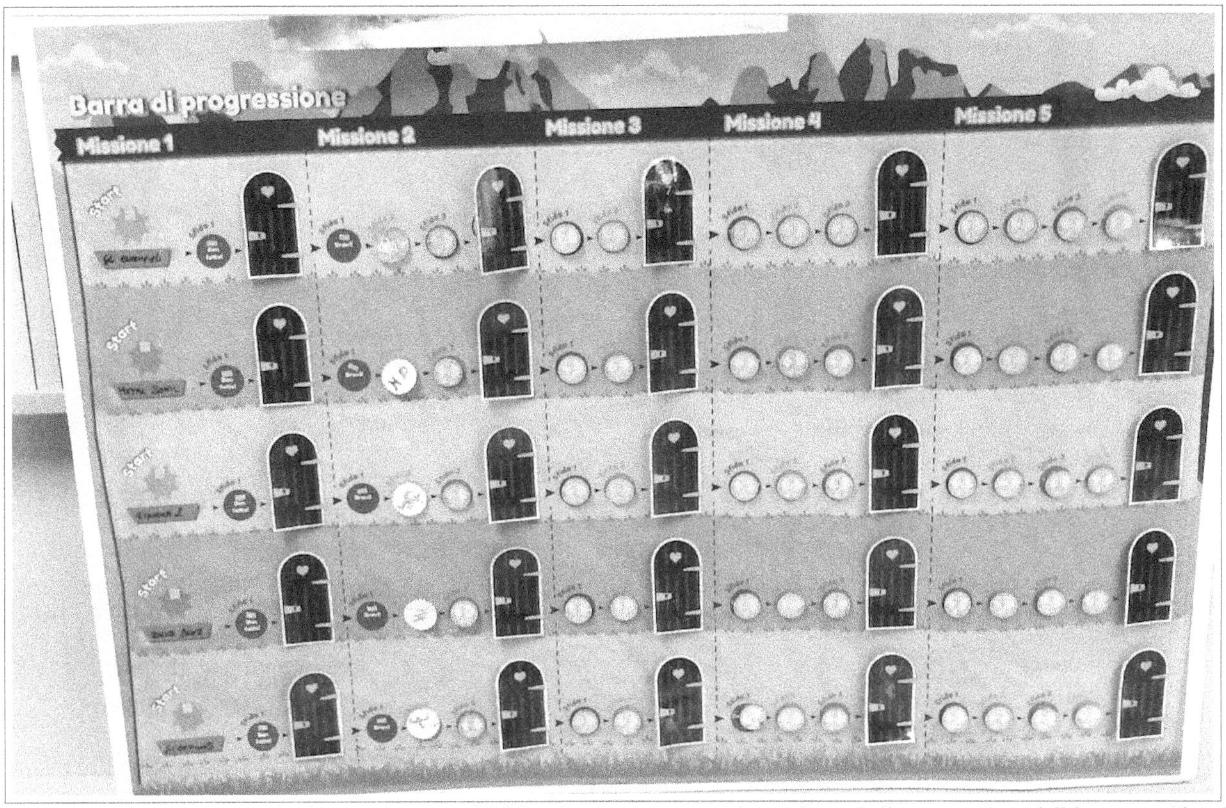

Figure 6. A screenshot of the progression bar: each group of children has its own row; each row shows challenges as coloured disks, grouped in missions

prototyping. Groups could buy objects of their daily mission by inserting their coin into the shop fissure. The objects on sell were 20, including a special card for the "help of the expert card". This card gave each group the right to ask the game designer for extra-help concerning their prototype.

Prototype frame (Figure 4). The last two missions were centred around a presentation of the co-designed prototypes. For their presentation, each group had a frame: an A0 poster with coloured shapes in which to insert pieces or information about their paper-based prototype, in a structured guided manner.

Signalling disks (Figure 9). In group challenges, at specific moment, each group member had to vote on proposals made by other group members by using his/her signalling disk, carved in wood. Using chalk, children drew smileys or wrote their feedback, positive or not, on their signalling disks in relation to the voting task.

Data Collection and Results

Again, a mixed-method approach was used for gathering data, taking care of triangulating as much as meaningful, like in the first study. In particular, the observer observed groups, coding their behaviour and engagement with challenges and mission material. The teacher feedback concerning behaviour and engagement was also sought with interviews after each mission. Moreover, each child self-reported their engagement in each mission by using a standardised questionnaire for children, see [21]. At the end of each mission, class feedback was also orally elicited at different levels, e.g., concerning " today's most beautiful challenge".

Hereby we focus on the first available results concerning the behaviour and engagement of children with the gamified material, focusing on their interest and enjoyment. Such results mainly come from the observer's notes, and from teachers' feedback.

Signalling disk (Figure 9). One of the elements that had the greatest success was the signalling disk for voting. Children were enthusiastic about this item, immediately showed the desire to use and re-use it, to draw and erase their opinion. They also tried voting with it even when they were not supposed to, satisfying their desire to use it but showing to do it in a creative and functional manner. Other times children were reproached for using it exceedingly by their teacher, which suggested that this risked to become too pervasive an object.

Shop (Figure 8). After the signalling disk, the object that received major interest was the shop for buying components for their game design. We observed smiling faces lightening up at the sight of the shop, and interest in observing the different objects on display in the shop. We also noted that, whereas in the first missions children were more interested in buying an item for its aesthetic value, while they were advancing through missions they bought items more and more relevant and useful to the design of their game.

Expert-help card. It is also worth reporting observations concerning the expert-help card, which children could buy at the

Figure 7. The tree map with trees, showing that each group had grown their own game prototype idea

shop. Groups behaved differently with respect to this item, albeit the majority of them bought and used it in each mission.

Progression bar and coins (Figure 6). As for the progression bar, following the study protocol, teachers used it upon starting a mission in a twofold manner: to recap what children had done in previous missions; to give an overview of the structure of the mission about to start. Children immediately grabbed how to use this item, looking at it when they needed to figure out how many challenges were missing and how much time they still had to complete their current challenge. Also, every time they finished a challenge, they were very solicit in asking the expert's feedback on their work in order to be allowed to go to the progression bar, move their place card and hence collect their coin. An extreme case happened when a fire alarm sounded for training purposes. Knowing that it was for training, a child asked to be allowed to progress on the bar and get his coin, because the group was approaching the end of the challenge and "the training would take too long a time"—and the child wished to have his coin as soon as possible.

Tree map (Figure 7). At the end of each mission, each group was eager to stick their portion of their tree on the tree map. However, after the first two missions in which they had shown surprise and interest for the piece hidden in the progression bar, their curiosity dropped: they had figured out that rewards hidden in the bar would be the subsequent pieces of the tree. In the last mission, instead, children were pleased to have completed their tree, and joyfully discovered that each group's tree had its own foliage, different than the others. Being in a hurry to complete the tree puzzle before the others, not every group bothered to wait for the green light of the expert and, in a lively and joyful manner, rushed for sticking their foliage on the tree map, discussing their achievements along the way.

Discussion

The first study was concerned with a short term co-design, of circa 2 hours per class. The second study was designed by leveraging on the results of the first study, and with 6 co-design missions, each of circa 2 hours and a half, split across different days. The classroom was also gamified with tangible objects typical of games. According to the preliminary results, children showed to enjoy and be interested in such objects, and could grab their intended usage for co-designing. In particular, children showed a preference for signalling-disks, which allowed them to express their opinions by drawing their own smileys, and the shop, which allowed them to buy objects for enriching their game prototype aesthetics.

Further analyses are on-going, also concerning the evaluation of the produced game prototypes.

CONCLUSIONS

Co-design is an ideal approach to designing with users. When moved in nowadays school, it faces school-dependent challenges [6]. One of them is how to promote positive engagement for co-designing products. This paper presents gamified

Figure 9. Signalling disk usage

Figure 8. The shop in the classroom for buying objects for game prototypes or the expert help

co-design as a viable solution for engaging school classes and producing products together. It does so via two studies in primary schools with gamified co-design: one run in 2013 as a short term study; one run in 2014 as a long term study.

Results of the first study show the viability of the approach as follows: all children managed to produce prototypes and were generally engaged with short term gamified co-design. However, children complained that short timings made them feel under pressure, constraining their ability to fully express themselves.

The second study picked up the challenge of allowing children to better express their ideas, and spread gamified co-design missions across several days. Engagement in such a long term fragmented co-design was more challenging to achieve, therefore gamification was moved one step further: tasks and environment were tangibly gamified with material for co-designing at school.

This paper ends by presenting preliminary results in relation to the behaviour and engagement of children with such material, showing that they grabbed the intended usage of the material and tended to enjoy it for co-designing.

ACKNOWLEDGMENTS

We thank all participating schools, Naomi Mastachi, working as industrial designer on the production of the gamification material, as well as the financial support provided by the DARE project, funded by the Province of Bozen-Bolzano.

REFERENCES

1. Adams, E. *Fundamentals of Game Design, Third Edition*. Pearson - Allyn and Bacon, 2009.
2. Albert, W., and Tullis, T. *Measuring the User Experience*. Morgan Kaufmann, 2013.
3. Bloom, B. S., Engelhart, M. D., Furst, E. J., Hill, W. H., and Krathwohl, D. R. Taxonomy of Educational Objectives: The Classification of Educational Goals. In *Handbook I: Cognitive Domain*. David McKay Company, 1956.
4. Common Sense Media Research Study. Zero to Eight: Children's Media Use in America 2013. Tech. rep., 2013.
5. Deci, E. L., and Ryan, R. M. *Intrinsic Motivation and Self-determination in Human Behavior*. Plenum, New York, 1985.
6. Dodero, G., Gennari, R., Melonio, A., and Torello, S. Gamified Co-design with Cooperative Learning. In *Proc. of alt chapter of the Conference on Human Factors in Computing Systems (CHI 2014)*, ACM (2014).
7. Druin, A. Cooperative Inquiry: Developing New Technologies for Children with Children. In *Proc. of SIGCHI Conference on Human Factors in Computing Systems*, CHI '99, ACM (New York, NY, USA, 1999), 592–599.
8. Druin, A. Children as Co-designers of New Technologies: Valuing the Imagination to Transform What Is Possible. *New Directions in Youth Development: Theory, Practice, and Research: Youth as Media Creators 128*, 1 (Jan. 2010), 35–43.

9. Fails, J. A., Guha, M. L., and Druin, A. Methods and Techniques for Involving Children in the Design of New Technology for Children. *Foundations and Trends in Human–Computer Interaction 6*, 2 (2013), 85–166.

10. Garzotto, F. Broadening Children's Involvement as Design Partners: from Technology to "Experience". In *Proc. of 7th Conference on Interaction Design and Children*, IDC '08, ACM (New York, NY, USA, 2008), 186–193.

11. Giaccardi, E., Paredes, P., Díaz, P., and Alvarado, D. Embodied Narratives: a Performative Co-design Technique. In *Proc. of Designing Interactive Systems Conference*, DIS '12, ACM (New York, NY, USA, 2012), 1–10.

12. Guha, M. L., Druin, A., Chipman, G., Fails, J. A., Simms, S., and Farber, A. Working with Young Children as Technology Design Partners. *Communications of the ACM 48*, 1 (Jan. 2005), 39–42.

13. Hamari, J., Koivisto, J., and Sarsa, H. Does Gamification Work?: A Literature Review of Empirical Studies on Gamification. In *Proc. of 47th Hawaii International Conference on System Sciences* (2014).

14. Hunicke, R., Leblanc, M., and Zubek, R. MDA: A Formal Approach to Game Design and Game Research. In *Proc. of Challenges in Games AI Workshop, 19th National Conference of Artificial Intelligence*, Press (2004), 1–5.

15. Kagan, S., and Kagan, M. *Cooperative Learning*. 1994.

16. Kapp, K. M. *The Gamification of Learning and Instruction*. San Francisco: Pfeiffer, 2012.

17. Lazzaro, N. Why We Play Games: Four Keys to More Emotion Without Story. Player Experience Research and Design for Mass Market Interactive Entertainment, 2004.

18. Merriam, S. B. *Qualitative Research: a Guide to Design and Implementation*. John Wiley & Sons, 2009.

19. McGonigal, J. *Reality is Broken*. Penguin, 2011.

20. Prensky, M. Engage Me or Enrage Me: What Today's Learners Demand. *Educause Review 40(5):60*, (2005).

21. Raccanello, D., Brondino, M., Pasini, M., and De Bernardi, B. The Assessment of Motivation for Technology-based Learning Environments: The Italian Version of the Achievement Goal Questionnaire-Revised. In *Proc. of Methodologies and Intelligent Systems for Technology Enhanced Learning*, Springer, 37–44 (2014).

22. Rogers, Y., Sharp, H., and Preece, J. *Interaction Design*. John Wiley and Sons, 2011.

23. Romero, M., Usart, M., Ott, M., Earp, J., de Freitas, S., and Arnab, S. Learning Through Playing For or Against Each Other? Promoting Collaborative Learning in Digital Game Based Learning. In *Proc. of 20th European Conference on Information Systems (ESADE)* (2012).

24. Sanders, E. B., and Stappers, P. J. Co-creation and the New Landscapes of Design. *CoDesign: International Journal of CoCreation in Design and the Arts 4*, 1 (2008), 5–18.

25. Sauro, J., and Lewis, J. *Quantifying the User Experience*. Morgan Kaufmann, 2012.

26. Shell, J.. *The Art of Game Design: a Book of Lenses*. Elsevier, 2008.

27. Shernoff, D. J., Csikszentmihalyi, M., Shneider, B., and Shernoff, E. S. A Student Engagement in High School Classrooms from the Perspective of Flow Theory. *School Psychology Quarterly 18*, 2 (2003), 158–176.

28. Sleeswijk Visser, F., van der Lugt, R., and Stappers, P. Participatory Design Needs Participatory Communication. In *Proc. of 9th European Conference on Creativity and Innovation* (2005), 173–195.

29. Slegers, K., and Gennari, R. State of the Art of Methods for the User Analysis and Description of Context of Use. Tech. Rep. D1.1, TERENCE project, 2011.

30. TERENCE consortium. http://www.terenceproject.eu.

31. Vaajakallio, K., Lee, J., and Mattelmäki, T. "It Has to Be a Group Work!": Co-design With Children. In *Proc. of 8th Conference on Interaction Design and Children*, IDC '09, ACM (New York, NY, USA, 2009), 246–249.

32. Walsh, G., Druin, A., Guha, M., Foss, E., Golub, E., Hatley, L., Bonsignore, E., and Franckel, S. Layered Elaboration: a New Technique for Co-design with Children. In *Proc. of SIGCHI Conference on Human Factors in Computing Systems*, CHI '10, ACM (New York, NY, USA, 2010), 1237–1240.

Exploring the Effect of Achievements on Students Attending University Orientation

Zachary Fitz-Walter, Peta Wyeth, Dian Tjondronegoro, Daniel Johnson
Queensland University of Technology
Brisbane, Australia
z.fitz-walter@qut.edu.au, peta.wyeth@qut.edu.au, dian@qut.edu.au, dm.johnson@qut.edu.au

ABSTRACT
University orientation is a key event for new students that aids in the transition from a school to a university environment. A smartphone orientation application was built to aid students attending the event. Achievements were added to the application in an attempt to engage students further with the orientation activities and application. An exploratory field study was undertaken to evaluate the effect of the achievement system on participants attending orientation. Forty-six new students were recruited to test the orientation application. Twenty-six participants used a gamified version of the orientation application and twenty participants used a non-gamified version. While the gamification was generally well received, no impact on user experience was evident. Some effect on engagement with orientation activities was shown. Participants who used the gamified system reported the game elements as fun, but some negative issues arose, such as cheating.

Author Keywords
Gamification; Achievements; Badges; Student Engagement; University Orientation; Smartphone; User Experience

ACM Classification Keywords
H.5.m. Information interfaces and presentation (e.g., HCI): Miscellaneous.

INTRODUCTION
A key event for new university students is orientation, which aids in the transition from a school to a university environment and introduces students to many important aspects of university life. In Australia, a weeklong event is often run during orientation with different days and activities tailored for students studying different courses. These events aim to not only introduce students to university life and the services available, but also introduce them to other students in their course. All of these events and activities are aimed at making the student feel like they are part of the university community, which in turn helps to create a comfortable place for learning.

Many universities have started to use smartphone applications to provide information to university students at open day and orientation events. Mobile-delivered event applications can be more convenient and personalised compared to traditional tools, such as paper-based event schedules and physical maps. However, they do not necessarily motivate students to engage with the event. As university orientation is important for new students, there is a need to encourage students to engage with the events and activities as much as possible.

The following research study investigates the use of achievements added to a smartphone university orientation application. We aimed to investigate if the addition of achievements to the application led to a more positive user experience, greater perceived motivation and behaviour change. In addition to these aims we also investigated if the addition of game elements was well received by university students.

Contributions of this research include a procedure for creating achievements based on the goals of an activity and also results that indicate using achievements in this context may affect engagement, without greatly affecting the user experience.

PREVIOUS RESEARCH
Current university students are more than likely to be gamers [4], and orientation games like scavenger hunts have had a history of being used to introduce new students to university [17]. Previous research studies have indicated positive results when combining games and smartphone technologies for orientation events. This includes the *MobiLearn Project*, which was an educational scavenger hunt aimed at introducing new students to a university campus [21]. Another example is *Scavenger Hunt*, a scavenger hunt around campus for new students, delivered on a mobile device [24]. The use of gamification at university has also been explored as a way to engage students with learning [15].

Gamification, or gameful design, is a design strategy where game elements are used in non-game systems to promote engagement with an activity. The idea is that if video games

CHI PLAY'14, October 19–21, 2014, Toronto, ON, Canada.
Copyright © 2014 ACM 978-1-4503-3014-5/14/10...$15.00.
http://dx.doi.org/10.1145/2658537.2658700

can create such engaging experiences, then other systems can adopt similar design techniques to engage users as well. This research study adopts the definition of gamification as the use of game design elements in non-game contexts [8]. Where a game design element could include anything from game aesthetics, such as graphics and progress bars, to complete games with an overarching goal, rules, story, levels, quests and achievements.

Achievements and the gamification blueprint

It has been common for gamification implementations in both industry and research to use competitive and reward-based game elements, such as points and leaderboards (e.g., [5]) or achievements (e.g., [18]). Combined with incentives, these elements have been described as the industry blueprint for gamification [7]. Badges, points and social leaderboards have been applied to many different computer applications [1]. These particular elements can be relatively easy and cheap to implement on top of existing systems, such as websites or mobile applications. However, the use of these game elements has been criticised as focusing on rewards and not representing the intrinsically motivating aspects of games [3, 19]. Research has also indicated that intrinsic motivation may be reduced through the use of extrinsic motivators [20].

While some research results indicate that badges can be used to influence user behaviour in different contexts [6, 11] other studies show that the addition of badges does not automatically lead to an increase in use activity [13]. Another study found participants responded differently to the use of achievements in a photo-sharing mobile application [18]. Some users appreciated the achievements, while others were either indifferent to their inclusion or were confused by them. These mixed results, combined with the continued use of badges in industry implementations indicate that further research is needed to investigate the effect of achievements in different contexts.

Investigating the effect of gamification

Previous empirical gamification research has generally investigated the effect of game elements on the construct of engagement. However, adding game elements to a non-game context can affect other aspects of the experience as well. For example, one study [18] found that some users got nothing out of added game elements, and thought they could lead to unwanted patterns of use. Another study [12] found that adding a fantasy roleplaying game to a market research survey led to low completion rate of 58% compared to three other non-gamified surveys that had completion rates of around 94%.

The addition of gamification to some applications can also lead to unwanted, and potentially dangerous, behaviour. Study participants have indicated both considering cheating [10] and also actually cheating when using gamified systems [22]. In the same study [22] participants suggested that the competitive nature of the leaderboard used, although effective, was not entirely comfortable for them. Participants have also been concerned that the use of competitive game elements to encourage exercise in another study [25] may be dangerous, leading to excessive exercise. And finally, a health game intervention deployed at a school led to rivalries forming between schools [26]. One student also admitted to finding and keeping a pedometer from another school until the end of the game to disadvantage them. Further research is needed to explore the effect of gamification on not just behaviour change, but also on other constructs, such as user experience.

USING GAMIFICATION TO ENGAGE NEW STUDENTS

A review of two previous student orientation surveys was undertaken in order to isolate areas of the orientation event where potential improvements could be made. The surveys were from semester 1 and 2 in 2010, with the goal of both being to help determine what students thought of the orientation program in the respective semester. The survey results suggested a number of areas could be improved upon including encouraging attendance, campus exploration and social networking.

A review of current orientation services was also undertaken. The review found that services available for new students include an online event planner, which students are encouraged to print out and bring along to orientation. There are also a number of navigation tools that currently exist for students. Physical maps and signposts have been set up at various locations around the university campus. Online maps of each campus are available, which can be accessed via a web browser or printed if the user requires a physical copy. An iPhone application was also released in December 2010, which provides a location-aware map with campus information.

Interviews and a focus group with orientation staff

Semi-structured interviews were undertaken with two staff members of the orientation engagement team. The orientation event was discussed, including areas of the event that could be improved. The results of the interviews helped support the findings from the surveys, with the staff members agreeing that new students could often feel lost, may have trouble meeting new friends, and may have difficulty finding what events were available. The interviews also revealed that the printed event list could be troublesome for both students and staff. They reported that students could easily forget or lose their printout, which led to confusion and an increase in workload for staff. They would need to handle additional enquiries from students asking about events. Presenting this information to the student via a mobile application could help to improve this situation.

The issues identified in the surveys and interviews were then discussed in a focus group with eight staff members from the orientation-planning group. An affinity diagram exercise was used to establish goals that would address these issues. These were grouped into three different areas, and were then discussed further. Three different themes emerged: administration, engagement, and information. The results of the focus group suggested that engagement was a key issue, specifically delivering orientation information to students, encouraging them to explore the campus, and encouraging them to meet people.

APPLICATION DESIGN AND DEVELOPMENT

To replace the paper-based event planner a smartphone application was developed. This application provided new students with personal orientation event information, a campus map, and a friend list for storing contact details of other students. The application was developed for the Apple iOS platform, targeting iPhone, iPod Touch and iPad devices. At the time of development this platform was (and still is) popular in Australia [14]. iOS devices were also the most popular mobile devices used to access the university website at the time. To the application achievements were added that aimed to engage students with the issues identified in the focus group and interviews.

An iterative design approach was used to design the gamified application, where three iterations of rapid prototype development and evaluation were undertaken. A paper prototype was first created and presented to orientation staff for feedback. A digital mockup was then designed and created based on the results. The digital prototype was presented to a focus group of staff and after receiving feedback, a working prototype was designed and developed that could run on iPhones and iPod Touches. A usability study was then run with four university students to identify any usability issues with the application. The study tested both technical and usability aspects of the application in a laboratory setting. The users were introduced to the application and had to complete five different achievements. They then could use the application freely and were asked questions about the application design. A number of design changes were made based on the results of the study.

GAMIFICATION DESIGN

Our gamification design was inspired by techniques used in previous research studies [9, 18, 21]. Our study shared a similar context to an earlier study [21], which focused on engaging students with a mobile scavenger hunt. To design achievements a process was used that identified the goals for gamification, explored available mobile sensing options for these goals, and then these were used to design the achievements.

Gamification goals

Three gamification goals were identified:

1. Encourage campus and service exploration
2. Encourage participation at orientation events
3. Encourage social networking between students

With the aid of the orientation engagement team, each goal was broken down into more specific and measurable activities. For example, important university locations were identified that students should explore (e.g., the library for borrowing books and for study spaces, the Information Technology helpdesk for help with any computer related issues), as well as important services (e.g., security phone number for emergencies).

Sensing the activities

Sensing options were explored to determine if these activities could be automatically measured by technology. Location information could be accessed through the use of the iPhone's Global Positioning System (GPS) sensor, cellular and Wi-Fi sensors, or by using the camera to scan a Quick Response (QR) code placed at a specific university location. Barcodes on books and other items can also be read using the camera. Time information could be obtained from the iPhone's internal clock. Movement data could be obtained from the iPhone's accelerometer sensor. Students could also provide input using the phone's keyboard.

Activity	Different sensing cues
Provide information regarding a university service	Keyboard input, list of important university services and details (e.g., campus security phone number).
Scan a collected object with a barcode	Camera input, an object with a barcode (e.g., library book, student card), a list of orientation objects with barcodes and their barcode numbers.
Find a location marker on campus	Camera input, unique QR code placed at the physical, list of QR codes and their locations.
Check-in to a scheduled orientation event	Using location sensor (GPS, Wi-Fi, cellular), internal clock, event schedule with location and time information.
Meet another student	List of contacts where new contacts are added using the Bump API (http://bu.mp - now decommissioned). This API triggered a connection between two users when a "bumping" motion was detected (Uses location, accelerometer and time sensors).

Table 1. Student activities that could be identified using available sensors.

University information was also available for use in the application. This information included details of scheduled orientation events, a list of library books and their barcodes, student identification cards with barcode numbers, university service details, university locations and a list of contacts that the student had added to their contact list. By combining the phone sensors with the university information, sensing cues could be created to identify if students had completed the desired activities (see Table 1).

Achievement design

Achievements were the primary game design element used in our system to challenge and reward students for completing orientation activities. The achievement design was drawn from industry game and gamification implementations, as well as research into achievements in non-game contexts [18]. A review of achievement systems from two popular game networks was undertaken (Xbox Live Achievements and Steam Achievements) as well as two popular gamified systems at the time (GiantBomb website and Foursquare). An anatomy of an achievement was defined, as well as different types of achievements. Using these findings, challenges were created by picking an orientation goal and choosing an activity that could be identified using the smartphone (see Table 2).

Goal →	Activity →	Challenge
Encourage exploration of the campus and services available	Learn about the free campus shuttle bus	- Find out the bus number of the campus shuttle bus and enter it
	Visit the library	- Find the library and scan the QR code there
Encourage participation in the orientation events	Attend a scheduled orientation event	- Check-in to one scheduled event
	Collect your student ID card	- Scan the barcode on your student ID card
Encourage students to meet other students	Meet people from the same year	- Add your first contact to the contact list from the same year

Table 2. Examples of linking goals to challenges via measurable activities.

These challenges were then used to create a total of 20 achievements. Clues, images, and unlock text were made for each achievement and these achievements were then organised into different sets, which focused on different orientation goals. Consideration was given to the experience of the entire achievement system by drawing on previous research [9, 16, 23]. Immediate feedback was provided via an alert message when an achievement was complete. Some achievements were very easy to complete, aiming to introduce the users to the gameplay. Achievements then became progressively more challenging to complete. This was done by requiring students to complete more activities (e.g., *Attend your third event*), by providing hints instead of giving exact locations (e.g., *this place will fulfill all your sugary desires*), or by having cryptic clues (e.g., *Title: 025.344 15. Clue: ???* - in this case the title was a catalog code of a book in the library which students had to find and scan with the application).

Another feature was added that allowed students to compare the number of achievements they had completed with others when they shared their contact information with another student. This aimed to encourage friendly competition between students. Students were also given a rank ranging from Orientation Newbie to Orientation Master, with each consecutive level requiring more achievements to be completed. This level was displayed in their profile and also shared with friends when they bumped phones.

Final application design

After a number of iterations the design was finalised and ready to be evaluated in a field study. The features of the application included an event list, map, friend list, profile and the list of achievements (see figure 1). The event list provided a personalised list of orientation events that the student had registered for. Students could view their schedule, along with detailed information about each event. Students could also check-in to each event, but only if they were on campus at the time of the event.

The map provided students with an overview of the campus and the locations of all the buildings. It also displayed the student's current location on campus. The friend list allowed students to easily add the contact details of any new friends they made on campus. Students simply pressed the 'add' button and then 'bumped' phones together with another student to share contact details, university course information and number of achievements completed.

The profile view provided the student with an overview of their personal details and the number of achievements they had completed. Students could edit their profile, limiting the information they shared with other students. Finally, the achievements list provided the list of twenty achievements that students could complete while at university orientation.

The achievements were organised into a number of different sets, each with different themes. Clicking on an achievement revealed detailed information about it, such as a clue that hinted at how to complete the achievement, and also an action button if the achievement required active input (e.g., scanning a QR code or barcode). When an achievement was completed, congratulatory text and an image were revealed as a reward. The text provided extra information for students to read which was often humourous, and the image was different for each achievement.

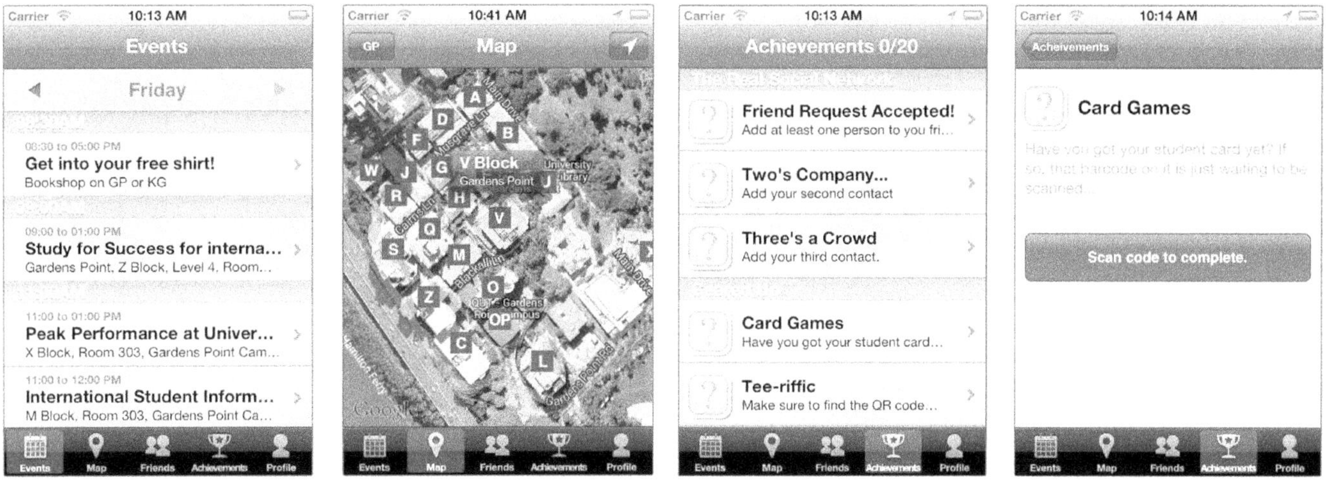

Figure 1. Screens from the final application design from left to right – Events, Map, Achievement List, and Achievement

FIELD STUDY

An exploratory field study was undertaken during university orientation week in order to evaluate the potential effectiveness of the gamified application compared to a non-gamified version.

Study Overview

The aim of the field study was to evaluate the effect the addition of achievements had on user experience, engagement and behaviour change. The study also looked at investigating the reception of the added gamification. Three hypotheses were formed:

1. We predict that participants using the gamified application will have a more positive user experience compared to participants using the non-gamified application.
2. We predict that participants using the gamified application will feel more motivated compared to participants using the non-gamified application.
3. We predict that the gamified application will encourage behaviour change compared to the non-gamified application.

In addition to these three hypotheses, a research question was also investigated:

1. Is the addition of game elements well received by university students?

Study Measures

To measure the constructs usage data was captured during the field study and a questionnaire was administered to participants at the end of the field study. The questionnaire design was informed by questionnaires used in similar studies [9, 21]. Five-point Likert-type questions were used with responses on the following scale (Strongly Disagree (1), Disagree (2), Neither Agree or Disagree (3), Agree (4), and Strongly Agree (5)).

To measure user-experience a four-item Likert-scale was developed (*"I found the application to be overall useful", "I found the application easy to use", "I enjoyed using the application", "The design of the application was attractive"*). To measure the perceived motivation of participants a nine-item Likert-scale was developed (*"The application motivated me to explore more of the campus", "I found and visited new places on campus that I would not have visited without the application", "By using the application I got to know the university campus well", "The application helped me to learn about the different locations on campus", "The application encouraged me to meet new people", "This application would encourage me to meet other students in my faculty and course", "The application encouraged me to attend events", "The application encouraged me to check-in to events", "The application helped to engage me in the orientation event"*).

To assess the reliability of the scales, Chronbach's alpha was calculated for both the gamified and non-gamified responses, the two scales were found to have acceptable reliability (alpha 0.768 for the perceived motivation scale and 0.765 for the user-experience scale).

Five-point Likert-type questions were used to measure the usefulness of specific application features with responses on the following scale (Not at all useful (1), Very little use (2), Useful (3), Very Useful (4), and Extremely Useful (5)). Specific features included the campus map (*"How useful was the map of the campus?"*), check-in function (*"How useful was the ability to check into an event?"*) and bump function (*"How useful was adding friends by bumping phones together?*).

The application also captured usage data including number of events checked-in to, the number of friends added to the friend list and if participants were using the gamified version, the total number of achievements completed was also captured. Short answer questions gathered qualitative data to support the quantitative findings.

Also, for those using the gamified application, their subjective gamification experience was measured using Likert-type questions with the same scale as the user experience and perceived motivation questions (e.g., *"The achievement system was fun to use", "The clues in the achievement system were easy to understand", "The achievement system motivated me to explore the campus"*), multiple choice questions (e.g., *"What did you like the most about the design of the achievement system?", "What was your favourite type of achievement to complete?"*) and short answer questions (e.g., *"Of all the achievements you completed pick your two favourite and tell us why you like them", "Do you think the difficulty level of the achievements was appropriate? If no, why not?"*).

Study Procedure

Participants were recruited online via an advertisement and at the event using flyers. They were met by the researcher at the library and provided with a link to download one of two versions of the application onto their smartphone. The non-gamified version provided exactly the same features as the gamified version but had the achievement list removed.

Participants were provided with a customised orientation event list, which listed the events to which they had signed up. The researcher then introduced them to the application features. Participants were asked to use the application while at the orientation event, and then return at the end of the day to provide feedback on their experience. When participants returned they were asked to complete the questionnaire about their use and experience of the application. Usage data was then sent to the researcher via email and each participant was given two movie vouchers at the end of the session to reward them for their participation.

RESULTS

To test the hypotheses and explore the research question, non-parametric methods were used to study the results of the survey and logged usage data. Likert-type and Likert-scale questions were compared using Mann-Whitney U tests. Mann-Whitney U tests were also used to analyse the logged usage data from both groups. As a function of the small sample size it can be expected that the current study had relatively low statistical power. Given this and the exploratory nature of the work we judged the application of a bonferonni correction to be overly conservative. However, given the resulting increase in the experiment-wise error rate and likelihood of Type I errors, these results must be interpreted with caution.

Participant Demographics

Forty-six students were recruited to participate in the field study (male = 31, female = 15). Participants were aged from 17 to 45 (mean = 20.76, SD = 5.824). All the participants were first year students, new to university. Each participant was from one of seven different university faculties, with the majority from three faculties: Business, Built Engineering and Environment, or Science and Technology.

Participants had been using an iPhone from anywhere between 0 to 44 months (mean = 12.5 months, SD = 10.893). Reported iPhone usage varied from 5 minutes to 2 hours a day. Reported video game usage varied widely as well, with participants reporting that on average they played computer and home console games for 4.70 hours a week (SD = 7.738) and mobile games for 3.89 hours (SD = 4.667). Twenty-three of the participants had used a video game achievement system before and all but one of these reported that they enjoyed using it. Only one participant had used an achievement system in a non-game context before (foursquare). This participant reported it as being enjoyable to use.

Participants were randomly divided into two groups to trial the two versions of the orientation application. Twenty-six participants used the gamified application, and 20 participants used the regular, non-gamified version. A series of independent groups t-tests found no statistical difference between the two groups in terms of age, previous number of campus visits, months using a smartphone, hours a day using a smartphone, hours a week playing games and hours a week playing mobile games.

User Experience Results

User Experience Measures	**Gam. (n=26)**	**Non-Gam. (n=20)**	U	z	p
User Experience Scale	4.50	4.50	247.5	-.283	.777
Check in feature	3.00	3.00	277.5	.400	.689
Bump feature	4.00	3.00	345.5	1.965	**.049**
Campus map feature	5.00	4.00	350.5	2.168	**.030**

Table 3 – Median User Experience and Usefulness Scores for Gamified and Non-Gamified Versions

A Mann-Whitney U test was run to determine if there were differences in user experience between participants who used the gamified version and participants who used the non-gamified version. The median user experience score was not significantly different between the two groups.

A Mann-Whitney U test was run to determine if there were differences in usefulness of specific features of the gamified version compared to the non-gamified version. The bump feature was statistically significantly different between the two groups (with the gamified version rated as more useful).

The median map feature was statistically significantly different between the two groups (with the gamified version rated as more useful). The median check-in feature was not statistically significantly different between the two groups.

Motivation and Behaviour Change Results

Motivation Measure	**Gam. (n=26)**	**Non-Gam. (n=20)**	*U*	*z*	*p*
Perceived Motivation Scale	3.944	3.944	254.5	-.122	.903
Behaviour Change Measures	**Gam. (n=22)**	**Non-Gam. (n=13)**	*U*	*z*	*p*
Total Check-ins	3.00	0.00	207.5	.023	**.026**
Friends Added	1.00	0.00	217.0	.007	**.011**

Table 4 – Median Motivation and Behaviour Change Scores for Gamified and non-Gamified Versions

A Mann-Whitney U test was run to determine if there were differences in perceived motivation between participants who used the gamified version and participants who used the non-gamified version. The median perceived engagement score was not statistically significantly different between the two groups.

Application usage data was only successfully captured from 13 participants who used the non-gamified application and from 22 participants who used the gamified application. The missing data resulted from participants who did not already have their email client set up on their device (predominantly users of iPod touch devices). None of our key outcome measures were expected to be related to the type of device used, and hence, this issue is unlikely to have introduced any systematic bias. Using the available data, a comparison was made to see if any differences occurred. Both versions of the application captured the number of events each participant checked-in to, as well as the number of friends added to the friend list.

Event check-ins

A Mann-Whitney U test was run to determine if there were differences in the number of event check-ins between participants who used the gamified version and participants who used the non-gamified version. The median number of check-ins was statistically significantly different between the two groups (with more check-ins completed by participants using the gamified version). It is important to note also that both the mode and median number of event check-ins by those using the gamified application was three events – the same number required for the final event related achievement.

Participants who used the gamified version were administered an additional Likert-type question which asked if the achievement system motivated them to attend events. The median response (n = 24) for this question was 3.5 (between the "Neither Agree nor Disagree" and "Agree" responses) and the mode was 3 ("*Neither Agree nor Disagree*").

Friends added

A Mann-Whitney U test was run to determine if there were differences in the number of friends added to the friend list between participants who used the gamified version and participants who used the non-gamified version. The median number of friends added was statistically significantly different between the two groups (with more friends added by users of the Gamified version). However, the average number of friends added was not particularly high in the gamified version (1.54, SD = 1.103).

Participants who used the gamified version were administered an additional Likert-type question which asked if the achievement system motivated them to add friends. The median and modal response (N=24) for this question was 4 ("Agree").

Campus engagement

An additional Likert-type question asked participants who used the gamified application if the achievement system motivated them to explore the campus. The median and modal response (N=24) for this question was 4 ("Agree"). Representative short answer responses reported that these types of achievements "*made me want to find where things are*", "*led me to places I enjoyed and that I otherwise wouldn't have seen*", and that they "*were the most motivating part of the application, it caused me to walk all around the university.*"

Gamification Experience Results

A multiple-choice question asked participants who used the gamified application to suggest the most motivating aspect of the achievement system. Of the five available options (Completing all the achievements, collecting points, gaining levels, competing with others, or working with others) the two most popular responses were '*completing all the achievements*' (10 responses) and '*gaining levels*' (10 responses). Another multiple-choice question asked the same participants to record what additional elements may have motivated them to complete more achievements. Of the four available options (More competitive elements, time limit to complete achievements within, more game elements, or a physical reward) the most popular response was a '*physical reward*' (11 responses), followed by '*more competitive elements*' (9 responses).

A Likert-type question asked participants if the achievement system was fun to use. The median and modal response for this question was 5 ("Strongly Agree"). Participants reported in representative short answer responses that the achievements were "*such a fantastic twist*" and "*were genuinely fun*", "*great for killing time productively*", "*very fun*" and that "*unlocking the achievements made it [the application] interesting*". Participants also reported that they liked the integration of achievements with orientation activities "*because it was simple and part of existing activities*" and because they were "*based on existing activities*" at orientation.

A Likert-type question asked participants if they found the achievement system aesthetically pleasing. The median and modal response for this question was 4 ("Agree"). Thus, participants who used the gamified application generally agreed that the achievement system was aesthetically pleasing. Another Likert-type question asked participants if the achievement system was easy to understand and use. The median and modal response for this question was 5 ("Strongly Agree"). Therefore, participants who used the gamified application generally strongly agreed that the achievement system was easy to understand and use.

A number of participants reported that for achievements that required numerical input (e.g., finding how many levels a building had, or entering the university bus number) they could simply guess the answer. It was also found that because of the large radius compensating for the GPS location sensor limitations, two students admitted in the questionnaire to cheating by checking-in to multiple events at the same time.

Finally, achievement completion data was captured from 24 participants who used the gamified application. Every participant completed at least one achievement. Of an available 20 achievements, the mean number completed by participants was 12.88 achievements (SD = 4.504). Both the modal and mean number of achievements completed were 14. One participant managed to complete all 20 achievements.

DISCUSSION

While acknowledging the need to interpret the results with caution given the small sample size and lack of correction for type I errors, the findings suggest that the achievement system influenced the perceived usefulness of some features, including the map and bumping phones. Results also suggest that the achievements had some influence on the number of check-ins made and friends added, but these could have been influenced as well by cheating. It was also found that those who used the gamified version reported that the achievement system was fun to use. An interesting finding as well was that on average, participants who used the gamified version completed over half of the achievements available. However, the results indicate that adding an achievement system did not have a significant effect on user experience.

There was little effect on user experience

The results suggest that adding an achievement system did not enhance the user experience, but at the same time it also did not negatively affect it.

It was hypothesised that the addition of game elements would enhance user enjoyment, similar to other previous research (E.g., [9]). However, there no difference was found in terms of reported enjoyment between the two groups. The novelty factor of both versions of the application may have contributed to this, especially when compared to the previously available paper-based orientation event planner participants would have received. Mean response values for both groups was high suggesting that a ceiling effect may have occurred, thus making it difficult to compare the two groups. However, the results from this study suggest that the addition of an achievement system did not negatively affect the user experience. Including game elements into a non-game context has the potential to add an extra layer of complexity, which in turn, has the potential to affect user experience (e.g., [12]).

Results also suggest that some application features were considered to be more useful by those participants who used the gamified version. These features included the campus map and the ability to bump phones to add new contacts. This may have been because the map feature helped participants complete the achievements and bumping phones was also necessary to complete some of the social achievements.

There was some effect on orientation behaviour change

There was no difference in reported subjective motivation between the two groups. However, results suggest that participants who tried the gamified version used some features of the application more than the other group, at least until the related achievements were completed.

Participants who used the gamified version did report that the achievement system motivated them to explore the campus and it was found that on average, participants who used the gamified application completed more than half of the achievements available. This suggests that participants using the gamified version were motivated to complete achievements and by completing this number it is possible that the participants would have exposed them to orientation activities and university information.

The results also suggest that participants who used the gamified version used the check-in and add friend functions of the application more than those using the non-gamified version. This is likely to have occurred because some achievements required the use of these functions in order to complete them. For example, an achievement was awarded to participants who checked into three events. However, the majority of participants stopped using the check-in function once this achievement was completed. This suggests that achievements did motivate some participants, but after these achievements were completed the function lost value.

Also a few participants admitted to cheating by checking-in to events they did not attend. Event-related achievements made up three of the 20 available achievements. This may have affected the check-in results.

The gamification experience was positive

The majority of the participants who used the gamified application reported that it was fun to use, aesthetically pleasing, easy to understand and to use. These findings were similar to another study [21] that found most players considered their application fun as well. It was interesting to note that different player preferences emerged and also some design issues arose that need to be considered in future implementations.

When Montola et al. [18] studied the effect of achievements on user experience they found that three different user groups emerged, those that appreciated the achievements, those that did not, and those that were confused by them. These three groups did not appear in this study. This could have been because of the demographic difference between participants in the two studies, or it may be that these groups may have emerged in the current study if a larger sample had been used. Although these groups did not emerge, it was found that different participants did like different aspects of the achievements. Some participants liked challenging achievements, while others preferred simple achievements. Some participants enjoyed achievements that supported orientation tasks, while others thought these were pointless. Different aspects of the achievement system motivated different participants as well. These results indicate that there were different player preferences amongst participants, and these should be considered in future gamification design.

Another notable finding was that very few participants added friends to their contact list. This is likely to have occurred because this feature required participants to 'bump' phones with each other. This meant that participants could only add others who were also taking part in the study, thus reducing the usefulness of this feature until more students started using the application. Allowing participants to add friends without having to bump phones could be more useful. However, this may lead to more cheating if participants could just manually enter a contact to complete an achievement. This balance between usability and enjoyment needs to be considered further.

Cheating can negatively affect the experience for players and a way is needed to address it when designing gamification. The GPS sensor used by the application had accuracy issues, especially when used indoors, and to counter this problem the application increased the location radius needed for a participant to check-in to an event. Because of this some users found they could cheat and complete achievements that required them to check-in to events without having to attend them. Some participants also reported that for achievements that required numerical input (e.g., finding how many levels a building had or entering the university bus number) they could simply *"guess the answer through trial and error"*. This ability to guess the answer meant that a number of students thought this activity was *"useful but not fun"*. For these cases, alternate sensing options could be explored, such as placing QR codes at locations. Otherwise these problematic achievements could be removed altogether.

Limitations

There are a number of limitations of the current study. Most notably the small sample size and lack of correction for experiment-wise error rate means that future research should seek to replicate these findings with a larger sample and more conservative statistical analysis. Additionally, it may be that the relatively novelty to students of the applications used in the current study influenced the results. Future research should aim to explore these questions over a longer timeframe. Finally, the current study utilised a number of single-item measures and non-standard scales. Future research should seek to confirm these findings using established and validated scales.

CONCLUSION

This paper outlined the results of a field study that explored the effect of adding achievements to a non-game context. While the gamification was generally well received, no impact on user experience was evident. Some effect on engagement with orientation activities was shown. Similar findings to previous gamification studies were also found, including issues relating to cheating and the emergence of different player preferences.

This study contributed a procedure for creating achievements based on the goals of an activity and also initial evidence that achievements may influence engagement without greatly affecting the user's experience. The results of this study help us better understand the effect of achievement usage and thus, hopefully aid in future gamification design.

ACKNOWLEDGMENTS

This research was carried out as part of the activities of, and funded by, the Smart Services Cooperative Research Centre (CRC) through the Australian Government's CRC Programme (Department of Innovation, Industry, Science and Research). The authors wish to thank the QUT Student Engagement Team for their input and support.

REFERENCES

1. Antin, J., & Churchill, E. Badges in Social Media : A Social Psychological Perspective. In *CHI 2011 Gamification Workshop Proceedings*, (2011).

2. Benford, S., Rowland, D., Hull, R., Reid, J., Morrison, J., Facer, K., & Clayton, B. Savannah: designing a location-based game simulating lion behaviour.

In *International conference on advances in computer entertainment technology*, (2004).

3. Bogost, I. Gamification is Bullshit. http://www.bogost.com/blog/gamification_is_bullshit.shtml
4. Bond University. Interactive Australia 2009. http://www.igea.net/wp-content/uploads/2009/08/IA9-Interactive-Australia-2009-Full-Report.pdf
5. De Oliveira, R., Cherubini, M., & Oliver, N. MoviPill: improving medication compliance for elders using a mobile persuasive social game. In *Proc. UBICOMP,* ACM Press (2010), 251–260.
6. Denny, P. The Effect of Virtual Achievements on Student Engagement. In *Proc. CHI 2013,* ACM Press (2013), 763–772.
7. Deterding, S. From Game Design Elements to Gamefulness: Defining "Gamification." http://www.slideshare.net/dings/from-game-design-elements-to-gamefulness-defining-gamification
8. Deterding, S., Dixon, D., Khaled, R., & Nacke, L. From game design elements to gamefulness: defining "gamification." In *Proc. MindTrek*, ACM Press (2011), 9-15.
9. Flatla, D. R., Gutwin, C., Nacke, L. E., Bateman, S., & Mandryk, R. L. Calibration games: making calibration tasks enjoyable by adding motivating game elements. In *Proc. UIST,* ACM Press (2011), 403–412.
10. Froehlich, J., Dillahunt, T., Klasnja, P., Mankoff, J., Consolvo, S., Harrison, B., & Landay, J. A. UbiGreen: investigating a mobile tool for tracking and supporting green transportation habits. In *Proc. CHI 2009*, ACM Press (2009), 1043–1052.
11. Grant, S., & Betts, B. Encouraging user behaviour with achievements: An empirical study. In *proc. MSR*, (2013), 65-68.
12. Guin, T. D.-L., Baker, R., Mechling, J., & Ruylea, E. Myths and realities of respondent engagement in online surveys. *International Journal of Market Research, 54,* 5 (2012).
13. Hamari, J. Transforming homo economicus into homo ludens: A field experiment on gamification in a utilitarian peer-to-peer trading service. *Electronic Commerce Research and Applications, 12,* 4 (2013), 236-245.
14. Hanlon, J. Apple first in Aussie phone market: IDC. http://www.cnet.com.au/apple-first-in-aussie-phone-market-idc-339317492.htm
15. Iosup, A., & Epema, D. An Experience Report on Using Gamification in Technical Higher Education. In *Proc. of the 45th ACM Technical Symposium on Computer Science Education*, ACM Press (2014), 27–32.
16. Malone, T. W. Heuristics for designing enjoyable user interfaces: Lessons from computer games. In *proc. CHI 1982*, ACM Press (1982), 63–68.
17. Martin, A. Ready-to-use simulation: THE CAMPUS INFORMATION GAME. *Simulation & Gaming 37,* 1 (2006), 124 –133.
18. Montola, M., Nummenmaa, T., Lucero, A., Boberg, M., & Korhonen, H. Applying game achievement systems to enhance user experience in a photo sharing service. In *Proc. MindTrek,* ACM Press (2009), 94–97.
19. Robertson, M. Can't play, won't play. http://hideandseek.net/2010/10/06/cant-play-wont-play/
20. Ryan, R. M., & Deci, E. L. Self-determination theory and the facilitation of intrinsic motivation, social development, and well-being. *American Psychologist 55*, 1 (2000), 68–78.
21. Schwabe, G., & Göth, C. Mobile learning with a mobile game: design and motivational effects. *Journal of Computer Assisted Learning*, *21*, 3 (2005), 204–216.
22. Singer, L., & Schneider, K. It was a bit of a race: Gamification of version control. In *2012 2nd International Workshop on Games and Software Engineering (GAS)*, (2012), 5–8.
23. Sweetser, P., & Wyeth, P. GameFlow: a model for evaluating player enjoyment in games. *Computers in Entertainment (CIE) 3*, 3 (2005).
24. Talton, J. O., Peterson, D. L., Kamin, S., Israel, D., & Al-Muhtadi, J. Scavenger hunt: computer science retention through orientation. In *ACM SIGCSE Bulletin 38,* (2006), 443–447.
25. Toscos, T., Faber, A., An, S., & Gandhi, M. P. Chick clique: persuasive technology to motivate teenage girls to exercise. In *Ext. Abstracts CHI 2006,* ACM Press (2006), 1873–1878.
26. Xu, Y., Poole, E. S., Miller, A. D., Eiriksdottir, E., Catrambone, R., & Mynatt, E. D. Designing pervasive health games for sustainability, adaptability and sociability. In *Proc. DIGRA*, ACM Press (2012), 49-56.

Decreasing Sedentary Behaviours in Pre-adolescents using Casual Exergames at School

Yue Gao[1], Kathrin M. Gerling[2], Regan L. Mandryk[1], Kevin G. Stanley[1]

[1]Department of Computer Science
University of Saskatchewan, Saskatoon, Canada
firstname.lastname@usask.ca

[2]School of Computer Science
University of Lincoln, Lincoln, UK
kgerling@lincoln.ac.uk

ABSTRACT

There are risks to too much sedentary behaviour, regardless of a person's level of physical activity, particularly for children. As exercise habits instilled during childhood are strong predictors of healthy lifestyles later in life, it is important that schools break up long sedentary periods with short periods of physical activity. Casual exergames are an appealing option for schools who wish to engage adolescents, and have been shown to provide exertion levels at recommended values, even when played for only 10 minutes. In this paper we describe a preliminary survey with teachers of a local school that informed the deployment of a casual exergame with a group of pre-adolescent students from the same school. We show that students preferred the game to traditional exercise, that the game was able to generate appropriate levels of exertion in pre-adolescents, and that students have a sophisticated understanding of the role of exercise in their lives. Overall, we establish the feasibility of casual exergames for combating sedentary behavior in preteen classrooms.

Author Keywords

Exergames; school; children; physical activity; sedentary.

ACM Classification Keywords

K.8.0 [Personal Computing]: General - *Games*.

INTRODUCTION

Recent work among health researchers has shown that alongside the variety of physical, cognitive, and emotional benefits provided by regular physical activity, there are also negative consequences associated with sedentary behaviour [33]. Interestingly, these consequences are distinct from those that result from a lack of physical activity [33]. Although it may seem surprising, physically-active people who exercise each day (e.g., biking to work) can also be at risk from sedentary behaviour if the remainder of their time is spent in sedentary activities (e.g., sitting at a desk) [22].

CHI PLAY'14, October 19–21, 2014, Toronto, ON, Canada.

http://dx.doi.org/10.1145/2658537.2658693

The potential health outcomes are of particular relevance to information workers who spend large amounts of time working on computers, and schoolchildren, who spend many hours a day sitting at their desks, and many groups are now exploring the need for anti-sedentary guidelines to exist alongside guidelines for physical activity [34].

Although parents and recreation workers can help children receive the recommended levels of physical activity [34] in the mornings or after school, schools themselves are critical for preventing harmful sedentary behaviours during the day. Providing physical activity breaks for students is important. Younger children will often engage in spontaneous physical activity if given the opportunity; however, as children age, changing social dynamics often discourage physical activity during break times. This change in behavior tends to emerge during the 'tweens' when children are aged 9-13 [19, 28] and sedentary habits adopted during this critical period can have lifelong consequences [27]. While educators can encourage short bursts of physical activity throughout the day, these 'body breaks' can be difficult to administer to adolescents, who are not as thrilled by the vertigo of simply moving through space.

To encourage physical activity, researchers and developers have created a variety of exergames, by integrating exercise into the game mechanics (e.g., [18, 25, 37]). Moreover, casual exergames – computer games that players can learn easily and access quickly, using simple rules and special game mechanics, to motivate them to exercise at a moderate intensity for short periods of play [10] – are specifically designed to encourage small 'exerbreaks' throughout the day. Casual exergames could be used to decrease sedentary time amongst students by providing exercise experiences that are more compelling than traditional body breaks in a form that is socially acceptable to a tween audience, who have significant experience with computer games.

For a casual exergame to be deployed in a school setting, we feel that it should be acceptable to educators, enjoyable for students, provide sufficient – but not excessive – levels of physical activity, and not significantly interfere with students' workflow. In this paper we present the design and analysis of such a system.

We begin by conducting a series of semi-structured interviews with educators of 9-13 year olds at a local elementary school to identify the requirements of casual exergames that would make them useful in the classroom, to codify what has and has not worked in their classrooms in the past, and to understand the teachers' perceptions of the changing sedentary habits of their tween students. We then conducted a study of their students' responses to playing an existing and validated casual exergame, called GrabApple [10]. We compared physical activity levels and affective responses after students played GrabApple, a sedentary version of the game, and participated in a traditional body break led by a physical education instructor. Students also provided answers to surveys about their attitude to exercise and sedentary behavior before and after the experiment. Finally, students and teachers returned several months later to evaluate how the students' attitudes towards exercise had changed with the passage of time. The interviews were meant to establish the acceptability of exergames in the classroom, and the experiment to confirm the game's ability to engage students and provide appropriate levels of activity, satisfying our four goals.

Our results showed that casual exergames could be a promising method for combatting sedentary behavior in schools amongst tween populations. Students found the game more engaging than traditional exercise and were better able to maintain a target activity intensity. In addition, the game required little supervision and motivated target levels of physical activity through the game mechanics, alleviating the burden on teachers who are already overextended. Combined, the qualitative and quantitative results obtained through our research provide support for the future design and deployment of casual exergames in for use by schoolchildren.

RELATED WORK

The goal of our research is to consider the introduction of efficacious casual exergames into the classroom. As such, we cover literature on the general benefits of exercise, children's and adolescents' attitudes towards exercise, and related literature on exergames including casual exergames.

Physical Activity during Childhood and Adolescence

Regular physical activity is crucial during childhood and adolescence, as it has a large impact on an individual's ability of maintaining a healthy lifestyle during adulthood [27]. The National Association for Sport and Physical Education (NAPSPE) recommends that children engage in more than 60 minutes of moderate to vigorous exercise a day. Exercise can be carried out in multiple short bouts lasting at least 15 minutes, including rest and recovery time [6]. However, only about half of US children meet the exercise recommendations on five or more days per week [39]. Physical exercise can help prevent chronic disease, reduce the cholesterol ratio, increase bone density [30] and reduce obesity [8] in children. It has been shown that fitness through physical activity can also enhance measures of children's psychological well-being, such as self-satisfaction and self-esteem [30], and has been shown to improve mood [20]. Finally, short bursts of exercise can result in acute (i.e., short and temporary) cognitive benefits, including improvements on the Working Memory Task [26], the Rey Auditory-Verbal Learning Test [24], which measures recall, and the Stroop test [20,38], which executive functioning.

While the research community has primarily focused on the positive effects of physical activity, it has recently been suggested that there may not only be benefits of being physically active, but also distinct negative effects caused by sedentary lifestyles [11, 33]. For instance, sedentary people might experience differences in carbohydrate metabolism [4] and vascular health [15]. This suggests that the effects of generally sedentary lifestyles are different than those caused by a lack of intense physical activity [16, 23], and that people who regularly engage in exercise may still be at risk of negative effects of if they are mostly sedentary during the day, e.g., while working an office job or attending school. In response to these findings, different organizations that previously focused on guidelines for physical activity have recently released anti-sedentary guidelines that specifically encourage activity throughout the day, for example, the Canadian Society of Exercise Physiologists has published guidelines that address sedentary lifestyles among adolescents [34].

The games research community needs to re-think the way it approaches games as an intervention for encouraging healthier lifestyles. If intense physical activity as currently provided by many exergames is not sufficient to address activity-related health issues among children and teenagers, new game concepts should explore the integration of short bursts of activity throughout the day to counteract negative implications of extended periods of inactivity [22].

Attitudes about Physical Activity

Related work reports a decline in children's participation in physical activity in early adolescence [19, 28]. One of the important predictors of people engaging in physical activity is attitude towards exercise [7]; in particular children will participate in physical activities when they have a positive attitude towards physical activity [14]. Several studies have shown that integrating health education in classes, labs and readings can have positive impact on children's health attitude [5, 12]. However, many schools (particularly in the U.S.) intend to improve students' academic scores by increasing time for core curricular subjects and decreasing physical education (PE) [36], or other scheduled physical activity. Therefore, it is challenging for schools to allocate more time for physical activity during the school day [3].

Casual Exergames

Casual exergames are based on the insight that the daily amount of exercise necessary to obtain health benefits can be broken down into smaller chunks, while maintaining the positive effects [6, 17]. To help people add these small chunks of physical activity throughout the day, casual exergames [10] apply the principles of casual game design to the design of exergames: most importantly, they allow players to engage in physical activity in short bouts. Specifically, casual exergames are defined as *computer games that players can learn easily and access quickly, using simple rules and game mechanics, to motivate them to exercise at a moderate intensity for short periods of play* [10]. Research on casual exergames has shown that as little as ten minutes of casual exergame play can produce moderate-intensity exertion levels, improving players' affective states and providing significant levels of acute cognitive benefits compared to sedentary casual games [9] (i.e., can improve post-play ability of players to focus attention). While these results are promising, prior work has only explored the benefits of casual exergames with adults in lab settings. This paper expands on the approach by introducing casual exergames in a classroom setting, investigating whether benefits still exist when casual exergames are applied in a less controlled environment.

Exergames in Schools

Lwin and Malik [21] argue that incorporating exergaming into PE lessons is more beneficial than regular physical education (PE) as it can improve physical activity beliefs and behaviors. However, Sun [32] claims that incorporating exergames into PE may not produce health benefits, as some commercial exergames may not provide appropriate levels of physical activity. Beyond applying commercially available games in schools, researchers have introduced exergames using mobile phones to help students at school to fight sedentary lifestyles [18, 25, 37], and the PlayFit project aims to persuade teenagers through playful interventions and ambient interaction based on four design principles []. Although results suggest that these games can motivate students to become more active in the short term, instrumenting each user with body-mounted sensors is complex, which might create challenges in deploying such games in schools.

EXPERIMENTS

We conducted an experiment to examine how casual exergames can be deployed in school settings. Our experiment proceeded through three phases. First, we deployed a survey to Grade 7 teachers from a local school to understand their perception of casual exergames as a classroom activity, student attitudes and the appropriateness of technology. Second, we conducted a single day study with the Grade 7 class from the same school, collecting quantitative and qualitative data. Finally, we administered a follow-up questionnaire five months later to determine how student perceptions of exercise and exergames had changed over time. We describe each of these in turn.

TEACHERS' PERCEPTION OF EXERGAMES

We invited four grade seven teachers (three men) responsible for the students' program to provide insights into their students' attitudes towards physical activity. Two taught physical education (in addition to other subjects) and one taught dance in addition to other subjects. Their previous teaching experience spanned from kindergarten to grade eight. We provide a summary of the responses to the semi-structured interviews according to the topic.

Age-Related Changes in Physical Activity

All of the teachers pointed out that students become less active when they grow older. "*Students seem more apathetic toward teacher directed/organized activity. They want to be in charge of their own activity; however, unfortunately they still need guidance and motivation"*, and that they are less motivated to exercise: *"less motivated, less interested in getting sweaty, less interested in working hard, slower"*, "*They move less and stop running places. They used to run just because they wanted to get to places as fast as possible. When they get older they slow down and tend to only move fast when playing a game. The worst thing is they seem to require organized sport to motivate them to play hard."* All teachers noticed older students are more sedentary than younger students. They also provided possible explanations for this change: *"longer classes, we expect older ones to sit and work longer - attention span longer*", "*Body changes, less time because many will start a part time job, more homework in high school, friends"*.

Two teachers mentioned that students start to worry about their image, pointing out how *"they become more social and worry about image"*, and that *"other things become more important to them, image!!!!*" Two teachers suggested that girls are more concerned about their image and avoid physical activity: *"They would be just as content to do nothing for fear of how they will be viewed by their peers. This is especially true for girls. I think they refrain from being physical as a result of how they might be perceived"*.

Integration of Physical Activity in the Classroom

Three out of four teachers reported that they integrated physical activity into classroom activities, such as cardio, relays, combative, strength, stretch and dance. One teacher said s/he encouraged her/his students to try new activities every day and did body breaks twice a day. When asked whether they noticed whether or not students enjoyed the activities, teachers reported that most students liked it, but some were reluctant to participate. The teacher who frequently integrated physical activity into classrooms pointed out that his/her students "*loved when we counted and did certain jumping activities; they also loved stretching to quiet music*".

Three out of four teachers claimed positive effects of PE on their students, reporting that they are "*ready to learn, almost energized in a way that they are charged up*", "*when they really push hard and have fun they seem to come back to class relaxed with less behavioral problems", "I feel they are calmer after they have had a chance to burn off some steam"*. Only one teacher who did not integrate any physical activities in classroom claimed that after PE, students are fidgety, and "*it is difficult to settle them back into the classroom setting*".

Integration of Exergames in the Classroom

Three out four teachers stated that they would like to integrate exergames in the classroom. Teachers expected benefits such as *"increased motivation towards getting physically active"* and *"increased focus"*. Furthermore, they saw advantages such as an *"increased heart rate, increased muscle memory,* and *motivation to score better than the last time"*. Teachers also noticed potential drawbacks of exergames, such as "*cheating, lack of motivation to those that are jocks*", and games being distractive, and a "*disruption of others*".

When asked how they would integrate casual exergames in the classroom, they came up with solutions such as "*setting up a station, whole class approach where one or 2 or 6 people are active and rest of class is holding a pose while they are doing the challenge. Almost like a relay race*", "*probably as body breaks as the students see as necessary for their own personal wellness*" and "*might need to play it by ear but could set up a rotation or allow sign up to be used by those who enjoy it as a body break*".

When comparing casual exergames to regular exercise, teachers saw advantages of exergames, expecting them to "*increase confidence to those lacking skill in certain areas*", pointing out that *"students will have more personal control and responsibility over their body breaks"*. Regarding students' attitudes towards exercise, teachers pointed out that they *"think it is something the students are more open to. It is an excellent way to disguise exercise"*.

These results show that the teachers who participated in our survey are generally open towards the integration of physical activity in the classroom. Their statements show that they are aware of benefits of activity, but that they also recognize potential problems, such as the disruption of other students if exercise units are not well-integrated into the schedule. Furthermore, the results underline the change in students' attitudes towards physical activity at the transition from childhood to adolescence, particularly highlighting the increasing sedentary habits among girls.

USER STUDY WITH ADOLESCENTS

To follow-up on the survey with teachers, we conducted an experiment on how casual exergames compare to sedentary games and traditional PE activities.

Participants

During the user study, 63 grade seven children (29 boys) from a local elementary school participated. Data from 3 participants were excluded (three children were unable to participate for the experiment's duration). Participants ranged from 11 to 13 years old (M=12). Seventeen of the participants reported that they played video games at least 5-6 days a week, six participants almost never played video games, and the majority of participants played 1-2 or 3-4 days per week. The majority of participants were familiar with games that require physical activity (e.g., Xbox Kinect, PlayStation Move and Nintendo Wii).

Our participants were physically active. When asked about exercise, 22 of the 63 participants reported engaging in daily physical activity outside of school, and only one participant almost never performed exercise outside of school. The remaining participants did exercise several days a week outside of school. In general, our participants were aware of the benefits of physical activity. At school, they participate in the *Healthy Bodies Active Minds* (HBAM) program, which provides extra PE classes and teaches students about nutrition and activity, and the physical and cognitive benefits of an active lifestyle.

The GrabApple Game

GrabApple (Figure 1) is a casual game that can be played in a 10-minute session. For a complete description, see [10]. The goal of the game is to pick up falling red and green apples and avoid touching the falling bombs using a virtual hand on the screen. In the exergame version of the game, the virtual hand is controlled through the movement of the player's body (sensed using a Microsoft Kinect), using the player's body weight as resistance to generate exercise, requiring jumping, ducking and movement. If players keep picking the same color of apple, a score multiplier that encourages additional movement is engaged. The hand can hold five apples. To empty the hand, players need to jump to the apple bag. In the sedentary version of the game, a mouse is used to control the virtual hand on the screen. We have previously used GrabApple in studies with young adults, and have shown that it is capable of producing moderate-intensity exercise [9,10].

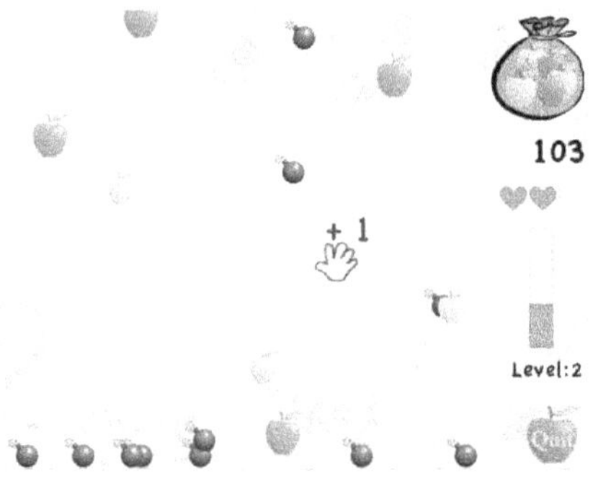

Figure 1. Screenshot of the GrabApple game.

Experimental Conditions

Our study had three conditions. In the *exergame condition*, participants were asked to play the casual exergame GrabApple. In the *sedentary condition*, participants played GrabApple using the keyboard and mouse. In the *exercise condition*, participants performed traditional exercise (e.g. rope skipping, climbing stairs and running short distances while avoiding obstacles) guided by a PE teacher. In all three conditions, participants wore a heart rate monitor.

Procedure and Methods

The study methods and instruments were first approved by ethics offices at the University of Saskatchewan, Saskatoon, Canada, and the Saskatoon School District. All students and students' parents filled out informed consent and assent forms prior to arriving at the University campus. Students arrived at the university on the morning of a school day. Each student received an envelope with worksheets for recording their heart rate, surveys and a pencil. Students filled out demographic, exercise attitude, and affective state surveys. Finally, we divided the students into two groups: one group participated in the experiment in the morning, while the other group participated in the afternoon. When students were not participating in the experiment, they completed a half-day workshop on Scratch programming.

The experimental group began the experimental protocol watching a two-minute video explaining GrabApple. Afterwards, each participant put on a heart rate monitor (chest strap with wrist band display) with the help of their teachers and wrote down their resting heart rate on the worksheet. We divided the participants into three subgroups (8-12 students per group) and assigned each subgroup to a different condition (exergame, sedentary, exercise). The order of conditions was fully counterbalanced. Each group was accompanied by at least two teachers and three volunteers to supervise participants and administer the surveys. Participants in the exercise condition were in a separate room and guided by a PE teacher to ensure comparable levels of activity across groups. In each condition, participants performed one activity for ten minutes. After each condition, participants reported their heart rate on the worksheet and filled out the post-condition surveys, including questions of player experience, affective state, and the Borg Rating of Perceived Exertion (RPE) [1]. At the end of each condition, volunteers collected the surveys. When all groups from both sessions had finished all the conditions, students returned to the lecture theatre and filled out the post-experiment surveys.

After five months, the same group of children returned to the university for a follow-up survey and to learn about the results of the study. They then filled out another exercise attitude survey.

Measures

Exertion was measures through heart rate and the Borg Rating of Perceived Exertion (RPE) [1]. Player experience was collected through Likert scale questions about how fun, exciting, challenging, easy to learn, and frustrating the game was to play. To measure affective state, we used the Self-Assessment Manikin (SAM) scale [2], a pictorial 9-point scale that is commonly used to self-report affective states via valence (feelings of pleasure or displeasure) and arousal (activation of feeling).

Apparatus

We arranged two computer labs at a local university to run the experiment. Both the sedentary and exergame conditions were held in the same computer lab with 12 computers available for each condition. The game was played on a Windows PC with a 20-inch widescreen monitor. For the exergame condition, participants stood approximately 1.2m from the display.

Data Analyses

Although all participants engaged in all three experimental conditions, the time between each condition did not allow for heart rates to reliably return to resting levels. As such, we treated the data as a between-subjects experiment, using data from only the first condition played for the measures %maxHR and perceived exertion. A one-way ANOVA was conducted with condition as a factor (exergame, sedentary, exercise), and we used the Tukey HSD test for post-hoc measurements. Questionnaire responses (affective state, player experience, and attitude) were analyzed using the Friedman Test for multiple related samples.

Results

We present results for exertion, experience, affect, and attitude during the experiment.

Physical Exertion

The American College of Sports Medicine defines moderate-intensity exercise as 64-76% of maximum heart rate (maxHR=220-age) [35], vigorous-intensity exercise as 77-93% of maximum heart rate and very hard intensity exercise as greater than 94% of maximum heart rate. Figure 2 shows the average percentage of maximum heart rate (%maxHR) of the participants. While the values for the exergame condition are within the range of moderate to vigorous-intensity exercise, heart rates for the exercise condition are within the range of vigorous to very hard-intensity exercise. A one-way ANOVA showed that the differences in %maxHR were significant ($F_{2,56}$=150.2, $p\approx.000$). Tukey's test showed that exercise intensity in the sedentary condition was significantly lower than intensity produced in the exergame condition ($p\approx.000$) and exercise condition ($p\approx.000$), and that the exergame condition was significantly lower than the exercise condition ($p\approx.000$).

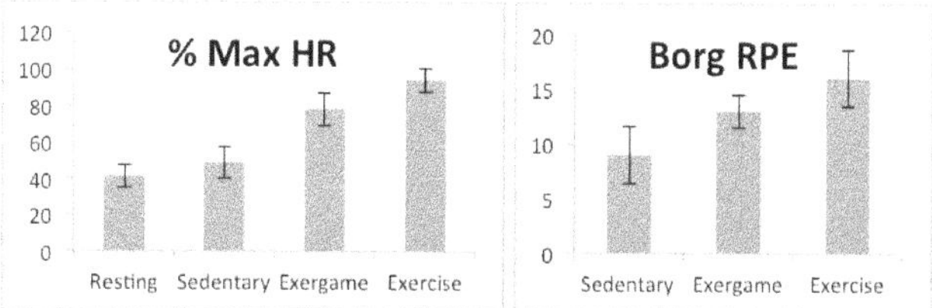

Figure 2. Means and SD for measures of exertion.

The results for Borg Ratings of Perceived Exertion (Borg RPE) are consistent with participants' heart rates. The exergame condition produced perceived exertion values within the recommended intensity: 12-13 (somewhat hard) to 15-16 (hard) [35]. The differences in perceived exertion between conditions were significant ($F_{2,53}$=44.9, p≈.000). Pairwise comparisons showed that the sedentary condition produced significantly lower levels of perceived exertion than the exergame (p≈.000) and traditional exercise (p≈.000), and that exergame was significantly lower than exercise condition (p=.001).

Our observations revealed that the PE teacher supervising the exercise condition pushed the students to give a lot of effort. She tailored the activities for individuals and offered encouragement and support, often participating with the students. This support is reflected in the exertion results and may not transfer to other environments with teachers who are not as committed to promoting physical activity.

From both a physiological and perceived exertion perspective, the exergame provided the appropriate amount of physical activity for an effective anti-sedentary body break. This result provides evidence that exergames can meet the physical requirements of a body break amongst our target tween demographic, our second requirement for establishing the utility of casual exergames as an antisedentary activity in the classroom.

Affective Benefits

Results for the effects of the different conditions on valence and arousal are displayed in Figure 3. Across all three conditions, results for valence were rather high, suggesting a positive mood among participants. A Friedman's Test for 3-related samples showed no significant difference in valence (χ^2_2=3.3, p=.195), but there was a significant difference in arousal (χ^2_2=34.3, p≈.000). Pairwise comparisons using Wilcoxon Signed Ranks Test revealed that players felt more aroused after the exercise condition than after the exergame condition (p=.001) or the sedentary condition (p≈.000), and more aroused after the exergame condition than the sedentary condition (p=.031). Although the SAM is designed to measure psychological arousal, it is likely that participants were also reflecting on the physiological arousal resulting from exercise intensity.

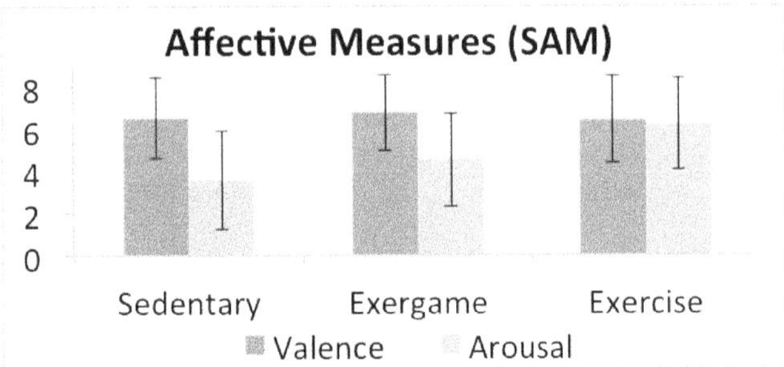

Figure 3. Means and SDs for valence and arousal as measured by SAM (1 is low, 9 is high).

Player Experience

We asked participants to rate six core aspects of the activities (fun, ease of learning, excitement, challenge, frustration, and whether they would consider playing it if they had a 10-minute break) on a 5-point Likert scale. The results show that participants' experience with the exergame and sedentary game as well as in the traditional exercise condition were generally positive. A Friedman test for 3-related samples showed significant differences in the ratings for challenge (χ^2_2=24.7, p≈.000) and ease of learning (χ^2_2=19.8, p≈.000) and marginally-significant differences for fun (χ^2_2=5.8, p=.055), excitement (χ^2_2=6.0, p=.051), and whether they would consider playing it (χ^2_2=5.7, p=.059). Pairwise comparisons using the Wilcoxon Signed Rank Test revealed that participants rated the exergame condition as significantly more fun than the exercise condition (p=.045) and would consider playing the exergame in the future rather than engage in traditional exercise (p=.008). Results for challenge mirror our findings regarding physical exertion with exercise being the most challenging, followed by the exergame condition, and the sedentary condition (all differences significant with p<.05). The sedentary game was seen as easier to learn than the exergame (p=.007) and the exercise condition (p≈.000). Finally, the exergame condition was rated as more exciting than the sedentary condition (p=.005).

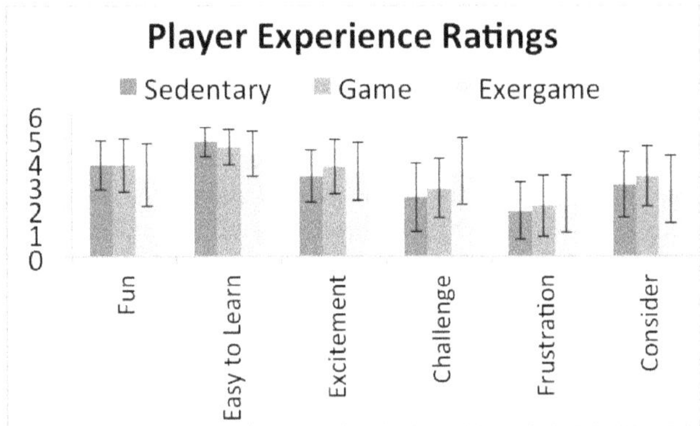

Figure 4. Means and SDs for player experience ratings (on a scale from 1 to 5; 5 is highest).

Given the player experience results, we can conclude that a sufficient number of players found the exergame sufficiently more enjoyable than traditional exercise and easy enough to learn to warrant its consideration for inclusion in the classroom.

FOLLOW-UP SURVEY ON ATTITUDE ABOUT EXERCISE

To gain further insights into the potential application of exergames in a classroom setting, at five months post-study, the same group of children provided ratings and explanations of their exercise attitudes gathered during the experiment (but reported below).

We posed a series of questions about the perceived attentional benefit of exercise because teachers felt that exercise can help students focus on subsequent classwork and research results show benefits of casual exergames on attention in adults [9]. We wished to determine if the students' perceptions matched that of educators and the literature. Participants answered the questions three times:

prior to the study (baseline), right after the study (post), and five months after the study had been completed (follow-up). Results (Figure 5) show that participant attitudes are neither overly positive nor negative towards exercise.

"I can concentrate better shortly after I exercise."

A Friedman Test for related samples showed significant differences in the ratings for agreement with this statement at three different times (χ^2_2=18.9, $p\approx$.000). Pairwise comparisons showed that agreement with this statement was significantly lower in the 5-month follow-up survey than in the baseline survey (p=.042) or post experiment ($p\approx$.000). There was no difference between the baseline and post-experiment surveys (p=.118).

Participants were generally able to observe what is going on in their bodies during and shortly after exercise. They gave reasons such as *"I am happy after I exercise"*, *"It helps get blood flowing to my head"* or *"I feel awake"*. Participants holding negative opinions often mentioned that exercise made them tired, such as *"I am tired after exercising and can't think straight"*. Other reasons included that they found exercise makes no difference *"It doesn't really change"* or they forgot what they were doing before exercise *"Not really because I usually forget what I was doing before exercising sometimes"*. Participants with neutral opinions mentioned that whether short bursts of exercise can improve concentration depended on the type and intensity of activity and length of recovery: *"It depends how hard I exercise"*, *"Depends on what the exercise is"*, *"If I am tired I can't concentrate so it depends on what I did"* and *"Right after an exercise, you're still recovering, so you will concentrate fairly after a exercise"*.

"Playing an exercise game can help me to improve my concentration."

We found a main effect of agreement with this statement at the three different survey times (χ^2_2=8.1, p=.018). Again, pairwise comparisons showed that agreement in the 5-month follow-up survey was significantly lower than in the post-experiment survey (p=.047), and marginally lower than in the baseline survey (p=.066). There was no difference between the baseline and post-experiment surveys (p=.878).

Some participants mentioned playing exercise games could give them a break: *"I just "exercise" my brain, gives it a break sometimes"*. Some participants mentioned games are fun, can make people compete and help in learning things: *"Exercising will improve your concentration but the game will make you compete more"*, *"Helps me learn things"* and *"They are usually fun and I will continue thinking about it"*. Most participants who held negative views explained they did not notice the difference between playing an exergame or sedentary activities on their ability to concentrate. One participant mentioned he/she prefers other activities: *"I prefer to just play silent ball or something less extravagant"*. Similar to previous statements on the effects of traditional exercise, participants with neutral opinions mentioned that whether an exercise game could improve concentration depended on the type of game and the intensity of physical activity required to engage in play: *"It depends on how much exercising this game gives to me"*.

"I concentrate better if I exercise regularly."

We found a main effect of agreement with this statement for all surveys times (χ^2_2=14.8, p=.001). Again, pairwise comparisons showed significantly lower agreement with this statement in the 5-month follow-up survey than in the baseline survey (p=.014) or the post-experiment survey (p=.006). There was no difference between the baseline and post-experiment surveys (p=.759).

Many participants agreed with the statement through experience. *"My dancing classes stop usually around June or July. This year they have stopped in May and I am finding it harder and harder to concentrate in my class"*, *"If I exercise half an hour before I need to concentrate I work well"*. The explanation for most participants who held negative options was they did not notice the difference between exercising regularly *"I don't think it makes much of a difference"*. Again, participants with neutral opinions mentioned that the impact of regular exercise on concentration depended on the context: *"It depends on the exercise and the time of the day"*, *"Usually depends on the day and if I am feeling tired or not"*.

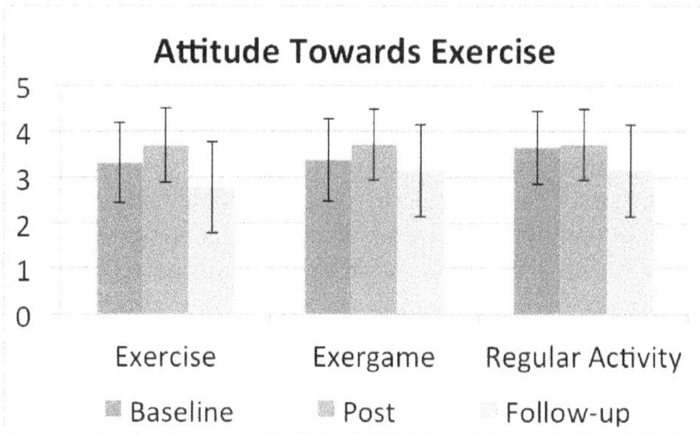

Figure 5. Means and SDs for questions related to perceived attentional benefits of being physically active (on a scale from 1-5; higher indicates more agreement).

Summary

On a general level, the five-month follow-up explanation surveys showed a range of opinions. Many participants stated that they do believe that exercise can have a positive effect on concentration, while some claimed that they did not notice any effects of exercise on concentration. Those who reported a negative impact of exercise or exergames on concentration frequently stated that it made them feel tired, thus reducing their ability to concentrate and potentially interrupted their workflow. This suggests that students have insight into the effects of physical activity on their ability of participating in cognitively challenging tasks, which needs to be taken into account when designing casual exergames to be played in a classroom setting.

Student perception of exergame-based impact on their attention was mixed and produced no significant differences between activities. This result then satisfies our final requirement, that the game not be disruptive to students. The exergame was no better or worse than sedentary or body break activities on perceived ability to concentrate. The decrease in attitude towards exercise could be a manifestation of age-related attitude changes noted by both the teachers and the literature, as discussed earlier.

DISCUSSION

We present our contributions and findings, followed by a discussion of casual exergame deployment in schools.

Contributions and Findings

The teachers' observations about their students' physical activities at school provided valuable opinions both on the nature of exercise in pre-adolescence and on the potential for casual exergames to help improve physical activity among schoolchildren. The teachers noted that students become more sedentary, less motivated and less interested in exercise when they grow older and most teachers already integrate physical activities into classroom activities, such as stretches and dance, to help students reenergize between class breaks. Teachers also noted that students enjoy short chunks of physical activity, which anecdotally seems to have positive effects on concentration. Similarly, teachers found that after PE class, students were often ready to learn.

Our results show that the exercise and exergame condition both provided intense workouts. The exergame condition demonstrated moderate to vigorous exertion, and the exercise condition created workouts at near maximum intensity, both in terms of objectively-measured heart rate and subjectively-measured exertion. The similarities in heart rate and ratings of perceived exertion show that students were able to rate the intensity at which they exercised, suggesting that they understood the physiological signals of exertion, and were able to subjectively evaluate exercise intensity. This is an important insight for exergame design: if students can accurately self-rate exercise intensity, then self-paced exergames can tailor the physical challenge necessary to produce optimal levels of exertion for health benefits and player engagement. They also show that exertion levels in the exercise condition were very high, exhausting students physically after 10 minutes, which the students felt affected their ability to concentrate.

The results of the player experience survey showed that students had more fun playing the exergame than doing traditional exercise. Moreover, students would consider playing an exergame during a break more than they would consider doing traditional exercise. Our participants rated traditional exercise as a fun activity as our sample consists of children who are generally fond of exercise, and the PE teacher made the exercise session fun and motivating. The students enjoyed the exergame more than traditional exercise and indicated they would play the exergame more than traditional exercise if they had 10-minutes of free time in a day, such as in breaks between classes.

We noted a significant decrease in opinions on exercise after the study, but no significant difference between any of the activities themselves, indicating that exergames should not have negatively impact concentration.

Overall we have successfully demonstrated that exergames are acceptable to teachers, provide sufficient and targeted exercise needs, are more enjoyable and easier to learn than traditional exercise and have a negligible effect on student concentration. In aggregate, we believe we have demonstrated that properly designed exergames can be used in the future as antisedentary interventions in classrooms.

The Deployment of Casual Exergames in Schools

The goal of our work was to explore how casual exergames can be deployed in schools to give kids the physical activity they require, and the cognitive advantages that result. Contrary to earlier work [13], our findings demonstrated that self-paced exergames can produce exertion levels in the children that meet current guidelines of physical activity.

The students' explanations of their attitudes demonstrated that they understand the cognitive advantages of exercise, and that they felt that too much exertion without sufficient time for recovery negatively affected their ability to concentrate. Some of the students mentioned that this problem could be addressed in the design of casual exergames, ensuring an intensity level within recommended guidelines. Our causal exergame produced exertion levels within the recommended guidelines, suggesting that the students paced themselves effectively.

Teachers were also interested in integrating casual games in the classroom to increase students' physical health and increase their focus after playing such games, and to decrease long stretches of sedentary time. Teachers noted that casual exergames have advantages over exercise by allowing students to have more control and being able to track students' physical activities individually. Teachers provided practical concerns, such as lack of space, disruption of others and cheating when playing the game. For example, classroom space varies among schools, so the location of an exergame system within the school (e.g. in a classroom or common area) must be addressed on a case-by-case basis. Teachers noted that students might cheat during play, so exergames should be robust enough to prevent students from gaming the input device or game mechanic. Finally, teachers reported different ideas on how exergames might be integrated into the classroom, such as letting students take turns like a relay race, letting interested students sign up, or using these games as a reward.

Limitations and Future Work

Our results show the potential possibilities of casual exergame deployment at schools; however, there are limitations in what we can infer from our studies leading to new research opportunities.

Our participants may not be representative of the general population of pre-adolescent schoolchildren. They come from a privileged neighbourhood, are high achieving, and are in a pilot educational program on staying healthy. Our results may not extend to children who are physically inactive or who have a different socioeconomic status.

The students in our study played the casual exergame for only ten minutes and the novelty of the Kinect-based game may have affected the players' perceptions of its fun. Outside of the context of our study, we do not know how motivated students would be to play a casual exergame over the longer term. Our study is the first step to investigate the potential of casual exergames in schools; the next logical step will be to develop casual exergame design guidelines for classroom use and deploy a suite of casual exergames in a classroom as a longitudinal study to determine the long-term efficacy of casual exergames as a pre-adolescent school-mediated health intervention for reducing sedentary time, and long-term player engagement, particularly during voluntary breaks such as recess.

Our work used a single casual exergame. It would be worthwhile to investigate the inclusion of other properly designed motivational elements, such as leader boards, classroom competition, or cooperative multiplayer games in a social context [18, 31].

Finally, the ultimate success of this work would be to evaluate the longitudinal health effects of a suite of well designed exergames and demonstrate measurable health effects by reducing sendentary behavior. This would be a sophisticated and difficult experiment to conduct to meet the burden of proof expected in the medical community. However, the results we have presented here indicate that it may be worth working towards this type of investigation.

CONCLUSIONS

Although the physical importance of breaking up sedentary time and the positive effects of physical activity on learning processes are widely known, schools struggle to provide sufficient opportunities for physical activity to their students. This effect is particularly apparent as students transition from childhood to adolescence. Casual exergames may be a means of encouraging physical activity amongst pre-adolescences and breaking up long stretches of sedentary behaviour. Due to the special characteristics of these games (interruptible, short chunks of play, easy setup routines), they are well suited for deployment in schools for play during natural breaks in the school day, such as at lunch or recess. We have demonstrated that students see the benefits of moderate physical activity throughout the day, and that they enjoy engaging with a casual exergame as a preferable alternative to traditional exercise.

Casual exergames have also been applied to help people regain focus during crucial periods of their day and yield acute cognitive benefits. Students demonstrated a mature understanding of the relationship between cognition and activity level. Further evidence of the utility of casual exergames in a school environment was provided by teachers who noted several methods where exergames could be successfully deployed in a classroom setting. This work in aggregate makes a strong case for the utility of casual exergames in a classroom setting to help break up sedentary time, thus avoiding the negative health outcomes that can result from sitting still for too long at school.

ACKNOWLEDGMENTS

We thank the GRAND NCE (GAMFIT) for funding, the members of the Interaction lab at the University of Saskatchewan for assisting with the experiment, Shakiba Jalal and Brittany Melnyk for conducting the Scratch workshop, and Silverspring School for their participation.

REFERENCES

1. Borg, G.A. Psychophysical bases of perceived exertion. *MSSE 14*, 5, 1982, 377-381.
2. Bradley, M.M. and Lang, P.J. Measuring emotion: the Self-Assessment Manikin and the Semantic Differential. *JBTEP 25*, 1, 1994, 49-59.
3. Centers for Disease Control and Prevention. *The association between school-based physical activity, including physical education, and academic performance*. U.S. Department of Health and Human Services, US, 2010.
4. Chilibeck, P.D., Bell, G., et al. Functional electrical stimulation exercise increases GLUT-1 and GLUT-4 in paralyzed skeletal muscle. Metabolism, 48(11), 1999, 1409-1413.
5. Christodoulos, A.D., Douda, H.T., Polykratis, M., and Tokmakidis, S.P. Attitudes towards exercise and physical activity behaviours in Greek schoolchildren after a year long health education intervention. *BJSM, 40*, 4, 2006, 367-371.
6. DeBusk, R.F. et al. Training effects of long versus short bouts of exercise in healthy subjects. *AJC 65*, 15, 1990, 1010-1013.
7. Deforche, B.I., De Bourdeaudhuij, I.M., and Tanghe, A.P. Attitude toward physical activity in normal-weight, overweight and obese adolescents. *Journal of Adolescent Health 38*, 5, 2006, 560-568.
8. Epstein, L.H., Coleman, K.J., and Myers, M.D. Exercise in treating obesity in children and adolescents. *MSSE, 28*, 4, 1996, 428–435.
9. Gao, Y. and Mandryk, R. The acute cognitive benefits of casual exergame play. *Proc. CHI*, 2012, 1863-1872.

10. Gao, Y. and Mandryk, R.L. GrabApple: the design of a casual exergame. *Proc. ICEC*, 2011, 35-46.

11. Garber, C. E., et al. American College of Sports Medicine position stand. Quantity and quality of exercise for developing and maintaining cardiorespiratory, musculoskeletal, and neuromotor fitness in apparently healthy adults: guidance for prescribing exercise. *MSSE*, 43(7), 2011, 1334-1359.

12. Goldfine, B.D. and Nahas, M.V. Incorporating health-fitness concepts in secondary physical education cirricula. *Journal of school health. 63*, 3, 1993, 142-146.

13. Graves, L. et al. Energy expenditure in adolescents playing new generation computer games. *BJSM 42*, 7, 2008, 592-594.

14. Hagger, M., Cale, L., Almond, L., and Krüger, A. Children's Physical Activity Levels and Attitudes Towards Physical Activity. *European Physical Education Review 3*, 2, 1997, 144-164.

15. Hamburg, N.M., et al. Physical inactivity rapidly induces insulin resistance and microvascular dysfunction in healthy volunteers. *ATVB*, 27(12), 2007, 2650-2656.

16. Hamilton, M.T., et al. Too little exercise and too much sitting: inactivity physiology and the need for new recommendations on sedentary behaviour. *Current Cardiovascular Risk Reports*, 2(4), 2008, 292-298.

17. Haskell, W.L. et al. Physical Activity and Public Health: Updated Recommendation for Adults from the American College of Sports Medicine and the American Heart Association. *MSSE 39*, 8, 2007, 1423-1434.

18. Kiili, K., et al. Designing mobile multiplayer exergames for physical education. Mobile Learning, 2010.

19. Kohl, H.W., 3rd and Hobbs, K.E. Development of physical activity behaviors among children and adolescents. *Pediatrics 101*, 3 Pt 2, 1998, 549-554.

20. Lichtman, S. and Poser, E.G. The effects of exercise on mood and cognitive functioning. *JPR 27*, 1, 1983, 43-52.

21. Lwin, M.O. and Malik, S. The efficacy of exergames-incorporated physical education lessons in influencing drivers of physical activity: A comparison of children and pre-adolescents. *JPSE, 13*, 6, 2012, 756-760.

22. Mandryk, R.L., Gerling, K.M., Stanley, K.S. Designing Games to Discourage Sedentary Behaviour. In: A. Nijholt (Ed.): Playful User Interfaces, Gaming Media and Social Effects. Springer, 2014, 253-274.

23. Owen, N., Healy, G.N., Matthews, C.E., & Dunstan, D.W. Too much sitting: the population health science of sedentary behaviour. Exercise and Sport Sciences Reviews, 38(3), 2010, 105-113.

24. Pontifex, M.B. et al. The Effect of Acute Aerobic and Resistance Exercise on Working Memory. *MSSE 41*, 4, 2009, 927-934.

25. Poole, E.S., et al. The place for ubiquitous computing in schools: lessons learned from a school-based intervention for youth physical activity. *Proc. Ubiquitous computing*, 2011, 395-404.

26. Potter, D. and Keeling, D. Effects of Moderate Exercise and Circadian Rhythms on Human Memory. *JSEP* 27, 1 2005, 117-125.

27. Rowland, T.W. and Freedson, P.S. Physical Activity, Fitness, and Health in Children: A Close Look. *Pediatrics 93*, 4, 1994, 669-672.

28. Sallis, J.F. Epidemiology of physical activity and fitness in children and adolescents. *Critical reviews in food science and nutrition 33*, 4-5, 1993, 403-408.

29. Sluis-Thiescheffer, R.J.W., et al. An Active Lifestyle for Youths through Ambient Persuasive Technology. Implementing Activating Concepts in a School Environment. *Games for Health*, 2013, 293-308.

30. Sothern, M.S., et al. The health benefits of physical activity in children and adolescents: implications for chronic disease prevention. *European Journal of Pediatrics 158*, 4, 1999, 271-274.

31. Stach, T., Graham, T.C.N., Yim, J., and Rhodes, R.E. Heart Rate Control of Exercise Video Games. *Proc. GI 2009*, 125-132.

32. Sun, H. Exergaming Impact on Physical Activity and Interest in Elementary School Children. *Research Quarterly for Exercise and Sport 83*, 2, 2012, 212-220.

33. Tremblay, M.S., Colley, R., Saunders, T.J., Healy, G.N., & Owen, N. Physiological and health implications of a sedentary lifestyle. *Applied Physiology, Nutrition, and Metabolism, 35*(6), 2010, 725-740.

34. Tremblay, M.S., et al. New Canadian physical activity guidelines. *Applied Physiology, Nutrition, and Metabolism, 36*(1), 2011, 36-46.

35. Whaley, M.H. et al. *ACSM's Guidelines for Exercise Testing and Prescription*. Lippincott Williams & Wilkins 7th Edition, 2006.

36. Wilkins, J.L.M., Graham, G., Parker, S., Westfall, S., Fraser, R.G., and Tembo, M. Time in the Arts and Physical Education and School Achievement. *Journal of Curriculum Studies 35*, 6, 2003, 721-734.

37. Xu, Y., Poole, E.S., Miller, A.D., Eiriksdottir, E., Catrambone, R., and Mynatt, E.D. Designing pervasive health games for sustainability, adaptability and sociability. *Proc. FDG*, 2012, 49-56.

38. Yanagisawa, H. et al. Acute moderate exercise elicits increased dorsolateral prefrontal activation and improves cognitive performance with Stroop test. *NeuroImage 50*, 4, 2010, 1702-1710.

39. *Youth Risk Behavior Surveillance — United States, 2011.*

Playfully Learning Visual Perspective Taking Skills with Sifteo Cubes

Luc Geurts, Vero Vanden Abeele, Kevin Van Keer, Ruben Isenborghs
KU Leuven – e-Media Lab
Andreas Vesaliusstraat 13, 3000 Leuven, Belgium
{luc.geurts, vero.vandenabeele}@kuleuven.be,
{kevin.vankeer, ruben.isenborghs}@student.kuleuven.be

ABSTRACT

In this paper we describe the design, development and testing of two computer games using Sifteo Cubes that help children to train their visual perspective taking (VPT) skills, i.e. the ability to see the world from another person's perspective. The challenge was to design an enjoyable and usable game that takes into account the huge variability in the perspective taking skills within the target group (preschoolers at the age of five, and older children with learning disabilities). Sifteo Cubes can be considered as digital or intelligent manipulatives that are often used in instruction. We advocate that these type tangible objects can help children performing VPT related tasks since they allow for actions in the real world that aid their thinking. Pre-test and post-test results revealed a short term learning effect on VPT skills after playing the two games.

Author Keywords

Sifteo Cubes; digital manipulatives; tangible interaction; serious games; visual perspective taking

ACM Classification Keywords

H.5.2. Information interfaces and presentation (e.g., HCI): User Interfaces – *Input devices and strategies*.

INTRODUCTION

The last decade has been characterized by the emergence of novel interaction technologies. Well-known commercial examples are Nintendo Wii, PlayStation Move and Microsoft Kinect. These technologies offer the opportunity to design new types of games, based on physical motion, and a have broadened the application area to 'serious games' and more particularly games for health; adults play exertion games to maintain their physical conditions, seniors play motion based games for fall rehabilitation, and children play these type of games to improve their psycho-motor skills.

CHI PLAY '14, October 19 - 22 2014, Toronto, ON, Canada

http://dx.doi.org/10.1145/2658537.2658706

Also more graspable or tangible objects have been suggested as a way to extend interaction [3,9]. When tangible interfaces make use of multiple interactive objects, the input is called space-multiplexed[1]; different tangibles, dispersed over the environment, can represent different actions or hold different information. These different tangible objects can come in different shapes, sizes and locations [16], which supports epistemic actions. Epistemic actions are unplanned actions that distribute some of the work of problem solving to the environment [6]. Epistemic actions do not directly bring a person closer to its goal but rather change the world in order to simplify the problem-solving task [1]. Clearly, space-multiplexed tangibles allow for epistemic actions: tangibles can be moved around; pieces can be shifted, individually or in group; objects can be touched or pointed at; blocks can be partitioned and recomposed in subsets, etc. Epistemic actions precede pragmatic actions, the latter directly bring the child closer to its goal, i.e. solving the problem. The division between epistemic versus pragmatic actions also underpins Physically Distributed Learning (PDL) [10]. Yet PDL emphasizes that actions and interpretations coevolve; actions and interpretations develop each other, and over time people develop stable ideas and solve problems using mental strategies.

In this manner, space-multiplexed tangibles also particularly lend themselves to PDL. Not surprisingly, the theory of Physically Distributed Learning has been built alongside research involving physical manipulatives for mathematics learning [11]. Manipulatives are concrete materials aimed to benefit children's learning [2,12,13].

Space-multiplexed tangibles could be considered digital manipulatives [15], and possibly can provide several benefits compared to popular platforms such as in recent years tablets. Intelligent manipulatives blur the boundary between the real and the digital world, and exploit the sense of touch as opposed to e.g. touch interaction: users can feel edges, curves, and ridges; different textures, pliability,

[1] Space-multiplexed interfaces are juxtaposed to time-multiplexed interfaces such as GUIs and computer mice, where a user can only interact with one object at a time.

temperature; distribution of weight; as opposed to the "glass plate" that exists between the user and the digital content in a tablet [20].

A recent popular game platform are the Sifteo Cubes that can be considered as intelligent manipulatives as well. Each cube has a touch sensitive display and contains sensors to detect motion and identify adjacent cubes. This leads to several interaction modes such as tilting, flipping, shaking, neighboring and pressing, as illustrated in Figure 1.

Several researchers have explored the potential of the Sifteo Cubes in various application areas. Hunter et al. presented two language-learning applications for children between 4 and 7 years old. The focus of one application is to teach children spatial concepts and basic sentence-construction skills through creative play, while the other game was designed to teach vocabulary and reading [8]. CogCubed (www.cogcubed.com) developed a diagnostic tool for testing for symptoms of Attention Deficit Hyperactivity Disorder [6]. Vandermaesen et al. presented 'PhysiCube', a rehabilitation system that provides motivating physical training for the upper limbs. Instead of manipulating daily objects, the patients play a game by lifting and reaching to Sifteo Cubes [19]. Pillias et al. developed and tested a collaborative game and advocate that the cubes' properties "provide players with more freedom and relatedness, while helping to create an easy-to-learn and customizable gameplay [14]."

Another application area where Sifteo Cubes might be of particular use is Visual Perspective Taking (VPT). Visual Perspective Taking is the ability to see the world from another person's perspective, taking into account what they see and how they see it [4,5,17] (see Figure 2). Children gradually acquire this skill during kindergarten and are assumed to have mastered this skill when they leave preschool for primary education. However, many five- or six-year olds still have difficulties identifying their own left and right, and identifying another person's left and right presents an even greater challenge. In this case, it might be beneficial to see a psychomotor therapist. Typically, psychomotor therapists rely on exercises and drawings on paper for the children to train these skills. Generally, children find these paper-based exercises quite boring. Incorporating these exercises in a game is likely to increase the children's motivation.

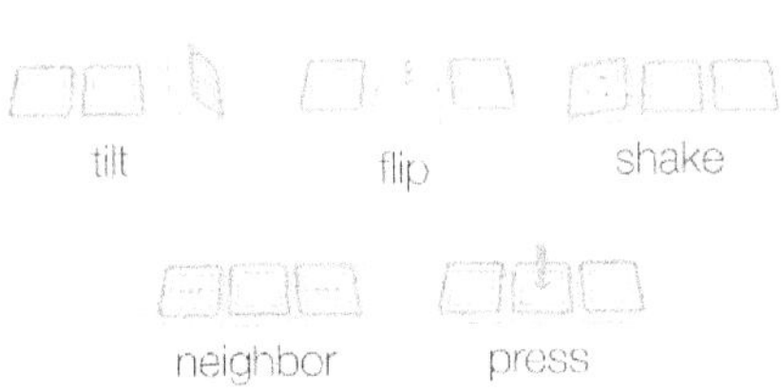

Figure 1 Possible interaction modes with Sifteo Cubes

Research question

The main objective of our project was to explore the benefits that digital manipulatives, and in particular Sifteo Cubes, might offer for young children learning or improving VPT skills. The challenge was to design games that are enjoyable and usable and that train VPT in five-year-olds.

As aforementioned, the main motivation to choose the Sifteo platform to train VPT, is Sifteo system's potential to enable physically distributed learning. While exercises on paper or tablet still require the child to think and operate in a 2D world, cubes can be distributed and manipulated in 3D space, by grasping, lifting and replacing them. These actions are very natural to these children, so the necessary manipulations are supposedly intuitive, they do not need to be learned. Also, as opposed to paper exercises, children can perform epistemic actions: they can take and replace cubes in order to help their thinking. Finally, digital manipulatives offer the opportunity to create interactive systems that provide immediate feedback to the player's actions. In conclusion, we postulate that games can be designed that can be learned very quickly, so that most mental effort has to go to the real challenge (i.e. VPT).

In the next section we will first discuss our iterative design process, and the two games we developed. Next, we will present and discuss the results of an experiment in which we investigated the usability of the games, the response from the players, and possible short term learning effects.

DESIGN

As is evident when designing games for young children, we adopted an iterative player-centered approach [18]. There is indeed a large discrepancy between the cognitive abilities of the game designers and those of the target group, resulting in a risk that incorrect preconceptions influence the game design.

Therefore, a psychomotor therapist was involved in this project. Her job consists of helping children with learning disabilities, varying from assisting in reading, writing, and mathematics, problem solving and performing daily activities. Her major contributions in this study were giving feedback on initial game concepts and assisting in and commenting on the intermediate user studies with children with learning disabilities. In addition to the psychomotor therapists, six children were involved as well, aged between 5 and 7. Three of these children were clients of the psychomotor therapist having problems with VPT, whereas the three other children were recruited via relatives of the researchers, and did not have known VPT-related problems.

Over a period of 7 weeks, game concepts and later interactive prototypes were designed and evaluated by the therapists and these children during formative usability tests. From these iterations we derived the following guidelines for training VPT skills.

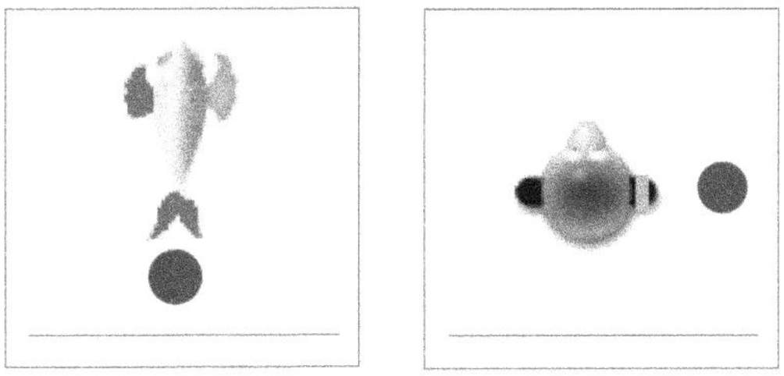

Figure 2 Visual perspective taking refers to the ability to identify another person's left, right, front or back. A typical question in a test would be: "If you were the fish, where would in the black dot be? In front of you, behind you, at your left, or at your right?"

General Guidelines for training Visual Perspective Taking Skills

The goal of the games is to train the child in its VPT skills. More specifically, the child should learn to identify another person's left, right, front and back. The challenge is two-fold: some of these children already have difficulties identifying their own left and right, and taking the perspective of another person makes the task even more challenging. Therefore, the game should add no additional complexity or other problem solving task, but focus on maintaining a high motivation of the child to keep on training his or her VPT skills. In consultation with the therapist and children, the following requirements were formulated:

1. Difficulty levels should increase progressively through all levels, starting with a very basic level where the orientation of the child and the 'other person' (aka the avatar in the game) is identical.
2. When mistakes are made, immediate feedback should be given, with clear information on the error that has been made.
3. The games should include immediate rewards, and few or no punishments should be given, in order to maintain the child's motivation.
4. The children should be able to play the games by themselves, without the aid of someone else.

During the course of the design process we decided to develop and test two games, each exploiting a different interaction style of the Sifteo Cubes. One game, the Fish Game, is mainly based on the neighboring function of the cubes and offers the advantage that the player always has a visual overview on all cubes involved. The other game, the Penguin Game, uses the shake function, but more importantly, in this case, the cubes are distributed in space, at several meters from each other. The idea is that the player has to move through the physical space, and has to perform bodily actions that are related to the challenge at hand. This might enlighten the mental rotation that has to take place when performing a VPT task. In [17] it was indeed concluded that *"embodied self-rotations, through which we actively imagine ourselves assuming someone else's position in the world can subserve not only reasoning about where objects are in relation to someone else but also how the objects in their environment appear to them."*

Fish Game

The main goal of the Fish Game is to help the fish to collect candy (see Figure 3, top left cube). The fish appears initially on one of the cubes. A bar of bubbles on the cube's display indicates at which side the player should be. The child is instructed to always place itself at the side with the bubbles.

One or more other cubes show a generic shape (circle, square…). When pressing on one of these cubes, a spoken instruction is given by the fish, e.g. *"Put the square at my left side"*. The player then has to "neighbor" this cube at one of the sides of the fish cube. In case this is done correctly, a candy is revealed, and the fish swims toward it. In case of an incorrect response, no candy is gained, and feedback is given, e.g. *"You placed the square at my right side. Please put it at my left side."* The cube with the fish is not allowed to be manipulated. An alarming sound will play when the player moves this cube (detected by the cube's accelerometer). The sixth cube shows a box with all the collected candy.

The Fish Game contains five levels, in increasing complexity. There is a "zero" tutorial level that explains all relevant rules of the game. Only when no mistakes are made, the player moves on to the next level. During the first three levels, the fish is oriented in the same direction as the player. Four cubes have to be positioned around the fish in

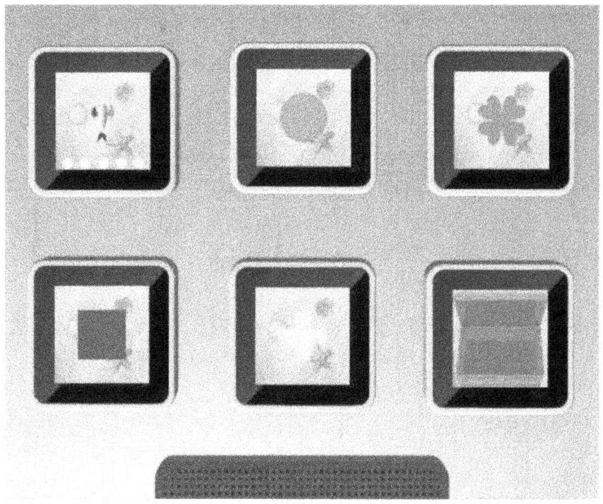

Figure 3 Six cubes are used in the Fish Game. One shows the main character, a fish that has to collect candy. The bubble bar on that cube shows where the player should be located. Four blocks show generic shapes revealing candy when placed at the correct side of the fish' cube. The sixth cube shows a box with all the collected candy.

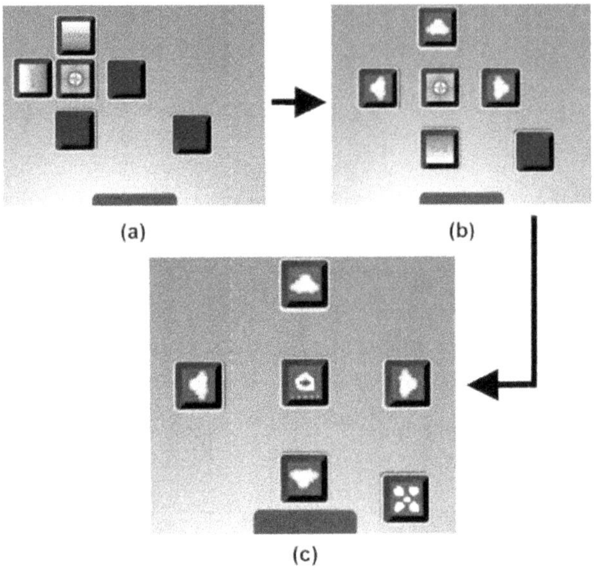

Figure 4 The cubes of the Penguin game are distributed in space in the four directions (north, east, south, west), at several meters from the middle block with the Penguin. The Penguin tells the player where the bird is hiding (e.g. "at my left"). The birds can be frightened away by shaking the correct cube.

the first level, two times two cubes are to be positioned during the second level (only left and right), four times one cube has to be positioned in the third level (left or right). Hence, the difficulty increases in each level since there are less options to exclude in higher levels. In the last two levels, the fish is oriented with its tail towards its previous cube, so differing from the player's orientation. Level 4 tests on front/back discrimination, level 5 on left/right. Hence, in these last two levels we come across the more challenging Visual Perspective Taking through another's person (in this case a fish) eyes.

Penguin Game

The main goal of the Penguin Game is to prevent the birds from stealing the Penguin's fish. To set-up the game, five cubes have to be placed in a cross (see Figure 4). The middle one is the Penguin's cube, the four others have to be placed a few meters away in the four directions (north, east, south, and west). Similar to the row of bubbles in the fish game, the player has to be aligned with the row of snowflakes at one side of penguin's cube. The other four cubes initially show a cloud behind which a pestering bird might be hiding. Then the game can start: the player presses the Penguin cube, and hears an instruction from the Penguin, e.g. "*The bird is hiding in front of me*". The player has to scare away the bird by shaking the correct cube out of the four possible cubes. In case the correct cube is shaken, the cloud will disappear, and the bird will fly away. In the other case, the bird will show up on another cube (the correct one) and steal a fish. A sixth cube shows the total amount of fish. A snowflakes bar on one of the sides of the display indicate at which side the player should be located.

The levels are very similar to the Fish game. This way it is assured that the complexity of the task is identical in each level, and so it allows a fair comparison between both games. The Penguin game has a sixth level though. In this level, the snowflakes bar is positioned at the side pointing to the cube that was last shaken, so it changes after every task. The motivation to include this level is the fact that children are constantly moving around and may arrive from different directions to the cube, ending up at another side.

To conclude, the main difference with the Fish Game is that the player has to move in space, which might be more fun, and more importantly, might encourage the child to perform physical rotations with its own body in order to align with the Penguin (as opposed to mental rotations). On the other hand, the task might be more complex, since the player has no clear overview on all cubes.

Lessons learned

During the formative user tests we made several observations that lead to improvements in the game design:

1. We observed a huge variability in the children's competences. Some children still had difficulties identifying their own left and right, so even at the lowest level, the game was too difficult. We decided to provide an extra cue by coloring the fish' right fin and the penguin's right wing red (see Figure 2).
2. Initial designs made use of 3D characters. However, the clearest view is the top view, so we chose objects that are easily recognizable from the top. This also ensured a clear indication on the object's orientation.
3. The player should always be located at the correct side of the Fish cube or the Penguin cube, indicated by a bubble bar or a snowflakes bar. Certainly in the first levels, where the orientation of the fish or the penguin is similar to the player, this is an extra help.
4. In the Penguin game we initially changed the position of the snowflakes bar, so that it appeared at the side from which the player returned after shaking a cube. We thought this would a more logical approach but it turned out to confuse the player even more, who was expecting the bar to stay at the same side.

EVALUATION

Rationale

In order to evaluate the two games, an experiment was conducted with eight preschoolers (age five years). We wanted to evaluate several aspects. The first question was whether the games are enjoyable and that no obstacles prevented game play. Given the great variability in the children's VPT skills at the age of five [5], some children might find the games too difficult. It was also our aspiration to create games that can be played without assistance, and that a few instructions would suffice in order to be able to play the games. A second question was whether the games yield any learning effect, in other words: do the children's VPT skills improve after playing the games? A third question was what strategies children use when playing the game: Do they profit from the tangibility that the games offer? Are epistemic actions observed? Can we see physically distributed learning in that actions and interpretation coevolve? And are these different for the two games? The final question was whether the children have a preference for one of the games and what motives they might have for this preference.

Methodology
Eight preschoolers participated in the experiments that were conducted in a separate room of their school. None of them participated in the formative tests. After a short introduction by the two experimenters and the goals of the experiment, a pre-test was taken consisting of 10 questions related to VPT (see example in Figure 2). This test was an adaptation of a paper test often used by the psychomotor therapist. Answers were either correct or wrong. The scores would provide insight in the initial level of VPT skills. Then two games were played. In order to compensate for possible ordering effects, four children started with the Fish Game, the other four with the Penguin Game. Each game was explained with the tutorial level (level 0), and help was provided when needed. Then the game was played during 10 minutes without interruption or pauses between the levels, and without any intervention from the experimenter. The number of mistakes were counted, as also the obtained level. Both experimenters observed the children while playing, thereby focusing on the used strategies. After playing the games, a post-test similar to the pre-test was taken in order to investigate a potential learning effect. Note however that we did not include a control group in this

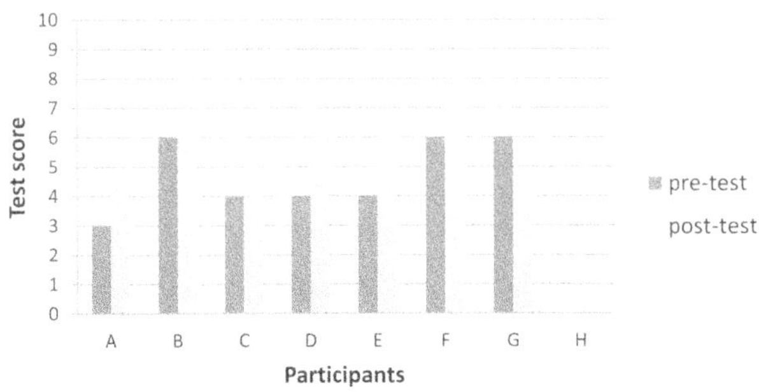

Figure 5 Results for the pre-test and the post-test for all participants. Note that subject H was not able to answer the questions.

study, e.g. with children playing a non-VPT related game between the pre-test and the post-test. So, it cannot be concluded that any statistical effect is induced by the games only. Finally, the children were asked which of the two games they preferred and why.

Results
Figure 5 shows the results of the pre-tests (dark bars). Scores vary from 0/10 (subject H) to 6/10, illustrating a large variety in initial VPT skills. Subject H indicated that he had no idea what the answers should be.

On the other hand, all participants were able to play the games. There were no drop-outs, the children kept on playing in upper concentration during 10 minutes. They gave no indication of boredom nor frustration, even though they had to perform difficult tasks. Figure 6 shows the obtained levels for all participants for both games. Two children completed all levels of one game. There is also a trend that the children were more successful in the second game, which is probably due to a higher acquaintance with the Sifteo cubes and the similar game mechanics in both games. Note also that subject H, who indicated not to be able to do the paper test, was able to reach at least level 4 in our games. We can conclude from these results that both games are playable, regardless the initial VPT ability.

The number of mistakes was very similar for both games. Across all participants, 19% of the instructions yielded an incorrect answer for the Fish game, while this number was 18% for the Penguin game. As also indicated by the children, the games had equal difficulty, even though they have different interaction styles.

A comparison between the results of the pre-test and the post-test revealed a moderate but significant effect (Figure 5). A one-tailed paired t-test revealed a significance difference between the scores ($p = 0.0437\%$). This might imply that the children indeed improved their VPT skills by playing the game, and were able to make the transfer to the paper test. However, as stated before, since no control group was included, this increase might be due to other effects, such as practice effects of the tests.

Observations during the playing confirmed that the children took their time to "think with their body" about the actions they had to perform. In case the fish' or penguin's orientation was different from the players', they tend to spontaneously turn their head or their whole body (in case of the Penguin Game), to align their orientation with that of the avatar. This phenomenon manifested itself more in the Penguin Game than in the Fish Game, so this could be an indication that provoking whole-body action has an advantage. In the Fish Game, children moved cubes around in different positions, before neighboring them to the fish cube. These movements indicate that they spontaneously performed epistemic actions.

No agreement was observed in the children's preference. Three children preferred the Fish Game, because they thought it was easier to play, or for less relevant reasons ("I like candy, so I like the Fish Game more."). Three other children preferred the Penguin Game because they liked moving around. The two remaining children could not make up their mind. This confirms that players should not be treated as a monolithic group and that it might be beneficial to design different games depending on the player type, instead of adopting a one-size-fits-all approach.

DISCUSSION

The results seem to suggest that tangible games do offer several advantages compared to traditional exercises. Even children performing poorly on the paper test were able to complete several levels of the games, thereby confirming that they were able to answer VPT related questions correctly. Although a fair comparison between the number of mistakes on the paper test and those on the games is quite impossible, there is a trend that less mistakes were made when playing the game. This is an encouraging observation, for it might have turned the other way around. Indeed, one could argue that embedding challenging tasks in a game environment adds complexity, since the player should not only focus on the task at hand, but also to other game-related aspects (e.g. knowing which cube to handle, when, and how). An obvious explanation for the better performance with the Sifteo Cubes is the incorporation of feedback in the games. This way children were able to correct their mistakes, a possibility not incorporated in the paper test. A second explanation is the more ecological setting of the game. Instead of having to make judgments based on static drawings on a 2D paper surface, the children operated in a more realistic setting, with 3D objects that were presented in a 3D environment. Note that even the child (participant H) that was unable to perform the paper test, could solve the VPT related questions when playing.

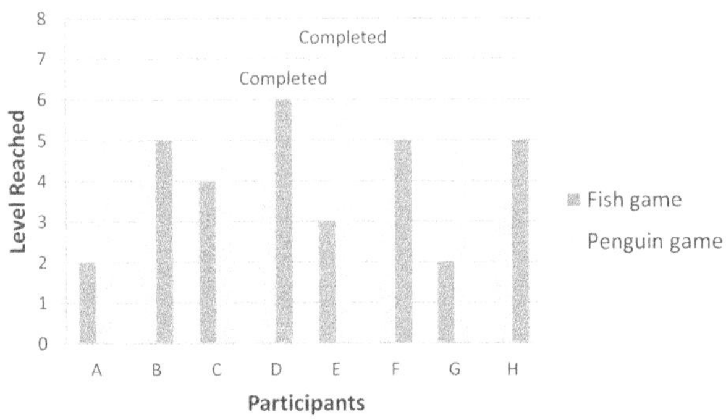

Figure 6 Levels reached after 10 minutes of playing for all participants, and for both games. Subject D completed all levels of the Fish Game (indicated as non-existing level 6), subject E completed all levels of the Penguin Game.

Also the fact that epistemic actions were observed probably contributes to the good performance of the children. In the case of the Penguin Game, such an epistemic action could be the player turning himself in the direction the penguin is looking. This action does not actually bring the player to the correct solution, but lightens the cognitive burden of replacing himself in the place of the penguin. These epistemic actions were used more in the Penguin Game than in the Fish Game, however, the mistake rate is about the same in both games. A possible cause of this is that the player in the Fish Game always has an overview on all cubes. This visual overview is lacking in the Penguin Game, which could counteract the beneficial effect of the epistemic actions. A hybrid approach, which would e.g. include a display with an overview in the Penguin Game, could then combine the best of both worlds [7].

Another encouraging observation were the short-term learning effects. This suggests that the children were able to transfer the skills they learned by playing the games (in a 3D environment) to the tasks at hand on the (2D) paper test. However, we acknowledge that the small sample (8 children) and the lack of a control group necessitates caution with respect to broad claims. More research with more children is necessary to strengthen our findings. In addition, it would be interesting to measure long term effects by allowing the children to play the games regularly during a few weeks. Bigger and more significant effects might be observed then.

CONCLUSION

We developed and tested two games that allow children to train their visual perspective taking skills. Besides the motivating environment that every computer game offers, the games offered manipulations of objects in a 3D world. This enabled epistemic actions, which facilitate thinking and problem solving. All children performed well in the games, although there was a large variety in VPT skills among them. A small but significant learning effect was observed, again revealing the potential of tangible games in learning.

ACKNOWLEDGMENTS

We would like to thank our psychomotor therapist, Sabine Plessers for her valuable input during this study. Her expertise in the domain of visual perspective taking was essential for this work. We are also grateful to the children who participated patiently in this study, and their parents for giving the necessary permissions.

REFERENCES

[1] Antle, A.N. Exploring how children use their hands to think: An embodied interactional analysis. Behaviour & Information Technology 32, 9 (2013), 938–954.

[2] Bruner, J.S. Studies in Cognitive Growth. John Wiley & Sons Inc, 1966.

[3] Fitzmaurice, G.W. Graspable user interfaces. 1996. http://portal.acm.org/citation.cfm?id=925309.

[4] Flavell, J.H. The development of knowledge about visual perception. Nebraska Symposium on Motivation. Nebraska Symposium on Motivation 25, (1977), 43–76.

[5] Frick, A., Möhring, W., and Newcombe, N.S. Picturing perspectives: development of perspective-taking abilities in 4- to 8-year-olds. Developmental Psychology 5, (2014), 386.

[6] Heller, M.D., Roots, K., Srivastava, S., Schumann, J., Srivastava, J., and Hale, T.S. A Machine Learning-Based Analysis of Game Data for Attention Deficit Hyperactivity Disorder Assessment. Games for Health Journal 2, 5 (2013), 291–298.

[7] Horn, M.S., Crouser, R.J., and Bers, M.U. Tangible Interaction and Learning: The Case for a Hybrid Approach. Personal Ubiquitous Comput. 16, 4 (2012), 379–389.

[8] Hunter, S., Kalanithi, J., and Merrill, D. Make a Riddle and TeleStory: Designing Children's Applications for the Siftables Platform. Proceedings of the 9th International Conference on Interaction Design and Children, ACM (2010), 206–209.

[9] Ishii, H. and Ullmer, B. Tangible bits: towards seamless interfaces between people, bits and atoms. Proceedings of the SIGCHI conference on Human factors in computing systems, ACM (1997), 234–241.

[10] Martin, T. A theory of physically distributed learning: How external environments and internal states interact in mathematics learning. Child Development Perspectives 3, 3 (2009), 140–144.

[11] McNeil, N.M. and Uttal, D.H. Rethinking the use of concrete materials in learning: Perspectives from development and education. Child development perspectives 3, 3 (2009), 137–139.

[12] Montessori, M. The montessori method. Transaction Publishers, 2013.

[13] Piaget, J. The Psychology of Intelligence. Routledge, 2001.

[14] Pillias, C., Robert-Bouchard, R., and Levieux, G. Designing Tangible Video Games: Lessons Learned from the Sifteo Cubes. Proceedings of the 32Nd Annual ACM Conference on Human Factors in Computing Systems, ACM (2014), 3163–3166.

[15] Resnick, M., Martin, F., Berg, R., et al. Digital Manipulatives: New Toys to Think with. Proceedings of the SIGCHI Conference on Human Factors in Computing Systems, ACM Press/Addison-Wesley Publishing Co. (1998), 281–287.

[16] Shaer, O. and Hornecker, E. Tangible User Interfaces: Past, Present, and Future Directions. Found. Trends Hum.-Comput. Interact. 3, 1–2 (2010), 1–137.

[17] Surtees, A.D.R., Apperly, I.A., and Samson, D. The use of embodied self-rotation for visual and spatial perspective-taking. Frontiers in Human Neuroscience 7, (2013), 698.

[18] Vanden Abeele, V., Schutter, B., Geurts, L., et al. P-III: A Player-Centered, Iterative, Interdisciplinary and Integrated Framework for Serious Game Design and Development. In S. Wannemacker, S. Vandercruysse and G. Clarebout, eds., Serious Games: The Challenge. Springer Berlin Heidelberg, 2012, 82–86.

[19] Vandermaesen, M., de Weyer, T., Luyten, K., and Coninx, K. PhysiCube: Providing Tangible Interaction in a Pervasive Upper-limb Rehabilitation System. Proceedings of the 8th International Conference on Tangible, Embedded and Embodied Interaction, ACM (2013), 85–92.

[20] Victor, B. A Brief Rant on the Future of Interaction Design. 2011. http://worrydream.com/ABriefRantOnTheFutureOfInteractionDesign/.

Using Video Games to Facilitate Understanding of Attention Deficit Hyperactivity Disorder: A Feasibility Study

Thomas Goldman
Digital Media
Drexel University
Philadelphia, PA, USA
tg439@drexel.edu

Frank Lee
Digital Media
Drexel University
Philadelphia, PA, USA
fjl@drexel.edu

Jichen Zhu
Digital Media
Drexel University
Philadelphia, PA, USA
jichen.zhu@drexel.edu

ABSTRACT

This paper presents an approach for facilitating understanding of Attention Deficit Hyperactivity Disorder (ADHD) through the procedural rhetoric of our persuasive video game *Drawn to Distraction*. Different from realistic simulations, our game is designed to convey a message about the disorder primarily through game mechanics. To test the feasibility of this approach, we conducted a series of studies involving caregivers of ADHD-affected children and the general public. The results, especially in Experiment 3, show promising trends on the feasibility of using persuasive games to promote understanding of psychological disorders.

Author Keywords

Game for Health; Procedural Rhetoric; Persuasive Game; ADHD Caregivers

ACM Classification Keywords

K.8.0 Personal Computing: Games

INTRODUCTION

Understanding psychological disorders can be difficult for those who are not affected by them. This is particularly true for Attention Deficit Hyperactivity Disorder (ADHD). ADHD is currently one of the most controversial psychological disorders in terms of diagnosis and validity [7], though a great deal of scientific research suggests it is a real and non-trivial disorder that may be under-diagnosed in certain populations [3]. This controversy and a related lack of understanding amongst caregivers are perhaps most impactful upon ADHD-affected children, as caregivers can strongly influence quality of life, social activity, and success in school environments [6, 11]. Furthermore, research has linked ADHD symptoms to greater parental stress, and parental stress to negative parental practices [11, 10]. To break this chain, possibly improving life quality of ADHD-affected children, it is useful to research effective strategies to facilitate understanding of ADHD, especially for caregivers.

CHI PLAY '14, October 19 - 22 2014, Toronto, ON, Canada

http://dx.doi.org/10.1145/2658537.2658707

A key challenge for caregivers is understanding the behavioral symptoms of ADHD patients from an *internal perspective*. Recent studies have shown that video games may be a promising tool for facilitating understanding through role-taking and other psychological impacts on players [2, 1, 9]. While it is possible to describe internal, psychological perspectives through media such as written text, image, and speech, video games offer a new way to involve players through interaction.

This paper presents our approach for studying how serious video games can be used to facilitate understanding of psychological disorders such as ADHD. In particular, we use Bogost's framework of *procedural rhetoric*, that is, the practice of using processes persuasively [5], in order to foster ADHD caregiver understanding. Based on research of symptoms and diagnosis, we identified a certain message (rhetoric point) about the disorder that we intended to convey. We then iteratively developed the message along with a persuasive game called *Drawn to Distraction*. To evaluate the game's effectiveness, we conducted a pilot feasibility study consisting of three experiments recruiting both caregivers of ADHD-diagnosed children and non-caregiver adults familiar with video games.

Our results showed that non-game playing populations had difficulty with our current design. Scope may have limited our ability to appeal to populations unfamiliar with video games. Game-familiar adults in both categories responded in a more intended manner, acknowledging our intent to facilitate understanding of ADHD's psychological effects through game mechanics.

In the rest of the paper, we first present our theoretical framework on procedural rhetoric and challenges of understanding ADHD. We then describe the design rationale and procedural rhetoric for *Drawn to Distraction*. Next, we present our design for the feasibility study and present our results. Finally, we conclude with suggestions for future work.

BACKGROUND AND RELATED WORK

This section presents a review of literature on the major concepts and research forming the background of our work.

The Challenge in Understanding ADHD

Misunderstanding related to ADHD may start with its title, which was created when the disorder was believed to be primarily of attention. However, research has shown ADHD to be a problem more of *self-regulation* [3]. Many symptoms of ADHD, such as impulsiveness or inattention, are also present in unaffected individuals, creating a commonality between the affected and unaffected. As a result, ADHD patients, who suffer from a much greater intensity of multiple symptoms over a long period of time, are often misunderstood as those who simply can't pay attention. Because of this commonality, ADHD's title, and other factors such as controversial over-diagnosis, ADHD remains misunderstood by a majority of the population [7].

This misunderstanding may cause increased negative perceptions of individuals affected by ADHD [8], leading to greater caregiver stress [12]. In turn, research has established a link between high levels of parental stress and dysfunctional parenting, including increased use of negative parental practices due to lowered perceived efficacy [11]. Dysfunctional parenting has further been linked to child underachievement [10], showing a vicious cycle for ADHD children where ADHD negatively influences caregivers, and caregiver stress can negatively influence children. On the other hand, positive perceptions of ADHD have been linked to a lessened impact of ADHD-related behavior on caregivers and positive relationships with children [12]. Hence, improving understanding of ADHD, especially amongst caregivers, may help to break the cycle and improve quality of life for each involved party.

Procedural Rhetoric

Procedural rhetoric, a term coined by Ian Bogost, describes the practice of "using processes persuasively" [5, p.28]. Compared to traditional forms of rhetoric such as speech, writing, and imagery, procedural rhetoric lends itself particularly well to making claims about *how things work* by highlighting the steps of a process through simulation. For example, Bogost analyzed Molleindustria's *The McDonald's Game* where players make difficult decisions about how to run the business. For example, will they choose to preserve rainforest but decrease availability of cow pastures? Will they bribe officials to secure profits? By letting players experience intertwined processes, the game embodies "a procedural rhetoric about the necessity of corruption in the global fast food business, and the overwhelming temptation of greed, which leads to more corruption" (p.31).

Bogost further unpacks a number of persuasive games in the domains of politics, advertising and learning. Like all rhetoric, procedural rhetoric and the video games that embody it are designed for persuasion. This makes them a potentially powerful tool to cause change in players.

Related Work

A particularly active area in the realm of representing psychological disorders through media is virtual schizophrenia simulation. In the 1980s, researchers used audio recordings to simulate auditory hallucinations. In the 1990s, head-mounted displays and 3D virtual worlds were developed to simulate visual hallucinations as well [4]. More recently, other types of simulations were created such as a multi-sensory interactive film in 2007 [13]. The intention of these simulations is to provide a greater understanding of schizophrenia for those not affected. They can show how overwhelming schizophrenia can be, potentially increasing the level of support provided by a caregiver [13]. Compared to these approaches, we intend to focus on representing ADHD symptoms through procedural rhetoric, an *interactive process*, rather than purely audio or visual representation.

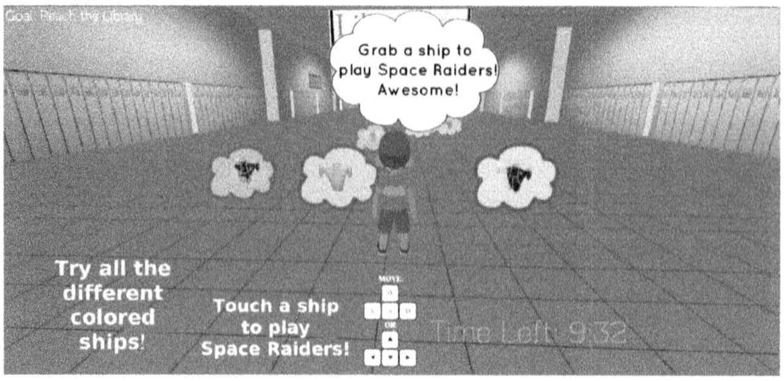

Figure 1. Distraction Objects in the Main Gameplay

DESIGN RATIONALE

Our work aims to convey some aspects of the psychological effects of ADHD through procedural rhetoric. In other words, we intend to recreate the "feeling" of ADHD through game mechanics. In essence, we are attempting to recreate the psychological processes of ADHD through the technical processes that affect a video game player.

It is important to note that our goal is NOT to recreate a *simulation* of ADHD in a realistic and comprehensive manner. Instead, we aim to convey a specific message about the internal condition of ADHD-affected children to their caregivers and the general public. As in other forms of rhetoric, this means we may emphasize certain aspects of ADHD while down-playing certain other aspects in order to make the point clear.

Intended Procedural Rhetoric

Based on current scientific theory and understanding, some of which is described above, ADHD can result in a psychological weakening to resistance of more immediately rewarding activities while individuals attempt to complete less-stimulating tasks. For example, while completing chores such as organizing the room, children affected by ADHD may be increasingly drawn to toys within the surrounding environment [3].

Therefore we developed the following message to be conveyed through procedural rhetoric: *As a result of ADHD, affected individuals have an increased drive to engage in immediately rewarding activities, despite knowledge of their long term harm.*

It was our intent to convey the above message through gameplay, in order to facilitate players' understanding of the related real-world behavior caused by the disorder. Our primary target audience was caregivers of ADHD-affected children, such as family members. However, we would also like to use our game to broaden understanding of ADHD amongst the general public.

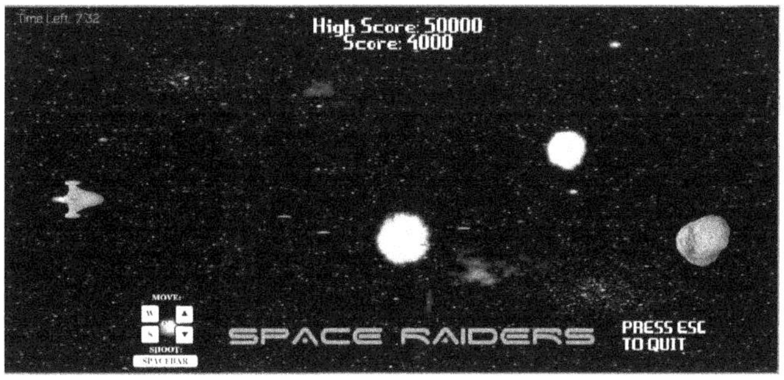

Figure 2. Mini-Game: Space Raiders

Figure 3. Distractions with a Greater Intensity

Game Design of Drawn to Distraction

We developed a third-person 3D video game called *Drawn to Distraction*. To our target audience of caregivers, we intended to convey that when children with ADHD fail to perform a seemingly simple yet unstimulating task, such as a homework assignment, the reason may be influential symptoms of ADHD rather than intentional negligence.

To convey our message, core game mechanics were designed to attract players toward options with immediate reward, despite knowledge that these actions would be harmful in the long term. In other words, we designed the game to cause frustration or mental exhaustion in our players, just as an ADHD-affected child completing a task might become frustrated or mentally exhausted due to the psychological effects of the disorder [3].

Players of *Drawn to Distraction* take on the role of a child whose goal is to reach a school library at the end of a linear, winding hallway. To win the game, the player must control the player character's (PC) movements and reach this library within 10 minutes of in-game time or he will not have enough time to study for an impending test. The player is informed by the game that he may not have enough time to study if he gets distracted along the way. Through an on-screen timer, the player can make a willful choice in how he uses his time. As our target audience may not be very familiar with computer games, we designed the control scheme to be simple, using the arrow keys and spacebar or an attached controller.

There are several elements in the game designed to gear the player toward distraction. First, we intentionally made the PC move very slowly, thus making movement toward the library a long and tedious endeavor. A key design challenge we faced was *how to make visible the condition of ADHD to people who are not affected by it*. By making this game design decision, we hoped to "translate" the mental exhaustion that children with ADHD feel into a similar reaction within ordinary players during certain tasks that may seem relatively effortless to the unaffected.

Second, we constantly create dynamic thought bubbles - narrating the PC's nagging inner thoughts - above the character (Fig. 1). These thoughts convey the PC's desire to play a game called *Space Raiders* (see Fig. 2). As the game progresses, the thought bubbles appear more frequently, making it increasingly difficult to stick to the main goal and avoid thinking about in-game distractions (details below).

Third, the main distractions in the game are manifested as miniature spaceships that appear out of thin air, filling up the area in which the player has to move. As the PC moves further through the hallway, these spaceships also appear more frequently. Once the PC touches one of them, the player is transported into a mini-game called *Space Raiders*, a favorite of the PC. In it, the player earns a separate score by shooting incoming asteroids. In contrast to the bland appearance and slow pace of the main game goal (within the hallway), *Space Raiders* is designed to be colorful, fast and more engaging. *Space Raiders* offers the player an immediately rewarding activity but distracts from the main goal of reaching the library. The player leaves the mini-game by being hit by an asteroid or by pressing the ESC key, resetting the *Space Raiders* score.

In addition, playing *Space Raiders* causes *Drawn to Distraction*'s main timer to tick down much faster than normal. Although we leave the timer visible throughout the mini-game, we did not stress this fact. This design decision was made to echo how an ADHD-affected child affected can easily lose track of time and fail a task due to distraction.

Therefore, the *conflict* in *Drawn to Distraction* is between short-term and long-term reward. The only way to win the game is to move to the library and avoid touching distractions for around 6-7 minutes, a relatively long time for an unstimulating task. As mentioned earlier, distractions become harder to avoid over time. This in-game conflict is designed to mirror the real-world conflict faced by ADHD-affected individuals while completing tasks that are not immediately rewarding.

Drawn to Distraction has two outcomes. The player can reach the library before the timer runs out and the PC receives an A grade on his test. Alternatively, when time is up, the game will immediately end with a poor grade of D+. Both outcomes were intended to cause frustration in the player. In the former case, the player likely endured a lengthy and unstimulating experience. In the latter case, he will likely become frustrated from failure, especially if he was only distracted for a short time. These outcomes could potentially express the psychological feelings that ADHD-affected children face in their everyday lives.

Through the above game mechanics, we intend to convey the message *"As a result of ADHD, affected individuals have an*

No.	Question
1	*In your opinion, how aware are ADHD-diagnosed individuals in terms of how ADHD affects their actions?*
2	*How well do you feel you understand the effect that ADHD has on an individual?*
3	*How much do you feel ADHD changes an individual's day-to-day decision-making process?*
4	*How much ability does an individual affected by ADHD have to change their own behavior patterns?*
5*	*How personally do you take it when the individual under your care does not respond to an immediate request (i.e. does not immediately complete chores, homework, etc.)?*
6	*How effective do you think a video game could be at expressing a message to the player and fostering his/her understanding of real world issues?*

Table 1. Survey Questions Used in Experiment 1 & 2 (*Question 5 only used in Experiment)

	M		SD			
Question	Pre	Post	Pre	Post	t(6)	p
1	4.86	5.14	1.86	1.95	-0.795	0.457
2	5.00	4.71	2.08	2.36	1.000	0.356
3	5.71	5.29	1.25	1.38	1.441	0.200
4	4.86	5.00	1.57	2.08	-0.311	0.766
5	4.72	5.43	1.80	1.51	-1.000	0.356
6	5.86	5.00	1.07	1.41	1.867	0.111

Table 2. Mean and Standard Deviation on Questionnaire from Caregivers in Experiment 1.

increased drive to engage in immediately rewarding activities, despite knowledge of their long term harm."

EXPERIMENT 1

We designed a series of experiments to 1) test how effectively our procedural rhetoric conveyed the intended message and 2) to collect preliminary data related to the use of procedural rhetoric to facilitate understanding of psychological disorders. More specifically, our hypothesis is that *after playing our game, participants will change their understanding of ADHD and will think favorably of our approach.*

Participants

The first experiment group consisted of caregivers of individuals affected by ADHD (N = 7). Seven caregivers were recruited through a Philadelphia-area psychologist as volunteers and were not compensated financially. The participants' ages ranged from 21 to 33, with an average age of 27.5. Amongst them, one participant spent 15+ hrs/week playing video games, and a second participant 3-6 hrs/week. The remaining 5 participants had no video game experience.

Procedure

After a short demographic survey, participants answered six questions on a 7-point Likert scale (Pre), in which 1 represented the most negative end of answers such as "zero understanding" or "zero effectiveness" and 7 represented the most positive end. Next, participants played *Drawn to Distraction* under the observation of an investigator. Once a participant finished the game with either outcome (i.e. reached the library or time ran out), she then completed the same six questions given previously to measure change in attitude and understanding (Post). These questions, which focus on understanding of ADHD aspects, are given in Table 1.

Results

Table 2 summarizes the results of pair-wise t-tests on the Pre and Post answers of the questionnaires from participants. Our hope was that there would be meaningful change in their answers after having played *Drawn to Distraction*. Unfortunately, as can be seen, none of the changes from Pre to Post were significant at alpha level 0.05.

One critical issue that we believe led to the lack of positive results in Experiment 1 was how most caregiver participants had little to no experience with video games. Only one participant, whom had most video game experience, reached the game's successful outcome. All other participants ran out of time, some within the distraction mini-game, and others by playing the distraction game for too long. No participant quit before reaching either outcome, but some participants exhibited confusion in what they were supposed to do within the game despite on-screen text explanations. We believe that in order for our message to be expressed, the player may need a certain level of familiarity with how video games generally work. This issue led us to carry out Experiment 2 with a population that was more familiar with and experienced in playing video games.

EXPERIMENT 2

To address lack of video game experience as a potential obstacle to *Drawn to Distraction's* procedural rhetoric in Experiment 1, we carried out a second experiment using the exact same procedure as the first but with a participant group more familiar and experienced with video games.

Participants

The second experiment consisted of thirteen undergraduate students recruited from the Digital Media Program at Drexel University. Within this group, all but two of the participants knew a family member or friend diagnosed with ADHD. All participants had significant exposure to video games, with video game playing time averaging 3-6 hours per week. Their average age was 19.8.

Procedure

The procedure in Experiment 2 followed the exact procedure as Experiment 1. However, we removed question 5 from the pre/post questionnaire because it was designed for caregivers and did not apply to this population.

Results

Table 3 lists the results of the pair-wise t-tests on the Pre and Post answers of the questionnaires from participants. Because question 5 was not given, it is missing from the table. We preserved question numbering to mirror Table 2 for ease of

	M		SD			
Question	Pre	Post	Pre	Post	t(12)	p
1	4.15	4.31	1.57	1.25	-0.485	0.636
2	3.85	4.31	1.57	1.03	-1.032	0.323
3	4.77	4.69	1.09	0.95	0.433	0.673
4	3.62	4.15	1.33	1.35	-1.849	0.089*
6	5.92	5.69	0.06	0.95	0.898	0.387

Table 3. Mean and Standard Deviation on Questionnaire from Students in Experiment 2.

comparison. As can be seen, none of the changes from pre to post were significant at alpha level 0.05.

However, we do see a hint of a positive change at least in one of the questions. At $p < 0.1$, question 4 shows moderate significance at $p = 0.089$, suggesting that after having played the game, participants were more likely to believe that an individual with ADHD had the ability to change their behavior.

ANALYSIS AND DISCUSSION

Our quantitative results from Experiment 1 and 2 are inconclusive. However, qualitative results from both experiments seem to support that we at least partially succeeded in conveying our message through procedural rhetoric. The open-ended comments in both experiments acknowledged that *Drawn to Distraction* was meant to send a message, and players from both groups (though primarily the non-caregiver group) understood that message. In some comments related to our game design, participants pointed out that the message about ADHD was derived from a comparison between an unstimulating main goal to a more stimulating distraction mini-game, which aligned with our intent.

Lack of video game experience appeared to be an immediate and significant factor for our caregiver participants. Some caregivers appeared confused about on-screen prompts and the game's main goal. We believe that this lack of experience significantly affected their responses. For the two caregiver participants with video game experience, including the only one who completed the game, both responded very favorably in terms of enjoyment.

In their open-ended comments, one participant suggested that the game should be "more comprehensive" because she "felt like [she] was lost." Another participant liked that there was a goal involved for the player. A third participant said she enjoyed how the game was a challenge for her as someone diagnosed with ADHD herself. We believe that this is an indication that our game had some success in capturing the psychological effects of ADHD.

In contrast, our non-caregiver student participants were familiar with games and responded well to the procedural rhetoric of our game. They expressed that it was interesting to turn a psychological problem into a physical one, and the game made them think about ADHD in a new way. They all indicated an understanding of the game's main goal without verbal explanation from researchers. However, this experience also turned out to be partially detrimental to our procedural rhetoric. Multiple students responded that they found distractions unappealing because they knew these objects would cause failure. Some of them also said they wished we could make our point in less time, and that there should be more fun activities besides the *Space Raiders* mini-game. One student even said that as a game player he tends to go against direction, so guidance toward distraction had the opposite effect. There appears to be a fine line between directing certain video game players toward an action and pushing them away from it entirely.

We noted that most participants believed ADHD to be a disorder primarily affecting focus and attention before engaging in our study. Because our game focuses on these common symptoms, it makes it more difficult to fully assess the effect of our approach. Still, a game such as *Drawn to Distraction* may have a place in attempting to replicate the feeling of already understood notions for greater empathy.

Additionally, most of our main questionnaire items may not have been appropriate for our specific purpose, as they were focused on general understanding of ADHD concepts. On the contrary, we wanted to send a message about a very specific aspect of ADHD. We believe our questionnaire items should have been focused more intently on the concept of our procedural rhetoric. This led us to Experiment 3.

EXPERIMENT 3

In this experiment, we sought to address our concerns with previous questionnaires. We revised our questions to focus more closely on the intended procedural rhetoric.

Participants

In this experiment, we recruited eight undergraduate and graduate Computer Science students at Drexel University ranging in age from 20 to 29, with an average age of 23.0. They all have substantial previous video game experience.

Procedure

The procedure followed the exact procedure as Experiments 1 and 2, but with a revised questionnaire as provided in Table 4. The responses also use a 7-point Likert scale, ranging from "entirely disagree" (1) to "entirely agree" (7).

Results

Table 5 lists the results of the pair-wise t-tests on questionnaire answers from pre and post. As can be seen, questions (1), (3), and (6) were found to be significant at alpha level = 0.05. First, this indicates that our concern about question quality was valid, and second, we feel that it also shows *Drawn to Distraction* successfully conveyed the intended procedural rhetoric to participants. In addition, question 7, while not significant at alpha level 0.05, is moderately significant at $p < 0.1$, at least hinting that participants believed video games could be effective at facilitating understanding of psychological disorders. In addition, it is notable that questions (1), (3), and (6), those in which we found significant change, were questions dealing with empathy for people affected by ADHD. This was significant in that the core procedural rhetoric of *Drawn to Distraction* was designed to increase player empathy/understanding of people affected by ADHD.

No.	Question
1	*I understand what it feels like to be affected by ADHD.*
2	*I understand the behavior exhibited by those affected by ADHD.*
3	*I understand the frustration that can be felt by those affected by ADHD.*
4	*I feel it is more challenging for ADHD-affected individuals to complete long-term goals.*
5	*I understand why ADHD-affected individuals might neglect long-term goals in favor of more immediately rewarding actions.*
6	*I understand the impact that ADHD has on an individual's time management skills.*
7	*I feel a video game can be effective at increasing understanding of psychological disorders.*

Table 4. Survey Questions Used in Experiment 3

	M		SD			
Question	Pre	Post	Pre	Post	t(7)	p
1	3.00	4.25	1.20	1.04	-2.546	0.038**
2	4.50	4.75	0.76	1.04	-0.798	0.451
3	4.75	5.63	0.89	0.92	-2.497	0.041**
4	5.00	5.13	1.41	1.25	-0.552	0.598
5	5.25	5.00	0.71	1.07	0.798	0.451
6	5.00	5.50	1.20	0.93	-2.646	0.033**
7	5.25	6.00	1.49	0.93	-2.049	0.08*

Table 5. Mean and Standard Deviation on Questionnaire from Students in Experiment 3.

CONCLUSION AND FUTURE WORK

We designed and developed *Drawn to Distraction*, a serious game that uses procedural rhetoric to facilitate understanding of ADHD. Instead of a realistic simulation of the disorder, as in many related projects, our game was designed to convey a message through gameplay. To test our approach, we conducted a series of studies on two populations. The results, especially Experiment 3, show promising trends on the feasibility of using persuasive games to promote understanding of psychological disorders.

There were multiple limitations of our studies. First, due to small sample size, our study does not offer conclusive evidence. In future work, we intend to recruit a larger number of participants. Second, our questionnaires used in Experiments 1 and 2 focused too heavily on general, factual-knowledge about ADHD. However, as indicated by the results of Experiment 3, a revised questionnaire that focused on empathy showed great promise. For future studies, we suggest using a more empathy-based instrument.

ACKNOWLEDGEMENT

The authors would like to thank Dr. Jenny Starosta and Dr. Connor Kerns for their help in developing our study, in addition to helping us with participant recruitment.

REFERENCES

1. Bailenson, J., Baughman, S., and Rosenberg, R. Virtual Superheroes: Using Superpowers in Virtual Reality to Encourage Prosocial Behavior. *PLoS ONE 8*, 11 (2013), e55003.
2. Banakou, D., Groten, R., and Slater, M. Social Impacts of Computing: Codes of Professional Ethics. *PNAS 110*, 31 (2013), 12846–12851.
3. Barkley, R. *Taking Charge of ADHD: The Complete Authoritative Guide for Parents, 3rd Ed.* Guilford Press, 2013.
4. Barley, E., Clement, S., Thornicroft, G., and Shuntaro, A. The simulation of hallucinations to reduce the stigma of schizophrenia: A systematic review. *Schizophrenia Research 133*, 1 (2011), 8–16.
5. Bogost, I. *Persuasive Games: The Expressive Power of Videogames*. MIT Press, 2007.
6. Clare, L., Harborne, A., and Wolpert, M. Making Sense of ADHD: A Battle for Understanding? Parents Views of Their Children Being Diagnosed with ADHD. *Clinical Child Psychology and Psychiatry 9*, 3 (2004), 327–339.
7. Fine, M., Frigerio, A., and Montali, L. Attention deficit/hyperactivity disorder blame game: A study on the positioning of professionals, teachers and parents. *Health (London) 17*, 6 (2013), 584–604.
8. Hallowell, E. *Driven to Distraction (Revised): Recognizing and Coping with Attention Deficit Disorder*. Anchor Books, 2011.
9. Heeter, C., Lee, M., and Peng, W. The Effects of a Serious Game on Role-Taking and Willingness to Help. *Journal of Communication 60*, 4 (2010), 723–742.
10. Marton, I., Rogers, M., Tannock, R., and Wiener, J. Supportive and Controlling Parental Involvement as Predictors of Childrens Academic Achievement: Relations to Childrens ADHD Symptoms and Parenting Stress. *School Mental Health 1*, 2 (2009), 89–102.
11. Pimentel, M., Santos, V., Vale, M. C., and Vieira-Santos, S. Mothers of children with attention deficit/hyperactivity disorder: relationship among parenting stress, parental practices and child behavior. *ADHD Attention Deficit and Hyperactivity Disorders 3*, 1 (2011), 61–88.
12. Podolski, C., and Nigg, J. Parent stress and coping in relation to child ADHD severity and associated child disruptive behavior problems. *Journal of Clinical Child Psychology 30*, 4 (2001), 503–513.
13. Tabar, P. Mindstorm: simulating psychosis. A new virtual reality experience depicts hallucinations in 3-D. *Behavioral Healthcare 27*, 10 (2007), 31.

Instructional Objectives to Core-Gameplay: A Serious Game Design Technique

Joshua Hall
School of EECS
QLD University of Technology
Brisbane, Australia
joshua.hall@qut.edu.au

Peta Wyeth
School of EECS
QLD University of Technology
Brisbane, Australia
peta.wyeth@qut.edu.au

Daniel Johnson
School of EECS
QLD University of Technology
Brisbane, Australia
dm.johnson@qut.edu.au

ABSTRACT
This paper explores a gap within serious game design research. That gap is the ambiguity surrounding the process of aligning the instructional objectives of serious games with their core-gameplay i.e. the moment-to-moment activity that is the core of player interaction. We propose a core-gameplay focused design framework that can work alongside existing, more broadly focused serious games design frameworks. The framework utilises an inquiry-based approach that allows the serious game designer to use key questions as a means of clearly connecting instructional objectives to core-gameplay. The paper describes the use of this design framework in the context of a small section of gameplay from an educational game currently in development. This demonstration of the framework demonstrates how instructional objectives can be embedded into a serious games core-gameplay.

Author Keywords
Game Design; Gameplay; Instructional Objectives; Human Computer Interaction; Serious Games.

ACM Classification Keywords
K.8.0. Personal Computing: General – *games.* K.3.1. Computers and Education: General.

INTRODUCTION
Designing educational games can be a complex and challenging endeavor. The challenge comes from finding a balance between achieving player engagement and meeting learning outcomes [31]. Failure in finding this balance can result in a game becoming "chocolate-dipped broccoli" [5] i.e. forcing the integration of educational tasks with game design in the hope that it can be awkwardly molded into an engaging experience.

CHI PLAY 2014, October 19–October 22, 2014, Toronto, Ontario, Canada.

ACM 978-1-4503-2473-1/14/04...$15.00.
http://dx.doi.org/10.1145/2658537.2658696

There are a number of educational game design frameworks that can assist with the design of educational games [2,6,13,30]. These frameworks offer various guidelines and structured processes to ensure developers make informed pedagogical decisions when creating educational games. The common theme with these frameworks is the importance of clearly defined learning objectives. Whilst these frameworks are useful in guiding the entire game design and development cycle, there exists a common gap with respect to the translation of high-level guidelines and criteria into practical game design elements. The gap appears with the design of gameplay – that is the challenges faced and actions performed to achieve the goals of a game [1]. More specifically the issue resides within the design of *core-gameplay* i.e. the moment-to-moment activity that is the core of player interaction. The core-gameplay should align with the learning content to ensure maximal learning and engagement [14]. However, there seems to be no clear guidance on how to systematically approach and produce good design decisions for the purposes of learning. There are some frameworks that have provided useful matrices designed to highlight similarities between learning outcomes and types of core-gameplay [3,11,13,26]. However, the connection between instructional objectives and core-gameplay design, i.e., how gameplay can be intentionally, systematically and methodically designed to meet the learning objective, remains ambiguous.

A design framework is required that can work alongside existing educational game design frameworks, and provide additional support in guiding designers to create core-gameplay that is based on clearly defined instructional objectives. Using this framework can clearly identify how and why educational games will meet the desired learning outcomes. The potential of educational games is in its ability to illustrate educational content and harness motivational characteristics of the player. The framework presented provides a method for systematically aligning core-gameplay.

This paper is a *design exploration* grounded in the field of game design, education and human-computer interaction. We outline techniques for designing core-gameplay and provide details on the process that links core-gameplay interactivity to specific instructional objectives.

The resultant framework is presented in the context of a small section of gameplay from an educational game currently in development. The design method aims to bring clarity to the process of identifying and molding game activities that align with desired learning outcomes for the player. In turn, it is intended that this knowledge will contribute to the wider educational games industry in their desire to build effective and engaging serious games.

LEARNING FROM GAMEPLAY

Serious games are digital games that have been designed to allow users to learn or demonstrate skills, knowledge and/or behaviors that have value beyond the game itself [19]. One of the most-powerful characteristics that digital games can bring to learning is the ability to increase motivation to engage with learning content [23]. Designing games to support autonomy, competence, relatedness [9] and Flow [8] can help facilitate enjoyment, ongoing gameplay [23,28] and consequently result in meaningful learning outcomes. With a pedagogical perspective, Habgood and Ainsworth [14] recommend that harnessing the motivational pull of digital games for learning can be achieved by tightly coupling the learning content with the core mechanics i.e. the series of mechanisms that are designed to be repeatedly used during gameplay. Evidence of this approach has shown that learning content coupled with core mechanics can create more effective learning outcomes [14]. Serious games are a valuable tool within a larger program containing a range of instructional techniques and tools [15].

Serious games can be used to facilitate a number of different pedagogical approaches such as constructivism, constructionism, situated cognition, deduction and hypothesis testing, complex concepts, abstract thinking, and visual and spatial processing [12]. Serious games also facilitate a number of different types of learning outcomes. In a systematic literature review of the evidence on serious games, Connolly et al. [7] categorised the behavioral and learning outcomes of serious games as affective and motivational, behaviour change, knowledge acquisition /content understanding, motor skills, and perceptual and cognitive, physiological and social/soft skill outcomes. This paper primarily discusses the design of games that have the goal of behavioural change and knowledge acquisition /content understanding.

Transfer of knowledge is based on the relationship between a person's sensing and memory systems. Short-term memory receives instructional content via the senses, is then processed by working memory and is potentially stored in long-term memory [22]. The qualities and design of the instructional content will determine if that new knowledge will be assimilated with existing knowledge (meaningfully) or will only exist as a separate concept (rote) in long-term memory [4].

The benefit to knowledge being learned meaningfully is that it is stored in long-term memory for longer and has potential to be used in further learning or problem solving contexts i.e. used outside of the learning context in real life [22]. These meaningful qualities consist of conceptually clear learning material, existing relevant prior knowledge to facilitate assimilation, and internal motivation to learn [22].

INSTRUCTIONAL OBJECTIVES

There is a need to understand how people learn in meaningful ways and it is necessary to examine how to create appropriate instructional objectives to meet this aim. Instructional objectives are statements that clearly outline intended instructional outcomes [18] and designing clear instructional objectives is an essential step when creating effective educational experiences [20]. Instructional objectives should outline three specific qualities that describe the outcome of the learning experience: performance, condition, and criterion. Creating statements that include these qualities starts by answering a series of questions.

- What should the learner be able to do? (Performance)

  E.g., *the student will be able to ride a bike*

- Under what conditions do you want the learner to be able to do it? (Conditions)

  E.g., *whilst in slippery conditions* [the student will be able to ride a bike]

- How well must it be done? (Criterion)

  E.g., [whilst in slippery conditions the student will be able to ride a bike] *for 5 minutes without falling over*

Based on these questions an instructional objective could be *"whilst in slippery conditions the learner must ride a bike for five minutes without falling over."*

During the serious game design process many instructional objectives might be formulated. However, not all objectives may be incorporated into one game experience. The core-gameplay framework offers designers a way to identify, synthesise and embed key instructional objectives within core-gameplay i.e. identifying instructional objectives that can be transformed into interesting choices and engaging interaction sequences.

SERIOUS GAME DESIGN FRAMEWORKS

Within a serious games context, motivation to play may be determined by the way the game's core mechanic links to the educational purposes of a game [14]. There are a number of educational game design frameworks that can assist with designing educational games and gameplay with guidelines, mapping tools and tables.

Some design frameworks take a holistic approach, encompassing many different elements that aim to guide the design of the entire game from start to finish [2,6,13,30]. These game design frameworks offer various guidelines and structured processes to ensure developers make informed pedagogical decisions when creating educational games.

Other gameplay frameworks provide useful matrices that highlight similarities between learning outcomes and types of gameplay as defined by genre [11,25,26]. The mapping of learning objectives to game elements during the design has been explored in research using pedagogical foundations such as Bloom's revised taxonomy [16] as a lens to see how different game elements can be viewed in regards to the cognitive processes that occur during gameplay [26]. A typical gap in all these frameworks is the justification and reasoning behind the mapping of desired learning objectives to the designed gameplay in order to enable the player to reach those objectives.

The Learning Mechanic to Game Mechanic (LM-GM) framework [3] aims to address this gap by mapping learning content elements to elements within game mechanics. Applying this framework to the analysis of educational games helps to understand the relationship between learning objectives and gameplay. However, ambiguity remains in understanding how to design *core gameplay*, defined as the moment-to-moment activity within the game, to meet learning objectives. With applied design in mind, further investigation and clarity is required to ensure the core gameplay is guided by the desired learning outcomes.

CORE-GAMEPLAY AND INTERACTION MODELS

Gameplay fundamentally consists of two components: the challenges that a player must face arriving at the objective of the game, and the action that the player is permitted to take to address these challenges [1]. There is a close relationship between the gameplay within the game and its core mechanics, with the core mechanics being the "data and algorithms that precisely define the games central rules and internal operations" [1].

Interpretations of the precise nature of game mechanics vary across the academic and game design literature [1,3,17,27]. Sicart [27] discussed different types of game mechanics such as core, primary and secondary mechanics. The core mechanics can often be the combination of various activities that are repeatedly used to progress towards a rewarding end state. The experience that emerges from repeatedly interacting with the core mechanics is viewed as core-gameplay.

Understanding the interaction loop that occurs during the moment-to-moment experiences within the game is required to design core-gameplay. A common framework for dissecting interaction into stages is Norman's Seven Stages of Action [21]. The cycle can be used to understand the stages that occur leading up to the execution of an action (feed forward) and the impact of the action (feedback) [21]. An important way to use stages of action as design aids can be to base questions around each step in the interaction cycle e.g. (Goal) "What do I want to accomplish?", (Specify) "What can I do?", (Perceive) "What happened?" [21].

The answers to questions such as these can provide a useful insight into how to design activities to meet predefined principles and guidelines e.g. Norman's Seven Fundamental Design Principles of discoverability, feedback, conceptual model, affordances, signifiers, mapping and constraints [21]. It is important to note that within the Seven Stages of Action there may be numerous sequences of interactions that occur before the original goal is met. In the context of a game example, a player may start by heading towards their goal of saving the princess, which can be achieved through the gameplay of defeating enemies leaping gaps. However, it is not until a deep understanding of core-gameplay is explained (e.g., jumping on top of enemies to kill them) that the Seven Stages of Action become an invaluable tool to explain what the player needs to do, what they have done, and how the system should respond.

It is important to understand that more than one core-gameplay interaction may occur in parallel or sequentially. It is during these moments that higher order cognitive processes may be facilitated such as analysis or evaluation [16]. For example, identifying (pointing out) threats, may transition into evaluative interactions (triaging threats) by attending to them in order of severity.

Whilst the Seven Stages of Action can help to understand the moment-to-moment interaction, the aim is to develop a game design process. Merging an understanding of interaction and core-gameplay into a framework allows the design of both. The elements used within this framework are based around the same interaction cycle found in the Seven Stages of Action; however, the language used speaks more clearly to the design of core-gameplay.

The constructed framework (see Figure 1) focuses on designing the elements of goals, choice, action, rules, and feedback. These essential elements of gameplay, game mechanics and the interaction cycle can be manipulated and sequenced by designers to form core-gameplay.

The framework works on the basis that players are presented with a goal, which involves a choice to be acted upon in order to progress towards their objective. Based on the player's previous knowledge and skill, the player determines the correct action to take and performs it. That action is evaluated by the system's rules and feedback is then sent back to the player. The player then interprets the feedback and potentially learns to adjust any further decisions made when presented with similar choices. The design of these qualities will determine if the player can utilise this new knowledge beyond the game-based situation.

The strength of the analysed gameplay is its relationship to how desired learning objectives maybe be represented in the game. Similarities can be drawn between the qualities required creating a learning objective and the elements required when constructing gameplay, game mechanics and the interaction cycle. These similarities are discussed in the following section.

FRAMEWORK ELEMENTS

Goals:

A core-gameplay goal can be guided by the instructional objective developed i.e. we wish the player to interact with and demonstrate a competent level of knowledge or skill in the form of a task performance. This performance is displayed by interacting with the core-gameplay. If players do not currently have the knowledge or skill to perform the task at the expected competency level, then either they can be supported through instructional techniques separate to the game. Alternately, the game could be incrementally developed using feedback during the various gameplay cycles. For example, when first interacting with the core-gameplay, the player may need to be guided using supportive feedback to determine the mechanisms of the core-gameplay. This feedback is often seen as a tutorial that explicitly outlines how the player can perform actions in the game. Strategies to overcome challenges may also be presented during this time. Therefore, if the core-gameplay is a mirror of instructional objectives then the player will inadvertently learn the knowledge and skills required to overcome the games challenges. Through various progressive iterations of the core-gameplay, feedback and support can be reduced to allow the player's knowledge and skills to be tested to the point where they are matching the expected level of competency.

The framework builds on this understanding of goals and specifies a question to be asked during the design process:

G1: What performance should I be able to achieve? [18].

This question allows the game designer to clearly articulate the instructional objective within a particular game context. The answer to this question will outline what the learner should be able to do competently by the end of the game.

Choice:

Choice is an integral cognitive process that occurs during the lead up to performing a task. During the planning and specifying stages of Norman's Seven Stages of Action [21] it is important to identify what alternatives are available when deciding to perform a task. Salen & Zimmerman [24] also discuss the anatomy of a choice utilising five fundamental questions. Of these five, the question of "How is the possibility of choice conveyed?" fits within our choice component of the framework.

Whilst discussing the components that form the absolute difficulty of a challenge/task, Adams [1] identifies that the intrinsic skill is an essential component that when combined with stress, creates a level of difficulty. Intrinsic skill is the "level of skill needed to surmount the challenge if you give the player an unlimited amount of time in which to do it" [1]. This level of skill can be seen as the amount of mental or physical effort required to perform a task. The amount of physical effort in digital games is relatively low, and the amount of cognitive effort is relatively high. This cognitive effort can be viewed as the difficulty in determining the most acceptable option amongst the different task states and associated options [29]. Therefore, it is important to choose an instructional objective that can offer the player an adequate number of interesting and meaningful choices that are deserving of their effort.

Based on this understanding of choice two questions are included in the framework:

CH1: What can I do and what are my alternatives? [21]

CH2: How is the possibility of choice conveyed? [24]

The answers to these questions will outline the choices and the way in which choices are presented to the player.

Action:

Within the Seven Stages of Action [21] the result of enacting a choice occurs during the "perform" stage. Norman [21] proposes the question of "How do I do it?" can aid in detailing exactly how the user will interact with the system. How the user will "do it" may be either an individual or series of actions. From the perspective of core-gameplay, this observation is the detection of player actions by the system after a choice has been presented. Adams [1] recommends that verbs be used to reflect what the player does. These actions may not always map exactly to how they might appear in a real situations. Therefore, it is important when choosing actions that they conform to usability principles such as those found in Norman's Seven Fundamental Design Principles [21] so that they will still remain intuitive and easy to use.

Based on this understanding of action a question to ask during the design process has been incorporated into the framework:

A1: What series of action (verbs) will indicate I am making a choice? [1,18,21]

The answer to this question should be a series of verbs/steps that outline the player's interaction with the games interface.

Rules:

The rules in the framework are used as an evaluative method to ascertain the performance level during the core-gameplay. The learning objectives will outline the various elements that make up the "criterion" i.e. level at which someone has to be at to be considered competent [18]. These elements consist of the speed, accuracy and quality of the performed task and relate very closely to the elements that make up difficulty in games. Adams [1] identifies intrinsic skill and stress (time pressure) as qualities that determine the amount of effort required overcoming the challenge. It is also important to outline the conditions and constraints under which the learner must perform the task e.g. what are the things they can/can't use and what setting, or physical environment does the performance need to be in [18].

There will be other game mechanics that also have rules; however the primarily focus is on the core-gameplay and the related core-mechanics/rule systems that go with it. It is important to ask questions that identify the characteristics that form the basis of the rules that govern if a learner is competent enough to overcome the designed gameplay.

Based on this understanding of rules five questions to consider during the design process have been included in the framework:

R1: (Speed) How quickly do I need to make my choice and perform the actions to achieve my desired goal? [18]

R2: (Accuracy) To what degree or level of precision do I have to demonstrate to achieve my desired goal? [18]

R3: (Quality) What standards/criteria do I have to meet whilst I perform the actions to achieve my desired goal? [18]

R4: (Conditions) In what conditions will my performance occur? [18]

R5: (Constraints) What can/cannot I use whilst making a choice performing the actions? [18]

The answers to these questions will outline the criterion, conditions and constraints that will set the standard level of competency. Whilst the core-gameplay is being used to build up knowledge and skill, it is expected that this criterion level will start lower and buildup as the player progresses until they reach the standard outlined in the instructional objective.

Feedback:

While Mager's [18] learning objective structure does not identify how to construct feedback, there is a critical role feedback has in both the interaction cycle and learning. It is through feedback, both internal and external to the game, that learning can occur i.e. corrective feedback on previous task performances or through contextual events triggered by the system. To design feedback based around the choices a player makes, Salen and Zimmerman [24] identified certain questions as part of their anatomy of choice. In the Seven Stages of Action, Norman [21] also discusses questions that can be asked when designing for the three stages that form feedback.

We use this understanding of feedback to formulate key feedback-related questions within the core-gameplay framework:

F1: What is the result / new state of the environment once the choice and actions are made? [24]

F2: How do I know I made the correct/incorrect choice? [21,24]

F3: How will this affect my choices in the future? [24].

The answers to these questions will outline the system events that occur after players have made their choice and how they are expected to respond to future choices. It is at this point that constructive feedback can be given, and learning can be re-enforced.

FRAMEWORK USE

The framework developed is comparable to a user interaction framework, similar to those established in human-computer interaction (e.g., the Seven Stages of Action [21]). The purpose of articulating a core-gameplay framework is to establish a process whereby key game design strategies can have an apparent impact on learning. The process can be applied in a systematic way. By questioning every design decision raised by the framework it is anticipated that critical design thinking and idea generation that is guided by the required instructional outcomes will be stimulated. This type of thinking, in turn, leads to designed educational games that align to the instructional objectives, where each design decision can be clearly justified. This process is not context specific and is aimed at being flexible enough to fit in with existing educational game design frameworks that support the development of any educational game.

The usable representation of the working framework is structured around an open inquiry process where learning objectives, interaction design and gameplay questions are used to drive the design. These questions are aimed at investigating the desired outcome of performing a task at a level of competency. The answers then form the building blocks of the goals, choices, actions, rules and feedback. The following section outlines how this design process can be used to map one instructional objective to core-gameplay.

Design Brief: General Fire Evacuation Safety

Office based workplace safety training was the educational focus of this design exercise. An existing workplace safety training implementation, in the form of an e-learning module, already existed. This instructional method delivered relevant information via audio and visual presentation. The module was a self-paced slideshow that concluded with a short multiple-choice quiz.

Numerous consultations with workplace safety management staff highlighted the limitations of the current e-learning system and some key topics that would be useful to explore in a game-based experience. A prevalent workplace safety issue is that of injuries resulting from slips, trips and falls. These accidents lead to personal injury costs to the injured employee and a loss in productivity and liability costs to business.

Expert discussions, existing training material, and various related safety documents were analyzed. From this analysis, instructional objectives to be pursued in the game were developed. Guided by the framework, a design process was then followed that allowed the alignment of core-gameplay with the instructional objectives.

The Game Example

At the time of development, the game was titled "Catastrophe". Catastrophe is a top down crisis management game where the player manipulates the environment to keep non-player characters (NPCs) safe in normal working situation (Figure 1). Players can interact with in-game objects that are represented as potential safety hazards. These hazards all relate to those resulting in slips, trips and falls e.g. boxes or rubbish left in walkways, spilt liquid and loose cords. The NPCs will primarily act on their own, traveling between tasks such as working at a computer to handling boxes, rubbish or using the kitchen.

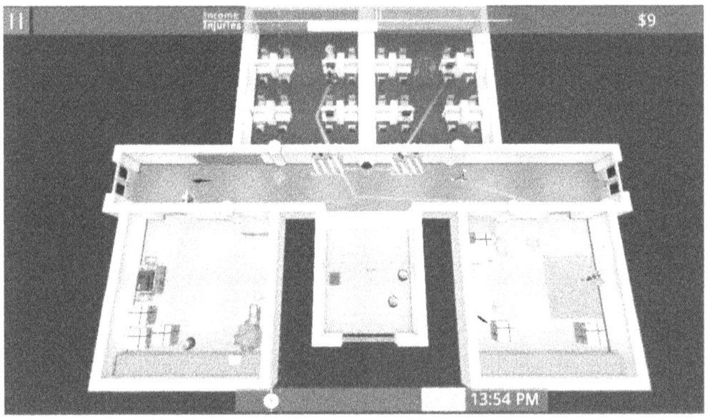

Figure 1: Catastrophe Crisis Management Game

The core-gameplay (moment-to-moment experience) requires the player to prevent injuries from occurring e.g. removing any hazards before an accident occurs. Game goals and concise safety information is delivered to the player via an advisor. If NPCs collide with a potential hazard, they will injure themselves. This will affects the player's final game score through loss of productivity and injury costs. The game has been specially designed to be extendable if further learning goals are to be pursued e.g. evacuation planning, emergency communication (alarms), and the use of hazard fighting equipment (fire extinguishers).

A series of instructional objectives were designed based upon the following learning goal. "After the training, the learner will be able to identify various trips and falls within an office environment and know how to respond". Whilst relatively open-ended, this learning goal gives an ideal starting point to develop a cognitive walkthrough that identifies the discrete steps and choices made when identifying and responding to hazards. From this map, critical, yet interesting task decision points could be identified as the focus. These could then be developed into instructional objectives that clearly explain what the learner should be able to do after they play the game. An example of one of those instructional objectives will be the focus of the following example.

- What should the learner be able to do? (Performance)

  Respond (applying control measures)

- Under what conditions do you want the learner to be able to do it? (Conditions)

  Presented with a potential hazard in an office environment [the learner will respond (applying control measures)]

- How well must it be done? (Criterion)

  [Presented with a potential hazard in an office environment the player will respond] *choosing the ideal control measures to reduce the level of risk*

The formed instructional objective might look like this: "*When presented with a potential hazard in an office environment the learner will respond by choosing the ideal control measures that could reduce the level of risk.*"

As part of the inquiry approach, the instructional objective is considered through a framework with questions that break down a task into its sub-components and qualities. The answers to these questions can then be used as building blocks to form the core-gameplay. Design challenges related to mapping learning to game elements becomes clear once the relationships between the instructional objective and core-gameplay are broken down.

The following tables outline how the elements of goals, choice, action, rules and feedback were constructed based around this specific instructional objective. The real life and game examples are focused on the desired level of competency i.e. the core-gameplay cycle experienced towards the end of the game.

Goal		
Question	**Real Life**	**Game**
G1: What performance should I be able to achieve? [18]	Respond to hazards by applying different control measures.	Respond to hazards by applying different control measures.

Table 1. Goal Mapping Table

G1: Within a real life context, the learner should be able respond to potential hazards. In an Occupational Health and Safety context, this response is known as applying control measures. The application of different control measures in the game allows the user to learn from the effect they have in a simulated environment and to develop a greater depth of understanding. This application allows a tighter coupling of the decisions and actions experienced within the game so that they can may be transferred into a real situation.

Choice		
Question	**Real Life**	**Game**
CH1: What can I do, and what are my alternatives? [21]	Determine the ideal control measure/s to apply from the list of existing control measures.	At least 2-3 meaningful choices/control measures available to the player.
CH2: How is the possibility of choice conveyed [24]?	The perceived affordances of objects in the environment and the internally imagined actions taken with objects not currently present.	Menu of buttons with each available control measure present. Menu buttons will have tool tips to identify the future effects it will have.

Table 2. Choice Mapping Table

CH1: The focus of this cycle of core-gameplay is presenting the user with similar choices to those choices available when facing hazards in the real world. Realistically there will often be two-three control measures that could be applied. Therefore, the game offers the player the same types of choices that are core to responding to a hazard and ultimately helps to re-enforce making the most effective decisions. In the game, each hazard will have at least two or three choices that could have some effect on the hazard.

CH2: In real life, choices to interact with objects at hand are often conveyed by their perceived affordances [21], or some decisions could be made based on an understanding of objects that are not immediately available. For example, choosing to place a barrier around a hazard first requires an understanding that things nearby could be used as a barrier or that barriers are found elsewhere. The game simplifies the decision-making process by clearly conveying if the necessary actions and tools can or cannot be used. This design decision ensures the core-gameplay focuses on making the critical decision of choosing effective control measures. This choice will be visually conveyed via a menu of buttons that represent applying a control measure. Tooltips over each button will identify the future events that will occur once the button is pressed.

Action		
Question	**Real Life**	**Game**
A1: What series of action (verbs) will indicate I am making a choice? [1,18,21]	Series of steps that represent applying a particular control measures.	Click the hazard, then click the control measure button.

Table 3. Action Mapping Table

A1: The real life performance involves completing a sequence of tasks for each control measure that will achieve the goal e.g. cleaning up a spill requires fetching a sign to warn others, fetching cleaning products, applying cleaning products, and storing the sign and cleaning products when done. Direct mapping of these real actions would push the scope and focus of the game beyond the requirements. Therefore, the majority of actions taken for this core-gameplay cycle consist of clicking on the hazard, and then clicking on a control measure button.

Rules		
Question	**Real Life**	**Game**
R1: (Speed) How quickly do I need to make my choice and perform the actions to achieve my desired goal? [18]	Respond to a hazard as soon as it identified visually.	Respond to a hazard as soon as it identified visually.
R2: (Accuracy) To what degree or level of precision do I have to demonstrate to achieve my desired goal? [18]	One or more control measures will reduce the level of risk.	One or two control measures out of the six will significantly reduce the risk of a hazard injuring an NPC.
R3: (Quality) What standards/criteria do I have to meet whilst I perform the actions to achieve my desired goal? [18]	Apply the correct ordering of control measures based on an evaluation of the time a control measure might take to perform.	Evaluate what controls should have been chosen first based on each hazard. i.e. higher order controls may not always be the ideal first response.

R4: (Conditions) In what conditions will my performance occur? [18]	Real office environment, presented with a real hazards and workers.	Simulated 3D office environment presented with simulated hazards and workers.
R5: (Constraints) What can/cannot I use whilst making a choice performing the actions? [18]	Can't use reference material. Could ask for assistance if hazards cannot be immediately eliminated.	Can't use interactive safety reference material. Assistance could be provided when making and applying a choice.

Table 4. Rules Mapping Table

R1: The NPC AI routines will travel to office tasks that bypass hazards frequently. This design decision ensures that the player is motivated to respond to all hazards quickly before an NPC is injured. Some control measures will not immediately reduce the level of risk, re-enforcing the idea that temporary control measures may also be required.

R2: The accuracy criterion of the task is based on the predefined control measures that should be used for each hazard. For example, a hazard will have various control measures that can and cannot be applied. The game will always expect that at least one or two control measures are correctly chosen before the hazard no longer poses a risk of injuring the NPC.

R3: Players will be evaluated on the quality of their response based on their ability to determine the ideal control measure to apply first. Often lower order short term controls need to be put in place until higher order controls can be effectively applied. Some of the control measures will be more effective at reducing the risk of injury than others. For example, cleaning up a spill takes time but is more effective than placing a barrier around it. Ideally the barrier should be placed first to reduce the level of risk immediately.

R4: An environmental condition that could present the player with a multitude of hazards to respond to was used i.e. a 3D simulated office environment with animated workers, hazards and responses. The camera perspective used was a top-down view that offered the player a greater sense of choice to perform various actions as well as giving the player the ability to spot hazards immediately. It was also important to include NPC moving about the environment as this emphasized the importance or responding to hazards quickly and effectively.

R5: When performing the task at a level of competency in real life it is expected that the learner would not have any physical reference material them to aid in determining the ideal control measures to implement. In some cases, not all hazards can be eliminated immediately. Assistance is often necessary to apply lower order control measures. The game reflects these constraints by implying some hazards require assistance and time to be resolved that is outside of the abilities of the player. As the player is learning about how to respond to hazards, the amount of helpful information can be structured to taper off as the game progresses in difficulty.

Feedback		
Question	**Real Life**	**Game**
F1: What is the result / new state of the environment once the choice and actions are made? [24]	A hazards risk will increase, decrease or remain the same.	The chance of an NPC being injured will increase, decrease or remain the same.
F2: How do I know I made the correct/incorrect choice?[21,24]	Feedback to convey a correct choice is often implicit. Incorrect choices are often explicitly conveyed through injury reports or workplace announcements.	Audio-visual effects, and removal of the hazard will convey that the player made correct choices. Injured NPCs and end game scores will convey incorrect choices.
F3: How will this affect my choices in the future? [24]	Without clear, explicit feedback or relevant prior knowledge, my future choices will likely remain unchanged.	Immediate and delayed explicit feedback will encourage the player to makes correct choices when presented with similar situations.

Table 5. Feedback Mapping Table

F1: The events that occur after a control measure is applied in the game will update the chances of an injury occurring. The aim is to encourage the player to re-engage in a new cycle of interaction with either the same or similar hazards.

F2: Feedback that a hazard is responded to correctly is limited in real life situation. The benefit to using a game-based learning approach is correct choices can be immediately re-enforced with feedback. Negative feedback in the game has been delayed i.e. an NPC injures themselves to show the real implications of failing to apply effective control measures. Auxiliary audio and visual feedback mechanisms are also used to show that the user has performed an action the system recognises. It is expected that the player's motivations to improve the safety of the virtual environment will transfer to real motivations to improve the safety real workplaces they enter.

F3: In real life contexts, it is rare that an individual would have faced and responded to many different hazards in the workplace. Games can allow players to learn from their actions in a safe manner. The design of the game ensures the player regularly interacts with the core-gameplay cycle consisting of identifying and responding to hazards. This design decision ensures the resulting explicit feedback is received more readily and built upon so that future choices in the real world may be influenced by the experience.

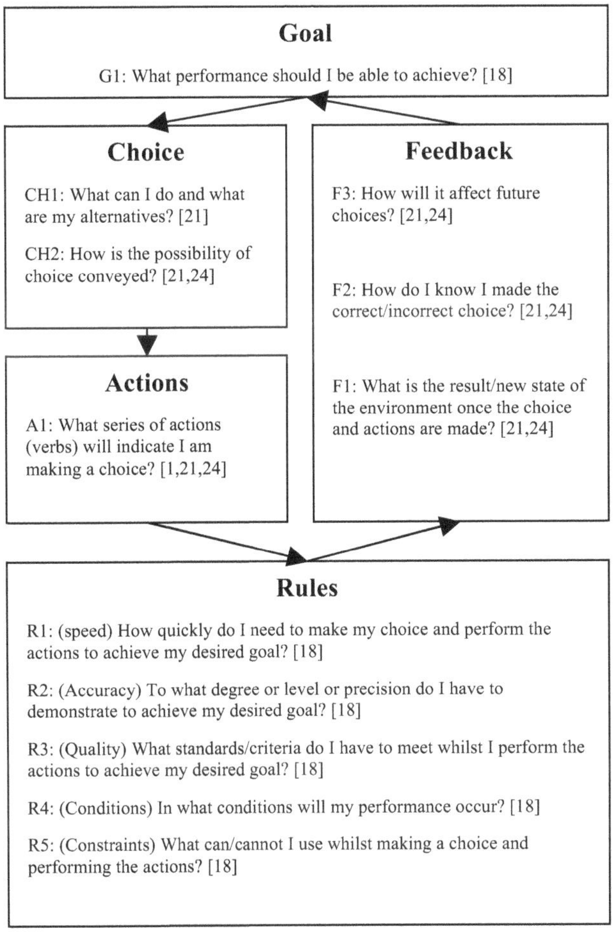

Figure 2. Core-Gameplay Framework with Design Questions

DISCUSSION AND CONCLUSION

The framework presented in this paper provides a clear process to map instructional objectives to core-gameplay activity. This design framework can work alongside existing frameworks and allows designers to systematically design core-gameplay that embeds educational objectives by using an inquiry design process. This inquiry design process asks questions relating to the core-gameplay elements of goals, choices, actions, rules and feedback in relation to the instructional objectives (see Figure 2). As demonstrated in the example mapping tables, the answers to these questions form design criteria that allow designers to justify the learning potential of the game.

A limitation of this research is that the game example used has not been empirically tested to determine the extent to which it meets the identified learning objectives. Future research will aim to provide this empirical evidence. Additionally, there has been limited use of the framework in other case examples. In the future the framework could be applied to not just a training purpose, but also to the purposes of game-based awareness and assessment [10].

It is planned to apply a similar approach adopted by Arnab et al., [3] who repurposed their framework to focus on the analysis of serious games. The framework can be used as a flexible plug-in to add clarity to the design and analysis process articulated in existing frameworks such as LM-GM [3] or the Game Object Model 2 [2]. Therefore, future research may focus on the ease with which the framework can be used in conjunction with existing frameworks. Feedback from observing how others come to use the framework will only strengthen and enhance it to ensure it can significantly improve the way educational games are designed.

REFERENCES

1. Adams, E. *Fundamentals of Game Design*. New Riders, Berkeley, CA, 2013.
2. Amory, A. Game object model version II: A Theoretical Framework for Educational Game Development. *Educational Technology Research and Development 55*, 1 (2006), 51–77.
3. Arnab, S., Lim, T., Carvalho, M.B., et al. Mapping Learning and Game Mechanics for Serious Games Analysis. *British Journal of Educational Technology*, (2014).
4. Ausubel, D.P. *Educational Psychology: A Cognitive View*. Holt, Rinehart and Winston, New York, NY, USA, 1968.
5. Bruckman, A. Can Educational be Fun. *Proc. Game Developers Conference 1999*, (1999).
6. Chamberlin, B., Trespalacios, J., and Gallagher, R. The Learning Games Design Model. *International Journal of Game-Based Learning 2*, 3 (2012), 87–110.
7. Connolly, T., Stansfield, M., and Hainey, T. Development of a General Framework for Evaluating Games-Based Learning. *Proc. 2nd European Conference on Games Based Learning*, Academic Conferences Limited (2008), 105–114.
8. Csikszentmihalyi, M. *Flow: The Psychology of Optimal Experience*. Harper and Row, New York, 1990.

9. Deci, E.L. and Ryan, R.M. The " What " and " Why " of Goal Pursuits : Human Needs and the Self-Determination of Behavior. *Psychological Inquiry 11*, 4 (2000), 227–268.

10. Djaouti, D., Alvarez, J., and Jessel, J. Classifying Serious Games : the G / P / S model. In *Handbook of Research on Improving Learning and Motivation through Educational Games: Multidisciplinary Approaches*. 2011, 118–136.

11. Dondi, C. and Moretti, M. A methodological proposal for learning games selection and quality assessment. *British Journal of Educational Technology 38*, 3 (2007), 502–512.

12. Dondlinger, M.J. Educational Video Game Design : A Review of the Literature. *Journal of Applied Educational Technology 4*, 1 (2007), 21–31.

13. Gosper, M. and Mcneill, M. Implementing Game-Based Learning: The MAPLET Framework as a Guide to Learner-Centred Design and Assessment. In *Assessment in Game-Based Learning*. Springer New York, New York, 2012, 217–233.

14. Habgood, J. and Ainsworth, S. Motivating Children to Learn Effectively: Exploring the Value of Intrinsic Integration in Educational Games. *Journal of the Learning Sciences 20*, 2 (2011), 169–206.

15. Hays, R.T. *The Effectiveness Of Instructional Games : A Literature Review And Discussion*. Orlando, FL, 2005.

16. Krathwohl, D.R. A revision of Bloom's taxonomy: An overview. *Theory into practice 41*, 4 (2002), 212–218.

17. Lundgren, S. and Björk, S. Game Mechanics : Describing Computer-Augmented Games in Terms of Interaction. *Proc. Technologies for Interactive Digital Storytelling and Entertainment (TIDSE)*, (2003).

18. Mager, R. *Preparing Instructional Objectives: A critical tool in the development of effective instruction*. Center for Effective Performance, 1997.

19. Martin, M.W. Serious Game Design Principles : The Impact Of Game Design On Learning Outcomes. 2012, 163.

20. Marzano, R.J. *Designing & teaching learning goals & objectives*. Marzano Research Laboratory, Bloomington, IN, 2009.

21. Norman, D. *The Design of Everyday Things: Revised and Expanded Edition*. Basic Books, 2013.

22. Novak, J.D. and Canas, A.J. The theory underlying concept maps and how to construct and use them. 2008. http://cmap.ihmc.us/Publications/ResearchPapers/TheoryUnderlyingConceptMaps.pdf.

23. Przybylski, A.K., Rigby, C.S., and Ryan, R.M. A motivational model of video game engagement. *Review of General Psychology 14*, 2 (2010), 154–166.

24. Salen, K. and Zimmerman, E. *Rules of play: Game design fundamentals*. The MIT Press, Cambridge, MA, 2004.

25. Shelton, B.E. and Scoresby, J. Aligning game activity with educational goals: following a constrained design approach to instructional computer games. *Educational Technology Research and Development 59*, 1 (2011), 113–138.

26. Sherry, J. and Pacheco, A. Matching Computer Game Genres To Educational Outcomes. *Electronic Journal of Communication 16*, (2006), 10–14.

27. Sicart, M. Defining Game Mechanics. *Game Studies*, 2008. http://gamestudies.org/0802/articles/sicart.

28. Sweetser, P. and Wyeth, P. GameFlow: a model for evaluating player enjoyment in games. *Comput. Entertain. 3*, 3 (2005).

29. Sweller, J. Element Interactivity and Intrinsic, Extraneous, and Germane Cognitive Load. *Educational Psychology Review 22*, 2 (2010), 123–138.

30. Tang, S. and Hanneghan, M. Designing Educational Games : A Pedagogical Approach. In *Design and Implementation of Educational Games: Theoretical and Practical Perspectives*. IGI Global, Hershey, PA, 2010, 108–125.

31. Watson, W.R. Formative Research on an Instructional Design Theory for Educational Video Games. 2007, 203.

Player Strategies: Achieving Breakthroughs and Progressing in Single-player and Cooperative Games

Ioanna Iacovides	Anna L. Cox	Ara Avakian	Thomas Knoll
UCL Interaction Centre, Gower Street, London, WC1E 6BT, UK.	UCL Interaction Centre, Gower Street, London, WC1E 6BT, UK.	Hutchison 3G UK Ltd., Star House, 20 Grenfell Road, Maidenhead, SL6 1EH, UK.	Amberlight Partners Ltd., 58 Bloomsbury Street, London, WC1B 3QT, UK.
i.iacovides@ucl.ac.uk	anna.cox@ucl.ac.uk	ara.avakian@three.co.uk	tom@amber-light.co.uk

ABSTRACT
Challenge is considered to be one of the key components of game-play, where game designers face the tricky task of getting the balance right so that game-play is neither too easy nor too difficult. Through attempting in-game challenges, players experience cycles of breakdown and breakthrough, where breakthroughs involve moments of insight in which learning occurs. However, little attention has been given to how players actually overcome challenges to progress during game-play. Across two studies, we explore the ways in which players attempt to achieve breakthroughs in relation to single-player and co-located multiplayer games. We identified a number of strategies that are used by players, which illustrate how learning occurs during play. For instance, while "*Experiment*" involves forming an informal hypothesis, "*Trial & error*" occurs when the player tries to find out what, if anything, will happen when they carry out an action. These strategies are considered in relation to supporting player progress and engaging game-play when designing commercial and educational games.

Author Keywords
Games; learning; engagement; player strategies.

ACM Classification Keywords
H.5.3 Information interfaces and presentation (e.g., HCI): Miscellaneous ; K.8.0. General: Games.

INTRODUCTION
Digital games now appeal to large audiences of both "hardcore gamers" and more "casual" players [17] and are being produced for a variety of purposes including entertainment and education. However, despite their increasing popularity, creating a successful game is not an easy task - up to 80% of titles fail commercially [12]. Further, while it has been argued that learning is what makes games fun [18], outside the realm of education, there has been little examination of how players learn during play and how this relates to the experience of achieving game progress. Investigating these processes will not only improve our understanding of learning but is also likely to contribute to the design of more engaging educational and commercial games.

CHI PLAY '14, October 19 - 22 2014, Toronto, ON, Canada
Copyright 2014 ACM 978-1-4503-3014-5/14/10…$15.00.
http://dx.doi.org/10.1145/2658537.2658697

Within the field of HCI, games research has focused mainly on enjoyment in digital games, e.g. [24], and on how to evaluate game-play experiences, e.g. [25]. Learnability is sometimes considered in relation to design, e.g. [2], but rarely beyond the scope of grasping initial controls and mechanics. Furthermore, while cognitive challenge is considered a key component of game-play [5; 23] and there has been some consideration of how learning results from game-play breakdowns [14; 16; 26], little attention has been paid to the different strategies adult players employ to overcome game play obstacles.

This paper addresses this issue through reporting on two studies. A preliminary analysis of the first study was previously reported as a work-in-progress [15]. Participants played two different games for up to 20 minutes each and the data collected was used to develop a standardized set of strategy types that players employed to overcome breakdowns during play. This paper also presents a second study; in which pairs of players played a cooperative game for up to 40 minutes. The analysis also extends the initial strategies in order to account for multiplayer co-located play and learning within a social context. The findings of both studies are drawn together and considered in terms of game design implications.

RELATED WORK

Learning and games
Gee's seminal book on video games [8] lays out numerous ways in which well-designed games are able to support learning. Essentially, Gee argues that through increasing rewards and scaffolding progress, games are able to push players "to operate within, but at the outer edge of, his or

her resources, so that at those points things are felt as challenging but not 'undoable'" [p. 71; ibid]. In this way players are continuously learning, practicing and mastering skills, and adapting their knowledge to deal with the challenges presented to them. Further, Gee notes how game knowledge and meanings are distributed across objects, tools, technologies and other players.

Gee [8; 9] is mainly concerned with games as a metaphor for learning in the digital age, and how education can learn from commercial game design. However, his semiotic analysis is based on his own observations so there is a need for further empirical evidence to substantiate his account.

Game-play breakdowns and breakthroughs

A range of work has examined breakdowns that occur during game-play. For instance, Pelletier and Oliver [26] point out that while Gee [8] provides a strong account of how learning may occur, it is not clear what researchers should focus on if they do want to study game-play. As a result, they present an approach based on Activity Theory [19], where player activities were decomposed into actions and operations, with particular attention paid to "contradictions" within the activity system. "Contradictions" refer to problematic moments that occurred during play, such as failures or mistakes i.e. breakdowns. The authors studied 3 cases (one involving *Harry Potter & the Chamber of Secrets*; the other two *Deus Ex*). Their analysis enabled an identification of the strategies players adopted (such as "spot unusual objects and click on them") but relying on observation alone meant inferences were made about player objectives. Further, the aim was to present a method for studying game-play rather than generalisable findings so it is unclear how applicable the strategies they identified are to other contexts.

Ryan and Siegel [27] also focus on breakdowns as a way to understand game-play, relying on a previously identified distinction between *interaction* and *illusion breakdowns* [22]. Breakdowns are described by Ryan and Siegel as occurring when actions carried out by players no longer seem to work; where breakdowns in interaction refer to "natural breakdowns" that lead to new strategy development, and breakdowns in illusion refer to a loss of immersion (in terms of absorbed attention). They argue that the former are part of normal game-play, but unlike the latter, they do not disrupt the experience of flow. Flow [6] occurs when there is an appropriate match between someone's skills and the challenge presented to them, resulting in an experience of intense engagement.

As a result of their heterophenomenological analysis across 17 games, Ryan and Siegel [27] present four main categories of breakdown and 17 heuristic guidelines for design. The categories relate to Perceiving the Environment, Developing Strategy, Taking Action, and Meaning Making. An example guideline under Developing Strategy is: "Keep tasks and instructions focused towards the current goal." However, while certain player strategies are implied, e.g. trial and error, this was not their focus.

The concept of breakdowns has also been utilized in other design contexts. For instance, as part of research that elicited educational mobile technology requirements, Sharples [29] defines breakdowns as "observable critical incidents where a learner is struggling with the technology, asking for help, or appears to be labouring under a clear misunderstanding" and adds the concept of breakthroughs: "observable critical incidents which appear to be initiating productive, new forms of learning or important conceptual change" (p. 10).

These concepts have been modified in order to investigate the relationship between learning and involvement within game-play. Iacovides and colleagues argue that breakdowns and breakthroughs can occur in relation to player *action* (e.g. problems with the controller, performing a new attack); *understanding* (e.g. not knowing what to do next, figuring out a solution a puzzle); and *involvement* (e.g. getting frustrated, experiencing satisfaction) [14; 16]. While this approach provides a more nuanced appreciation of how learning and involvement relate to each other, the research reported by Iacovides and colleagues does not explicitly consider the different strategies players adopt in attempting to overcome breakdowns and achieve breakthroughs.

Problem-solving and player strategies

There has also been some interest in problem-solving in games and the strategies players adopt from a psychological perspective. For instance, Blumberg et al. [4] conducted a think-aloud study that examined how frequent and infrequent players negotiated impasses within *Sonic the Hedgehog 2*. The authors describe an impasse as "a catalyst for the acquisition of new knowledge and problem-solving strategies" while games are described as a venue for examining the specific problem solving strategies that facilitate 'expert' performance during game play" (p. 1531). They found that frequent game players generally made more references to insight and game strategies than infrequent players, though all players tended to comment on game progress and potential game strategies after reaching an impasse. While their study indicates that expertise may lead to different kinds of problem solving, the strategies used by players were not classified during the analysis so it is unclear how they actually overcame impasses.

In order to investigate the strategies novices adopt when playing a new game (*Return of the Incredible Machine: Contraptions*), Alkan & Cagiltay [1] integrated eye-tracking equipment within a usability study. Perhaps unsurprisingly, the results indicated fixation times were lowest in relation to the menu and highest in the area where participants had to focus on solving problems. During the post-play interview, participants suggested the main strategies they use to learn games are "trial and error" and using "friends as sources of information". No serious usability issues were uncovered though the authors note that while the game offers a hint function that provides explicit instructions to the player, these were never heeded by the participants. This suggests that players do not always pay attention to help provided by the game, though, given that the participants reported that they "prefer more complex action and strategy games" (p. 541) they may have found the instructions boring and preferred to ignore them.

The previous studies mentioned have focused on single-player games. Adopting a different emphasis, El-Nasr et al. [7] present a method for evaluating cooperative game design. While not explicitly focusing on player strategies, some of Cooperative Performance Metrics (CPMs) presented suggest certain types of strategies that occur during cooperative play. These include examples such as "Worked out strategies" (where players discuss how to solve problems, divide up game zones, and/or consult each other while navigating the game world) and "Helping each other" (where players discuss controllers and game mechanics, dictate how an obstacle should be overcome, and/or rescue a player who is failing). However, these metrics are presented as a tool for evaluating game-play in relation to cooperative design patterns, not for understanding how learning occurs in relation to the player. For instance, other CPM examples are "Laughter or excitement together" and "Got in each other's way".

While the research discussed above has examined the challenges and problems that can occur during play, it lacks comprehensive investigation into the variety of strategies players adopt to overcome challenges across different games. In order to further explore these issues, we describe two observational studies of game-play (supplemented by post-play interviews) that explore learning in the form of the different types of strategies people adopt within single-player and multi-player contexts.

STUDY 1

Method

Design: This was an observational study of game-play that included a post-play interview, where a recording of the game-play session was reviewed by participants.

Participants: Twenty participants (F=5; M=15; Mean age = 25.2) were recruited from a university participant pool. Participants were paid £10 for taking part, and consisted of an equal mix of hardcore and casual players so that the strategies would reflect a range of player ability. Hardcore players are those who have played a large number of games, invest large amounts of time and resources towards games, and enjoy higher levels of difficulty, while casual players play fewer games, commit little time and few resources towards games and prefer lower levels of difficulty [17]. Player categorization was established through a combination of self-identification and a brief questionnaire about their gaming habits and preferences.

Materials: Each participant played two games of different genre, to improve the generalizability of the research. Both games were sourced from Independent Games Festival finalists [13] to ensure they had a reasonable level of quality and that, being independent games, it was unlikely that participants would have played them before.

Figure 1: Screen shot from *Wonderputt* (2012 finalist)

Wonderputt (*WP*) is a crazy golf game (Figure 1). The player completes 18 holes using the mouse to adjust the angle and the speed of the ball. The holes gradually get harder requiring more precision and creative approaches.

Figure 2: Screenshot from *Rocketbirds: Revolution!* (2010 finalist)

The second game, *Rocketbirds: Revolution!* (*RR*), is a 2D third person action/strategy game, where the player has to negotiate their way through an enemy base end of the level solving basic puzzles, killing enemies and managing their health and ammunition (Figure 2).

RR and *WP* are web-based games, which means they were accessible and did not require extended tutorial sessions to acquire basic proficiency. This was ideal as it ensured that players could become familiar with the gameplay mechanics within a short space of time. Simple instructions sheets were also provided.

The gaming session was recorded on a high definition video camera positioned on a tripod behind the participant, which captured the participant's interaction with the game. The post-play cued interview was recorded using the iPhone memo software and a computer monitor was used to play the gaming session back to the participant.

Procedure: Participants were given the same instructions and played through the same two games, counterbalanced in order over two sessions (split to minimize the effects of fatigue). During the first session, participants completed a questionnaire about their gaming habits and preferences. They were then provided with a brief overview of the game and were given 20 minutes to play (unless they finished the game earlier). At the end of the session, the experimenter interviewed the participant and played back a recording of the game-play session to stimulate their recall [as in 14]. During this time, the participant was asked to explain what they were doing and thinking with particular emphasis placed on how they dealt with the problems they encountered during the session.

Analysis

The video and interview data was coded for critical incidents. An incident was defined as a point in the game where the participant found themselves in a situation where they were unable to progress through lack of proficiency with the controls (action breakdowns), a lack of understanding about their current objective (understanding breakdowns) or reduction of their level of interest in the game (involvement breakdowns). In addition, any significant changes in a participant's strategies were also recorded even when this change in behavior was not accompanied by a breakdown. In order to develop the categories of strategies, these incidents were then examined in relation to the actions the player took to overcome breakdowns and achieve breakthroughs. Similar to a thematic analysis [3], the strategy categories were developed iteratively in a bottom up approach and discussed among the researchers until a definitive set was able to account for all different actions observed.

Findings

Player strategies

The strategies are defined below with examples provided for illustrative purposes. Participants are referred to by number e.g. Participant 1 is P1.

1. Trial & error

This approach consists of exploring what the game allows, how to carry out actions and finding out which actions lead to progress. Essentially, after carrying out a specific action, the player is trying to find out what, if anything, will happen. For instance, P10 (Hardcore) in *RR* is having trouble picking up a key, so resorts to pressing different buttons on the keyboard to find out whether any translate to in game-actions. Similarly, P2 (Casual) in *WP*, did not know what to do next so tried hitting the ball hard against the rocks to see what would happen. In this case, the action resulted in deactivated a force field, allowing for further progress. While P2 learnt from this experience, P8 (Casual) on the same level accidentally caused the force field to deactivate when repeatedly aiming at the hole, but failed to notice what had occurred. For P8, *Trial & error* was not accompanied by an understanding breakthrough and subsequent progress was accidental.

2. Experiment

On the basis of previous knowledge and/or understanding breakthroughs resulting from *Trial & error*, the player forms an informal hypothesis, takes a subsequent action and, depending on the outcome, either proceeds in the game or reforms the hypothesis. For instance, after taking an exploratory shot (*Trial & error*) to see how the crane works in *WP*, P19 (Casual) uses this information to direct his next shot and is able to use the crane to progress within the level. This strategy can also involve transferring knowledge from the real world, from experiences with other games or from earlier experience within the same game. For example, in *WP*, P7 (Casual) realizes the ball needs to cross a section of water. Through their understanding of real world physics, they assume they will need to hit the ball harder than normal so that it will skim over the water and this approach proves successful. However, inappropriate transfer can lead to further breakdowns. For example, in *RR*, P6 (Hardcore) misses several jumps by assuming the character will grab onto a ledge automatically as in the case of *Mario* and *Zelda* games.

3. Repetition

Initially called *Practice* [15], this strategy was renamed to cover both when a player's aim was to gain proficiency with the controls (and so rehearsed or refined a technique on an obstacle or in a safe area of the game) and when they proceeded to repeat the same action several times in an effort to progress. For instance, in *RR*, P14 (Casual) decides to practice within the first screen of the game, where there were no enemies and no risks. They gain basic proficiency in moving, jumping and firing the gun before proceeding with the level. Similarly, in *WP*, P3 (Hardcore) knows that the only way to proceed is to hit the ball up the hill, so they attempt the same shot several times until they succeed.

4. Stop & Think

Play is suspended briefly (either by pausing or not acting within the game) while the player considers how best to proceed. While reflection may occur "in action" as part of the *Experiment* strategy, this category is reserved for reflection "on action" [28]. For instance, in *RR*, P12 (Hardcore) accidently unequipped their gun so when they came across an enemy they were unable to return fire. They retreat to the previous screen and pause to consider what has gone wrong. A variant of this strategy involves pausing the game to check for external resources or to look for in-game help. For instance, in *WP*, P4 (Hardcore) looks at the information sheet provided to find out more about the controls work. Similarly, P15 (Casual) in *RR* initially consults the information sheet before attempting to practice different combinations of actions (*Repetition*).

5. Take the Hint

Games often provide explicit hints and tips at various points in the game – this strategy involves the player choosing to carry out the suggested action. In *WP*, this was only observed at the introduction screen when players would attempt to interpret the arrows provided to them on screen and translate them to the mouse controls. In *RR*, hints are provided at various points e.g. the player is told they can hide behind certain objects in the environment. However, further breakdowns can occur if the player misses these instructions or does not understand them. For instance, P15 (Casual) in *RR* does not notice the hint about using the action button to access the lift and ends up exploring other parts of the game for clues instead.

Discussion

The findings illustrate how multiple strategies were often employed to achieve a single breakthrough, as one would lead on from the other. For instance, while a player would start exploring the game through *Trial & error,* knowledge would be gained via understanding breakthroughs that fed into the *Experiment* strategy. Alternatively, action breakdowns as a result of *Trial & error* could lead to *Repetition* as players aimed to develop their abilities. *Stop & think* tended to occur after repeated breakdowns and the failure of other strategies. In contrast, *Take the hint* usually led to breakthroughs without breakdowns but only if the hint was noticed in the first place.

However, as these strategies were developed on the basis of single-player games, it is not clear to what extent they would apply when people are playing a game together. This is important to consider as the "people factor" [20] is a key reason for why we play games. Gameplay can be an inherently social phenomenon and as Stevens and colleagues argue [30], multiplayer games allow for additional opportunities for learning and engagement to emerge from the interactions between players. Social factors are especially important to consider given the popularity of co-located games [7].

In addition, while breakdowns are an important source of learning, it was also clear from the analysis in Study 1 that player strategies could lead to breakthroughs without a preceding breakdown. As such, study 2 aims to validate the existing strategies and extend them in relation to breakthroughs that occur during co-located play.

STUDY 2

Method

Design: An exploratory case-study approach was [31] employed where multiple pairs of participants were observed playing a co-located cooperative game for approximately 40 minutes. The participants were interviewed briefly about their experience after the session. A recording was not played back as the conversation between participants provided a rich source of data.

Participants: 11 pairs were recruited for the study (M= 20, F = 2; Mean age = 25.9). Participants were paid £10 each for taking part and recruited from a university participant pool, and from advertisements placed around campus and video game shops. The adverts asked for participants to bring in someone they felt comfortable playing with and had played with before. A screening questionnaire was used to assess how experienced players were with of the game being used in the study, *Portal 2*. Participants were classed as experts if they had played a game in the *Portal* series before or had experience of the cooperative mode in *Portal 2*. Novice participants were those who had limited or no experience with the series. In total, there were 5 pairs of Experts, 4 pairs of Novices and 2 Mixed pairs (containing one expert and one novice). As in Study 1, a mix of players were included so that the strategies would reflect a range of player ability.

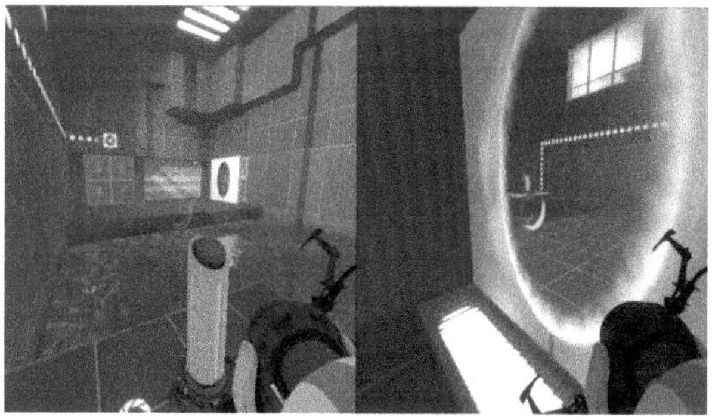

Figure 3: Screenshot of *Portal 2* spilt screen

Materials: Portal 2, was created and published by Valve and is available through the Steam gaming platform. The game employs a 3D first-person perspective, where players have to overcome a variety of puzzles in self-contained 'test chambers' using portals. The portals, projected on surfaces with a "portal gun", create a pathway that allows players to cross between spaces instantly. The levels often contain hints via visuals on the ground and walls, while the voice of GLaDOS (Genetic Lifeform and Disk Operating System), a robotic AI, sarcastically directs and berates the players within each chamber. The participants were asked to play through three different sections of the game:

1. *Calibration Course*: This tutorial level introduces players to the basics of playing in cooperative mode,

including an in-game communication method called the "Ping tool", with which players can point at place of interest and "ping" to draw attention to it.
2. *Team Building (Sections 1-3)*: This is the first level in which players have to work through a number of test chambers that require team work and the use of portals.
3. *Friendship is Magic 3*: *Portal 2* has an active online community where people create and share their own test chambers using the games inbuilt tools. This map was rated easy-medium difficulty and 5/5 stars by 8334 players. Including a custom test chamber ensured that even experienced players would be playing something they had not done before.

The sessions took place in a lab that was furnished like a living room, containing a comfortable sofa, coffee table and TV. The game was running on an Intel i5 gaming PC with a dedicated graphics card. The PC was connected to a large screen LCD TV where the game was presented in a split screen format (Figure 3). Participants interacted with the game via wireless Xbox 360 controllers. A camera was placed above the TV to capture the participants sitting on a sofa and a microphone was positioned on a table in front of the sofa. Morae Recorder by Techsmith was used to capture the game-play feed from the PC.

Procedure: Piloting with three pairs before the main study ensured that an appropriate custom community map was selected and that the game was playable by players with varying experience. Novice pairs had more trouble with some of the core mechanics so a more detailed information sheet was supplied. In the main study, participants were introduced to the game, before starting the calibration course. The experimenter observed the session from a separate room and took note of important events that occurred. The participants were stopped after completing the three sections, or until 40 minutes had passed. After the session a brief semi-structured interview was conducted to review and discuss some of the key events that occurred.

Analyses

The primary source of data was the video recordings, synchronized with game footage of the participants playing the game and talking to each other. This data was supplemented by the post-play interviews.

This study focused on critical incidents where breakthroughs occurred. These related to action (when the player performed a new action via the controller), understanding (when a participant realized how to progress in the puzzle or learnt about a game mechanic), and involvement (when participants were visibly happy or interested in the game). The strategies developed in Study 1 were applied but it was soon found that they did not account for all aspects of cooperative co-located play. Similar to a thematic analysis [3], new categories were developed iteratively, in a bottom up approach and discussed among the researchers until a definitive set was able to account for the different actions observed.

Findings

Short examples of the initial strategies are provided for illustrative purposes, before presenting the cooperative strategies. Participants are referred to as P1 or P2 (referring to Player 1 and Player 2 within a single pair) in "Session X", where X denotes which session the pair took part in.

Initial strategies

1. Trial & error

As in Study 1, *Trial & error* was coded when players explored the game environment and mechanics. This strategy was also found to be source of fun for the players and applied without a specific goal in mind. For instance, after starting the final map, P2 in Session 1 (Mixed), places a portal on the ceiling and floor and jumps through them, creating a continuous loop. P1 notices this and says "What happens if I jump in with you?". After doing so, for a short while they are both falling through the portals, before crashing into each other. They laugh and then continue with the game. While there is no initial breakdown in this case, arguably the players are experiencing an involvement breakthrough as they probe how the game works.

2. Experiment

Experiment was evidenced in a co-located setting through players thinking out loud and referring to transfer of knowledge. For instance, in Session 7 (Expert), after entering a new area where a receptacle drops from the ceiling after pressing a button, P2 wonders "If I press this [the button], will that one [the receptacle] go?". He proceeds to press it again and watches while the previous receptacle disappears and a new one drops from the ceiling. This is a recurring mechanic in the *Portal* games, where only one item is allowed at a time, and it is something P2 appears to be aware of but wanted to test out.

3. Repetition

Repetition was usually utilized in *Portal 2* when players were trying to get a sequence of tasks correct or to get the timing of certain actions right. An example of this occurred in Session 2 (Expert), where P1 pressed a button to release a cube that drops into a body of water. P2 was not able to catch it in time so says "You've got to do it again, I missed it". P1 then presses the button a couple of times until P2 is able to grab the cube before it disappeared into the water. They are then able to proceed to the next task.

4. Stop & think

The *Stop & think* category was most commonly coded when one player would stop playing in order to observe the other. For example, in Session 11 (Expert), the players encounter a problem in the custom community map which requires them to split off to perform different tasks. They were initially in the same room, but soon realize that one of them needs to investigate the effect of their action within another room (since there is no direct line of sight). P1 ventures out to the other room while P2 is inactive and focuses solely on P1's screen. As one player investigates the environment, the observer chimes in with suggestions e.g. referring to the location of P1's portals "No wait, from the other side? ... Oh, no, there." (P2).

Similar to Study 1, participants would also occasionally consult the information sheets provided about the game. For example, in Session 7 (Expert), P1 stops to check the sheet and tells P2 what the Ping button is. The post-play interviews corroborated the fact that players would sometimes consult external resources, e.g. an online guide, when they got stuck playing games outside of the lab.

5. Take the Hint

Portal 2 contains many hints in the environment. For instance, in Figure 4, the symbols on the ground indicate that the button will release a cube from the ceiling but that the player should watch their head! However, players rarely seemed to refer to these pictorial clues, and it is not clear whether they actually paid attention to them or not. Arguably, these hints would be easier to interpret only after having had some experience of playing the game.

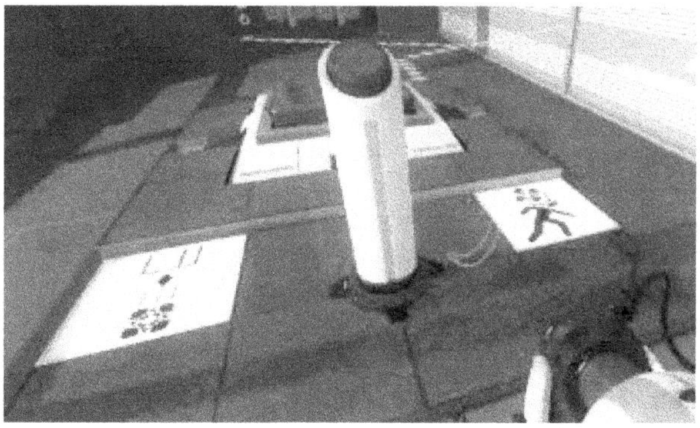

Figure 4: Screenshot of floor symbols in *Portal 2*

The Calibration course was designed to introduce players to the basic game mechanics. However, particularly for those who had not played the Portal series before, the instructions were not always clear. For instance, in Session 9 (Novice) while P1 understood the instructions for getting his avatar to wave, P2 was confused, until P1 showed him what to do. Similarly, in Session 6 (Novice) players had trouble using the "Ping Tool", not realizing it was for communication and confusing it with their portal guns.

Cooperative strategies

The additional strategies identified within the data set are defined below with illustrative examples.

6. Knowledge exchange

Players often chatted about the game challenges and environment, providing feedback about what they are doing, through sharing (and sometimes arguing!) about the knowledge and ideas they gained from other strategies such as *Trial & error* and *Experiment*. For instance, in Session 9 (Novice), P1 and P2 are trying to figure out how to cross over a pool of water and go through a timed door. The solution involves one of the players staying behind to control the door timer while the other player crosses over and creates portals for the player left behind. P1 and P2 are in a constant conversation, asking each other questions and sharing ideas e.g. P2: "Yeah, create a portal there", P1: "But then you can't press the button". The ensuing discussion leads P2 to achieve an understanding breakthrough and then to dictate the solution to P1 in the form of *Guidance* (see below).

Another example of this strategy concerns how players would split up to explore the game. Though *Portal 2* sometimes enforces a division of labor to solve puzzles, there were occasions when players would divide up responsibility when they didn't have to. For instance, in Session 3 (Expert), the players need to align a cube with a laser beam but are having trouble doing so. P1 goes to the cube and re-aligns it slightly asking P2 to go over the far node to provide feedback about how close the laser is.

7. Guidance

This category refers to instances where a player directly asks for help, or where one player explicitly provides guidance in the form of dictating instructions. For example, in Session 4 (Novice), P2 asks P1 "What should I do?"; P1 tells P2: "you see, first here, and then first out here, and then go in here and last here [He pings at the walls whilst saying this and continues with more explicit instructions] ...Ok so, first cancel all of them...you create one here and uh, here [pings at the location he wants the portal]". In this instance, P2 follows the guidance and they finish the puzzle successfully.

As the last example also indicates, the "Ping Tool" was sometimes used by players. However, given that they were in a co-located environment, players would often resort to physical gesturing and pointing to provide emphasis. For instance, in Session 8 (Novice), during the 'Calibration Course', both players are confused about how to get up to a ledge. P2 starts describing a solution, eventually standing up and pointing at the TV screen to illustrate what needs to be done:

P2: "So shoot the thingy and then look at me, in front of me there is a... there is something you can..."
[P1 fires portal at incorrect place]
P2: "No, not in front of me, in front of.... [Stands and walks to the TV] You should shoot here...if you shoot there you can go up".

8. Surrender control/take over

Unlike *Guidance* where advice is offered verbally, this strategy involves a physical taking over of control by one of the players. This included occasions where one player would allow the other to take the controller - e.g. in Session 5 (Expert), P2 asks P1 beforehand: [Laughs] "Do you want me to do it?" (referring to making a selection with the "Ping Tool"). However, there also were also occasional yet nonetheless surprising examples when taking over occurred without permission. For instance, in Session 6 (Novice), P1 was waiting for his partner to get up on a ledge. P2 is confused about what to do and P1 becomes impatient, eventually reaching over to press P2's controller buttons to create a portal without saying anything. P2 then points at the screen to try and encourage P1 to create the second portal and walk through. When P1 is unable to do this, P2 takes the controller away to perform the action. During the whole process, P1 looks visibly disinterested and is no rush to get the controller back. Despite the fact that this strategy led to progress, this example shows how being told what to do and losing control is likely to lead to an involvement breakdown.

Discussion

Similar to Study 1, the findings show how one strategy led on to another but also how different strategies were used by each participant within a pair. For instance, while working on the same problem one player may have been engaged in *Trial & error*, whilst the second player would be using *Stop & think* to observe them and subsequently formulate a possible solution through *Experiment*, before communicating this back to the first player through *Knowledge exchange*.

Interestingly, the findings also indicate how involvement breakthroughs can be achieved through testing the limits of the game. In addition to the players jumping through portals together in Session 1 (Mixed), in Session 2 (Expert) the pair attempted to shoot each other with lasers (P2: "I expect you to die Mr.Bond!"). P2 also teases P1 by repeatedly stepping on and off a button to briefly open a door but not for long enough to walk through. Again, while these types of breakdowns are not engineered by the game, they illustrate how playing around with the mechanics can lead to an increase in involvement. Though perhaps in some cases for only one of the players!

In Study 2, a recording of the game-play video was not played back to the participants as the dialogue between the players was considered a rich source of data. While the dialogue was helpful for developing the cooperative strategies, the lack of insight into players' internal thought processes meant it was sometimes hard to code for the previously established strategies e.g. a player may have been using *Experiment* but unless they verbalized this to their companion it was difficult to pinpoint. Nonetheless, there were still examples within the data of all the categories that were developed in the previous study. This point is raised however as a caution to those who would like to attempt a quantitative comparison of the categories and how often different types of players used each strategy on the basis of observation and the conversational data.

GENERAL DISCUSSION AND CONCLUSIONS

There is lack of research on how people adopt different types of strategy as part of learning through gameplay. We addressed this issue by examining the strategies players use to overcome breakdowns and achieve breakthroughs. Given that learning is often a social process, the initial set of strategies was applied and extended to account for cooperative play. The result is a set of eight strategy types; three of which apply only within cooperative games, while five apply to both single and multi-player games.

The strategies adopted by players are likely to relate to the type of game being played (or even to particular sections of the same game), as well as their level expertise. To account for a range of player behavior, both studies included players of different ability levels. Study 1 recruited hardcore and casual players and asked them to play a game they had not played before. Study 2 recruited players who differed in terms of their experience with the *Portal* series. However, expertise can be difficult to define in the context of gaming. Does expertise relate to gaming in general or one game specifically? There is scope for further research to examine the impact of different types of expertise in relation to strategy choice and progress. The challenge for designers is how to support players with different levels of ability while avoiding major involvement breakdowns that lead to players quitting the game altogether.

The findings of the studies indicate multiple strategies are often employed to achieve a breakthrough in single-player and multiplayer games. For single players, one strategy would lead on to the next (sometimes quite rapidly). In a multiplayer co-located context, players would use different strategies at the same time e.g. P1 would *Stop & think* to observe P2 as they offered *Guidance* or P2's *Knowledge exchange* would lead to P1 to *Experiment* etc.

Regarding each of the strategies, *Trial & error* has been referred to in other studies [1; 4; 30], though it is not always clearly defined. In Gee's analysis of games [8], he describes how players are continually probing the game-world, reflecting on actions, forming a hypothesis, testing through re-probing and then accepting or rethinking their initial hypothesis. However, the *Trial & error* strategy indicates that there are times when players are more playful and haphazard; trying out actions just to see what, if anything, will happen and sometimes just for fun. Unlike Gee's "Probing principle" suggests [8], an explicit hypothesis is not always formed. However, in *Experiment*, the player does need to have a more developed understanding about the game-world in order to be able to test it.

In terms of design considerations, the distinction between these two strategies is particularly important to consider in relation to educational games where it is key to ensure that there is an alignment between the game mechanics and the intended learning [10; 11]. While *Trial & error* may lead to progress, subsequent understanding is not guaranteed, and progress in itself is not an indication of learning [16; 21]. Essentially, designers should avoid situations where action breakdowns lead to progress without understanding breakthroughs.

A further consideration relates to the need to ensure that players are given an opportunity to *Repeat* actions either in a safe part of the game, or in terms of allowing for gradual improvement of skills throughout the game e.g. through a tutorial. As suggested by Gee [8], players should be able to take risks in game sections where the consequences of failure are minimal. However, consideration should also be given to when the same actions are repeated several times but do not lead to progress e.g. through providing advice to the player about the strategy they are using when they seem stuck after a certain time limit.

In addition, *Stop & think* should be supported and encouraged as reflection is an integral component of the learning process [8; 28]. Though the studies took place outside of a home context, the fact that the information sheets provided were consulted (if only occasionally) as part of *Stop & think* highlights the fact game information can be distributed across modalities and that players do look outside a game for help. There is scope for designers to consider how to provide further information to players or ways in which the game itself can suggest strategies to players who are taking a long time to progress.

Knowledge is also distributed across players, as the cooperative strategies indicate. These strategies do echo some of the Cooperative Performance Metrics presented by El-Nasr and colleagues [7]. Like "Worked out strategies", *Knowledge exchange* represents how player discuss the game-play with each other while *Guidance* relates to "Helping each other". However, these strategies should be viewed in relation to others such as *Experiment* and *Stop & think* to understand how players move from individual actions to cooperative behaviors. Furthermore, the CPMs are presented as a way to evaluate good design practice rather than as a tool for discussing how learning taking place during game-play through achieving breakthroughs.

However, while *Guidance* did seem to be a useful strategy to players, there was no guarantee that players would actually take the advice they were given. Arguably, such interactions show that players are in control of constructing their own learning environment as and when required [30]. An inability or unwillingness to carry out the instructions would occasionally lead to *Surrendering control/Taking over* though this was quite rare.

The *Surrendering control/Taking over* strategy is not necessarily a negative when the surrendering is voluntary and learning occurs as part of observation during *Stop & Think*. However, learning may not always result from this action and the non-active player is likely to experience an involvement breakdown due to not feeling responsible for subsequent progress [16]. One possible way to avoid this is to provide mechanisms that allow for a kind of "Quantum Leap" mode (Quantum Leap was a TV show where the main character would jump into the body of someone else and live their lives for a short period of time). This mode could offer a temporary switch in control of avatars, to allow the more experienced player to demonstrate the solution but without the action being permanent. The less experienced player would thus get a chance to observe the action, get an explanation, and most importantly, carry out the action themselves once control is given back. Thus, the player could consolidate a breakthrough by developing the procedural skills they require, without losing any agency.

Through considering these strategies, we argue that designers can produce experiences which are able to support both learning and player involvement. Furthermore, the strategies can also help develop games that appeal to a broad audience since they account for the ways in different types of players respond to a variety of challenges. Though players with varying levels of expertise were included in studies, to capture a range of behaviors and develop the categories, a consideration of how expertise impacts patterns of strategies, and how social dynamics influence strategy choice was beyond the scope of this research.

In addition, while the studies covered more than one type of game, further research is required to establish the extent to which the strategies apply to other genres e.g. role playing games. While the strategies were applied and developed in relation to co-located multiplayer games, they do not cover online play or competitive contexts (e.g. they do not account for sharing of resources in games like *World of Warcraft*). Finally, future work could investigate how strategies are combined in different ways and further examine the strategies in more depth e.g. by looking at hypothesis formation within *Experiment* in terms how knowledge transfers from the real world, from other games and/or from the same game.

ACKNOWLEDGMENTS

We thank all the volunteers who took part in both studies. This research was supported by the EPSRC funded CHI+MED project (EP/G059063/1) and EU project Citizen Cyberlab (317705).

REFERENCES

1. Alkan, S., and Cagıltay, K Studying computer game learning experience through eye tracking. *British Journal of Educational Technology*, 38, (2007), 539-543.

2. Andersen , E., O'Rourke, Liu, Y., Snider, R., Lowdermilk, J., Truong , D., Cooper, S., & Popovic, Z. The impact of tutorials on games of varying complexity, In *Proc. CHI 2013*, ACM Press (2013), 59-68.

3. Braun, V., & Clarke, V. (2006). Using thematic analysis in psychology. *Qualitative Research in Psychology*, 3(2), 77–101.

4. Blumberg, F. C., Rosenthal, S. F., & Randall, J. D. Impasse-driven learning in the context of video games. *Computers in Human Behavior*, 24(4), (2008), 1530-1541.

5. Cox, A.L., Cairns, P., Shah P., & Carroll, M. Not Doing But Thinking: The Role of Challenge in the Gaming Experience. In *Proc. CHI 2012*, ACM Press (2012), 79-88.

6. Csikszentmihalyi, M. *Flow: The Psychology of Optimal Experience.* Harper Perennial, New York, 1990.

7. El-Nasr, M.S., Aghabeigi, B., Milam, D., Erfani, M, Lameman, B., Maygoli, H., & Mah, S. Understanding and Evaluating Cooperative Games. In *Proc. CHI 2010*, ACM Press (2010), 253-262.

8. Gee, J. P. *What video games have to teach us about literacy and learning.* New York: Palgrave Macmillan, 2004.

9. Gee, J. P. Games, learning, and 21st century survival skills. *Journal of Virtual Worlds Research*, 2(1), (2009), 3-9.

10. Habgood, M.P.J., and Ainsworth, S.E. Motivating children to learn effectively: Exploring the value of intrinsic integration in educational games. *Journal of the Learning Sciences*, 20 (2), (2011), 169-206.

11. Harpstead, E., MacLellan, C. J., Aleven, V., & Myers, B. A. Using Extracted Features to Inform Alignment-Driven Design Ideas in an Educational Game. In P*roc. CHI 2014*, ACM Press (2014), 3329-3338.

12. Hollins, P., & Whitton, N. (2011). From the Games Industry: Ten Lessons for Game-Based Learning. *International Journal of Virtual and Personal Learning Environments*, 2(2), 73-82.

13. Independent Games Festival. www.igf.com

14. Iacovides, I., Aczel J.C., Scanlon, E., & Woods, W.I.S. What can breakdowns and breakthroughs tell us about learning and involvement experienced during game-play? In *Proc. of the 5th European Conference on Games Based Learning,* ACI (2011), 275-281.

15. Iacovides, I., Cox, A.L., & Knoll, T. Learning the game: breakdowns, breakthroughs and player strategies. *CHI '14 Extended Abstracts on Human Factors in Computing Systems* (2014), 2215-2220.

16. Iacovides, I., Cox, A.L., McAndrew, P., Aczel, J.C., & Scanlon, E. (submitted). Game-play breakdowns and breakthroughs: Exploring the relationship between action, understanding and involvement.

17. Juul, J. *A Casual revolution: Reinventing video games. Cambridge*, MA: The MIT Press. 2010.

18. Koster, R. *Theory of fun for game design*. Scottsdale, AZ: Paraglyph Press, 2005.

19. Kuutti, K. Activity theory as a potential framework for human computer interaction research, in: Nardi, B.A. (Ed.) *Context and consciousness: activity theory and human computer interaction*, MIT Press, (1996), 17-44.

20. Lazzaro, N. (2004). Why we play games: Four keys to more emotion without story. [Technical report]. Oakland, CA: XEO Design Inc.

21. Linderoth, J. Why Gamers Don't Learn More. *Journal of Gaming and Virtual Worlds*, 4(1), (2012), 45-62.

22. Marsh, T., Wright, P., & Smith, S. Evaluation for the design of experience in virtual environments: modelling breakdown of interaction and illusion. *Cyberpsychology & Behavior*, 4(2), (2001), 225–238.

23. Malone, T. W., and Lepper, M. R. Making learning fun: A taxonomy of intrinsic motivations for learning. *Aptitude, Learning, and Instruction*, 3, (1987), 223-253.

24. Mekler, E. D., Bopp, J. A., Tuch, A. N., & Opwis, K. (2014, April). A systematic review of quantitative studies on the enjoyment of digital entertainment games. In P*roc. CHI 2014*, ACM Press (2014), 927-936.

25. Mirza-Babaei, P., Nacke, L.E., Gregory, J., Collins, N., & Fitzpatrick, G.A. How Does It Play Better? Exploring User Testing and Biometric Storyboards in Games User Research. In *Proc. CHI 2013,* ACM Press (2013), 1499-1508.

26. Pelletier, C. and Oliver, M. Learning to play in digital games. *Learning, media and technology*, 31, (2006). 329-342.

27. Ryan, W., and Siegel, M. A. Evaluating interactive entertainment using breakdown: Understanding embodied learning in video games. In *Proc. of DiGRA,* (2009).

28. Schön, D. A. (1987). *Educating the reflective practitioner*. San Francisco: Jossey-Bass.

29. Sharples, M. Methods for Evaluating Mobile Learning. In Vavoula, G.N., Pachler, N., & Kukulska-Hulme, A. (eds), *Researching Mobile Learning: Frameworks, Tools and Research Designs*. Oxford: Peter Lang Publishing Group, (2009), 17-39.

30. Stevens, R., Satwicz, T. and McCarthy, L. In-game, in-room, in-world: Reconnecting video gameplay to the rest of kids' lives. In K. Salen (Ed.) *The ecology of games: Connecting youth, games, and learning.* Cambridge, MA: MIT Press, (2008), 41-66.

31. Yin, R. K. (2009). *Case study research: Design and methods.* 4th edition. Thousand Oaks, CA: Sage

The Edge of Glory: The Relationship between Metacritic Scores and Player Experience

Daniel Johnson
Queensland University of Technology
Brisbane, Queensland
dm.johnson@qut.edu.au

Christopher N. Watling
Queensland University of Technology
Brisbane, Queensland
christopher.watling@qut.edu.au

John Gardner
CSIRO Ecosystem Sciences
Brisbane, Queensland
john.gardner@csiro.au

Lennart E. Nacke
University of Ontario Institute of Technology, Canada
lennart.nacke@acm.org

ABSTRACT
This study sought to examine how measures of player experience used in videogame research relate to Metacritic Professional and User scores. In total, 573 participants completed an online survey, where they responded the Player Experience of Need Satisfaction (PENS) and the Game Experience Questionnaire (GEQ) in relation to their current favourite videogame. Correlations among the data indicate an overlap between the player experience constructs and the factors informing Metacritic scores. Additionally, differences emerged in the ways professionals and users appear to allocate game ratings. However, the data also provide clear evidence that Metacritic scores do not reflect the full complexity of player experience and may be misleading in some cases.

Author Keywords
Videogames; player experience; Metacritic; Psychology; Player Experience of Need Satisfaction; Game Experience Questionnaire

ACM Classification Keywords
J.4 [**Computer Applications**]: Sociology, Psychology – Social and Behavioural Sciences; K.8.0 [**Personal Computing**]: General – games;

INTRODUCTION
Review scores sell videogames. However, little is known about how much aggregated reviewer and user scores reflect the actual player experience. Videogame reviews are, for some consumers, an important source of information that can guide purchasing of videogame titles [6, 8]. In fact, research has shown that reviews (when read before playing a game for the first time) can actually influence player experience [20, 21]. In essence, videogame reviewers summarise and quantify their own subjective player experience. They provide a benchmark for consumers. This benchmark has a critical impact on video game sales and publisher deals in an increasingly competitive environment of videogame development. Score aggregators like the Metacritic website[1] provide an aggregation of a number of different reviews for major videogame releases. Videogame publishers have used Metacritic scores to adjust developers' monetary compensation tied to specific video game titles[2]. The relationship between sales and Metacritic scores is still debated. However, an important research question that arises from this debate is how representative Metacritic scores are of different facets of player experience.

Scientific studies increasingly recognize the potential impact (both positive and negative) of videogames on personal wellbeing [2, 10, 18, 37]. To study this impact, a growing number of psychometric scales or questionnaires for measuring player experience have been developed. These measures represent attempts to better understand the engagement and enjoyment associated with player experience as well as the factors that motivate people to play videogames.

A noteworthy distinction between psychometric measures of player experience and game reviews is that the former generally assume player experience is a multidimensional construct. This multidimensionality is important, because it allows for the possibility that a videogame might do some things well and other things poorly. Different players might enjoy different aspects of the same game. It is counterintuitive to reduce a videogame to a single score as a measure of quality and success. However, this is common practice when a videogame is reviewed and it is also a result of Metacritic's review aggregation process. This inevitably hides some of the complexities of player experience.

We can assume that the quality of a reviewer's player experience directly informs review scores. However, to date, little is known about which facets of player experience influence how a game is judged in a review.

CHI PLAY '14, October 19 - 22 2014, Toronto, ON, Canada
Copyright 2014 ACM 978-1-4503-3014-5/14/10…$15.00.
http://dx.doi.org/10.1145/2658537.2658694

---

[1] http://www.metacritic.com

[2] VentureBeat: http://venturebeat.com/2009/08/27/the-influence-of-metacritic-on-game-sales/

Validated psychometric scales are not necessarily designed to measure the same components of player experience as review scores. However, players use reviews and review scores to choose which games they are going to play and hence any overlap between review scores and the player experience is of interest. This study explores how two, commonly used, player experience scales relate to aggregate game review scores (from both professional reviewers and consumers). Our study explicitly aims to identify which components of player experience relate to game review scores.

Quantifying Player Experience

As a result of the increasing popularity of studying videogames in experimental settings, many questionnaires have emerged, designed to measure the general engagement and enjoyment associated with playing videogames [5, 7, 9, 13, 14, 32, 39] and the extent to which specific states or experiences occur – for example, flow [38]. The Player Experience of Need Satisfaction [32] and the Game Experience Questionnaire [13] were chosen for use in the current study. We selected them on the basis that they offer multiple subscales designed to assess different components of player experience and they have been widely used in previous research (as detailed below).

The Player Experience of Need Satisfaction Questionnaire

Ryan et al. [32] applied an established psychological theory of motivation – Self-Determination Theory (SDT) – to videogame player motivations. SDT is primarily concerned with the potential of social contexts to provide experiences that satisfy universal needs of people. SDT has been successfully applied in research on sports, education and leisure domains. Przybylski and colleagues explored how videogames fulfill or thwart psychological needs and thus promote or discourage sustained engagement and either positive or negative outcomes for players. Based on SDT and other relevant theories (e.g., Presence), Przybylski and colleagues developed the Player Experience of Need Satisfaction (PENS) measure. This questionnaire assesses player experience in the dimensions: Competence (perceived efficacy playing the game), Autonomy (sense of freedom and independence), Relatedness (connectedness within the game), Intuitive Controls (perception of the in-game controls) and Presence/Immersion (sense of being in the game world, as opposed to experiencing oneself as a person outside the game, manipulating controls or characters).

The initial validation of the PENS was performed in experimental contexts with participants, who may or may not have been experienced video game players and in a non-experimental context with a sample of MMO players [32]. The PENS has been used successfully in different settings and with many videogames [15, 22, 27-29, 32]. The five factors measured by the PENS have been shown to be associated with aspects of videogame experiences, including: videogame sales, game series loyalty, duration of videogame interest, positive affect and enjoyment [3, 30, 35]. As part of their initial validation Ryan and colleagues showed that the PENS accurately distinguished between a game that had received very positive reviews and a game that had received largely negative reviews.

The Game Experience Questionnaire

The Game Experience Questionnaire [GEQ: 13] is designed to provide a comprehensive evaluation of the gameplay experience. Unlike the PENS, the GEQ structure is not based around a specific theory. Rather, the GEQ is based on conceptual accounts of player experiences and focus-group explorations with a range of gamers. The GEQ is comprised by seven factors, which are: Positive Affect (experiencing positive emotions during gameplay), Negative Affect (experiencing negative emotions during gameplay), Frustration (irritation from negative experiences of gameplay), Flow (holistic sensation of acting within the confines of the game), Challenge (feelings of being tested within the gameplay experience), Immersion (perception of being absorbed in the game environment), and Competence (perceived efficacy playing the game).

Concerns have been raised regarding the GEQ's psychometric properties because the preliminary validation work (leading to the creation of the scale) has never been published [see 26]. Nevertheless, the GEQ has been applied in many game research studies. The GEQ has been used in psychophysiological studies of player experience [16, 24, 25], studies of social experiences of videogaming [11], studies that experimentally explored how player experiences vary across genres [17] and the designing of videogames for unique user populations [1].

Metacritic Scores

The Metacritic website typically produces a Metacritic *Professional Score* and a Metacritic *User Score* for a videogame. Metacritic professional scores are calculated by collating a number of professional reviews (from various online videogame review sources), converting the associated individual review scores into a score out of 100 (e.g., 4 out of 5 stars becomes a score of 80) and then weighting the scores to produce a final aggregated Metacritic professional review score. It is stated that weighting is given to critics and publications as function of their quality and overall stature (with greater weighting given to those outlets judged to be higher quality [23]). Unfortunately, the weighting that is applied to the collated reviews is not available to the public. In contrast to professional Metacritic scores, Metacritic user scores are simply the unweighted average of all ratings provided by visitors to the Metacritic website. User scores are provided anonymously (or pseudonymously) with reviewers identifiably only by a self-chosen username.

The use of the Metacritic Professional Scores varies, but it is substantial in some cases. For instance, it has been reported that contracts between game developers and publishers include clauses that tie key deliverables and outcomes to Metacritic scores [8, 33]. Metacritic scores that fall short of pre-determined benchmarks can lead to bonuses or royalties not being paid to a game's developer by the game's publisher [36]. Additionally, a game developer's track record of Metacritic scores can be used by game publishers to negotiate reduced royalties and expenditure for the developer [33]. Moreover poor Metacritic scores can lead to a drop in a game development company's stock price [8]. In these ways, Metacritic scores can be a substantial financial influence on game development.

Metacritic scores have become so important to the gaming industry that, in some cases, it has been suggested that game developers are seeking to influence who publicly reviews their games and thus which professional game reviewers can contribute to Metacritic scores [33]. This means that game publishers and developers can hire professional game reviewers to review their unreleased games to provide feedback. Games user research studios sometimes – but rarely – use professional reviewers for early user testing. This feedback is then used to improve the game prior to its public release. However, once the professional game reviewer has been paid to provide feedback on a game, they cannot ethically provide a consumer review of that game. This conveniently excludes them from contributing to the overall Metacritic professional score for that particular game [33].

The utility of professional Metacritic scores is equivocal for benchmarking the videogame experience. Research has shown that non-player characters from videogames with higher professional Metacritic scores are more believable and enjoyable than those from videogames with lower Metacritic scores [19]. Additionally, Metacritic professional scores have been shown to be strongly correlated with videogame sales [12]. While player experience should arguably be the primary driver of both review scores and sales, Metacritic scores should not drive sales independent of game quality. However, it has been suggested that a Metacritic Professional Score, particularly scores over 90 out of 100, can become the primary driver of videogames sales, [4, 8, 40] rather than the influence of the actual quality of player experience.

The reliability of the Metacritic professional scores is also ambiguous. For instance, a reviewer's scores of a videogame sequel can be influenced by both the commercial success and player experience of the prequel videogame [34]. In such cases, experiencing a videogame brand (e.g., a game franchise with many sequels) seems to strongly influence the attitudes brought to experiencing an individual game. Professional videogame reviewers are likely to have a systematic approach for reviewing videogames. Nevertheless, the subjective nature and the potential for bias for or against a videogame's genre, platform, producer, and series [31] are likely to affect the reliability of the Metacritic aggregation. Moreover, the undisclosed procedure by which reviewers' scores are weighted to create the professional Metacritic score could also impact the reliability and validity of the aggregated professional review scores.

With respect to Metacritic user scores, other issues arise that potentially influence validity and reliability. It is possible that those who feel strongly about a game (either positively or negatively) are more likely to take the time to rate it than those who feel less strongly. Thus, it may be that Metacritic user scores disproportionately sample extremely negative and extremely positive opinions about a particular game. Relatedly, there is evidence – in terms of the written reviews submitted by users on the Metacritic website – that negative reviews for some games are written in an attempt to make other games appear relatively more popular in comparison. For instance, there exists rivalry between fans of the Call of Duty and Battlefield franchises, and fans of either series can be seen to post negative reviews for the other series. Regardless of these potential bias sources, it is not clear how Metacritic user scores relate to player experience (as measured by psychometrics) or which facets of player experience are most strongly associated with user scores.

The Current Study

Professional videogame reviewers are an established and influential source of information for consumers. However, to the best of our knowledge, no studies have yet addressed the relationship between videogame reviewer scores and gameplay experience measures. Therefore, we wanted to study how commonly used measures of player experience (i.e., PENS and GEQ) relate to the aggregated review scores of Metacritic. Metacritic scores were chosen over any individual source of reviews as a means of avoiding any idiosyncrasies associated with specific review websites. By examining the relationships between the PENS and GEQ and Metacritic scores, we can identify player experience facets that are most important to professional videogame critics and to Metacritic website users, who review and rate games. Therefore, we pose the following research questions:

RQ1: Which subscales of the PENS and GEQ are associated with the Metacritic Professional scores?

RQ2: Which subscales of the PENS and GEQ are associated with the Metacritic User scores?

METHOD

Participants

For this study, we selected only participants that had an interest in videogames and that played videogames at the time of the study. No other selection criteria were applied for participation in the study. The research protocol received ethical as well as health and safety approval from the host University.

In total, 573 participants took part in the study. The average age of the participants was 20.7 years (*SD* = 5.1; range = 13-54), with the majority of participants being male (81.7%). On average, the participants played videogames 16.6 hours per week (*SD* = 12.5; range = 1-100 hours) and played their favourite game for an average of 9.5 hours per week (*SD* = 9.6; range = 1-100 hours).

An extensive list was generated from the participants' favourite game titles; over 200 different titles were listed. For the sake of brevity, the game titles will not be listed but rather the proportions of game genres that were represented. The most common genre of participants' current favourite game was first-person shooter games (24.9%), followed by action role-playing games (13.6%), action adventure games (11.9%), role-playing games (9.6%), massively multiplayer online role-playing games (8.7%), multiplayer online battle arenas (5.8%), real-time strategy (5.6%), and other various games genres (19.9%).

The measures of player experience used in the current study were not provided by the same sample that provided the Metacritic scores (i.e., the professional or user scores). However, we can expect a relationship between the two measures of player experience on the basis that the same games were being analysed with each measure. The qualities of each game exist independent of who is playing them. This is our core assumption.

Measures

Player Experience of Needs Satisfaction Questionnaire

The PENS questionnaire [PENS: 32] is a self-report measure of an individual's experiences while playing a videogame. Participants indicate their agreement with 21 items on a seven-point Likert scale (1 – "do not agree" to 7 – "strongly agree"). The PENS measures different aspects of player experience with five subscales: Competence, Autonomy, Relatedness, Presence and Intuitive Controls (as described above). Higher scores on each scale indicate greater agreement. The PENS subscales have been found to have good reliability, as determined by Cronbach's alpha. The initial examination study of the utility of the PENS, reported a Cronbach's alpha statistic between 0.7–0.8 [32]. Subsequent work has reported Cronbach's alpha statistics between 0.7–0.9 for multiplayer videogaming sessions [16]. Based on these previous studies, we consider the PENS a reliable instrument.

Game Experience Questionnaire

The GEQ [GEQ: 13] is another self-report measure of an individual's experience during gameplay. Participants indicate their agreement with 33 items on a five-point Likert scale (1 – "not at all" to 7 – "extremely"). The GEQ is designed to measure seven facets of player experience: Positive Affect, Negative Affect, Frustration, Flow, Challenge, Immersion, and Competence (as described above). Higher scores on a particular subscale indicate greater experience of that facet during gameplay.

As discussed, the scale's authors have not published any formal studies assessing the structure and performance of the GEQ. On that basis, exploratory factor analysis was undertaken to examine the performance of the GEQ in the current sample. The full 33 items were subject to exploratory factor analysis via principal axis factoring, using oblique rotation. Initial analyses suggested the existence of 5 or 6 factors, but there were split loadings in both solutions, and the hypothesized scale structure did not clearly emerge. Items with no loading higher than .4, and items with loadings of higher than .3 on two or more factors, were dropped from the analysis. In total, seven items were dropped, and a final 6-factor solution (which explained 50.4% of the variance) was chosen as best reflecting the underlying structure. In contrast to the original factor structure, negative affect and tension/annoyance items were found to load on a single factor, which was renamed *Frustration*. Another item was dropped because it lowered the associated scale reliability. The GEQ competence subscale was not used in the current study given its conceptual overlap with the PENS measure of the same construct.

Procedure

The majority of participants (81.7%) were drawn from a first-year university videogame study course. A snowball procedure was used to gather additional participants via gaming forums, social media web pages and through personal contacts of the researchers. Participants completed the study questionnaires online. There was no way to control for the time that had elapsed since participants had last played videogames, because participants completed the survey at a time of their own choosing. To address this issue, a guided recall process was used to prime respondents before they answered questions about their gameplay experiences. Respondents were asked to recall and describe in detail what was happening when they were most recently playing their current favourite game. Participants then responded to the PENS and GEQ with regard to their experience of playing that game. Participants were offered the chance to win a $100 voucher in return for their participation. For each game nominated by participants, Metacritic Professional and User scores were obtained from the Metacritic website (CBS Interactive Inc, 2014). These variables were used as the dependent variables for the study.

Statistical Analyses

The internal consistency of the scale scores was evaluated with Cronbach's alpha coefficient. The variables of Metacritic Professional Score, Metacritic User Score, and "Hours of Playing Favourite Game" had non-normal distributions. To account for this non-normality, Spearman's rho correlations were used to examine the bivariate associations between study variables.

RESULTS

Descriptive Statistics

The means, standard deviations, and – where applicable – Cronbach's alphas for the study's main variables are displayed in Table 1 (below). The participants nominated favourite games tended to be rated highly by others, as demonstrated by high mean values for both the Metacritic Professional and User Scores.

Study variable	Mean	SD	α	Actual Range
Metacritic Pro Score	86.84	6.95	-	55.00-99.00
Metacritic User Score	7.38	1.43	-	2.40-9.40
Hours Play Fav Game	9.50	9.62	-	1-100.00
PENS Competence	5.80	0.94	.71	2.00-7.00
PENS Autonomy	5.52	1.10	.68	1.00-7.00
PENS Relatedness	3.95	1.49	.71	1.00-7.00
PENS Presence	4.30	1.31	.87	1.11-7.00
PENS Int Controls	5.86	0.90	.57	2.00-7.00
GEQ Positive Affect	4.25	0.56	.84	2.40-5.00
GEQ Frustration	1.48	0.52	.85	1.50-5.00
GEQ Flow	3.50	0.90	.81	1.00-5.00
GEQ Challenge	3.37	0.82	.66	1.00-5.00
GEQ Immersion	3.57	0.92	.72	1.00-5.00

Table 1.Means, standard deviations (SD), Cronbach's alphas (α), and actual range of the study variables.

Correlations

Table 2 (below) displays the Spearman correlation coefficients for the Professional and User Metacritic scores, Hours Playing Favourite Game and the PENS and GEQ subscales. Many significant correlations were found between the study variables. Clear differences between what professionals and users are responding to showed in their ratings of games. Regarding the correlations with the Metacritic Professional Scores, all of the PENS subscales had significant and positive correlations with the Metacritic Professional Scores. The two largest correlations were between the Metacritic Professional scores and Intuitive Controls and Autonomy. Somewhat smaller correlations were found between the Metacritic professional scores and the PENS measures of competence, autonomy, relatedness and presence. The GEQ subscales were less aligned with the Metacritic Professional scores. Specifically, only three of the GEQ subscales (Positive Affect, Immersion and Competence) were correlated with the Metacritic Professional Scores.

Study variable	Pro Score	User Score
Metacritic Pro Score	-	
Metacritic User Score	.26**	-
Hours Play Fav Game	-.03	-.13**
PENS Competence	.18**	.08*
PENS Autonomy	.22**	.11*
PENS Relatedness	.16**	.05
PENS Presence	.20**	.13**
PENS Int Controls	.25**	.07
GEQ Positive Affect	.15**	.18*
GEQ Frustration	-.05	.01
GEQ Flow	.02	.05
GEQ Challenge	-.06	.09*
GEQ Immersion	.20**	.12**

**$p < .01$, *$p < .05$

Table 2. Spearman rho correlation coefficients for the Metacritic scores, Hours Playing Favourite Game, and subscales of the PENS and GEQ

Slightly fewer significant correlations were found between the Metacritic User Scores and the measures of player experience. The PENS subscales of Competence, Autonomy and Presence were significantly associated with the Metacritic Users scores. Regarding the correlations between Metacritic Users scores and the subscales from the GEQ, only three significant correlations were found. These were for Positive Affect, Challenge and Immersion. Interestingly, the variable "Hours of Playing Favourite Game" was negatively correlated with the Metacritic Users score (that is, lower Metacritic User scores were associated with higher hours of play and high Metacritic User scores were associated with lower hours of play).

DISCUSSION

Overall Patterns

Overall, it can be seen that both professional and user Metacritic scores relate to player experience facets that are measured by the PENS and the GEQ. This generally indicates there is overlap between player experience constructs being assessed in videogame research and the videogame aspects to which professional critics respond. Professional Metacritic scores (and to a lesser extent, player Metacritic scores) are more strongly associated with the components of the PENS than the GEQ. All five components of the PENS were positively associated with professional Metacritic scores. This means that higher Metacritic scores are indicative of higher PENS scores. However, only two of the five components of the modified, more reliable, version of the GEQ used were associated with Metacritic Professional scores: Positive Affect and Immersion.

These results could reflect the relative importance of the satisfaction of self-determination theory related needs in creating a rewarding player experience. At the very least, the constructs measured by the PENS measure seem to be of high importance for people (reviewers and users) that rank videogames on Metacritic. It may also be that the PENS is a relatively stronger measure in terms of psychometric properties, having been formally validated and refined in various settings.

With the exception of Positive Affect, all the measured components of player experience show a stronger association with Metacritic Professional scores than with Metacritic User scores. This pattern may reflect a greater ability on the part of professional critics to identify how well a game will satisfy player needs and provide a pleasing experience. Professional reviewers arguably have developed a game literacy through playing many games that allows them to accurately judge aspects of player experience that are important for most people when playing a game. User generated scores, in contrast, might reflect more idiosyncratic opinions, which relate less well to typical player experiences. There might be a difference between the formalized idea of player experience developed in academia and the subjectively voiced player experience of Metacritic users. It might also point to a bias in reporting experience. The number that Metacritic users give in their rating might reflect an opinion or an attitude toward a game rather than a marker of the quality of player experience. What players experience and what they report to have experienced might not be the same thing. However, a quantitative analysis of user game ratings is limited here because it distils their possibly complex feelings about gameplay to a single numeric quality indicator. However, this pattern provides an important starting point for a necessary discussion of the relationship between game ratings and player experience.

Furthermore, it is interesting to note that only a moderate correlation exists between Metacritic professional and user scores. This supports the idea that professional critics and everyday players view the same games in different ways and perhaps respond to different things when rating a game. It may be that professionals are more objective than players, or perhaps, more critical. Alternatively, it may be that professional critics are required to provide a more superficial rating of some games, because of constraints in available playing time. This would not apply in the case of games that primarily consist of single-player campaigns, because most reviewers play such games in full before publishing a final review. Generally, both the required professionalism and available playing time might drive professional reviewers to adopt a more formalized reviewing approach. It may also be that the low correlation is partially a function of the aforementioned issues with user scores related to bias (e.g., scoring less favoured games with extremely negative ratings). Since we looked at aggregate Metacritic scores, outliers could be having a strong influence on these results. Without knowing the score distribution for each game, we cannot know for sure how much influence these factors might be having.

Strength of Associations

The strongest relationships for Metacritic Professional scores were found with Intuitive Controls, Autonomy, Presence and Immersion. The strongest relationships for Metacritic User scores were found with Positive Affect, Presence, Immersion and Autonomy. Thus, some clear differences and similarities exist between what professionals and users are responding to as components of player experience measured in the current study. It seems that the experience of positive affect is similarly influential to both professionals and players. This is not surprising – enjoyment and associated positive emotions are a universal component of videogame play. Similarly, Immersion and Presence are related to the scores given by both professional reviewers and users. It seems likely that these are universally positively regarded components of player experience. For both Presence and Immersion, the relationship is stronger for professional reviewers. It may be that professionals place greater importance on these components of player experience.

Competence and Autonomy are more strongly related with Metacritic Professional scores than Metacritic User scores. These stronger associations with professional scores (Presence, Immersion, Competence and Autonomy) may reflect that professional critics are more clinical or objective than regular players – focussing on these formal aspects of the game, while regular players are relatively more influenced by their emotional response to the game (as shown in the relationship between Metacritic User scores and Positive Affect).

Differences between Professional and User Scores

Some key differences emerged in terms of elements of the player experience associated with one Metacritic score but not the other. Intuitive Controls and Relatedness are related to Metacritic Professional scores but not to Metacritic user scores. With respect to Intuitive Controls, a relatively large relationship with Metacritic Professional scores is evident. This most likely reflects the fact that the understandability and ease of controls in a game is a key issue for a reviewer aiming to provide a rating that is useful and informative for consumers with varying skills levels and prior experience. Given their personal game literacy (built through playing many different games) with genre-based controls, professional reviewers might also be less forgiving when a game does not handle player controls well. Alternatively, if we assume that players spend longer playing a game than professional reviewers, then it may be that players have more time to become familiar with controls even if they are not intuitive. However, it should be acknowledged that the reliability for the Intuitive Controls subscale was relatively low in the current study and this result should thus be interpreted with some caution.

With respect to Relatedness, professional reviewers may place greater importance on games that are enjoyable when played with others, because their focus (when reviewing a game) must in some ways take place with reference to all other games. As a result, a game that offers greater connection with others can be seen as deserving of a higher score. In contrast, a user might not be concerned with this aspect of player experience, as some games (and arguably genres of games) do not attempt to provide relatable characters or to create connections between players. Players, who favour such games, may disregard relatedness when judging a game they like for other reasons.

Challenge was only related to Metacritic User scores. This may reflect the fact that players are more influenced by whether the game offers them a suitable level of challenge. Professional reviewers, on the other hand, are aiming to give a review that is relevant to users of varying skill levels, so the degree of challenge offered is less likely to be directly influential. Alternatively, it may be that greater challenge in a game sometimes interferes with the process of reviewing it in a timely fashion, resulting in reviewers adjusting game difficultly (and thus challenge) to a level that allows them to complete the game quickly. In contrast, for user, the game is a purely recreational task wherein challenge is directly related to the quality of player experience. A challenging game could also be likely to influence player attitudes more strongly, because players have to invest more time into more challenging games. The more time invested could lead to stronger game attachment and a greater likelihood of rating the game on a website like Metacritic. Separately, it may be that professional game reviewers are so experienced with and proficient at playing games that few games provide high levels of challenge, and hence the notion of challenge does not directly inform their rating of a game.

The lack of a relationship between Flow and Challenge with Metacritic Professional scores may reflect a "ceiling effect" in that these components of player experience are "givens" in popular games. Hence, they do not inform the score unless the game is particularly poor (unlikely in a sample made of players' current favourite games). However, this interpretation is not well supported by the relatively low Flow scores found in the sample (see Table 1). Similarly, the lack of relationship between Metacritic scores and frustration may be a "floor effect" in that a low level of frustration is commonly required for a game to become a players' favourite game.

It is interesting to note how "hours of play" relates to the Metacritic scores. The lack of relationship between Metacritic Professional scores and hours of play suggests that professional review scores do not provide an indication of how long people play a particular videogame. It is likely that variations associated with different genres (e.g., MMORPGs are structurally longer games than platformers or action adventure games) hide any connection between review scores and play time. The negative relationship between Metacritic User scores and hours of play is at first glance, counter-intuitive. However, it may be that shorter games are easier to make in a way that appeals to players as (other things being equal) greater development time and energy can be placed into the production of all aspects a shorter game than a longer game. Alternatively, it may be that players of longer games are more critical of them because of the relatively greater amount of time they have invested in playing them.

Limitations and Future Research

Overall, the effect sizes associated with the relationships identified in the present study are relatively small. This suggests that the factors identified by researchers as being key components of player experience are having only a small impact on review scores. It may also be that the influence of these factors is weakened as part of the weighting process of professional scores undertaken on the Metacritic website. For example, if specific critics treated as less influential (and therefore apportioned relatively less weight as part of the overall professional Metacritic score) are more influenced by these factors than critics considered more influential then the strength of the relationship would be partially hidden. This might be the case if more influential critics are, for example, more jaded, more cynical or more subjectively critical than less influential or less experienced critics. However, this explanation is not relevant to the relatively small effect sizes between player experience factors and Metacritic User scores. In this case, the effect sizes are relatively small most likely because of the previously discussed noise or bias associated with user scores (resulting from extreme opinions being more likely to motivate providing a review score and some users posting low scores for games that are perceived to compete with their own preferred games).

However, for both Metacritic Professional and User scores there are three likely explanations for the relatively small effect sizes: Firstly, the sample of people, who completed our player experience measures (PENS, GEQ) is not necessarily the same sample of people, who provided ratings towards the Metacritic scores. The strength of the relationship is inevitably reduced by this difference. Secondly, a large variety of factors can potentially influence the rating of a game. It is probable that different people respond to games in different ways – factors of personal taste, preferences for or against different games types based on prior experiences and personality differences among players and reviewers are all likely to contribute meaningfully to how each individual person responds to any particular game. As a result, the player experience factors measured in the current study – while directly relevant to the experience of play – and associated ratings of a game cannot account for the full range of variability in an individual's player experience. Future research should seek to incorporate a larger range of relevant measures of the player experience to better explore this possibility. An option could be the textual analysis and exploration of the content of user reviews on Metacritic. Finally, it should be noted that the full range of values on the measurement scales was not included in the current study. For example, games with a professional Metacritic score below 55 were not assessed (this is a function of participants evaluating their current favourite game). This reduced range of the scales may have caused the correlations we reported above to underestimate the true relationships. Future research should extend to games that are relatively less popular.

It should also be acknowledged that the player experience metrics used in the current study are far from perfect and the small effect sizes may also relate to noise and variability introduced through the use of these metrics. In particular, the psychometric properties of the GEQ are difficult to judge because of the lack of factor structure validation studies published to date. Future research could attempt to explore these relationships using other measures of player experience or incorporate larger samples, which would allow for more extensive assessment of the validity and structure of the component measures.

Conclusion

Overall, the findings in the current study suggest that there is a degree of overlap and commonality between measures of player experience used by researchers and Metacritic scores. However, Metacritic Professional scores, though potentially useful in some situations (e.g., getting a sense of the majority critical opinion of a game or distinguishing particularly well received games from particularly poorly received games) do not reflect the full complexity of the experience of playing a game. Arguably, Metacritic scores may be being given too much weight in some situations such as negotiations between developers and publishers or purchasing decisions being made by players. Our findings support the notion that Metacritic scores may be influencing videogame sales irrespective of game quality, because people basing their purchasing decisions on Metacritic scores may inadvertently miss out on games they would greatly enjoy. This is particularly likely if players respond strongly to specific aspects of player experience (e.g., feelings of relatedness or the experience of challenge) that are not necessarily fully reflected in Metacritic scores.

REFERENCES

1. Al Mahmud, A., et al. Designing and evaluating the tabletop game experience for senior citizens. In *Proceedings of the 5th Nordic conference on Human-computer interaction: building bridges* 2008, ACM press (2008), 403-406.

2. Anderson, C.A., et al., Violent video game effects on aggression, empathy, and prosocial behavior in eastern and western countries: a meta-analytic review. *Psychological bulletin 136*, 2 (2010), 151-173.

3. Birk, M. and R.L. Mandryk. Control your game-self: effects of controller type on enjoyment, motivation, and personality in game. In *Proceedings of the SIGCHI Conference on Human Factors in Computing Systems* 2013, ACM press (2013), 685-694.

4. Bower, B., *Valuing a Video Game: Does Score Determine Value?* 2009.

5. Brockmyer, J.H., et al., The development of the Game Engagement Questionnaire: A measure of engagement in video game-playing. *Journal of Experimental Social Psychology 45*, 4 (2009), 624-634.

6. Cox, J., What Makes a Blockbuster Video Game? An Empirical Analysis of US Sales Data. *Managerial and Decision Economics 35*, 3 (2013), 189-198.

7. Dauphin, B. and G. Heller, Going to other worlds: The relationships between videogaming, psychological absorption, and daydreaming styles. *Cyberpsychology, Behavior, and Social Networking 13*, 2 (2010), 169-172.

8. Everiss, B. Metacritic has changed the games industry. 2008, Available from: http://www.bruceongames.com/2008/06/04/metacritic-has-changed-the-games-industry/.

9. Fang, X., et al., Development of an instrument to measure enjoyment of computer game play. *Intl. Journal of Human–Computer Interaction 26*, 9 (2010), 868-886.

10. Ferguson, C.J., The good, the bad and the ugly: A meta-analytic review of positive and negative effects of violent video games. *Psychiatric Quarterly 78*, 4 (2007), 309-316.

11. Gajadhar, B., Y. De Kort, and W. Ijsselsteijn. Shared fun is doubled fun: Player enjoyment as a function

of social setting. In *Fun and Games* 2008 (2008), 106-117.

12. Greenwood-Ericksen, A., S.R. Poorman, and R. Papp, On the Validity of Metacritic in Assessing Game Value. *Eludamos. Journal for Computer Game Culture 7*, 1 (2013), 101-127.

13. IJsselsteijn, W.A., K. Poels, and Y.A.W. de Kort, *The Game Experience Questionnaire: Development of a self-report measure to assess player experiences of digital games*. Eindhoven University of Technology: Eindhoven. 2008.

14. Jennett, C., et al., Measuring and defining the experience of immersion in games. *International Journal of Human-Computer Studies 66*, 9 (2008), 641-661.

15. Johnson, D. and J. Gardner. Personality, motivation and video games. In *Proceedings of the 22nd Conference of the Computer-Human Interaction Special Interest Group of Australia on Computer-Human Interaction* 2010, ACM press (2010), 276-279.

16. Johnson, D., et al., Cooperative Play with Avatars and Agents: Differences in Brain Activity and the Experience of Play. *Computers in Human Behavior under review*, (2014).

17. Johnson, D., et al. Personality, genre and videogame play experience. In *Proceedings of the 4th International Conference on Fun and Games* 2012, ACM press (2012), 117-120.

18. Jones, C.M., et al., Gaming well: links between videogames and flourishing mental health. *Frontiers in psychology 5*, (2014), 1-8.

19. Lee, M.S. and C. Heeter, What do you mean by believable characters?: The effect of character rating and hostility on the perception of character believability. *Journal of Gaming & Virtual Worlds 4*, 1 (2012), 81-97.

20. Livingston, I., L. Nacke, and R. Mandryk, *Influencing Experience: The Effects of Reading Game Reviews on Player Experience*, in *Entertainment Computing – ICEC 2011*, J. Anacleto, et al., Editors. Springer Berlin Heidelberg. p. 89-100, 2011.

21. Livingston, I.J., L.E. Nacke, and R.L. Mandryk. The impact of negative game reviews and user comments on player experience. In *ACM SIGGRAPH 2011 Game Papers* 2011, ACM press (2011).

22. McEwan, M., et al. Videogame control device impact on the play experience. In *Proceedings of The 8th Australasian Conference on Interactive Entertainment: Playing the System* 2012, ACM press (2012), 1-3.

23. Metacritic. How we create the metascore magic. 2014, Available from: http://www.metacritic.com/about-metascores.

24. Nacke, L. and C.A. Lindley. Flow and immersion in first-person shooters: measuring the player's gameplay experience. In *Proceedings of the 2008 Conference on Future Play: Research, Play, Share* 2008, ACM press (2008), 81-88.

25. Nacke, L.E., M.N. Grimshaw, and C.A. Lindley, More than a feeling: Measurement of sonic user experience and psychophysiology in a first-person shooter game. *Interacting with Computers 22*, 5 (2010), 336-343.

26. Norman, K.L., GEQ (Game Engagement/Experience Questionnaire): A Review of Two Papers. *Interacting with Computers 25*, 4 (2013), 278-283.

27. Przybylski, A.K., C.S. Rigby, and R.M. Ryan, A motivational model of video game engagement. *Review of General Psychology 14*, 2 (2010), 154-166.

28. Przybylski, A.K., R.M. Ryan, and C.S. Rigby, The motivating role of violence in video games. *Personality and Social Psychology Bulletin 35*, 2 (2009), 243-259.

29. Przybylski, A.K., et al., The ideal self at play: the appeal of video games that let you be all you can be. *Psychological Science 23*, 1 (2012), 69-76.

30. Rigby, C.S. and R.M. Ryan, *The Player Experience of Need Satisfaction (PENS) Model*. Immersyve Inc. 2007.

31. Rollings, A. and E. Adams, *Andrew Rollings and Ernest Adams on game design*. New Riders. 2003.

32. Ryan, R.M., C.S. Rigby, and A.K. Przybylski, The Motivational Pull of Video Games: A Self-Determination Theory Approach. *Motivation and Emotion 30*, 4 (2006), 344-360.

33. Schreier, J. Metacritic Matters: How Review Scores Hurt Video Games. 2013, Available from: http://kotaku.com/metacritic-matters-how-review-scores-hurt-video-games-472462218.

34. Situmeang, F.B.I., M.A.A.M. Leenders, and N.M. Wijnberg, History matters: The impact of reviews and sales of earlier versions of a product on consumer and expert reviews of new editions. *European Management Journal 32*, 1 (2014), 73-83.

35. Tamborini, R., et al., Defining media enjoyment as the satisfaction of intrinsic needs. *Journal of Communication 60*, 4 (2010), 758-777.

36. Totilo, S. Low Metacritic scores cause game publishers to withhold developer royalties. 2008, Available from: http://multiplayerblog.mtv.com/2008/05/29/low-metacritic-costs-developers/.

37. Vella, K., D. Johnson, and L. Hides. Positively playful: when videogames lead to player wellbeing. In *First International Conference on Gameful Design, Research and Applications* 2013, ACM press (2013).

38. Wang, L.C. and M.P. Chen, The effects of game strategy and preference-matching on flow experience and programming performance in game-based learning. *Innovations in Education and Teaching International 47*, 1 (2010), 39-52.

39. Wiebe, E.N., et al., Measuring engagement in video game-based environments: Investigation of the User Engagement Scale. *Computers in Human Behavior 32*, (2014), 123-132.

40. Wingfield, N. *High scores matter to game makers, too.* The Wall Street Journal, 2007.

Engaged By Boos and Cheers: The Effect of Co-Located Game Audiences on Social Player Experience

Dennis L. Kappen, Pejman Mirza-Babaei, Jens Johannsmeier, Daniel Buckstein, James Robb, Lennart E. Nacke

HCI Games Group, Faculty of Business and IT, University of Ontario Institute of Technology, 2000 Simcoe St. N, Oshawa, ON, Canada

dennis.kappen@humber.ca, pejman@uoit.ca, jjohannsmeie@uos.de, daniel.buckstein@uoit.ca, james.robb@uoit.ca, lennart.nacke@acm.org

ABSTRACT

Little is currently known about the influence of co-located player audiences on gameplay experience. Social player experiences are important to understand in co-located gaming scenarios, because these experiences relate to player performance. Player-audience relationships have been studied before, but prior research focused on player attributes and typology. In our study, we investigated the effect of different *co-located* audience types (silent, positive, negative) and no audience on player experience. For the study, we contribute a video game specifically developed for two-player, co-located gameplay and findings from questionnaires and semi-structured interviews. Our findings show that both – negative and positive audience activity – drove players to become more engaged in the video game. In contrast, silent audiences made players feel unnerved and less engaged in gameplay. Our paper is the first to study of the relevance of co-located audience influence on player experience, which is important for understanding the design of co-located games.

Author Keywords

Audience Influence; Game Design; Social Interaction; Player Experience; Multiplayer Game; Co-located Gaming

ACM Classification Keywords

H.5.2. Information interfaces and presentation K.8.0 [Personal Computing]: General – Games

INTRODUCTION

The continued success of co-located games, which rely on interaction between players when they play a game, can be seen in the multiplayer focus of top-selling games. In particular, co-located gaming in front of an audience (as often done in co-located games like *Wii Sports* or *Just Dance*) always has a performance aspect to it, where the interaction between players and their audience shapes the overall gameplay experience. However, we currently know very little about the effect of different kinds of audiences on players when playing co-located games. Our ability to design for audience influence (as well as for social interactions) during gameplay would improve, if we had a better understanding of the effect that audiences have on players. A first necessary step towards this is to investigate different audience responses during co-located gameplay.

Audience responses have been studied in different environments before. For example, in art and performance [19] or during multimedia presentations [31]. Prior research has focused on social facilitation and choking effects in gaming on the performance of good players [16] and on the player-onlooker relationship [21]. However, these studies are limited to player attributes and typology [2]. Recently, effects of game physicality on turn anticipation of audience members [8] was studied. However, the player-audience relationship (especially during co-located gameplay in video games) is currently not well studied. Supportive audiences have been shown lead to performance decrements compared to non-supportive audiences in skill-based activities [4] and in sports activities, where skill is learned with higher levels of explicit knowledge [20]. However, both these past studies consider the audience influence on only a *single* performer. In this paper, we are building on and extending this line of research by investigating the influence of an audience presence in a *multiplayer*, *co-located* gaming environment. Hence, we conducted a study to compare the presence and influence of an audience on player experience in a co-located performance-type game to determine how different types of audience activity influence player experience.

To investigate this audience influence, we developed a two-player co-located video game called *Magic Duel* (MD). The game uses *Kinect* input (a camera-based tracker) and facilitates drop-in gameplay. People can walk up to the gaming setup and participate in a quick game with each other. We chose this setup because we believe that these types of multiplayer games naturally get an audience and that the effect of an audience is important for their design.

CHI PLAY '14, October 19 - 22 2014, Toronto, ON, Canada

Copyright 2014 ACM 978-1-4503-3014-5/14/10...$15.00.

http://dx.doi.org/10.1145/2658537.2658687

We conducted two exploratory studies: an initial pilot study in a co-located space, where the game was put in front of players in an open and co-located environment. We investigated how audience presence influenced gameplay. This informed a follow-up study in a controlled environment within a laboratory setting. In the follow-up study, we aimed to understand the effect of different *audience types* (i.e., none, silent, positive, negative) on player experience.

Our findings present evidence that positive and negative audiences drove players to be more engaged in a game in different ways. In our study, a positive audience led to player distraction, but this in turn forced the player to be more concentrated and engaged in the game. Similarly, a negative audience led players to improve their effort in gameplay and hence also increased player engagement and concentration. In contrast, a silent audience led to less engagement and unnerved players with an uncanny feeling of being watched.

To the best of our knowledge, our paper is the first to show that negative and positive audience activity engages players *more*, while silent audiences engages them *less* in co-located multiplayer games. A better understanding of the influencing role of the audience on co-located gaming can help designers to use this knowledge in their game design to build engaging games. Our paper provides an important first step in understanding player experience in co-located games involving audience participation.

RELATED WORK

Co-located games create engaging social interactions, where players, audience and their level of experience are important for shaping the gameplay experience. Games can encourage play between intergenerational populations [1] and enable players with varying skill levels to play together.

In this section, we provide an overview of prior research in co-located gaming, audience influence and user experience in co-located game settings. The *iGamefloor* [10] was an interactive floor platform that engaged players in a social game involving multiple individual players in a co-located collaborative game environment. The game was specifically designed for school children to track the movement of limb contact points. However, none of these game examples were evaluating the impact of different audience types.

The level of engagement with a game ranges from passive game spectatorship to active – even transformational – play. Innovative interaction paradigms have enabled a freedom of experiences through body movements, gestural controls and social interaction between players within co-located game settings. Games are more often incorporating performance aspects into them, moving from home environments to public settings involving gaming tournaments and exertion games. "Sports over a distance" explored exertion interfaces [24], which helped to connect people socially over distances. Research on full-body experience indicated that body movements led to stronger and affective experiences [3]. Another example is adding an interactive display to a public basketball hoop can motivate players and foster community [6]. Researchers also explored the potential of facilitating social awkwardness to investigate social player experiences during physical co-located gameplay [12].

Video game design often relies on player to system interaction from the personal spaces of players or their interaction with an online community. This leads to players navigating games on their own or collaboratively playing with their friends in a co-located setting or an online environment. Roccetti et al. [27] define *context accessibility* and *player heterogeneity* to be two variables distinguishing between gaming at home versus in a public space. This means that in public-space gaming, the contextual relationship of the game is accessible to any or all players in situ, and anyone can step in and play the game. For example, contemporary city [30] shows how non-instrumental actions are relevant. Spatial opportunities and encounters with strangers were key influencers for play in public spaces.

Player experience is exciting because of the spatial relationship between onlookers and player. Engagement in games stems from encouraging dynamic social interactions [21]. In another study, the precision of player body movement recognition increased players' immersion levels in exertion games [25]. The emotional content expressed by players [28] added a dynamic and complex context in a body-movement game. *Physicality of an experience* introduces an added dynamic to any play activity that involves players engaged in physical interaction through gameplay. For example, player engagement increased when the game mechanics afforded body movements [22]. However, this physical experience transcends beyond the player into the realm of social presence [18] when the game system is deployed in a co-located space. Furthermore, gestural interactions as studied using a Kinect controller, facilitate the opportunity of fun, laughter and gentle mocking gaze [11] from observers, which influences the participants engagement. This shows that a relationship between players and their audience exists, which contextualises player experience at any given point in time during gameplay.

Spontaneity and fluidity of information sharing between people in a communal space has been compared in physical media and digital media. Designing a spectator experience [26] is a key challenge in a co-located game with audience present. The synergy between spectators and a performer interacting with a computer affords multiple levels of interactions. Previous research proposed design strategies to be secretive, expressive, magical and suspenseful [26] in a taxonomical matrix – four approaches that explained a spectators perception of a performer's interaction.

One of the main challenges for a game installation in a co-located space with audience presence for us was how to define the desired interaction type. This Social Experience (SX) of play can be defined as the relationship between player, game system and audience; a symbiotic relationship [14] between these domains affecting play in co-located spaces. We define game interaction in this context: between *players and the game system*, between *players and the audience* and between *the audience and the game system*.

Audience participation and engagement has been a topic of interest to researchers in previous studies. For example, the *WeINteract* [5] system introduced the quantification of audience approval activities in a venue-based game as a measure of athletes' performance, leading to greater audience engagement. There is also a differentiation between passive engagement and active participation of an audience. As such, a study about Starcraft spectators [7] explored the audience relationship with a real-time strategy game being played online. Kimble et al. [16] investigated social facilitation and choking when playing games before an audience. Presence of supportive audiences as opposed to non-supportive audiences has also led to degradation of performance in previous studies [4] of a single player in a skill-based activity. In addition, supportive audiences had a negative effect [20] on performance in single player sporting conditions. Building on these related works, our focus is to explore the effect of audience types on player engagement and experience in a two player co-located gaming situation.

MAGIC DUEL: A FULL-BODY PERFORMANCE GAME

The success of a co-located collaborative game is dependent on the levels of interaction and enjoyment. For our study, we were interested in the influence of audience on player experience. In addition we were also interested in understanding audience effects on the design of co-located games in relation to social play and social affordances (e.g., as discussed by de Kort et al. [18]).

Hence, we focus on answering two research questions here:

1. Does the presence of an audience affect player experience in a multiplayer co-located game?
2. How do different characteristics of an audience's behaviour affect player experience in a multiplayer-co-located game?

To identify the challenges and relationships between players, audiences and the game system, we used the game Magic Duel (MD). MD was designed as a co-located two-player game to entertain and draw an audience in its socio-spatial environment. The relevance of an audience watching players duel in a video game could be similar to an audience watching a sporting arena match between players or teams. We used this game (as a stimulus) to understand the effect of a co-located audience on player experience.

In MD (see Figure 1), players act as magicians that conjure spells with their hand gestures. The game can be played with two people, who are co-located, so that they can see their own gestures and the feedback from their avatar in the game world. Hand movements are used by the players to cast spells at each other and at the same time hand gestures enable blocking spells from the opponent player.

Players duel each other by casting spells back and forth and at the same time dodging each other's attacks. They play until one of the players is completely depleted of magic. Each player – displayed on screen as a sorcerer avatar – can cast spells of three different elemental types (i.e., fire, earth and ice) by changing the orientation of their hands. The spells cast are visualized as either a bolt of an elemental type or a corresponding shield spell that absorbs or blocks incoming bolts. Whenever a sorcerer is unable to block an incoming projectile, the avatar gets hit and loses some of its magic. Magic is used as a health indicator. When one of the sorcerers loses all their health, the player loses the match.

Figure 1. Magic Duel screenshot in the view for one player.

At the top right of the screen, the hand positions are indicated (e.g., metaphorically represented in an east west direction for the fire spell; north-east to south-west hand position for the earth spell and the north-west to south-east hand position for the ice spell). Blocking the spells for fire, earth and ice is done by moving one's hands outwards in the directions mentioned above for corresponding spells.

We conducted two studies with this game; the first (pilot) study was in a public space at a conference in a Toronto, Canada; and the second study was in a controlled environment at our dedicated game research lab.

PILOT STUDY

We deployed MD at a games conference to gauge player reactions and understand audience engagement effects on player performance. Conference attendees were invited to play the game and fill out a brief survey after playing.

Our main goal was to understand whether or not MD was a good candidate for assessing the impact of an audience on player experience. We wanted to find out, if MD's setting naturally gets an audience and to observe the effect of an audience on players' gameplay experience. Moreover, we studied (from a player's perspective), whether the game was easily usable and satisfying, so that these factors would not interfere with their reports in our following exploratory lab study, which we detail later in this paper.

Procedure

People visiting the games conference were invited to play the game with other people watching, often cheering (unguided) and supporting their gameplay. Prior to participating, they were informed about the study and filled out a consent form. Eighteen adults took part in this pilot study (N=18, 16 males, 2 females) aged between 15 and 40 years (M= 25.6, SD=3.1).

All participants were familiar with digital gaming. After playing the game, the participants were asked to fill out an extended version of the usefulness, satisfaction and ease of use (USE) questionnaire [23]. We used this questionnaire, because we wanted to assess how well this game would work as a stimulus in our later experiments. The questionnaire comprised of questions in the categories: ease of learning, ease of use and satisfaction, to which we added additional questions about audience influence. In addition to the USE questionnaire, participants were also rated their experience on a 7-point Likert scale (1= strongly disagree and 7= strongly agree). These questions were about: being conscious of the presence of an audience, nervousness because of an audience, being watched by an audience, inhibitions to play by audience presence, distraction due to noise from audience and effect of audience presence as a distraction to gameplay. We refer to and discuss these questions as *audience influence* in the following sections.

Results

Responses to questions corresponding to each of the three categories *ease of learning*, *ease of use* and *satisfaction* were averaged and the resulting category average values analyzed using Wilcoxon signed-rank tests (using a normal approximation with continuity correction due to ties in the data) to see if they are significantly different from the neutral response (4; "Neither agree nor disagree"). A conservative non-parametric test was chosen because the data was not normally distributed. Box-whisker diagrams of the distributions are shown in Figure 2.

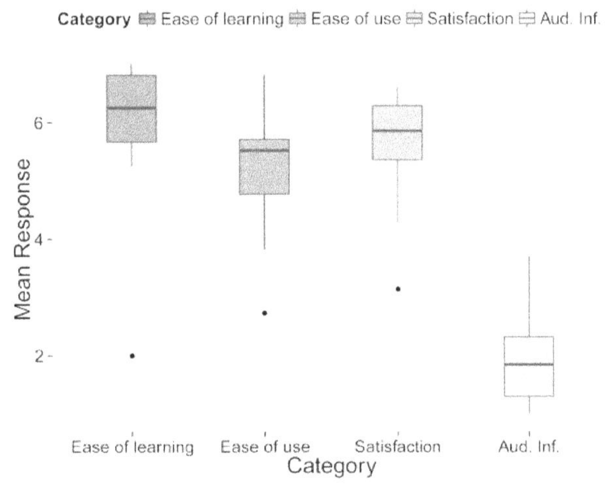

Figure 2. Box-whisker diagrams showing distributions for each of the category scores in the extended USE questionnaire.

Our results show that participants found the game easy to learn (Mdn = 6.25, $z = -3.17$, $p < 0.01$, $r = 0.79$), and also easy to use (Mdn = 5.52, $z = -3.35$, $p < 0.001$, $r = 0.79$). Furthermore, they seemed to be satisfied playing it (Mdn = 5.86, $z = -3.62$, $p < 0.001$, $r = -0.85$). For the *audience influence* category, all questions but one were aimed at negative (e.g., distracting) audience effects. We averaged responses on these questions (inverting answers on one because it had positive wording instead of negative wording like the others), which showed that participants did not feel negatively affected by an audience being present (Mdn = 1.85, $z = -3.71$, $p < 0.001$, $r = 0.87$). Responses on the individual questions show, for example, that players did not feel nervous playing in front of an audience (Mdn = 1, $z = -3.70$, $p < 0.001$, $r = 0.87$). Also, audience was not perceived as a distraction (Mdn = 1, $z = -3.98$, $p < 0.0001$, $r = 0.94$). Responses on a question about positive effects of an audience ("Audience encouragement helped me to play better") were not significant (Mdn = 4, $p > 0.05$).

Discussion and Take Away

Our pilot study provided us with the initial finding that people playing a game in a public co-located space – surrounded by onlookers – do not seem negatively affected by this fact compared to playing games without an audience. This finding surprised us, because humans are affected by an audience being present in many activities and functions [17][16]. We thought that this could point to gameplay taking a different place in the spectrum of human activities. Following the pilot study, we expanded our research into an exploratory study where we focused on categorizing the audience into *audience types* and studying their influence on player experience.

Our pilot study findings also showed that – from the player's point of view – the MD game was easily usable and satisfying to play (i.e., we continued using it as a stimulus). Based on the pilot study, MD itself being a newly designed game should not be considered a limitation in the exploratory study. One of our main takeaways from this pilot study was that our game setup seemed to work well as a game deployed for performing in front of an audience.

EXPLORATORY STUDY

The layout of the experimental setup is shown in Figure 3.

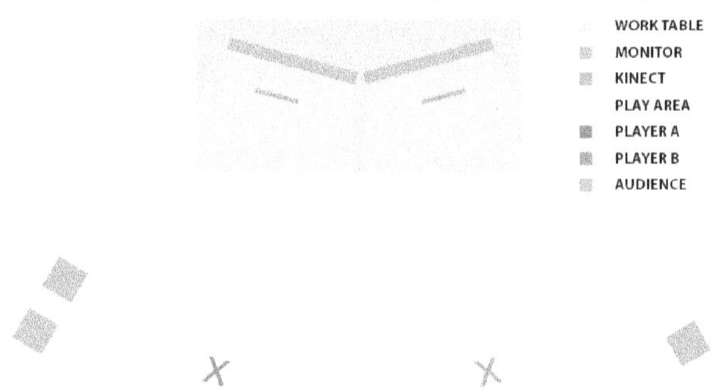

Figure 3. Experimental setup for the exploratory study.

This study was conducted in a University lab. Our leading question was whether positive or negative audience reactions would influence player experience in any way. MD was set up on two Dell computers. The Kinects were placed in front of Dell monitors and the game was started. Players were allowed to interact and talk to each other. We checked for interference of the gestural movements of both players with their arms extended so that the Kinect did not respond to the other player's movements. The spots marked "X" demarcate the suggested location of players.

We had three audience members who remained a constant throughout the study. Based on prior evidence of scripting responses for supportive (positive) audience and non-supportive (negative) audience [4],[20], the comments for positive and negative audience were scripted. As an example a positive script was: *"You are doing great, keep focusing on the spells"*; and a negative script was: *"Your game is poor, you should quit!"* The intonations and comments order were rehearsed with the audience members to sound authentic.

Research Questions

We were interested in whether the audience excitement level and enthusiasm (or lack thereof), affected the performance of a player while playing a game. After a lack of audience influence on gameplay in our pilot study, we wanted to understand if player experience can be positively or negatively influenced by an audience being present and them being in a certain pre-defined mood.

Based on the pilot study, we modified our exploration to investigate the effects of audience influence on player experience. Following from the contextual relationship between the player and the audience, we established the following exploratory research questions:

RQ1: Would the presence or absence of an audience affect the player experience in the game?
RQ2: Does the presence of a "positive" audience increase the player experience in the game?
RQ3: Does the presence of a "negative" audience decrease the player experience in the game?

Method

Using a repeated-measures (within-subjects) design, audience types corresponded to different levels on a four-level independent variable with the following conditions:

A. No Audience (i.e., Control)
B. Silent Audience
C. Positive (Cheerful) Audience
D. Negative (Booing) Audience

Pairs of participants were asked to play MD in all four conditions, equally balanced using a Latin-square design. All participant pairs played all four conditions of the independent variable. We had a set of questions to determine the demographics of the population. Player experience, as approximated by questionnaires and interviews, was the dependent variable to be studied. To determine factor of player experience for each of the above four conditions, we use the Flow Short Scale (FSS) [9], the Immersion questionnaire [13] and an extended version of our own pre-interview questions to identify players reactions to Audience Influence (AI) (see *Table 1*). These questions had positive and negative questions about audience presence, silent audience, positive audience and negative audience. The questions are shown in the following table.

Item	Audience Influence (AI) Questions
1	Did the presence of an audience make you self-conscious?
2	Did the presence of an audience make you nervous?
3	Did the audience inhibit your play?
4	Was the audience noise distracting?
5	Was the audience a distraction?
6	Did the audience affect your concentration?
7	Did the audience encouragement help you play better?
8	Was the presence of an audience watching you play acceptable?
9	Did you prefer to play the game with audience present?
10	Did the audience motivate you to play better?
11	Did the audience demotivate your gameplay?
12	How engaged were you in the session?

Table 1. Audience Influence (AI) questions on a 5-point Likert scale (1 = strongly disagree; 5= strongly agree)

Additionally, once participants played all four conditions, they were asked to fill in our 5-point Likert scale (1= very poor; 5= very good) Final Game Rating Questions (FGRQ), to evaluate the player's reaction to the game itself. We used these questions to evaluate MD based on the aspects of experience, quality, fun, visuals and sounds.

Participants

Participants were recruited from a pool of University students. The study was run with pairs of participants. Recruitment was done via mailing lists, notices and word of mouth. Sixteen participants, all male students between the ages of 18 and 23, participated in the study. Three audience members were chosen, of which one female and two male persons, and stayed as constants for the study.

Materials

Two Dell workstations were used to run MD – connected to each other via a network switch and assigned a static IP address. The game was displayed on two separate Dell 21 inch monitors. Microsoft Kinect controllers were connected to each workstation and placed in from of the monitors. A Sony HD 250 GB video camera was used to record the player activities. Evernote software was used to record player interviews at the end of the study.

MD was designed for a co-located installation to have the players facing each other separated by a screen. However, in our study setup, the players did not face each other. They faced their individual monitors in a sector formation (see Figure 3). This was done to accommodate the play in a small controlled experimental room as opposed to a larger co-located space. Audience members were positioned around the players within their peripheral vision area.

Procedure

Participant pairs were welcomed. Players were informed that they would be playing four conditions. Details of the type of four conditions were blinded from the participants. Then, they filled out a consent form and a demographic questionnaire. They were given time to get accustomed with their location in the study area – with reference to the Kinect – to check for their screen avatar's response to their corresponding movements in their own physical space. The participants were given detailed information about the gestures being used in the game to duel each other and block the spells from opposing players. They were allowed to try out these gestures for casting and blocking spells, which enabled the experimenter to check for the responsiveness of the game avatar to gestural movements of players.

Participant pairs played each condition for five minutes and the number of deaths of each player was noted. After each condition, each player independently completed the questionnaires (FSS, Immersion and Audience Influence questions). This also accounted for rest between conditions to accommodate fatigue effects. After playing in all of the conditions, each player filled out our Final Rating Game Questions (FRGQ). Each player was interviewed to gain insight into their individual, subjective gameplay experience.

Interview Protocol

The 16 participants who took part in the study were interviewed independently to elicit responses towards player experience. Interviews were semi-structured and questions were categorized into game experience (game usability, gameplay, game story), motivation to play and audience influence. Participants were asked to elaborate on their experience based on their performance in the game, their ability to navigate the gesture controls, their reactions and feelings towards audience influence, and their motivation to play the game. The verbal data was categorized and documented into an Excel spreadsheet. Additional themes emerging from the iterative process were identified and documented for comparison.

Results

Results of the data from the Immersion questionnaire, FSS, AI questions are discussed first, followed by the results from our Final Game Rating Questions (FGRQ). Finally, we last report qualitative data from player interviews.

Immersion, FSS and AI questions

Responses by the two participants in each pair were averaged as recommended in previous work [15] to achieve independent observations. For each participant and condition, we divided the questionnaire responses into five categories and computed the average category scores.

The scale measures were in particular: Audience influence (Positive), Audience influence (Negative), Immersion and two categories corresponding to the FSS (which uses two different response scales), named FSS10 and FSS3 according to the number of questions in the category. Before averaging, we inversed responses on negatively worded questions. We excluded the *no audience* condition from all audience influence questionnaire analyses.

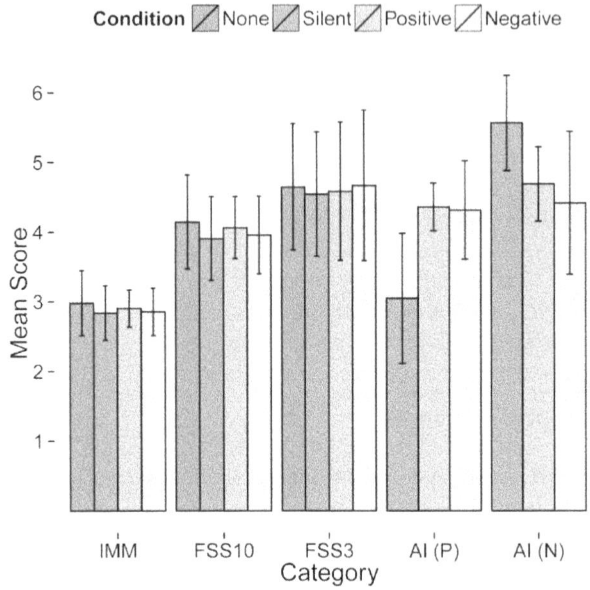

Figure 4. Bar plots showing scale averages for each condition. Error bars indicate 95% confidence intervals of the mean.

Figure 4 shows the means and their 95% confidence intervals for the resulting distribution. For each of the category scores, we compared answers in the four conditions via repeated-measures analyses of variance (ANOVA) after confirming that all assumptions had been met. Significant effects were found for the two categories on audience influence: positive influence, $F(2,14) = 10.45$, $\eta_p^2 = 0.37$ and negative influence, $F(2,14) = 9.78$, $\eta_p^2 = 0.24$ (both $p < 0.01$).

Subsequent pairwise comparisons (dependent t-tests using Holm correction) revealed significant differences between Silent and Negative and Silent and Positive conditions for both types of audience influence, but not between Positive and Negative conditions. For positive influence, means are Silent M: 3.05 Positive M: 4.36, Negative M: 4.31. For negative influence, means are: Silent M: 5.56, Positive M: 4.69, Negative M: 4.41. Note that – because scores for negatively worded questions were inversed – high scores indicated a "good" score for the negative influence category.

Final Game Rating Questions (FGRQ)

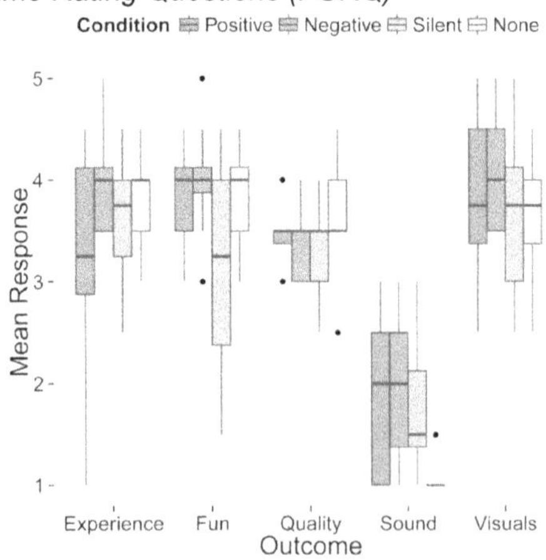

Figure 5. Box plots for Final Game Rating Questions (FGRQ)

Participants rated the five game attributes on a Likert scale of 1 (very poor) to 5 (very good) for each audience influence condition (see Figure 5). Friedman's test was conducted on the data and revealed significant effects of condition (positive, negative, silent, none) for the variables Experience ($\chi^2(3) = 7.84$), Fun ($\chi^2(3) = 12.05$), Visuals ($\chi^2(3) = 9.86$) and Sounds ($\chi^2(3) = 12.77$), all $p<0.05$. The Quality variable was not significant. However, subsequent multiple comparisons only revealed significant differences between Negative and Silent conditions for the variable Fun ($p<0.05$).

Player Interviews

We analyzed the audio interviews using coding techniques based on thematic analysis. Notes from the recorded interviews were analyzed for the categories mentioned in the interview protocol. Additional themes, which originated along the course of data analysis, are further explained in this section. We analyzed categorized audience influence into *audience presence*, *encouragement* and *discouragement*.

Audience Presence. Regarding a silent audience, player P7-1 indicated, *"When they were just watching me play, I felt that it was eerie. An active audience (-ve or +ve) immersed me in the game as opposed to having an audience that was silent."* Player P6-2 indicated *"having people watching me while playing was distracting. From time to time my conscious thought would go to wondering what they are looking at."* Player P2-1 stated, *"I noticed them more that they were around when they were not talking. I am conscious about people watching me play, as it makes me want to do better."* A few participants preferred an active audience over a silent audience as indicated by P7-2, *"Presence of an audience affected my game a bit, because I preferred the audience to be lively watching me game as opposed to be silent as in watching a chess game."*

Audience Encouragement. For the positive audience, many participants indicated that they tended to "tune out" the comments from the positive audience because they felt the comments to be distracting. One player (P7-1) mentioned, *"When the audience was cheering me positively or negatively, [...] I felt more immersed. However with the positive audience I felt more distracted"*. On the other hand player (P6-2) mentioned *"from time to time, I did pay attention to the cheers from the audience which gave me some tips and clues to play better."* Player P5-1 indicated regarding the positive audience that *"their comments were distracting hence I was trying to tune them out."* A few participants were affected positively by the positive audience as indicated by participant P7-2 *"I like the cheering audience because I like to entertain people when I game, and I was motivated to play more and better."*

Audience Discouragement. We also noted from the interviews that a greater percentage of players were more in focus of the game with a negative audience as opposed to a positive audience. The negative audience did not bother some players. Player P6-1 indicated *"with the negative audience, I felt more inclined to block them out as opposed to listening to them."* However three participants were affected by the negative comments in that it caused a deterioration of their scores. Participant P2-2 indicated, *"the booing made me a bit conscious that I was not doing well"*. Participant P6-2 stated, *"The negative audience did contribute to the downplay in the game, you do not actually hear what they were saying, but you could feel the negativity in the air."* At-times the comments tended to lower the morale of the player as participant P1-1 indicated, *"The negative comments from the audience pulled the experience in the negative direction, because they are saying nasty things, I was already not feeling good about myself, and I did not need these comments."* Some participants tended to filter the negative comments out of their *"mindspace"* as participant P7-2 said, *"When they were booing, I just pushed them aside from my mental space; I'm playing and I was just filtering them out. At the same time when they were negative, I was trying to get them onto my side by making them laugh."*

Motivation to Play. The positive audience, negative audience and/or silent audience also influenced player motivation. Player P7-1 indicated, *"The negative audience did not demotivate me at all! In fact they were more motivating."* Physical tiredness from playing the game repeatedly also contributed to the players losing interest in playing the game. As stated by participant P1-1 *"I was physically tired after the third game session. Towards the end of each session, I was, when my opponent was about to finish me off, I was more ready to take the final hit rather than trying to defend myself."*

DISCUSSION

Motivated based on the results from the questionnaires, we want to focus our discussion mainly on the rich qualitative insights from our interviews, because we think that we got the most inspiring understandings from this part of our study. Being qualitative in nature, the broad findings from these interviews have the following characteristics:

- **Silent** audience posed an eerie and **uncomfortable** feeling that affected player engagement.
- **Positive** audience was a **distraction** that affected player engagement.
- **Negative** audience afforded player engagement **challenges** from the usage of gesture controls, which affected gameplay experience and player experience.
- **Cognitive load** from the gesture controls because of poor game control design affected gameplay experience.
- **Motivation** to play was also affected by physical **abilities** that also influenced player experience.

When analyzing the results, further classification of the audience into silent, positive and negative audience types helped us to understand the effect of this multi-level independent variable on player engagement. Our results show that an audience as small as three people can influence game players. On average, participants felt that an active audience both posed a distraction and yet influenced them in a good way, pushing them to perform better (RQ1). It should be noted, however, that the quantitative data does not reveal differences in the influence of a positive or negative audience. In fact, both audience types seem to increase player engagement as measured by the "positive audience influence" category. Our initial research question asking if a negative audience will decrease player engagement (RQ3) seems to have a negative answer. However, our research question about the presence of a positive audience (RQ2) seems to be positively answered for this category. The FSS and Immersion questionnaires did not produce any significant results. Implications are discussed further below.

Relating Subjective Responses and Quantitative Data

The value that an active audience provides compared to a silent or passive audience is an insight that we gathered from our interviews. Comparing the analysis of our subjective interviews to the quantitative data analysis, we were surprised to find that players tended to "tune out" the comments of the negative audience to concentrate better and be more immersed in the game. The fact that some participants mentioned the eerie feeling when the audience was silent can be an important fact for designing games as performances (e.g., a game performance becoming creepier at some points because the audience receives explicit instructions to be quiet). It tells us that not only does an audience need to be present, but also it needs to be active, to have impact in those who take part of the game. Imagining, for example, an artist who is about to play a live piece for the first time, the uneasy feeling of being observed, rather than appreciated, might be due to the same factors. The lack of feedback from those who are watching – the silence in the concert room, or in the play area in our case – reveals itself to be perhaps worse than having an audience cheering negatively, since participants found them easier to block out.

Consequently, for an active audience of positive or negative audience types quantitative results were significant. Comments from the negative audience also forced the players to try and improve their effort in the game, increasing player engagement, to overcome the negative comments, which are contrary to our research question (RQ3) regarding negative audience. The will to succeed, show that the players were able to "tune out" and overcome the negativity to focus on their game. On the other hand the comments from the positive audience was more of a distraction for most of the players and did not do much for the players except help them focus more on playing the game itself. This supports our research question (RQ2) regarding positive audience indirectly, meaning that the presence of a positive audience does increase player engagement. Perhaps because the players were already aware of their success, the positive reinforcement became more of a nuisance. These results support the findings of Butler et al., [4] and Law et al., [20] and further extends the influence of audience types in the context of a two-player co-located game installation.

Social Experience in Relation to Player Experience

From the results we gathered, players seem to perceive the audience as a performance gauge. They benefit from the audience when they are being scolded – pushing harder to success – but do not want too much attention when they are already performing well. Players can use the audience to assess how well they are doing, and that is particularly observable when players report discomfort in front of a silent audience. This same silence indicates the lack of feedback, breaking one of the main domains of the social experience relationship: the audience to player relationship.

Gameplay experience as defined to be a contextual relation between the game system, player experience and socio-spatial condition, provides another dimension in this study of audience influence on player engagement. The challenges with game system usability in reference of the gesture controls; the confusion between the short time intervals between the attacks versus defense gesture controls presented additional cognitive load on the players. Some players discovered a simple method of "spamming" the attack gestures to gain advantage over their opponent.

Prior experience in gaming might have also been a limiting factor in the social experiences in this study. The level of previous experience with games of the participants (skillfulness) might influence different reactions or responses from the audience. Contrary to what we discovered in regards to positive active audiences – instead of becoming a distraction for a more novice player – the audience might increase performance and help enjoy the experience in a co-located space. The fun aspects of the game did facilitate player experience in this study. However, there was a starting inertia to engaging in play because of the need for the players to understand the relationship between the attack and defence mechanisms with their hands. A characteristic that is often taken care of in games by a process called onboarding, where the player learns the controls of a game while the gameplay starts.

From a social interaction perspective, our studies indicate that presence of an audience is the first step towards establishing a socio-spatial interrelationship between the player, audience and the game system in a co-located space gaming installation. However an active audience (positive or negative) is preferred over a silent audience (passive audience). While game controls play an important role in establishing a player to game system interrelationship; audience-player relationship enhances the immersion within the game via social experience.

In our study, our aim was to explore our research questions with a smaller group of audience members. Quite possibly the size of the audience may have been rather small to have a measurable impact on player experience, because the audience may go unnoticed while in play. Spontaneity of the audience, authenticity of the audience's comments and the tone of the comments could influence player engagement from the perspective of immersion and flow within gaming. The participants might assume that the audience was just there for the study's sake. In the end, they might have perceived that the audience might not have been authentically rooting for them. It is possible they perceived it as fake cheering, which can deter overall performance.

On the other hand, when an audience gathers around someone in a spontaneous manner by accident – for example, when finding a peculiar street musician that is extremely good – cheering is felt as being more authentic and potentially more effective. While critical audience characteristics like audience size and variation in audience demographics were beyond the scope of this study, it is an interesting follow-up opportunity for this study.

Game Design for Multiplayer Co-located Installations

For future designers of multiplayer co-located games, care must be taken to design games that are not too difficult to play. Difficulty might be ideal for seasoned gamers, but for the general population or a novice gamer, it might prevent them from returning to play the game.

In our case, player experience was critically informed by the gesture controls used in MD. Ease of understanding how to use the gesture controls contributed to a greater engagement in the game. Difficulty in using the gesture controls was predominantly due to the Kinect not being able to recognize the location of the players' hand positions quickly. The need for the players to orient their hands rapidly in these positions to cast spells posed challenges for the players to be immersed in the game. Once the Kinect was synchronized with a player's hand positions, they were excited to play the game.

Player P5-1 mentioned *"the gesture control type is good but not reliable, they do not always work, as I still do not understand if I have to move the hands in a specific way, this affected my concentration in the game."* There were three types of hand position for attacks with spells and three types of hand positions for blocking spells. This variety of hand gestures posed additional cognitive load on the participants to remember their gestures correctly, because a fire spell had to be blocked by a fire block and so on. Participant P7-1 indicated, *"the attack and defense was clear, however the types of attacks and the types of blocks for hand orientation posed a mental challenge."*

Even though the game was supposed to be a duelling match, we noticed player-to-player interaction for supporting each other's play in overcoming some of the issues of the gesture controls. Participant P5-1 mentioned *"You need to move your hands wider along the directions of fire, ice or earth to block my spells."* Participant P2-2 indicated to the opponent: *"Perhaps you can try to dodge and jump out of the way to escape being hit by the spells."* This indicates to us that players, who found the best use of the controls, wanted a worthy opponent to duel against.

Designers should leave some room for failure within the game, so that the audience has a good chance to reproach the player. In this manner, the player will, according to our findings, try even harder to overcome the challenges of the game, harder than if they were playing with an audience influencing them positively. Design of games for co-located spaces must be inclusive of the audience allowing for participatory interaction between player-audience and game system. Games with gestural controls and full-body movements afford the possibility of role reversals between the player and the audience [3].

LIMITATIONS AND FUTURE WORK

Our audience characteristics do not fully represent the wide spectrum of all audience characteristics possible. An inquiry into a detailed taxonomical framework of characteristics other than silent, positive and negative types is beyond the scope of our paper. Our exploratory experiment was conducted with an audience sample size of three members. While this might be a low number, studies on audience size and social facilitation attributed to presence of an audience used audience sizes of 2, 4, or 8 people [17]. Other studies, which considered audience size on blushing [29] had audience sizes from 1 to 4. While these references are not necessarily representative of an audience size in a co-located gaming installation, our selection of three audience members is potentially low. In addition, the demographic profile of the audience could also be changed to relate between a younger audience groups to a mature or an older audience group.

Our study used only male participants, and including female participants would help to understand audience influence effects on female gamers in co-located spaces.

The fact that questionnaire data results for the exploratory study were always close to the median "neutral" response (3 for immersion; 4 for FSS10 and audience influence; 5 for FSS3) indicates a need for revising one or several characteristics of the study design for future work in this direction. For example, audience size could be increased.

One could also try measuring audience influence with measures that do not rely on subjective player reports. For example, we could use game performance measures or measure cognitive functioning, both of which can be affected by arousal, flow or immersion experiences [13].

CONCLUSION

In this paper, we presented findings and insights from rich qualitative and quantitative data relating the effects of audience influence on player engagement. Our study contributes to human-computer interaction and game research in the following ways: Firstly, this study helps us understand the effects of silent, positive and negative audience on player engagement. Secondly, we found that positive audience at times tends to be distractive in nature compared to a negative audience that drives player focus. Thirdly, we postulate social experience in the gaming context as connected with player experience. Finally, we identify important criteria of games designed for co-located gaming with audience participation. We presented a study that showed that (positive or negative) audience activity fosters game engagement, while a silent audience makes players feel eerie. It is our hope, based on this contribution, game designers for co-located games are able to understand some challenges of designing social game interactions.

ACKNOWLEDGMENTS

We thank all the participants involved in this study. We would also like to thank João P. Costa and everyone, who provided helpful comments on previous versions of this document. We are grateful to our support from NSERC, GRAND NCE and SSHRC (IMMERSe, 895-2011-1014).

REFERENCES

1. Vanden Abeele, V. and Schutter, B. Designing intergenerational play via enactive interaction, competition and acceleration. *Personal and Ubiquitous Computing 14*, 5 (2010), 425–433.
2. Bateman, C., Lowenhaupt, R., and Nacke, L.E. Player Typology in Theory and Practice. *DIGRA'11*, (2011).
3. Bianchi-Berthouze, N., Kim, W.W., and Patel, D. Does Body Movement Engage You More in Digital Game Play ? and Why ? *ACII 2007*, (2007), 102–113.
4. Butler, J.L. and Baumeister, R.F. The trouble with friendly faces: skilled performance with a supportive audience. *J Pers Soc Psychol 75*, 5 (1998), 1213–30.
5. Chandrasekaran, V., Mohan, S., Pathipaka, O., and Saxena, S. WeINteract – A Pervasive Audience Participation System. *CHI '04*, (2004), 1700–1704.
6. Chatham, A. and Mueller, F. "Floyd." Adding an interactive display to a public basketball hoop can motivate players and foster community. *Proc. of UbiComp '13*, ACM (2013), 667–676.
7. Cheung, G. and Jeff, H. Starcraft from the Stands : Understanding the Game Spectator. *Proc. of CHI'11* (2011), 763–772.
8. Downs, J., Vetere, F., Howard, S., Loughnan, S., and Smith, W. Audience Experience in Social Videogaming: Effects of Turn Expectation and Game Physicality. *Proc. of CHI '14* (2014), 3473–3482.
9. Engeser, S. and Rheinberg, F. Flow, performance and moderators of challenge-skill balance. *Motivation and Emotion 32*, 3 (2008), 158–172.
10. Grønbæk, K., Iversen, O.S., Kortbek, K.J., Nielsen, K.R., and Aagaard, L. iGameFloor - A Platform for Co-Located Collaborative Games. *Proc. of ACE '07*, (1907), 64–71.
11. Harper, R. and Mentis, H.M. The Mocking Gaze : The Social Organization of Kinect Use. (2013), 167–180.
12. Huggard, A., Mel, A. De, Garner, J., Toprak, C.C., Chatham, A., and Mueller, F.F. Musical Embrace : Exploring Social Awkwardness in Digital Games. *Proc. of UbiComp '13*, (2013), 725–728.
13. Jennett, C., Cox, A.L., Cairns, P., et al. Measuring and defining the experience of immersion in games. *Int J Hum-Comput St 66*, 9 (2008), 641–661.
14. Kappen, D.L., Gregory, J., Stepchenko, D., Wehbe, R.R., and Nacke, L.E. Exploring Social Interaction in Co-located multiplayer games. *CHI EA'13*, ACM (2013), 1119–1124.
15. Kenny, D.A., Kashy, D., and Cook, W.L. *Dyadic Data Analysis*. Guilford Press, 2006.
16. Kimble, C.E. and Rezabek, J.S. Playing Games Before an Audience: Social Facilitation or Choking. *Social Behaviour and Personality 20*, 2 (1992), 115–120.
17. Knowles, E.S. Social physics and the effects of others: Tests of the effects of audience size and distance on social judgments and behavior. *J Pers Soc Psychol 45*, 6 (1983), 1263–1279.
18. Kort, Y.A.W.D.E. and Ijsselsteijn, W.A. People , Places , and Play : Player Experience in a Socio-Spatial Context. *ACM Comp. in Entertainm. 6*, 2 (2008), 1–11.
19. Latulipe, C., Charlotte, C., Carroll, E.A., and Lottridge, D. Love , Hate , Arousal and Engagement : Exploring Audience Responses to Performing Arts. *Proc. of CHI '11*, (2011), 1845–1854.
20. Law, J., Masters, R., Bray, S.R., Eves, F., and Bardswell, I. Motor Performance as a Function of Audience Affability and Metaknowledge. *Journal of Sport and Exercise Psychology 25*, (2003), 484–500.
21. Lin, H. and Sun, C.-T. The Role of Onlookers in Arcade Gaming: Frame Analysis of Public Behaviours. *Convergence 17*, 2 (2011), 125–137.
22. Lindley, S., Couteur, J. Le, Place, A., and Bianchi-Berthouze, N. Stirring up Experience through Movement in Game Play : Effects on Engagement and Social Behaviour. *Proc. CHI 2008*, (2008), 511–514.
23. Lund, A.M. Measuring usability with the USE questionnaire. *STC Usability SIG Newsletter 8*, 2 (2001).
24. Mueller, F., Agamanolis, S., and Picard, R. Exertion Interfaces : Sports over a Distance for Social Bonding and Fun. *CHI '03*, (2003), 561–568.
25. Nijhar, J., Bianchi-Berthouze, N., and Boguslawski, G. Does Movement Recognition Precision affect the Player Experience in Exertion Games? In *INTETAIN'2011, LNICST 78,* 73–82.
26. Reeves, S., Benford, S., O'Malley, C., and Fraser, M. Designing the Spectator Experience. *Proc. of CHI '05*, ACM Press (2005), 741.
27. Roccetti, M., Marfia, G., and Semeraro, A. Playing into the wild: A gesture-based interface for gaming in public spaces. *J Vis Commun Image Represent 23*, 3 (2012), 426–440.
28. Savva, N., Scarinzi, A., and Bianchi-Berthouze, N. Continuous Recognition of Player's Affective Body Expression as Dynamic Quality of Aesthetic Experience. *IEEE Transactions on Computational Intelligence and AI in Games 4*, 3 (2012), 199–212.
29. Shearn, D., Bergman, E., Hill, K., Abel, a, and Hinds, L. Blushing as a function of audience size. *Psychophysiology 29*, 4 (1992), 431–6.
30. Stevens, Q. *The Ludic City: Exploring the Potential of Public Spaces*. Taylor & Francis, 2007.
31. Webster, J. and Ho, H. Audience engagement in multimedia presentations. *ACM SIGMIS Database 28*, 2 (1997), 63–77.

Playing with Strangers: Understanding Temporary Teams in League of Legends

Yubo Kou and Xinning Gui
Department of Informatics
Donald Bren School of Information and Computer Sciences
University of California, Irvine
{yubok, guix}@ics.uci.edu

ABSTRACT

Game researchers have extensively studied how players form long-term social organizations such as guilds and clans to accomplish complex tasks such as raiding in online games. Few studies have been done to understand how temporary teams (or pickup groups) composed of strangers fulfill complex tasks. Riot Games' League of Legends, a team-based competitive online game, is played by two temporary teams. Players must collaborate with strangers in a relatively short time (about 30-50 minutes). How do players interact and collaborate with their teammates in temporary teams? To answer this question, we conducted an ethnographic study within the League of Legends community. We conducted 30 semi-structured interviews with experienced players. We found that rich social interaction exists within temporary teams. Players want to collaborate with strangers through communication and coordination. They discipline their own ways of interaction to facilitate collaboration. They try to exert influence over their teammates. We further discuss design implications for facilitating collaboration among strangers.

Author Keywords

Temporary team; pickup group; collaboration; regulation; social interaction; deviant behavior; Multiplayer online Games; League of Legends

ACM Classification Keywords

H.1.2 Human factors

INTRODUCTION

Collaboration is a key theme in MMOGs (Massively Multiplayer Online Games). Players collaborate through various social organizations to accomplish different tasks. Players form long-term teams such as guilds and clans to accomplish large-scale, complex tasks [1, 7, 8, 19]. For example, Bardzell et al. reported an extensive study of two guilds that made deliberate strategies to raid in World of Warcraft [1]. On the other hand, collaboration between strangers is usually lightweight and informal. For example, players of *There* could only chat with strangers [4]. Star Wars Galaxy provided a relatively low level of interactivity between players, characterized by short interactions centered on instrumental purposes (e.g. getting healed and purchasing services) [6]. World of Warcraft players engage in informal, unplanned collaborations with strangers such as casting a beneficial spell or helping beat a monster [19]. Ducheneaut et al. reported that players enjoyed strangers' "countless antics and humorous interactions," such as impromptu dance [7].

Some online games provide mechanisms that allow strangers to form temporary teams to fight non-player characters (NPCs). For example, World of Warcraft (WoW) supports players from different servers to form a temporary team to do an instance or a quest. Studies of these temporary teams reported a low level of social interaction between players. For example, Ekbia and Nardi commented that "*Players served primarily to fill out the roles in the trinity so that contests could be completed and items of equipment won; the social dimension transmogrified to minimal instrumental interaction, and sometimes no interaction at all*" [9]. Eklund and Johansson noted that players held communication to a minimum and focused primarily on fulfilling their roles [10].

Recent years have seen the rise and prosperity of many team-based competitive online games, such as Riot Games' League of Legends [24], Valve's DOTA 2 [28], Blizzard Entertainment's Heroes of the Storm [3], etc. In these games, strangers form a temporary team, collaborate intensively, and achieve complex goals – defeating another team. How do strangers interact and collaborate in temporary teams?

To answer this question, we conducted a qualitative study of League of Legends (LoL). LoL is one of the most popular games in the world with more than 27 million gamers each day [26]. We found that temporary team in LoL is characterized by rich and complicated social interactions. Temporary teams meet various challenges in communication and coordination, such as lack of organization and deviant behavior. To achieve success,

CHI PLAY '14, October 19 - 22 2014, Toronto, ON, Canada

ACM 978-1-4503-3014-5/14/10…$15.00.
http://dx.doi.org/10.1145/2658537.2658538

players must discipline themselves as well as influence their teammates.

RELATED WORK

Game researchers have extensively studied player collaboration in Massively multiplayer online role-playing games. Yee pointed out that collaboration is one of player motivations in online games [31]. Nardi and Harris argued that collaboration makes World of Warcraft more fun and yields rich learning opportunities [19]. Lindtner et al. reported that players' collaboration formed an ecology with their real life friends and physical environment [17]. Zhong reported that collaboration positively influences players' online social capital and online civic engagement [32].

People collaborate in different social organizations. Guild, as a form of social organization, has been widely studied. Ducheneaut et al. examined group dynamics within guilds, in terms of their demographics, structure and life cycle [8]. Pisan examined players' identity within guilds [22]. Bardzell et al. investigated how guilds made strategies to progress in game [1]. People can socialize with each other within guilds and clans, which contributes to the successful collaboration.

Several studies pointed out the importance of friendship in collaboration. For example, Xu et al. reported that people are more willing to play with their friends in Halo 3, a first person shooter game [30]. Mason and Clauset reported that friendships exert a strong influence, leading to "both improved individual and team performance and increased pro-social behaviors" [18]. Bardzell reported that in World of Warcraft's instance runs, players preferred to play with established friends, rather than strangers, and the primary reasons were insecurity about being judged by strangers and a desire to avoid people with poor social skills [2].

Collaboration is fundamental to the success of MMOGs. Scholars have examined non-strangers' collaboration from different angles, such as social organization and friendship. Little is known about strangers' collaboration. We want to understand how strangers collectively accomplish complicated tasks in League of Legends.

LEAGUE OF LEGENDS

League of Legends is a free-to-play match-based game. Each match lasts about 30 – 50 minutes. A team usually consists of five players who do not know each other. Within each match, players defend their own base and try to destroy their opponents'.

To play a game, a player first enters "champion select lobby," where he meets his teammates for the first time and determines the champion and the role he wants to play (see Figure 1). Currently there are more than 110 champions. Each champion has a unique set of abilities. A team comprises three different roles: carry, which deals damage, tank, which absorbs damage, and support, which can buff teammates or debuff enemies. An optimal team composition needs players to fill all of these three roles. During the champion select phase, players can communicate with their teammates through a text-based channel at the lower middle part of the game client. Players cannot communicate with their opponents at this phase.

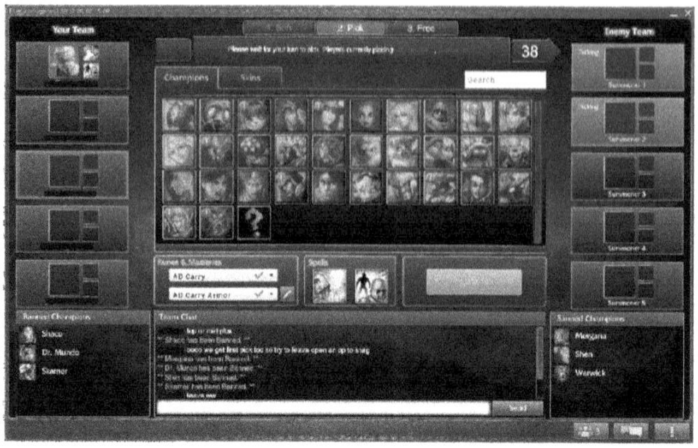

Figure 1. Champion select lobby.

A match begins after every player has determined their champion (see Figure 2). As the match goes on, the champion gains experience points and gold by killing opponent minions and monsters in the wild. The character gets stronger by learning or upgrading his abilities when he levels up and purchasing items with his gold. A match ends whenever one side's base is destroyed. Players can talk with their teammates as well as opponents through an in-game text-based channel.

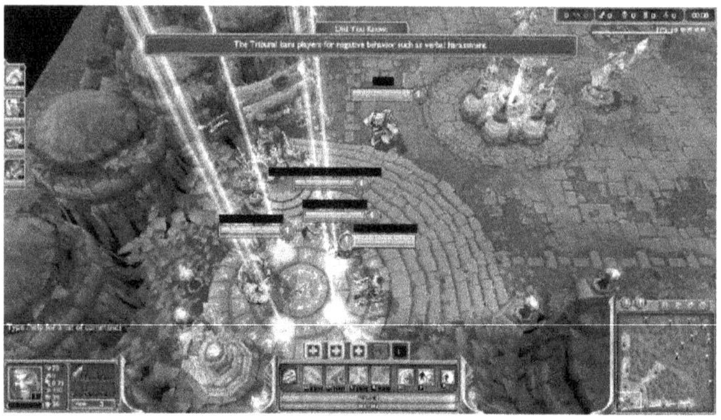

Figure 2. The beginning of a match.

LoL has two game modes: normal game and ranked game. Ranked game is paired with a ranking system that measures players' skill levels and assigns them into one of six leagues: Challenger, Diamond, Platinum, Gold, Silver, and Bronze. LoL matches players with similar skills. Players can rise to the next higher league if they keep winning games. Players can be demoted to the next lower league if they keep losing games or stop playing games for a long time.

Riot Games have developed several systems that promote collaboration or sportsmanship in Riot Games' own terms. The "Tribunal" system is a punitive system that allows players to identify and punish deviant behavior [33]. With the help of the Tribunal, players have evolved a hybrid system of governance within the LoL community [14]. The "Honor" system is a reputation system that encourages players to give a positive rating to whoever they consider to be a good player [23].

METHODS

We conducted an ethnographic study within the League of Legends community from January 2012 to January 2014. The first author has played League of Legends since October 2011. We collected and analyzed documents from Riot Games' official websites, including Riot Games' official announcements, official blogs, and code of conduct for the LoL community. We analyzed player discussion about collaboration on Riot Games' official forums. We analyzed 200 matches' chat logs, which we randomly selected from Riot Games' Tribunal system. We read through these chat logs to find out how deviant behavior happened, how players responded to such behavior, and how such behavior affected players' collaboration.

We conducted 30 semi-structured interviews with players on LoL's North America server. We recruited players through directly contacting them in game, posting recruiting message on the official forums, and snowballing. Our interviewees ranged between 18 and 30 years old. There were 28 males and 2 females. All of our interviewees were experienced players who played LoL for at least one year. Their in-game rankings ranged from Bronze to Diamond during the period when the interviews were conducted.

The interviews were conducted in person, over Skype, and through in-game chat. Each interview lasted between 30 minutes to one hour. We asked them what they liked and disliked about playing with strangers, how they communicated with strangers, and what efforts they made to collaborate with strangers. When we report quotes from interviews and forum posts, we retain the original orthography and punctuation.

FINDINGS

Social interaction plays an important role in LoL's temporary teams. Successful interaction upholds promising collaboration between strangers. However, the social interaction can be problematic, which hinders collaboration. To facilitate social interaction, promote collaboration, and win game, players discipline themselves within the team and influence their teammates proactively.

Unpacking the Role of Social Interaction

Players acknowledge the significance of social interaction within temporary teams. A player said, "*Every aspect of the game needs communication. Positioning of the jungler, rotations, movement predictions, warding, etc. Even counter jungling. The only things that don't involve teamwork is farming and outplaying solo lanes.*" During a match, each player associates with the rest team. One action influences several teammates. Communication at "every aspect" is necessary to keep a team work closely.

Another player said, "*You really have to make sure everyone is on the same page. And you need to work with your team to make sure they understand their strengths and weaknesses, and make sure they know when to fight or run.*" The situations a temporary team faces are constantly changing. There is no fixed strategy for a player to follow. Players must keep communicating with their teams to ensure that they share mutual understanding as well as the same goals ever since the champion select lobby.

Players agree that collaboration outweighs individual skill in this game. For example, a player said, "*If your team works together correctly you can beat five individuals just trying to win with 'skill.'*" By emphasizing "skill," the player was trying to say merely individual skill is not enough for this game.

However, interacting with strangers is not easy and straightforward. A player admitted that, "*From progressing from lvl 1 and learning the basics I've come to notice that people tend to tunnel vision, blame others for their mistakes and not communicate at least untill you start winning more and get better players on your team.*" The player pointed out that in-game situations heavily influence people's social interaction.

Many players reported the challenges of giving direct feedback to their teammates. For example, below is a conversation between the first author and an interviewee.

> *[11:23] Inteviewer: Do you give advice to your teammate so that they can make fewer mistakes in game?*
>
> *[11:24] Player: I try to, but most of the time they just get offended and rage at me.*
>
> *[11:25] Interviewer: So giving advice is generally not welcome in this game, right?*
>
> *[11:26] Player: Usually it is just seen as an insult and most people think they know better.*
>
> *[11:27] Interviewer: Is there any way you can help when one teammate is keeping doing one risky move and getting killed?*
>
> *[11:28] Player: Ask them to ward and to play safer, but even that is an "insult" to most of the community.*

Similar to this player, many interviewees reported the difficulties of giving others advice. They agreed that players could hardly take advice in a peaceful manner within an intense, competitive gaming atmosphere.

Problematic social interaction such as griefing and flaming exists in LoL. Griefing refers to player behaviors that intentionally disrupt the gaming experience of other players [11]. Flaming indicates aggressive, hostile, sometimes profanity-lace interaction [20]. A player told us that: "*What I dislike is all the shit talking! The bad attitudes, players who blame other players for their own mistakes, trolls, etc.*" Kou and Nardi noted that flaming often occurs when players are losing the game [13]. Shores et al. reported that problematic social interaction is more likely to happen when players play in ranked game mode, play damage dealer, or play longer tend to behave aggressively towards other players in social interaction [27]. In our study, players considered problematic social interaction detrimental to temporary team's successes. A player said, "*I am totally distracted and can't focus on play whenever someone on my team is trolling*." Another player wrote in his blog, "*Flaming is perhaps the biggest reason for defeat in this game. Telling a person that he has made a mistake in a rude way, as if he doesn't know that he made it, this helps no one at all*."

Disciplining the Self

Players understand that the way they interact with teammates affects collaboration. They must communicate with teammates in an appropriate way. They must discipline themselves to facilitate successful social interaction with their team.

Our interviewees suggested that the first thing is to adjust to the right mood while playing. For example, a player said, "*Playing while angry or stressed makes you surprisingly bad at League of Legends. Take a break from time to time.*" Another player told us: "*Do your best not to let your emotions from a game with an AFK in it carry over to the next. If my emotions could get carried away, I would never have been able to focus on improving my gameplay to get diamond*." "AFK" is short for "away from keyboard."

More importantly, people underlined the importance of keeping a positive attitude. A player said, "*I try to keep quiet and keep a good attitude and make sure everyone else is content with what they're doing*." The player associated individual attitude with team satisfaction.

Another player said:

> *Attitude is one of the most important differences I see when I am playing in Diamond as opposed to other ranking brackets. The players in here usually never rage and always try their best to win games. This makes a lot of sense because the only way you can get to the top .01% of players is by never giving up and allowing yourself to have comebacks. People do not realize that your attitude plays a massive role in whether or not you win some games. It's not even about raging at this point, but you have to be positive and always try to win even when games look bleak.*

The player pointed out several important characteristics of good attitude, such as anger management, endeavor, hope, and persistence.

Self-discipline also includes behaving appropriately towards your teammates. Flaming at teammates can only cause trouble to teamwork. A player said, "*Toxicity just doesn't do anything but negatively impact your team*." Toxicity is a term Riot Games uses to denote problematic player behavior. Another player said:

> *Never rage or say negative things about your teammates. It might not seem like a big deal when you call out your teammates for doing something bad or making a mistake but you are actually killing their morale and making your chances for a comeback a lot less possible. You always want to have the ability to win games, even if you are behind which is why it is important that you never give up right away or be negative. In League of Legends there is always a possibility that the other team is going to mess up and hand you the game. Do not miss out on these opportunities by raging at your team.*

The player stressed acting properly by pointing out the consequences of conducting toxic behavior. On the other hand, players can choose to interact with teammates in a more constructive way. For example, a player wrote, "*If you get mad at another player because of their skill, don't be an ass, help their lane, talk them up, don't ping them a trillion times either. Honestly that ****'s annoying for everyone. It's a team game and requires teamwork to win*." This player listed the appropriate and inappropriate ways to approach teammates that performed badly.

Proactively Influencing Teammates

A successful temporary team builds on players' proactive endeavors to create a harmonious atmosphere for communication, to take the leadership, and to deal with deviant players.

Creating a Harmonious Atmosphere

Players know that little communication and problematic social interaction destroy teamwork. They want to promote smooth communication by creating and maintaining a harmonious atmosphere.

Creating a positive and constructive atmosphere starts at the very beginning when strangers first meet each other. A player said:

> *At the beginning of the game, say something along the lines of "gg, hf" or "Let's have a good game, shall we? ^_^" Whether that's during champion selection, or in all chat as the game begins, saying something as simple as that and getting responses from your team and the enemy team along the same lines makes for a nicer game.*

"Gg" and "hf" are abbreviations for "good game" and "have fun." The player recommended that greeting teammates, and even opponents, can make a difference in the gaming atmosphere. Early communication is not limited to greetings. For example, a player said:

> *This is your first meeting with your team. As was stated, it is important to get to work with morale as soon as*

possible. Introduce yourself, give a friendly greeting to the team, and get right to work on stating which role you would prefer. Introductions are important to open up communication with teammates, and build a sense of familiarity.

This player pointed out that early communication also includes self-introduction and role preference, which can help teammates understand each one's strength and weakness, leading to the optimal utilization of five strangers. The player further noted that early communication contribute to harmony between players. We also observed nonverbal communication between players during early stage. For example, players can type "/dance" to command their characters to dance in front of their teammates (see Figure 3). Such actions represent a friendly gesture and break the ice.

Figure 3. A character that is dancing.

Similarly, Dabbish et al. reported that communication early in a group's history encourages members to talk more later on and that the early communication increases people's commitment through its influence on group atmosphere rather than through increased member participation [5].

Players also pay attention to maintaining a positive atmosphere as a match proceeds. They support and encourage teammates who perform poorly. For example, a player said:

What I do when I notice a teammate is performing poorly is to try and get their head back into the game. The vast majority of people were not "boosted" to where they are. They are simply having a bad game but can play well. If a person is clearly feeling down and I have the choice between taking a kill or giving it to them then I'll give it to them. While climbing to diamond I did not once allow myself to bring my teammates down. I make sure that I create the most family-loving environment possible.

The player suggested that trusting and helping teammates are the way to promote a positive atmosphere. Another player explained the impact of supporting teammates. He said:

Being friendly is probably your best bet in a solo q environment. With gamers everyone thinks they are right and everyone has there own opinions on what to do and what not. Being friendly to your teammates will keep them more focused on the game and more likely....to be there when you need them instead of getting frustrated and losing interest.

Besides helping teammates who perform poorly, players also verbally praise teammates' contribution. For example, our interviewees reported typing "gj" whenever their teammates make an evident contribution, such as killing an opponent. "gj" is short for "good job." When asked why they do this, a player said:

Positive reinforcement is always good imo [in my opinion]. If you keep your team's spirits high then generally there is less griefing and people won't doubt themselves. That second hesitation because you wonder "Will this really work?" can cost quite a bit. So yeah when I see a good play happen I drop the Gj guys.

This player talked about the influence of praising teammates from a psychological perspective. He also underlined the timely manner of the praising action. Another player said:

Every chance I get, I type gj...I think most of the times people like being complimented on their play.

Leadership

LoL does not force a leadership structure within temporary teams. Leadership emerges as a match proceeds. A temporary team needs leader especially when the team is in bad situations. For example, a player said:

When you're behind, someone has to step up make a big play, people will follow when someone is making the right decisions.

The player emphasized the skill of a leader – he must be able to make a "big play," an unexceptional contribution. Besides the ability of making a big play, good in-game scores also help foster leadership. A player said:

People tend to look at scores over everything else. So generally good effort and showing a good score gets people to follow what you say...With a better kda you do make a larger impact since you will do more damage, be tankier or heal better but if people see you are 10/0 and you say "Let's go." They are going to follow the fed person. Generally following the stronger player snowballs a team if they know what they are doing.

Players also look for people who have a good attitude towards the game. For example, when asked what characterizes a leader, a player answered:

> *People who are calm and respectful and who care about winning the game.*

Leaders in LoL's temporary teams determine strategic moves. A player who often makes calls said:

> *I'm a shot caller. I keep timers on dragon and if I'm jangling I'll time buffs if you just remind your team of the timers in chat you can usually get teamwork on invades and dragon re-spawns.*

Leadership in LoL is dynamic and evolving. Anyone can step up to make calls. A player told us:

> *I like taking charge of late game objectives, but otherwise I leave decision making to the person who makes good calls. [For example] I say we should group mid and shove cause need turrets, or we can siege, we have control etc. something that's a positive for everyone and that gives everything the feeling that we're strong and we can win this game easily.*

The player introduced when and how he tended to take the leadership. He also pointed out that good leadership helps develop a team's confidence.

Dealing with Deviant Players

Players sometimes encounter problematic social interaction. They have to deal with deviant players. Players hope deviant players can again focus on cooperating with teammates instead of flaming or griefing. They take actions towards deviant players. For example, a player said:

> *If it's really bad I mute them otherwise Ill say things to calm them down and regain order*

Another player said:

> *If my teammates are ever trolling each other I'll try to get them to stop.*

When deviant behavior happens, players should step up rather than possessing a passive attitude. A player said:

> *You'd be surprised how many games you can win by telling a rager to shut up, or making a play that turns the game when two people are yelling at each other. Emotions run high in games, and you have to control the pace, or you get left behind in the complaints.*

The player pointed out that the key to dealing with deviant players is to actively intervene through text chat. He supported having a firm stance against deviant players.

DISCUSSION

In LoL, temporary teams must accomplish fast-paced and dynamic tasks to eventually win a game. There is no fixed strategy. Players have to reach mutual understanding of the changing situations, work closely, and continuously make new strategies together. Therefore, LoL players engage in a variety of social interaction with their teammates. They proactively influence their teammates rather than passively fulfill a given role.

A well-functioning team relies on smooth social interaction among teammates. Players must cautiously choose the ways to communicate with strangers, because the relationships between them are temporary and fragile. They must carefully choose the words they use to avoid irritating their teammates. For example, players often apologize right after they accidentally type capital letters in the communication channel.

Eklund and Johansson divided temporary team's interaction into two categories: instrumental and sociable. The former deals with strategies and achievements, while the latter refers to "*greetings and goodbyes, jokes, out of game discussion and discussion concerning game but not necessary for the progression of the session*" [10]. In LoL, these two types of interaction exist. But the boundary between them is ambiguous. LoL players see the instrumental value of sociable interaction. They also emphasize the importance of conducting instrumental interaction in a friendly and pleasant way.

Playing with strangers provide people novel experiences different from playing with friends. Sometimes, playing with strangers can be disturbing. The once-friendly teammates suddenly behave aggressively when the game does not proceed as expected. Yet, playing with friends can also bring players unexpected gaming experience, compared to playing with friends. A player said, "*One part [of this game] I like most is I can always meet amazing people.*" Another player told us a story where he was "*extremely happy*" because he received an in-game gift from a stranger he just played with. A third player said:

> *I think I'm more used to play with strangers, ... A lot of time, when I'm playing with someone I know, he's gonna not play very well, like that will influence way more than playing with random people. I just assume random people are gonna be good, and a lot of times they're not. But I like to assume they're gonna be good. It' harder to not have biases with people when you know how they're going to play already.*

In this case, the friendship this player owned became a burden to his game experience. Playing with strangers offers the player a sense of freshness and expectation of average teammates.

By studying temporary teams in World of Warcraft, Bardzell et al. noted: "*For groups with effective leaders, strong communication, tight social bonds, and competent role execution, player satisfaction rose*" [2]. Similarly, these elements are important in LoL. However, with a different team setting, the way these factors become prominent in LoL teams differs from that in WoW. First, LoL does not predefine a captain for a team. Every player has equal access to team resources. Leadership can, but not always, emerge. People generally follow those who perform well, have positive attitude, and make meaningful calls. However, leadership does not always emerge. People play games with vastly different motivations and styles [31]. The behavior of playing in an uncooperative way exists. A player expressed his frustration:

> *Sometimes people just won't listen no matter what I say and how I try. In this case I would rather leave the game and call it a day.*

Second, people do not have existing social bonds with teammates they just meet in game. Third, competent role execution is less guaranteed in LoL. LoL players must collectively arrange roles in champion select lobby in a short time, while WoW players decide roles before joining a team. Successfully arranging roles is challenging. Quarrels can arise when people do not handle conflicts over roles smoothly (To improve player experience, Riot Games released a beta game mode where people can select roles before joining a team in 2014 [16].). Besides these elements, our study highlights the importance of a positive team atmosphere. To sum up, players have fewer constraints in LoL's team setting than in WoW. Such setting brings more challenges to successful collaboration.

In League of Legends, players have developed strong social norms that value teamwork [14]. After decades of studying cooperative behavior within offline communities, Ostrom noted that:

> *Norms seem to have a certain staying power in encouraging growth of the desire for cooperative behavior over time, while cooperation enforced by externally imposed rules can disappear very quickly* [21].

Similarly, the norms LoL players have developed are influencing them in a positive way. Players' two endeavors, disciplining the self and influencing teammates, have inherent connections. Both of them are players' ways to apply the community norms. To be specific, disciplining the self is a means of internalization, "*the incorporation of values within the self as guiding principles*" [25]. Players identify with norms such as keeping a positive attitude, friendliness, maintaining hope, and persistence. Influencing teammates is to enforce these norms – encourage teammates to comply with them. By creating a harmonious atmosphere, players expect teammates to possess a positive attitude and be friendly to each other. Leadership emerges with players who have positive attitude and are willing to encourage teammates. Players intervene in deviant behaviors to promote friendliness and cooperation. Therefore, disciplining the self and influencing teammates are inherently consistent.

DESIGN IMPLICATIONS

Kiesler et al. noted that people are less likely to behave appropriately online because of reduced social cues and anonymity [12]. Such phenomenon happens often in MMOGs where players perceive little social constraints. Some scholars have argued that a way to improve players' willingness to cooperate is to create a rich context for players to interact with each other. For example, Williams et al. suggested that the addition of voice increases liking and trust among players [29]. Yet, other scholars reported that voice chat did not necessarily result in better collaboration. For example, Kuznekoff and Rose found that female players received three times more negative comments once other players recognized their gender [15]. Our findings suggest that adding new communication channels does not simply better or worsen collaboration. Players have the agency to creatively use the available communication channels either positively or negatively.

Our study suggests that players can help promote a positive atmosphere with sociable interaction. Designers should consider how to facilitate such interaction. For example, currently players have to type "gj" to praise his teammates' actions. Typing can be distracting during a fast-paced game. Designers can provide multiple convenient ways for a player to compliment his teammates' contribution, such as designing hotkeys for some common complimentary phrases.

CONCLUSION

This paper presents a study of how strangers collaborate within temporary teams in League of Legends. Strangers' collaboration poses various challenges that do not happen in friends' collaboration. Players must figure out the right way to communicate and coordinate. They must carefully handle in-game conflicts and maintain a positive atmosphere. Players have the agency to discipline themselves and manage their teammates.

More research needs to be done to uncover player experience of playing with strangers and dynamics within temporary teams. For example, to what extent do players enjoy playing with strangers? How much does the temporary team setting contribute to LoL's enormous popularity? Since being successful in LoL requires not only competent in-game skill but also necessary social skills, how do players learn these skills? How do Riot Games' efforts, such as the Tribunal and the Honor systems, affect players' in-game interaction?

ACKNOWLEDGMENTS

We thank all the interviewees who generously provided their experiences and opinions. We are grateful to the anonymous reviewers for their valuable and insightful feedbacks.

REFERENCES

1. Bardzell, J., Nichols, J., Pace, T., and Bardzell, S. Come meet me at Ulduar: progression raiding in world of warcraft. *Proceedings of the ACM 2012 conference on Computer Supported Cooperative Work - CSCW '12*, ACM Press (2012), 603.
2. Bardzell, S., Bardzell, J., Pace, T., and Reed, K. Blissfully productive: grouping and cooperation in world of warcraft instance runs. *Proceedings of the ACM 2008 conference on Computer supported cooperative work - CSCW '08*, ACM Press (2008), 357.
3. Blizzard Entertainment. *Heroes of the Storm*. 2014.
4. Brown, B. and Bell, M. CSCW at play: 'there'as a collaborative virtual environment. *Proceedings of the 2004 ACM conference on Computer supported cooperative work - CSCW '04*, ACM Press (2004), 350.
5. Dabbish, L., Kraut, R., and Patton, J. Communication and commitment in an online game team. *Proceedings of the 2012 ACM annual conference on Human Factors in Computing Systems - CHI '12*, ACM Press (2012), 879.
6. Ducheneaut, N. and Moore, R.J. The social side of gaming: a study of interaction patterns in a massively multiplayer online game. *Proceedings of the 2004 ACM conference on Computer supported cooperative work - CSCW '04*, ACM Press (2004), 360.
7. Ducheneaut, N., Yee, N., Nickell, E., and Moore, R.J. "Alone together?": exploring the social dynamics of massively multiplayer online games. *Proceedings of the SIGCHI conference on Human Factors in computing systems - CHI '06*, ACM Press (2006), 407.
8. Ducheneaut, N., Yee, N., Nickell, E., and Moore, R.J. The life and death of online gaming communities. *Proceedings of the SIGCHI conference on Human factors in computing systems - CHI '07*, ACM Press (2007), 839.
9. Ekbia, H. and Nardi, B. Inverse Instrumentality: How Technologies Objectify Patients and Players. In *Materiality and Organizing: Social Interaction in a Technological World.* MI: University of Michigan Press., Ann Arbor, 2011.
10. Eklund, L. and Johansson, M. Social Play? A study of social interaction in temporary group formation (PUG) in World of Warcraft. *DiGRA Nordic*, (2010).
11. Foo, C.Y. and Koivisto, E.M.I. Defining grief play in MMORPGs: player and developer perceptions. *Proceedings of the 2004 ACM SIGCHI International Conference on Advances in computer entertainment technology - ACE '04*, ACM Press (2004), 245–250.
12. Kiesler, S., Siegel, J., and McGuire, T. Social psychological aspects of computer-mediated communication. *American Psychologist*, 39 (1984), 1123–1134.
13. Kou, Y. and Nardi, B. Regulating Anti-Social Behavior on the Internet : The Example of League of Legends. *iConference 2013 Proceedings*, (2013), 616–622.
14. Kou, Y. and Nardi, B. Governance in League of Legends: A Hybrid System. *Foundation of Digital Games*, (2014).
15. Kuznekoff, J.H. and Rose, L.M. Communication in multiplayer gaming: Examining player responses to gender cues. *New Media & Society 15*, 4 (2012), 541–556.
16. KWOH, S. Announcing Team Builder two-day live beta! http://na.leagueoflegends.com/en/news/game-updates/features/announcing-team-builder-two-day-live-beta.
17. Lindtner, S., Nardi, B., Wang, Y., Mainwaring, S., Jing, H., and Liang, W. A hybrid cultural ecology: world of warcraft in China. *Proceedings of the ACM 2008 conference on Computer supported cooperative work - CSCW '08*, ACM Press (2008), 371.
18. Mason, W. and Clauset, A. Friends FTW! friendship and competition in halo. *Proceedings of the 2013 conference on Computer supported cooperative work - CSCW '13*, ACM Press (2013), 375.
19. Nardi, B. and Harris, J. Strangers and friends: collaborative play in world of warcraft. *Proceedings of the 2006 20th anniversary conference on Computer supported cooperative work - CSCW '06*, ACM Press (2006), 149.
20. O'Sullivan, P.B. and Flanagin, A.J. Reconceptualizing 'flaming' and other problematic messages. *New Media & Society 5*, 1 (2003), 69–94.
21. Ostrom, E. Collective Action and the Evolution of Social Norms. *The Journal of Economic Perspectives 14*, 3 (2000), 137–158.
22. Pisan, Y. My Guild, My People: Role of Guilds in Massively Multiplayer Online Games. RMIT University (2007), 20:1–20:5.
23. Riot Games. The Honor System. http://gameinfo.na.leagueoflegends.com/en/game-info/get-started/honor/.
24. Riot Games. *League of Legends*. 2008.
25. Shamir, B., House, R.J., and Arthur, M.B. The Motivational Effects of Charismatic Leadership: A Self-Concept Based Theory. *Organization Science 4*, 4 (1993), 577–594.
26. Sherr, I. Player Tally for 'League of Legends' Surges. 2014. http://blogs.wsj.com/digits/2014/01/27/player-tally-for-league-of-legends-surges/.
27. Shores, K.B., He, Y., Swanenburg, K.L., Kraut, R., and Riedl, J. The identification of deviance and its impact on retention in a multiplayer game. *Proceedings of the 17th ACM conference on Computer supported cooperative*

work & social computing - CSCW '14, ACM Press (2014), 1356–1365.

28. Valve. *"DOTA 2."*2013.

29. Williams, D., Caplan, S., and Xiong, L. Can You Hear Me Now? The Impact of Voice in an Online Gaming Community. *Human Communication Research 33*, 4 (2007), 427–449.

30. Xu, Y., Cao, X., Sellen, A., Herbrich, R., and Graepel, T. Sociable killers: Understanding Social Relationships in an Online First-person Shooter Game. *Proceedings of the ACM 2011 conference on Computer supported cooperative work - CSCW '11*, ACM Press (2011), 197.

31. Yee, N. Motivations for Play in Online Games. *CyberPsychology & Behavior 9*, (2006), 772–775.

32. Zhong, Z.-J. The effects of collective MMORPG (Massively Multiplayer Online Role-Playing Games) play on gamers' online and offline social capital. *Computers in Human Behavior 27*, 6 (2011), 2352–2363.

33. The Tribunal. http://na.leagueoflegends.com/Tribunal.

Whom are you looking for?

The Effects of Different Player Representation Relations on the Presence in Gaze-Based Games

Michael Lankes
University of Applied Sciences Upper Austria
Softwarepark 11, 4232 Hagenberg, Austria
michael.lankes@fh-hagenberg.at

Thomas Mirlacher
Marx-Reichlich Straße 6, 5020 Salzburg, Austria
thomas@mirlacher.at

Stefan Wagner
Wüstenrotstraße 9, 4020 Linz, Austria
stefan.wagner_privat@gmx.at

Wolfgang Hochleitner
University of Applied Sciences Upper Austria
Softwarepark 11, 4232 Hagenberg, Austria
wolfgang.hochleitner@fh-hagenberg.at

ABSTRACT
In this paper, we investigate the influence of different loci of manipulation relations (position of the player's ability to assert control) on presence. Novel game input devices (such as Microsoft Kinect or PlayStation Move) contribute to presence, and allow a broad range of game interactions, such as using facial expressions, gaze or head movement. This increase of complexity has led to some interesting design challenges: in a typical game design the setup of the locus of manipulation is quite simple as there is only one. For instance, the player uses a gamepad to move a game character through an obstacle course. However, design decisions get more complicated, when a game design includes more than just one input device and a second locus of manipulation. Does the relation of the two loci of manipulation have an impact on the perceived presence? To address this topic we utilized eye tracking technology, and carried out a comparative study consisting of four scenarios based on a 2D platform game. Three scenarios are controlled using an eye tracking device and a gamepad. They differ in their relation between the player character and the avatar. The 4th scenario is solely controlled with the gamepad. Results revealed that the inclusion of gaze input to investigate this issue proved to be very effective. It was discovered that the relation between the loci of manipulation has a strong influence on the perceived presence and its sub-dimensions.

Author Keywords
Gaze-based interaction; locus of manipulation; presence; games; eye tracking

ACM Classification Keywords
H.5.m. Information Interfaces and Presentation (e.g. HCI): Miscellaneous; K.8.0. General: Games

INTRODUCTION
In recent years, the diversity of game input devices has increased dramatically. Game controllers, such as the Oculus Rift[1] or the Leap Motion[2], allow players to experience digital worlds in a way that previously required expensive equipment. The current generation of controllers are now attractive for a broad consumer market, and promise players to interact with games "in simpler, more natural ways" [19]. The term *natural mapping* is frequently used in this context to imply how closely actions performed by the player in a game situation match the actions carried out in a real environment [22]. In other words, natural mapping can be defined as "the ability of a system to map its controls to changes in the mediated environment in a natural and predictable manner" [20]. By using natural mapping the gap between the player and the game world should be reduced.

Several studies show that game controllers with natural mapping have a positive impact on the phenomenon called *presence* (e.g. [23]). According to Lombard and Ditton [13], presence can be understood as the perceptual illusion of non-mediation. In artificial established environments, such as games, it refers to the sense of "being there" and has an crucial impact on the game experience [18].

Research efforts within the field are still only at the beginning: a high degree of presence does not automatically emerge when a game input device with natural mapping is applied to an existing game. To achieve presence, deep knowledge about the quality of individual game mechanics in regard to the input devices is required. This is especially relevant when more than just one device is utilized during the interaction with a game (e.g. a gamepad together with an eye tracking device). This paper addresses one specific issue in this context: how to set up the relation between several different player input channels (the loci of manipulation) defined by the employed input devices, in order to foster the feeling of presence, and thus create a more satisfying experience. The locus of manipulation can be understood as a description of the in-game position of the player's ability to assert control

[1] `http://www.oculusvr.com/`
[2] `http://www.leapmotion.com/`

over the game world, whether this is a character, an implied avatar, or a user interface cursor [1] (see Figure 1).

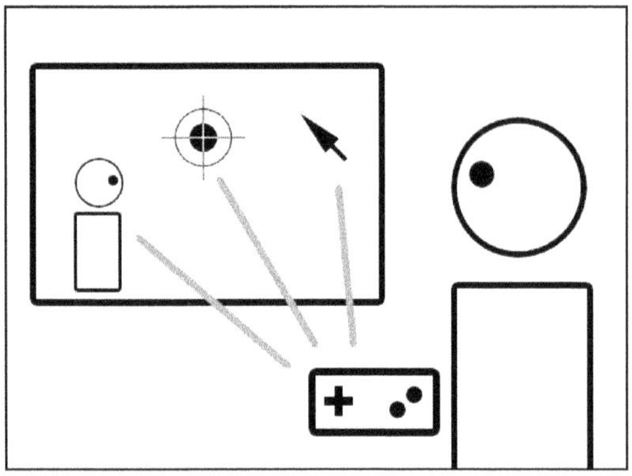

Figure 1. The locus of manipulation: a description of the in-game position of the player's ability to assert control over the game world.

It is obvious, that not every combination of game controllers is suitable for a specific game design: e.g. it is difficult (if not impossible) to use a mouse and a gamepad at the same time. Gaze-based interaction however offers a solution to this issue.

PRESENCE

Presence originated from the term "tele-presence" coined by Minsky [15] in 1980 and has undergone several developmental processes. When looking at available definitions for presence today, it becomes apparent that there is confusion about its precise meaning [5]. One effort to define presence was undertaken by Lee [12]: in general, presence can be understood as a psychological state in which the artificiality of an experience is not noticed by the subject. In computer-mediated environments authors frequently state, that the term refers to the sense of existing or of "being there" in a virtual space [18]. Lombard and Ditton [13] define presence as the perceptual illusion of non-mediation. The phenomenon includes responses "...sensory, cognitive, and affective processing systems to objects and entities in a person's environment" [13]. Presence is a multi-faceted phenomenon composed of various dimensions [18]. Several authors share the opinion that it is composed of the three dimensions: social presence, spatial presence, and self presence [22].

According to Lee [12], *social presence* can be identified when users "successfully simulate other humans or non-human intelligences". In such a scenario users do not notice the artificiality of the experienced social actors. Participants within a technologically mediated environment communicate as in a real human-to-human communication [2]. This can be observed as users frequently interact in artificial spaces by applying social rules that they also utilize in the real world.

The second dimension, *spatial presence*, describes the sensation of a user being "there" in the mediated environment [2]. It is frequently associated with the immersive experience of a user in the mediated environment, which occurs on a psychological and sensorial level. Referring to Wirth et al. [26], spatial presence can be further subdivided into two dimensions. The first sub-dimension is coined *self-location*, which is the perception of being physically situated within the environment simulated by the technology. The second one deals with the perceived possibilities to act within the environment. Users who are experiencing a feeling of spatial presence will perceive and employ only those actions that are possible in a mediated surrounding, but will not be aware of actions that are related to their real environment [26].

Self presence, the third dimension, can be defined as a psychological state in which users perceive their mediated self as if it were their actual self in the real world [12]. In the context of self presence, the virtual representation (the locus of manipulation) of users plays a vital role [6]. The locus of manipulation refers to "...the in-game position of the player's ability to assert control over the game-world, whether this is a visible character, an implied avatar, or a graphical user interface cursor" [1]. This is an obvious necessity as users cannot simply enter the virtual world through the screen—i.e. they exist in dual realities [8].

As users cannot directly interact with the virtual world, all actions are mediated through avatars. They are representations of the user and appear as an embodiment of their identity within a virtual environment [6]. Researchers, such as van Looy et al. [24], use the term *Embodied Presence (EP)* in this context. EP is the degree to which players feel like being their avatar when playing the game. With this definition the embodied nature of a mediated experience is emphasized.

PRESENCE AND GAME CONTROLLERS

In recent years, research on presence has also received an increased interest in games. This may be rooted in the technological advancements that have transpired within this field. Games as a medium offer unique experiences supported by game mechanics, art and level elements as well as in- and output devices. Referring to [4], game controllers contribute to presence—especially when it comes to spatial and embodied presence. These devices serve as the foundation to get in contact with the game world and have a critical impact concerning the embodiment within the setting. Biocca [3] claims that there are three bodies present when interacting with games: the objective body, the virtual body, and the body schema. The objective body forms the physical and observable body of the player, while the virtual body represents the player's body inside the game world. The third component, the body schema, is the user's mental representation of his or her body. All these elements are related to the game experience and are, furthermore, moderated by various game elements (input, output, design, etc.).

Several research activities were carried out in the field of presence and game controllers with a focus on natural mapping. Nacke [17], for instance, presents a study dealing with the impact of interaction modes (PS2 game controller vs. Wii remote and Nunchuk) on the subjective experience (one of the factors being spatial presence) and the brain activity of players. The researchers discovered that the spatial presence (self-location) was rated differently on the Wii and the PS2. Spatial presence was emphasized significantly more while using the Wii remote controller compared to the PS2 controller. Following the authors, the interaction with the (more natural mapped) Wii remote positively influences the experience of spatial presence through self-location.

Similar to Nacke [17], McEwan et al. [14] investigated the influence of the control interface on the experience of players. Three game control devices (controller, speed wheel, racing wheel), that differed in their type of mapping (natural vs. non-natural mapping), were evaluated. The introduced experimental design consisting of 64 participants was set up to measure differences in play experience within groups. Results showed that players performed best with the controller, followed by the speed wheel and the racing wheel. According to the authors, natural mapping has a strong influence on the feeling of presence: the more naturally mapped a device's control interface is, the higher the average ratings of presence. Interestingly, the players' positive responses to the played games were not dependent on their play performance or their capability to play with the device, but rather on the degree of natural mapping the device offered.

Apart from fairly well-established devices with natural mapping such as the Kinect or the Wiimote, alternative ways of interaction, as offered by eye tracking technologies, can also be employed to investigate presence in games. Nowadays, eye trackers can be efficiently integrated into games as the the technology has become affordable, more accurate, and less intrusive to players [21]. Companies, such as Tobii[3], offer developers eye tracking technology for an affordable price and encourage them to identify and create concepts for future gaze-based games.

Currently, a large portion of gaze-based games is developed in research projects. Ekman et al. [7], for example, developed a gaze-based game, called *Invisible Eni*, which uses gaze, blinking and pupil size to affect game state. In their game, the pupil size can be controlled by strong emotional experiences and cognitive effort. The design maps the size of the pupil variations and allows players to control game objects through the use of will-power. Smith and Graham [19] present games that utilize the eye tracker in a variety of ways. They integrate eye tracking in a first-person shooter game, a role playing game, and a classic arcade game called *Missile Command*. They state that eye tracking can increase spatial presence and can significantly alter the gaming experience and believe that "this is due to the continuous nature of eye-based control". When using a pointing device such as a mouse, players, as a first step, will typically look at the target. Afterwards, the players decide to select a given game entity or not. When utilizing eye tracking, pointing and selecting are merged into a single action.

Investigating gaze-based games in the context of presence is fairly new. Important contributions were made by Nacke et al. [16], who found out that the challenge of controlling the game through gaze leads to a positive spatial presence among players (as well as other game experience related factors). The results are in line with that found by Hartescu and Oikonomou [10]. Although the eye tracking devices are not as effective as their traditional counterparts (e.g. a mouse), players have a more pleasant experience and a higher degree of presence. Similar results were also found by Gowases et al. [9], who used gaze-based games in an educational setting.

Although important steps were taken to investigate the topic, further research is required. A common issue of many experiments lies in the focus on input hardware comparison (mouse, keyboard, controller, eye tracker, etc.). Research on mapping-variations of input devices (eye tracking integrated in different ways into game design) and their impact on presence are hard to find. Little is known about how these novel interaction devices should be employed to create positive experiences. At the moment, the overall game design, the specific game mechanics, or even the relation between game entities are of minor importance. Birk and Mandryk [4] for instance mention, that their game used in an experiment was intentionally designed to be without any dramatic elements. Therefore, elements such as story, character attachment were not part of their investigation. They add though that the inclusion of dramatic and other game design-related elements appears to be an interesting research direction.

EXPERIMENT DESCRIPTION

The previous section highlighted the lack of research in certain aspects concerning the impact of natural mapped input controllers on the phenomenon of presence. It was stated that it is not sufficient to simply integrate natural-mapped devices into an existing design in order to create a high degree of presence. The relation between the player and the game world established by the game controllers and a specific game design has to be considered. Therefore we want to investigate the influence of the relations defined by game design and input devices (gaze-based interaction in combination with a gamepad) on the presence experienced by players.

Game design mechanisms (mechanics, goals, etc.) in conjunction with controllers offer a tremendous amount of research possibilities and cannot be investigated in one single experiment. Thus, in this paper we are only able to assess specific aspects in this field. We will focus on the relation of the loci of manipulation defined by the game mechanics. The locus of manipulation is a key element in games; without it, the player would be just an observer with no means to interact with the game world.

In a typical game design the setup is usually quite simple as there is only one locus of manipulation. The player uses a gamepad to maneuver a game character through an obstacle course, or makes use of a steering wheel to drive a car in a racing game. However, things can get more complicated, when a game design includes more than just one input device. For example, body gestures, facial expressions or voice input can be used in combination with other devices such a mouse or keyboard input. In most cases the loci of manipulation are sub-parts of the virtual body: in an action adventure game, the player may navigate his or her character using a gamepad. He or she can carry out actions through the press of a button and use the analog stick to move the virtual body in the desired directions. Furthermore, the game could also include the tracking of facial expressions and the position of the eyes, which may be utilized in game dialogue situations. With this

[3] `http://www.tobii.com/`

constellation the game world is perceived through one entity supported by two or more loci of manipulation. Based on the existing research results it could be assumed that the more natural game input devices are, the stronger a feeling of presence would be. In most cases the assumption might be true. However, what happens when there is not just one, but two entities that represent the player? A player might control an avatar using a gamepad, while using his or her eyes to alter certain elements within the game.

Consequently, the question arises: will the degree of presence be influenced if the relation between the two loci of manipulation is changed?

Scenarios

To investigate and answer the stated research question we created four scenarios, which are all based on the same game design. The first three scenarios only differ in the modification of one game mechanic—the relation between the loci of manipulation (between the avatar and the gaze position of the player). The 4th scenario is played only with a traditional game input device (gamepad) without any gaze-support. A fifth scenario (interaction only through gaze) was canceled as it was not compatible with the chosen genre (changes to the game would have been too significantly compared to the other scenarios).

As a first step, the basic game design will be presented. Our game is called *Limus and the Eyes of the Beholders* and references several mechanics used in the game *Super Mario World*, which is a typical 2D platform game. We chose this type of game as it represents a well known genre with simple game mechanics. We took inspiration from the ghost house stages in Super Mario World: while exploring the level, Mario is confronted with an enemy called *Boo*. This type of enemy can only be avoided but not defeated by Mario. When the ghost detects him, it moves towards his position to catch him. The only way to stop the ghosts is by having Mario look at them. When they are being watched they are scared and are not able to move. The player is constantly in the dilemma of either moving forward to reach the end of the level, or looking back to freeze the chasing enemies.

This mechanic served as the basic component for the game design of our prototypes: our hero, called *Limus*, has to escape a dark cellar by reaching a magic portal. To grant players a certain amount of challenge, several obstacles, such as pits and small platforms, have to be mastered. The lives of Limus are limited but can be refilled by collecting light ghosts (*Lumees*) that are also present in the cellar.

Additionally sphere-shaped enemies with spikes, called *Spikees*, chase the player. Their behavior patterns are similar to the previously described Boos. When they see Limus, they try to catch him. A scene including all the main actors of our game can be seen in Figure 2. As in Super Mario World the player controls the avatar (Limus) using a gamepad. In contrast to the ghost stages of Super Mario world though, players are not only required to use the eyes of Limus, but also their very own to stop the Spikees. The way this works is different for each scenario:

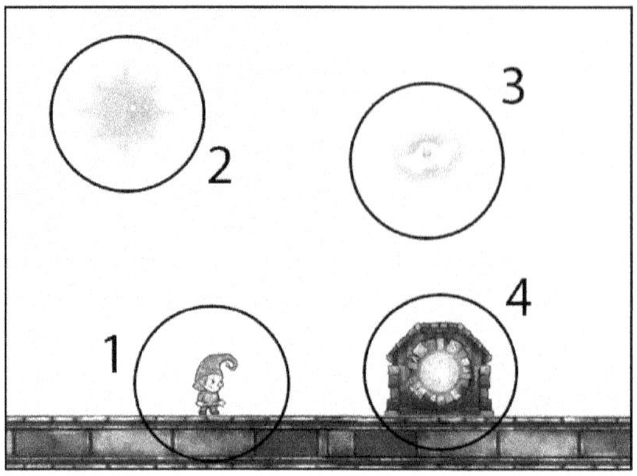

Figure 2. Screenshot of the game *Limus and the Eyes of the Beholders*: 1. Limus, 2. Spikee, 3. Lumee, 4. respawn point.

In *Scenario No Relation (Sc1NoR)* (see Figure 3, left picture) there is no connection between the two loci of manipulation (Limus and gaze position of the player). This means that Limus is controlled through the gamepad: he can run and jump, but he is not able to stun enemies with his gaze. This task is done solely using the player's eyes. When the player fixates a Spikee on the screen, the enemy is immediately frozen for a certain amount of time. This gives the player time to navigate Limus towards the end of the level using the game pad. What distinguishes this scenario from the other three is the fact that the player does not have to take care where Limus is currently looking—both act as independent entities.

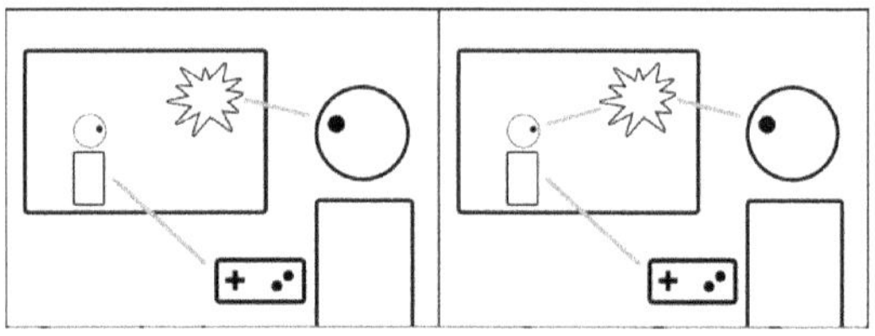

Figure 3. Left: Sc1NoR (no relation), and Right: Sc2PoR (positive relation).

Scenario Positive Relation (Sc2PoR) see Figure 3, right picture) offers the same game features as Sc1NoR—with only one exception: the loci of manipulation depend on each other. To stun the Spikees the players do not only have to look at them, but have to make sure that Limus also faces towards the enemies. This has the effect that players have to adapt to certain game situations as platforms or other obstacles might interfere with the reorientation of the avatar.

In *Scenario Negative Relation (Sc3NeR)* (see Figure 4, left picture) the stun effect is inverted. The enemy is frozen when players fixate a Spikee and Limus does *not* look at it. This should reveal the effects of contradicting loci of manipulation. In this scenario the two elements do not work as a single unit, but oppose each other.

Scenario No Gaze-Based Interaction (Sc4NoG) (see Figure 4, right picture) includes the mechanics that were also used in Super Mario World. No gaze input is required in this scenario, players control Limus using only the gamepad. When

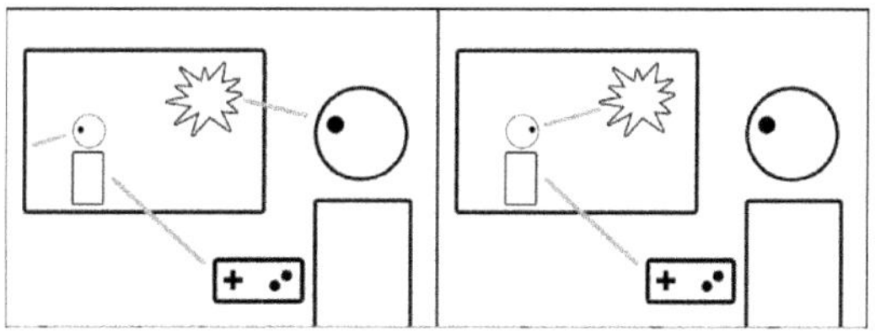

Figure 4. Left: Sc3NeR (negative relation), and Right: Sc4NoG (no gaze-based interaction).

Limus looks at enemies they are stunned—if he looks away the Spikees will again pursue him.

Hypotheses

We assume that each of the proposed scenarios should arouse a different feeling of presence. As our scenarios are based on on a very simple (single-player) game design, we will focus only on the aspects of embodied and spatial presence. Consequently, the dimension social presence will not be examined in the study. The following hypotheses are formulated:

H1 – Embodied Presence (EP): If there is a positive connection between the loci of manipulation (Sc2PoR) then the player experiences a stronger embodied presence within in a game situation compared to no (Sc1NoR) or negative relations (Sc3NeR) to loci of manipulation. Sc4NoG will have a stronger perceived embodied presence than Sc1NoR and Sc3NeR.

H1 addresses the question if the player has the impression that he or she is their avatar when playing the game. It is anticipated that the consistent design concerning the loci of manipulation (player *and* game character) will have a positive impact on the perceived embodied presence. Through the design a bridge is built that connects the player with the character. The player and the character have to carry out the same actions (look at the Spikees to stun them) and are dependent on each other. The feeling should be supported by the the natural mapping defined by the eye tracking device. In Sc1NoR there is no connection between the two loci of manipulation: thus, the player does not have the possibility to get directly in contact with Limus. Sc3NeR should have the lowest emotional presence, as actions granted by the loci of manipulation contradict each other. Therefore, it should be very hard for players to build up a contact with the game character. In Sc4NoG the perceived embodied presence should be fairly high as the interaction solely focuses on the Limus character and is consistent with the game world. However, Sc4NoG should receive lower scores than Sc2PoR, since Sc4NoG does not include the natural mapping of the eye tracker.

Concerning spatial presence we focus on two aspects: first, the perceived spatial presence of being part of the game world (Spatial Presence: Self Location (SPSL)), and secondly, the feeling of being able to act in the game world (Spatial Presence: Possible Actions (SPPA)). This categorization is based on the research carried out by Vorderer et al. [25]. In the following we propose the two hypotheses:

H2 – Spatial Presence: Self Location (SPSL): If there is a positive connection between the loci of manipulation (Sc2PoR) then the player experiences a stronger feeling of being part of the game world compared to no (Sc1NoR) or negative relations (Sc3NeR) to loci of manipulation. Sc4NoG should have the lowest perceived spatial presence.

As in H1 it is deemed that the consistent design of the loci of manipulation will foster the feeling of being part of the game world. Furthermore, the gaze-based interaction should have a significant influence on this dimension, as it allows players to act directly and naturally with the game environment. As in H1 it is assumed that Sc1NoR should receive higher scores than Sc3NeR. Concerning Sc4NoG, we anticipate that the perceived spatial presence should be fairly low, as players are not able to directly interact with the game world as they have only the possibility to control the character using the gamepad.

H3 – Spatial Presence: Possible Actions (SPPA): If there is no connection between the loci of manipulation (Sc1NoR) then the players share a stronger impression of being able to act in a game world compared to no (Sc2PoR) or negative relations (Sc3NeR) to loci of manipulation. It is deemed that Sc4NoG receives the lowest spatial presence scores.

In H3 it is assumed that Sc1NoR (no relation) leads to a higher perceived spatial presence, followed by Sc2PoR, Sc3NeR and Sc4NoG. The missing relation between the loci of manipulation in Sc1NoR offers the players a high amount of freedom, as they are not depending on the game character. Through the inclusion of the eye tracker, this effect should be emphasized. In the other scenarios players can also make use of their eyes, leading to a more complex gameplay. The most inconsistent scenario—Sc3NeR—should arouse a feeling of being limited, as the player has to act with the game character in a counterintuitive way. Nonetheless, Sc3NeR should have higher scores than Sc4NoG, as it includes the natural-mapped input device.

Participants and Procedure

The study was conducted at the University of Applied Sciences Upper Austria. The sample consisted of 24 participants, age 20 to 34 years (M: 24.6, SD: 3.5). Women, however, were significantly underrepresented in our sample (7 female and 17 male). All participants are students of the University of Applied Sciences Upper Austria and were recruited via e-mail. Most of the participants (19 persons) play video games at least several times a week.

The procedure itself took between 25 to 30 minutes per participant. The experimental setting was made up of a desktop PC and a Tobii Rex eye tracker.[4] The prototypes were created using the software Construct 2.

As a first step, the experimenter welcomed the participants and provided a short introduction text that gave an overview of the procedure and purpose of the study. The evaluation was divided into four major parts based on the previously described four scenarios. By choosing a *within-subject design*, all participants had to play each of the mentioned scenarios

[4] `http://developer.tobii.com/rex-technical-specs-faq/`

(average play time: 4 minutes). As the control scheme and the genre itself (platform game) were very easy to comprehend, subjects had no difficulties to get into the game. Additionally it was decided to set up a compressed level design (many entities in the level space) which led to the short interaction time per scenario. The order in which participants were confronted with the prototypes was randomized to take possible interaction effects into account.

Each evaluation part started with a tutorial showing the basic means of interaction. Participants were instructed about the setting and the game goals. When subjects confirmed that every aspect was clear to them the evaluation began. When the interaction with one scenario was completed, the experimenter instructed the participants to fill out the questionnaire (questions on the spatial and embodied presence and some demographic questions). After participants were finished with the first scenario, the other three were played and evaluated. Afterwards, participants had the possibility to give comments on the perceived spatial and embodied presence.

Measures

All dependent measures were collected by using validated scales. To measure the spatial presence dimensions the MEC Spatial Presence Questionnaire (MEC-SPQ) by Vorderer et al. [25] was employed. It is designed to measure spatial presence and consists of nine scales. Four of the scales feature process factors, two scales refer to states and actions and three scales include trait-like personality characteristics. As in [11], two of the process scales, spatial presence: SPSL and SPPA, were utilized in the study. SPSL specifically reflects the physical quality of presence (example: "I had the feeling that I was in the middle of the action rather than merely observing.", or "I felt like I was a part of the environment in the presentation."). It measures the impression of the subject to be physically in the middle of the virtual game environment. The other sub-scale, possible actions, assesses the impression of being able to act (example: "The objects in the presentation gave me the feeling that I could do things with them.", or "I felt like I could move around among the objects in the presentation."). Due to the fact that the reported reliability of the scales was good, we decided to make use of the stated short versions (4 items) of the scales (Cronbach's α for SPSL: 0.92 and for SPPA: 0.81) [25]. Our own findings show acceptable Cronbach's α values from 0.69–0.88. The items are rated using a five-point Likert scale (ranging from "strongly disagree" to "strongly agree"). Finally the selected items have been merged in order to create a score.

The other dimension, embodied presence, was measured by using a part of Player Identification (PI) scale by van Looy et al. [24]. It was used to measure identification in Massively Multiplayer Online Role-Playing Games (MMORPGs), but can also be employed in other genres. The PI consists of three main dimensions: avatar (character) identification, group (guild) identification and game (community) identification. Avatar identification is made up of three subcomponents: perceived similarity, wishful identification and embodied presence. For our study we only made used of the embodied presence sub scale (examples: "When I am playing, it feels as if I am my character", or "When playing, it feels as if my character's body becomes my own"). The internal consistency is very good (according to the different scenarios Cronbach's α ranges between 0.88 and 0.97). As in MEC-SPQ, five-point Likert scale items range from "strongly disagree" to "strongly agree" and finally the acceptable items have been merged to an index-variable.

Data Analyses

In order to examine the underlying hypotheses, all analyses were conducted using repeated-measures ANOVA. A benefit of the repeated-measures ANOVA is the limited number of subjects required. All parametric tests were performed after validating the data for assumptions of ANOVA use. Degrees of freedom were corrected using the Greenhouse-Geisser method, if the condition of sphericity was not satisfied. Pairwise comparisons used the Bonferroni method of adjusting the degrees of freedom for multiple comparisons (post-hoc-tests). All statistic tests were carried out with SPSS 20. Significance was set at $\alpha = 0.05$.

RESULTS

In the following section results of the study are presented. Insights are provided if the various scenarios (with different loci of manipulation relations) have an influence on the perceived presence (dependent variable: spatial and embodied presence). Information on the dimensions embodied presence, spatial presence: self location, and spatial presence: possible actions are be presented. It has to be noted that the aspect of gender does not have any significant differences concerning the mean values of EP, SPSL, and SPPA ($p > .05$).

Embodied Presence

Results of the ANOVA indicate a significant effect of the scenario on the perceived EP ($F_{3,69} = 11.29$, $p \approx .000$, $\eta^2 = 0.33$) (see Figure 5). 33 % of the variation in the dependent variable (EP) can be explained by the independent variable loci of manipulation. Sc2PoR (positive relation) has a higher perceived EP than Sc1NoR and Sc3NeR (each: $p = .001$). However, it has to be noted that no significant difference was found when looking at Sc2PoR and Sc4NoG. Although Sc2PoR (M: 3.41, SD: 1.12) received higher scores in total than Sc4NoG (M: 3.16, SD: 0,93) the inclusion of the eye tracking device did not have the anticipated effect. Similar to Sc2PoR, in Sc4NoG subjects had a significantly stronger perception of EP, when compared to Sc1NoR ($p = .034$) and 3 ($p = .005$). With one exception (no significant difference between Sc2PoR and Sc4NoG) all assumptions formulated in H1 were confirmed.

Spatial Presence: Self Location

Concerning the SPSL, results show that the chosen scenarios have a significant impact on the perceived spatial presence: self location ($F_{2,46.3} = 30.9$, $p \approx .000$, $\eta^2 = 0.57$) (see Figure 6). The proportion of the variation in the dependent variable (SPSL) that is explained by the independent variable loci of manipulation is 57%. Pairwise comparisons show that Sc1NoR and Sc2PoR have the strongest influence on SPSL. Surprisingly, no significant difference between the two scenarios could be identified.

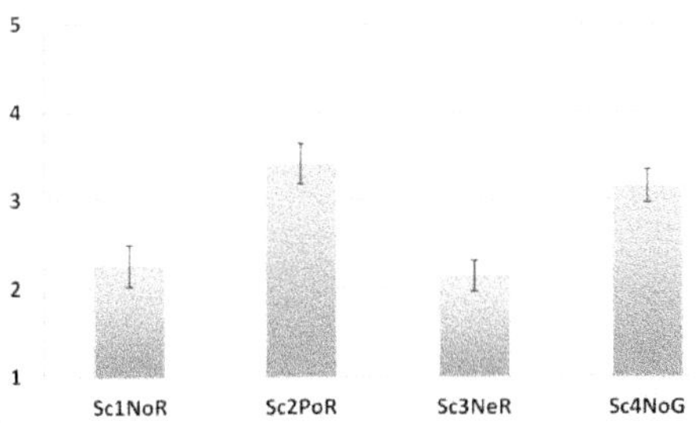

Figure 5. Means for Embodied Presence (EP) of all scenarios on a scale from 1 ("strongly disagree") to 5 ("strongly agree").

However, a significant difference is shown between Sc2PoR and Sc3NeR, as well as between Sc3NeR and Sc4NoG ($p = .009$ and $p \approx .000$). This means that in Sc2PoR SPSL is perceived more strongly than in the other two scenarios. Furthermore, Sc3NeR and Sc4NoG differ significantly ($p = .008$). SPSL has a higher value in Sc3NeR (M: 3.54, SD: 1.05) than in Sc4NoG (M: 2.56, SD: 0.94).

Hypothesis H2 (Sc2PoR has a higher SPSL than the other three scenarios) does only apply to Sc3NeR and Sc4NoG. Although the differences between Sc1NoR and Sc2PoR are not significant, Sc1NoR (M: 4.22, SD: 0.72) received more positive answers than Sc2PoR (M: 4.16, SD: 0.71). The assumption that Sc2PoR has a higher SPSL than the other scenarios has to be rejected.

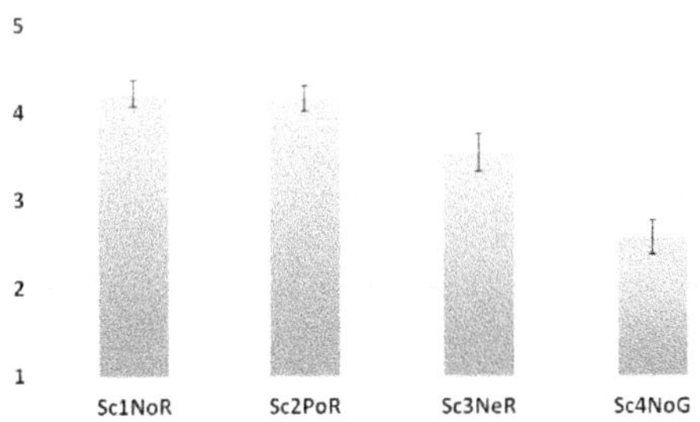

Figure 6. Means for Spatial Presence: Self Location (SPSL) of all scenarios on a scale from 1 ("strongly disagree") to 5 ("strongly agree").

Spatial Presence: Possible Actions

The third dimensions SPPA reveals a significant effect ($F_{2,46.6} = 21.5$, $p \approx .000$, $\eta^2 = 0.49$, see Figure 7). 49% of the variation in the dependent variable (SPPA) can be explained by the independent variable loci of manipulation. As hypothesized in H3, Sc1NoR has the strongest influence on the perceived SPPA. When compared with the other scenarios a significant effect can be identified ($p \leq .001$).

Additionally, the SPPA score in Sc2PoR as well as in Sc3NeR is significantly higher than in Sc4NoG ($p = .003$ and $p = .03$). Surprisingly, no significant difference could be found between Sc2PoR and Sc3NeR.

A summary of the results (mean values and standard deviations of EP, SPPA, and SPSL) is shown in Table 1.

DISCUSSION

Our study shows that small changes in the game design, regardless of the natural mapping, have a strong influence on

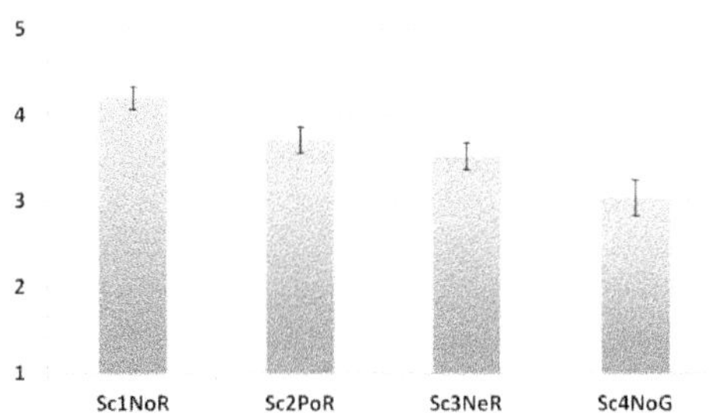

Figure 7. Means for Spatial Presence: Possible Actions (SPPA) of all scenarios on a scale from 1 ("strongly disagree") to 5 ("strongly agree").

	EP	SPPA	SPSL
Sc1NoR	2.26 (1.14)	4.20 (0.66)	4.22 (0.72)
Sc2PoR	3.41 (1.12)	3.71 (0.73)	4.16 (0.71)
Sc3NeR	2.14 (0.85)	3.52 (0.77)	3.54 (1.05)
Sc4NoG	3.16 (0.93)	3.03 (1.02)	2.56 (0.94)
Cronbach's α	0.88–0.97	0.69–0.82	0.82–0.87

Table 1. Means and Standard Deviation for Spatial (SPSL and SPPA) and Embodied Presence (EP) on a scale from 1 ("strongly disagree") to 5 ("strongly agree") per scenario. The internal consistency of the scales is shown by Cronbach's α.

the perceived presence. By altering the mechanics that regulate the relation between the loci of manipulation, players get a different impression of "being there" in the game world. Additionally the modification of mechanics influences how strong players feel if they are their avatar when playing the game. In the following we describe the findings and discuss them in detail.

A majority of assumptions was confirmed by the conducted experiment. However, especially Sc1NoR led to some interesting results that were not anticipated. Concerning SPSL no significant difference between Sc1NoR and Sc2PoR could be found. One explanation for this can be seen in the fact that some subjects felt that, without the relation between them and the Limus character, they experience themselves as autonomous entities. In Sc2PoR participants articulated a negative SPSL in one particular situation: they looked at the Spikee, and the enemy was not stunned. Immediately they focused on Limus and noticed that he was not facing the Spikee. This insight pulled them out of the game world.

Of course this situation cannot occur in Sc1NoR as it does not matter, where Limus is looking. One solution to this issue would be to include a visual or audio cue if Limus and the player focus a Spikee. As predicted in H3, the highest SPPA scores appeared in Sc1NoR. Subjects had the possibility to act freely by using their gaze, independent from the Limus character. Some of them had the impression of having a high degree of control over the current game situation. A subject noted that he had the feeling that he had god-like abilities within the game (stunning enemies by just looking at them). This imagination serves also as an indicator for the relatively low EP score. On several occasions subjects reported to act on a meta level: they see themselves as a powerful guardian force, who has to protect Limus. Consequently, the distance between the player and the game character is greater than in most other scenarios (with the exception of Sc3NeR).

Sc2PoR, on the other hand, was rated with the highest EP score. By employing gaze-based interaction in conjunction with a positive relation towards the game character, EP is fostered. It has to be noted, however, that Sc2PoR and Sc4NoG do not show any significant differences. It seems that the inclusion of the eye tracking device in Sc2PoR was not sufficient to obtain optimal results. A solution to this issue might be to utilize an additional visual element that emphasizes the positive relation between the character and Limus. One design strategy would be to integrate a visual representation of the line of sight (or a similar element like a magic spell with a target component linked to Limus) to overcome this issue. When looking at SPSL and SPPA results, Sc2PoR led to a better impression when compared with Sc3NeR and Sc4NoG (with the exception of Sc1NoR). This effect is based on the dependency between the player and Limus, which restricted and, in some cases, hampered the stunning of the Spikees.

In general, Sc3NeR received negative ratings on all presence dimensions. A negative relation led to low EP scores. Subjects mentioned that it felt very counterintuitive to control the game in this particular manner. A participant noted that this concept has an inverted logic, and it was really hard for him to get in contact with character. Thus, it received similar negative results as Sc1NoR. The comparison of SPPA ratings of Sc2PoR and Sc3NeR led to a unexpected result: no significant difference could be found. The employed level has a tower-like design structure, where players can navigate without any restrictions: the player starts in left corner of the level, and has to climb the steps to reach the magic portal. In order to advance he or she has to switch directions, meaning that in some cases he or she has to run from left to right or vice versa. This aspect has an influence on how Limus faces the Spikees. First, they appear in front of him. When he turns around, the Spikees are behind him, which makes the stunning of the Spikees much easier for players. This had the effect that in some situations the negative constellation was not noticed by the players.

Finally, Sc4NoG, with its traditional game design had the lowest scores in regard to SPPA and SPSL. Many participants mentioned that they did not have the feeling of being powerful and described the experience as conventional as well as too easy. In terms of EP, Sc4NoG was rated higher than Sc1NoR and Sc3NeR. Due to the lack of another locus of manipulation it was rather easy for subjects to relate to the game character. Sc2PoR had a slightly better rating than Sc4NoG: it was not sufficient, however, to reveal any significant difference. A stronger visual reference between the loci of manipulation would solve the issue.

The results of the study lead to some practical implications: designers can make use of the gathered findings. As it was shown, a game design with no relation between the loci of manipulation fosters a feeling of acting on a meta layer. Subjects might play a character with the gamepad, while, on the other hand, support him or her with their gaze input. Thus, a protector/protected relationship can be established. However, one has to bear in mind that this design choice has also a negative effect on the perceived EP. If a designer aims for a strong bond between the player and the game character, and wants to include additional input, than he or she should try to establish a bridge between the two loci of manipulation through specific game mechanics. However, it has to be noted that the presented scenarios need to be evaluated in other genres (such as role-playing games, action shooter games, etc.) in order to be generally applicable. Relevant factors that have to be considered in regard to the evaluation of other genres are the mechanics (simple/complex), the art style (abstract/realistic) or the degree of collaboration (single player/multiplayer).

CONCLUSIONS

It has been shown that gaze input promises great potential for game designers. In comparison to traditional approaches, gaze input facilitates presence on different dimensions (Embodied Presence (EP), Spatial Presence: Self Location (SPSL), Spatial Presence: Possible Actions (SPPA)). However, the relation between the loci of manipulation (positive relation, no relation, negative relation) has a strong influence on the perceived presence. By setting up a positive relation between the loci of manipulation (player's gaze, gaze of the game character), EP is fostered, whereas when employing an unrelated design approach, SPSL and SPPA are more pronounced. While this paper focused on a platform game with a basic game design, it would be interesting to carry out further studies based on different genres such as action adventures or role playing games. Furthermore, the type of the perspective (2D, 3D, first or third person) is an intriguing topic for future studies. Since some anticipated differences could not be shown (e.g. no significant difference between Scenario Positive Relation (Sc2PoR) and Scenario No Gaze-Based Interaction (Sc4NoG) with regards to EP) it might make sense to adjust various visual elements. One approach could be to emphasize the relation between the player and the game character through visual cues.

Another area for further investigation is the length of a play test session. The average playtime for each scenario was about 4 minutes (which was sufficient for the chosen game and level design in the employed scenarios). The question arises, if differences with regards to presence appear, when subjects play the game for a longer time span. A further area of improvement concerning the design of the experiment is the inclusion of structured or semi-structured interviews (in conjunction with the research tools utilized in the study) in order to get a better understanding of the design space.

ACKNOWLEDGMENTS

We would like to thank all of our survey participants for their time and for the data they generously provided.

REFERENCES

1. Bayliss, P. Beings in the game-world: Characters, avatars, and players. In *Proceedings of the 4th Australasian Conference on Interactive Entertainment*, IE '07, RMIT University (Melbourne, Australia, Australia, 2007), 4:1–4:6.

2. Behm-Morawitz, E. Mirrored selves: The influence of self-presence in a virtual world on health, appearance, and well-being. *Computers in Human Behavior 29*, 1 (2013), 119–128.

3. Biocca, F. The cyborg's dilemma: Progressive embodiment in virtual environments. *Journal of Computer-Mediated Communication 3*, 2 (1997), 0.

4. Birk, M., and Mandryk, R. L. Control your game-self: Effects of controller type on enjoyment, motivation, and personality in game. In *Proceedings of the SIGCHI Conference on Human Factors in Computing Systems*, CHI '13, ACM (New York, NY, USA, 2013), 685–694.

5. Calleja, G. *In-Game: From Immersion to Incorporation.* The MIT Press, Cambridge, Massachusetts, 2011.

6. Ducheneaut, N., Wen, M.-H., Yee, N., and Wadley, G. Body and mind: A study of avatar personalization in three virtual worlds. In *Proceedings of the SIGCHI Conference on Human Factors in Computing Systems*, CHI '09, ACM (New York, NY, USA, 2009), 1151–1160.

7. Ekman, I. M., Poikola, A. W., and Mäkäräinen, M. K. Invisible Eni: Using gaze and pupil size to control a game. In *CHI '08 Extended Abstracts on Human Factors in Computing Systems*, CHI EA '08, ACM (New York, NY, USA, 2008), 3135–3140.

8. Gazzard, A. Player as parent, character as child: Exploring avatarial relationships in gamespace. In *Proceedings of the 14th International Academic MindTrek Conference: Envisioning Future Media Environments*, MindTrek '10, ACM (New York, NY, USA, 2010), 25–31.

9. Gowases, T., Bednarik, R., and Tukiainen, M. Gaze vs. mouse in games: The effects on user experience. In *In Proc. of the International Conference on Computers in Education (ICCE) 2008* (2008), pp. 773–777.

10. Hartescu, D., and Oikonomou, A. Gaze tracking as a game input interface. In *CGAMES*, Q. H. Mehdi, A. S. Elmaghraby, R. Moreton, R. V. Yampolskiy, and J. Chariker, Eds., IEEE (2011), 126–133.

11. Havranek, M., Langer, N., Cheetham, M., and Jäncke, L. Perspective and agency during video gaming influences spatial presence experience and brain activation patterns. *Behavioral and Brain Functions 8*, 34 (2012).

12. Lee, K. Presence, explicated. *Communication Theory 14*, 1 (2004), 27–50.

13. Lombard, M., and Ditton, T. At the heart of it all: The concept of presence. *Journal of Computer-Mediated Communication 3*, 2 (1997), 0.

14. McEwan, M., Johnson, D., Wyeth, P., and Blackler, A. Videogame control device impact on the play experience. In *Proceedings of The 8th Australasian Conference on Interactive Entertainment: Playing the System*, IE '12, ACM (New York, NY, USA, 2012), 18:1–18:3.

15. Minsky, M. Telepresence. *OMNI magazine* (June 1980).

16. Nacke, L., Stellmach, S., Sasse, D., and Lindley, C. A. Gameplay experience in a gaze interaction game. In *Proceedings of the 5th Conference on Communication by Gaze Interaction – COGAIN 2009: Gaze Interaction For Those Who Want It Most*, A. Villanueva, J. P. Hansen, and B. K. Ersbøll, Eds., The COGAIN Association, The COGAIN Association (Lyngby, Denmark, 2009), 49–54.

17. Nacke, L. E. Wiimote vs. controller: Electroencephalographic measurement of affective gameplay interaction. In *Proceedings of the International Academic Conference on the Future of Game Design and Technology*, Futureplay '10, ACM (New York, NY, USA, 2010), 159–166.

18. Schultze, U. Embodiment and presence in virtual worlds: a review. *JIT 25*, 4 (2010), 434–449.

19. Smith, J. D., and Graham, T. C. N. Use of eye movements for video game control. In *Proceedings of the 2006 ACM SIGCHI International Conference on Advances in Computer Entertainment Technology*, ACE '06, ACM (New York, NY, USA, 2006).

20. Steuer, J. Defining virtual reality: Dimensions determining telepresence. *Journal of Communication 42* (1992), 73–93.

21. Sundstedt, V. Gazing at games: Using eye tracking to control virtual characters. In *ACM SIGGRAPH 2010 Courses*, SIGGRAPH '10, ACM (New York, NY, USA, 2010), 5:1–5:160.

22. Tamborini, R., and Bowman, N. Presence in video games. In *Immersed in Media: Telepresence in Everyday Life*, C. Bracken and P. Skalski, Eds. Routledge, New York, NY, USA, 2010, 87–109.

23. Tamborini, R., and Skalski, P. The role of presence in the experience of electronic games. In *Playing video games - motives, responses, and consequences*, P. Vorderer and J. Bryant, Eds. Lawrence Erlbaum, 2006, 225–240.

24. van Looy, J., Courtois, C., and De Vocht, M. Player identification in online games: Validation of a scale for measuring identification in MMORPGs. In *Proceedings of the 3rd International Conference on Fun and Games*, Fun and Games '10, ACM (New York, NY, USA, 2010), 126–134.

25. Vorderer, P., Wirth, W., Gouveia, F. R., Biocca, F., Saari, T., Jaencke, F., Böcking, S., Schramm, H., Gysbers, A., Hartmann, T., Klimmt, C., Laarni, J., Ravaja, N., Sacau, A., Baumgartner, T., and Jäncke, P. MEC spatial presence questionnaire (MECSPQ): Short documentation and instructions for application. report to the european community, project presence: MEC (IST-2001-37661), 2004.

26. Wirth, W., Hartmann, T., Böcking, S., Vorderer, P., Klimmt, C., Schramm, H., Saari, T., Laarni, J., Ravaja, N., Gouveia, F. R., Biocca, F., Sacau, A., Jäncke, L., Baumgartner, T., and Jäncke, P. A Process Model of the Formation of Spatial Presence Experiences. *Media Psychology 9* (Dec. 2007), 493–525.

Learning Curves: Analysing Pace and Challenge in Four Successful Puzzle Games

Conor Linehan, George Bellord, Ben Kirman
University of Lincoln,
Lincoln, LN6 7TS, UK
clinehan@lincoln.ac.uk

Zachary H. Morford
University of Reno, Nevada
1664 N. Virginia Street Reno, NV
zachary.morford@gmail.com

Bryan Roche
National University of Ireland,
Maynooth, Maynooth,
Co. Kildare, Ireland
bryan.t.roche@nuim.ie

ABSTRACT
The pace at which challenges are introduced in a game has long been identified as a key determinant of both the enjoyment and difficulty experienced by game players, and their ability to learn from game play. In order to understand how to best pace challenges in games, there is great value in analysing games already demonstrated as highly engaging. Play-through videos of four puzzle games (*Portal, Portal 2 Co-operative mode, Braid* and *Lemmings),* were observed and analysed using metrics derived from a behavioural psychology understanding of how people solve problems. Findings suggest that; 1) the main skills learned in each game are introduced separately, 2) through simple puzzles that require only basic performance of that skill, 3) the player has the opportunity to practice and integrate that skill with previously learned skills, and 4) puzzles increase in complexity until the next new skill is introduced. These data provide practical guidance for designers, support contemporary thinking on the design of learning structures in games, and suggest future directions for empirical research.

Author Keywords
Education; Gamification; Learning Curve

ACM Classification Keywords
K.8.0 [Personal Computing]: Games – *General;* J.4 [Computer Applications]: K.3.1 [Computers and Education]: Computer Uses in Education – *Computer-assisted instruction.*

INTRODUCTION
There has been a great deal of interest in recent years in exploring the use of games design techniques to augment and improve people's motivation for learning [31]. Good games are challenging, encourage players to spend large amounts of time on a specific task, and allow players to learn through exploration and failure [18, 27,37,39]. It is suggested that if the same type of focused, tenacious behaviour were observed of people while learning, educational outcomes would be greatly improved. Distinct sub-themes have emerged from this research domain, addressing topics such as gamified educational technology [14, 16, 28], educational games [4, 29, 30], and games to promote behavioural change [3, 6]. However, we are only beginning to see rigorous analyses of what it is about the design of video games that we should transfer to these contexts in order to best harness games design elements as motivational tools for learning.

This paper examines one specific aspect of game design that is central to both learning and enjoyment during game play; the question of how to best pace the challenges presented by games [10, 39, 2, 38]. This question has been discussed and analysed many times by games designers and academics, using a range of different perspectives. The general understanding is that challenges should be matched to a player's individual level of skill, and that challenges should increase as players skills increase. While much has been written about this concept, and some experimental studies have been undertaken [2, 30, 38], what is missing in the literature is an understanding of the design features of games that successfully achieve this effect.

Our approach to analyzing pace and challenge in this paper is based on a pragmatic approach to the understanding of problem solving taken from the behavioural psychology literature. Specifically, behavioural psychologists argue that the behavior that solves a problem is rarely a brand new insight, but is more often a combination (or chaining together) of already learned behaviors [40, 42]. In order for a games' design to support people in solving in-game challenges in this manner, it seems that a number of structural game design features must be present. For example, when learning a complex skill, players should first learn the discrete components of that skill individually, before practicing 'chaining' them together in combinations. These are precisely the structural design features examined in the games analysed in this paper. Specifically, we analyse how complexity fluctuates over the sequence of challenges presented in those games and how complexity

CHI PLAY '14, October 19 - 22 2014, Toronto, ON, Canada
Copyright 2014 ACM 978-1-4503-3014-5/14/10···$15.00.
http://dx.doi.org/10.1145/2658537.2658695

correlates with the points at which new skills are introduced.

Since we are interested in understanding games design elements useful in the context of education, we chose to focus our analysis on commercially successful puzzle-based video games. We define puzzle-based games as those in which the fun is derived primarily from learning and applying specific skills to progress. The commercial success of the games chosen indicates that the designers of these games have successfully integrated and balanced the learning and game play elements (i.e. achieved good structures that support both learning and enjoyment). We believe that studying demonstrably engaging puzzle games can provide a wealth of information to help understand the usefulness of game design elements in wider educational contexts, where the aim is similarly on the acquisition and application of specific skills. Essentially, instead of postulating game design features that may be useful for education, or analysing participant's subjective experience of a game, we reverse engineer games that have been observed as demonstrating good design, in order to learn about their structures.

The contribution of the paper is threefold. 1) We present a novel analysis of four commercially successful puzzle games, which identifies a number of shared structural features between those games. These findings may be of immediate use to all game designers, and are particularly useful for those interested in applying game design to education. 2) Findings are coherent with previous work published by both game designers and academics regarding the pacing of challenges in games. Our paper supports and adds to that that work by providing an interesting data set that may encourage future discussion. 3) We present a simple but robust methodology for understanding, measuring and analyzing complexity in game play.

BACKGROUND

Many commentators have suggested that game design elements have the potential to improve motivation and engagement in educational contexts. However, work that specifically examines which game design elements have useful effects in which educational contexts is only beginning to emerge. In this section, we first present a brief review of literature on games and learning, focusing particularly on recent studies that examine the effects of specific game elements on measurable behaviour. We then discuss how pace and challenge have been analysed and discussed in previous game design literature. We provide a brief introduction to behavioural psychology, and the behavioural approach to understanding problem solving, as a means for providing context for our method of analysis. Finally, we justify the choice of commercially successful puzzle games as a topic worthy of study and a source of insight into the use of games in educational contexts.

Games and learning

There has been much discussion and commentary recently about how games design can be used as a tool to improve peoples motivation for learning [31,18]. Researchers and commentators demonstrate excitement at the prospect of developing educational tools and environments that maintain the motivational effects of video games, while supporting learning. Notably, while much has been written about why games should or could prove useful in improving engagement in educational contexts [18], we are only beginning to see work emerge that offers practical guidance to designers on how to recreate the motivation seen in entertainment games when designing specifically for the context of education [20, 29].

Historically, the majority of studies that have explored the effectiveness (or, more commonly, the "potential"), of games to function as educational tools, have goals other than understanding and improving the design process. Those studies rarely investigate the specific effects of specific design features on player behaviour. Rather, they typically report summative trials of specific games designed to teach specific skills or knowledge (see [5, 17, 32, 36, 45] for comprehensive reviews of empirical studies). Typically the question asked in these studies is something like "can games improve adherence to medical treatment" (i.e., [6]) or "can games teach simple mathematics" (i.e., [28]). Indeed, the term "game" is often used in a vague way that implies that games are a homogenous category, all instances of which contain common features [20]. Thus, even when the evaluation methodology is rigorous, it is difficult to learn generalisable lessons about game design from these studies.

More recently, studies have emerged that examine the effects of gamified systems on user behaviour. For example, Christy and Fox [9] examine how the use of leaderboards can evoke social comparisons and influence academic performance, sometimes negatively so. De-Marcos et al., [14] found that both gamification and social networking, when integrated with an e-learning programme, resulted in higher skill acquisition by participants. Conversely, those participants demonstrated better knowledge acquisition when using the basic e-learning programme. Koivisto & Hamari [26] examine the long-term effects of gamification on exercise behaviour, studying the service *Fitocracy*, and found that the perceived enjoyment and usefulness of gamification features decline with use, suggesting a novelty effect. Thus, while much research is being carried out, results are rarely straightforward. It is difficult to identify from studies of complete systems how discrete components of those systems effect player behaviour.

In contrast to the studies mentioned above, a small amount of recent research does analyse specific qualities of games that may be useful in the context of education. For example, Hamari [21] found that the implementation of achievement badges in a peer-to-peer trading service improved user activity, but only for those users who actively monitored their achievements. Hamari et al., [22] report a literature review of all studies that empirically examine the effects of gamification on user behaviour, finding that any positive effects of gamification were greatly dependent on context, and that gamification generally improves motivation only for those users already interested in those gamified elements. It seems that there may be differences between the types of design features necessary to draw in new users, and those necessary to maintain engagement. In summary, we are only beginning to see empirical work that provides practical direction to designers aiming to use game design as part of educational programmes and the results of those early studies are often difficult to interpret by designers.

Pace and Challenge

Game 'challenge' is one feature that is regularly discussed as important in influencing player motivation. There seems almost unanimous acceptance that games should present challenges that are matched to the players individual skill level, and that playing games is fun only if a sufficient proportion of the game challenges are mastered by the player [7, 25, 37, 39]. It is also suggested that players will not be motivated to play a game that they do not find challenging. The concept of 'appropriate challenge' is central to the idea of designing for 'flow' [12], so influential on the practice of many game designers [39].

While 'appropriate challenge' is a useful design goal, we are only beginning to see analyses of what represents an 'appropriate' level of challenge in a computer game, or how a game designer can approach the problem of ensuring that players experience it. For example, Lomas et al., [30] report two studies, featuring tens of thousands of participants, which experimentally analysed how challenge affects motivation in educational games. Both studies found that less challenging games engendered greater motivation in players than more challenging games. Alexander et al., [2] conducted an experiment with 90 participants, and found that players enjoy a game more if the difficulty provided is reflective of their gaming experience. Sampayo-Vargas et al. [38] in a study with 234 particiapnts, found that an educational game that adapted its difficulty level based on player performance produced better learning outcomes.

In this paper we suggest that the structure and pace through which challenges are introduced to players (or, the learning curve) is a feature that can be analysed objectively through examining game play. We suggest that commercially successful and well-regarded puzzle games manage this pacing in an effective manner. By analyzing the structure of these successful games we can unpick successful strategies for managing complexity and designing appropriate learning curves in games.

Behavioural Psychology

For the purposes of the current paper, we are not interested in player's subjective experience of challenge in games. Rather, we are interested in how demonstrably successful games are designed in order to present challenges to players over the course of play. Essentially, we are reverse engineering successful games that have been observed as demonstrating good design in order to learn about their structures. In order to analyse game challenge in an observational manner (i.e., through analyzing features of the game design, rather than features of player experience) we adopt an approach to understanding challenge and problem solving derived from behavioural psychology.

Behaviorism is an approach to psychology that assumes, for pragmatic reasons (see [24]), that behaviour is learned through experience. It is intentionally not concerned with hypothesised internal states such as feelings, thoughts and intentions, as those cannot currently be measured and recorded accurately in experimental conditions. The work of a behavioral psychologist therefore lies in investigating which specific features of the environment lead to particular behaviors [8]. In the current paper we are analyzing how design features of games support problem solving. Problem solving here is understood as a synonym for the actions necessary for completing puzzles in a game.

Behaviourism and Problem solving

Over the past century, many explanations have been offered to account for the apparently novel, insightful and creative behaviour exhibited by people when solving problems [33]. One explanation, offered by behavioural psychologist B.F. Skinner, seems to offer some practical guidance for the design of the structure and pacing of learning in games. Skinner [40,42] suggests that, contrary to appearances, the behavior that solves a problem is rarely a brand new insight, but is more often a novel combination of already established behaviors. For instance, a child who has been taught to pull a chain on the ceiling to flush a toilet, and also to climb on a step to reach objects, may one day climb on a step to pull a chain that is out of reach. This behaviour appears to be insightful, but it might be more simply described as the chaining together of previously learned responses (or, response chaining). Since people seem predisposed to solve problems in this way, we suggest that it would be useful for game designers to structure games to allow for this type of problem solving. This leads to one of our research questions; whether the design of highly successful games support this type of problem solving.

Notably, Gingold [19], in explaining the appeal of the game *Wario Ware* [34], describes a form of response chaining, without naming it such. Gingold proposes that the process of gradually learning simple behaviors individually and combining these as the game progresses explains the appeal of the game. Indeed, anecdotally, the structure of puzzle games, such as *World of Goo* [1] seem optimized to take advantage of the human capacity for problem solving in terms of response chaining. Game designer Dan Cook, in explaining his own practice, presents an in-depth analysis of how to structure 'skill chains' [10] over the course of game play. While not referring specifically to the behavioural psychology understanding of response chaining, he is clearly describing the same phenonmenon.

Thus, one of the goals of the current study is to examine the structure of puzzle games in order to verify whether response chaining appears important in the design of these games. Specifically, we will examine the number of individual actions necessary to complete each puzzle in each game, and whether those are new actions, or new combinations of old actions. This will allow us to chart, on a line graph [11, 41], the pace with which new information is introduced in these games. Thus, there are two basic metrics used in the analysis used in the current study:

1. The number of player actions necessary to solve an in-game problem. This represents a behavioural definition of complexity. The higher number of distinct actions necessary, the more complex the problem.

2. Whether each of those actions had been required previously in the game.

Using these two metrics we can build a picture of when new skills are introduced, how game complexity correlates with those new skills, and whether games provide space for players to practice chaining those skills with other skills before encountering the next novel skill.

Puzzle games

We define puzzle games as those video games where problem solving is the central mechanic. We suggest that studying the design of commercially successful puzzle games can teach us valuable lessons about designing game based educational technology. This is because the design goals of puzzle games are so similar to those of education. While all games must teach players the skills necessary to succeed at that game, puzzle games focus on generating fun primarily from problem solving. Hence, in order to produce successful products, designers of puzzle games must focus on ensuring that game challenges (i.e., the learning) is structured in a manner that is engaging and fun, and which ensures most players can attain the necessary skills without unreasonable frustration. These are precisely the challenges that designers must overcome in order to create useful learning experiences.

People working in game based learning rarely have the resources to do the type of rapid, iterative, player-centered development process necessary to perfect the balance and pace of a commercial game [23]. By studying the structure of puzzle games that have been hugely successful (this can be seen as a way of validating the "fun" component of these designs), we can learn some general, practical lessons about making fun games that focus on learning and applying skills. While this study does not present a massive theoretical leap forward, it helps us to generate some practical evidence-based guidance for games designers.

METHOD

Materials

It was necessary to decide upon a set of games appropriate for this study. We were interested specifically in how learning is structured in puzzle games widely experienced as fun. Thus, it was important to choose popular games. We distributed a brief online survey, to which 52 participants replied, inquiring as to the puzzle games that people found most fun, most challenging, and which made them feel most competent or intelligent. Based on participant responses, four games were chosen: *Portal* [43], *Portal 2 Co-operative mode* [44], *Braid* [35], and *Lemmings* [15].

Procedure

In order to carry out an objective analysis of the structure of those four games, we followed an observational research methodology. Specifically, "Let's Play" videos (videos where a player records and narrates gameplay experience for the benefit of spectators through online video-sharing services) were observed. The researcher took notes on game play according to a carefully defined set of metrics (see below). The raw data generated through this process is available as auxiliary material, published simultaneously with the paper. Please see that material in order to understand the process through which observations were used to generate the analysis below. In summary, each video was first watched carefully, the researcher identifying each individual skill asked of players in that game (i.e., Appendix 1, Table 2). Next, the researcher identified which of those skills were used in each individual game section (i.e., Appendix 1, Table 4). The researcher observed each of these videos a number of times in order to ensure reliability of measurement and to ensure that the optimal solution was noted. These data were used to generate an analysis of the points at which new skills were introduced (i.e, Appendix 1, Table 5) and the minimum number of actions required to complete that game section. In this way, an objective picture of puzzle complexity is built based on the puzzle design itself, rather than a subjective measure of player performance (e.g. time taken), despite the subjective nature of the play experience.

Metrics

Defining the 'puzzle' as a unit of analysis

Puzzle games typically are engaged with in a linear fashion, where simpler challenges are faced first and more complex challenges are faced after experience and skill has been gained. Thus, in order to analyse the specific way in which learning is structured and scaffolded in a puzzle game, it is useful and valid to represent specific game characteristics on a line graph. This provides a sense of how pacing is constructed in the game; how quickly the game introduces new challenges, and how it allows space for practice. It is also coherent with the methods used by behaviour analysts, both experimental [41] and applied [11]. However, in order to present data on a line graph, there must be an agreed-upon unit of analysis for the x-axis.

It was deemed inappropriate to use game 'level' demarcations provided in the narrative of the games as units of analysis in our study as 'levels' often involve a series of puzzles, particularly in the later stages of the games (see figures 1 and 2 for evidence of this in the games we analysed). Since we were interested in analysing the composition and complexity of the puzzles themselves, it was felt necessary to divide these longer levels into their constituent parts. Otherwise, longer levels would inherently seem more complex, regardless of the complexity of individual tasks they presented to players. Two categories were used to separate game sections into individual puzzles; 1) puzzles must be clearly separated geographically within the game world, either by being in different 'rooms' or by being separated by a significant distance, and 2) the actions required within each of these areas must not affect the puzzles within the other areas. In order to be considered a separate unit of analysis, both conditions must be met.

Number of actions required for the completion of a puzzle

In order to analyse how learning is structured in games, it is essential to have an objective measure of the complexity of the tasks presented throughout the game. While we recognize that there are many ways that this could be defined, in this paper, and for pragmatic reasons [24], we are interested in a simple, observable definition. We define the complexity of individual puzzles as the minimum number of actions required by the player to complete that puzzle. The higher number of distinct actions necessary, the more complex the problem.

Presentation of a novel skill

Another metric important for characterising both the complexity of an individual puzzle, as well as the overall pacing of a game, is an indication of whether or not actions required of players are novel (i.e., whether or not they have been encountered previously in the game). The point at which novel skills are introduced can be easily visualised. We also recorded each specific skill needed in to solve each puzzle in every game. However, due to space restrictions we do not report the results of this measure in full in this paper. Please refer to the auxiliary material for these data.

Using these metrics we can build a picture of when new skills are introduced, how game complexity correlates with novel skills, and whether games provide space for players to practice chaining those skills with other skills before encountering the next novel skill.

RESULTS

We discuss the results obtained from analysing each of the four puzzle games in turn. Please note that raw data is published as Appendices.

Portal

Game play in Portal is split into two main sections. Firstly the player plays through a series of 20 'test chambers' labelled from 0 to 19. Test Chambers in the game are designed to have a definite start and end point, whereas the sections after the 19th Test Chamber do not. Test chambers are also used to teach all of the skills used in the game. Considering this, the analysis will focus on those Test chambers.

Number of actions required for the completion of a puzzle

Figure 1 presents the results of our analysis of the minimum number of actions required to solve each of the puzzles in the game. Some of the test chambers were split into component puzzles, in accordance with the criteria outlined above. These are indicated with decimal numbers on the x-axis. The data within this graph shows a number of peaks and troughs in the number of skills required throughout the game. There is also a general increase in the number of actions required per test chamber something which is shown in the gradual increase in multi-section test chambers as the game progresses. This shows a distinct pattern in which the puzzles within the game get gradually more difficult before suddenly becoming much easier at distinct points within the game.

Presentation of a novel skill

Figure 1 also illustrates the points at which novel skills are introduced in the game, represented here by dots on the line graph. For Portal, this ranges from basic skills such as "moving" and "jumping" through to more advanced and specific learning such as "Re-entering a portal can further increase the player's exit momentum". Notably, there seems to be a correlation between the introduction of a novel skill, and puzzles that require a small number of player actions. The results for the 6th point at test chamber 11 however do not follow the trend. Within this chamber the player must collect the orange Portal, but is required to complete a puzzle in order to do so. Once the orange Portal is collected the player is required to complete a further four actions before the chamber is completed.

The general correlation between the troughs in the graph and the point at which the player is presented with a novel skill, suggests that upon the presentation of a novel skill the difficulty of the level is reduced. This appears to be an intentional design strategy to allow the player to understand the basics of how that skill works, before applying it in more complex contexts. The analysis shows a number of interesting ways in which the game structures learning; 1) each of the main skills are introduced separately, 2) they are typically introduced in puzzles that require few other actions, 3) from the point at which a new skill is introduced, puzzles increase in complexity up until the point at which the next new skill is introduced. It is interesting to see whether the other games follow or diverge from this pattern.

Portal 2 Co-operative Mode

In Portal 2 Co-op mode, game play is split into a number of 'courses,' each of which has a specific focus (e.g., Mass and Velocity, Hard-Light Surfaces). The sections analysed are the introduction chamber at the very beginning of the game, and the first three courses the player is required to

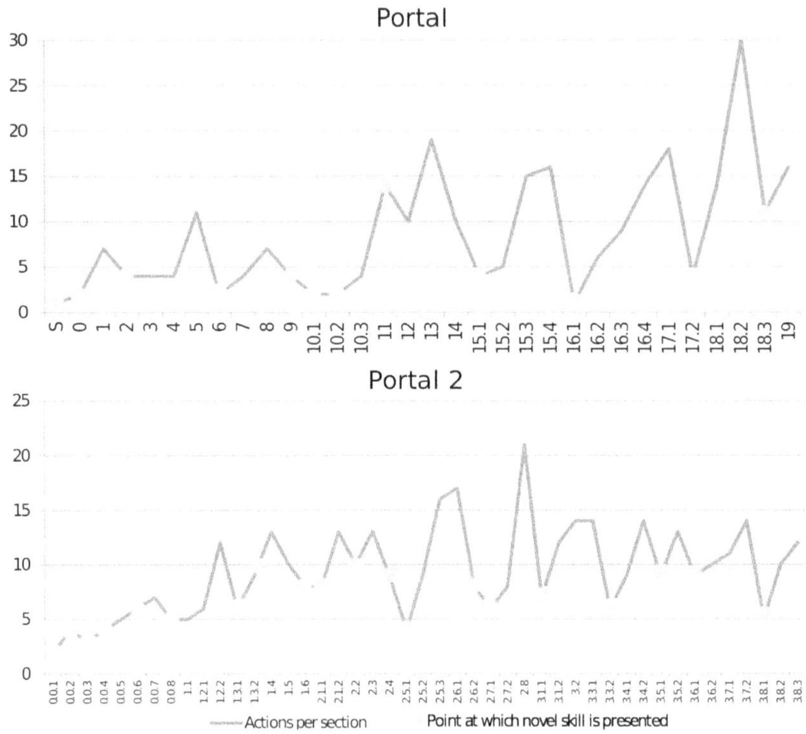

Figure 1. Minimum number of player actions required to solve successive puzzles in Portal (top panel) and Portal 2 (bottom panel).

complete. This will provide data on 23 test chambers, and 45 individual puzzles, which should be sufficient to determine how learning is structured in the game.

Number of actions required for the completion of a puzzle

Portal 2's Co-op mode includes checkpoints between puzzles, meaning the definition of puzzles as units of analysis was relatively straightforward. It should be noted that this is a two-player game, and puzzles are solved through co-operation between both players. Thus, the figure given for the *number of steps required for completion of a puzzle* is a combination of the actions made by both players. The exception to this rule are the introduction sections, where for simplicity a number of the puzzles require the two players to work separately whilst solving separate but identical puzzles. In these cases, since the puzzles are identical, we have only analysed one set of actions.

Figure 1 displays the number of actions required for the completion of the first 45 puzzles in Portal 2 Co-op mode. Results are similar to that of Portal's single player, with a number of peaks and troughs throughout the data. Across the game, puzzles show a trend of increasing numbers of actions required by the player as the game progresses.

Presentation of a novel skill

Figure 1 also illustrates the points at which novel skills are introduced in the game, represented here by dots on the line graph. Results are similar to those found with Portal 1. Specifically, most of the skills are presented at troughs in the graph, which represent puzzles that require a relatively small number of actions from players. Notably, however, during the introductory test chamber, a number of skills are taught in successive simple puzzles. This series of puzzles seems to be designed to familiarise players with the games basic controls, perhaps as a catch-up for players who have not played portal 1 or the single player mode of portal 2. Either way, it is notable that the pattern is markedly different in this section.

In summary, the three conclusions made about the structure of Portal are also true for Portal 2. This should not be a huge surprise, since the same studio produced both games. However, it is interesting to note the differences between games. Specifically, the pattern of introducing novel skills in very simple puzzles before gradually combining them with previously learned skills is even more pronounced in Portal 2 co-op mode. Indeed, the latter is explicitly divided into separate "courses," each of which focuses on a specific set of skills.

Braid

Braid is a platform puzzle game based around a variety of time mechanics, such as reversing time, pausing time and slowing time. Braid is designed in a similar way to Portal 2's co-op mode. The game has the player move through a series of 'worlds' with each one introducing the player to a variety of different mechanics the player has to use to solve the puzzles within that world. Game levels were divided into individual puzzles for analysis, based on the criteria outlined above.

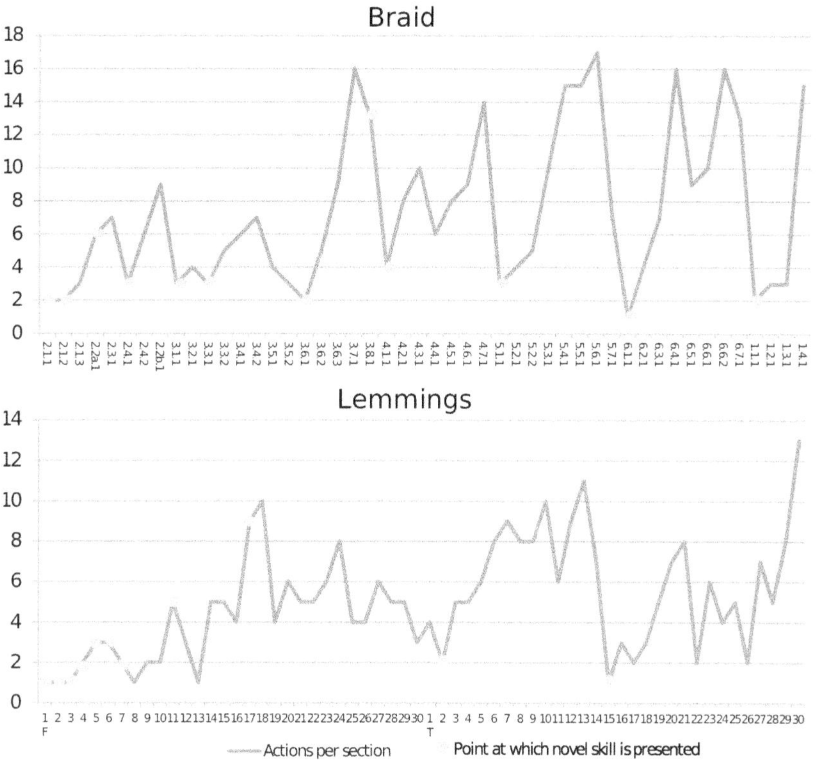

Figure 2. Minimum number of player actions required to solve successive puzzles in Braid (top panel) and Lemmings (bottom panel).

Since Braid is a platform game, many of the actions the player is required to perform involve movement around the world, such as jumping and climbing, and often a series of jumps or a series of climbs are necessary. We found that noting down each instance of movement created massive amounts of data. Thus, we simplified the analysis. Movement actions are included in our analysis as one action, as long as they are not interrupted by the performing of another type of action. So, if the player must climb, jump three times and then climb again, this is noted as three actions, not five.

Number of actions required for the completion of a puzzle

Figure 2 presents the number of actions required to complete the puzzles presented throughout Braid. Please note that in game narrative player starts at level 2 and continues through to level six before finishing on level 1. This is the reason why the numbering of the x-axis is counter-intuitive. Each of the six game worlds demonstrates a pattern where earlier puzzles in that world require less player actions, and later puzzles require more actions. There is also a pattern where puzzles in the later game worlds generally require more actions than those presented earlier in the game.

Presentation of a novel skill

Figure 2 also illustrates the points at which novel skills are introduced in the game, represented here by dots on the line graph. Similarly with the previous games, novel skills are presented during simple puzzles that do not require many player actions. The number of actions required of the player to solve puzzles gradually increases until the next new skill is introduced.

Notably, however, there are a couple of anomalous points that don't quite fit with the rest of the data, these are at section 2.2a.1 and section 3.8.1. Section 2.2a.1 is the first point of the game in which the player is required to use a key to open a door. This happens at the very start of the level, after which the player is required to do a number of actions they have previously encountered. As there is not a significant divide between these areas, our definition of a puzzle does not allow us to divide the areas into separate puzzles. Section 3.8.1 is a similar situation, except the new skill is introduced at the end of a complex puzzle. Again, while it is quite separated from the rest of the puzzle, it cannot be defined as a separate puzzle according to our definition. However, these are only two exceptions and the pattern is quite clear throughout the rest of the game.

The analysis of Braid has shown many similarities between this game and the games within the Portal series, more specifically Portal 2's Co-op. This game has the player play through a series of different worlds, each based around a different mechanic, which the player is required to learn. Each of these worlds involves a series of puzzles which become progressively more complex as the player is exposed to more of the games mechanics.

Lemmings

This game comprises of a series of levels in which the player has to guide a group of 'Lemmings' through a series of obstacles, saving as many as possible in the process. The game has four difficulty settings, each containing 30 levels that players have to complete in sequential order. For the analysis, the first two difficulty categories will be used, consisting of a total of 60 levels. The two difficulty categories within the game are represented by the F and T on the graph, representing the fun and tricky categories respectively.

Number of actions required for the completion of a puzzle

Figure 2 presents the number of actions required to complete the puzzles presented throughout Lemmings. There is a general trend where the puzzles earlier in the game require fewer actions, while those later in the game require more actions. However, the pattern is not as obvious as in the other games. Also, like the previous games, there are quite a number of peaks and troughs as pacing of challenges is varied.

Presentation of a novel skill

Figure 2 also illustrates the points at which novel skills are introduced in the game, represented here by dots on the line graph. Interestingly, the pattern in Lemmings is very different to the previous three games. Specifically, the majority of skills that players use throughout the game are actually presented in the first seven levels of the first difficulty category, and instead of being practiced immediately, are only explored later in the game. Another difference is that some of the puzzles in which a novel skill is presented (F11 and F17) also require a very large number of actions. F11 involves the introduction of rocks that can only be dug through from one direction, while F17 introduces indestructible stone. These are obstacles that specifically require a series of player actions to overcome. Notably, when novel skills are introduced later in the game, the pattern is similar to that observed with the other three games.

The analysis of Lemmings shows that the learning curve of this game is very different to Braid and both Portal games and Braid. Lemmings introduces the player to all of the basic skills within the first 7 levels of the game. After this, the player plays through another 23 levels in which those skills are practiced in a variety of situations, before moving onto the next difficulty level. Each of these levels requires the player to use a different set of skills to overcome a different problem, but a number of the levels are ordered to encourage the player to re-use the same skills they used in the previous level, either in a different situation or with a single added skill, before moving onto a different skill.

Another interesting aspect of the game design within Lemmings is found in how some levels provide the player with an almost unlimited supply of the 8 skills within the game, and others provide the player with a small number of a specific group of skills. Within the first few levels of the game the player only has access to one or two of these skills so that the player is forced to solve the puzzle with that specific skill. This design helps the player to learn what each skill does by simplifying the skills available to them.

Of course, while it was still popular with our survey respondents, it must be noted that Lemmings is a significantly older game (i.e., 1991) than the other three games (Portal, 2007; Portal 2, 2011; Braid, 2008). Certainly, the theory and practice of designing puzzle games has advanced in the time since Lemmings was released, and as such, if it were designed today, it might follow more closely the structure seen in the other games.

DISCUSSION

The findings of this paper suggest that popular (i.e. considered fun and well-designed) puzzle games, whose core game play centres around the learning and application of skills, tend to follow a very structured way of teaching players how to use the skills available in the game. While there are some exceptions, it seems that there are some findings that are relatively consistent across all four games; 1) each of the main skills are introduced separately in the game, 2) they are introduced through a simple puzzle that requires little more than the basic performance of the new skill, 3) after the introduction of a new skill, a number of puzzles are presented in which the player is given the opportunity to practice that skill and to integrate it with previously learned skills, and 4) from the point at which a new skill is introduced, puzzles increase in complexity up until the point at which the next new skill is introduced. These findings may be of immediate use to all game designers, and are particularly useful for those interested in applying game design to education.

This paper supports design thinking emergent from the best practices of the game design community. For example, Canossa [7], Hullett [25], Schell [39], and especially Cook [10] offer guidelines for designing for complexity in games. Those authors all point to the importance of breaking complex skills into simpler components and introducing them gradually, as well as increasing complexity over the course of game play. Our findings support these suggestions on both a micro and macro level. Challenge increases both on a small scale, from the point at which a new skill is introduced, as well as on a larger scale, over the entire course of game play.

The analysis presented here, combined with previous work in the game design literature, suggests an optimal model for structuring the pace with which tasks are introduced in commercially successful games. It seems that designers should follow a pattern where the player is presented with a new skill, and then required to practice this skill along with all previously learnt skills, slowly building up the number of skills that are chained together until players are expected to use all of those in a single puzzle. While this concept is by no means a novel contribution of our paper, we have found no similar previous attempts in the literature to establish a rigorous theoretical framework for analyzing learning curves in games. In this way, this article lends empirical evidence to what is essentially a practice emergent from "popular wisdom" among game designers.

Notably, findings are also consistent with a basic behavioural psychology account of problem solving and the behavioural approach to education. Since people seem predisposed to solve problems through the type of response chaining observed in these games, future games that structure tasks chronologically so as to allow for this type of problem solving should prove successful. Indeed, applied behaviour analysis (ABA), which adopts exactly this type of approach to structuring learning, has proved incredibly successful in many different contexts in recent years [11].

Of course, the current study does not attempt to present a comprehensive analysis of learning in all puzzle games. The findings reported here are based on one study carried out with four games. These games were subjected to a rigorous, detailed analysis consisting of hundreds of hours of observation. Thus, the findings of this study are generalisable because of their depth and their ecological validity, rather than their breadth. Future work should aim to replicate these findings through application of our methodology with other popular games, in order to draw conclusions about the generalisability of the findings.

It must also be noted that, while the paper provides a clear analysis of good practice in game design, it does not suggest that the design patterns revealed here are necessarily the best way of structuring learning curves in games. Rather, these data reveal the best practice currently observed in game design. The question of whether this is indeed the optimal design strategy is an empirical question. We believe that the methods used here can inspire future work on this topic.

CONCLUSION

Four commercially successful puzzle games were analysed, using an observational methodology derived from experimental behavioural psychology research. Findings suggest that successful, fun puzzle games very carefully control the pace with which challenges are introduced chronologically (i.e., the learning curve) throughout a players interaction with the game. The findings of this study provide practical guidance for games designers, especially designers of game-based educational activities (i.e., context where instructional design is of equal importance as entertainment). They support contemporary thinking on the design of learning structures in games, and suggest future directions for empirical research.

REFERENCES

1. 2D Boy. *World of Goo.* PC. 2D Boy, 2008.
2. Alexander, Justin T., John Sear, and Andreas Oikonomou. An Investigation of the Effects of Game Difficulty on Player Enjoyment. *Entertainment Computing, 4* (2013), 53–62.
3. Baranowski, T., Buday, R., Thompson, D. I., & Baranowski, J. Playing for real: video games and stories for health-related behavior change. *Am. J. Preventive Medicine, 34* (2008), 74-82.
4. Barzilai, S., & Blau, I. Scaffolding game-based learning: Impact on learning achievements, perceived learning, and game experiences. *Computers & Education, 70* (2014), 65-79.
5. Blakely, G., Skirton, H., Cooper, S., Allum, P., & Nelmes, P. Educational gaming in the health sciences: systematic review. *J. Advanced Nursing, 65* (2009), 259-269.
6. Brown, S. J., Lieberman, D. A., Gemeny, B. A., Fan, Y. C., & Pasta, D. J. Educational video game for juvenile diabetes: results of a controlled trial. *Informatics for Health and Social Care, 22* (1997), 77-89.
7. Canossa, A. *Play-Persona: Modeling Player Behavior in Computer Games.* Copenhagen, Danish Design School Press, 2009.
8. Catania, C.A. *Learning, 4th ed.* Cornwall-on-Hudson. NY: Sloan Publishing, 1998.
9. Christy, K. R., & Fox, J. Leaderboards in a Virtual Classroom: A Test of Stereotype Threat and Social Comparison Explanations for Women's Math Performance. *Computers & Education 78* (2014), 66-77.
10. Cook, Daniel. 2007. "The Chemistry Of Game Design." *Gamasutra.* http://www.gamasutra.com/view/feature/129948/the_chemistry_of_game_design.php?print=1.
11. Cooper, J. O., Heron, T. E., & Heward, W. L. *Applied behavior analysis, 2nd ed.* NJ: Prentice Hall, 2006.
12. Csikszentmihalyi, M. *Flow: The psychology of optimal experience.* New York: Harper Perennial, 1991.
13. Deterding, S., Dixon, D., Khaled, R., & Nacke, L. From game design elements to gamefulness: defining gamification. In Proc. Mindtrek 2011, ACM Press (2011), 9-15.
14. de-Marcos, L., Domínguez, A., Saenz-de-Navarrete, J., & Pagés, C. An empirical study comparing gamification and social networking on e-learning. *Computers & Education, 75* (2014), 82-91.
15. DMA Design. *Lemmings.* Amiga. Psygnosis, 1991.
16. Domínguez, A., Saenz-de-Navarrete, J., De-Marcos, L., Fernández-Sanz, L., Pagés, C., & Martínez-Herráiz, J. J. Gamifying learning experiences: Practical

implications and outcomes. *Computers & Education,* 63, (2013), 380-392.
17. Dondlinger, M.J. Educational Video Game Design: A Review of the Literature. *Journal of Applied Educational Technology, 4* (2007), 21-31.
18. Gee, J.P. *What Video Games Have to Teach Us About Learning and Literacy*. NY: Palgrave Macmillan, 2003.
19. Gingold, C. What warioware can teach us about game design. *The International Journal of Computer Game Research, 5* (2005), online article.
20. Girard, C., Ecalle, J., & Magnan, A. Serious games as new educational tools: how effective are they? A meta-analysis of recent studies. *Journal of Computer Assisted Learning, 29* (2013), 207-219.
21. Hamari, J. Transforming homo economicus into homo ludens: A field experiment on gamification in a utilitarian peer-to-peer trading service. Electronic commerce Research and Applications, 12 (2013), 236-245.
22. Hamari, J., Koivisto, J., & Sarsa, H. Does Gamification Work? A Literature Review of Empirical Studies on Gamification. In System Sciences, IEEE Press, (2014) 3025-3034).
23. Harpstead, E., MacLellan, C. J., Aleven, V., & Myers, B. A. Using Extracted Features to Inform Alignment-Driven Design Ideas in an Educational Game. In *Proc. CHI 2014*, ACM Press (2014), 3329-3338.
24. Hayes, Stephen C. Why environmentally based analyses are necessary in behavior analysis. *J. Exp. Analysis of Behavior, 60* (1993), 461–463.
25. Hullet,K. *The Science of Level Design.* University of California Press, 2010.
26. Koivisto, J., & Hamari, J. Demographic differences in perceived benefits from gamification. *Computers in Human Behavior, 35* (2014), 179-188.
27. Koster, R. *A theory of fun for game design.* Scottsdale, AZ: Paraglyph Press, 2005.
28. Lee, J., Luchini, K., Michael, B., Norris, C. and Soloway, E. More than just fun and games: Assessing the value of educational video games in the classroom. In *Proc. CHI 2004*, ACM Press (2004), 1375-1378.
29. Linehan, C., Kirman, B., Lawson, S., & Chan, G. Practical, appropriate, empirically-validated guidelines for designing educational games. In *Proc. CHI 2011,* ACM Press (2011), 1979-1988.
30. Lomas, D., Patel, K., Forlizzi, J. L., & Koedinger, K. R. Optimizing challenge in an educational game using large-scale design experiments. In *Proc. CHI 2013*, ACM Press (2013), 89-98.
31. Malouf, D.B. The effect of instructional computer games on continuing student motivation. *Journal of Special Education, 21* (1987), 27-38.
32. Moreno-Ger, P., Burgos, D., Martínez-Ortiz, I., Sierra, J.L., and Fernández-Manjón, B. Educational game design for online education. *Computers in Human Behavior, 24* (2008) 2530–2540.
33. Munoz Blanco, M.I. *A naturalistic analysis of creativity in terms of the creator and the critic.* PhD dissertation, University of Reno, Nevada, 2014.
34. Nintendo R&D1. *Wario Ware.* Game Boy Advance. Nintendo, 2003.
35. Number None Inc. *Braid.* PC. Number None Inc, 2009.
36. O'Neil, H.F., Wainess, R. and Baker, E.L. Classification of learning outcomes: evidence from the computer games literature. *The Curriculum Journal, 16* (2005), 455 - 474.
37. Salen, K. and Zimmerman, E. *Rules of Play: Game Design Fundamentals.* MIT Press, Cambridge, 2004.
38. Sampayo-Vargas, S., Cope, C.J., He, Z., and Byrne, G.J. The Effectiveness of Adaptive Difficulty Adjustments of Students' Motivation and Learning in an Educational Computer Game. Computers & Education 69 (2013): 452–462.
39. Schell, J. *The Art of Game Design: A book of Lenses.* CRC Press, 2008.
40. Skinner, B. F. *Science and human behavior.* Simon and Schuster, 1953.
41. Skinner, B.F. *Cumulative Record.* New York: Appleton Century-Crofts, 1959.
42. Skinner, B. F. *About behaviorism.* Random House, 1974.
43. Valve. *Portal.* PC. Valve Corporation, 2007.
44. Valve. *Portal 2.* PC. Valve Corporation, 2011.
45. Wouters, P., & Van Oostendorp, H. A meta-analytic review of the role of instructional support in game-based learning. *Computers & Education, 60* (2013), 412-425.

Natural Mapping and Intuitive Interaction in Videogames

Mitchell McEwan
School of EECS
QUT, Australia
m1.mcewan@qut.edu.au

Alethea Blackler
School of Design,
QUT, Australia
a.blacker@qut.edu.au

Daniel Johnson
School of EECS
QUT, Australia
dm.johnson@qut.edu.au

Peta Wyeth
School of EECS
QUT, Australia
peta.wyeth@qut.edu.au

ABSTRACT

Videogame control interfaces continue to evolve beyond their traditional roots, with devices encouraging more natural forms of interaction growing in number and pervasiveness. Yet little is known about their true potential for intuitive use. This paper proposes methods to leverage existing intuitive interaction theory for games research, specifically by examining different types of naturally mapped control interfaces for videogames using new measures for previous player experience. Three commercial control devices for a racing game were categorised using an existing typology, according to how the interface maps physical control inputs with the virtual gameplay actions. The devices were then used in a within-groups (n=64) experimental design aimed at measuring differences in intuitive use outcomes. Results from mixed design ANOVA are discussed, along with implications for the field.

Author Keywords

Intuitive Interaction; Game Control; Natural Mapping; Control Devices; Games User Research.

ACM Classification Keywords

H.5.2. Information interfaces and presentation: User Interfaces – *evaluation/methodology, input devices and strategies, interaction styles.* K.8.0. Personal Computing: General – *games.*

INTRODUCTION

The growing study of intuitive interaction with user interfaces offers definitions for intuition, means to measure occurrence of intuitive interaction, and guidelines for designers to maximise their interface's potential for intuitive use. The focus of research in this field has largely been on interfaces with a utilitarian purpose, and application of these techniques to evaluate the intuitive potential of interfaces for systems with other purposes, such as videogames, is not available in the current literature. This is despite the fact that motion control and tangible interfaces for games are becoming more pervasive, are often claimed to be 'intuitive' [8, 11, 18, 19, 20], and the accessibility of these interfaces has been identified as one of the key drivers for growth in the industry [21, 23]. These control devices employ natural mapping to leverage embodied knowledge by capturing control actions that mimic the simulated real-life activity. This offers players the chance to bypass the expertise requirements usually demanded to execute challenging virtual control actions with traditional interfaces. While it appears these interfaces use natural mapping to broaden their accessibility and enable a higher potential for intuitive use, these assumptions have yet to be empirically tested. This paper seeks to verify these claims by applying and adapting existing intuitive interaction theory and tools to evaluate naturally mapped control interfaces (NMCIs) for videogames. It presents newly developed instruments to measure intuitive potential and fulfilment, which were applied in an experiment that examined the intuitive use outcomes for players using three different types of NMCIs with a racing videogame.

CHI PLAY '14, October 19 - 22 2014, Toronto, ON, Canada
Copyright 2014 ACM 978-1-4503-3014-5/14/10...$15.00.
http://dx.doi.org/10.1145/2658537.2658541

Naturally Mapped Control Interfaces for Videogames

Naturally mapped control interfaces (NMCIs) for videogames involve interactions with less abstraction between the task to be virtually achieved and the action required to achieve it. As such it is hypothesised that these control interfaces are more accessible, provide the potential for more nuanced virtual control, and remove barriers to enjoyment of the game [2, 9, 21]. Additionally, if the interface mapping (and the supportive technology) is strong enough players should be able to achieve much more freedom in how they execute control actions, with potentially a much finer degree of control than with a traditional controller. In theory, the barriers to performing well in a game move from mastery of a control device to the mastery of one's own actions as relevant to the game mechanics. For example, making the main game character swing a sword a particular way should be easier to remember, provide greater proprioceptive feedback, and be more satisfying to perform if the player physically swings a control wand (like the Playstation Move) the way the player wants the character to do it rather than having to recall and execute specific stick and button combinations.

Early research on NMCIs for videogames focused on the performance impacts and player preferences for natural controllers and peripherals [8, 11, 14]. Recently the impact of different NMCIs on the player experience has also started to be explored more widely [1, 3, 9, 12, 13, 20, 21].

Generally, researchers have found that more naturally mapped interfaces provide a greater response to some play experience measures, particularly measures related to game engagement such as presence and flow [1, 3, 9, 13, 20, 21]. Broad measures for enjoyment have also been positively linked with the use of NMCIs as compared to traditional interfaces [2, 3, 14, 20], yet some research challenges this claim [12]. The youth of this field of research, however, inevitably leads to discrepancies in experimental approach and control. For instance, due to the limited field of available commercial products to test some studies test games and controllers across different platforms, limiting their ability to directly compare conditions [12]. Attempts to address this have been made by developing custom game environments for testing [3, 9], yet this requires greater investment and development skills and raises additional questions around ecological validity. There is also inconsistency of approach in terms of how to measure a player's previous experience and whether to consider exposure to the equivalent real-life activities that are being naturally mapped. Some researchers use measures such as hours of play with the tested game or videogames generally [7, 9, 11, 14, 21], while some ask participants to select from broad categories [3, 8, 9, 12]. Examples of the equivalent real-life activity being measured are limited and also vary in approach [8, 12, 20]. Work in this field initially only broadly categorised NMCI types, grouping all NMCIs together using terms such as 'natural' or 'realistic' when comparing them to their 'non-natural' counterparts [7, 11, 14, 20]. The level of body motion required to interact with the interface has been used as a defining factor in some research [2, 15, 16], and has been applied in defining NMCIs along with the social context of use [1, 2, 15, 16].

Skalski et al. [21] also examined perceived enjoyment and preference for NMCIs, yet helped explicate differences between different types of NMCIs and traditional controls by developing an initial typology of NMCIs for videogames. The typology consists of four categories of natural mapping: directional, kinesic, incomplete tangible, and realistic tangible. Directional natural mapping occurs when there is a 'correspondence' with direction between physical control and virtual result, such as when a control stick makes a character turn left when pushed left. Kinesic natural mapping occurs when natural body movements are captured and translated into equivalent actions in the game space without a tangible component (for example, making a kicking motion in the real world in order to kick a ball in the virtual world). Incomplete tangible natural mapping is when the player is provided with a physical object to manipulate that 'partially simulates' the form and function of the equivalent virtual object, such as with using the Wii Remote as a tennis racket. Realistic tangible natural mapping takes place when the tangible object looks, feels and responds like the virtual object in the real world, such as a spring loaded leather-bound racing wheel controller. Skalski et al. [21] admit this typology is only starting to explicate the variables around control mapping in games, and suggest its use as a starting point for further research. They highlight that types may overlap in a single control device, which means an NMCI type is defined by a specific instance of mapping of control actions between a control device and a game.

The hypotheses of Skalski et al.'s [21] research are that the realistic and tangible NMCIs will sit at the top of the scale of perceived controller naturalness, provide a greater sense of spatial presence, and in turn predict videogame enjoyment. To confirm their hypotheses, controllers falling into different categories in the typology were tested for both a racing and a golf game. While the relationship with enjoyment was not confirmed, NMCI types were found to powerfully modify responses to videogames as otherwise predicted. Additional validation of the NMCI typology has been published [9, 13], with Cairns et al. [9] examining the effects of NMCI type on immersion in mobile games. Here Skalski et al's hypotheses are again broadly confirmed, with more naturally mapped control types generally leading to greater immersion. Yet more research is needed to clarify the definition and broader play experience impacts of NMCIs [9, 21], both across genres/platforms and for different player groups.

Intuitive Interaction

The source of knowledge for an intuitive action can be difficult to identify, yet two groups of researchers building on decades of research and theory in cognitive science have helped tie intuition to previous experience [4, 6, 10, 17]. According to these researchers, intuition is the end result of a cognitive process that matches current stimuli with a store of amalgamated experiential knowledge, built up through time in similar situations. Strictly speaking, a device or interface is not 'intuitive' in and of itself, however, the information processing applied to it can be [6]. Intuitive interactions should also be, at least subjectively, the correct action in the context of use and can be much faster due to the increased speed of subconscious rather than analytical processing. It is for these reasons that response time and accuracy are common measures for intuitive interaction [6].

A product can have a high potential for intuitive use if it is designed to take advantage of experiential knowledge that is broadly possessed by its target audience. The two groups of intuitive interaction researchers developed distinct theory about the types of experiential knowledge accessed during intuitive interaction, and how designers could maximise an interface's potential for intuitive use, yet there is significant overlap between these two models. The German-based Intuitive Use of User Interfaces (IUUI) Research Group presented a 'continuum of knowledge in intuitive interaction' (shown as the upper square in Figure 1) with types of experiential knowledge accessed during intuitive interaction based upon their frequency of cognitive encoding and retrieval [10]. Blackler's intuitive interaction continuum suggested the means by which intuitive use can be supported in product design [6], and is shown in Figure 1 as it relates to IUUI's continuum. In IUUI's continuum the most basic and broadly possessed knowledge identified is innate knowledge, which has genetic origins and manifests in responses such as reflexes. In Blackler's continuum the most accessible design strategy is to use *physical affordances*, which take advantage of embodied knowledge of the world established early in life. This fits within IUUI's *sensorimotor* level, which also includes knowledge applied during basic analytical processes (such as determining direction or identifying faces). Blackler classes the next level of knowledge as *population stereotype*, which relates to IUUI's *culture* and *sensorimotor* levels and includes knowledge broadly possessed yet limited by societal bounds (such as different meanings for hand gestures between cultures). The level with the lowest frequency of encoding and retrieval in IUUI's continuum is *expertise*, which is knowledge held only by those adept at a particular speciality (such as the knowledge a programmer uses to code a game). To enable intuitive interaction for this group Blacker suggests using *familiar features from the same domain*, yet if unavailable the designer may have to leverage *familiar features from another domain*. If the technology or context of use is completely new then designers can leverage metaphor to communicate the intended interaction protocol. In this way both research groups highlighted how targeting different types of knowledge in the design of an interface might modify the potential for intuitive use.

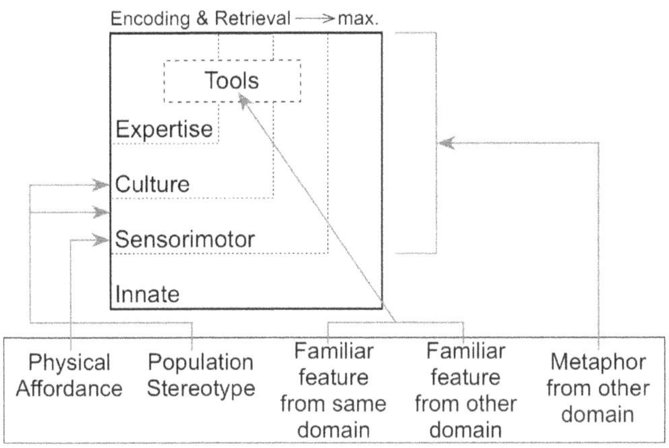

Figure 1: The Intuitive Interaction Continua, adapted from [4]

Blackler also devised the Technology Familiarity (TF) questionnaire as a tool to quantify the relevant experience of users that may contribute to intuitive use with a particular interface. This survey compiled a range of products and interfaces with similar features to the device being studied and asked participants to rate how often they have used them and how many of the features they used. Responses were then given a score (with greater frequency and breadth of use receiving higher scores) and tallied to determine the user's TF score for that device. In four experiments focusing on interfaces from microwaves, universal remote controls and a digital camera, where the percentage of intuitive uses was established through codified observational measures, Blackler found significant correlations between TF scores and percentage of intuitive uses as well as other measures such as correct uses and time to complete set tasks. Overall, Blackler was able to conclude that related amalgamated experiential knowledge, as measured by Technology Familiarity, is an accurate predictor for intuitive use [5]. In other words, an interface enables intuitive use if its design includes features that the intended users have had previous experience with.

In intuitive interaction research the focus has largely been on interfaces for functional interactive systems, where usability and efficiency have been given priority during evaluations. While games research into the impact of NMCIs is diverse and growing, exploration of the role of NMCIs in facilitating intuitive interaction is limited. Specifically, intuitive interaction theory, and its associated tools and measures, have not yet been applied in the games research space. This is despite 'intuitive' control devices being recognised as fundamental to play motivation and experience [19]. Since the main goal of videogames is to engage users in an emotionally motivating way (produce enjoyment through the application of skill to overcome challenge), the impact of control devices designed for intuitive interaction may extend beyond usability and efficiency gains into uncharted territory.

METHOD

The primary aims of the experiment presented here were to develop targeted measures of technology familiarity for videogames, and evaluate the intuitive interaction potential of different types of naturally mapped control interfaces (NMCIs) for videogames for different demographic groups. Sixty-four participants (43 male) voluntarily took part in the within-groups study. The study was conducted with participants individually and took around one hour to complete. Participant age ranged from 17 to 76, with an average age of 29.7 years (SD = 10.5). Study recruitment methods included online social networking, personal and professional networking (in person and via email), and an announcement in a first year undergraduate computer games studies unit. The chance to win a $100 gift card was offered as a recruitment incentive to all participants.

Manipulation

Participants were asked to indicate their age bracket and on this basis were randomly assigned to a counterbalanced order of the study conditions – three control devices (shown in Figure 2) used for play sessions with *Forza Motorsport 4* (Turn 10 Studios, 2011), a racing game on Microsoft's Xbox 360 gaming console. Each device had full native support within the main mode of the game and represented a distinct type from Skalski et al.'s typology of NMCIs [21], as shown in Figure 2. The categorisation of the naturally mapped control device was thus determined by the NMCI type represented by the mapping between the physical and virtual representations of the main control actions for this specific game context. The Controller is the primary control device for the Xbox 360 games console (released 2006), and is recognised as a traditional control input. In this study players used the left analogue stick for steering, the right analogue trigger for accelerating, and the left analogue trigger for braking/reversing. The Controller was used as an example of a device with directional natural mapping, as only the direction of the player's input is mapped to the in game action (e.g. pushing left on the control stick causes the car to turn left).

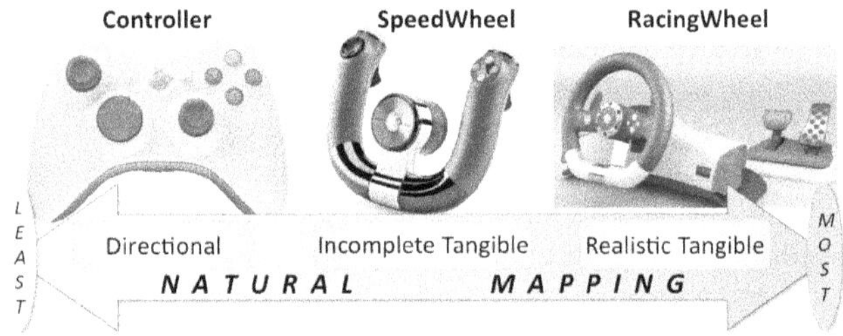

Figure 2: Naturally Mapped Control Types Tested

The SpeedWheel (*Wireless Speed Wheel for Xbox 360*, released by Microsoft in 2011) uses internal accelerometers to detect tilt manipulation. In this study players used tilt-based motion controls for steering, the right analogue trigger for accelerating, and the left analogue trigger for braking/reversing. The SpeedWheel is an example of incomplete tangible natural mapping as players manipulate the device like the real-life equivalent interface (i.e. turning the wheel to the right turns the car right), yet its U-shape only partially simulates the look and feel of a steering wheel and pedal motions are still assigned to analogue triggers. The RacingWheel (*Xbox 360 Wireless Racing Wheel*, released by Microsoft in 2006) features a leather-bound racing wheel with wired pedals. In this study players rotated the wheel for steering, and pressed down on the right analogue pedal for accelerating and the left analogue pedal for braking/reversing. The RacingWheel is an example of realistic tangible natural mapping because it is manipulated as if driving a real car and also simulates the look and feel of the real-life interface. The RacingWheel was mounted to a table that, along with the wired pedals, was moved in front of the seated participant and adjusted if necessary. The setting for the vibration and force feedback motors remained in the default state for all devices.

Procedure

Upon arrival at the laboratory participants were given a brief scripted verbal overview of how the study session was to be conducted. Following this, the demographics and Game Technology Familiarity (GTF) questionnaires were administered by the researcher as a guided online survey. The guided survey approach was utilised, as with previous applications of Technology Familiarity measurement [6], to ensure that all participants had the highest chance of fully understanding the questions being asked, many of which referred to very specific devices and technological features. This section of the study concluded with participants filling in additional demographic details, and in total took between 5-15 minutes. Participants were then asked to play the racing game using their first assigned control device. To play the game participants were asked to sit approximately 2.5 metres in front of a 55-inch TV connected to the game console and screen recording equipment. The track and car selected within the game was the same for all study conditions - *Fuji New Down Hill* and the *Seat Leon Supercup* respectively. The track was chosen as it was linear and so offered a percentage complete score, as well as decreased learning effect between conditions (in comparison to a race in which the same lap was repeated multiple times) and required a good mix of control actions (accelerating, braking, and steering in both directions). The car was chosen as it offered a good balance between a racecar and a regular automobile (high acceleration and top speed yet also a reasonable level of handling).

Upon commencement of each experimental condition the researcher gave a limited overview of what participants could expect to encounter in the play session, including a description of the basic controls along with the objectives - to relax, have fun, and try to progress as far down the mountain as possible before the race was stopped. The participants were not informed exactly how long they would be racing for, and were not given any practice using the control devices. This was necessary to meet our experimental aim of measuring intuitive interaction, allowing us to assess how the participants were transferring their previous experience into playing the game rather than how quickly they could be trained to use the devices [6]. Once the participant confirmed their understanding the game screen was activated and the countdown to the start of the race began. After four minutes of race time the participant's progress through the course, represented in the game as a percentage complete score, was recorded and the screen was switched off. Participants were then asked to fill out an online play experience survey alone based on their time playing the game with the control device. Next, participants were asked to complete an interview regarding their experience using the control device. The interview took one to two minutes and captured qualitative data about participants' likes and dislikes of using the device and whether the device worked as expected. Following the interview, participants were asked to play the race again with the next assigned control device and the above process was repeated for the second and third conditions. After the third interview regarding the device just used, an additional interview was undertaken that captured general feedback and device preferences before the study session was concluded.

MEASURES

Demographics and Subjective Response

The demographic questionnaire captured Gender and Age as well as items to gauge general gaming experience, such as average hours per week spent gaming in the last year, most hours ever spent gaming in a single week, genre exposure and current play preferences. An 18 item version of the Player Experience of Need Satisfaction (PENS) instrument [19], with the Relatedness component removed, was completed after each condition. Initial descriptive analysis of some play experience measures has already been published [13], however statistical analysis of these measures are in preparation for publication. Analysis of the Intuitive Controls measure from PENS is included in this publication as a subjective measurement of the intuitive interaction potential of each control device as compared to objective measures such as Progress and Errors. The other play experience variables are withheld for later publication since they are less conceptually relevant to an examination of intuitive interaction in videogames. Intuitive Controls consists of three items and is high when the controls make sense and do not interfere with game involvement. An example item from Intuitive Controls is "When I wanted to do something in the game it was easy to remember the corresponding control". The PENS implementation asked participants to think about their time playing the game with each control device and rate their agreement on a seven-point Likert scale between '1-do not agree' and '7-strongly agree'. Item order for the PENS survey were independently randomised upon presentation to participants, and component scores calculated as the mean of its items.

Game Technology Familiarity (GTF)

The game technology familiarity (GTF) questionnaire is a new measure intended for application in the game control interface space that is adapted from the technology familiarity (TF) instrument developed by Blackler [6]. Four game technology familiarity (GTF) scores were calculated for each participant – one relating to their familiarity with each naturally-mapped control device type tested ('Directional GTF' relating to Controller familiarity, 'Incomplete Tangible GTF' relating to SpeedWheel familiarity, and 'Realistic Tangible GTF' relating to RacingWheel familiarity), and 'RacePlay GTF' relating to previous play with racing games. GTF scores are a weighted average of relevant item scores derived from participants' pre-play indication of their degree of familiarity with the actual game and devices used in the experiment, and similar games, devices or device features. A 'RaceLife familiarity' score was also calculated that consisted of items relating to racing and driving a motorised wheel-controlled vehicle in real-life. For each GTF/ familiarity item, three questions were asked: the initial and most recent time the participant used/did the item (to determine the approximate length of item exposure), and the peak frequency of item use/exposure. Scoring of question responses within each item were determined in a linear manner with escalating and proportional values assigned to the broad time categories that participants selected from. This approach to the design of question responses and scoring was adapted from the technology familiarity (TF) questionnaire, where time categories were broad (e.g. "at least once a week") yet the scores for each category were not proportional to the temporal distance between them [6]. Each item score was calculated using the following formula, where T_I = 'initial time *used*', T_R = 'most recent time *used*', and F = 'peak frequency of *use*':

$$\text{GTF item score} = ((T_I + 1) - T_R) * (2 / T_R) * F$$

Full GTF metrics, including item contents and weights, along with justification for the final formula, are detailed in the supplementary materials. Question metrics were set consistently across all items so that calculation with the GTF formula ensured that no familiarity always equalled an item score of zero. The next possible smallest item score was 0.4 (if the participant only used the item more than 10 years ago and less often than every few months). The highest possible item score was 25 (if the item was initially used more than 10 years ago, most recently used in the last few days, and was used daily at the time the participant was using it the most). For the mixed ANOVA analysis presented in results the three GTF scores related to the control device conditions were converted into a percentage of their maximum potential score for each device. This was undertaken to enable a demographic analysis and repeated measures comparison between participant scores for each device, since the original GTF scores had different potential maximums that were logically limited by the temporal commercial availability of some of their items.

Objective Measures for Intuitive Interaction

Two measures were used to objectively assess the intuitiveness of each control interface, acting in place of traditional intuitive use measures such as time to complete set tasks, codified intuitive uses and accuracy [6]. The first measure, titled Progress, was the percentage of the race that was complete as shown on the game's visual interface at four minutes through play in each condition. As the race was on a linear track, this represents the players' progress towards their main goal – to race as far down the hill as possible before play was interrupted. The second measure aimed to assess intuitive interaction during play by counting the number of significant errors committed by the participant when using each control device to play the game. Errors were codified for each device post-play using observational analysis of videogame screen footage captured during play. This required errors to be visually apparent, representing substantial mistakes in judgement or performance that negatively impacted achievement of the in-game goal. Specifically, the errors count increased for participants when one of the following conditions was satisfied: the car spun around, flipped over or onto its side, stopped for no apparent reason, was put into reverse, or the player's in-game point of view was changed). If part of the same event (i.e. if one error was causally linked to another) the combined event was only counted as one error. A coding scheme covering the types of errors identified is included in the supplementary materials.

RESULTS

A series of repeated measures analyses of variance (RM ANOVA) were conducted using 'Control Device' as the within-subjects factor. Age, RacePlay GTF and RaceLife familiarity were split into three groups for use as between-subject factors along with Gender. The between-subjects factors were then individually used to conduct mixed design repeated measures ANOVA's with the dependent variables [Game Technology Familiarity device percentage scores (device GTF), Progress, Errors and perceived Intuitive Controls (pIC) from PENS]. Descriptive statistics (such as age ranges and gender percentages) for these between-subject factors and their groups, as well the full the mean and standard error results, are detailed in the supplementary materials. Wilks' Lambda and an alpha level of $p < .05$ was used as the significance test for the mixed ANOVA results, while a Bonferroni adjustment with the same alpha level was used for all multiple pairwise comparisons. An experiment-wise Bonferroni correction was not applied due to the exploratory nature of the study, and so results should be interpreted with some caution.

During data cleaning one score was removed from each condition of the Progress measure due to participants travelling the wrong direction for more than a few seconds. No other missing values required intervention as missing data was below the accepted threshold [22]. Assumptions of normality were satisfied as in all instances there are both more cases than dependent variables and more than 20 cases per cell [22]. The only exceptions were age and gender by Control Device for Progress, where only 17 and 18 cases remained in the oldest and female categories respectively after data cleaning. However, Progress was expected to be skewed in the population and on this basis no transformations of the variables were performed. Three outliers were identified manually for both device GTF and Progress, however they were retained in both cases on the basis that they did not cause differences in the results when transformed and were representative of real demographic groups in the broader population (males with high RacingWheel familiarity and older females respectively). Investigation of the assumption of homogeneity of variance and covariance matrices was violated for Progress and Errors with age and gender as between-subjects factors. Further analysis found that variance and covariance was higher for the oldest group and females, and so significant findings related to gender and age for Progress and Errors should be interpreted with caution [22]. Violations to the assumption of Sphericity are highlighted within each relevant dependent variable, and in all cases were corrected with Greenhouse-Geisser adjustments.

Device Game Technology Familiarity (GTF) percentage

In the mixed ANOVA results for the device Game Technology Familiarity (device GTF) percentage a significant main effect of Control Device on device GTF ($F(2, 122) = 56.8$, $p < .001$, $\eta_p^2 = .482$), was qualified by interactions between Control Device and Age ($F(4, 122) = 6.39$, $p < .001$, $\eta_p^2 = .173$) and Control Device and RacePlay GTF ($F(4, 122) = 5.91$, $p < .001$, $\eta_p^2 = .162$) for device GTF. A significant between-subjects effect of Gender on device GTF ($F(1, 62) = 4.32$, $p < .05$, $\eta_p^2 = .065$) was also revealed, such that males ($M = 21.7$) reported higher familiarity across devices than females ($M = 14.6$). No significant effects were shown for RaceLife familiarity.

For the interaction between Age and Control Device for device GTF (shown in Figure 3A) the youngest group showed significant differences between all devices, such that they reported significantly more familiarity with the Controller ($M = 40.5$) than they did with the SpeedWheel ($M = 32.8$, $p < .05$) or RacingWheel ($M = 8.71$, $p < .001$), and also significantly more familiarity with the SpeedWheel than the RacingWheel ($p < .001$). The middle age group reported significantly less familiarity with the RacingWheel ($M = 7.31$) than both the Controller ($M = 22$, $p < .001$) and SpeedWheel ($M = 22.7$, $p < .001$), while the oldest group only reported significantly less familiarity with the RacingWheel ($M = 6.17$) than the SpeedWheel ($M = 16.8$, $p < .01$). For the within-device results for Age, the youngest group reported significantly more familiarity with the SpeedWheel than the oldest group ($p < .01$), as well as significantly more familiarity with the Controller than both the middle ($p < .01$) and oldest ($p < .001$) Age groups. All other multiple pairwise comparisons for the effect of Age on device GTF percentage were non-significant.

For the interaction between RacePlay GTF and Control Device for device GTF (shown in Figure 3B), all groups had significantly more device familiarity with the SpeedWheel [(LOW $M = 13.8$, $p < .05$), (MEDIUM $M = 27.8$, $p < .001$), (HIGH $M = 32.8$, $p < .001$)] than the RacingWheel [(LOW $M = 4.94$, $p < .05$), (MEDIUM $M = 6.38$, $p < .001$), (HIGH $M = 11.41$, $p < .001$)]. However, only the medium and high RacePlay GTF groups also reported significantly more familiarity with the Controller (MEDIUM $M = 31.5$, HIGH $M = 37.8$) than the RacingWheel (both $p < .001$). Within device results revealed that the medium and high RacePlay GTF groups had significantly more familiarity with the Controller (MEDIUM $p < .01$, HIGH $p < .001$) and SpeedWheel (MEDIUM $p < .05$, HIGH $p < .001$) than the low group (CONTROLLER $M = 11.5$). For the RacingWheel, the high RacePlay GTF group showed more familiarity than the both the medium ($p < .05$) and low groups ($p < .01$). All other between and within device effects of RacePlay GTF on device GTF percentage were non-significant.

Progress

Results from the mixed ANOVA for Progress (race percentage complete at four minutes) revealed a main effect of Control Device on Progress ($F(2, 116) = 24.1$, $p < .001$, $\eta_p^2 = .293$), that was qualified by a significant interaction between Age and Control Device ($F(4, 116) = 2.46$, $p < .05$, $\eta_p^2 = .078$). While no significant interactions were found for

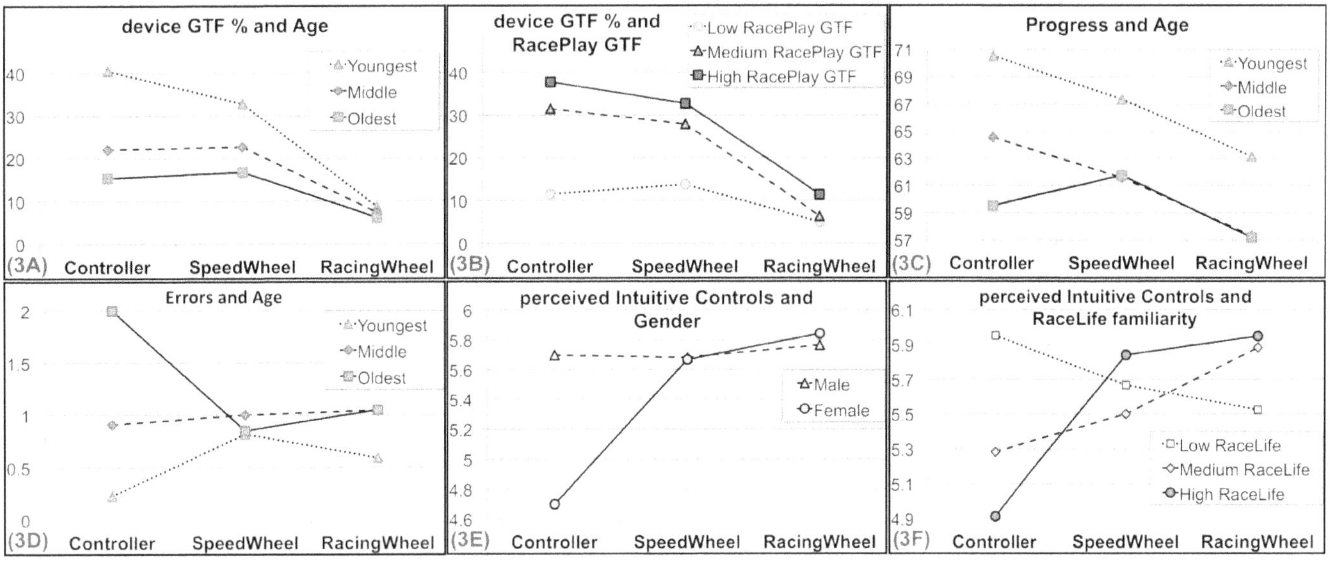

Figure 3: A Range of the Significant Interactions Revealed for device GTF, Progress, Errors and perceived Intuitive Controls

the other between-subject factors, significant between-subject factor effects were revealed for both Gender ($F(1, 59) = 13.9, p < .001, \eta_p^2 = .19$) and RacePlay GTF ($F(2, 58) = 9.78, p < .001, \eta_p^2 = .252$). For the Gender effect, across devices males (M = 65.5) progressed significantly further through the course than females (M = 56.5). For the significant between-subjects of RacePlay GTF on Progress, the low RacePlay GTF group (M = 56.1) made less progress than the other RacePlay GTF groups [($_{\text{MEDIUM}}$ M = 66.3, p < .01), ($_{\text{HIGH}}$ M = 65.8, p < .01)].

For the interaction between Age and Control Device for Progress (shown in Figure 3C), all age groups progressed significantly further with the SpeedWheel ($_{\text{YOUNGEST}}$ M = 67.4, $_{\text{MIDDLE}}$ M = 61.6, $_{\text{OLDEST}}$ M = 61.8) than the RacingWheel [($_{\text{YOUNGEST}}$ M = 63.1, p < .01), ($_{\text{MIDDLE}}$ M = 57.3, p < .01), ($_{\text{OLDEST}}$ M = 57.2, p < .05)]. For the oldest group Progress differences between other devices were non-significant. Only the two younger groups progressed significantly further with the Controller ($_{\text{YOUNGEST}}$ M = 70.6, $_{\text{MIDDLE}}$ M = 64.6) than the RacingWheel ($_{\text{YOUNGEST}}$ p < .001, $_{\text{MIDDLE}}$ p < .001). Within device, the only significant result revealed that for the Controller the youngest group made more Progress than the oldest group (M = 59.2, p < .01), with all other differences non-significant.

Errors

For the mixed ANOVA results for Errors, Mauchly's Test indicated that the assumption of sphericity had been violated for Errors with Age ($W = .9, \chi^2(2) = 6.25, p < .05$) and Gender ($W = .88, \chi^2(2) = 8.06, p < .05$) as between-subject factors, and so adjustments ($_{\text{AGE}}$ ε = .91, $_{\text{GENDER}}$ ε = .89) were used for their within-subjects analyses. Significant interactions were found between Age and Control Device ($F(3.64, 111) = 3.74, p < .01, \eta_p^2 = .109$) and Gender and Control Device ($F(1.78, 110.3) = 3.35, p < .05, \eta_p^2 = .051$) for Errors. A significant between-subjects effect of RacePlay GTF on Errors ($F(2, 61) = 6.83, p < .01, \eta_p^2 = .183$) revealed that the low RacePlay GTF group (M = 1.45) made more errors than the other RacePlay GTF groups [($_{\text{MEDIUM}}$ M = 0.64, p < .01), ($_{\text{HIGH}}$ M = 0.65, p < .01). Interaction and between-subjects effects of RaceLife familiarity on Errors were non-significant.

For the interaction between Age and Control Device for Errors (shown in Figure 3D), the difference in Errors between devices was only significant for the oldest group, such that they had significantly more errors with the Controller (M = 2) than the SpeedWheel (M = 0.85, p < .05) or RacingWheel (M = 1.05, p < .05). For the within-device effects, only the Controller yielded a significant difference between Age groups, with the oldest group producing significantly more errors than the youngest group (M = 0.28, p = .001). All other between and within-device results for Age were non-significant. For the interaction between Gender and Control Device for Errors, males and females showed no significant difference between devices. However, females did show significantly more Errors than males on both the Controller (p < .001, $_{\text{FEMALES}}$ M = 2.1, $_{\text{MALES}}$ M = 0.49) and RacingWheel (p < .01, $_{\text{FEMALES}}$ M = 1.48, $_{\text{MALES}}$ M = 0.61). The difference between genders on the SpeedWheel, however, was non-significant.

Perceived Intuitive Controls (pIC) (PENS)

For the mixed ANOVA results for perceived Intuitive Controls (pIC) from PENS, Mauchly's Test indicated that the assumption of sphericity had been violated for Gender ($W = .84, \chi^2(2) = 10.6, p < .01$) and RaceLife familiarity ($W = .83, \chi^2(2) = 10.9, p < .01$), and so adjustments (both ε = .86) were used for their within-subjects analysis. A significant main effect of Control Device on Intuitive Controls ($F(1.73, 106.9) = 4.55, p < .05, \eta_p^2 = .068$), was qualified by interactions between Control Device and Gender ($F(1.73, 106.9) = 3.99, p < .05, \eta_p^2 = .06$) and

Control Device and RaceLife familiarity ($F(3.43, 104.6) = 2.93$, $p < .05$, $\eta_p^2 = .088$) for pIC. While interactions for Age and RacePlay GTF were non-significant, a significant between-subjects factor effect across devices was revealed for Age ($F(2, 61) = 3.6$, $p < .05$, $\eta_p^2 = .105$), yet step-down analysis failed to reveal any significant pairwise comparisons (all p > .05).

For the interaction between Gender and Control Device for perceived Intuitive Controls (shown in Figure 3E), the difference between devices was only significant for females, such that the Controller ($M = 4.7$) was reported as significantly less intuitive than the RacingWheel ($M = 5.84$, $p < .01$). The difference in pIC between genders was also significant for the Controller ($p < .05$), such that males ($M = 5.7$) reported the device to have significantly higher pIC than females ($M = 4.7$), yet the differences between genders for PIC were non-significant for the SpeedWheel and RacingWheel. For the interaction between RaceLife familiarity and Control Device for perceived Intuitive Controls (shown in Figure 3F), the difference between devices was only significant for the high RaceLife group, such that the Controller ($M = 4.91$) was perceived to be significantly less intuitive than the RacingWheel ($M = 5.95$, $p < .01$). Differences between and within devices for the other groups were all non-significant.

DISCUSSION

Device GTF percentage and Progress

While results for device GTF indicate participants' past familiarity with the control devices tested, Progress reveals their empirical skill level with these devices during the experiment. Overall, however, the device GTF results show similar patterns of results for the Age and RacePlay GTF groups, with a general trend towards higher familiarity with devices with the least natural mapping (Controller and SpeedWheel). All groups showed more familiarity with the SpeedWheel than the RacingWheel, perhaps reflective of the recent pervasiveness of accelerometer-based motion control devices for racing games as compared to the larger, older arcade racing devices. Only the younger age groups and those with more racing game familiarity were more familiar with the Controller than the RacingWheel, suggesting that the oldest and lowest racing game familiarity groups lack experience with traditional controls. The within-device results also reflect this trend, with the older and lowest racing game familiarity groups reporting less familiarity than other groups with the Controller and SpeedWheel. Familiarity differences between these two controllers were only shown in the youngest/higher racing game familiarity groups reporting more familiarity with the Controller than the SpeedWheel, perhaps indicative of the pervasiveness of traditional devices for those that play the most.

Progress results generally reflect previous experience as measured through device GTF, with the same Age groups that had higher familiarity also making more Progress. The only exceptions to this were that the youngest group did not make more Progress with the SpeedWheel than the other groups and also did not make more Progress with the Controller than the middle Age group. All other between and within device GTF differences for Age accurately predict the resulting performance differences as measured by Progress, such that the same age groups that had higher familiarity with a specific device also performed better with that device (and vice versa). Males also reported higher device GTF and progressed further than females, further strengthening the relationship between the two measures. These gender differences could be reflective of heavier game play patterns for males in society, or representative of a gender preference for racing games. While the same patterns revealed by the different racing game experience groups in device familiarity were not shown in Progress, those with more racing game experience did make further Progress through the course across devices than the least experienced group. Altogether, the correspondence in results between device GTF and Progress provides evidence of the value of GTF as a measure of previous experience that can reliably predict performance. Since Progress in this study also represented the intuitive interaction measure for 'time to complete set tasks', GTF also appears to have been successful for replicating some of the technology familiarity (TF) measure's ability to predict intuitive use outcomes.

Perceived Intuitive Controls (pIC) and Errors

The perceived Intuitive Controls (pIC) measure from PENS and the Errors measure represent a newer subjective and a more traditional objective approach to measuring intuitive interaction. The interactions for Gender and Age for Errors help to explain some of the equivalent interactions for Gender and RaceLife familiarity for pIC. For instance, males showed no difference in Errors or pIC between devices. Females, however, produced more Errors with the Controller than males and also found that device less intuitive (pIC) than males. Likewise, the oldest group had more Errors with the Controller than the other devices and those with the most real-life racing/driving experience reported that the Controller offered lower perceived Intuitive Controls. Age and RaceLife familiarity have a significant positive correlation (Pearson's $r(64) = .514$, $p < .001$), which is understandable given that older participants have had more time and opportunity to become familiar with racing/driving in real-life. A relative lack of experience with traditional control devices for the oldest and high real-life racing groups could explain their higher Errors and lower perceived Intuitive Controls, however it also might suggest that higher natural mapping in the SpeedWheel and RacingWheel are enabling intuitive interaction to take place. This is further strengthened by Errors and pIC indicating either the same or higher levels of intuitive use for the more naturally mapped devices for all between-subject factor groups (except for female errors with the RacingWheel) despite most groups having less device familiarity with the SpeedWheel and RacingWheel. That more naturally mapped devices produced a higher level of pIC only for those with the most real-life racing/driving experience also emphasises the importance of accurately measuring familiarity with real-life equivalent interfaces when measuring intuitive use outcomes in games. However, lack of differences for device GTF, Progress and Errors for the RaceLife familiarity groups indicates that real-life racing/driving experience does not automatically lead to higher racing game familiarity or performance.

Not all results were reflected cleanly between perceived Intuitive Controls and Errors, strengthening the argument for a multi-modal (subjective and objective) approach to measuring intuitive interaction in games. For instance, the oldest group produced significantly more Errors with the Controller than the youngest group, yet there were no differences between any of the real-life racing/driving familiarity groups regarding the perceived intuitiveness (pIC) of any device. Additionally, while females produced more Errors with the RacingWheel than males there was no difference in pIC between genders for this device, yet females did report that the RacingWheel was more intuitive (pIC) than the Controller. That is, although females produced more Errors on the RacingWheel and Controller than males, and both genders showed no difference in Errors between devices, females still indicated that the more naturally mapped devices were more intuitive (pIC) than the Controller. Combined with the other between-subject results for females and those with the least racing game experience (less device Familiarity, lower Progress and more Errors), this may lend support to the argument for naturally mapped controls as a means to provide accessibility through increased potential for intuitive interaction. The contradictions between device familiarity and the intuitive use outcomes for different age groups may add further weight to this argument. For instance, most age groups reported less familiarity with each of the more naturally mapped devices, yet the only difference between devices for Errors was that the oldest group produced more errors with the Controller. Once again, it appears that familiarity as measured through GTF may provide a good indicator of intuitive use outcomes, yet natural mapping (or transferring knowledge across domains) might compensate for lack of previous experience, especially for those with less experience in the domain.

Natural Mapping and the Intuitive Interaction Continua

Tying these results back to the continua for intuitive interaction shown in Figure 1, stronger natural mapping takes advantage of lower (more base and pervasive) levels of knowledge (sensorimotor/physical affordance), whereas devices that employ weaker natural mapping rely more on specialised knowledge (such as Culture / Population Stereotypes and Expertise/Knowledge from same domain). The difficulty of naturally mapping an activity depends on both the pervasiveness of the knowledge being leveraged, which in turn depends on the frequency of encoding/retrieval for the mapped activity, and how directly the actions to be mapped can be transferred. Put another way, it depends on both the cultural penetration of the activity and the level of metaphor required to naturally map its action to an available interface. This may explain why certain activities are more frequently simulated in videogames using Naturally Mapped Control Interfaces (NMCIs). For instance, driving as a skill has a high level of cultural penetration not only because a majority of adults learn it but also since children are encouraged to participate in activities using similar skills from an early age (riding on trikes, go-karts, etc.). Thus the conceptual model for the activity has a high level of penetration in society, and the basic control actions for this activity also easily map to accessible and pervasive tilt-based and mechanical control input technologies. NMCI types for videogames that use a high level of natural mapping for such activities can hope to encourage a higher potential for intuitive use. However, this potential is only greater than the potential for intuitive interaction leveraged through expertise knowledge (e.g. by traditional control inputs with lower natural mapping levels) when targeting those either with low game device familiarity or high relevant real-life experience. Users with a high level of experiential knowledge using traditional interfaces in the same domain/genre (or able to transfer these skills from a similar domain/genre) will be primed for intuitive use with traditional interfaces leveraging their expert knowledge of tools. Since "...intuitive use is most beneficial for first, early and intermittent use of interfaces" [6], the accessibility benefit or intuitive potential of NMCIs may only be applicable to casual or intermittent gamers (those with low same domain familiarity) or those approaching the genre for the first time. This possibility needs to be explored further, along with the question of whether there are additional factors, such as broader play experience outcomes, related to the use of control interfaces for videogames that might influence the design of interfaces with the potential for intuitive interaction in this space.

SUMMARY AND FUTURE WORK

Different types of naturally mapped control interfaces in a racing game, classified using Skalski et al.'s typology [21], produced distinctly different intuitive use outcomes between devices. The lack of an experiment-wise Bonferonni correction in the current study resulted in a elevated chance of Type I errors and future work should aim to confirm these findings with a larger sample and more conservative statistical analysis. While more naturally mapped devices may offer a higher degree of control more closely equivalent to the real-life activity, they also provide greater potential for intuitive use for those with less gaming experience and/or higher familiarity with the real-life activity. While this increased potential for intuitive use may be limited for high familiarity gamers, due to their overwhelming familiarity with traditional interfaces, this does not automatically make naturally mapped controls detrimental for this group. It does, however, allow for first time or occasional gamers to leverage experiential knowledge to make gaming more accessible. Further definition of these player familiarity types and of naturally mapped control device types, as well as broader exploration of related play experience outcomes, will form the focus of our future work.

This paper presented a new approach to measuring previous gaming experience. Evolved from similar measures to help predict intuitive interaction [6], Game Technology Familiarity (GTF) provides a deep and reliable previous experience measure that can be adapted for unique combinations of control interfaces and game types. Drawing on intuitive interaction theory, GTF also emphasises the importance of measuring familiarity with similar devices and activities, given that these form an amalgamated pool of experience referenced for intuitive use that may also influence other play experience outcomes. Measurement of accuracy and time to complete tasks as employed in intuitive interaction research was also adapted for games research using Errors and Progress. Future work should test implementation of these measures, and their potential to predict and explicate intuitive use, against traditional measures of previous play experience and across different videogame genres. While research in genres with a clear potential for naturally mapped controls is needed, such as in sports and actions games, future work should also seek to explore motion controls where the in-game activity is not so clearly mapped to the real world.

REFERENCES

1. Abeele, V. Vanden, Schutter, B. De, Gajadhar, B., Johnson, D., and Geurts, L. More naturalness, less control: The effect of natural mapping on the co-located player experience. *Proc. FDG'13*, (2013), 174–182.
2. Bianchi-Berthouze, N. Body movement as a means to modulate engagement in computer games. *Proc. Workshop on Whole Body Interaction, HCI'08*, (2008).
3. Birk, M. and Mandryk, R. Control your game-self: effects of controller type on enjoyment, motivation, and personality in game. *Proc. CHI 2013*, ACM (2013).
4. Blackler, A. and Hurtienne, J. Towards a unified view of intuitive interaction: definitions, models and tools across the world. *MMI-interaktiv 13*, (2007), 36–54.
5. Blackler, A., Popovic, V., Lawry, S., et al. Researching intuitive interaction. *Proc. IASDR2011*, (2011), 562–73.
6. Blackler, A.L. *Intuitive Interaction with complex artefacts: empirically-based research.* VDM Verlag, Saarbrücken, Germany, 2008.
7. Bowman, N. and Boyan, A. Cognitive Skill as a Predictor of Flow and Presence in Naturally Mapped Video Games. *Proc. ICA 2008*, ICA (2008), 25.
8. Brown, M., Kehoe, A., Kirakowski, J., and Pitt, I. Beyond the Gamepad: HCI and Game Controller Design and Evaluation. In R. Bernhaupt, ed., *Evaluating User Experience in Games*. Springer London, 2010, 197–219.
9. Cairns, P., Li, J., Wang, W., and Nordin, a. I. The influence of controllers on immersion in mobile games. *Proc. CHI 2014*, ACM Press (2014), 371–380.
10. Hurtienne, J. and Israel, J.H. Image schemas and their metaphorical extensions: intuitive patterns for tangible interaction. *Proc. TEI 2007*, ACM (2007), 127–134.
11. Johnson, D., Wiles, J., Sweetser, P., Hollingsworth, K.M., and Gardner, J.A. The inherent appeal of physically controlled peripherals. *Proc. IWEC 2002*, Kluwer (2002), 371–378.
12. Limperos, A.M., Schmierbach, M.G., Kegerise, A.D., and Dardis, F.E. Gaming across different consoles: exploring the influence of control scheme on game-player enjoyment. *Cyberpsychology, behavior and social networking 14*, 6 (2011), 345–350.
13. McEwan, M., Johnson, D., Wyeth, P., and Blackler, A. Videogame control device impact on the play experience. *IE 2012*, ACM (2012), 3.
14. McMahan, R.P., Alon, A.J.D., Lazem, S., et al. Evaluating natural interaction techniques in video games. *Proc. 3DUI 2010*, IEEE (2010), 11–14.
15. Mueller, F. "Floyd" and Bianchi-Berthouze, N. Evaluating Exertion Games. In *Evaluating User Experience in Games*. Springer, 2010, 187–207.
16. Mueller, F. "Floyd," Gibbs, M.R., and Vetere, F. Taxonomy of exertion games. *OZCHI'08*, ACM (2008).
17. Naumann, A., Hurtienne, J., Israel, J., et al. Intuitive Use of User Interfaces : Defining a Vague Concept. *EPCE, HCII 2007, LNAI 4562*, Springer (2007).
18. Nintendo. Search: Results for 'intuitive.'2014. www.nintendo.com/search/#/results/intuitive.
19. Ryan, R.M., Rigby, C.S., and Przybylski, A.K. The motivational pull of video games: A self-determination theory approach. *Motivation and Emotion 30*, 4 (2006).
20. Sah, Y., Ahn, B., and Sundar, S. Realistic mapping vs. symbolic mapping: Effects of controllers on video game experience. *Proc. AEJMC 2010*, All Academic (2010).
21. Skalski, P., Tamborini, R., Shelton, A., Buncher, M., and Lindmark, P. Mapping the road to fun: Natural video game controllers, presence, and game enjoyment. *New Media & Society 13*, 2 (2011), 224–242.
22. Tabachnick, B. and Fidell, L. *Using multivariate statistics*. Pearson, Boston, 2013.
23. Wada, Y. The Undercurrent of Revolution in the Games Industry. *Tokyo Game Show*, 2011. www.square-enix.com/eng/docs/TGSForum_2011_1.html.

Understanding Expectations with Multiple Controllers in an Augmented Reality Videogame

Pejman Mirza-Babaei[1], Nathan Gale[1], Joao P. Costa[1], Lennart E. Nacke[1], Daniel Johnson[2]
[1]HCI Games Group, Faculty of Business and IT, University of Ontario Institute of Technology, 2000 Simcoe St. N, Oshawa, ON, Canada
[2]Queensland University of Technology, Brisbane, QLD 4001, Australia
pejman.m@acm.org, nathan.gale@uoit.ca, joao.costa@uoit.ca, lennart.nacke@acm.org, dm.johnson@qut.edu.au

ABSTRACT
Player experiences and expectations are connected. The presumptions players have about how they control their gameplay interactions may shape the way they play and perceive videogames. A successfully engaging player experience might rest on the way controllers meet players' expectations. We studied player interaction with novel controllers on the Sony PlayStation Wonderbook, an augmented reality (AR) gaming system. Our goal was to understand player expectations regarding game controllers in AR game design. Based on this preliminary study, we propose several interaction guidelines for hybrid input from both augmented reality and physical game controllers.

Author Keywords
Games; User Experience; Player Experience; Games User Research; Controllers; Augmented Reality; Wonderbook;

ACM Classification Keywords
H.5.2 [Information Systems]: User Interfaces; K.8.0 [General]: Games – Personal Computing;

INTRODUCTION
Users are highly engaged by products or services they desire. Games provide some of the most desirable technical platforms of Human-Computer Interaction (HCI). Therefore, studying user experience in games, or more aptly called player experience, can provide great insights about player expectations and desires [11]. As part of player experience research, we are using evaluation methods from HCI to try and find optimally engaging game designs and to evaluate player experiences [20]. In games, play and enjoyment are the primary goals of the interaction taking place. The accomplishment of tasks remains secondary to, or integrated with, these primary fun goals. Thus, while a task may motivate engagement with productivity applications, engagement with videogames must be motivated by attractive, engaging or pleasurable interactions [15]. One of the main components of any interaction with a system, is the way its user interface works. For videogames, the experience outside of a game has traditionally revolved around the buttons, sticks, and discs featured on game controllers. In particular, the buttons of traditional video game controllers (e.g., a joypad or a gamepad) allow a player's intentions to be translated and mapped onto physical actions and game interaction.

CHI PLAY '14, October 19 - 22 2014, Toronto, ON, Canada

ACM 978-1-4503-3014-5/14/10...$15.00.
http://dx.doi.org/10.1145/2658537.2658705

Videogames have moved beyond the screen. Traditional consoles had to adapt as mobile phones created player experience in everyday contexts. New virtual reality hardware like the Oculus Rift allow for new forms of output that do not even necessarily involve the television screen as an output medium anymore. In addition, augmented reality (AR) games and new physical controllers are commonplace now for the gaming consoles of this generation (e.g., Microsoft's Xbox One, Sony's Playstation 4 or Nintendo's Wii U). We believe there is huge potential in designing games for these new input and output modalities. For example, we imagine that these modalities can offer existing players more intuitive and satisfying interactions. They also potentially offer easier access to videogames for new audiences, who are less experienced with traditional control methods. However, current game designers are lacking focused investigations that can help to establish interaction design guidelines for these novel games. We address this lack by providing an initial study of players using the Sony Wonderbook augmented reality system.

RELATED WORK
Studies have investigated the influence of control schemes of different consoles on player enjoyment [5, 9, 13] and support user preference for traditional button-driven controls compared to more advanced control schemes. One strong proposed influence on player experience is the user's perceived preference for a product or technique. Users appear to be more effective at using an interaction technique they prefer. For example, Nielsen and Levy [14] found problem solving was greatly improved when participants used their preferred interaction technique over any other.

An essential feature of game design is to break down goals and add tasks for players that lead them from onboarding toward mastery. Games have a clear set of goals for the challenges they present. A consequence of such clearness is the expectation for immediate feedback while the player engrosses in feelings of flow and immersion [12], progressing from one challenge to the next – more difficult – one, in the process accumulating greater skills and abilities. Hence, a core part of player experience would then be the interface through which a player interacts with a game and with other players. Immediate feedback from this interface is crucial for the player. The lack of feedback may break the state of flow that keeps the player engaged. Often, a central part of game interfaces and therefore of player experience is the game controller. Games have evolved over time, and so have the input controllers they require. The interactions with games and their level of abstraction, or naturalness, have changed in an attempt to create more engaging and fun experiences.

Interactions can thus be of different nature [3, 16]. Some can be of symbolic nature, by abstracting and reducing game actions like jumping to something as pressing a button to jump. In contrast to symbolic interactions, it is also possible to have iconic interactions, where natural motion of our body plays a central role, like performing the same actions for playing a tennis videogame (e.g., in *Wii Sport*) as in real life. Hence, these distinct interactions might create different controller shapes or affordances, which affect player expectations in regards to how they may differently operate [8]. For example, the Sony move controller suggests the affordance of being gripped and potentially being swung (like a racket or a sword). In contrast, a hypothetical controller, shaped like a disc might suggest to the player it can be interacted with by wielding it like a shield or throwing it like a discus.

Skalski et al. [19] provide a comparison between various game controllers regarding the naturalness of the mapped actions and how this correlates to enjoyment. The more natural the game controller feels, the greater the enjoyment should be for the player. Research exploring the impact of controller naturalness has shown that – while players of racing game may report greater flow, presence, autonomy and intuitiveness for naturally-mapped controllers (e.g., steering wheels) – players may still perform better with non-natural devices, such as traditional controllers [10]. The connection between more naturally-mapped controller interface and greater immersion has also been found in the context of mobile videogames [2]. Nevertheless, the way we feel if a controller is natural is different for each individual, and natural motion might not work equally well [9].

According to Gregersen and Grodal [6], the theme of a game and its representation in the game controller is equally important as a part of the gameplay experience. Accurately representing game actions in the game controller is important, but recreating certain elements of the game's theme in the controller itself can further increase the interest and engagement in the game, while meeting player expectations [17]. An example for a case of harmonious use of theme and affordances is Ishii et al.'s PingPongPlus [7]. It is an augmented game of table tennis that is played with real paddles, providing accurate physical and intentional affordances. These affordances also fit into the theme of the game.

Sony PlayStation's Wonderbook controller is an AR book featuring pages with different fiducial markers (see Figure 1). It also uses motion input objects like PlayStation Move controller and/or the player's hand gestures to interact with it. Few researches have looked at similar interaction paradigms, which would use two controllers in a similar fashion that Wonderbook and Move controllers do it. For example, Rohs in handheld AR games [18], and Billinghurst et al in the MagicBook with handheld display, which created at the Sony Computer Science laboratories in 2001 [1].

Yet, as these interaction paradigms become more popular, key issues remain to be explored. It is not yet fully understood how players perceive and experience the affordances of multiple controllers used together in a game. It is also not clear how well the controller combination in Wonderbook articulates the available mapped actions. One unique aspect of the Wonderbook system is the use of a physical book as an interaction channel. There is a potential to assume interacting with the book (as a game input device) may create some expectations for users [4] as most can be assumed to have a long and established relationship with books. However, it is not clear whether users' established expectations would be met during their interactions within an AR game.

We report here a study to that explores these issues. As an outcome of this study, we propose early design guidelines for interactions with these types of controllers, based on the observations we collected from our participants. Should there be increasing interest in utilizing controller combinations such as this when developing games, the insight that this article provides can help improve player experience. Moreover, game developers and designers may also find these insights helpful when utilizing a combination of such input systems when designing a new game.

WONDERBOOK STUDY

We conducted a study of the PlayStation Wonderbook and the PlayStation Move controllers (see Figure 1).

Figure 1. The Wonderbook and Move Controllers.

The Game: Book of Spells

Book of Spells is a game based in the *Harry Potter* universe that uses the Wonderbook and the PlayStation Move controller. The intent of the game is to make players feel as a part of the wizard world. The story itself is Miranda Goshawk's Book of Spells, an old textbook used to teach the readers a variety of different charms and spells. The Move controller takes on the look of wand, chosen by the player, and the Wonderbook takes on the look of the old spell book (see Figure 2). Players must learn each spell in the chapter and complete the chapter tests, which involve all the previously learnt spells, to advance in the game.

Figure 2. Book of Spells game screenshot, exhibiting the Wonderbook and Move controllers overlaid with 3D imagery.

The Controllers

As explained above, this game and its interactions are a hybrid combination of controllers. The Wonderbook acts as an interactive AR play mat, allowing the player to flip through the pages, rotate and fold the book while looking at the television to follow the gameplay (or its instructions). As the game uses the Playstation Move Camera, it is important for the player to keep the fiducial markers (Wonderbook) and the Move controller visible to the camera at all time.

In the case of the studied game, the Wonderbook adopts the appearance of an old spell book on the television, blending in with the theme of the game while hiding its more technological appearance (Figure 1 and Figure 2). Flipping through the pages of the books proceeds or retrocedes the level presented to the player, while moving it in certain angles allows the player to perform intended in-game actions, such as lifting the book to dry after soaking it with a water-making spell.

The PlayStation Move controller exhibits a wand-like appearance, which reinforces its integration into the theme of the game, features various buttons for input, while being motion-tracking capable. The players can interact with the Wonderbook through this wand, by pointing it at certain key directions exhibited in the game, while pressing specific buttons, or by flicking or drawing gestures. For most of these interactions, verbal, visual and haptic feedback is provided by the game.

The Participants and the Playtest

For the purpose of our case study, we recruited six participants [P1 to P6] who frequently played videogames and were familiar with the Harry Potter stories. Players were selected carefully so that none had used the Wonderbook before. They were recruited using our University's mailing list and their participation was voluntary. Individual user test sessions were conducted in our dedicated game laboratory. The participants played the game on a Sony PlayStation 3 connected to a 55" display. The participants were seated on a couch, while they had the Wonderbook resting on a coffee table directly in front of them. Video cameras captured the player, and real-time game footage was digitally streamed in a single screen for live viewing in an isolated observation room and recorded for analysis (Figure 2 shows a screenshot from recorded gameplay video and participants seating position).

Before starting the study, the players signed an informed consent form, and were provided with a brief explanation about the study. The players were asked to play both sections of the first chapter (about 45 minutes). They were told that the study is not about how well they can play the game and were asked to play the game as if they are at home in their own living room. Before the test started all the save files (from pervious study) were removed so each player would experience the game from the beginning (including a standard animated introduction about the Wonderbook and basic interaction as part of the game's loading process). After they finished both sections of the first chapter (all six players completed the test) the recording was stopped and the participant were asked questions (in the form of a semi-structured interview) about their experience with the game and controllers (e.g., features they liked and did not like). After this, the players were thanked for their participation and left.

Analysis

Two evaluators observed and analyzed the gameplay sessions separately, noting players' gameplay experience in regards to the observed interactions, the players' comments and their moments of notable satisfaction or frustration in a 'double-expert' approach. Their findings were collated and summarized with identical issues combined, providing our own list of findings.

RESULTS

We identify the following as overarching game design consideration in our findings:

- Accurate or inaccurate mapping of actions on the Move controller and the Wonderbook
- Positive or negative match between player expectations and game interactions
- Verbal communication's terminologies or language
- Storytelling

We observed that *accurately mapping* gestures to the Move controller was the most ambiguous area for the players. Some players had difficulty in performing the required motions, mostly caused by inaccuracy in tracking the spells gesture. This happened not only because players were executing the gestures too fast (or too slow) for it to be correctly tracked, but also because some required gestures were too complex for the players to remember and recall or they did not match to the players' expectation. Moreover, the camera angle required tracking of both book and controller on the same scene made it difficult for the players to cast certain spells or move the wand around to skip text. Finally, we observed inconsistencies in interactions between spells requiring flicking motions and those requiring reaching for objects.

Despite having more consistence performance in interactions when involving the Wonderbook (such as rotating, tilting or pointing to virtual object on the pages), similar issues were still observed across our players. For example, the game replaces the Move controller's image with that of a wand that is longer in size (as shown in Figure 2). This transfers players' focal point of interaction to the tip of the virtual wand and not the tip of the physical controller. We observed situations where this disparity led to some issues when players had to point to (interact with) virtual objects above the book's surface. There were also in-game situations where players had to use their hand to interact with virtual objects. This inconsistency between the sources of interactions also created issues for the players learning when to use their actual hands or the Move controller. Our result shows that in most cases players tend to try to use the controller until they are told otherwise explicitly.

Since our players were familiar with the Harry Potter universe, they had initial *expectations* about how a magic wand should work in game. *Expectations* were also present for how to interact with the book, as it is a well-known medium. For example, P4 felt that the books flipped imagery in the television screen was upsetting and caused a break in the believability of interacting with a real book.

Moreover, we observed several reactions in relation to *the match between players' expectations and in-game actions.* The value of matching player expectations in an in-game actions operated at mulitiple levels. At one level, when the actions required to complete a spell matched player expectations in terms of using real-world metaphors and existing knowledge/experiences that can help players understand game mechanics. For example in the water-making spell, where the players expressed satisfaction and pleasure. At another level of abstraction, players enjoyed the match between the game and their recollections of Harry Potter mythology from the books and films, for example, enjoying having to speak aloud a popular Harry Potter spell.

In contrast, when learning new incantations the game would sometimes recognize background noises as the correct pronunciation causing confusion and shattering expectations. Other ambiguities were also present in context specific situations. One of the players, P4, explicitly noted a false (or insincere) positive reinforcement within the game. When this player did not cast the spell correctly, the game positively reinforced this failure by saying "Well done! But try to do it again!". As another example, we observed participants frequently lifted the book towards themselves (instead of tilting the book towards the Move camera placed above television) to take a glance inside a virtual hole (as part of the game's storyline) (See Figure 3 below). Although they were interacting with the book in a different fashion, players reported that actions like this make this controller feel like something much more foreign than a traditional book.

Figure 3. Players need to tilt the book towards television

These types of issues can be seen as a consequence of controllers not matching with the players' *expectations* of using real-world metaphors and existing knowledge as explained earlier. The pre-conceived notion of how books, wands, or spells work influenced the expectations players had and shaped the way they interacted.

Various *mapped actions* used similar controller gestures, but different buttons, causing confusion among the players, and thus breaking the fun experience of the game. An example of this is that a button has to be pressed to cast a spell (as an action button) within a game scene, whereas a different button has to be pressed to interact with the book (as an action button), on a scene where no spells have to be cast. These feelings are attributed to the inconsistency of the actions that players have to perform, as well as to the lack of guidance provided by the game.

We also observed various issues related to how players perceived *language* in the given instructions during the game. For example, there is one spell within the game that creates light. Sometimes players had to cast this spell for the first time and were prompted to "turn on the lights". Given that this game uses computer vision technology to track both the book and the wand controllers, this instruction seemed to be confusing. Some players mistook this with having to turn on the lights of the room to improve the computer vision capabilities of the game.

Storytelling was equally considered to be an important factor, especially as the game involves a book as the controller. Even though the game relied heavily on trying to invoke memories of the books and movies only two participants showed any interest while the rest tried to skip through from reading story related texts (and narration commenting). P4, the player most interested in the story, turned off the narration commenting that if the game involves a book, it should be about reading and not having it read. P5 stated: "it would be more interesting and fun to have a spell sandbox, where player could cast the spells they wish"; instead of having limited interactions throughout the storyline.

DISCUSSION

This study was of an exploratory nature, trying to understand and provide initial guidelines for the design of games involving hybrid input from both AR and physical controllers.

Based on our results, we provide five primary points followed by detailed explanation for the implementation and integration of the two-part interaction paradigm, summarized in Table 1.

Guideline #1 - Interactions should be robust
Guideline #2 – Mapped actions should be consistent
Guideline #3 – Actions should match user expectations
Guideline #4 – Instruction Language should be clear and contextually supported
Guideline #5 – Storyline should bind the experience

Table 1. Proposed Initial Design Guidelines.

Guideline #1 – Interactions should be robust

We observed some situations where the interactions required by players were poorly supported by the technology and unsuccessful as a result. For examples, players had placed the book in certain positions that caused the fiducial markers to be blocked from the camera, causing the virtual imagery to disappear, leading to player confusion and broken gameplay. Similar issues were present when players had to perform a gesture with the Move controller in a way that was hard for the camera to track (e.g., in the edges of camera view). Exposing the players to these limitations impoverish the game experience and should be minimized by either changing designs (e.g., modifying the level design), or steering players away from these potential pitfalls (e.g., replacing these interactions).

Guideline #2 – Mapped actions should be consistent

By having an input system that consists of two controllers, we looked at how well the mapped actions of both were closely intertwined. Several issues arose due to irregularity in button mapping, and movement tracking with participants citing the use of the Move as inconsistent. We propose that the actions that are provided within a hybrid game are kept in a **consistent and natural** manner. They should not be a showcase of the technological capabilities, but should instead prioritize consistency as well as being directed towards players' expectations, another guideline that we propose.

Guideline #3 – Actions should match user expectations

Some of the mapped actions leveraged by the controllers, like brushing off dust from the virtual book, did not raise problems in the players' expectations. However, some interactions that involved moving or displacing the book, such as peeking at a virtual hole in the book, broke the players' expectations. Based on this we suggest that where games rely on player expectations it is important that these expectations be well established or commonly understood by players.

Guideline #4 – Instruction Language should be clear and contextually supported

Various interaction mistakes resulted from the poor prompting of actions. To increase the success of the game, these instructions should be understandable and contextualized. This requirement also extends to instructions regarding how to manipulate the controllers. By providing clear instructions that cannot be subject to multiple interpretations, player's dissatisfaction, confusion and frustration can be avoided. For example, as mentioned in the result section, players made some mistakes, in response to unclear language. This error could have been avoided by visually prompting the tilting motion. Designing games that rely on narrative, or on instruction and prompting, should not leave room for ambiguities and contextual interpretations.

Guideline #5 – Storyline should bind the experience

We recognize that storytelling is often a complementary element to player experience with this hybrid controller. Whenever the previous guidelines are met, the story of the game, and the recollection of memorable moments from another medium the game draws from, will increase both the success of the game and of the controllers. In the case of Harry Potter, which is a well-known story, whenever a recollection occurred, players exhibited joy and excitement.

LIMITATIONS AND FUTURE WORK

Future iterations could look at the variations of the interaction with younger players, larger sample size and in a more natural environment. We expect not only that they will interact differently, but also that they may show different interests in other aspects of gameplay. Looking at longer play sessions might identify different types of issues than those we observed.

The Wonderbook is supported by other games, which use it as the main controller. Our future interest is to study these new interactions, improving or enhancing our proposed guidelines. For future work, in order to create more general guidelines, it will be useful to analyze games, which use a similar controller combination, but do not use the Move controller (e.g., in Diggs Nightcrawler), the Wonderbook or even neither. A game that uses fiducial marker cards with the Move controller would be another example. Nevertheless, with our preliminary study, we have proposed primary initial guidelines on which future research can build on.

ACKNOWLEDGMENTS

This research was supported by UOIT, NSERC, SSHRC IMMERSe and GRAND NCE for supporting this research. We would like to thank our participants for their contributions to this study.

REFERENCES

[1] Billinghurst, M., Kato, H., Poupyrev, I. The magicbook-moving seamlessly between reality and virtuality - Computer Graphics and Applications, IEEE, 2001

[2] Cairns, P., Li, J., Wang, W. and Nordin, I. 2014. The influence of controllers on immersion in mobile games. In Proceedings of the SIGCHI Conference on Human Factors in Computing Systems (CHI '14). ACM, New York, NY, USA, 371-380.

[3] Familiant, M.E. and Detweiler, M.C. Iconic reference: Evolving perspectives and an organizing framework. International Journal of Man-Machine Studies 39, 5 (1993), 705–728.

[4] Gaver, W. and College, R. Affordances for interaction: The Social is Material for Design. Ecological Psychology 8, 2 (1996), 111–129.

[5] Gerling, K. M., Klauser, M. and Niesenhaus, J. Measuring the impact of game controllers on player experience in FPS games. In Proc. of MindTrek (Tampere, Finland, 2011). ACM, 2011.

[6] Gregersen, A. and Grodal, T. Embodiment and Interface. In B. Perron and M.J.P. Wolf, eds., The Video Game Theory Reader 2. New York, NY, USA, 2009, 65–83.

[7] Ishii, H., Wisneski, C., Orbanes, J., Chun, B., and Paradiso, J. PingPongPlus: design of an athletic-tangible interface for computer-supported cooperative play. Proc. of CHI'99, ACM (1999), 394–401.

[8] Herrewijn L and Poels K (2014) Recall and recognition of in-game advertising: the role of game control. Front. Psychol. 4:1023. doi: 10.3389/fpsyg.2013.01023

[9] Limperos, A.M., Schmierbach, M.G., Kegerise, A.D., and Dardis, F.E. Gaming across different consoles: exploring the influence of control scheme on game-player enjoyment. Cyberpsychol Behav 14, 6 (2011), 345–350.

[10] McEwan, Mitchell, Johnson, Daniel, Wyeth, Peta, & Blackler, Alethea L. (2012) Videogame control device impact on the play experience. In Cermak-Sassenrath, Daniel & Walker, Charles (Eds.) Proceedings of The 8th Australasian Conference on Interactive Entertainment : Playing the System, ACM, Aotea Centre, Auckland, New Zealand, 18:1-18:3.

[11] Mirza-Babaei, P., Nacke, L.E., Gregory, J., Collins. N. and Fitzpatrick, G. How does it play better?: exploring user testing and biometric storyboards in games user research. In Proceedings of the SIGCHI Conference on Human Factors in Computing Systems (CHI '13). DOI=10.1145/2470654.2466200

[12] Nacke, L.E. and Lindley, C.A. Flow and Immersion in First-Person Shooters: Measuring the player's game-play experience. Proc. of Future Play '08, ACM (2008), 81–88.

[13] Nacke, L.E. (2010). Wiimote vs. controller: electroencephalographic measurement of affective gameplay interaction. In Proceedings of the International Academic Conference on the Future of Game Design and Technology (Futureplay '10). ACM, New York, NY, USA, 159-166. DOI=10.1145/1920778.1920801

[14] Nielsen, J. and Levy, J. (1994). Measuring usability, preference vs. performance. Communications of the ACM, 37(4).

[15] Pagulayan, R. J., Keeker, K., Wixon, D., & Romero, R. L. (2003). User-centered design in games. Handbook for Human-Computer Interaction in Interactive Systems.

[16] Peirce, C.S. Logic as Semiotic: The Theory of Signs. Dover Publications, New York, NY, USA, 1955. 7

[17] Vicencio-Moreira, R., Mandryk, R., Gutwin, C. and Bateman, S. 2014. The effectiveness (or lack thereof) of aim-assist techniques in first-person shooter games. In Proceedings of the SIGCHI Conference on Human Factors in Computing Systems (CHI '14). ACM, New York, NY, USA, 937-946.

[18] Rohs, M. Marker-based embodied interaction for handheld augmented reality games. Journal of Virtual Reality and Broadcasting, 2007

[19] Skalski, P., Tamborini, R., Shelton, A., Buncher, M., and Lindmark, P. Mapping the road to fun: Natural video game controllers, presence, and game enjoyment. New Media & Society 13, 2 (2010), 224–242.

[20] Zammitto, V., Mirza-Babaei, P., Livingston, I., Kobayashi, M., and Nacke, L.E. Player experience: mixed methods and reporting results. In CHI '14 Extended Abstracts on Human Factors in Computing Systems (CHI EA '14). ACM, New York, NY, USA, 147-150. DOI=10.1145/2559206.2559239

Around the World in 8 Workshops: Investigating Anticipated Player Experiences of Children

Christiane Moser
Christian Doppler Laboratory for "Contextual Interfaces"
HCI & Usability Unit, ICT&S Center, University of Salzburg
Salzburg, Austria
christiane.moser@sbg.ac.at

Yoram Chisik
Madeira Interactive Technologies Institute, University of Madeira,
Funchal, Portugal
ychisik@uma.pt

Manfred Tscheligi
Christian Doppler Laboratory for "Contextual Interfaces"
HCI & Usability Unit, ICT&S Center, University of Salzburg
Salzburg, Austria
manfred.tscheligi@sbg.ac.at

ABSTRACT

Player experience describes the qualities of player-game interaction and is typically evaluated during or after the game has been developed. Different approaches exist to improve and optimize player experience during the design process (e.g., design guidelines). However, the anticipated or expected player experience of users can also guide game developers and researcher in order to develop better games. A series of game ideation workshops with children aged 8 to 15 years was conducted in eight different locations around the world. The workshops produced video snippets, in which children explain their thoughts on possible game play scenarios of a game idea (i.e., anticipations and expectations). An initial content analysis of the videos highlights the game elements and playful experiences that contribute to the anticipated player experience of the children that should guide game developers and researchers.

Author Keywords

Game Ideation Workshops; Anticipated Player Experience; Children; Game Design; Video Analysis; Annotation

ACM Classification Keywords

H.5.m. [Information interfaces and presentation (e.g., HCI)]: Miscellaneous.

INTRODUCTION

Addressing user needs and evaluating design ideas based on user feedback are the corner stones of user-centered design (UCD) and positively influence user experience (UX). Roto et al. [17] recommend that anticipated interactions with different concept ideas should be taken into account during the earliest ideation and conceptualization phase of the design process. This point is further stressed by Karapanos et al. [8], who claim "*the act of anticipating an experience resulting in the formation of expectations, happens prior to any actual experience of use*" and can thus influence UX positively or negatively in case there is a conflict between actual experiences and expectations. However, the majority of current design and evaluation approaches aim at capturing UX when a user interacts with a system, i.e., at advanced stages of the design process.

CHI PLAY'14, October 19–21, 2014, Toronto, ON, Canada.

http://dx.doi.org/10.1145/2658537.2658702

Schell [19] noted that games enable player experience (PX) through interaction with game elements and/or other players, but the imagined (i.e., anticipated) PX is the reason for people to play. PX describes the qualities of the player-game interactions and is typically investigated during and after the interaction with games [13]. Currently, there are different approaches to improve and optimize PX in the design phase (e.g., [6, 9, 14, 15]), but they do not take into account anticipated PX. Thus, it would be beneficial to gain insights on anticipated PX by capturing it in an early phase of game design, i.e., idea generation and conceptualization.

Children are an important user group, as they are frequent and experienced users of games and other technologies [6]. In order to meet their needs and provide them a positive PX, an adequate consideration of their expectations in the game design process is necessary [11]. This objective is best achieved by incorporating children (as informants, design partners, etc.) before the game is ready for evaluation, allowing game developers and researchers to learn from children's ideas, anticipations, and expectations.

In this paper, we focus on the investigation of anticipated PX in videos produced during game ideation workshops with children [12]. The workshops were conducted in eight locations all over the world (as part of a special track at ACE 2013). In the videos, children explain their thoughts on possible gameplay scenarios of an idea and describe playful experiences. The aim of the videos is to provide game developers and researchers insights on children's thoughts and expectations in order to guide the game ideation phase [12]. We will illustrate how the outcomes of a video analysis can contribute to an initial understanding of anticipated PX of children for a game idea by annotating game elements and playful experiences.

RELATED WORK

Anticipated User Experience

According to Roto et al. [17], the term UX has been in use since the mid-1990s and has many different definitions. Our work follows the ISO Norm 9241-210, which defines it as "*a person's perceptions and responses that result from the use and/or anticipated use of a product, system or service.*"

In order to establish a systematic procedure for evaluating UX, Roto et al. [17] outlined four steps that should be performed: 1) obtaining a good understanding of UX, 2) defining UX metrics, 3) developing UX evaluation methods based on these metrics, and 4) integrating UX evaluations into the product development process. They noted two problems when evaluating UX in early phases of the product development process, i.e., the absence of interaction with the systems results in incomplete experiences and, as UX is context-dependent, its early evaluation suffers from losing many contextual components (e.g., the social and physical contexts of use). However, they argued that with only a rough system concept available, the evaluation of UX is already possible through assessing the value of the outcome of anticipated interactions. Karapanos et al. [8] defined anticipation as an additional facet of the dynamics of UX over time representing users' anticipation of an experience that leads to the formation of expectations before any actual user-product interaction occurs.

Later, Roto et al. [18] differentiated four time spans: 1) anticipated UX (i.e., imagining experience before usage), 2) momentary UX (i.e., experiencing during usage), 3) episodic UX (i.e., reflecting on an experience after usage), and 4) cumulative UX (i.e., recollecting multiple periods of use over time). In the following section, possibilities to capture anticipated UX are described.

Investigating Anticipated User Experience

Davis [4] was one of the first researchers that investigated attitude and anticipate behavior/usage of a system as part of perceived usefulness after the interaction with a system in the work context. However, only a small percentage of existing methods can be utilized to evaluate UX before usage [1, 5, 21]. A well-established method commonly used for evaluating early product concepts is experience prototyping. Buchenau and Fulton Suri [3] first introduced experience prototyping, a technique that emphasizes the active participation of designers, users, and clients in appreciating the experience of a product concept through prototypes. They pointed out three critical design activities in which experience prototyping is useful: 1) understanding existing UX and context, 2) exploring and evaluating design alternatives, and 3) communicating design ideas.

Roto et al. [17] mentioned two methods for evaluating UX of early product concepts, i.e., expert evaluation (relying on experts' ability to evaluate UX as a subjective construct and predict how users will experience a certain concept) and remote online evaluation. Yogasara [22] explored ways in which users anticipate their experiences with a desired future product without the use of scenarios or prototypes, i.e., the design and usage contexts are entirely conceived by the users themselves. He discovered, for example, that the desired product and intended use of it are the most dominant aspects in the formation of anticipated UX and that the users' needs and expectation have a strong influence on the process of anticipating experiences. Therefore, he recommended exploring users' anticipated UX, as the insights derived from this exploration can help to predict users' underlying needs and obtain design ideas.

Anticipated Player Experience

PX or user's gameplay experience describes the qualities of the player-game interactions (e.g., the importance of different factors like enjoyment, flow, immersion, or curiosity). It can be investigated by assessing reflective and reflexive responses of players during and after the interaction with games [13]. Read [16], for example, assessed the willing to play the game again (anticipated usage) with the again and again table.

Mäyrä [10] argued that there is a need for a more comprehensive view on PX, as it should not only take place during actual gameplay (i.e., it is a more comprehensive phenomenon). Schell [19] explained that the anticipated experiences are the reason for people to play games. In order to gain a more holistic view on PX, the anticipated PX should also be investigated in early phases of game design (e.g., during ideation). Anticipated PX, in our understanding, is related to expectations created from previous experiences with games and other sources of information (e.g., brands).

Typically, designers try to anticipate and assess the users' experiences with the game being designed through empathizing with them when developing game concepts. While this ability to empathize is fast, not resource intensive (i.e., requiring no users), and easy to implement, its comprehensiveness is questionable from a UCD perspective, as designers are not the target users. For game developers and researchers, it would be beneficial to capture PX already in the game idea/concept phase in order to learn from the users' anticipated PX. In the following section, we will introduce how the outcomes of the game ideation workshops [12] can contribute to an initial understanding of anticipated PX of children for a game idea.

GAME IDEATION WORKSHOPS

While Roto et al. [17] defined one or more initial concept from designers (e.g., in the form of visual scenarios, draft UI specifications, or physical mock-ups) as a prerequisite for early concept evaluation of UX, we will illustrate how it is also possible to capture insights on anticipated PX with the help of game ideation workshops [12] in which users come up with game ideas (similar to [22]). The ideation workshop concept for the design of games, proposed by Moser [12], combines two child-centered game development approaches [11], which aim at 1) enabling participatory design with children and 2) creating creative and tangible low-fidelity prototypes of game ideas. The outputs are reported in the form of video snippets providing insights about children's thoughts on gameplay in order to better meet their expectations and needs [12].

Around the World in 8 Workshops

The concept for the game ideation workshop [12] was submitted to the kids' workshops at ACE 2013 (a special track for concepts to conduct creative workshops with children). The workshop chairs sought researchers and practitioners from all around the world, who would voluntarily organize a workshop in their own country before the conference and one in Enschede during in order to collect a large variety of video snippets reflecting a wide range of cultural perspectives and expectations. In total, 8 workshops were conducted in the following locations: Freilassing (Germany), Enschede (Netherlands), Funchal (Madeira, Portugal), Kingston (Ontario, Canada), Porto Alegre & São Paulo (Brazil), Nairobi (Kenya), and Lahore (Pakistan). Before the workshops, the children and their parents were provided with an information sheet about the workshops and asked for their informed consent.

An average of 25 to 35 children (average school class size in the different countries) attended the workshops with the exception of the large scale workshop conducted in Enschede (76 children) during the conference (see Figure 1) and the two small scale workshop conducted in Kingston and Nairobi (10 and 11 children respectively) before the conference. The Funchal, Lahore, Porto Alegre and Freilassing workshops were held in a school with the children from one or two classes. In Kingston and Nairobi the children were invited to visit a research lab. The workshops in Enschede and São Paulo were conducted in community centers. The age of the children ranged from 8 to 15 with some groups having a large variation in age and others being rather homogenous (e.g., the workshops in the schools). In Freilassing the workshop was conducted in an all-girls school, while all others were mixed gender.

Figure 1. Introduction in Enschede with 76 children

In all the workshops, the children were divided into groups of four to six children and asked to think of game ideas related to their favorite places in town that they would like to show to visiting children and explore in a playful way in their summer vacation. Each group created storyboards and a game idea prototype that was recorded in a 2-5 minute video snippet, illustrating the game idea and a gameplay sequence. In total, the ideation workshops produced more than two hours of video snippets that provide a broad spectrum of expectations and anticipations regarding gameplay for their game idea. The applied procedure in the workshops is explained in more detail in the following.

Procedure

In the beginning of each workshop, the topic for the game (favorite places in town) was explained to the children, providing them with a starting point for thinking of game ideas. A topic description consisting of a nondescript narrative (i.e., no concrete mechanics or setting) and several questions (e.g., what are your favorite places in town, where will you take visiting children? why? or how can you make other children curios to visit your favorite places?) was handed out. The sheet left enough room for imagination in order to easily come up with game ideas and provided a consistent starting point. Afterwards, groups of four to six children were formed, which started to brainstorm game ideas (see Figure 2). They then selected one idea to design within the workshop. In the following section, the different steps performed in the workshops are described.

Figure 2. Children in Nairobi (top) and Porto Alegre (bottom) brainstorming in small groups

Step 1: Game Progress Storyboards

In a first step, the groups were provided with empty storyboards (see Figure 3). The game progress storyboards [11] aimed at illustrating or highlighting certain aspects of the game idea (e.g., gameplay scenes). They illustrate a short sequence of interactions within the game for their idea, in order to build the game prototype.

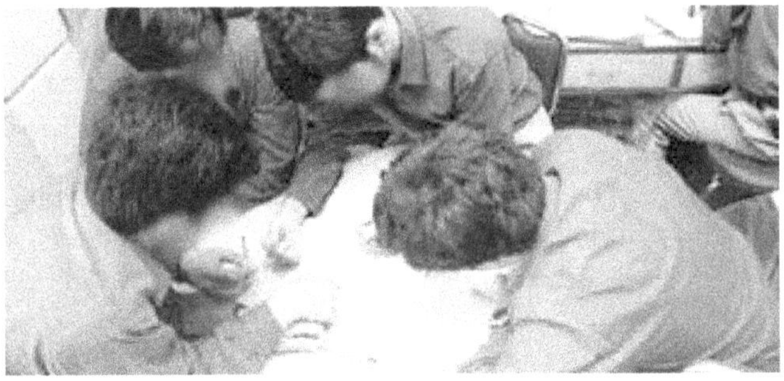

Figure 3. Children in Lahore creating storyboards

Step 2: Creative low-fidelity Prototypes

The creative low-fidelity prototypes [11] are sketchy, incomplete, and quickly built working models of game aspects to illustrate gameplay and describe what the player expects to happen in the game. Therefore, the children were provided with Playmais®, Playdough®, Lego®, and other creative material to create the prototypes (see Figure 4).

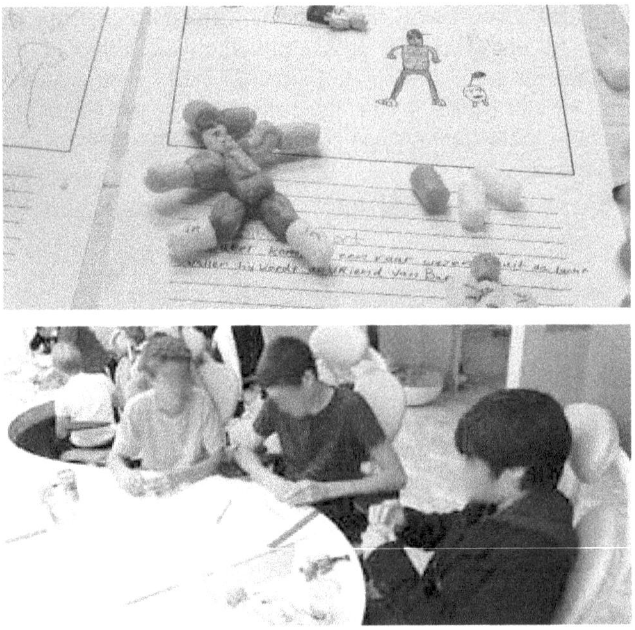

Figure 4. Children in Freilassing (top) and Kingston (bottom) creating prototypes

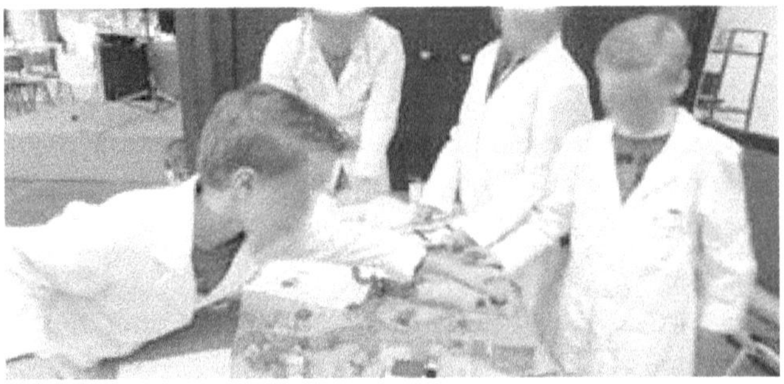

Figure 5. Children in Enschede trying out their prototypes

In playing with the prototypes the children could try out game mechanics (see Figure 5) and actively discover problems or challenges in the gameplay, which can affect their PX with the game later on.

Step 3: Video snippets

In the end, the creative, low-fidelity prototypes were filmed by the workshop organizers, while the children were playing (reenacting) the game sequence of the storyboard (see Figure 6). For filming, the children assigned roles to each other, i.e., one director (storyteller), one or more players (moving the character), and artists moving around the other game elements.

Figure 6. Producing the videos with the children in Freilassing

Finally, the workshop organizers edited the videos, e.g., cutting them, adding subtitles with English translations (if needed) and any additional contextual information about the location or the evolution of the idea. This should enable the developers and researchers watching the videos to understand the ideas of the children and avoid misinterpretation due to lack of local knowledge or skills.

Game Jam during ACE conference

The workshops culminated with a 16-hour game jam (held during the conference), in which a team of four students from the University of Twente developed a game prototype for mobile devices inspired by half of the videos. Due to the limited amount of time and lack of a defined strategy to process the videos, they were not able to watch and properly assimilate the large number of videos produced. The developed game prototype was provided to all conference attendees and later to all eight workshop organizers, whereof some shared it with the children.

In this paper, we focus on the analysis of the videos with regard to anticipated PX of the children in order to investigate elements and playful experiences that should guide the design process. We will not discuss the experiences of the game jam participants, the workshop organizers or participants, and conference attendees who had access to the game, as we are still collecting feedback.

INSIGHTS ON ANTICIPATED PLAYER EXPERIENCE

As game developers and researchers try to design for experiences, their goal is to decipher essential elements that define the experiences and find ways to make them part of the game design [19]. The videos of the game ideation workshops illustrate and report children's thoughts on possible gameplay scenarios, which can help to better meet their game expectations and guide the game design.

We believe that the short narrative videos provide insights on how children envision their experience with the game. As we had access to the videos, we were able to investigate the anticipated PX of children for game ideas around their favorite places in town. We used the lenses of game design of Schell [19] and the categories for playful user experience of Korhonen et al. [9] in order to annotate the videos for discovering game elements and experiences that contribute to the anticipated PX of children. The lenses of Schell [19] help game designers to focus on the different aspects of game design by providing questions to elaborate the aspect. The categories for playful user experience of Korhonen et al. [9] help game designers to come up with new game ideas by combining different experiences in the gameplay.

Two game researchers (authors of this paper) independently annotated the videos using VideoAnt (http://ant.umn.edu/), applying a topic coding strategy to find information related to a specific topic. We annotated game elements addressing lenses of game design and player experiences addressing playful user experience categories in order to investigate insights on anticipated PX.

For a first content analysis, 31 video snippets from six workshops (total 60.02 minutes) were watched and analyzed with a total of 370 annotations. Due to time constraints, we have not annotated the videos from Enschede and São Paulo. Annotations were assigned to one or more lenses of game design [19] and playful user experience categories [9] (indicated in *italic* in the findings below). Therefore, some findings are redundant. Possible cultural differences were not taken into account for this analysis, as we were not interested in a comparative analysis at this point. Below, we provide selected insights from the analysis. These are not presented as generalizations, but rather as an example of the potential of the game ideation workshop videos to capture insights on anticipated PX.

Lens of action (78 annotations) helps to understand what the player is able to do in the game and why, for example:

- Movement in the game incorporating directions (e.g., slide up for jump, left/right to go left/right, down for move), avoiding obstacles (addressing also the *lens of obstacles*), and sliding down objects (e.g., water pipes).
- Interaction with elements of the game world by, for example, grabbing artifacts (e.g., a treasure, coins, or token), putting them in specific places, clicking on and selecting items in order to get information (e.g., for sights or artifacts), or create elements.
- Making decisions in the game (often related to the *lens of challenge*) (e.g., where to go and search in the game for the treasure, accept a quest or not, which way to take in a maze, or to search for someone) or possibility to choose between options (e.g., in a menu), answer questions, unlock something (e.g., level or mini-games), or take pictures in the game (see example in Figure 7).
- Interaction with the child's own character (i.e., *nurture* through sleeping or eating) and other characters (e.g., talking).

Figure 7. Game to explore Lahore

Lens of Story (54 annotations) helps to find out in which stories children are interested and when a story was needed, e.g., to support the understanding of other parts of the game and explain the focus, for example:

- A lot of *hero's journeys* (also a lens of game design with 17 annotations) were introduced as a story (e.g., the king, who ruled over an archipelago of 9 islands – see Figure 8, gets kidnapped and the two players have to save him by travelling from island to island, or a foreigner settles in Lahore and has to visit different places by accepting and solving quests – see example in Figure 9).
- Others were treasure-hunting stories (e.g., the player has to go to different places in town to do missions and find the key for the treasure).
- Several stories were about companions in the game (e.g., the player has to travel with Mr. Butt – a game character – to different, legendary, and fun places to follow cues like the fortune letter).
- Some stories served as an overall story to build a link between a series of mini-games (e.g., the story was about getting to know the local nature of Germany with mini-games about animal sounds, plants, fruits, etc. see example in Figure 13).

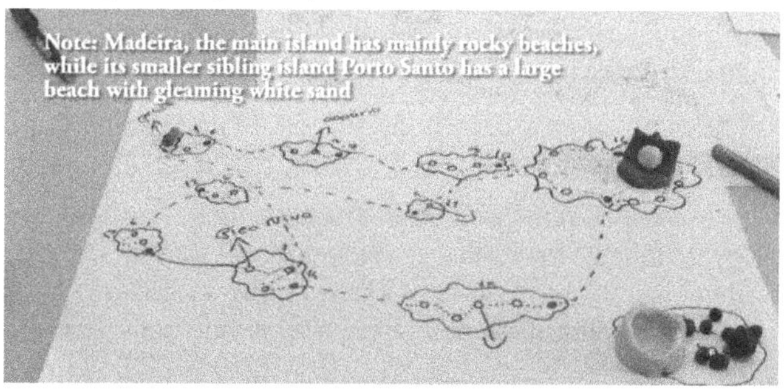

Figure 8. Game about a kidnapped king from Funchal

Lens of goals (48 annotations) helps to identify, which (series of) goals children want to achieve within games and how they are related to each other. Reaching a goal is closely related to *completion* (20 annotations), for example:

- Learn something about and get interested in local nature, food, historical places, or main sights through 1) exploring the game (strongly related to *exploration*) or 2) solving riddles or quests (strongly related to the *lens of puzzle*, see example in Figure 9).
- In a *hero's journeys* (also a lens of game design), the player has to get something back (e.g., the key to the treasure or the king that was kidnapped) or find a treasure, hidden places, and secrets in the game.
- Collect as many points as possible, for example, to buy something for your character (related to *lens of character transformation* and *lens of economy*).
- Get as far as possible by avoiding obstacles (e.g., in a car race through a city avoid other cars, people, etc., which is strongly related to the *lens of obstacle*) or find a safe path (being related to the *lens of triangularity*, i.e., giving the player the choice to play safe for low reward or take risk for big reward).
- Collaborate (related to *lens of cooperation*, 6 annotations) with other characters or players (e.g., talk to people in the game to get answers, save the king or local animals together with the other player).
- Finish a timed mini-game, such as one minute (related to the *lens of time* and the *lens of challenge*), in order to unlock new mini-games.

Figure 9. Game about solving puzzles about Lahore

Lens of challenge/challenge (36 annotations) is about developing and exercising skills in challenging situations and provides insights about how children want to be challenged in games, for example, by:

- The increase of difficulty by successful *completion* (e.g., for each mini-game, or the better the player gets).
- The combination with *lens of puzzle* (e.g., recognizing local animal traces/leaves/rinds/insects, answer quizzes about sights of Lahore - see example in Figure 9, or solving riddles in the real world to continue in the game).
- The hide and seek principle (e.g., quests with finding objects by exploring the game world).
- The avoidance of *obstacles* (also a lens with 15 annotations, see example in Figure 10) or finding the path through a maze to continue a journey.

Figure 10. Jump & run game from Kingston

Lens of the world (33 annotations) is the doorway to the magic place that exists only in the imagination of the players. The findings were not very surprising due to the chosen topic (favorite places in town). Examples are:

- Most of the game worlds consist of characteristics taken from the real world (e.g., the city center – see example in Figure 11, local surrounding of cities – see Figure 8). Other games copied certain details of the real world (e.g., sights or landmarks of cities – see Figure 9, famous, or exciting places like beneath the streets of Lahore).
- Most of the games incorporated other characters and fictious or exciting artifacts in the game world in order to solve quests and challenges (e.g., find the key for the treasure by talking to people, by looking beneath and behind objects, or avoid the quicksand).

Figure 11. Game about city center of Kingston

Lens of reward (23 annotations) helps to find out when and what kind of reward should be given in the game, for example:

- Achieve a reward to continue in the game or as a bonus (e.g., lives – see example in Figure 12, or health packs) when completing the game, level, quest, or challenge.
- Base rewards on performance (e.g., gold medal for the winner or ranking in the highscore list – related to *lens of competition*, 6 annotations) and unlock game parts.
- Earn points in order to customize the character (related to *lens of economy*).

Figure 12. Game under the streets of Lahore

Exploration (18 annotations) is about exploring or investigating the game world, affordances, or situations and provides insights about what children would like to explore in a game and how, for example:

- A virtual world or interactive map that shows a real city or country (related to the *lens of world*) in order to learn something about local nature (see example in Figure 13), food, historical , or main sights.
- Through playful exploration inside the game (e.g., solving quests with information available in the game, like text, pictures as well as stories from other characters, or finding the way through a maze).
- Through playful exploration outside the game (e.g., solving riddles with information available in the real world or by performing activities in the real world, like finding the oldest locomotion in a museum).

Figure 13. Game about animals and plants from Freilassing

Lens of avatar/Expression (17 annotations) helps to build up a special relationship with the character in the game. This was addressed by, for example:

- The possibility to choose a character (e.g., different characters from known games, or one for girls and one for boys) or to create a character.
- The possibility to buy/earn items for customization (e.g., the collected coins are used to customize the clothing of the character – see example in Figure 14)
- The possibility to upgrade a character (e.g., the collected points make the character stronger)

Figure 14. Game exploring the city of Porto Alegre

Lens of rules (14 annotations) helps to understand how children would structure the game in terms of game mechanics, for example:

- In most of the *hero's journey* games, the player lost lives for wrong behavior when failing to avoid obstacles, or even had to start all over again (also *lens of punishment*, 7 annotations).
- The possibilities to collect points, like combo items double the points or refill character traits when reaching certain gameplay points (e.g., on a certain level the energy of the character is refilled).
- Clicking on items provides extra information (e.g., click on a place/waypoint in the game to display information – related to *lens of virtual interface*).
- Multiple players have to do the same thing at the same time (e.g., completing a quest by dancing in the same rhythm – see example in Figure 15).

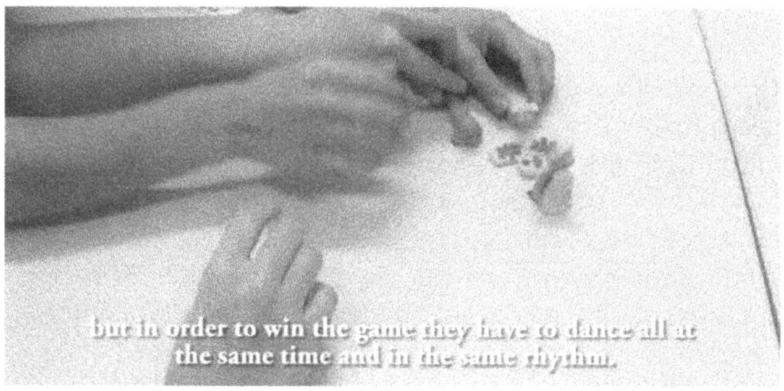

Figure 15. Game about finding the magic domino (Funchal)

Lens of economy (8 annotations) helps to understand how the children want to earn money in order to customize or upgrade the character (related to the *lens of character transformation*, 4 annotations), for example:

- Find and collect coins on the path to the goal, perform tasks (e.g., take pictures) or play mini-games in the game (see example in Figure 7) in order to earn money.

Several of the ideas were related to *Fantasy* (e.g., a cat and a dog searching for a magic domino). The children in these cases preferred to have a mix of fantasy and reality (i.e., a touch of fantasia is added to a realistic setting in order to make it more appealing or interesting).

The classification and annotation of the identified findings according to the lenses of game design [19] and playful user experience categories [9] helped to structure the findings in order to guide the game design. In the following sections, the described insights are discussed to reveal the potential of the game ideation workshops to investigate anticipated PX.

DISCUSSION

Below, we discuss the gained insights from the video analysis of the game idea workshops and what should be taken away from our research.

Capturing Experiences

The game idea workshops provide a similar outcome to experience prototyping [3], which is a technique that emphasizes the active participation of designers and users in appreciating the experience of a concept through prototypes. The game idea workshops enable children to come up with their own game ideas built upon their imagination and pre-experiences. In comparison to experience prototyping, the low-fidelity prototypes are created by children and contain essential game elements, which are dominant aspects influencing their expected or anticipated PX. The prototype can simulate certain aspects of what children want to experience while playing one sequence of the game. The produced videos enable children to describe their experiences with the prototype. These experiences are focused around specific artifacts, elements, or functions (i.e., game elements). By analyzing these experiences and according game elements, we gained insights on their anticipated PX.

In contrast to experience prototyping, designers are not necessarily part of the game idea workshops. Although, they might miss the opportunity to talk to the children or make discoveries themselves when interacting with the prototype, the videos enable designers to observe the interactive behavior and can provide inspiration. The video analysis of the workshops additionally enables capturing insights related to anticipated PX in a structured way to guide the game development. We intend to explore conducting a series of iterative workshops, which would build upon one another and allow the designers to engage in a more elaborate design process with the children.

Anticipations and Expectations

In interaction design, anticipations and expectations have been acknowledged to be important aspects of UX [22]. Anticipation is, thereby, the act of forming expectations before actual user-product interaction [8].

Typically, designers try to anticipate and assess the users' experiences with the game being designed through empathizing with them when developing the game concept. For the favorite places in town game they would try to solve questions, such as which genre should the game have (e.g., action, adventure, strategy, or role-play), should it be a serious game, why would children like to play the game, or how can children be challenged in the game.

We investigated which game elements (described with the lenses of game design) and playful experiences (described with the playful user experience categories) are important for children in their game ideas. These findings contribute the understanding about anticipated PX of children around the topic of favorite places and activities in town. The following examples illustrate what we learned about anticipations and expectations of children.

- The videos enabled the children to tell the story around the game ideas, which contained most of the anticipations about what will be happening in the game (e.g., describing the journeys of heroes). The story is very important for them in order to introduce the goal, challenges, etc. related to favorite places of a town.
- The interaction with the creative low-fidelity prototype revealed the importance of taking decisions in several game ideas that was often related to the goal of the game and the diverse challenges in it. This shows that children want to actively influence what is happening in the game and not just to follow the flow of the game (e.g., in jump & run games) when they explore favorite places.
- The goals of the games were related to the overall game topic (favorite places in town). The children expected to learn something from the game about culture, historical places, local sights, nature through puzzles, playful exploration inside and outside the game, or strolling around in the game world. These insights reveal the necessity for serious game aspects related to learning (which might be influenced by the context some workshops took place in, e.g., schools).
- The videos provided a lot of hints how children want to be challenged, like through increasing difficulty, avoiding obstacles, solving puzzles, or finding things. Strongly related are the rewards for successful challenges and the possibility to collect points for customizing the character. These findings show that children anticipate being challenged by a variety of different game aspects and want to play a customizable character.
- The interactions with the creative low-fidelity prototype also revealed some rules that children anticipated for the gameplay (e.g., what happens when the game character loses a life).

These examples illustrate the potential of the game ideation workshops to capture anticipation and expectation of children for their game ideas and, thereby, reveal important game elements contributing to the future anticipated PX of children. These elements and playful experiences should guide game developers and researchers in order to ensure that expectations of children are addressed.

Pre-experience matters

Anticipated PX is of course greatly influenced by previous experiences [18]. This supports with the observation we made, when annotating the videos. There is a divide of games ideas according to age. Many of the game ideas from 8 to 12 year old children dealt with fantasy and fairy tale worlds. If gameplay included killing other characters, it tended to be presented in a fairy tale or abstract symbolic form rather than being very realistic. This observation is in line with the rating of games approved for children aged 6 and above by the Entertainment Software Self-Regulation Body USK (http://www.usk.de/en/). These games mainly involve family-friendly games with exciting and competitive gameplay (e.g., via faster game speeds and more complex tasks), such as racing, simulation, jump & run, and role-playing games.

The game ideas gathered from 12 to 14 year old children are much more realistic, they reflect more upon real life than fantasy and can be easily transferred into everyday life (e.g., learn something about the local culture/history). The gameplay is structured in a more complex manner, requiring abstract and logical thinking or making decisions. If gameplay included killing other characters, it remained recognizably unrealistic, i.e., not capable of being transferred into everyday life (e.g., the game robots vs. zombies, defending fortresses in Lahore). This is also in line with the rating of games approved for children aged 12 to 16 by the USK.

This can be seen as a limitation in terms of inspiration, but the gained insights form the video analysis are based on the pre-experiences of children and reveal what children expect from a game in terms of game elements. In the end, the game developers and researchers can decide to which degree they want to build their game idea on the children's anticipated PX and their preferred game elements.

Video Analysis Approach

For the first content analysis of the videos, we applied a topic coding strategy using the lenses of game design of Schell [19] and the playful user experience categories of Korhonen et al. [9] to gather information about important game elements and playful experiences related to the anticipated PX of children. In our analysis, we did not want to annotate every single game element or playful experience, but rather the most important ones children put special emphasize on. When we watched the videos for the first time, we were also overwhelmed by the richness of the videos and we could only remember certain highlights. However, the summarized findings provided us a more structured overview of important game element and gameplay experiences. Thereby, we learned a lot about anticipated PX of children.

As both researchers were familiar with the work of Schell [19] and Korhonen et al. [9], they could easily annotate the findings. However, the large number of 100 lenses was difficult to handle even for us experienced researchers. Therefore, it is possible that we overlooked potential interesting finding for lenses not yet addressed. For our next analysis, we intend to explore ways of managing this complexity and explore other frameworks and methodologies for annotating the videos (e.g., [2]).

At this stage, we also did not look at the cultural differences between the workshops, nor did we attempt to evaluate the quality of our findings. We found assessing the quality of the creative work challenging and, therefore, focused on the potential of game ideation workshop videos to capture insights on anticipated PX of children. We intend to revisit the videos analyzed in this paper and those we have not had the opportunity to analyze yet and conduct a more comprehensive analysis of the videos and the reactions they generate by game designers and researchers.

CONCLUSION

The videos generated in the eight workshops all around the world vividly captured the envisioned gameplay of the game ideas proposed by the children. Some explicitly described anticipated PX (i.e., what the player want to experience), while others highlighted game elements contributing to anticipated PX. The game ideation workshops proved to be a source of great joy to the participating children and amazed, as well as fascinated the organizers. The game design and development students, who participated in the game jam, were overwhelmed by the number of videos (due to the short time period available to watch them during the game jam) and very fascinated about the content (same as we were when watching them for the first time). They regretted that they did not have more time to focus in more detail on the game elements and ideas expressed in the videos in their game prototype.

Our video content analysis illustrates the potential of the game ideation workshops to capture children gameplay anticipations and expectations in the earliest stages of the design process. We can conclude that the investigation of anticipated PX through annotating game elements and playful experiences in the videos worked out satisfyingly. The classification and annotation of the identified findings according the lenses of game design [19] and playful user experience categories [9] was adequate for us and fairly easy to perform (being familiar with the lenses and categories). We encourage other researchers to apply our analysis approach to investigate game elements and playful experiences children anticipate with a game idea in order to get a more holistic view on them and not just work with the most prominent observed issues after having watched the videos for the first time.

In light of the success of the workshops and the promising structured insights derived from the annotation and analysis of the videos, we plan to: 1) continue the work we have begun in analyzing the set of videos generated by the workshops, by annotating those we have not annotated yet;

2) explore other classification and annotation frameworks as well as analysis approaches; 3) investigate how these early stage findings support game developers and researchers to design for a better PX; and 4) conduct a second series of workshops and a game jam building up on what we have learned so far.

ACKNOWLEDGEMENTS

This works was partially funded by the Games4School Project of the Austrian Ministry of Science in course of the educational project "Sparkling Science" and by the Federal Ministry of Economy, Family and Youth, and the National Foundation for Research, Technology and Development (Christian Doppler Laboratory for Contextual Interfaces).

We owe a special debt of gratitude to the following individuals: António Gomes; Johannes van Staveren; Juliette Wanyiri; Kagonya Awori; Márcia Azevedo; Mônica Puoli; Rebeca Sá; Rui Branco; Shibli Mansuri; Thais Reali; and the following organizations; Escola Basica dos 2 e 3 Ciclos dos Louros, Funchal; Human Media Lab, Queens University, Kingston; iHub UX Lab, Nairobi; La Salle School, Porto Alegre; Liga Solidária, São Paulo; Mädchenrealschule Freilassing; Resource Academia, Lahore; University of Twente and Zabuki Enschede for helping us conduct the workshops and those who supported them for whom there is no space on this paper but there will always be space in our hearts. Last but not least we thank all the children who participated in the workshops and shared their imagination, exuberance and insights with us.

REFERENCES

1. Bargas-Avila, J.A. and Hornbæk, K. Foci and blind spots in user experience research. *Interactions*, 19, 6 (2012), 24-27.
2. Beck, E., Moser, C. and Tscheligi, M. Memoing and Lenses: Two Approaches for Exploring Player-Generated Game Ideas in Videos. In *Proc. ACE 2014*, ACM (2014).
3. Buchenau, M. and Fulton Suri, J. Experience prototyping. In *Proc. DIS'00*, ACM (2000), 424-433.
4. Davis, F.D. A technology acceptance model for empirically testing new end-user information systems: Theory and results (Doctoral dissertation, Massachusetts Institute of Technology), 1985.
5. Hassenzahl, M., Platz, A., Burmester, M. and Lehner, K. Hedonic and ergonomic quality aspects determine a software's appeal. In *Proc. CHI'00*. ACM (2000), 201-208.
6. Isbister, K. and Schaffer, N. Game usability: Advancing the player experience, Taylor & Francis US, 2008.
7. Jensen, J.J. and Skov, M.B. A review of research methods in children's technology design. In *Proc. IDC'05*, ACM (2005), 80-87.
8. Karapanos, E., Zimmerman, J., Forlizzi, J., and Martens, J.-B. User experience over time: an initial framework. In *Proc. CHI'09*, ACM (2009), 729-738.
9. Korhonen, H., Montola, M. and Arrasvuori, J. Understanding playful user experience through digital games. In *Proc. DPPI 2009*, ACM (2009), 274-285.
10. Mäyrä, F. The contextual game experience: On the socio-cultural contexts for meaning in digital play. In *Proc. DiGRA 2007*, (2007), 810-814.
11. Moser, C. Child-Centered Game Development (CCGD): Developing Games with Children at School. *Personal and Ubiquitous Computing,* 17, 8 (2013), 1647-1661.
12. Moser, C. Children Ideation Workshop. In *Proc. ACE 2013*. Springer International Publishing (2013), 592-599.
13. Nacke, L.E., Drachen, A., Kuikkaniemi, K., Niesenhaus, J., Korhonen, H. J., Hoogen, V.D.W., Poels, K., IJsselsteijn, W.A. and Kort, Y. Playability and player experience research. In *Proc. DiGRA 2009*, (2009).
14. Pedersen, C., Togelius, J. and Yannakakis, G.N. Optimization of Platform Game Levels for Player Experience. In *Proc. AIIDE 2009*, AAAI (2009), 191-192.
15. Pedersen, C., Togelius, J. and Yannakakis, G.N. Modeling player experience for content creation. *Computational Intelligence and AI in Games, IEEE Transactions on,* 2, 1 (2010), 54-67.
16. Read, J. C. Validating the Fun Toolkit: an instrument for measuring children's opinions of technology. *Cognition, Technology & Work*, 10, 2 (2008), 119-128.
17. Roto, V., Rantavuo, H., and Väänänen-Vainio-Mattila, K. Evaluating user experience of early product concepts. In Proc. DPPI'09, ACM (2009), 199-208.
18. Roto, V., Law, E., Vermeeren, A.P.O.S., and Hoonhout, J. User experience white paper: Bringing clarity to the concept of user experience. *Dagstuhl Seminar on Decraminting User Experience 2010*, published (2011).
19. Schell, J. *The Art of Game Design: A book of lenses.* CRC Press, 2008.
20. Vermeeren, A.P.O.S., Cremers, A.H.M., Kort, J., and Fokker, J.E. Comparing UX measurements, a case study. In *Proc. COST294-MAUSE International Workshop on Meaningful Measures: Valid Useful User Experience Measurement (VUUM)*, 18, (2008), 72-78.
21. Vermeeren, A.P.O.S., Law, E., Roto, V., Obrist, M., Hoonhout, J., and Väänänen-Vainio-Mattila, K. User experience evaluation methods: Current state and development needs. In *Proc. NordiCHI'10*, ACM (2010), 521-530.
22. Yogasara, T. Anticipated user experience in the early stages of product development. PhD Thesis (2014).

Beyond Designing for Motivation: The Importance of Context in Gamification

Chad Richards[1], Craig W. Thompson[2], T.C. Nicholas Graham[1]

[1]School of Computing
Queen's University
Kingston, ON, Canada

[2]Computer Science and
Computer Engineering Department
University of Arkansas
Fayetteville, AR, USA

chad.richards@queensu.ca, cwt@uark.edu, nicholas.graham@queensu.ca

ABSTRACT

Most design advice for the development of successful gamification systems has focused on how best to engage the end user while imbuing the system with playfulness. This paper argues that it is also critical for designers to focus on the broad context of the system's deployment, including the identification of stakeholder requirements, requirements from the hosting organization, deep understanding of the diversity of the target population, understanding of limits in the agency of the target users, and constraints arising from the post-deployment environment. To illustrate the importance of such contextual and stakeholder analysis, the paper presents issues and associated solutions that were discovered through the creation of a children's nutrition and fitness education gamification system. The problems identified through a broad analysis of context significantly altered the design of the system and led to the realization that the initially conceptualized project would have been unusable. The paper concludes with concrete lessons for designers.

Author Keywords

Gamification; contextual design; educational games.

ACM Classification Keywords

H.5.m [Information Systems and Presentations (e.g., HCI)]: Miscellaneous; K.8.0 [Personal Computing]: Games

Gamification, the use of design elements characteristic of games in non-game contexts [9], has become an increasingly popular research area. Gamification provides a novel way to engage users and solve real-world problems in areas such as defense [15], education [18], healthcare [11, 31], and scientific research [30]. Research into successful gamification techniques has primarily focused on how best to engage the end user [1, 8, 17, 27] using internal (autonomy, competence, and relatedness) and external (badges, point systems, leaderboards, levels, and quests) motivators [1, 8, 17, 27] and how to make the user's activity entertaining through gameplay [8, 19, 22, 25, 31]. In this paper, we argue that in addition to motivational constructs and entertainment value, gamification systems—tools used to gamify activities—need to consider their *context of deployment*. While this is well established in the field of computer-human interaction, context in design has, to date, received little attention in the field of gamification.

To illustrate the importance of context in designing a gamification system, we report on our experience in the design of *Edufitment*, a framework for educating children in nutrition and fitness. For instance, Edufitment was initially intended for deployment in school classrooms. We aimed to improve the diets of the targeted children by teaching nutrition using a game. However, investigations with our stakeholders revealed that 94% of the targeted children were eligible for free or reduced-cost lunch programs. This reduced the children's ability to choose what they ate during school hours. Had we designed the framework as initially intended, there could have been a large disconnect between the types of foods our program taught the children to eat and the types of foods the children had the option of eating.

This represents just one of numerous examples of how information gleaned from stakeholders and from consideration of the context of deployment was critically influential on the design of the system.

As another example, our experts in nutrition advocated that we follow the popular *We Can!* program due to its national support and proven effectiveness [16, 26]. *We Can!*, however, features a policy of reducing screen time for children [26]. To meet this screen time requirement, our stakeholders imposed a fifteen minute daily gameplay limit. This required us to completely rethink the structure of Edufitment, moving from a single, monolithic game to a framework encapsulating a set of smaller, shorter games, each with a focused educational message.

CHI PLAY '14, October 19 - 22 2014, Toronto, ON, Canada

ACM 978-1-4503-3014-5/14/10...$15.00.
http://dx.doi.org/10.1145/2658537.2658683

To facilitate a development process informed by broad investigation of context, our team involved experts in nursing, education, statistics, psychology, nutrition, kinesiology, and computer science. As suggested by Rojas et al., external factors, such as context and choice of platform, and internal factors, such as stakeholder requirements and project goals, necessarily make an iterative process out of a complex intervention involving gamification [28]. We followed an iterative process, meeting weekly for brainstorming and discussion sessions. Group members were assigned tasks involving gathering and interpreting contextual information such as which schools should be involved, the makeup of the student body at these schools, and what guidelines should be followed to provide nutritional advice for children. Each member reported their findings and highlighted any issues discovered. A designated member took minutes of the session to record design issues and solutions. These issues were tackled as a group, and we then assigned new tasks to group members.

This paper is organized as follows. We first consider related work in gamification, arguing that research in this area has focused on motivational constructs to support desired behaviors and techniques to enhance the entertainment value of gamification systems. We further argue that considerably less attention has been paid to the context of deployment. We then describe the background of the Edufitment project and briefly describe the design of the Edufitment system. The core of the paper then explores issues we discovered through our investigation of the broad context of the Edufitment project and discusses our solutions to these issues. Finally, we present lessons learned from this investigative process.

RELATED WORK

Gamification is an evolving term that is used to describe the process of taking motivational mechanics from games such as badges, leaderboards, levels and points and applying them in a non-game context. Gamification does not necessarily involve the creation of a game; a leaderboard can easily be added to a non-game activity, such as jogging [6, 11] or managing a to-do list [25]. Reasons for gamifying applications include motivating people to change behavior or develop skills, increasing brand loyalty, or increasing user engagement [4]. The guiding idea behind gamification is that the elements of games that make them engaging will still be motivational if they are moved to a new, non-game context.

To date, research in gamification has mainly concentrated on how to make gamification systems fun and engaging for the end user [1, 17, 27]. Advice is drawn from well-established game design principles. For instance, Liu et al. believe that gamification systems should be designed with fun in mind, through well-designed user interfaces and game-like flow [22]. Deterding suggests that systems should provide interesting challenges, clear goals that are varied and well-paced, and feedback that is presented in a fun and exciting, or *juicy*, manner [8].

An increasing number of gamification systems illustrate this approach. For instance, CARROT is a gamified to-do list application featuring an artificial personality that boasts being "built around character and story instead of meaningless badges and achievements" [25]. Zombies, Run! is a gamified fitness application that features a full game, including a gripping story, and "turns the player's runs into a post-apocalyptic action hero's fight for survival" [31]. These examples make use of game design concepts, such as story and flow, to create a playful experience for the end user.

Besides advice to make systems playful, designers have been encouraged to significantly focus on engaging the end user [1, 17, 27]. This follows from gamification's central premise that using game-like elements can increase participation and engagement in an activity [3]. Bunchball, for instance, believes that the "overall goal of gamification is to engage with consumers and get them to participate, share and interact in some activity or community" [3].

Advice for making gamification engaging to the end user has been grounded in psychology, particularly making use of the concepts of extrinsic and intrinsic motivation from self-determination theory [29]. Extrinsic motivators in gamification are game elements such as badges and points. Intrinsic motivators include autonomy, relatedness, and competence [29]. Gamification systems can provide autonomy by giving players a sense of freedom of play [8]. Mastery is provided when players feel as if they are accomplishing something and progressing toward their goals [8]. Relatedness connects players to the system in a way that plays to their goals and passions [8].

Though the bulk of gamification solutions make use of extrinsic motivators, an increasing number of gamification systems are also taking advantage of intrinsic motivators. For example, gamification has been seen as a way to improve student motivation and engagement in schools, where it can provide cognitive, emotional, and social benefits to students [21]. A successful example of this is Khan Academy, which gamifies education in areas including mathematics, science, history, and economics [18]. To engage the student, Khan Academy makes use of external motivators such as badges and quests. It also takes advantage of intrinsic motivators by allowing players to create their own goals, providing a sense of freedom to the player, and by providing real-time statistics to let the players know they are progressing towards their goals.

Additional examples that make use of these principles include Nike+ and Fitocracy, which gamify fitness. Nike+, used by approximately 11 million people, features a point system, challenges, leaderboards, and ways to challenge friends [6], while Fitocracy employs badges, quests, levels, points, and groups [11]. Like Khan Academy, Nike+ and Fitocracy allow players to create their own goals and provide feedback so that players can achieve a sense of mastery. They also bring together large, like-minded communities to promote a sense of relatedness.

While it is natural and necessary to focus on producing a fun and engaging experience, we argue that a third area is also critical to successful gamification—investigating the context of deployment. No matter how entertaining or motivational the system is, inadequate consideration of broader issues of the deployment environment and stakeholder needs can lead to failure.

For example, when Slalom Computing included a leaderboard with the goal of improving facial recognition between long-distance employees, only five percent participated, even with added incentives [20]. Stakeholder requirements were not studied before applying this gamification system, and the system failed. Thankfully, when this was changed to a group leaderboard using randomly assigned teams, the participation jumped from five percent to ninety due to the fact that employees did not want to let their teams down. But, the initial failure reinforces the idea that these systems should not be applied without forethought. Also, Slalom Computing's initial shortcomings may not have been so easily remedied if it had been applied to end consumers instead of employees, which is the typical case for most gamification systems.

The importance of understanding context will not be surprising to researchers in human-computer interaction. Participatory design, in particular, involves stakeholders in the design process, helping to ensure that their needs are met. For example, participatory design was used in developing a fitness game for children with cerebral palsy [14], with a team involving health professionals as well as the children themselves. This project reported the need to solve issues outside the game itself, including the need to design special-purpose cycling hardware and the need to support home play. However, the use of such design methods in gamification is uncommon.

Gartner, Inc. has identified the dangers of inadequately considering context of deployment, predicting that 80% of current gamified applications will fail, primarily due to poor design [4]. The 20% that are thought to succeed will be those that clearly identify business objectives and provide a thorough analysis of how gamification can fulfill those objectives [4]. This will take a thorough investigation of stakeholder requirements to accomplish. At least one successful gamification company, Bunchball, already follows this advice, beginning each project with a thorough investigation of business needs [7].

Leaders in the gamification area also share concern over the lack of broad context development. Gabe Zichermann, CEO of Gamification.co and Conference Chair of Gamification Summit, notes that corporations have used leaderboards and "employee of the month" programs for motivation for many decades. But, he and others would like to see research into how well gamification elements such as these work. Zichermann admits, "There aren't any long-term studies that support... broad, context-based solutions because this discussion didn't start until 2010" [20].

Theories are emerging to support studies that involve organizational context [27], and some researchers even feel that the purpose of gamification is to advance instrumental organizational goals [24]. But, focusing on the organization is still seen as a symptom of meaningless gamification [27].

Thus, there is much room for research into this important, as yet poorly understood, area of gamification. In this paper, we help to fill this gap by reporting on the broad contextual investigation underlying the design of our Edufitment system for teaching elementary school children about nutrition. We report on issues raised by this investigation that significantly threatened the success of the system. We now introduce the Edufitment project, and then discuss our study of its context of deployment.

EDUFITMENT

The goal of the Edufitment project was to combat childhood obesity in the southern United States. Obesity is a particular health challenge in this region, affecting over 40% of the children in our target schools [2]. We focused on children in fourth, fifth, and sixth grades, representing a total of 1,097 children at two elementary schools. There are many ways to tackle childhood obesity, such as providing healthier meals at school and at home and increasing daily exercise by requiring more frequent or longer physical activity classes at school. These and other approaches have already been attempted at the national and state levels, but the problem remains unresolved. Thus, there is significant motivation to find solutions that actually work.

From summer 2011 to spring 2012, our team of experts held collaborative brainstorming sessions that guided the iterative development of the project. Among their tasks, group members investigated and reported on the context of deployment and stakeholder requirements. For instance, our biostatistician was responsible for determining the makeup of the student body, while our nutrition expert researched what food the schools provided at lunch. These investigations were critical to the design of our system, helping us to avoid errors that would have rendered the system unusable in practice.

Through this process, we created Edufitment, a video-game based system for education in nutrition and fitness—the system's name is a combination of *education*, *fitness*, and *entertainment*. Edufitment is structured around a web-based gamification framework; it can take elements common to games and apply them in a non-game context. The system contains game elements common to gamification, such as experience points and redeemable points, leaderboards, and dashboards. Edufitment shares gamification mechanics between a set of modular serious games and non-game activities performed outside the system, including logging out-of-game physical activity to gain points in the system.

In addition to gamification mechanics, Edufitment contains several useful features. To aid user privacy, the system supports roles, each with its own set of permissions. The system is multilingual, initially supporting the German, English, Spanish, and French languages. A plugin game application programming interface (API) is provided for first and third-party games to be added into the system. A chat room allows players to connect to one another and spend earned coins by sending customized messages.

To improve diet at home, it is necessary for the child and, especially, their families to understand what constitutes a healthy meal. Our underlying hypothesis was that, consistent with the approaches described in the previous section, children would find gaming to be an engaging way of learning this material. Based on this hypothesis, we used video games to teach concepts related to fitness and nutrition to children, with the goal of affecting diet change and improving activity levels.

Our games build on a rich history of nutrition games for children. For example, Squire's Quest! II is a 10-episode online video game that promotes fruit and vegetable consumption to elementary school children [32]. Each episode provides a different mini-game, such as trivia and matching games, and focuses on specific educational goals related to fruits and vegetables, such as understanding portion size [32]. Other initiatives have researched different aspects of nutrition games, such as story immersion [23].

Despite significant research having been conducted around nutrition games, the vast majority of registered dietitians, considered leading experts in nutrition, have not played nutrition games [12]. They do, however, believe nutrition games can be valuable educational tools [12]. This suggests that the nutrition game field has the potential to benefit from the involvement of experts. This paper is, to our knowledge, the first to provide a detailed look at the multidisciplinary development process of a significant gamification system.

The Edufitment framework contains four initial games dedicated to nutrition education, an application for recording any activity performed outside the system, and a proof-of-concept exergame. The nutrition games include a quiz show game similar to *Jeopardy!*, featuring an expandable database of questions and categories. A matching game similar to *Bejeweled* (see Figure 1) helps children understand what types of foods belong to which food group. A hunting game similar to Nintendo Entertainment System's *Duck Hunt* allows for a variety of winning and losing conditions, such as shooting only foods that are high in Vitamin C. A poker-like card game (see Figure 2) teaches the number of Calories that are in different foods. The activity-recording application allows manual entry activities performed outside the game, such as walking or playing sports. Finally, the exergame requires players to keep their heart rate elevated to win. Through its plugin architecture, Edufitment allows additional games to easily be integrated.

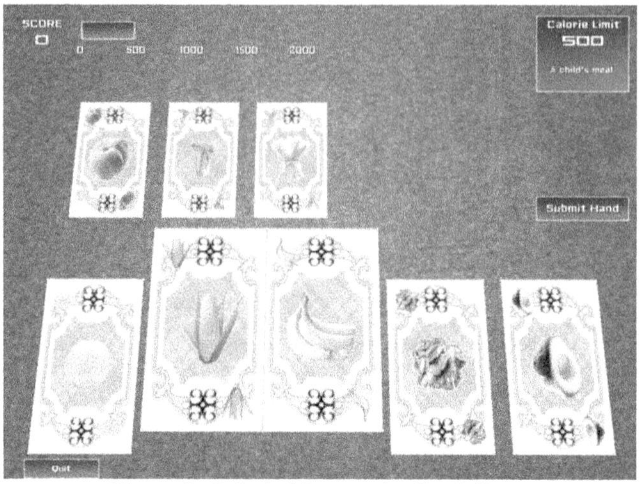

Figure 1: Calorie Meter—the Card Game

Figure 2: Food Group Match Up

Edufitment is currently a robust prototype, and further refinement and testing of the games will be required before it is ready for broad deployment. The design and development process underlying Edufitment allowed us to understand the critical importance of context in the design of gamification systems. In the next section, we explore issues that were brought to light by our detailed investigations and show how they affected many aspects of the project, including the framework, the deployment environment, and the games developed for the intervention.

THE IMPORTANCE OF CONTEXT IN THE DESIGN OF GAMIFICATION SYSTEMS

The complementary expertise of our multidisciplinary team members permitted investigation of stakeholder requirements, informed by the context in which the system was to be deployed. As we shall see, this process helped identify issues that could lead to significant problems in the deployment of the system. Specifically, we found five key areas where deep understanding of context was critical:

Issue	Example	Solution
Stakeholders may bring critical requirements	Stakeholders followed a nutrition program that advocates reduced screen time	Developed small, short games focused on specific educational messages
Hosting organization may bring critical requirements	School administrators set a high bar for demonstrated efficacy before being willing to allocate class time to intervention	Sought alternative venue for deployment
Target audience may lack means to change behavior	Elementary school children do not typically shop for or make their own food	Enabled parents / guardians to play along with their children
Diverse population may introduce critical requirements	Healthy meals presented by program may not be familiar to the targeted culture	Developed an expandable database of foods, allowing familiar foods to be easily integrated into the system
Addressing post-deployment may reveal key concerns	Team of IT professionals would not be available post system deployment	Developed full-featured, easy-to-use tools to allow new administrators to quickly become familiar with the system

Table 1: Summary of issues discovered and solutions

- The *stakeholders* in the process—for example, educators, experts in nutrition, parents, or the children themselves—may bring requirements that would be hard to predict without their input, but which are critical to the success of the system.
- The *organization hosting the intervention*—in our case the schools and eventually civic centers—may bring critical requirements.
- Members of the target audience may *lack the means to change their own behavior,* requiring designers to identify who has the agency to permit behavioral change and ensure that they are engaged in the intervention.
- The target population may be *diverse*, and some parts of the population may have specific and important requirements.
- The *intervention may last longer* than the availability of the initial research or development team. To be successful, the intervention may require identification and support of stakeholders who will continue the intervention into the future.

In the following sections, we discuss these issues, and illustrate them through our experience in the Edufitment project. A summary of these issues is listed in Table 1.

Stakeholders May Bring Critical Requirements

Stakeholders involved in the project can bring requirements that are hard to anticipate, but that may be critical to the success of the system. It is essential to understand these requirements early, before incorrect assumptions become deeply embedded in the design of the system.

An example arising from our project involves competing requirements around screen time. As mentioned in our introduction, the nutrition program agreed upon by healthcare experts promotes reduced screen time as one of its primary goals, yet our product was to be a video game. This demonstrates that there are times when two good initiatives can conflict in nonsensical ways, and this conflict must be resolved.

The nutrition program selected, *We Can!* (Ways to Enhance Children's Activity & Nutrition), is sponsored by the National Heart, Lung, and Blood Institute, the National Institute of Diabetes and Digestive and Kidney Diseases, the *Eunice Kennedy Shriver* National Institute of Child Health and Human Development, and the National Cancer Institute [26]. It has been successful in schools with similar demographics to our target schools, which is one of the primary reasons this program was selected [16]. The program has helpful tools, tips, and worksheets for parents and caregivers to encourage healthy eating and increased exercise in their children [26]. The problem is that the program also heavily advocates the reduction of screen time exposure for children.

Video games, such as those used in Edufitment, can support the *We Can!* goals of education around nutrition and fitness. But video games are played on a computer, game console, or smartphone, contradicting the requirement to reduce screen time. *We Can!* has only three primary objectives: eat right, get active, and reduce screen time [26]. Our health care experts argued that if we adhered to only two of the three requirements of the program, we would be unable to claim to be following it. The team concluded that the extensive press and positive public feeling about *We Can!* gave us little choice but to adhere to the initiative. Thus, we needed to find a way to reconcile these conflicting requirements, rather than considering our system to be an exception to the screen time requirement.

We solved this issue by imposing a system requirement that games must be playable within fifteen minutes. This required us to reconsider our original plan of creating one large game, instead creating several smaller, modular games that each addresses one focused area of knowledge. For example, the match-up game addresses the single question of understanding food groups. The requirement for games to be modular led to the development of a flexible and extensible gamification framework that can accommodate and link many games. This, in turn, allowed us to target different areas of knowledge, age groups, genders, ethnicities, and skill levels, and allowed us to add new games to the framework.

To further emphasize our support of *We Can!*, we provided an additional application as part of the suite of games that granted players the ability to record any activity performed outside of the game and to view the progress of that activity over time (e.g., if 20 push-ups are entered today and 25 the next day, they could see this on a graph).

These two solutions, developing short games and including an application that recorded activity performed outside the system, allowed us to adhere to the *We Can!* initiative and to the requirements of the stakeholders. Had this requirement been discovered after development, complete re-design and development of the game might have necessary, and the collaboration between the technical and healthcare team members could have been put in jeopardy. Stakeholders are not the only ones that can bring critical requirements to the gamification system, though. In the next section, we will demonstrate that the organization hosting deployment may also bring its own requirements that affect the development of the system.

Hosting Organization May Bring Critical Requirements

Initially, the system was targeted for deployment in classrooms or computer labs at schools. Target schools had been identified based on their demographics and proximity to the research team. We reasoned that delivery of the intervention within a school would help ensure a large degree of participation and would have given the children a convenient place to use the system. There is evidence that using educational games in schools can be advantageous, since gamification can promote classroom engagement and provide useful tools for teachers [21]. However, gamification can also take up valuable time and teaching resources and can promote to students the notion that external rewards are expected if they put forth effort to learn [21].

Ultimately, however, the school administrators were hesitant to fit use of the system into an already busy school schedule. They set a high bar for demonstrated efficacy before being willing to allocate class time to the use of Edufitment. This made the idea of deploying only in classrooms or computer labs at schools infeasible until trials had been successfully completed elsewhere, and as such, we needed to consider other venues.

We identified two free, school-based civic centers that were already highly popular with students and provided many services, including an on-staff nurse. Further investigations at the schools and the civic centers, though, led to the discovery of issues with the ability to effectively reach the target population, which will be discussed next.

Target Audience May Lack Means to Change Behavior

The core strategy underlying Edufitment was that increased knowledge in nutrition would lead to improved eating habits. Members of our target population of elementary school children typically do not shop for or prepare their own food, and so have limited choice in what they eat. Our team's investigations revealed that our target children may consume much of their daily Calories at school and at the civic center, and even in those venues, their choices are limited in a negative way.

Our intervention was particularly directed toward at-risk and special-needs populations. We discovered that approximately 94% of the children (1,097) being considered for deployment of the system were eligible for free or reduced-price lunch programs at school. Unfortunately, Gunderson at al. have shown that children in the National School Lunch Program receive a large portion of Calories from fat, which is associated with obesity [13]. This could result in a mismatch between the types of food provided at school lunches and the types of foods our system teaches the child to eat.

Additionally, the civic centers under consideration for hosting Edufitment provide food, but this food is not of the healthy form advocated by our program, again potentially undermining our educational program. To help improve the food provided at the centers, we reached out to Feed Fayetteville [10], a group dedicated to providing healthy food to the community. We soon realized that despite the desire to help of Feed Fayetteville, it would be difficult to raise the necessary funds to change the food offered to the approximately 1,100 children targeted by the intervention.

Since we could not change diet at the schools or civic centers, this left the home as the final area to influence nutritional choices for meals. Because children do not typically make their own meals, it was considered important to reach the children's families. The idea was to provide "stealth" education for parents by having them play along with their children in order to promote a positive change in the children's meals at home. This posed a problem, however.

Contrary to our expectations, we found that children who attend the civic centers after school are not typically accompanied by family members; therefore, children would not play with parents/guardians at those locations. While we wanted to host Edufitment at the civic centers in order to introduce the children to the games, we realized that it was going to be necessary to allow home play as well, to allow the parents/guardians to take part.

Thus, as requirements became clear, our vision of the system evolved from a standard PC-based application that could run on school computers to a centrally hosted online deployment that could be accessed both in the civic centers and at the children's homes. Computers with internet access would be available at the civic centers, supporting the choice of developing a web-based application.

Since our intervention was now targeted at involving parents and guardians in the home, we continued to investigate the home environment and discovered issues related to the diversity of our population.

Diverse Population May Introduce Critical Requirements

Diets differ from home to home, impacting the form of dietary suggestions that our system should make. Investigations of the target population led to the discovery that approximately 72% of students (837) being considered for deployment of the system were of Hispanic ethnicity. Analysis of public school student BMI data for a 5-year period in the targeted area shows that 36% of Caucasian children in grades K, 2, 4, 6, 8, and 10 are classified as either overweight or obese. As discouraging as this is, nearly half (48%) of children of Hispanic ethnicity are classified as overweight or obese in the same grades [2]. This suggests that diet may vary between the populations [5].

It was therefore important for our system to account for possible differences in diet due to culture. We wanted to influence at-home diet, changing the foods selected at home to healthier options. The diet suggested by our intervention, however, must not be so different from the participants' cultures that it has no chance of being accepted. Thus, we needed to find ways to suggest modifications to the participants' current diets that would be beneficial to their health but would also be within a familiar palette of food.

For example, a game might present, as an example of an unhealthy meal, traditional southern fare of fried chicken with macaroni and cheese, collard greens, breaded fried okra and cornbread. This may be a staple diet for some, but might not be a common main course of a Hispanic family. Taking into consideration the family's palette, a healthy meal recommendation might consist of a quesadilla using a corn tortilla filled with chicken, avocado, chopped onion, tomatoes, and cilantro. In order to allow healthier choices to be made from foods conventional to the families, we developed an expandable database of foods, containing names, images, and nutrition information of each food. This database was shared between all the games developed, allowing familiar foods to be easily integrated into the system.

Along with potential diet differences, language barriers may exist at the children's homes. Though only 7.1% of Arkansans ages five and up speak or hear a language other than English at home, in the targeted area, this number increases to 38.7% [33, 34]. Since we intended that families would play the games alongside their children, our system needed to ensure that language was not a barrier.

To provide a potentially more familiar language at home and to prevent any potential barriers to using the system, extensive attention to localization was prioritized early in the development of the gamification framework. Although multilingual capabilities were an eventual goal, the investigation of the children's home environment changed this to a high priority of the system. This led to the integration of multiple languages within the framework (English, Spanish, French, and German), using a flexible mechanism allowing simple future extension to additional languages.

Addressing Post-Deployment May Reveal Key Concerns

With development and deployment issues addressed, our teams began to investigate post-deployment concerns. Our development was performed by students in computer science and computer engineering programs, limiting our ability to provide a technical team to support the system post-deployment. We wanted to enable third-parties to add modules to our system in the future. We also knew that our target population was children, introducing particular sensitivities around privacy. Each of these observations led to issues that could affect post-deployment success had we not identified them during the development process.

Though our technical team would be available for modest ongoing support, it was not expected that a team of IT professionals would be available to provide expert-level support to the system once deployed. Having such a team available to maintain the system would significantly raise deployment costs. This led to two requirements. There would need to be stakeholders (such as teachers, members of the civic centers, or volunteer healthcare professionals) to take on the role of administrator, and administrative features would need to be developed to facilitate this role.

One of the difficulties of having a stakeholder act as administrator is that this is an add-on to their already existing job, limiting their available time [21]. To address these requirements, we developed administrative tools with ease-of-use as a primary goal. For administrators, a dashboard was created to view participant progress and allow participants to be added, modified, or removed from the system. Also, several games provided easy support for extensions, such as the Quiz Show Game that provided the ability to add new categories and questions. To remove additional constraints of the administrator role, features were provided to participant accounts so that they could easily change personalized settings such as their preferred language or system of units.

A second observation for a post-deployment Edufitment was that we wanted to allow third-parties, given approval, to be able to add additional games to the system. To address this requirement, a plugin game Application Programming Interface (API) was developed. This API provides access to the framework's features, and provides secure access to user data. Features provided by the API include the ability to submit a player's score, to submit game metrics measured after a round of play, and to retrieve language translations for the game.

One final observation, that our target population is composed of children, means that precautions must be taken by our system to keep the children's data private. Roles were developed with varying levels of access to user data. This prevents the general public or malicious parties from being able to access personal data of a child in the system. In all, seven roles were defined: administrators, developers, healthcare administrators, school administrators, teachers, students, and players.

LESSONS LEARNED

We have argued that understanding the context of deployment is a critical aspect in the design of a gamification system. We view this as the third important pillar of design, in addition to a consideration of user engagement and the entertainment value of the system. We have argued that this third pillar has to-date received comparatively little attention. Our examples from the design of Edufitment show just how significant requirements drawn from contextual analysis can be, and that a poor understanding of these requirements could lead to ultimate failure of the system during deployment. We now reflect on the lessons learned from this design exercise and on how these lessons might apply more broadly.

Design should be interdisciplinary and participatory. Human-computer interaction has long taught that it is important to include stakeholders in the design process, not just as people being consulted on occasion, but as full-fledged members of the design team. Our experience shows that in gamification, this advice is particularly important.

Through our development, we found that the set of people whose input is required in a design process can be extensive. End users are required for testing of the entertainment value and persuasive properties of the games. Domain experts are required to set requirements for the intervention and ensure that the content of the system is appropriate. Representatives of any organization hosting the deployment are required to participate; in our case this included members of the schools' administration and representatives of the civic centers. Experts with a broad understanding of the target users are required to ensure that the full diversity of the user group is captured. In cases where long-term support from the development group may not be available, champions must be identified who can help plan how the system will be deployed and maintained over time.

This leads to a concrete recommendation that members of the design team should be aware of HCI processes, such as participatory design, contextual analysis, and stakeholder identification and analysis, and should use these approaches early and throughout the design process.

It is important to foster positive collaborative efforts by ensuring the goals of the system and stakeholder objectives are aligned. We observed that requirements from some stakeholders may not be obvious to other stakeholders and may, in fact, conflict. We saw this in our design where the team of healthcare experts was committed to following the *We Can!* program, which limits daily screen time. This conflicted with the initial idea of having a single game that encompassed a large portion of nutrition and fitness knowledge. We resolved this by developing a suite of games that could be played in short bursts and were tied together by a central, shared gamification framework.

This example illustrates that two good initiatives can sometimes conflict. Design of a gamification solution, must, therefore be open to compromise, and designers should be careful not to inflexibly commit to a particular idea too early. Designers must be willing to adapt to stakeholder objectives and should seek ways to resolve conflicts that are satisfactory to all parties involved.

It is important for gamification systems to align with the objectives and constraints of the organization hosting deployment. In addition to stakeholders, the organization hosting deployment can bring forth its own set of critical requirements. In our case, these requirements were so stringent that we chose to change venues altogether, from the schools that we had initially targeted. It proved difficult to fit the system into an already busy school schedule, and the system needed to prove its efficacy before administrators would consider modifying the school schedule. Our solution was to use venues already popular with the target audience for deployment, school-based civic centers combined with home deployment.

Hosting organizations may not perfectly match the requirements of an intervention. In this case, it may be that the best that can be done is to identify and be aware of any such issues. For example, food available to children attending the civic centers was not of the healthy form that is recommended by our Edufitment system. Also, children attending the centers were usually not accompanied by their parents/guardians, and therefore do not receive the benefit of their families learning along with them. In any deployment environment, it is important to ensure that the requirements of the hosting organization are thoroughly researched so that the gamification system can effectively align itself with the organization's goals and constraints [4].

It is important to understand and work with the limitations of the target population. A population identified as the target of an intervention may have characteristics that significantly affect its ability to respond to the intervention. These could include access to computers and internet, physical, cognitive and linguistic abilities, ability to travel, or restricted availability due to work, scholastic, or family obligations.

Our target population, children in elementary schools, had limited ability to affect the desired change in diet on their own. For an intervention such as ours to be successful, nutritional education needs to lead to change in actual diet. Barriers to this change are that children do not typically make their own meals, the children we targeted had limited dietary options at school due to eligibility in free or reduced-price lunch programs, and the food available at civic centers was not consistent with the goals of our program.

We addressed this problem by enabling home-based play of

the games, to encourage parents to play along with their children. This required us to develop the framework and suite of games for web-based online play, supporting access at schools, civic centers, and home.

Other target groups could have similarly restricted agency; for example, meal planning may be restricted for populations such as prison inmates, members of the military, university students on meal plans, or people residing in retirement homes. It is important when designing gamification systems that aim to affect behavioral change to ensure that the target audience is actually capable of affecting the desired change, and to adjust the intervention in cases where it is not.

It is important to be sensitive to cultural differences within the target population. People's culture can influence their likes and dislikes, their frame of reference, and therefore may influence their engagement with a gamification system. Thus, it is important for designers to understand the cultural makeup of their target population and to be sensitive and inclusive in their design to how culture can impact the success of their system.

We found that diets differ significantly between homes within our target population, and that significant numbers of our population use languages other than English at home. We solved the issue with diet differences by including an expandable database of foods shared by our games in case, for instance, our targeted population is more familiar with foods such as sopes or barbacoas than poutine or sushi. To reduce language barriers, we prioritized multilingual capabilities early in the development of the system.

When designing any gamification system, it is important to understand that differences like these may exist within the target audience and to be sensitive to cultural differences. For example, gamifying a business that sells flowers may need to take into consideration that sending a red flower could be considered a romantic gesture in one culture but could be associated with death or funerals in another.

It is important to address post-deployment concerns during the development process. It is essential to investigate post-deployment concerns before deeply entering into the development of a gamification system. For example, our system relies heavily on the notion that a champion could be identified to take on the role of administrator post-deployment. It was therefore necessary to develop simple, yet powerful, administrative features that could be used by people with limited technical skills and limited time. To prevent malicious third-parties from tampering with children's data, we developed security layers that prevented unwarranted access to data and identified the party connecting to the framework. Finally, since our target population consisted of children, privacy was of high concern. Roles were developed with varying access to data so that malicious parties outside the system would not be able to easily access the children's data.

In general, it is important to consider who will maintain the system post-deployment. Will there be a team dedicated to troubleshooting players' problems and providing routine security patches, or do members of the target community need to take on these roles? It is also important to consider how the system can handle expansion. Systems can grow stale if they are not readily changed or if content remains static. There should be a plan in place to handle the addition of extra content to keep players engaged with the system. Finally, it is important to determine how the privacy of players will be addressed. Player privacy is a critical concern when gamifying. It is essential to investigate what types of data need to be passed from the players to the stakeholders, to determine who will have access to this data, and to inform the players about the types of data being shared.

CONCLUSIONS

Gamification is used to motivate users, and most of the research performed in the field to-date has focused on how to accomplish this. We have argued that in addition to considering the fun and engagement of the system, designers must also be concerned with the broad context of deployment and the stakeholder's requirements. We have provided examples showing how a process considering such context can lead to the discovery of significant problems that may not be found when focusing solely on user engagement.

Specifically, we identified that it is important to consider the requirements of both the stakeholders and the organization hosting the eventual deployment of the gamification system. We argued that the target population may have unexpected limitations on their ability to carry out behaviors advocated by the system. We have shown that it is requisite to identify who does have the necessary power and also engage them in the intervention. We discussed issues that can arise from diversity in the target group and considered the importance of planning for post-deployment maintenance of the system.

ACKNOWLEDGEMENTS

We would like to acknowledge the hard work of Taylor Yust for helping develop several of the games and to the multidisciplinary team of experts who made this project possible:

Jamie I. Baum, Nancy J. Smith-Blair, Karee Elise Dunn, Denise Garner, Marie-Rachelle Narcisse Jean-Louis, Kelly Vowell Johnson, Adrienne Shaunfield, Kristen N. Jozkowski, Marcia A. Shobe, and Angela Smith-Nix.

REFERENCES

1. Amir, B. and Ralph, P. Proposing a theory of gamification effectiveness. *Systems Research, 3, 1*, 60-95.
2. Arkansas Center for Health Improvement. *Arkansas Center for Health Improvement, Year Nine Assessment of Childhood and Adolescent Obesity in Arkansas*. 2012.
3. Bunchball. Gamification 101: An introduction to the use of game dynamics to influence behavior. 2010.
4. Burke, B. The Gamification of Business. *Forbes*, 2013.

5. Centers for Disease Control and Prevention. Overweight and Obesity. 2010. http://www.cdc.gov/obesity/childhood/problem.html.
6. Chou, Y. Top 10 Marketing Gamification Cases You Won't Forget. 2013. http://www.yukaichou.com/gamification-examples/top-10-marketing-gamification-cases-remember/.
7. Deterding, S. Gamification: designing for motivation. *interactions*, *19*, 4 (2012), 14-17.
8. Deterding, S. Meaningful play: Getting gamification right. *Google Tech Talk*, 2011.
9. Deterding, S., Dixon, D., Khaled, R., and Nacke, L. From game design elements to gamefulness: Defining gamification. In *Proc. of the 15th International Academic MindTrek Conference: Envisioning Future Media Environments 2011*, ACM Press (2011) 9-15.
10. Feed Fayetteville. Feed Fayetteville. 2013. http://www.feedfayetteville.org/.
11. Fitocracy, Inc. Fitocracy. 2014. https://www.fitocracy.com/.
12. Frederico, C. Results of a dietitian survey about nutrition games. *GAMES FOR HEALTH: Research, Development, and Clinical Applications*, *1*, 1 (2012), 51-57.
13. Gundersen, C., Kreider, B., and Pepper, J. The impact of the National School Lunch Program on child health: A nonparametric bounds analysis. *Journal of Econometrics*, *166*, 1 (2012), 79-91.
14. Hernandez, H. A., Ye, Z., Graham, T.C.N., Fehlings, D., and Switzer, L. Designing action-based exergames for children with cerebral palsy. In *Proc. Human Factors in Computing Systems*, ACM Press (2013), 1261-1270.
15. Hsu, J. Gamers are enlisted to battle bugs in military weapons. *Innovation News Daily*, 2012.
16. James, K. S., Connelly, C. D., Gracia, L., Mareno, N., and Baietto, J. Ways to enhance children's activity and nutrition (WE CAN)—A pilot project with Latina mothers. *Journal for Specialists in Pediatric Nursing*, *15*, 4 (2010), 292-300.
17. Kappen, D. L. and Nacke, L.E.. The kaleidoscope of effective gamification: Deconstructing gamification in business applications. In *Gamification 2013*, 1–4.
18. Khan Academy. Our Mission. 2014. https://www.khanacademy.org/about.
19. King, D., Greaves, F., Exeter, C., and Darzi, A. 'Gamification': Influencing health behaviours with games. *Journal of the Royal Society of Medicine*, *106*, 3 (2013), 76-78.
20. Korolov, M. Gamification of the enterprise. *Network World*, *9* (2012), 31-33.
21. Lee, J. J., and Hammer, J. Gamification in education: what, how, why bother? *Academic Exchange Quarterly*, *15*, 2 (2011), 146.
22. Liu, Y., Alexandrova, T., and Nakajima, T. Gamifying intelligent environments. In *Proc. Ubiquitous meta user interfaces*. ACM Press (2011), 7-12.
23. Lu, A. S., Thompson, D., Baranowski, J., Buday, R., and Baranowski, T. Story immersion in a health videogame for childhood obesity prevention. *Games for Health: Research, Development, and Clinical Applications*, *1*, 1 (2012), 37-44.
24. Mollick, E. R. and Rothbard, N. Mandatory fun: Gamification and the impact of games at work. *The Wharton School Research Paper Series*, 2013.
25. Mueller, Brian. CARROT presskit. 2014. http://www.meetcarrot.com/todo/presskit.html.
26. National Heart, Lung, and Blood Institute. About We Can!®. 2013. http://www.nhlbi.nih.gov/health/public/heart/obesity/wecan/about-wecan/index.htm.
27. Nicholson, S. A user-centered theoretical framework for meaningful gamification. *Games+ Learning+ Society*, 8 (2012).
28. Rojas, D., Kapralos, B., and Dubrowski, A. The missing piece in the gamification puzzle. In *Proceedings of the First International Conference on Gameful Design, Research, and Applications*, ACM Press (2013), 135-138.
29. Ryan, R. M. and Deci, E. L. Self-determination theory and the facilitation of intrinsic motivation, social development, and well-being. *American psychologist*, *55*, 1 (2000), 68.
30. The Scientific Research Society. Behind the Scenes of Foldit, Pioneering Science Gamification. *American Scientist*.
31. Six to Start. Zombies, Run! 2 presskit. 2013. https://www.zombiesrungame.com/press/.
32. Thompson, D., Bhatt, R., Lazarus, M., Cullen, K., Baranowski, J., and Baranowski, T. A serious video game to increase fruit and vegetable consumption among elementary aged youth (Squire's Quest! II): Rationale, design, and methods. *JMIR Research Protocols*, *1*, 2 (2012).
33. United States Census Bureau. State and County QuickFacts. 2012. http://quickfacts.census.gov/qfd/states/05/0566080.html.
34. United States Census Bureau. State and County QuickFacts. 2012. http://quickfacts.census.gov/qfd/states/05000.html.

Maze Commander: A Collaborative Asynchronous Game Using the Oculus Rift & the Sifteo Cubes

Pejman Sajjadi, Edgar Omar Cebolledo Gutierrez, Sandra Trullemans, and Olga De Troyer
Vrije Universiteit Brussel
Department of Computer Science, WISE, Pleinlaan 2, Building F, 10th floor, 1050 Brussels BELGIUM
{Ssajjadi,Ecebolle,Sandra.Trullemans,Olga.DeTroyer}@vub.ac.be

ABSTRACT
In this paper we present Maze Commander, a two-player game using two different types of interaction. One player uses the Oculus Rift and the other uses the Sifteo Cubes. The game requires effective and efficient communication to win. We also conducted an evaluation. The results show a positive evaluation for the game experience and collaboration, but no significant differences in game experience between the two modes of interaction. However, preferred interaction modalities were not yet taken into consideration for selecting the participants. We also present lessons learned from this experiment, and our future work.

Author Keywords
Collaborative; Game; Oculus Rift; Sifteo Cubes; User Experiment; Game Experience

ACM Classification Keywords
K.8.0 **[General]**: Games; H.5.2 **[User Interfaces]**: Input devices and strategies, Evaluation; K.3.1 **[Computer Uses in Education]**: Collaborative learning.

INTRODUCTION
Novel modes of human-computer interaction supported by novel controllers have appeared in the last years, the most well known being the gesture-based interaction supported by controllers such as the Microsoft Kinect[1] and the Nintendo Wii[2]. These new modes of interaction and associated controllers are also used in games, regardless of whether they are used for fun or for serious purposes. However, little is known about the effect of the interaction mode or controller on the player experience and performance. Having this information would not only allow choosing the most appropriate mode of interaction for a particular game, but could also be interesting in the context of serious games to increase the intended outcome.

[1]http://www.microsoft.com/en-us/kinectforwindows/
[2]http://www.nintendo.com/wii

CHI PLAY'14, October 19–21, 2014, Toronto, ON, Canada.

http://dx.doi.org/10.1145/2658537.2658690

The purpose of this work is to investigate whether the choice of interaction mode/controller has an impact on the game experience, in particular for two novel and less researched controllers. For this reason, we developed a two-player game, Maze Commander[3]. This game aims fostering communication and uses two novel interaction modalities, the virtual reality glasses of Oculus Rift [23] and a tangible interaction mode using Sifteo Cubes [19] [18]. Each player is using a different mode of interaction to play the game. Maze commander can be considered as a serious game since it promotes 21st century skills [7] such as communication and collaborative work. However, in the context of this paper, we do not focus on the effects of the interaction modes on improving communication and collaboration skills. We rather focus on effect on the game experience and collaboration. We first investigated whether the choice of interaction mode/controller has an impact on the game experience, as a good game experience is an important factor for a serious game. Without a good game experience, a serious game will not be successful.

We describe the game, as well as an experiment done to investigate whether the mode of interaction has an impact on the game experience. A positive evaluation was obtained for the game experience and collaboration, but we did not find significant differences in game experience between the two modes of interaction. We also formulate design recommendations based on the formative within-subject evaluation.

The rest of the paper is organized as follows. First, we provide background information about the collaborative games. Next, we discuss related work. Then, we present Maze Commander and subsequently the experiment performed and the results. This is followed by discussion and future work, and conclusions.

BACKGROUND
Collaborative serious games [32] are used for specific purposes such as team building, learning effective communication, and practicing collaborative tasks. In collaborative games players work together on shared tasks to achieve common goals [1], thus, in the context of serious games the term "work together" can have different meanings depending on the learning objectives of the game. In [1], three main groups of collaborative games are identified: Instructional collaboration in which collaboration is purely based on the instincts

[3]https://www.youtube.com/watch?v=55TaHKHgFDU

of the players, Supportive collaboration in which the players have the time and opportunity to discuss and strategise at a conscious cognitive level before the game commences; and Integrative collaboration that provides the context of making collaborative decisions while playing the game. Most digital sports games, such as FIFA[4] fall into the second category and games such as TeamUp[5] fall into the third. The game Maze Commander falls in between the second and third category.

There are numerous examples of successful collaborative games, starting from board games, e.g., Ghost Stories[6] to digital games, e.g., Portal[7] and more specifically serious games, e.g., Escape From Wilson Island [31]. However, to the best of our knowledge the mode of interaction with most of these games is the same for all the players whether they are physically in the same location or not.

Several attempts have been made in the literature to identify the building blocks and the essential components of collaborative games. In [32], the authors provide a series of guidelines for designing collaborative games based on an analysis of collaborative board games. On similar grounds, in [33] a series of guidelines for designing collaborative educational video games are provided by taking the cooperative working requirements introduced by Johnson & Johnson in [13] as starting point. Viktor Wendel et al. [31] combined the two sets of guidelines and augmented them with their own finding. This resulted into nine components that can be used in the design of collaborative games: Common goal/success, Heterogeneous resources, Refillable personal resources, Collectable and tradable resources, Collaborative task, Communication, In-game help system, Scoreboard, and Trading system. These components cover almost all the building blocks that can be found in collaborative games. Based on the purpose of a collaborative game, certain components from this list can be deployed in the design process. For the Maze Commander game, four components were deployed. We discuss them in the design section.

RELATED WORK

First, we discuss related collaborative serious games. Secondly, work related to collaborative games with the Sifteo Cubes is considered and thirdly, work related to games with the Oculus Rift that have the potential to be collaborative is discussed. To our knowledge, no work combining the Oculus Rift and the Sifteo Cubes exists. Finally, we discuss work that investigates the impact of different interaction modes or controllers on the game experience.

Collaborative serious games

To begin with collaborative serious games, we can refer to games such as TeamUp [2], Escape From Wilson Island [31], and HeatMeUp[22].

TeamUp is a collaborative serious game with the main goal of fostering teamwork [2]. Four players play this game; each player takes the role of one avatar. The game consists of several challenges that require close collaboration of the teammates. Each challenge is designed for a particular aspect of effective teamwork, including leadership and communication. The players of the game are physically present in the same location. They are allowed to communicate verbally but are positioned in such a way that they cannot look at each other's screens.

Escape From Wilson Island is another example of a serious game with a focus on collaborative gameplay that fosters the development of social skills such as team-work, communication, and coordination [31]. This game is an online role-playing game in which four players find themselves on an island where the goal is to escape from it by reaching a neighboring island and igniting a rescue sign through close collaboration.

HeatMeUp is a collaborative serious game with the goal of collaborative path finding. It is a two-player game with the roles of a fire fighter and a fire chief. The fire fighter interacts with the game using a gamepad and the fire chief is placed in the control room and is in charge of three screens. The collaboration of the players in this game does not take place through verbal communication but rather through game objects [22].

Collaborative games with Sifteo Cubes

Two collaborative games designed for the Sifteo Cubes will be discussed: Fat and Furious [25] and Tangicons [27].

Fat and Furious is a multiplayer collaborative game of the type runner. The main character of the game is a hamster that takes a path of the crossroad randomly, and its speed increases over time. The player loses the game when the hamster takes a path and there are no other cubes connected to that side of the current cube, or when it reaches an obstacle in a cube. Every time the hamster leaves a cube an element may appear on the cube, and the player then needs to use alchemy to get rid of this obstacle. Furthermore, certain hand motions (tilting, shaking, and repeatedly touching) can be performed in order to remove or transform the obstacles [25].

Tangicons is described as an educational non-competitive collaborative, targeting children between the ages of six and nine. Tangicons foster algorithmic construction and reasoning as well as discussions among the players [27]. This collaborative game is played in teams of four players with a total of six Sifteo Cubes and a laptop. Each player has a cube as a personal token that represents an action to be executed. Each player's cube represents an action, and the players have to discuss the order in which these actions are to be executed.

Collaborative games with Oculus Rift

The Oculus Rift can be used for traditional co-op or multiplayer games like Team Fortress 2 or Left 4 Dead 2 to provide a more immersive experience. But the Oculus Rift also isolates the player. This isolation has been used to create asymmetrical co-op experiences, where one player uses the Oculus Rift while the other player(s) use another way of interaction. Two games use the Oculus Rift this way.

[4]http://www.ea.com/fifa

[5]http://www.simxp.com/en/simulations-games/teamup/

[6]http://goo.gl/pBZxFG

[7]http://www.valvesoftware.com/games/portal.html

Black Hat Oculus[8] is a two-player heist co-op game. The player with the Oculus Rift is a bandit that navigates through a building while avoiding guards and looking for loot. The second player is a hacker that has access to a top-down view of the building. He has a greater field of view than the bandit, and can communicate with the bandit by using the keyboard. The player with the Oculus can read these messages at the center of the screen. The hacker needs to communicate the location of loot, enemies, and tactics to the bandit. The game is over when an enemy sees the bandit in the building.

In Keep Talking and Nobody Explodes[9] the goal is to defuse a bomb before it explodes. One player plays the role of the person in front of the bomb using the Oculus, while the rest of the players are the experts on bombs defusing. The player in front of the bomb can see and interact with the bomb using the Razer Hydra game controller[10], while the others have a set of instructions to defuse bombs. The player with the Oculus needs to describe the bomb to the experts, so that they can give proper instructions to diffuse it before the time runs out.

Impact of interaction modes on game experience

Previous work that investigated the effect of interaction modes or controller types on game experience is limited. If different input devices are compared, the focus is usually on differences in performance with respect to the selecting or tracking of objects, e.g., [21], [14], and [12]. In these works, devices such as the Nintendo Wii Remote, Xbox gamepad, a track mouse, and standard input (mouse and keyboard) are compared. With respect to comparisons of input devices regarding game experience, we can report the following work. Nacke [20] compared the Playstation 2 game controller with the Wii remote and Nunchuk on subjective experience and brain activity measured with electroencephalography (EEG). Limperos et al. [15] reported greater feelings of control and enjoyment with the Playstation 2 than with the more technologically advanced control of Nintendo Wii. Gerling et al. [10] examined the impact of mouse and keyboard versus gamepad control in first-person shooters using the PC and PlayStation 3. No significant impact on overall player enjoyment was found. McEwan et al. [17] compared a standard Xbox 360 controller (as an example of a directionally mapped device), the Wireless Speed Wheel for Xbox 360 (as an example of a device using incomplete tangible natural mapping), and the Xbox 360 Wireless Racing Wheel (as an example of a device using realistic tangible natural mapping) in a racing game. Generally, participants performed better with the controller, followed by the Speed Wheel and then the Racing Wheel. However, the more naturally mapped a device was, the higher results were on perceived levels of game involvement. The participant's positive response to the play experience seems to be related to the degree of natural mapping of the control device and not to their performance or capability with that device. Skalski et al. [29] showed that spatial presence and enjoyment were both affected by the perceived naturalness of the controllers. In their study, they used

[8]http://globalgamejam.org/2014/games/black-hat-oculus
[9]http://goo.gl/9aNlkv
[10]http://sixense.com/hardware/razerhydra

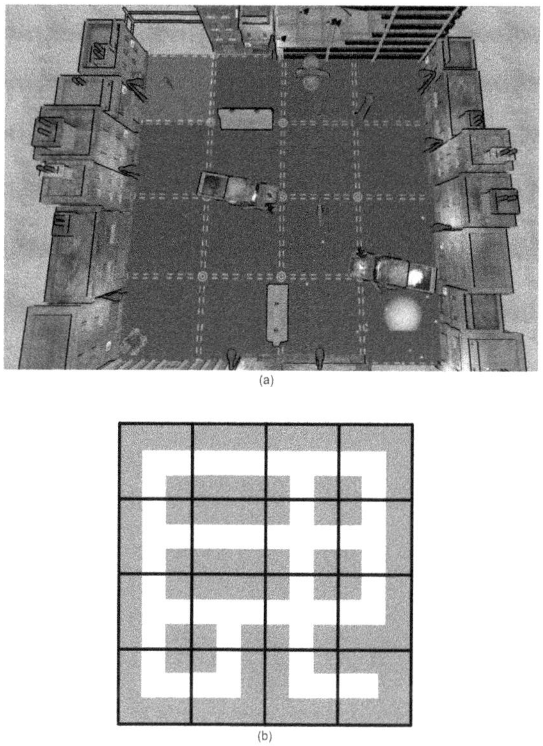

Figure 1. Maze as seen with the Oculus Rift (a) and the Sifteo Cubes (b)

a Nintendo Wiimote, a gamepad, a steering wheel, a keyboard, and a joystick. Pietschmann et al. [24] also conducted a study comparing the Nintendo Wii Remote and a classic gamepad controller with respect to immersion and presence. Birk and Mandryk [3] studied the effect of three controllers (Microsoft Kinect, Playstation Move, and Xbox GamePad) on the player's perception of themselves during play (in-game player personality) in a targeting game and found that the choice of the controller could affect the in-game personality. No work including the Oculus Rift or the Sifteo Cubes for comparison could be found.

MAZE COMMANDER

Maze Commander is a two-player collaborative tile-based maze game. The objective of the game is to escape from a maze while avoiding enemies and hazards (explosions and traps). The enemies are always patrolling over specific paths (they do not chase the character), moreover certain tiles explode after a certain time interval. Traps are tiles that kill the character upon contact. These traps are not visible until the character steps over it. The game is over when either the player ends up on the same tile as an enemy or a trap, or when the player is on a tile when it explodes.

As mentioned previously, the two players use different interaction modalities to play the game: one uses the Oculus Rift and the other uses the Sifteo Cubes. The game experience is different for each player since the view of the game as well as the possible actions are different for each interaction mode. The player using the Oculus Rift cannot move the character in the game, but has a 3D top down view of the whole maze and can see the enemies, the character, and the explosions.

Figure 2. A Sifteo Cube showing the tile where the character is

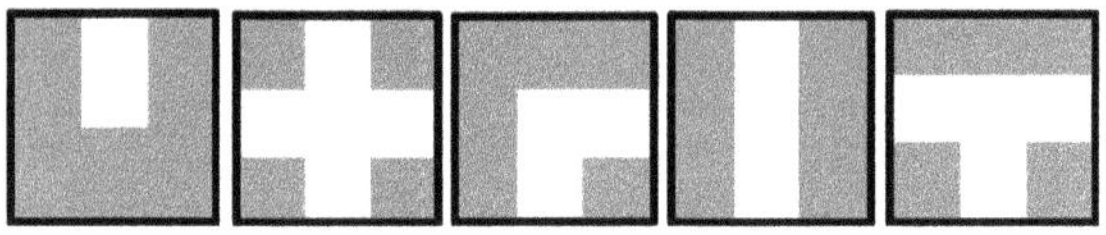

Figure 3. The 5 different patterns that the cubes can have

The maze is visualized to this player as a grid of tiles (see Figure 1 (a)). The Sifteo Cubes also visualize the maze but in a different way (see Figure 1 (b)). A Sifteo Cube can also visualize a tile, but mainly shows possible paths for moving (colored white). However, the player with the Sifteo Cubes does not get the view shown in Figure 1 (b). He only has four cubes: one showing the tile containing the character (i.e., the character cube, see Figure 2), the three other cubes can be used to move the character to the right direction.

The objective of the player with the cubes is to move the character through the maze by manipulating the cubes (see below for the rules) based on the instructions given by the player with the Oculus Rift. The objective of the player using the Oculus Rift is to provide detailed instructions to his/her team mate on what pattern to select on the Sifteo Cubes, which direction to move to and when to do so in order to reach the exit of the maze (indicated with a green light).

At the start of the game, the character cube shows the tile where the character is at the beginning of the game and the other three cubes show random patterns. There are five possible tile patterns (see Figure 3). In order to move the character to a new tile, the player needs to join the character cube with another cube showing the desired direction for the move. As part of the rules of the game, only one cube can be attached in either direction of the character cube (the motivation for providing three cubes for this is given in the design section). In order to change the pattern of one of the random tiles (if the desired pattern is not available), the player can pick up a cube and shake it. The shaking motion will switch between the different patterns. The cube can also be rotated in order to have the desired orientation.

When the player connects a cube to the character cube, and the pattern and orientation of the cube does not match the one of the maze for that position, then the cube color will switch to red (see Figure 4 (a)) to show the player that this is an invalid combination. If the combination is valid, the cube color will switch to green (see Figure 4 (b)). Once a correct combination is recognized, the player can observe the ongoing activities on the connected tile (e.g., the existence of an enemy, see Figure 4 (c)). The character will not move to the desired destination tile unless the player clicks on the destination tile (see Figure 4 (b)). Once this action is finished, the destination tile becomes the new character tile and the same procedure follows.

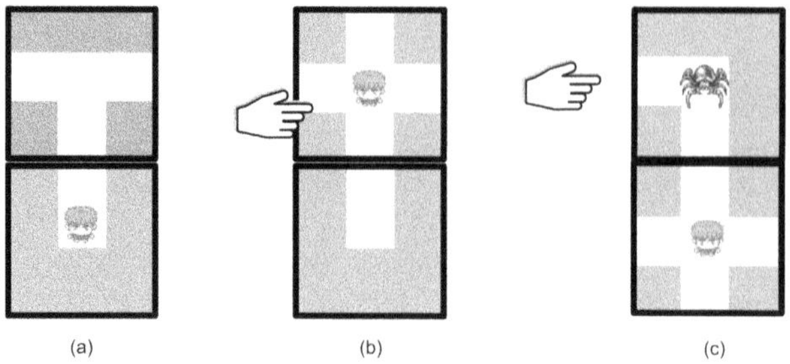

Figure 4. Character movement

Maze Commander has three levels with increasing difficulty. The difficulty is in terms of the size of the grid, the number of enemies, the amount of safe tiles, and the distance between them. A safe tile is a tile without hazards, so the player can stay on that tile as long as he wants and define a strategy.

The first level has 13 tiles, five of them are safe, and the shortest path between two safe tiles has a maximum distance of three. There are two enemies and one explosion hazard on this level. The first two tiles of the maze are safe to allow the player to get familiar with the tiles and moving. The second level has 16 tiles arranged in a 4x4 grid, five of them are safe, and the shortest path between two safe tiles has a maximum distance of four. There are two enemies and one explosion on this level. The player does not start on a safe tile and needs to move at least two tiles to reach a safe tile as soon as the game commences. The third level has 25 tiles arranged in a 5x5 grid, three of them are safe, and the shortest path between two safe tiles has a maximum distance of eight. There are four enemies, one explosion, and a trap. The player starts on a safe tile, and from that tile on there are only two additional safe tiles: the exit, and the center tile. The minimum distance from those two tiles to the exit is eight, so the players have to communicate and act fast in order to win the level.

DESIGN

Maze Commander was designed based on the collaborative game design guidelines proposed in [31]. Four of the proposed guidelines were considered relevant and were taken into account during the design process of this game. We list them below. For each guideline, a brief explanation of the guideline is given and how it is related to Maze Commander.

- **Common goal/success:** The game must be designed in such a way that both players have the same goal, and succeeding in the game means success for both. In Maze Commander both players have the same goal, i.e., escaping from the maze. Since accomplishing this requires rather close collaboration between the players, the success and failure in terms of achieving the objective is common.
- **Heterogeneous resources:** The game must be constructed in such a way that each player has a unique tool or ability that would enable that player to perform unique tasks. In Maze Commander, this guideline is clearly followed. The player who interacts with the game using the Oculus Rift is in possession of a unique resource, being an overview of the whole maze, enabling him/her to strategize and provide instructions to the other player. The player who interacts

with the game using the Sifteo Cubes, is in possession of a different unique resource, being the ability of moving the character and viewing patterns that can be used.

- **Collaborative tasks:** The game must contain tasks that are only solvable when the players collaborate. Maze Commander follows this guideline. It is virtually impossible for either player to finish a challenge without the help of the other. Although the player interacting with the Sifteo Cubes actually moves the character around, without a strategy and guidance from the player with the Oculus Rift, accomplishing the task would not be possible. These two roles are equally vital for accomplishing the task.
- **Communication:** Communication is a vital component in collaborative learning. In Maze Commander players have the possibility to communicate with each other in different ways, the most common one is verbal communication. On the other hand other modes of communication have also been observed in our evaluation, for example using hand gestures to describe the pattern of a tile that is required. This game is designed in such a way that bi-directional communication between the players is needed. The player with the Sifteo Cubes also needs to communicate certain information to the other player, for example describing the shape of the patterns he or she sees on the cubes in order to help the other player recognizing the tiles in the maze.

The decision to use only four cubes was made in order to make a balance between the levels of challenge the players would experience and their skills. If more than four cubes were given to the players, planning all the moves ahead would have become easier after a few tryouts of the game; this way the player has only a limited number of possibilities for prearranging the movements they want to make and therefore they have to act fast on finding the correct pattern and orientation while they are on the move. On the other hand, if less than four cubes were used, the game would have become extremely challenging, since the players had to switch between tile patterns and orientations extremely fast. Based on the difficulty levels we designed for this game, four Sifteo Cubes seemed to be the best trade-off after some trial sessions.

As mentioned in the previous section, a tile in each level explodes after a specific time interval, but the information about the frequency of the explosions is not given to the players, this choice was made deliberately, firstly to challenge the player with the Oculus Rift to find the timing in order to give the "go ahead" signal to the other player, as well as challenging the player with the Sifteo Cubes to act quickly on moving the character before a new explosion occurs; secondly to encourage the players to communicate effectively, efficiently, and in a timely manner.

Furthermore, as mentioned in the previous section, the game starts on a safe tile in levels one and on an unsafe tile in level two. This decision was taken to challenge the players to act faster in the second level in order to avoid losing the game. This decision was made based on the assumption that after finishing the first level, the players have already established an effective communication protocol and are able to communicate more effectively and efficiently.

Maze Commanders was designed with the aim of developing certain skills. For players interacting with the game using the Oculus Rift, these skills are visual perception [16], pattern recognition, strategising, and problem solving [7]. For those interacting with the Sifteo Cubes, skills such as spatial reasoning [16] and decision making [7] are targeted. These skills target the individual player, but team skills such as collaboration are also considered.

IMPLEMENTATION

Maze Commander consists of two applications running simultaneously: the Oculus Rift application and the Sifteo Cubes application. The Oculus Rift application is written in C# in Unity3d, while the Sifteo Cubes application is written in C# using the Sifteo SDK. In order to synchronize both applications, sockets using TCP/IP are used. Each application connects to two ports, one for sending information and one for receiving information. The communication between the two applications is in the form of a full duplex, meaning that both applications act as client and server.

The Oculus Rift application needs to notify the Sifteo application when a new level is loaded or when the game is over. It also constantly streams the position of the enemies. The Sifteo Cubes application receives the commands and executes the corresponding actions. If the enemies are on the tiles currently visible on the cubes that are rendered, the Sifteo application also streams the position of the character.

The graphics on the Sifteo Cubes have five different sprites, one for the character and four for the different enemies, the paths are generated using Sifteo SDK primitives. We did not include animations in this version to avoid lags on the cubes.

Although our tests were made using one computer, acting as both server and client, the network architecture chosen allows us to run the two applications on different computers, and we plan to do that in the future since we found it is too demanding for a single computer to run both programs at the same time, causing lags under certain circumstances.

EVALUATION

Although the Maze Commander was developed to investigate the effect of interaction modes on the learning experience, we first evaluate the overall game experience and the collaborative facet of the game. In addition, we explored the differences in game experience between the two modes of interaction. Based on our evaluation, we provide initial design recommendations for collaborative games combining Oculus Rift and Sifteo Cubes.

Methodology

In order to evaluate the game experience and the collaborative aspect of Maze Commander, we have chosen a formative evaluation design composed of three components. The first component evaluates the user's game experience and collaboration through a within-subject factorial research design. Secondly, we have further explored the collaboration and communication aspect by observation. In addition, a semi-structured interview and additional observation metrics were used. This gave us the possibility to determine how and why users experienced certain game experience factors and collaborative issues.

Data Collection

In the first component of the evaluation design, the game experience and social presence questionnaires developed by Kort et al. [6] were used. The questionnaires contain in average four to six questions on a 5-point Likert scale to measure the game experience in terms of competence, flow, immersion, tension, challenge, negative, and positive affect. Competence includes, among others, skillfulness and successful rate. A factor to determine flow is given by how much they forgot the world around them, where immersion includes for example how imaginative a user felt. Tension was partly constructed by the degree of annoyance, and negative affect by how much a player thought about other things. Finally, the level of effort contributed to the challenge factor and the degree of fun was included in the positive affect factor. The social presence is factorized by empathy, negative feelings, and behavioral involvement. Empathy is represented for example by being connected to the other player. The negative feeling factor included revengefulness, and behavioral involvement was measured, among others, by how close the player paid attention to the other player.

Besides the social presence measured by the questionnaire mentioned above, the evaluation of the collaborative aspect of Maze Commander is also achieved by the observation of collaborative metrics. We have used the collaborative metrics for cooperative games specified by El-Nasr et al. [28], which include excitement together, worked out strategies, helping, global strategies, waited for each other, and got in each others' way. In addition, we have paid significant attention to how players communicated during play sessions. This extra metric could give us more insight in the explanation of, for example, tension or negative affect since communication is essential in Maze Commander.

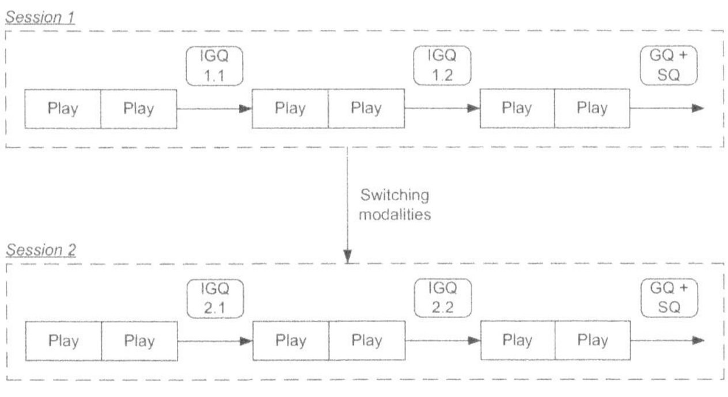

Figure 5. The evaluation study's setup. IGQ: Short in-game questionnaire, GQ: Core game experience questionnaire, SQ: Social presence questionnaire.

Procedure

Since we are interested in the overall game experience as well as the in-game experience with both modes of interaction in Maze Commander, the evaluation design includes two evaluation sessions with multiple rounds (see Figure 5). A round consists of two attempts to complete the level. In the first session one player plays with the Oculus Rift while the other plays with the Sifteo Cubes. Before starting the evaluation sessions the players could try the game. After the try-out, participants played three rounds where each round was followed by an in-game questionnaire (IGQ) except for the third round. This in-game questionnaire is a shortened version of the post-game questionnaire (GQ). After the third round, the post-game (GQ) and social presence (SQ) questionnaires were completed. Note that the in-game, post-game and social presence questionnaires were developed by Kort et al. [6]. Since we opted for a within-subject design, both players switched modalities and played again three rounds with the same procedure as in the first evaluation session.

Participants

We had sixteen participants aged between 19 and 36 years, with an average of 23.62 years. Twelve participants were male and four female. Furthermore, three users did not have any game experience while seven mentioned that they were intermediate frequent players and six participants had an advanced level of game experience. Finally, two out of the sixteen participants were colorblind.

Results

In the analysis of the results, we have used the mean of the relevant questions to construct the seven game experience and the three social presence factors. In addition, a t-test is applied to determine differences between the modes of interaction in each session. Cross-session statistical comparisons were not appropriate due to the learning effect and the increase of difficulty in the game's levels.

Overall Game Experience

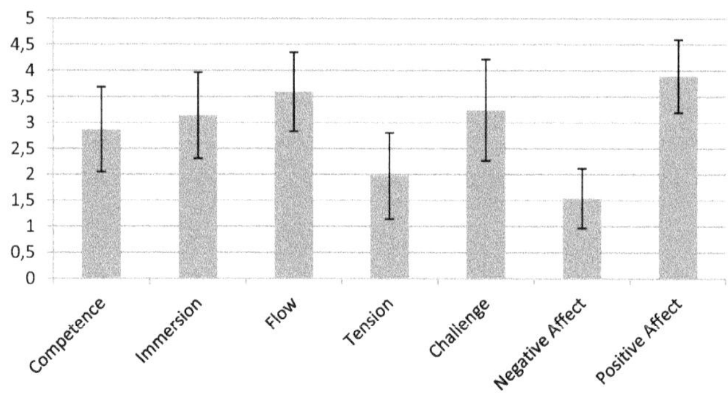

Figure 6. Overall Game Experience (GEX). The error bars indicate the standard deviation.

The overall game experience results indicate a promising positive evaluation of the Maze Commander game. Figure 6 shows the means with the standard deviation for all seven game experience factors. The overall game experience means are given by combining the factor's mean of the first and second evaluation session. Note that the lowest possible value is 1 since the results are based on a 5-point Likert scale. We can observe a positive evaluation for flow and challenge where competence is neutral. According to Csikszentmihalyi [5], a good game design should include closely related values of competence and challenge in order to keep the player in the flow of a game. As illustrated in Figure 6, we have achieved a positive flow by the flow value itself and by the minimal difference between competence and challenge. Furthermore, a positive evaluation is given for immersion and positive affect. It is worth to mention that, although the game is not using a first person view for the Oculus Rift, the immersion is still positive even though the Oculus Rift is often promoted to be used in first person view. The good score on positive affect was also observed during the play sessions. Participants had fun, they laughed, made jokes, and expressed their excitement verbally. Although some players looked quite serious and were utterly immersed in the game, upon completing a level they expressed their happiness and joy explicitly. Moreover, the results show a low but not "null" value for tension and negative affect (i.e 1.96 respectively 1.53 with lowest possible value 1). In the observation of several play sessions, we have seen that some pairs of players had some difficulty in verbally communicating with each other. Participants using the Oculus Rift described the scene in depth but did not provide the accurate information which was needed to form the path with the Sifteo Cubes. This sometimes lead to discussions between the two participants where the player with cubes became irritated. A second reason could be that two participants were taking a dominant role over the co-player. When the co-players did not tell them how they needed to arrange the cubes, or, in the other session, they did not place the cubes in the proper way, we could observe some frustration.

Social and Collaborative Aspects of Maze Commander

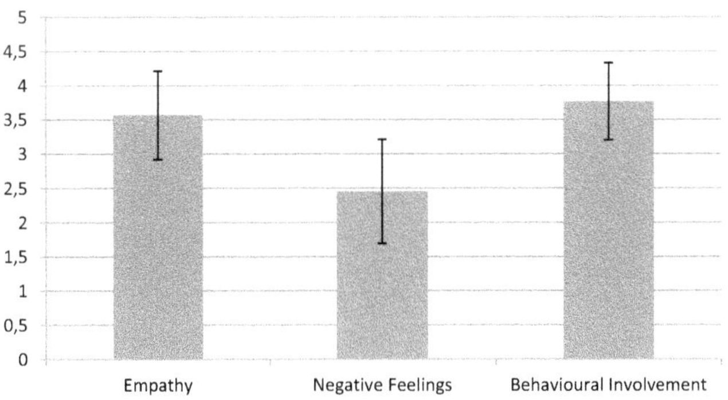

Figure 7. General social presence. The error bars indicate the standard deviation.

Since Maze Commander is a collaborative game, we have measured the social presence in terms of empathy, negative feelings, and behavioral involvement. The results are given in Figure 7. Empathy as well as behavioral involvement have a positive score. Due to the game design, the behavioral involvement's score could be expected since it measures factors as the degree of actions where players are dependent on each other. In Maze Commander one player needs to wait for instructions of the other player before he can continue in the game. On the other hand, the positive score for the empathy factor illustrates that players found it, among others, enjoyable to play with each other.

Besides the social presence quantitative results, we also have used the previously mentioned collaborative observation metrics. We could clearly observe the excitement-together metric where participants verbally expressed joy, and bodily expressions were noticed between play sessions and when accomplishing the challenges of the game. We could also observe that strategizing was a major activity in the game play. Only one pair played the game with an ad-hoc try and error strategy.

All other participants consulted each other in some degree. This leads us to the metric worked out strategies, which was definitely observed. Players consulted each other to determine a step by step strategy in order to reach the end goal. Furthermore, when a player waited for the other player to give comments or to do an action, the waiting player did not get frustrated or annoyed. Moreover, when players had to wait for the other player, they focused on their own responsibilities. For example, a player with the cubes waiting for instructions from the Oculus player, constructed the correct path with the cubes in the meantime. This is due to the fact that they had the knowledge about the patterns of the path from previous play sessions. A remarkable observation is the fact that they did not helped each other in the first evaluation session. In contrast, some participants helped the other player after switching modes of interaction in the second session. However, the majority of participants did not use their prior knowledge of the other modality to help the other player or to communicate in better terms. For example, a player which had played in the first session with the cubes started to describe tiles in terms of go straight, go left or right but they did not describe the pattern of the tile. Although they had played with the cubes and knew that they had to determine the path before the character can move, they did not use this knowledge in the second session.

Differences Between Interaction Modes

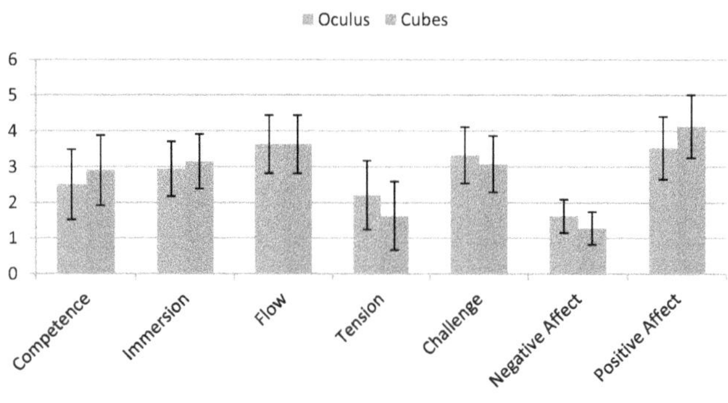

Figure 8. Game experience of the first session. Standard deviation is given by the error bars.

In addition to the game experience and collaborative evaluation, we have explored game experience differences between the two modes of interaction. The game experience results for each mode of interaction in both evaluation sessions are given in Figure 8 and Figure 9. We did not found any significant difference between the game experience of the Sifteo Cubes and the Oculus Rift within the two evaluation sessions. The results of the conducted t-test for both evaluation sessions are given in Table 1. This means that players experienced an equal level of game satisfaction. Note that we cannot provide

		First Session				Second Session			
GE Factor	Interaction Mode	Mean	SD (σ)	t-value	p-value	Mean	SD (σ)	t-value	p-value
Competence	Oculus Rift	2.500	0.979	−0.966	0.350	3.225	1.092	0.842	0.414
	Sifteo Cubes	2.900	0.641			2.825	0.781		
Immersion	Oculus Rift	2.937	0.760	−0.491	0.631	3.541	0.911	1.448	0.170
	Sifteo Cubes	3.145	0.927			2.916	0.811		
Flow	Oculus Rift	3.625	0.810	0.000	1.000	3.800	0.785	1.213	0.245
	Sifteo Cubes	3.625	0.795			3.300	0.861		
Tension	Oculus Rift	2.208	0.958	1.360	0.195	1.666	0.816	−1.747	0.103
	Sifteo Cubes	1.625	0.744			2.375	0.805		
Challenge	Oculus Rift	3.325	0.785	0.457	0.655	3.325	1.185	0.200	0.844
	Sifteo Cubes	3.075	1.334			3.225	0.766		
Negative Affect	Oculus Rift	1.625	0.462	1.389	0.187	1.437	0.691	−1.152	0.269
	Sifteo Cubes	1.281	0.525			1.812	0.608		
Positive Affect	Oculus Rift	3.525	0.874	−1.693	0.112	4.250	0.542	1.673	0.117
	Sifteo Cubes	4.125	0.489			3.675	0.806		

Table 1. Results of the two evaluation sessions' t-test between the two interaction modes for each game experience factor

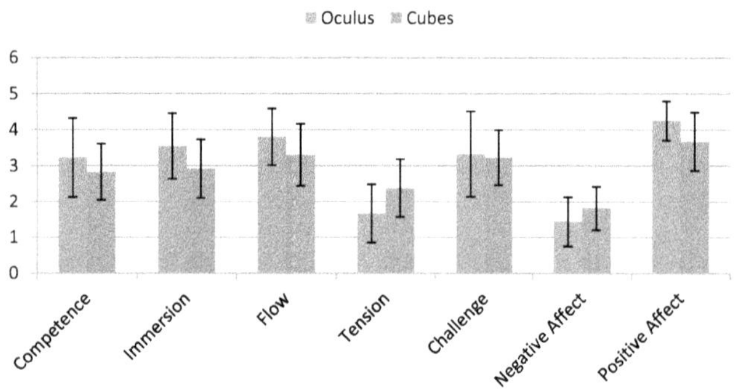

Figure 9. Game experience of the second session after switching the modalities (i.e. Oculus Rift and Sifteo Cubes). The error bars give the standard deviation.

a statement concerning differences between the two evaluation sessions due to the significant differences in baseline such as the increase of difficulty and learning effect.

Finally, the participants found the combination of the two modes of interaction very promising and innovative. Six participants preferred both modes of interaction and both modes were seen as a very fun alternative to keyboard and mouse. The Oculus Rift was preferred by six participants, mostly because of the imaginative immersion and the presence of a visual overview of the game scene. In contrast, four participants were in flavour of the Sifteo Cubes since they felt they had explicit control over the game by moving the character from one tile to the other.

Lessons Learned

Based on the evaluation, we can formulate some observations that might be taken into account when designing collaborative games with the Oculus Rift and the Sifteo Cubes.

Explicit control for the Oculus Rift

As illustrated earlier, some users preferred the Sifteo Cubes due to a lack on perceived explicit control when playing with the Oculus Rift. Although the person with the Oculus Rift implicitly has more control since they need to explain the next move and are responsible to determine the optimal path to the end goal, certain players did not experience being in control of the game when they were playing with the Oculus Rift. For these cases, one could adapt Maze Commander with the possibility to move the character in the Oculus Rift interaction mode. Nevertheless, the collaborative aspect and separation of responsibilities should be kept.

Allowing to communicate through different channels

Although we had expected to observe only verbal communication, almost all participants using the Oculus Rift also used gestures for communication. Gestures included drawing for example a cross in the air or small drawings on the table surface with a finger. Additionally, left and right directions were often not used but replaced by commands such as "to the wall" or "to the door". One participant, playing with the Oculus Rift, even mentioned *"I need a T-tile directed to your belly"* while pointing to his teammate's stomach.

The importance of strategizing moments

Most participants collaboratively strategized to some degree. We observed four categories of strategizing behavior. Only one group played the game without any strategy but with a try and error approach. All other pairs of participants strategized on three different moments. Some participants only consulted each other about strategies during the breaks between play sessions, while other participants used 'safe' tiles to discuss the next steps. Nevertheless, two pairs of players took their time on both 'safe' tiles and during the breaks. One group even took five times more time than the other players in each game session to determine a strategy.

Skills and personality adaptations

During the evaluation sessions it became clear that players significantly differ in their interaction with the two provided modes. Some players were very skillful with the Sifteo Cubes, while others could give very clear instructions when playing with the Oculus Rift. This indicates that the direction for our future work to relate the mode of interaction for an individual to their learning style or strong intelligences may be useful to explore.

Interacting with the Sifteo Cubes

When interacting with the Sifteo Cubes, some users experienced difficulties in finding the proper pattern. It was clear to them that they could join the cubes to form the path, but changing a cube's pattern by shaking the cube was not always perceived as a natural interaction. They had to shake the cube several times until the correct pattern was shown on the cube. Often the shaking was too fast or too slow which lead to skipping the correct pattern and eventually losing the game. Therefore, common or critical actions could be done by more common interactions such as placing the cubes together or clicking on the cube's screen. On the other hand, problems with the shaking-interaction could be solved by providing some learning time. Whether the problem with the shaking is a fundamental problem or only due to the inexperience of the player with the device should be investigated further.

DISCUSSION & FUTURE WORK

Based on the evaluation results, we can conclude that the players had an overall good game experience, which we associate with the game design as well as with the novel modes of interaction used. Furthermore, no significant difference in the overall game experience between the Oculus Rift and the Sifteo Cubes was observed, which suggests that both interaction modalities were perceived equally positive. However, personal characteristics, such as learning style, were not yet taken into consideration for selecting the participants. In comparison with other collaborative serious games with good gaming experience, our game managed to provide a good gaming experience for its players, although a different interaction modality for each player was deployed. This is of importance, since the combination of different interaction modalities have the potential of delivering a higher level of game experience.

In future work, we will evaluate both game experience and learning outcome (i.e., increase of communication and collaboration skills) of players in a setting in which each player would use an interaction modality that is in accordance with their learning style and/or strong intelligences. One way to measure the effectiveness of such experiment could be based on measuring the performance of players. In the context of this game, one measuring factor of performance is the quality of communication. Therefore, a closer study on the communication aspect of the game should also be performed.

CONCLUSIONS

In this paper, we have introduced a collaborative game called Maze Commander that uses two novel interaction modalities. The design of this game was explained and motivated. With an experiment, we have evaluated the game experience of 16 participants and observed that the game provided a good gaming experience in general. Furthermore, based on our evaluation, we have gained insight on design decisions important for collaborative games with the two given interaction modes.

REFERENCES

1. Azadegan, A., and Harteveld, C. Work for or against players: On the use of collaboration engineering for collaborative games. *Foundations of Digital Games* (2014).

2. Beznosyk, A., Quax, P., Coninx, K., and Lamotte, W. The influence of cooperative game design patterns for remote play on player experience. In *Proceedings of the 10th asia pacific conference on Computer human interaction*, ACM (2012), 11–20.

3. Birk, M., and Mandryk, R. L. Control your game-self: effects of controller type on enjoyment, motivation, and personality in game. In *Proceedings of the SIGCHI Conference on Human Factors in Computing Systems*, ACM (2013), 685–694.

4. Connolly, T. M., Stansfield, M., and Hainey, T. An alternate reality game for language learning: Arguing for multilingual motivation. *Computers & Education 57*, 1 (2011), 1389–1415.

5. Csikszentmihalyi, I. S. *Optimal experience: Psychological studies of flow in consciousness.* Cambridge University Press, 1992.

6. de Kort, Y. A., IJsselsteijn, W. A., and Poels, K. Digital games as social presence technology: Development of the social presence in gaming questionnaire (spgq). *Proceedings of PRESENCE* (2007), 195–203.

7. Dondlinger, M. J. Educational video game design: A review of the literature. *Journal of Applied Educational Technology 4*, 1 (2007), 21–31.

8. Fleming, N., and Baume, D. Learning styles again: Varking up the right tree! *Educational Developments 7*, 4 (2006), 4.

9. Gardner, H. *Intelligence reframed: Multiple intelligences for the 21st century*. Basic Books, (1999).

10. Gerling, K. M., Klauser, M., and Niesenhaus, J. Measuring the impact of game controllers on player experience in fps games. In *Proceedings of the 15th International Academic MindTrek Conference: Envisioning Future Media Environments*, ACM (2011), 83–86.

11. Gilleade, K. M., and Dix, A. Using frustration in the design of adaptive videogames. In *Proceedings of the 2004 ACM SIGCHI International Conference on Advances in computer entertainment technology*, ACM (2004), 228–232.

12. Isokoski, P., and Martin, B. Performance of input devices in fps target acquisition. In *Proceedings of the international conference on Advances in computer entertainment technology*, ACM (2007), 240–241.

13. Johnson, D. W., and Johnson, R. T. *Learning together and alone: Cooperative, competitive, and individualistic learning* . Prentice-Hall, Inc, (1987).

14. Klochek, C., and MacKenzie, I. S. Performance measures of game controllers in a three-dimensional environment. In *Proceedings of Graphics Interface 2006*, Canadian Information Processing Society (2006), 73–79.

15. Limperos, A. M., Schmierbach, M. G., Kegerise, A. D., and Dardis, F. E. Gaming across different consoles: exploring the influence of control scheme on game-player enjoyment. *Cyberpsychology, Behavior, and Social Networking 14*, 6 (2011), 345–350.

16. Loomis, J. M., Blascovich, J. J., and Beall, A. C. Immersive virtual environment technology as a basic research tool in psychology. *Behavior Research Methods, Instruments, & Computers 31*, 4 (1999), 557–564.

17. McEwan, M., Johnson, D., Wyeth, P., and Blackler, A. Videogame control device impact on the play experience. In *Proceedings of The 8th Australasian Conference on Interactive Entertainment: Playing the System*, ACM (2012), 18.

18. Merrill, D., Kalanithi, J., and Maes, P. Siftables: towards sensor network user interfaces. In *Proceedings of the 1st international conference on Tangible and embedded interaction*, ACM (2007), 75–78.

19. Merrill, D., Sun, E., and Kalanithi, J. Sifteo cubes. In *CHI'12 Extended Abstracts on Human Factors in Computing Systems*, ACM (2012), 1015–1018.

20. Nacke, L. E. Wiimote vs. controller: electroencephalographic measurement of affective gameplay interaction. In *Proceedings of the International Academic Conference on the Future of Game Design and Technology*, ACM (2010), 159–166.

21. Natapov, D., Castellucci, S. J., and MacKenzie, I. S. Iso 9241-9 evaluation of video game controllers. In *Proceedings of Graphics Interface 2009*, Canadian Information Processing Society (2009), 223–230.

22. Notelaers, S., De Weyer, T., Goorts, P., Maesen, S., Vanacken, L., Coninx, K., and Bekaert, P. Heatmeup: a 3dui serious game to explore collaborative wayfinding. In *3D User Interfaces (3DUI), 2012 IEEE Symposium on*, IEEE (2012), 177–178.

23. Oculus, V. Oculus rift, 2013.

24. Pietschmann, D., Valtin, G., and Ohler, P. The effect of authentic input devices on computer game immersion. In *Computer Games and New Media Cultures*. Springer, (2012), 279–292.

25. Pillias, C., Robert-Bouchard, R., and Levieux, G. Designing tangible video games: lessons learned from the sifteo cubes. In *Proceedings of the 32nd annual ACM conference on Human factors in computing systems*, ACM (2014), 3163–3166.

26. Sajjadi, P., Van Broeckhoven, F., and De Troyer, O. Dynamically adaptive educational games: A new perspective. In *Games for Training, Education, Health and Sports*. Springer, (2014), 71–76.

27. Scharf, F., Winkler, T., Hahn, C., Wolters, C., and Herczeg, M. Tangicons 3.0: an educational non-competitive collaborative game. In *Proceedings of the 11th International Conference on Interaction Design and Children*, ACM (2012), 144–151.

28. Seif El-Nasr, M., Aghabeigi, B., Milam, D., Erfani, M., Lameman, B., Maygoli, H., and Mah, S. Understanding and evaluating cooperative games. In *Proceedings of the SIGCHI Conference on Human Factors in Computing Systems*, ACM (2010), 253–262.

29. Skalski, P., Tamborini, R., Shelton, A., Buncher, M., and Lindmark, P. Mapping the road to fun: Natural video game controllers, presence, and game enjoyment. *New Media & Society 13*, 2 (2011), 224–242.

30. Szulborski, D. *This is not a game: A guide to alternate reality gaming*. Incunabula, (2005).

31. Wendel, V., Gutjahr, M., Göbel, S., and Steinmetz, R. Designing collaborative multiplayer serious games for collaborative learning. *Proceedings of the CSEDU 2012* (2012).

32. Zagal, J. P., Rick, J., and Hsi, I. Collaborative games: Lessons learned from board games. *Simulation & Gaming 37*, 1 (2006), 24–40.

33. Zea, N. P., Sánchez, J. L. G., Gutiérrez, F. L., Cabrera, M. J., and Paderewski, P. Design of educational multiplayer videogames: A vision from collaborative learning. *Advances in Engineering Software 40*, 12 (2009), 1251–1260.

Reducing the Negative Effects of Inconsistencies in Networked Games

Cheryl Savery
School of Computing
Queen's University
Kingston, Ontario, Canada
cheryl.savery@queensu.ca

T.C. Nicholas Graham
School of Computing
Queen's University
Kingston, Ontario, Canada
nicholas.graham@queensu.ca

ABSTRACT

Networking is a key component of digital games, with many featuring multiplayer modes and online components. The time required to transmit data over a network can lead to usability problems such as inconsistency between players' views of a virtual world, and race conditions when resolving players' actions. Implementing a good consistency maintenance scheme is therefore critical to gameplay. Sadly, problems with consistency remain a regular occurrence in multiplayer games, causing player game states to diverge. There is little guidance available on how these inconsistencies impact player experience, nor on how best to repair them when they arise. We investigate the effectiveness of different strategies for repairing inconsistencies, and show that the three most important factors affecting the detection of corrections are the player's locus of attention, the smoothness of the correction and the duration of the correction.

Author Keywords

Consistency maintenance; game development; usability

ACM Classification Keywords

H.5.3 Information Interfaces and Presentation: CSCW

General Terms

Human Factors

INTRODUCTION

Networking has become a key technology within digital games, as multiplayer interaction has become an almost ubiquitous feature. The time required to transmit data over a network can lead to usability problems in networked games, such as inconsistency between players' views of a virtual world and race conditions when resolving players' actions. Implementing a good consistency maintenance scheme is therefore critical to game play.

Sadly, problems with consistency remain a regular occurrence in multiplayer games, including some top-selling titles, and these problems can have a huge impact on player experience. For example, when Battlefield 4 [2] was released in November 2013, players protested about the numerous lag issues with the game. Sites such as IGN [12] and Reddit [18] were inundated with negative comments from users. Even today, the game continues to suffer from issues such as rubber-banding, where characters are pulled back to previous positions, and players being killed despite being under cover. While Battlefield 4 is one of the most egregious cases, it is certainly not unique. In a 2009 survey of 389 reviews of networked games, Pinelle et al. found that 49 of the reviews specifically cited gameplay problems related to network latency [17]. For example, in his review of Rainbow Six: Lockdown, William Harms commented that "*there were constant issues with ghosting, where an enemy would simply vanish right before you doubletapped him*" [11].

What is it about game networking that makes it so difficult to provide a consistent view of the game world to all players? The primary culprits are network latency, that is, the time required for updates to travel over the network, and limited bandwidth, meaning there is sometimes more data to be updated than can be transmitted without delays. To overcome these restrictions, games rely on a variety of techniques to maintain consistency, such as *dead reckoning* [16], which uses prediction to estimate the positions of remote players and other game objects between network updates, and *local lag* [13], which delays local updates in order to improve overall consistency. Regardless of the technique used, the fact that it takes time to transmit state updates over a network means that the game state can never be perfectly synchronized. Inconsistencies are thus inevitable.

Despite the large body of research on techniques for maintaining consistency in networked games, the issue of how to *repair* inconsistencies when they are detected has been largely overlooked. Inconsistencies can be repaired immediately, possibly resulting in a confusing or jarring experience such as seen in Battlefield 4. Or gameplay can be adjusted to mask the inconsistency until it can be repaired. There is little guidance available as to which of these broad approaches (and their many variants) best reduces the impact on player experience. To address this, we conducted an experiment that provides answers to three broad questions:

- How noticeable and annoying are corrections in networked games?

CHI PLAY'14, October 19–21, 2014, Toronto, ON, Canada.

http://dx.doi.org/10.1145/2658537.2658539

- How do different gameplay conditions affect a player's reaction to these corrections? and
- What techniques may make corrections less annoying to game players?

Our study tested 18 people in five variations of a custom game that implemented several techniques for error correction. For each correction, we recorded whether or not players noticed the correction, and if they did notice it, the degree to which they found the correction annoying. Some of our results were largely expected, but are confirmed here for the first time: corrections are most problematic when they occur within the player's locus of attention, and corrections are far more annoying when they impact the game situation. Other results were surprising. Smoothing corrections over even a 250 ms interval has an enormous effect on how frequently corrections are noticed. Performing corrections with a gradually changing velocity is surprisingly better than using constant velocity. And the likelihood with which a player sees that a correction has taken place depends more on the correction's velocity than its magnitude.

This paper represents the first study of the impact of error repair on player experience in networked games, and makes three important contributions. First, we provide a list of factors that influence how corrections affect player experience. Second, we evaluate techniques for reducing this impact. Third, we provide specific guidelines for the rate at which inconsistencies should be corrected.

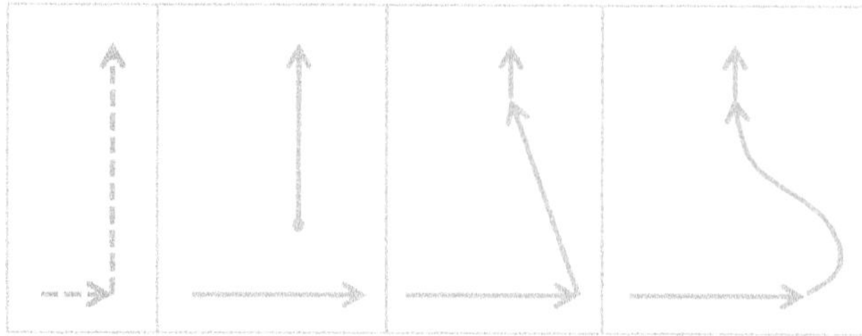

Figure 1. The dashed line (a) shows the motion of a game object that is travelling from left to right and then sharply turns upward. The next three images show the motion of that same object as viewed on a remote display when using (b) warping, (c) simple smooth corrections and (d) smooth corrections with a gradually adjusted correction rate.

BACKGROUND AND RELATED WORK

In networked games, inconsistencies arise due to a combination of network latency and the use of prediction by the game client to determine the local game state. Because of the real-time performance requirements of many networked games, some inconsistency must typically be tolerated in exchange for faster feedback to the player and quicker resolution of game events.

Inconsistencies can have a negative impact on player performance and experience [3, 15], such as the confusion caused by sudden warps in position, the frustration of shooting directly at another player and missing [4], or the bafflement of suffering damage from a grenade while protected by an invincibility shield [1].

When an inconsistency between the views of two players is identified (e.g., when a prediction algorithm has moved an avatar to the wrong location), the error must be repaired – and since errors often involve a visible object in the game, the repair must be visually understandable. As we describe in more detail below, some techniques provide smoother corrections (e.g., interpolating between the incorrect and correct locations over a time period) but at the cost of prolonging the inconsistency, in that it takes longer for the two players' views to reach the same state.

To get a better understanding of inconsistencies and how they can be repaired, let's consider two players, Alice and Bob. Alice is controlling her in game avatar. She is moving from left to right and then suddenly turns upward. We see this motion in Figure 1a. Bob is playing on another computer, and there is network latency between their two computers. In Figures 1b, c and d, we see three possible representations of what might be shown on Bob's screen. In all cases, Bob sees Alice's avatar moving from left to right, but when Alice's avatar turns, there is a delay before Bob's computer receives a message specifying that Alice's avatar has changed direction. Until this message arrives, Bob's computer continues to predict (incorrectly) that Alice's avatar is moving to the right. When the update arrives at Bob's computer, Bob's game client detects an inconsistency: since Alice's avatar has been predicted to be moving to the right, but was in fact moving up, her avatar is shown in the wrong location on Bob's screen.

This error can be corrected in one of three ways. (1) Alice's avatar can simply be drawn in the updated location. More precisely, the avatar will be drawn in a new predicted position based on the newly received positional update – the prediction is necessary, since the avatar may have moved during the time it took for this update to be transmitted over the network. Bob will see Alice's avatar jump (or "warp") to this new position (Figure 1b). (2) The update can be performed progressively, smoothly moving the avatar to the new location. Bob would see Alice's avatar speed up to join her newly predicted path (Figure 1c). (3) Or, the avatar can be moved with a gradually increasing speed to the new position. Bob would see Alice's avatar change speed more gradually to join its newly predicted path (Figure 1d).

There are significant tradeoffs between these solutions, and to-date, their impact on players' experience has received very little attention. Warping may affect players' immersion in the game world, since a player's attention may be drawn toward any sudden discontinuities in the position or motion of objects in the game [15]. A player may also lose context, for example, if an avatar that was in front of him is suddenly behind him, out of his field of view. Smooth corrections may reduce the jarring effect of corrections [20]; however, they prolong the inconsistency, which may be unacceptable in some game situations. Fiedler [8] suggests the rule of thumb of moving 10% toward the true position during each frame, but if the correction is large, simply warping to the new position.

Figure 2. In the Space Rock-it colouring game, players colour the asteroids by bumping into them with their ship.

More sophisticated forms of smooth correction are possible; e.g. varying priorities may be given to different objects in the game to ensure the objects of higher importance deviate the least from their true position [6]. While these algorithms are promising, and while ad hoc rules of thumb can be useful, there has been to-date no experimental validation of the impact of these techniques on user experience. There has been little effort to characterize when smooth corrections are effective, and to determine when and how they should be applied.

USER STUDY

As indicated previously, our research addresses three broad questions: how noticeable and annoying corrections are in networked games, how different gameplay conditions affect players' reactions to corrections, and what techniques make corrections less annoying for game players.

To address these questions, we conducted a user study using a custom-built game that allowed us to inject errors and corrections into the game and to obtain player feedback. The game – *Space Rock-it*, as shown in Figure 2 – features two space ships and asteroids moving about in a 2-D world. Participants played *Space Rock-it* under five separate gameplay conditions, where they either observed the motion of the objects on the screen or controlled the motion of one of the space ships. Consistency errors were periodically injected into the game, with varying magnitude and varying correction styles. *Space Rock-it* is intentionally simple in order to allow easy isolation of gameplay conditions and to emphasize the importance of corrections on player experience. We now describe how the game allowed us to address our research questions.

Q1: How Noticeable and Annoying are Corrections?

As participants played *Space Rock-it*, errors of differing magnitude were randomly injected into the game and then corrected using a variety of algorithms. Players were instructed to press the space bar when they saw a correction, and then rate how annoying they found the error. This allowed assessment of what magnitude of errors people perceive, under which conditions, and how annoying they found them.

Table 1. Summary of Game Conditions

Condition Name	Task	Game Entities	Ship Corrected
Observing - Single	Observe Only	One	Observed Ship
Observing - Many	Observe Only	Many	Observed Ship
Colouring	Colour Asteroids	Many	Other Ship
Controlling	Colour Asteroids	Many	My Ship
Shooting	Shoot Other Ship	Many	Other Ship

Q2: How Do Gameplay Conditions Affect Reactions to Corrections?

In addition to the question of how annoying people find corrections to be in general, we wished to investigate the impact of three key factors on how players notice and react to corrections. These factors are *distraction*, *locus of attention*, and *involvement with gameplay*. First, the amount of activity and number of objects or clutter in the game interface may *distract* players and affect their ability to notice corrections. Second, at any given time, people focus on a single area of the display, and the proximity of a correction to this *locus of attention* may affect how likely players are to notice it [21]. Finally, the very *act of playing a game* may affect a player's ability to notice corrections: playing a game may either distract players, causing them to not notice the corrections, or it may exacerbate the effect of a correction if it breaks immersion or affects gameplay performance.

To investigate these questions, we created five game conditions within the *Space Rock-it* game (see Table 1). The rationale behind each condition is discussed below.

First, to investigate whether or not a visually busy game might distract players and therefore mask corrections, we used two conditions which differed only in the number of potentially distracting objects on the screen. The task was simple: watching the screen and reporting corrections when they were observed. In the *Observing - Single* condition, the participants observed the motion of a single pink space ship on an otherwise empty display. In the *Observing - Many* condition, the participants again observed the motion of the pink space ship, but there were also a second green ship and 40 asteroids moving about on the screen. In both conditions, corrections were applied to the pink ship at random intervals. No corrections were applied to the green ship or the asteroids. Comparing the number of corrections detected by the participants in these two conditions allowed us to see whether the distractions had any effect.

In the *Observing* conditions described above, the participants were passive observers of the pink space ship, allowing them to fully focus their attention on it. By adding elements of game play to *Space Rock-it*, we manipulated the players' locus of attention. In the "Colouring Game", players control the green ship with the keyboard, and colour asteroids by bumping into them. At the start of the game, all of the asteroids are yellow in colour. If the green ship hits an asteroid, it turns green. If the pink ship hits an asteroid, it turns pink. This Colouring Game was used to create two conditions. In the *Controlling* condition, the corrections all occurred to the green space ship being controlled by the player, where we presumed the player would be focusing most of her attention. In the *Colouring* condition, the corrections all occurred to the pink, non-player controlled ship where we expected the player would be paying much less attention. The "Shooting Game" variant enable a third condition in which the player needed to pay attention to two locations on the display. In the *Shooting* condition, the player moved and aimed the green ship while attempting to hit the pink ship with missiles. Corrections were applied to the pink target ship. By comparing the number of corrections detected by the participants in the *Controlling*, *Colouring* and *Shooting* conditions, we determined the degree to which the player's locus of attention affected their ability to notice corrections.

Finally, to investigate how playing a game impacted a player's opinion of corrections, we compared the *Observing - Many* and the *Controlling* conditions described above. In both conditions, the player is focused on the ship being corrected. The conditions differ only in that in the *Observing - Many* condition, both ships move on their own, while in the *Controlling* condition, the player attempts to colour asteroids by controlling the green ship that is experiencing the corrections. We could thus determine how the act of playing a game affected player perceptions by comparing the number of corrections detected and the player ratings of the corrections for these two conditions.

Q3: How Do Error Repair Techniques Impact Player Experience?

Our third major question addresses the effect of different repair techniques on player experience. We implemented three repair strategies in *Space Rock-it*: warping, smooth corrections with a constant correction rate, and smooth corrections with a variable correction rate. To provide guidelines for repairing inconsistencies, we compared warping corrections to smooth corrections and we compared smooth corrections with a constant correction rate to those with a gradually adjusted rate. We also calculated detection limits for the various corrections based on the time interval over which the correction was performed.

When performing smooth corrections, the simplest approach is to pick a target location where the game entity should arrive at some point in the future and then adjust the entity's velocity to smoothly move to that location (Figure 1c). The problem with this approach is that, although there are no instantaneous jumps in the position of the entity, there is a sharp and sudden change in its velocity. Smed and Hakonen have suggested that gradually changing the velocity (Figure 1d) would make the correction less noticeable and thus be preferable [20]. We sought to confirm this by implementing two versions of smooth corrections. In the first version, we set a time interval (ranging from 250 ms to 1000 ms, refer to the *Procedure* section for specific values) over which the correction is to be completed and then move the entity toward the correct location at a constant rate. This is shown by the solid blue line in Figure 3. In the second version, we perform the correction over the same time interval, but initially move the entity slowly, increasing the correction rate over time as shown by the dashed red line in Figure 3. The correction

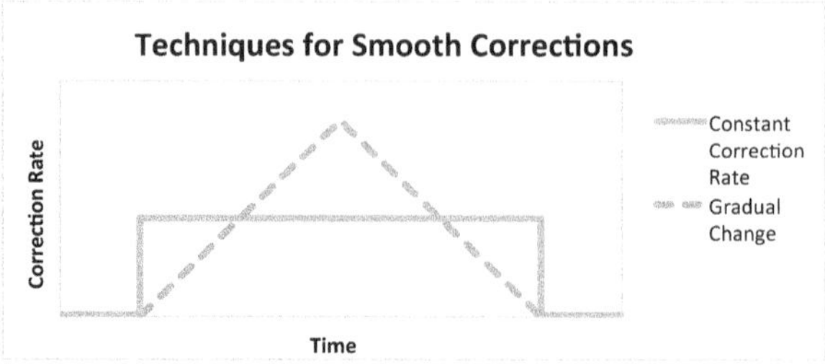

Figure 3. Corrections may be done using either a constant or variable correction rate

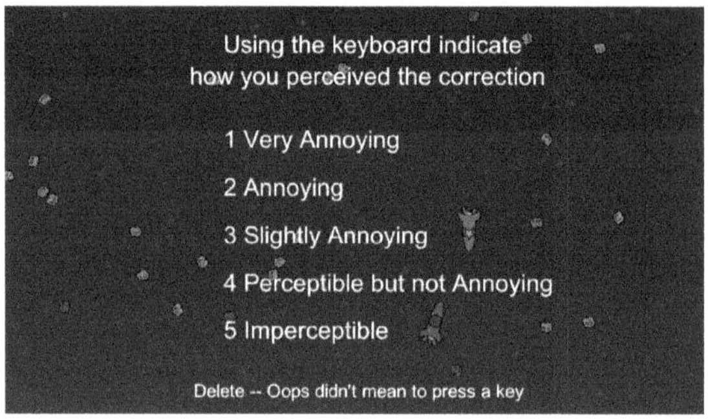

Figure 4. When the participants noticed a correction they rated the degree of annoyance on a scale of 1 to 5

rate increases linearly up to the mid point of the correction and then decreases linearly. In both cases, the correction is completed over in the same amount of time, and the average correction rates are identical. Note, however, that when the correction rate is changed gradually, the correction rate is actually higher in the middle of the correction. We compared the number of corrections detected and the player ratings for these two forms of smooth correction.

We expected that if smooth corrections are performed increasingly slowly, there eventually comes a point where the corrections are undetectable. In order to compute the detection limits, we included a range of correction sizes and correction times in the study. The specific values are listed in the *Procedures* section.

Method

18 participants (16 male and 2 female) were recruited from a local university. All of the participants were regular game players who played fast-paced action games for a minimum of four hours per week. We specifically recruited regular game players, as our earlier work has shown that non-gamers have significantly less ability to detect anomalies in games [19].

Procedure

The participants played the game seated at a computer with a 27 inch monitor and used the keyboard both to control their on screen avatar (a space ship) and to provide feedback when they observed a correction. Although the study investigated repairs to inconsistencies in networked games, we used a single player game in which errors and the subsequent corrections were synthetically generated. This allowed us to control the frequency and magnitude of repairs to inconsistencies.

The study began with a brief training session in which the participants observed the normal motion of the space ship for approximately thirty seconds. The ship then suddenly warped to a new position and the participants were asked to press the space bar when they saw this happen. At this point, the rating system (Figure 4) appeared on the screen and was explained to them. The participants continued to observe the space ship for an additional minute and pressed the space bar each time they noticed a correction.

Following this training period, the participants played the five different game conditions listed in Table 1, with each condition lasting approximately eight minutes. The conditions were always played in the same order:

- *Observing - Single*: Observing one ship
- *Observing - Many*: Observing two ships and asteroids
- *Colouring*: Colouring game with corrections occurring to the other ship
- *Controlling*: Colouring game with corrections occurring to the player controlled ship
- *Shooting*: Shooting game with corrections occurring to the target ship

We did not randomize the order of the conditions, because we wanted the players to become thoroughly familiar with the motion of the space ships and asteroids before beginning the game play conditions. The results indicate that any learning effect had little impact on the results, as we found no significant difference in the total number of corrections detected between the *Observing - Single*, *Observing - Many* and *Controlling* (first, second and fourth) conditions.

During each condition, corrections occurred to the position of one of the two space ships. The players were asked to indicate when they noticed a correction and to specify the degree to which they found the correction to be annoying. When the players noticed a correction, they pressed the space bar. The game then paused and the participant rated how annoying they would have found a similar correction had it occurred in an actual game (Figure 4). The rating scale was based on the *Mean Opinion Score* (MOS) [14], a metric established for subjective quality measurements of audio and video signals. The MOS is based on human perception and has values ranging from 1 to 5 with 1 indicating the poorest quality and 5 indicating no signal degradation. This scale has been adapted and used by researchers to measure video game quality, particularly when affected by network latency [7, 22, 23].

The participants also had the option of pressing the delete key to indicate that they had accidentally pressed the space bar. While the game was paused, the positions of the space ships and the asteroids were dimly visible in the background behind the text. This enabled the players to remain focused on the game while providing feedback about the corrections. The game resumed immediately after the player pressed a number key to rate the correction. The order of the errors was randomized and the errors and corrections were uniformly distributed over three to eight seconds.

Following the study, we conducted a semi-structured interview with each participant to elicit additional information about how they rated the corrections and the types of corrections they found most annoying.

During each condition, there were 60 corrections. We varied the corrections along three axes:

- the magnitude of the correction,
- the correction time – the time over which the error was repaired, and
- the smoothness of the correction

Each of these axes is described in more detail below.

Magnitude of the Correction

The magnitude of a correction is measured in centimetres on the display. The space ship was 4 cm long by 1.5 cm wide and travelled at a speed of 12 cm per second. This size was chosen based on aesthetics and the requirement that the ship be easily visible on the screen. The speed was selected to make the ship comfortable to control. In setting the magnitude of corrections, we considered the range of errors that might typically be found with modern network conditions and based the size of the correction on how far the ship could travel in 125, 250 and 500 ms. With a ship velocity of 12 cm/s, the correction magnitudes were thus 1.5, 3.0 and 6.0 cm respectively.

Duration of the Correction

When repairing inconsistencies, a game developer must choose between making the repair instantly with possibly jarring effects or prolonging the inconsistency and progressively fixing it over time. While it seems intuitive that repairing inconsistencies over time would be superior to warping, this had never been tested prior to this study, and there was no experimental data to indicate how quickly the repairs should actually be made. We performed a pilot study to determine repair times that ranged from very obvious to rarely detected, and based on these, we selected five duration values : 0 ms (warping), 250 ms, 500 ms, 750 ms and 1000 ms.

Smoothness of the Correction

When repairing inconsistencies using smooth corrections, the simplest solution is to adjust the speed of the entity and move it at a constant rate toward the corrected position, as shown in Figure 1c. This has the potential to be jarring for the player as the entity instantaneously changes speed and direction. As shown in shown in Figure 1d, "smoother" corrections gradually adjust the correction rate so that there are no sudden changes in velocity [20]. The actual correction rates for these two techniques are shown in Figure 3. When the correction rate is changed gradually, the actual rate is faster at the midpoint of the correction. In our study, we compared these two options of constant and variable correction rates.

Data Collection and Analysis

The *Space Rock-it* game was used to log data about the corrections and the participant responses. For each correction, we recorded *date and time*, *game condition*, *correction type* (constant or variable correction rate), *magnitude of correc-*

Table 2. Summary of Participant Responses

	Description	Number Reported	False Positives
1	Very Annoying	579	1
2	Annoying	660	5
3	Slightly Annoying	760	2
4	Perceptible but not Annoying	694	19
5	Imperceptible	3	0
	Not detected	2,704	
	Total	5,400	27

tion, correction duration, positions of the ships, participant response (or non-response if they did not detect the correction). We also recorded when participants incorrectly reported corrections when none had occurred.

We analyzed the data using one-way ANOVA to test for effects on the number of corrections observed. Player opinion of the corrections was analyzed with Wilcoxon tests on medians.

RESULTS

The results of our study allow us to address the three broad questions posed earlier in the paper: how noticeable and annoying do players find corrections; how do gameplay conditions affect reactions to corrections; and how do error repair techniques impact player experience?

During the study, participants were presented with a total of 5,400 corrections across all conditions. Participants noticed 2,696, or 50%, of these corrections. Table 2 summarizes the level of annoyance that participants assigned to each correction. There were a large number of reports at each level, indicating that participants used all available categories.[1]

We also collected data to measure the number of times a participant pressed the space bar when no correction had occurred (false positives). There were 27 false positives, representing 0.5% of the total corrections. We believe this to be a sufficiently small value as to not impact the overall results of the study and thus the false positives were simply discarded in the subsequent data analysis.

Q1: How Noticeable and Annoying are Corrections?

Participants noticed 50% of the corrections that occurred during gameplay, and rated 46% of the corrections they noticed as either "Annoying" or "Very Annoying". This is consistent with the anecdotal experience of games such as Battlefield 4 and Rainbow Six: Lockdown, where consistency issues were reported by players and reviewers as significantly negatively impacting player experience. This indicates that inconsistencies in video games are a real problem, and that corrections can be both noticeable and annoying for game players.

[1]Surprisingly, one participant rated three corrections as "Imperceptible", raising the question of why he flagged them at all. During the post-experiment interview, he explained that he had used the "Imperceptible" rating in cases where he was not sure whether he had observed a correction.

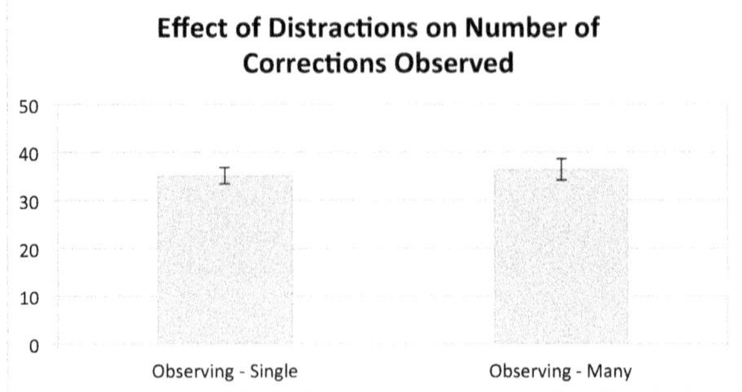

Figure 5. The addition of distractions did not show a significant effect on the number of corrections observed. The error bars shown represent the standard error for the number of corrections detected.

Q2: How Do Gameplay Conditions Affect Reactions to Corrections?

While the data from Table 2 shows that corrections are frequently noticed and are frequently considered annoying, we are primarily interested in what specific factors lead to corrections being more or less visible or annoying. We investigated the impact of three key factors on how players notice and react to corrections. These factors are *distraction, locus of attention*, and *involvement with gameplay*.

Distractions

We used the two "observing" conditions to evaluate how placing additional elements in the scene affects players' ability to notice when corrections occur. In both conditions, the players were merely observing the motion occurring in the scene. The first condition, *Observing - Single*, displayed a single pink space ship travelling around the screen, while the second condition, *Observing - Many*, showed two mobile space ships and forty asteroids. In both conditions, the participants were asked to focus their attention on the pink ship and all the corrections occurred to the position of the pink ship.

In each condition, a total of 60 corrections were displayed. In *Observing - Single*, the participants noticed on average 35 of the corrections, compared to 36 in the *Observing - Many* condition (see Figure 5). A paired-samples t-test failed to show a significant effect on number of corrections detected from adding the distraction of the second space ship and asteroids ($t(17)=0.98$, $p=0.342$).

Because we did not find a significant difference between these two conditions, for simplicity, we will present only the *Observing - Many* condition in all further discussion of the results, and we will refer to this condition as *Observing*.

Locus of Attention

In a game, a player's "locus of attention" is the point on the screen where the player's visual attention is focused. People direct their focus on a small portion of the visual world and their attention must be redirected to enable them to process information in another region [21]. In both the *Observing* and *Controlling* conditions, we directed participants to focus their attention on the ship to which the corrections were being applied. However, in the *Shooting* condition, the player was required to divide her attention between the ship she was

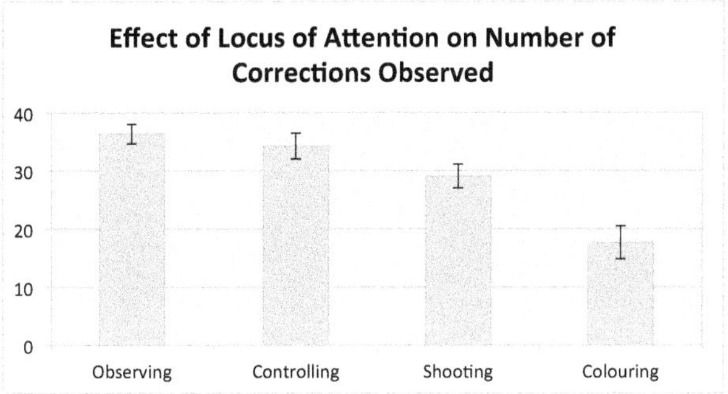

Figure 6. The participants noticed more corrections when their attention was focused on the game entity to which the correction was applied.

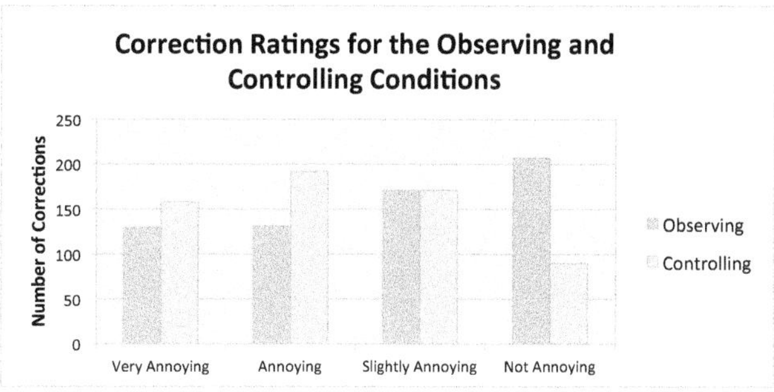

Figure 7. The participants rated the corrections as significantly more annoying when they affected the game play.

shooting at and the ship she was controlling. In the *Colouring* condition, the corrections all occurred to the AI-controlled ship, and the player needed to focus little attention on the motion of that ship. These four conditions therefore represented (1) locus of attention on the avatar being corrected (*Observing* and *Controlling*); (2) locus of attention split between the avatar being corrected and another avatar (*Shooting*); and (3) locus of attention on an avatar other than the one being corrected (*Colouring*).

The number of corrections detected in each of these conditions as well as the standard error is shown in Figure 6. One-way ANOVA showed a significant effect of the locus of attention on the number of corrections observed ($F(3,51)=48.17$ $p<0.001$). Follow-up pairwise t-tests using Bonferroni correction indicated that the number of corrections observed in the *Colouring* condition was significantly less than all the other conditions ($p<0.001$) and that the *Shooting* condition was significantly less than both the *Observing* ($p=0.001$) and the *Controlling* ($p=0.007$) conditions. No significant difference was found in the number of corrections observed between the *Observing* and *Controlling* conditions ($p=0.190$). The participants therefore saw most corrections in the cases where they were focused on the avatar being corrected, less in the split-attention case, and less yet when attention was focused on another avatar.

To investigate more deeply peoples' ability to perceive corrections while focused on another avatar, we performed further analysis on the *Colouring* condition, where players control a green ship that is not being corrected, while corrections are applied to a pink ship. We hypothesized that players would be more likely to notice corrections when the green ship that they control is close to the pink ship that is being corrected. We tested for a correlation between the distance between the two ships and the likelihood of observing corrections. We coded each correction as a 1 if it was detected and a 0 if it was not detected and correlated versus distance between the avatars. We found a weak negative correlation between distance and observation of corrections, ($r(1078)= -0.134$, $p<0.01$), establishing that indeed players were somewhat more likely to observe a correction when it occurred near to their locus of attention.

Involvement with Gameplay

We used the *Observing* and *Controlling* conditions to investigate whether corrections are more annoying when they impact gameplay. In the *Observing* condition, players simply watched the ship, while in the *Controlling* condition, they used the ship to colour asteroids. In both conditions, the player's attention was focused directly on the ship to which the corrections were being applied, and so the only difference between the conditions was whether the observation was passive, or whether the participant was engaged in the game-like colouring activity. In the *Controlling* condition, when a correction occurred, the player's ship moved location, often interfering with the player's intended movement. We hypothesized that this would cause players to rate the corrections as more annoying than in the *Observing* condition.

As described in the previous section, we found no significant difference between the *number of corrections* detected by the participants in each of these conditions. To test whether the corrections were more annoying when they impacted gameplay, we analysed players' ratings of the corrections using the Mean Opinion Score (Figure 4). A Wilcoxon signed rank test indicated that the corrections were rated as significantly more annoying in the *Controlling* condition than in the *Observing* condition ($z = -4.84$, $p<0.001$). Figure 7 shows the correction ratings for the *Observing* and *Controlling* conditions. More corrections were rated as "Annoying" or "Very Annoying" in the *Controlling* condition and more corrections were rated as "Not Annoying" in the *Observing* condition.

Q3: How Do Error Repair Techniques Impact Player Experience?

We now compare the three principle correction techniques of warping, smooth corrections with a constant correction rate and smooth corrections with a variable correction rate and calculate detection limits for the corrections based on the time interval over which the correction was performed. We begin by comparing warping to smooth corrections.

Smooth Corrections Versus Warping

Smooth corrections were performed over four time periods ranging from 250 ms to 1000 ms. We first consider the shortest repair period for smooth corrections, 250 ms. As shown in Figure 8, in all the conditions, fewer corrections were detected when they were performed smoothly over 250 ms than

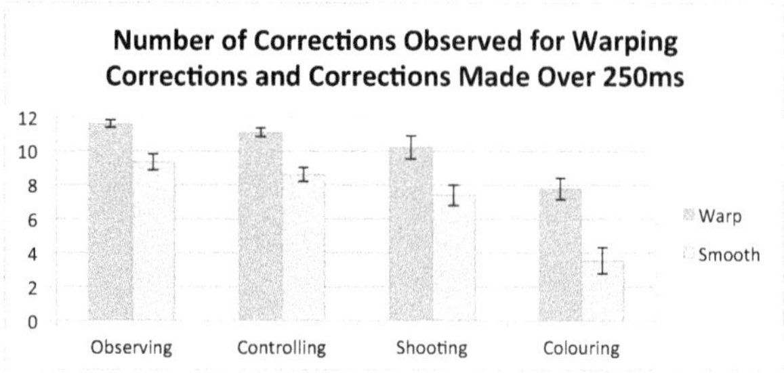

Figure 8. In all conditions, more corrections were noticed when warping was used

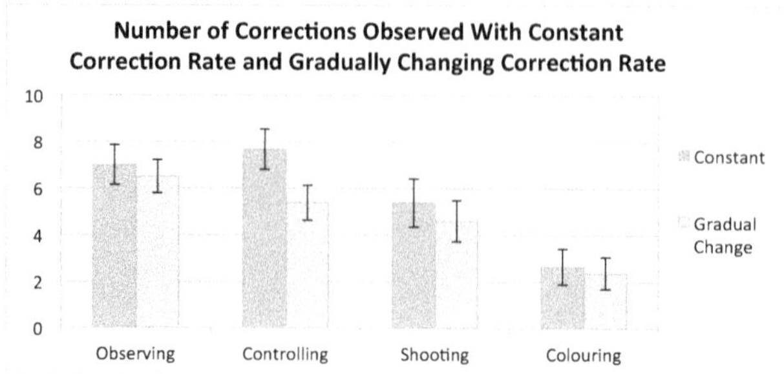

Figure 9. In all conditions, fewer corrections were noticed when the correction rate was adjusted smoothly

if warping was used. In all cases, the difference was significant ($p < 0.001$).

In addition to comparing the number of corrections detected, we also compared the participants' ratings of the corrections. For any correction the participants did not detect, we assigned a rating of 5, "Imperceptible". For each condition, we performed a Wilcoxon test to evaluate whether there was a difference between warping corrections and the corrections performed over a 250 ms window. In each case, the results indicated a significant difference: *Observing* ($z = -11.61$, $p < 0.001$), *Controlling* ($z = -9.72$, $p < 0.001$), *Shooting* ($z = -9.92$, $p < 0.001$) and *Colouring* ($z = -8.30$, $p < 0.001$). This indicates that players found smooth corrections to be less annoying than warping in all five game conditions, when smooth corrections were made over a 250 ms window.

Similar comparisons over longer correction windows (500 ms to 1,000 ms) yielded the same results, that in all cases, smooth corrections were preferred to warping, at the $\alpha < 0.05$ level.

Constant Versus Variable Correction Rate

To investigate the effect of the smoothness of corrections, we first looked at the number of corrections detected by the participants when the corrections were performed using a constant correction rate and when they were performed by gradually adjusting the correction rate (Figure 9). For each condition, there were a maximum of twelve corrections of each type that might have been detected by the participants: three correction sizes (1.5, 3.0 and 6.0 cm) and four durations (250 ms, 500 ms, 750 ms and 1,000 ms). Paired-samples t tests showed that the difference was significant for the *Controlling* condition ($t(17) = 5.25$, $p < 0.001$), with fewer corrections observed with variable correction rate. For the other conditions, the results were as follows: *Observing* ($t(17) = 1.23$, $p = 0.235$); *Shooting* ($t(17) = 1.44$, $p = 0.168$); and *Colouring* ($t(17) = 0.74$, $p = 0.472$). When we considered the different correction sizes, there was a significant difference between the number of corrections detected for the small (1.5 cm) and medium (3.0 cm) corrections for both the *Controlling* and *Shooting* conditions. For the large (6.0 cm) corrections, there was no significant difference between the number of corrections detected, likely because these larger corrections were easier to detect and the participants noticed in excess of 60% of the corrections in all of the conditions except *Colouring*.

We consulted the Mean Opinion Score ratings assigned under each condition to determine whether participants found a difference in annoyance of corrections using the constant versus variable algorithms. Wilcoxon tests indicated that there was a significant difference in all conditions except *Colouring*, indicating that variable rate corrections were less annoying in three of four conditions. The results were as follows: *Observing* ($z = -2.47$, $p = 0.014$), *Controlling* ($z = -6.69$, $p < 0.001$), *Shooting* ($z = -2.11$, $p = 0.035$) and *Colouring* ($z = -0.38$, $p = 0.702$).

A review of the number of positive and negative ranks reported by the Wilcoxon test for each correction size and correction duration were similar, indicating that this difference is applicable over the entire range of correction sizes and durations tested in our study.

Correction Detection Limits

We calculated the detection limits for each correction size and test condition. We use a standard psychophysical definition of detection limit as the level at which 50% of the participants notice the stimulus [9]. The detection limits were measured in milliseconds. That is, we sought the minimum correction duration in milliseconds where 50% of the participants detected the correction. In all cases, we noticed that the detection limit for the large (6 cm) corrections was approximately twice as large as for the medium size (3 cm) corrections. Similarly the detection limit for the medium size corrections was approximately twice as large as for the smallest (1.5 cm) corrections. For this reason, we report the detection limits in terms of the correction rate (cm/s) instead of in terms of the time over which the correction was performed and combine the detection limits for the three correction magnitudes. A correlation of the detection limits in cm/s versus the size of the correction validated this approach, showing no significant correlation for any of the conditions: *Observing* $p = 0.080$, *Controlling* $p = 0.575$, *Shooting* $p = 0.812$ and *Colouring* $p = 0.251$.

In Figure 10, we show the average detection limit for each condition. The *Observing* condition had the lowest detection limit ($M = 5.0$, $SE = 0.4$), followed by the *Controlling* condition ($M = 6.4$, $SE = 0.8$) and then the *Shooting* condition ($M = 7.5$, $SE = 0.7$). The *Colouring* condition had a much higher detection limit ($M = 26.2$, $SE = 4.1$). For the first three conditions, the detection limit is close to half the normal speed of the space ship in the game. In the *Colouring* condition, where the corrections occurred to the AI controlled ship and the player was paying less attention to that ship, the limit was much higher at over twice the normal ship speed.

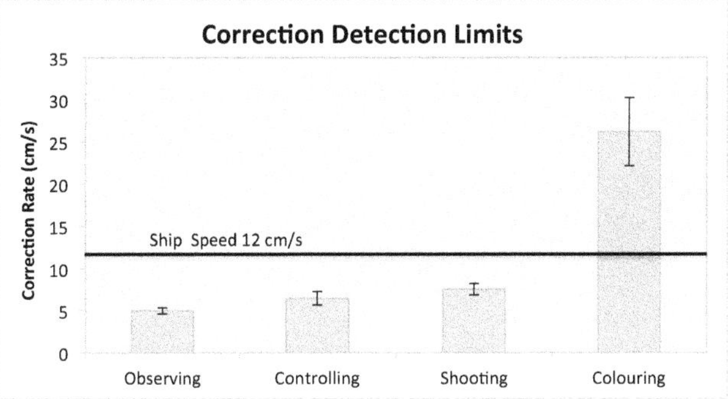

Figure 10. For the *Observing*, *Controlling* and *Shooting* conditions, the detection limit arose at a correction rate of approximately half the normal ship velocity.

SUMMARY OF RESULTS

We found that the primary factor significantly affecting the detection of corrections was the player's locus of attention. Distractions that did not shift the player's focus had little impact on the number of corrections detected.

We found that for the corrections in our study, smooth corrections were vastly superior to warping. Also, based on the player ratings of the corrections, we found that it was significantly better to make gradual adjustments to the correction rate rather than performing the correction at a constant rate.

Finally, we found that the ability of players to detect corrections is based on the speed of the correction, not its magnitude. When an entity is within the player's locus of attention, its speed can be adjusted by approximately 50% relative to its normal speed. Significantly higher adjustments can be made when the entity is outside the locus of attention.

DISCUSSION

The first objective of our study was to determine how noticeable and annoying corrections are. We found that corrections are a real problem in video games and players rated a significant proportion of them as either "Annoying" or "Very Annoying". All of the participants rated at least some of the corrections as "Very Annoying".

Our next objective was to determine which factors affected players' abilities to notice corrections and the degree to which they found the corrections annoying.

We were surprised to find no significant difference in the number of corrections detected as a result of adding distractions to the scene in our two observing conditions. In the first condition, the scene showed only a single space ship and in the other, a second ship and 40 asteroids had been added to the scene. In both conditions, the corrections all occurred to the same pink ship on which the participants were instructed to focus their attention. The additional objects all moved around the scene at a constant speed and did little to attract the participants' attention. Grad et al. [10] have shown that users tend not to notice peripheral information unless it is flashing or animated. Thus, we believe it is likely that the objects we added to the scene did not cause the participants to shift their focus away from the pink ship. It is quite possible that, if the motion of the other ship and asteroids was discontinuous or included some other unexpected motion, the distractions might have had an effect. This tells us that, in general, we cannot rely on distractions to mask the effects of repairs to inconsistencies.

Interestingly, during the post-hoc interviews, 11 of the 18 participants felt that the addition of the second space ship and the asteroids did distract them. It appears, however, that most of the participants thought that they were just momentary distracted; for example, participant 15 stated "*Once I got distracted 'cause I was looking at the green ship.... Then, I thought wait – I shouldn't be watching that.*" and participant 3 commented "*I would start wandering off and think let's see what that green ship is doing, but I am pretty sure I didn't miss anything.*"

The most significant factor we found in determining a player's ability to notice corrections was their locus of attention. Each of the three game-like conditions represented a different level of focus relative to the game object experiencing the corrections. In the *Controlling* condition, the players were controlling the space ship being corrected and their attention was almost completely focused on the point where the corrections occurred. In the *Shooting* condition, the corrections were applied to the target ship and the players were required to divide their attention between the target ship and the ship they were controlling. Finally, in the *Colouring* condition, the corrections were applied to the other ship, yet the position of that ship had little impact on the player. Thus, the players focused little attention on these corrections. Additionally, as the player's attention is shifted away from the point of the correction, fewer corrections were detected (although this distance correlation was weak). Together, these observations tell us that when developing games we need to pay close attention to where the player is looking and attempt to minimize the number and the visibility of corrections in that area.

In addition to knowing which corrections are most easily detected by players, it is also important to know what makes the corrections upsetting or disturbing. We found that corrections were more problematic when they interfered with the player's progress in the game. In the *Observing* condition, corrections were rated as significantly less annoying than those same corrections when they occurred in the *Controlling* condition. Warping corrections were also found to be significantly more annoying than smooth corrections, even when the smooth corrections were completed over a time window as small as 250 ms. In the post-hoc interviews, when the participants were asked which corrections they had found most annoying, they all described either the warping corrections or specific game situations that had affected them. Ten of the participants specifically mentioned the warping corrections; for example, participant 13 commented, "*The leaping one really bothered me a lot.*", and participant 9 stated "*The most annoying ones were when it flashed from one point on the screen to another.*" Eleven of the participants referred to specific gameplay situations that they found annoying; for example, participant 15 stated "*When I was shooting at the pink ship and tailing it, it glitched behind me*" and participant 2 mentioned "*The most annoying would be when you were trying to hit a ship or an asteroid and it just flies you somewhere totally different.*" Although the players in our study found the smooth corrections less annoying than the warping corrections, we note that corrections are not the only factor affecting player experience. For example, if the correction prolonged the duration of an inconsistency, it is possible that decisions such as who was shot might not be consistent with the players view of the world. Further research is required to study the interactions effects between these game critical decisions and error correction techniques.

In addition to minimizing corrections near the player's locus of attention, developers should attempt to eliminate warping corrections, and should reduce the impact of corrections that affect gameplay. For game developers, eliminating warping corrections can usually be accomplished by replacing them with smooth corrections. Minimizing corrections that might affect game play can be more challenging. One technique that can help is adaptive dead reckoning [5] in which the frequency of update messages for different game objects could be varied based on factors like where the player is focusing and whether or not the object is likely to be affected by game play. The use of remote lag [4] can almost eliminate the need for corrections to the positions of remote game entities, but adds the complexity of making game-critical decisions when players have diverging views of the game world [19].

When corrections are unavoidable, they should be performed as slowly as possible using a gradual change in velocity over time. We found that a correction rate equal to approximately half of the normal ship velocity resulted in only half of the participants detecting the correction. Further studies using different types of motion and different velocities would be required to determine the general applicability of such a guideline.

CONCLUSIONS AND FUTURE WORK

Problems with consistency are a regular occurrence in multiplayer games and these problems can have a huge impact on player experience. However, there has been until now little guidance available on how these inconsistencies impact player experience or how to repair inconsistencies once they are detected.

We have provided insight into how players perceive corrections in networked games and into techniques that can help to minimize the negative effects of corrections. We have performed a user study confirming that smooth correction techniques are significantly better than warping and that smooth corrections with a gradually changing correction rate are preferable over corrections with a constant correction rate. We found that players were most disturbed by warping corrections and corrections that directly affected them in the game, either moving them away from an asteroid they were about to hit, or spoiling their aim when shooting at another other ship. Finally, as a general guideline, we suggest that the speed of corrections should be based on the typical speed of the entity being corrected. We found that the detection limit for corrections was when the entity speed changed by 50%.

In future work, we plan to carry out additional studies, exploring other game situations, other types of avatar motion and other possible ways to distract players from the negative effects of corrections.

ACKNOWLEDGMENTS

We gratefully acknowledge the funding of the GRAND Network of Centres of Excellence.

REFERENCES

1. Aldridge, D. I shot you first! Gameplay networking in Halo: Reach. In *Game Developers Conference* (2011).
2. Battlefield 4. `http://www.battlefield.com/battlefield-4`.
3. Beigbeder, T., Coughlan, R., Lusher, C., Plunkett, J., Agu, E., and Claypool, M. The effects of loss and latency on user performance in Unreal Tournament 2003. In *NetGames*, ACM (2004), 144–151.
4. Bernier, Y. W. Latency compensating methods in client/server in-game protocol design and optimization. In *GDC* (2001).
5. Cai, W., Lee, F., and Chen, L. An auto-adaptive dead reckoning algorithm for distributed interactive simulation. In *PADS '99*, IEEE (1999), 82–89.
6. Chandler, A., and Finney, J. On the effects of loose causal consistency in mobile multiplayer games. In *NetGames*, ACM (2005), 1–11.
7. Dick, M., Wellnitz, O., and Wolf, L. Analysis of factors affecting players' performance and perception in multiplayer games. In *NetGames*, ACM (2005), 1–7.
8. Fiedler, G. Networked physics. `gafferongame.com/game-physics/networked-physics`, 2006.
9. Gescheider, G. A. *Psychophysics: the fundamentals*. Psychology Press, 2013.
10. Grad, K., Graham, T.C.N., and Stewart, J. Effective use of the periphery in game displays. In *Future Play*, ACM (2007), 69–76.
11. Harms, W. Review of Rainbow Six: Lockdown. `http://pc.gamespy.com/pc/rainbow-six-4-tentative-title/690399p2.html`, 2006. Accessed: 1-Apr-2014.
12. IGN. `http://ca.ign.com/articles/games/battlefield-4/xbox-one-161397`. Accessed: 9-Apr-2014.
13. Mauve, M., Vogel, J., Hilt, V., and Effelsberg, W. Local-lag and timewarp: Providing consistency in replicated continuous interactive media. *IEEE Transactions on Multimedia 6*, 1 (2004), 47–57.
14. ITU-T Recommendation P.800. Methods for Subjective Determination of Transmission Quality, 1996".
15. Murphy, C. Believable dead reckoning for networked games. In *Game Engine Gems, Volume 2*, E. Lengyel, Ed. CRC Press, 2011.
16. Pantel, L., and Wolf, L. C. On the suitability of dead reckoning schemes for games. In *NetGames*, ACM (2002), 79–84.
17. Pinelle, D., Wong, N., Stach, T., and Gutwin, C. Usability heuristics for networked multiplayer games. In *GROUP'09*, ACM (2009), 169–178.
18. Reddit. `http://www.reddit.com/r/battlefield_4`. Accessed: 9-Apr-2014.
19. Savery, C., Graham, T.C.N., Gutwin, C., and Brown, M. The effects of consistency maintenance methods on player experience and performance in networked games. In *CSCW*, ACM (2014), 1344–1355.
20. Smed, J., and Hakonen, H. *Algorithms and Networking for Computer Games*. Wiley, 2006. ISBN: 9780470018125.
21. Treisman, A. M., and Gelade, G. A feature-integration theory of attention. *Cognitive psychology 12*, 1 (1980), 97–136.
22. Wattimena, A., Kooij, R. E., Van Vugt, J., and Ahmed, O. Predicting the perceived quality of a first person shooter: the Quake IV G-model. In *NetGames*, ACM (2006), 42.
23. Zander, S., and Armitage, G. Empirically measuring the QoS sensitivity of interactive online game players. In *Proc. ATNAC* (2004), 511–518.

Interaction Design and Cognitive Gameplay: Role of Activation Time

Kamran Sedig **Robert Haworth**
Western University
London, Ontario, Canada, N6A 5B7
{sedig, rhaworth}@uwo.ca

ABSTRACT
Currently, there are no frameworks or methods for the systematic design of cognitive gameplay, the cognitive processes that emerge from the gameplay experience. In this paper, our aim is to contribute to the understanding of how to systematically design interaction for cognitive gameplay. The quality of the essential interactions between the player and the game—the sum of the operational forms of several structural elements of interaction—is the heart of cognitive gameplay. One such element is activation time, the timing of the action response of an interaction. We conducted a study to investigate the effect of different operational forms of activation time on cognitive gameplay. Two puzzle games were developed, each with one version for immediate activation time and another for on-demand activation time. The on-demand version of both games engaged participants in more effortful and reflective cognitive gameplay, while the immediate version was not conducive to such engagement.

Author Keywords
Cognition; Cognitive Gameplay; Core Mechanic; Games; Game Evaluation; Interaction Design; Interactivity Design

ACM Classification Keywords
H.5.2 [Information Interfaces]: User Interfaces; J.4 [Computer Applications - Social and Behavioral Sciences]: Psychology; K.3.1 [Computer Uses in Education]; K.8.0 [Personal Computing - General]: Games

INTRODUCTION
Recently, there has been increasing interest in using computer games for more than just entertainment. For instance, games have been designed with a focus on engaging players in deep and meaningful cognition—e.g., learning content, improving working memory, practicing spatial reasoning, or developing problem-solving skills. For

CHI PLAY '14, October 19 - 22 2014, Toronto, ON, Canada

http://dx.doi.org/10.1145/2658537.2658691

such games, cognitive gameplay has a very important role. In general, gameplay refers to the experience that emerges from the player interacting with a game [18]. Cognitive gameplay, then, signifies the emergent cognitive processes within the overall gameplay experience. In other words, it is the cognitive component of the game-playing experience.

Cognitive gameplay is the primary factor that determines how well games engage the player in cognitive tasks and activities [8]. For example, if we want to design a game for the cognitive activity of learning mathematics, we need to attentively design cognitive gameplay so that it is conducive to deep reflection focused on the mathematical concepts embedded in the game [21]. Since cognitive gameplay is emergent, we must design it indirectly [18] by designing the interaction from which it can emerge. Thus, to design cognitive gameplay in a systematic manner we need to be guided by a conceptual framework that clarifies the relationship between interaction and cognition. Currently, however, there are no such frameworks.

There are some frameworks and methods for the design of gameplay (e.g., [6, 10, 27]); but they focus on how to design for usability or enjoyment. As such, the cognitive aspects of gameplay are either ignored (e.g., [27]) or considered in relation to the enjoyment or challenge it causes (e.g., [5, 6]). Such frameworks and methods are necessary for designing effective and enjoyable games, and for analyzing games to understand what makes them enjoyable. However, they do not assist in understanding how to make players think more deeply or meaningfully.

There are also numerous frameworks for design in the context of learning (e.g., [1, 2]; see especially [6]), some of which even relate learning outcomes to specific game features (e.g., [2]). While these are certainly more useful for determining how to make players think, they have several limitations. First, the features are often very broad in scope, such as narrative or the right level of challenge [2]; this information is important for macro-level design, but it is less useful for micro-level design, especially micro-level design of interaction. Second, these frameworks are focused on a given activity (i.e., learning), and thus do not always generalize to other high-level activities that emerge in the context of cognitive gameplay—e.g., planning, problem solving, or decision-making. And, third, it is uncommon for these frameworks to be empirically supported [6, 17]. Little empirical support is a problem for research about general gameplay though, with randomly-controlled trials and properly qualitative studies seemingly lacking [6]. Existing studies on cognitive gameplay have mixed conclusions; some suggest there are cognitive benefits to playing games (e.g., [16]), while others suggest that cognitive benefits are limited in scope (e.g., [15]). Such confusion is reached because of the way in which games have been studied (see [17]). Furthermore, these studies are often disconnected from any design-related theory; in other words, the study indicates the kind and/or depth of cognitive gameplay that playing a game seems to have but has little to say about how to potentially duplicate this effect in other games.

Despite the significant work conducted in cognition for games, most especially in the area of learning, what is lacking from existing studies and frameworks is some way to identify and investigate the relationship between specific components of the interaction in a game and the resulting cognitive gameplay. [25] have recently developed a framework to inform the design of the micro-level interaction elements that affect the interactivity of visual tools. Since games are also visual tools, in this paper, we will use one element of this framework, activation time, to study cognitive gameplay. Each interaction in a game can be considered as a composite of a set of elements that collectively determine its structure. One of these structural elements is activation time. This element refers to the timing of the action response of an interaction. All the structural elements of interaction can take on different operational forms, depending on how the interaction itself is designed. Two operational forms which activation time can assume include: immediate and on-demand. When activation time is operationalized as immediate, the action response occurs as soon as the player performs an action. When activation time is operationalized as on-demand, the action response does not occur until after the player explicitly requests it. For example, consider a game in which the essential interaction is arranging shapes in some container. If the activation time element of this interaction is operationalized as immediate, whenever the player acts on a shape to move or rotate it, the shape will immediately change its position or orientation. If activation time is operationalized as on-demand instead, whenever the player acts on a shape, it will not change. The player will have to apply the changes separately, such as by clicking a "move shapes" button. Once that button is clicked, all the shapes on which the player has acted will change their position or orientation accordingly.

Since previous research has examined other aspects of interaction (e.g., [12, 21, 23]), we decided to explore the usefulness of activation time for the systematic design of cognitive gameplay, which is the focus of this paper. We will discuss how we investigated the relationship between different operational forms of activation time and cognitive gameplay, particularly the effect of activation time on deep and reflective planning. First, we designed two 2D puzzle games, each of which had two versions that only differed in the way that activation time was operationalized. We hypothesized that operationalizing activation time as immediate would promote a fragmentary and reactionary approach to planning, while operationalizing activation time as on-demand would promote a more holistic and reflective approach to planning. We then conducted an empirical study with these versions to test the difference between the cognitive gameplay that participants experienced, with the results confirming our hypothesis.

Therefore, we will discuss three things in this paper: 1) a summary of our conceptual framework for the design of cognitive gameplay as it pertains to the studied games, 2) the games that we developed, and 3) the study that we conducted and its results. Thus, the key contribution of this paper is to further our understanding of interaction design for computer games, particularly in relation to cognitive gameplay.

THEORETICAL FOUNDATIONS

In this paper, our sole interest is computer games—that is, games that are implemented on some form of computation technology. The exact form of this technology is irrelevant as a computer game could use any software or hardware platform (e.g., a tablet, game console, personal computer, or cell phone). In other words, by computer game we mean a game in which computational technology is the means through which the player interacts with the game, and not simply a game functioning on a personal computer. Several other terms are used in the literature to describe this medium (e.g., video game, digital game, electronic game), but we will treat them as synonymous with computer game.

Computer games are more suitable for cognitive gameplay than non-computer games (e.g., board games, physical sports) because of the greater interactive potential that computational technology provides [19, 24]. For example, consider a computer game version of *Soccer*. The player could act in the game by directing a player and pressing buttons to click the ball, which would result in similar interaction as non-computer game versions. However, the player could also interact by typing the velocity for the ball each time it is kicked, or by arranging the path that the ball will take each time it collides with a specific team member. These forms of interaction are relatively simple to design for computer games but are impractical or impossible for non-computer games. It is this greater range of possibilities for interaction that allows computer games to facilitate more appropriate forms of cognitive gameplay, since the design of interaction plays the greatest role in how cognitive gameplay unfolds [8].

Interaction

Computer games are interactive, meaning that there is a two-way dialogue between the player and the game. Thus, interaction can be divided into two components: an action that the player performs on some object at the user interface (UI) level of the game, and a reaction from the game. The reaction typically includes some perceivable effect, such as an object on the UI changing in size or position. It is also synonymous with other terms such as action response and visual feedback, though these terms may have more specific meanings than the general one intended by reaction.

Interaction can refer to low-level software or hardware events, such as clicking the mouse, pressing a key, or tapping a touch-sensitive surface. In this paper though, the term interaction refers to a general pattern of interaction, such as arranging a set of tiles, transforming one or more shapes, navigating through a game space, or assigning some behavior to game entities. Although the designer can choose patterns appropriate for the goal of a game, each pattern also differs in the cognitive engagement that it provides (for a comprehensive list of such action patterns and their cognitive utility, see [24]).

The Core Mechanic

Computer games often have several interactions that are incidental, such as pausing, saving the current game state, or adjusting the sound volume. Yet, there is usually a set of one or more interactions that are essential for playing the game. The term core mechanic typically refers to these essential interactions [18, 26]. When playing the game, the player performs these essential interactions repeatedly, forming a cycle of action-reaction. In other words, the core mechanic of a game is the continual pattern of essential interactions in which the player and the game are engaged.

For example, consider the computer game *Tetris*. There are two essential interactions in this game: rotating and sliding. As such, *Tetris* has a very simple core mechanic: the repeated cycle of acting on a shape and it reacting by moving or rotating.

For usability reasons, the incidental interactions should be carefully designed. However, the core mechanic forms the heart of gameplay; it is the repeated performance of these essential interactions that gives rise to the experience called gameplay [7, 18]. Therefore, the design of the core mechanic will have the greatest effect on cognitive gameplay (e.g., [21, 23]).

Cognitive Gameplay

Over the past few decades, cognitive scientists have largely departed from models of cognition as discrete information processing that occurs within the brain to models that encompass a broader system (e.g., [4, 9]). This is due to increasing evidence that objects external to the brain not only mediate and facilitate the operation of cognitive processes but also are integral parts of what can be viewed as an extended and distributed cognitive system (see [3]).

Cognition in the context of computer games can therefore be understood as the player-game cognitive system, which is composed of a player and a computer game. Although the player is engaged in some cognitive task, the task itself is enabled, mediated, and supported by the game [8, 12]. Thus, cognition is the mutual coordination and cooperation between the player and the game. This occurs as a result of the core mechanic. It is through the core mechanic that the player and the game are coupled together in a mutual and dynamic dialogue [11, 19, 23]. In other words, it is through the cognitive coupling enabled by the core mechanic that cognitive processes and activities (e.g., planning, problem solving, decision-making, pattern recognition) can emerge.

For example, consider again the computer game *Tetris*. Through the core mechanic the player is continually moving and rotating shapes. However, the goal of the game is to form solid rows so that the components of the row will be removed from the play area. The player must identify optimal positions for the current block, in anticipation of future ones, in order to succeed. This is entirely facilitated by the core mechanic. In other words, the player can move and rotate shapes to aid the process of identifying possible and optimal locations, and to aid the task of planning the positions of blocks [12]. This is a simple illustration of the cognitive coupling between the player and the game. An important research question involves the quality of this cognitive coupling—that is, how should the core mechanic be designed to create desired forms of coupling?

Therefore, the term cognitive gameplay refers to the cognitive processes that emerge through the mutual dialogue between the player and the game, enabled by the core mechanic. In considering the quality of cognitive gameplay though, a number of factors could be involved such as: the kinds of processes in which the player is engaged (e.g., [2, 24]), how deeply or consciously the player performs these processes [20], and the amount of mental effort that these processes require [23, 28]. As such, these could be the factors that designers consider in order to promote desired kinds of cognitive gameplay.

Interactivity

Since cognitive gameplay is an emergent phenomenon, it cannot be designed directly. Design of cognitive gameplay is a second-order activity and must be done indirectly. It is the core mechanic that is designed directly, enabling the desired cognitive gameplay to emerge. The term interactivity refers to the quality of interaction, and thus the quality of the cognitive coupling between the player and the game [25]. The operational form of the interaction elements that make up the core mechanic of a game affect the game's interactivity and hence the quality of its cognitive coupling and its cognitive gameplay.

As previously mentioned, each interaction in the core mechanic has a set of structural elements. [25] have identified twelve such elements, some of which include: agency, context, flow, focus, granularity, and timing. These elements have various operational forms that affect the quality of the cognitive coupling between a user and any visual tool, including games. Hence, designing interactivity of a game at a micro-level involves determining how each of these elements should be operationalized.

An example of one of these elements that has been studied is focus. This element can be operationalized as direct or indirect. In the former the player acts on an interface object directly, whereas in the latter the player acts on an intermediary interface object to influence the target object. In a study of a game dealing with mathematical concepts, a comparison of these two operationalizations of focus resulted in different cognitive gameplay. The results showed that indirect focus led to deeper and more effortful learning among the subjects than direct focus [23]. Careful operationalization of this interaction element in one version of the game led to cognitive gameplay that was characterized by reflective, mindful learning as opposed to the other version of the game that promoted experiential cognition and shallow learning.

Activation Time

The interaction element investigated and reported in this paper is activation time. As previously mentioned, this element is concerned with the commencement of the reaction after the player has committed an action. Two operational forms of activation time are: immediate and on-demand. If activation time is immediate, the reaction occurs instantaneously after an action is committed. If activation time is on-demand, the reaction does not occur after an action is committed but only once the player requests it.

The operationalization of this element may promote different degrees of mental effort and engagement. For example, if activation time is on-demand, the player may be forced to engage in deep, reflective thought before committing an action, since the feedback from the action (i.e., the reaction) is not immediate. However, to test whether and how different operationalizations of activation time affect cognitive gameplay, we conducted a study.

STUDY METHODOLOGY

To investigate the role of activation time in cognitive gameplay we created two simple 2D puzzle-based computer games: *Temple Swap* (TS) and *Laser Dilemma* (LD). One game may be insufficient for proper generalization and validation of the study [17], so we developed two. We used puzzle games so that some cognitive effort would already be required; hence, we could measure difference of, and not existence of, cognitive gameplay. We used simple games to reduce the likelihood that game factors other than activation time would influence cognitive gameplay, and because simple games were easier to produce and learn how to play.

To test the different operationalizations of activation time, we created two versions for each game. Following the procedure outlined in [22], the only change between the two versions was the way in which activation time was operationalized. Although at the surface level these two versions are different games, they are still the same game at a higher level of abstraction [see 22]. As differences in the versions are due to the design decisions that we are interested in studying (i.e., activation time), it is reasonable to correlate any differences in cognitive gameplay to the operationalization of activation time. Two versions were thus necessary to study within-game effects of activation time, while two games were necessary to study between-game effects of activation time [see 17].

Game 1: Temple Swap (TS)

TS has 20 levels of slowly increasing difficulty. In each level, the player is given a grid of tiles. Each tile has one of four different symbols on it. The goal of the game is to arrange the tiles so that each one is in a horizontal or vertical set of three or more with matching symbols. A level is complete when all its tiles are in a set.

The core mechanic includes one interaction: swapping the position of two adjacent tiles. Tiles can be vertically or horizontally adjacent, but not diagonally adjacent (i.e., connected at the corner). One incidental interaction is also included: resetting the level, which returns all the tiles to their original position. The player is awarded points for completing each level, with the number of points based only on the difficulty of the level. The same levels were used in both versions of the game and were play-tested to ensure a similar increase in difficulty across both versions.

Temple Swap – Immediate Activation Time (TS-I)

In this version, the activation time element of the core mechanic was operationalized as immediate. This was implemented as follows. The player selects one tile by clicking on it and then selects another adjacent tile by clicking on it. Then, the tiles move so that their positions are swapped. The movement is gradual, taking just under one second to complete, and is accompanied by a sound effect. The player cannot select tiles while this movement is occurring. After each swap, the game checks if a correct solution has been found and rewards the player accordingly.

Figure 1. A screenshot of game TS-D.

Temple Swap – On-Demand Activation Time (TS-D)

In this version, the activation time element of the core mechanic was operationalized as on-demand. This was implemented as follows. The player selects tiles exactly as described for TS-I. Once the player has selected a pair of tiles, this pair is added to the end of a queue. The queue lists all the locations on the grid that will be swapped and in the order that this swapping will occur. The player can click on a "go" button to request the reaction. Then, each pair in the queue, in its appropriate order, will swap exactly as described for TS-I. The player cannot select tiles until all pairs in the queue have been swapped. If the sequence of swaps in the queue does not result in a correct solution, then the level resets as though the player had pressed the reset button. In other words, once the player clicks the "go" button, the proposed solution must correct or else a whole new solution will have to be created.

Game 2: Laser Dilemma (LD)

LD has 20 levels of slowly increasing difficulty. In each level, the player is given a maze-like arrangement of objects: goal rings, a laser gun, walls, and reflector blocks. The laser gun fires an energy ball in a certain direction. This ball travels in a straight line until it collides with a wall, which destroys it, or a reflector block, which changes its direction. When the ball collides with a goal ring, the ring becomes activated. The goal of the game is to have the energy ball activate all the goal rings on the level before the ball is destroyed.

The core mechanic includes two interactions: the player can move reflector blocks around on the level, and she can change the orientation of these blocks. Only certain reflector blocks in each level are interactive. These are marked with a thick black border around their edge, and are placed in a box on the left-hand side of the UI at the start of each level. There is also one incidental interaction: the player can reset the level, which returns all the interactive reflector blocks to their original position.

The player is awarded points for completing each level, with the number of points based only on the difficulty of the level. The same levels were used in both versions of the game and were play-tested to ensure a similar increase in difficulty across both versions.

Laser Dilemma – Immediate Activation Time (LD-I)

In this version, the activation time element of the core mechanic was operationalized as immediate. The activation time in this case does not refer to the placing or rotating of reflector blocks, which is also immediate, but to the laser gun firing to test the solution. In other words, every time the player places a reflector block on the play area, the laser gun will fire and the solution will be tested. Thus, the player can always and immediately see whether her current solution is correct and, if not, continue to revise it.

Laser Dilemma – On-Demand Activation Time (LD-D)

In this version, the activation time element of the core mechanic was operationalized as on-demand. As above, the activation time refers to when the laser gun fires. In this version, the player can place and rotate as many reflector blocks as desired and the laser gun will never fire. To fire the gun, the player must click the "fire" button, at which point the game will test the solution exactly as it occurs in LD-I. However, if the solution is not correct then the level resets as though the player had pressed the reset button, and she will have to create a whole new solution.

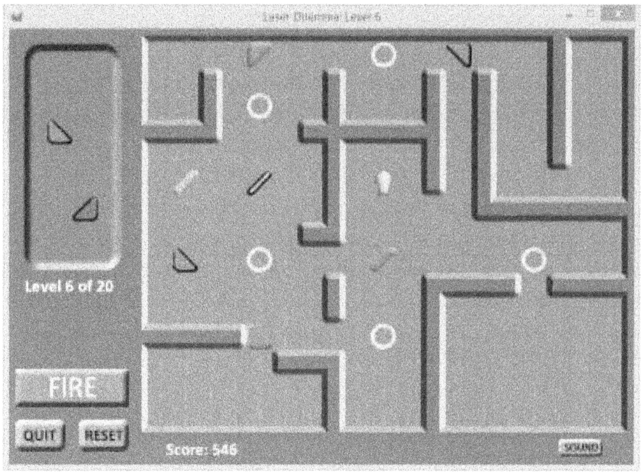

Figure 2. A screenshot of game LD-D.

Study Procedure

We conducted the study with a mixed-methods approach that emphasized qualitative data, and divided the study into two sessions: a play session and an interview session (both are described below). We recruited 40 university students (n=40) using on-campus posters and in-class presentations. Two randomly chosen participants won a cash prize, but the rest were not compensated. This method of compensation was mentioned during recruitment but the size of the prize ($150 CA) was not mentioned in accordance with ethical requirements. Participant demographics are described in the participants sub-section below. We randomly assigned each participant to one game version: TS-I, TS-D, LD-I, or LD-D. At least one male and female played each version, but the number of each gender varied in each version. All 40 participants performed the play session, while 12 of them were chosen to participate in the interview session. Interview criteria included: the quality of their comments during the play session and their preference and availability for being interviewed. Most participants were excluded from the interview due to being uninterested or unavailable.

Play Session

Each play session was approximately 60 minutes in length, involving three steps in the following order: 1) participants filled out a demographics survey on paper, 2) they played their assigned game version for about 25 minutes, and 3) they filled out a design questionnaire on paper. They only played the version to which they were assigned, and they received the same instructions as others who were assigned to their version. The game provided the instructions, though the researchers answered questions from participants.

We collected four sources of data: 1) video-recordings of the game screen, to capture in-game interaction; 2) audio-recordings, to capture verbal comments of the participants;

3) two paper surveys, to capture specific opinions and experiences; and 4) direct observations obtained from watching participants interact with the game.

We constructed the two surveys, using previous HCI-based computer game studies [e.g., 21] as examples. The demographics survey gathered demographic data, previous game-playing behavior, and game-playing preferences. The design questionnaire gathered participants' opinions of different aspects of the game and gameplay—e.g., whether there were usability problems, the degree of challenge the game provided and the nature of this challenge, the kind of cognitive tasks in which they engaged, and the mental effort involved in these tasks. Some questions in both surveys used a 5-point Likert scale, such as "Do you think the game interface made it easier for you to create plans for each level?" with a scale from "Absolutely" to "Definitely No". Most of the questions were open-ended or contained an open-ended portion, such as "What did or didn't you find challenging in the game," and "If you ever reset one of the levels, why did you reset it?"

Interview Session

The purpose of the interview session was to let participants experience the other version of their assigned game so that they could compare the two versions. The interview was separate so that the original session time could be kept short but participants would still have sufficient time to discuss their thoughts on the two versions in detail. Each interview session was performed two to three weeks after the participant had performed the play session. The interview session was approximately 60 minutes in length, during which time the participants were shown both versions of their assigned game, were asked several questions about both versions, and were given a brief opportunity to play. The interview was semi-structured in format (see [13]). The questions were mostly open-ended, and were intended to gather opinions of each version from several perspectives—e.g., perceived difficulty or challenge, anticipated effort required for planning and cognitive load for memory, and the way in which they would think while playing it. The interview was audio-recorded, and the game screen was video-recorded to capture any playing by the participants.

Participants

In this sub-section, we will present a summary of some data gathered from the demographics survey. Participants were equally split in terms of gender (20 male, 20 female), came from a variety of disciplines[1], and were both graduate (17) and undergraduate (23) students. When asked to list the kinds of games which participants had experience, only 5 wrote puzzle games; most wrote games or categories that were reaction-oriented in nature (e.g., First-Person Shooter, apps like Fruit Ninja). The most commonly mentioned games that participants preferred playing[2] were Tetris (8), Candy Crush Saga (4), and Call of Duty (4). Most participants considered themselves non-gamers and either a total novice or slightly experienced gamer (see Table 1).

Self-identification of gamer status[3]					
NG	C	C-A	A	A-H	H
23	3	5	3	5	1

Self-assessed game-playing experience level[4]				
N	SE	E	VE	X
11	14	7	6	2

Table 1. Participant demographics summary.

STUDY RESULTS

In this section, we will present some results from the study. This section is divided into four sub-sections, one for each treatment group. Each sub-section begins with a summary of the findings for that group. Since the data was merged during the analysis phase, the results include a combination of observations, recordings, verbal comments from both sessions, and survey responses. Participants were encoded using P<#> (e.g., P4, P27) when the study was conducted, and are referred to accordingly when they are quoted.

Game TS-I

In this version, the cognitive gameplay that participants experienced included fragmentary planning, undirected planning, and a low degree of mental effort relative to effort in TS-D.

Fragmentary Planning

The participants who played this version attempted to solve each level by moving tiles around until they found a correct solution. In some cases, this movement was part of a larger strategy for solving one part of the puzzle: "*I just moved pieces around, for the most part. If I knew a certain set was supposed to be somewhere, I stuck it there. Like, I didn't move the keys once they were there ... unless I really needed to.*" (P23) In other cases, the tiles were moved because the attempted solution was incorrect and the

[1] Including: biology, business, chemistry, computer science, economics, education, engineering, English, health science, kinesiology, law, library science, mathematics, media studies, medicine, modern language studies, psychology.

[2] In response to: "List some of the computer games that you most prefer playing." Participants wrote between 1 and 4 games or game-genres. Over 80 unique entries were given.

[3] "Do you consider yourself ..." Choices are: NG=non-gamer, C=causal gamer, C-A=between C and A, A=average gamer, A-H=between A and H, H=hardcore gamer.

[4] "In general, how experienced are you with playing games?" Choices are: N=novice, SE=slightly experienced, E=experienced, VE=very experienced, X=expert.

participant was exploring other possibilities. When P4 was asked how he recovered from an incorrect solution, he responded: "*I still tried to make sets of three. I just kept trying different shapes, kept moving things around until it worked.*" However, just randomly moving pieces around to get through the game was a possible strategy. For instance, P34 wrote in the design questionnaire that the game had low difficulty because "*one could try and try and move tiles randomly until they matched.*"

Undirected Planning

All the participants sometimes performed actions that had little pragmatic utility. For example, they would move a tile from one location on the grid to another and then move it back to its original position. Other times they would swap two tiles that had the same symbol. P34 did this a few times, and one of those times commented "*Oh, that was pointless.*" At some point, all of them realized that a solution they were building was incorrect. Some of them also developed a correct solution without realizing it. This occurred to P23 three times, and on the second time he remarked: "*I didn't see that coming either. [The game] said it was right though, so fair enough.*"

Low Mental Effort

In the questionnaire, one participant wrote that the UI 'maybe' supported memory because "*immediately after [I made] a move I could undo it*" (P34). Another answered 'maybe' to the same question because "*I didn't remember the steps or action I performed in the game.*" (P4) Participants were observed repeating similar actions when attempting to solve one puzzle. For instance, P23 found one incorrect solution and then attempted to create a new one. However, once this solution was complete the participant exclaimed with a laugh "*I just did the same thing [but] on the other side!*"

Game TS-D

In this version, the cognitive gameplay that participants experienced included effortful visualizing and a high demand on working memory. Furthermore, the cognitive gameplay of TS-D was deemed superior to that of TS-I.

Effortful Visualizing

The participants indicated that the game engaged them in visualizing the sequence of moves and state of the board: "*I'm trying to mentally see all the swaps.*" (P6) For some of the participants, this activity was the very difficult. For instance, P2 said "*The hard thing is I can't visually imagine what happens next. If I could do it one at a time and have them swap, I could see it but I have to think instead.*" P18 echoed this sentiment:

"*It's hard to plan ahead, I can't see everything. I do one move in my head, and then the next one, but then I begin to forget what I did. You don't see it as you do it, you have to do it all in your head and then press go. It's hard to remember all that. If it was one move at a time it would be a lot easier for me.*"

Similarly, when asked in the design questionnaire whether the UI made it easier to know the outcome of their actions, the most common answer (60%) was 'not really.' Some reasons why included: "*Because I had to perform all steps and did not see intermediary actions on the board,*" (P8) and "*You had to visualize your moves as opposed to seeing them one by one.*" (P6)

High Memory Demand

The participants also indicated that they needed to remember the mental visualization created and/or the sequence of actions. This was also a difficult and demanding task, as explained by P7: "*The most difficult part is to remember where the pieces are [...] that's why I keep failing and trying again. I keep forgetting my moves. I forget one step in my plan or where I moved one thing.*" The high memory demand was also reported in the design questionnaire. When asked whether the UI made it easier to remember things, the most common answer (70%) was "not really." The main reason repeated by the participants was similar to P32's response: "*I was holding the information in my head to figure out what to do next.*"

In response to the high memory demand, some participants created partial solutions, tested them, and then revised them. For example, when working through part of a solution, P6 said "*I need this here, and I need to swap those to get it ... I think it will be helpful to see it,*" after which the participant tested the solution. When the solution was completed the participant carefully looked at the screen to see the end state, but exclaimed when the level reset shortly after that: "*Oh no! I needed to see that longer.*"

Other participants broke the puzzle down into sections and solved the sections one at a time. The value of this strategy was explained by P9: "*I divided the puzzle into smaller parts, and that makes it much easier to solve. [...] Because memorizing all of those places is hard.*" A more detailed explanation of this strategy was given by P3:

"*I tried to break it down into smaller parts. For this puzzle, you've got three birds down at the bottom, and I said 'Ah, my first two moves would be to get those birds down.' I can now forget about those birds, because I've logically sealed then off. [...] So now I've almost started a fresh game in my head, because I made that one logical move. So that's how I try to break it down into smaller and smaller parts.*"

Superior Cognitive Gameplay Compared to TS-I

When the interview participants were shown version TS-I they all thought that it had inferior cognitive gameplay than TS-D, based on their experiences with TS-D:

"*My thoughts are that you've broken any need to play the game. You've eliminated any memory issues. [...] You still have to figure out the end state [...] but now you can just fool around and try things and get there eventually. [...] If playing this game has any exercise benefits to the mind, [...] this state of the game would ruin all of it.*" (P29)

"*Now it's become a clicky game, it's really simple. Because I don't have to track my moves anymore [...] I'm just playing a clicky game now. [...] A game like this I'd get tired of very quickly. [...] I don't think this would push you as much as the other versions, [even if] you had a maximum number of moves.*" (P3)

"*You don't have to remember anything [in TS-I]. You make a step, and then based on that you make a new plan. [...] [But,] there's no planning. You're not planning three or four steps ahead, you're not having to think of the bigger picture [...] because the moment you click it, it switches. [...] I think it's not as fun because it's so easy.*" (P8)

Game LD-I

In this version, the cognitive gameplay that participants experienced included wayfinding and planning, but the participants found themselves restricted from fully performing those activities.

Hindered Wayfinding

All of the participants engaged in the cognitive activity of wayfinding; they were trying to find a path through the level. This activity was externalized by tracing the path with their hand and with the mouse. However, the participants reported that wayfinding was influenced by the way that activation time was operationalized:

"*[The laser firing after each block] kind of hinders me a bit. [...] I would rather plan it and map it out first and fire when I'm done. Then I'd see where I went go wrong and take that singular one out.*" (P22)

"*Here I lose a lot of time for a misplaced piece or just mentally thinking things through, and for every single piece I don't need to test the entire system.*" (P16)

Occasionally, participants would move a reflector block to a desired location but instead of placing it, and triggering the reaction, they would leave it and trace a path using their hand. One participant also placed blocks in front of the laser, to shorten the reaction time. Sometimes, participants would intentionally pick up a block and place it in the same location to trigger the reaction, and watch the result.

Hindered Planning

The participants were also engaged in planning; they had to place a sequence of reflector blocks in order to proceed through the game. When P22 was asked whether he had to do much planning, his response was "*not really. I mean, it shoots every time so I just go with whatever it's doing.*" When the participants were asked how the well they could plan with immediate activation time, their responses were largely negative:

"*I found it frustrating. I wish I could have said 'ok, execute', or had a button to say 'go now.' [...] Also, it was not helpful because it was slow, it shoots then it goes 'bom... bom...', but I'm working faster than that. I know what many of the contingencies are, I know what's going to happen in the event that I do that, so I don't need you to play it all out for me.*" (P13)

"*I guess by it going step-by-step this forces me to—it almost solves it for you or works in a certain sequence. Because I have to put one down each time, and it shows me the solution each time, this is a step-by-step process.*" (P16)

Inferior Cognitive Gameplay Compared to LD-D

When the interview participants were shown version LD-D they thought it required more effortful planning and supported memory better:

"*There is definitely more effort in planning, since I only have essentially one shot at it. And so, instead of putting a few pieces and figuring it out later, I basically have to map it all out by moving the mouse around.*" (P16)

"*In this one you put [reflector blocks] all there, you can offload your memory onto [the game], and then test it. Whereas in [LD-I], you're keeping them in your memory. You're offloading them but you have to offload them one at a time. At any time you could forget one of them. Whereas [in LD-D] you can put them all there at one time, and that helps memory.*" (P13)

Game LD-D

In this version, the cognitive gameplay that participants experienced included effortful visualizing and a moderate memory demand.

Effortful Visualizing

As in LD-I, all the participants engaged in wayfinding. They externalized this activity by tracing the path with their hand and with the mouse. However, they also put significant effort into mentally visualizing the path:

"*I'm attempting to predict the entire path [...] I'm trying to simulate the entire thing in my mind, based on where it's going to go before I make a change, and then what changes I can make to get it to go where I want.*" (P10).

"*[My strategy is to] predict the way the ball's going to go. It's tough to visualize it. I'd say [my strategy is] maybe a combination of trial-and-error and just like intense forethought before I press the actual fire button.*" (P20)

In the design questionnaire, P24 explained his strategy: "*I did not really make plans. For certain levels, it seemed like it would be easy and beneficial for me to make plans first, but I just did 'trial-and-error' in my mind a lot, which was why it was so demanding on my memory!*"

At some point, all the participants started creating partial solutions and testing them. For instance, while explaining the path being developed, P21 said "*if I place this here it will go up like this... no. I need to try this first to see how it works, because I have no idea.*" Some of the participants tested their plan quite frequently while others did not. For P29, for example, it was the latter: "*I check that it works; when I'm sure that it works [then] I click the fire button.*" For some participants it was necessary to test the solution to help them visualize the path, while others were able to mentally visualize it unassisted. For instance, compare P21's comment above with that of P25: "*Wow, I just don't even know what to do [for this level]. Part of me just wants to press fire and see where it goes, but I know exactly where it will go.*"

Moderate Memory Demand

When trying to build partial solutions and test them, some participants experienced difficulty remembering the solution they tested: "*It's hard to remember what I just did. I totally saw [the correct solution], if this could just come back down there. ... It's hard, this is really hard.*" (P25) When asked in the design questionnaire whether the UI made it easier to remember things, the responses were mixed. Half agreed, "*I can see it. I don't need to remember everything,*" (P26) while the other half disagreed, "*I had to press reset a lot, and for levels with a lot of pieces I sometimes forgot where things were before I pressed reset.*" (P15) This memory demand was involved in both the visualizing, as shown in P24's comment above, and planning. P31 wrote in the questionnaire that planning was difficult because "*The [background] lines helped, but much of the state had to be maintained in working memory.*"

DISCUSSION AND CONCLUSION

In this paper we discussed activation time, one micro-level interaction element, and its role in cognitive gameplay. To further investigate this role, we developed two computer games each with two versions corresponding to the two operationalizations of activation. We then conducted a study to test the effect on cognitive gameplay. The results indicated that a difference in cognitive gameplay occurred across both games. The game versions with on-demand activation time engaged participants in more comprehensive planning and demanded more mental resources (e.g., working memory). The versions with immediate activation discouraged the participants from engaging in effortful cognitive gameplay and, in one of the games, interfered with their ability to plan in a comprehensive manner.

This study has several limitations, of which four will be mentioned. First, the sample size is small with very diverse backgrounds. This diversity assists generalizability [17] but needs a larger sample size than what we used. However, our current sample size is typical for usability studies [13] and, at the very least, is sufficient to identify that something warranting further study with a larger sample is occurring.

Second, our study gathered primarily self-report measures for the depth and kind of cognitive engagement. This was sufficient, since we were not interested in measuring gains from playing (e.g., improvement in working memory) but whether participants felt engaged in certain cognitive activities. Future studies that include objective measures of cognitive performance would more precisely indicate the cognitive processes that are affected by activation time.

Third, very little in the way of standard usability or game-enjoyment testing was incorporated into the study. This was intentional, since the focus was on cognitive gameplay. Informal usability testing was performed on the games, but it was not part of the study nor was it reported in this paper. Future studies incorporating usability testing would help to rule out extraneous UI issues that might confound the effect of activation time. As well, cognitive gameplay is known to have an effect on enjoyment [e.g., 5, 6]. Hence, measuring enjoyment more thoroughly would give finer granularity to the effects of activation time on gameplay. This may be difficult, especially considering the current problems with measuring enjoyment in games (see [14]), and is another reason why such testing was not included in our study.

Fourth and finally, the games we tested were both puzzle games. This was intentional, so that we could first identify whether similar effects occur across different games in the same genre. In theory though, the effects of activation time should occur regardless of the game genre. However, puzzle games inherently require some cognitive effort, so our results may be limited to puzzle games. Future studies with games of different genres should be conducted to eliminate such bias.

The results of the study presented in this paper have implications for interaction design of computer games. They suggest that incorporating on-demand activation time into the core mechanic of puzzle-based games may result in more engaging, effortful, and reflective cognitive gameplay. They also suggest that incorporating immediate activation time in the core mechanic may result in less optimal forms of thinking, planning, problem solving, and visualizing. Therefore, if designers are not aware of activation time, the game they design may not be conducive to the intended cognitive gameplay. If designers want to systematically design cognitive gameplay, they should carefully consider how activation time is operationalized in the core mechanic.

ACKNOWLEDGMENTS

This research has been financially supported by the Natural Sciences and Engineering Research Council of Canada.

REFERENCES

1. Aleven, V., Myers, E., Easterday, M., and Ogan, A. Toward a framework for the analysis and design of educational games. In *Proc. DIGITEL 2010*, IEEE (2010), 69-76.
2. Bedwell, W.L., Pavlas, D., Heyne, K., Lazzara, E.H., and Salas, E. Toward a taxonomy linking game attributes to learning: An empirical study. *Simulation & Gaming 43*, 6 (2012), 729-760.

3. Clark, A. *Supersizing the mind: Embodiment, action, and cognitive extension*. Oxford University Press, New York, NY, USA, 2008.
4. Clark, A., and Chalmers, D. The extended mind. *Analysis 58*, 1 (1998), 7-19.
5. Cox, A., Cairns, P., Shah, P., and Carroll, M. Not doing but thinking: The role of challenge in the gaming experience. In *Proc. SIGCHI 2012*, ACM Press (2012), 79-88.
6. Connolly, T.M., Boyle, E.a., MacArthur, E., Hainey, T., and Boyle, J.M. A systematic literature review of empirical evidence on computer games and serious games. *Computers & Education 59*, 2 (2012), 661-686
7. Ermi, L., and Mäyrä, F. Fundamental components of the gameplay experience: Analysing immersion. In *Proc. DiGRA 2005*, DiGRA, (2005).
8. Haworth, R., Parsons, P., and Sedig, K. Design of digital cognitive games: Some considerations. *Journal of Cognitive Technology 18*, 1 (2013), 22-27.
9. Hutchins, E. *Cognition in the Wild*. MIT Press, Cambridge, MA, USA, 1995.
10. Isbister, K., and Schaffer, N. *Game Usability*. Morgan Kaufmann, Burlington, MA, USA, 2008.
11. Kirsh, D. Metacognition, distributed cognition and visual design. In P. Gardinfas and P. Johansson, eds., *Cognition, Education and Communication Technology*. Lawrence Erlbaum, Mahwah, NJ, USA, 2005, 1-22.
12. Kirsh, D., and Maglio, P. On distinguishing epistemic from pragmatic action. *Cognitive Science 18*, (1994), 513-549.
13. Lazar, J., Feng, J.H., and Hochheiser, H. *Research Methods in Human-Computer Interaction*. Wiley and Sons, West Sussex, UK, 2010.
14. Nacke, L., Drachen, A., and Göbel, S. Methods for Evaluating Gameplay Experience in a Serious Gaming Context. *International Journal of Computer Science in Sport 9*, 2 (2010).
15. Owen, A.M., Hampshire, A., Grahn, J.A., Stenton, R., Dajani, S., Burns, A.S., Howard, R., and Ballard, C.G. Putting Brain Training to the Test. *Nature 465*, 7299 (2010), 775-778.
16. Quiroga, M.Á., Román, F.J., Catalán, A., Rodríguez, H., Ruiz, J., Herranz, M., Gómez-Abad, M., and Colom, R. Videogame Performance (Not Always) Requires Intelligence. *International Journal of Online Pedagogy and Course Design 1*, 3 (2011), 18-32.
17. Ravaja, N., and Kivikangas, M. Designing game research: Addressing questions of validity. In U. Ritterfeld, M.J. Cody, & P. Vorderer, eds., *Serious games: Mechanisms and effects*. Routledge, New York, NY, USA, 2009, 404-410.
18. Salen, K., and Zimmerman, E. *Rules of play: Game design fundamentals*. MIT Press, Cambridge, MA, USA, 2004.
19. Salomon, G., and Perkins, D. Do technologies make us smarter? Intellectual amplification with, of, and through technology. In R. Sternberg and D.D. Preiss, eds., *Intelligence and technology: The impact of tools on the nature and development of human abilities*. Lawrence Erlbaum, Mahwah, NJ, USA, 2005, 71-86.
20. Schneider, W., and Chein, J.S. Controlled & automatic processing: Behavior, theory, and biological mechanisms. *Cognitive Science 27*, 3 (2003), 525-559.
21. Sedig, K. From play to thoughtful learning: A design strategy to engage children with mathematical representations. *Journal of Computers in Mathematics and Science Teaching 27*, 1 (2008), 65-101.
22. Sedig, K., and Haworth, R. Creative design of digital cognitive games: Application of cognitive toys and isomorphism. *Bulletin of Science, Technology & Society 32*, 5 (2012), 413-426.
23. Sedig, K., Klawe, M., and Westrom, M. Role of interface manipulation style and scaffolding on cognition and concept learning in learnware. *ACM Transactions on Computer-Human Interaction 8*, 1 (2001), 34-59.
24. Sedig, K., and Parsons, P. Interaction design for complex cognitive activities with visual representations: A pattern-based approach. *AIS Transactions on Human-Computer Interaction 5*, 2 (2013), 84-133.
25. Sedig, K., Parsons, P., Dittmer, M., and Haworth, R. Human-centered interactivity of visualization tools: Micro- and macro-level considerations. In W. Huang, ed., *Handbook of Human Centric Visualization*. Springer New York, New York, NY, USA, 2014, 717-743.
26. Sicart, M. Defining game mechanics. *Game Studies 8*, 2 (2008).
27. Sweetser, P., and Wyeth, P. GameFlow: A model for evaluating player enjoyment in games. *Computers in Entertainment 3*, 3 (2005), 1-24.
28. Sweller, J. Element interactivity and intrinsic, extraneous, and germane cognitive load. *Educational Psychology Review 22*, 2 (2010), 123-138.

A Framework for Cooperative Communication Game Mechanics from Grounded Theory

Zachary O. Toups[1], Jessica Hammer[2], William A. Hamilton[3], Ahmad Jarrah[1], William Graves[4], Oliver Garretson[5]
[1]Dept. Computer Science / [4]Physical Science Laboratory, New Mexico State University
[2]HCI Institute / Entertainment Technology Center, Carnegie Mellon University
[3]Dept. Computer Science & Engineering / [5]Dept. Sociology, Texas A&M University
ztoups@nmsu.edu, hammerj@cs.cmu.edu, bill@ecologylab.net,
jarrah@nmsu.edu, wgraves@psl.nmsu.edu, olivergarretson@tamu.edu

ABSTRACT
A rich element of cooperative games are mechanics that communicate. Unlike automated awareness cues and synchronous verbal communication, *cooperative communication mechanics* enable players to share information and direct action by engaging with game systems. These include both explicitly communicative mechanics, such as built-in pings that direct teammates' attention to specific locations, and emergent communicative mechanics, where players develop their own conventions about the meaning of in-game activities, like jumping to get attention. We use a grounded theory approach with 40 digital games to identify and classify the types of cooperative communication mechanics game designers might use to enable cooperative play. We provide details on the classification scheme and offer a discussion on the implications of cooperative communication mechanics.

Author Keywords
Game design; analysis; cooperation; communication; teams

ACM Classification Keywords
H.5.3. Group and Organization Interfaces: Computer-supported cooperative play

INTRODUCTION
In cooperative digital games, *communication is a core mechanic*, an activity that players explicitly regularly invoke in play. While synchronous verbal communication via voice or text chat is common for online games, either directly or through an external program, rich alternate channels for communication to teammates exist: *cooperative communication mechanics*. These in-game systems enable players to direct attention and provide information in ways that are difficult or impossible verbally. The present research investigates game mechanics that players actively invoke to provide information to other players in the game and support team situation awareness. Using a grounded theory approach on a corpus of game mechanics selected from 40 cooperative games, we develop a framework of game mechanics for cooperative communication. The present framework can be used to identify the types of communication available in a game, which has implications for cooperative play. The framework is also used to identify areas of potential for new and innovative mechanics for team communication.

The present research focuses on game mechanics explicitly invoked by players in synchronous PC and console games. We exclude both synchronous verbal communication and automated awareness mechanisms, such as those in groupware systems [17]. Many games include automated awareness cues; however, we are interested in the opportunity cost of communicating versus other in-game actions. Verbal communication is already well-studied in groupware [17], group work [18], and games [5], but cooperative communication mechanics have not yet been investigated.

This paper is structured as follows: we synthesize background on teams, game design, collaborative virtual environments, and embodied cognition. Next, we provide details on our grounded theory methodology, from which we constructed a framework of cooperative communication game mechanics. We discuss the framework, describing each component and providing examples. Finally, we discuss the implications of the framework, highlighting gaps in existing designs and seeds for future research.

BACKGROUND
The background for cooperative communication mechanics is diverse, drawing on research in teams, game design, collaborative virtual environments, and embodied cognition.

Teams
The fields of situation awareness, distributed cognition, and team cognition influence the present research, providing a framing for understanding how cooperative communication mechanics are used and why they are valuable. Teams are "a distinguishable set of two or more people who interact dynamically, interdependently, and adaptively toward a common or valued goal/object/mission, who have each been assigned specific roles or functions to perform, and who have a

CHI PLAY '14, October 19–22 2014, Toronto, ON, Canada.

limited life span of membership" [28]. Cooperating players form teams during play; they develop and maintain situation awareness to succeed at a game.

Situation awareness refers to the ability of individuals to understand their environment and how it will likely change [8, 9]. A high level of situation awareness supports an individual in making intelligent decisions about how to act in an environment and support her/his team in problem solving.

In a *distributed cognition* environment, such as cooperative game play, information is used to make decisions and enact change; it is transferred throughout a cognitive system consisting of people, interfaces, and objects [19, 21, 22]. As information is translated among media and through time, its form and values change. Distributed cognition accounts for how information form is altered to ensure its usefulness for a task or its ability to be transferred further. A team player might need to observe multiple components of a game's state and communicate it to teammates using her/his avatar.

Team cognition theory [12, 24, 29] posits a team (as defined above) as a unit capable of thought. Team members share information and develop an understanding of one another's roles, capabilities, and knowledge as these are needed to accomplish the team's objectives. Teams must contend with *communication overhead* [10, 24], the cost in terms of time, cognitive bandwidth, and technological bandwidth of sharing information with other team members. Communication is thus *not "free"* and highly efficient teams develop strategies and understanding that limit their need for communication. These efficient teams *implicitly coordinate* [10, 11, 24, 35], anticipating and fulfilling one another's information needs.

Game Design

Salen and Zimmerman characterize games as systems of interrelated *rules* and *play* [30]. Rules are the structures that constrain player action, while play is the freedom to make decisions within the rules. A *game mechanic* is a moment at which a player makes a choice and observes the outcome [23, 30]. *Core mechanics* are the essence of a game, and are engaged with repeatedly. Game scholars have created frameworks to analyze subsets of game mechanics, such as Consalvo's review of social mechanics in social games [6]. The present research develops a framework that identifies game mechanics that support cooperative communication.

Prior work has investigated cooperation in game play. Much of this is centered around the design of cooperative game mechanics [2, 15, 31, 34], the verbal practices of teams [33], or how people play in co-located settings [5]. Communication channels and awareness cues are critical to keep players engaged in game play in a challenging teamwork environment while maintaining situation awareness.

Importantly, Chuang et al. [5] found that co-located players collaborate not only through explicit communication channels but also an implicit awareness of each other; this can be likened to the work of high-performance teams. One key communication channel they and Tomi and Tony [34] identify are "virtual gestures": players use avatar movement to send information to partner(s). This research suggests the importance of investigating other potential communication channels that are unique to games.

Collaborative Virtual Environments

Collaborative virtual environments (CVEs) are shared, persistent computer-simulated spaces. Users interact in a virtual environment with each other in real-time [39]. Zutshi et al. [39] identify key features of virtual environments, some of which are relevant to cooperative play: user presentation (e.g. using avatar to present the player), gesture (e.g. avatar gestures [5, 34]), and communication (e.g. voice or text chat).

CVEs enable groups to work on a common task, where they benefit from sharing resources, sharing ideas, and learning from each another [39]. Games represent one such context. Players in a cooperative games work together to solve problems, where the game highlights contribution, challenge, and fun [1, 39]. Playing in a CVE has been recognized as increasing technical playing ability; the collaborative aspect allows players to explore games with the backing of a social infrastructure, which creates a strong bond between players [3].

Embodied Communication

Embodied communication occurs in real life between individuals when they cannot communicate through a direct method of transferring meaning [13]. Language is not static; it evolves as individuals are exposed to new settings and need to convey novel meanings [27]. Embodied communication is not restricted to the physical world, but has expanded into the virtual realm, as seen in the present and prior [5, 34] research.

Despite voice and text communication availability in games, designers and players have devised communication methods that use neither. Players are frequently exposed to novel settings and mechanics where their language and conceptual understanding adapt to cope with new problems. This has implications in digital game play where voice or text communication are not available or are not viable (e.g. playing a first person shooter game without a headset). One player does not inherently know what others know; a disconnect of perspectives occurs. Each player's viewpoint gives one set of information; information is distributed [37]. Players must use the communication channels available to them—the mechanics and affordances of the game itself—to share information.

Summary

These bodies of literature explain the information needs of team members, which are met through other team members in the shared CVE of the game. Teams can and do use game mechanics as collaborative tools to accomplish in-game goals and to communicate. No review of cooperative game mechanics separate from synchronous verbal communication exists. As researchers, we believe this work will provide tools for future investigation of collaboration patterns in online play; as designers, we are interested in how we can enable players to have rich, game-centric communication.

METHODOLOGY

We conducted a qualitative study to investigate the game mechanics players may use to communicate with others in lieu

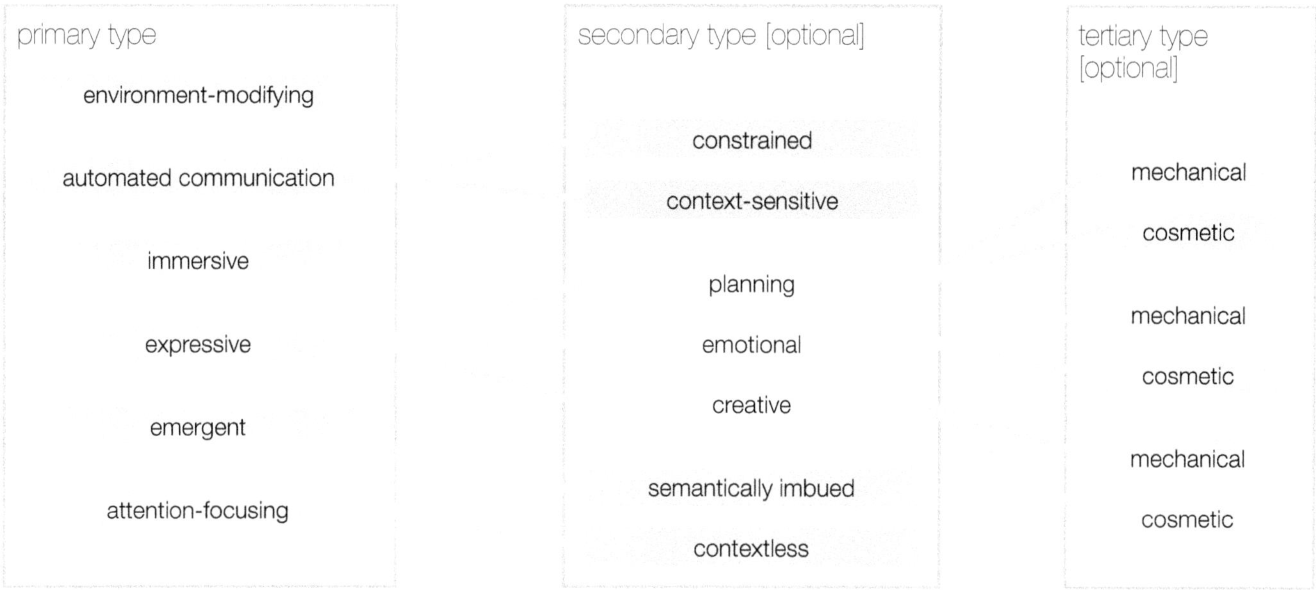

Figure 1. Framework for cooperative communication game mechanics produced from a grounded theory analysis of game designs. There are up to three levels of classification for game mechanics: primary, secondary, and tertiary.

of, or in addition to, synchronous verbal communication. We engaged in grounded theory methodology [4, 14, 32], iterating between data collection and analysis. Beyond identifying the mechanisms of communication in play, we developed a framework to classify patterns of cooperative mechanics.

Four researchers independently identified cooperative games from prior experience, ultimately developing Table 1. Data was drawn from personal play experiences and oberservations of players, both in person and through sites such as Twitch.tv. Within these games, the researchers identified the specific game mechanics that support cooperative communication in play, samples of which are discussed later and listed in Table 2[1]. The researchers independently open coded their experiences with cooperative game mechanics. Within this context of coding the data was conceptualized and classified independently [32]. During this process, researchers developed theoretical memos [32] to further refine emerging ideas.

Initially, we independently developed an 8-code, single-layer scheme and a two layer scheme with 4-codes on the top layer and two sub-codes for each super-code to identify mechanics. Then we compared codes, merging similar categories or developing new ones; we compiled a list of interesting game contexts where the identified coordination mechanisms occur. Codes and phenomena were categorized; the independently conceptualized codes were integrated and reiterated to form the beginning of a framework. This new intermediate framework was similar to the final version. An additional round of comparison, merging, and developing codes followed to produce the present three-level framework shown in Figure 1 and discussed in detail in the next section.

A selective coding process followed: fieldwork was done to verify certain codes and phenomena by playing the games in question and/or observing gameplay through internet sources. This selective coding was done within the emerging framework allowing for a more focused investigation of communication mechanisms. This process allowed us to see an array of ways players communicate within specific games as well as where communication mechanisms are lacking.

FRAMEWORK FOR COOPERATIVE COMMUNICATION

Based on a grounded theory approach, we present a framework for classifying cooperative communication game mechanics based on the way they provide information to teammates. There are three layers of classification, primary, secondary, and tertiary, that correspond to deepening levels of specification for some of the types. Figure 1 diagrams the framework. The primary types of mechanics, discussed in detail below, include environment-modifying, automated communication, immersive, expressive, emergent, and attention-focusing. A game mechanic may fit into multiple types.

We note that the player behaviors we describe below are a representative, rather than exhaustive, set of ways that players use cooperative communication mechanics. These play techniques are supported by the cooperative communication mechanics, and as such are available to all players of a given game. However, we do not claim that *all* players use a particular mechanic in a particular way. Rather, we argue that these cooperative behaviors are *enabled* by the cooperative communication mechanics, and that based on our observations are used on a regular basis by at least some players.

Environment-Modifying

Environment-modifying game mechanics allow the player to permanently or semi-permanently change some component of the game world to convey information to other players.

[1]Table 2 includes the final coding, based on Figure 1, which was not developed until the final cycle of theory generation.

game	play mode(s)	genre(s)
1.) *Army of Two*	coop	TPS
2.) *Assassin's Creed III*	free-for-all	Ac, Ad, St
3.) *Castle Crashers*	free-for-all	BEU, RPG, Ac
4.) *Counter-Strike: Global Offensive*	team comp.	FPS
5.) *Counter-Strike: Source*	"	"
6.) *Dark Souls*	single player	Ac, RPG, metroidva-nia, DC
7.) *Dark Souls II*	"	Ac, RPG, HS
8.) *DayZ*	free-for-all	Su
9.) *Destiny*	coop	Ac, RPG, FPS
10.) *Diablo*	coop	Ac, RPG, HS
11.) *Diablo II*	"	"
12.) *Diablo III*	"	"
13.) *The Elder Scrolls Online*	team comp., coop	MMO, RPG
14.) *Final Fantasy: Crystal Chronicles*	coop	Ac, RPG
15.) *Halo: Combat Evolved*	team comp.	FPS
16.) *Halo 2*	team comp., coop	"
17.) *Halo 3*	"	"
18.) *Halo 4*	"	"
19.) *Hearthstone: Heroes of Warcraft*	1-vs.-1	collectible card game
20.) *Journey* [2012]	single player	Ad
21.) *League of Legends*	team comp.	MOBA
22.) *Legend of Zelda: Four Swords Adventure*	free-for-all	AcAd
23.) *Little Big Planet*	coop	PP
24.) *Little Big Planet 2*	"	"
25.) *Mass Effect 3*	team comp.	Ac, RPG, TPS
26.) *Minecraft*	free-for-all	Sa, Su
27.) *Monaco: What's Yours is Mine*	coop	Ac, St
28.) *Payday: The Heist*	coop	FPS
29.) *Payday 2*	"	"
30.) *Planetside 2*	team comp.	MMO, FPS
31.) *Portal 2*	coop	PP
32.) *StarCraft*	team comp.	RTS
33.) *StarCraft 2*	"	"
34.) *Super Mario Galaxy*	coop	platforming
35.) *Rust*	free-for-all	Ac, Ad, Su
36.) *Titanfall*	team comp.	FPS
37.) *Starseige: Tribes*	team comp.	FPS
38.) *Tribes 2*	"	"
39.) *Tribes Ascend*	"	"
40.) *World of Warcraft*	team comp., coop	MMO, RPG

Table 1. List of games considered in analysis. All cooperative games considered as data sources; not all games were found to include cooperative communication mechanics. Genres derived from games' Wikipedia.org entries. Genre abbreviations: Ac: action; Ad: adventure; BEU: beat 'em up; DC: dungeon crawl; FPS: first-person shooter; HS: hack and slash; MMO: massively multiplayer online; MOBA: multiplayer battle arena; PP: puzzle platformer; RPG: role-playing game; Sa: sandbox; St: stealth; Su: survival; TPS: third-person shooter.

Such mechanics may function as cairns, marking out a safe trail to other players, or might be used to store lore created by players. Although we are interested in cooperation, environment-modifying mechanics can also be abused to grief or troll players. These game mechanics may not be for a *team* per se, as environment-modifying mechanics are often asynchronous, but they may be used to provide help to others facing similar in-game challenges in the future. Environment-modifying game mechanics were among the rarest observed in our sample, but function as cooperative communication mechanics and are thus included in the framework.

Exemplar Mechanics: Signposts. Signposts allow players to leave persistent text messages in the game environment, an **environment-modifying** game mechanic. Some games allow only messages that are pre-generated by the designers, while others allow players to input arbitrary text. Signpost mechanics may be synchronous—players building signs in front of other players—but they are more commonly asynchronous. Players create messages and choose where to leave them in the game world; they must make assumptions about how other players will later see it and react.

Signpost mechanics generally involve the signpost-making player taking a break from other gameplay to interact with a messaging sub-system. Players who read the signpost, on the other hand, may need to take much less of a break from other in-game activities. This asymmetry means that signpost creation may be best suited for non-urgent moments or tasks, but the messages can be relevant for even critical situations.

Games with signpost mechanics include *Dark Souls* and *Dark Souls II*, in which players can write messages on the ground to be read later by others. *Minecraft* is another example, in which players can create signs that other players can later read. Built environments in *Minecraft* can also be understood as signpost mechanics, such as buildings shaped like arrows to indicate to other players where resources can be found.

Automated Communication

Automated communication game mechanics enable efficient communication among teammates, reducing the burden on the player to provide context or detail. The subtypes of automated communication are constrained and context-sensitive.

Automated Communication/Constrained

Automated communication/constrained takes the form of predefined announcements or responses that the player invokes to explicitly indicate something to teammates. These types of cooperative communication mechanics require the player to decide what information to share with teammates, accounting for context manually, activating it through a game mechanic. The game must have an expressive-enough interface to support the kinds of automated communication/constrained that the player needs to provide teammates.

Exemplar Mechanics: Message Macros. Message macros allow the player to efficiently select from a limited set of pregenerated messages and share them with teammates, a form of **automated communication/constrained**. The player issues a command (for example, by typing a three-key combination) that is translated into an audio or text message shared with other players. The messages in question may be aimed at allies or at enemies. The former tend to be either informational or instructive, such as "I need help" or "Follow me!" The latter include taunts and threats to disrupt opponent concentration.

Message macros are quick and easy to access, once learned. They minimize the time it takes for players to call up a particular message, so that players can use the macros even in high-stress, high-speed scenarios. However, players are limited to the messages chosen by the game designer, which may not cover every situation in which the player finds him/herself. Additionally, message macros rely heavily on player recall for access.

Games with message macros include the *Tribes* series of team-based first-person shooters and the *Diablo* series of action role-playing games. *Journey* is a corner case here: there is just one message macro, the ability to sing. Singing is a core mechanic for interacting with the environment in addition to being an **emergent** communication mechanic.

Automated Communication/Context-Sensitive

Automated communications/context-sensitive rely on game state to parameterize a communication to teammates. They reduce the burden on players, effectively allowing the player to transmit information that the avatar is presumed to "understand" from the current situation. In these types of mechanics, players make decisions about when at what to share, but the game handles some of the cognitive burden.

Exemplar Mechanics: Contextual Macros. Contextual macros are like message macros, but include contextual information in addition to a pregenerated message; these are **automated communication/context-sensitive**. The player selects an in-game object, then issues a macro command. Information related to the context selected is then sent to other players in the game, either by voice or by text. For example, *Diablo III* allows players to automatically send the extended description of a piece of treasure to allies, which is ordinarily only visible to the player carrying it. This allows allies to quickly evaluate whether found treasure is desirable—for example, if it is a more powerful weapon than the one they are using—without putting an undue burden on the player sharing the information.

Contextual macros, like message macros, are quick and easy to access. They minimize the time it takes for players to share information that relates to a particular game situation, such as needing to evaluate whether an item is useful to any of the players on a team. They also rely less on memory, as they are often linked to contextual behaviors rather than arbitrary command triggers. For example, in the PC version of *Diablo III*, players activate item linking by clicking on the item—a contextually sensible action—while holding shift.

However, players are more limited than with message macros, as contextual macros often cannot even be evoked except outside the specific context for which the designers planned. They also function in a specified manner. If the player is unfamiliar with how the macro works, s/he may also find it does not function in the way intended, or that what the game design considers context differs from the player's intent.

Games with contextual macros include the ability to share item information with teammates in *Diablo III*, sending a visual readout of information about a selected enemy to teammates in the *Tribes* series, and voice macros that incorporate enemy-specific information in *Tribes Ascend*.

Immersive

The purpose of immersive game mechanics is to provide information to players in a way consistent with the game's fiction, deepening the player's experience of being in the world and enhancing the play experience. These game mechanics highlight elements of the game's narrative as a component of play. Rather than directing other players toward specific game-winning behavior, immersive game mechanics invite teammates to join in a shared experience.

Exemplar Mechanics: In-Character Emotes. Many games include the ability to *emote*, or act dramatically, in character. Hailing from the early years of MUD (Multi-User Dungeon) text-based multiplayer games [7] and recommended by Tomi and Tony [34], emotes allow players to deepen the immersive experience with other players (and, possibly, communicate to support situation awareness) as **immersive** cooperative communication mechanics. Emotes may be single player, such as waving to others, dancing, etc., or involve multiple players, such as high-fives in *Portal 2*. Emotes are found in many games, including *Destiny*, *World of Warcraft*, the *Little Big Planet* series, *Hearthstone*, and *Portal 2*.

Expressive

The expressive tree of game mechanics is the deepest and most complex. It includes mechanics that support players in sharing information about themselves. Expressive mechanics are used for planning and sharing emotion; each of these may be more deeply classified by whether they enact state change on the game (mechanical) or if they are only cosmetic.

Expressive/.../Mechanical or /Cosmetic

The tertiary component, the leaves of the expressive tree, classifies each mechanic as either mechanical or cosmetic. Mechanical subtypes meaningfully modify the state of the game. Cosmetic subtypes do not change the state of the game directly, but change how the game environment is perceived by other players. Cosmetic subtypes thus may change the game mechanically indirectly, as they potentially change how teammates play.

Expressive/Planning

The expressive/planning subtree includes game mechanics that are used to express future intent in play. Planning mechanics may be used to direct teammates. Mechanically, this generally means enacting some change to the player's interface (such as a waypoint with HUD indicator or using an automated communication to transmit enemy data). Cosmetic expressive/planning mechanics provide less formal or temporary directive information, such as an avatar gesture. Expressive/planning mechanics might support team situation awareness by indicating what a player will do in the near future.

Exemplar Mechanics: Holding. Holding mechanics limit how many in-game items the player can have active at a given moment, and determine how long it takes to swap between items. While many games have holding mechanics, holding mechanics for joint communication allow other players to see what item a player is holding, and how it is being held (e.g. holding a weapon in a stance ready for combat, or sheathed in peace). When the item held is visible to other players, the holding player can signal her/his own intentions and plans. Such game mechanics are thus **expressive/planning**.

This is particularly true when holding an item has a mechanical impact. For example, in the game *Rust* it takes time for players to switch between items. A player holding a non-aggressive item, such as a torch, is at a clear disadvantage should violence erupt. As a result, a player holding a torch is signaling a commitment to non-violence, or at least that they believe they can salvage the situation should violence occur. Since no deception is possible about what item a player is holding, other players can trust that the torch-holding player is truthfully signaling and willing to accept any mechanical penalties that might arise.

Other games with holding mechanics include *DayZ*, in which others can see if the player is holding a weapon, which weapon they are holding, and where the weapon is pointed. Physical signals such as weapon-pointing, which have mechanical consequences and which are visible from a distance, are a critical part of establishing initial trust in a game where any player could potentially be an enemy.

Expressive/Emotional

In the expressive/emotional subtree, players indicate to one another their emotive state, supporting team cohesion. Known to be important in stressful environments, such as firefighting [35], conveying emotion supports team members in situation awareness, enabling team members to understand the readiness of fellow players. Expressive/emotional cooperative communication mechanics may support emotional contagion [20], causing positive emotions to cascade through the team.

Exemplar Mechanics: Gesturing. Gesture mechanics, a form of **expressive/emotional** cooperative communication mechanics, allow players to press a key or key combination, and to have their avatar respond with a virtual gesture in the game world. These gestures might include solitary gestures, like a fist-pump, or collaborative ones, like attempting to high-five a nearby player. Gestures can be triggered by simple key presses, or by typing commands to the character like `/wave`.

All nearby players can see gestures performed by the player, allowing players to use gestures to broadcast how they are feeling. Since gestures are a constrained set of pre-defined animations, that means players are selecting their emotional expressions from a small set of options. On the other hand, gestures do not require players to articulate how they feel in words, and constraints can help players decide on an emotion to express quickly.

Observed games with gestures include *Portal 2*, *DayZ*, *Army of Two*, *Elder Scrolls Online*, and *World of Warcraft*.

Emergent

The category of emergent [30] cooperative communication mechanics include game mechanics not expressly constructed for communication, but that have been appropriated by small groups or whole communities as a meaningful way of communicating. These are the most common type of game mechanic encountered in the analysis. Emergent cooperative communication typically uses some capability of the avatar to move or intervene in another player's environment (such as Cheung et al.'s virtual gestures [5]). The information communicated through emergent cooperative communication mechanics may have to be learned, and may exist only within certain communities of practice. Prior to learning, players may find that they do not know what the intended communication is.

Exemplar Mechanics: Jumping. Because jumping does have in-game meaning, there is a difference between jumping to play and jumping to communicate. This is a game design decision, as jumping mechanics may be designed to happen automatically as needed, rather than be under player control.

Jumping without an immediate purpose for the jump can mean anything from "Pay attention to me" to "I am impatient." The semantic meaning of the jump varies between play communities, and is usually highly dependent on the specific context of the particular situation in which the players find themselves. While the ability to jump without purpose is a game design decision, the exact messages conveyed by apparently purposeless jumping are emergent and situational.

Games with the option of communicative jumping include *Journey*, *Portal 2*, the *Halo* series, *Elder Scrolls Online*, and *Minecraft*.

Attention-Focusing

Attention-focusing game mechanics enable one player to provide another with a directive, calling attention to someone or something in the game environment. Deictic reference can be difficult in game play, especially using verbal communication mechanisms without embodied communication. Attention-focusing game mechanics enable deictic reference, as well as embed actionable intelligence into the game environment or interface for other players. Subtypes of attention-focusing mechanics are unbound and semantically imbued.

Attention-Focusing/Unbound

Attention-focusing/contextless mechanics do not provide any additional information. A ping on a map or in the environment, which requires additional data to decode by teammates, were the most common of this mechanic type observed.

Exemplar Mechanics: Map Pings. Map ping mechanics allow players to identify locations to one another by placing icons on a map or in the virtual space of the game. The pinging player must select the location they wish to ping, then indicate that they wish to ping it. Some games combine these steps by providing a mini-map on which players can click to automatically set up a ping at the clicked location. Map pings are an example of **attention-focusing/unbound** cooperative communication mechanics.

For example, in the *StarCraft* series, a player can ping the map for an ally. This ping carries no information beyond its location, so understanding the meaning of a ping requires disambiguation.

Other games with pinging mechanics include the *Tribes* series and *Diablo III*.

Attention-Focusing/Semantically Imbued

Attention-focusing/semantically imbued game mechanics provide some shared meaning, encoded in the game's rules. These somehow identify a characteristic of the thing indicated, or provide a call to action for one or more teammates, attaching semantic information to an indicator in the game environment.

Exemplar Mechanics: Augmented Environment Pings. Augmented environment pings operate like standard map pings, but include contextual or directive information, making them **attention-focusing/semantically imbued**. Because the game world is not uniform, the pings can respond to the features of the location in the game world that was clicked, conveying more information with the same amount of effort on the part of the player. Of course, as with contextual messaging systems, contextual pings also lock the player into *needing* to send that additional, contextual information even if they do not wish to.

Pings in *League of Legends* are an excellent example of augmented environment pings. Five-player teams battle for control of a virtual space that contains objects like allied turrets (in-game structures that aid the player and their team), enemy turrets (the same structures, but fighting for the enemy), and enemies controlled both by other players and by the game's AI. When players ping a location on the map, their teammates see a different response depending on what they have targeted. If they target an enemy character, whether controlled by players or the game's AI, a red exclamation point appears above the target to indicate it was selected. If they target an allied structure, such as a turret, a green shield appears above the structure indicating it needs to be defended. If they ping a location without either enemies or allies, a simple blue dot appears in the game world and on the minimap, indicating to allies that some action needs to be taken at that location.

Other games include different types of pings. For example, *Portal 2*'s collaborative mode includes two different ping types that players can choose between. The *Look Ping* displays an eye icon on both players' screens, indicating where the pinging player wishes the other player to look. The *Timer Ping* displays a countdown timer icon, starting at three seconds, that appears on both players' screens when it is initiated. These pings serve different functions, but both provide functionality that would be difficult to achieve by speaking. The Look Ping accurately, concisely, and specifically identifies a particular location in the game; the Timer Ping ensures that players can perfectly synchronize their actions.

DISCUSSION

In this section, we discuss the ways in which future game designers might leverage cooperative communication mechanics to construct new and exciting ways to play. We also discuss how cooperative communication mechanics may be used to analyze player performance, guiding game design and providing a means to analyze game experiments. We close by highlighting how cooperative communication mechanics should be designed and leveraged to be effective.

Potential for Future Design

Through this research, we have made a number of discoveries about cooperative communication mechanics that may aid designers in building future games. We see that players have many ways to offer, but little ability to request, information from their teammates; that environment-modifying game mechanics are not well-represented; and that players may develop emergent cooperative communication mechanics when the existing design fails to provide what they need.

Ability to Request Information

Nearly every game mechanic analyzed offers a means for a team member to *push information* to teammates. While effective teams *are* proactive about providing information, reducing the number of requests for information to reduce communication overhead [10, 11, 24, 35], the ability to *pull information* is still essential. We observe a dearth of game mechanics that provide players the ability to poll teammates for information, or to interrogate the game environment or state through teammates. Only one data source provides such ability: the *Tribes* Voice Game System, which allows players to request, "What's my assignment?", "I need a target painted!", or "Is our base secure?"

In the current designs, players can *only* be proactive about communicating needed information to players. The act of communicating through these game mechanics may not become elevated to core mechanic, as two-way communication among teammates to discover meaningful information about game state is not something in which players can engage. Instead, players much rely on verbal communication to make requests, to which other players might respond with an attention-focusing mechanic. The ability to request information potentially opens up new and exciting game designs where sharing and exchanging information is a key component of play and teammates scout game environments and engage in interesting, two-way communication.

Modifying Environments

The ability to modify game worlds were among the rarest game mechanics observed in the sample, yet a rich area for future work. *Minecraft* provides the largest collection of such instances, enabling players to not only leave signs with verbal communication on them, but also to physically alter the environment so that it signifies affordances and constraints [25,

game	mechanic	details	type
Army of Two	gesturing	avatars can "fist bump" on command	expressive/ emotional, immersive
Dark Souls series	signposts	write and post text on the ground in the game world	environment-modifying
DayZ	holding	avatars can hold objects, switching objects takes time	expressive/ planning, emergent
Diablo series	message macros	number keys trigger character to speak a command or taunt in-character	automated communication/ constrained, immersive
Diablo III	contextual macros	player can hold a modifier key and click a piece of loot to share its statistics with allies	automated communication/ context-sensitive
Journey	message macros	avatars can "sing" as a core mechanic for interacting with the environment, but cooperative players also use it to grab attention	automated communication/ constrained, attention-focusing/ unbound, emergent
League of Legends	augmented environment pings	players may ping map to indicate needs or details about enemies to teammates	attention-focusing/ semantically imbued, automated communication/ constrained
Minecraft	signposts	write and post persistent sign objects in the game world	environment-modifying
Minecraft	jumping	avatars can jump to interact with the environment, which is also used to grab attention	emergent, attention-focusing/ unbound
Portal 2	augmented environment pings	players may use a timer ping or a look ping to indicate to an ally when/where to perform an action or where to look, respectively	attention-focusing/ semantically imbued, automated communication/ constrained
Portal 2	gesturing	avatars can perform a number of cooperative gestures, such as high-fives	expressive/ emotional, immersive
Rust	holding	avatars can hold objects, switching objects takes time	expressive/ planning, emergent
StarCraft series	map pings	players may cause a sound to play and a highlight to appear on the map by clicking in the game's minimap	attention-focusing/ unbound
Tribes series	message macros	Voice Game System (VGS): voice macros triggered by 3- to 4-character commands	automated communication/ constrained
Tribes Ascend	contextual macros	identify enemy mechanic: context-specific voice macros and HUD information sent to teammates, triggered by looking at an enemy and pressing a key	automated communication/ context-sensitive, attention-focusing/ unbound
World of Warcraft	in-character emotes	avatars may dance or gesture, performing scripted animations in character	immersive

Table 2. Data sources for grounded theory analysis connected to the resulting cooperative communication game mechanics. Interpretation may require familiarity with the game in question.

26] on action directly. The *Dark Souls* series of games does this in a more subtle manner, as other players may modify the environments in a single player game to provide advice or cause trouble.

We suggest that the modifying environment cooperative communication mechanics are a rich area for future work. There is great potential in using these mechanics to construct interesting new forms of play. Their biggest drawback is the asymmetric nature of their use—creating requires significant investment, yet using them does not. At the same time, once created, a modification to the environment may be used by many players. The creator also sometimes never receives feedback regarding their modification's ultimate impact.

Need for More Cooperative Communication Mechanics

Emergent cooperative communication mechanics were the most prevalent observed in the analysis. This suggests that players are finding existing, designed cooperative communication mechanics insufficient (or missing altogether). Players working together need to communicate with one another, and game designers should consider carefully in what situated ways players will want or need to do this.

Analyzing Team Coordination

Effective team coordination is generally assessed by analyzing the communication between team members [10, 24, 16]. By applying a coding scheme to the utterances of team members, a researcher or educator can produce an anticipation ratio for the team, which compares the amount of communication that provides information to teammates versus the amount of communication that requests information. A high anticipation ratio means that the team is overcoming communication overhead and acting efficiently [10, 16, 24, 37, 38]. Anticipation ratio is generally calculated only on verbal (or text) utterances between teammates. A similar technique is used by El-Nasr et al. [31] by observing and coding Cooperative Performance Metrics during play, where players engage in observable behaviors outside of the game.

Analyzing communication for anticipation ratio or cooperative performance is a work-intensive and slow process. The present framework functions as a means to analyze team coordination automatically and efficiently. Once these mechanics have been identified, game developers and researchers can easily log use of cooperative communication in play, possibly to analyze anticipation ratio, or to get a more nuanced understanding of how players are explicitly coordinating with one another.

Communication Tools

Beyond gameplay, in the real world, teams need to communicate with one another. The present framework and exemplar mechanics can function as inspiration for real-world communication systems. As we advance to combinations of human-robot teams, where real-world situations look even more similar to games, this becomes even more compelling.

Designing for Communicability

Prior work has discussed the need to design game interfaces to support communicability [36], that is, render information so that it can be easily verbally communicated to teammates. The present work identifies cooperative communication mechanics that help to alleviate this need by making non-verbal communication a component of game play. Still, interfaces must be expressive enough to enable players to transmit the information they need to transmit, otherwise it must be sent verbally.

The game designer must carefully consider not only the range of expressiveness of cooperative communication mechanics, but also how they are to be invoked in play. Context-sensitivity is key to making game mechanics easy to access in intense play. As an alternative, the designer may also wish to restrict the ease-of-use of such mechanics, as gameplay is often about challenge.

CONCLUSION

In this paper, we discuss designing for communication as a game mechanic, using commercial systems as data sources for a grounded theory analysis and framework. Communication between players in these games is something about which they make decisions that affect the outcomes of the game. The game designer's primary tool to construct game mechanics is to provide rules that constrain player action.

The present framework provides six trees of cooperative communication mechanic types. Environment-modifying mechanics are used to alter the game environment to make it informative for other players. Automated communication mechanics simplify the communicator's job in intense gameplay, so that they can supply complex game-specific information to teammates. Immersive mechanics enhance the game experience by deepening the players' involvement in the game's story or world. Expressive mechanics support players in suppling information about their own state during gameplay, including their plans and emotions. Players create their own meaning through emergent mechanics, adopting their own meanings for game actions that were not primarily designed for communication. Finally, attention-focusing game mechanics allow players to point out components of the game environment to others, supporting a call to action or providing information.

A future research agenda will investigate the ways in which cooperative communication mechanics are invoked by players, how their use impacts game play, and how effective they are as a communication channel. We plan to use the present framework to code our observations of cooperative play, and look for connections across games.

REFERENCES

1. Arroyo, E., Righi, V., Tarrago, R., Santos, P., Hernández-Leo, D., and Blat, J. Remote collaborative multi-user informal learning experiences: Design and evaluation. In *Proc. 6th European Conf. on Technology Enhanced Learning: Towards Ubiquitous Learning* (2011), 43–56.
2. Beznosyk, A., Quax, P., Coninx, K., and Lamotte, W. The influence of cooperative game design patterns for remote play on player experience. In *Proc. 10th Asia Pacific Conf. on Computer Human Interaction* (2012), 11–20.
3. Brown, B., and Bell, M. CSCW at play: 'There' as a collaborative virtual environment. In *Proc. ACM Conf. on Computer Supported Cooperative Work* (2004), 350–359.
4. Charmaz, K. *Constructing grounded theory: A practical guide through qualitative analysis*. Pine Forge Press, 2006.
5. Cheung, V., Chang, Y.-L. B., and Scott, S. D. Communication channels and awareness cues in collocated collaborative time-critical gaming. In *Proc. ACM Conf. on Computer Supported Cooperative Work* (2012), 569–578.
6. Consalvo, M. Using your friends: Social mechanics in social games. In *Proc. International Conference on Foundations of Digital Games* (2011), 188–195.
7. Curtis, P. Mudding: Social phenomena in text-based virtual realities. *High noon on the electronic frontier: Conceptual issues in cyberspace* (1992), 347–374.
8. Endsley, M. R. Toward a theory of situation awareness in dynamic systems. *Human Factors 37*, 1 (1995), 32–64.
9. Endsley, M. R. Theoretical underpinnings of situation awareness: A critical review. In *Situation Awareness Analysis and Measurement*, M. R. Endsley and D. J. Garland, Eds. Lawrence Erlbaum Associates, Mahwah, NJ, USA, 2000, 3–6.
10. Entin, E. E., and Serfaty, D. Adaptive team coordination. *Human Factors 41*, 2 (June 1999), 312–325.
11. Espinosa, J. A., Lerch, F. J., and Kraut, R. E. Explicit versus implicit coordination mechanisms and task dependencies: One size does not fit all. In Salas and Fiore [29], 107–130.

12. Fiore, S. M., Cuevas, H. M., Schooler, J. W., and Salas, E. Cognition, teams, and team cognition: Memory actions and memory failures in distributed team environments. In *Creating High-Tech Teams*, C. A. Bowers, E. Salas, and F. Jentsch, Eds., no. 4. American Psychological Association, Washington, DC, USA, 2006, 71–87.

13. Galantucci, B., and Steels, L. The emergence of embodied communication in artificial agents and humans. *Embodied communication in humans and machines* (2008), 229–256.

14. Glaser, B. G., and Strauss, A. *The Discovery of Grounded Theory: Strategies for Qualitative Research.* Aldine Publishing Company, Chicago, IL, USA, 1967.

15. Golder, S. A., and Donath, J. Hiding and revealing in online poker games. In *Proc. ACM Conf. on Computer Supported Cooperative Work* (2004), 370–373.

16. Gurtner, A., Tschan, F., Semmer, N. K., and Nägele, C. Getting groups to develop good strategies: Effects of reflexivity interventions on team process, team performance, and shared mental models. *Organ. Behav. Hum. Dec. 102* (2007), 127–142.

17. Gutwin, C., and Greenberg, S. A descriptive framework of workspace awareness for real-time groupware. *Comput. Supported Coop. Work 11*, 3 (Nov. 2002), 411–446.

18. Heath, C., and Luff, P. Team work: Collaboration and control in London Underground line control rooms. In *Technology in Action*, R. Pea, J. S. Brown, and C. Heath, Eds. Cambridge University Press, Cambridge, UK, 2000, 88–124.

19. Hollan, J., Hutchins, E., and Kirsh, D. Distributed cognition: Toward a new foundation for human-computer interaction research. *ACM Trans. Comput.-Hum. Interact. 7*, 2 (2000), 174–196.

20. Hsee, C. K., Hatfeild, E., and Chemtob, C. Assessments of the emotional states of others: Conscious judgements versus emotional contagion. *Journal of Social and Clinical Psychology 11*, 2 (1992), 119–128.

21. Hutchins, E. *Cognition in the Wild*. MIT Press, Cambridge, MA, USA, 1995.

22. Hutchins, E. How a cockpit remembers its speeds. *Cognitive Science 19*, 3 (1995), 265–288.

23. Juul, J. *Half Real: Video Games between Real Rules and Fictional Worlds*. MIT Press, Cambridge, MA, USA, 2005.

24. MacMillan, J., Entin, E. E., and Serfaty, D. Communication overhead: The hidden cost of team cognition. In Salas and Fiore [29], 61–82.

25. Norman, D. *The Design of Everyday Things: Revised and Expanded Edition*. Basic Books, 2013.

26. Norman, D. A. Signifiers, not affordances. *interactions 15*, 6 (2008), 18–19.

27. Pickering, M. J., and Garrod, S. Toward a mechanistic psychology of dialogue. *Behavioral and brain sciences 27*, 02 (2004), 169–190.

28. Salas, E., Dickinson, T. L., Converse, S. A., and Tannenbaum, S. I. Toward an understanding of team performance and training. In *Teams: Their Training and Performance*, R. W. Swezey and E. Salas, Eds. Ablex Publishing Corporation, Norwood, NJ, USA, 1992, 3–29.

29. Salas, E., and Fiore, S. M., Eds. *Team Cognition: Understanding the Factors that Drive Process and Performance*, 1st ed. American Psychological Association, Washington, DC, USA, 2004.

30. Salen, K., and Zimmerman, E. *Rules of Play: Game Design Fundamentals*. MIT Press, Cambridge, MA, USA, 2004.

31. Seif El-Nasr, M., Aghabeigi, B., Milam, D., Erfani, M., Lameman, B., Maygoli, H., and Mah, S. Understanding and evaluating cooperative games. In *Proc. SIGCHI Conf. on Human Factors in Computing Systems* (2010), 253–262.

32. Strauss, A., and Corbin, J. *Basics of Qualitative Research: Techniques and Procedures for Developing Grounded Theory*, 2nd ed. Sage Publications, Inc., 1998.

33. Tang, A., Massey, J., Wong, N., Reilly, D., and Edwards, W. K. Verbal coordination in first person shooter games. In *Proc. ACM Conf. on Computer Supported Cooperative Work* (2012), 579–582.

34. Tomi, K., and Tony, M. Supporting visual elements of non-verbal communication in computer game avatars. In *Level Up Conf. Proc.*, U. Utrecht (2003).

35. Toups, Z. O., and Kerne, A. Implicit coordination in firefighting practice: Design implications for teaching fire emergency responders. In *Proc. SIGCHI Conf. on Human Factors in Computing Systems* (2007), 707–716.

36. Toups, Z. O., Kerne, A., and Hamilton, W. Game design principles for engaging cooperative play: Core mechanics and interfaces for non-mimetic simulation of fire emergency response. In *Proc. 2009 ACM SIGGRAPH Symp. on Video Games* (2009), 71–78.

37. Toups, Z. O., Kerne, A., and Hamilton, W. A. The Team Coordination Game: Zero-fidelity simulation abstracted from fire emergency response practice. *ACM Trans. Comput.-Hum. Interact. 18* (Dec. 2011), 23:1–23:37.

38. Toups, Z. O., Kerne, A., Hamilton, W. A., and Shahzad, N. Zero-fidelity simulation of fire emergency response: Improving team coordination learning. In *Proc. SIGCHI Conf. on Human Factors in Computing Systems* (2011), 1959–1968.

39. Zutshi, A., and Sharma, G. A study of virtual environments for enterprise collaboration. In *Proc. 8th International Conf. on Virtual Reality Continuum and Its Applications in Industry* (2009), 331–333.

Problematizing Cultural Appropriation

Asimina Vasalou[1], Rilla Khaled[2], Daniel Gooch[1] and Laura Benton[1]

[1] London Knowledge Lab
Institute of Education
{a.vasalou, d.gooch, l.benton}@ioe.ac.uk

[2] Institute of Digital Games
University of Malta
rilla.khaled@um.edu.mt

ABSTRACT

Cultural appropriation in games entails the taking of knowledge, artifacts or expression from a culture and recontextualizing it within game structures. While cultural appropriation is a pervasive practice in games, little attention has been given to the ethical issues that emerge from such practices with regards to how culture is portrayed. This paper problematizes cultural appropriation in the context of a serious game for children inspired by Día de los Muertos, a Mexican festival focused on remembrance of the dead. Taking a research through design approach, we demonstrate that recontextualised cultural elements can retain their basic, original meaning. However, we also find that cultural appropriation is inevitable and its ethical implications can be far reaching. In our context, ethical concerns arose as a result of children's beliefs that death affects prominent others and their destructive ways of coping with death. We argue that revealing emergent ethical concerns is imperative before deciding how and in what way to encourage culturally authentic narratives.

Author Keywords

cultural appropriation; game narrative; research through design; serious games; death; children

ACM Classification Keywords

H.5.m. Information interfaces and presentation (e.g., HCI): Miscellaneous – Design.

INTRODUCTION

Games can create new and unfamiliar experiences that extend players' knowledge and challenge their beliefs. While this is considered to be a strength of games, it also introduces challenges. In the case of games that convey new *cultural* knowledge and representations, game designers must be cognizant that their choices offer a lens through which a particular culture may be viewed in the future, influencing the public's attitudes and behaviors toward the culture being portrayed [8].

Cultural appropriation is "the taking – from a culture that is not one's own – of intellectual property, cultural expressions or artefacts, history and ways of knowledge" [21]. Cultural appropriation occurs when game designers decontextualize cultural history, expressions or artifacts that belong to a culture that is not their own, in turn recontextualizing them into game structures. Even though culturally-sensitive game designers might seek to formalize cultural elements within game structures such that cultural authenticity is retained, control over the experiential nature of a game narrative is rarely possible [4]. Both formal and experiential aspects of narrative foster the construction of cultural knowledge that may be offensive to the original culture. Therefore, we argue that in taking social responsibility seriously, designers must strive to understand how games encourage cultural interpretations toward capturing and responding to emergent ethical concerns.

The aim of this paper is to problematize cultural appropriation in the context of a serious game whose goal is to teach literacy skills to children with dyslexia. Our game world is inspired by Día de los Muertos, a Mexican festival with origins traceable to the Aztec period, that is focused on celebrating and remembering the dead. This game design context introduced two particular challenges in relation to retaining cultural authenticity: first, the nature of our game prioritized learning literacy aspects, over the cultural richness of the narrative; second, our players were children whose cognition on death is already shaped by their development and local culture. In acknowledging how the particularities of our context might shape cultural interpretations, we adopted a research through design approach to understand how cultural appropriation and cultural authenticity co-exist and are experienced by children. This research does not aim to reduce cultural appropriation in all its complexity to a set of definitive game design recommendations. Rather, it attempts to foster a better understanding of cultural appropriation and the considerations it raises in the context of game design and in light of design methods involving cultural outsiders.

The contributions of our research are the following: First, we show that recontextualised cultural elements can be interpreted in culturally authentic terms if they convey core values through symbolic rituals and interactions. This helps to inform design strategies that may promote cultural authenticity in the context of games. Second, we show that cultural appropriation is hard to avoid, especially when the cultural rituals refer to concepts of universal concern, as was the case with our game. Our findings highlighted the

CHI PLAY'14, October 19 - 22 2014, Toronto, ON, Canada
Copyright 2014 ACM 978-1-4503-3014-5/14/10…$15.00.
http://dx.doi.org/10.1145/2658537.2658689

importance of understanding cultural appropriation as the interpretive product of children's development and local culture. Third, we find that striving for cultural authenticity introduces new design concerns, ranging from the ethical to the methodological. Even though our research was initially motivated by ethical responsibilities towards cultures represented with a view to limit cultural appropriation, children's appropriation of the festival raised different ethical issues and designer responsibilities toward them. Importantly, some of their interpretations required us to rethink the consequences and complications of both cultural authenticity and appropriation.

BACKGROUND

Culture in Games

Work on culture within the games research community has most often concerned cultural representations. For the last decade, researchers have pointed out the lack of cultural diversity present, and the over-representation of white, male characters. For example, Williams et al. write that "the world of game characters is highly unrepresentative of the actual population and even of game players" [25]. Furthermore, when culturally diverse characters are present in games, often they present negative or problematic cultural stereotypes. For example, in considering representations of black males, after studying 149 games, Burgess et al. found that all black male characters were either athletic, violent, or both [2]. With respect to representations of Native American cultures, Lameman points out that male characters are frequently portrayed as vengeful warriors or mystics, and otherwise as generic warrior types, while female characters are excessively sexualized and tend to play minor roles [13, 14].

The lack of diversity and stereotypes within games might be less troubling if games truly were enclosed "magic circles", where meaning within a game was separate from meaning outside of it. Various scholars have refuted this notion, however [3, 7]. Indeed, serious games in particular are premised on evidence that games encourage meaning making, foster knowledge and develop transversal skills that are transferable beyond the game [6]. In reflecting on what this means for cultural representations, Leonard argues that games serve as a form of tourism, allowing us to "try on other bodies and experiences" so that players can "indulge in the other" [16]. Nakamura suggests that due to heavy stereotyping, identity tourism in games is currently more about supporting experiences that are "entertaining, nonthreatening, and committed to sustaining racial hierarchies" than it is about being enlightening [17]. Through the process of becoming a game character and interacting with other stereotyped characters, Deskins posits that games can serve as a form of reinforcement of prejudicial, if not racist beliefs [8].

Cultural appropriation, a specific form of cultural representation, has as yet been largely overlooked by the games research community. Cultural identity, culture, and appropriation can all be contextually defined, thus it is sometimes difficult to tell when cultural appropriation is taking place [21]. Often, the "taking" also involves a transformation process, during which the representation, interpretation, meaning, and context of the cultural elements can change. In games, cultural appropriation can be argued as taking place whenever elements of a culture are decontextualised and recontextualised to fit within a game's world, narrative, and mechanics, by designers not from that culture. The *Turok* games, for example, appropriate Native American cultures in the service of entertainment, representing Native American characters as warriors who fight with bows, arrows and tomahawks, and possess connections to spirit worlds and almost alien tracking and sneaking abilities [11].

This transformation process has been viewed as potentially problematic, as it can lead to appropriations that are considered inappropriate and wrong by the members of the "original" culture [27]. For example, in Native American cultures, feather headdresses hold special meaning, and the right to wear them must be earned by the wearer. Yet, Native American-inspired feather headdresses have frequently been appropriated by members of other cultures as fashion accessories and costumes [19]. Often, the culture that has been taken from also constitutes a minority culture. Due to a lack of knowledge, members of the majority culture who experience the recontextualised cultural elements may have little idea of the "original" meanings associated with them. Thus, we should not expect majority culture members to easily identify instances of cultural appropriation. But as Eglash et al. point out in the context of ethnocomputing, cultural appropriation is not always negative, potentially supporting empowerment and two-way cultural shifts in both people and technology [9]. The different perspectives on cultural appropriation highlight the important role of the designer in considering the benefits and ethics of cultural appropriation in games, in order to proceed accordingly.

Strategies for Conveying Cultural Characteristics

In turning our attention to practical design strategies related to how culture is portrayed in games, given the globalized nature of the games industry, many games undergo a process of localization prior to local distribution. "Localisers" end up mediating our knowledge of the world, and "filter the images and narratives that are sold and marketed to global consumers" [5]. This localization can range from modification for clarity — e.g. changing user interface metaphors to ones that are culturally familiar — to modification for cultural appropriateness — e.g. making nude characters clothed. Carlson and Corliss present two strategies that localizers use: *domesticating*, in which they swap details deemed too culturally specific to another culture for culturally familiar ones, and *foreignizing*, in which they seek to retain the cultural and historical provenance of the source text [5].

Both techniques come with disadvantages: domesticating potentially runs the risk of cultural appropriation and sacrificing the character of the original text, while foreignizing potentially runs the risk of culturally alienating players, exoticising and drawing undue attention to details which, in the original text might have been mundane. A third technique commonly used by Japanese game developers might be described as *ambiguifying*. This technique embraces *mukokuseki* or statelessness as a design strategy, in which characters have ambiguous racial and cultural backgrounds (for example, having blue hair), in order to appeal to the broadest market possible [5].

MOTIVATION AND RESEARCH QUESTIONS

In general, cultural representations in games currently leave much to be desired. Especially in the context of serious games, where the intention is for players to reflect on game experiences and for learning transfer to occur, we should approach the representation of different cultures thoughtfully. In light of the global games industry and other forms of transcultural exchange, cultural appropriation in games is an additional phenomenon of which we should be cognizant, facing many of the same difficulties as cultural representations in games, as well as additional ethical issues concerning the recontextualisation of cultural elements for use in games. Domesticating and foreignizing are two approaches that have been used in game localization for addressing cultural elements, but both have their weaknesses. Adopting blanket rules to not represent elements of other cultures is not an ideal solution either. Amongst other reasons, it hugely limits people's exposure to other cultures, and cultural ownership is frequently not a cut-and-dried affair. Clearly, there is a need for designers to consciously reflect on how to represent culture in games respectfully, while taking into account the characteristics of their players to avoid alienation. The present work focuses on and problematizes cultural appropriation in the context of the design of a serious game for literacy featuring a Mexican festival celebrating death. It has a particular focus on children's meaning making processes, and the issues that arise from deeply considering player participation in design.

The objective of the game we are designing is to strengthen the literacy skills of players. Our target audience concerns late primary school aged children (ages 9-11) who live in England with reading difficulties, many of whom find reading to be a demotivating activity. Previous research shows that best practice teaching for dyslexia involves 'explicit phonics teaching', which is often performed through multisensory drill and practice activities [20]. Part of our design challenge therefore became to present versions of these activities within a motivating frame. In particular, we sought to pique enough interest in players such that they would return to the activities repeatedly, with the game featuring no set ending point. We wished to situate the game within a world that was both familiar and unfamiliar, in which the player's role would be a heroic one involving language decoding, and the other characters would be reliant on the player. Having decided to foreground maintenance of friendships with characters as a means of encouraging replaying of activities, we also needed a world that would feature a multitude of interesting characters.

We eventually chose a world inspired by Dia de los Muertos, or the Day of the Dead (DotD). The core message of DotD, a two-day festival that is observed in Mexico and other central American cultures, is of remembrance and acceptance of death, with death being viewed as a continuation of life [1]. On these days, friends and family gather to celebrate the lives of the departed. The living build shrines for their loved ones. They honor the dead by giving offerings to them such as sugar skulls, marigold flowers, traditional foods and beverages, by praying for them, and by writing and performing humorous poems and songs about them. It is believed that over those days, the souls of the dead awake to visit the living. DotD is associated with a particular aesthetic, characterized by bright colours and cheerful, playful representations of the dead as skeletons. We initially became interested in DotD because of its aesthetics. On further exploration of what the festival signified, particularly, reflecting on the central role of communication in DotD, we decided to draw on it to inform our game world as it could be interpreted as aligning with the pedagogical goals of our game.

A guiding value of our work was to maintain the cultural authenticity of DotD in the game world. However, in designing a culturally faithful account of the festival, we faced challenges. One such challenge arose from the primary purpose of our game, which was to strengthen literacy. The world setting played a secondary role of support in motivating learners to continue playing the game. This meant that as designers we could not privilege a rich cultural exploration of the DotD. Such narrative constraints are inherent to serious games. *Socialdrome*, for example, aimed at developing children's social skills acquired in a fictional island called Cascara. While the island provided the context for numerous learning activities, its role was to motivate the learning goal of the game [23]. Thus, our first research question was: *can cultural authenticity in game design be maintained by presenting children with a narrow perspective of the festival that retains its core message and rituals?*

A second challenge emerged from the fact that neither we, nor our target players, are Mexican, and concerned the meanings, interpretations, and practices surrounding death in the cultural context of childhood in the UK. While cultural appropriation debates have focused on ownership of particular cultural artefacts or knowledge, death affects everyone and is not tied to any specific culture; indeed every culture interprets death in its own ways.

Previous research provides some insight into children's cognitive and cultural understanding of death. Children understand the natural causes of death by middle childhood

[10, 15, 22]. This understanding is in part mediated by the media's persistency in reporting death. Challenging a sociological claim that death has become a private matter, Walter et al. argue that death is at the centre of public life, with the British media 'trespassing' into the family realm on a daily basis [24]. They argue that the media privilege the reporting of the deaths of public members of society, or deaths that have occurred under extraordinary circumstances. Their analysis also demonstrates the media's fascination with the feelings, emotions and grief associated with death, which they call 'emotion invigilation'. As children's understanding of the natural causes of death evolve, supernatural explanations also begin to develop; such explanations go beyond what can be explained by natural laws. In a meta-review of relevant empirical work, Woolley and Ghossainy show that despite the common belief that children display credulity, compared to adults, children are less supernatural in the way they conceive of death [26]. Even though children and adults both agree that biological functions cease upon death, adults tend to propose that cognitive processes continue beyond death. Crucially, culture plays a central role in this belief shift. Testimonials from loved ones, such as parents and teachers, foster children's belief in the supernatural [10] with supernatural explanations of death increasing with children's age [15].

The research described above thus claims that children already have understandings of death, which are strongly culturally situated. In exploring how to approach cultural appropriation in the game design process, it was important to examine to what extent children contributing to the design would seek to appropriate DotD to make it more familiar to their ways of understanding, despite designers' best efforts to maintain cultural authenticity. Our second research question was: *will the festival mediate children's understanding of death and how?*

To address these questions, we adopted a *research through design* approach undertaken through a participatory, constructivist game design method described below.

METHOD

Participants

We undertook two design workshops with two classes (year five and six) at a single mainstream primary school in south-east London. The school is located in a socially and ethnically diverse area with a higher than average proportion of students whose first language is not English. The children were all within our target age group (ages 9-11). A total of 37 children participated (20 boys and 17 girls), with 22 children within the year five class (aged 9-10) and 15 children within the year six class (aged 10-11). The children were divided into groups of four or five, with a total of five groups in the year five class and four groups in the year six class.

Materials and Procedure

Each workshop lasted for about one hour and was facilitated by three to four researchers. The children's class teacher was also present throughout the session. We based the workshop on a constructivist approach. Through children's development of stories, we explored their cultural beliefs, understanding and experiences of death.

The workshop involved three related phases. The activity structure within each phase, along with adult facilitation when necessary, provided scaffolding for children's development of stories. The activities were designed to encourage the children to actively construct stories in collaboration with their peers and imbue them with their own meanings. Moreover, to ensure that children's stories aligned with game structures, workshop activities required an incremental building up of a game system, as recently proposed by Khaled and Vasalou [12]. For instance, children designed game characters before they went on to design events that took place between these characters. Importantly, we chose to retain the festival's cultural authenticity by highlighting the core values it expressed (indicated in small caps within the text), ensuring in turn that these values were an intrinsic and central part of the activities. To derive the values, prior to the workshop, the authors conducted research on the festival. After each researcher had read numerous secondary sources, namely online articles written about the festival, they convened to discuss their understanding of the festival and to define a first core set of values. These values were later verified in discussion with two cultural insiders who served as informants to our method. Thus, workshop prompts and activities were based on this preliminary research aiming at building a design method that reflected the cultural authenticity of the festival.

Presentation of design context: we explained to the class that we were designing a game based on the DotD festival, and that we welcomed their ideas for game characters and stories. First, we highlighted the purpose of the festival in celebrating the lives of those who have died, exemplifying the UNIVERSALITY of death to all humans and living organisms. We then showed the students a 3-minute animated film of a young girl's experience of the festival[1]. The film had been created by art and design students and had received a Student Academy Award. It started with the girl's visit to her mother's grave on the DotD. As tears flowed down her face, she was drawn by a sudden force into the world of the dead. Even though she was initially afraid, the girl slowly joined the festivities dancing with one skeletal figurine in particular, whom she recognized as her mother. As mother and daughter held each other with love, the girl found herself back at the grave site. The story ended as the girl skipped with joy away from the graveyard. The video encapsulated the festival's core message of

[1] https://www.youtube.com/watch?v=jCQnUuq-TEE

REMEMBRANCE and ACCEPTANCE. It also served as an introduction to the aesthetic style of the DotD. Next, one researcher told a 5-minute story about a girl and her dead dog using a PowerPoint deck featuring photos of Mexican DotD festivities to support the storytelling process. This story was built upon our research on the festival and was purposefully designed to introduce children to values, customs and traditions for honoring and calling on the dead, including customary foods, marigold flowers, poetry written for the dead and dedicated shrines. These customs expressed the INTIMACY fostered on the day between the dead and the living.

Development of characters: we then asked the children to create their own characters in groups for a story about this festival featuring one living, and one dead character. Each group was provided with paper templates for each character, which they could fill in with details such as their hobbies/interests, job, and relationship to the other character. Example templates based on the story told to the children at the start of the workshop were displayed on an interactive whiteboard as a prompt for groups who were struggling with ideas. Once the children had agreed on their two characters, they were provided with modeling clay as well as a selection of other art materials including paper, beads, and other accessories. Using these materials, they built or drew each of their characters.

Narrative construction: we invited children to create a story about their characters. In supporting the children in developing stories that described relationships and communication between characters, they were asked to consider the following questions: *Why does one of your characters want to contact the other character? How do they contact them? What are they saying? How does the story end?* Through this narrative, children were able to explore all three emotive and cognitive components fostered by the festival: INTIMACY, REMEMBRANCE and ACCEPTANCE. Each group was provided with a blank paper storyboard on which they could document their ideas for their story. Lastly, each group was given a Flip video camera and asked to capture their story on it. This activity required children to integrate all of the ideas they had developed into a cohesive narrative.

To summarize, our method closely defined some parts of the narrative with a view to promote cultural authenticity, while other parts were left ambiguous and open, such as for example character roles. We intentionally included this underspecificity in order to invite, capture, and understand children's cultural interpretations of DotD values, and their proposals for suitable game design elements.

DATA CAPTURE AND ANALYSIS

Where possible during the workshop, researchers took written notes about events taking place, and took photos. Post-workshop, the notes were compiled into full written accounts of what happened within each group, and the videos recorded by the children were transcribed. The notes and transcripts were transferred to an online qualitative analysis tool and were analyzed according to thematic analysis drawing out key themes in conjunction with the photos, videos, character profiles, drawings, models and storyboards produced during the workshop.

RESULTS

Aesthetics of Death

Children connected the concept of death to characters and physical properties of the world to create playful combinations. Using the aesthetics of the festival as a point of departure, dead characters were often designed as skeletons putting to use the modeling clay we had provided. Children proposed a 'skeleton orchestra'. They envisioned the 'dead playing football with their skulls'. All of them perceived the world of the dead as a place of both decay and mystery, with little light, homes made out of bones, and moldy food. Children were fascinated by the strangeness in the world's decay as they envisioned it.

Aesthetic and creative choices were also prompted by opportunities suggested by the arts materials made available. One team first identified a shiny heart icon in their arts packet before deciding to attach it on their living character's body to express love for her dead dog. Overall, it appeared that children's engagement was sustained through the constructivist approach taken where aesthetic expression and meaning making was encouraged. Figure 1 displays several clay models that children made.

Figure 1: Clay models of dead and living characters

Actors, Causes and Interpretations of Death

In most of the stories developed, children depicted dead characters to occupy an important status in the world of the dead. For instance, a dead dog acted as protector of dead inhabitants and their animals. Status was also acquired during the transition to the world of the dead. A character who used to be a schoolgirl in life became a doctor upon entering the world of the dead. Another group of children created a story between an uncle, Pedro, and his niece, Pearly. Upon meeting in the world of the dead, an evil leader, Zorgon, arrived and told them that Pearly was not allowed to leave. Pearly defended her uncle and defeated the leader, leaving Pedro as king of the world of the dead.

Figure 2: Pedro, the king of the world of the dead

Children made sense of death through both natural and supernatural explanations. Those who focused on the natural cessation of biological functions tended to sensationalise and dramatize death through gruesome details. One team described the killing of a living character, while enacting it by disassembling the physical props: 'A car came out and hit Johnny. Blood poured and her heart fell out and then her body was split in half. She got buried in her grave piece by piece.' In a similar fashion, another team described a fight erupting between two characters in the world of the dead: 'She takes Pedro's gun, shoots Zorgon in the eye sockets and bones start falling out of them. She then punches Zorgon's skull off and kicks it away'. While natural causes of death emerged in children's stories, many children made reference to supernatural causes that did not adhere to natural laws. Some discussed the continuation of life after death. Drawing on their own religious ideologies, they compared the world of the dead with heaven. Moreover, dead characters were envisioned to continue praying and thinking of their loved ones, suggesting a continuing bond between the dead and the living. One team designed a Facebook application called 'Ghostbook' that was proposed to sustain this communication. Highlighting the importance of the supernatural, another team discussed the role of fate in dying: they talked about a living pirate who had travelled

Figure 3: A 'Ghostbook' message sent by a dead to a living character

the world and taken many risks only to die at the same spot as his grandfather.

As Walter et al. caution, children in England are exposed daily to media portrayals of death that privilege and sensationalise both the deaths of public figures as well as extraordinary causes of death [24]. Indeed, the influence of culture was evident in children's construction of stories. Moreover, we note that violence and status in relation to death are frequent tropes in the context of games. Game heroines are comparable to public figures as they almost always occupy an important status in game narratives. Additionally, coping with violence in games is perceived to be a rite of passage by younger children, with in-game violence seen as unrealistic compared to their real world experiences [18]. The perceived lack of realism associated with games could have thus served to foster the violent accounts of death that children provided. Turning our focus to the supernatural, our participants belonged to an age group that has begun to incorporate religious beliefs into their reasoning processes. Even though the exploration of the supernatural was encouraged through the festival and its rituals, children interpreted the supernatural from the lens of their own religious and fatalistic perspectives.

Cultural Rituals as an Entry Point for Exploring the Supernatural

As noted above, the workshops explicitly invited children to consider supernatural elements through the lens of Mexican cultural rituals for communicating with the dead (e.g. marigold flowers). As mentioned earlier, researchers provided an example story for inspiration that described a living child being drawn into the world of the dead as she stood over her mother's grave. Although "novel" ideas did feature in the children's stories, when designing the initial communication act between the living and the dead, most children relied on the cultural rituals we had provided. Communication often began at a three-tier shrine, it was encouraged by marigold flower petals and through placing customary food at graveyards. Similarly children mimicked the example given by researchers as inspiration with most of them describing a sudden force pulling the living character into the world of the dead.

Figure 4: A young girl leaves marigold flowers at the site of her dog's grave

Only two teams provided new ideas for character communication. The first team of children described a dead father who used to be barrister. The father appeared in his son's bedroom with a special mist flowing into his wig. The second team described the importance of mutual gaze between a dead father and his living daughter. The characters acknowledged each other's presence only when simultaneously looking into a body of water. In interpreting these findings, we recognize that the DotD served as a novel and legitimizing cultural lens from which children could explore the supernatural. In light of the cultural unfamiliarity of the concept of directly communicating with the dead, they drew on Mexican cultural rituals and practices to establish their stories. To continue the stories, they then moved to more culturally familiar tropes and practices, shedding light on their own culturally-relevant explanations and meaning making processes.

Emotions and Death

Children's narratives described a series of emotionally charged events whose sequence was directed by the narrative structure we had guided them to follow through the storyboarding activity. Most stories began by expressing the living's state of longing, sadness and nostalgia for the dead. Stories went on to describe the moment where the dead and the living met again. Living characters typically experienced fear and shock when first facing their loved one. After fear subsided, children proposed interactions in which characters expressed their love for each other and shared meaningful moments. Upon the living's exit of the world of the dead, they talked about growing acceptance and peace with death. This composure was often maintained through yearly meetings between characters at the time of the festival. One team for example narrated a story between a father and a daughter who both shared a love for swimming: 'Well Philip died when he went to the Olympic stadium. He had a competition and accidentally drowned. His daughter (Elizabeth) tried to save him, dived in but it was too late and the daughter was very, very sad… Ok, they communicate by Elizabeth saying a poem to her father and… She goes underground and gets grabbed by a hand, a bone hand, she screams but then her father shows her his swimming move and they are both happy and when they hug each other, the daughter is back saying her poem'. Most notably these emotional narratives aligned with the festival's message of celebrating and accepting death.

Figure 5: A living and a dead sister communicate through a mirror

While the majority of stories started with emotions of sadness, which progressed into acceptance and relief, two teams constructed this emotional journey in different terms. The first focused on the living character's revenge and anger about the death of her friend who had been killed in a road accident: 'Lucy stamped on the car, and crushed it and was very angry with the driver. She ended up putting the driver in the hospital and ended in prison behind bars'. This group of children went on to describe the meeting between the dead and the living character, after which the living made sure that cars could harm no child by casually killing other drivers she encountered. In contrast, the second team emphasized the living character's feelings of guilt and the external pressures imposed on the bereaved in suppressing their emotions. Upon hearing of the death of his father, a young child Lucas thought 'it is not my fault'. After asking 'when is he going to be back?', Lucas was told that his father is never coming back. He was so upset that he began to jump on his bed and broke it. His mother said in disdain: 'why are you jumping on the bed like that? You just broke the bed. That's £150. Learn to be a good boy, a good boy.. now you're going to sleep on a broken bed'. These two groups of children deviated from exploring the festival's message and expressed responses to death that could be viewed as problematic if not further discussed: the first game character expressed revenge, while the second was punished for showing grief in his own way.

In summary, our workshops revealed how children interpret death in the cultural context of our game concept. Their characters and stories embodied the tension between strict cultural authenticity in games and involving cultural outsiders as game design participants. We used their interpretations to reflect on the role of the game as a 'cultural artifact' that encourages certain ways of thinking about death through its narrative and interactive values. We explore their design implications next alongside how they advanced our understanding of cultural appropriation.

DISCUSSION

Co-Existence of Cultural Authenticity and Appropriation

When the children were asked to engage with new perspectives on the supernatural, they drew on cultural knowledge that the researchers had given them. We found that children could not easily conceive how the dead and the living communicate. Lacking their own points of reference, they strongly relied on the cultural rituals and customs of the DotD for proposing how this could happen. Our findings echoed one of the concerns associated with foreignizing as a localization approach, namely, that it led to the exoticizing of particular details [5]. In our case, those details concerned being pulled into the world of the dead, which encapsulates only a small part of the DotD. At the same time, we did not find much evidence that the other significant disadvantage of foreignizing, cultural alienation, was taking place. While children heavily relied on our descriptions of DotD rituals, they simultaneously utilized the rituals as a vantage point for understanding the meaning of the festival. Indeed, the festival's emphasis on remembrance, intimacy and acceptance were understood and enacted by most of the teams. In directing children's construction of stories by providing the purpose and outcomes of the festival, we were able to maintain some cultural authenticity. In drawing this conclusion, however, it is important to recognize that the workshops were run with participants from an ethnically diverse school. Children's pre-existing exposure to cultural diversity might help to explain why they were open to exploring the rituals and narratives of other cultures. Nevertheless, in line with our first research question, our findings are encouraging for games such as our own where narrative exploration is not an end, but serves as a means for motivating another primary objective. We thus argue that game narrative can communicate cultural authenticity as long as it retains components that exemplify its core cultural values.

At the same time, establishing cultural authenticity was not a straightforward process. Despite our efforts to direct them toward culturally authentic stories, children appropriated the festival and imbued it with their own meanings. Leonard writes of games enabling people to "try on other bodies and experiences" and to "indulge in the other" [16]. Conversely, we observed that children sought to make the experiences more familiar. Certain elements and narratives associated with the DotD festival had resonance with them, including relationships between characters, responses to death and causes of death. In those cases, children tended to construct stories in the context of their own cultural, social, and religious background and experiences. To give one example, children engaged in what Walter et al. call emotion invigilation where they elaborated and dramatized the emotions of the deceased [24]. Therefore, while cultural authenticity was retained and benefited children in understanding death in different terms, children also naturally gravitated towards cultural appropriation. As Calleja argues, game narrative is not only formalized by the designer, but also interpreted, reshaped and experienced by the player [4]. In the special case of cultural representations of death, given the universality of death as a phenomenon, it may be argued that appropriation is not only inevitable but also imperative if children are to make sense of death and bereavement. With respect to our second research question, our findings demonstrated that children's cultural understanding of death played a determining role in shaping their understanding of the festival.

Ethics of Cultural Appropriation

Observing children's cultural appropriation of the festival raised several ethical questions. While children of the age group involved have been shown to understand both natural and supernatural aspects of death, our findings question the extent to which they have accepted death. DotD addresses the universality of death to all human beings and living organisms. In contrast to this view, our participants explicitly avoided describing death as an event that touches all people: those living in the world of the dead were mostly assumed to be people of status. One explanation advanced earlier was that children might be mimicking the way that death is portrayed culturally in the media [24] or in relation to game protagonists. However, it is also likely that they believe death is not of relevance to them, or a distant event, a finding that has been shown in previous empirical research [22]. In maintaining the cultural authenticity of DotD, our game would need to promote a universal view on death, potentially demanding children to confront their own mortality and that of close others, thereby facilitating a change in cognition.

Additionally, DotD foregrounds closure as a means of accepting and coping with death. Some children departed from this perspective on coping to experiment with different ways of thinking and acting. They described counterproductive and detrimental ways of coping with death, including revenge and the suppression of emotions, thus missing the message of emotional acceptance mediated through the festival. Exposing such ways of coping might help children explore when, how and if to regulate emotions during grief [24]. However, neither the workshop, nor our initial game concept, included provisions to encourage reflection on these kinds of interpretations of death. Finally, while participating children had not suffered bereavement, grieving children will undoubtedly understand the game in different terms raising further ethical considerations.

The present work was motivated by an ethical obligation toward the originating culture, in which cultural appropriation in games was viewed as problematic. Our findings broadened this ethical obligation by exploring design conflicts that can arise as a result of children's cultural appropriation. This highlighted the importance to design for cultural authenticity such that clashes with children's existing beliefs are handled with sensitivity.

Design as a Mechanism to Mitigate Cultural Appropriation and Related Ethical Concerns

In the context of games, mukokuseki has been used as a means of appealing to the widest possible audience, as mukokuseki design is ambiguous and cannot be clearly associated with any particular culture [5]. Within our workshop, we observed that ambiguous aspects were interpreted in culturally familiar ways and thus paradoxically invited cultural appropriation. Some designers might argue in favor of unambiguous, closed representations of other cultures that maintain as much cultural authenticity as possible. Nonetheless, as our findings show, the experiential nature of narrative suggests that cultural appropriation will happen. Studies such as our own that take a research through design perspective to understand how cultural events, artifacts or knowledge are interpreted by end users and assimilated into their own cultural knowledge will be vital to determine the ethical issues that might arise, and to design opportunities for further mitigating these concerns within and outside of the game. In the context of our game, our findings have sensitized us to the importance of exploring and acknowledging children's ongoing reflections on death during an educational intervention focused on literacy.

Design Participation For Cultural Authenticity

Acknowledging children's interpretive role in games, in the present work we set out to observe their interpretations of the festival with a view to understand if and how cultural appropriation happens. This research demonstrated the ever-shifting balance between cultural appropriation and authenticity, while also helping us to reflect on how to mitigate emergent ethical issues. Although we engaged our participants in storytelling activities during the workshops, our aim was to generate knowledge about cultural appropriation rather than to share design control with them. Yet, our findings suggest that attempts to co-design in light of cultural appropriation concerns will introduce new methodological challenges, especially with regards to who participates and what participation means. Participatory design in particular foregrounds the needs and perspectives of end users. In understanding users' cultural beliefs, needs and values, designers aim to create appropriate tools and systems. Both pragmatically and ethically, it stands to reason that users should be directly involved in design activities. Games and virtual worlds can feature cultural representations of diverse cultures, human and non-human alike. These cultures may be new to intended players. In the context of our workshop, if we had drawn largely on children's ideas to design the game world and narrative, we would have largely relied on domesticating as an approach for representing culture, as well as cultural appropriation. Therefore, in cases where designers want to share control with users for applications and systems that represent other cultures, new considerations arise.

Within our workshop, we presented children with cultural rituals and encouraged them to embed them into their stories. Children balanced the use of such cultural resources, and the meaning making encouraged through them, with their own stories about death. Thus, the cultural context of the workshop empowered them to make meaning of a sensitive topic [9]. As discussed earlier, this strategy was used by children to understand the core values of the festival. Future work could develop this approach further through participatory methods that support children to acquire cultural expertise before their input to design. A further approach that balances cultural authenticity with children's experiences would be to involve cultural experts and consultants in working together with children. Such a design team could establish shared understandings of death that accommodate cultural authenticity and at the same time are sensitive to children's development and culture.

CONCLUSION

The present work drew attention to the implications of cultural appropriation arguing that it can influence how the originating culture is perceived, while changing the nature and meaning of important cultural rituals. Our research focused on how cultural appropriation can arise during the design process of a serious game. Targeted at primary school children, the game's narrative was based on the Mexican festival, Día de los Muertos or Day of the Dead, celebrating the lives of those who have died. Taking a research through design approach, we set out to explore how cultural authenticity can be retained through game structures and narrative, while capturing if and how cultural appropriation may happen given children's contextual, cultural understandings of death.

Our findings demonstrated that cultural authenticity can be fostered if designers foreground rituals and relational dynamics that allow users to make sense of the underpinning cultural values. However, we also found that in the case of cultural rituals that implicate universal concerns, cultural appropriation is unavoidable. Most importantly, we showed that cultural appropriation can extend designers' ethical considerations beyond members of the originating culture, to include end users. A key outcome of our research was to gain insight into children's new beliefs, understandings and ways of coping with death. Cultural appropriation became an issue of ethical concern not least due to the subordinate role of our game narrative, highlighting the importance of creating space for exploration and discussion on death within the context of our educational intervention. Our work also served as a springboard for discussing methodological implications for those espousing co-design approaches to game design. Given children's tendency toward cultural appropriation, we emphasize the importance of developing children's cultural knowledge before they assume an active role in design. Finally, we hope that this work has raised attention to an important design consideration, shedding light into research processes that may support designers to better understand the occurrence and implications of cultural appropriation within their respective domains.

ACKNOWLEDGEMENT

This work was funded by the ILearnRW (project no: 318803) FP7 ICT EU project. We gratefully acknowledge the children who participated in this workshop contributing with their creativity and enthusiasm.

REFERENCES

1. Andrade, M. J. Dìa de Muertos en Mèxico: Ciudad de Mèxico, Mixquic y Morelos. San Jose, CA, 2000.
2. Burgess, M. C. R., Dill, K. E., Stermer, S. P., Burgess, S. R., and Brown, B. P. Playing with prejudice: The prevalence and consequences of racial stereotypes in video games. Media Psychology 14, 3 2011, 289–311.
3. Calleja, G. Erasing the Magic Circle. Philosophy of Engineering and Technology 7, 3 2012, 77-91.
4. Calleja, G. Narrative Involvement in Digital Games. ACM Press, New York, 2013..
5. Carlson, R., and Corliss, J. Imagined commodities: Video game localization and mythologies of cultural difference. Games and Culture 6, 1 2011, 61–82.
6. Connolly, T. M., Boyle, E. A., MacArthur, E., Hainey, T. and Boyle, J. M. A systematic literature review of the empirical evidence on computer games and serious games. Computers & Education 59 2012, 661-686.
7. Consalvo, M. There is no magic circle. Games and Culture 4, 4 2009, 408–417.
8. Deskins, T. G. Stereotypes in video games and how they perpetuate prejudice. McNair Scholars Research Journal 6, 1 2013.
9. Eglash, R., Bennett, A., O'Donnell, C., Jennings, S., and Cintorino, M. Culturally Situated Design Tools: Ethnocomputing from Field Site to Classroom. American Anthropologist 108, 2 2006, 347-362.
10. Harris, P.L. and Koenig, M.A.. Trust in Testimony: How Children Learn About Science and Religion. Child Development 77, 3 2006, 505-524.
11. Entertainment, I. Turok: Dinosaur Hunter. Acclaim Entertainment, City, 1997.
12. Khaled, R., and Vasalou, A. Bridging Serious Games and Participatory Design. International Journal of Child-computer Interaction, In press.
13. Lameman, B. A. The Good, the Bad, and the Sultry: Indigenous Women in Video Games. Retrieved from http://www.abtec.org/docs/IndigenousWomenInVideoGames.pdf, 2010.
14. LaPensée, B. A. Native Representations in Video Games. Retrieved from http://indiancountrytodaymedianetwork.com/2011/08/14/native-representations-video-games-47243, 2011.
15. Legare, C. H., Evans, E.M., Rosengren, K.S. and Harris, P.L. The coexistence of natural and supernatural explanations across cultures and development. Child Development 83, 3 2012, 779-793.
16. Leonard, D. J. "live in your world, play in ours": Race, video games, and consuming the other. SIMILE: Studies In Media & Information Literacy Education 3, 4 2003, 1–9.
17. Nakamura, L. Cybertypes: Race, Ethnicity, and Identity on the Internet. Routledge, 2002.
18. Olson, C. K. Children's Motivations for Video Game Play in the Context of Normal Development. Review of General Psychology 14, 2 2010, 180-187.
19. Polacek, J. Heidi Klum's Redface Photo Shoot Is a Massive Insult to Native Americans. Retrieved from http://www.policymic.com/articles/87351/heidi-klum-s-redface-photo-shoot-is-a-massive-insult-to-native-americans, 2014.
20. Rose, J. Identifying and Teaching Children and Young People with Dyslexia and Literacy Difficulties. Department for Education, Retrieved from http://webarchive.nationalarchives.gov.uk/20130401151715/http://www.education.gov.uk/publications/standard/publicationdetail/page1/dcsf-00659-2009, 2009.
21. Schneider, A. On 'appropriation'. a critical reappraisal of the concept and its application in global art practices. Social Anthropology 11, 2 2003, 215–229.
22. Speece, M.W. and Brent, S.B. Children's understanding of death: A review of three components of a death concept. Child Development 55, 5 1984, 1671-1686.
23. Tan, J. L., Goh, D.H., Ang, R.P. and Huan, V.S. Child-Centered Interaction in the Design of a Game for Social Skills Intervention. Computers in Entertainment 9, 1 2011.
24. Walter, T., Littlewood, J. and Pickering, M. Death in the news: the public invigilation of private emotion. Sociology 29, 4 1995, 579-596.
25. Williams, D., Martins, N., Consalvo, M., and Ivory, J. D. The virtual census: representations of gender, race and age in video games. New Media & Society 11, 5 2009, 815–834.
26. Woolley, J.D. and Ghossainy, E. M. Revisiting the fantasy-reality distinction: children as naïve skeptics. Child Development 84, 5 2013, 1496-1510.
27. The Ethics of Cultural Appropriation. Wiley-Blackwell, 2009.

Know Before you Go: Feelings of Flow for Older Players Depends on Game and Player Characteristics

Laura A. Whitlock, Anne Collins McLaughlin
Dept. of Psychology,
North Carolina State University
Raleigh, NC
lawhitlo@ncsu,edu,
acmclaug@ncsu.edu

William Leidheiser
Dept. of Psychology,
Clemson University
Clemson, SC
wleidhe@clemson.edu

Maribeth Gandy
Interactive Media Technology Center,
Georgia Institute of Technology
Atlanta, GA
maribeth@imtc.gatech.edu

Jason C. Allaire
Dept. of Psychology,
North Carolina State University
Raleigh, NC
jason_allaire@ncsu.edu

ABSTRACT

The success of therapeutic games has received recent attention in the research literature, particularly for health issues frequently experienced by adults over age sixty-five. However, less is known about the experience of older adults after interaction with these games and what may promote their adoption and use. We measured the development of flow in a study of over 100 older adults who played a video game for 15 hours across three weeks. Findings indicate that flow development was affected by both individual differences between participants, measured prior to any game experience, and to characteristics of the game, particularly those related to usability of the interface and input device. We conclude with discussion of the flow experience in games for older adults and guidelines for the design of engaging and immersive therapeutic games.

Author Keywords

Aging; usability; digital games; flow; user experience; therapy; cognitive training; rehabilitation

ACM Classification Keywords

H.5.m [**Information Interfaces and Presentation** (e.g., HCI)]: Miscellaneous.
K.8.0 [**Personal Computing**]: General—games.
J.4 [**Social and Behavioral Sciences**]: Psychology.

INTRODUCTION

Digital games are increasingly used as therapeutic tools across domains important to the well-being of older adults. From improving cognitive function in older age [2, 29] to rehabilitation [16] and pain management [16], digital games have shown positive effects in health and wellbeing, including for older players.

There are however challenges associated with designing and administering effective therapeutic games for older persons [29]. Fewer older adults play digital games compared to other age groups [26], although one study of adults aged 55 and older found that approximately one third had played games for over 10 years [24]. However, games used for therapy may push users' capabilities, often past the point of enjoyment. For example, older participants assigned to play a game found to produce cognitive gains in younger adults did not adhere to the training program due to lack of enjoyment [5]. Thus, promoting long term effort in voluntary games may require an especially careful balance between the game's challenge and players' frustration [29].

While much effort is being put towards understanding the types of activities that result in cognitive change, less thought is given to the game design and player experience. The design of computer games that are both compelling and accessible to an older player needs further exploration [21]. Whitlock et al. found the massively multiplayer online role-playing game "World of Warcraft" to yield cognitive benefits in older players, yet the participants struggled with the complexity of the game. The participants in that study required two hours of in-person training and extensive remote support [34]. The Lumosity team highlighted the critical role that engagement and reward played in effective brain games [16]. The realities are that, given the amount of time players must engage with these games to achieve results, people may not get the maximum value out of these interventions if they are bored, frustrated, unmotivated, or if they play the game in an unintended manner. As Hanson et al. noted, it is critical for technology design to address older adults' values and not just their usability requirements [15]. While prior work has addressed the issue of individual differences (player type: achiever, socializer) to inform the tailoring of persuasive health games [30], age differences were not examined as part of the study.

CHI PLAY '14, October 19 - 22 2014, Toronto, ON, Canada

http://dx.doi.org/10.1145/2658537.2658703

It is therefore important to better understand the way in which older adults experience digital games by measuring enjoyment, immersion, and whether there is a match between game challenge and player skill. Higher levels of such attributes have been linked to use of and adherence to therapeutic games for younger players [23]. These game-related attributes are important and are situated within the individual player differences in function, ability, and skill.

Immersion, engagement, and skill balance are all attributes connected to feelings of "flow." First described by Csikszentmihályi & Csikszentmihályi [9], flow is a state in which a person experiences enjoyment through meeting a challenge that matches his or her skill and during the process becomes absorbed in the experience to the point of total focus. Flow has most frequently been assessed using a questionnaire with 9 subscales: challenge-skill balance, action-awareness merging, clear goals, unambiguous feedback, concentration on task at hand, sense of control, loss of self-consciousness, transformation of time, and autoelic experience [22]. Flow has been used to study experience in domains including work [10] and digital games [6, 8] and is generally seen as a measure of immersion, enjoyment, and engagement.

Relatively little is known, however, about the experience of flow for older adults in the context of games. In the few studies specific to flow, it has been found that 1) older adults experienced more flow when playing other humans online, compared to playing against other humans disguised as computer controlled players [12], 2) a match between older adult ability/experience and game challenge has been related to feelings of flow [20], 3) clear goals and feedback in a game may foster a sense of mastery associated with flow in older adults [4], and 4) flow in games for older adults has been related to better therapeutic outcomes [35]. These studies suggest benefits for flow, but there is a paucity of studies concerning user experience outcomes, including flow, for older players. In sum, flow appears to be important to therapeutic use of games and may be a good measure of motivation, user experience, and immersion for older adults. However, questions remain concerning the individual- and task-related variables that promote such immersion in older players.

One method for considering the totality of game experience is to study the game environment as a system that depends on the interaction between game design and the characteristics of the player. Such a model includes human factors methods for formative evaluation, design, and iterative evaluation with considerations of person attributes that affect the capabilities and limitations expected of a player. These capabilities and limitations then match or mismatch the knowledge, skills, and abilities required by the task. The original model was designed for creating training programs [31] and has been adapted here to game design, focused on user experience as an outcome.

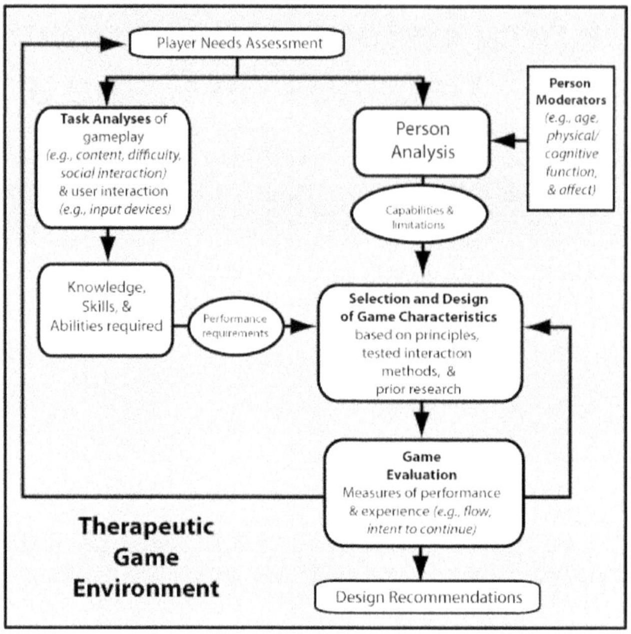

Figure 1. The systems approach adapted to suggest a game design cycle focused on the match between player and game with performance in the game and user experience as outcomes.

The difference between the systems approach and most game development models [32] is the explicit focus on person analysis, including group and individual variables that predict eventual experience with the game, and the feedback loops between evaluation/needs analysis and evaluation/selection and design of game characteristics. For example, the capabilities and limitations of older adults' emotions are more heterogeneous than younger adults, making for a larger effect on how a game might be experienced [25]. In the example model presented in Figure 1, person-related moderators are suggested, such as affect and health, that would be likely to interact with the game attributes, though they must be empirically tested before basing game design on such recommendations.

Affect is a person-level characteristic that may be especially important and is generally measured as two scales: positive and negative affect. Positive affect reflects the extent to which a person feels enthusiastic, active, and alert and relates to the personality factor of extraversion [33], and is also associated with experiences like engagement in social activity [7]. Positive affect may therefore influence players' emotional reaction to a game as well as their reaction to social interaction during play. The positive affect scale has previously been used to measure transient mood improvements due to gameplay for older adults [14].

Health is also likely to play a role in how older adults experience therapeutic games, particularly as the result of health-related physical limitations. For example, hand pain is common in adults over the age of 50 [11] and may worsen during use. As a consequence older adults with greater physical limitations due to health may be expected to experience greater usability problems during play that could affect their experience.

Study Overview

The goal of this study was to investigate the development of flow in a digital game in an older adult sample after interacting with a game for fifteen hours. To understand:

- ...individual differences in flow experience, we measured levels of physical functioning, positive affect, and other person level variables prior to having them play the game.
- ...the effect of game difficulty on flow and its subscales, we manipulated the difficulty of the game.
- ...the effect of social interaction on flow and its subscales, we manipulated whether participants played the game individually or paired with another participant.

METHOD

Participants

Participants were 103 adults between the ages of 65 and 96 recruited from senior living centers, religious centers, and the community to participate in a randomized study of cognitive training via digital games (Table 1.)

Participant Characteristics

Gender		
Females	66	
Males	37	
Video Game Play Frequency[1]		
Non-gamers	35	
Occasional gamers	29	
Regular Gamers	35	
Did not report frequency	4	
	M	*SD*
Age	77.75	7.49
Education[2]	4.08	1.40
PANAS-Positive Affect[3]	34.62	7.75
SF36-Physical Functioning[4]	64.81	25.55
Mean Flow	3.62	0.52

Table 1. [1]Frequency was categorized based on reported play.[1]Education was measured on a scale (1=less than high school, 2=high school or GED, 3=some college, 4=Bachelor's degree, 5=some graduate work, 6=Master's degrees, 7=MD, JD, PhD, or other advanced degree). [2][27]. [3][23].

Materials

Questionnaires

A demographics questionnaire was administered at pre-test to collect age, gender, education, and frequency of video game play. Participants were categorized into three levels; those not currently playing games were "Non-gamers," those playing less than once a month to a couple times a month were "Occasional gamers," and those playing once a week to every day were "Regular gamers."

After the last day of play participants completed an exit survey assessing their experience with the game through a series of statements on a 7-point scale from "Strongly disagree" to "Strongly agree." One statement ("If I had the opportunity, I would be likely to continue playing the game in the future") measured desire to continue. Two statements ("It was difficult to use the game controller that I held in my hand"/"It was difficult to see what was going on in the game") were summed to create a usability problems score.

Flow State scale

Flow on the last day of play was measured with 5-point 36-item Likert scales [22] split into nine subscales: challenge-skill balance, action-awareness merging, clear goals, unambiguous feedback, concentration on task at hand, sense of control, loss of self-consciousness, change in perception of time, and autoelic experience. Higher scores indicated greater experience of flow.

Positive and Negative Affect Schedule (PANAS)

PANAS [33] consisted of 10 items to measure the extent to which a person experiences positive mood states. Because the PANAS measurement took place at the very start of the study prior to any experience with the game, positive affect scores in this study represent a trait of the person. In other words, it describes the individual's tendency to respond emotionally to different situations, not a measure of transient moods or emotions in response to game play.

In the current study, positive affect scores were used in analyses because positive affect - but not negative affect - has been shown to be associated with experiences such as engagement in social activity [7] as well as used in other studies of older adult digital game experience [14]. Higher scores indicated greater experience of positive affect.

Medical Outcomes Study Short Form-36 Health Survey

Physical health was assessed through the SF-36 subscale of Physical Functioning [28], which measured the extent to which participants' physical health limited their activities through questions about a range of activities. Higher scores indicated greater physical function and fewer limitations.

Game

BoomBlox 1 & 2 for Nintendo Wii were selected for the study; because the two games have nearly identical game play and interaction methods they will be discussed as a single game. The nature of the study required a game that required a number of cognitive abilities during play but that

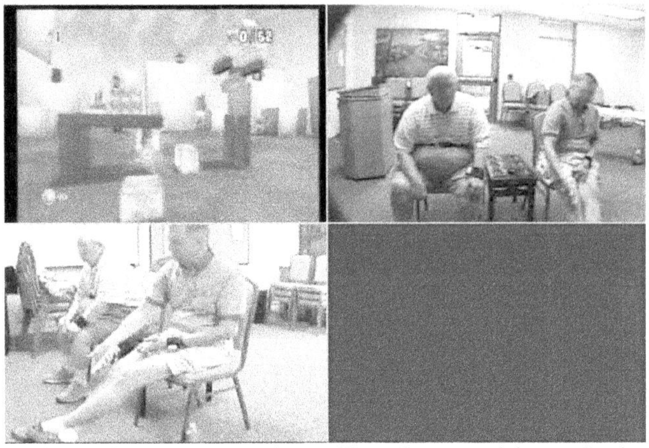

Figure 2. Screen capture from video of two participants in the social condition playing the game. Upper left shows the game as they saw it, other camera angles recorded movements, comments, and interactions with the game.

could also be customized to include a low difficulty condition that required less cognitive effort during play. Boomblox met these criteria by having gameplay that required the player to think ahead for many puzzles, but also allowed for a low difficulty version that maintained the same interaction and visuals on the screen without requiring thinking ahead or complex cognitive processes, which we confirmed via a cognitive task analysis of its gameplay. The game must be able to be played socially or individually, which BoomBlox fit due to being turn-based. Last, the game must be acceptable to older adults. Prior to selecting the game we collected feedback from focus groups with older adults demonstrating BoomBlox and three other games that fit our criteria [29]. In the focus groups BoomBlox scored highly in interest, challenge, and fun.

BoomBlox was a 3-D puzzle game in which players manipulated blocks using various tools. Blocks had both realistic properties such as gravity and fantastic ones, such as exploding upon contact. For example, one level required the player to knock down a tower of blocks in only three throws using a baseball. One of the benefits of using BoomBlox as an intervention game was that it could be manipulated to have higher or lower cognitive demands for each level in the game. For example, a level could be simple with a clear path to a goal that did not require holding past actions in human memory or planning far ahead during play or a level could require a player to consider numerous possible paths toward the goal of the level, mentally playing each before choosing to take action. All game interactions were conducted using a handheld remote. All participants played on an LCD TV (Vizio 37" HDTV) in a controlled setting. Sessions took place in a community room at the senior living centers and religious centers, or in a room in office space used for psychological research. Figure 2 shows the set-up of the game and players from two viewpoints.

Design and Procedure

After providing informed consent participants completed ~2 hours of pre-tests, including measures of health, emotion, and affect. They were then randomly assigned to either the treatment or control conditions. Those in the treatment conditions were further randomly assigned to play with a partner or alone and were assigned to a game version with lower difficulty or a game version with higher demands. Play sessions commenced and continued for 15 days, one hour of play each day. Sessions took place on consecutive weekdays except when participants' schedules required postponing a day due to other time commitments. On the last day of play participants completed a flow questionnaire, exit interview, and were scheduled for ~2 hours of post-tests similar to their pre-test session. All participants used in this analysis were in the treatment group, as only those who played the game completed the measure of flow.

RESULTS

Manipulation Check

One-way multivariate analysis of variance (MANOVA) was performed to determine if participants randomly assigned into difficulty and social conditions differed at pre-test. This manipulation check revealed no significant differences between participants in the social and individual conditions or between participants in the high and low difficulty conditions for age, education, video game play frequency, positive affect, or physical function (all $p>.05$).

Flow

	M	*SD*
Mean flow	3.62	0.52
Change in perception of time	3.20	0.72
Action-awareness merging	2.94	0.88
Paradox of control	3.56	0.81
Loss of self-consciousness	3.75	0.72
Skill balance	3.71	0.75
Autoclic	3.75	0.96
Unambiguous feedback	3.73	0.74
Clear goals	3.86	0.64
Concentration	4.09	0.68

Table 2. Subjective flow experienced by older participants after fifteen hours of video game play.

In general, participants reported experiencing flow (Table 2) and their reported flow differed across the 9 subscales. We next investigated which person-level characteristics predicted the experience of flow.

Person Characteristics

Multiple regression analysis was used across all groups to test if participants' level of positive affect and physical

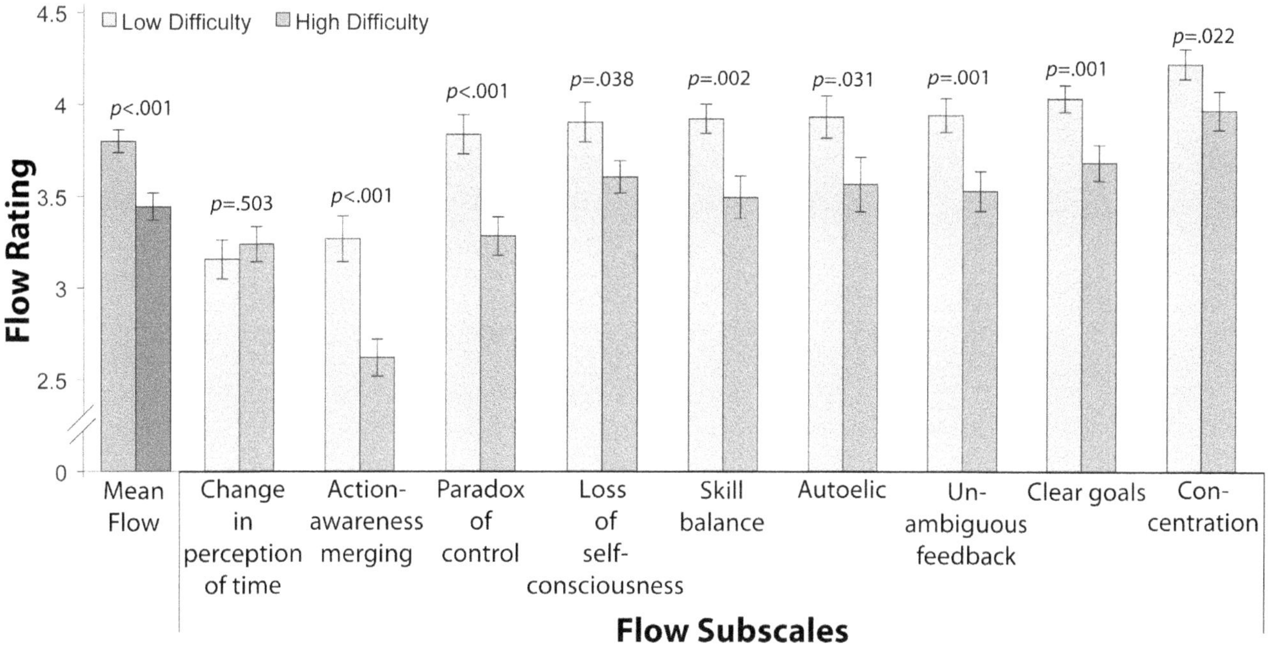

Figure 3. Comparison of flow for high and low difficulty groups. Significance values provided by subscale - bars represent standard error.

function significantly predicted mean flow experienced during the game. The results of the regression indicated that the two predictors together accounted for 18.6% of the variance, R^2=.19, $F(2,94)$=10.71, p<.001. Both positive affect (β=.35, p<.001) and physical function (β=.20, p<.05) were independent predictors of mean flow. No significant relationships (ps>.05) were found between gender, age, and mean flow, despite significant findings in previous work [10]. In sum, positive mood - measured as positive affect - was significantly and positively correlated with reporting more feelings of flow, even though mood was measured prior to any game play (and at least fifteen days prior to measuring flow.)

Game Characteristics

After investigating the person-level characteristics most likely to influence flow, we turned to an examination of the experimentally manipulated game characteristics. A Difficulty condition x Social condition (2x2) multivariate ANOVA was used to examine the effects of these conditions on mean flow and its subscales. There was a main effect of Difficulty such that for mean flow and all subscales (except 'change in perception of time'), participants in the low difficulty condition reported higher flow than in the high difficulty condition (Figure 3).

A main effect of social condition ($F(1,99)$=5.54, p<.05) was found for the clear goals subscale where social participants reported greater clear goals flow (M=3.96, SD=.50) than did participants in the individual condition (M=3.71, SD=.77). A significant Difficulty x Social interaction was found for clear goals ($F(1,99)$=4.89, p<.05) and unambiguous feedback ($F(1,99)$=4.55, p<.05) and a marginal interaction for concentration ($F(1,99)$=3.67, p=.059). On these subscales, participants in the high difficulty and social condition experienced greater flow than participants in the high difficulty and individual condition. (Figure 4).

In sum, two flow subscales (clear goals, unambiguous feedback) were lower for those in the high difficulty condition who played alone. Those in the social condition reported flow similar to those in the low difficulty condition.

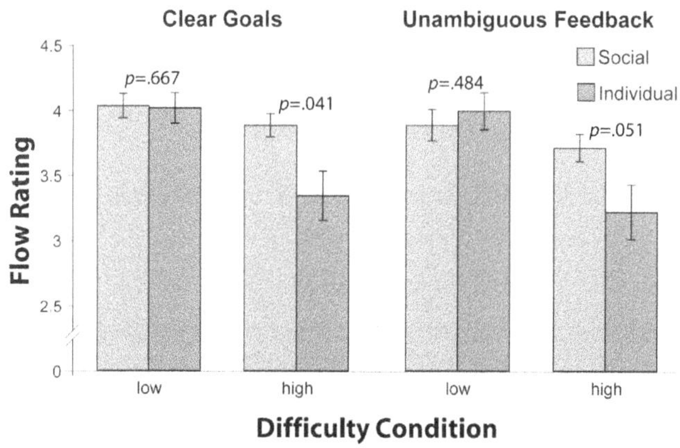

Figure 4. Flow subscales where difficulty and social conditions interacted significantly. *p* values represent *post hoc* contrasts. Bars represent standard error.

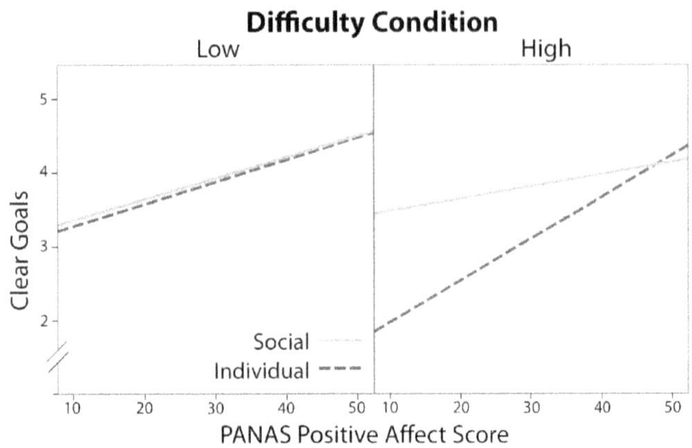

Figure 5. Regression lines showing the relationships between positive affect, game difficulty, and social condition for the clear goals subscale of flow.

Effects of Game and Person Characteristics

A multiple regression analysis including positive affect was conducted to further examine the Difficulty x Social interactions found for the subscales of clear goals and unambiguous feedback. For clear goals, the model accounted for 27.5% of the variance (R^2=.28, F(3, 93)=11.75, p<.001). Difficulty (β=-.28, p<.01), social interaction (β=-.23, p<.05), and positive affect (β=.37, p<.001) were unique and significant predictors of flow (Figure 5). For unambiguous feedback, the same model accounted for 16% of the variance (R^2=.16, F(3, 93)=6.02, p<.01) but only difficulty condition (β=-.27, p<.01) and positive affect (β=-.16, p<.05) were significant predictors.

In sum, individual differences in positive mood contributed to perceiving clear goals in the game beyond the contributions of game characteristics (difficulty, interacting with another player).

Self-Reported Difficulties

A regression analysis found greater reported usability problems related to lower experience of flow (R^2=.15, F(1,80)=14.12, p<.001). A subsequent mediation analysis examined if this relationship between usability problems and flow accounted for the relationship between physical functioning and mean flow.

The relationship between physical functioning and mean flow was significantly mediated (Sobel's test: p<.05) by usability problems reported on the exit survey. The standardized regression coefficient between physical functioning and mean flow decreased substantially when controlling for reported usability problems (Figure 6).

The impact of physical functioning on flow therefore related to usability problems - those with problems in physical function were more susceptible to usability issues and this impacted their flow.

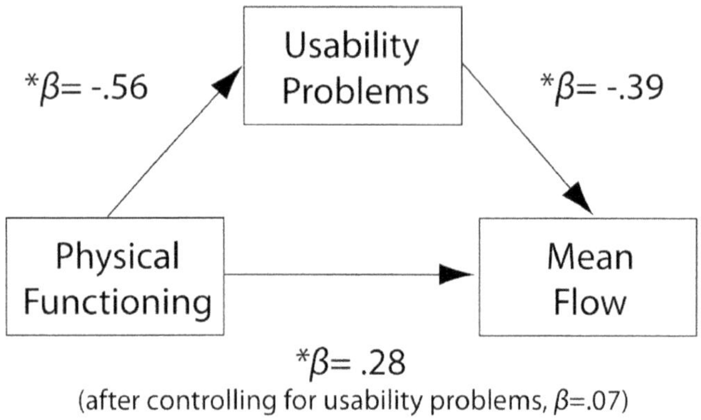

Figure 6. The relationship between physical functioning and mean flow as mediated by usability problems with standardized regression coefficients for the effects of physical functioning on usability problems, usability problems on mean flow, and physical functioning on mean flow both with (β=.07) and without (β=.28) controlling for usability problems. *p<.05

Predictions of Future Play

We were interested in examining if flow experienced during the game predicted participants' desire to continue playing the game after the end of the study. Regression analysis found that mean flow significantly predicted desire to continue playing the game (β=.41, p<.001). To investigate which subscales might be most responsible for this effect we performed a stepwise multiple regression analysis. Included in the model were the three flow subscale items most correlated with desire to continue playing: autoelic, skill balance, and change in perception of time. Only autoelic was retained in the model and it significantly predicted 57.0% of the variability in desire to continue playing (R^2=.57, F(1,83)=112.26, p<.001), suggesting that the relationship between flow and desire to continue playing is driven primarily by autoelic experience.

DISCUSSION

The unique contributions of the current study were as follows:

- Many studies of therapeutic game interventions sample from 7 to 24 older players. Here we provide data from over 100 older participants, all of whom learned to play in a controlled setting over the same period of time. This level of experimental control, paired with validated measures of individual difference, extends the internal and external validity of our study.
- Many studies of therapeutic game interventions measured the effect of the game on individual difference measures, such as mood [14], but in this study we found that even when measured *before play* such variables predict game experience, meaning that measures to adapt the game to the individual can be taken prior to play.

- Game difficulty affected the flow experience of our older players, and more interestingly, this effect was moderated by social interaction. In older adults, cooperative interactions between players may facilitate flow even in challenging games by compensating for player difficulty in clearly perceiving goals and understanding feedback.

- When analyzed together, positive affect, game difficulty, and social interaction all contributed uniquely to explaining the variance in a subscale of flow. This is the first study we know of that has included both experimental manipulation and individual difference measures together to examine flow state.

In this discussion, we address the implications of these findings along with some caveats about generalizing our results. We close with practical guidelines for game designers interested in making immersive and engaging therapeutic games.

First, our finding that participants in the low difficulty condition reported greater flow than participants in the high difficulty condition was in line with the results of prior work by Lomas et al. which found greater player engagement in a lower difficulty condition of a game designed for elementary and high school children [27]. The authors proposed several potential mechanisms behind this effect, notably the effectance motivation hypothesis [18], where player success is the driving force behind motivation, and the expertise hypothesis, where challenge-seeking behavior only occurs after players have reached a significant level of expertise. The effectance motivation hypothesis may explain our finding of greater flow under low difficulty if participants experienced a fewer successes in the high difficulty condition due to a mismatch between game and player characteristics. Furthermore, because 15 hours of exposure to a complex new game does not result in expertise, our participants may not have reached a challenge-seeking state in which higher difficulty results in greater engagement. A prior study found an association between greater challenge and greater enjoyment in an online game with participants who had likely already developed some level of expertise [1].

Second, the flow subscales most affected by individual differences and game characteristics were those most closely linked to usability: understanding how to form clear goals in the game and interpreting feedback from the game. These two aspects of flow have been highlighted in prior work as characteristics that foster flow in older adults [4]. In essence, flow in these areas may be linked to good instructions and well-designed feedback in the game. We speculate that having a social partner protected these flow areas due to collaborative cognition by our participants, defined as a state in which two or more people work together to complete a cognitive task. It is possible that for the more difficult version of the game, where goals tended to change more frequently and feedback could be for a variety of actions, having a social partner meant having another perspective available for on-screen information. This may also have been true for those with lower initial positive affect scores - a partner helped them understand game functions they were unable or unwilling to understand by themselves. Anecdotally, our observations of social play support this hypothesis - a human partner could help a player overcome the usability hurdles inherent in BoomBlox. Of course, thorough analysis of the behavior and game play data is needed, but it is possible that the human partner provided continuous tutorials and scaffolding [14]. We caution designers that these data came from a single game and it is possible that a game with instructions and feedback more suited to older adults would not have seen a benefit for social play: this would mean that social play is only protective when there is a mismatch between the characteristics of the game and the characteristics of the players. This is however an important consideration given the heterogeneity of cognitive abilities in older adults, since a game that is the appropriate level of challenge for an older adult with a higher level of ability may be too challenging for an older adult with a lower level of ability. Our results suggest that integrating social play may help mitigate the cost to flow associated with a challenging game.

In addition to issues with the goals and feedback given by BoomBlox, flow was affected by difficulties with physical or perceptual interactions. Again, anecdotal observation of our players was that the game changed frequently enough to disturb the perceptual and motor skills they needed to develop for success. For example, the number of points available changed for every level: one might be judged on taking the least amount of time while another would be judged by how many blocks were knocked over. Indeed, a player commented "*I go along and I have no earthly idea how well or how poorly I'm doing on these things until the final score comes up.*" Even when they achieved a new goal, we observed that sometimes players did not know they did well until the finishing animation, because they did not understand the goal of the level (e.g. one player commented difficulty came from "*Not knowing the point of the game and when the game was over, except for the fireworks [animation]*").

There is a general belief that the Nintendo Wii is more accessible to older players than conventional controllers. For example, Wiis have been placed in nursing homes and rehabilitation centers [21] because of their reputation as being friendly to older adults. However, the Wii controller is not a panacea for usability problems and our players struggled with aspects of the motion control interface for BoomBlox, which is less forgiving than games such as Wii Bowling. The main challenge was the amount of precision pointing required. They also struggled with the throwing interaction that was the main game mechanic. Although motion control interaction seems more "natural" and intuition leads us to surmise that an inexperienced player would find it more user friendly than a standard game controller, the interactions of BoomBlox required precise hand/eye coordination and careful timing (releasing the "A" button to trigger a throw) that caused our players to struggle. In sum, the majority of our findings and our anecdotal observations point to the importance of usability in interface and carefully designed game mechanics for therapeutic games.

A Last Thought Concerning Flow

Throughout this paper we have assumed that more feelings of flow in therapeutic games are desirable. We do believe this is the case for therapeutic games focused on goals such as pain management [19]. However, it is possible that for physical and cognitive therapies the challenge in a game would need to be so high that a flow state may not be possible. In that case we believe the findings from the current study should be broken down according to the goals of the designer. For example, usability issues affected flow. We believe this means that game challenge should come from the game content rather than from operating the display or input device. Improvements in usability-related areas may *allow* for more difficult gameplay.

CONCLUSION

We have linked individual differences in mood and function to experimentally manipulated game characteristics in terms of player feelings of flow. Although study of adaptive games is extensive, we have rarely if ever seen use of such predictive measures in altering games to suit an individual prior to play.

Although we found social interaction to be beneficial, we hesitate to prescribe social play as a prerequisite for older adult games. When a game is social, it introduces other requirements that may not be desirable. For example, a critical mass of players is required - there must be someone to play *with*. Older players in particular might struggle to find a physically located cohort and they may be intimidated by online play with strangers [12]. It is also important to understand what it was about social play that added benefit (i.e., Do players need to be co-located? Does play need to be synchronous? Can the benefits found for social interaction be instead achieved by improving game usability?) A game that provides the support that (in our study) came from the human partner may provide the same protection against play difficulties. It should be possible to design a game that detects when a player is confused or struggling (e.g., random choices, non-strategic play, long pauses between actions, or repeating ineffective strategies) and then provides help. Another approach would be to allow the player to explicitly query the game when he or she needs guidance. Modern digital games already provide simple versions of these recommendations (e.g., Donkey Kong Country for the Wii provides scaffolding after several failures; Gears of War suggests inverting the mouse after a period of inaccurate aiming). A game designed for older adults could be more transparent about why they were successful or not by providing explicit feedback on how player choices affected the outcome.

We close with the following recommendations based on our analyses and observations.

General game design recommendations:

- Games for older adults should be evaluated with a sample of users that represents the heterogeneity of physical, cognitive, and emotional function in that population.
- Consider individual differences when designing games. For example, if the targeted players are likely to have lower positive emotions or physical functioning, options to make the game more social could be protective of feelings of flow. If the game needs to be challenging, social support may also compensate for added difficulty.
- The formal elements that comprise the game (e.g. procedures, rules, win conditions etc.) should to be purposefully designed to be consistent and approachable to older players. When possible the scoring metric should be grounded in reality. Ideally, the game should leverage the players' previous experiences [13] and knowledge of the real world. This allows them to utilize their intuition about how the game world operates and focus on *how* to achieve in the game rather than on comprehending *what* determines success.
- There were no measures where social interaction was harmful to the play experience. We present this guideline with some reservation, as the world of social play still needs to be explored (such as asynchronous play or social play in the presence of a highly usable game interface).
- The autoelic flow subscale was highly predictive of intent to continue play after the conclusion of the study and may be a good scale to include in evaluation of a new game. Although subjective assessment of intent to continue is not the same as measuring behavior, forming intentions is accepted as a close link to actual behavior (i.e., in the theory of planned behavior [2]). Some participants told us they purchased a Nintendo Wii because of their experience in the study, but this is anecdotal evidence.

Specific game interaction recommendations:

- Make the instruction and goals provided by the game explicit, and employ user testing to make sure older players, who may or may not have prior experience with games, understand both.

- Design the game to assist players when they behave in ways that suggest they are confused. Allow players to explicitly indicate confusion and receive assistance from the game, similar to how they could ask for help from a social partner during play.

- Similarly, have the game detect when players are repeating the same ineffective strategies and intervene with assistance. Due to the heterogeneity of the older adult population, some older players may need a good deal more assistance than do others. Just-in-time assistance helps those who need more guidance without burdening those who do well without it.

- Have the game provide explicit feedback that relates the actions of the player to the game outcomes. For example, convey to the player "this is the action you took, this is the outcome in the game, and this is why you received that outcome." Remember that the type of feedback in a game that is immediately comprehensible to a younger audience may not necessarily translate well to an older audience, but that playing the game under social conditions may help players better interpret the game's feedback.

FUTURE DIRECTIONS

Along with the pre and post-test test/questionnaires, we collected a variety of data from each play session (e.g. video, audio, galvanic skin response, movements of the remote) that will allow us to fully characterize each player's experience, helping us to understand why specific types of players, game play, or behaviors resulted in different outcomes (cognitive changes, flow, etc.). We are in the process of analyzing these data, but have provided here some initial anecdotes that begin to give insight into what elements of the user interface and game mechanics might have contributed to our flow results. In particular, our early observations suggested that a source of usability issues was the motion control interface and that inconsistent goals and methods of evaluation between levels might have frustrated players. The user interface challenges caused by the motion control interface also appear to account for participants with lower physical functioning experiencing reduced flow in the current analyses. Also, social groups may have utilized collaborative cognition to overcome the opaque and unpredictable nature of the scoring system, which might explain why social play preserved flow, but further investigation is necessary.

ACKNOWLEDGEMENTS

This research was supported by Grant #0905127 from the National Science Foundation.

REFERENCES

1. Abuhamdeh, S., & Csikszentmihalyi, M. The importance of challenge for the enjoyment of intrinsically motivated, goal-directed activities. Personality and Social Psychology Bulletin 38, 3 (2012), 317-330.
2. Ajzen, I. Perceived behavioral control, self-efficacy, locus of control, and the theory of planned behavior. *Journal of Applied Social Psychology 32*, 4 (2002), 665-683.
3. Basak, C., Boot, W. R., Voss, M. W., & Kramer, A. F. Can training in a real-time strategy video game attenuate cognitive decline in older adults? *Psychology and Aging 23*, 4 (2008), 765-777.
4. Belchior, P., Marsiske, M., Sisco, S., Yam, A., & Mann, W. Older adults' engagement with a video game training program. *Activities, Adaptation & Aging*, *36*, 4 (2012), 269-279.
5. Boot, W., Charness, N., Champion, M., Blakely, D., Wright, T., & Souders, D. Improving the cognition of older adults: Video games as a tool to reverse age-related decline? In *Proc. APA 2012*, (2012).
6. Chen, J. Flow in games (and everything else). *Communications of ACM 50*, 4 (2007), 31-34.
7. Clark, L. A., & Watson, D. Mood and the mundane: Relations between daily life events and self-reported mood. *Journal of Personality and Social Psychology 54*, 2 (1988), 296-308.
8. Cowley, B., Charles, D., Black, M., and Hickey, R. Toward an understanding of flow in video games. *Computers in Entertainment 6*, 2 (2008).
9. Csikszentmihályi, I., & Csikszentmihályi M. *Optimal Experience: Psychological Studies of Flow in Consciousness*. Cambridge University Press, New York, NY, USA, 1988.
10. Demerouti, E. Job characteristics, flow, and performance: The moderating role of conscientiousness. *Journal of Occupational Health Psychology 11*, 3 (2006), 266-280.
11. Dziedzic, K., Thomas, E., Hill, S., Wilkie, R., Peat, G., & Croft, P. R. The impact of musculoskeletal hand problems in older adults: findings from the North Staffordshire Osteoarthritis Project (NorStOP). *Rheumatology 46*, 6 (2007), 963-967.
12. Gajadhar, B. J., Nap, H. H., de Kort, A. W., & IJsselsteijn, W. A. Out of sight, out of mind: co-player effects on seniors' player experience. In *Proc. Fun and Games 2010*, ACM Press (2010), 74-83.
13. Gamberini, L., Alcaniz, M., Barresi, G., Fabregat, M., Ibanez, F., & Prontu, L. Cognition, technology and

games for the elderly: An introduction to ELDERGAMES Project. *PsychNology Journal 4*, 3 (2006), 285-308.

14. Gerling, K. M., Livingston, I. J., Nacke, L. E., & Mandryk, R. L. Full-body motion-based game interaction for older adults. In *Proc. CHI 2012*, ACM Press (2012), 1873-1882.
15. Hanson, V. L., Gibson, L., Bobrowciz, A., & MacKay, A. Engaging those who are disinterested: Access for digitally excluded older adults. In *Proc. CHI 2010*, ACM Press (2010).
16. Hardy, J., & Scanlon, M. *The Science Behind Lumosity*. (2009). http://www.lumosity.com/documents/the_science_behind_lumosity.pdf
17. Harley, L., Robertson, S., Gandy, M., Harbert, S., & Britton, D. The design of an interactive stroke rehabilitation gaming system. In *Proc. HCII 2011*, Springer-Verlag Press (2011), 167-173.
18. Harter, S. Effectance Motivation Reconsidered: Towards a developmental model. *Human Development;Human Development*, (1978), 34–64.
19. Hoffman, H. G., Patterson, D. R., Seibel, E., Soltani, M., Jewett-Leahy, L., & Sharar, S. R. Virtual reality pain control during burn wound debridement in the hydrotank. *Clinical Journal of Pain 24*, 4 (2008), 299-304.
20. Hwang, M., Hong, J., Hao, Y., & Jong, J. Elders' usability, dependability, and flow experiences on embodied interactive video games. *Educational Gerontology 37*, 8 (2011), 715-731.
21. Ijsselsteijn, W., Nap, H. H., Kort, Y. d., & Poels, K. Digital game design for elderly users. In *Proc. Future Play 2007*, ACM Press (2007), 17-22.
22. Jackson, S. A., & Marsh, H. W. Development and validation of a scale to measure optimal experience: The flow state scale. *Journal of Sport & Exercise Psychology 18*, 1 (1996), 17-35.
23. Kato, P. M. Video games in health care: Closing the gap. *Review of General Psychology 14*, 2 (2010), 113-121.
24. Kaufman, D. Aging well: Can digital games help older adults? In World Conference on E-Learning in Corporate, Government, Healthcare, and Higher Education, 1 (2013), 1943-1949.
25. Kliegel, M., Jäger, T., & Phillips, L. H. Emotional development across adulthood: differential age-related emotional reactivity and emotion regulation in a negative mood induction procedure. *International Journal of Aging & Human Development 64*, 3 (2007), 217-44.
26. Lenhart, A., Jones, S., & Macgill, A. R. Pew Internet and American Life Project. *Video Games: Adults are Players Too.* (2008). http://pewresearch.org/pubs/1048/video-gamesadults.
27. Lomas, D., Patel, K., Forlizzi, J. L., and Koedinger, K. R. Optimizing challenge in an educational game using large-scale design experiments. In Proceedings of the SIGCHI Conference on Human Factors in Computing Systems, ACM Press (2013), 89–98.
28. McHorney, C. A., Ware, J. E., & Raczek, A. E. The MOS 36-item short-form health survey (SF-36): II. Psychometric and clinical tests of validity in measuring physical and mental health constructs. *Med Care 31*, 3 (1993), 247-263.
29. McLaughlin, A. C., Gandy, M., Allaire, J. C., & Whitlock, L. A. Putting fun into video games for older adults. *Ergonomics of Design: The Quarterly of Human Factors Applications 20*, 2 (2012), 13-22.
30. Orji, R., Mandryk, R. L., Vassileva, J., and Gerling, K. M. Tailoring persuasive health games to gamer type. In Proceedings of the SIGCHI Conference on Human Factors in Computing Systems, ACM Press (2013), 2467–2476.
31. Rogers, W. A., Campbell, R. H., & Pak, R. A systems approach for training older adults to use technology. In *Communication, Technology, and Aging*. Springer, (2001), 187-208.
32. Tang, S., & Hanneghan, M. Game content model: An ontology for documenting serious game design. In *Proc. Developments in E-systems Engineering (DeSE) 2011*, (2011), 431-436.
33. Watson, D., Clark, L. A., & Tellegen, A. Development and validation of brief measures of positive and negative affect: The PANAS scales. *Journal of Personality and Social Psychology 54,* 6 (1988), 1063-1070.
34. Whitlock, L. A., McLaughlin, A. C., & Allaire, J. C. Training requirements of a video game-based cognitive intervention for older adults: Lessons learned. In *Proc. HFES 2010*, SAGE Press (2010), 2343-2346.
35. Yin, L., Ring, L., & Bickmore, T. Using an interactive visual novel to promote patient empowerment through engagement. In *Proc. FDG 2012*, ACM Press (2012), 41-48.

A Model of Game Design Activity: New Perspectives on Creativity and Innovation

Laureline Chiapello
Faculty of Environmental Design
University of Montreal
Québec, Canada
laureline.chiapello@umontreal.ca

Abstract
Innovation and creativity seem to be mere buzzwords, but the quest for innovation and creativity by game companies is very real. This Ph.D. dissertation suggests adopting a new perspective on these concepts by abandoning a managerial attitude and favoring a design approach. The design process of video games is under-studied, and this research aims to create a model of video game design activity, using the already existing literature in the field of design, and the observation of actual game designers in Montreal.

CHI PLAY '14, Oct 19-22 2014, Toronto, ON, Canada
ACM 978-1-4503-3014-5/14/10.

http://dx.doi.org/10.1145/2658537.2659011

Author Keywords
Game design; design thinking; innovation; creativity

ACM Classification Keywords
K.8.0 [Personal Computing]: General – Games

Research Situation
The Ph.D. in Environmental Design studies at the University of Montreal is a two-phased process. During two to three years, students take different courses and prepare their comprehensive exam, after which they can start their data collection and dissertation. I am currently at the end of my second year and I plan on taking my comprehensive exam soon.

Environmental Design (as it is translated from *Aménagement* in French) is a broad field: I am working with Prof. Rabah Bousbaci from the Design School, and my specialty is video game design. The University of Montreal also has a video game department that is part of Cinema studies, but I chose the Design School in order to provide new and original insights about video game creation. The faculty is currently building this video game design department, and I am one of the first two Ph.D. students in the program. This situation leads me to feel rather isolated, and the doctoral consortium would be a valuable opportunity to interact with students and experts in the field of interaction design, and to challenge my approach.

Context and Motivation

Creating new Intellectual Property (IP) in the video game industry appears challenging [1]. For example, in 2012, Funcom launched a new IP: *The Secret World*. Unfortunately, the game did not take off. This situation has been assessed mainly in terms of poor commercial and managerial decisions. The point of view of creators was not considered as a determining factor [2].

Around the same time, I was meeting game designers from the Montreal game area for my Master's research. My interviews presented attention-grabbing results: game designers from different companies, responsible for the core features of games, were encountering trouble understanding their role. They often feel powerless when they need to justify their work. This reinforces the literature acknowledging that management or marketing departments often challenge creative employees' decisions [3]. This was particularly clear when my participants were working on projects with new elements, such as a new audience, or new Intellectual Property. More specifically, my results pointed out a lack of theory about game design activity. What does a game designer do? How do game designers think in action? What is the "creative process" of game designers? How and when does "creativity" happen? This conjunction of events brings me to the hypothesis that tackling the problem of innovation from a design point of view might offer new insights about video game projects. Instead of blaming marketing or production choices, I would like to start documenting how designers work. I hope this will empower game designers, and give us new insights about creativity and innovation in the video game industry.

Background and related work

Innovation and creativity issues in the video game industry have primarily been defined and assessed by economic and management studies [1, 3-5], focusing mainly on product innovation (radically different video games) and ways to foster employee creativity. While much debate exists around the definitions of innovation and creativity, the fact I would like to underline is that authors insist on the importance of game design, and the lack of knowledge concerning creative processes: "*The field still lacks an integrated view that more fully describes the creative process of a technological artifact*" [5].

Innovation has also been studied from the perspective of game studies, especially by Annakaisa Kultima and her colleagues [6-8]. These studies acknowledge the importance of innovation and creativity as core value in the video game industry, even when their definitions are unclear. Once again, creativity is seen as the territory of game designers: *"Furthermore, games are said to be idea-based products, where ideas can be seen as the outputs of creative acts and processes of game designers" [8].*

However, game studies did not seem to have conducted any thorough study of game design activity. While a large number of game design books exist nowadays, literature reviews [9, 10] show that these works are mainly focused on the games themselves, and Kuittinen and Holopainen conclude that *"the activity called design is left with too little attention"* [10]. Video game design is like a black box. Kuittinen and Holopainen suggest borrowing concepts from design studies to bridge this gap, but this remains to be done. A similar bridging started in Human-Computer Interaction: for example, Erik Stolterman [11] insists that the very nature of design practice should have an influence on interaction design research.

Statement of Thesis and Research Goal

Video game research needs to encompass innovation and creativity challenges from the point of view of design. This implies a better understanding of game design activity and creative processes, and a clearer view of the manifestation of creativity in those processes. This could be achieved by bridging the gap between video game studies and design studies, and by diving into current practice.

The main research goal is to theorize video game design activity, with a focus on the creative dimension of the design process. The theorization will take the form of a model of video game design activity. Two main steps are guiding the elaboration of such a model:

1. Diving into existing literature to elaborate a conceptual model. This model not only has to give a rich vision of design activity, but also must define and highlight the creativity behind game designers' actions.
2. Collaborating with actual game designers to enrich the model. Observation and interviews will allow for confirming, modifying and transforming current design theories.

These steps will be taken iteratively to produce a descriptive model. The goal is not to produce a recipe to enhance designers' creativity, but to accurately depict their actual practices and better understand the creative dimensions of what they do.

Dissertation Status

I am currently gathering the existing literature to elaborate a first draft of the conceptual model, which I would like to discuss at the doctoral consortium.

The study of designers' creative process has been regrouped under the term "design thinking", and design thinking research already considers innovation. However, there are now two radically different understandings of design thinking: one is drawing from design studies, while the other from the managerial field. The management discourse is very popular nowadays and tends to shatter the design discourse. This is a problem, as the management discourse tends to have "*a more superficial and popular character and is less academically anchored than the designerly one.*"[12]. However, the design discourse is fragmented with several visions of design thinking, making it difficult to grasp.

Using my Master's research experience, I chose to draw from one of the most important design approaches of design thinking: Schön's model of reflexive practice [13]. He constructed a theoretical model of design activity as a *reflective conversation with a situation*. According to Dorst [14], studying the framing of design situations is a promising track to foster innovation. However, creativity issues are not directly dealt with in Schon's model. Thus, I am revisiting the literature surrounding Schön's work, especially the work of the pragmatist John Dewey. According to the philosopher Hans Joas [15], pragmatism is a philosophy that allows taking the creativity of human action into account, and defining it in contrast with a rational vision of human action. I am trying to bring these pragmatist influences in Schön's work to the foreground, in order to enrich and further Schön's conceptual model. I would therefore like to discuss this work at the CHI doctoral consortium, since interaction design has a well-known interest in pragmatism, experience (for the users but also for the designers) and creativity.

Expected Contributions

The model of video game design activity will show how and when creativity occurs in game designers' design processes. I hope this will help in understanding how video game projects can rely on designers' creativity, and in creating innovative products. The model will be specially designed for video game design, but it might also be useful for interaction designers, or any form of design.

The author would like to thank Rabah Bousbaci, Amy Oliver and Nada Toueir for their comments and support.

References

[1] Hotho, S. and Champion, K. Small businesses in the new creative industries: Innovation as a people management challenge. *Management Decision*, 49, 1 (2011), 29-54.

[2] Prell, S. *Life after layoffs: the former lead designer of Secret World looks back on the game's struggles*. http://www.penny-arcade.com/, 2012.

[3] Tschang, F. T. Balancing the tensions between rationalization and creativity in the video games industry. *Organization Science*, 18, 6 (2007), 989-1005.

[4] Zackariasson, P., Walfisz, M. and Wilson, T. L. Management of Creativity in Video Game Development. *Services Marketing Quarterly*, 27, 4 (2006), 73-97.

[5] Tschang, F. T. *When does an idea become an innovation? The role of individual and group creativity in videogame design*. In Proc. DRUID 2003.

[6] Kultima, A., Köönikkä, J. and Karvinen, J. *The Four Different Innovation Philosophies Guiding the Game Development Processes*. In Proc. Games and Innovation Research Seminar 2011.

[7] Kultima, A. and Alha, K. *"Hopefully everything I'm doing has to do with innovation"* In Proc. Games Innovations Conference, IEEE 2010.

[8] Kultima, A. *The organic nature of game ideation: game ideas arise from solitude and mature by bouncing*. In Proc. Future of Game Design and Technology, IEEE 2010.

[9] Djaouti, D., Alvarez, J. and Jessel, J.-P. *Concevoir l'interactivité ludique: une vue d'ensemble des méthodologies de «Game Design»*. In Proc. Ludovia 2010.

[10] Kuittinen, J. and Holopainen, J. *Some notes on the nature of game design*. In Proc. DiGRA 2009.

[11] Stolterman, E. The Nature of Design Practice and Implications for Interaction Design Research. *International Journal of Design*, 2, 1 (2008), 55-65.

[12] Johansson-Sköldberg, U., Woodilla, J. and Çetinkaya, M. Design Thinking: Past, Present and Possible Futures. *Creativity and Innovation Management*, 22, 2 (2013), 121-146.

[13] Schön, D. *The Reflective Practitioner : How Professionals Think in Action*. Basic Books, New York, 1983.

[14] Dorst, K. The core of 'design thinking' and its application. *Design Studies*, 32, 6 (2011), 521-532.

[15] Joas, H. *The creativity of action*. University of Chicago Press, 1996.

Examining the Impact of Game Interventions on Depression among Older Adults

Jinhui Li
Nanyang Technological University
31 Nanyang Link, Singapore
637718
jli020@e.ntu.edu.sg

CHI PLAY'14, October 19–21, 2014, Toronto, ON, Canada.
ACM 978-1-4503-3014-5/14/10.
http://dx.doi.org/10.1145/2658537.2659009

Abstract
My dissertation research aims to investigate the feasibility and effects of game interventions as depression treatment for geriatric depression. More specifically, I will examine the effects of both game types and settings on older adults' depression. A between-subject factorial design experiment will be conducted to address the main purpose. Results from the study will contribute to existing literature on the influencing mechanisms of games for depression, and provide practical knowledge of game design for mental health purposes.

Author Keywords
Depression; Game intervention; Elderly; Mental health

Introduction
Motivation for dissertation research

Population ageing becomes a worldwide problem, and has led to increasing concerns on elderly's mental health in recent decades. Depression is one of the highest prevalent mental disorders appeared in late life, affecting approximately 10.3% of elderly population around the world [1]. Geriatric depression significantly decreases quality of life, and is reported to be a major risk factor for suicide. Besides medications, researchers and health professionals are trying to identify

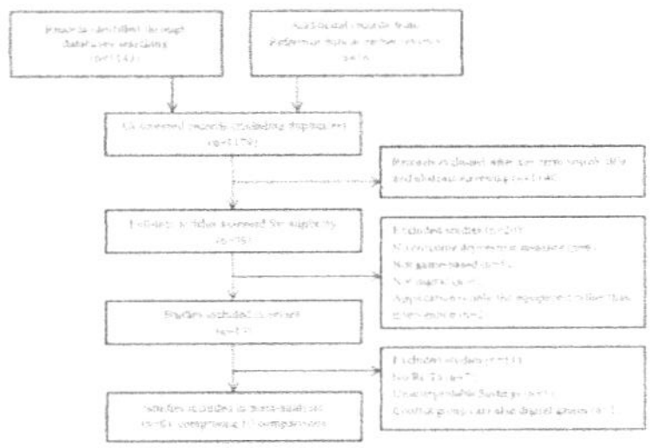

Figure 1. Selection process of inclusive studies

acceptable and effective psychosocial treatments for geriatric depression, due to the low treatment-seeking rate amongst older adults [2].

Game interventions were found to have practical effects in enhancing treatment adherence and accessibility in the healthcare domain, particularly for the young. Increasing number of studies has also supported the mental benefits of game interventions for older adults [3]. Evidence from neuropsychological research further suggests that positive game-playing experiences may lead to mood improvements, such as reducing depression [4]. However, far less was known on the feasibility and effectiveness of game interventions when applied into treating depression among older adults. Consequently, my dissertation research aims to contribute to this new research domain of game for health. The main objective is to investigate the effects of game intervention on geriatric depression via a between-subject factorial design experiment.

A Systematic review and meta-analysis

In order to have an overview of extant literature and identify current research trends in this new research domain, I have conducted a systematic review and meta-analysis of existing randomized controlled trials (RCTs). A search of seven main health and technology databases was conducted to identify studies published in English before May 2013. The search yielded a total of 1,179 articles, with 19 studies meeting the criteria for inclusion in the final review. Eight studies involving 10 RCTs were eligible for inclusion in the final meta-analysis. Figure 1 shows a flowchart of the selection of studies. Detail of this review was described in one of my previous paper [5]. The findings suggest that game applications in general have a moderate effect size (d=0.47) as depression therapy. This overall effect size was found to be slightly higher that other forms of computerized depression therapy [6]. Nevertheless, it was much higher than the effectiveness of traditional psychotherapy [7]. Taken together, the game interventions are estimated to have high potential to be effective therapy for treating depression.

Research Gaps

Digital vs. Non-digital Games

Studies from Rendon et al. [8] and Rosenberg et al. [9] have supported the therapeutic values of exercising video games on reducing depression among elderly players. Compared to the games in real context, digital games may have the advantages of high accessibility, less cost and therapist support. Since most previous research on games interventions have applied 'passive' treatments as control conditions (e.g., waiting list, treat-as-usual, or placebo), few studies were found to compare the direct effects of digital and non-digital games in treating depression.

Physical vs. Cognitive Games

A systematic review by Blake et al. [10] indicated the short-term benefits of physical activities in reducing clinically defined depression in older adults. Some scholars have investigated the effects of another type of game – cognitive games – on depression. Although they are defined as the game activities that practice players' mental functions, cognitive games were also found to be able to lower depressive symptoms in older adults [11, 12]. Although both physical and cognitive games are associated with depression, it is far less known about the comparison of these two types of games. Investigation on this unclear domain will open the discussion on the type effect of game interventions

	Physical	Cognitive	TAU
Digital	Wii blowing	Wii Chess	Treat as usual
Non-digital	Real blowing	Board game	

Table 2. Selection process of inclusive studies

on depression, and lead to guidelines for mental health game development.

Increasing evidences in the field have shown that high percentage of older adults aged 65 years or above actively paly digital videogames in their daily life. Elderly population is becoming another important group to receive attention from therapeutic game developers. Nevertheless, in my previous systematic review, only 2 out of 19 studies were found to focus on elderly. Therefore, there is a research demand for investigating what and how game interventions can be applied to address elderly depression.

Research approach and methods

Realizing the gaps, I proposed a between-subject experiment to investigate the effects of game intervention on geriatric depression. More specifically, I intend to examine the impact of the type effect (physical vs. cognitive) and setting effect (digital vs. non-digital) in game interventions.

Participants. Around 270 participants will be recruited from several senior activity centers in Singapore, after a screening process. They will be eligible for inclusion in the study if: 1) aged 65 years or above; 2) experiencing mild depression.

Study Design and Procedure. Potential participants will be identified in the depression screening assessment by Geriatric Depression Scale before the study. Those in the mild to moderate range will be told about the study and invited to take part. Full measurement of depression and other key psychosocial variables will conducted both in the pre-test and post-test period. In addition, a shorten form of depression measurement will be issued in each week. The study will use a 2 (physical game vs. cognitive game) × 2 (digital vs. non-digital) between–subject factorial design. One additional control group under treat as usual will be involved for comparison. Participants will be randomized into five treatment conditions, with around thirty elderly in each condition. Table 1 illustrates the six conditions. Nintendo Wii's sport game 'Brunswick Pro Bowling' and board game "Wii Chess" will be used respectively in the two digital game conditions. A familiarized section (half day) will be conducted to teach participants how to play the games before actual test. Consisted with previous trials on game interventions, participants will be asked to perform the activities in each condition for half an hour, three times a week for 12 consecutive weeks.

Measurements. Geriatric Depression Scale (GDS) will be used as both a screening tool for admission into the study, and an assessment of the depression symptoms among participants in intervention period. Center for Epidemiologic Studies Depression Scale (CES-D) will be employed as secondary measure for depression in the study. GDS and CES-D will be also issued in the last session of each week. I will also measure treatment acceptability in the post-test section by using the Client Satisfaction Questionnaire.

Expected contributions

As it is still the early stage, scientific knowledge and evidences are largely absent on investigating the adoption of game interventions for depressive patients in their late life. According to my previous systematic review [5], only 2 studies were conducted on examining the effects of game interventions for geriatric depression. Both of them were based on U.S. participants.

To my knowledge, my dissertation research is the first study studies exploring the acceptability and feasibility of game interventions on older adults in Asian context. Compared with western aging population, older adults in Asia have reported to have a higher depression prevalent rate. My study will therefore contribute to the extant literature and extend the 'game for depression' research to a new culture context. More importantly, I will investigate the mechanism of how game interventions affect geriatric depression, through a 2X2 between-subject experiment. The findings will lead to more suitable interventions implemented in the future to better address the mental problems of this group of older adults.

Acknowledgement

I would like to express my sincere gratitude to my supervisors, Prof. Theng Yin-Leng and Prof. Schubert Foo, for their helpful comments on the work.

References

[1] A. Barua, M. K. Ghosh, N. Kar, and M. A. Basilio, "Prevalence of depressive disorders in the elderly," *Annals of Saudi Medicine,* vol. 31, pp. 620-624, 2011.

[2] J. N. Trollor, T. M. Anderson, P. S. Sachdev, H. Brodaty, and G. Andrews, "Prevalence of mental disorders in the elderly: The Australian Mental Health and Well-Being Survey," *American Journal of Geriatric Psychiatry* vol. 15, pp. 455-466, 2007.

[3] A. K. Hall, E. Chavarria, V. Maneeratana, B. H. Chaney, and J. M. Bernhardt, "Health benefits of digital videogames for older adults: A systematic review of the literature," *Games for Health Journal,* vol. 1, pp. 402-410, 2012.

[4] I. Granic, A. Lobel, and R. C. M. E. Engels, "The benefits of playing video games," *American Psychologist,* 2013.

[5] J. Li, Y. L. Theng, and S. Foo, "Game-based digital interventions for depression therapy: A systematic review and meta-analysis," *Cyberpsychology, Behavior, and Social Networking,* vol. 17, pp. 519-527, 2014.

[6] G. Andersson and P. Cuijpers, " Internet-based and other computerized psychological treatments for adult depression: A meta-analysis," *Cognitive Behaviour Therapy,* vol. 38, pp. 196-205, 2009.

[7] P. Cuijpers, R. F. Muñoz, G. N. Clarke, and P. M. Lewinsohn, "Psychoeducational treatment and prevention of depression: The "coping with depression" course thirty years later," *Clinical Psychology Review,* vol. 29, pp. 449-458, 2009.

[8] A. A. Rendon, E. B. Lohman, D. Thorpe, E. G. Johnson, E. Medina, and B. Bradley, "The effect of virtual reality gaming on dynamic balance in older adults," *Age and Ageing,* vol. 41, pp. 549-552, 2012.

[9] D. Rosenberg, C. A. Depp, I. V. Vahia, J. Reichstadt, B. W. Palmer, J. Kerr, *et al.*, "Exergames for subsyndromal depression in older adults: A pilot study of a novel intervention," *American Journal of Geriatric Psychiatry,* vol. 18, pp. 221-226, 2010.

[10] H. Blake, P. Mo, S. Malik, and S. Thomas, "How effective are physical activity interventions for alleviating depressive symptoms in older people? A systematic review," *Clinical Rehabilitation,* vol. 23, pp. 873-887, 2009.

[11] C. V. Russoniello, K. O'Brien, and J. M. Parks, "EEG, HRV and psychological correlates while playing Bejeweled II: A randomized controlled study," *Studies in Health Technology and Informatics,* vol. 144, pp. 189-192, 2009.

[12] S. T. Cheng, P. K. Chow, E. C. Yu, and A. C. Chan, "Leisure activities alleviate depressive symptoms in nursing home residents with very mild or mild dementia," *American Journal of Geriatric Psychiatry,* vol. 20, pp. 904-908, 2012.

Gamified Co-design with Cooperative Learning at School

Alessandra Melonio
Faculty of Computer Science
Free U. of Bozen-Bolzano
Piazza Domenicani 3, 39100
Bolzano, Italy
alessandra.melonio@unibz.it

CHI-PLAY'14, October 19–21, 2014, Toronto, ON, Canada.
ACM 978-1-4503-3014-5/14/10.
http://dx.doi.org/10.1145/2658537.2659010

Abstract
This paper reports on the Ph.D work of A. Melonio. The work deals with co-design for learning contexts. Since co-design with children should be engaging, the Ph.D. work proposes to gamify learning contexts with game ideas and elements for playfully engaging learners and teachers alike. Moreover, since co-design requires to create a sense of partnership, the Ph.D. research proposes the adoption of cooperative learning strategies for fostering the inclusion of all in the design process. In the opening, the main research area and the motivation of this Ph.D. work are overviewed. The paper continues presenting the research method of the Ph.D. work and the related goal, objectives and questions. The paper ends recapping the result to date and the next steps to reach.

Author Keywords
gamification, co-design, cooperation, playful engagement

ACM Classification Keywords
H.4 [Human-centred computing]: Interaction design

Introduction
This paper outlines the Ph.D work of A. Melonio at the Faculty of Computer Science of the Free University of Bozen-Bolzano (UniBZ), under the supervision of Prof. G. Dodero and Dr. R. Gennari. The PhD is supported by a

three-year full-time grant. Melonio resulted among the top six candidates in Computer Science who applied for the PhD programme. The research area this Ph.D. fits in is *human machine interaction* (HMI) with applications in the area of *technology enhanced learning* (TEL). In particular, this Ph.D. focuses on co-design methods and techniques of HMI [4] that allow designers to prototype interactive products with users in their natural environment. The products under consideration are interactive games. The primary research goal of the Ph.D. is to adapt and refine co-design for nowadays' learning contexts, by mixing it with cooperative learning and gamification of learning. The resulting approach is baptised GaCoCo, which stands for *GAmified CO-design with COopeartive Learning*. This Ph.D. requires designing and running empirical studies in order to assess and refine GaCoCo for prototyping in learning contexts. The remainder of this paper explains the specific research area, method and goal of this Ph.D.

Main Research Area and Motivation

Co-design [10] is an HMI comprehensive design approach that allows designers to work with any user. In case the products are games for children, having children as co-designers should help in producing playable games that meet the requirements of nowadays' children [3]. This Ph.D. work adopts such a view and refines co-design for prototyping games for children, with children and in a learning context, so as to foster inclusion and playful engagement. In the remainder, the paper outlines the background literature necessary for the Ph.D. work.

Co-design

Sanders and Stappers in [10] characterised co-design as an approach that extends participatory design and co-creation, involving all stakeholders as co-designers. When these are children, specific methods are used, depending on the product design activity [4]. Co-design at school, albeit not new, has received increasing attention in recent years. However, co-design in current formal learning contexts, such as schools, presents several challenges, e.g., see [2]. For instance, a relevant issue is **how to effectively include all children in co-design**. In particular, if the organisation of group-work is completely handed over to teachers and they are not sufficiently acquainted with learning theories promoting group-work, the effects on co-design studies can be detrimental, e.g., see [12]. The idea of this Ph.D. is to use cooperative learning for organising group work and hence including all as co-designers. Moreover, as the work of [6] and others stress, co-design at school should be engaging, possibly fun, for children. However, **how to design fun engaging tasks** for wide and diverse groups of school learners, who are used to interactive digital tools and games, and often equate school with boring rote? This Ph.D. proposes gamification of learning for playfully engaging all learners and their teachers alike in co-designing.

Cooperative Learning

Cooperative learning is a specific instructional methodology promoting group work [11]. Empirical evidence suggests that use of cooperative learning at school seems to improve social inclusion of learners in class [7]. When co-designing, co-designers need to develop a sense of partnership, leveraging on everybody's skills. The organisation of a cooperative team is the main taking of cooperative learning in this Ph.D. work, for allowing all to work as partners, and hence for fostering the social inclusion of all learners.

Gamification of Learning

Gamification means applying game-design thinking [1] for non-game activities and in a non-game context to make them more fun and engaging. Several psychology motivation theories and empirical studies support the use of specific game elements for gamification purposes [8]. In this Ph.D., gamification is used for playfully engaging learners and teachers in co-design as games can do, see [9, 2]. For instance, in this Ph.D., co-design tasks are presented as missions, with a valuable clear goal for children and contingent-completion rewards, e.g., objects for prototyping that children can acquire at their co-design shop. According to their complexity, missions are structured into smaller progressive challenges. Each comes with its own timing, clear rules and contingent-completion rewards. Most importantly, gamification of co-design is done fostering cooperation, so as to be faithful to the co-design partnership principle, e.g., rewards should not increase competition within groups. Such a constraint is met by keeping competition inter-groups, and providing rewards so as to enhance intra-group cooperation.

The Research Method

This Ph.D. work proposes and promotes GaCoCo for traditional learning contexts, by refining co-design for prototyping interactive products via gamification and coopeartive learning. The proposed HMI research can be explained as exploratory in nature [5], leading to a novel approach for co-designing interactive products in learning contexts, in which the data collected are hybrid, both qualitative and quantitative. GaCoCo was thus used within this Ph.D. in empirical studies with schools and at school, and refined after each study. In those studies of the first and second Ph.D. years, the co-designed products were interactive games for children. However the GaCoCo methodology is more general and, in principle, allows anybody to use it for any interactive product and goal.

Research Goal, Objectives and Questions

The **research goal** is to adapt and refine co-design for prototyping interactive games in learning contexts, with cooperative learning and gamification of learning. The related objectives and questions are as follow.

O1: analysing the context of use. The first research objective is to explore if and how learners, teachers and designers can cooperatively work and be engaged in a traditional school context. How can one adopt co-design to work in such a setting? What are the constraints that such a setting imposes on co-design? How can one playfully engage nowadays' children and teachers in co-design? How can one include all learners in co-design?

O2: promoting, using and revising GaCoCo. By answering the above questions, one can craft GaCoCo according to school contexts, and tackle the following related questions. How shall researchers organise a GaCoCo session? What are the roles of participants, that is, teachers, learners and designers? Does GaCoCo engage learners? And teachers? Does GaCoCo promote inclusion? And engagement? What is the quality of the resulting products?

O3: refining GaCoCo. Abstracting from lessons learnt by tackling the above objectives, finally, this Ph.D. work aims at refining GaCoCo for learning contexts, in order to foster inclusion and engagement for co-designing quality interactive products for schools.

Result to Date and Next Steps

The first Ph.D. year saw an extensive and in-depth study of the literature concerning co-design, game design and gamification. Melonio became also knowledgable of specific cooperative learning strategies, being guided through them by an expert of pedagogy. Several GaCoCo pilot studies were then conducted for achieving the first objective (O1) and refining GaCoCo. In particular, performance results, concerning children's behavior, show that GaCoCo can be effectively used at school. Such studies, which were planned as short-term ones, had also positive inclusion and engagement results, mainly due to class feedback and evaluators' observations. For instance, the majority of children perceived mission challenges and the entire activity as quickly passing by, to the point of feeling this as too short—and so did teachers.

Strengthened with the first year's results, the first half of the second Ph.D. year saw a revision of GaCoCo for primary schools for O2. Firstly, the co-design of game prototypes was replanedd as a long-term activity, so as to provide children with a more lasting experience, which would allow them to better express their ideas. Therefore the new study protocol had to be planned for running in different days, and be even more integrated within school activities. Secondly, in order to maintain participants' engagement, a step further was to gamify the co-design protocol and classrooms even more, e.g., enriching these with game-like tangible interactive objects. These were designed so as to be low-cost and reusable, so that classes may in the future use them and adapt them to their learning needs. The next step of this Ph.D. sees a refined integration of paper-based material and low-cost technology so as to create an even more engaging experience.

References

[1] Adams, E. *Fundamentals of Game Design, Third Edition*. Pearson - Allyn and Bacon, 2009.

[2] Dodero, G., Gennari, R., Melonio, A., and Torello, S. Gamified Co-design with Cooperative Learning. In *In Proceedings of alt CHI 2014*, ACM (2014).

[3] Druin, A. The Role of Children in the Design of new Technology. *Behaviour and Information Technology 21* (2002), 1–25.

[4] Druin, A. Children as Co-designers of New Technologies: Valuing the Imagination to Transform What Is Possible. *New Directions in Youth Development: Theory, Practice, and Research: Youth as Media Creators 128*, 1 (Jan. 2010), 35–43.

[5] Edmondson, A. C., and McManus, S. E. *Methodological Fit in Management Field Research*, vol. 32. Academy of Management Review, 2007.

[6] Garzotto, F. Broadening Children's Involvement as Design Partners: from Technology to "Experience". In *Proceedings of the 7th Conference on Interaction Design and Children*, IDC '08, ACM (New York, NY, USA, 2008), 186–193.

[7] Johnson, D., and Johnson, R. An Overview of Cooperative Learning. *Creativity and Collaborative Learning* (2002).

[8] Kapp, K. M. *The Gamification of Learning and Instruction*. San Francisco: Pfeiffer, 2012.

[9] Melonio, A. Game-based Co-design of Games for Learning with Children and Teachers: Research Goals and a Study. In *CEUR Proc. of the Doctoral Consortium of CHItaly 2013* (2013).

[10] Sanders, E. B., and Stappers, P. J. Co-creation and the New Landscapes of Design. *CoDesign: International Journal of CoCreation in Design and the Arts 4*, 1 (2008), 5–18.

[11] Slavin, R. Cooperative Learning. *Cooperative learning: Theory, Research, and Practice Englewood Cliffs, NJ: Prenrice Hall.* (1990).

[12] Vaajakallio, K., Mattelmäki, T., and Lee, J. Co-design Lessons with Children. *Interactions 17*, 4 (July 2010), 26–29.

Using an Invisible Coach to Help Players Achieve Fitness Goals in Exergames while Retaining Immersion

Chad Richards
School of Computing
Queen's University
Kingston, ON, Canada
chad.richards@queensu.ca

CHI PLAY '14, Oct 19-22 2014, Toronto, ON, Canada
ACM 978-1-4503-3014-5/14/10.
http://dx.doi.org/10.1145/2658537.2659015

Abstract
Two approaches to designing exergames exist: design a *game* with incidental exercise, or design an *exercise program* with an incidental game. We aim to combine the advantages of these approaches by developing an *invisible coach* that modifies gameplay in order to guide workouts while maintaining game immersion. This opens opportunities to guide players toward focused exercise goals, such as cycling at a desired intensity, or strengthening a weak muscle group, while allowing players to retain the sense of *playing a game*. We are investigating the design and efficacy of an invisible coach in the context of a novel strength training game.

Author Keywords
Virtual coach; exergaming

ACM Classification Keywords
H.5.m. Information interfaces and presentation (e.g., HCI): Miscellaneous.

Introduction
The exergaming field aspires to increase exercise participation and adherence in a novel manner, by combining games and exercise. Currently, two major approaches exist to designing exergames. In the

exercise-first approach, exercise is at the forefront of the program, while the game is incidental and usually consists of simply earning points for performing exercises. The *game-first* approach puts the game at the forefront, while the exercise is incidental. An *exercise-first* example is Nike+ Kinect Training, while Dance Dance Revolution follows the *game-first* approach.

Both approaches have strengths and weaknesses. Exercises that have many requirements or are more dangerous to perform without proper instruction, such as muscle-strengthening exercises, can be implemented more readily using the *exercise-first* approach. But *exercise-first* games lack the immersive gameplay of the *game-first* approach. *Game-first* exergames can provide a more entertaining experience, but may not lead to sufficiently vigorous exercise for health benefits to result.

Our research aims to combine the advantages of these two approaches. An *invisible* coach modifies gameplay to nudge the player to the required form and intensity of exercise-first exergames while providing the fun experience seen in *game-first* exergames. By guiding gameplay, we aim to improve the quality of exercise in exergames.

Coaches and Virtual Coaches

Traditionally, we meet specific exercise goals by asking an expert *coach*, such as a personal trainer or a physical therapist. This coach is primarily responsible for developing a safe and effective workout program for and with clients, setting goals and providing feedback to clients, and measuring clients' strengths and weaknesses with fitness assessments [1].

Figure 1. Ubisoft's Your Shape: Fitness Evolved game, with an on-screen avatar trainer demonstrating a Bicep Curl in a gym environment [5].

The advantages of utilizing expert guidance from a coach have prompted the development of virtual coaches in exergames. The term *virtual coach* refers to a program and/or device that guides users through tasks to promote positive behavior or assists with learning new skills [2]. Virtual coaches are usually presented as trainers in the form of on-screen avatars. For instance, Ellis et al. and Eyck et al. have developed virtual coaches that provide positive feedback to participants during exercise, both of which have been well received by users in their studies.

Commercial games have also included virtual coaches. For example, in EA Sports Active NFL Training Camp, a coach avatar provides instructions to the player. Several other commercial games also provide a virtual coach, such as Nike+ Kinect Training, Ubisoft's My Fitness Coach and Your Shape: Fitness Evolved (see Figure 1), EA Sports Active: Personal Trainer, and UFC Personal Trainer: The Ultimate Fitness System. While these games each provide a virtual coach in some form, their primary concern is to replicate a gym atmosphere, not to provide an entertaining game for players. The games are, in fact, examples of gamification instead of traditional games. Points are earned for exercising, but that typically comprises the entirety of the game. In addition, the efficacy of these virtual coaches has yet to be tested [2].

Invisible Coach

Our research aims to test the efficacy of a virtual coach in a game environment. We hypothesize that using an embodied coach will reduce immersion in the game. Embodied coaches make it clear to the player that they are involved in an exercise program instead of playing a game. Instead of having an explicitly embodied coach to help achieve specific exercise goals, our idea is to have an *invisible* coach evaluate performance relative to the player's workout goals and subtly modify gameplay to make sure the goals are being met.

As an example, imagine that an expert cyclist wants to improve cycling performance. At some point in the season, the cyclist may need to work on speed and endurance using interval training. In real life, the cyclist observes her or his cadence using a device, and attempts to reach targets provided by a coach. A straight racing exergame performed on a stationary bike would not be good for this purpose. We could build interval training into the exergame using verbal coaching cues (e.g., "Speed up now", "Slow down now"). Our argument is that this reduces immersion, leading to an experience that feels more like a workout than a game.

Instead, our invisible coach modifies gameplay to make adherence to workout goals feel like a natural part of the game. Players should be unaware they are being guided. This will let players focus on the game while still being coached. For instance, when the cyclist reaches the point in the interval when the high-intensity burst should occur, a dog could start chasing the cyclist, and the cyclist must pedal faster to avoid the dog. This, in turn, drives heart rate higher for the faster burst. After the burst is over, the dog stops chasing the cyclist, allowing her or him to return to normal pedaling speed.

Research Contributions

Fitness goals, such as improving cycling performance, are difficult to meet without some form of guide to plan workouts, monitor progress, and provide feedback. At the same time, most exercise has specific goals in mind:

- Exercising to improve general health focuses on the intensity of exercise and amount of exercise performed. The goals of a healthy adult are to perform aerobic exercise at least 150 minutes a week at a moderate intensity (or 75 minutes a week at a vigorous intensity), along with including muscle-strengthening activities that are moderate or high intensity and involve all major muscle groups on two or more days a week [6].

- Interval training combines short, high intensity bursts of speed with longer and slower recovery phases. Interval training can lead to improving exercise performance, speed, and endurance. The goal of the participant during interval training is to achieve specific heart rate targets during the slow and fast bursts of each interval.

- Muscle-strengthening exercise aims to build strong muscles and bones to prevent osteoporosis and reduce risk of injury from falls in later life, as well as rehabilitate weakened or injured muscles. The participant's goal is to train specific muscle groups by performing exercises at an intensity and frequency, as set by a health practitioner, with specific rest and recovery periods during and between workouts to prevent injury and maximize effectiveness.

- Exercising to improve sports performance has sport-specific goals in mind. For instance, boxing requires a different training regimen than professional cycling, but each of these are typically guided by a coach.

While these goals may be achieved using exercise-first exergames, the invisible coach has the potential to extend these goals to game-first exergames and still maintain their level of immersion. An expected contribution of our research is to improve the quality of exercise in exergames by combining the advantages of exercise that includes incidental games and games that include incidental exercise. The research, being conducted as part of Queen's University's Computer Science doctoral program, will involve the development and testing of an invisible coach for exergames that guides a player's workout.

We are addressing the following research questions. Is it possible to design games where by influencing gameplay we can guide players into meeting workout goals without the guidance of an expert? Do players enjoy this type of game, or do they find it intrusive? Do players find this more immersive than being presented with explicit instructions? Can this technique lead to sufficient success in meeting workout goals in comparison to being expertly guided?

Since there are many different goals the invisible coach can achieve, such as increasing sports performance and strengthening weak muscle groups, there are a variety of ways in which the coach can be tested. This leaves room for a great deal of valuable information that can be discovered in this area. We are investigating the concept of the invisible coach in the context of a novel strength training game.

References

[1] American Council on Exercise®. *ACE Personal Trainer Manual* (4th. Ed.). American Council on Exercise, San Diego, CA.

[2] Ding, D., Liu, H. Y., Cooper, R., Cooper, R. A., Smailagic, A., and Siewiorek, D. Virtual coach technology for supporting self-care. *Physical Medicine and Rehabilitation Clinics of North America*, *21*, 1 (2010), 179-194.

[3] Ellis, T., Latham, N. K., DeAngelis, T. R., Thomas, C. A., Saint-Hilaire, M., and Bickmore, T. W. Feasibility of a virtual exercise coach to promote walking in community-dwelling persons with Parkinson disease. *American Journal of Physical Medicine & Rehabilitation*, *92,* 6 (2013), 472-485.

[4] Eyck, A., Geerlings, K., Karimova, D., Meerbeek, B., Wang, L., IJsselsteijn, W., Kort, Y., Roersma, Y., and Westerink, J. Effect of a virtual coach on athletes' motivation. In *Persuasive Technology 2006.* Springer Berlin Heidelberg (2006), 158-161.

[5] GameZone. Screenshots and Images for Your Shape: Fitness Evolved.

[6] U.S. Department of Health & Human Services. *2008 Physical Activity Guidelines for Americans: Be Active, Be Healthy and Happy*.

Understanding Difficulty, Your Brain and Challenge

Rina R. Wehbe
HCI Games Group
Faculty of Business and IT
University of Ontario Institute of Technology
2000 Simcoe Street North
Oshawa, ON, Canada
rina.wehbe@uoit.ca

CHI PLAY '14, Oct 19-22 2014, Toronto, ON, Canada
ACM 978-1-4503-3014-5/14/10.
http://dx.doi.org/10.1145/2658537.2659014.

Abstract
My thesis proposes to use physiological measures with a focus on electroencephalography (EEG) to examine user-centered difficulty in games and user interfaces. The thesis specifically looks at both intended sources of difficulty and unintended sources of difficulty.

Author Keywords
Electroencephalography (EEG); Physiological measures; Mixed-methods; Human-computer interaction (HCI); Brain-Computer Interfaces (BCI)

ACM Classification Keywords
H.5.2 [Information Systems]: User Interfaces; K.8.0 [General]: Games – Personal Computing

Introduction
Both productivity applications and games may have different sources of difficulty. However, the difficulty originating from these diverse sources are fundamentally different. Productivity applications seek to give the user the smoothest possible experience with no points of confusion or frustration; the end goal of these applications is to have a user interface that elicits no negative feelings and provide a pleasant user experience. In contrast, games need difficulty (and to a certain extent frustration) to facilitate a pleasant user experience. Games seek to challenge the player to

ensure they remain in a flow state, where challenge and skill are equal. Keeping players in this state increases immersion and causes players to ignore the passing of time (while in the game), thereby improving the player experience.

Research Program

In September 2015, I will begin my Ph.D. under the supervision of Dr. Lennart E. Nacke at University of Ontario Institute of Technology, Canada and Dr. Stephen H. Fairclough at the Liverpool John Moores University, UK. Under their combined supervision, I plan to complete my Ph.D. in Computer Science. The focus of my Ph.D. will center on understanding where difficulty arises in games and how to design and evaluate user interfaces for non-gaming applications. I will do this by looking at difficulties stemming from the user interface in games and intentional difficulty in games themselves. I will look at both: productivity applications and game applications.

Motivation

In traditional Human computer Interaction (HCI), difficulty is reduced to creating a seamless interaction. The goal is to create an interface that is useful, usable or easy to use and enjoyable to use. When we say something is enjoyable to use, we are describing the user experience positively. The user experience is the description of the thoughts and feelings of the player while using this application [1].

HCI and HCI for games both focus on different aspects of user experience. HCI for productivity applications focuses on reducing difficulty, barriers of entry as well as ensure communication between the user and application is clear. As previously stated, games intentionally add difficulty to create a better gameplay experience. In games, we want to keep the user challenged without frustrating or boring them too much by balancing challenge and skill. This is called the flow state and can lead to what some researchers believe is an optimal experience [2].

Both of these perspectives handle difficultly in computer games and applications differently. Both views have significant impact on games user research. Although games need difficulty and problems to overcome, game designers acknowledge that difficulty stemming from the interface or instructions can detract from the game experience. This motivates the need to understand how and where difficulty arises in games to ensure the only difficulty in the game is intended to be there (i.e., "difficulty by design"). For example, if the game has a puzzle component the puzzle should be the source of challenge and not the instruction set or the controls.

Therefore, I will be looking at the origin of difficulty in both productivity applications and in games. The first step in my research plan is to conduct an in-depth review of the literature. Following, I will look at difficult arising from interfaces as well as games. The end goal is to separate the difficulty in games arising from problems with the interface versus intentional difficult designed to create challenge for the user. In the end the separation of these two forms of difficulty can be used to design games to optimize player experience.

The goal of my research is to improve user experience (UX) in games. UX is arguably at the heart of games [3]. UX is considered important, because it takes players beyond the game as a product to creating the game UX to become part of our own self-definition [1]. This is why players get engaged with games. Finally, creating a good player experience will improve games and likely create lasting relationships among players.

Research Question

Difficulty and challenge arises from many different sources such as being unable to understand the interface's requirements of the user. Before tackling this bigger question the questions such as: how do we define difficulty in games and applications? How do we separate difficulty and challenge in games? What causes mistakes in games? Does difficulty arise due to a lack of communication? Furthermore, once we have an understanding of difficulty how can we adjust games dynamically in response to the user's perceived level of difficulty, maintaining the optimum balance of challenge and skill?

Literature Review

Physiological measures have been used to assess the brain and body state during gameplay in real-time. Researchers have been able to gain insight on learning [4], social environment [5], as well as, the user's emotional response [6].

The literature has often focused on dynamic difficulty adjustment systems. These systems are designed to keep the player engaged by balancing the skill level and challenge presented to each player [7]. Difficulty adjustments have both advantages and disadvantages. No difficulty dynamic systems have been perfected. For example, if the system has two players playing multiple games, the system will have difficulty adjusting dynamically. This is the case if the players are not well matched by skill level [8].

Methodology

Before attempting to study difficulty, I will review the literature to come up with a study plan and methodology. I will use physiological measures including electroencephalography (EEG) to understand the player's reactions during interactions with the interface or during gameplay. This methodology may include using error related negativity (ERN) responses to understand mistakes [9]. Or using mu rhythms to understand observed learning [10]. Additionally, cardiovascular measures and skin conductance can be used to better understand the participants reaction to game events [11], [12]. At this stage, I am still conceptually developing my methodology and would benefit from the input in the Doctoral Consortium.

Dissertation Status and Next Steps

Currently, I have not started my Ph.D. program. However, the work from my M.Sc. feeds directly into the proposed Ph.D. project.

Results to Date

In my previous research, I used EEG to understand learning in games [10]. Learning is important to difficulty, because game designers want the puzzles to be challenging due to the design of the puzzle and not due to an inability to understand the rules.

Additionally, I am currently working on an ERN study to help understand how changes in game design elements affect mistakes made by the user.

Contributions

The expected contributions of this research include a greater understanding of the difficulties and challenges in games and applications. Additionally, I hope to learn more about how the human brain experiences difficulty. Moreover, I hope to design a dynamic difficulty adjustment system, which takes into account physiological brain data. Furthermore, I hope to have solid takeaways for game designers and help improve user/player experiences in games.

Acknowledgements

I would like to thank my supervisors, Dr. Lennart E. Nacke and Dr. Stephen H. Fairclough, for their support. As part of Dr. Nacke's HCI games research group, I would like to thank the GRAND NCE for partial funding from the CONNECT and G4HLTH projects and for the GRAND HQP scholarship, SSHRC IMMERSe (895-2011-1014), Dr. Nacke's NSERC Discovery Grant and my Ontario Graduate Scholarship for partially funding this research. Thank you to everyone at UOIT and the graduate students in the GAMER Lab for their support.

References

1. M. Hassenzahl, "The Thing and I: Understanding the Relationship Between User and Product," in *Funology SE - 4*, vol. 3, M. Blythe, K. Overbeeke, A. Monk, and P. Wright, Eds. Springer Netherlands, 2005, pp. 31–42.
2. M. Csikszentlmihalyi, *The Psychology of Optimal Experience*. New York: Harper and Row, 1990.
3. R. Pagulayan and K. Keeker, "User-centered design in games," *Handb. Comput. Interact.*, pp. 1–46, 2003.
4. S. H. Fairclough, L. Venables, and A. Tattersall, "The influence of task demand and learning on the psychophysiological response.," *Int. J. Psychophysiol.*, vol. 56, no. 2, pp. 171–84, May 2005.
5. N. Ravaja, T. Saari, and M. Turpeinen, "Spatial presence and emotions during video game playing: Does it matter with whom you play?," *Presence*, pp. 327–333, 2006.
6. N. Ravaja, M. Turpeinen, T. Saari, S. Puttonen, and L. Keltikangas-Järvinen, "The psychophysiology of James Bond: phasic emotional responses to violent video game events.," *Emotion*, vol. 8, no. 1, pp. 114–20, Feb. 2008.
7. S. Bateman, R. L. Mandryk, T. Stach, and C. Gutwin, "Target assistance for subtly balancing competitive play," *Proc. 2011 Annu. Conf. Hum. factors Comput. Syst. - CHI '11*, p. 2355, 2011.
8. J. Payton, E. Powell, A. Nickel, K. Doran, and T. Barnes, "GameChanger: A Middleware for Social Exergames," pp. 36–39, 2011.
9. C. B. Holroyd and M. G. H. Coles, "The neural basis of human error processing: Reinforcement learning, dopamine, and the error-related negativity.," *Psychol. Rev.*, vol. 109, no. 4, pp. 679–709, 2002.
10. R. Wehbe, D. Kappen, D. Rojas, M. Klauser, B. Kapralos, and L. E. Nacke, "EEG-based assessment of video and in-game learning," *Proc. CHI'13 Ext. Abstr.*, 2013.
11. J. Kivikangas, G. Chanel, B. Cowley, I. Ekman, M. Salminen, S. Jarvela, and N. Ravaja, "A review of the use of psychophysiological methods in game research," *Proc. Nord. DiGRA'10*, vol. 3, no. 3, pp. 181–199, 2011.
12. P. Mirza-Babaei, L. E. Nacke, J. Gregory, N. Collins, and G. Fitzpatrick, "How does it play better?: exploring user testing and biometric storyboards in games user research," *Proc. CHI'13*, no. May, 2013.

Using Play as a Lens to Bridge the Physical with the Digital

Gavin Wood
Culture Lab
School of Computing Science
Newcastle University, UK
g.wood2@ncl.ac.uk

CHI PLAY '14, Oct 19-22 2014, Toronto, ON, Canada
ACM 978-1-4503-3014-5/14/10.
http://dx.doi.org/10.1145/2658537.2659012

Abstract
When you play, you are deeply involved which is why interaction designers and game designers are increasingly creating playful experiences. However, a pitfall in these digital designs is to focus too much on the game rules and goals. In doing so, we miss the opportunity to design around the more open and self-expressive play that we might relate to our childhoods. In response to this problem, we will explore new digital designs using a lens of play. In treating play as something aspirational, we believe our designs will be able to change our relationships with each other and give new meaning to the spaces around us.

Author Keywords
Game design;play;playful design;playfulness

Introduction
Play is engaging, creative, encourages self-expression, requires the use of the imagination (or make-believe), often involves physical movement and is inherently social [7][15]. Where play has been considered as the focus in the design process, such as in ludic design [5], games-for-learning [17] and body space games [16], there is evidence that the resulting experiences are engaging and fun. In particular, they benefit from being open, free form, expressive and social [4].

In these examples, designers are successful in bridging the physical and the digital world. However, when these same worlds are connected in pervasive games and locative games (described [13]) it has been assumed that something akin to gamification [3] (the use of game design elements such as goals and rewards) can make activities in real world locations more engaging and fun. A typical example of such a *gamification* strategy when applied to museums, heritage sites and public spaces could be to create a treasure hunt activity [11]. However, such games are predictable and uninspiring with gameplay that does not achieve the enviable level of immersion that some games manage. A further criticism is that designers are often more interested in exploring the capabilities of technologies rather than creating engaging experiences [8].

Instead, we propose that a lens of play can be used inform the design of digital experiences that bridge the virtual world and the real world. Our aspiration in exploring play is our belief that it will encourage designers to create and explore a more open design space with a more varied palette of interactive possibilities than those in familiar gameful strategies.

Background and Related Work

In games studies, the distinction between games and play is usually tied back to Callois [2] who placed the terms ludus and paidia at opposite ends of a play continuum. Ludus (or gamefulness) consists of formal play which is bounded by rules and has defined winners and losers. In contrast, Paidia (or playfulness) and our focus for design, is typified by activities that involve improvisation, expressiveness, spontaneity, and uncontrolled fantasy (described [7] and [12]).

PLEX [12] is one example of a design framework which has taken a play-centric approach to the design of digital technologies. PLEX expanded an earlier framework of pleasurable experience by considering characteristics of play from video games. However, this has meant PLEX is mostly designed around positive experiences of play. We believe this is a problem since negative aspects of play, for example, shame and tragedy (suggested [12]) could provide interesting provocations for imaginative and creative play. In addition, the characteristics of play were identified through an analysis of play engendered by console-styled video games, which for the most part fails to take account of social and physical play. In contrast, we are informed by the play embodied by other genres of games such as JS Joust [16].

Montola [13] argues that pervasive games are one example of genre that can be approached with a stance toward paidia, a position they recognise that sets them apart from most ludologists. Montola analyses different pervasive games with respect to Huizinga's magic circle as it is expanded temporarily, spatially and socially [13]. However, there is only an implicit connection to theories of play (such as those in [15]) and we are frustrated by the lack of a starting point for these games. This can also be said of other game design resources such as [14]. We are currently seeing new exciting technologies emerge and new games will need to be designed from the ground up and therefore a starting point is invaluable.

Pervasive games such as those described in Benford's work with the Mixed Reality Lab [1] are successful in bridging the physical world with the digital world. However, these experiences are curated like works of

Figure 1. i-dentity: a digital game based upon childhood play.

Figure 2. The Wild Man game with an artist's impression of the digital experience.

art, they are costly to produce and often deliver prescriptive game play. Instead, a lens of play will allow us to explore experiences where the onus is on the participant to create and control the play. As in Benford's work we undertake our research through our key activities of practice, studies and theory. Our practice is games studies but similarly, each activity informs one another. We are inspired by Benford's use of ethnographic methods and employ qualitative methods in evaluating our designs. Finally, we are also looking to sensitise designers to new concepts; albeit our focus will be concepts relating to play.

Early Results

In the first eighteen months of our research we have created two pervasive games: The Department of Hidden Stories [17] and a mobile phone game to engage families in play at a heritage space. In addition, we explore play as a starting point for design in our game i-dentity (with Exertion Labs [4]).

Department of Hidden Stories (DoHS): In our DoHS paper [17] we describe the design and evaluation of DoHS, a mobile-based game developed to support 8 to 10 year old children in playful digital storytelling and engagement with books in public libraries (see Figure 1). Our game motivates the children to use traditional writing materials while encouraging the child to explore the whole space of the library as they get their hands on as many different books as they want. In our findings, we conclude that we should design tools that act as conduits and mediators for play. We also suggest guidelines that can help designers create playful digitally based activities that encourage children to challenge their preconceptions of their cultural spaces.

i-dentity: In our paper i-dentity [4] (pictured Figure 1), we report on our body-space game that is played with a tangible interface. i-dentity was designed in the Game Jam at CHI 2013 and inspired by traditional play. We were motivated by advocates of the New Games Movement, such as Bernard De Koven [9] who suggests that designers should reconsider old playground games and how we play together. i-dentity used childhood games such as *Sleeping Lions* and *What Time is it Mr. Wolf*[1] as a starting point for design. Through role-play and experimentation with digital prototypes we explore how the core elements of these games can be represented digitally and these changed during development of the game. Our paper describes how this crossover from physical play to a digital game created new compelling and social gameplay.

This initial work has informed us in three areas which will continue to shape our future research. We will focus on: 1) how designers can mediate (and scaffold) play through digital technology, 2) how to engage users with the space and the context of the game, and 3) identifying how user interactions can afford play.

Next Steps

The Wild Man Game: We have created a mobile phone game (pictured Figure 2) that lets visitors experience a heritage site from the perspective of a "wild man". In our game we prompt players to involve themselves in untypical and sometimes embarrassing play, for example, creeping around, dancing wildly or even mimicking wild animals. As such, our game provides an invitation to play and a convenient alibi for behaviour that challenges the social norm of these spaces.

[1] Activity Village - http://www.activityvillage.co.uk/

We hope that by engaging visitors through play that we can give these places personal meaning or what Harrison and Dourish [6] describe as a sense of place (discussed [10]). A positive sense of place can mean different things to different places, for example, in a library it might mean we visit and borrow books more often and in the case of a heritage site it means we can change visitor's attitudes so they can become future custodians of these spaces.

Acknowledgements

I would like to thank my supervisory team: Madeline Balaam, Peter Wright and Patrick Olivier.

This research is funded by the UK's Arts & Humanities Research Council as part of the Creative Exchange knowledge exchange hub between Newcastle and Lancaster Universities, and the Royal College of Art.

References

[1] Benford, S., et al., Performance-Led Research in the Wild. ACM Trans. Comput.-Hum. *Interactions*, 20, 3 (2013), 14:1-14:22.

[2] Caillois, R. *Man, Play, and Games*. Thames and Hudson, UK, 1962.

[3] Deterding, S., Khaled, R., Nacke, L., & Dixon, D. (2011). Gamification: Toward a definition. Proc. CHI'11.

[4] Garner, J., Wood, G., et al., F. i-dentity: Innominate Movement Representation as Engaging Game Element. Proc. *CHI '14*, ACM (2014), 2181-2190.

[5] Gaver, W. Designing for homo ludens, still, *(Re)searching the digital Bauhaus*. Springer, London, 2009, 163–178.

[6] Harrison, S., Dourish P., *Re-Place-ing space: the roles of place and space in collaborative systems*, http://www.dourish.com/publications.html, 2010.

[7] Hinske, S., et al, Classifying Pervasive Games: On Pervasive Computing and Mixed Reality, *Concepts and technologies for Pervasive Games*. Shaker, Aachen, Germany, 2007.

[8] Kirman, B., Linehan, C. and Lawson, S. Blowtooth: A Provocative Pervasive Game for Smuggling Virtual Drugs Through Real Airport Security. *Personal Ubiquitous Computing*, 16, 6 (2012), 767-775.

[9] Koven, B. 2013, *The Well-Played Game: A Player's Philosophy*. The MIT Press.

[10] Lentini, L., Decortis, .F. Space and places: when interacting with and in physical space becomes a meaningful experience. *Personal Ubiquitous Computing*, 14, 5, July 2010, 407-415.

[11] Linehan, C., Bull, N. and Kirman, B. BOLLOCKS!! Designing Pervasive Games That Play with the Social Rules of Built Environments. Proc. *Lecture Notes in Computer Science*, Springer (2013), 123-137.

[12] Lucero, S., Karapanos, E., Arrasvuori, J., Korhonen. , H., Playful or Gameful? Creating delightful user experiences. *Interactions*, ACM (2014), 34-39.

[13] Montola, M., Stenros, J. and Waern, A. 2009, *Pervasive Games: Theory and Design*. Morgan Kaufmann Publishers Inc. Elsevier.

[14] Salen, K. and Zimmerman, E. *Rules of play: Game design fundamentals*. Cambridge, MIT Press, 2003.

[15] Verenikina, I., et al. Child's play: computer games, theories of play and children's development. Proc. *CRPIT '03*, ACS (2003), 99-106.

[16] Wilson, D. (2012). *Designing for the Pleasures of Disputation -or- How to make friends by trying to kick them! PhD Dissertation*, IT University of Copenhagen.

[17] Wood, G., Vines, J., Balaam, M., et al. The Dept. Of Hidden Stories: Playful Digital Storytelling for Children in a Public Library. Proc. *CHI '14*, ACM (2014), 1885-1894.

PoetryLab: A Close Listening Game For iOS

Ian Arawjo
Research Assistant
Department of English
Concordia University
Montreal, QC, Canada
ian@alkemieatelier.com

Jason Camlot
Associate Professor
Department of English
Concordia University
Montreal, QC, Canada
jason.camlot@concordia.ca

Christine Mitchell
Postdoctoral Fellow
Department of Media, Culture, and Communications
NYU Steinhardt
New York, NY, USA
christletine@gmail.com

CHI PLAY '14, Oct 19-22 2014, Toronto, ON, Canada
ACM 978-1-4503-3014 5/14/10.
http://dx.doi.org/10.1145/2658537.2662972

Abstract
PoetryLab is a close listening game for iOS in which players manipulate a virtual reel-to-reel tape machine and learn editing techniques to solve sound puzzles featuring recorded poetry. Gameplay teaches players about poetry and recording media from both auditory and archival perspectives. Players are trained to listen to and interact with recorded speech in new and unfamiliar ways as they discover the provenance of the poetry excerpts — a university reading series held in 1960-1970s Montreal.

Author Keywords
Game interaction; close listening; sound archive; sound recording; poetry

ACM Classification Keywords
K.8.0 Personal Computing: Games; J.5 Computer Applications: Literature; J.5 Computer Applications: Performing Arts.

Introduction
In this paper we present PoetryLab, a close listening game for iOS devices in which players learn reel-to-reel playback and editing techniques to solve sound puzzles featuring recorded poetry. The player adopts the dual roles of 1960s sound technician and present-day digital archivist, traveling through technological and literary

Figure 1: Slicing up audiotape with a razor blade.

timeframes to listen and learn about a historical event while working to literally splice it back together.

PoetryLab was developed to exploit the SpokenWeb digital poetry archive in innovative ways [7, 8]. The archive features an avant-garde poetry reading series that was held in Montreal between 1966 and 1974, and which was recently re-discovered as a series of reel-to-reel tapes [4]. SpokenWeb responds to growing interest in the study of oral performance and sound recordings of poetry, breaking with the tradition of seeing poetry primarily as a textual medium. It aims to train listeners in what Charles Bernstein has called "the denser linguistic field" of literary prosody [1], by using the sound archive as a means to discover the complex musicality of poetry and its rich microtones: its intensity, duration, pitch, intonation, accent, modulation, resonance and vocal mode [4]. Players make these discoveries using their ears, instead of relying on descriptive information.

But the sound archive is not "live." With archival close listening the driver of gameplay, PoetryLab also highlights the role of sound recording media in the production of poetry, and builds gameplay mechanics out of virtual reel-to-reel playback and editing.

Core Gameplay

The player selects from a shelf of reel-to-reel tape boxes. The box opens, revealing a tape reel, which loads onto a simulated tape machine. The tape holds audio fragments spliced together from the poetry archive, as well as listening puzzles – these are sections of poetry that have been incorrectly spliced together. The player can advance and rewind tape using buttons or play forward and in reverse by "rocking the reels" with their finger, physically controlling the tape speed. When a puzzle reaches the playhead, it jams the recorder, routing the player to the centerpiece of the game: the editing screen. Here, a razor blade slices up audiotape, scattering sound for players to listen to (tap to play), to re-order and resplice [Figure 1]. If the pieces are correctly respliced, the player revisits the reel-to-reel screen and playback resumes. Once all the puzzles are discovered and solved on a single reel, the reel is returned to its tape box, and to the shelf, this time with an identifying label.

At early levels, the speech sounds encountered are familiar, and players use semantic knowledge to piece together solutions that make linguistic sense. As players advance in the game, they are presented with audio puzzles whose tape pieces have been altered with digital tools (e.g. dropped out frequencies, Auto-Tune effects, etc.). Solutions to higher-level puzzles hinge on closer and closer listening — not to the meaning of what is being said, but to sound as signal.

Innovating Poetics and Play

A priority for the SpokenWeb project is to emphasize the media used to record, store and bring past poetry readings to present day ears. A major theme of our game is therefore the discovery of older media, in particular the reel-to-reel machine. This is an innovation for younger users, who are unfamiliar with tape recorders and the affordances of tape.

In designing PoetryLab we opted against digital representations and functions of audio where possible (e.g. waveforms, seeking, ID3 tags, etc). This forced us to consider the materiality of audio on tape. Although we could have supplemented pieces of tapes with

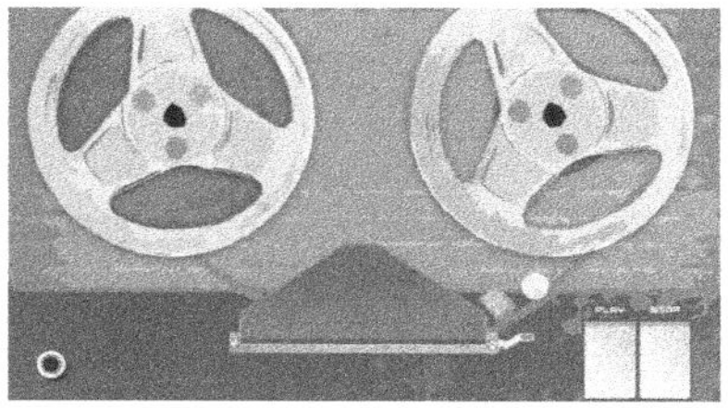

Figure 2: The simulated reel-to-reel machine.

words or other indicators, we chose to stick as close as possible to the analog medium. As a result, tape pieces are visually indistinguishable for two-thirds of the game.

Whereas some apps gamify poetry by having users memorize and/or recite poetry aloud [6, 9] — or read and play with poetry-as-text [11, 12] — PoetryLab players interact exclusively with existing audio content. In contrast to audiobooks, this content is poetry-as-performance (in front of a live audience) rather than poetry merely spoken aloud. Our design is closer to games that rely on audio cues to drive game narratives [3, 10], which eliminate visuals and disorient users. In short: to play such games is to listen. In line with those approaches, PoetryLab highlights listening over visual- and haptic modalities, which are nonetheless necessary to help contextualize the audio from the twin perspectives of media and history [Figure 2].

Finally, PoetryLab enacts Ian Bogost's "procedural rhetoric," which sees games as devices for expressing points of view and making arguments through the interactive procedurality of software [2]. As players listen to historical documentary audio and fix carefully designed editing snafus (puzzles) — using old tech in new media — players come to see sound archives as malleable, not fixed, sites.

Audience
The primary audience for the game is poetry enthusiasts, poetry instructors and students of poetry (university, college, high school). PoetryLab could be adapted to focus on a single poet for a particular course, or integrate audio from other poetry sound archives (e.g. PennSound, UbuWeb). At the same time, we do not conceive of our app only as a poetry app, but as a language, voice and sound app. We therefore downplayed more typical (and textbook) signposts for poetry, such as titles and texts of poems, dates and bibliographical information. The result, we hope, is an app that appeals to that giant swath of word-puzzle devotees, who will see PoetryLab as an audio complement to their love for crosswords, jumbles and word-finds. The emphasis on recording media, again, with the literary and biographical details downplayed, will be a draw for techie types.

In preliminary tests with players, we have found the tape reconstruction mechanic immediately accessible. Most people were able to solve our simplest 4-piece ordering puzzle in one to three tries, with no prior playing experience. Further tests proved that some puzzles could be ordered "correctly," from a semantic perspective, in several different ways. We are currently engaged in more extensive user testing in order to perfect our puzzle designs.

Technical Innovations
A design process innovation was necessary to streamline game testing and support PoetryLab's collaborative workflow. A protocol was created that enabled compressed folders containing ordered audio files to be parsed into the game via the "Open In..." feature on iOS devices. This allowed the team's puzzle-makers to test and tweak their creations as soon as they designed them, sharing their creations easily with testers via email or cloud-sharing services. This feedback mechanism saved time, skirting the need to re-build the code with every new content update. Moreover, this approach has the positive side-effect that players can create their own tapes and puzzles.

PoetryLab's major in-game technical challenge was to emulate a reel-to-reel machine on a mobile device, staying true to the linearly winding nature of tape by letting players rotate reels with their fingers to navigate. Initially we used rope physics to articulate the tape (with Apple's SKPhysics classes), but encountered too many problems with maintaining the code, and therefore moved to a less dynamic approach. We applied the FMOD Ex API to enable real-time bidirectional "scrubbing" of sound sentences [5], with a few modifications. Reels loaded into the virtual tape machine can consist of an arbitrary number of gapless audio segments, each loading asynchronously as the tape spins. These innovations help emphasize features of analog playback; they leave out from PoetryLab several customary digital "comforts" such as instantaneously jumping to the end of a tape (as in SoundCloud, iTunes or other common MP3 players).

We chose to program in Objective-C instead of a proprietary engine such as Unity (unity3d.com), because simulation of a reel-to-reel required low-level access to the mobile sound hardware. We used Apple's SpriteKit and CoreAnimation frameworks for the game's 2D physics and 3D visuals, respectively.

Acknowledgements

The authors gratefully acknowledge SSHRC IG and Grand-NCE, under grant numbers 435-2012-1245 and G-CI-11-C0-03, respectively, as well as Concordia University Records Management and Archives for support of this project, and thank PoetryLab team members for their creative and technical contributions: A. Clarkson, T. Fitzmaurice, P. Hamou, L. Hannigan, A. Lemay and M. Stein.

References

[1] Bernstein, C. Introduction. Close Listening: Poetry and the Performed Word. Ed. Bernstein. NY: Oxford UP, 1998. 3-26.

[2] Bogost, I. Persuasive games: the expressive power of videogames. Cambridge: MIT Press, 2007.

[3] Brown, G. (2013). Blindscape. [Mobile application software].

[4] Camlot, J. "The Sound of Canadian Modernisms: The Sir George Williams University Poetry Series, 1966-1974." Journal of Canadian Studies 46 (2012): 26-59. (Published in 2013).

[5] FMOD Ex API. Version 4.44. (2013) Firelight Technologies Pty Ltd. http://www.fmod.org/

[6] LudicVoice. (2011). Victorianator. [Mobile application software].

[7] Murray, A. and J. Wiercinski, "A Design Methodology for Web Based Sound Archives." DHQ: Digital Humanities Quarterly 8 (2014).

[8] Murray, A. and J. Wiercinski. "Looking at archival sound: visual features of a spoken word archive's web interface that enhance the listening experience." First Monday 17(4), April 2012.

[9] Penguin Group USA. (2013). Poems By Heart by Penguin Classics. [Mobile application software].

[10] Playground Publishing B.V. (2014). Papa Sangre II. [Mobile application software].

[11] The Poetry Foundation. (2012). POETRY from The Poetry Foundation.

[12] Tiny Mobile Inc. (2012). Poetry Creator | Verses - Poetry, Poems & Poets. [Mobile application software].

Tag and Seek
A Location-Based Game in Tainan City

Caroline Arkenson
KTH Royal Institute of Tech
100 44 Stockholm, Sweden
arkenson@kth.se

Chun-Yen Huang
National Cheng Kung University
70101 Tainan City, Taiwan
p38001067@ncku.edu.tw

Yin-Yu Chou
National Cheng Kung University
70101 Tainan City, Taiwan
p38001075@ncku.edu.tw

Yi-Chin Lee
National Cheng Kung University
70101 Tainan City, Taiwan
f34009014@mail.ncku.edu.tw

Figure 1: Tag and Seek

CHI PLAY '14, Oct 19-22, 2014, Toronto, ON, Canada
ACM 978-1-4503-3014-5/14/10.
http://dx.doi.org/10.1145/2658537.2662986

Abstract
Tag and Seek is a location-based game which leads a traveler through Tainan City in Taiwan. The traveler's task is to find Harry's friends who are hiding at different sites in the city. Once at the site, the traveler has to scan a Near Field Communication (NFC) tag placed on a board looking like Harry's friend. When the NFC tag is scanned the lost friend is found, information about the site is presented and instructions to the next site will be available. The game lets the traveler experience culture, gain knowledge about sites in the city and meet local citizens – without the traveler having to plan the trip ahead. By implementing NFC technology as check points the interaction with the game differs from regular tourist guides and the threat of privacy which comes with location-based services is greatly lowered as the traveler is not being tracked by GPS. From our user evaluation we found that both the interface and interaction with the boards could use some improvements to increase the usability.

Author Keywords
Location-based game; NFC technology; educational game; tourist guide; interaction

ACM Classification Keywords
H.5.2. Information interfaces and presentation: User Interfaces

Figure 2: The instruction screen - the traveler is presented with instructions to the site and the option to show site location on a map, a hint about Harry's friend or to scan a tag.

Introduction

Tag and Seek (Figure 1) is a location-based game developed for Android which leads the user, a traveler, around Tainan City in Taiwan. The storyline includes a guy named Harry who has lost his friends around the city and needs someone's help to find them, because Harry feels very lonely without his friends!

The traveler sets up the game by first choosing a level - *short walk*, *stroll* or *challenge* - and then the desired package of sites to visit from the available categories *parks*, *historical sites*, *restaurants*, *cafés* and *museums*. A "stroll" package, for example, contains five sites. Harry provides the traveler with instructions (Figure 2) to the first site and hints about who and where his friend is (Figure 3). Once at the site the traveler must use his/her smartphone to scan a Near Field Communication (NFC) tag placed on a board that looks like Harry's friend (Figure 4). When the NFC tag is scanned the lost friend is found (Figure 5), information about the site is presented and instructions to the next site will be available. Upon completion of the route, the traveler receives a coupon which can be exchanged to a specific item in a specific store.

As the route leads the travelers to interesting sites in the city and presents information about the sites, Tag and Seek works as an educational game with an element of surprise. By playing Tag and Seek, the traveler gets to experience culture, gain new knowledge, meet local citizens and get the chance try typical local food. By implementing NFC technology the traveler is also provided with a different way of interacting with a digital tourist guide.

Our hope is to with Tag and Seek provide a fun way to experience, learn about and interact with a new city and the digital tourist guide – without the traveler having to plan the trip ahead.

Related work

Similar applications are the WHAIWHAI guides in which the user has to solve clues on sites in order to get the missing pieces of a story, initially found in a book, and to keep playing. The clues are answered by SMS. [6] REXplore is another location-based game with the aim to make history learning fun and influence the tourists' path through the city. The tourists have to find historical buildings and then a waving motion with the phone is required to continue playing. [2] Seoul Museum of History has implemented QR codes and NFC tags which provide the visitors with additional information when scanned with smartphones. While it is not a game, it implements the same technology. [5]

Location-based services

User needs and behaviors are important factors to keep in mind while designing location-based services. Along with location-based services arise questions of privacy issues. Since people are concerned with abuse of technology and location data, the way the application handles such data affects the user's will to use it. [3]

Location-based games mostly focus on entertaining the user while sometimes learning is a part of the game. The purpose of location-based learning games is to help the visitor experience the environment in a better way. By incorporating an application as a multimedia companion, for example in tourist guides or at museums, traditional visits to interesting sites can be improved. [1]

Figure 3: The hint shows the shape of the friend and hints where the board is placed.

Figure 4: The board, Harry's friend, on which the NFC tag is placed.

User studies

To understand the needs and behaviors of our target audience *travelers*, we sent a survey to Taiwanese asking them how they plan a trip, find information about a city and about their smartphone usage while traveling. The survey received 20 answers through which we learnt that the respondents often search information online before going on a trip. When arriving in a city the respondents either try to find a tourist information office or information boards, for example at Metro stations. 16 respondents use their smartphones while traveling, and Google Maps is a common navigator to use when traveling through the city. The smartphone is used to find online information about sites, food and how to travel within a city. Pictures are also taken for documentation of the trip.

Game implementation

Tag and Seek was developed and tested on an Android device running Android version 4.4.2. It uses a cloud database service, Parse.com, to store data related to the sites. GPS is used only once to find the traveler's current location when setting up the game in order to find the closest site. This is with the traveler's convenience in mind, as the route will be optimized to start close to the traveler's current location. By allowing the traveler to easily set up a game once the application is installed, the need for researching and planning the trip ahead is lowered. Google Maps for Android API is used to show the location of the site on a map. As we found that travelers often are familiar with Google Maps, it is a good tool for displaying the location of a site.

To detect NFC tags a device has to be equipped with an NFC scanner, which Android devices are. Amongst the advantages with implementing NFC technology is the simple interaction between the tag and the user, the low battery drainage as well as user safety since tags only can be detected on a very close distance when the smartphone's screen is turned on. [4]

In Tag and Seek, the NFC tag works as a check point which both lets the traveler continue the game and as a prompt for the application to fetch site data from the database. By implementing NFC technology in Tag and Seek, the concern of privacy issues is overcome as no user data is stored – the traveler is not tracked while playing the game – and the traveler makes an active choice to scan a tag. The design of the interaction boards have been chosen to be a fun element in pictures from the trip.

User evaluation

In order to find usability issues in Tag and Seek, we decided to conduct a user evaluation with a small set of test users to quickly find usability issues. Three Taiwanese university students were, one by one, given a brief introduction to the game before they were asked to complete a route with the boards placed in a room. The evaluation was followed by a short interview with each test user.

None of the test users had previously encountered NFC technology and for user A the biggest issue when using the application seemed to be the scanning of the NFC tag, as user A did not know where to place the phone in relation to the tag. User B did not know how close to the tag the phone had to be in order to scan it. Neither user B or C did at first realize that they after scanning the tag were being displayed with new instructions, as the different instruction pages only differ in text and thus look very similar. The site instructions and hints given in the game were perceived as clear but the user flow, i.e. what button to click and when, was not always clear to the test users.

While user A and B found the interaction with the NFC tag quite inconvenient as the tag is small, user C did enjoy it as it provided feedback and a sense of accomplishment. To user C it was easy to understand why a tag had to be scanned as it is hinted by the name *Tag and Seek*. User A thought that it was good that privacy is protected, but none of the three users did mind being tracked by GPS. User A and B would not want to travel this way but user B thought it would be fun to play together with children. User C found it to be fun and interesting to interact with a board but that perhaps the requirements for finishing the route should not be so strict. A suggestion from user C was that more tips could be included in the site information, e.g. "at this café, this type of coffee is the most popular".

Figure 5: When the NFC tag is scanned the friend is found and the traveler is presented with this screen. From here, the traveler can either choose to read info about the current site or see instructions to the following site.

Conclusions

In this paper we presented Tag and Seek, a location-based game implementing NFC technology. Through our user study we found that travelers use their smartphones to find information online and find their way through a new city. Our hope with Tag and Seek was to provide a fun way to experience, learn about and interact with a new city and the digital tourist guide – without the traveler having to plan the trip ahead. We conducted a quick user evaluation to find usability issues in Tag and Seek. The interaction with the NFC tag was by the test users, who had never encountered NFC technology before, either perceived as inconvenient since the scanning area is small or as providing a sense of accomplishment. The interaction with the NFC tag could be improved to reduce friction for those who might find it inconvenient. One way to do so could be to use a larger tag or clearly mark where to place the smartphone. The interface and its structure could use some improvements in order to facilitate the user flow and make it clear when the user is being presented with new instructions.

A video of the Tag and Seek experience can be found here: http://tinyurl.com/tagandseek

Acknowledgements

We would like to thank our professors and classmates for their feedback throughout the course.

References

[1] Ardito, C. et al. Design Guidelines for Location-based Mobile Games for Learning. *Social Appl. For Lifelong Learning* (2010), 4–5.

[2] Ballagas, R. et al. REXplorer: a mobile, pervasive spell-casting game for tourists. *Ext. Abstracts CHI 2007*, ACM Press (2007), 1929-1934.

[3] Jiang, B. & Yao, X. Location-based services and GIS in perspective. *Comp., Environm. and Urban Systems, 30,6* (2006), 712–725.

[4] Milette, J. & Stroud. A.,*Professional Android Sensor Programming.* John Wiley & Sons, Inc. (2012).

[5] Seoul Museum of History http://eng.museum.seoul.kr/eng/visit/audioGuide.jsp

[6] WHAIWHAI – Play the storyline through the city http://www.whaiwhai.com/en/game/howtoplay/

BloxAR: Augment Your Social Life!

Niels C. Bakker,
Jehan R. S. da Camara,
Maarten van Elsas,
Leon J. Helsloot, Gert Spek,
Isha J. van Baar,
Rafael Bidarra,
Ben A. Kybartas
Delft University of Technology
Delft, The Netherlands
n.c.bakker | j.r.s.dacamara |
m.vanelsas | l.j.helsloot | g.spek
| i.j.vanbaar@student.tudelft.nl
r.bidarra |
b.a.kybartas@tudelft.nl

CHI PLAY '14, Oct 19-22 2014, Toronto, ON, Canada
ACM 978-1-4503-3014-5/14/10.
http://dx.doi.org/10.1145/2658537.2662989

Abstract
Many people who own a smartphone spend a large amount of time playing mobile games. Despite the technological capabilities and social potential of these devices, the majority of mobile games make limited use of available technologies and contain little or no multiplayer elements. *BloxAR* is an augmented reality mobile game that aims to provide a fun and engaging social experience. In this game, players compete in teams to be the first to build a virtual block structure within a set time. Play consists of physically exploring the structure in an augmented reality environment, building the structure by placing blocks and cooperating with teammates to combine blocks together.

Author Keywords
augmented reality; collaborative gaming; social gaming; mobile gaming

ACM Classification Keywords
H.5.1 [Information interfaces and presentation (e.g., HCI)]: Multimedia information systems;; K.8.0 [Personal Computing]: Games

Introduction
Despite the large number of sensors modern smartphones are equipped with, most mobile games use few or none of these possibilities. *BloxAR* makes use of the mobility and

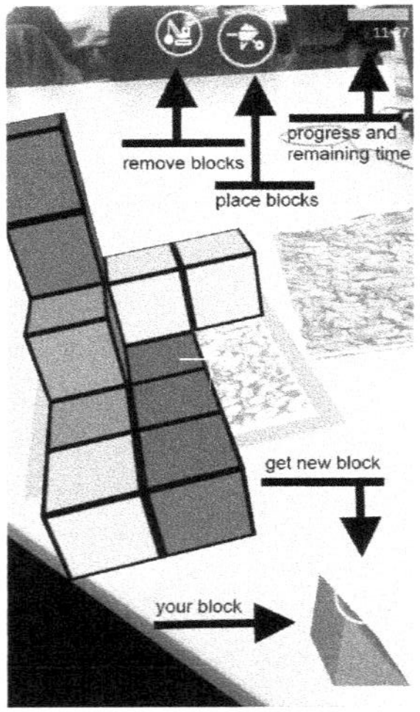

Figure 1: The interface of *BloxAR*.

Figure 2: An image target with a block structure drawn on top.

sensory capabilities of smartphones to let players interact with their environment and with other players. *Augmented Reality* (AR) is used to display virtual structures as if they exist in the real world, binding all players to a single physical location. Players have to bump their phones together to mix two different color blocks. This way, real-life movement, augmented reality and team play combine into a fun and challenging game experience.

Game Concept

The objective of *BloxAR* is for each team to replicate a structure of blocks that is shown on a public screen within a set time. Figure 3 shows an example of a public screen, with the target structure in the middle.

Figure 3: The public screen, with the target structure shown in the middle. The progress and structure of each team is shown on either side of the target and the QR code to join the game is at the bottom.

To join a game, a player has to scan a *Quick Response* (QR) code. Most smarthpone users are familiar with QR codes, which makes scanning such a code an intuitive means for joining a game.

After joining the game, a player will get a block in one of the three primary colors (yellow, red or blue). A player can tap the refresh button in the lower right corner of the screen to get a new block if they cannot use the block they currently have. Figure 1 shows the user interface as it appears on the smartphone screen.

Apart from blocks in the three primary colors, target structures may also contain blocks in the three secondary colors (orange, green and purple). Players have to create blocks in secondary colors by combining their own block with the block of another player. Combining is done by "bumping" the phones of two players back to back, as in Figure 6. After combining, both players receive a new block with a mix of the colors of the combined blocks. An orange block, for example, is formed by combining a red block with a yellow block.

Players can see the structure they are building by aiming the camera of their phone at a specific AR image target, as shown in Figure 2. The structure will be drawn on top of the image target on the phone's screen. By moving the phone around, a player can aim at the location where they wish to place their block. Tapping the screen places the block at the location highlighted in the structure. Removing blocks is also possible by switching to a 'destroy mode' at the top of the interface. In this mode, players first target a block to destroy and then tap the screen to remove that block from the structure. At the top right of the interface, the player may see the remaining time and the progress of the current structure.

Players of *BloxAR* are divided into two teams. The team that finishes the target structure first or has most progress when a set time has elapsed wins the game.

Figure 4: A structure nearing completion.

Figure 5: The structure as seen through a phone

The public screen, seen in Figure 3, shows the progress of both teams, the structure each team has built so far, as well as a progress bar showing how complete each structure is. This allows sby to enjoy watching the game. Furthermore, it allows both teams to see the progress of their opposing team, increasing the competitive element of the game.

A gameplay video showing the basics of *BloxAR* can be found at `http://youtu.be/p8bu2bqPSKQ`

Target Audience

Although most building block toys target younger players, *BloxAR* was designed to appeal to a wide age group. Ideally, people who have never met before can play the game together regardless of age and background. User tests with a group of people of mixed ages, from early teens to early twenties, have shown that this is a realistic scenario.

BloxAR is a fairly simple game that forces its players to communicate and cooperate and it can even be used at events where people have to get to know each other or learn to work together. The main difficulty is that the game requires some setup, requiring both a server, public screen and one image target for each team. Once people start playing, however, the public screen will make others want to join or watch. In testing, we found people who had not spoken a word to each other before playing the game having elaborate conversations afterwards.

User Experience

The most important aspect of a social game is of course the people playing. *BloxAR* draws attention with its prominent appearance including a public screen, players bumping their phones together and people aiming their phones at image targets. The fun environment created by the game makes people want to join in. The QR code on the public screen provides an easy way to do so.

Bumping phones back to back is not an intuitive action for most people and therefore the game provides a short tutorial explaining the concept of mixing blocks. In testing, some players initially had difficulty mixing, either because they bumped the phones too rapidly or because they were not aware of the possible color combinations. After a few minutes of practice, however, there were no further confusions.

The fun and social experience delivered by the game keeps players hooked. So far, every user test resulted in people playing until either their phones ran out of energy or the server was shut down.

Innovations

Although the technologies used in *BloxAR* are not new by themselves, the innovation comes from combining those technologies into a social game. Collaborative and competitive gaming, augmented reality and real-world movement provide a unique gaming experience.

BloxAR is also unique with regard to the amount of interaction players have with their surroundings. In a time where many people focus more on the screen of their smartphone than on the world around them, *BloxAR* uses that very same screen to make people who might have never met before interact with one another.

The basic concept described above allowed us to provide the following three innovative gameplay features:

- Augmented reality, which leads to an immersive gaming experience. Players see the world around them with the game state drawn on top, making them feel more connected to their environment. Being able to modify the structure in the augmented reality environment enhances this experience.

- Players are bound to a specific location by the public screen and the image targets. Because players of the game are physically together, they will be more inclined to interact verbally. Likewise the public screen allows passersby to watch and possible be drawn into playing the game for themselves.
- All team members share the same augmented reality state. Any member of a team can modify the shared structure of their team. Changes to the structure will be visible for every player, through their phones or on the public screen. The collaborative element is increased by being able to see the actions of other team members in real time.

Technical Aspects

BloxAR relies on various existing technologies. The game is built using the *Unity* [2] game engine. For recognizing image targets and extended tracking, *Qualcomm® Vuforia™* [3] is used. The *ZXing* library [1] is used for generating and reading QR codes.

Near Field Communication (NFC), a technique to communicate between devices in close proximity, is currently not supported on many smartphones. Therefore, *BloxAR* uses a custom bump detection algorithm. The algorithm uses the phone's accelerometer input to detect peaks in acceleration, as would occur when bumping phones together. Furthermore, raw compass data is used to detect changes in the magnetic field possibly caused by another phone. The sensor data is combined with timing information to detect phones being bumped together.

Figure 6: Testers combining blocks.

Related Games

Paintrix [4] is a social game in which teams have to color figures in a matrix by scanning QR codes with their smartphone. Like *BloxAR*, players have to mix colors. The mixing mechanic used by *Paintrix* is to first color a cell with one primary color, followed by another primary color.

References

[1] Official ZXing ("Zebra Crossing") project home. https://github.com/zxing/zxing.

[2] Unity - Game engine, tools and multiplatform. https://unity3d.com/unity.

[3] Vuforia - enable your apps to see. https://www.vuforia.com.

[4] Slappendel, D., Lie, F., de Vos, M., Kopla, A., and Bidarra, R. Paintrix: Color up your life! In *Advances in Computer Entertainment*, D. Reidsma, H. Katayose, and A. Nijholt, Eds., vol. 8253 of *Lecture Notes in Computer Science*. Springer International Publishing, 2013, 576–579.

HIDDEN LION: A Location Based APP Game of Sword Lion Searching

Kuo-Ping Chang
Department of Industrial Design
National Cheng Kung University
Tainan, Taiwan
p36024069@mail.ncku.edu.tw

Yu-Wei Huang
Institute of Creative Industries Design, National Cheng Kung University, Tainan, Taiwan
pa6024031@ncku.edu.tw

Shu-Yin Hsueh
Institute of Creative Industries Design, National Cheng Kung University, Tainan, Taiwan
pa6021067@ncku.edu.tw

Yuh-Tyng Chen
Institute of Creative Industries Design, National Cheng Kung University, Tainan, Taiwan
pa8021039@ncku.edu.tw

Shun-Nung Huang
Institute of Creative Industries Design, National Cheng Kung University, Tainan, Taiwan
pa8021055@ncku.edu.tw

Chien-Hsu Chen
Department of Industrial Design
National Cheng Kung University
Tainan, Taiwan
chenhsu@mail.ncku.edu.tw

Sheng-Fen Chien
Institute of Creative Industries Design & Department of Architecture, National Cheng Kung University, Tainan, Taiwan
schien@mail.ncku.edu.tw

CHI PLAY '14, Oct 19-22 2014, Toronto, ON, Canada
ACM 978-1-4503-3014-5/14/10.
http://dx.doi.org/10.1145/2658537.2662975

Abstract
Hidden Lion is a Location Based Service (LBS) with an APP game to promote the sword lion culture in Anping, Taiwan. We combine elements of geocaching, cultural tourism, and arcade-style gameplay in Hidden Lion. Players wander in Anping to find the sword lions, and when they find one, they are directed to an interactive game and learn the background story of the particular sword lion as well as connections to local cultural organizations. Furthermore, Hidden Lion is a service system that integrates the public sector of Anping district office, the commercial sector of local business association, and the cultural sector of Sword Lion School. Hidden Lion demonstrates a service framework of city and cultural tourism that is enabled by multi-touch, sensing and geo-location technologies through gaming and gameplay. The service framework may be applicable beyond cultural tourism to onsite learning as well.

Author Keywords
Location based game; APP; sword lion; service design.

ACM Classification Keywords
H.5.2. [Information Interfaces and Presentation]: User Interfaces; H.5.1. [Information Interfaces and Presentation]: Multimedia Information Systems.

Figure 1. One of the sword lions

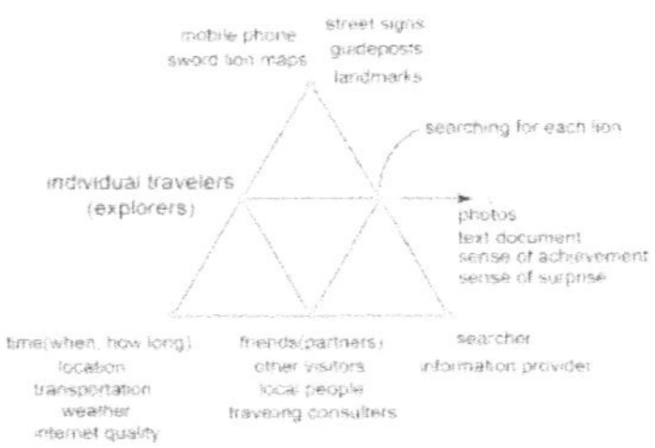

Figure 2. Activity structure of sword lion searching

Figure 3. Persona of target users

Introduction

Sword Lion symbolizes the protector god in Anping. In the old days, local people put sword lions in front their houses because they believed that the stone plated statues (Figure 1) might keep evil spirits away. For decades, the statues weathered and decayed, and some destroyed. In recent years, with the revival of local cultural heritage, Anping visitors are attracted to search for the remaining sword lions and learn the cultural stories of these protectors.

However, sword lion searching has some problems:

1. Sword lions are scattered and difficult to identify.
2. The searching activity may disturb local residents.
3. Visitors do not know stories of various sword lions.

Thus, we design Hidden Lion to assist sword lion searching. The aim is to develop a LBS APP game that has a connection with the local culture. Three types of methods are employed in the design process: user and activity study, service design and game design. Important technologies such as Google map, compass, image recognition and multi touch and sensors (e.g. Apple iBeacon) are also adopted to help the implementation. By integrating all these design methods and practical technologies, Hidden Lion is created and the whole service system is constructed.

Related Work

We design Hidden Lion to combine elements of geocaching, cultural tourism, and arcade-style gameplay. Our searching mechanism is similar to Geocaching, a game of treasure-hunting using GPS [1]. For cultural tourism, Time Treks [2] is a history based LBS game that posts questions before players visit target historical sites. After arriving sites and answering the required questions, players are given clues before traveling to the next site. Thus, players can track clues and learn historical stories while playing the game. Combine geocaching and cultural tourism, O'Munaciedd [3] is a GPS treasure hunting game. Players travel along the tourist route in the city of Matera, and follow the clues to find treasures to earn rewards. Thus, players learn about local culture by playing games and visiting the heritage and landscape. Our on-location, arcade-style gameplay is similar to PiNiZoRo [4], a LBS game on mobile device to encourage obese children to conduct physical activities. Parents plan purposeful neighborhood walking by creating custom quests for their kids; kids walk and explore in the neighborhood to conquer the quests. In evaluation, parents showed enthusiasm for the concept, implementation, and gameplay.

Methodology

User Study

We interviewed people who have done sword lion searching in Anping. We adopted activity theories [5, 6] to analyze the details of sword lion searching activity (Figure 2). Through interviews and activity analysis, we identified our users to be parents with kids, and couples. We designed two personas for these two groups. For Hidden Lion, we identified target users as parents and kids, and the respective persona is Mrs. Hsueh (Figure 3).

Service Design

We used a set of service design tools (cf. [7]). With the help of these tools, we realize the needs of users and stakeholders, as well as the connections between touch

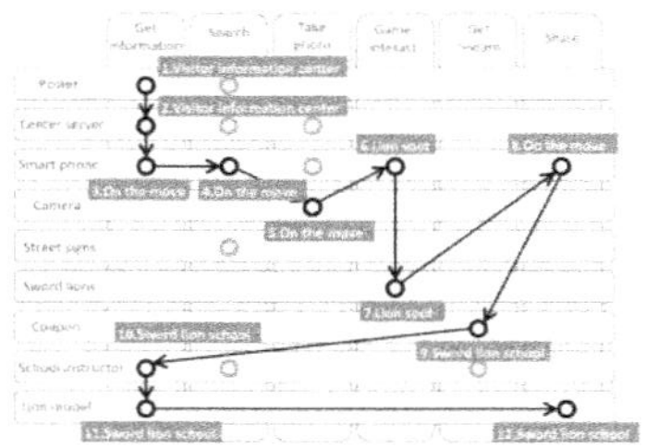

Figure 4. Touch-points and the journey of Mrs. Hsueh

Figure 5. Anping island in Hidden Lion

Figure 6. Detailed view of Hidden Lion: Empire City zone

points [8] (Figure 4). Thus, we were able to come up with more design ideas.

Game Design
We added dramatic elements to create the game story. Since Anping was an island in the past and sword lions could fend off evils, our story starts with that "Anping is attacked by evil spirits and powerful lions are imprisoned..." Therefore, players need to locate the imprisoned lions and play onsite mini games to set them free, and thus defeating evils and bringing peace in Anping again.

Implementation

Technological support
The Hidden Lion LBS game is implemented as an iOS App. The system uses the Google map service as the main navigation view and connects to the Parse data-cloud service. The Moodstocks plugin is used to perform image recognition. The system also employs the iBeacon technology for distance tracking onsite. All technologies used in Hidden Lion are listed in Table 1 below.

Technology	Purpose
Google GPS	Map guide
Electronic Compass	Direction orientation
Image recognition	Scan sword lion to trigger onsite mini game
Multi-touch	Touch event to click or swipe items
iBeacon	Distance detection between objects and players

Table 1.Technologies used in Hidden Lion

For example, in one onsite mini game, Apple iBeacon is used to detect if players actually pass through five spots to form a star-shape figure. The spots are marked with boxes of bagua symbols. Each box contains an iBeacons so that the system may infer if players are at the correct spot. In another onsite mini game, players are require to clean up bubbles covering a lion. We use multi-touch functions to allow various types of wiping/mobbing.

User Interface Design
In Hidden Lion, Anping is presented as an island divided into four zones. Each zone consists of five to six sword lions. Each zone is designed specifically according to the real environment with features in the respective region of Anping (Figure 5). The style of the detailed view for searching sword lions and looking up information also follows the style of each zone (Figure 6). In the searching process, players focus on the detailed view to find locations of sword lions. In addition, the view also shows historical sites and famous restaurants in Anping.

In Hidden Lion, players begin by choosing a desired zone, where detailed map is shown guiding players to search for sword lions. Once discovering a lion, players press "catch" to take a photo of the lion, and in the same time, the system uses image recognition to match the with the target lion stored in the database. A successful match triggers the mini game of that particular site. For example: players need to clean bubbles for the Bath sword lion, or they need to run a star-figure route to release the Yu Jian Er sword lion. These mini games are related to the background story of each sword lions. After finishing all the games, players receive a coupon from the Sword Lion School

Figure 7. Main playing process of Hidden Lion

where they can make their own sword lion status (Figure 7).

Evaluation

Four users (a student and three families) were invited into the evaluation. We asked them to think aloud while playing Hidden Lion. They are all fond of Hidden Lion, but with common complaints: poor in-game instructions. Some places, more instructions are needed. Other places, too much information confuses players of what they have to do next. Therefore, we are revising in-game instructions to achieve clarity.

Conclusion

Hidden Lion is a service system that integrates the public sector of Anping district office, the commercial sector of local business association, and the cultural sector of Sword Lion School (Figure 8). The service framework may be applicable beyond cultural tourism to onsite learning as well.

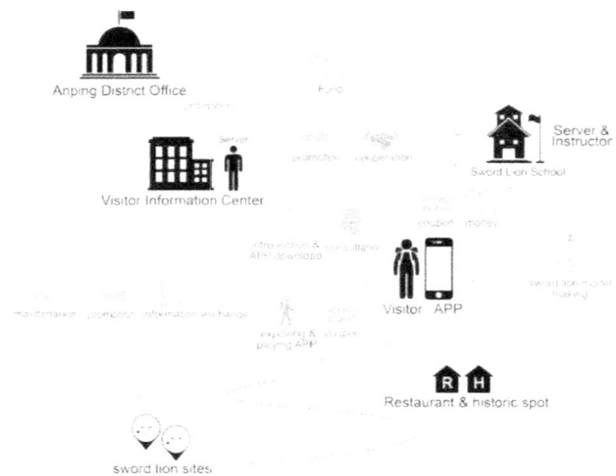

Figure 8. Hidden Lion service system

Acknowledgements

We thank the reviewers for invaluable comments. The development of Hidden Lion is partially sponsored by a grant from the Smart Seed Union (under Talent Cultivation Program for Smart Living Industry, MOE Taiwan).

References

[1] Lynch, M., *Location, Location, Location - A Review Of Location Based Gaming.* Journal of International Computer Science, 2012. **18**(15).

[2] Kim, H. and J. Schliesser, *Adaptation of Storytelling to Mobile Entertainment Service for Site-Specific Cultural and Historical Tour.* Information and Communication Technologies in Tourism, 2007: 97-108.

[3] Guardia, D.L., M. Arrigo, and O.D. Giuseppe, *A Location-Based Serious Game to Learn About the Culture.* International conference the future of education, 2010.

[4] Stanley, K.G., et al., *PiNiZoRo: A GPS-based Exercise Game for Families.* Proceedings of the International Academic Conference on the Future of Game Design and Technology. ACM, 2010.

[5] Kuutti, K., *Activity Theory as a Potential Framework for Human-Computer Interaction Research.* Context and consciousness: Activity theory and human-computer interaction, 1996: 17-44.

[6] Uden, L., *Activity theory for designing mobile learning.* Mobile Learning and Organisation, 2007. **1**(1): 81-102.

[7] Tassi, R., Service Design Tools. http://www.servicedesigntools.org

[8] Brugnoli, G., *Connecting the Dots of User Experience.* Journal of Information Architecture, 2009. **1**(1).

ASPECT Sinking and Floating: An Interactive Playable Simulation for Teaching Buoyancy Concepts

Shengyen Tony Chen
North Carolina State University
890 Oval Drive
Raleigh, NC 27695 USA
stchen@ncsu.edu

Ryan Grady
North Carolina State University
College of Design
Raleigh, NC 27695 USA
regrady@ncsu.edu

David Borland
University of North Carolina at Chapel Hill
RENCI
100 Europa Drive Suite 540
Chapel Hill, NC 27517 USA
borland@renci.org

James Minogue
North Carolina State University
Department of Elementary Education
Campus Box 7801
Raleigh, NC 27695 USA
james_minogue@ncsu.edu

Marc Russo
North Carolina State University
College of Design
Campus Box 7701
Raleigh, NC 27695 USA
marc_russo@ncsu.edu

CHI PLAY '14, Oct 19-22 2014, Toronto, ON, Canada
ACM 978-1-4503-3014-5/14/10.
http://dx.doi.org/10.1145/2658537.2662978

Abstract
Traditional methods of teaching concepts relating to buoyancy (sinking and floating) to elementary students are often ineffective. With the development of new const-effective haptic controllers, we may be able to improve upon traditional teaching methods. Data was gathered during focus groups with both teachers and students to develop a list of misconceptions to target. In addition to targeting misconceptions, we use a Novint Falcon [1] haptic force feedback controller to enable direct feeling of forces. To effectively merge the haptic controller into the system usability testing was performed. This paper presents the initial findings of our interactive playable simulation.

Author Keywords
Games; Simulation; Haptics; Elementary School Education; Buoyancy; Conceptual Physics; Intelligent Tutoring Systems; HCI

ACM Classification Keywords
H.5.2 [Information interfaces and presentation]: Haptic I/O; K.3.1 [Computers and Education]: Computer-assisted instruction (CAI); K.8.0 [General]: Games

Introduction

Haptics can be defined as the study of touch and/or human interaction using touch [6]. The use of haptics in K-12 is relatively new. Williams[9] stated that prior to the publication "literature regarding the use of haptics in K-12 education seems to be nonexistent." Even though there have been advances in haptic controllers in education since, only a few have discussed teaching concepts of physics [8]. Our design focuses on creating an interactive playable simulation that will teach buoyancy-related concepts to elementary school students. Some inspirations come from Loverude's experimental design [5].

With little research regarding haptics in K-12 education, we wanted to know if haptics will have a positive impact on learning. First we looked at traditional methods of teaching buoyancy in elementary school. In traditional methods students are given a ball of clay and a tub of water. The students are then asked to create an object using the ball of clay that will not sink. This concept of making a hypothesis and experimenting is well documented in Klahr et al's theory of scientific discovery as dual search (SDDS) [4]. Using the idea of SDDS, De Jong et al. [3] discuss how to create computer simulations to encourage scientific discovery learning.

Following the concepts of De Jong et al., designing the experiments is crucial. We hypothesized that being able to interact with objects in controlled simulations targeting common misconceptions using haptics, students will be able to develop a better understanding of buoyancy.

Methodology

Designing the simulation was a four step process. First we conducted a focus group study to determine if the traditional method of teaching buoyancy was effective.

Using the results from the focus group study we then designed parts of the simulation to correct common misconceptions. Then usability testing was conducted to improve simulations. Lastly, we refined parts of the simulation and turned it into a fluid interactive playable experience.

Figure 1: Student performing experiment in focus group.

For our focus group, gave a pretest to ten fifth-grade students asking them why things sink or float. After the answers were recorded, we used the traditional method of teaching buoyancy. Students were given a clay ball and a tub of water to experiment with. Each student was instructed to create an object that will float. After the session was completed, many students were able to design an object that will float. We then asked each student again why things sink or float. During the pretest all students stated that heavy things sink and light things float with only two students suggesting either material or size. The post test result showed that six out of ten students (60%) still believed that weight was the only

Figure 2: Four objects same size different material.

Figure 3: Four objects different size same weight.

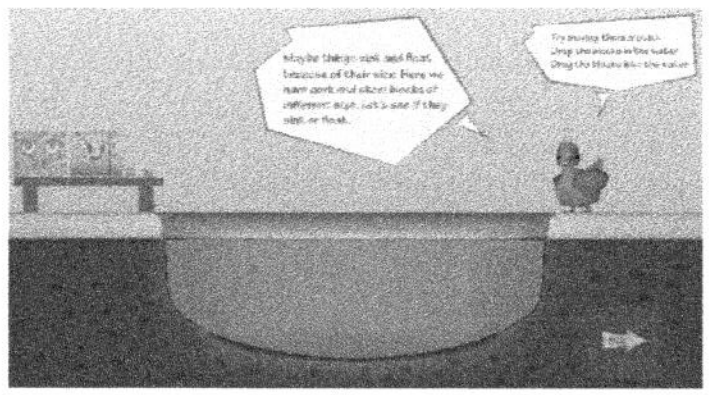

Figure 4: Four objects, two materials with two sizes.

Figure 5: Two materials multiple different shapes.

factor with the remaining four (40%) discussing shape, mass, material, and water content as determining factors.

This misconception of heavy things sink and light things float was something that traditional methods did not address. During our design phase we wanted to target three dimensions of sinking and floating. These dimensions are material, size, and shape. We designed a series of experiments (Figures 2-4) that showed how these three dimensions can affect why things sink or float[1]. Using these four scenes, students are able to experiment with different objects while using a Novint Falcon device as shown in Figure 6.

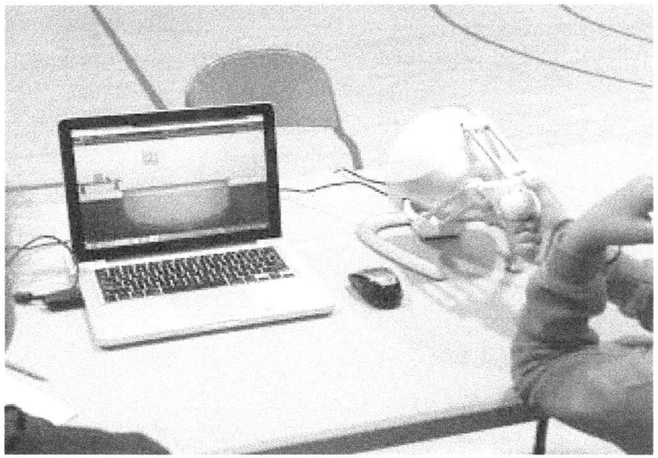

Figure 6: Students using a Falcon device.

We tailored the scenes in this order to target misconceptions one at a time. First we designed a scene in which all objects have the same size but different material. When experimenting in this scene students might realize that material and/or weight are factors. To target the misconception of weight by itself being a contributing factor, the second scene presents objects that have the same weight but different sizes. Next, the student can play with objects that have the same material but different sizes. Lastly, we present different shapes to try to get students to consider that combination of each dimensions affect buoyancy.

The three degree of freedom force-feedback controller enables the students to feel both the weight of the object and the net weight and buoyant force when submerged if force feedback is turned on. We hypothesized that being able to directly feel the forces involved in sinking and floating will help students think about more abstract concepts. A pool of 48 third and fifth graders were asked to play through the simulation. To establish a comparison of the benefits of haptics, roughly half the population (23 out of 24) played through the simulation using the Falcon device without force feedback. As the students played through the simulation, we collected data regarding time spent on different experiments as well as doing pre and post tests. The pre and post tests were scored based on the following SOLO Taxonomy [2]:

- 1 point for having no aspect of buoyancy used in response.
- 2 points for a single aspect of buoyancy used in response (weight/mass, size, shape, material, and force).
- 3 points for having two or more aspect of buoyancy used in response.
- 4 points for having two or more aspect of buoyancy used in response as well as some explanation of aspects.

[1]Download game play video: http://tinyurl.com/m29ejgw

- 5 points for reflecting applications/extensions beyond the immediate context including abstract concepts such as density, volume, and/or water displacement in response.

Results

Our results from the experiment has shown that our simulation increases student understanding, haptics are more effective in third graders than fifth graders (for this simulation), and haptics increase time spent during the simulation.

When evaluating pre and post test, the consensus estimate of interrater reliability was 73% (as a simple percent-agreement figure) [7]. The resulting discrepancies were discussed in person and final SOLO taxonomy scores were assigned. The results showed mostly positive benefits of haptics. On average third graders gained 0.75 point and fifth graders gained 1 point from pre test to post test. Third grade students with force feedback showed and average of 2.64 on the post test compared to 2.08 from students without force feedback. The resulting average for fifth graders was 3 with or without force feedback. And finally, we see that on average students who had force feedback spend longer in the simulation than students who did not have force feedback.

Future Work

ASPECT is a three year long project that will look at the effects of haptics in elementary education. With our preliminary results there are many questions left to answer. One major question is why haptics seemed to have little or no effects on fifth graders. Another question is how can we pinpoint and increase the effects of haptics in educational simulations.

Acknowledgements

This material is based upon work supported by the National Science Foundation under Grant No. 1316473.

References

[1] Novint Falcon. http://www.novint.com/index.php/novintfalcon.

[2] Biggs, J., and Collis, K. Evaluating the quality of learning. *New York* (1982).

[3] De Jong, T., and Van Joolingen, W. R. Scientific discovery learning with computer simulations of conceptual domains. *Review of educational research 68*, 2 (1998), 179–201.

[4] Klahr, D., and Dunbar, K. Dual space search during scientific reasoning. *Cognitive science 12*, 1 (Jan. 1988), 1–48.

[5] Loverude, M. E., Kautz, C. H., and Heron, P. R. L. Helping students develop an understanding of Archimedes principle. I. Research on student understanding. *AJP 71*, 11 (2003), 1178.

[6] Robles-De-La-Torre, G. Virtual Reality: touch/haptics. *Encyclopedia of* (2009).

[7] Stemler, S. E. A comparison of consensus, consistency, and measurement approaches to estimating interrater reliability. *Practical Assessment, Research & Evaluation 9*, 4 (2004), 66–78.

[8] Wiebe, E. N., Minogue, J., Gail Jones, M., Cowley, J., and Krebs, D. Haptic feedback and students learning about levers: Unraveling the effect of simulated touch. *Computers & Education 53*, 3 (2009), 667–676.

[9] Williams Ii, R. L., Chen, M.-Y., and Seaton, J. M. Haptics-augmented simple-machine educational tools. *Journal of Science Education and Technology 12*, 1 (2003), 1–12.

Herbert – A Motion-Controlled Mobile Game

Alexander M. Duff
Drexel University
Computer Science Department
amd435@drexel.edu

Jun Ma
Drexel University
College of Media Arts and Design
jm3675@drexel.edu

Shannon Sepelak
Drexel University
College of Media Arts and Design
sls386@drexel.edu

Alberto Uriarte
Drexel University
Computer Science Department
au49@drexel.edu

Wenjie Wu
Drexel University
College of Media Arts and Design
ww342@drexel.edu

Jichen Zhu
Drexel University
College of Media Arts and Design
jichen@drexel.edu

CHI PLAY'14, October 19–21, 2014, Toronto, ON, Canada.
ACM 978-1-4503-3014-5/14/10.
http://dx.doi.org/10.1145/2658537.2662982

Abstract
Smartphone games lack the hardware interface afforded by other gaming platforms like gamepads, keyboard, mouse or joysticks. Therefore, many popular games for smartphones focus on puzzle mechanics using the touch screen interface, such as *Angry Birds*[1] or *Cut the Rope*[2]. We focused on skill-based, reactionary gameplay with an intuitive control scheme in *Herbert*, where the player moves the character around the world by tilting the device and free oneself from traps by shaking the device to exploit all the possibilities of the accelerometer sensors. We did this in order to minimize on-screen GUI clutter found in other games such as *OMG Pirates!*[3], *Street Fighter IV*[4] and *Zombieville, USA*[5] while retaining the challenge enjoyment, and intuitiveness of skill based gaming.

Author Keywords
Mobile devices; Accelerometer; Shake; Skill game; Chasing; Kiting; Intuitive controls; Motion controls

Introduction
Generally, being infected with a virus is a bad thing, but what if there were a virus that just wanted to live peacefully within the body? In this game, the player takes on the role of Herbert the virus. Herbert is an unlikely hero who leads the White Blood Cells depicted as the body's internal police force to the dangerous

Figure 1 A comic-book styled cutscene explains the premise to the player

germs named Sal Monella. Possessing only the ability to move and to enter his dormant state where he cannot be detected by the White Blood Cells, Herbert cannot destroy his enemies alone. Being a virus, he also must avoid capture by the same white blood cells he must lead to the enemy.

The game is played on mobile devices and controlled using the device's accelerometer as well as touch-screen controls and features an original score.

Target Audience

As of 2012, 46% of adults in the USA own a smartphone, and of cell phone users, 19% own an iPhone[6]. This fact means the iPhone is a prevalent gaming platform to which many people have access. Since a wide array of gamers with different skillsets have access to the platform, *Herbert* is designed to be casual and easy to learn, yet challenging, allowing for players to play as much or as little as they want. Since the game is mobile, it lends itself to short gameplay sessions, such as down time between other activities like when one is waiting for the bus. Due to its relative simplicity in its control scheme and difficulty curve, the target audience is casual smart phone gamers.

Technical Innovations

As we wanted *Herbert* to be accessible to a large audience, it had to be relatively easy to learn the control scheme. We decided to use the features unique to the smartphone platform. We devised a unique control scheme whereby the character's movement was determined entirely by the tilt of the device as measured by the iPhone's accelerometer. In doing so, we were able to give users an experience where they could intuitively control the player character by tilting the phone in the direction in which they wanted the character to move. The sharper the angle at which the user tilts the phone, the faster his movement speed in that direction will be. The character's movement can be thought of as similar to how a ball rolling on a flat surface will behave when the surface is tilted.

When stuck on a sticky surface or stuck to a special sticky enemy, the player can free Herbert by shaking the device. This is also accomplished using the accelerometer by detecting abrupt changes of direction.

Lastly, the player activates Herbert's "dormant" or hiding power by tapping anywhere on the touch screen, except for the pause button, while the game is not paused and Herbert has energy to use the ability.

By not having on-screen virtual controls like up/down/left/right buttons, a button to shake off sticky surfaces, a button to activate his dormancy power, etc., the user interface is very Spartan and uncomplicated. There are only 3 parts of the heads up display (HUD): the remaining time, the pause button, and Herbert's energy bar. This is critical to the user experience as an iPhone 5 has a relatively small display compared to other gaming media, so screen space is precious.

Gameplay Innovations

Many skill-games feature the player winning by directly attacking and defeating his or her enemies. This can be seen in such early games as *Pac-Man*[7], where the player must control Pac-Man in order to eat ghosts and collect pellets, or even *Super Mario Bros.*[8], where the player takes on the role of Mario or Luigi to defeats Goombas and Koopas by jumping directly on them. We, instead, took a different approach.

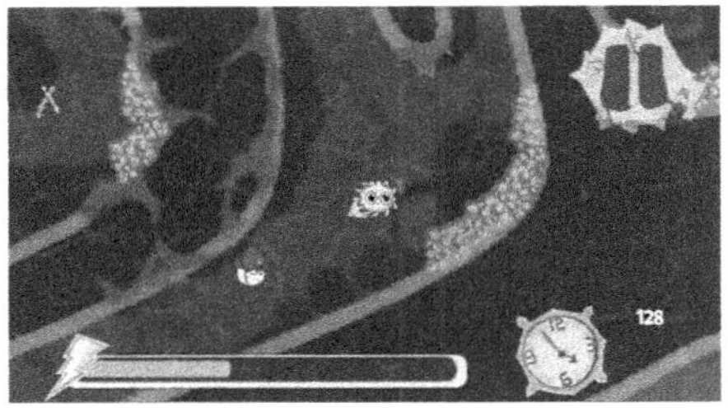

Figure 2 Above, the GUI elements such as pause, energy level, and time as well as Player-Controlled Character Herbert (center), Non-Player-Character WBC, Cholesterol, and Plaque Spikes as well as DNA collectable.

Herbert is a virus hero with absolutely no offensive capabilities who is highly vulnerable to the enemies in his environment like the White Blood Cells. All he can do is move, hide, and shake his way out of traps. Herbert cannot directly attack the enemy germs in the body and he can't defend himself against the White Blood Cell "cops" patrolling the level. Instead, he must attract the attention of the cops and lead them to the more dangerous germs and then hide himself so the cops will attack the more dangerous germs.

This mechanic of using one's enemies to eliminate one's other enemies is something that is distinctly unique to our game. In the following subsections we explain each object of the game and how they influence the gameplay/mechanics.

Main Character (Herbert)

The playable character is a benign virus living peacefully within his host. He is an unlikely hero, timid and classically nerdy. His graphical depiction is designed to reinforce the game's main kiting and hiding mechanics.

Non Playable Characters

The *White Blood Cells or WBCs* are units in the game that are used to destroy the germs in order to progress to the next level. However, they will apprehend Herbert if they catch him, as he is a virus. Herbert must "kite" (approaching the target unit closely enough so as to cause it to attack and then flee outside of its attack range, causing it to give chase, staying far enough to avoid being caught while remaining close enough to keep the enemy chasing)[9] to the germs and then hide so as not to be caught. They can be guarding a location or patrolling. Since it is a skill-game the camera is so close that you cannot oversee the patrol routes and plan a strategy. Therefore we aid the player with a green arrow pointing the nearest WBC.

This will reinforce our goal to make a reactive game rather than a tactical game.

Sal Monellas are the true enemies of the game. The objective is to remove every one of them from a given level before the player can proceed to the next stage.

Environmental Hazards

We added some environmental hazards with two objectives: first we can increase the difficult of the level adding objects that can kill immediately the player (*Plaque Spikes and Calcified Spikes*); and secondly we can reduce the mobility of the player by totally immobilizing it (through sticky green stuff aka "*Cholesterol*") or little dark creatures (*Platelets*) that they will stick to the player and slowing his movement. If the player wants to release himself, they should shake the device (adding a new mechanic and making the game more fun).

Graphical User Interface

Pause Button

Since tapping the screen puts the player in the dormant, state a separate pause button was added. The pause menu also features a way back to the level select screen allowing a player to restart the current level or revisit any previously unlocked level.

Energy Bar

Utilizing the dormant state consumes energy. Energy consumption and collection is displayed along the bottom of the GUI interface housed in a lightning bolt container.

Time Indicator

Each level features a countdown timer represented by a graphical clock and white text that ticks down.

Mechanics and Controls

Movement

The player moves Herbert by tilting the device in the direction they would like Herbert to move. Data from the accelerometer is read in and the x and y values are combined to form a two dimensional vector that governs his movement direction and speed.

Dormant State

Herbert can enter his dormant stat when he has energy and the player taps the phone. In this state, the WBCs will ignore Herbert and he is invulnerable.

Shaking the Device

The accelerometer can detect when the device is shaken. This is used to get out of sticky traps or shake platelets off of Herbert.

Conclusion

Herbert is a unique game play experience for the iPhone 5 or newer. Its novelty comes from both the skill involved in the mastery of the tilt-based movement controls, and the unique kiting techniques the player must perform in order to win the game. The tilt-based movement system is intuitive harkening back to days of playing with ball bearings in wooden mazes.

Playing as Herbert, the timid hero of the story, players can appreciate the way they are able to achieve their goals without directly attacking. This is a unique position in video games with few exceptions such as *Oddworld: Abe's Oddysee*[10] and the results of such gameplay are novel.

REFERENCES

[1] *Angry Birds*.[Online].Finland: Rovio Entertainment, 2009.

[2] *Cut the Rope*.[Online].United Kingdom: ZeptoLab UK Limited, 2010.

[3] *OMG Pirates!*.[Mobile]. Marin County CA United States: Mika Mobile, Inc., 2011.

[4] *Street Fighter IV*.[Format For Your Source???]. Chuo-Ku, Osaka, Japan: Capcom, 2010.

[5] *Zombieville, USA*.[Mobile]. Marin County CA United States: Mika Mobile, Inc., 2009.

[6] A. Smith. "46% of American adults are smartphone owners."[BlogEntry]1 May 2012. *Pew Internet & American Life Project*. Available http://www.pewinternet.org/2012/03/01/nearly-half-of-american-adults-are-smartphone-owners/[Accessed: 23 June 2014]

[7] *Pac-Man*.[Arcade]. Tokyo Japan: Namco, 1980.

[8] *Super Mario Bros.*[Nintendo Console]. New York United States: Nintendo, 1985.

[9] A. Uriarte and S. Ontañón. "Kiting in RTS games using influence maps.": *Eighth Artificial Intelligence and Interactive Digital Entertainment Conference*, AAAI Conference, Stanford, CA, USA, October 12, 2012, AAAI Press. United States: Palo Alto, 2012. pp31-36.

[10] *Oddworld: Abe's Oddysee*.[Play station Console]United Kingdom: Oddworld Inhabitants, 1997.

ASCENT: A First Person Mountain Climbing Game on the Oculus Rift

Tristan Dufour
ENJMIN, Cnam
Angoulême, France
dufour.tristan@gmail.com

Théo Torregrossa
ENJMIN, Cnam
Angoulême, France
torregrossatheo@gmail.com

Ricardo Ibarra Cortes
ENJMIN, Cnam
Angoulême, France
rd.ibarrac.859@gmail.com

Vincent Pellarrey
ENJMIN, Cnam
Angoulême, France
vincentpellarrey@gmail.com

Vladimir Nachbaur
ENJMIN, Cnam
Angoulême, France
vizigr0u@gmail.com

Jonathan Clermont
ENJMIN, Cnam
Angoulême, France
joooclermont@gmail.com

Philippe Chagnon
ENJMIN, Cnam
Angoulême, France
ph.chagnon@gmail.com

Cheng Li
ENJMIN, Cnam
Angoulême, France
vue@gmx.fr

Florent Dumas
ENJMIN, Cnam
Angoulême, France
dumasflo@gmail.com

Ahmed Majdoubi
ENJMIN, Cnam
Angoulême, France
ahmed.majd@gmail.com

CHI PLAY '14, Oct 19-22, 2014, Toronto, ON, Canada
ACM 978-1-4503-3014-5/14/10.
http://dx.doi.org/10.1145/2658537.2662969

Abstract
ASCENT is a first person mountain climbing game on the Oculus Rift (PC). The player attempts to ascend the highest peaks of each continent. Equipped with two ice axes, he challenges the breathtaking slopes of mountaineering legends such as the Eiger, Denali and Mount Everest. His ascents are captured by his GoPro and watched by millions on the web. Thanks to his sponsors and his fans, the player will be able to test himself on new mountains and upgrade his equipment.

Author Keywords
Student game; oculus rift; virtual reality;

Features
- Feeling of the mountaineer: a precise and fluid climbing mechanic
- 35 missions to reach seven famous summits
- Total immersion in the extreme environments of high altitude mountaineering
- Tailor made for Virtual Reality

Overview
- Platform: PC + Oculus Rift
- Genre: Mountain climbing game
- Setting: Extreme sport

- Target: VR enthusiast, Extreme Sports enthusiast
- Status: Preproduction

Intentions

Be a mountaineer

ASCENT is a mountain climbing game. The ambition of the team has always been to put the player in the shoes of a mountaineer, by using a set of iconic climbing characteristics while neglecting other, as we did not want to make a simulation game. The goal was to make the player live the fantasy. To this end, our core gameplay revolves around the mountaineer's main activity: climbing. This choice is one of the originalities of the project but also its major challenge. Our game system, from which stems the challenge of ASCENT, and that has to be rich enough to fascinate the player for hours, is mountain climbing. Secondary and exotic mechanics do come to enrich the core gameplay, but the game never steers away from what it does best: mountain climbing.

The mountain as if you were there

Before the player starts to feel like a mountaineer, he has to have the impression of being on a real mountain. Several elements in Ascent contribute to this illusion. NASA satellite maps were used to recreate the true topology of mountains such as Himalayas, Alps, Alaska Chain... The visual rendering of ASCENT is realistic. The sound was not neglected with the establishment of a binaural sound system.
This will to enhance the immersion of ASCENT is also one of the main reasons for the choice of the Oculus Rift. From the first test of the virtual reality headset, the team was unanimous in its enormous immersive potential. But playing demos and games that used the device, we realized we could not simply add a few lines of code to our game to make it compatible with virtual reality. To be successful the game should be tailored for the device as it demands considerations in game design, ergonomics and very specific visual design (motion sickness strongly related to the game design itself and user interface considerations). As of today, most games compatible with the Oculus Rift are not taking into account these new challenges and deliver poor experiences. Our ambition is to create a product that fully exploits virtual reality. As such ASCENT is not playable without the Oculus Rift.

Game User Research

Our research on the usability of the Oculus Rift is charting new territory, as few developers have seriously worked with the device. We spent the necessary time testing the device and benchmarking as much VR games as possible. The two main issues that plague the Oculus Rift experience are motion sickness and accessibility/legibility of information. Consequently we put these considerations at the heart of ASCENT's conception. To this end, it became necessary to emit a new set of guidelines that would frame the game designer's decision model, and underline at each step of the development the importance of usability.
In order to observe how much players were affected by motion sickness we chose a questionnaire widely used in the aeronautic industry: the Simulation Sickness Questionnaire by Kennedy, Lane, Berbaum & Lilienthal (1993). The score comparison obtained with this questionnaire before and after the experimentation showed a slight degradation of Oculo-Motor and Nausea dimension (average of +1.25). Those results validated

the design decisions that stemmed for guidelines and in our opinion enhanced the user experience.

Game World

The Seven Summits are the highest mountains of each continent. There are seven of them (from the highest to the lowest): Mount Everest, Acongua, Mount McKinley, Kilimanjaro, Mount Elbrus, Mount Vinson, Puncak Jaya. To have a chance of accomplishing this feat, the player will have to complete missions to legitimize his status, attract sponsors, develop his fan base and upgrade his equipment.

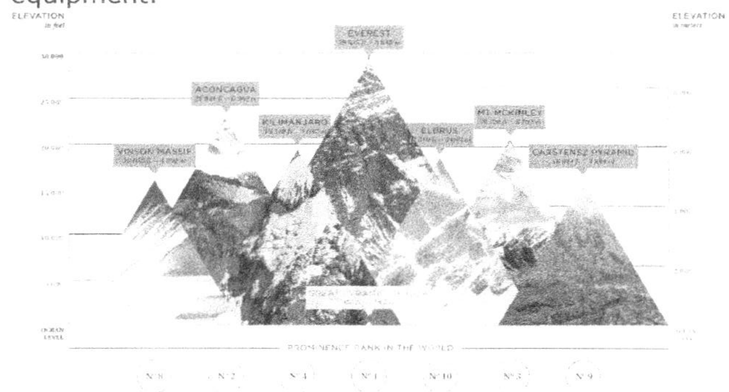

Global Structure

Player progression in ASCENT is relatively linear. Once the player reaches the summit of one mountain, he goes on to tackle the next one. Each mountain constitutes a chapter of the game. A series of missions kicks of the chapter. The player must complete these to unlock the "Summit Push", the grand finale during which the player reaches the summit.
The missions underline different aspects of the core climbing mechanic and introduce new challenges. The "Summit Push" is the heart of ASCENT: the player will have to apply everything he has learned during the missions.

Main objective

The main objective determines the behavior the player is going to have to take during the mission, while informing him of the various choices he can make. The main objective can insist on different player skills (precision, reflexes, management, tactical). The forms of the mission and its mode have a great influence on which player skills will be tested. If the player doesn't complete the main objective he fails the mission.
Special variables can affect a great variety of elements. They enable us to propose new challenges to the player and call forth his mastery of a specific skill:

- Stamina: lower/augment the player's base amount of stamina
- Surface properties: change amount of swings it takes to anchor ice axe, not allowed to anchor in soft surfaces
- Focus system: modify regen of streaks and stamina loss mitigation, player must reach streak 3 and never break it.
- Consumables: limit use of consumables (energy oxygen)

Precise and fluid climbing

In ASCENT, climbing can be reduced to a succession of ice axe anchors in the mountain face. An ice axe anchor is the positive output of an ice axe swing, where the player securely attaches himself to the mountain face. Through this sequence of actions the player can explore the game environment.

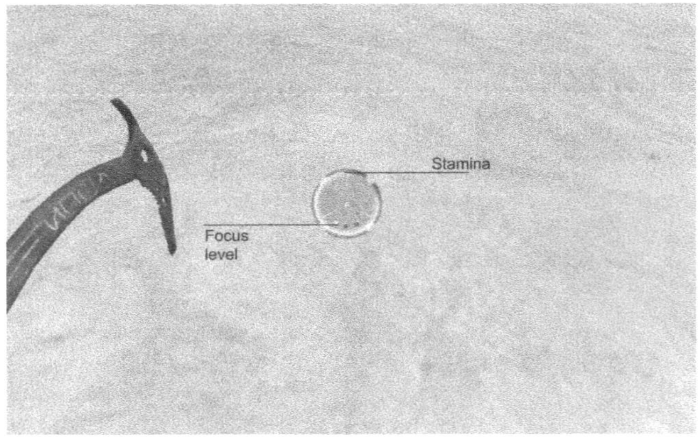

Because the player embodies one of the world's finest mountaineers, the game feel of climbing has to support his expertise. Through our controls we have attempted to convey a feeling of mastery. The control scheme of ASCENT (in vertical situation) is original. It relies on the gyroscopes and accelerometer of the VR headset for camera control and ice axe aiming. The rest of the inputs, like the jump, are mapped to a gamepad, in this case an Xbox 360 controller.

Managing your effort: stamina

Mountaineers must be careful not to burn all their energy before reaching the summit. Exhaustion can have dire consequences high up on the mountain. We wanted to incorporate this aspect of the sport in ASCENT.

To this end we implemented a stamina gauge. When the gauge is depleted the climber is in a state of exhaustion and will fall off of the mountain. Because each of the player's actions have a stamina cost, stamina management is often required of the player if he hopes to reach the end of the level.

Through the necessity of stamina regeneration we also introduced a system that rewards mastery of the primary climbing mechanic. Each time the player performs five successful and swift ice axe anchors, his stamina is regenerated and he enters a level of Focus. To reach the highest Focus level the player must perform fifteen consecutive perfect ice axe anchors. If the player ever slows down or misses an ice swing, his Focus level is reset.

The Focus system incentivizes risk taking. The higher Focus level the player reaches the faster he goes, the more views he gets but the more stamina his actions cost. This means that an error at a high Focus level is more costly that an error at a lower level. The increase in speed also raises the difficulty of the game, as the player has less time to aim (precision skill), must be quicker at dodging rock and snow fall (reflex skill) to determine his route (tactical) and to watch his stamina (management).

UnderControl an Educational Serious-Game for Reproductive Health

Victor Guana
University of Alberta
Edmonton, Alberta. Canada.
guana@ualberta.ca

Ella Schepens
University of Alberta
Edmonton, Alberta. Canada.
sella@ualberta.ca

Tracy Xiang
University of Alberta
Edmonton, Alberta. Canada.
xxiang@ualberta.ca

Eleni Stroulia
University of Alberta
Edmonton, Alberta. Canada.
stroulia@ualberta.ca

Hannah Zhang
University of Alberta
Edmonton, Alberta, Canada.
chzhang@ualberta.ca

CHI PLAY'14, October 19–21, 2014, Toronto, ON, Canada.
ACM 978-1-4503-3014-5/14/10.
http://dx.doi.org/10.1145/2658537.2662983

Abstract
Educational serious games are effective tools to communicate topics of interest to diverse audiences through well defined gameplay designs. In recent years, reproductive health has become an area of special interest for government and health organizations when designing educational programs for teens and young adults. In this paper we present UnderControl, a multi-level mobile serious game that educates players about contraception and STI prevention in an elegant, yet straightforward fashion.

Author Keywords
video game; reproductive health

ACM Classification Keywords
H.4 [Information Systems Applications]: Miscellaneous

Introduction
According to the World Health Organization (WHO) reproductive health focuses on the reproductive mechanisms, behaviors and functions at all stages of human life[1]. Furthermore, two of the major components within the WHO framework for reproductive health are birth control, and Sexual Transmitted Infections (STI) prevention. Indeed, the promotion of informed birth

[1] http://www.who.int/reproductivehealth/en/

control practices, and STI prevention mechanisms, is a big concern for governments and health organizations around the globe [1]. In [2], Gabarron et al. studied how a gamified applications can be used to raise public awareness of STI prevention and reproductive health. Following a similar principle, we created UnderControl, a mobile game for Android and iOS devices that employs interactive gaming to educate players about contraception methods, and STI prevention mechanisms.

Related Work

Educational games on reproductive health are very limited on mobile platforms, particularly in terms of the quality of content they provide during their gameplay experience. UnderControl covers a variety of topics surrounding contraception and safe sex, offering great educational value while effectively engaging players through a real-time strategy model. Let us now review some the games available for mobile platforms that involve reproductive health content.

Spermys Journey[2] and *Sperm Race*[3] are both endless-running games where the players tilt their device left or right to move the character on the screen and collect coins, while avoiding obstacles. Although information about the real life's mechanics of some contraceptives methods is presented in both games, a concrete educational message is not conveyed. Unlike UnderControl, both games lack information about a complete range of available contraceptives and STI prevention mechanisms. Other web-based sexual education games, such as *Avert Games*[4], are arcade quiz games. Despite they great educational value, it is difficult for young players to obtain a high degree of motivation as they may not find their gameplay particularly engaging.

Gameplay Design

The main goal of UnderControl's gameplay is to palace a variety of contraceptives with different defensive capabilities around a female egg, in order to stop the sperms from reaching it (see Figure 1). Contraceptives have to be acquired using the game currency. Currency units can be obtained every time a sperm is captured Currently, UnderControl has four levels, each one introduces different contraceptive methods (as defense mechanisms), and new STIs (as enemies that have to be blocked).

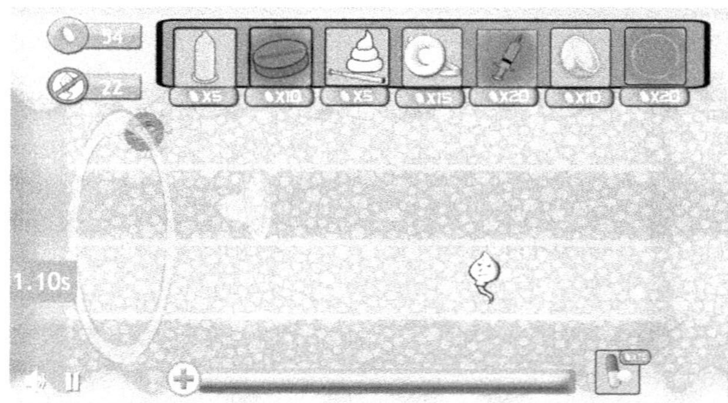

Figure 1: UnderControl Level 4 - Gameplay Design

Birth Control Education Gameplay Elements: The methods of contraception presented in UnderControl are analogous to their roles in real life.

STI prevention Gameplay Elements: An overview of the STIs that the player will encounter in the game is presented at the beginning of each new level. Also, the

[2]https://itunes.apple.com/ca/app/spermys-journey-race-to-egg!/id741293412
[3]https://itunes.apple.com/ca/app/sperm-race/id824478616
[4]http://www.avert.org/games/sex-education-game

player is expected to realize that the usage of condoms is the most effective way of advancing to the next level.

Level 1: The three most common birth control methods are introduced, namely condoms, oral contraceptives, and spermicide. The player must capture 30 sperm to advance to the next level.

Level 2: The contraceptive sponge and birth control shots are introduced. Furthermore, emergency contraceptives such as the "morning after pill" are also presented, giving the player another chance to continue the level if (s)he fails to protect the egg from the invading sperm.

Level 3: The player unlocks the diaphragm as a new contraceptive method. STIs are also first introduced in this level. The player will encounter Chlamydia, Syphilis and Herpes. Furthermore, the player's "health" is reflected in the health-bar at the bottom of the screen (see Figure 2).

Figure 2: UnderControl Level 3-4 - Gameplay Design

Level 4: The player is given the birth control ring as a new contraceptive method. In this level, three new STIs are introduced, namely Hep-B, HIV and HPV. The player is also introduced to the treatable, but not curable nature of HIV. In this case the player is only able to regain half of their health-bar value using the "medications" button.

User Study

An informal survey composed by five questions was conducted with eleven game testers in order to improve the UnderControl's player experience, and to determine the its potential player demographics.

Player Experience

Regarding the player experience, the survey covers three important aspects of gameplay design, namely perceived difficulty, playability, and visual aesthetics (Questions 1 to 3, see Figure 3).

Question 1 (Figure 3 - Q1) asked participants to rank UnderControl's difficulty on a scale of 1-5: 1=very easy - 5=very difficult. The results show that most players found the difficulty of the game suitable for an engaging game experience. However, the wide range of the responses received indicates that the parameters needed to be adjusted to offer appropriate challenges to players of different skill levels. The games's difficulty level is moderated by three attributes a) number coins provided in the beginning of the level, b) the travelling speed of the enemies, particularly the "sperm actor" and the "STI actors" in later levels, and c) the spawning frequency of the enemies.

The playability of the game was assessed based on the players' satisfaction, learning process, as well as the game's efficiency. Question 2 (Figure 3 - Q2) asked participants to rate their user experience using the following five-point likert scale: 1=poor, 2=acceptable, 3=good, 4=very good, and 5=excellent. Survey results exposed that most players perceived UnderControl's playability in a positive manner. However the results also warranted certain concerns as there were more people giving lower ratings such as "acceptable" and "good". A review of player comments revealed that two actions of the game should be modified, a) the spawning mechanism of the "condom actor" –*"I didn't realize that I should drag and drop the items..."*– and b) the lack of a tutorial level –*"there should be an interactive tutorial, because just with the description, it didn't make a lot of sense"*–. These issues have since been fixed.

When asked about their perception of the game's character and user interface design (Figure 3 - Q3) , the majority of respondents rated UnderControl "4– very good" and "5– excellent".

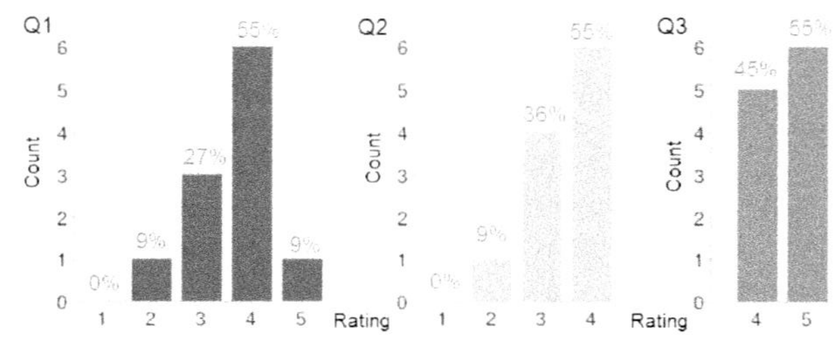

Figure 3: Q1: How difficult do you find this game? Q2: Was this game user-friendly and the instructions relatively easy to understand? Q3: Was this game visually appealing to you?

Demographic Assessment
For Question 4 –*what age group do you consider UnderControl is best suited for?*– the survey results revealed that the large majority of respondents consider UnderControl suitable for youth, especially in the age groups of 13-15 (43%) and 16-20 (35%). Furthermore, 13% of the participants felt that the game is also suitable for age groups 21-29 and 30+. The results point out that although UnderControl is created to appeal to youth, a more mature audience can also benefit from the game's contents. Regarding the perceived gender alignment of the game, investigated in Question 5 –*which gender do you feel this game is best suited to?*– only 36% of the respondents considered that UnderControl is best suited to female players, the majority of respondents (64%) agreed that UnderControl is appropriate for both male and female players.

Game Availability
In this paper we introduced UnderControl, a multi-level mobile serious game that educates players about contraception and STI prevention mechanisms in an elegant, yet straightforward fashion. Furthermore, we presented the results of an informal survey performed with eleven game testers that investigated the perceived player experience, and UnderControl's potential player demographics. UnderControl is available in both Android and iOS application markets.

Android: http://bit.ly/1wqu2Mg
iOS: http://bit.ly/1o3Sr5b
Gameplay Video: http://bit.ly/1u1zE1q

References

[1] G, M., CE, C., and JC, A. Teenagers in the united states: sexual activity, contraceptive use, and childbearing 2006-2010. *Vital and Health Statistics 23*, 31 (2011).

[2] Gabarron, E., Schopf, T., Serrano, J. A., Fernandez-Luque, L., and Dorronzoro, E. Gamification strategy on prevention of stds for youth. *Studies in health technology and informatics 192* (2012), 1066–1066.

CHI PLAY 2014: The Bellman: Subtle Interactions in a Linear Narrative

Daniel Harley
Ryerson University
350 Victoria St
Toronto, ON
M5B 2K3
dharley{at}ryerson.ca

Richard Lachman
Ryerson University
350 Victoria St
Toronto, ON
M5B 2K3
richlach{at}ryerson.ca

CHI PLAY'14, OCTOBER 19–21, 2014, TORONTO, ON, CANADA.
ACM 978-1-4503-3014-5/14/10.
http://dx.doi.org/10.1145/2658537.2662988

Abstract
This paper presents an Internet adaptation of a novella called *The Bellman*. The design is inspired by unconventional video games, particularly with regard to how interaction affects a narrative. *The Bellman* explores how simple mechanics can be part of the storytelling, and can have an impact on the player's emotional response. *The Bellman* is available at www.thebellman.ca.

Author Keywords
Internet; narrative; interactive; games; storytelling.

ACM Classification Keywords
K.8.0 Personal Computing: Games

Introduction
This paper presents some of the concepts behind the Internet adaptation of a novella called *The Bellman* [6]. The adaptation is difficult to categorize. *The Bellman* could be called linear interactive fiction, but many aspects of its design were inspired by unconventional video games. In this paper, *The Bellman* is considered a game in order to explore how mechanics and available interactions can affect a game's narrative.

The adaptation of *The Bellman* is a website that includes text, photographs, and interactivity. It is programmed with a JavaScript scrolling mechanism known as parallax scrolling, which is essentially a method of controlling the pacing and positioning of objects on the screen. The adaptation focuses on the titular character only, leaving open the possibility of future adaptations for the other characters of the novella. The core mechanics of the website are scrolling and clicking. As the player scrolls down, text and images fade in and out. White bars enter and pass across the screen, delineating space, sometimes revealing photographs. When the mouse cursor is on a clickable photograph, the white bar turns red. Clicking the left mouse button displays the next picture in a sequence. Clicking the right mouse button displays the previous picture. The pictures show the titular character sitting or standing, surrounded by black space (Figure 1). Music plays in the background: intersecting pulses of tones. The first click on a set of images produces another tone, adding to the score.

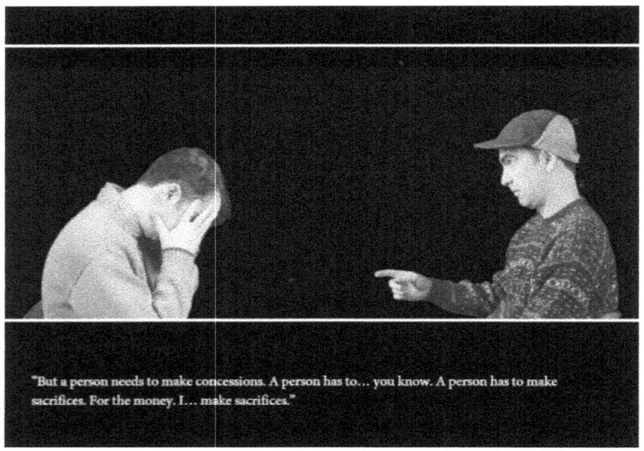

Figure 1. As the player scrolls, text and images fade in and out. The player can click on the images to direct the actor's reactions.

The Bellman is not explicit about what it asks from its audience. The subject matter is slightly absurd, and the presentation is minimalist. The player will not immediately know that they are contributing to the music by clicking on a set of images, or that the right mouse button does not operate as it does on an ordinary webpage, or know what it means when the white bar turns red. These are elements that must be discovered by the player before they can be interpreted. If this creates a sense of unease, it may initiate a parallel between the player and the struggling protagonist of the story. But soon these mechanics are learned, and the player is able to direct the protagonist's reaction to the events. The narrative will remain linear and unchangeable. What changes is a subtle level of control, which may lead to a change in the player's emotional response.

Choice and Emotional Response

The design of *The Bellman* experiments with implied choices in games, choices that are linked to the unassuming act of learning and using the mechanics. These choices, whether meaningful to the narrative or not, can be important for the emotional connection between the player and the story. A similar design consideration can be seen in some recent experimental video games. The following examples show how the mechanics and available interactions in a game can affect the player's interpretation and emotional response.

Dys4ia is a game that uses 8-bit graphics, four short levels, and arrow keys to guide the player through a story about hormone replacement therapy [1]. The player's choices do not alter the outcome of the game, but the gameplay and the interactivity are essential to the player's immersion in the narrative, and the simplicity of the graphics and game design are disarming. *Save the Date* is a comically hopeless dating simulation. Choices usually lead to disaster; the girlfriend dies every time but the player can start over and make dialogue choices that keep her alive a little longer [3]. In a "film for computer" called *BlaBla* [8], the player clicks on and around characters without a clear indication of what the result will be: the characters sometimes respond negatively to the clicking. In *Dinner Date*, the player listens to a character's monologue and can choose how the character fidgets [10].

In *The Bellman,* the player chooses how the protagonist reacts to the text by clicking through a set of images. The goal of this interaction is to involve the player in the emotional state of the protagonist. In many other Internet narratives, choices are primarily related to exploration [e.g. 2, 7, 9]. For *The Bellman*, as for *BlaBla* or *Save the Date,* available interactions are not always positive. The fact that the player can interact does not necessarily mean that they should. The choices in *The Bellman* will not change the text of the story, but the player must implicitly assess their effect and their meaning.

Stout, the creator of *Dinner Date,* argues that in mainstream narrative games, many of the player's choices are essentially meaningless [11]. The player asserts control over puzzles, or challenges, or fighting, but for the most part, the way these tasks are completed will not affect the narrative. Stout's argument is rhetorically reductionist; there is, of course, a lot that can be emotionally rewarding about many in-game choices. But his argument raises important questions about what constitutes meaningful interaction, and how an available interaction can affect a player's experience. The player's choice to use a mechanic to engage with the world can lead to a variety of emotional responses, perhaps especially when the mechanic is aligned with the narrative.

In *BlaBla*, the emotional response might come from a feeling of doubt: is my interaction a form of torment for these characters? In *Dinner Date,* it might come from a feeling of futility: we know that we cannot affect the outcome, but we try anyway. In *Dys4ia*, it might come from the juxtaposition of simple play with difficult subject matter. In *Save the Date,* it might come from a feeling of playful compromise: as we play, we come to an understanding of the game world, but have to accept the repeated sacrifice of a virtual character in exchange. In *The Bellman*, the emotional response might come from an odd feeling of complicity: our clicking on the character, whether aimless or purposeful, will mirror the casual manipulation that the protagonist experiences throughout the story.

The type and range of emotional responses will vary from player to player. What makes this emotional content effective is that it depends on the player as much as the game. The simple mechanics in a game like *The Bellman* belie the importance of the player's interaction. It is not obvious, and it is not meant to be obvious, but the very act of playing the game, of doing what the mechanics offer, will affect the player's relationship with the protagonist.

Conclusion

There is room to explore the emotional impact of such subtle design. The media literacy of the digital audience is increasing [see 4, 5], and works that experiment within genres and formats can diversify the audience's expectations for content. The way that an interaction can add to a narrative will depend on the player and on the story. *The Bellman* was designed through careful consideration for how the medium and the available interactions might affect a player's interpretation.

Acknowledgements

We would like to thank Luke Garwood, Claire Harvie, and Adam Harley. They were indispensable in the making of *The Bellman*. Thanks also to Alexandra Mazalek for her advice and support.

References

[1] Anthropy, A. "Dys4ia." Newgrounds.com. 9 Mar. 2012. Web. 20 June 2014.

[2] Cizek, Katerina. "Highrise/Out My Window." NFB Interactive, 2010. Web. 20 June 2014.

[3] Cornell, Chris. "Save the Date." Paper Dino Software. 2013. Web. 20 June 2014.

[4] Jenkins, Henry. "Convergence Culture: Where Old and New Media Collide." NYU Press, 2006.

[5] Jenkins, Henry. "Confronting the challenges of participatory culture: Media education for the 21st century." Mit Press, 2009.

[6] Harley, Daniel. "The Bellman." Unpublished, 2011.

[7] Mendes, Jeremy and Leanne Allison. "Bear 71." NFB Interactive, 2012. Web. 20 June 2014.

[8] Morisset, Vincent. "BlaBla." NFB Interactive, 2012. Web. 20 June 2014.

[9] Shoebridge, Paul and Michael Simons. "Welcome to Pinepoint". NFB Interactive, 2011. Web. 20 June 2014.

[10] Stout, Jeroen. "Dinner Date." Stout Games, 2011.

[11] Stout, Jeroen. "The Lie of the Grandfather Clock." *Vimeo*. Indiedevelopment. 25. April, 2013. Web. 01 July 2014.

WORD BLASTOFF: A Physics Word Game for iOS

Nook Harquail
149 Division St.
Sartoga Springs, NY
12866
nook@wordblastoff.com

Michelle Khare
11015 Seville Quarters,
Shreveport, LA
71106
michelle@wordblastoff.com

CHI PLAY '14, Oct 19-22, 2014, Toronto, ON, Canada
ACM 978-1-4503-3014-5/14/10.
http://dx.doi.org/10.1145/2658537.2662970

Abstract
Word Blastoff *is a single-player word game app in which players are challenged to create 2 to 7 letter words from a pool of randomly-generated letters that enter the screen and gravitate towards a central black hole. With each letter that it zaps, the hole expands in size and ultimately explodes once it is too large for the screen, ending the game.*

Author Keywords
iOS; word game; physics-based game; casual game design; interface design; nonlinear gameplay; dynamic music

ACM Classification Keywords
D.2.10 Software Engineering, Design; D.2.0 Software Engineering, General

Introduction
Word Blastoff aims to capture the casual gamer audience, those who enjoy playing short games on mobile devices. As an additional goal, we strove to make the game appealing for middle school students who can use the game as an educational tool.

Technological Innovations

This application was written in Objective C over the course of three terms for our senior theses at Dartmouth College. Apple's SpriteKit framework provides a basis for drawing, animation, and physics simulation. Although this does much of the heavy lifting, Apple's code is sparsely documented and somewhat buggy. The situation improved as we developed the app; however, seemingly simple features (such as pausing the physics animation) required hacky workarounds.

Because the app was produced over nine months, we designed and programmed rapidly, testing prototypes with playtesters at each stage. Although we had several false starts and major redesigns, the evolved product is far stronger now, having been tested with players at every stage of the process. Prior to app store launch, we used the TestFlight framework to facilitate the distribution of beta versions of our app to users.

We considered performance primarily in areas where inefficiencies affected gameplay. For example, the game preloads textures and sounds to avoid jumping frames when new letters spawn or hit the black hole. We make heavy use of threading to load large resources such as textures, word lists, and sounds. Other practical considerations include giving players a good distribution of letter types, smoothly increasing difficulty (gravitation attraction to the black hole, letter speed, number of letters, etc.), and changing sound as the player's score and health change. In order to perform fast validation of submitted words, we store words in a Trie data structure — a multi-way tree that allows for very fast word lookup.

Although we spent a good deal of time balancing gameplay and creating a strong word list, the game is also designed to be remotely changeable. The major balancing aspects (level difficulty, score thresholds for unlocking new levels, and the word list) are all fetched remotely when there is a new version available on our servers. Thus, we can adjust the game (e.g. by analyzing rejected words to see if some should be added to the dictionary or increasing level difficulties) in response to data about how the app is being used — without users having to download an update from the app store. In the future, some of these adjustments may be automated.

The ability to define words spelled in the game is provided by the Wordnik API. We use this API because the local dictionary does not contain many of the words in our list. In order to provide better definitions through their API, we lemmatized our dictionary (organized it based on root words). This was accomplished through Apple's NSLinguisticTagger library, analysis of "see also" entries in Wordnik definitions, and open source word lists. The word list is organized based on rarity, so that the game can reward players for spelling uncommon words.

Word Blastoff also functions seamlessly without an Internet connection. Without internet, the app will use the local dictionary rather than the Wordnik API.

Gameplay Innovations

Word Blastoff is a new kind of physics-based word game that rejects the grid-based structure of traditional word games like *Scrabble* (and digital equivalents such as *Words With Friends*). It provides a challenging experience to players of many ages and skill levels.

The majority of word games in the App Store are spin-offs of Parker Brothers' *Scrabble* and *Boggle*, both of which have built a historical significance, nostalgia, and fan culture which originate in the physical media of their respective board games. Roughly 150 million sets of Scrabble board games have been sold worldwide and roughly one-third of American homes have a Scrabble set. This cross-media exposure provides a market advantage that allows the app equivalents of these games to capture the older, less tech-savvy generation segment, in addition to younger tech gurus. Few apps in the word game category have taken risks to break free from these playing norms; the well-ranked spin-offs succeed in capturing the *Scrabble/Boggle* audiences by adding to the games features like social media integration that appeal to younger audiences[1].

These traditional apps and their spin-offs follow a gridded, square, rigidly-structured playing board. To this end, the graphics of each of these games are what architecture, art, and design scholars would call "inorganic." Inorganic shapes, such as squares, triangles, rectangles, are rarely found in nature; they are designed by humankind and are often buildings, furniture, and landscape elements, often demonstrating an aura of "control over nature." None of the graphics employed in these games are organic[3]. Organic shapes are shapes found in nature. They are rounded, serpentine; often they are asymmetrical in form. Aside from simply following the example set by Parker Brothers' *Scrabble* and *Boggle*, we could not find a specific reason as to why this design choice has consistently been made. *Word Blastoff*, on the other hand, uses rounded shapes and a circular, "gravity-free" gameplay, in which round letters move in a circular orbit around the black hole. Players have consistently commented positively on the game's design and aesthetic as one of their favorite aspects of the game.

Perhaps the most critical insight lay in the ubiquitous feeling that a good word game has the pleasant surprise of self-satisfaction. It makes the player feel as though they are intelligent as well as able to learn new words with ease. A key playing tactic which differentiates *Words With Friends / Scramble With Friends* from *Scrabble / Boggle* is the ability to blindly attempt multiple word options without punishment, a quite common and fun strategy; it feels good to discover a new word "by accident." Just as in Words With Friends and other popular word games, we wanted players to experience accidental learning. Employing a similar tactic, players of *Word Blastoff* can attempt words and rearrange letters until a word submits. Additionally, because there is no board or opponents to affect possible words, players can spell any possible word from the available letters without hindrance, thus inciting more "aha!" moments. In this same vein, at the end of the game, the player can view his performance, a list of words submitted and their definitions. Even though the game always ends by losing to the black hole, the post-game experience is one of positivity and recognition of the player's accomplishments. Additionally, from the menu screen, players can access a full analysis of their statistics, including: Best Word (highest scoring), Favorite Word (most used), Vocabulary (variety of words submitted). Players find these features highly encouraging and rewarding; per analytics, many players check their statistics multiple times per day.

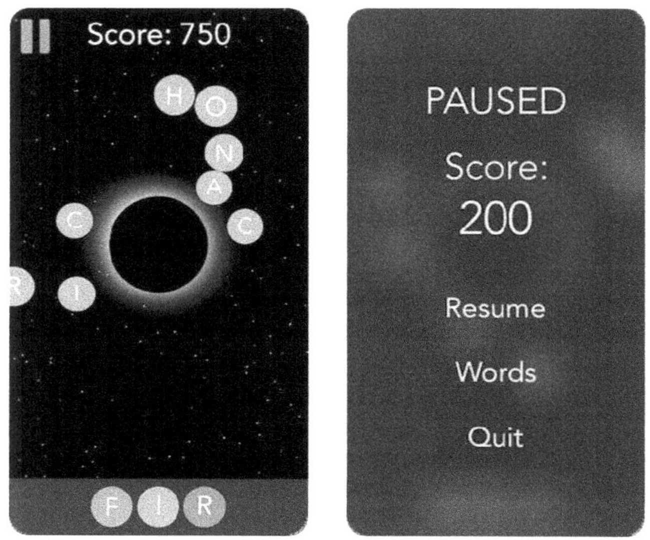

Figure 1: Typical Gameplay.

In designing *Word Blastoff*, we aimed to create a game that takes full advantage of the affordances of the phone. Unlimited by the structure of traditional word games, we can take full advantage of the touch screen — allowing players to form words quickly and efficiently. We also take advantage of several iOS specific features: players can track high scores in Game Center, and shaking the device removes all letters the player has placed on the dock. (This convention of "shaking to clear" is commonly employed by other iOS applications and is familiar to users.)

Figure 2: Statistics and Dictionary Views

Acknowledgements

We are very grateful for the financial support, advice, and guidance of the Neukom DALI Lab at Dartmouth throughout this process. Additionally, we would like to extend a heartfelt thanks to our advisor Professor Lorie Loeb for her unconditional, positive support throughout our galactic journey to create *Word Blastoff*.

Video of Gameplay

http://youtu.be/I74wKAWd-zE

References

[1] "Spell Bound." *The Guardian*. Guardian News and Media, 28 June 2008. Web. 1 May 2014.

[2] Harquail, Nook. "An Annotated List of Word Lists." N.p. Web. 1 May 2014. *http://digitalscholarship.herokuapp.com/*.

[3] "MoMA Learning." MoMA. N.p., n.d. Web. 26 June 2014. *http://www.moma.org/learn/moma_learning/glossary*.

Little Newton: An Educational Physics Game

Natalie Lyon
Drexel University
3501 Market St.
Philadelphia, PA 19104 USA
nel35@drexel.edu

Josep Valls
Drexel University
3501 Market St.
Philadelphia, PA 19104 USA
jv384@drexel.edu

Caroline Guevara
Drexel University
3501 Market St.
Philadelphia, PA 19104 USA
cjg89@drexel.edu

Ning Shao
Drexel University
3501 Market St.
Philadelphia, PA 19104 USA
ns684@drexel.edu

Junyu Zhu
Drexel University
3501 Market St.
Philadelphia, PA 19104 USA
jz464@drexel.edu

Jichen Zhu
Drexel University
3501 Market St.
Philadelphia, PA 19104 USA
jz435@drexel.edu

CHI PLAY '14, Oct 19-22, 2014, Toronto, ON, Canada
ACM 978-1-4503-3014-5/14/10.
http://dx.doi.org/10.1145/2658537.2662985 /or a fee.

Abstract
Little Newton is a 3D defense game in which the player learns about basic physics concepts by controlling physical attributes of projectiles. The mechanics of the game require the player to learn the basics of parabolic arcs, and friction in order to make use of the projectiles. Educational and learning theories are applied to the design in order to increase the ability of the player to learn how to play the game itself and therefore learn physics concepts in the process, balancing entertainment and educational content.

Author Keywords
Games; Educational

ACM Classification Keywords
H.5.2

Introduction
Games possess an innate motivational potential. They are an activity that the player engages in for no other reason than for the sake of the play itself. According to self-determination theory, if an activity can become self-motivating to the participant, he or she will experience increased incentive to continue the activity for its own sake [1]. When the action of the player is a new skill the player did not have before, the player has gone through an act of learning. In order to harness

the potential of these acts of learning for a purpose other than the gameplay itself, educational games can be designed with mechanics that use educational content as the core action.

Little Newton is a 3D defense game that seeks to teach the player about the basic physics concepts of parabolic motion and friction by controlling physical attributes of projectiles. The player character is Little Newton, who defends himself from an army of evil toys by using apples as ammunition and traps. The mechanics at the core of the game require the player to learn the basics of parabolic arcs, and friction. This connection between physics educational material and the physics of the game itself function to take advantage of the learning potential of the game design, harnessing the motivational properties of play mechanics integrated with an activity that increases learning of the targeted concepts. A version of the game playable through the Unity Web Player extension is available at: http://natalielyon.com/LittleNewton.html

Target audience

The target audience of the game is children in schools at the beginning of their physics education. The age at which a student first begins learning physics concepts can vary in the U.S., especially since physics education can begin in a mixed-science format, typical of middle or junior high schools, or in a first class devoted entirely to physics, more typical of high schools. Therefore, *Little Newton* has been designed with a broad age range of children in mind, but focusing primarily on ages 12 to 16.

In order to fit this demographic, the difficulty level has been balanced to provide an appropriate level of challenge for the age range. The level of challenge increases with one concept at a time, and the progression requires players to master one skill before moving on to the next and ultimately combining skills they have learned. A young student may initially find a level challenging, but sufficient information is provided so that the player can solve each level. When a level is failed, it may be immediately replayed, allowing the player to attempt to find the solution over however much time is needed for the individual. To aid with ease of use, the language is sufficiently simple that reading level should not typically provide a barrier to gameplay.

Furthermore, the art style and narrative content of the game are meant to be age appropriate. The colorful world frames a narrative that supports learning as a fun activity. The villains are made extremely cartoon like through both the story of toys coming to life to try to distract the player character, and through the visual style of the bright colors, simple shapes, and cartoonish outlined rendering. These narratological elements are integrated with the ludological focus of the game, the combination of which has been shown to maximize the enjoyment and immersiveness of educational video games [2].

Throughout *Little Newton* gameplay, the player adjusts the force, mass, and angle of impulse of the parabolic in real time to see the effects and defeat enemies of different types.

Figure 1. Parabolic arc control in gameplay of *Little Newton*

Technological and Game Play Innovations

Good video games are "learning machines," or constructions aimed with the purpose of providing the space and tools for learning to take place. Video game design can use educational concepts like giving information "on demand" and "just in time" in order for the players to learn how to play the game easily and intuitively, without undue frustration. They operate at the outside edge of the player's competency, remaining challenging but doable. They also present information in order, allowing the player to make generalizations to solve increasingly complex problems [3].

Little Newton employs these design features for allowing the player to learn the game mechanics as easily as possible. Since the game mechanics themselves are exercises in adjusting the physics properties of friction and force, mass, and angle of impulse for controlling a parabolic arc, the player can therefore learn these basics physics concepts more easily through playing the game. If a player learns to master the mechanics of the game, he or she has also inevitably learned how to manipulate a parabolic arc and the property of friction, combining the effort usually required for pure learning with the effort expended playing the game. The intersection of design constraints with whatever intention the player brings to the game creates a designed experience, which can be effective learning environments [4].

Typically, when a student is learning these same physics concepts of parabolic arc and friction in a classroom, the primary method of teaching these concepts is through diagrams in a textbook.

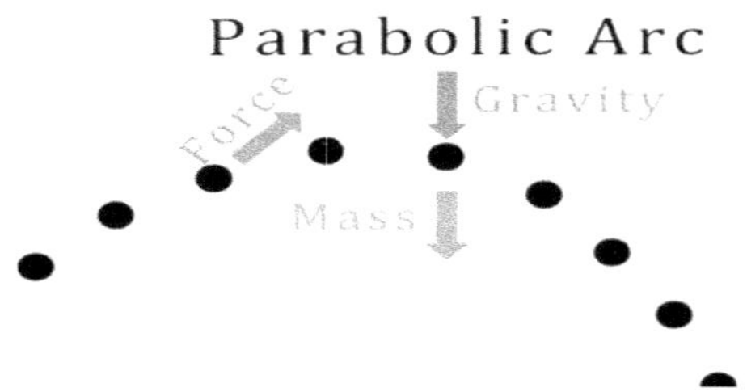

Figure 2. Parabolic arc diagram, typical of physics textbooks.

It is nearly impossible to convey the effects of parameters like Force and Mass on the speed of the object over the course of the arc by this method. By contrast, the method of teaching these concepts through the gameplay of *Little Newton* allows the player to explore what effect each one has on the arc in real time. The player can easily see the effect of each on the shape of the arc previewed by the dotted line when force, mass, or angle of impulse is adjusted. The effect on the speed can be seen in real time as well.

Furthermore, the player must master the control of each of these parameters in real time order to advance past increasingly difficult and nuanced sets of enemies. The combination of the real time controls and the puzzle-like combinations of enemies of different types creates gameplay that is similar to that of traditional tower-defense, but with elements of a real-time strategy game. This unique blend of puzzle and real-time mechanics fosters a fast-paced sense of fun during gameplay. Furthermore, limited ammunition is given to the player on each level, encouraging players to figure out what strategy is most efficient quickly rather than simply by trial and error. Some enemies require precise arc and speed control because of small hit boxes. Some enemies are stationed behind walls, requiring further precision of the arc to reach over the wall. Some must be hit in combination with others, requiring a high amount of control over the speed of the arc. All of these parameters make for many combinations of levels that allow the player the fun of shooting down the enemies in real time with the satisfaction of solving the puzzle of the level.

Additionally, the introduction of new concepts is added one at a time, in a short tutorial type instruction. The concept is then tested by the player in a short level before another concept is introduced. The series of concepts follows a logical progression through the process of learning about parabolic arc and friction.

Through this schema of direct control over physics properties, the gameplay of Little Newton creates a new way to combine learning and entertainment for elementary physics education.

References

[1] R. M. Ryan and E. L. Deci. Self-Determination Theory and the Facilitation of Intrinsic Motivation, Social Development, and Well-Being. *American Psychologist 55*, 1 (2000), 68-78.

[2] C. S. Ang and R. K. Rao. Computer Game Theories for Designing Motivating Educational Software: A Survey. *International Journal on E-Learning 7*, 2 (2008), 181-199.

[3] Gee, J.P. What Video Games Have to Teach Us About Learning and Literacy. *Computer in Entertainment 1,* 1 (2003), 20-20.

[4] K. Squire. Front Content to Context: Videogames as Designed Experience. *Educational Researcher 35,* 8, 19-29.

OHR

Zeno Menestrina
DISI - University of Trento
Via Sommarive, 9
Open Space 11
38123, Trento, TN - Italy
zeno.menestrina@unitn.it

Michele Bianchi
DISI - University of Trento
Via Sommarive, 9
Open Space 11
38123, Trento, TN - Italy
jazzinghen@gmail.com

Adriano Siesser
DISI - University of Trento
Via Sommarive, 9
Office 177
38123, Trento, TN - Italy
adriano.siesser@gmail.com

Raul Masu
DISI - University of Trento
Via Sommarive, 9
Open Sapce 11
38123, Trento, TN - Italy
raul.masu@gmail.com

Andrea Conci
DISI - University of Trento
Via Sommarive, 9
Office 177
38123, Trento, TN - Italy
andrea.conci.1@studenti.unitn.it

CHI PLAY '14, Oct 19-22 2014, Toronto, ON, Canada.
ACM 978-1-4503-3014-5/14/10.
http://dx.doi.org/10.1145/2658537.2662987

Abstract

OHR is a puzzle and platform game, based on both classical mechanics and tangible interaction, powered by *Unity3D* and a custom-built hardware interface called *Radiant Square* (Radiant^2). OHR tells the tale of *Spark*, an electronic life form, which wakes up in an electronic components dump, trying to exit from it. Players will help Spark to solve puzzles placed throughout the game world using the provided game elements, represented as physical electronic components, by placing them on the Radiant^2. Thanks to both the game design and Radiant^2 each puzzle can be solved in different ways, allowing the players to explore various solutions. A video presentation of OHR and Radiant^2 can be found at: http://youtu.be/OGhOtuTHAXk

Author Keywords

Game Design Document; Tangible Interaction; Exploration; Platformer; Puzzle; Open Source; Unity3D

ACM Classification Keywords

K.8.0 [PERSONAL COMPUTING]: General; H.5.2 [INFORMATION INTERFACES AND PRESENTATION (e.g., HCI)]: User Interfaces.

General Terms

Game Design Document

Figure 1: Matrix evocation and subsequent positioning of a ground component (i.e. strip)

Introduction

OHR is a puzzle and platform game telling the tale of *Spark*, an electronic life form that wakes up in an electronic components dump, trying to reach the exit of a wasteland. The landscape shows the passage of others like Spark, highlighted by the presence of various contraptions along the way, devised to stop anyone without the proper tools. Spark, however, can evoke electronic components to interact with these contraptions and solve them to continue with its journey.

Figure 2: Radiant^2 and Radiant Blocks in action

OHR is a game developed in Unity3D[1], designed to be played with Radiant^2, a tangible interface designed and built by the team. Radiant^2 is an electronic game board on which the players can place *Radiant Blocks* (both shown in Figure 2), which represent in-game elements. Some Radiant Blocks provide an additional analogical interface with which the players can interact, influencing the game. Radiant^2 communicates with the player by lighting up in accordance to the game status (e.g. by showing where it is possible to place Radiant Blocks).

The game targets players in the age range of 15 to 50, with any level of gaming experience, focusing on Explorers and Achievers player types[2]. OHR is designed to mainly elicit three pleasures[3]: Sensation, Discovery and Expression.

Background

The game takes inspiration from art, animation and game industry. The game graphics are designed to simulate a hand-drawn style, similar to *Amanita Design*'s[4] games (e.g. *Samorost*, *Botanicula*), *Braid* and *Rayman Origins*.

In order to express all the possibilities that the group envisioned for Radiant^2 we developed a game based on both exploration and sandboxing, leaving the players the possiblity to experiment with the Radiant Blocks. This was partly influenced by Rude Godberg simulator games such as *The Incredible Machine*.

The background of the game setting borrows some graphical and story inspirations from various sources: *9*, Paul Klee (Figure 4) and Hieronymus Bosch.

Gameplay

OHR is a puzzle and platform game based on the exploration of the game world and the solution of proposed enigmas. While the proposed game mechanics are not new, they have been designed to be as integrated as possible with the game setting. Puzzles have been designed following Schell's guidelines [7], avoiding evident solutions. This has been chosen to elicit both the Discovery and Expression pleasures, following also the concept that a too easy game bores the players [3]. In order to foster additional creativity OHR was designed to use a custom-built tangible interface [1].

[1] http://unity3d.com/

[2] http://mud.co.uk/richard/hcds.htm
[3] http://8kindsoffun.com/
[4] http://amanita-design.net/

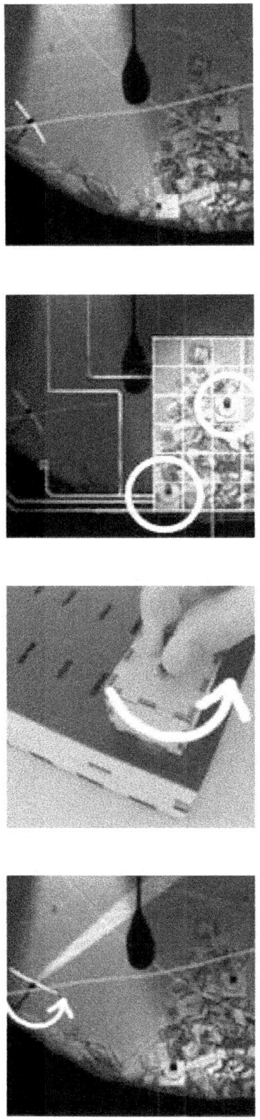

Figure 3: Potentiometers and how Radiant Blocks influence the game world

Solving puzzles revolves around a core mechanic: the matrix evocation. When players evoke the matrix (Figure 1), a 6 x 6 (i.e. the size of the Radiant^2) is superimposed on the game world. The matrix can be moved both vertically and horizontally, provided that it is always on top of Spark. When the matrix is evoked the Radiant^2 is activated, showing information based on the position of the matrix on screen, allowing the players to place Radiant Blocks, representing electronical components, on it. Some components can be placed on the ground (e.g. the strip block shown in Figure 1), while most of them require specific hotspots, called *Universal Sockets* (as the ones shown in Figure 3). Universal Sockets are highlighted on the Radiant^2 with a specific colour (the bright blue cell in Figure 2) and are connected with in-game elements through power lines that light up if electricity flows through them. Most of the components that require a Universal Socket are interactive and provide additional inputs and outputs (e.g. the potentiometers shown in Figure 3). Once the players suppress the matrix all the electronical components, placed on any position they are allowed to, materialize in the game world (Third panel of Figure 1). Electronical components influence elements they are connected to based on their physical status (e.g. an in-game button is pressed only when its physical counterpart on the Radiant^2 is pressed) and disappear from the game as soon as the matrix is evoked again. Puzzles have been designed with internal consistency in mind, mimicking real-world behaviour of electronical devices, making them solvable using various approaches (e.g. a button pressed has the same effect of a potentiometer set at maximum).

The available electronical components (and where they can be placed) are:

Strip (ground) Grows a pin strip ladder

Chip (specific elements in background) Evokes a chip to be used as a platform

Cable (walls and Universal Sockets) Evokes a cable that can be walked, or connects two Universal Sockets

Button (Universal Sockets) A simple button

Potentiometer (Universal Sockets) Allows the players to choose how much current flows through a Socket

Switch (Universal Sockets) If placed on a socket with a single connection acts as a switchable button If placed on a Socket with two connections switches the current flow from one connection to the other

Triple switch (Universal Sockets) Allows the control of three values, such as RGB or a 3-bit number

LED (Universal Socket) A simple LED

E^{2}PROM (Universal Socket) Allows Spark to leave a backup copy, effectively saving the game status

Aesthetical Choices

OHR aesthetics have been created following a single guideline: "The right music coupled with the right visuals is pure magic" [4].

Graphical aesthetics were conceptualised and drawn to resemble as much as possible realistic electronic components, starting from the main character, Spark (Figure 5), to background elements (Figure 6). In order to maintain consistency throughout the game all the puzzles were designed and drawn using electronic components with behaviours coherent to what was the desired in-game effect.

The entire soundtrack of OHR has been composed with the aim of being organic and dynamic. In order to achieve this goal, all the sounds of the game are organized as a *soundscape* [6], and, to guarantee the constituency of the

Figure 4: Paul Klee, *Flagged pavilion (Landscape and yellow church tower)*, 1927

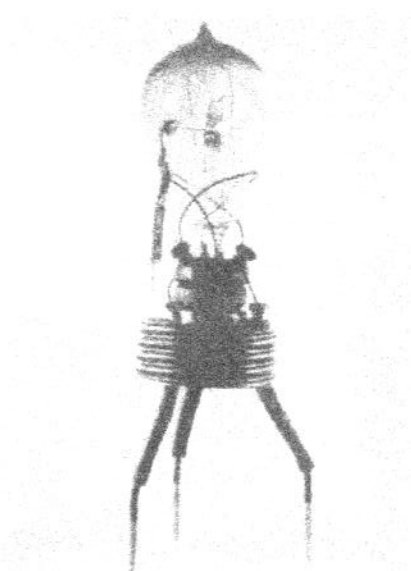

Figure 5: One of the first Fleming valve prototypes, October 1904

Figure 6: Comparison between in game graphics (left) and real world inspirations (right)

design, have been synthesized using the same algorithm (white noise processed with 8 filters and reverb). The audio is organized in a multilayered structure. Each different ambient has is own *background*, representing the environmental noise of the game world. The *foreground* is composed by melodies and effects, both of them can be either *sound signals* or *soundmarks* [6]. Soundmarks may be environmental sounds (e. g. electricity flowing) or gameplay melodies unrelated to specific game events, while the "Win" melody [4] and the "new challenge" melody or sound effects like "right block" and "wrong block" are sound signals. Sound signal melodies have been composed exploiting the mapping between musical parameters and emotions. (e. g. "new challenge" melody should increase the arousal level in the player). [2] [5]

Technical and gameplay innovations

OHR is based on classical gameplay and the use of Radiant[2], which introduces the main innovation. The game allows the player to decide which game elements to use to solve the puzzles and where to place them based on the on-screen location of the matrix. This permits the configuration of a custom physical controller by the players every time a new solution is envisioned.

Future works

We believe that Radiant[2], given its nature, can be used in more applicationts than just OHR, such as other videogames, artistic installations or musical interfaces. These applications will be explored, requiring the design of new Radiant Blocks. One of the possible evolution of OHR, instead, is the removal of spatial constrains for electronic components (i.e. Universal Sockets are not required anymore), increasing the freedom of the player.

Acknowledgements

The authors would like to thank all the people of the MUSE's FabLab (Trento, Italy) and of the electronics lab at the University of Trento (Physics department) for giving us precious insight, along with the access to the tools needed to create Radiant[2]. Cheers also go to Antonella De Angeli, head of the HCI research group at the University of Trento; Marìa Menèndez and Silvia Bordin who helped us with the initial QA and our two under-grad studends, Mattia Digilio and Luca Miozzo, who helped us in design and run usability tests of Radiant[2].

References

[1] Catala, A., Jaen, J., van Dijk, B., and Jordà, S. Exploring tabletops as an effective tool to foster creativity traits. In *Proceedings of the Sixth International Conference on Tangible, Embedded and Embodied Interaction*, ACM (2012), 143–150.

[2] Juslin, P. N., and Sloboda, J. *Handbook of music and emotion: Theory, research, applications*. Oxford University Press, 2011.

[3] Juul, J. *The art of failure: An essay on the pain of playing video games*. MIT Press, 2013.

[4] Marks, A. *The complete guide to game audio: for composers, musicians, sound designers, and game developers*. Taylor & Francis, 2001.

[5] Morreale, F., Masu, R., De Angeli, A., and Fava, P. The effect of expertise in evaluating emotions in music. In *Proceedings of the 3rd International Conference on Music & Emotion (ICME3)* (2013).

[6] Schafer, R. M. *The soundscape: Our sonic environment and the tuning of the world*. Inner Traditions/Bear & Co, 1993.

[7] Schell, J. *The Art of Game Design: A book of lenses*. CRC Press, 2008.

IRC Quest: Using the Commons Dilemma to Support a Single-Screen Game for Hundreds of Players

Dan John Moran
Queen's University
Kingston, ON K7L 3N6 Canada
9djm13@queensu.ca

Carey Metcalfe
Queen's University
Kingston, ON K7L 3N6 Canada
8caom@queensu.ca

T.C. Nicholas Graham
Queen's University
Kingston, ON K7L 3N6 Canada
nicholas.graham@queensu.ca

CHI PLAY'14, October 19–21, 2014, Toronto, ON, Canada.
ACM 978-1-4503-3014-5/14/10.
http://dx.doi.org/10.1145/2658537.2662991

Abstract
In this paper we describe the challenges of creating a game that can be played by large groups on a single display. Our solutions include the use of smart phones as game controllers using the standard IRC protocol, voting-based turn interaction, and automatically customized avatars allowing hundreds of players to appear on the display simultaneously. To provide meaningful gameplay for large numbers of people, the game is designed around a series of commons dilemmas.

Author Keywords
Game Design; Commons Dilemma; Massively Multiplayer Game

ACM Classification Keywords
K.8.0. [Personal Computing]: General - Games

Introduction
Since the earliest generations of home game consoles, players have enjoyed multiplayer games on a shared screen. Many of these games feature split screen, a graphics technique that divides a single screen into multiple rectangles to simulate multiple displays on a single screen. Coupled with the need for a game console controller in each player's hand, the prevalent

techniques for multiplayer games on a shared screen greatly limit how many players can play simultaneously. In IRC Quest, we demonstrate how literally hundreds of players can enjoy a game on a shared display. Players control an avatar by issuing commands from a smartphone or tablet that they likely already own. All players' progress through the game as a group to avoid having to divide up the screen. To coordinate players' actions, the gameplay is turn-based, based on a simple voting mechanism. To provide meaningful gameplay for large numbers of players, the game is based on a series of *commons dilemmas,* which put each player's best interests at odds with the group as a whole. This clash of individual strategy versus group strategy creates a unique gameplay experience.

Many Players on a Single Display

Supporting groups larger than the two to four players permitted in traditional games introduces several challenges. Most important is the control scheme. The early days of home game consoles had players stretching controller wires across their living room floor to support four players. Even with the recent transition to wireless controllers, requiring users to purchase a controller for each additional player limits how many players can play simultaneously. To counter this, we enabled any smartphone or tablet to become a controller, thus allowing people to play with a device that is likely already in their pockets. The game is controlled through Internet Relay Chat (IRC). Players join the game by adding themselves to the appropriate IRC channel. When a user joins, an avatar will be created for them and subsequent commands will control that avatar. Once the game has started, all of the avatars move together as a group.

Figure 1. The group moving together across the world

The group comes across choice nodes as they move. A binary choice is presented by game visuals and a text prompt (Figure 2). Players have thirty seconds at each choice node to make a decision by entering a keyword prefixed by a number sign in IRC. Players' choices are visualized by a bar graph that displays the ratio of one choice versus another.

Figure 2. The screen that appears at each choice node

For large groups, it can be difficult for an individual to keep track of their own avatar. To help players find the avatar they control, each avatar has floating text above its head with the corresponding player's name as it appears in IRC. Avatars are also given a random assortment of equipment so that they vary in appearance. Once a player has identified their own avatar, they can recognize it later by its appearance or by its floating name tag.

The Commons Dilemma

Engaging players through binary decisions and text input is challenging. To create more consequential decisions we give the group a shared goal of defeating a dragon while promoting individual success for those who survive the encounter. An individual cannot succeed without the group, but helping the group may also lead to a player's demise. Example: The players come across a choice node where they must either fight a powerful enemy or attempt to sneak past. A few players can successfully sneak past while the rest of the group confronts the enemy, but if too many choose to sneak and the enemy isn't defeated, all players will be penalized.

Figure 3. Several players attempt to sneak past while the rest face a dangerous enemy

Such choices are labeled as a Commons Dilemma [1], in which short-term interests of the individual contradict the long-term interests of the collective. During the timed choice nodes, implicit negotiation takes place between players as they decide who will serve the group and who will help themselves. Players see a visualization of each other's choices, updated as players make or change their choice. This visualization provides meaningful communication for large groups that otherwise could not effectively communicate in a chat window. Creating friction between members of the group is what makes IRC Quest's gameplay compelling even with many players sharing a screen and limited to simple text inputs.

Implementation

IRC Quest has several major components: the IRC Bot, the Command Parser, the Avatar Manager, and finally the game world itself. The IRC Bot is a simulated user that connects to the IRC Channel just as any other user would. The bot idles in chat and reads all messages posted to the channel and passes them along to the Command Parser. The parser interprets players' messages and propagates valid commands to the Avatar Manager. This is a centralized manager of all player avatars that uses actions from the Command Parser to control player avatars. The avatars then move through the game world interacting with other game elements such as a way point system and enemies.

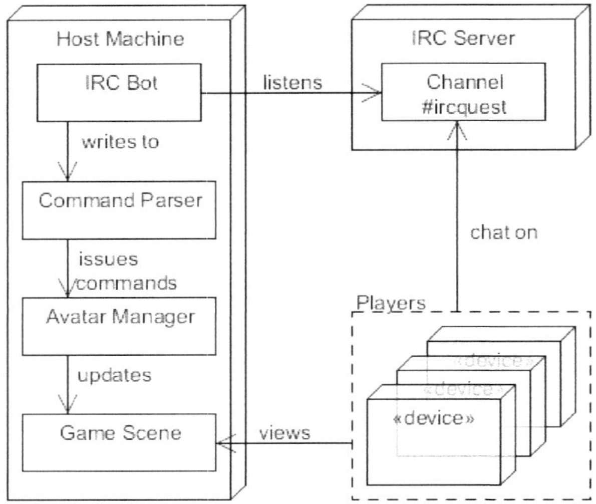

Figure 4. Architecture diagram of IRC Quest

The game itself was created using the Unity Engine and irc4net, an IRC library for the .NET framework. The IRC Bot and Command Parser were designed modularly, to allow use in any game implementing a multiplayer IRC based control scheme.

Experience

IRC Quest has been tested with as many as one hundred simulated users. This tested the amount of traffic that the IRC Bot and Command Parser can handle. Both components performed well under this load, providing feedback with no observable latency. Even with 100 users, individual players' avatars could be distinguished. We also trialed the game with several groups of up to ten real users. For these groups, we played on a large television, and players joined the IRC channel from their own smartphones, tablets and laptop computers. Players were enthused, engaging in vigorous discussion around decision-making, and laughing and cheering at the results. This experience provides early evidence of the success of the techniques we used to support large groups of players. Players reported that the randomized avatar appearance was useful in recognizing their own avatar, more so than the floating name text.

During the game's development, we considered the possibility of playing the game over a wide area network. To accomplish this, the host machine would stream the visual output to a popular media streaming service. Users could join the stream to view the game and participate by joining the associated IRC channel. We tested this using Twitch.tv: a streaming service primarily for games that includes an IRC chatroom with each stream. Unfortunately this service exhibited latency as high as fifteen seconds, making it impractical for real-time networked play.

In summary, IRC Quest demonstrates a new paradigm for multiplayer games. The success of the techniques we used encourages us to continue developing multiplayer games that don't conform to the definition outlined by the early generations of home video games.

Reference

[1] Cass, Robert C., and Julian J. Edney. "The commons dilemma: A simulation testing the effects of resource visibility and territorial division." *Human Ecology* 6.4 (1978): 371-386.

The Trial of Galileo: A Game of Motion Graphs

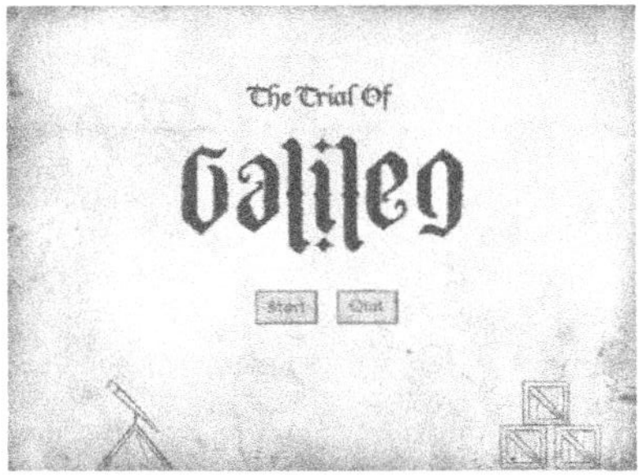

Ian Pommer[1]
pommeri7448@my.uwstout.edu

Alicia Griesbach[1]
griesbacha2565@my.uwstout.edu

John Leitner[1]
leitnerj2504@my.uwstout.edu

Dylan Tepp[1]
teppd0638@my.uwstout.edu

[1] University of Wisconsin-Stout
Menomonie, WI 54751 USA

Michael Flaherty[1]
flahertym@my.uwstout.edu

Bryant Seiler[1]
seilerb5922@my.uwstout.edu

Kenneth Patterson[1,2]
pattersonk@uwstout.edu

Brent Dingle[1]
dingleb@uwstout.edu

[2] Big John Games
dba Digital Content, LLC
7483 Cahill Road
Edina, MN 55439 USA

CHI PLAY '14, Oct 19–22 2014, Toronto, ON, Canada.
ACM 978-1-4503-3014-5/14/10
http://dx.doi.org/10.1145/2658537.2662977

Abstract
This paper presents a 2D game designed to assist students in better understanding motion graphs. In this game the player's character is not controlled by a joystick or control pad. Instead the game employs a unique interface enabling the player to control the actions of a character by creating a motion graph. The motion graph represents the desired position, velocity, or acceleration of the player's character over time. The graph must be fashioned to move the character through various puzzle environments. Through trial and error the player may achieve a better understanding of what motion graphs depict in the real world.

Author Keywords
Educational game; physics; motion graphs; interface design; 2D platform game; game design.

ACM Classification Keywords
H.5.m. Information interfaces and presentation: Miscellaneous; J.2. Physical Sciences and Engineering; K.3.m Computers and Education: Miscellaneous.

Introduction
A game's content is just one educational component of the game. Its interface also can be used as an educational tool. For example it was shown board games based on a number line representation offer

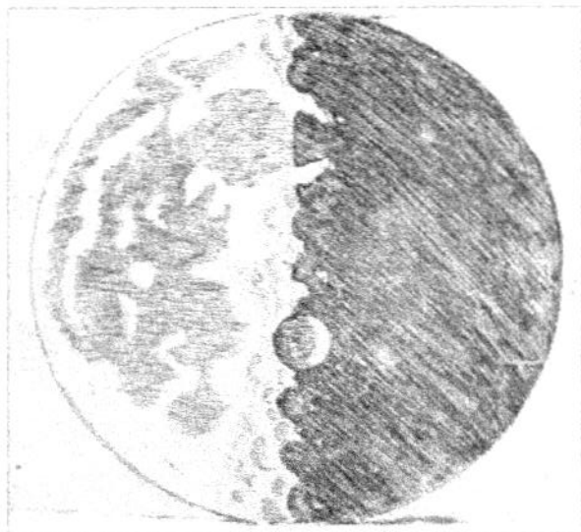

Figure 1: Galileo's Moon Sketch

Figure 2: Concept Gameplay Art

greater advantages to numerical understanding than the same games implemented using a color based representation [16]. This implies the interface to a game can offer explicit enhancements to the educational value of the game. This can also be inferred from other evaluation methodologies [7, 9, 13].

This paper presents a 2D game designed to assist students in understanding physics and how motion graphs relate to that understanding. The game implements an interface of motion graphs to move the game character. This interface allows the player to experiment with the creation and manipulation of position, velocity, and acceleration graphs to move the character through increasingly difficult obstacle courses and puzzle environments.

Background and Motivation

Understanding motion graphs is important to animation and game design. In animation they have been used to create realistic, controllable motion from a captured set of data [11], to develop control policies to animate characters [6], and for real-time interactive character animation [4]. In game design they have been used to develop path planning algorithms to move characters through complex environments [5, 14], and have been used for in-game animation of characters [8, 18].

However, before such advanced application there must be basic understanding. Early exposure to motion graphs and the relation between position, velocity, and acceleration typically occurs while taking a math or physics course. Intuitively these relations make sense by definition and experience. Yet, for many, coming to understand and relate a set of graphs to real world behavior is difficult [12, 15]. Perhaps a game can help.

Most games use a joystick, control pad, keyboard, or mouse as an input device to allow the user to control the motion of a game character. The visual feedback is easily understood. This type of interface has become the default to use. However it does not have to be the only interface.

Games such as *Rabbit Wants Cake* [2] use an interface allowing the player to alter a graph of position relative to time. We propose this type of interface, in a suitable context, can be used to educate players on motion graphs and how they relate to real world behavior. The following describes a gaming environment designed to encourage exploration and understanding of how to use such graphs.

Game Concept and Setting

The player of the game controls a character named Galileo. At the beginning of the game, Galileo has used scientific methods and careful observation to resolve some controversial ideas; however, he is brought to trial to prove his findings and avoid heresy charges. Fortunately his evidence is strong enough that he avoids immediate sentencing. However, he must prove himself in further trials where he navigates deadly obstacle courses using only his (or rather the player's) understanding of physics.

Main Gameplay

The game is composed of levels. Each level is an obstacle course puzzle. To solve the puzzle the player must construct a motion graph to move Galileo from one place to another while avoiding obstacles. Points are awarded based on how well the player's motion graphs compare to a hardcoded solution. Additional points are given if the player can draw all three graphs

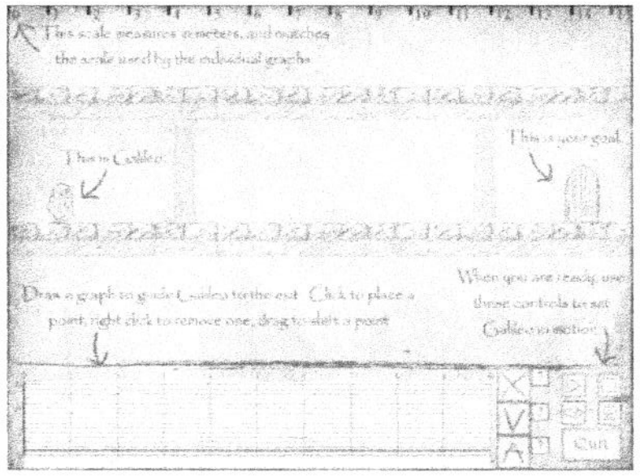

Figure 3: Actual Gameplay Screen

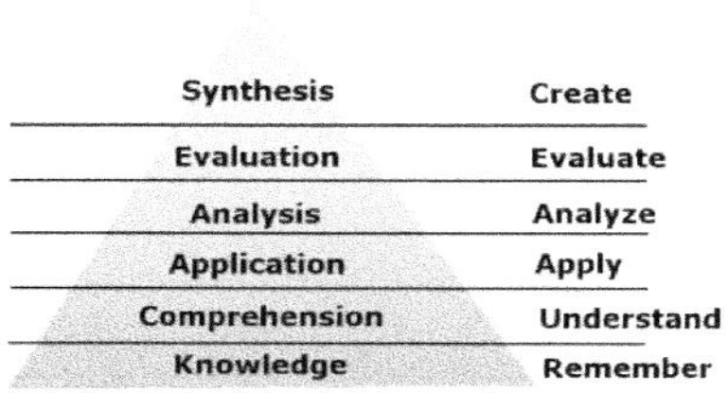

Figure 5: Bloom's Taxonomy

relative to each other (position, velocity, acceleration). Bonus points can be earned if the player opts to collect extra objects within a given level. Successful acquisition of these bonus objects, of course, requires more sophisticated motion graphs.

Game Aesthetics

The game aesthetics are intended to give the feel of the time of Galileo. So the background appears to be aged paper and the objects are displayed from a side view perspective with a hand drawn appearance. The general art style is based on Galileo's sketch of the Moon.

User Interface

The interface, as mentioned in previous sections, is a key educational component of the game to assist in understanding how motion graphs relate to actual, real, motion of objects. This interface allows the creation and exploration of motion graphs, providing visual feedback via the game character's motion.

The layout of the game's interface is such that the user is presented the puzzle space in the upper portion of the screen. In the lower portion the user is allowed to draw a motion graph by placing points on a piece of graph paper. The horizontal axis of the paper represents time and the vertical axis represents Galileo's position, velocity, or acceleration in the horizontal direction. Gravity and other game features automatically affect and adjust his vertical position.

Experiments were conducted allowing the player to have vertical control of Galileo using additional motion graphs. User feedback surveys indicated this made the interface too complicated. In response to the surveys we added a jump feature that can be placed on the motion graph at a desired point in time. This feature causes Galileo to be given an increased velocity in the vertical direction at the time indicated. Gravity then automatically reduces it which creates the appearance of jumping. Throughout this the player's motion graph still controls Galileo's horizontal movement. In later testing and user surveys, this feature was commented on for its ease of understanding. And it still maintained the basic premise of the interface.

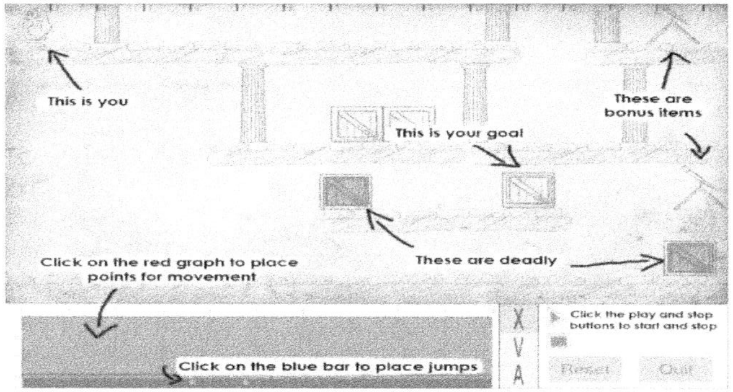

Figure 4: Conceptual Gameplay Screen

Another improvement in the usability of the interface, again based on test-user feedback, was the addition of a ruler-like metric to the top of the screen. This serves to establish the positive and negative direction of position as well as a visual indication of the unit of measure for distance.

Learning Retention

The educational merit of this game is based on Bloom's Taxonomy [1, 3]. We assume the player has an existing knowledge and comprehension of basic physics relative to position, velocity, and acceleration as well as definitional knowledge of motion graphs.

Game players (students) are given the opportunity to apply, analyze, and evaluate their knowledge and understanding of motion graphs. Over time players should achieve a higher level of understanding of the nature of motion graphs as well as physics in general. It is believed, players may then reapply this experience to other fields of interest and problem domains. While we do not yet have empirical results to explicitly indicate this, other studies on experimentation with graphs and visual feedback imply a positive result should be expected [10].

Summary

This paper has presented a game which uses a unique interface based on motion graphs. It serves to demonstrate how a game may capture the interest of a student and assist in teaching. It also emphasizes a point: The content of a game is not the only educational part of a game. The interface of the game is also a key component of the learning experience.

References

[1] Anderson, L.W. and Krathwohl, D.R. *A Taxonomy for Learning, Teaching, and Assessing: A Revision of Bloom's Taxonomy of Educational Objectives*, (2001).

[2] Armor Games, *Rabbit Wants Cake*, http://www.notdoppler.com/rabbitwantscake.php

[3] Bloom B.S. *Taxonomy of Educational Objectives, Handbook I: The Cognitive Domain*, (1956).

[4] Casas, D., Tejera, M., Guillemaut, J. and Hilton, A. 4D parametric motion graphs for interactive animation. *Proc. I3D 2012*, (2012).

[5] Choi, M.G., Lee, J. and Shin, S.Y. Planning biped locomotion using motion capture data and probabilistic roadmaps. *ACM Trans. Graph.* 22, 2 (April 2003).

[6] Coros, S., Beaudoin, P. and van de Panne, M. Robust task-based control policies for physics-based characters. *SIGGRAPH Asia 2009*, (2009), Article 170.

[7] Griffiths, M.D. The educational benefits of videogames. *Education and Health*, 20, 3, (2002).

[8] Heck, R. and Gleicher, M. Parametric motion graphs. *Proc. I3D 2007*, (2007).

[9] Isbister, K., Flanagan, M. and Hash, C. Designing games for learning: insights from conversations with designers. *Proc. CHI 2010*, (2010).

[10] Jeong, Allan C. Teaching Motion Graphs with Real-Time Notations and Methods of Computer Graph Manipulation. Master Thesis. UW-Madison, (1996).

[11] Kovar, L., Gleicher, M. and Pighin, F. Motion graphs. *ACM Trans. Graph.* 21, 3 (July 2002).

[12] Larkin, J., Understanding, problem representations, and skill in physics. In Problems of Representation in the Teaching and Learning of Mathematics (Janvier, C.) Hillsdale, NJ: L. Erlbaum Associates, (1987), 154-155.

[13] Looi, Q.E. and See, S.L. Effectively engaging students in educational games by deploying HCI evaluation methods. *Proc. WCECS 2010*, (2010).

[14] Mahmudi, M. and Kallmann, M. Fast path planning using motion graphs. *Proc. I3D 2008*, 13, (2008).

[15] Mokros, J. R. and Tinker, R. F. The impact of microcomputer-based science labs on children's ability to interpret graphs. Journal of Research in Science Teaching, 24, (1987), 369-383.

[16] Ramani, G.B. and Siegler, Robert S. Promoting broad and stable improvements in low-income children's numerical knowledge through playing number board games, *Child Development*, 79, 2, (2008).

[17] Wampler, K., Andersen, E., Herbst, E., Lee, Y. and Popovic, Z. Character animation in two-player adversarial games. *ACM Trans. Graph.* 29, 3, (July 2010).

Jelly Polo: Increasing Richness and Competition in Sports Games Using Small-Scale Exertion

Mike Sheinin
University of Saskatchewan
110 Science Place
Saskatoon, SK S7N 5C9 Canada
mike.sheinin@usask.ca

Carl Gutwin
University of Saskatchewan
110 Science Place
Saskatoon, SK S7N 5C9 Canada
gutwin@cs.usask.ca

CHI PLAY '14, Oct 19-22 2014, Toronto, ON, Canada
ACM 978-1-4503-3014-5/14/10.
http://dx.doi.org/10.1145/2658537.2662981

Abstract
Sports video games should be inherently competitive, but they fall short in providing true competition for the players. The emphasis on statistical simulations in traditional sports video games has taken away the ability for players to gain expertise development, differentiate how they play from other players, and change the way they play throughout the course of the game. Jelly Polo, a 2D 3-on-3 sports video game uses small-scale exertion to counter the drawbacks stated above. By providing impulse-based movement and precision passing, players can gain expertise in running and passing, differentiating how they play. The small-scale exertion aspect also makes players fatigued, forcing them to strategize how they play throughout the course of a game. Jelly Polo is the first game to show that small-scale exertion can increase the richness and competitiveness in sports video games.

Author Keywords
Sports video games; physical controls; exertion games; small-scale exertion

ACM Classification Keywords
H.5.2. Information interfaces (HCI): Interaction techniques

Introduction

Real life sports are not the same as sports video games. This statement is actually very true in many ways. In real life, sports are largely about competition. The winner of the competition is determined by things like who can run faster, shoot better, or maybe who is less fatigued. Sports video games, however, are different. Take running for example. How can a player make the in-game character they are controlling run faster, other than by using something like a sprint button? The answer is: they can't. If the in-game character the player is controlling has the exact same speed statistics as another in-game character, they will be the same speed.

At the moment, in traditional sports video games, there is no way for the player to increase simple skills like running through being *better* at using the game controller. This is because to move your in-game character, all you can do (in most cases) is hold the thumbstick over to one side. There is no real way to do this *better* than anyone else.

Currently, sports video games try to be some of the best simulations possible of the real thing. Characters look like real people, the animations are more life-like, and each in-game character is given different stats based on how good they are in real life. The fact that each character is given a set of predefined statistics is the problem. Sports video games are too much of a statistical simulation. Passes and shots are automatically aimed, statistics determine outcomes of certain situations and teams with better players technically have a better chance at winning a game, simply because they have higher in-game statistics.

This leads to three drawbacks of sports video games compared to real life sports:

- Limited opportunity for *expertise development* in simple skills like running and throwing;
- Little *differentiation* between players, again, in terms of running and throwing;
- *Fatigue* is not a factor in the outcome of a game.

Our solution to these drawbacks is to add small-scale physical exertion to sports video games. To show that our solution works, we built a 2D sports game with small-scale exertion called *Jelly Polo*. Through our research that is discussed in detail below, we found that adding small-scale exertion to a sports game fixed all three drawbacks [2]. It enables the opportunity for expertise development, increases differentiation between players, and allows fatigue to become an important gameplay factor.

Jelly Polo

Game Concept

Jelly Polo is a 3-on-3 top-down 2D sports game that is similar to hockey or soccer. Two teams play against each other to see who can score the most points by shooting a ball into the opposing team's net. Games are 10-40 minutes long depending on what the players choose at the beginning of the game. There is also a half-time break where teams switch sides and have a short rest. Jelly Polo is an exergame, which is a game that uses an interface that causes exertion [1]. The movement mechanic, discussed below, is what makes Jelly Polo an exergame.

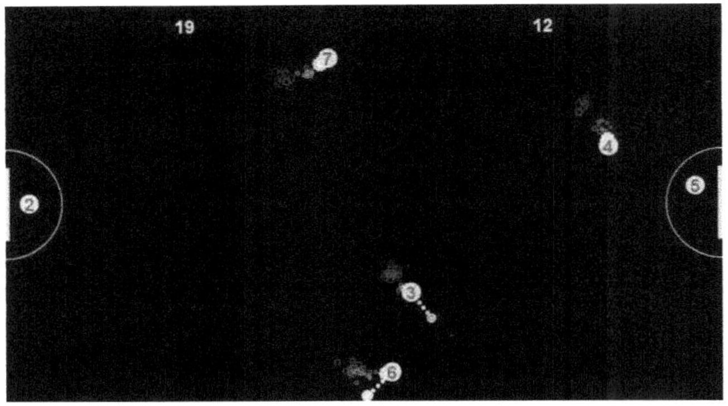

Figure 1. Jelly Polo game in progress (from [2]).

There are only two controls in Jelly Polo, the left and right thumbsticks on a standard gamepad controller. The left thumbstick controls movement and the right thumbstick controls an arm for throwing. The gameplay 'innovations' that will be discussed in its own section below are both the movement and throwing mechanics.

Target Audience
Part of our target audience is male sports fans. This is because recent research has shown that about 95% of all sports video game players are male sports fans [3]. However, we also feel as though our target audience is focused towards any competitive video game player. With small-scale exertion added to the game, competition is much higher between the players. This could lead to players training to compete at their highest levels. Since Jelly Polo is very sport-like and competitive, eSports would be a perfect fit for Jelly Polo.

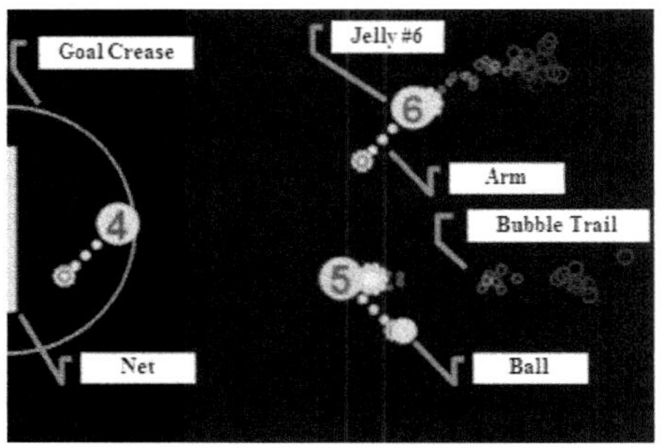

Figure 2. Jelly Polo close-up with annotations (from [2]).

Gameplay Innovations
Moving in traditional sports games usually involves rate-based movement. Rate-based movement is when the player can hold the thumbstick over to one side and their in-game character moves at a constant rate in that direction. Jelly Polo, however, uses impulse-based movement where the player has to constantly flick the thumbstick in the direction they want to move. The faster the player flicks the thumbstick, the faster they move. This is what causes small-scale exertion in Jelly Polo.

With impulse-based movement, players have very different top speeds and levels of endurance. This leads to certain situations that would not be found in most traditional sports games. For example, in Jelly Polo, players switch positions in the middle of the game to strategize against fatigue (e.g., switching to the goalie position because it is less fatiguing).

Another phenomenon that happens in Jelly Polo is that players can catch up to other players that are on a breakaway. In traditional sports games, only if the character you are controlling has a higher speed statistic than the character on the breakaway can you have a chance at catching up to them. In Jelly Polo, if you are physically faster (i.e., better) at flicking the thumbstick, then you can catch up to another, slower, player if they are on a breakaway. With this control scheme, we switch the competitive aspects of the game to be controlled by the player rather than by the statistics of characters in the game.

The other control mechanic in Jelly Polo is precision throwing. Using the right thumbstick, if the player has the ball, flicking the thumbstick will cause the ball to be thrown in the exact direction the thumbstick is pointing. The speed of the ball as it is thrown is determined by how hard the thumbstick is flicked. This leads to much more skill development in passing and shooting as opposed to some traditional sports video games which only need a single button press to make a perfect pass.

We want to stress, though, that these mechanics (i.e., impulse-based movement and precision passing) are by no means original control mechanics. They have been around for many years, but seem to have been lost in the world of ever-increasing graphics and realistic simulations [2].

Research

Research Question

To determine if small-scale exertion in a sports video game can fix the three drawbacks stated above: limited expertise development, differentiation and fatigue.

Methodology

We ran a four week long Jelly Polo league with four consistent teams of three. Each team played three games a week and each game was 20 minutes long. We kept track of each player's statistics (e.g., goals, shots, assists, saves, etc.), gave likert scale questionnaires and performed interviews with each team at the end of the study.

Implementation

Jelly Polo was built with Processing using the proControll library for the controllers. We used the same desktop PC and the same Logitech Dual Shock controllers for each game session.

Results

Through both qualitative and quantitative data analysis, we found that with small-scale exertion, the three drawbacks were fixed. Expertise development was made in running and passing; differentiation was made in the players' abilities and the way each player played; and fatigue was found to be a big factor in the outcome of a game. All these were found in both the qualitative and quantitative data in some way [2].

Conclusion

Overall, we found that by using small-scale exertion in a sports video game, we can make sports games truly competitive and sport-like. Players are given the ability to train and get better at simple skills like running and passing, they also found niches in which they could play (e.g., a goalie as opposed to an offensive player), and team strategy became a huge part of the gameplay because of fatigue. Fatigue changed the way players played throughout the course of a game because the small-scale exertion kept them from moving at top speed throughout the entire game. Players had to consciously strategize against the fatiguing aspects [2].

There were many unique situations that we found with Jelly Polo that cannot be seen in any other current video game. It is truly a unique experience and we hope players and developers alike will embrace what we have learned and use it to their own benefits.

References

[1] Mueller, F. Gibbs, M.R. Vetere, F. Taxonomy of exertion games. *OZCHI 2008*, 263—266.

[2] Sheinin, M. Gutwin, C. Exertion in the small: improving differentiation and expressiveness in sports games with physical controls. *CHI '14*, 1845—1854.

[3] Stein, A. Mitgutsch, K. Who are sports gamers? A large scale study of sports video game players. *Convergence,* 19(3), 2013, 345—363.

"Generic Shooter 3000": A Realistic First Person Shooter Powered By Biofeedback

Gonçalo Amaral da Silva
Faculty of Engineering of
University of Porto
Rua Dr. Roberto Frias
Porto, 4200-465 Portugal
goncalofsilva.25@gmail.com

Pedro Alves Nogueira
Artificial Intelligence and
Computer Science Laboratory
(LIACC)
Rua Dr. Roberto Frias
Porto, 4200-465 Portugal
pedro.alves.nogueira@fe.up.pt

Rui Rodrigues
INESC-TEC
Rua Dr. Roberto Frias
Porto, 4200-465 Portugal
rui.rodrigues@fe.up.pt

CHI PLAY '14, Oct 19–22 2014, Toronto, ON, Canada
ACM 978-1-4503-3014-5/14/10.

Abstract
"Generic Shooter 3000" is a First-Person shooter with semi-realistic interaction, where actions such as firing a gun or diving through underwater sections are performed with your own body- through the use of biofeedback technology. This prototype is the idealised version of a research game developed for a master's thesis project on "biofeedback interaction in video games".

Author Keywords
Biofeedback game design; direct multimodal biofeedback; physiological control.

ACM Classification Keywords
K.8.0 [Personal Computing]: Games; H.5.2 [Information Interfaces and Presentation]: User Interfaces; H.1.2 [Models and Principles]: User/Machine Systems - *Human Factors*

General Terms
Measurement, Design, Experimentation, Human Factors.

Introduction
"Generic Shooter 3000" is a prototype of a first person shooter where all in-game actions are portrayed as closely as possible to reality, by using the player's entire body as input to the game.

Instead of relying solely on the well-known keyboard and mouse devices (used for movement, aiming and shooting), players are also connected to a biofeedback device which captures their body data over time. This allows the game to recognise even the smallest body movements of the player and to trigger appropriate actions inside the game, such as influencing gun recoil while firing, when players contract their arm or hold their breath. A second example is to simulate underwater diving when players hold their breath.

Biofeedback interaction
In the context of video games and Human-Computer Interaction, biofeedback is the process of capturing a player's physiological data and using it to modify the behaviour of a game. Here, we use direct biofeedback, where players manipulate *intentionally* their body to perform an action inside the game: for example, closing their hand to grab an object or to open a door.

This work is mostly inspired by the interaction potential demonstrated by previous research-based games using biofeedback [1, 3]. The idea was to bring the player as close as possible to the game, and making them "feel" what the game character is facing at the moment. We believe that biofeedback is the ideal technology to implement such design, and attempted to do so using the following equipment:

Respiration sensor (RESP). Worn by players around their chest, it is used to approximate the amount of air held in wearer's lungs.

Temperature sensor (TEMP). Attached to a headset worn by the player, it is activated in the game by blowing air on it.

Electromyography sensors (EMG). Used can be used to know if a muscle is contracted or relaxed.

Glove tracker (GLOVE). Monitors the position and bending of each finger, and can be used to detect different hand poses.

Game Concept
In our test scenario, which takes place at a dungeon, the player has to make way through enemies inside the building and retrieve three gold keys in order to escape. Enemies are equipped with guns and have basic *shoot-and-pursuit* AI. The player can run, jump, crouch and use two combat guns, along with a Physics Gun to move heavy objects. All the remaining actions make use of the biofeedback interaction.

Gun Recoil Control. While players are firing at enemies, aim can be stabilised by contracting the arm and by breathing in a small amount of air - making for a close simulation of "good posture" while firing a gun. The RESP sensor and an EMG sensor placed on the player's arm are used here.

Underwater Breathing. To dive underwater, players will have to sustain breath as if diving in real life (using the RESP sensor). This is one of the mechanics that we wanted to test with real players, as it provides a great impact on the overall game experience.

Sprinting. Players can run for a short period of time by raising one of their heels (or both), activating the leg muscles both inside and outside of the game. These are connected to 2x EMG sensors.

Invisibility. This is activated by combining two actions. Players have to close their fist (using the GLOVE) to gather magical power and breathe in using the RESP sensor, becoming instantly invisible to enemies. They will remain invisible as long as they sustain breath or until the power runs out.

Possession. Here, players are allowed to control an enemy while leaving their own body behind, and vulnerable to other enemies in the vicinity. This is activated by performing a special hand pose (using the GLOVE) and *whisper their soul out of their body* (using the TEMP sensor) - taking control of the enemy's body.

Fire Blow. Currently, the player can interact with fire objects by blowing out through the temperature sensor. Depending on the intensity/size of the fire object, they may need to gather air first using the RESP sensor.

Usable Objects. Players can use levers, buttons or items can be used or equipped by closing their fist (using the tracker glove).

Grab/Move Objects. Occasionally, players will find obstacles represented by physics-based objects. These are meant to be moved with the Physics Gun. Players move them by closing their fist (the same as "Use objects"). Depending on the weight of the object, they may need to use more strength by contracting the arm equipped with the EMG sensor.

Biofeedback Interaction - Empirical Study

It is our belief that direct biofeedback games can leverage multimodal biofeedback - the use of multiple sensors contributing to one game mechanic - and open up the possibilities to combine different inputs in creative ways, rather than constraining game designers too much when attempting to give "meaning" to a single input sensor. In the scope of the original master's thesis project [2], it was our initial intention to introduce this concept in research, as well as to study the pros and cons of placing this design into practice (versus standard games and unimodal biofeedback games).

32 players who play games regularly were recruited to test three distinct versions of our game (no biofeedback, unimodal, multimodal biofeedback) and to evaluate each one using both objective (Fun, Ease of Use, Originality) and subjective measures (associating keywords with each version and open-ended commentaries). A repeated-measures experimental design was employed using the three versions as the within subjects factor. From the entire set of results presented in the full study [2], we discuss here those which we consider most relevant to the current state of the game: Fun, Ease of Use, and a reflection on the different game experiences provided by the three interaction types.

Overall in terms of Fun, both biofeedback versions were considered more fun than the "no biofeedback" version. Informally, a good game presents challenges to the player and allows he/she to master new abilities in order to overcome those challenges. In this case, players can effectively enjoy the challenge of experimenting with new technologies and dominating them in a game. The obtained results confirm the potential to use of this technology in video games.

Regarding Ease of Use, the "no biofeedback version" was considered the easier to use when compared to its biofeedback counterparts (the latter were still rated positively in the "easy" range). This poses no surprise as despite very simplistic, the current devices produce great satisfaction in players by allowing them to express themselves with little effort. Instead, Ease of Use was measured to ensure that the biofeedback controls were not an obstacle for players and allowed them to enjoy the game and positively express themselves. Steve Swink describes this as part of the larger concept of *Game Feel* [4]. For immersion and a positive game feel to exist, the game needs to have quality controls that are able to deliver fun to players.

Although the idea of direct multimodal biofeedback did not exist previously in research, we consider that multimodal biofeedback is not the definitive solution to the problem of creating engaging games using this technology. Instead, the key is to balance both unimodal and multimodal types to achieve a strong design.

Target Audience

Based on the feedback that we got from the players and the data that we collected [2], we believe that **this game is best targeted at players who enjoy games focused on exploration and interaction with the surrounding environment**. With the current technology, players are able to see and hear aesthetically pleasant environments in games - and also manipulate them, to a certain degree, using the traditional gamepads and mouse/keyboards. Using biofeedback, players have the chance to experience the same environments using an unexplored dimension, where their physiological characteristics can play a role in the game as well.

Lastly, based on the feedback provided by two of our players, direct biofeedback might not be appropriate for highly competitive games. This is because although easy to use after a while, may prove difficult to be fully mastered, as there are more input variables to be controlled. Current shooter games require from players a certain degree of eye-hand coordination to aim perfectly, and "game intelligence" so they know exactly when and where they should take action in order to win. The added dimension of physical control can make this task more difficult and become a source of frustration for some players. Additionally, they may feel tired due to the repeated use of their body.

Credits and Acknowledgements

The gameplay footage demonstrating our game can be seen at https://vimeo.com/104439652. All credits regarding the original map design and 3D modelled objects of the dungeon map goes to Chris Holden.[1] The biofeedback prototype was developed using Unreal Development Kit. With the exception of the pre-made scripting code that ships with the engine, all code was written by our development team.

References

[1] Ambinder, M. Biofeedback in gameplay: How valve measures physiology to enhance gaming experience. In *Game Developers Conference* (2011).

[2] da Silva, G. A. Multimodal vs. unimodal physiological control in videogames for enhanced realism and depth. Master's thesis, Faculty of Engineering of the University of Porto, http://hdl.handle.net/10216/72289, 2012.

[3] Nacke, L. E., Kalyn, M., Lough, C., and Mandryk, R. L. Biofeedback game design: using direct and indirect physiological control to enhance game interaction. In *Proceedings of the SIGCHI Conference on Human Factors in Computing Systems*, ACM (2011), 103–112.

[4] Swink, S. *Game Feel*. Morgan Kaufmann, 2009.

[1]Permission was given by the author to use the map in both the original master's thesis project and to submit this biofeedback prototype to the "Student Game Design Competition". The original map can be accessed at http://www.chrisholden.net/05.htm.

"Toru": A Game that Reverses the Wisdom of Age Using Mosquito Sound

john smith
Institute of Advanced Media Arts
and Sciences
4-1-7 Kagano, Ogaki-shi, Gifu
503-0006, JAPAN
johnsmith13@iamas.ac.jp

Kazuhiro Jo
Institute of Advanced Media Arts
and Sciences
4-1-7 Kagano, Ogaki-shi, Gifu
503-0006, JAPAN
jo@iamas.ac.jp

CHI PLAY '14, Oct 19-22, 2014, Toronto, ON, Canada
ACM 978-1-4503-3014-5/14/10.
http://dx.doi.org/10.1145/2658537.2662973

Abstract
We propose "Toru," a game that reverses the game skills developed as a person ages using ultra-high-frequency (mosquito) sound. The game has its origin in the computer game Simon (1978), which we interpret from visual to auditory form using the mosquito sound (i.e., ultra-high-frequency sound) for its difficulty settings. Because of individual variations in hearing, the Toru game transforms its character from Mimicry (simulation) to Alea (chance), and provides an opportunity to reverse the wisdom of age (i.e., game skills advantage) developed by adults over the years.

Author Keywords
Sound Game; Play; Cognitive Science

ACM Classification Keywords
J.5 ARTS AND HUMANITIES

Introduction
The motivation to create this game comes from the personal experience of one of the authors with regard to games in his childhood. At that time, both of his parents were experienced programmers with excellent skills in computer games. Consequently, he was not able to defeat his parents in any game. This asymmetry/unfairness based on skills developed over a period of years became deeply engraved in his memory as a very frustrating experience. As a result of the frustration, we developed the "Toru" game, which

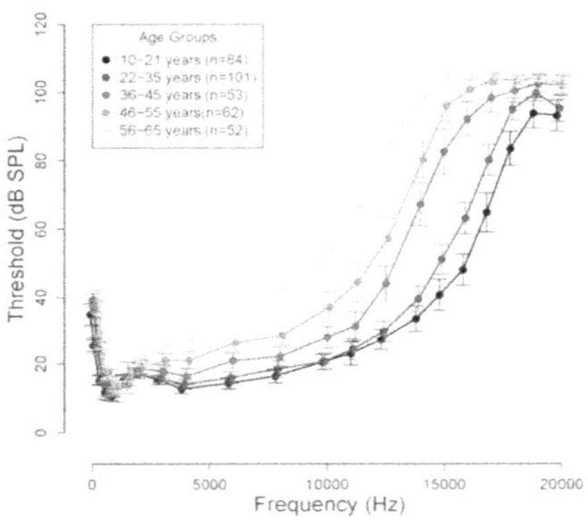

Fig. 1 Average hearing thresholds for different age groups [1].

reverses this asymmetrical situation using the mosquito sound (i.e., ultra-high-frequency sound).

The mosquito sound has individual variations in hearing, which occur naturally as a result of ageing (Fig. 1) [1]. A UK company, COMPOUND SECURITY, Inc. (http://www.compoundsecurity.co.uk/), used the sound to produce discomfort in younger people in order to prevent loitering on streets. They used a 17,000 Hz sine wave, a frequency that is typically difficult for persons in their late 20s and the elderly to perceive.

We apply the sound in our game such that even if people play the same game, we produce an environment with a different gaming experience for individuals primarily arising from age. When the frequency of the sound is increased according to the progress of the game, the degree of difficulty remains low for people who can hear the sound; however, for people who cannot hear it, the game shows an alternative aspect that makes it a gambling situation. In particular, for persons in their 20s and 30s, the generation that has diversity in their hearing because of not only age induced hearing loss but also from their individual noise-induced hearing loss (e.g., headphones), the sound provides an opportunity to improve the variety in their play.

THE "TORU" GAME

The "Toru" game itself has its origin in the 1970's computer game Simon [2]. Simon is a game in which one or more players memorize the order of light and sound of four buttons, and then press the buttons in the order remembered. Difficulty settings are defined by the speed and the number of trials. The speed and number increase each time the player is successful in the trial. Simon emerged from the children's game "Simon says," in which people follow instructions beginning with "Simon says" (and do not follow any instructions with any other name). In the computer form of the game, instead of a voice, players mimic the instruction from a computer.

In this game, we re-interpret Simon with the mosquito sound. Instead of using speed and numbers, we use different frequencies as difficulty settings. The idea to use the mosquito sound instead of light comes from our previous research into the use of auditory representations in the Tower of Hanoi problem [3], influenced by Zhang and Norman's research into representations in distributed cognitive tasks [4]. The basic settings/rules of the "Toru" game are as follows:

Settings (Fig. 2):
- Two handheld boxes with cables.
- Each box has a button and a speaker.

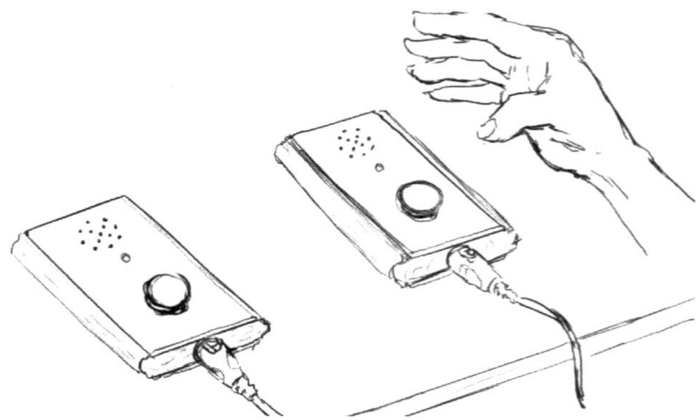

Fig. 2 Settings in "Toru"

Fig. 3 Hearing difference according to age

Rules:
- Follow the order of the sound generated randomly from each box by pushing the buttons.
- The game consists of five sets with four trials.
- Following each trial, the number of sounds is increased from one to four (i.e., one sound in the first trial, to four sounds in the fourth trial).
- After each set, the frequency range of the sound is expanded in the following series: 4000 Hz, 10000 Hz, 14000 Hz, 16000 Hz, and 18000 Hz (i.e., 4000 Hz for every four trials in the first set, 4000, and 10000 Hz in the second set, to every five frequencies in the final set).
- The game ends after five sets.

We choose the range of frequencies based on the average hearing threshold of ultra-high frequency sound [5]. In the first set, we use highly audible sound (i.e., 4000 Hz), then we proceed over the range with diversity according to age group. With this setting, for each player, the game has a moment for inaudible sound in a set. The timing is different from player to player; however, for all players, the game suddenly requires a gamble in order to decide on the source of the inaudible sound from the two choices (i.e., boxes) (Fig. 3).

SYSTEM CONFIGURATION

The game consists of two boxes connected to a PC with openFrameworks (http://www.openframeworks.cc/) through Arduino (http://www.arduino.cc/) (Fig. 4). Each box comprises a set of a button and a speaker. The set allows players to adjust their listening position by handling the boxes. Throughout the game, openFrameworks checks not. openFrameworks provides feedback on whether a push is correct (the original sound) or not (beep sound) through the speakers. When a player fails the trial, the system returns to the initial set (i.e., 4000 Hz). When a player masters all five sets, openFrameworks presents a celebratory sound.

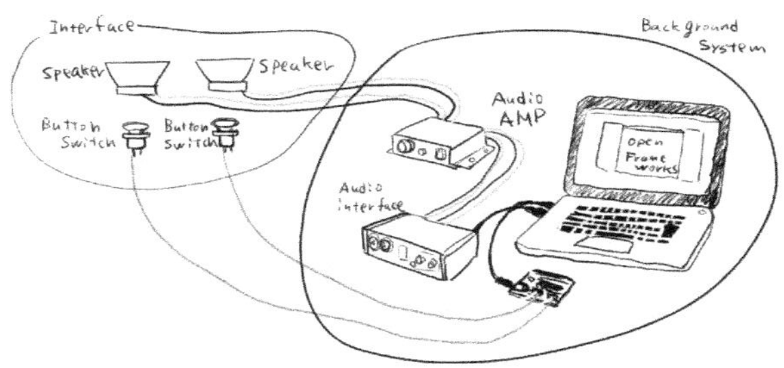

Fig. 4 Toru's system configuration

DISCUSSION

A French philosopher, Roger Caillois, classified the phenomenon of play into four categories: Mimicry (simulation), Alea (chance), Agôn (competition), and Ilinx (vertigo) [6]. From his perspective, we observed a shift from Mimicry to Alea in the "Toru" game at the moment the sounds became inaudible. The timing of the shift itself is specific to each player according to his/her hearing threshold. However, in general, the game provides an opportunity to reverse the wisdom of age (i.e., game skills advantage) developed by adults over the years, particularly in the relationship between children and parents (i.e., the motivation of the "Toru").

From this point of view, we are also interested in how Agôn emerges in the "Toru" game. According to Caillos, Agôn is an appearance of desire to have one's superiority recognized, and the superiority requires a distinction within the space of a game. In this regard, we could embody the desire among the players by showing their results each other (e.g., a scoring function) through the game. However, at the same time, the embodiment may veil the another form of innate competition within the game. 1: A competition within the player him/herself. Within an extended time scale, the game could be regarded as a challenge as the player ages. As mentioned at the beginning, the game emerged from the frustration felt as a result of the advantage of age. If the game had been present at that time, it would have been a suitable solution to defeat experienced parents by using the asymmetry of audible/inaudible ability. However, as a matter of fact, we are already in our 20s and 30s; therefore, for each of us, the game would appear almost in the form of Alea (chance). Our next step might be a time travel to bring the game back to our childhood.

ACKNOWLEDGEMENTS

We would like to thank Ryota Kuwakubo and Masahiro Miwa for their valuable comments. We also would like to thank the members of the "Reinventing the wheel" project and other members at IAMAS for their support.

One of the author, john smith would like to thank his parents for the childhood memory. This work was supported by JSPS KAKENHI Grant Number 24652029.

References

[1] Lee J, Dhar S, Abel R, Banakis R, Grolley E, Lee J, Zecker S, Siegel J. Behavioral hearing thresholds between 0.125 and 20 kHz using depth-compensated ear simulator calibration. Ear Hear (2012). 315-29.

[2] Simon, Milton Bradley Company (1978).

[3] Kazuhiro Jo, Kazuyuki Yamada, and Kumiyo Nakakoji, Sound Attributes and the Ease of Problem Solving in Auditory Interaction Design, IPSJ SIG Technical Report (2005) 83-90. (In Japanese).

[4] Jlaje Zhang and Donald A. Norman, Representation In Distributed Cognitive Tasks, Cognitive Science Volume 18, Issue 1 (1994) 87-122.

[5] D. W. Robinson and G. J. Sutton, Age Effect in Hearing—A comparative Analysis of Published Threshold Data, Audiology 18 (1979) 320-334.

[6] Roger Caillois, "Man, Play, and Games," University of Illinois Press (2001).

Extended Abstract for *Canvas Obscura*

Sam Snodgrass
Computer Science
Drexel University
Philadelphia, PA 19104 USA
sps74@drexel.edu

Brandon Packard
Computer Science
Drexel University
Philadelphia, PA 19104 USA
btp36@drexel.edu

Benjamin Goldberg
Digital Media
Drexel University
Philadelphia, PA 19104 USA
bag74@drexel.edu

Cathy Lu
Digital Media
Drexel University
Philadelphia, PA 19104 USA
cyl33@drexel.edu

Ariel Evans
Digital Media
Drexel University
Philadelphia, PA 19104 USA
ale43@drexel.edu

Jichen Zhu
Digital Media
Drexel University
Philadelphia, PA 19104 USA
jz435@drexel.edu

CHI PLAY'14, October 19–21, 2014, Toronto, ON, Canada.
ACM 978-1-4503-3014-5/14/10.
http://dx.doi.org/10.1145/2658537.2662982

Abstract
Canvas Obscura is a survival-horror game where the player must locate objects within an ever-changing environment. *Canvas Obscura* pushes the boundaries of the survival-horror genre by including procedurally generated levels.

Author Keywords
Survival Horror; procedural content generation; level generation

ACM Classification Keywords
K. 8. Games, I.2.1 Artificial Intelligence: Applications and Expert Systems - Games

Introduction
Since the early days of their development, video games have had a close relationship with the horror genre [5]. Legaspi and Numao [4] describe survival horror as, "a sub-genre of action-adventure where the player leads an avatar character through uncanny and hostile environments, reminiscent of horror fiction or movie." Seeking to continue with this tradition, as well as push the boundaries of technological innovation in gameplay, our team developed the survival-horror game, *Canvas Obscura.*

The game was built using the Unity engine with C# and JavaScript. The models were created with Autodesk Maya and ZBrush and textured with Adobe Photoshop.

Concept

Canvas Obscura pays homage to acclaimed survival horror games, such as *Amnesia*[1] and *Slender: The Arrival*[2], while also acting as a test bed for procedural content generation. Procedural content generation (PCG) is the process of creating game content (e.g., maps [6], quests [1], etc.) algorithmically with minimal manual intervention [6]. For more information about PCG, Hendrikx et al. [3] provides an overview of many techniques and applications.

Set in the shell of a once thriving estate, *Canvas Obscura* follows the journey of a struggling painter in his desperate search for inspiration. The painter travels to the estate because of its dark history, thinking that exploring a place with such a brutal past might rekindle his passion for painting, but he soon finds himself just trying to survive. Inspiration for the game's creatures was derived from a combination of the surrealist painting style as well as the game's own narrative.

The narrative of *Canvas Obscura* relies on horror motifs such as murders, ghosts and the living dead. In the background of the game, the creatures and setting are all linked to violent histories. The player's objective is to collect artifacts related to these backstories, such as a noose and a bloody hammer, in order to escape the building.

Gameplay Innovation

Wishing to promote an inherent replay value not traditionally attributed to horror games, we decided to procedurally generate a varied layout for each level on every play-through. The player must navigate these labyrinthine hallways while using kiting or avoidance techniques to bypass the patrolling enemies. However, no two levels will be the same, preventing the player from memorizing the level layout for future plays; the player character's death also results in a new level layout. The ever-changing layout encourages the player to explore the environment and seek out new paths for avoiding enemies. In addition to the level layouts, the placement of the monsters is also unique to each generated level. The player cannot anticipate where a creature may pop out of the floor to strike her, or where an enemy may be patrolling. Lastly, in an effort to follow a narrative arc of rising tension, the level sections themselves are constructed such that they become successively darker, more decrepit, and harder to navigate as the story progresses.

Although a few recent horror games, such as *SCP Containment Breach*[3], have experimented with PCG as a primary component of the gameplay, we argue that there are differences that set our game apart. *SCP Containment Breach* also uses PCG to generate a map at start-up, but allows the player to save her game at any point during gameplay, preserving the map layout. The player dies immediately when caught by any enemy, but upon death, the player restarts from the last save and the map remains the same. This allows the player to remember landmarks throughout the level and have multiple chances at getting through the same map. For *Canvas Obscura,* we have chosen not to allow the player to save at all, and we completely regenerate the level upon death. This approach puts more pressure on the player, because of the harsher

[1] http://www.amnesiagame.com/#main

[2] http://www.slenderarrival.com/

[3] http://www.scpcbgame.com/

consequences. The player also has a health bar and does not die immediately from enemy attacks. The health bar adds rising tension to game (i.e., the less life the player has the more pressure she is under). Conversely, dying from a single hit from an enemy can lead to flat tension, because the player will constantly have the same consequences for getting hit by an enemy. That is, the player has a constant amount of pressure on her, leading to flat tension. These mechanics add a different level of difficulty to the game and teach the player to not perform high risk activities to complete each level. The player must remain vigilant and carefully navigate around enemies, or learn to kite enemies once spotted by them. This player-enemy dynamic provides the main tension in the game (like most horror games), but also discourages the player from resorting to death as a means of escape. Though our game puts more pressure on the player, through harsher consequences and rising tension, it is our intention to keep the game fresh and enjoyable through procedural content generation.

Technological Innovation

Canvas Obscura explores the use of procedural content generation (PCG). PCG, as explained above, is the automatic generation of content with minimal user intervention.

Canvas Obscura uses a designer authored probability distribution and adjustable width and height values in order to place interlocking level sections in the level. We use a set of 8 level sections: **four-way intersections**, **3-way** (or **T**) **intersections**, **straight halls**, **end-rooms**, **halls with doors**, **bedrooms**, **sitting rooms**, and **corners**. The probability distribution gives the designer some control over which level sections he would like to show up more often. For instance, the designer can increase the likelihood of four-way intersections and decrease the likelihood of straight hall sections if he wants a more connected level. The width and height values dictate the dimensions of the generated level. This gives the designer another method of control over the level generator by allowing him to decide if he wants, for example, a long and narrow level or an expansive level. In addition to the probability distribution, our method contains several hard constraints to ensure that all levels generated are playable and well-formed. To increase the diversity of the levels generated, our method chooses from several options for each level section each time a section type is chosen. The options for the level sections have differing objects and object layouts. This helps prevent levels from getting repetitive and breaking player immersion. Once the structure of the level is generated, the algorithm randomly distributes enemies, interactive objects (i.e. notes and books), and special events, such as texture changes intended to startle the player. The entire process is repeated if the player character dies.

Canvas Obscura also features relentless enemy AI. Implementing this system advances the game in two key ways. First, the ability of the enemies to chase and damage the player gives a sense of danger to the game, which in turn makes it more frightening. Second, the indefatigable enemies give *Canvas Obscura* more tension and conflict. The player attempts to escape, but quickly discovers that the enemy will follow her no matter where she tries to flee. This combination of tension, the feeling of being hunted, and the disorientation from the generation of the maps creates a powerful sense of panic and fear in the player.

The relentlessness of the enemies in *Canvas Obscura* was achieved in the following way. An enemy, upon seeing the player, transitions into an attack state and takes chase. This is accomplished by giving the enemy a vision cone and a simulated sense of smell. As the player moves through the level, traces of her position are repeatedly stored. Once the player is noticed by an enemy, that enemy will continually check to see if any trace of the player is within its range. If a trace is found, the enemy will move towards the newest tracked position, making it very difficult for the player to kite around or outrun the enemy. Due to the advanced tracking system, once an enemy has locked onto a player it will not relent until it has either caught her or the player has ended the level.

Target Audience

Canvas Obscura is designed for followers of the super genre "adventure," and more specifically of the survival-horror genre, which has seen an increase in followers in recent years [2, 5]. We targeted this group by throwing the player headlong into the game and story, after giving her a description of the controls. We increase immersion into the story, an important aspect in any horror game, by including a brief narration in the beginning. The first-person camera view also adds to the immersion of the player. In addition to immersion into the story, our game offers more replayability than many other horror games. The replayability of *Canvas Obscura* stems from the use of procedurally generated levels, which ensures that no two play-throughs are the same. Additionally, consumers of the puzzle genre may also show interest in *Canvas Obscura* because of the puzzle-like levels introduced by the procedural level generation.

References

[1] Bakkes, Sander, and Joris Dormans. Involving player experience in dynamically generated missions and game spaces. *Eleventh International Conference on Intelligent Games and Simulation*. 2010. 72-79.

[2] Entertainment Software Association. (2014 April) 2014 Essential Facts About the Computer and Video Game Industry. Entertainment Software Association. Washington, DC. [Online.] Available: http://www.theesa.com/facts/pdfs/esa_ef_2014.pdf

[3] Hendrikx, Mark, et al. Procedural content generation for games: A survey. *ACM Transactions on Multimedia Computing, Communications, and Applications*. 2013. 1:1-1:23.

[4] R. Legaspi and M. Numao. Towards the Design and Development of Anticipation-Based Event Selection Modeling for Survival Horror Games. *Proc. In Information and Communications Technology. Vol. 7.* 2013. 184-194.

[5] R. Rouse. Match Made in Hell: The Inevitable Success of the Horror Genre in Video Games. *Horror Video Games: Essays on the Fusion of Fear and Play*. 2009. Chapter 2, 15-25.

[6] Togelius, Julian, et al. Search-based procedural content generation: A taxonomy and survey. *Computational Intelligence and AI in Games, IEEE Transactions on 3.3*. 2011. 172-186.

Immaculacy: A Game of Privacy

April Suknot
Department of Computer Science
University of New Mexico
Albuquerque, NM 87131
asuknot@cs.unm.edu

Tim Chavez
Department of Computer Science
University of New Mexico
Albuquerque, NM 87131
tchavez22@unm.edu

Nathan Rackley
Department of Computer Science
University of New Mexico
Albuquerque, NM 87131
nprackley@gmail.com

Patrick Gage Kelley
Department of Computer Science
University of New Mexico
Albuquerque, NM 87131
pgk@unm.edu

CHI PLAY '14, Oct 19-22 2014, Toronto, ON, Canada
ACM 978-1-4503-3014-5/14/10.
http://dx.doi.org/10.1145/2658537.2662971

Abstract
With the intent of addressing growing concerns regarding online privacy, *Immaculacy* is an interactive story that immerses the player in a slightly dystopian world littered with privacy issues. Events unfold in the narrative based on hidden scores kept during gameplay and calculated based on specific decisions made by the player. Ultimately, we hope to create an engaging environment that helps players consider the decisions they are making in their own lives. We give the player experience with many privacy issues through their explorations of a world of hyper surveillance and connectivity.

Author Keywords
privacy; security; interactive story; game design;

ACM Classification Keywords
K.4.1. Public Policy Issues

Introduction
The continuous evolution in the pervasiveness and connectedness of technology is a subject of growing concern. Databases, smartphones, tablets, laptops, wearables are all united through a single global network—the Internet. This growth has resulted in social networks and other data-collecting applications becoming a major part of everyday life for many

people. Consequently, new threats have emerged which are capable of harming people professionally, financially, personally, and even physically. With medical, educational, financial, and other personal data available online, exploited vulnerabilities have the potential to devastate large numbers of people, with a single attack. Because of this, it is easy to see how privacy and security are among top concerns for many people around the world.

Game Concept

Immaculacy is a game that takes the player to a near-future society, New Washington, with an overbearing city government. The New Washington government keeps constant watch on its citizens through various means of surveillance, in the name of maintaining the "immaculacy." The player will be exposed to many consequences that can arise from this type of governing. There will be instances of citizens being unfairly accused of wrongdoings and sometimes becoming rebellious. Some people will abuse the power or access that they are given. Such abuse, among other vulnerabilities, can result in sensitive information ending up in malicious hands and may also put innocent people in danger. In many cases, the player will find him or herself in the middle of sensitive situations and will be forced to make decisions that may have major consequences in the future.

This interactive story takes the player on a journey, through a world in which personal information is in constant jeopardy. The player is placed in the role of an eighteen-year-old girl, Sydney Carlisle. Sydney is a high-school graduate who grew up in the small town of Danville. Although Sydney and her best friend have

Figure 1: With the narrative interface, making decisions is the primary game mechanic and will affect the player's score and elements of the story.

been dreaming of moving to New Washington since grade school, rumors of the oppressive government and technological advancement in the big city cause Sydney to have second thoughts about moving there. When her friend is given a full ride to New Washington University, the pressure builds on Sydney to join her in the peculiar city. Upon arriving in New Washington, Sydney realizes that the watchful eye of the city government is just one of many threats. In order to survive in her new home she must learn how to protect her information and be cautious when trusting others.

Because the intent behind *Immaculacy* is to communicate both the seriousness and the range of attacks that can be used against Internet users, the target audience is very broad. In general, any smartphone owner or person who uses the Internet on a regular basis can benefit from and enjoy this game. We estimate that if submitted to the Entertainment Software Rating Board, the rating given could

Events unfold in *Immaculacy* based on two types of hidden scores:

SECURITY SCORES

Data Leaking: Determined by how much sensitive information the player gives when questioned by any NPC.
City Suspicion: Determined by how much information the player withholds when questioned by city officials.

PERSONAL SCORES

Individual NPC Scores: Determined by how the player treats the individual NPC, in addition to other NPCs that are somehow related to the individual NPC's story arc.
Karma Score: Determined by overall treatment of other characters either directly or indirectly.

These scores affect the main character's:

- relationships with other characters;
- extent of government surveillance;
- vulnerability to criminals;
- employment and community status.

potentially be up to the Teen rating level due to the psychological nature of the game. The narrative game is presented with a comic book art style, as can be seen in Figure 1. This style offers an experience that can be enjoyable and familiar for people with ranging interests.

Game Design and Mechanics

Sydney, the character controlled by the player, will have the ability to interact with people, devices, and items in the world through a narrative interface. Certain interactions will present the player with decisions that are tracked and maintained by the game using hidden score metrics.

The primary novel quality associated with *Immaculacy* is the nature of the game within its own genre. Rather than creating a game revolving around quizzing players on their knowledge of privacy issues, this dialogue-based role-playing game is designed to present the player with realistic situations in which Sydney's privacy, and sometimes safety, can be compromised. Furthermore, this game is intended for the average Internet user and is not tailored to a player working within a specific field.

Game Goals

The online games presented in [1] and [2] educate the average Internet user on several threats that they may encounter on the Internet. The game in [1] is intended to help users identify phishing attacks by studying web addresses, whereas [2] focuses more on general security like virtual and physical handling of sensitive data. Both games however, do present the information similarly, utilizing a quiz-based format where players are asked questions that have a right or wrong answer.

Several other games exist that use a more story or situation based approach to teach a player about security concepts. In contrast to *Immaculacy*, these games are intended to train personnel who are or will be working in an information assurance related field. The games presented in [3] and [4] consist of simulations, which were used to train personnel who are or will be working in a cyber-security, or information assurance related field. Similarly, the game introduced in [5] is a card game and is used in a similar fashion to train people for a privacy related job position. Each of these games presents the player with a variety of scenarios that a professional in the information assurance field may encounter. Depending on the way a player handles a certain encounter; they are met with the appropriate consequence in game. User studies for many of these games have shown some success in training computer users in privacy and security related topics.

We have created a privacy themed mobile game for the average Internet and smartphone user. With this game, our goal is to raise awareness of different types of Internet related threats and the impact they can have on someone's life. Through an interactive story, we have simulated many real situations concerning privacy topics. We hope to give the user some experience with these threats and issues as a result of playing *Immaculacy*.

The studies conducted in [6] and [7] not only reveal concerns that users have with different privacy issues, but they also show where there are still large vulnerabilities for average users. Pilot studies performed for the game described in [1] helped the authors to review the development of the full version of

Privacy topics that will be encountered in *Immaculacy*:

Smartphones
Smartphone Surveillance
Smartphone Hacking
Application Permissions

Social Networking
Oversharing Information
Cyber-stalking
Cyber-bullying

E-Mail
Phishing Attacks
Viruses

General Internet Use
Internet Scams
Internet Surveillance
Malware
Spyware
Social Engineering
Adware
Censorship
Selling or Leaking Data
Identity Theft
Website Privacy Policies

the game to have a larger impact on its players. Similarly, the study conducted in [8] included user testing with privacy policy visualizations to optimize the appearance and layout of the visualization for average users.

We hope to build on the studies in [6] and [7] by addressing some of the issues discussed in these works within the story for *Immaculacy*. We will be conducting upcoming playtests on a demo of the first part of the game. From these tests, we hope to learn more about privacy concerns of Internet users and whether *Immaculacy* is effective in helping players address and consider such concerns. We also plan to use a similar approach to the user studies in [1] and [8] by using the tests that we will be conducting to assist in determining our approach in implementing the full version of the game.

Conclusion

With the security threats facing Internet and smartphone users today, *Immaculacy* is a game about Internet privacy that gives players the opportunity to play through events that they could potentially encounter on their connected devices. By assessing various studies and evaluating known threats, we have created a storyline that provides its players with topics and situations to consider when revealing personal information online. While *Immaculacy* is currently in the very early stages of development, we aim to further build on the foundation that we have created. Ultimately, hope to provide an enjoyable, informative, and thought provoking experience. A video of the gameplay demo can be found at: exit.cs.unm.edu/immaculacy.

References

[1] Sheng, S., Magnien, B., Kumaraguru, P., Acquisti, A., Cranor, L. F., Hong, J., and Nunge, E. Anti-phishing phil: the design and evaluation of a game that teaches people not to fall for phish. *In Proceedings of the 3rd symposium on Usable privacy and security*, ACM (2007), 88-99.

[2] Office of Justice Programs. Mission: Laptop Security. http://www.onguardonline.gov/media/game-0008-mission-laptop-security.

[3] Jordan, C., Knapp, M., Mitchell, D., Claypool, M., and Fisler, K. CounterMeasures: a game for teaching computer security. In *Proceedings of the 10th Annual Workshop on Network and Systems Support for Games*, IEEE Press (2011), 7.

[4] Irvine, C. E., Thompson, M. F., and Allen, K. CyberCIEGE: gaming for information assurance. *Security & Privacy,* IEEE, *3*(3) (2005), 61-64.

[5] Denning, T., Kohno, T., and Shostack, A. Control-Alt-Hack™: a card game for computer security outreach and education. In *Proceeding of the 44th ACM technical symposium on Computer science education*, ACM (2013), 729.

[6] Felt, A. P., Egelman, S., and Wagner, D. I've got 99 problems, but vibration ain't one: A survey of smartphone users' concerns. *Technical Report UCB/EECS-2012-70*, EECS Department, University of California, Berkeley (2012).

[7] Young D., and Quan-Haase, A. Information revelation and internet privacy concerns on social network sites: a case study of Facebook. In *C&T '09: Proceedings of the 4th International Conference on Communities and Technologies*, New York, NY, USA (2009), 265-274.

[8] Kelley, P.G., Bresee, J., Cranor, L.F., and Reeder, R.W. A "Nutrition Label" for Privacy. *Symposium On Usable Privacy and Security (SOUPS)* (2009).

Taxi Trouble: Communication is Key

Rob van Bekkum, Thijs L.M. Brands, S.Soheil Jahanshahi, Aidan C.A. Mauricio, Joost J.E. van Oorschot, Fanny Lie, Ben Kybartas, Rafael Bidarra
Delft University of Technology,
Delft, The Netherlands
R.vanBekkum | T.L.M.Brands | S.S.Jahanshahi | A.C.A.Mauricio |
J.J.E.vanOorschot | F.F.Lie@student.tudelft.nl
B.A.Kybartas | R.Bidarra@tudelft.nl

CHI PLAY '14, Oct 19-22, 2014, Toronto, ON, Canada
ACM 978-1-4503-3014-5/14/10.
http://dx.doi.org/10.1145/2658537.2662994

Abstract
We present the Android game ***Taxi Trouble***, an interactive, competitive and collaborative multi-player game focusing on stimulating social interaction, effective communication and entertaining groups of four to eight people for a short timeframe.

Author Keywords
Competitive gaming; Collaborative gaming; Social Interaction; Social gaming; Mobile gaming

Overview
Taxi Trouble is a racing game developed to entertain groups of four to eight people who are together in the same area. It is designed with the purpose of stimulating social interaction between players. The game requires that players verbally communicate within teams of two in order to be successful.

Background Research
In various situations, large groups of people will be together for long periods of time, e.g. parties, festivals, etc. This is a great potential for social interaction, which may be difficult especially when surrounded by complete strangers. Sellar [1] argues that computer games are not simply a means of individual entertainment. Allowing players to participate in an interactive, competitive and cooperative computer game is thus a well-fitting, but also challenging way of improving social interactions between individuals.

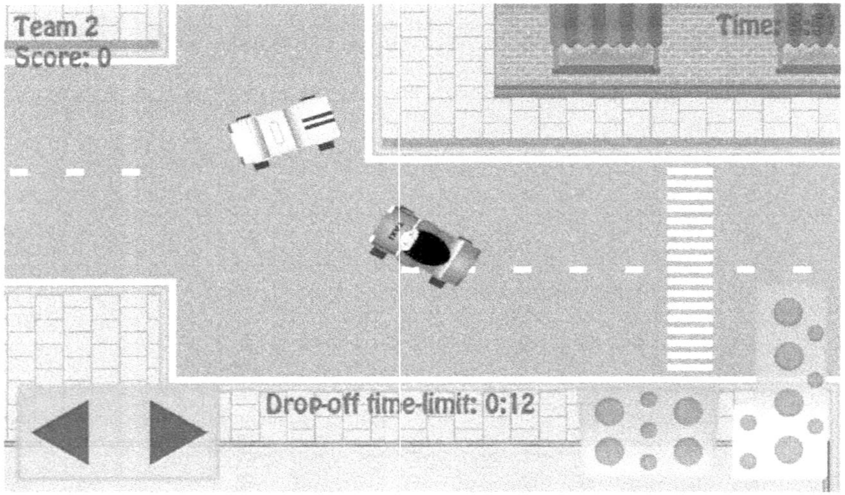

Figure 1. Driver view: Team 2's taxi carrying a passenger, with the first team's taxi visible above it.

Collaborative games are becoming more and more popular. Ducheneaut and Moore [2] describe three elements that make a social game stand out, which are collaborative activities, a shared experience of playing the game and getting satisfaction as a result of socializing with a group of people. Granic et. al. [3] further state that an entertaining game should make players feel in control, but at the same time have an element of unpredictability, resulting in a sense of satisfaction and pride when the players' shared goal has been reached.

Competition in computer games has always taken an essential role in multiplayer games. According to Vorderer et. al. [4], including competitive elements in games allows active player engagement and yields in getting direct feedback on the players' actions. Cairns et. al. [5] add that playing a game against human players results in more involvement than playing against computer opponents.

Design and Development

Following the results of the background research, as discussed in the previous section, we designed a game in which players are assigned to teams of two, with one player taking the role of a taxi-driver and the second taking the role of navigator. The goal of the game is to pick up passengers and take them to a specific location to score points while racing against the clock. Collaboration exists between teammates while competition occurs between teams.

When a player decides to start a new game, they can decide on the total number of players (either 4, 6 or 8). The player must then wait for the total number of players to join. As soon as the game starts the players are randomly assigned into teams of two and get either the role of taxi-driver or navigator. The taxi-driver controls the taxi and only has a limited view of the city, as shown in *Figure* 1. The navigator on the other hand has a much wider overview of the city, as shown in *Figure 2* and can further explore it by swiping the screen and zooming in or out. The navigator's job is to verbally guide the driver to the right locations to pick up passengers and drop them off at their destinations within a given time limit. Without the help of the navigator, the driver will not know the location of passengers or other teams. This makes the game difficult to win without effective communication between the driver and navigator. Each passenger must be delivered to a specific location within a certain time limit, and points are scored based on how quickly the passenger is delivered. To make the gameplay even more entertaining and competitive, it is possible to steal a passenger from another taxi by bumping into it. We also introduced power-ups that can be picked up and activated by the navigator. These provided benefits such as shields from other taxis, and speed boosts to make the taxi faster. We opted for short games to increase tension, so each game takes five minutes. The team with the highest score at the end of the five minutes is declared the winner.

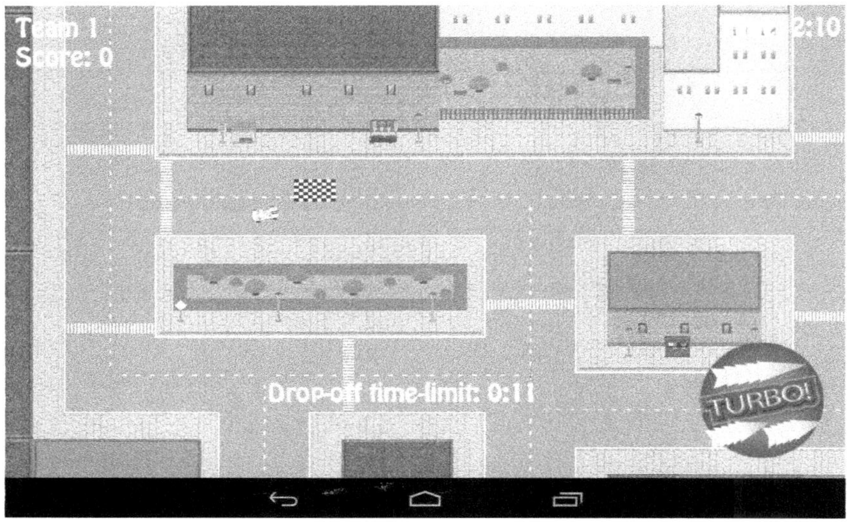

Figure 2. Navigator view: The taxi is shown approaching the passenger drop-off area, represented as a checkered box.

Gameplay Testing and Evaluation

Just before our product entered the beta stage, we held a gameplay test at the *Science Centre Delft*. We choose this location on purpose as it tends to attract a large technically-oriented crowd between the ages of twelve and thirty.

Our tests indicated that it is a bit troublesome figuring out how to play the game, as nearly half of the players said that it took too long to completely understand the game. Once users understood the game, they began to communicate with each other. This showed that the collaborative elements of the game were effective at stimulating social interaction.

The time-limit for a passenger drop-off actually emerged due to results of this study. We found that, while the game was fun to play, players felt that it was a little bit too easy to score points. By adding the time-limit, there is now a heightened tension associated with scoring points. We found that this additional feature made our game more challenging and fun to play, and also forces the navigator and taxi-driver to communicate more, to quickly determine where the driver needs to go in order to drop off the passenger.

Despite the initial absence of this time constraint, all players found our game a huge success, as nearly everyone said that they would like to own the game.

Figure 3. Gameplay tests: Players communicating with each other as driver and navigator.

Game trailer

A trailer for Taxi Trouble has been created showing the most important and distinguishing aspects of its gameplay in comparison to existing games. The video can be viewed at: http://goo.gl/3CnKV3

Acknowledgements

We thank Jan-Willem van Velzen for his work on the artwork for our logo. We further wish to thank the *Science Centre Delft* for facilitating our player tests.

References

[1] Sellar, T. (2004). User experience in interactive computer game development. In Computer Human Interaction, pages 675-681, Springer Berlin Heidelberg.

[2] Ducheneaut, N. and Moore, R. J. (2004). The social side of gaming: a study of interaction patterns in a massively multiplayer online game. In Proceedings of the 2004 ACM conference on Computer supported cooperative work, CSCW '04, pages 360-369, New York, NY, USA. ACM.

[3] Granic, I., Lobel, A. and Engels, R. C. M. E. (2013), The Benefits of Playing Video Games. Radboud University, American Psychological Association.

[4] Vorderer, P., Hartmann, T., and Klimmt, C. (2003). Explaining the enjoyment of playing video games: the role of competition. In Proceedings of the second international conference on Entertainment computing, ICEC '03, pages 1-9, Pittsburgh, PA, USA. Carnegie Mellon University.

[5] Cairns, P., Cox, A. L., Day, M., Martin, H., and Perryman, T. (2013). Who but not where: The effect of social play on immersion in digital games. In International Journal of Human-Computer Studies, pages 1069-1077, Duluth, MN, USA, ACM.

Shynosaurs: A Game of Attention Dilemma

Melodie Vidal
Lancaster University
Lancaster, UK
m.vidal@lancaster.ac.uk

CHI-PLAY'14, October 19–21, 2014, Toronto, ON, Canada.
ACM 978-1-4503-3014-5/14/10.
http://dx.doi.org/10.1145/2658537.2662979

Abstract
Shynosaurs is a game designed to harvest the full range of the natural behaviour of the eyes. On one hand, players need to use their eyes to aim where they direct the mouse, click and drop characters into a safe zone (the cuties). This is the usual behaviour of the eyes, as sensors to gather information. On the other hand, players can choose to use their eyes to stare at and intimidate the enemies (the shynosaurs) in order to slow them down and send them away. This is also a natural behaviour of the eyes, which we sometimes use as means to win a battle of wills. The Shynosaurs game is developed with eye-tracking in mind and aims to embrace the delicate balance needed to use the eyes as both sensors and controllers.

Author Keywords
Game controllers, Eye-tracking, Visual Attention

ACM Classification Keywords
H.5.m [Information interfaces and presentation (e.g., HCI)]: Miscellaneous.

General Terms
Interaction Modalities

Figure 1: An idle cutie.

Figure 2: A shynosaur pretends to not be doing anything wrong when looked at.

Introduction

The eyes are good indicators of what a person's attention is focused on. They are also remarkably fast, which is another reason why they have attracted interest for their use as game controllers, in particular for people with disabilities. However, there has been extremely few games written with eye tracking as the main modality in mind, such as Isokoski's penguin shooting game [4]. Instead, eye-tracking is often used as a replacement for the original modality in pre-existing games [3], such as controlling commands in World of Warcraft [5], navigating in Mario Bros [6], orienting the camera or aiming in First-Person Shooter (FPS) games like Quake2 [7].

The eyes are one of our main sensors to comprehend the world around us and we need to move them very often in order to continuously gather visual information. In daily life, they are thus mainly used as passive sensors to bring visual information to the brain. However, we do occasionally use our eyes as ways to influence the world around us. Humans possess an awareness of when and how they are being looked at by another person and it tends to modify their behaviour depending on their personality. For example, it has been found that people behave better when they think they are being observed [1]. Using the eyes and the knowledge that one is being observed (and that one can "misbehave" while not being observed) is for example used in children's games, such as "Red light, Green light".

Another example of the effect of the eyes is the fact that a glance can be made into a stare to intimidate someone. Humans and animals alike are very sensitive to staring and reportedly feel discomfort when stared at [1]. In this light, we can see the eyes not only as sensors but also as actuators that have influence on another being. Humans are used to staring and know the effects that it can have on other people. It can thus be seen as a natural controller that we might occasionally use, for example as means of intimidation or for a battle of wills. It has been found that comfortable eye contact lasts around 1.5 to 3.6 seconds, after which the gaze becomes uncomfortable and turns into a stare [2].

Game concept

Bringing a player's stare in a gaming context has very interesting effects on gameplay. Characters can be intimidated and stared down, which may be interesting for means of immersion since the virtual characters present the same reaction that one might expect from real, living beings. However, staring down characters presents another interesting challenge: While players need to keep their eyes still, they can not gather detailed information about what is happening elsewhere on the screen. As a consequence, they also may not be able to properly click on a target with a mouse. Shynosaurs is specifically built to take advantage of this dilemma between information gathering and interaction.

We chose to embrace this duality in order to create a fast-paced, exciting game that requires users to balance how they choose to use their eyes. We wish to investigate whether players choose different strategies. In Shynosaurs, players need to save as many cuties (see Figure 2) as possible by dragging and dropping them with the mouse into a safe fenced zone. The player competes against shynosaurs (see Figure 6) that come from the woods to steal the cuties away. However, the shynosaurs are shy and easy to intimidate. If the player glances at a shynosaur, it will first stop and start to whistle (Figure 3) as if it was doing nothing wrong, as if it "feels" it is being observed. After two seconds, past the point where a glance becomes

Figure 3: When it realises it is stared at, the shynosaur becomes pale for a second.

Figure 4: An intimidated shynosaur runs away crying.

a stare, the shynosaur will turn pale (Figure 4) then run away crying (Figure 5). This means the shynosaur has been effectively intimidated by the player's stare.

The game also gradually increases in difficulty. Players have three lives in total, and lose a life when the shynosaurs have stolen more than half of the initial number of cuties. When the player is successful, a new level is loaded, with more cuties, faster shynosaurs and a smaller safe zone.

Figure 5: A screenshot of the game. Two cuties are in the safe zone, a shynosaur is being looked at and another one has captured a cutie and is carrying it away.

Implementation details
Shynosaurs was developed using Unity3D and custom graphics and sounds. The game requires an eye-tracker in order to track the player's gaze. Eye-trackers generally consist of infrared cameras pointing at the eyes. The image is then processed to extract the pupil position from the camera's point of view. A calibration of the eye-tracker is needed before playing the game, which takes only seconds. The pupil position data is then streamed to the game using custom software.

Implications

The duality of using the eyes both as sensors and actuators is the core lever of the gameplay. The fact that it will be difficult for the player to keep a shynosaur away and drag and drop a cutie in the safe zone at the same time creates a fast-paced, challenging environment. Players need to carefully manage the way they choose to use their eyes, to handle the constant stream of shynosaurs coming from the woods and take the cuties to safety at the same time.

The shrinking of the safe zone area is particularly challenging, as dragging and dropping the cuties requires more precision. In addition, players might at first be able to drop cuties in the safe zone while their eyes are busy looking at shynosaurs by using their peripheral vision, but as the safe zone becomes smaller their chances of dropping the cutie out of the safe zone increase. Players from a pilot study reported being more aware of their peripheral vision, which is used to aim the mouse at cuties and dropping them in the safe zone while they are staring at shynosaurs. We are in the process of conducting a more detailed investigation about players' strategies, perceived immersion and effect over time.

Conclusion

Shynosaurs is a fast-paced, challenging game developed around the duality of using two natural behaviours of the eyes: Sensing the environment and controlling (or, more accurately, intimidating). While there have been some games adapted for eye tracking as means of control, Shynosaurs is one of the very few games specifically developed around the possibilities and natural behaviours of the eyes. Instead of trying to work around the fact that the eyes cannot view the entire visual scene at the same time, we aimed to create a game that takes advantage of this fact and integrate it into the gameplay.

Acknowledgements

We wish to thank Rémi Bismuth for the graphic design and his invaluable advice and Jensen Forshaw for the sound design of the game.

References

[1] Frischen, A., Bayliss, A. P., and Tipper, S. P. Gaze cueing of attention: visual attention, social cognition, and individual differences. *Psychological bulletin 133* (2007).

[2] Helminen, T. M., Kaasinen, S. M., and Hietanen, J. K. Eye contact and arousal: The effects of stimulus duration. *Biological Psychology 88*, 1 (2011), 124 – 130.

[3] Isokoski, P., Joos, M., Spakov, O., and Martin, B. Gaze controlled games. *Universal Access in the Information Society 8*, 4 (Oct. 2009), 323–337.

[4] Isokoski, P., and Martin, B. Eye tracker input in first person shooter games. *Proceedings of the 2nd Conference on Communication by Gaze Interaction - COGAIN 2006: Gazing into the Future* (2006), 78–81.

[5] Istance, H., Hyrskykari, A., Vickers, S., and Chaves, T. For your eyes only: Controlling 3d online games by eye-gaze. In *Proceedings of the 12th IFIP TC 13 International Conference on Human-Computer Interaction: Part I*, INTERACT '09 (2009), 314–327.

[6] Muoz, J., Yannakakis, G. N., Mulvey, F., Hansen, D. W., Gutierrez, G., and Sanchis, A. Towards Gaze-Controlled Platform Games. In *Proceedings 2011 IEEE Conference on Computational Intelligence and Games* (September 2011).

[7] Smith, J. D., and Graham, T. C. N. Use of eye movements for video game control. In *Proceedings of the 2006 ACM SIGCHI International Conference on Advances in Computer Entertainment Technology*, ACE '06 (2006).

PowerFall - A Voice-Controlled Collaborative Game

Marco Filipe Ganança Vieira
Entertainment Technology Center, Carnegie Mellon University
Pittsburgh, PA, USA
Madeira Interactive Technologies Institute
Funchal, Portugal
mvieira@andrew.cmu.edu

Hao Fu
Entertainment Technology Center, Carnegie Mellon University
Pittsburgh, PA, USA
haof@andrew.cmu.edu

Chong Hu
Entertainment Technology Center, Carnegie Mellon University
Pittsburgh, PA, USA
chongh@andrew.cmu.edu

Nayoung Kim
Entertainment Technology Center, Carnegie Mellon University
Pittsburgh, PA, USA
nayoung1@andrew.cmu.edu

Sudhanshu Aggarwal
Entertainment Technology Center, Carnegie Mellon University
Pittsburgh, PA, USA
sudhansa@andrew.cmu.edu

CHI-PLAY'14, October 19–21, 2014, Toronto, ON, Canada.
ACM 978-1-4503-3014-5/14/10.
http://dx.doi.org/10.1145/2658537.2662993

Abstract
In this extended abstract, we present PowerFall, a 2D arcade-style voice-controlled two-player collaborative game. In the game, two players control two cartoon characters tied back-to-back under a falling parachute. The players shout into smartphone microphones, and the volume of their voice is used to navigate the parachute horizontally. The objective of the game is to avoid various hazardous obstacles and safely land on the ground.

Author Keywords
Game; Voice Control; Living Room; Smartphone; Collaborative.

ACM Classification Keywords
H.5.2 [Information Interfaces and Presentation]: User Interfaces; J.5 [Arts and Humanities]

Introduction
PowerFall is a 2D arcade-style two-player collaborative game where two players have to shout to control a falling parachute in order to help the main characters survive various hazardous obstacles.

The story of the game begins with two main characters piloting a plane with severe mechanical malfunctions, which consequently lead to an explosion. As there was only one parachute on the plane, the characters had to share it by tying themselves back-to-back. While the characters are falling, different types of dangerous objects, such as hot-air balloons, rockets, meteorites and birds, appear in their way (shown in Figure ??). In order to survive, they have to pilot the parachute to avoid them. Each time they hit an object, the parachute will get damaged until it reaches a threshold resulting in a parachute failure and a fatal free fall.

Figure 1: PowerFall game screenshot.

PowerFall is a collaborative game. The fact that the two characters are tied back-to-back in the game allows one player to control the parachute to move either left or right, not both. It requires the two players to cooperate and accurately control their shouting volume to navigate the parachute to avoid dangerous objects.

Target Audience

PowerFall is a game made for everyone. With abstract and cartoonish art style, the game is easily received by people from all age groups. In order to attract different demographics, we designed characters as cute and funny creatures, which create a comic style within the game that players will feel spontaneous to laugh and enjoy. Although PowerFall is a simple game, it has strong emotional impact to the players. As screaming releases stress, players can gain more much fun shouting out loud with their friends or family members.

Technological Innovations

In the design stage of PowerFall, we decided not to let the standard gaming platform (e.g., PC, game console) to limit the gaming experience. As a result, we chose to explore the living room form factor consisting of large panel displays and smartphones. Figure **??** shows the setup of PowerFall, in which the main game program is running on a PC and shown on a large panel display. Each player holds a smartphone and shouts into the microphone to play. This setup imposed two technological challenges: acquiring players' shouting; transmitting the shouting data to the main game program.

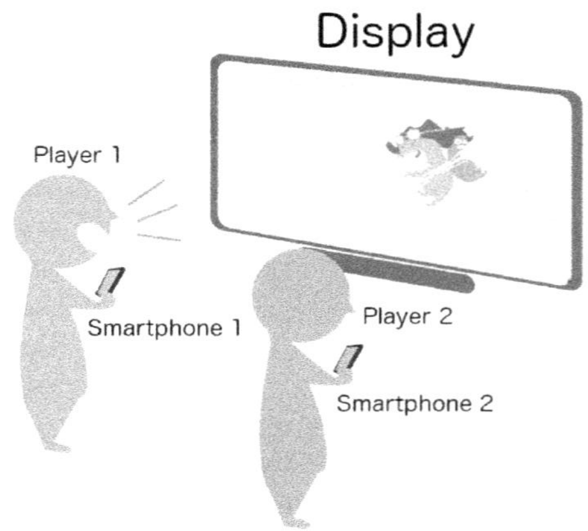

Figure 2: PowerFall setup.

To solve the first challenge, we implemented a native Android application to capture the players' shouting by sampling the amplitude of the waveform. We implemented a calibration mechanism in the application such that players with different volume ranges could produce similar results in the game. To solve the second challenge, a UDP server module was implemented in the main game program. The Android application constantly transmits UDP packets containing players' shouting data to the server module. The main game program parses the packets and converts shouting into force applied on the main characters. A hinge-joint structure (shown in Figure **??**) was created to faithfully reflect the effects of the force.

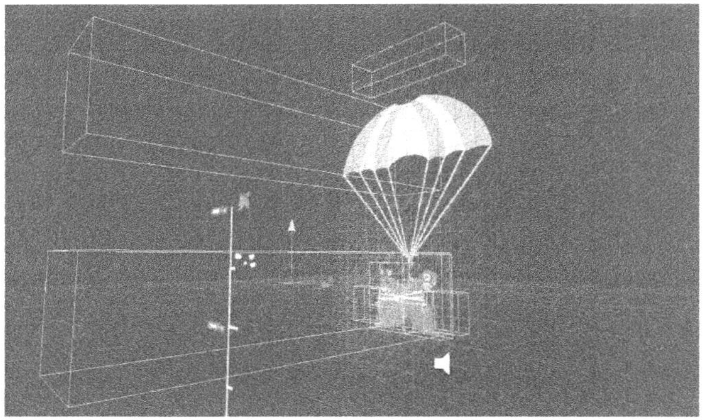

Figure 3: The parachute and characters structure.

Game Play Innovations
PowerFall uses smartphone microphone as the only controller. By detecting the volume of players' shouting volume, it converts and maps shouting to sound wave blasting out of the mouths of the main characters, which exert counterforce to the parachute to push it horizontally.

To indicate the strength of the force, four levels of distinct representation (shown in Figure **??**) were created to give players intuitive visual feedback.

Figure 4: Four sound wave blast levels.

As each player only controls one character, a player can only cause the parachute to move in one specific direction, which makes PowerFall a collaborative game. The most interesting fact about collaboration is that it requires verbal communication, which contradicts the shouting. As a result, we observed in most playtest cases that players had lots of fun struggling with instructing their teammates while shouting to navigate the parachute.

Game Concept Formulation
The concept of the game was formulated in the first week of entire three-week development process. We set out to make a simple and fun game. During the early stage of brainstorming, we wanted to develop a "silly puzzle" game where the solution of the puzzle would contradict players intuition. However, we failed to narrow the scope of the game, so we decided to start with a simple game

mechanism and develop a game around it. During the silly puzzle game ideation, we all agreed that shouting could be an interesting way to play a game, so we extended the idea and let players shout to control main characters falling with a parachute.We continued to use the essence of silly puzzle games - irony, as the theme of the game.

As the development of the game only took two weeks, we chose flat design in hope to achieve the most appealing visual style. After we finalized art style, we proposed two candidate designs of main characters. The first one was two boy pilots, and the second one was two monsters. Because our target audience spanned all age groups, we decided on the second design to minimize the idea of gender, race and age. Realizing the monster design was too abstract, we added pilot hats to the main characters to fit the background story. In terms of animation, we focused on immediate feedback and exaggeration. Four levels of distinct representation of sound wave blasts were created to give players accurate visual feedback. We also exaggerated the obstacles and character expressions to make the game experience fun.

Playtest

Throughout the development of PowerFall, we conducted three rounds of playtests. In each playtest, we collected valuable feedbacks from our playtesters and made observations that could be improved in the next iteration.

The first playtest was done right after we had a working game prototype with the main characters and basic game mechanism finished. Ten groups of playtesters played our game. The feedbacks were mostly positive as most people feel the game is fun to play and visually appealing. However, some playtesters told us that there is no indication of the game progress and little visual feedbacks for the main characters.

In the next iteration, we added an altitude meter and ten small parachutes on the game user interface to indicate the game progress and number of hits left to win the game. We also added sound waves to indicate the force generated by shouting and screen vibration when the main characters hit obstacles. In the second playtest, we found the previous problems were successfully solved with these modifications, but we did notice that the interest curve of the game was not exciting because of the arrangement of different types of obstacles.

We spend some time categorizing the obstacles into different difficulty levels and arranged them to appear in a specific order such that it would become more challenging to avoid obstacles as the game progressed. In the final playtest, all the playtesters shout more often and more loudly as the game advanced. Most of the playtesters told us that the game experience was so enjoyable that they felt happy no matter they won or lost the game. We also noticed during the playtest that audiences were entertained by simply watching other people playing.

Acknowledgments

We would like to express our gratitude to Jesse Schell, David Culyba and Brenda Bakker Harger, who are all faculty members of Entertainment Technology Center at Carnegie Mellon University, for their insightful help during the development of the game PowerFall. Also we would like to thank Fiona Jiayue Yu for voice acting.

Dodging Stress With A Personalized Biofeedback Game

Rami Al Rihawi
Texas A&M University
Doha, Qatar
rami.al_rihawi@qatar.tamu.edu

Beena Ahmed
Texas A&M University
Doha, Qatar
beena.ahmed@qatar.tamu.edu

Ricardo Gutierrez-Osuna
Texas A&M University
College Station, TX, USA
rgutier@cse.tamu.edu

ABSTRACT

We present a personalized biofeedback game that trains subjects to relax during gameplay. Training is achieved by increasing the game difficulty if the subject's breathing rate differs from a prescribed target. Personalization is achieved by adapting game difficulty to the subject's skill level, thus keeping the game challenging over long periods. Validation on a small group of users indicates that the game is effective at training players to acquire deep breathing skills and reducing arousal in a subsequent stress-inducing task.

Author Keywords

Games for health; stress; biofeedback; wearable sensors.

ACM Classification Keywords

J.2.3 [Computer Applications]: Life and Medical Sciences –Health; K.8.0 [**Computing Milieux**]: Personal Computing –General –Games.

INTRODUCTION

Chronic stress is becoming the "silent killer" due to the hidden dangers that it poses to our health. Commonly prescribed stress reduction techniques include meditation, deep breathing (DB), relaxation and biofeedback [1], with DB being the easiest and most commonly used. Unfortunately, these treatments have high attrition rates due to decreasing motivation levels with time and fail to train subjects to engage in relaxation-inducing behavior in the presence of stressors. Thus, there is a need for treatments that help individuals learn to regulate their stress response under duress while keeping them motivated.

We present Dodging Stress, a biofeedback game where subjects are trained to slow down their breathing (i.e. breathe deeply) to induce relaxation by modulating game difficulty. The game is then personalized by further adapting game difficulty based on the subject's skill level to maintain engagement. We also present results from a pilot study to test the effectiveness of the approach.

CHI PLAY '14, Oct 19-22 2014, Toronto, ON, Canada
ACM 978-1-4503-3014-5/14/10.
http://dx.doi.org/10.1145/2658537.2661310

RELATED WORK

Due to their broad appeal and interactive nature, video games have been explored to help regulate the impact of stress. In early work, Leahy et al. [2] developed a game to teach deep relaxation to patients with irritable bowel syndrome, an ailment to which stress is a major contributor. More recently, Reynolds et al. [3] developed a game to help players cope with fear; to succeed, players had to lower their psychological arousal, as measured with a heart rate sensor. Parnandi et al. [4] developed Chill-Out, a game that trains players to relax by penalizing high breathing rates with increased game difficulty. When compared to traditional DB and a non-adaptive version of the game, Chill-Out was found to be more effective in transferring DB skills and reducing arousal during a subsequent stress-inducing task.

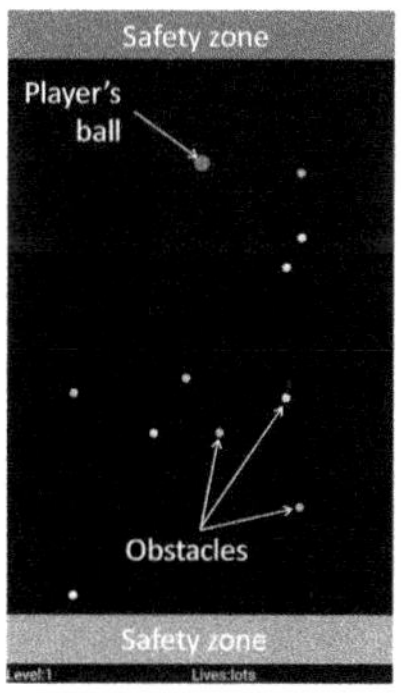

(a)

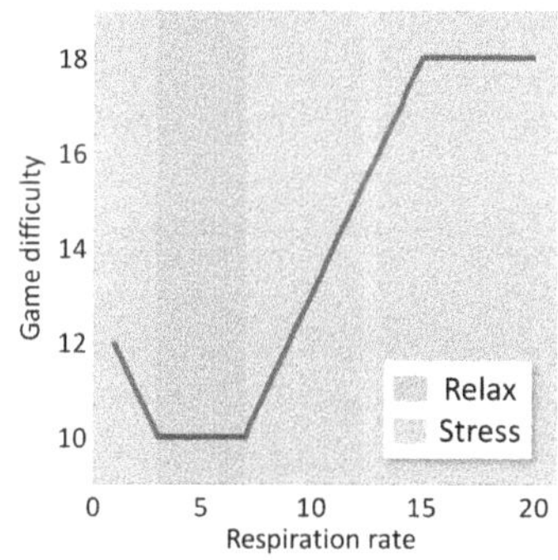

(b)

Fig. 1. (a) The goal of the game is to move the blue ball from one side of the screen to the other without hitting the smaller obstacles. (b) Mapping breathing rate into game difficulty.

GAME DESIGN

Dodging Stress is an adaptation of Dodge [5], an open source Android game under GNU-GPL. Shown in Fig. 1(a), the goal in Dodge is to steer a ball from one side of the field to the other side without hitting any obstacles, as many times as possible. We adapt Dodge for game-biofeedback purposes by introducing a positive feedback control law that increases the game difficulty in proportion to the player's breathing rate deviating from the ideal of five breaths per minute. Namely, given the player's breathing rate (b_t), game difficulty (d_t) at time t follows a piecewise-linear U curve; see Fig. 1(b). In contrast with [5], however, the game difficulty is not tied to an intrinsic parameter of the game but to the player's skill level, as measured during gameplay. This allows the game to adapt to each player, keeping them engaged regardless of their skill levels. Namely, the game maintains an estimate of the player's probability of success (p = successful/overall attempts) over a 45-sec window and then adjusts the number of obstacles n_t as:

$$n_t = \begin{cases} n_0 + 2 \times d_t & 3 > b_t \vee b_t > 7 \\ n_{t-1} + 2 & 3 < b_t < 7 \wedge p_t > \tau + 0.05 \\ n_{t-1} - 2 & 3 < b_t < 7 \wedge p_t < \tau - 0.05 \\ n_{t-1} & otherwise \end{cases} \quad (1)$$

where $n_0 = 10$ is the initial number of obstacles and $\tau = 0.75$ is the threshold (i.e. 75% chance of success).

PILOT USER STUDY

We evaluated Dodging Stress through a user study (N=5 male participants, ages 20–23 years) with the protocol [5]:

- Training (4 min): Subjects watched a video describing deep breathing (DB), and then practiced DB with an auditory pacing signal at 6 brpm for 2 minutes.
- Stressor (4 min): Subjects performed a modified Stroop color word test (CWT) as a pre-treatment stressor.
- Treatment (8 min): Subjects played Dodging Stress.
- Stressor (4 min): Subjects repeated CWT post-treatment.

To evaluate the game's effectiveness in teaching relaxation, we recorded heart rate variability (HRV) and electrodermal activity (EDA), both of which are proven physiological indicators of stress [6, 7]. EDA was measured with a Shimmer GSR sensor, whereas heart and respiration rate were measured with a Zephyr BioHarness.

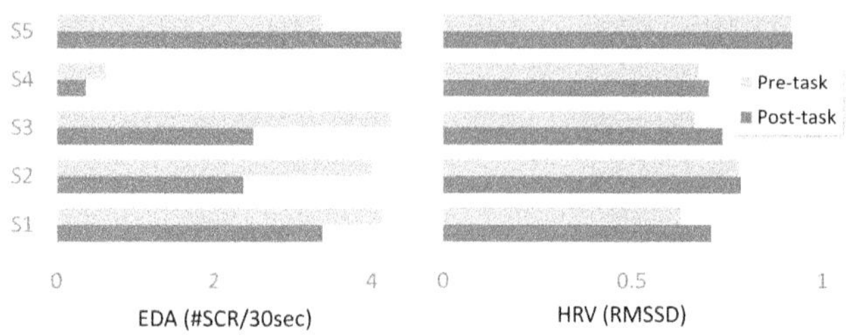

Fig. 2. Pre- and post-task HRV (root mean square of successive differences in a 30-sec window) and EDA (number of skin conductance responses above 2μS in a 30-sec window)

RESULTS

Fig. 2 shows the HRV and EDA pre- and post-tasks for all participants in the study. Overall, subjects showed a decrease in EDA and an increase in HRV between the pre- and post-tasks (both measures indicative of relaxation), except for subject 5. Fig. 3 shows the trajectory of game difficulty and breathing rate for one subject in the study; game difficulty closely follows changes in respiration rate, peaking at the 50-sec mark, when $b > 7$. Between 170 – 425 seconds, the difficulty level tracks the subject's success rate while $3 < b < 7$. User feedback was also positive, with subjects expressing an interest in continuing to play the game.

CONCLUSION AND FUTURE WORK

Our work shows that it is feasible to use biofeedback games to acquire relaxation skills while performing an engaging activity. Work is underway to compare the effectiveness of Dodging Stress against traditional relaxation techniques (i.e., deep breathing), and investigate the effect of game difficulty (e.g. easy vs. hard settings) on skill transfer on a larger subject pool. Alternative measures of stress (i.e. salivary cortisol) and game effectiveness (i.e. subjective experience) are also being pursued at this time. Personalization may also be improved by tracking performance over repeated attempts to better predict the subject's optimal level. This will maintain game appeal over longer periods, thus reducing attrition rates and enabling continuous improvement in relaxation skills.

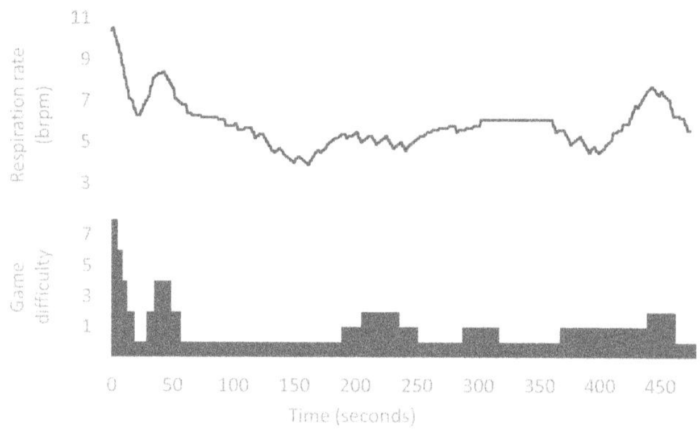

Fig. 3. Respiration and game difficulty for subject 1

ACKNOWLEDGEMENT

This publication was made possible by NPRP grant # 5-678-2-282 from the Qatar National Research Fund (a member of Qatar Foundation). The statements made herein are solely the responsibility of the authors.

REFERENCES

1. Richardson, K. M. and Rothstein, H. R. Effects of occupational stress management intervention programs: A meta-analysis. *J. Occ. Health Psy. 13*. 1 (2008). 69-93.
2. Leahy, A. et al. Computerised biofeedback games: a new method for teaching stress management and its use in irritable bowel syndrome. *J. RCP London 32*. 6 (1998). 552-6.
3. Reynolds, E. Nevermind: creating an entertaining biofeedback-enhanced game experience to train users in stress management. In Proc. *SIGGRAPH '13*, ACM, (2013).
4. Parnandi, A. et al. Chill-Out: Relaxation Training through Respiratory Biofeedback in a Mobile Casual Game. In Proc. *MobiCase 2013*, (2013), 252-260.
5. Dodge by Dozing Cat Software. https://code.google.com/p/dodge-android/
6. Martini, F. and Bartholomew, E. *Essentials of anatomy and Physiology*. Benjamin Cummings, 2010.
7. Freedman, L., et al. The relationship of sweat gland count to electrodermal activity. *Psychophysiology 31*. 2 (1994). 196-200.

Ad Hoc Genre Switching: A Concept for Generalized Parametrizable Game Mechanics

Daniel Apken
TZI, University of Bremen
dapken@tzi.de

Marc Herrlich
TZI, University of Bremen
mh@tzi.de

Rainer Malaka
TZI, University of Bremen
malaka@tzi.de

ABSTRACT
Game designers have to satisfy the needs of different player types. This paper presents a generalizable concept for switching between different play styles or genres without changing the basic game elements. As an example we employ specific combinations of parametrized game elements to emulate well-known genres: platformer, shooter, and puzzle games that can be switched at run-time by the player. We discuss first insights gained through a preliminary study.

Author Keywords
multi-genre games; genre blending; parametrizable game mechanics; game mashups

ACM Classification Keywords
H.5.m. Information Interfaces and Presentation (e.g. HCI): Miscellaneous; K.8.0. Personal Computing: General – Games

INTRODUCTION
When creating video games, designers have to satisfy the needs of many different player types [1]. They might have to provide multiple difficulty levels, game mechanics for various play styles and lots of content to be explored [6]. A system that gives players the choice to interfere with a game's flow in a meaningful and playful way could greatly benefit game developers and players alike. In this work we present a generalizable concept and a concrete example based on that concept for adjusting and switching between different play styles or genres without changing the basic game elements and the overall look and feel of the game. Our prototype game demonstrates different parametrizable game mechanics and elements, which in specific combinations map to certain genres: platformer, shooter, and puzzle games. We discuss first insights gained through a preliminary study that was conducted to evaluate the feasibility and player acceptance of our concept.

RELATED WORK
Procedural content generation is a common feature of so called Rogue-like games [3] and procedural level generation has been studied extensively [4]. Bjork et al. discuss a pattern approach to game design that may be used to formalized game mechanics and their relationships to a certain degree [2]. The MDA framework is intended to aid game designers by abstracting the intended player experience evoked through runtime behaviors, which are in turn implemented by low-level mechanics [6]. While dynamic difficulty adjustment (DDA) modifies game mechanics at run-time for balancing the difficulty [5], our approach modifies game mechanics to change the play style.

CHI PLAY'14, October 19–21, 2014, Toronto, ON, Canada.
ACM 978-1-4503-3014-5/14/10.
http://dx.doi.org/10.1145/2658537.2661324

GENERALIZED PARAMETRIZABLE GAME MECHANICS
One of the main goals of a concept for generalized parametrizable game mechanics is to provide players with additional choices and make them feel empowered when utilizing them. Therefore, switching or adapting the game mechanics should have a strong, noticeable impact on gameplay but ultimately switching the genres should not be forced on the players in order to succeed.

We developed a theoretical system (Figure 1) in which the players progress is monitored constantly and game mechanics are adapted accordingly. This system requires a basic game concept that provides primary and secondary game mechanics. Primary mechanics are those actively used by the player to reach her goal, while secondary mechanics might either be supportive, opposing or both.

During gameplay, the currently dominant (primary) game mechanics are altered to be slightly less powerful, while other subordinate (secondary) mechanics gain impact. This leads to a periodically increase in difficulty, which eventually makes it harder to progress in the game. The players choice at any point is to switch the primary game mechanic with a different one, creating new relations between primary and secondary mechanics. Suddenly, previously opposing mechanics might become supportive and vice versa. This can greatly benefit the players progress in the game and will also drastically change the play style.

Our concept is intended to facilitate the design process by clearly highlighting the important decision points, however, the concrete nature of and the balancing between game mechanics is subject to an iterative design process and requires conscious choices and trade-offs by the game designers.

We implemented a prototype game with parametrizable primary and secondary game mechanics following our theoretical framework. We chose a 2D casual game in order to minimize the threshold and access a potentially large and diverse

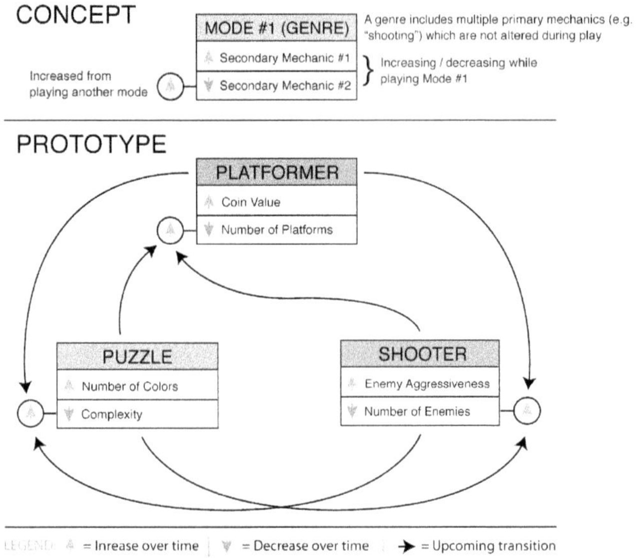

Figure 1. Top: General concept of defining different modes or playstyles by increasing and decreasing secondary mechanics. Bottom: Example modes and mechanics implemented by the prototype. Arrows show how modes influence each other's mechanics. Increasing difficulty is intended to motivate tactical mode swichting. However, a switch is never forced nor automatically performed by the game but is left to the player.

player base. Through iterative informal game testing we empirically determined the parameters for three game modes in order to map the basic mechanics to three common game genres.

The primary mechanics for each mode (or genre) are as follows: *Platformer:* Jumping, moving upwards and collecting coins. *Shooter:* Automatically moving sidewards and shooting enemies. *Puzzle:* Free movement in any direction, shooting puzzle pieces to trigger them and chaining puzzles for better results.

In the current prototype, the player's choice of switching the primary game mechanics is limited in such a way that she may only switch to a randomly preselected mode. However, she may switch repeatedly and through the underlying concept it is ensured that after successfully playing a certain mode for some time, switching to a different game mode is beneficial to the player's progress in the game.

Figure 1 shows the relations between each genre and the secondary mechanics. While each mode always affects mechanics typical to its own genre, it also tweaks one mechanic from the previously selected mode over time (shown as a green arrow outside of the box).

In the platformer mode, the player starts off with a high number of platforms and coins with a low value. As she progresses, these secondary mechanics are continuously altered. While the platforms decrease in frequency, the coins gain value. While playing the platformer mode, actions which increase the coin value and decrease the platform amount will also increase the otherwise decreasing parameter of the puzzle mode (here: puzzle complexity).

USER STUDY

In order to evaluate our concept, a preliminary user study with six participants was conducted. The main goal was to collect formative user feedback in order to iterate the concept and prepare both the prototype game and the study setup itself for a larger summative study. We were particularly interested if players would perceive the transition mechanic as a beneficial game element and in their satisfaction with the overall game experience. After explaining the basic elements and game controls, we observed each participant playing the game for roughly 10-15 min. without intervention. Afterwards, we collected subjective feedback through questionnaires and semi-structured interviews.

Despite the small sample and the preliminary setup of the study, the collected observations and player feedback already provided valuable insights. Specifically players that characterized themselves as playing often and being very competitive understood the strategic value of changing the game mode at the right time. Players describing themselves as casual players on the other hand commented negatively on the absence of a clear goal and stated that they lacked the motivation to switch the mode at all or only after staying in one mode until they felt they had explored everything.

CONCLUSION AND FUTURE WORK

In this paper we presented a generalizable concept and a prototype for parametrized game mechanics that allow to switch between different play style at run-time. Switching the current mode is not only a matter of personal preference but is also intrinsically motivated (but not forced) during play.

While we received positive feedback from experienced players, results of a preliminary test setup suggest that our current concept and prototype might exclude casual players by not providing a clear enough goal. In the future, we will modify the concept and the prototype accordingly, e.g. by providing clearer hints and feedback on the goals and the potential tactical value of switching the mode. Furthermore, we plan to conduct a larger formal evaluation.

REFERENCES

1. Bateman, C., Lowenhaupt, R., and Nacke, L. E. Player typology in theory and practice. In *Proc. of DiGRA* (2011).
2. Bjork, S. *Patterns in Game Design*, 1st ed. ed. Charles River Media, Hingham Mass., 2005.
3. Compton, K., and Mateas, M. Procedural level design for platform games. In *AIIDE* (2006), 109–111.
4. Hendrikx, M., Meijer, S., Van Der Velden, J., and Iosup, A. Procedural content generation for games: A survey. *ACM TOMCCAP 9*, 1 (2013), 1.
5. Hunicke, R. The case for dynamic difficulty adjustment in games. In *Proc. of ACE'05*, ACM (2005), 429–433.
6. Hunicke, R., LeBlanc, M., and Zubek, R. Mda: A formal approach to game design and game research. In *Proc. of AAAI Workshop on Challenges in Game AI* (2004), 04–04.

IC-CRIME Snapshots: Training Crime Scene Photographers Using Procedural Content Generation in Games

Julio César Bahamón, Maxim Litvinov, Phillip Wright, Roderick Gayle, Kurt Lippert, and R. Michael Young
Liquid Narrative Research Group, North Carolina State University
Raleigh, NC, USA
{jcbahamo, malitvin, pcwright, rcgayle, klipper}@ncsu.edu, young@csc.ncsu.edu

ABSTRACT
Modern day crime scene investigation methods are continually being enhanced by the application of new technologies to improve the analysis and presentation of crime scene information, helping to solve and prosecute crimes. The IC-CRIME Snapshots system provides a games-based tool to help train forensic photographers in a virtual environment.

Author Keywords
Serious Games; Artificial Intelligence; Planning; Forensic; Evidence; Virtual Reality; Mixed Reality.

ACM Classification Keywords
H.5.1 Information Interfaces and Presentation (e.g. HCI): Multimedia Information Systems—*Artificial, augmented, and virtual realities*; K.3.1 Computer Uses in Education: Computer Assisted Instruction (CAI)

INTRODUCTION
The IC-CRIME system is a game-based tool for use by crime scene investigators to model real-world crime scenes, link objects in the virtual scene to real world databases (e.g., fingerprint, hair and fiber) and collaborate with detectives and criminologists within a 3D virtual environment. A potential new feature for IC-CRIME is the ability for crime scene photographers to make use of the system to practice skills needed to produce effective photographs while obeying rules regarding preservation of evidence [1, 7].

The IC-CRIME Snapshots project focuses on the development of a novel game-based tool to train crime scene photographers within the IC-CRIME system. Crime scene photographers often must enter unfamiliar locations where crimes have occurred, locate evidence within the location without assistance of police or lab technicians and photograph the evidence in the context of the scene. These photographs must obey particular framing and content guidelines to maximize evidentiary value [7]. The photographer must also take these photographs without disturbing additional evidence within the scene.

CHI PLAY '14, Oct 19-22 2014, Toronto, ON, Canada
ACM 978-1-4503-3014-5/14/10.
http://dx.doi.org/10.1145/2658537.2661312

Figure 1. Capturing evidence and navigating the scene

RELATED WORK
The most significant applications of multimedia technologies to the area of criminal justice have fallen into two broad categories: the development of systems for the presentation of information in the courtroom and the implementation of software tools to assist in the investigative procedures related to the processing and analysis of the crime scene. The focus of our research is on the latter; however, the IC-CRIME system has potential applications in both contexts. Consequently, in this section we describe work in both areas.

One of the key applications of 3D technology that several researchers have focused on is the presentation of evidence to jurors, investigators, forensic scientists and other parties that are involved in the legal process [5, 4, 2]. Systems that apply augmented reality to provide additional information about a crime scene have been used successfully in court cases in the United Kingdom to assist in the prosecution and conviction of criminals [2, 5]. Work by Schofield [5] on the reconstruction of criminal incidents provides evidence of the applicability of virtual crime scene reconstructions in real crime scenarios. Research in the area of augmented crime scenes by Gee, et al. [3] has focused on implementing systems to help in the collection and processing of evidence at the crime scene.

SYSTEM OVERVIEW
IC-CRIME Snapshots is a game-based training tool that uses procedurally-generated content to provide a standalone 3D virtual environment to train forensic photographers. The system generates crime scenes—interiors of houses and apartments—that contain variations which allow for a unique environment on each play through. The player can walk through the scene and photograph objects. Photographs are saved to a file and also tagged with metadata to enable their examination in-game through an inventory system. At the end

of the game session, photo metadata and scene information are exported to an XML-formatted file to enable the system to recreate the training session at a later time. Additionally, the system provides the player with an assessment of her performance in the form of detailed feedback about each photograph taken as well as about any evidence that was *contaminated* in the process of navigating the scene. Data recorded from the session enables the system or a human instructor to asses the quality of the photographs collected by the player.

USER INTERACTION

Players experience the game in the role of a forensic photographer who interacts with the scene in a first-person mode. The game simulates the experience of walking through the crime scene while observing and cataloging its contents. To this effect, we implemented basic physics and collision detection with evidence items (e.g. victims' bodies and weapons).

Players can switch between a navigation mode and a photo capture mode. The former allows them to move throughout the scene while observing its contents and the latter simulates the use of a digital camera to capture still images of elements that are visible in the scene. Additionally, players may select from different levels of difficulty to accommodate varying degrees of proficiency. An administrator mode provides more detailed information about the evidence captured to help instructors assess the performance of the player.

GAME MECHANICS

The player's main objective is to capture a photographic record of all the evidence present in the crime scene while preserving its integrity. Evidence may include elements such as victims' bodies, blood spatter, broken windows, bullet casings, and weapons. The game evaluates the quality of photographs taken by the player based on the percentage of the item that is captured in the frame without being occluded by other objects. Additionally, since players must navigate the scene to find all the evidence, the game keeps track of their movements and records any instance when they collide with or walk over evidence. Note that players do not know in advance the number of evidence items available or their location, part of their objective is to discover them.

At the end of the game session, a score is computed based on the number of evidence items that were successfully photographed and the quality of the photographs. The score is adjusted to subtract points for any items *contaminated* by the player. The game displays a letter grade (A to F scale).

PROCEDURAL CONTENT GENERATION

The game uses procedural content generation (PCG) to create a variety of training scenarios while reducing the effort of manually creating individual instances. One of the key requirements for this component was ensuring that the procedural system always generates meaningful room layouts that can be correctly rendered and successfully navigated by a player. Additionally, the resulting content needed to allow for the future integration of an AI subsystem used to develop more interesting and complex training situations. To this effect, the system produces an XML representation of the scene, its contents, and the crime scenario used during the training session.

AI COMPONENT FOR CRIME SCENE GENERATION

Currently we use a small knowledge base of crime scenarios that are randomly selected and adapted to the level created by the PCG. A future version of the game will be integrated with a planning system [8] that utilizes the scene produced by the procedural content generator and applies a detailed knowledge base of the forensics domain to create more realistic crime scenes that can achieve specific training objectives.

LOGGING AND RETRIEVAL OF PLAYER PERFORMANCE

An important component of the system is the ability to record the play-through session to allow its later recreation and analysis. Essential elements of the user interaction are stored in a set of XML files. The system is designed to use these to recreate the scene exactly as it was created by the procedural content generator. Additionally, important elements of the user interaction such as player location, the time when interactions took place, and relevant metadata are also recorded.

IMPLEMENTATION

IC-CRIME Snapshots is built on top of the Unity3D game engine [6], a tool used for many commercial video games and to teach games-specific courses to computer science students.

ACKNOWLEDGMENTS

Support for this work was provided in part by NSF award number 0941421.

REFERENCES

1. Bahamón, J. C., Cassell, B. A., Young, R. M., Thomas, J. M., Hinks, D., Litzsinger, Z. E., and Lang, E. W. IC-CRIME: A Collaborative, Web-Based, 3D System for the Investigation, Analysis, and Annotation of Crime Scenes. In *5th Int. Workshop on Computational Forensics (in conj. with ICPR 2012)* (Tsukuba, Japan, 2012), 88–99.
2. Burton, A. M., Schofield, D., and Goodwin, L. M. Gates of global perception: forensic graphics for evidence presentation. In *Proc. of MULTIMEDIA '05*, ACM (New York, NY, USA, 2005), 103–111.
3. Gee, A. P., Escamilla-Ambrosio, P. J., Webb, M., Mayol-Cuevas, W., and Calway, A. Augmented crime scenes: virtual annotation of physical environments for forensic investigation. In *Proc. of MiFor '10*, ACM (New York, NY, USA, 2010), 105–110.
4. Gibson, S., and Howard, T. Interactive reconstruction of virtual environments from photographs, with application to scene-of-crime analysis. In *Proc. of VSRT'00*, ACM (New York, NY, USA, 2000), 41–48.
5. Schofield, D. Animating and Interacting with Graphical Evidence: Bringing Courtrooms to Life with Virtual Reconstructions. In *Proc. of CGIV '07*, IEEE CS (Washington, DC, USA, 2007), 321–328.
6. Unity3D. http://www.unity3d.com.
7. Waggoner, K., Suchma, K. H., and Holliday, S. D. *Handbook of Forensic Services*. US Dept. of Justice, Federal Bureau of Investigation, Laboratory Div., 2007.
8. Weld, D. S. An introduction to least commitment planning. *AI Magazine 15*, 4 (1994), 27–61.

ASPECT: Sinking and Floating Haptics for Elementary School Students

Shengyen Tony Chen[1], David Borland[2], Marc Russo[1], Ryan Grady[1], James Minogue[1]
[1]North Carolina State University
[2]RENCI, University of North Carolina at Chapel Hill
{stchen | marc_russo | regrady | james_minogue }@ncsu.edu, borland@renci.org

ABSTRACT
Traditional classroom methods of teaching concepts relating to buoyancy (sinking and floating) to elementary students are often ineffective. Incorporating haptic force-feedback controllers may help to improve traditional teaching methods. *ASPECT: Sinking and Floating*, targets student misconceptions via an interactive playable simulation. In addition to targeting misconceptions, *ASPECT: Sinking and Floating* also uses a Novint Falcon (http://www.novint.com/index.php/novintfalcon) haptic force-feedback controller to enable direct feeling of forces. This paper presents our design process and initial findings.

Author Keywords
Games; Simulation; Haptic; Elementary School Education; Conceptual Physics; Intelligent Tutoring System; HCI

ACM Classification Keywords
H.5.2 Information Interfaces and Presentation: Haptic I/O; K.3.1 Computers and Education: Computer-Assisted Instruction; K.8.0 General: Games

INTRODUCTION

Haptics can be defined as the study of touch and/or human interaction using touch [8]. The use of haptics in K-12 is relatively new. Williams[12] stated that prior to the publication "literature regarding the use of haptics in K-12 education seems to be nonexistent." Even though there have been advances in using haptic controllers in education since , only a few have discussed teaching concepts of physics [2, 7, 11]. Our design focuses on creating an simulation that teaches buoyancy-related concepts to elementary students.

The true efficacy of haptics in learning about "invisibile" science ideas remains unknown due to the lack of studies that have directly examined haptic interfaces for teaching and learning science concepts [2, 7, 11]. These studies set a precedent for using haptic interfaces to study cognitive processes. However, taken together their mixed findings and theoretically-based explanations of observed results speak to the complexity of the issue at hand and underscore the need for more work in this area. The ASPECT project is attempting to unravel the complex issues of the nature, persistence, and utility of visual-haptic information in memory.

We challenge the assumption that elementary school students cannot learn about abstract, often invisible, content. Traditional methods of teaching buoyancy involve students using a ball of clay to create a non-sinking object. This concept of making a hypothesis and experimenting is well documented in Klahr et al's theory of scientific discovery as dual search (SDDS) [6]. De Jong et al. [3] discuss how to create computer simulations to encourage scientific discovery learning. The design of the experiments are crucial. ASPECT adopts an informant design approach [4, 9]. Our key informants are children, expert STEM teachers, and content experts that form an Advisory Committee. We then use what we learn via testing with students to iteratively revise our simulation.

METHODOLOGY

Designing the simulation was a four step process. First we conducted a focus group study to determine if the traditional method of teaching buoyancy was effective. Using the results from the focus group study we then designed parts of the simulation to correct misconceptions. Then usability testing was conducted to improve our simulations. Lastly, we refined the simulation and turned it into a playable experience.

For our focus group, we employed a pre-test asking ten fifth-grade students to tell us why things sink or float. After the answers were recorded, we used the traditional method of teaching buoyancy. Each student was instructed to create an object out of clay that will float. Many students were able to design an object that will float. We then asked each student again why things sink or float. During the pretest all students stated that heavy things sink and light things float with only two students suggesting either material or size. The post test result showed that six out of ten students (60%) still believed that weight was the only factor with the remaining four (40%) discussing shape, mass, material, and water content as determining factors. Prior research [5] "suggests that novices often focus on only one dimension of sinking and floating." During our design phase we wanted to target three dimensions of sinking and floating. These dimensions are shape, size, and material. We designed a series of experiments that showed how these three dimensions can affect why things sink or

CHI PLAY '14, Oct 19-22 2014, Toronto, ON, Canada
ACM 978-1-4503-3014-5/14/10.
http://dx.doi.org/10.1145/2658537.2661319

float. Using four experimental scenarios (same size different weight, same weight different size, same material different size, and different shapes), students are able to experiment with different objects while using a Novint Falcon.

This three degree of freedom force-feedback controller enables the students to feel both the weight of the object and the combined weight and buoyant force when in water if force feedback is turned on. A pool of 48 third and fifth graders were asked to play through the simulation. To allow for a comparison of the relative impact of haptics, roughly half the population (23 out of 48) played through the simulation using the Falcon device without force feedback; the remaining 25 received both visual and haptic feedback. As the students played through the simulation, we collected data regarding time spent on different experiments as well as doing pre and post tests. The pre and post tests were scored based on the following SOLO Taxonomy [1]:

- 1 point for no aspect of buoyancy used in response.
- 2 points for a single aspect of buoyancy used in response (weight/mass, size, shape, material, and or force).
- 3 points for two or more aspects of buoyancy used in response.
- 4 points for two or more aspects of buoyancy used in response as well as some explanation of these aspects.
- 5 points for reflecting applications/extensions beyond the immediate context including abstract concepts such as density, volume, and/or water displacement in response.

PRELIMINARY FINDINGS

Using the SOLO Taxonomy outlined above, we have started the initial data analysis of the pre and post tests. When evaluating pre- and post-test, the consensus estimate of interrater reliability was 73% (as a simple percent-agreement figure) [10]. The resulting discrepancies were discussed in person and final SOLO taxonomy scores were assigned.

Independent t-tests (alpha = .05) that were conducted using the gain scores on the pre and post tests. The results showed that third graders as a whole gained 0.75 points and fifth graders gained 0.95 points on our SOLO taxonomy. These result suggests that our simulation does help students learn about buoyancy. Third grade students with force feedback averaged 2.92 on post-test compared to 2.27 without force feedback (gains of .846 and .636 respectively). The Cohen's d of 0.35 suggests a modest effect of haptics on our third graders. Fifth grade students averaged 2.80 with haptics and 3.00 without (gains of .900 and 1.00 respectively). This results suggests no significant difference due to having haptics.

CONCLUSION AND FUTURE WORK

ASPECT is a three year long project that will look at the impact of haptics in elementary science education. Our preliminary results have open up some new questions that we can try to answer with future simulations. Currently we are looking at two major questions. First question is why haptics seemed to have little or no effects on fifth graders in our sample. The other question is how can we better pinpoint the differential impact of haptics in educational simulations. In addition to the data described above (pre and post test), we have used screen capture and in game prompts. We will develop a typology of user behaviors to help us pinpoint any differences in user actions across the treatment groups (haptics vs. no haptics). We are also looking at evaluating the development of knowledge through the simulation scenes. The hope is that we can trace learning through the scenes and see how knowledge is being gained throughout the simulation. In future years, ASPECT will create simulations based on chemical bonds and magnetism.

ACKNOWLEDGMENTS

This material is based upon work supported by the National Science Foundation under Grant No. 1316473.

REFERENCES

1. Biggs, J., and Collis, K. Evaluating the quality of learning. *New York* (1982).
2. Bivall, P., Ainsworth, S., and Tibell, L. A. Do haptic representations help complex molecular learning? *Science Education 95*, 4 (2011), 700–719.
3. De Jong, T., and Van Joolingen, W. R. Scientific discovery learning with computer simulations of conceptual domains. *Review of educational research 68*, 2 (1998), 179–201.
4. Druin, A. Cooperative inquiry: developing new technologies for children with children. In *Proc. SIGCHI*, ACM (1999), 592–599.
5. Hardy, I., Jonen, A., Möller, K., and Stern, E. Effects of instructional support within constructivist learning environments for elementary school students' understanding of" floating and sinking.". *J. of Educational Psychology 98*, 2 (2006), 307.
6. Klahr, D., and Dunbar, K. Dual space search during scientific reasoning. *Cognitive science 12*, 1 (1988), 1–48.
7. Minogue, J., and Jones, M. G. Haptics in education: exploring an untapped sensory modality. *Review of Educational Research 76*, 3 (2006), 317–348.
8. Robles-De-La-Torre, G. Virtual Reality: touch/haptics. *Encyclopedia of* (2009).
9. Scaife, M., and Rogers, Y. Kids as informants: Telling us what we didnt know or confirming what we knew already. *The design of childrens technology* (1999), 27–50.
10. Stemler, S. E. A comparison of consensus, consistency, and measurement approaches to estimating interrater reliability. *Practical Assessment, Research & Evaluation 9*, 4 (2004), 66–78.
11. Wiebe, E. N., Minogue, J., Gail Jones, M., Cowley, J., and Krebs, D. Haptic feedback and students learning about levers: Unraveling the effect of simulated touch. *Computers & Education 53*, 3 (2009), 667–676.
12. Williams, R. L., Chen, M.-Y., and Seaton, J. M. Haptics-augmented simple-machine educational tools. *J. of Science Education and Technology 12*, 1 (2003), 1–12.

ASPECT: Sinking and Floating Haptics for Elementary School Students

Shengyen Tony Chen[1], David Borland[2], Marc Russo[1], Ryan Grady[1], James Minogue[1]
[1]North Carolina State University
[2]RENCI, University of North Carolina at Chapel Hill
{stchen | marc_russo | regrady | james_minogue }@ncsu.edu, borland@renci.org

ABSTRACT
Traditional classroom methods of teaching concepts relating to buoyancy (sinking and floating) to elementary students are often ineffective. Incorporating haptic force-feedback controllers may help to improve traditional teaching methods. *ASPECT: Sinking and Floating*, targets student misconceptions via an interactive playable simulation. In addition to targeting misconceptions, *ASPECT: Sinking and Floating* also uses a Novint Falcon (http://www.novint.com/index.php/novintfalcon) haptic force-feedback controller to enable direct feeling of forces. This paper presents our design process and initial findings.

Author Keywords
Games; Simulation; Haptic; Elementary School Education; Conceptual Physics; Intelligent Tutoring System; HCI

ACM Classification Keywords
H.5.2 Information Interfaces and Presentation: Haptic I/O; K.3.1 Computers and Education: Computer-Assisted Instruction; K.8.0 General: Games

INTRODUCTION
Haptics can be defined as the study of touch and/or human interaction using touch [8]. The use of haptics in K-12 is relatively new. Williams[12] stated that prior to the publication "literature regarding the use of haptics in K-12 education seems to be nonexistent." Even though there have been advances in using haptic controllers in education since , only a few have discussed teaching concepts of physics [2, 7, 11]. Our design focuses on creating an simulation that teaches buoyancy-related concepts to elementary students.

The true efficacy of haptics in learning about "invisibile" science ideas remains unknown due to the lack of studies that have directly examined haptic interfaces for teaching and learning science concepts [2, 7, 11]. These studies set a precedent for using haptic interfaces to study cognitive processes. However, taken together their mixed findings and theoretically-based explanations of observed results speak to the complexity of the issue at hand and underscore the need for more work in this area. The ASPECT project is attempting to unravel the complex issues of the nature, persistence, and utility of visual-haptic information in memory.

We challenge the assumption that elementary school students cannot learn about abstract, often invisible, content. Traditional methods of teaching buoyancy involve students using a ball of clay to create a non-sinking object. This concept of making a hypothesis and experimenting is well documented in Klahr et al's theory of scientific discovery as dual search (SDDS) [6]. De Jong et al. [3] discuss how to create computer simulations to encourage scientific discovery learning. The design of the experiments are crucial. ASPECT adopts an informant design approach [4, 9]. Our key informants are children, expert STEM teachers, and content experts that form an Advisory Committee. We then use what we learn via testing with students to iteratively revise our simulation.

METHODOLOGY
Designing the simulation was a four step process. First we conducted a focus group study to determine if the traditional method of teaching buoyancy was effective. Using the results from the focus group study we then designed parts of the simulation to correct misconceptions. Then usability testing was conducted to improve our simulations. Lastly, we refined the simulation and turned it into a playable experience.

For our focus group, we employed a pre-test asking ten fifth-grade students to tell us why things sink or float. After the answers were recorded, we used the traditional method of teaching buoyancy. Each student was instructed to create an object out of clay that will float. Many students were able to design an object that will float. We then asked each student again why things sink or float. During the pretest all students stated that heavy things sink and light things float with only two students suggesting either material or size. The post test result showed that six out of ten students (60%) still believed that weight was the only factor with the remaining four (40%) discussing shape, mass, material, and water content as determining factors. Prior research [5] "suggests that novices often focus on only one dimension of sinking and floating." During our design phase we wanted to target three dimensions of sinking and floating. These dimensions are shape, size, and material. We designed a series of experiments that showed how these three dimensions can affect why things sink or

CHI PLAY '14, Oct 19-22 2014, Toronto, ON, Canada
ACM 978-1-4503-3014-5/14/10.
http://dx.doi.org/10.1145/2658537.2661319

float. Using four experimental scenarios (same size different weight, same weight different size, same material different size, and different shapes), students are able to experiment with different objects while using a Novint Falcon.

This three degree of freedom force-feedback controller enables the students to feel both the weight of the object and the combined weight and buoyant force when in water if force feedback is turned on. A pool of 48 third and fifth graders were asked to play through the simulation. To allow for a comparison of the relative impact of haptics, roughly half the population (23 out of 48) played through the simulation using the Falcon device without force feedback; the remaining 25 received both visual and haptic feedback. As the students played through the simulation, we collected data regarding time spent on different experiments as well as doing pre and post tests. The pre and post tests were scored based on the following SOLO Taxonomy [1]:

- 1 point for no aspect of buoyancy used in response.
- 2 points for a single aspect of buoyancy used in response (weight/mass, size, shape, material, and or force).
- 3 points for two or more aspects of buoyancy used in response.
- 4 points for two or more aspects of buoyancy used in response as well as some explanation of these aspects.
- 5 points for reflecting applications/extensions beyond the immediate context including abstract concepts such as density, volume, and/or water displacement in response.

PRELIMINARY FINDINGS

Using the SOLO Taxonomy outlined above, we have started the initial data analysis of the pre and post tests. When evaluating pre- and post-test, the consensus estimate of interrater reliability was 73% (as a simple percent-agreement figure) [10]. The resulting discrepancies were discussed in person and final SOLO taxonomy scores were assigned.

Independent t-tests (alpha = .05) that were conducted using the gain scores on the pre and post tests. The results showed that third graders as a whole gained 0.75 points and fifth graders gained 0.95 points on our SOLO taxonomy. These result suggests that our simulation does help students learn about buoyancy. Third grade students with force feedback averaged 2.92 on post-test compared to 2.27 without force feedback (gains of .846 and .636 respectively). The Cohen's d of 0.35 suggests a modest effect of haptics on our third graders. Fifth grade students averaged 2.80 with haptics and 3.00 without (gains of .900 and 1.00 respectively). This results suggests no significant difference due to having haptics.

CONCLUSION AND FUTURE WORK

ASPECT is a three year long project that will look at the impact of haptics in elementary science education. Our preliminary results have open up some new questions that we can try to answer with future simulations. Currently we are looking at two major questions. First question is why haptics seemed to have little or no effects on fifth graders in our sample. The other question is how can we better pinpoint the differential impact of haptics in educational simulations. In addition to the data described above (pre and post test), we have used screen capture and in game prompts. We will develop a typology of user behaviors to help us pinpoint any differences in user actions across the treatment groups (haptics vs. no haptics). We are also looking at evaluating the development of knowledge through the simulation scenes. The hope is that we can trace learning through the scenes and see how knowledge is being gained throughout the simulation. In future years, ASPECT will create simulations based on chemical bonds and magnetism.

ACKNOWLEDGMENTS

This material is based upon work supported by the National Science Foundation under Grant No. 1316473.

REFERENCES

1. Biggs, J., and Collis, K. Evaluating the quality of learning. *New York* (1982).
2. Bivall, P., Ainsworth, S., and Tibell, L. A. Do haptic representations help complex molecular learning? *Science Education 95*, 4 (2011), 700–719.
3. De Jong, T., and Van Joolingen, W. R. Scientific discovery learning with computer simulations of conceptual domains. *Review of educational research 68*, 2 (1998), 179–201.
4. Druin, A. Cooperative inquiry: developing new technologies for children with children. In *Proc. SIGCHI*, ACM (1999), 592–599.
5. Hardy, I., Jonen, A., Möller, K., and Stern, E. Effects of instructional support within constructivist learning environments for elementary school students' understanding of" floating and sinking.". *J. of Educational Psychology 98*, 2 (2006), 307.
6. Klahr, D., and Dunbar, K. Dual space search during scientific reasoning. *Cognitive science 12*, 1 (1988), 1–48.
7. Minogue, J., and Jones, M. G. Haptics in education: exploring an untapped sensory modality. *Review of Educational Research 76*, 3 (2006), 317–348.
8. Robles-De-La-Torre, G. Virtual Reality: touch/haptics. *Encyclopedia of* (2009).
9. Scaife, M., and Rogers, Y. Kids as informants: Telling us what we didnt know or confirming what we knew already. *The design of childrens technology* (1999), 27–50.
10. Stemler, S. E. A comparison of consensus, consistency, and measurement approaches to estimating interrater reliability. *Practical Assessment, Research & Evaluation 9*, 4 (2004), 66–78.
11. Wiebe, E. N., Minogue, J., Gail Jones, M., Cowley, J., and Krebs, D. Haptic feedback and students learning about levers: Unraveling the effect of simulated touch. *Computers & Education 53*, 3 (2009), 667–676.
12. Williams, R. L., Chen, M.-Y., and Seaton, J. M. Haptics-augmented simple-machine educational tools. *J. of Science Education and Technology 12*, 1 (2003), 1–12.

ASPECT: Sinking and Floating Haptics for Elementary School Students

Shengyen Tony Chen[1], David Borland[2], Marc Russo[1], Ryan Grady[1], James Minogue[1]
[1]North Carolina State University
[2]RENCI, University of North Carolina at Chapel Hill
{stchen | marc_russo | regrady | james_minogue }@ncsu.edu, borland@renci.org

ABSTRACT
Traditional classroom methods of teaching concepts relating to buoyancy (sinking and floating) to elementary students are often ineffective. Incorporating haptic force-feedback controllers may help to improve traditional teaching methods. *ASPECT: Sinking and Floating*, targets student misconceptions via an interactive playable simulation. In addition to targeting misconceptions, *ASPECT: Sinking and Floating* also uses a Novint Falcon (http://www.novint.com/index.php/novintfalcon) haptic force-feedback controller to enable direct feeling of forces. This paper presents our design process and initial findings.

Author Keywords
Games; Simulation; Haptic; Elementary School Education; Conceptual Physics; Intelligent Tutoring System; HCI

ACM Classification Keywords
H.5.2 Information Interfaces and Presentation: Haptic I/O; K.3.1 Computers and Education: Computer-Assisted Instruction; K.8.0 General: Games

INTRODUCTION
Haptics can be defined as the study of touch and/or human interaction using touch [8]. The use of haptics in K-12 is relatively new. Williams[12] stated that prior to the publication "literature regarding the use of haptics in K-12 education seems to be nonexistent." Even though there have been advances in using haptic controllers in education since , only a few have discussed teaching concepts of physics [2, 7, 11]. Our design focuses on creating an simulation that teaches buoyancy-related concepts to elementary students.

The true efficacy of haptics in learning about "invisibile" science ideas remains unknown due to the lack of studies that have directly examined haptic interfaces for teaching and learning science concepts [2, 7, 11]. These studies set a precedent for using haptic interfaces to study cognitive processes. However, taken together their mixed findings and theoretically-based explanations of observed results speak to the complexity of the issue at hand and underscore the need for more work in this area. The ASPECT project is attempting to unravel the complex issues of the nature, persistence, and utility of visual-haptic information in memory.

We challenge the assumption that elementary school students cannot learn about abstract, often invisible, content. Traditional methods of teaching buoyancy involve students using a ball of clay to create a non-sinking object. This concept of making a hypothesis and experimenting is well documented in Klahr et al's theory of scientific discovery as dual search (SDDS) [6]. De Jong et al. [3] discuss how to create computer simulations to encourage scientific discovery learning. The design of the experiments are crucial. ASPECT adopts an informant design approach [4, 9]. Our key informants are children, expert STEM teachers, and content experts that form an Advisory Committee. We then use what we learn via testing with students to iteratively revise our simulation.

METHODOLOGY
Designing the simulation was a four step process. First we conducted a focus group study to determine if the traditional method of teaching buoyancy was effective. Using the results from the focus group study we then designed parts of the simulation to correct misconceptions. Then usability testing was conducted to improve our simulations. Lastly, we refined the simulation and turned it into a playable experience.

For our focus group, we employed a pre-test asking ten fifth-grade students to tell us why things sink or float. After the answers were recorded, we used the traditional method of teaching buoyancy. Each student was instructed to create an object out of clay that will float. Many students were able to design an object that will float. We then asked each student again why things sink or float. During the pretest all students stated that heavy things sink and light things float with only two students suggesting either material or size. The post test result showed that six out of ten students (60%) still believed that weight was the only factor with the remaining four (40%) discussing shape, mass, material, and water content as determining factors. Prior research [5] "suggests that novices often focus on only one dimension of sinking and floating." During our design phase we wanted to target three dimensions of sinking and floating. These dimensions are shape, size, and material. We designed a series of experiments that showed how these three dimensions can affect why things sink or

CHI PLAY '14, Oct 19-22 2014, Toronto, ON, Canada
ACM 978-1-4503-3014-5/14/10.
http://dx.doi.org/10.1145/2658537.2661319

float. Using four experimental scenarios (same size different weight, same weight different size, same material different size, and different shapes), students are able to experiment with different objects while using a Novint Falcon.

This three degree of freedom force-feedback controller enables the students to feel both the weight of the object and the combined weight and buoyant force when in water if force feedback is turned on. A pool of 48 third and fifth graders were asked to play through the simulation. To allow for a comparison of the relative impact of haptics, roughly half the population (23 out of 48) played through the simulation using the Falcon device without force feedback; the remaining 25 received both visual and haptic feedback. As the students played through the simulation, we collected data regarding time spent on different experiments as well as doing pre and post tests. The pre and post tests were scored based on the following SOLO Taxonomy [1]:

- 1 point for no aspect of buoyancy used in response.
- 2 points for a single aspect of buoyancy used in response (weight/mass, size, shape, material, and or force).
- 3 points for two or more aspects of buoyancy used in response.
- 4 points for two or more aspects of buoyancy used in response as well as some explanation of these aspects.
- 5 points for reflecting applications/extensions beyond the immediate context including abstract concepts such as density, volume, and/or water displacement in response.

PRELIMINARY FINDINGS

Using the SOLO Taxonomy outlined above, we have started the initial data analysis of the pre and post tests. When evaluating pre- and post-test, the consensus estimate of interrater reliability was 73% (as a simple percent-agreement figure) [10]. The resulting discrepancies were discussed in person and final SOLO taxonomy scores were assigned.

Independent t-tests (alpha = .05) that were conducted using the gain scores on the pre and post tests. The results showed that third graders as a whole gained 0.75 points and fifth graders gained 0.95 points on our SOLO taxonomy. These result suggests that our simulation does help students learn about buoyancy. Third grade students with force feedback averaged 2.92 on post-test compared to 2.27 without force feedback (gains of .846 and .636 respectively). The Cohen's d of 0.35 suggests a modest effect of haptics on our third graders. Fifth grade students averaged 2.80 with haptics and 3.00 without (gains of .900 and 1.00 respectively). This results suggests no significant difference due to having haptics.

CONCLUSION AND FUTURE WORK

ASPECT is a three year long project that will look at the impact of haptics in elementary science education. Our preliminary results have open up some new questions that we can try to answer with future simulations. Currently we are looking at two major questions. First question is why haptics seemed to have little or no effects on fifth graders in our sample. The other question is how can we better pinpoint the differential impact of haptics in educational simulations. In addition to the data described above (pre and post test), we have used screen capture and in game prompts. We will develop a typology of user behaviors to help us pinpoint any differences in user actions across the treatment groups (haptics vs. no haptics). We are also looking at evaluating the development of knowledge through the simulation scenes. The hope is that we can trace learning through the scenes and see how knowledge is being gained throughout the simulation. In future years, ASPECT will create simulations based on chemical bonds and magnetism.

ACKNOWLEDGMENTS

This material is based upon work supported by the National Science Foundation under Grant No. 1316473.

REFERENCES

1. Biggs, J., and Collis, K. Evaluating the quality of learning. *New York* (1982).
2. Bivall, P., Ainsworth, S., and Tibell, L. A. Do haptic representations help complex molecular learning? *Science Education 95*, 4 (2011), 700–719.
3. De Jong, T., and Van Joolingen, W. R. Scientific discovery learning with computer simulations of conceptual domains. *Review of educational research 68*, 2 (1998), 179–201.
4. Druin, A. Cooperative inquiry: developing new technologies for children with children. In *Proc. SIGCHI*, ACM (1999), 592–599.
5. Hardy, I., Jonen, A., Möller, K., and Stern, E. Effects of instructional support within constructivist learning environments for elementary school students' understanding of" floating and sinking.". *J. of Educational Psychology 98*, 2 (2006), 307.
6. Klahr, D., and Dunbar, K. Dual space search during scientific reasoning. *Cognitive science 12*, 1 (1988), 1–48.
7. Minogue, J., and Jones, M. G. Haptics in education: exploring an untapped sensory modality. *Review of Educational Research 76*, 3 (2006), 317–348.
8. Robles-De-La-Torre, G. Virtual Reality: touch/haptics. *Encyclopedia of* (2009).
9. Scaife, M., and Rogers, Y. Kids as informants: Telling us what we didnt know or confirming what we knew already. *The design of childrens technology* (1999), 27–50.
10. Stemler, S. E. A comparison of consensus, consistency, and measurement approaches to estimating interrater reliability. *Practical Assessment, Research & Evaluation 9*, 4 (2004), 66–78.
11. Wiebe, E. N., Minogue, J., Gail Jones, M., Cowley, J., and Krebs, D. Haptic feedback and students learning about levers: Unraveling the effect of simulated touch. *Computers & Education 53*, 3 (2009), 667–676.
12. Williams, R. L., Chen, M.-Y., and Seaton, J. M. Haptics-augmented simple-machine educational tools. *J. of Science Education and Technology 12*, 1 (2003), 1–12.

Reindeer & Wolves: Exploring Sensory Deprivation in Multiplayer Digital Bodily Play

Daniel J. Finnegan[1], Eduardo Velloso[2], Robb Mitchell[3], Florian 'Floyd' Mueller[4], Richard Byrne[4]
[1]Centre for Digital Entertainment, University of Bath, UK
[2]School of Computer Communications, Lancaster University, UK
[3]SDU Design, University of Southern Denmark, Kolding, Denmark
[4]Exertion Games Lab, RMIT University, Melbourne, Australia
[1]djf32@bath.ac.uk, [2]e.velloso@lancaster.ac.uk, [3]robb@mci.sdu.dk, [4]{floyd,rich}@exertiongameslab.org

ABSTRACT
Games designed around digital bodily play involve bodily movement and expression to create engaging gameplay experiences. Most feedback in these games takes the form of visual stimuli. To explore the gameplay mechanics afforded by depriving players from these visual cues, we designed *Reindeer & Wolves*, a role-playing game where blindfolded players capture other players relying on their hearing alone. Based on our design and play testing, we devised four strategies for designing games that incorporate sensory deprivation as an element of the core mechanic.

Author Keywords
Bodily Play; Sensory Deprivation; Social Play; Experiential Play; Movement-Sensed Play; Sensory Substitution;

ACM Classification Keywords
H.5.m. Information Interfaces and Presentation (e.g. HCI): Miscellaneous

INTRODUCTION
For centuries children (and adults) have played games that deprive players of their sight (e.g. *Piñata*, *Blind man's Buff*, *Marco Polo*). Navigating the physical environment without seeing can be a challenging but stimulating experience for players, requiring them to perceive the game world through non-visual stimuli. Recently, digital bodily play research has explored novel interaction design such as open-ended play [6], blurring movement and its digital representation [2] and most recently remote, creative play [3].

An established domain of research in HCI is that of sensory substitution, defined as "...the use of one human sense to receive information normally received by another sense" [4].

CHI PLAY '14, Oct 19-22 2014, Toronto, ON, Canada
ACM 978-1-4503-3014-5/14/10.
http://dx.doi.org/10.1145/2658537.2661309

Sensory substitution has been explored predominately in rehabilitation [1], but has been applied to make *single* player motion based video games accessible [5].

To better inform the design of sensory *substitution* in *multiplayer* digital bodily play, we contribute an initial exploration of designing for *sensory deprivation* (SD) in this context. Through observing and evaluating *Reindeer & Wolves*, we also provide a set of design strategies for incorporating SD in multiplayer digital bodily play.

HOW TO PLAY
In *Reindeer & Wolves*, five players break into two groups; three players assume the roles of reindeer while the remaining two assume the roles of wolves (see Figure 1). The reindeer are equipped with PlayStation Move controllers; these sensors detect movement and are coupled with RGB LEDs. Wolves are blindfolded throughout the game with opaque scarf ribbons. In our prototype, the sensors each have a small box of nails attached so that when shook, a 'rattle' noise is made. The goal of the reindeer is to gain points by shaking their sensor; the more vigourously they shake, the more points they accumulate. While reindeer aren't shaking the sensor, their points reduce gradually. Reindeer are restricted to only shaking in designated 'feeding zones' of the game area. The goal of the wolves is to capture the reindeer, aided by the rattle sound made as the reindeer shake their sensor.

During the course of the game, the sensor's LED will change colour. When blue, the reindeer must freeze in place. As they accumulate points, their sensor will gradually become a brighter red colour. Upon accumulating enough points, the sensor's LED flashes green to signify victory for the reindeer. If the wolves capture (come in contact with) all reindeer before this, the wolves win the game.

EVALUATION
The game was designed as part of a one week workshop on designing bodily play, held at the UBI Summer School in Oulu, Finland. Over 30 people played the game for a total of 12 rounds of play testing, each lasting 3-5 minutes. Almost all participants experienced playing as both a wolf and a reindeer. We conducted unstructured open-ended interviews

Figure 1. A game consisting of 2 Wolves (blindfolded, in cyan) pursuing 3 Reindeer (holding a PlayStation Move controller each, in magenta). Taped markers (in green) indicate feeding grounds.

with each player after each round and we derived four strategies for incorporating sensory deprivation into the design of multiplayer digital bodily play, based on them.

DESIGN STRATEGIES FOR DIGITAL BODILY PLAY

Challenge players through sensory deprivation

We observed an amusing challenge for the coordination between wolves. Sometimes they would bump into each other and become entangled, thinking they had caught a reindeer, when they had in fact caught another wolf. Using this observation as a strategy, it is possible to design a game mechanic involving SD (e.g a physical game that challenges players to co-operate to achieve a goal, where all five human senses are distributed (via SD) among the players).

Sense simple gestures for greater freedom of movement

Our technology only senses a vigorous shake of the reindeer sensor. This gives the reindeer great autonomy in terms of choosing how, when and where they might run, walk, jump, or crawl etc. Games involving sensory deprivation can be cognitively demanding. Thus we suggest that designing for simple gestures as game input can lead to games which give players an enjoyable feeling of agency in the game's digitally enhanced physical environment.

Sensory deprivation provokes expressive ludic activity

Reindeer frequently used the blindness of the wolves as an opportunity for playful activities outside the intended scope of the game. For instance, pulling irreverent faces at a wolf and performing mocking gestures. The intended audience for such acts was varied; sometimes it seemed to be a shared joke between reindeer whilst at other times these actions were either more for the benefit of spectators or the personal amusement of the individual reindeer. This leads us to suggest that designers utilizing sensory deprivation should support bodily expression with minimal digital intervention.

Juxtapose frantic movement with tense stillness

Reindeer reported feeling exerted not only from the shaking action required by the game, but also from the interaction with other players, namely avoiding capture from wolves. Wolves grew tired from frantically chasing reindeer. Such frenetic activities were also interspersed with some very quiet moments when a wolf became so close to a reindeer that their only hope of escape seemed to be remaining still and thus silent and undetectable. We suggest that designers should consider how combining sensory deprivation with motion detectors can facilitate and exploit different exertive rhythms in gameplay. In our game, the blue state of the LED signalling that a reindeer must freeze offers an example of how digital feedback can enforce stillness in a movement based game.

CONCLUSION

The positive feedback from players encourages us to pursue the topic of sensory deprivation in games further. Future work will include a formal user study to test the validity of our design strategies by applying them in additional SD-based games and novel multiplayer experiences.

In this game, we assigned the deprivation to some players only (namely, the wolves). We hope to explore how SD can be used in games where more players are deprived. Moreover, we have only explored the deprivation of sight, but other senses, as well as dynamic manipulations of such senses, can also be explored in the future.

Digital technologies' ability to transform perceptual information seems to give great potential for developers to further exploit the engagement of sensory deprivation in games. Finally, in future work we hope to relate our findings about *sensory deprivation* to understand how *sensory substitution* can be incorporated into digital bodily play.

ACKNOWLEDGEMENTS

The authors would like to thank the UK's EPSRC Centre for Doctoral Training in Digital Entertainment (CDE) for funding Mr. Finnegan's studentship.

REFERENCES

1. Bach-y Rita, P., and W Kercel, S. Sensory substitution and the human–machine interface. *Trends in cognitive sciences 7*, 12 (2003), 541–546.
2. Garner, J., Wood, G., Pijnappel, S., Murer, M., and Mueller, F. i-dentity: innominate representation as engaging movement game element. In *CHI'14 EA*, ACM (2014), 375–378.
3. Hunter, S. E., Maes, P., Tang, A., Inkpen, K. M., and Hessey, S. M. Waazam!: Supporting creative play at a distance in customized video environments. In *CHI'14*, ACM (2014), 1197–1206.
4. Kaczmarek, K. A., Webster, J. G., Bach-y Rita, P., and Tompkins, W. J. Electrotactile and vibrotactile displays for sensory substitution systems. *Biomedical Engineering 38*, 1 (1991), 1–16.
5. Morelli, T., and Folmer, E. Real-time sensory substitution to enable players who are blind to play video games using whole body gestures. *Entertainment Computing 5*, 1 (2014), 83–90.
6. op't Hof, L., de Pee, J., Sturm, J., Bekker, T., and Verbeek, J. Prolonged play with the colorflares: How does open-ended play behavior change over time? In *Fun and Games '10*, ACM (2010), 99–106.

intangle: Exploring Interpersonal Bodily Interactions through Sharing Controllers

Jayden Garner[1], Gavin Wood[2], Sandra Danilovic[3], Jessica Hammer[4], Florian 'Floyd' Mueller[1]

[1] Exertion Games Lab
RMIT University
Melbourne, Australia
{ jayden, floyd }
@exertiongameslab.org

[2] Culture Lab
Newcastle University
Newcastle Upon Tyne,
United Kingdom
g.wood2@newcastle.ac.uk

[3] University of
Toronto
Ontario, Canada
{ s.danilovic }
@mail.utoronto.ca

[4] HCI Institute
Carnegie Mellon
University
Pittsburgh, USA
hammerj@cs.cmu.edu

ABSTRACT
Multi-player computer games are increasingly being designed to engage with interpersonal bodily interactions, however, their focus is often limited to facilitating direct body contact. In contrast, we propose that designers foster varying levels of body contact through the design of shared controller interactions to introduce new types of gameplay that affords players a more nuanced engagement with the concept of socially and personally mediated body-space in games. We explore this through our game *intangle*, where participants follow computer-generated vocal instructions on how to operate shared controllers that results inevitably into players weaving their bodies together. This game embeds strong social values in the gameplay such as collaboration, empathy and inclusivity.

Author Keywords
Whole-body interaction; bodily play; game design; agency; engagement; ambiguity; proxemics; social values

ACM Classification Keywords
H.5.2. Information interfaces and presentation (e.g., HCI): Interaction Styles.

INTRODUCTION
HCI and games increasingly place the body at the forefront of the interaction, drawing inspiration from research on embodiment [2] and proxemics [6]. This corresponds with an emerging shift towards engaging with interpersonal bodily interactions in digital games in order to create new, unexpected and engaging experiences, as seen in games like *Musical Embrace* [8] and *JS Joust* [10]. While digital games that involve physical movements typically have each player's controller interacted with by only one player, we see an opportunity to explore the design of shared controller interactions. We present our game *intangle* as a research vehicle to explore the design of shared controllers to encourage interpersonal bodily interactions between players to occur gradually through the trajectory of a play experience. We further propose that the ambiguity resulting from players' contact forces onto a shared controller can be a valuable resource for designers to know about.

CHI PLAY '14, Oct 19-22 2014, Toronto, ON, Canada
ACM 978-1-4503-3014-5/14/10.
http://dx.doi.org/10.1145/2658537.2661306

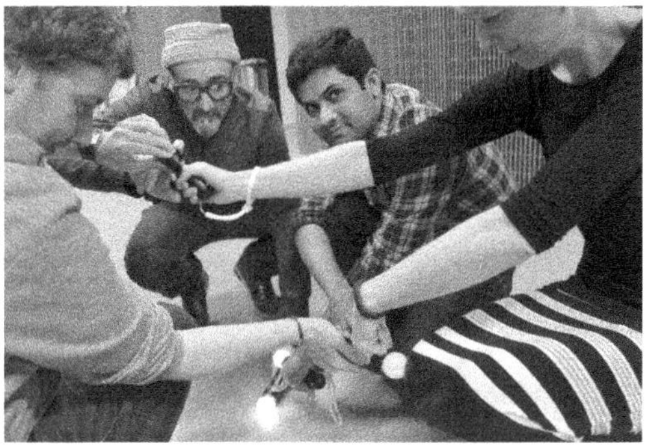

Figure 1: Playing *intangle*

INTANGLE
intangle (Figure 1) is a collaborative game involving a group of four or more players, where each player is given a Sony Move controller. Each player's controller shows a different colored LED light to illustrate his or her role, for instance "red player" is the player whose controller displays a red light. Gameplay involves the game giving the group procedures via a series of computer-generated vocal instructions, which must be then carried out. For example, players might hear, "Two players press a button on someone else's controller". The group has to complete each instruction to progress. Time constraints are enforced by the game, with visual, auditory and haptic sources of feedback given via the controller's light and vibration as well as beeping sounds, to alert everyone that the time to complete the current instruction is nearly up. Upon completing an instruction on time, the group is given the next instruction, however they must also continue to fulfill the requirements of the previous instructions, otherwise the game will end. The game also gives feedback if these requirements are not fulfilled. For example, if a button is no longer held down on one of the controllers, that controller will flash and vibrate. The game gives a moment of time for someone to push back down the button, otherwise the game will end. Players gradually become more entangled with one another as more and more buttons are pressed down. Over the course of the game, a more complex range of procedures is introduced, like crouching down or placing a controller onto the floor.

DISCUSSION
We focus the discussion of our design experiences with *intangle* on the intersection of two key themes for designing games that facilitate interpersonal bodily interactions through shared controllers: body contact and ambiguity.

Facilitating varying levels of body contact to occur through the trajectory of a play experience

Body contact can be an outcome of shared controller experiences. In body-space games [7] we can often find a continuum between 'up-close and personal' contact, to games where contact is used sparingly. For example, *Musical Embrace* [8] explores uncomfortable interactions as players squeeze a shared pillow to progress through the game. In *JS Joust* [10], a player intentionally keeps out of reach of other players until they can see an opportunity to strike the other's controllers. However, the amount of body contact in these games is always imposed by the rules of the game. Instead, in *intangle* we suggest that varied actions can encourage different amounts of body contact, for example, one action might be, "Put white controller in someone's pocket", whereas another might be "Everyone, jump together". This variation could allow players to regain personal space, or more provocatively seize an opportunity and find themselves closer to another player. We observed that gameplay often started with little to no body contact being experienced during the early stages, however over time we made it progressively more challenging for the players to avoid body contact as bodies become entangled and controllers harder to reach, often resulting in body contact occurring indirectly. As the experience reached its climax, we gave some instructions where body contact was a more direct outcome, like "two players touch someone else's leg with their controllers". In our early evaluation of playtests held during our game jam design process [1], we find *intangle* encourages players to playfully and safely test social and personal boundaries of contact through game play. We allow room for these explorations to occur by inviting rather than enforcing body contact. This can allow players to decide upon the level of body contact that feels personally comfortable; this important distinction in the rules can give players a greater sense of agency as players configure the rules of engagement on their own individual terms. The game's premise of agency is partially informed by self-determination theory (SDT), which posits human needs for autonomy, competence and relatedness as crucial to motivation [9]. In our game, agency is a social value set within the objectives of having fun, building connections among players and meaning making. We designed *intangle* so players could gradually engage with a full extent of this continuum of contact over the trajectory of the experience.

Utilizing ambiguity from contact force onto controllers to engage players with each other's movements

As ambiguity in the design of interactive systems can encourage thoughtful reflection on interactions with technology [5] and stimulate engagement with digital bodily play [4], we believe that ambiguity can enable opportunities for new types of engaging gameplay experiences. Through our design experiences with *intangle* we propose that the ambiguity of contact force can be a useful design resource for designers of shared controller experiences. We use contact force to describe the physical force in which a person or object comes in contact with another person or object. Contact forces are responsible for most interpersonal bodily interactions between people and with people and objects, such as kicking a ball to another player. Interpersonal bodily interactions in digital games typically occur with gamepads or touchscreens most often situated in fixed and stable positions (e.g. *Fingle* [3]) or have these forces applied directly to another's body, (e.g. *Musical Embrace* [8]). However, with *intangle* the players must apply bodily pressure onto other players' controllers, rather than their own controllers or through direct contact with the body itself. The resulting contact forces introduce a sense of ambiguity that makes it more challenging for the group to keep the controllers (and thus one another's bodies) steady. This ambiguity becomes more apparent as the game progresses, when several players' contact forces become situated at the source of a single controller. In sum, we believe the ambiguity of contact force resulting from players' shared controller interactions has much potential for further game design research that is yet to be explored.

CONCLUSION

We presented *intangle* as a research vehicle to explore body contact and ambiguity as two key design themes for shared controller experiences. By providing an initial understanding of how designers can engage with interpersonal bodily interactions through a shared controller to design engaging gameplay experiences, we believe we can extend our knowledge on concepts such as proxemics and ambiguity for the benefit of engaging a form of game design that integrates a variety of social values in the gameplay, which the conceptual category of 'agency' engenders. Ultimately, we aim to expand the range of shared bodily play in order to better understand how to foster meaningful connections between players.

REFERENCES

1. Deen, M., Cercos, R., Chatman, A., et al. Game Jam: [4 Research]. *Proc. CHI '14 EA*, ACM (2014), 25–28.
2. Dourish, P. (2001). *Where the Action is: The Foundations of Embodied Interaction*. MIT Press.
3. Fingle. Game Oven (2011). http://fingleforipad.com/
4. Garner, J., Wood, G., Pijnappel, S., Murer, M. & Mueller, F. 2014. i-dentity: Innominate Movement Representation as Engaging Game Element. *Proc. CHI '14*, ACM (2014), 2181-2190.
5. Gaver, W.W., Beaver, J. & Benford, S. Ambiguity as a Resource for Design. *Proc. CHI '03*, ACM (2003) 233–240.
6. Hall, E.T. (1966). *The hidden dimension*. Doubleday.
7. Isbister, K. How to Stop Being a Buzzkill: Designing Yamove!, a Mobile Tech Mash-up to Truly Augment Social Play. *Proc. MobileHCI '12*, ACM (2012), 1-4.
8. Mueller, F., Stellmach, S., Greenberg, S., et al. Proxemics Play: Understanding Proxemics for Designing Digital Play Experiences. *Proc. DIS '14*, ACM (2014), 533–542.
9. Ryan, R. M. & Deci, E. L. (2000). Self-determination theory and the facilitation of intrinsic motivation, social development, and well-being. *The American Psychologist*, 55, 1, 68-78.
10. Wilson, D. (2012). Designing for the Pleasures of Disputation -or- How to make friends by trying to kick them! *PhD Dissertation*, IT University of Copenhagen.

Last Tank Rolling: Exploring Shared Motion-Based Play to Empower Persons Using Wheelchairs

Kathrin Maria Gerling
University of Lincoln
Brayford Pool, LN6 7TS, UK
kgerling@lincoln.ac.uk

Laura Buttrick
University of Lincoln
Brayford Pool, LN6 7TS, UK
laurabuttrick@gmail.com

ABSTRACT
This paper presents *Last Tank Rolling*, a collaborative motion-based military survival game in which players using wheelchairs are invited to apply their assistive device to control a tank. The game offers a strong in-game metaphor for the wheelchair, and invites joint physical interaction that encourages able-bodied players to perceive their peer as a competent collaborator. Ultimately, this project aims to explore the value of shared video game play as a means of empowering people with disabilities, and connecting players of all abilities to foster inclusion.

INTRODUCTION AND BACKGROUND
Connecting people using wheelchairs and able-bodied persons in a positive context is an important step towards fostering inclusion [8]. Research on video games suggests that they can be a tool to promote positive relationships among players by increasing empathy and engagement [2, 3]. Findings on motion-based games demonstrate that players become more engaged not only with the game but with each other if movements are natural [7]. However, developing games with wheelchairs specifically in mind has usually been a single-player process [1, 4]. Recently, projects like Liberi [6] have begun to explore the value of collaborative motion-based play for persons with mobility disabilities, and work on player balancing in a competitive context [5] has demonstrated that incorporating wheelchairs in motion-based games provides an opportunity for engaging players of all abilities.

In this project, we explore whether collaborative motion-based games can be leveraged to empower persons using wheelchairs, and connect them with able-bodied peers. We present *Last Tank Rolling*, a collaborative motion-based military survival game in which players are invited to apply their wheelchair to control a tank, and players need to work together to withstand enemy troops. The game aims to empower persons using wheelchairs by offering a strong in-game metaphor for the wheelchair, and through joint physical interaction that encourages players to perceive their peer as a competent collaborator.

CHI PLAY '14, Oct 19-22 2014, Toronto, ON, Canada
ACM 978-1-4503-3014-5/14/10.
http://dx.doi.org/10.1145/2658537.2661303

LAST TANK ROLLING: SHARED MOTION-BASED PLAY TO EMPOWER PERSONS USING WHEELCHAIRS
To explore the integration of wheelchairs in shared motion-based game interaction, we created *Last Tank Rolling*.

Design Rationale
Last Tank Rolling was developed with a focus on providing an empowering experience for the player using wheelchair input; it is a 2D vertical scrolling military survival game, players need to collaborate to withstand enemy troops. The basic game concept was developed by an interdisciplinary team consisting of researchers in human-computer interaction, sports and exercise science, practitioners, and persons using wheelchairs at an AHRC workshop on performance and games at the University of Lincoln.

Game Concept and Joint Player Actions
In *Last Tank Rolling*, players need to work together to defeat waves of enemy forces and reach their military base. The game implements two player roles: the person using wheelchair input controls a tank, the other player controls a soldier. The game leverages differences between the roles to create a complimentary set of skills and abilities; while the solider is agile, but vulnerable, the tank has a higher resistance to enemy fire, but depends on the soldier for repairs. To underline this reciprocal relationship, players need to overcome a number of in-game challenges, each associated with a specific combination of player input.

Both players need to *navigate the territory* by avoiding obstacles, e.g., abandoned vehicles, the tank driver needs to ensure that the soldier is safe. If an enemy air strike occurs, the soldier needs to *seek shelter* behind the tank to stay alive. While the soldier's health is replenished automatically, *tank maintenance* after enemy fire has to be performed by the soldier. Both players can individually *fight enemy troops*. The solider can fire at a higher frequency but deals little damage; the tank has a low firing rate, but enemies take extensive damage. Players can combine strength by entering a *joint firing mode* (Figure 1).

Figure 1. Collaborative input in Last Tank Rolling: Seeking shelter (left), tank maintenance (middle), and joint firing mode (right).

Prototyping Phase

The prototyping phase focused on interaction design to reinforce the idea of empowering players using wheelchair input, and highlighting reciprocity between both players.

Interaction prototyping: Collaborative input. We followed a Wizard-of-Oz approach to identify suitable forms of shared player interaction that would strengthen the role of the player using wheelchair input. Figure 1 gives an overview of collaborative physical player input. The goal of these interactions is to implement the wheelchair in a way that adds value to the game and empowers the player by offering an important and powerful in-game role, and to emphasize reciprocity through synchronous player actions.

Interaction prototyping: Individual input. We created a digital prototype (Figure 2) to assess the feasibility of individual body-based and wheelchair-based game input. The prototype was implemented using Game Maker, the Kinect SDK, and the KINECT^{Wheels} toolkit [4]. Basic wheelchair movements control the tank (moving back and forth, turning to sides), weapons can be fired by extending one arm to the front. Tank speed controls game speed.

NEXT STEPS AND CONCLUSION

Last Tank Rolling is currently being implemented into a fully playable game. It is planned to evaluate the game in terms of player experience as well as its potential to connect players together with St. Francis School for children and young adults with special needs in Lincolnshire. The goal of the next phase of this project is to validate the potential of collaborative motion-based play to empower persons using wheelchairs, and to study whether it is possible to foster inclusion through positive shared experiences. The first study will explore whether persons using wheelchairs can be empowered by experiencing physical competence through motion-based play. In a second study, we will focus on the able-bodied player, and whether shared motion-based play that puts persons using wheelchairs in a strong in-game role has the potential of positively influencing the way able-bodied persons perceive peers with mobility disabilities. We believe that motion-based games could be a new tool to empower persons using wheelchairs. This project is a first step towards exploring whether shared video game play has the potential of empowering people with disabilities, promoting positive attitudes towards them, and connecting people of all abilities to foster inclusion.

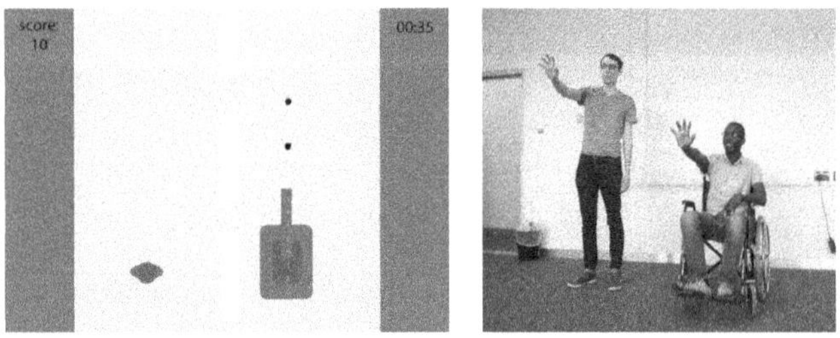

Figure 2. Digital prototype and interaction prototyping.

ACKNOWLEDGMENTS

We would like to thank all workshop participants for their contribution to our game concept, and Kieran Hicks for implementation support.

REFERENCES

1. Cuzzort, S., and Starner, T. Astro Wheelie: A wheelchair based exercise game. In *Proc. of ISWC'08*, IEEE (2008).
2. De Kort, Y.A.W. and IJsselsteijn, W.A. People, Places, and Play: Player Experience in a Socio-Spatial Context. *Computers in Entertainment* 6, 2 (2009).
3. Emmerich, K., Masuch, M. Helping Friends or Fighting Foes: The Influence of Collaboration and Competition on Player Experience. In *Proc. of FDG'13*, ACM (2013).
4. Gerling, K.M., Kalyn, M.R., and Mandryk, R.L. KINECT^{Wheels}: Wheelchair-Accessible Motion-Based Game Interaction. In *Proc. of CHI EA'13*, ACM (2013).
5. Gerling, K.M., Miller, M., Mandryk, R.L., Birk, M., and Smeddinck, J. Effects of Balancing for Physical Abilities on Player Performance, Experience and Self-Esteem in Exergames. In *Proc. of CHI'14*, ACM (2014).
6. Hernandez, H., Ye, Z., Graham, N., Fehlings, D., Switzer, L. Designing action-based exergames for children with cerebral palsy. In *Proc. of CHI'13*, ACM (2013).
7. Lindley, S., Le Couteur, J., and Bianchi-Berthouze, N. Stirring up Experience through Movement in Game Play: Effects on Engagement and Social Behaviour. In *Proc. of CHI'08*, ACM (2008).
8. Krahé, B. and Altwasser, C. Changing Negative Attitudes Towards Persons with Physical Disabilities: An Experimental Intervention. *Journal of Community & Applied Social Psychology* 16, (2006), 56-69.

"Beam Me 'Round, Scotty!": Exploring the Effect of Interdependence in Asymmetric Cooperative Games

John Harris
Games Institute
University of Waterloo
John.Harris@UWaterloo.ca

Mark Hancock
Games Institute
University of Waterloo
Mark.Hancock@UWaterloo.ca

Stacey Scott
Games Institute
University of Waterloo
Stacey.Scott@UWaterloo.ca

ABSTRACT

In this paper, we explore *interdependence through asymmetry* as a possible game design tool for enriching player experience. We describe a prototype game we developed called "Beam Me 'Round, Scotty!" which alternately tightly or loosely couples the cooperation of two heterogeneous groups of players in an action-oriented science fiction survival game. Future studies will examine the effects of interdependence on player experience and explore whether deliberately symbiotic player relationships can serve as a shortcut to enhanced socialization between players.

Author Keywords

Cooperative games; game design; asymmetric games; interdependence; symbiotic play.

ACM Classification Keywords

H.5.2 [User Interfaces]: Evaluation/Methodology

INTRODUCTION

It has been argued that many online multi-player games are often much less social than originally estimated. Despite the potential millions of other players sharing the same online world, individualistic and egocentric play remains typical and interaction with other players can often be fleeting, anonymous, and unnecessary for success [3].

In contrast, traditional tabletop games, party games, and recreational sports exhibit much richer socialization and bonding between participants; even during impromptu "pick-up" games between strangers in public. Players negotiate custom "house rules", assume unique roles within the group (leader, narrator, banker, goalie), jockey with and taunt each other playfully, and rejoice and commiserate with each other during victory and defeat.

This disconnect between the inherent togetherness of traditional games and the unexpected aloofness of many multiplayer video games is underscored by research showing that gamers are happier, perform better, and play longer when playing with friends they know personally [4] and whose interactions are tightly coupled with their own [2]. Designers could thus emphasize cooperative play, which has been shown to quickly overcome social barriers and lead to more prosocial behavior, even between strangers [6].

In our current work, we propose that by creating reciprocal imbalances between game players in a cooperative play scenario, our fundamental human motivation to belong to productive groups [1] can jumpstart the desire to cooperate in video game play and act as a shortcut to improved socialization and bonding between players.

We explore this interdependence through asymmetry as a design tool in video games for enriching player experience and leading to unique forms of engagement and enjoyment for heterogeneous groups of players.

Although some commercial video games exhibit rich asymmetry and cooperation (e.g. Unknown Worlds' *Natural Selection,* Ubisoft's *Watch Dogs,* Nintendo's *Super Mario Galaxy*), differences across titles in interface, content, pacing, and aesthetic make comparison with more symmetric games difficult. Instead, we have developed our own prototype game which affords control of these confounding factors and modification of only those game design elements which most directly impact interdependence.

PROTOTYPE GAME

Called "Beam Me 'Round, Scotty!'" (BMRS), our prototype game is modelled on the science fiction scenario of a starship crew exploring an alien planet while their spaceship remains in orbit. All players observe a single communal display that shows a small area of the planet's surface from an overhead perspective, the player characters exploring it, and the status of the starship.

The Away Team

The majority of players assume the role of the intrepid "Away Team" that has travelled down to the planet's surface to explore dangerous alien ruins in search of artefacts and treasure. Each game session, the Away Team is quickly set upon by violent native creatures that they must fight off using their handheld blaster pistols. If an Away Team character takes too much damage from enemies, they fall to the ground incapacitated and must wait for medical assistance from their teammates.

CHI PLAY '14, Oct 19-22 2014, Toronto, ON, Canada
ACM 978-1-4503-3014-5/14/10.
http://dx.doi.org/10.1145/2658537.2661311

Away Team players can move their on-screen characters around the game world and fire their weapons in any direction using individual smartphone devices as handheld controllers. Each device affords the display of personalized character information such as colour, health, and score, as well as vibration and audible feedback when their in-game character is injured.

With the need for fast reflexes and the threat of becoming incapacitated, playing as an Away Team member is designed to appeal to action-oriented players with a desire for high-tension combat and fast, agile action [5].

Scotty

One other player assumes the role of the starship's plucky engineer "Scotty" who observes the game world from an overhead perspective and can use the starship's various systems to support his or her teammates on the planet's surface. Using a mouse and keyboard, Scotty can send down supplies such as health kits and ammunition, create temporary shield walls to protect the Away Team, and teleport teammates out of (and into) danger.

Scotty's abilities are limited by a gradually replenishing pool of energy generated by the starship. The rate of energy regeneration can be set before the game begins to generate alternately strong or loose coupling between player teams. Rapid energy regeneration allows the Scotty player to make fairly reckless use of their powers with little consequence. A more limited rate of regeneration forces the Scotty player to make more judicious choices on when and where to spend their energy lest their teammates be left without support at a critical moment.

Scotty's abilities are designed to cater to a more collaborative and support-oriented player who prefers lower-stress, strategic thinking and "big picture" challenges [5]. Since the surface-dwelling alien enemies do not have any means by which to attack the starship, there is no immediate threat to the Scotty player. They cannot fail the game directly and their continuously replenishing pool of energy always allows them to contribute to the party of players, given sufficient patience.

INTERDEPENCE AND SYMBIOSIS

The degree of symbiosis between Scotty and the Away Team players can be modified through a number of game mechanic design parameters.

In the "Loose Coupling" condition, the interdependence between the Away Team and Scotty can be essentially eliminated by, for example, allowing the Away Team players to collect their own healing power-ups on the surface of the planet. If the Away Team's weapons are sufficiently powerful such that the Away Team can manage to survive on their own through skillful game play, the Scotty character becomes a helpful but not mission-critical contributor to the group play session.

Alternatively, in the "Tight Coupling" condition, the Away Team can *require* Scotty's intervention in order to heal their wounds and rearm their weapons. Similarly, Scotty could *require* the Away Team to collect 'energy modules' on the planet's surface in order to recharge the starship's abilities or to activate localized 'stabilizer beacons' on the planet surface before Scotty is able to help the Away Team within a limited proximity of the active beacon.

An even more tightly-coupled three-way relationship can be introduced whereby injured players must first be 'diagnosed' by Scotty before being 'treated' by another member of the Away Team. In order to revive the player, their smartphone screen (displaying a QR code) must be appropriately scanned by another player who is physically nearby both in-game and in the real world.

FUTURE WORK

Using "Beam Me 'Round, Scotty!'" as an experimental platform, we plan to study the effects of interdependence and asymmetry on player experience in different gameplay contexts: both online and offline and between strangers and existing friends. We hypothesize that well-designed asymmetric game mechanics can generate unique challenge and symbiosis between players, improving engagement and socialization. We also anticipate that poorly designed or excessive interdependence between players can be frustrating and detrimental to player experience. Ultimately, we hope to generate a set of design recommendations and guidelines for successfully incorporating interdependence and asymmetry into other practitioners' game designs.

REFERENCES

1. Baumeister, R., & Leary, M.. "The need to belong: desire for interpersonal attachments as a fundamental human motivation." *Psychological bulletin* , 117.3: 4. APA 1995
2. Beznosyk, A., Quax, P., Lamotte, W., & Coninx, K., "The effect of closely-coupled interaction on player experience in casual games". *In Proc. ICEC* '12, pp. 243-255. Springer Berlin Heidelberg
3. Ducheneaut, N., Yee, N., Nickell, E., & Moore, R. J. "Alone together?: exploring the social dynamics of massively multiplayer online games". *In Proc.CHI* '06, pp. 407-416. ACM
4. Mason, W., & Clauset, A. "Friends ftw! friendship and competition in halo: Reach". *In Proc CSCW* '13. pp. 375-386. ACM 2013
5. Stewart, B. "The Four Bartle Types." *Gamasutra*. www.gamasutra.com, 1 Sept. 2011. Web. 14 July 2014.
6. Velez, John A., et al. "Ingroup versus outgroup conflict in the context of violent video game play: The effect of cooperation on increased helping and decreased aggression." *Communication Research* 2012: 0093650212456202. SAGE

TouchPoints: An Exertion Game with Strategy

Yasaman Hashemian
Interactive Media & Games Division
School of Cinematic Art
University of Southern California
yhashemi@usc.edu

Ding Wang
Highwire CTD,
Lancaster University
LA1 4YW, UK
d.wang4@lancaster.ac.uk

ABSTRACT
Using video games in rehabilitation has proven the potential to provide patients with fun and motivating exercise systems [1,8,10]. The main question therefore is how to design body-based video games to improve a rehabilitation experience. This work-in-progress paper introduces *TouchPoints*, a full body exertion experience designed for stretching exercises in rehabilitation centers as part of a series of short-duration design studies. Our concept is to provide patients with a scenario where a stretching exercise routine could be accomplished in a playful and pleasant way. Lo-fi prototypes were used to demonstrate the game-play and gather valuable feedback from users' experience, which later informed the design of the *TouchPoints*. In addition, we propose further user-centric developments for *TouchPoints* involving both rehabilitation patients and therapists on how to increase patients' motivation. This paper is intended to read alongside the game demo video.

Author Keywords: Exertion Game; Wearable Sensors; Touch Screens; Physical Therapy; Rehabilitation

ACM Classification Keywords
H.5.m. Information interfaces and HCI: Miscellaneous.

INTRODUCTION
Motivating game-based exercises have the potential to revolutionise therapy for people with neurological impairments such as stroke, spinal cord injury and traumatic brain injury [1,6,7,11]. Our prototype *TouchPoints* is an exertion game that contains strategy elements. *TouchPoints* is the first game that uses multiple touch screens to facilitate collaborative stretch exercise for rehabilitation. The initial step was to explore a wide range of concepts that are essential for therapeutic use, in order to create an interactive game that is engaging and appropriate for stretching exercises. For example, *TouchPoints* can be personalized to the player's physical abilities and provide appropriate levels of challenge throughout the rehabilitation process. As a multiple-player game, users are provided with the ability to collaborate and support the opponent's moves or compete and try to constrain the opponent's moves. In a real-life setting one of the players will be the therapist and the other the patient, so that the therapist can choose to either support or constrain the patient's moves and assist them to stretch certain parts of the body. Repetitive skilled practice is crucial for rehabilitation [2,7,9] as well as various metrics such as game scores and performance data that are saved to the computer and can be further analysed by the therapist after the completion of a therapy session or over longer periods of time. In this paper we outline the design concept for *TouchPoints,* and then we discuss future implementations of *TouchPoints* in physical therapy. All game's features and actual clinical use will be evaluated in future work with experts in rehabilitation involved.

CHI PLAY '14, Oct 19-22 2014, Toronto, ON, Canada
ACM 978-1-4503-3014-5/14/10.
http://dx.doi.org/10.1145/2658537.2661313

CONCEPT DESIGN PROCESS
The design intuition behind TouchPoints is to create a playful and social environment for people to experience a physical connection with each other while stretching their body. The idea of making TouchPoints a social game came from the consideration of rehabilitation patients' mental health factors. For example, stroke survivors sometimes fall into a severe depression and decline of social activities [12, 13]. TouchPoints could potentially help to reinforce a healthy social involvement for rehabilitation patients. Our first step towards designing an exerting interactive experience is to obtain and analyze the impact of each movement within the context of the application. The importance lays at capturing both the quality (trajectory and speed) and the quantity (number of repetitions) of the movements. Therefore, it is essential to answer different set of questions regarding the range and the trajectory of each movement, the alignment and the position of player's body. Finally the design challenge is how to incorporate all of them into an engaging interactive play. Feedback from a series of elementary user experiences guides us towards implementing a broader goal for this application rather than just stretching exercises. In addition we recognized the potential of this experience in social play, self-expression, and the promotion of physical therapy as a joyful and playful activity in rehabilitation centers. Games by nature enable social engagement and interactions in new ways and such experiences offer greater motivation and engagement to patients and therapists during and after physical therapy [5]. During the play we promote the setting of TouchPoints in such a way that players have the opportunity to interact with each other and encourage

them to express their feelings and emotions during gameplay [3,4]. TouchPoints was designed with its targeted audiences in mind. The sophisticated movement in TouchPoints serves as feature but also makes the game more appropriate for certain audiences. Taking stroke survivors as an instance, TouchPoints would work better for patients in their later rehabilitation stage or younger patients. Overall our long-term interest is to incorporate physical therapy protocols into TouchPoints and serve the need of body-based therapeutic games for rehabilitation centers.

GAME FLOW

TouchPoints requires a set of wireless wearable pressure sensors for each player – patient and therapist. Each set of sensors is responsive to any connection the other set of sensors. When one of the sensors from the patient's set, get connected to another sensor from therapist's set, a signal will be sent to the system that will start the game (see Figure 3).

The physical set up of the game starts with players wearing the sensors and place them on their joints (ankles, knees, wrists, elbows, and head). Players face each other while a large touch screen is placed behind each player in reach distance (See Figure 1). The screen contents are separated into a grid-fashion and divided into 9 spaces.

The game starts by lighting up and blinking two or three squares on the screen with a color that represent which one of them will be the target space to hit (See Figure 2). This brings more challenge to the players as they do not know which one will be the next space that they need to touch. The actual target square won't reveal until both players get two pairs of their wearable sensors connected with each other and keep connection to start the game (see Figure 3). As soon as players connect the sensors with each other, the target space starts blinking and players have 10 sec to make their move and hit the target on the screen behind them for hold on for at least 5 sec. The touched target will stay lighted as a reward for players.

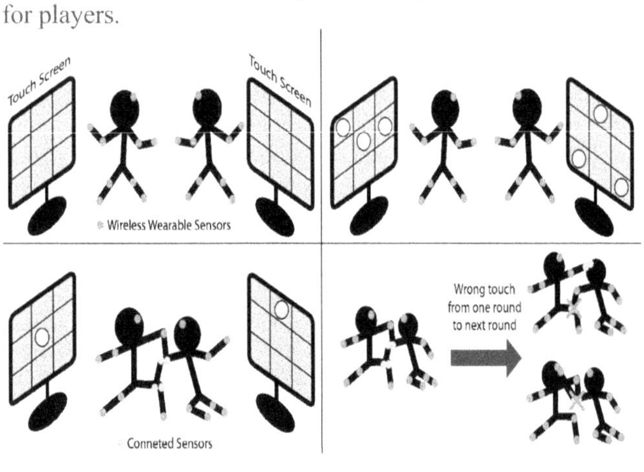

Figure 1. Physical set up of the game (Top left)
Figure 2. Possible hitting squares (Top right)
Figure 3. Connected Sensors (Bottom left)
Figure 4. Wrong moves (Bottom right)

To mitigate boredom during game play the sensors that are connected in the previous round will be deactivated in the next round, which conveniently enable us to provide different body postures and alignment for players (See Figure 4). The end of the game is when players are able to light up all 9 spaces on their wall. The layout of the screen and the randomly appeared target spaces allow players to stretch their body in different directions and at various heights. In addition plays can choose any part of their body (e.g. hands, feet, head etc) to touch the screen for their convenience. Here is also where strategy in TouchPoints kicks in, the therapist could strategically chose their movement to either support or constraint the patient's movement do meet the stretching goal.

In our prototyping layout the software receives data from the wearable sensors and the touch screens, processes them in real-time and send clear control data to Processing to enable interaction, graphics rendering, and sound generation.

CONCLUSION

The customization that was implemented into our game design makes this experience a potential toolset for physical therapy at a rehabilitation center. Patients and their therapists can collaborate with each other to reach their maximum abilities in stretching in the physical therapy context. *TouchPoints* was somewhat enjoyable based on the feedback we received from participants. The next steps are to equip the game with more sophisticated gesture-controlled movements to address more needs of physical therapists and engage patients in a personalized rehab exercise program. Therefore, in future studies, there will be involvement of both rehabilitation therapists and patients to ensure the game would truly work in the rehabilitation context.

REFERENCES

1. Gotsis, M., Lympouridis, V., Requejo, P., Haubert, L., Poulos, I.C., Frangoudes, F., Turpin, D., Jordan-Marsh, M. :Skyfarer: Design Case Study of a Mixed Reality Rehabilitation Video Game. HCI (9) 2014: 699-710
2. Blom, L.A., Chaplin, L.T.: The intimate act of choreography. University of Pittsburg Press, Pittsburg, PA (1982).
3. Nadia Bianchi-Berthouze, Whan Woong Kim, and Darshak Patel. 2007. Does Body Movement Engage You More in Digital Game Play? and Why?. In *Proceedings of the 2nd international conference on Affective Computing and Intelligent Interaction* (ACII '07). Springer-Verlag, Berlin, Heidelberg, 102-113.
4. W.D. Russell and M. Newton, Short-Term Psychological Effects of Interactive Video Game Technology Exercise on Mood and Attention. ;In Proceedings of Educational Technology & Society. 2008, 294-308.
5. Regina Bernhaupt, 2010. Evaluating User Experience in Games: *Concepts and Methods* (1st ed.). Springer Publication Company, Incorporated
6. Lang B.S., Requejo P., et al (2010), The Potential of Virtual Reality and Gaming to Assist Successful Aging with Disability. Phys Med Rehabil Clin N Am. 21, pp.339-356
7. Khen, M., & Kroll. T. (2009). Staying physically active after spinal cord injury: A qualitative exploration of barriers and facilitators to exercise participation. BMC Public Health. 9, 168, pp. 1-11
8. Chun-Ming Chang, Yen-Ching Chang, Hsiao-Yun Chang, and Li-Wei Chou (2012). An interactive game-based shoulder wheel system for rehabilitation. Patient Prefer Adherence, 6, pp. 821-828
9. Mantovani, F. & Castelnuovo, G. (2003). Sense of presence in virtual training: Enhancing skills acquisition and transfer of knowledge through learning experience in virtual environments. Ios Press, pp. 167-179
10. Annesi, J. & Mazas, J. (1997). Effects of virtual reality-enhanced exercise equipment on adherence and exercise-induced feeling states. Perceptual and Motor Skills, 85, 3, pp.835-844
11. Nawoczenski, D., Ritter-Soronen, J., et al (2006). Clinical trial of exercise for shoulder pain in chronic spinal injury, Physical Therapy, 86, 12, pp. 1604-1618
12. op Reimer, W. S., De Haan, R. J., Rijnders, P. T., Limburg, M., & Van Den Bos, G. A. M. (1998). The burden of caregiving in partners of long-term stroke survivors. *Stroke*, *29*(8), 1605-1611.
13. Becker, G. (1993). Continuity after a stroke: Implications of life-course disruption in old age. *The Gerontologist*, *33*(2), 148-158

Synthetic Perception for Intelligent Virtual Agents

Tobias Haubrich, Sven Seele, Rainer Herpers*†, Peter Becker
Institute of Visual Computing,
Bonn-Rhein-Sieg University of Applied Sciences
Grantham-Allee 20, 53757 Sankt Augustin
tobias.haubrich@h-brs.de

Christian Bauckhage‡
University of Bonn
Wegelerstraße 10, 53115 Bonn
bauckhage@bit.uni-bonn.de

ABSTRACT
Perception is one of the most important cognitive capabilities of an entity since it determines how an entity perceives its environment. The presented work focuses on providing cost efficient but realistic perceptual processes for intelligent virtual agents (IVAs) or NPCs with the goal of providing a sound information basis for the entities' decision making processes. In addition, an agent-central perception process should provide a common interface for developers to retrieve data from the IVAs' environment. The overall process is evaluated by applying it to a scenario demonstrating its benefits. The evaluation indicates, that such a realistically simulated perception process provides a powerful instrument to enhance the (perceived) realism of an IVA's simulated behavior.

Author Keywords
Intelligent virtual agents; perception; virtual environments

ACM Classification Keywords
I.2.11 Artificial Intelligence: Distributed Artificial Intelligence, Intelligent Agents; I.3.7 Computer Graphics: Three-Dimensional Graphics and Realism, Virtual Reality;

INTRODUCTION
One aspect affecting a player's sense of immersion is the behavior of certain NPCs, which is often restricted by simplified perception processes. Commonly NPCs or intelligent virtual agents (IVAs) residing in game worlds or virtual environments (VEs) have access to the whole environment. One reason is that there does not need to be a difference between the environment and an IVA's representation of the environment [3]. In contrast, restricting the perceivable information of an IVA to more closely represent reality causes additional effort for developers and increases the complexity of the simulation. The focus of our research is to provide simulated IVAs with an agent-central perception process, providing an independent *view* of the environment. The IVAs' distinct information basis formed by this process is consequently providing a more realistic basis for simulated behavior enhancing a player's perceived realism. Another motivation is that a uniform interface for retrieving data from the environment eases the work of developers and designers. To restrict complexity, a synthetic perception is applied, which is only applicable in VEs, because it is not about deducing information from signals from the environment, but is concerned with extracting existing semantic information from virtual objects.

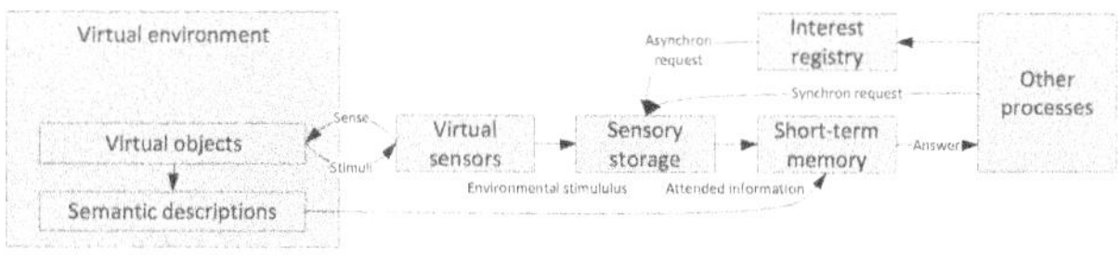

Figure 1. Architecture of the SynPeA framework. The parts on the left represent the ESC, while the parts on the right represent the IAC. Information is acquired from the VE through virtual sensors and stored in a sensory storage. Attention is expressed by requesting specific information, causing that information to be moved to the short-term memory.

SYNTHETIC PERCEPTION FOR AGENTS
A framework for simulating an IVA's perception process called SynPeA (synthetic perception for agents) is being developed. The SynPeA architecture (see Figure 1) is composed of three distinguishable processes: sensation, memory, and retrieval. Additionally, it contains two cycles, an environmental stimulus cycle (ESC) at the boundary between agent and environment and an internal information attention cycle (IAC). To simulate the ESC the environmental stimulus is reproduced. This is realized by a physical filtering which determines the objects whose real counterparts' signals could reach the sensor. To simulate the IAC, the attended information is to be determined from the environmental stimulus. Therefore, a cognitive filtering is applied.

Sensation
Initially, the sensation processes are simulated. This is usually achieved through a set of virtual sensors, which gather stimuli from the VE. A uniform interface was integrated that allows attaching different virtual sensors and aggregating their data (cf. [2]). As a proof of concept two sensors for visual sensation were realized. One uses a ray cast-based synthetic vision where a visibility check is performed by casting rays to a target. The other uses a depth buffer-based synthetic vision where a false colored image is rendered from an agent's point of view (cf. [4]). The image is subsequently analyzed to retrieve information about objects in view.

---
*University of New Brunswick, Fredericton, E3B 5A3, Canada
†York University, Toronto, M3J 1P3, Canada
‡Fraunhofer IAIS, Schloss Birlinghoven 1, 53757 Sankt Augustin

CHI PLAY '14, Oct 19-22 2014, Toronto, ON, Canada
ACM 978-1-4503-3014-5/14/10.
http://dx.doi.org/10.1145/2658537.2661302

Memory

A memory concept was integrated to provide the possibility to store the acquired information and realize further retrieval functionality. The memory model was adapted from [5]. It is based on a memory model from psychology and includes several memory stages of which a short-term sensory storage (STSS) and a short-term memory (STM) were integrated into our model. Information is moved from the STSS to the STM when it is attended, e.g., by our retrieval functionality. The entries in every memory stage are affected by memory decay, i.e. unattended entries are discarded after a given time.

Retrieval

The retrieval process includes a request interface which realizes a cognitive filtering. The requests themselves represent a form of attention. Synchronous requests are directly submitted to the request interface of the memory. Asynchronous requests are represented as interests (cf. [6]), which can be registered in an interest registry. A reply is sent in case the subject of an interest is detected. Requested information is filtered according to given constraints based on ideas from [1]. A positive request causes an entry to be moved from the STSS to the STM.

EVALUATION

The synthetic perception process was evaluated by applying it to a sample scenario. In the scenario an agent (embodied as car) drives along a street where several challenges have to be tackled. At first a traffic sign has to be recognized and the desired speed has to be adjusted. Subsequently, the car reaches a pedestrian crossing which has to be recognized. Additionally, pedestrians have to be recognized and it needs to be evaluated if the pedestrians are critical for passing the crossing.

While driving, the agent perceives the VE through SynPeA's processes. The functionality for overcoming the challenges was realized in separate tasks. The task for perceiving speed limit signs queries the request interface for entries which imply a restriction of the speed limit on the current lane. If the agent reaches a given distance to a speed limit sign, its desired speed is adjusted. The task for perceiving the pedestrian crossing first queries all pedestrian crossings to determine if there is one. If there is, all pedestrians are queried and it is evaluated whether the agent needs to stop or not.

The perception system allowed the integration of both situations without requiring a developer to think about perception mechanisms. However, it has to be considered that the information to be perceived must have been modeled previously. The benefits of our system become obvious when considering certain situations, e.g., a pedestrian is occluded while approaching a crossing. An IVA stopping because of full world knowledge might cause a user to wonder how the IVA knew about the approaching pedestrian. Our system would cause the IVA to perceive the pedestrian with delay resulting in different and more realistic behavior.

Different modifications were applied to the scenario to determine current limitations of our system. The problem of occlusion is already solved through the virtual sensors' approaches. Internal (e.g., myopia) and external (e.g., fog) restrictions of the view range are also covered, but so far with a fixed threshold. Prospectively, the clarity with which something is perceived will drop off due to these effects and distance. Future challenges lie in the integration of mechanisms to cover dysfunctions of sensation (e.g. glare) as well as mechanisms for predictive perception. Another existing limitation is that it cannot be perceived that something is possibly occluded, e.g., that a pedestrian crossing's entrance is occluded and the agent thus should limit its speed.

CONCLUSIONS

A simplified perception causes simplified and thus more or less unrealistic behavior that might confuse a player, especially if he expects perception to function like in reality. Thus enhancing the realism of IVAs or NPCs perception mechanisms (like in stealth games) helps to improve player experience and in addition enables advanced gameplay mechanisms. We presented a generic framework for virtual perception that helps to include more realistic perceptual processes. While occlusion is already considered, future improvements deal with the reproduction of further effects like myopia, fog, glare or prediction, as well as the integration of further modalities. One important question is whether a system like SynPeA would be accepted by developers. Therefore, it needs to be determined which processes increase the realism of agent behavior and can also be realized effectively. As shown in the evaluation, the presented agent-central perception process already provides a sound basis to retrieve plausible information from the environment. Thus, following decision making processes are improved resulting in more realistic behavior of simulated entities and in more valuable player experiences.

ACKNOWLEDGMENTS

The associated AVeSi project is being funded by the BMBF's FHprofUnt program (grant 17028X11).

REFERENCES

1. Bordeux, C., Boulic, R., and Thalmann, D. An Efficient and Flexible Perception Pipeline for Autonomous Agents. *Computer Graphics Forum 18* (1999), 23–30.
2. Kuiper, D. M., and Wenkstern, R. Z. Virtual Agent Perception Combination in Multi Agent Based Systems. In *Proc. of the 2013 Int. Conf. on Autonomous Agents and Multi-agent Systems* (2013), 611–618.
3. Luck, M., and Aylett, R. Applying Artificial Intelligence to Virtual Reality: Intelligent Virtual Environments. *Applied Artificial Intelligence 14* (2000), 3–32.
4. Noser, H., and Thalmann, D. Synthetic Vision and Audition for Digital Actors. *Computer Graphics Forum 14* (1995), 325–336.
5. Peters, C. An Object-Based Memory for Supporting Attentive Virtual Agents. In *AISB Convention, Symposium: Remembering Who We Are – Human Memory For Artificial Agents* (2010).
6. van Oijen, J., La Poutré, H., and Dignum, F. Agent Perception within CIGA: Performance Optimizations and Analysis. In *Agent-Oriented Software Engineering XIII*. Springer, 2013, 99–117.

RedWire: A Novel Way to Create and Re-Mix Games

Jesse Himmelstein[1], Mikael Couzic[1], Charlene Jennett[2], Anna L. Cox[2], Raphael Goujet[1], Ariel Lindner[1], François Taddei[1]
[1]Center for Research and Interdisciplinary, 10 rue Charles V, 75004 Paris, France
[2]University College London, Gower Street, London WC1E 6BT, UK
jesse.himmelstein@parisdescartes,fr, mikaelcouzic, raphael.goujet @ gmail.com
charlene.jennett, anna.cox @ ucl.ac.uk, francois.taddei, ariel.lindner @ inserm.fr

ABSTRACT
More and more researchers want to use games as a way of engaging the general public in their research; however game development takes time and requires significant programming knowledge. The goal of RedWire is to enable researchers to create games faster without starting from scratch each time. By encouraging re-mixing and mash-ups, we hope to provide users with an easy way of sharing games and creating variations of games.

Author Keywords
Game design; Game creation; Re-mix.

ACM Classification Keywords
H.1.2. User/Machine Systems: Human Factors; D.2.2 Design Tools and Techniques: Structured programming; D.2.6 Programming Environments: Graphical environments, interactive environments; D.2.13 Reusable Software: Reuse models; D.3.2 Language Classifications: Applicative (functional) languages

INTRODUCTION
Researchers are increasingly using games - as a means of educating players [8], collecting research data [1], and encouraging behaviour change [3]. Game development can take an extensive amount of time, even for experienced game studios. In this paper we present RedWire, a new game engine for the design and creation of games. The goal of RedWire is to enable people to create games faster without starting from scratch each time. By encouraging re-mixing and mash-ups, users are provided with an easy way of creating variations of the same game. Additionally, all games will be open source and available to play and re-mix on RedWire.

RELATED WORK
The inspiration for RedWire comes from the intersection of a number of fields: remixing, browser-based game engines, visual programming, and functional programming.

CHI PLAY '14, Oct 19-22 2014, Toronto, ON, Canada
ACM 978-1-4503-3014-5/14/10.
http://dx.doi.org/10.1145/2658537.2661315

Remixing is the act of adding to and modifying material from someone else in order to create something new. We draw heavily from insights of Rich Hickey, who is best known as the inventor of the Clojure programming language [4]. His analysis of the conditions that make certain programs easier to compose than others demonstrates the advantages of "untying", or decoupling, program elements from each other. The more decoupled the elements are, the "simpler" the resulting program is, and easier it will to take the program apart and recompose it [5].

Using this metric, Rich Hickey evaluates the simplicity of a number of common programming practices. Two practices that fare particularly poorly from this point of view are mutable state and object-oriented programming, which are almost universally present within game engines. Mutable state is complex because code that reads and or writes it cannot depend on it keeping its value between executions (or even during, in the case of multithreaded programs). Object-orientation, is also complex, because objects contain mutable state, and reference each other directly.

Existing visual programming environments that explore the easy access design space include Scratch [7] and Alice [2] – both allow users to create games and share their projects with others. However we argue that these environments are limited because they are object-oriented with mutable state. Another relevant example is Max/MSP [6] which offers users a dataflow architecture [9] to create interactive audio and video exhibits. This system does not include common functionality for game development, and is rarely used for that purpose.

REDWIRE INTERNALS
The goal of RedWire is to let developers remix games in a *simple* (in Rich Hickey's sense) and visual way, within the browser. We are targeting existing game and web developers who are accustomed to imperative programming languages. We decided to build RedWire as a functional *framework* that executes small blocks of imperative code in a manner that isolates, or "sandboxes", them from directly modifying state. In order to explain both the goals and operation of this novel approach to developers, we chose to compare it to a common prototyping tool used in electronics, the breadboard. Following the electronics metaphor, a RedWire game is made of components called *chips* that are connected to each other on a *board.* A *chip* communicates with the rest of the game via its *pins.* The

chip only has access to the values provided via its pins, and cannot store its own state.

In order to avoid the "visual spaghetti" that plagues large graphs, the user doesn't wire chips directly to one another, but to shared *buffers*. There are two kinds of buffers. The *memory buffer* stores "plain-old data", which allows the user to store state and hook up chips to one another. The *IO buffers* enable the purely functional system of chips to interact with the outside world. For example, there is a *keyboard IO buffer* that provides the list of keyboard keys that are currently pressed down, and a *mouse IO buffer* that gives the current mouse position. There are also output IO buffers such as the *canvas* buffer that draws the list of provided shapes to the screen.

USER JOURNEY

When a user finds a game that she would like to remix, she "forks" the game to create her own identical copy. Similar to other live coding environments, the user can keep the game playing while they make changes. Inspired by Brett Victor's work [10], RedWire supports "recording". When the user toggles the recording button and then presses play, RedWire memorizes all the data generated by the input IO services. This includes all input from the player, such as mouse movements, clicks, and keyboard presses. After stopping the recording, any changes the user makes can be retroactively applied to the recording, so that the user can directly see the results of the changes without having to play the game again.

Another feature that allows the user to experiment with the game is *muting*. When a user mutes a chip, it is temporarily deactivated. This draws from the strengths of the RedWire architecture, which ensures that muting the chip does not prevent the rest of the game from functioning.

HACKDAY EXAMPLE

Earlier this year at the Citizen Cyberscience Summit 2014 we included Redwire as a hack day challenge. The person that completed the challenge created a game that he called "Shoot sleeping computers and earn professor hats."

The creator of the re-mixed game had little programming experience. He created this game by re-mixing an existing game called "Stupendous Side Scrolling Space Shooter". Instead of a space ship shooting asteroids, he changed the images so that the player is shooting un-used computer cycles. He added a point system consisting of "professor hat" badges that are won by destroying the spare computer cycles. He explained that his idea was to illustrate the idea of volunteer computing, where volunteers donate their spare computer processing power to be used in scientific research. This example illustrates the potential of Redwire for the design and creation of games.

CONCLUSION

In this paper we have presented RedWire, a new game engine for the design and creation of games. RedWire is the first game engine to adopt an architecture specifically designed for re-mixing and mash-ups. The engine provides researchers with an easy way of sharing games and creating variations of games for comparative study. With further development work, we predict that RedWire will be a useful tool for creating research games. In future work, we will add a number of features to help designers share code across games. We will also integrate advanced metrics, remote game recording, and multiplayer capabilities.

ACKNOWLEDGMENTS

This research was funded by the EU project Citizen Cyberlab (Grant No 317705).

REFERENCES

1. Von Ahn, L. Games with a Purpose. *Computer 39*, 6 (2006), 92–94.
2. Cooper, S., Dann, W., and Pausch, R. Alice: a 3-D tool for introductory programming concepts. *Journal of Computing Sciences in Colleges 15*, (2000), 107–116.
3. Fogg, B.J. *Persuasive Technology: Using Computers to Change What We Think and Do*. Morgan Kaufmann, 2003.
4. Hickey, R. The Clojure Programming Language. *Proceedings of the 2008 symposium on Dynamic languages*, ACM New York, NY, USA (2008), 1.
5. Hickey, R. Simple Made Easy. *InfoQ*, 2011. http://www.infoq.com/presentations/Simple-Made-Easy.
6. Place, T. and Lossius, T. Jamoma: A Modular Standard for Structuring Patches in Max. *Proceedings of the 2006 International Computer Music Conference*, (2006), 143–146.
7. RESNICK, M., MALONEY, J., MONROY-HERNÁNDEZ, A., et al. Scratch: Programming for All. *Communications of the ACM 52*, (2009), 60–67.
8. Ritterfield, U., Cody, M., and VORDERER, P. Serious games: Explication of an oxymoron - introduction. In *Serious Games - Mechanisms and Effects*. 2009, 4–9.
9. Sousa, T. Dataflow Programming Concept, Languages and Applications. *Doctoral Symposium on Informatics Engineering*, (2012).
10. Victor, B. Inventing on Principle. 2012. https://vimeo.com/36579366.

Designing an Immersive and Entertaining Pervasive Gameplay Experience with Spheros as Game and Interface Elements

Brennan Jones, Kody Dillman, Setareh Aghel Manesh, Ehud Sharlin, Anthony Tang
Department of Computer Science, University of Calgary
{bdgjones, kody.dillman, setareh.aghelmanesh}@ucalgary.ca, ehud@cpsc.ucalgary.ca, tonyt@ucalgary.ca

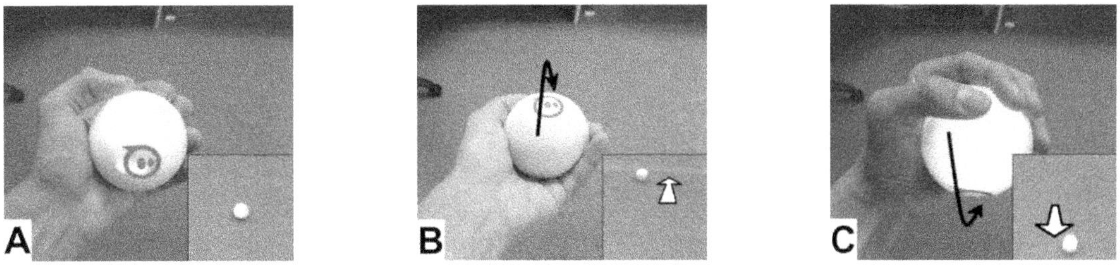

Figure 1: A control scheme that allows a player to roll a Sphero on the floor by tilting another in their hand.

ABSTRACT
The Sphero is a robotic remote-controlled ball capable of rolling around on its own in any direction at multiple speeds. Numerous games have been designed for the Sphero for smartphones and tablets. However, most of these games provide an interface for controlling the Sphero that is far from natural. These games also do not put a strong focus on the physical environment around the Sphero. This work discusses a control scheme used to control a Sphero with another Sphero, and a pervasive game leveraging this scheme that emphasizes physical properties of the environment to create an immersive experience.

Author Keywords
Sphero; robotic ball; pervasive gaming; controllers; natural mappings; immersion; gaming experience

ACM Classification Keywords
H.5.0. Information interfaces and presentation (e.g., HCI): General

INTRODUCTION
Pervasive gaming is a growing form of interactive entertainment that is being further realized through the use of robotic toys such as the Sphero. The Sphero is a robotic ball designed by Orbotix that is capable of rolling around in any direction at multiple speeds [1]. It can be controlled using a smartphone or a tablet.

There are several games available for the Sphero for iOS and Android, including augmented reality games, party games, and tabletop games. Most of these games allow players to control a Sphero via their smartphone or tablet by tapping buttons or tilting the device. While the main focus of most of these games is the Sphero, much of the interface is on the smartphone or tablet, and not on the Sphero itself.

CONTROL SCHEME
Previous work by Skalski et al. [4] and Cairns et al. [2] has shown that natural controller mappings lead to more enjoyable and immersive gameplay experiences than unnatural mappings. An example of a "natural" controller mapping, as defined in [4], would be a baseball bat controller used to swing a virtual baseball bat in a video game. In this case, the mapping is from a physical object to a virtual object of the exact same form factor. Players tend to find this control scheme more natural, and thus more enjoyable, than using a traditional game controller.

The Sphero device is typically controlled through an on-screen gamepad with "accelerate" and "turn" controls. Yet this style of control is very far from Skalski's "natural" mapping. The control scheme that we introduce here for the Sphero (the roller) employs a second, paired Sphero (the controller) that a player holds in their hand. We define the *starting position* of the controller, as shown in Figure 1(a), as the position with the tail light pointed toward the player and the lit-up hemisphere pointed up. From the starting position, the player tilts the controller in any direction to

CHI PLAY '14, Oct 19-22 2014, Toronto, ON, Canada.
ACM 978-1-4503-3014-5/14/10.
http://dx.doi.org/10.1145/2658537.2661301.

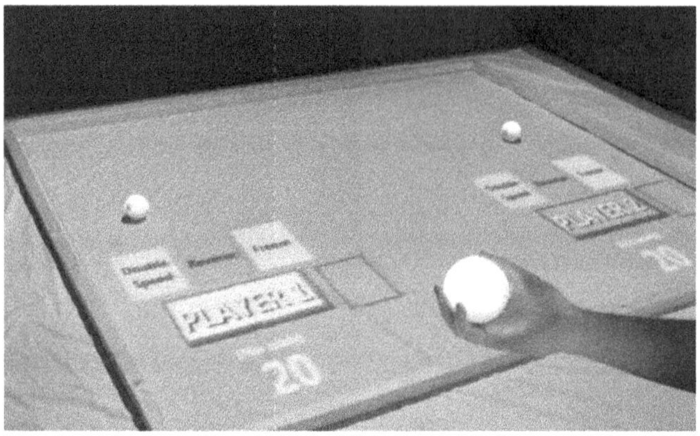

Figure 2: Sphero Sumo's play arena with the rollers in their starting positions.

move the roller in that direction relative to the player's initial position (Figures 1(b) and 1(c)). The degree to which the controller is tilted in any given direction, starting at 15 degrees and up to 100 degrees, positively and linearly affects the roller's speed in that direction. When the controller is tilted less than 15 degrees from its starting position, the roller does not move. This is to allow the player to easily stop the roller by holding the controller steady at its starting position. The roller's speed maxes out when the controller is tilted past 100 degrees.

Our design rationale is that the controller provides a natural and intuitive mapping to the roller because both objects have the exact same form factor. Although the movements of the controller and the roller are not the same (the roller is rolling while the controller is simply tilted), the directions of their movements are.

SPHERO SUMO

We designed a two-player game, called *Sphero Sumo* that leverages this control scheme. *Sphero Sumo* is a fighting game that requires two players to each control a Sphero in an arena and square off against each other. The rules of this game are simple: players one and two constantly hit each other to take health points from one another. The last player with health remaining wins.

The game's graphical interface is projected onto the floor, as shown in Figure 2. Each player starts with 20 health points. Players' rollers do damage to each other through collisions with their opponents. At the point of a collision between two rollers, the roller that is moving faster "wins" the collision, while the roller that is moving slower "loses" the collision and loses three health points.

Players must also avoid hitting walls; hitting a wall causes a player to lose one health point. A player's health is displayed both as a number on the scoreboard and through the roller as a steady transition in the brightness of the ball, with bright meaning at full health and dim meaning almost dead. Whenever a player's roller is involved in a collision, either with the wall or with another roller, that player's controller vibrates and flashes, and their roller also flashes. The game also utilizes special attacks by allowing a player to slap their controller once to load an attack and then again to use that attack.

EFFECTS OF PHYSICAL PROPERTIES ON PLAYER EXPERIENCES

The experience of a game can be made more enriching and immersive by emphasizing physical aspects of it [3]. The physical domain of a game can include both tangible interfaces and real-world properties that are also game elements or representations of game state. In contemporary video games, the game logic, game state (e.g., score), and game world all exist in what Magerkurth et al. [3] define as the "virtual domain." They are all within the computer and are not existent or represented in the physical world. Many traditional Sphero games for iOS and Android go beyond the virtual domain by including Spheros as physical game elements in order to increase immersion and enjoyability. Sphero Sumo does this as well, but takes it a step further by also including physical arena bounds, a physical stage, and a projector. The projector plays two roles: (1) augment additional information such as score values and player statuses onto the game arena, and (2) provide lighting to the game arena that is similar to stage lighting in a theatre, thus drawing focus (and emphasis) on the game stage.

FUTURE WORK

In the future, we plan on running user studies that compare the control scheme we presented to controlling a Sphero with a smartphone to see if our control scheme is perceived as more natural or more enjoyable than the smartphone. We are also interested in comparing Sphero Sumo to a similar fighting game played without Spheros but with only virtual game elements to see if emphasizing physical aspects of the game in this case affects the perceived immersiveness of the game.

REFERENCES

1. Sphero Robot Ball | Game System for iOS and Android. http://www.gosphero.com.
2. Cairns, P., Li, J., Wang, W., and Nordin, A.I. The Influence of Controllers on Immersion in Mobile Games. In *Proc. CHI 2014*, ACM (2014), 371-380.
3. Magerkurth, C., Engelke, T., and Memisoglu, M. Augmenting the Virtual Domain with Physical and Social Elements: Towards a Paradigm Shift in Computer Entertainment Technology. In *Proc. ACE 2004*, ACM (2004), 163-172.
4. Skalski, P., Tamborini, R., Shelton, A., Buncher, M., and Lindmark, P. Mapping the road to fun: Natural video game controllers, presence, and game enjoyment. *New Media & Society 13*, 2 (2011), 224-242.

A Bottom-up Method for Developing a Trait-based Model of Player Behavior

Mikhail Kabakov
Research Assistant
mikhail.a.kabakov@gmail.com

Alessandro Canossa
Associate Professor
a.canossa@neu.edu

Magy Seif El-Nasr
Associate Professor
m.seifel-nasr@neu.edu

Jeremy B. Badler
Postdoctoral Fellow
jbadler@ski.org

C. Randall Colvin
Professor
rcolvin57@gmail.com

Stefanie Tignor
Research Assistant
smtignir@gmail.com

Zhengxing Chen
Research Assistant
czxttkl@gmail.com

Kunal Asarsa
Research Assistant
kunal.asarsa@gmail.com

All authors are from:
Northeastern University, 360 Huntington avenue, Boston, MA

ABSTRACT
Understanding player behavior through telemetry logs is an important yet unresolved problem. Interpreting the meaning of players' low-level behaviors over time is important due to its utility in (a) developing a more adaptive and personalized game experience, (b) uncovering game design issues, and (c) understanding the human cognitive processes in a gaming context, not to mention its use and application to learning, training, and health. In this paper, the authors describe a work in progress developing a quantified model of player behavior for interpreting telemetry data from a first-person roll-playing game (RPG). This kind of model constitutes a grammar that will allow us to make sense of low-level behavioral data to assess personality, decision-making, and other cognitive constructs through behavioral measures.

Author Keywords
Gameplay telemetry; game analytics; player typology; behavior analysis and classification.

INTRODUCTION
Digital games have become a widespread form of entertainment. How people engage with the game needs to be described in a concise, quantifiable way – before it can be studied with scientific methods. In other words, there is a need for a player model. To create such a model, an interpretive grammar must be established, which is the goal of this work. We take a bottom-up approach to derive the model using a qualitative process where expert researchers are involved.

PREVIOUS WORK
There has been considerable research work aimed at developing and understanding players' behaviors within games. In this section, due to space limitations we will only mention a few representative studies. Bartle's seminal work [6] dates back to 1996. Based on research within the Multi-User Dungeons community, he categorized players into four types: Explorer, Achiever, Socializer and Killer. This was the first work in the field, and Bartle empathized that using it for classifying any other type of players or users in general was akin to *"using a hammer on screws."* Bateman and Boon [7] followed Bartle's work by creating another model, using the Myers-Briggs personality framework. They postulated that Myers-Briggs provided a psychometric basis for player types. They also categorized players into four classes: Conqueror, Manager, Wanderer and Participant. Additionally, Bateman [9] created the "BrainHex" classification, consisting of seven different player archetypes: Seeker, Survivor, Daredevil, Mastermind, Conqueror, Socializer and Achiever. However, this system was not empirically validated. Tuunanen and Hamari [4] did a meta-analysis of various player typologies. They concluded that a type-based approach is very limited, because types provide only a small piece of information about a player. Even that is blurred if a player falls into more than one category, as is very often the case with the typologies above. Similarly, Another meta-analysis done by Bateman, Lowenhaup, &, Nacke [8] concluded that "type theories have, except in rare cases, proven inadequate and have made way for alternative trait theories.". Thus, there is a need for a method for developing trait-based models of player behavior.

METHOD
For our project we used a custom-designed RPG mod for the game "*Fallout: New Vegas*" (Bethesda Softworks, 2010; Figure 1). The game was designed to give players a variety of choices eliciting different behaviors. For example, it offers a main quest with a variety of methods to achieve it, including strategic planning, bribery, deception, stealth, diversion, etc. There is also the option to become a turncoat and join the game's antagonists. Additionally, aside from the main quest there are four side quests, as well as several non-quest opportunities such as searching for treasure or crafting items. Many encounters can be resolved in more than one way. We chose to take an expert-driven

CHI PLAY'14, October 19–21, 2014, Toronto, ON, Canada.
ACM 978-1-4503-3014-5/14/10.
http://dx.doi.org/10.1145/2658537.2661320

approach to develop a list of factors that characterize play styles. While we used behaviors from within our game, the behaviors were abstracted from our mod's specifics to ensure generalizability of these factors to other RPGs.

Figure 1. A screenshot from the VPAL mod.

To derive the factors, we first developed a behavioral card deck consisting of 250 cards, each describing a situation and a behavior that a participant may take within the game. The intent was to cover as much as possible all *significant* situation-behavior pairings within our specific game, but that could also be generalized across first-person RPG games. An example card is: *"Leaving the basement location immediately after fulfilling the quest of killing the rat, without any exploration of what is there on the shelves and floor."* We then needed to derive 10-15 general factors that between them could encompass all 250 cards. To do this, we asked eight researchers, all experts in game behavior analysis and/or psychology, to categorize all 250 cards independently. They were told to use any linguistic variable to label the categories they came up with, and to create as many behavioral clusters as they would find best. All produced 8-20 behavior categories. We then held two meetings to discuss the resulting categories with the objective of coalescing differences and combining the results to produce an agreed-upon set. For example: all participants came up with a behavior category representing exploration though the exact names varied: "Explorative attitude", "Inquisitive, curious, explores possibilities", "Exploring" (twice), "Exploration" (twice), "World exploration: high" and "Adventurous/exploratory". Other categories were joined as opposite poles of a single factor: for example, "cautiously approaches encounters" and "boldly rushes into combat" both fit into a Strategic ⇔ Impulsive scale. Not all categories had broad agreement. Any category supported by 3 or fewer participants was either omitted or merged into others. Other categories were dropped because they required limited, highly specific behaviors (e.g., "*Looting lots of items, acquiring wealth / top-level items*"). There was also some debate whether to separate categories according to their domain; for example, should behaviors such as "explores different areas" and "asks questions during dialog to obtain information" be separated or grouped? In the end, we came up with a model featuring the following seven factors:

1. Strategic action ⇔ Impulsivity: denotes whether behaviors taken by the player is impulsive or strategic in nature.
2. Acquisition: describes players' need to collect items.
3. Approach ⇔ Avoid: is concerned with behaviors that are geared towards approaching something in the game or avoiding it. This can be approaching a quest, an enemy or avoiding them.
4. Explorative attitude: describes how much the behaviors that players engage in is exploratory vs. not. These can be through dialog or navigation.
5. Compliance ⇔ Independent activity: denotes whether the player follows quests given by the NPCs.
6. Social warmth ⇔ Rudeness, being sarcastic: is concerned with players' dialog choices warm vs. rude.
7. Morality ⇔ "Renegade" behavior: denotes the level of morality in players' choices.

CONCLUSION

In this paper we presented a list of factors that can be used as a starting point for a grammar that can be used to understand player behaviors over time, and characterize individual differences among players. Such a grammar could have a large impact on many areas, including player modeling, analytics, and adaptive designs. Our next step is to validate and verify the derived factors through several methods including statistical factor analysis, currently underway. We also plan to cross-validate the model across other RPG games, to ensure that the defined behaviors and categories are sufficiently generalizable.

REFERENCES

1. Przybylski, A., Rigby, C., Ryan, R. A Motivational Model of Video Game Engagement. *Review of General Psychology 14, 2* (2010), 154–166.
2. Ryan, R. M., Rigby, S. C., Przybylski, A The Motivational Pull of Video Games: A Self-Determination Theory Approach. *Motivation and Emotion 30, 4* (2006), 347–363.
3. Tamborini, R., Bowman, N. Defining Media Enjoyment as the Satisfaction of Intrinsic Needs. *Journal of communication 60* (2010), 758-777.
4. Tuunanen, J., Hamari, J. Meta-synthesis of player typologies *DiGRA Nordic* (2012).
5. Lankveld, G. Quantifying individual player differences Tilburg: *TiCC Ph.D. Series 25* (2013).
6. Bartle R. Hearts, Clubs, Diamonds and Spades: players who suit MUDs *Journal of MUD research* 1, 1 (1996).
7. Bateman, C., Boon, R. DGD1 ("Demographic Game Design") *International Hobo* (2004).
8. Bateman, C., Lowenhaup, R., Nacke, L. Player Typology in Theory and Practice. *DiGRA* (2011).
9. Bateman C., Boon R., Bundy N. BrainHex http://brainhex.com, accessed July (2014).

Flappy Voice: An Interactive Game for Childhood Apraxia of Speech Therapy

Tian Lan[1], Sandesh Aryal[1], Beena Ahmed[2], Kirrie Ballard[3], Ricardo Gutierez-Osuna[1]
[1]Texas A&M University, USA, {welkinlan, sandesh, rgutier}@tamu.edu
[2]Texas A&M University, Qatar, beena.ahmed@qatar.tamu.edu
[3]Faculty of Health Sciences, The University of Sydney, Australia, kirrie.ballard@sydney.edu.au

ABSTRACT
We present Flappy Voice, a mobile game to facilitate acquisition of speech timing and prosody skills for children with apraxia of speech. The game is adapted from the popular game Flappy Bird, and replaces touch interaction with voice control. Namely, we map the child's vocal loudness into the bird's position by means of a smoothing filter. In this way, children control the game via the duration and amplitude of their voice. Flappy Voice allows the therapist to create new exercises with different difficulty levels, including an assisted mode for children with limited skills, and a free mode for advanced players. Results from a pilot user study with children support the feasibility of the game as a speech training tool.

Author Keywords
Childhood apraxia of speech; games for health

ACM Classification Keywords
H.5.2 [Information Interfaces and Presentation]: User Interfaces –Voice I/O. **J.2.3 [Computer Applications]:** Life and Medical Sciences –Health.

INTRODUCTION
Childhood apraxia of speech (CAS) is a neurological pediatric disorder that can delay the acquisition of skills, including prosody control (pitch, loudness, and duration) and the production of speech units (phones, syllables and words) [1]. Treatment of CAS requires frequent, intensive, individualized, and naturalistic motor-based interventions [5]. However, the high ratio of children with CAS to speech language pathologists (SLPs) makes such intensive treatments unviable – CAS is estimated to affect 5-6 % of children. Thus, there is a need for cost-effective interventions to complement face-to-face therapy.

As a step towards this goal, Parnandi et al. [6] developed a remote therapy system that allows children to practice CAS exercises on a mobile app in the comfort of their homes, and the SLP to assign exercises and monitor progress remotely through a server. Results from the study showed that children, parents and SLPs prefer tablet-based delivery over paper-based activities, but also highlighted the need for interactive activities to keep children engaged.

In response to this need, we present Flappy Voice, a voice-driven game for speech motor acquisition. Adapted from its eponymous game, Flappy Voice replaces touch input with a speech detection algorithm that allows users to control the game with the duration and intensity of their voice.

RELATED WORK
Computer-based interventions have been shown to lead to higher levels of engagement and reduced error responses in children, as compared to traditional therapy. Umanski et al. [7] developed a voice-based game to promote the development of speech rhythm skills for children with speech disorders. The player controls an avatar skiing down a slalom slope in a way that each syllable onset causes a change in direction. Hailpern et al. [3] developed a real-time voice visualization tool for children with autism and speech delays. The clinician and child take turns to utter the same word, and the system provides a visual representation of the two utterances on a screen. Various other speech therapy apps have been developed for children, including PocketSLP, ArtikPix, Speech with Milo; and Apraxiaville; see [6] and references therein.

SYSTEM DESCRIPTION
While the causes for CAS are not well understood, recent studies have suggested that a central deficit in timing of speech sound production and prosodic variations may be implicated [2, 7]. Accordingly, Flappy Voice is designed to allow repeated practice of timing and vocal loudness exercises. As illustrated in Fig 1, Flappy Voice is a side-scrolling game whose goal is to fly a bird through a sequence of obstacles. Our implementation is adapted from an open-source Android clone of the original game known as "Zombie Bird" [4], replacing its apocalyptic theme with one more appropriate for children.

Voice Control
To control the game, the child's voice activity is mapped into the bird's height H_t via a low-pass filter:

$$H_t = s \times H_{t-1} + (1 - s) \times A_t \qquad (1)$$

where A_t is the speech amplitude at time t, computed as the logarithm of the root-mean-square of the speech signal over a 200 msec window, and s is a sensitivity parameter that controls how quickly the bird reacts to the speech input.

CHI PLAY '14, Oct 19-22, 2014, Toronto, ON, Canada
ACM 978-1-4503-3014-5/14/10.
http://dx.doi.org/10.1145/2658537.2661305

Calibration

To accommodate for individual differences in voice loudness, microphone characteristics or ambient noise, the speech amplitude A_t is normalized relative to the maximum and minimum amplitudes observed thus far in the session:

$$A_t = (A_t - A_{min})/(A_{max} - A_{min}) \quad (2)$$

This allows Flappy Voice to adapt to changes in the child's amplitude or ambient noise levels from session to session.

Free and Assisted Play

Flappy Voice offers two different play modes: free, and assisted. In *free* mode, crashing into an obstacle ends the game, which can severely disrupt practice. Thus, we have also developed an *assisted* mode, in which the bird's height is maintained within a "flight envelope" defined by tracing lines between consecutive obstacles –see Fig. 2a. This prevents the bird from ever hitting the obstacles, and allows endless play. To maintain player engagement, points are only awarded for clearing the obstacles without hitting the upper or lower soft barriers. In the free mode, a highest-scores board (not shown) provides an element of challenge over multiple sessions.

Customization

Flappy Voice can be customized to meet the needs of individual children. In addition to selecting between the two play modes, the SLP can also modify the sensitivity parameter in eq. (1) and the width of the vertical clearance at each obstacle –see Fig. 2b, which in turn affect the game's difficulty. Finally, Flappy Voice provides an interface that allows the SLP to create new screens with an arbitrary number of obstacles –see Fig. 2c.

USER STUDIES

We performed a pilot study in which children (N=6; 5 male; ages 4-12 years; 3 CAS, 3 control) were allowed to play with the game and then asked to complete a short survey describing their experience. When asked *What did you think about the exercises?*, children unanimously responded that the game was "fun" and that they enjoyed it, though one child responded that the bird was a "bit hard to control at times." When asked *What did you like about the exercises?*, one child replied that "Not as hard as the actual flappy bird and I don't think many people would get very angry," whereas another child replied "That he didn't die." Interestingly, children with CAS liked the assisted mode, whereas control children expressed preference towards the free mode. When asked *What did you not like about the exercises?*, three children replied that they did not like having to wear a headset microphone –a necessity in our study due to the poor quality of speech recorded from the tablet's built-in microphone. Altogether, the user study provides encouraging results, suggesting the game is fun to play and well-suited for CAS therapy.

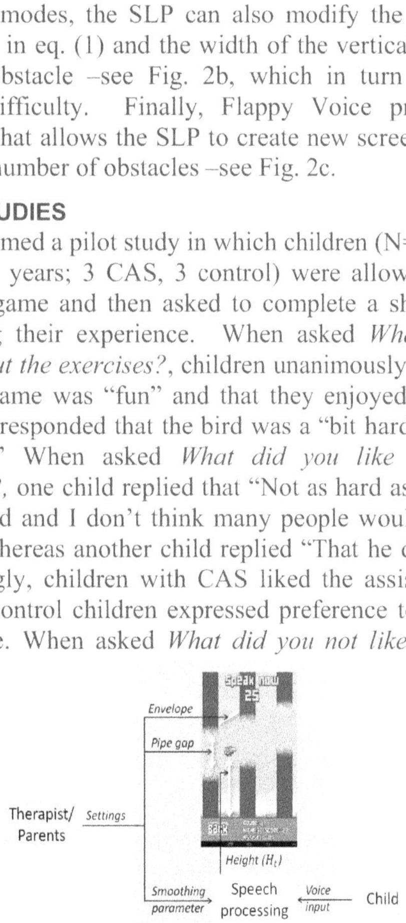

Fig 1. System diagram of Flappy Voice

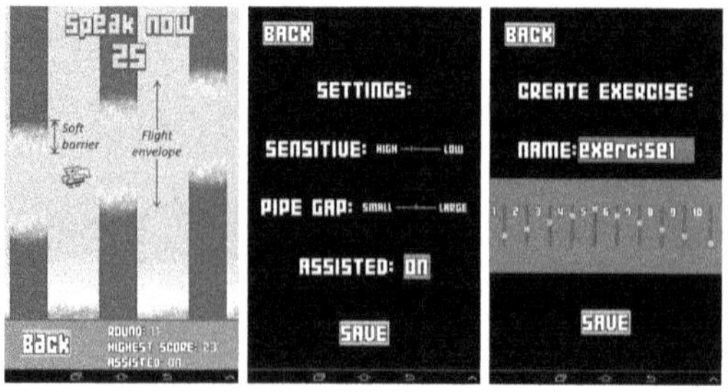

(a) (b) (c)

Fig. 2. (a) Flappy Voice in *assisted* mode shows the flight envelope; (b) Settings menu (c) Exercise editor.

FUTURE WORK

Work is underway to allow the game to be controlled by pitch; this would broaden the range of prosodic activities beyond amplitude control. Visual cues may also be added to each obstacle, e.g., an image of a lion to represent low pitch vs. a chipmunk for high pitch, or images of objects the child is to name. At present, Flappy Voice is a standalone app; additional work is needed to integrate the game with remote therapy systems [6]. User studies are also needed to test the games' effectiveness as an intervention for CAS.

ACKNOWLEDGEMENTS

This work was made possible by NPRP grant # [4-638-2-236] from the Qatar National Research Fund (a member of Qatar Foundation). The statements made herein are solely the responsibility of the authors.

REFERENCES

1. ASHA. *Childhood Apraxia of Speech,* 2007; Available from: http://www.asha.org/policy/TR2007-00278/.
2. Ballard, K.J., et al., *A treatment for dysprosody in childhood apraxia of speech,* J Speech Lang Hear Res, 2010, **53**(5): 1227-1245.
3. Hailpern, J., et al. *Designing visualizations to facilitate multisyllabic speech with children with autism and speech delays*, in *Proc. DIS,* 2012, 126-135.
4. Kilobolt, L. *Zombie Bird,* 2014; Available from: http://jamescho7.com/zombiebird/.
5. Maas, E., et al., *Motor-based intervention protocols in treatment of childhood apraxia of speech,* Curr Dev Disord Rep, 2014, **1**: 1-10.
6. Parnandi, A., et al. *Architecture of an automated therapy tool for childhood apraxia of speech*, in *Proc. ASSETS,* 2013, 1-8.
7. Umanski, D., et al. *Development of a voice-based rhythm game for training speech motor skills of children with speech disorders*, in *Proc. ICDVRAT,* 2010, 255-262.

Gingerman Challenge: A Persuasive Game for Promoting Adequate Sunlight Exposure for Office Workers

Hajin Lim[1] **Jaehyeon Park**[2] **Bongwon Suh**[3]
Human Centered Computing Lab[1 3], Game Media Lab[2]
Seoul National University, Republic of Korea
akal@snu.ac.kr, jaehyeonpark@snu.ac.kr, bongwon@snu.ac.kr

ABSTRACT
In this paper, we present *Gingerman Challenge*, which is a persuasive mobile game designed to promote moderate sunlight exposure. The design goals of *Gingerman Challenge* are to help players to recognize the merits of sunlight exposure and to promote maintenance of healthy vitamin D levels. We aim to accomplish these goals by incorporating both casual gaming features and the design principles drawn from preliminary user interviews.

Author Keywords
Persuasive game; casual game; health game; behavior change; vitamin D; sun exposure; design for moderation

ACM Classification Keywords
H.5.m. Information interfaces and presentation (e.g., HCI): Miscellaneous.

INTRODUCTION
Vitamin D deficiency has become a worldwide problem. The National Health and Nutrition Examination Survey (NHANES III) [3] revealed that three-quarters of U.S. teens and adults are deficient in vitamin D. The sun's UV-B rays enable skin cells to manufacture vitamin D, which is essential to absorb calcium and phosphorus from diet. A lack of vitamin D can cause bones to become weak, which might lead to bone deformities.

To reach the recommended level of vitamin D, people should expose themselves to a moderate amount of sunlight. However, it is complicated to determine **'How much sunlight is adequate?'**, because not only environmental factors such as weather and location, but also individual factors such as skin color and sunscreen use can affect the amount of ultraviolet radiation received and vitamin D synthesis [4]. Thus, even though individuals feel the necessity of sun exposure, it is difficult to recognize 'how long they need to be exposed' and 'how to minimize the risk of sun exposure such as skin cancer' at the same time.

To address this challenge, we propose a persuasive game, *Gingerman Challenge* (*GC*), which aims to encourage players to get adequate sunlight exposure in more playful and less complicated ways. Previous research and applications, such as *Sundroid* [1] and *SunSmart* [2] have mainly focused on protecting users from overexposure to sunlight and on informing the current UV index and its dangers. *GC* provides personalized recommendation, the adequate time range (e.g. 11AM to 3PM) and duration (e.g. 30mins) for sun exposure, by integrating real-time environmental data (weather, location) and individual characteristics (age, skin color, sunscreen use). We use a 'Baking Oven' metaphor in game design, in which the sunlight exposure is regarded as the heat for baking a gingerman cookie. The mission of this game is to bake a gingerman by getting the adequate amount of sunlight: not to let it burn (overexposure to the sun) nor under baked (insufficient exposure). After comparing the recommended sun exposure time and the actual exposure duration at the end of each day, only a player with the adequate amount of sunlight is awarded for his/her achievement.

CHI PLAY '14, Oct 19-22 2014, Toronto, ON, Canada
ACM 978-1-4503-3014-5/14/10. http://dx.doi.org/10.1145/2658537.2661308

DESIGN PRINCIPLE
Four design principles to develop *GC* were drawn from user interviews. Because there is limited amount of research on managing sun exposure, we think it is essential to obtain opinions of potential users. We recruited five full-time students and five full-time office workers who spent most of their daytime indoors. (5 Females, Average 26 yrs. old)

1) Provide personalized and practicable information
Most interviewees were fairly aware of the benefit and the necessity of the adequate sun exposure. However, they did not know how exactly they could put this knowledge into practicable action. Thus, *GC* should provide practicable and personalized information for each player after collecting environmental and personal data in unobtrusive ways.

2) Design for moderation: sun block vs. sun exposure
Because both blocking and catching the sun are equally important, keeping to the middle between them is tricky. The female interviewees were especially afraid of getting freckled or sunburnt by overexposure to the sun. Thus, it should help players to exercise the moderation, which enables them to enjoy the merits of sun exposure as well as stay safe from the harmful effects of the sun.

3) Integrate with daily routines
Some interviewees hinted that it would be hard to make them adopt and engage in new target behavior. Thus, *GC* should be integrated into the daily routines of players. Therefore, we select one of daily routines of potential users, *checking up the daily weather,* which should mingle well with our game because daily weather usually determines the optimal daily sun exposure duration.

4) Provide alternative options to supplement vitamin D

Interviewees pointed out several unavoidable situations for playing *GC*, such as bad weather conditions, business duties and class works. Therefore, when a player inevitably misses a chance to get sunlight, *GC* should suggest alternatives to supplement insufficient vitamin D, by recommending the food that contains vitamin D, such as fish oils, milk or vitamin D supplements.

GINGERMAN CHALLENGE

Gingerman Challenge is a persuasive mobile game aiming to promote players to get moderate amount of sunlight for maintaining healthy vitamin D levels.

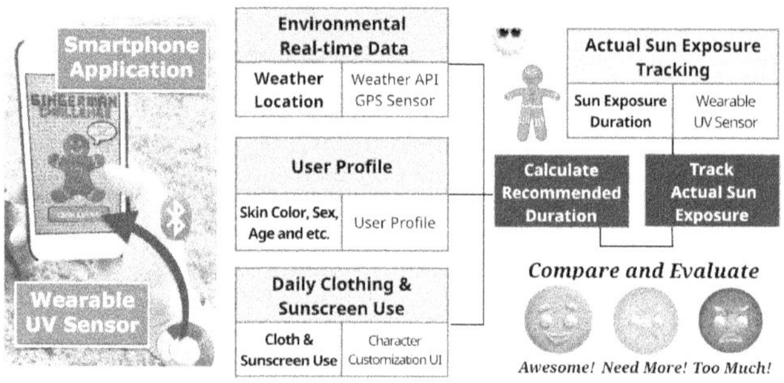

Figure 1. System Components (Left) / Algorithm (Right)

The *GC* architecture (Figure 1) is composed of two components. The first is a wearable UV sensor that tracks the actual sun exposure time of players and transmits it to an Android client via Bluetooth. The second is the Android application that includes (1) the gameplay UI and (2) the algorithm for estimating the optimum exposure durations for a healthy vitamin D status [5]. This algorithm utilizes the following data to elicit the accurate optimal exposure duration: (a) real-time environmental data: weather and location data using GPS sensor and weather API, (b) user characteristics: skin color, age, sex, and etc., from user generated profiles, and (c) daily clothing and sunscreen use from the character customization interface (Figure 2-Left).

Gameplay

When a player starts the game, *GC* provides today's weather information and introduces today's gingerman to bake. If players want to participate in the challenge, s/he should decorate the gingerman using cloth and sunscreen powders in accordance with how they actually dress and put on sunscreen (Figure 2-Left). *GC* requires this information because body exposure is contingent upon clothing and sunscreen use and changes every day, which is important to calculate the daily optimal sun exposure duration. Along with this information, *GC* utilizes player's current location/weather data and user profile to calculate the personalized sun exposure time and duration. Then, *GC* gives players a mission: optimal sun exposure time and duration to bake the gingerman successfully.

During the day, a UV sensor tracks player's actual sun exposure time and duration. When the player takes in sunlight, *GC* displays current progress (Figure 2-Middle). On the other hand, when the player does not take in sunlight, *GC* displays a drained gingerman with warning messages about vitamin D deficiency.

At sunset, when a user cannot take in sunlight anymore, *GC* evaluates each player's performance by comparing the actual sun exposure duration and the recommended duration (Figure 2-Right). Only when a player takes the appropriate amount of sunlight and bakes a gingerman properly, s/he can be awarded with virtual coins to buy items to decorate gingerman further. If a player does not reach the recommended sun exposure duration, s/he will receive a food list to supplement vitamin D. When a player is overexposed to the sunlight, s/he will receive a warning message about the harmful effects of the sun.

Figure 2. Gameplay UI (Left: Character Customization UI, Middle: Tracking UI-*Daytime*, Right: Result UI-*Sunset*)

CONCLUSION AND FUTURE WORKS

Because sun exposure is beneficial and detrimental at the same time, moderating between them can be quite tough. Thus, we propose a persuasive mobile game, *Gingerman Challenge,* to promote players to expose themselves to the moderate amount of sunlight with practicable and personalized recommendations. The current contribution of this study is the design principles and the game design aiming to encourage players to get adequate sunlight exposure, which could inform the design of various persuasive systems that needs to consider deficiency and overdose. In the future, we plan to complete the whole components of *GC* and conduct the field evaluation study to test its efficacy and appeal.

Acknowledgement: This work is supported by BK21 Plus Program, Smart Humanity Convergence Center.

REFERENCES

1. Fahrni, T. et al. 2011. Sundroid: solar radiation awareness with smartphones. *Proc. UbiComp '11*, 365-374
2. Free SunSmart app: http://www.sunsmart.com.au/tools/interactive-tools/free-sunsmart-app. Accessed: 2014-06-23.
3. Ginde, A.A. et al. 2009. Demographic differences and trends of vitamin D insufficiency in the US Population, 1988-2004. *Arch Intern Med.*2009;169(6):626-632.
4. Deborah, K. 2008. Time in the Sun: How Much Is Needed for Vitamin D? - US News: http://health.usnews.com/health-news/family-health/heart/articles/2008/06/23/time-in-the-sun-how-much-is-needed-for-vitamin-d. Accessed: 2014-06-23.
5. Webb, A.R. and Engelsen, O. 2006. Calculated Ultraviolet Exposure Levels for a Healthy Vitamin D Status. Photochemistry and Photobiology. 82.6, 1697-1703.

A Diary Study Exploring Game Completion and Player Experience

Elisa D. Mekler, Alexandre N. Tuch, Anja Lea Martig, Klaus Opwis
University of Basel, Department of Psychology, Center for Cognitive Psychology & Methodology
Missionsstrasse 62a, 4055 Basel, Switzerland
elisa.mekler@unibas.ch, a.tuch@unibas.ch, anja.martig@unibas.ch, klaus.opwis@unibas.ch

ABSTRACT
This work-in-progress describes a three-month diary study, exploring how 25 players experienced the puzzle platformer *FEZ* over several gaming sessions. Following each 30 - 60 minute gaming sessions, players wrote a diary entry describing their game experience and rated their intrinsic motivation. Preliminary findings showed that intrinsic motivation significantly decreased over the course of several sessions. Interestingly, while all players reported comparable experiences during the first few sessions, players who would later finish the game, were less likely to experience this loss of motivation, even before actual completion of the game. Further steps for data analysis are discussed.

Author Keywords
Player Experience, Games User Research, Diary Study

ACM Classification Keywords
K.8.0 Personal Computing: Games

INTRODUCTION
Players are often willing to invest numerous hours into a single game. However, many players do not actually finish the games they bought [1]. To date, few studies have explored how the player experience develops and fluctuates over the playthrough of a single game [5] and to our knowledge, none have looked into the phenomenon of players not completing games. Several studies have investigated what keeps players engaged over several gaming sessions by analyzing game metrics (e.g., [2, 8]). But while the analysis of objective gameplay data is valuable for learning "what" player behavior occurs, the data is not always able to answer "why" a behavior (e.g., playing a game to completion) emerges [6]. Diary studies, which may consist of open-end diary entries and/or rating scales, may provide insight into how players' thoughts and emotions about a game change over time and help identify what players look forward to experiencing in their next gaming session [4]. These findings may then inform game designers on how to keep players engaged till the end of a game. The present work-in-progress introduces preliminary findings of an online diary study, which combined questionnaires and open-end diary entries to explore how the player experience shapes over several gaming sessions.

CHI PLAY '14, Oct 19-22 2014, Toronto, ON, Canada
ACM 978-1-4503-3014-5/14/10.
http://dx.doi.org/10.1145/2658537.2661304

METHOD
Twenty-five university students (13 female, 12 male, age 22 - 28 years, mean age = 24.45) played the non-linear puzzle platformer *FEZ* through Steam. None of them had heard of the game before. They were asked to generate at least 6 diary entries in total, but were encouraged to keep up the diary, if they continued playing the game after that. More precisely, players were instructed to write an entry immediately after every 30 to 60 minutes of gameplay. However, players were free to choose when they wanted to play the game. We deliberately decided to have players choose themselves the play duration and the moment of play. Firstly, a fixed schedule might have interfered with players' experience of the game. Secondly, due to gaming being an activity that people usually engage in voluntarily [7], this allowed us to study players' experience with the game "in the wild" [4]. The only exception was the first entry, which players had to complete after finishing the tutorial section of the game. Overall, the data collection phase lasted from February 25 to June 1st 2014.

Each diary entry consisted of an open-end written section, where players had to describe what they did in the game and how they felt while playing, followed by several questionnaires. Players rated their game session on the Player Experience Need Satisfaction scale (PENS) [7], which has previously been employed to study puzzle platformer games [3], as well as on the Enjoyment/Interest construct from the Intrinsic Motivation Inventory, which has often been used to assess player enjoyment [5, 7]. A week after completion of the data collection phase, players had to write a short review of *FEZ* and retrospectively evaluate it on the PENS and intrinsic motivation scales, as well as state whether they would recommend the game and whether they would play the game again in the future.

RESULTS
On average, players generated 8.2 diary entries (range 6 - 13) and spent 7.88 hours (range 6 to 13.7) on *FEZ*. Eight players completed the game during the data collection phase (which could be verified, as they had unlocked the corresponding Steam achievement). However, they did not invest significantly more time into the game. An independent samples Mann-Whitney U Test showed that players who had finished *FEZ*, rated it significantly better in the retrospective evaluation and were more likely to recommend it (p = .011) (Table 1). They also tended to rate it as more intrinsically mo-

tivating than players who had not completed the game, although the difference was not significant ($p = .086$).

Table 1. Descriptive statistics of the retrospective evaluation

	Game completed M (SD)	Game not completed M (SD)
IM*	5.71 (.82)	4.87 (1.69)
Recommend	5.88 (.83)	4.29 (1.61)
Future play intent	4.75 (1.9)	3.88 (1.69)
Good	5.88 (.64)	4.65 (1.17)

Note. All scales employed a 7-point Likert scale.
* Intrinsic motivation

A repeated measures ANOVA revealed that intrinsic motivation decreased significantly over the course of 6 sessions ($p < .001$, $\eta_p^2 = .199$). The course was comparable for all players during the first three gaming sessions. Still, players who would later go on to complete the game (note that at the time of the fifth and sixth gaming session, none of the players had yet completed the game), already tended to experience less of a decrease in intrinsic motivation by the fifth gaming session (Figure 1), although the difference was not significant due to the small sample size ($p = .08$, $\eta_p^2 = .081$). Lending further evidence to these findings, the open-end diary entries suggest that although all players reported frustration due to getting lost in the game world and due to the difficulty of the puzzles, players who would eventually complete *FEZ*, seemed more willing to experiment and simply explore the various levels and puzzles.

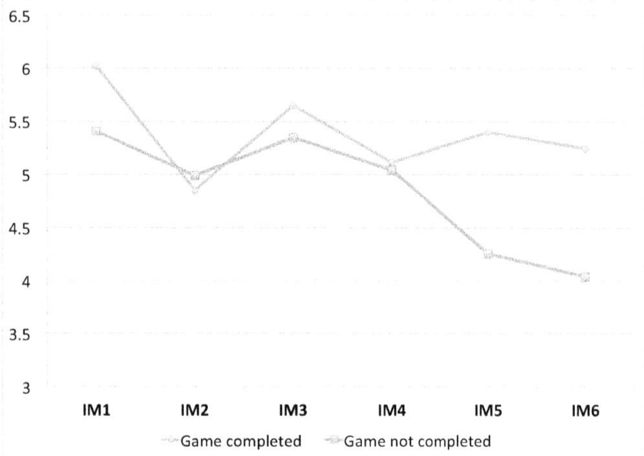

Figure 1. Intrinsic motivation over the course of 6 gaming sessions.

OUTLOOK

While it may come to little surprise that players who completed *FEZ* also rated the game more favourably in retrospective, it is interesting to note that this trend already established itself several sessions before players were actually close to game completion. In order to identify potential predictors for why some players did complete *FEZ*, whereas others did not, we plan on investigating the fluctuations over the course of individual player experiences. In particular, we believe that systematic examination of the open-end diary entries will shed more light on what kept these players motivated to complete the game. Especially the entries of players that generated more than the six required entries might provide a better understanding of what characterizes longer-term motivation to play. By applying Inchamnan and Wyeth's [3] gameplay activity checklist, we hope to identify particular gameplay aspects, such as (lack of) feedback or clear goals, that may have boosted or thwarted players' intrinsic motivation to play *FEZ* to completion. Additionally, we will attempt to link the qualitative data to the PENS scores [7], in order to map certain gameplay aspects with the satisfaction of autonomy and competence needs. Finally, it could also prove interesting to compare the player experiences of several, consecutive sessions, compared to players, who spaced out their gaming sessions over several weeks. These findings will hopefully prove insightful for game designers, who wish to engage players until game completion, as well as generate more concrete research questions about the nature of motivation and player experience over time.

REFERENCES

1. Abernathy, T., and Rouse III, R. Death to the three-act structure: Toward a unique structure for game narratives, 2014. Retrieved July 1, 2014 from `http://www.paranoidproductions.com/writings.html`.
2. Bauckhage, C., Kersting, K., Sifa, R., Thurau, C., Drachen, A., and Canossa, A. How players lose interest in playing a game: An empirical study based on distributions of total playing times. In *Computational Intelligence and Games (CIG), 2012 IEEE Conference on*, IEEE (2012), 139–146.
3. Inchamnan, W., and Wyeth, P. Motivation during videogame play: analysing player experience in terms of cognitive action. In *Proceedings of The 9th Australasian Conference on Interactive Entertainment: Matters of Life and Death*, ACM (2013), 6.
4. Kobayashi, M., and Iloreta, J. Diary studies: A method for games user research "in the wild". In *CHI'13 Workshop – Games User Research: Practice, Methods, and Applications* (2013).
5. Mekler, E. D., Bopp, J. A., Tuch, A. N., and Opwis, K. A systematic review of quantitative studies on the enjoyment of digital entertainment games. In *CHI '14*, ACM (2014), 927–936.
6. Nacke, L. E., Drachen, A., Kuikkaniemi, K., Niesenhaus, J., Korhonen, H. J., Hoogen, v. d. W., Poels, K., IJsselsteijn, W., and Kort, Y. Playability and player experience research. In *Proceedings of DiGRA*, Brunel University (2009).
7. Ryan, R., Rigby, C., and Przybylski, A. The motivational pull of video games: A self-determination theory approach. *Motivation and Emotion 30*, 4 (2006), 344–360.
8. Sifa, R., Drachen, A., Bauckhage, C., Thurau, C., and Canossa, A. Behavior evolution in tomb raider underworld. In *Computational Intelligence in Games (CIG), 2013 IEEE Conference on*, IEEE (2013), 1–8.

Developing Iconic and Semi-Iconic Game Controllers

Lennart E. Nacke, João P. Costa, Dennis L. Kappen, James Robb, Daniel Buckstein
HCI Games Group, Faculty of Business and IT, University of Ontario Institute of Technology, 2000 Simcoe St. N, Oshawa, ON, Canada
lennart.nacke@acm.org , joao.costa@uoit.ca, dennis.kappen@humber.ca, james.robb@uoit.ca, daniel.buckstein@uoit.ca

ABSTRACT
We propose the notion of *semi-iconic* game input (i.e., sharing some properties of game objects instead of being a complete iconic representation of them) and investigate influence of controller representation on player experience. In particular, we developed game controllers at different degrees of realism (*symbolic*, *semi-iconic*, and *iconic*). We present the developed controllers and initial usability findings.

Author Keywords
Games; Player Interaction; Controllers; Player Experience

ACM Classification Keywords
H.5.2. Information interfaces and presentation; K.8.0 Personal Computing – General: Games.

INTRODUCTION
Some of the most successful recent video games are based on non-traditional controller concepts, which map game objects to real-world objects. These controllers have a strong aesthetic representation of game objects and there is a lack of research addressing whether these novel controllers provide a better player experience. Game designers strive to create more realism for their games. Therefore, it is important to understand whether realistic (or iconic) representations of game objects as part of controllers have a greater impact on player experience or if they are just eye candy for players.

Past research has made a distinction between symbolic and iconic controllers of tabletop games. Researchers have explored how iconic and symbolic [2,3] game tokens affect the enjoyment of a game and how these tokens maximize or deter the learning process of game rules for a digital tabletop board game [1]. In this particular study, two sets of custom game tokens were created: iconic and symbolic play pieces. However, these researchers did not explore or design controllers as icons or symbols of in-video-game objects. Therefore, we designed our own sets of iconic and semi-iconic controllers for a game called Balloon Fight (Nintendo). We define semi-iconic game controllers as input devices that share a common feature with an in-game object (e.g., shape) without being a complete (or iconic) representation of them.

CHI PLAY '14, Oct 19-22 2014, Toronto, ON, Canada
ACM 978-1-4503-3014-5/14/10.
http://dx.doi.org/10.1145/2658537.2661327

To develop semi-iconic and iconic controllers for Balloon Fight, we used the *MakeyMakey* controller prototyping hardware (available at http://www.makeymakey.com) to create representative game interactions using three balloons to represent iconic game objects and three balls to represent semi-iconic game objects, representing a game element controllable by the player. Thus, our definition of game controller iconism is *the overlap and sharing of representational (i.e., aesthetical) properties between an object used as input and a game element controlled by the player.* This definition is grounded in the works of Familiant and Detweiler [2] as well as Gregersen and Grodal [4]. In contrast, we understand symbolism as a lack of overlap or sharing of aesthetical properties.

We contribute new knowledge to the design of game controllers by documenting our process of implementing the design of novel game controllers that represent specific game objects. This contribution is relevant for product designers and game designers when creating game controllers.

ICONIC, SEMI-ICONIC AND SYMBOLIC CONTROLLERS
We developed game controllers that had different levels of metaphorical representations of game elements (i.e., more iconic than a standard symbolic game controller). To study these controllers, we chose to develop controllers for a game with modest interactions to make it easier to simplify the controllers, thus reducing possible usability issues. We used a Nintendo Entertainment System (NES) game because the control scheme uses only two action buttons and directional input, which was easy to map to different tested controllers. The player controls a character that has balloons tied to its back. The character flies around in consecutive platform levels by flapping its arms and changing directions. A level is completed once the player pops the balloons on the back of the opponents and lands on them while they are either falling or on the ground. The game ends when both of the player's balloons have been popped three times.

Controller Design
We compared three controllers: (1) a Microsoft Xbox 360 gamepad, representing a standard controller. This is a highly symbolic controller and the most traditional form of input; a type of input that the game was originally developed for.

(2) A 3-balloon controller, representing an iconic game controller (see Figure 1) because it maps visual game objects on the actual game controller. The balloons on the controller represent the balloons in the game.

Figure 1. The 3-Balloon Controller.

(3) A 3-ball controller, representing a semi-iconic game controller (see Figure 2). We consider it a semi-iconic aesthetical representation of a game controller for this game, because it is similar to the 3-balloon controller in its control scheme. However, it does not represent any game object in particular, but maintains iconic properties (i.e., the round shape).

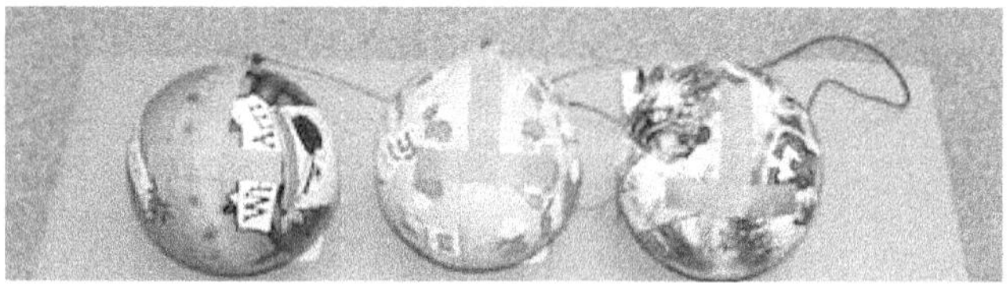

Figure 2. The 3-Ball Controller.

The two last controllers were developed using a fast controller prototyping device called *MakeyMakey*. We deliberately chose to use balloons and a similar round object because they are tied to the character's avatar, and thus were controllable elements in the original game interaction.

The *MakeyMakey* is an electronic hardware device that – when plugged in via Universal Serial Bus (USB) – can be connected to any object that conducts electricity to simulate keyboard inputs. By using cables linked to the *MakeyMakey* and conductive objects, it is possible to map those objects to specific key presses and play a game with such arbitrary objects as a *controller*. Furthermore, pieces of electrically conductive adhesive tape can be attached to crocodile cables to make surfaces responsive to touch, acting as input devices.

Three red balloons, resembling the ones that the player character has attached to their back in the game, were connected to the *MakeyMakey,* so that touching these balloons would map to game input (similar to a button press). The balloons were laid out in a line along a long piece of cardboard, where the middle balloon controlled the *flapping* action, while the left and right two balloons represented the directional controls. This constitutes the iconic controller version, because the controller represents a game object (i.e., red balloons). The second controller that we created is similar to the three balloons and represents the semi-iconic representation, consisting of a controller with three beach balls. It is a semi-iconic controller because – instead of using red balloons – we broke the direct reference to game objects by replacing them with balls of different colours that are only similar to the game objects in their shape.

PILOT STUDY RESULTS

After a pilot study, the two controllers that we designed were often criticized because of the lack of action affordances. Players often struggled and became frustrated when controlling the game with our new controllers. Shifting from the traditional gamepad input mapping to the new mapping caused some interaction problems, because players had to move their arms and change around hands often to efficiently control the character using a control scheme not immediately perceptible or intuitive to them. To address this issue, we changed order of actions mapped to the input objects (more precisely, the flap input action) to meet the recommendations of the pilot study participants. Instead of the pilot study configuration, where the middle object makes the character flap and the others makes the character change directions, the flap action balloon and ball were changed to be on the right-hand side of the controllers, as suggested by the players. This change reproduced an experience similar to the gamepad input. After changing the control scheme, and looking at the actions involved with all the controllers, each hand is related to one action alone: the left hand changes direction, the right hand elicits the character action (i.e., arm flapping).

LIMITATIONS AND FUTURE WORK

This pilot study is limited in the controller designs, since we developed a semi-iconic and iconic controller to the best of our knowledge for one particular game: Balloon Fight, but could not find proper representations for all in-game actions. Future work should focus on evaluating gameplay experience with these different controller types to understand the impact of different game controllers. It is important to investigate whether semi-iconic or iconic controllers are more engaging than standard controllers. This is an important design consideration, because if it is possible to design semi-iconic game controllers that are equally engaging for players, this could mean less production cost than iconic controllers.

ACKNOWLEDGMENTS

We thank all the participants involved in this study. We would also like to thank everyone, who provided helpful comments on previous versions of this manuscript. We are grateful to our support from NSERC, GRAND NCE and SSHRC (IMMERSe, 895-2011-1014).

REFERENCES

1. Bakker, S. and Vorstenbosch, D. Tangible interaction in tabletop games: studying iconic and symbolic play pieces. *Proc. of ACE'07*, ACM (2007), 163–170.
2. Familiant, M.E. and Detweiler, M.C. Iconic reference: Evolving perspectives and an organizing framework. *Int J Man Mach Stud 39*, 5 (1993), 705–728.
3. Ullmer, B. and Ishii, H. Emerging frameworks for tangible user interfaces. *IBM Systems Journal 39*, 3.4 (2000), 915–931.
4. Gregersen, A. and Grodal, T. Embodiment and Interface. In B. Perron and M.J.P. Wolf, eds., The Video Game Theory Reader 2. New York, NY, USA, 2009, 65–83.

ADAGE: An Open API for Data Collection in Educational Games

Mark Stenerson, Allison Salmon, Matthew Berland, Kurt Squire
Games + Learning + Society, University of Wisconsin - Madison
stenerson@wisc.edu, allisonmariesalmon@gmail.com, mberland@wisc.edu, kurt.squire@gmail.com

ABSTRACT

In an attempt to provide academic game development studios with an efficient and low-cost data collection system that can be used across multiple games, the *Assessment Data Aggregator for Gaming Environments* (ADAGE) framework is currently being designed and developed by the *University of Wisconsin* and the *Learning Games Network*, in tandem with the *Play Data Consortium* [1, 8]. The developers of ADAGE hope that the open-source nature of the project will encourage collaboration across the multiple academic institutions currently developing and investigating the use of video games as educational tools.

Author Keywords

Gameplay Visualization; Playtesting; Data Logging; Educational Games; Player Behavior

ACM Classification Keywords

H.5.m. Information Interfaces and Presentation (e.g. HCI): Miscellaneous; H.5.2 User Interfaces: Evaluation/methodology; K.3.1 Computer Uses in Education: Computer-assisted instruction (CAI); H.8.0 Personal Computing: Games

INTRODUCTION

As with all educational interventions, showing that a video game is an effective learning tool can be a complicated task [2, 5, 10]. Although many might suggest that a pre/post-test analysis would be a sufficient form of measurement, it is important to note that games are complex environments containing a wealth of measurable information that can be applied to learning. In-game player activities such as social interactions with other players, world or level exploration patterns, and player usage of in-game tools have the potential to provide a deeper insight into player experience and knowledge. Although commercial tools [3, 7] exist to assist the complex assessment of games, many of these tools have fundamental drawbacks that make them less desirable in an academic setting. For instance, while they claim to provide secure and unlimited data storage, most commercial applications that track in-game player data also require that the data be stored on third-party servers. From an academic standpoint, the ethical and security implications of using third party, offsite data storage cannot be ignored.

CHI PLAY'14, October 19–21, 2014, Toronto, ON, Canada.
ACM 978-1-4503-3014-5/14/10.
http://dx.doi.org/10.1145/2658537.2661325

In order to provide educational game development studios with an efficient, low-cost data collection system that can be used across multiple games, the *Assessment Data Aggregator for Gaming Environments* (ADAGE) framework is currently being designed by the *Games+Learning+Society* group at the *University of Wisconsin* in conjunction with the *Play Data Consortium* while an ADAGE implementation is being developed in tandem by the *Learning Games Network* [1, 8].

ADAGE Implementation

As Schell notes, a user experience cannot be observed without disturbing the nature of that experience [9]. Therefore, a primary design requirement for ADAGE was to ensure that the system collected information from play sessions without disrupting the user experience of the game. While this can be achieved, it requires that game researchers and developers communicate with one another to determine what aspects of the user experience need to be recorded for analysis. This may appear contrary to the work done by Harpstead [6] – where every piece of data from a game, no matter how insignificant, would be recorded – but the designers of ADAGE privilege consistency of communication over low information data (such as momentary mouse position). This ensures that game researchers and game developers receive cleaner datasets and minimizes any effect on game performance while background data is compressed and recorded.

To achieve this, ADAGE provides developers with base ADAGE event objects, then accepts and logs custom data objects that inherit from those base events. This allows developers to customize the data that is stored while remaining conformant. For example, a game developer logging an event where a player initiated a conversation with a non-player character (NPC) could create a subclassed event object that logs pertinent information regarding an NPC conversation (location, NPC ID, etc). Since this object inherits from the ADAGEData object, the system automatically records basic information (e.g., version, timestamp) and stores the entire event on the ADAGE server.

Researcher Portal

The researcher portal for ADAGE contains a suite of tools for collecting, querying, and analyzing data from ADAGE enabled games. Researcher accounts have the ability to quickly and easily create large cohorts of player accounts for use in

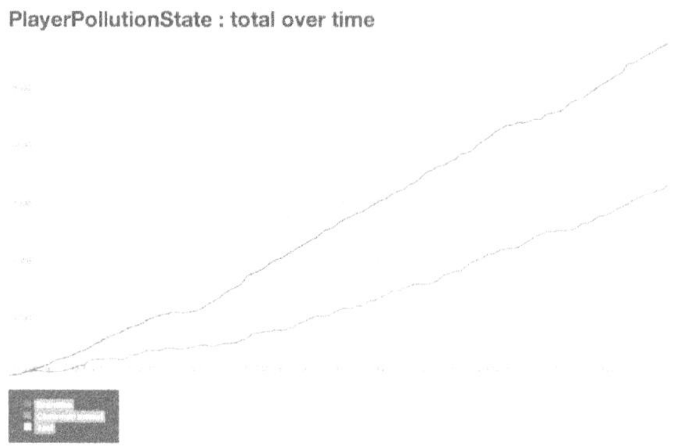

Figure 1. With easy-to-use online tools, ADAGE can make plotting data fast and easy.

formal education, informal settings, and for free play. As more than a dozen ADAGE-enabled games are already being used in classrooms, researchers can compare learning goals and player data across games. The data-querying interface of the portal allows researchers access to player data in various formats. Researchers are able to construct queries to filter and aggregate log entries to not only download raw data but also to create reports and graphs (Figure 1).

Custom Visualizations

ADAGE also provides endpoints for developers to query data into custom data visualizations. For example, player activity was logged and displayed next to pollution creation for the real-time strategy game Econauts for iPad [4] (Figure 2). These maps are currently being used in student playtests to determine if access to real-time information about the game world will impact a player's decision-making processes. Preliminary work is currently being conducted on how these real-time visualization affect player thought processes and decision making while playing a game (Figure 3).

ACKNOWLEDGMENTS

We thank the National Science Foundation for their continued

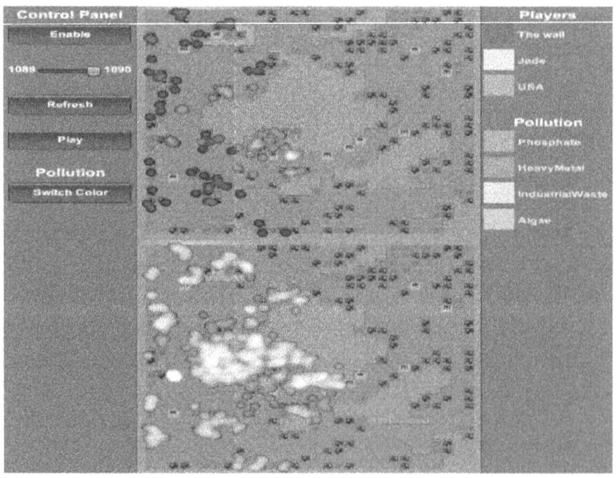

Figure 2. An example of the ADAGE data being used to generate a heat map of player activity in the game Econauts [4]

Figure 3. Students play Econauts while data visualizations provide real-time feedback

support in funding ADAGE (DRL-1119383) as well as Econauts, although the views expressed herein are those of the authors and do not necessarily represent the funding agency. We also thank all the developers, artists, and researchers on both ADAGE and the Econauts projects.

REFERENCES

1. Berland, M. Play Data Consortium. `http://playdataconsortium.org/`, 2014. Accessed: 2014-08-27.
2. Bransford, J. D., and Schwartz, D. L. Rethinking transfer: A simple proposal with multiple implications. *Review of research in education 24* (1999), 61–100.
3. GameAnalytics. `http://www.gameanalytics.com/`. Accessed: 2014-08-19.
4. Games Learning Society. Econauts. `http://www.gameslearningsociety.org/econauts_microsite/`. Accessed: 2014-06-15.
5. Gee, J. P. Game-like learning: An example of situated learning and implications for opportunity to learn. *Assessment, equity, and opportunity to learn* (2008), 200–221.
6. Harpstead, E., Myers, B. A., and Aleven, V. In search of learning: facilitating data analysis in educational games. In *Proceedings of the SIGCHI Conference on Human Factors in Computing Systems*, CHI '13, ACM (New York, NY, USA, 2013), 79–88.
7. HoneyTracks. `https://honeytracks.com/`. Accessed: 2014-08-19.
8. Owen, V., and Halverson, R. Adage (assessment data aggregator for game environments): A click-steam data framework for assessment of learning in play. In *Proceedings of the 9th Annual Games+Learning+Society Conference*, ETC Press (Pittsburgh, PA, USA, 2013).
9. Schell, J. *The Art of Game Design: A book of lenses*. Taylor & Francis US, 2008.
10. Steinkuehler, C. A. Why game (culture) studies now? *Games and Culture 1*, 1 (2006), 97–102.

Playing with Emotions: Sentiment Design for Public Space

Emily Sun, Mark Matthews, Geri Gay,
Cornell University Information Science
219 Gates Hall, Ithaca, NY
{es765, mark.matthews,
gkg1}@cornell.edu

Margaret Morris, Douglas Carmean
Intel Corporation
Hillsboro, OR
{margaret.morris,
doug.m.carmean}@intel.com

ABSTRACT
This design research explored ways to support emotional expression in interactive games played in a public, social setting. Affective gaming has incorporated emotional assessment to tailor feedback during gameplay, but as a result, distills complex emotional states into simple inputs. Our research focused not on measuring affect but on designing games to evoke emotional expression and sharing of personal experiences. This work centered on games in public spaces as a particularly rich area to explore how people's emotions might influence each other. We present the design and initial play-testing results of four games that draw on a player's idiosyncratic experience and feelings as part of the game. These designs were based on internal paper prototyping sessions, naturalistic observation of the testing space and design and enactment sessions with researchers as participants and designers. Our design sessions indicate that image-based games are a rich element for these types of games, and the importance of ambiguity and disagreement amongst players to promote sharing of personal stories. Other design principles that emerged include affordances for short interactions, individual or multiple players, and forms of "cheating" as game play.

Author Keywords
affective gaming, public space

ACM Classification Keywords
D.2.2. Design Tools and Techniques; H.5.2. User Interfaces

INTRODUCTION
Affective gaming is the application of affective computing, "computing that relates to, arises from, or influences emotions," [3] to games. Researchers have explored providing responsive game feedback based on physiological inputs where computer characters and the environment can respond to players' emotions. These techniques allow for dynamic games, but also require the simplification of complex emotional states through the synthesis of emotion data [2]. As opposed to acquiring users' emotional states, Sengers argues that affective computing should provide opportunities for users to experience, interpret, and reflect on their emotions. This approach acknowledges "the human emotional experience is to some degree fundamentally unknowable" [4, p. 348]. We argue for a similar approach to affective gaming; since games naturally elicit emotional reactions, the goal was to allow players to embrace this complexity of emotional expression rather than simplify it.

Instead of *measuring* affect, our intent was to illuminate how to *design* for affective expression in game design. The focus was on the design of sentiment games in public spaces as a particularly rich area to exploration. While there is evidence that players react emotionally to games in public spaces [1], little work has considered how to evoke emotional expression in public space games. As opposed to games played in isolation, the inherent sociality in public spaces presents an opportunity for emotional communication among players/strangers.

CHI PLAY '14, Oct 19-22, 2014, Toronto, ON, Canada
ACM 978-1-4503-3014-5/14/10.
http://dx.doi.org/10.1145/2658537.2661317

DESIGN
To ground our design, we began with ethnographic observations of individual behavior in two public café spaces. These observations provided requirements for the games that were designed following an iterative process that included multiple sessions of paper prototyping within the research team. Once a game had been brainstormed and tested internally, the prototype was brought to a group of four or five students and researchers and observed in an informal setting. From this, we developed four game concepts. We further refined our idea based on an enactment session where we adopted roles of strangers and acted out potential scenarios.

Escalating Emotions
This is a publicly projected game in the genre of tile-matching games like Bejeweled and Candy Crush. Players are each presented with a different emotion word and try to gain points for their word before their opponent does. Players gain points by correctly matching images that have been pre-labeled with the same sentiment. Images could be pulled from Instagram and Twitter with a certain emotion hashtag. Once one player reaches a certain number of points from matches, new sentiments and images appear. Players win once they fill up their emotion meter.

Make a Face

Two players are seated on either side of a partition with a screen and camera on both sides. For each round of this game, players have 10 seconds to make as many facial expressions that represent their reaction to a picture. If players make the same facial expression then they advance to the next image. The game ends once players fail to match facial expressions for an image within the allotted time.

Clairsentience

Players compete to see who can correctly identify an image by using as few sentiment tags as possible. In the first part of the game, players view images and add multiple emotion tags to them. These get added to a list of other tags from previous players, and the aggregated data is used in the second part of the game. For the second part, a grid of 16 images is presented on a large touchscreen with one emotion tag associated with one of the 16 images revealed initially. An additional emotion tag for the same image is revealed every 10 seconds, giving more hints as to the correct image. Players receive more points for correctly guessing the image that has been tagged with fewer hints.

Mood Match

People try to match images displayed on a wall with emotion tags. One person picks a photo that was projected on a wall that best fit a given sentiment (e.g. happy) and then another person is given the picture and has to pick an adjective from a list to see if they match. Points are awarded for correct matches. The design of this game was modified during the design process where people in two different locations could try to match the same sentiment to a given image. We believed this design would minimize hesitancy to interact with a system someone else was using while still creating the opportunity for a shared experience.

DISCUSSION

Through our paper prototyping sessions, it was revealed that failure in the game, which normally is a singularly negative experience, actually was an interesting part of the social interaction. Instead of being a point of frustration, disagreements in emotion called for an explanation, invariably leading to disclosure of a personal story. In one session of *Clairsentience*, one player rated a picture of a stuffed dinosaur with a negative emotion whereas the other rated it with a positive emotion, eliciting humor between participants. In another session, there was some consensus amongst players who tagged a picture of donuts with words like "Happy," but there were also tags like "Hate" that stimulated discussion around individual preferences.

When designing for public spaces, we realized the importance of allowing for the game to be played in a short amount of time. As these are places when people may not intend on lingering, the games were designed to encourage people to play through brief interactions. Similarly, because of this short duration of attention, it was important that the visual display was inviting of interactivity and that the game was intuitive to navigate without needing instructions.

Since the design was for public spaces, we wanted to allow for a single-player mode in all of our designs. In *Make A Face*, for example, single-player mode could compare people's facial expressions with those people who had played before, creating an asynchronous social interaction. Given that many of the people coming to the cafe only stayed in the space for the time that it took them to get their drink, it was a conscious design decision to support short interactions that could also be lengthened if people had more time.

Because we were designing games, we wanted to allow for playful uses of the system, including cheating. For example, using live images in *Escalating Emotions* would potentially elicit cheating behavior where people may intentionally tag images with inappropriate hashtags for their benefit in the game. Instead of designing to make this behavior impossible, we decided to allow it to occur since it could be a point of emotional discussion.

CONCLUSION AND FUTURE WORK

In this paper, we proposed a novel method for affective gaming that integrates emotion into game design to allow for a more nuanced interpretation of emotional expressions. We drew on players' experiences and sentiments to create games that used ambiguity and disagreement to create connections between players through sharing of stories for their choices. Initial play-testing observations provided support for the expectation that ambiguous, controversial images would evoke emotional communication. The games should also be fast interactions, able to be played single- or multi-player, and allow for cheating behavior. Future work will analyze the results of ongoing installations and explore whether players' affective labels could be used to annotate existing image databases.

REFERENCES

1. Finke, M., Tang, A., Leung, R., & Blackstock, M. (2008, September). Lessons learned: game design for large public displays. In *Proceedings of the 3rd international conference on Digital Interactive Media in Entertainment and Arts* (pp. 26-33). ACM.
2. Hudlicka, E. (2008). Affective computing for game design. In *Proceedings of the 4th Intl. North American Conference on Intelligent Games and Simulation (GAMEON-NA), Montreal, Canada.*
3. Picard, R. W. (2000). *Affective computing*. MIT press.
4. Sengers, P., Boehner, K., Mateas, M., & Gay, G. (2008). The disenchantment of affect. *Personal and Ubiquitous Computing*, *12*(5), 347-358.

Predicting the Metascore with a Subjective User Experience Data

Jari M.E. Takatalo
University of Helsinki
P.O. Box 9, 00014 Helsinki, FI
jari.takatalo@helsinki.fi

Jukka P. Häkkinen
University of Helsinki
P.O. Box 9, 00014 Helsinki, FI
jukka.hakkinen@helsinki.fi

ABSTRACT
The aim of this study is to test how well a subjective user experience (UX) data predicts the Metascore of a digital game. The Metascore calculated by the Metacritic.com is one of the most important indicators of a game's commercial success. Thus, game companies are interested in finding reliable in-house tools to estimate the Metascore before releasing their product. We utilized subjective survey data to test a preliminary regression model for Metascore. The model explained over 50% of the variance between the Metascores. Practically, this means that we can predict a correct Metascore class (e.g., universal acclaim) with 75% accuracy. These promising results provide good grounds for future research on the topic.

Author Keywords
User experience; game-user research; metascore

ACM Classification Keywords
K.8.0 Personal Computing: General: Games; I.6.8 Gaming

INTRODUCTION
Game developers and publishers aim to sell as many games as possible. Optimizing user experience (UX) in a game and immersing the gamers to play the game is one obvious way to reach desirable sales figures. When a game is published, specialized gaming journals evaluate it. The evaluations are collected by Metacritic (www.metacritic.com), which combines them into a single Metascore, which strongly affects gamers' decisions to buy the game [2]. In the current market situation where gamers have hundreds of options to choose from, a trustworthy single number provides a secure guideline to follow. Predicting the Metascore and optimizing the game accordingly would give game developers a clear advantage in the crowded marketplace.

Although game companies try to figure out the forthcoming Metascore by in-house panels and expert evaluations, the challenge of the Metacritic magic hasn't been solved. The in-house nature of the pre-release product evaluation prevents utilizing the "big" behavioral data. Thus, the game developer faces a typical laboratory experiment setting, in which the research question is clearly stated but the method needs some pondering. In any case, the chosen method needs to be valid, reliable and efficient to use.

Academic researchers have studied the connection between subjective UX evaluations, and an aggregate meta-review score on gamerankings.com, which is similar to Metascore [1]. Unfortunately, they couldn't find connection between evaluations and gamerankings score. However, they provide a list of possible reasons for the failure: 1) reviewers typically finish the game before they write their reviews but the participants played the game in the lab for only 45 minutes. 2) The amount of games (two) and participants ("a handful") was not enough. 3) The poor validity of the scales used, which assessed usability and player frustration more than UX. Nevertheless, collecting gamers' evaluations after a game-play session always provides information about important UX. The value of this increases substantially, if it can also be used to predict Metascore or the like.

We used a large pool of experienced participants who evaluated multiple games based on a reliable and valid questionnaire designed to measure UX in games. Based on this data we were able to find clear connections between one game-play session and the Metascore.

METHODS

Participants, Data Collection and Games
A total of 1384 participants (1295 males, 89 females) filled-in our online survey, which consisted of 139 questions. The survey was administered to an individual gamer after a playing session that took place at gamer's home. The gamers were encouraged to reflect on their subjective experiences of the game they just played. The data was then factored into fifteen multivariate subcomponents (factor-scores) forming the Presence-Involvement-Flow framework (PIFF) (Table 1), as suggested by Takatalo et al. [4-6].

The participants played 60 different PC or console games, which belonged to the following game genres: first-person shooters(23), strategy(3), role-playing(13), driving(3), 3rd person action(13), MMORPG(3), and simulators(2). The Metascores of the studied games were based on 2385 game reviews and ranged between 59-96. These Metascores cover three highest Metasore classes (universal acclaim, generally favorable reviews, and mixed or average reviews).

CHI PLAY'14, October 19–21, 2014, Toronto, ON, Canada.
ACM 978-1-4503-3014-5/14/10.
http://dx.doi.org/10.1145/2658537.2661299

Name and number of items	ρ	Description
PRESENCE		
Role Engagement (12)	.80	Enclosed by the role and place provided by the story
Attention (12)	.88	Time distortion and focusing on the game world
Co-Presence (14)	.89	Feeling of sharing a place with others
Arousal (5)	.70	Level of emotional arousal
Physical Presence (17)	.82	Feeling of being in a real and vivid place
INVOLVEMENT		
Interest (6)	.72	Value-related valences towards the game
Importance (8)	.89	The meaning and relevancy of the game
FLOW-COGNITION		
Competence (11)	.86	Skilled with positive feelings of effectiveness
Challenge (5)	.76	Game was challenging and required my abilities
Interaction (9)	.72	Speed, range, and mapping of the interaction
FLOW-EMOTION		
Valence (10)	.77	Positive valence, happy, not bored or anxious
Impressiveness (9)	.79	Amazed and astonished by the game
Enjoyment (7)	.77	Playing was pleasant and somewhat special
Playfulness (9)	.78	Feelings of flow and ease of doing
Control (5)	.74	Feeling of being in control and independent

Table 1. Name, number of questions, Tarkkonen's rho reliability coefficient (values >.70 are acceptable), and short description from each subcomponent of the PIFF.

RESULTS

We utilized linear regression to predict Metascore with the individual PIFF subcomponents. In regression analysis, the preferred ratio between predictor variables and observations is 1/20. With 60 games we could have utilized 3 predictors. Considering the explorative nature of our work, we took the liberty to test up to 5 predictors in one analysis. Thus, we run individual analyses with presence (5), involvement (2), cognitive flow (3) and emotional flow (5) subcomponents. Based on these analyses, we chose five subcomponents for the final model (Figure 1.). Taken together, *importance, interest, valence, arousal,* and *challenge* explained a significant proportion of variance in Metascores, $R^2 = .57$, $F(5, 54) = 14.41$, $p < .001$. The Variance Inflation Factor measures were less than 1.8, which indicates the absence of multicollinearity.

Furthermore, we used a nominal regression to investigate how well the model predicts different Metascore classes. The overall classification accuracy was 75%. The individual Metascore classes varied in the following way: universal acclaim 64,0%, generally favorable reviews 80,3%, and mixed or average reviews 80%.

CONCLUSION AND FUTURE WORK

The aim of this study was to test how well subjective UX data collected after one game-play session predicts the Metascore of a game. The preliminary results are promising: five UX subcomponents, composed of 34 questions enabled us to predict game's Metascore relatively well. When we predicted the Metascore class, the practical value of the model became even clearer. The potential of the methodology is increased by the fact that the data is a random sample of one game-play session. Encouraged by the current findings, we will continue our work.

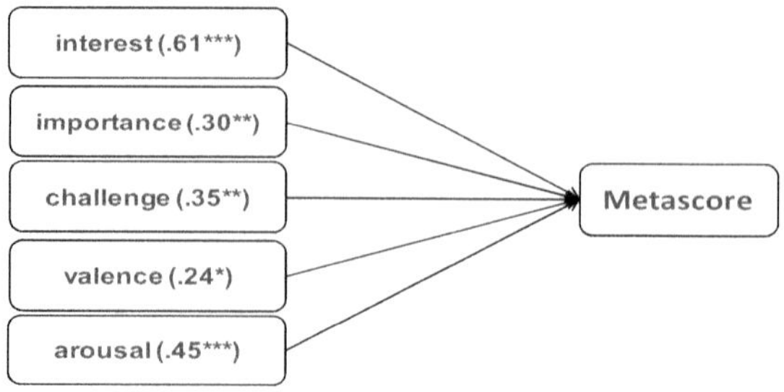

Figure 1. The five significant predictors and their standardized beta coefficients (*** = p < .001; ** = p < .01; * = p < .05).

Our future studies will start with refining the current model with sophisticated statistical and machine learning methods (e.g., support vector regression). The current data enables us to refine the model by analyzing genre-level differences, for example. These additional analyses will provide a better predictive model, which will be then tested with a new data set that will be collected. The new data will include balanced gender (here 95% of males), multiple platforms, and details about the game session. We will also assess participants' prior knowledge about the game's reviews, which may affect the UX [3]. The aim of this research will be to pinpoint the right time to get the player's descriptions and to develop the best set of questions that would yield a valid and reliable prediction of a Metascore. In this research we will look for collaboration with game distributors and developers who are interested in finding the psychological bliss-point of a game that mesmerizes both the gamers and the reviewers.

REFERENCES

1. Chen, M., Kolko, B. E., Cuddihy, E. and Medina, E. Modeling but NOT measuring engagement in computer games. In *Proc. Games Learning Society,* ETC Press (2011), 55-63.
2. Greenwood-Ericksen, A., Poorman, S. and Papp, R. On the Validity of Metacritic in Assessing Game Value. *Eludamos Journal for Computer Game Culture 7,* 1 (2013), 101-127.
3. Livingston I., Nacke L. and Mandryk R. Influencing experience: the effects of reading game reviews on player experience. In *Proc. Entertainment Computing–ICEC 2011.* Springer, 2011, 89-100.
4. Takatalo, J., Nyman, G. and Laaksonen, L. Components of human experience in virtual environments. *Computers in Human Behavior 24,* 1 (2008), 1-15.
5. Takatalo J. *Psychologically-based and content-oriented experience in entertainment virtual environments.* PhD Thesis, Helsinki: Unigrafia, 2011.
6. Takatalo J., Häkkinen J., Kaistinen J. and Nyman G. Presence, involvement & flow in digital games. In Bernhaupt R. ed. *Evaluating user experiences in games: concepts and methods.* Springer-Verlag, London, 2010.

Design Guidelines for Audio-Based Game Features

Tiffany Tong
University of Toronto
5 King's College Road
Toronto, ON, M5S 3G8
tiffany.tong@mail.utoronto.ca

Daniel Zingaro
University of Toronto Mississauga
3359 Mississauga Road
Mississauga, ON, L5L 1C6
daniel.zingaro@utoronto.ca

Steve Engels
University of Toronto
40 St. George Street
Toronto, ON, M5S 2E4
sengels@cs.toronto.edu

ABSTRACT
The game design process integrates visual, audio, gameplay, and control elements into a single experience. Of these, the audio component is often treated as a secondary concern in both the design and research arenas. Our research seeks to remedy this, by focusing on audio elements of games, their impact they can have, and how audio design can be integrated in the overall design process. This poster will present the audio games we have created to test these elements, and our current research findings on how audio features can affect overall gameplay. We will also propose the configuration of these audio features for effective audio-based games.

Author Keywords
Audio Game, Auditory Interface; Game Audio; Games; Usability; User Interaction; User Experience

ACM Classification Keywords
K.8.0 [General]: Games; H.5.1 [Information Interfaces and Presentation]: Multimedia Information Systems—audio input/output; H.5.2 [Information Interfaces and Presentation]: User Interfaces—auditory (non-speech) feedback, theory and methods, user-centered design

INTRODUCTION
Game audio design and research are in their infancy and are often overshadowed by video and control components of games [3,4]. However, audio has the potential to carry a game on its own. Audio cues can communicate a variety of information, including location, enemies, objects, and interaction elements. Audio games illustrate this point by creating experiences that are based entirely on audio elements. While these games work well, the understanding of these elements has not been explored deeply. Previous research on audio games focuses on the design and evaluation of the games themselves, rather than on the evaluation of individual audio features that influence overall game play and user experience [1,2,5]. We seek to understand the importance and use of audio elements to inform our understanding of how to use audio effectively in audio and mainstream games.

CHI PLAY '14, Oct 19-22 2014, Toronto, ON, Canada
ACM 978-1-4503-3014-5/14/10.
http://dx.doi.org/10.1145/2658537.2661307

BACKGROUND INFORMATION
In order to understand the effect of various audio components on games, the first stage of our study focuses on these audio components in isolation, independent of video or control aspects. This is done through the creation of audio games on which we received feedback from blind players. Audio games are games designed primarily using an auditory interface as opposed to a graphical interface, which make them appealing to visual impaired users [2].

In our research, this first stage involved four audio-based features, which we isolated and tested using four separate games. The next stages involve testing the effects of these audio games on sighted players, and then testing the effect of these games after they have been enhanced with a video component. Our overall goal is to determine which audio elements should be featured and to what degree when designing games. The findings from this work will generate a set of design guidelines for future audio games in addition to audio interface design to complement video games.

METHODS
A series of user studies was conducted at the University of Toronto. We have divided our research study into three phases. In the first phase of the experiment, we are evaluating the audio games with a blind sample population. The purpose is to explore which games and features are most appealing to an audience that relies primarily on non-visual user interaction methods to interact with a game (e.g. haptic and audio feedback). The data collection for this phase is currently in progress. Based on these findings, the games will be re-iterated upon and re-evaluated in the second phase of the study.

In the second phase of the experiment, we are interested in evaluating the games with a larger sample including both blind and non-blind users. Finally, in the third phase, we are interested in evaluating the same games except this time designed with a graphical user interface. These games will be evaluated with both a blind and non-blind sample. The goal is to compare the user experience and performance on games designed with emphasis on both the audio and visual elements compared to the same games developed with a primary focus on the visual interface.

Participants

The first phase of our study includes six blind male participants between the ages of 18 and 40 years.

Study Design

Each user study is conducted with one participant at a time. The participant is asked to play-test each game and use a think-aloud protocol. Following the play-testing session, the user is interviewed on the usability and their experience with each game. The experimenter takes notes while observing the participant.

Games

Below are the four audio games under investigation in this research study.

1. **Sandwich Making:** The objective is to assemble a sandwich in the correct order.
2. **Text Fighter:** The objective is to defeat an opponent using a series of fighting moves.
3. **Stealth Exploration:** The objective is to navigate to a goal point without being detected by enemies.
4. **Text-Based Adventure:** The objective is to follow a series of text clues from one location to another.

Game Features

The game features we are interested in evaluating are described below.

- **Feedback:** The amount and frequency of the audio feedback provided during game play.
- **Volume:** The contrast in volume between loud and soft audio elements, and the effect on game performance.
- **Information speed:** The influence of information speed on the user.
- **Game speed:** This feature evaluates the influence of game speed on user experience.

RESULTS

The results discussed will focus on the findings from the first phase of our study. Our results highlight design principles that apply to audio games with emphasis on the interface devices, the expectations for the audio interface and the gameplay interaction, as well as game and level design in general. Each principle will be discussed below.

Extent of sound cues

There is a tradeoff between insufficient sound cues (making the game very difficult to play) and overusing sound cues (harming realism and widening the gap between accessible games and mainstream games). We also observed that creating sounds for objects such as tables or walls was an unnatural abstraction for our participants, and led to confusion when interpreting game sounds. Based on these findings, we recommend that games for blind users be designed with different sound cues for elements such as player location and objects that are pertinent to gameplay and assist in describing the environment to the user.

Communicating instructions

We observed that users are unwilling to sit through a tutorial session, as they are familiar with friends who learn to play a game by playing the game itself. One technique is to provide considerable information at a slow speed as the user begins, then fade the feedback once the basic controls and gameplay are understood. Another method is to allow the user to adjust the information speed, which parallels the ability to adjust screen readers. In addition, during beginning levels, we found that allowing more time for users to respond during gameplay was desirable. As with feedback, once the user is acquainted with the game, we suggest increasing the game speed.

Spatial awareness

Our participants expressed frustration in not knowing their current position. More feedback and area-specific sound cues help, as do configurations that encourage players to the navigational process. In one case, round rooms prevent players from getting stuck in particular areas. Instead, a player who "runs into a wall" simply traverses the perimeter of the room using volume-specific feedback until they reach an opening and a new set of sound cues.

CONCLUSION

Based on our current research study, we found that designing audio games for both sighted and non-sighted users relies on different design principles than those in mainstream games. These principles can be incorporated into the design of future audio games, and have wider implications in general game design as well. In continuation of this work, we will be conducting further user studies with both blind and non-blind users with our revised games.

REFERENCES

1. Atkinson, M.T., Gucukoglu, S., Machin, C.H.C., and Lawrence, A.E. Making the mainstream accessible. *Proceedings of the 2006 ACM SIGGRAPH symposium on Videogames*, ACM Press (2006), 21–28.
2. Eriksson, Y. and Gardenfors, D. Computer games for children with visual impairments. *International Journal on Disability and Human Development*, (2005).
3. Grimshaw, M. Game Sound Technology and Player Interaction. In M. Grimshaw, ed., *Game Sound Technology and Player Interaction: Concepts and Developments*. IGI Global, 2010, 362–383.
4. Peres, S.C., Best, V., Brock, D., et al. Auditory interfaces. In P. Kortum, ed., *HCI Beyond the GUI: Design for Haptic, Speech, Olfactory, and Other Nontraditional Interfaces*. Morgan Kaufman, Burlington, 2008, 147–195.
5. Targett, S. and Fernström, M. Audio games: Fun for all? All for fun. *ICAD*, (2003).

A Theory of Game Mechanic Signaling for Interface Design

Zachary O. Toups[1], **Igor Dolgov**[2], **Elizabeth M. Bonsignore**[3]
[1]Dept. of Computer Science / [2]Dept. of Psychology, New Mexico State University
[3]HCI Lab, University of Maryland, College Park
[1]ztoups@nmsu.edu, [2]id@nmsu.edu, [3]ebonsign@umd.edu

ABSTRACT

We introduce a theory of how game mechanics are signaled through interfaces. Game mechanics may be signaled through player-perceived affordances, player-interpreted signifiers, avatar-perceived affordances, avatar-interpreted signifiers, arbitrary signifiers, or metagame signifiers, and may be obscured with hidden affordances and false signifiers. Each has implications for immersion, narrative coherence, and player frustration. Designers can use game mechanic signaling to understand how a player will perceive action opportunities in play, suggesting alternate designs to support or inhibit discovery and game mechanic engagement.

ACM Classification Keywords

H.5.2. Information Interfaces & Presentation: GUIs

Author Keywords

Game interface design; affordance; signifier.

INTRODUCTION

The game designer must communicate how to engage game mechanics—points of player decision-making [11]—without breaking immersion or reducing optimal challenge [2, 11]; this contrasts with traditional user interface design, in which the goal is *not* to challenge the user [8]. Avatar bodies may be wildly incongruent with the player's, yet, the avatar becomes an incorporated extension of the player in the game world [1].

In the physical world, an *affordance* is an objectively real relational mapping between an element of the environment and an actor's ability to interact with that element [5, 9]. *Perceivable affordances* and *signifiers* of imperceptible affordances signal how to interact with physical, and, through mental models, virtual interfaces [9]. As mastery with affordances and signifiers develops, users *cognitively grip* [6] them, invoking them without thought.

Our central question is, "how can designers render game mechanic affordances perceptible, and what are the implications of the various techniques?" A designer might wish to make certain elements of play easy [7], and use clear affordances to enable smooth play; in other cases, the designer may obfuscate the way forward with hidden affordances that align with the game's narrative. The present theory, developed from a design research approach [4], explains how players understand the activities afforded by play environments and avatars, helping designers avoid pitfalls and enabling them to design for specific experiences.

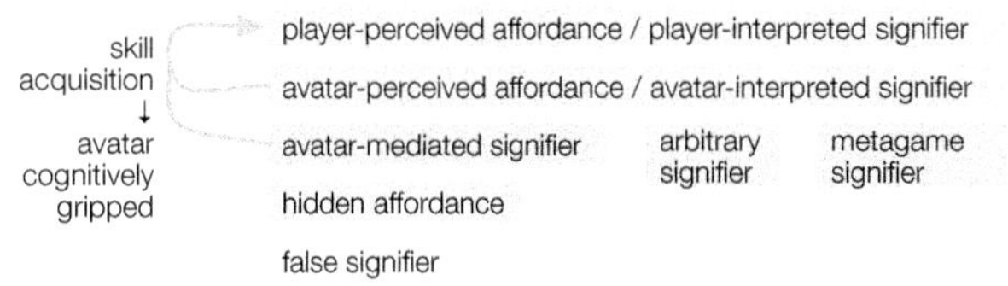

Figure 1. Theory of game mechanic signaling. As an avatar becomes cognitively gripped, game mechanic signals are interpretable by the player.

A THEORY OF GAME MECHANIC SIGNALING

Game designers must attune themselves to the ways in which players perceive an object's function in a game world. At the same time, a tension may exist in that, to immerse players, game worlds and narratives must be consistent and believable. A problem with structuring in-game objects to make affordances obvious is that, even if they are visible, they may not be *understandable* to the player [3, 9]. Such affordances might be designed for the avatar, consistent with the avatar's world and not designed for the player. Actions made visible may thus be un-knowable. At the same time, signifiers may function easily where affordances do not.

Player-Perceived Affordance (PPA) / Player-Interpreted Signifier (PIS). To make use of *player-perceived affordances / player-interpreted signifiers* the player's body image suffices to understand the game mechanics. While the avatar may be differently abled from the player, the avatar acts in a way consistent with the player's model of the function of her/his body and knowledge of the functioning of the physical world. In such a design, the player's life experience suffices to make the affordances and signifiers understandable.

Avatar-Perceived Affordance (APA) / Avatar-Interpreted Signifier (AIS). In an *avatar-perceived affordance / avatar-interpreted signifier*, the player's body image or knowledge differs from that of the avatar. The player needs an additional step to understand how to invoke game mechanics, provided through narrative, instruction, tutorial, etc. A learned APA / AIS may become a PPA / PIS as the player develops mastery and incorporates a new set of affordances into her/his repertoire through cognitive gripping [6]. Narrative conceits about the way in which the UI presents avatar knowledge to

CHI PLAY '14, Oct 19–22 2014, Toronto, ON, Canada
ACM 978-1-4503-3014-5/14/10.
http://dx.doi.org/10.1145/2658537.2661318

game	mechanic	type
Assassin's Creed series	avatar automatically interacts with any object that he can	PPA
Burnout Paradise	cars can super jump over ramps with flashing blue barricades across them	ArS
Halo series	label indicates potential interaction	MGS
Mario series	jumping clears obstacles	PPA
Metroid Prime series	HUD overlays perspective → draws icons over interactive objects	AIS
Mirror's Edge	interact-able objects are red → avatar "knows" how to act on them (player may not)	AMS
Prince of Persia [2008]	claw marks indicate to use claw thematically, but make no sense narratively	ArS
Thief [2014]	objects sparkle → avatar "knows" what objects are worth stealing (player may not)	AMS
Vanquish	QTEs to complete parts of the game by responding to visual prompts	MGS
Zelda series	cracked walls can normally be destroyed / some cannot / some that can are not cracked	AIS/FS/HA

Table 1. Game mechanic signals types in various games and game series. These games, among others, are sources of data for the theory.

the player may support the transition. How well signifiers are tied into the narrative has implications for player immersion.

Avatar-Mediated Signifier (AMS). In some cases, the designer must provide additional indicators to an APA or AIS in the environment to trigger the player to understand how the environment affords action using a *avatar-mediated signifier*. Unlike an APA/AIS, an AMS is *not* "understood" by the avatar, but by the player tapping into the knowledge of the avatar. An AMS provides a player-readable UI element that interprets an APA/AIS. As a designer, it may be necessary to provide additional UI support to make clear the signifiers.

Arbitrary Signifier (ArS). An *arbitrary signifier* is neither tied to the player's body nor the avatar's body, but is incorporated into the world. Arbitrary signifiers must be memorized. Arbitrary signifiers rely on an acquisition process characterized by the player becoming familiar with an avatar's capabilities. As a player becomes adequately familiarized with the game interface, the avatar becomes an extension of the player's body, something that is used in-order-to, and can directly interpret arbitrary signifiers.

Metagame Signifier (MGS). *Metagame signifiers* are UI constructs that do not tie into the knowledge of the player or the avatar. They replace affordances with a signifier not built on the environment, but on *metagame information*. Metagame signifiers are typically labels tell the player what to do to play. *Quick Time Events* (QTEs) are an example of metagame signifiers, game mechanics in which the player observes non-interactive game play, and must engage an appropriate action at an appropriate time, as indicated by an icon [10]. These designs potentially break immersion, but offer a way to make clear how to engage a game mechanic.

Hidden Affordance (HA). One game design choice is not to signal how to interact with the environment at all, leading to hidden affordances. Hidden affordances have a place in game design, even if they may be frustrating to players. They may not inhibit immersion; for example, a secret door may be highly internally consistent for a game world, while challenging, or even frustrating, to the player.

False Signifier (FS). Affordances, either player- or avatar-perceived, can inhibit play. Many game objects may not be interact-able, but may be interpreted as such through this lens as *false signifiers*. If non-interact-able objects appear useful to the player, player mapping can misdirect and frustrate. In this case, the player may mis-apply her/his understanding of the game and attempt an action that is not possible.

CONCLUSION

We provide a theory of game mechanic signaling for understanding and informing UI design in games from the perspective that game mechanics are intimately linked to UIs. We note that all types of affordances and signifiers have a place in game design and many good games combine them; the theory is not a value judgement. Each provides advantages and disadvantages, depending on the designer's intent. Our theory forms the basis of a new analytic framework; it functions as both a tool for evaluating game UIs and for developing them. Future work will develop the framework further, assembling concrete design implications and testing with gamers.

ACKNOWLEDGEMENTS

Thanks to Don Norman, Jessica Hammer, and Andruid Kerne for their feedback, insight, and thoughtful provocation.

REFERENCES

1. Bayliss, P. *Videogames, Interfaces, and the Body: The importance of embodied phenomena to the experience of videogame play*. PhD thesis, RMIT University, 2010.
2. Csikszentmihalyi, M. *Creativity: Flow and the Psychology of Discovery*. Harper Collins, 2009.
3. Forlizzi, J., and Battarbee, K. Understanding experience in interactive systems. In *Proc. DIS* (2004), 261–268.
4. Gaver, W. What should we expect from research through design? In *Proc. CHI* (2012), 937–946.
5. Gibson, J. J. *The Ecological Approach to Visual Perception*. Lawrence Erlbaum Assoc., 1986.
6. Kirsh, D. Embodied cognition and the magical future of interaction design. *ACM ToCHI 20*, 1 (2013), 3:1–3:30.
7. Lazzaro, N. Why we play games: Four keys to more emotion without story. Tech. rep., XEODesign, 2004.
8. Löwgren, J. Fluency as an experiential quality in augmented spaces. *Int'l J. Design 1*, 3 (2007), 1–10.
9. Norman, D. *The Design of Everyday Things: Revised and Expanded Edition*, 2013 ed. Basic Books, 2013.
10. Rogers, S. *Level Up!: The Guide to Great Video Game Design*. Wiley, 2010.
11. Salen, K., and Zimmerman, E. *Rules of Play: Game Design Fundamentals*. MIT Press, 2004.

Exercising Playfully: Co-designing Fun Ways of Keeping Active in the Park

Emmanuel Tsekleves
Imagination Lab, LICA,
Lancaster University
LICA Building, LA1 4YW, UK
e.tsekleves@lancaster.ac.uk

Andy Darby
Highwire Centre for Doctoral Training, Lancaster University,
LA1 4YW, UK
a.darby@lancaster.ac.uk

Adrian Gradinar
The Creative Exchange, LICA,
Lancaster University,
LA1 4YW
a.gradinar@lancaster.ac.uk

Marcia Smith
Highwire Centre for Doctoral Training, Lancaster University,
LA1 4YW, UK
m.smith10@lancaster.ac.uk

ABSTRACT
In this work in progress paper we present our work in the co-design of a playful interactive artifact that encourages people to engage in casual physical activity in the park. The initial testing of our proof-of-concept prototype received extremely positive feedback as a potential way of motivating people to keep active in the park and in bridging the generation gap.

Author Keywords
Playful design; Co-design; Digital-Physical interaction.

ACM Classification Keywords
H.5.2 User Interfaces: User-centered design; I.2.1 Applications and Expert Systems: Games.

INTRODUCTION
In the Active Parks project we are exploring how to engage older and sedentary park users in taking casual physical activity through playful interactions. Working together with local community groups who look after the park, the Lancaster City Council and NHS Lancashire Public Health, we have co-designed a playful 'digital health trail', which offers a new way of motivating and taking casual physical activity specific to local people in their park (using Ryelands Park in the city of Lancaster, in the UK as a use case).

RELATED WORK
Playful design has been a subject of recent research [1, 2] but has not been explored as widely in engaging older and sedentary people with physical activity. A few pieces of research work, such as that of Romero et al. [3] have explored playful experiences for older people in care home facilities by following a traditional user-centred design methodology. There is a great potential, therefore, to go beyond user-centred design and explore how more participatory design methodologies, such as co-design can create playful 'phygital' experiences that encourage sedentary and older people in taking casual physical activity [1, 2] in public urban spaces, such as in parks.

METHODOLOGY
A co-design process [4] incorporating a number of workshops and events in the park was the starting point of our research. The co-design activities were focused on initially capturing people's values, needs, vision and aspirations on the type of physical activities they enjoy doing and would like to do in the park. The key values identified were activities that are playful, help bridge the generation gap, and are available for and accessible to everyone. Looking at the affordances and constraints of creating an interactive and playful casual activity trail, our co-designers started generating very rich ideas and prototypes of potential activities.

One of the best ideas, which epitomized the co-design values expressed by workshop participants, was an interactive xylophone idea. Instead of interacting with it in the same way one would do with the traditional instrument, digital technologies were employed to make it more playful, interactive and musical.

Interaction is facilitated in two different ways. One of the interactions allows the users to use an NFC enabled mobile phone to scan hidden RFID tags (embedded into the design) and play, note by note, 'Twinkle, Twinkle Little Star', by following the numbers displayed on the phone. In order to play the tune correctly, one has to scan the correct notes as fast as possible, making into a very challenging game.

CHI PLAY'14, October 19–21, 2014, Toronto, ON, Canada.
ACM 978-1-4503-3014-5/14/10.
http://dx.doi.org/10.1145/2658537.2661316.

The second type of interaction allows the players to directly interface with the xylophone by placing and holding one hand on the large painted hand, and with the other free hand, touch any of the other smaller hands scattered around the xylophone (all hands are painted using conductive paint). Due to the use of conductive technology multiple players can play provided there is a physical connection between them.

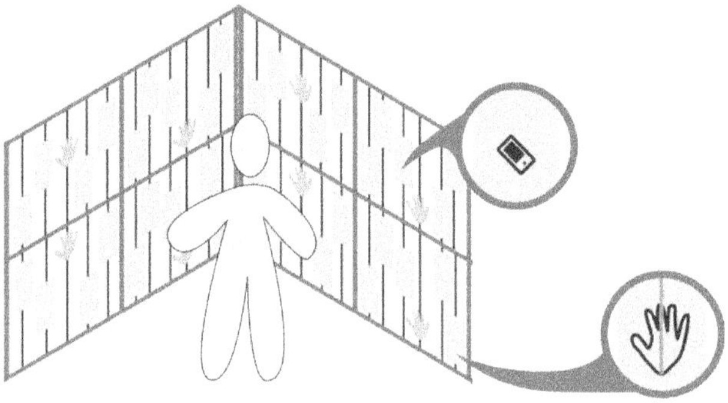

Figure 1. Sketch diagram of the interactive xylophone concept.

PRELIMINARY RESULTS AND FEEDBACK

The interactive xylophone proof-of-concept prototype was tested in the park during a community event in late June 2014, receiving over 150 visitors. Users left written feedback in our 'Graffiti walls' on what they liked the most about it and how it could be improved. Video observations and informal discussion were also made with several users.

Figure 2. Community members pilot testing the 1st prototype of the interactive xylophone in the park.

We gathered that playfulness is ageless. It was great to see people across all age groups interacting together, learning from each other and having fun. The artifact provides a focus for intergenerational bridging, which directly relates to the participants stated values.

Playful interactions aimed at public health and exercise in public spaces could offer significant benefits to park users. Developing this approach would facilitate connectedness between people and across ages.

When the exercises are incorporated within a playful environment (an interactive toy or game) we noticed people increasing their physical exertion. Such experiences can be made more enjoyable through multisensorial interactions that involve touch, audio and vision. Having artifacts designed at a large scale is important in order to facilitate and encourage moment and physical exertion.

CONCLUSION

The interaction mode through the conductive technology received a lot more attention and was seen as a more natural way of interaction. Although the mobile interaction mode allows for more games incorporation there are issues around accessibility. The most interesting element of the xylophone was that concepts such as this can encourage parents and children, grandparents and grandchildren to interact together, bridging in this way the generation gap.

Following the feedback received we are looking at concepts that gamify it further with focus on the multiplayer interaction and to conduct more pilot tests. We also plan to conduct a pilot with our health-related project partner to investigate the health outcomes of such intervention for public health.

ACKNOWLEDGMENTS

We thank all the members of the community who participated in the project, our project partners. We also thank our funders, the FASS-Enterprise Centre and the Catalyst research project at Lancaster University, funded by the EPSRC.

REFERENCES

1. Deterding, S., Björk, S., Nacke, L. (2013) Designing gamification: creating gameful and playful experiences. CHI'13 Extended Abstracts on Human Factors in Computing Systems. 3263-3266.
2. Bekker, T., Sturm, J., Eggen, B. *Designing playful interactions for social interaction and physical play 14*, (2010), 385-39.
3. Romero N., Sturm J., Bekker T., de Valk, L., Sander K. (2010) Playful persuasion to support older adults' social and physical activities. Interacting with Computers. 22:485–495.
4. Sanders, E and Stappers, P. Co-creation and the new landscapes of design. *Co-Design 4, 1* (2008), 5-18

PLEX as Input and Evaluation Tool in Persuasive Game Design: Pilot Study

Marierose M.M. van Dooren[1]*
m.m.m.vandooren@tudelft.nl

Renske Spijkerman[2]
renske.spijkerman@brijder.nl

Richard H.M. Goossens[1]
r.h.m.goossens@tudelft.nl

Vincent M. Hendriks[2]
vincent.hendriks@brijder.nl

Valentijn T. Visch[1]
v.t.visch@tudelft.nl

ABSTRACT
One of the main objectives in game design is to create game experiences that enhance the motivation to start and continue to play the game. To gain insight into which game experiences can be evolved by the game, designers have been using PLEX cards in the user input phase or in the product evaluation phase of the design process. However, to our knowledge, no research has been conducted to check if the PLEX gathered design input experiences matches the experiences that are evolved by the game in the final design. This study checks if such a use of PLEX is possible in a game design procedure for youngsters in treatment for drug addiction. Youngsters firstly selected their preferred PLEX experiences. Secondly, a game designer created a prototype based on the user's motivating experiences and a prototype based on the user's least motivating experiences. Thirdly, other youngsters from the addiction clinic evaluated both prototypes by selecting the PLEX cards that matched their game experiences best. Results suggested that motivating PLEX experiences resulted in a better tailored prototype. However, PLEX experiences derived in the user input phase could not be matched one-on-one to the ones in the evaluation phase. This can problematize the usage of PLEX as a general tool for experience-based game design.

Author Keywords
Design method; gamification; PLEX; paper prototyping; youth addiction care

ACM Classification Keywords
J.4: Computer Application: Social and Behavioral Sciences

INTRODUCTION
This pilot study is part of a larger project on implementation guidelines for persuasive game design in youth addiction care: how to align the design to the user and how to implement it to the user context. Persuasive Game Design aims to create a user experienced game world to change the user behavior in the real world [4].

[1] Industrial Design Engineering, TU Delft: Delft University of Technology, 2628 CE Delft, the Netherlands

[2] Parnassia Addiction Research Centre (PARC), Brijder Addiction Care, Parnassia Group, PO Box 53002, 2505 AA The Hague, the Netherlands

CHI PLAY '14, Oct 19-22 2014, Toronto, ON, Canada
ACM 978-1-4503-3014-5/14/10.
http://dx.doi.org/10.1145/2658537.2661314

In order to adjust the user experience by game design, it is necessary to align user's game-related experiential preferences. In order to verify if the design of a game is matched to the user's preferences, it is important to use one tool that generates and evaluates the input from users. The playful experiences (PLEX) framework [2] is one example of such a tool. It consists of 22 PLEX cards and has two proposed design techniques for the user research input phase: a 'brainstorming'- and a 'scenario' technique [1]. Also, PLEX cards have been used without these techniques in the evaluation phase [3], but not in both phases together.

Currently, it is not clear yet whether one specific tool can be used for verification in the design process by applying it in both the user research input- and evaluation phase. In this study, PLEX experiences were used as a tool to map game experiences in both phases.

METHODS
This study consisted of three phases: user research input phase, design phase and evaluation phase. In the user research input phase it was studied which PLEX cards motivated and which PLEX cards did not motivate addicted youngsters to continue playing a game for a longer period of time. Youngsters (*N*=7), in treatment at Mistral addiction clinic, participated in this phase and differed in age and comorbid problems. Mistral is part of Brijder, an addiction-care organization in the Netherlands. It is an open clinic that provides group treatment for approximately 14 youngsters who have stopped using substances. The participants received the PLEX cards, which presented motivating game experiences, and were asked to divide the cards into 'motivating' or 'not motivating' cards. In the design phase, a professional external game designer was asked to design two prototype games: one aiming to elicit the most motivating PLEX experiences and another to elicit the least motivating PLEX experiences In the evaluation phase another group of youngsters (*N*=5) in treatment at Mistral, evaluated both prototypes on the presence of PLEX experiences.

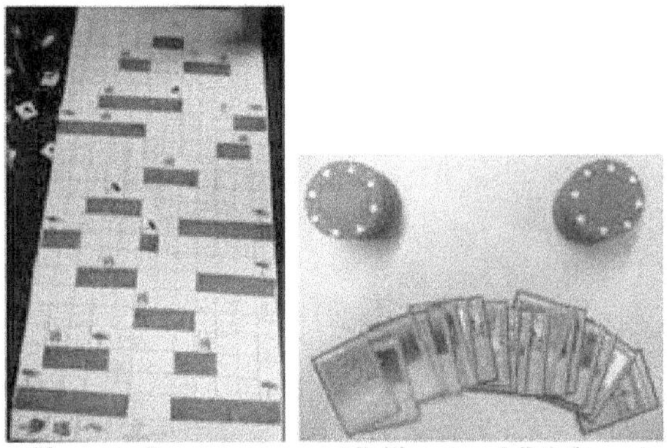

Figure 1: Paper prototype "Falling Angels" (left) and paper prototype "Evolution Battle" (right)

RESULTS

In the user research input phase, the most motivating experiences were "competition" and "thrill" and the least motivating ones were "nurture" and "suffering". The most motivating experiences resulted in the paper prototype "Evolution Battle", where 10 organisms on cards, e.g., human and ranked from 1 to 10, battled for a survival of the fittest. The game was played in rounds of 10 seconds. The first round was started with betting one coin. In each round, a player could raise his/her bet, swap the organism or pass. After a pass the other player had one round to swap, raise or also pass. In the end, the cards with the organisms were compared. The fittest: the player that had the card with the highest number, received all the bets placed (see Figure 1).

The paper prototype based on the least motivating experiences, resulted in "Falling Angels". Angels fell from the sky onto a world filled with platforms. The platforms contained all kinds of danger which made the angels suffer. Angels had to be guided safely towards heaven. Players could protect the angels with help from the "hands of God" represented by three symbols, i.e. a fist, an open hand and a pointing finger (see Figure 1).

PLEX Evolution Battle	
Competition	**9**
Thrill	**2**
Challenge	6
Completion	4
Relaxation	3
Control	3
Exploration	2
PLEX Falling Angels	
Nurture	**6**
Suffering	**1**
Completion	7
Humor	6
Control	4
Challenge	4
Competition	3
Fantasy	2
Exploration	2
Submission	2

Table 1: Evaluation of PLEX experiences in prototype "Evolution Battle" and prototype "Falling Angels". A higher score indicates a higher presence of a PLEX experience.

To evaluate the game experiences of the paper prototypes, five youngsters played and rated both prototypes by means of PLEX. In line with expectations, our results showed that the prototype based on the most motivating PLEX experiences was preferred by four out of five participants. However, other experiences than those derived from the user research input phase were also reported. Furthermore, in the Falling Angels prototype, participants experienced other PLEX more strongly than the ones from the user research input phase (see Table 1).

DISCUSSION

Our preliminary findings suggest that using motivating PLEX experiences for game design resulted in a better tailored prototype, since the prototype based on the most motivating PLEX experiences was preferred by a majority of the participants. However, the PLEX experiences derived in the user research input phase did not correspond one-on-one with the experiences reported in the evaluation phase, problematizing the application of PLEX as a general design tool for experience-based game design.

A possible explanation could be that the PLEX experiences may be multiple interpretable and can show overlap [3]. Furthermore, a game designer may interpret the PLEX experiences differently in comparison to naïve users of the game. Finally, designers might base their choices in the design process not solely on information about game experiences derived from the user research input phase.

More research is needed to draw more in depth conclusions on PLEX as a possible tool in both phases and to verify if the two prototypes differ significantly on motivation.

ACKNOWLEDGEMENTS

We would like to thank all the staff of PARC Brijder and TU Delft, who wrote and provided helpful comments in this study. We would especially like to thank all the participants and staff of the youth clinic of Brijder as well as Michaël Bas (RANJ Serious Game). This research is funded by NWO (314-99-102).

REFERENCES

[1] Arrasvuori, J., Boberg, M., Holopainen, J., Korhonen, H., Lucero, A., and Montola, M. Applying the PLEX framework in designing for playfulness. In Proc. of DPPI'11. ACM Press.

[2] Korhonen, H., Montola, M., and Arrasvuori, J. Understanding playful user experience through digital games. In. Proc. of DPPI'09. ACM Press, 274-285.

[3] Lucero, A., Holopainen, J., Ollila, E., Suomela, R., and Karapanos, E. The Playful Experiences (PLEX) Framework as a Guide for Expert Evaluation. In Proc. of DPPI'13. ACM Press, 221-230.

[4] Visch, V.T., Vegt, N., Anderiesen, H., and van der Kooij, K. Persuasive Game Design: A model and its definitions. CHI '13 Gamification Workshop proceedings. ACM press (2013), 978-1.

Designing a Gameful System to Support the Collection, Curation, Exploration, and Sharing of Sports Memorabilia

Diane Watson[1] Computer Science
Deltcho Valtchanov[1] Management Sciences
[1]University of Waterloo
first.last@uwaterloo.ca

Mark Hancock[1] Management Sciences
Regan Mandryk[2] Computer Science
[2]University of Saskatchewan
first.last@usask.ca

ABSTRACT

Collectors often attach memories and stories to the objects they collect. These stories can be lost over time, and particularly when the collections are digitized. In this paper, we present semi-structured interviews with collectors of hockey memorabilia to inform a set of design guidelines for creating games and playful interfaces that support collectors. Our interviews highlighted the importance of narrative, organization, and authenticity to collection, and identified the need to support emergent behaviour. Our work provides an example of gameful design principles that could motivate collectors to digitize and share their collections.

INTRODUCTION

Artifacts play a significant role in the sharing of memories between people, across cultures, and throughout time. At a personal level, people assign meaning to objects, such as rocks from a beach in a faraway land, or a gift given to symbolize relationships (e.g., wedding rings, friendship bracelets). At a cultural or historical level, people associate artifacts with ancestry or heritage, such as totem poles (Native Americans), clogs (Dutch), or more specific historical artifacts, such as King Tut's tomb or the Crown of Napoleon [2]. However, with the shift to digital records, such as photographs and 3D scans, it is not clear if the stories associated with these artifacts will be maintained the same way.

The digitization of collections allows collectors to easily share memories and stories about the artifacts with a wide audience, and also allows non-collectors to access information about these collections that might otherwise be inaccessible. In addition, the creation, curation, and exploration of digital collections of artifacts are activities that would benefit from interfaces that employ gameful design—designing for the experiential and behavioural quality of games, typically by using game design elements [3]. However, there is little guidance on how to design gameful systems that support the behaviours collectors engage in.

In this paper, we investigate the possibility of allowing the sharing of memories and the assignment of meaning to digital contents and records. In particular, we focus on collectors of sports (hockey) memorabilia and develop a set of design guidelines to encourage collectors to share stories and memories about their digitized collections.

CHI PLAY '14, Oct 19-22 2014, Toronto, ON, Canada
ACM 978-1-4503-3014-5/14/10.
http://dx.doi.org/10.1145/2658537.2661322

We have two main contributions: First, we present empirical data from semi-structured interviews with collectors. Second, we create design guidelines for supporting collection, with narrative as a central part of this process.

SPORTS MEMORABILIA COLLECTOR INTERVIEWS

While other researchers have discussed collectors and reasons for collecting, the intent of previous studies was not focused on how to design technology to support collection, but rather to investigate the psychology of collection [4].

Participants & Methods

We recruited 4 participants (male) who met the following criteria: collect hockey memorabilia, have at least 500 items on display, and have 10+ years of experience as a collector.

We used affinity diagramming [1] to determine themes for the interviews. The audio of the interviews was then coded. Frequency counts and quotations for each theme were extracted and used to inform our design guidelines.

ANALYSIS & DESIGN GUIDELINES

Our analysis revealed several themes that evolved from the interviews and coding process. In this section, we describe the results of our study in terms of the design guidelines that emerged from this analysis.

Stories Must Be Shared

Narrative became an important theme throughout the interviews. The stories about an item often added to the intrinsic value. These could be stories about the original function, event, location, athlete, or stories that were created post-acquisition, such as getting the item signed by the athlete.

P2: "I won't buy anything off anybody if there's no story. If there's no story to it, I don't want it. Because the most important thing about it is the history of the piece, where it's come from, the route it's travelled."

The design of gameful systems for collecting should focus on the importance of stories, both in the past and in the present. Often an item will collect multiple stories as it passes between collectors, and these stories should be preserved.

Organization is Key

Photos of the collections showed that physical organization of the collection is important as those with large collections like to "show and tell". Objects were organized spatially

Figure 1. Highly organized display of memorabilia (left) and a display created with our game prototype (right).

(Figure 1), and lighting of the collection was used as a visual hint of importance (e.g., a spotlight).

The careful organization of items (Figure 1) suggested that developers should allow for the organization of items in the collections. Video content was also very important, with collectors using televisions to display pre-recorded content or live games. Audio from radio broadcasts had also been recorded and played in some spaces.

Authenticity Should Be Supported

The authenticity of objects is valued by collectors. Physical signatures add to their authenticity, creating a physical connection and official recognition between athletes and the item (i.e., the athlete had to physically sign the item).

P4: "I remember thinking: I don't know what either of these things is worth, but I do know that something is out of whack. There's no way that an original document signed by Hap Day is only worth three times what a card is."

While digital copies may not be viewed as being as authentic as their physical counterparts, developers should ensure that when procuring digital copies of items, the resolution is sufficient to maintain signature integrity.

Collecting Behaviours are Emergent

There are few agreed-upon rules around when a collector can acquire an item, what items are considered collectable, and how stories may be created. The items that are desirable vary vastly from person to person, and often items are destroyed or discarded by someone who does not value them or who is unaware of the item's value.

P4: "There are many [athletes] whose contracts have never seen the light of day. What happened was those documents didn't get pulled out of the garbage, so they just got destroyed. It's very sad."

Designers should create a system that does not restrict collectors or narrative, as narrative may grow with time.

Future Work

We are actively developing a prototype game (Figure 1) based on these design guidelines and past research on sandbox games [1], which will allow players to build trophy rooms, similar to the way collectors do with their physical collections. We plan to deploy the game to obtain feedback on the experience and on how the sandbox game motivates people to create, curate, and explore digital collections.

While players may come into the game with existing narratives about the items that they collect, it is our hope that the game itself helps to create new narratives. For example, the trophy rooms themselves could have a story associated with the room (e.g., a specific athlete or game). We also hope that items will collect narratives from players other than the one who submitted the item, or will have new stories over time as the physical copy of the item trades hands or is signed by an athlete, for example.

Research Enabled by a Digital Archive of Memorabilia

Collecting a digital archive of memorabilia that has not lost its connection to the original narrative is important. Other than the social value it provides to the public, there are several research questions that will be able to be addressed. Researchers will be able to look at the difference between physical and digital trophy rooms, which may inform designers about the differences between physical and virtual play. Also, narrative has not been extensively explored in the collecting literature, and our game will enable us to investigate how and when artifacts become associated with a narrative, and how these narratives change over time.

ACKNOWLEDGEMENTS

We thank the Tom Jenkins Foundation, Natural Sciences & Engineering Council of Canada (NSERC), Social Sciences & Humanities Research Council of Canada (SSHRC), Graphics Animation & New Media (GRAND) NCE, University of Waterloo Games Institute, Neil Randall, Kent Aardse, Jason Hawreliak, Ian Milligan, Michael Hancock, Kirk Goodlet, and members of the Hockey History Team.

REFERENCES

1. Babbar, S., Behara, R., & White, E. Mapping product usability. *International Journal of Operations & Production Management*, *22*(10), pp. 1071-1089, 2002.
2. Danet, B. & Katriel, T. No two alike: Play and aesthetics in collecting. In *S. M. Pearce (Ed.), Interpreting objects and collections,* (pp. 220-239), 1994.
3. Deterding, S., Dixon, D., Khaled, R., & Nacke, L. From game design elements to gamefulness: defining gamification. In *Proc. MindTrek: Envisioning Future Media Environments* (pp. 9-15), 2011.
4. McIntosh, W. D., & Schmeichel, B. Collectors and collecting: a social psychological perspective. *Leisure Sciences*, 2004, *26*(1), 85-97.
5. Squire, K. 2008. Open-ended video games: A model for developing learning for the interactive age. In *The Ecology of Games: Connecting Youth, Games, and Learning*, K. Salen (ed.), MIT Press, Cambridge, MA, 167-198

Toward Interactive Social Stories for Children with Autism

Jichen Zhu
Digital Media
Drexel University
Philadelphia, PA, USA
jichen@drexel.edu

James Connell
A.J. Drexel Autism Institute
Drexel University
Philadelphia, PA, USA
jec338@drexel.edu

Connor M. Kerns
A.J. Drexel Autism Institute
Drexel University
Philadelphia, PA, USA
cmk352@drexel.edu

ABSTRACT

This paper proposes *Interactive Social Stories* (ISS), a new approach for enhancing traditional autism interventions to promote stimulus *generalization*. Using interactive narrative techniques of variability and branching structures, we designed a tablet-based ISS app called *FriendStar* to teach 9-13 year old children on the autism spectrum the social skills of greeting in the school context.

Author Keywords

Games for Health; Autism Intervention; Interactive Narrative

ACM Classification Keywords

H.5.2 INFORMATION INTERFACES AND PRESENTATION: User Interfaces

INTRODUCTION

Autism is one of the fastest-growing serious developmental disorders in the U.S. Deficits in social communication and reciprocity reflect a key feature of the autism disorder. Such deficits are associated with significant functional impairment and growing public health costs. It is estimated that nationwide each year 50,000 individuals with ASD turn 18, many lacking adequate social skills to function or live independently. There is thus a pressing need to understand how to improve the social skills of the youth so that they can better integrate into their family and community.

This paper proposes *Interactive Social Stories* (ISS), a new interdisciplinary approach for enhancing traditional autism interventions through computer games, especially interactive narrative. In particular, we aim to promote *stimulus generalization*, that is, helping children learn the behavior in response to varied stimuli as opposed to in one discrete circumstance or in response to a single cue [3]. How to promote stimulus generalization is a key challenge for teaching social skills. By incorporating interactive narrative techniques of variability and branching structure in the traditional ASD intervention of Social Stories, we aim to help children practice certain behavior in response to various similar, but not identical cues/ settings and hence help them generalize to the outside world.

CHI PLAY'14, October 19–21, 2014, Toronto, ON, Canada.
ACM 978-1-4503-3014-5/14/10.
http://dx.doi.org/10.1145/2658537.2661321

Here, we describe our preliminary work in designing *FriendStar*, a mobile tablet-based ISS app that aims to help children on the autism spectrum to practice how to initiate social interaction, i.e., greeting, in the context of schools. We also briefly describe the design of our on-going feasibility study.

BACKGROUND

Among evidence-based interventions, Social Stories are commonly used to help individuals on the autism spectrum better understand the process of interpersonal communication [4, 7]. However, traditional Social Story formats lack flexibility as most of them are linear. These stories depict one particular sequence of events, leaving little space for variations or agency. For instance, when a Social Story teaches how to greet a classmate in school, a child with ASD may not understand how the same greeting can be generalized to others (e.g. a cousin at home) or comprehend how different behaviors (e.g., choosing not to greet) may result in different social consequences. As a result, these linear Social Stories have limited *generalizability* to novel, real-world social interactions with unexpected outcomes.

There have been many efforts to adapt Social Stories into digital media, by using video and computer graphics. Authoring tools such as StoryMaker^{TM} have been developed for caregivers, educators, and clinicians to create their own Social Stories. While most digital Social Stories remain linear, researchers have looked into interactivity. For instance, the "I can Problem-Solve" program, with the help of human instructors, allows children to choose solutions or propose novel ones to problem situations[1]. The Refl-ex system, paired with its authoring tool, aims to help children with High-Functioning Autism through obstacle-based branching[2].

However, very little, if any, Social Story intervention has been designed to promote the *stimulus or response generalization*. Generalization is needed for social skills known to be difficult for ASD youth, such as responding to a variety of greetings in a variety of settings across multiple groups of people. We hence propose to extend Social Stories with interactive narrative techniques such as variability and branching structures [6]. Examples of interactive narrative are modern computer games that use the branching structure to model different user choices and their consequences in the fictional world.

INTERACTIVE SOCIAL STORIES

We built an interactive social story mobile app called *FriendStar*, as a prototype of our new approach. Our goal is to 1) explore a new way of modeling social skills in a fluid and flexible manner, 2) develop an interactive social simulation

Figure 1. A Screenshot from *FriendStar* on a Tablet.

wherein children can learn, test and adjust their generalization of the specific social skills in a less threatening environment, and most importantly, 3) promote stimulus generalizability.

Our target audience is children on the autism spectrum between the age of 9 and 13. They can use the app either with caregivers or on their own. We focus on teaching the social skill of greeting in the school context. Following the convention of traditional social stories, the user plays the role of himself. In order to help the user to identify with the cartoonish character, we incorporate a character personalization function where the user can adjust the skin tone, hair style, and clothing of the character to better match himself.

In order to facilitate generalizability, we divided the instructional content of *FriendStar* into three components, each represented as a week. A week is composed of five days. Following the errorless learning design paradigm [5], the user cannot move on to the next day unless he completes the current day's social challenge correctly.

In Week 1, the user practices how to greet the *same person in different contexts*. In Week 2, he practices greeting skills with *different people in the same context*. In Week 3, the user will encounter new combinations of person and context for further practice. It also allows us to measure how much he has formed a generalized understanding of greeting (generalization over people vs generalization over context) based on examples shown in the first two weeks.

Each day is a self-contained interactive social story, where the user can practice how to greet a particular person in a particular context. The user controls the development of the story by selecting different actions on the screen (Fig. 1). These choices, marking the branching points in the story, lead to different consequences. Different from many digital Social Stories, we incorporate a cascade of choices, allowing the player to "recover" from early mistakes. Every time a correct action is selected, it is reinforced through sound and animation (indicated by the star on the upper right corner of Fig. 1).

FEASIBILITY STUDY DESIGN

As our next step, we are designing a feasibility study to test the effectiveness of the ISS intervention. We plan to collect data from children, their caregivers, and clinicians. Parents and children will be invited to attend an hour-long session to play with *FriendStar*, where each child's interaction with the app will be logged to identify issues and potential interaction patterns. They will then be asked a series of questions by research staff about the usability and learnability of the ISS app in order to assess child comfort and rapport. Clinicians will participate in a focus group to discuss their impressions of the app. In addition, parents and clinicians will also be asked to complete a standard intervention acceptability measure: the Intervention Rating Profile (IRP-15).

CONCLUSION

In summary, we propose a new framework of Interactive Social Story to help children with autism to learn social skills. We focus on incorporating techniques from interactive narrative, particularly its branching structure and variability, to promote stimulus generalization. We designed and developed a tablet-based ISS application called *FriendStar*.

ADDITIONAL AUTHORS

Natalie Lyon (nel35@drexel.edu), Nicole Vecere (nmvecere@gmail.com), Desiree Lim (ddl38@drexel.edu), Chelsea Myers (chelsea.m.myers@drexel.edu), Digital Media, Drexel University, Philadelphia, PA USA

REFERENCES

1. Bernard-Opitz, V., Sriram, N., and Nakhoda-Sapuan, S. Enhancing social problem solving in children with autism and normal children through computer-assisted instruction. *Journal of autism and developmental disorders 31*, 4 (2001), 377–384.
2. Boujarwah, F. A., Riedl, M. O., Abowd, G. D., and Arriaga, R. I. React: intelligent authoring of social skills instructional modules for adolescents with high-functioning autism. *ACM SIGACCESS Accessibility and Computing*, 99 (2011), 13–23.
3. Cooper, J. O., Heron, T. E., and Heward, W. L. *Applied behavior analysis*. Prentice Hall, Upper Saddle River, NJ, 2007.
4. Gray, C. A., and Garand, J. D. Social stories: Improving responses of students with autism with accurate social information. *Focus on Autistic Behavior* (1993).
5. Jones, R. S., and Eayrs, C. The use of errorless learning procedures in teaching people with a learning disability: A critical review. *Mental Handicap Research 5*, 2 (1992), 204–212.
6. Murray, J. H. *Hamlet on the Holodeck: The Future of Narrative in Cyberspace*. MIT Press, Cambridge, 1998.
7. Reynhout, G., and Carter, M. Evaluation of the efficacy of social stories™ using three single subject metrics. *Research in Autism Spectrum Disorders 5*, 2 (2011), 885–900.

Towards Balancing Learner Autonomy and Pedagogical Process in Educational Games

Jichen Zhu
Digital Media Department
Drexel University
Philadelphia, PA USA
jichen.zhu@gmail.com

Aroutis Foster
School of Education
Drexel Universit
Philadelphia, PA USA
aroutisfoster@gmail.com

Glen Muschio
Digital Media Department
Drexel Universit
Philadelphia, PA USA
muschio@drexel.edu

ABSTRACT
We present the preliminary work in the TAEMILE project, which aims to co-regulate the learning process in educational games by automatically balancing learners autonomy and the pedagogical processes intended by educators. We focus on our design rationale and the initial results from our user study.

Author Keywords
Educational Game, Player Modeling, Co-Regulation

ACM Classification Keywords
H.5.2 INFORMATION INTERFACES AND PRESENTATION: User Interfaces

INTRODUCTION
Interactive learning environments, such as educational games, allow learners tremendous amounts of autonomy to take responsibility over their actions based on their own preferences. However, studies have shown that unchecked learner autonomy and pure-discovery based learning are not the best strategies. As most students in the initial stages of the learning process do not have the necessary declarative, procedural, and conditional knowledge to be metacognitively aware of what needs to be done nor adequate strategies to direct their learning, they still need a "more advanced other" such as a teacher to aid the learning process [4]. By contrast, guided-discovery-based learning has many advantages over traditional didactic and pure-discovery-based learning pedagogies in scaffolding active learning and nurturing complex understanding of content [1, 8].

A key challenge to support guided-discovery-based learning in game-based learning environments is to provide the appropriate co-regulation. As each student has a different learning orientation, play style, and domain knowledge, the balance between learner autonomy and desired pedagogical processes should also adapt to individual needs. A central challenge for educational games is thus how to adjust this balance over time according to both the content and the individual student's needs, and then effectively communicate the level of scaffolding to the player in unobtrusive ways.

In this paper, we present the on-going work in the TAEMILE project, which aims to co-regulate the learning process by automatically balancing learners' autonomy and the pedagogical processes intended by educators. In particular, we focus on how we designed the game environment to support different play styles and our preliminary results of the first user study, which aims to analyze how players interact in the game through gameplay traces.

BACKGROUND
Co-regulation provides guidance without completely removing students' autonomy. Hadwin and Oshige [6] described the co-regulation process as "the temporary sharing or distributing of self-regulatory processes ... between a learner and a more capable other while the learner is in transit toward becoming a self-regulator in that domain." They emphasize that during the period of transit, in the zone of proximal development, self-regulatory processes need to be scaffolded.

Motivation research has shown that there are generally two types of orientations for learning — performance and mastery. Students with performance goal orientation focus on external goals such as scores and grades to validate their success. By contrast, students with mastery approach orientation achieve a sense of satisfaction from the detailed understanding of the work and are not influenced by extrinsic factors such as scores or grades [9, 3] and there are students who avoid mastery, but are not performance oriented.

Based on mastery and performance orientations from Achievement Goal Theory [2], we focus on two general categories of play types: explorers and goal seekers [5, 7]. When applied to educational games, explorers are inclined to experience a wider range of in-game content while goal seekers tend to focus on content necessary for winning. The gameplay in *Solving the Incognitum* supports both play types. A goal seeker can take on three main quests necessary to win the game, and an explorer can roam around the virtual museum exploring different subjects of interest.

DESIGNING "SOLVING THE INCOGNITUM"
Solving the Incognitum is a point-and-click-based interactive learning environment for teaching the relationships between geological time and fossil records. In an environment based on the historical Charles Willson Peale's Museum of Art and Science, the largest U.S. natural history museum of its day,

CHI PLAY'14, October 19–21, 2014, Toronto, ON, Canada.
ACM 978-1-4503-3014-5/14/10.
http://dx.doi.org/10.1145/2658537.2661326

Figure 1. A Screenshot from *Solving the Incognitum*

the player can locate and assemble the bones of a mastodon by answering questions about the museum exhibits (Fig. 1). In particular, the educational goal of the game is to teach 1) Law of Superposition, 2) Geological Time, and 3) Mastodon life. After a brief tutorial, the player can explore the virtual space, examine different exhibits (e.g., fossils, soil samples, portraits of geologists) and answer questions about them.

In order to support the different play styles a player may adopt, the game provides different gameplay options. For goal seekers, the main objective for winning the game is to locate and assemble the skeleton of a mastodon by completing four main quests. Each quest requires the player to visit several exhibits and apply the knowledge they learn to answer related questions. For explorers, the environment contains a range of other exhibits, grouped based on their association, which the players can explore based on their own interest. There are also badges that a player can earn by exploring.

USER STUDY DESIGN

In our first user study, we intend to understand how learners with different play styles interact with the game as well as how much they learn from the game. In order to measure learning outcome, we designed a knowledge test about the subject that each participant takes before and after the gameplay session. The difference is measured as an indicator of how much she has learned in the game. In order to understand a particular learner's play style, we use the instrument of *Achievement Goal Theory Survey*, which measures her alignment to the Achievement Goal Theory framework, and *Gaming Preference Survey*, which gathers information about how she plays games. The participants complete the surveys before and after the gameplay session.

PRELIMINARY RESULTS

In our recent study, we recruited 27 undergraduate students from Drexel University. Our observation and initial results from analyzing gameplay traces show that participants took up a wide range of play styles. For example, one participant systematically explored all the exhibits in order, whereas another visited only the exhibits needed for the four main quests. This indicates that the design of the game supports both play styles of explorers and goal seekers. An interesting finding we observed from the focus group discussions is that it is common that players switch between play styles as they play the game. A number of participants described how they started with exploration and once they figured out how the game worked, they switched to focus on winning the game. This is a new finding, which has not been fully discussed in the literature.

CONCLUSION AND FUTURE WORK

This work-in-progress paper presents our work towards balancing learner autonomy and pedagogical process through providing appropriate co-regulation to learners with different play style. We discuss the design of our *Solving the Incognitum* game and preliminary results from our first user study.

ADDITIONAL AUTHORS

Justin Patterson[1](jhpatt33@gmail.com), Josep Valls-Vargas[2] (jv384@drexel.edu), and Daniel Newman[1] (djn38 @drexel.edu). [1]Digital Media, [2]Computer Science, Drexel University, Philadelphia PA

ACKNOWLEDGEMENT

This material is based upon work supported by the National Science Foundation under Grant Numbers IIS-1349082.

REFERENCES

1. Alfieri, L., Brooks, P. J., Aldrich, N. J., and Tenenbaum, H. R. Does discovery-based instruction enhance learning? *Journal of Educational Psychology 103*, 1 (2011), 1.
2. Ames, C. Classrooms: Goals, structures, and student motivation. *Journal of educational psychology 84*, 3 (1992), 261.
3. Aylett, R., and Louchart, S. Towards a narrative theory of virtual reality. *Virtual Reality 7*, 1 (2003), 2–9.
4. Boekaerts, M. What have we learned about the social context-student engagement link? *Teachers College Record 113*, 2 (2011), 375–393.
5. Foster, A. N. The process of learning in a simulation strategy game: Disciplinary knowledge construction. *Journal of Educational Computing Research 45*, 1 (2011), 1–27.
6. Hadwin, A., and Oshige, M. Self-regulation, coregulation, and socially shared regulation: Exploring perspectives of social in self-regulated learning theory. *Teachers College Record 113*, 6 (2011), 240–264.
7. Heeter, C., Magerko, B., Medler, B., and Fitzgerald, J. Game design and the challenge-avoiding, self-validator player type. *International Journal of Gaming and Computer-Mediated Simulations (IJGCMS) 1*, 3 (2009), 53–67.
8. Mayer, R. E. Should there be a three-strikes rule against pure discovery learning? *American Psychologist 59*, 1 (2004), 14.
9. Riedl, M. O., Stern, A., Dini, D., and Alderman, J. Dynamic experience management in virtual worlds for entertainment, education, and training. *International Transactions on Systems Science and Applications 4*, 2 (2008), 23–42.

Participatory Design for Serious Game Design: Truth and Lies

Rilla Khaled
Institute of Digital Games
University of Malta
rilla.khaled@um.edu.mt

Asimina Vasalou
London Knowledge Lab
Institute of Education
a.vasalou@ioe.ac.uk

Vero Vanden Abeele
e-Media Lab
KU Leuven
Vero.VandenAbeele@kuleuven.be

Maarten Van Mechelen
CUO | Social Spaces, iMinds
KU Leuven
Maarten.vanmechelen@kuleuven.be

CHIPLAY 2014, October 19–21, 2014, Toronto, ON, Canada.
ACM 978-1-4503-3014-5/14/10.

Abstract

While the importance of participatory design has been acknowledged broadly within the field of HCI, its use in serious games is less frequent. This workshop will explore the underpinning reasons for this gap and advance the identification of philosophical, methodological and pragmatic opportunities as well as challenges. The workshop will serve as a venue for synthesizing productive practices and a future agenda that will benefit serious game design processes.

Author Keywords

Serious games; learning games; game design, participatory design; user-centered design, co-creation

ACM Classification Keywords

H.5.m. Information interfaces and presentation (e.g., HCI): Miscellaneous

Introduction

Serious games, games with an agenda alongside entertainment [11], are paradoxical. They are *games*, which Suits has defined as voluntary attempts to overcome unnecessary obstacles [10]. Yet they are used instrumentally, thus their obstacles are often necessary. In some cases, serious games are not even played voluntarily. Serious games owe much of their lineage to entertainment-oriented games, frequently borrowing not only their design tropes and mechanics, but also their design processes. As entertainment-oriented game design has traditionally been perceived as closer to artistic practice and more definitively serving aesthetic – or at least – hedonic rather than utilitarian ends, "designer-led" design has remained the norm, with players frequently only contributing once a testable prototype exists.

In light of the duality of expectations associated with serious games, strictly adopting the design processes of entertainment games will rarely yield effective serious games. General game design processes neither shed much light on how to embed and communicate particular 'serious' content within gameplay, nor on how to design for the values and expectations of specific audiences, both of which hold paramount importance in the design of serious games. While the former concern has essentially been the core focus of numerous serious and persuasive game design approaches, e.g. [11], the latter concern has typically been the focus of Participatory Design (PD).

PD activity is extraordinarily diverse and this diversity has not lent itself to a single theory or paradigm of study or approach to practices. At the same time, many PD researchers and practitioners agree on the importance of the value of democracy in civic, educational and commercial settings. Democracy has been seen as means to empower disempowered groups, to improve internal processes and to combine diverse knowledge to produce better services and products [9]. Reciprocity and symmetry of knowledge are also widely viewed as important; it is taken as a given that designers cannot, from the outset, understand the needs of end users. Thus, non-designer stakeholders should participate in, and contribute towards decisions that affect them [2] .

A number of PD methods concern gaining insight into stakeholder perspectives. For example, *design games* have been used as a means for designers and users to develop shared vocabulary [3]. Other methods concern how to engage users in co-creation. For example, in *future workshops* designers and users collaboratively identify current problems, propose future solutions, and identify ways to bridge the distance between the two [6]. We point out, though, that it is not just the use of these methods that characterizes design efforts as PD. Rather, it is when, how and why these methods are used that renders efforts as PD [5].

Philosophically and methodologically, participatory design has much to offer to serious game design. Indeed, in recent years growing numbers of researchers have reported adopting PD-inspired methods during serious game design processes. For example, Danielsson and Wiberg used PD-inspired approaches with teenagers to design a learning game about gender identity [4]. The authors of this proposal devised a game-specific PD method for engaging game-literate users in the design of learning game mechanics [7] as well as a participatory player-centered serious game design framework [1]. Unfortunately, these reports provide only limited details of how exactly (and if) design concepts were co-created between designers and players. Other reports emphasize that attempts to employ PD in serious game design processes happen neither smoothly nor automatically [1][7][8].

In fact, these difficulties of fit between PD and serious game design are not surprising: characteristic qualities of PD and serious game design are, along certain dimensions, in explicit tension with one another. PD posits that design should be a reciprocal activity and that users should co-create artifacts destined for them.

In contrast, serious game design requires the translation of specific domain knowledge and rhetorical perspectives into game systems, which have traditionally been designed via designer-led approaches.

Workshop Goals

In this workshop, we reflect on the reciprocal influence of PD and serious game design. Employing PD in serious game design requires us to extend conceptualisations of both PD and serious game design; a core workshop goal is to establish what happens within these extended spaces. We intend to explore and map out the ways in which researchers and practitioners of the games and PD communities have approached this in academic and industry settings alike. We will seek *case studies* of how PD has been used in different stages of serious game design processes, specific *methods* appropriated or developed for doing so, and details of problematic *dynamics* between PD processes and serious game design. We are interested in *critical reflections* on how and when PD approaches were helpful for serious game design, and new forces and considerations that the inclusion of PD may have introduced. We also wish to examine how PD can create *new forms of empowerment* for players in serious game design contexts. Case studies will be encouraged to address, while not being limited to, the following questions:

- How does expertise influence power dynamics between different stakeholders? How should future players be involved in the design of game systems if they do not understand how game systems work, or equally if they don't possess domain expertise?
- How should we build on the perspectives, values, and ideas of players if, as politically incorrect as it sounds, these are not game-friendly, clash with the design aesthetics of game designers or contravene evidence from learning theories?
- Given the type of stakeholders involved in serious games design, what are the value dilemmas that can occur and how can these be overcome by fostering intragroup or co-design dynamics?
- What do researchers and users expect from PD and are these expectations realized in PD projects?
- In light of the empowerment focus of PD, how can we use game design processes to empower users, and what do we do when users do not want to be empowered?
- How might we use PD to foster an accountability culture in relation to the promise of serious games? How do we identify and address tokenism?

Workshop Outcomes

The workshop will define and prioritize a future agenda for PD and serious games design. This will be fostered before, during and after the workshop through a number of forums. A dedicated website will serve as a portal for forming and discussing this agenda within and outside the workshop. A special journal issue will be organized after the workshop and a SIG will be established to build a community of researchers with this shared interest. SIG meetings and follow up workshops at related venues will be discussed and planned during the workshop.

Tentative Plans and Schedule

Before the Workshop

The call for participation will be distributed via HCI, child-computer interaction, games and entertainment related mailing lists as well as specialized ones (e.g. ACM SIGCHI, British HCI News, etc.). The workshop organizers will also publicize the workshop via a

WordPress website. Submissions will consist of narratives on key workshop questions (appr. 500 words). Accepted participants' narratives will be made available and shared with other participants through the website. All participants will be asked to read the narratives and to add comments, questions or sum-up what they took away from each contribution.

During the Workshop

Themes explored during the day will be identified from participants' narrative submissions. The workshop will be structured to explore and discuss each theme. Emerging concepts and patterns will be identified and documented. In the second part of the workshop, the concepts identified earlier in the day will be explored in a more focused format. Participants will be asked to pick a concept they affiliate with. The resultant sub groups will lead on particular concepts. The purpose of this will be twofold: (1) teams will be encouraged to find cross links between their case studies toward collaborating on joint submissions for the special issue; (2) given the expertise within teams we will push the agenda further by formulating new research questions and plans to advance the respective themes.

After the Workshop (Dissemination)

The website will be maintained past the workshop to foster a community of interest for those who seek to apply PD processes in serious game design. The website will allow interested parties to contribute their own stories and share relevant events. Additionally, the workshop organizers are planning to propose a special issue. The call will be advertised to the serious games, HCI and PD communities.

References

[1] Abeele, V. et al. (2012). P-iii: A player-centered, iterative, interdisciplinary and integrated framework for serious game design and development. In Serious Games: The Challenge. Springer, 82–86.

[2] Bødker et al. (1988). Computer support for cooperative design. *In Proceedings of the Conference on Computer Supported Cooperative Work*. Portland, Oregon.

[3] Brandt, E. (2006). Designing exploratory design games: a framework for participation in participatory design. *In Proceedings of the Ninth Conference on Participatory design*, 57–66.

[4] Danielsson, K. and Wiberg, C. (2006). Participatory design of learning media: Designing educational computer games with and for teenagers. *Interactive Technology & Smart Education* 3 (4), 275–291.

[5] Iversen et al. (2010). Rekindling Values in Participatory Design. *In Proceedings of the 11th Biennial Participatory Design Conference*. ACM, NY.

[6] Kensing, F. and Madsen, K. H. (1992) *Generating visions: future workshops and metaphorical design*. L. Erlbaum Associates Inc., Hillsdale, NJ, USA, 155–168.

[7] Khaled, R. and Vasalou, A. (In Press). Bridging Serious Games and Participatory Design. *International Journal of Child-Computer Interaction*.

[8] Moser, et al. "Let's Talk about Failures: Why Was the Game for Children Not a Success?," *In Proceedings of Human Factors in Computing Systems*, Extended Abstracts, Paris, France, 3199-3202.

[9] Spinuzzi, C. (2005) The methodology of participatory design. Technical Communication 52 (2), 163-174.

[10] Suits, B. and Hurka, T. (2005). The Grasshopper: Games, Life and Utopia. Broadview encore editions. Broadview Press.

[11] Winn, B. (2008). The design, play, and experience Framework. In Handbook of Research on Effective Electronic Gaming in Education. IGI Global Publication, Hershey, Philadelphia, 1010-1024.

Game Idea Jam for Sport and Exertion Games

Christiane Moser,
Manfred Tscheligi
ICT&S Center,
University of Salzburg
Salzburg, Austria
{firstname.lastname}@sbg.ac.at

Mark Magnusson
EA Sports
Vancouver, Canada
markmagnusson@ea.com

Florian 'Floyd' Mueller
Exertion Games Lab
RMIT University
Melbourne, Australia
floyd@exertiongameslab.org

CHI PLAY'14, October 19–21, 2014, Toronto, ON, Canada.
ACM 978-1-4503-3014-5/14/10.
http://dx.doi.org/10.1145/2658537.2659017

Abstract
Game Jams have successfully been introduced to the CHI Community during the past two years. Game developers meet to plan, design, and create one or more games within a short time span (ranging from 24 to 48 hours). We propose a Game Idea Jam focusing on the opportunity to draw on researchers' and developers' own experiences when developing creative game ideas for sport or exertion to combat physical inactivity. Game Idea Jams focus on brainstorming and conceptualizing of one or more game ideas within seven hours. Due to time constraints, the final game idea will be produced in the form of a conceptual video, trying to demonstrate the player experience. We aim to enable game researcher with no development skills to participate in the Game Idea Jam and support them with different creative approaches to choose from.

Author Keywords
Game Jams; Ideation; Sports; Exertion;

ACM Classification Keywords
H.5.m. Information interfaces and presentation (e.g., HCI): Miscellaneous.

Introduction
In 2013, the Game Jam workshop [2] introduced the CHI community to the collaborative method of designing game ideas, which is a successful practice in game design communities. Following up this success, the 2014 Game Jam [4Research] CHI Workshop [3]

enabled researchers and practitioners to design a game where the design process and resulting game artifact served as a case study, situated in a research-through-design tradition. In particular, we want to highlight how the collaborative nature of Game Jams provides participants, from varied backgrounds, the possibility to network and cooperate across institutions, research, and industry through a shared experience.

The proposed Game Idea Jam invites researchers and practitioners to develop ideas for sports and exertion games, which improve physical health by combating physical inactivity. Addressing this is important, as according to the World Health Organisation's (WHO) global health report[1], physical inactivity is one of the greatest public health problems of our century (see also Figure 1).

Figure 1. Insufficient physical activity[2]

There is also evidence that regular physical activity (i.e., reduction of physical inactivity) has important and wide-ranging health benefits (ranging from reduced risk of chronic diseases such as heart disease, type 2 diabetes, and specific cancers to enhanced function and preservation of function with age) [1]. This inspired our topic for the Game Idea Jam.

[1] http://www.who.int/whr/2013/report/en/
[2] http://gamapserver.who.int/gho/interactive_charts/

Motivation

The motivation of the Game Idea Jam is to combine the potential of sport and exertion games with game jams in order to come up with new and creative ideas to improve physical health by combating physical inactivity.

Sport and Exertion Games

Computer games can address a central human desire to engage in entertaining activities. Sport games without physical activity, like FIFA, have been around for many years. This has changed since Nintendo Wii, Sony Playstation Move, and Microsoft XBOX Kinect have been introduced, as they offer home video gaming systems involving player movement to control game play. Interestingly, the boundaries between game genres are not clear, meaning there is rather a continuum between games that use physical, full body input and fitness programs.

Malaka [6] states that the motivational power and the immersion of exertion games can lead to sustainable motivation for doing exercises and thereby affecting health status. However, there are three big challenges, which are addressed in the Game Idea Jam: 1) reaching sustainable motivation, 2) enabling physiologically positive movements, and 3) adapting to users.

Game Jam

Recent years have shown the popularity of game jams all around the world and also at conferences such as CHI. Game jams have proven to be a successful approach for rapid prototyping of game ideas developed by participants from diverse backgrounds (e.g., art, programming, design, and scholars) in a pre-defined time span [4]. Every year, the Global Game Jam[3]

[3] http://globalgamejam.org/

attracts thousands of game developers and the Games [4Health] Jam[4] in the Netherlands explores ways to trigger physical activity amongst youngsters in different situational contexts. Due to time constraints we will only focus on the game ideation in our Game Idea Jam.

Objectives

The objectives of the Game Idea Jam for sport and exertion games are:

- Enable game researchers and practitioners with and without development skills to participate;
- Explore jamming through a practice-based collaboration between game researchers and practitioners;
- Develop creative ideas for sport or exertion games combating physical inactivity;
- Provide the experience of a game jam to our participants in order to get confidence to integrate this approach into their own practice.

Workshop Format

As no particular game development skills are required for the participation, the participants are supported with different creative approaches to choose from.

Creative Approaches

EA Sports developed extensive personas based on their user (experience) data. Excerpts of these personas will provide (background) information about different user groups and can be used as a starting point for the game idea development.

Exertion Game Cards [10] are a set of design cards to help participants break down the game design tasks into individual elements covering a spectrum of themes valuable for exertion games.

PLEX Cards [5] were created to communicate the 22 categories of a playful experiences framework to designers and other stakeholders, who wish to design for playfulness.

Video snippets of Game Ideation Workshops (e.g., [8] or **Fehler! Verweisquelle konnte nicht gefunden werden.**) provide insights from users on possible game ideas, relevant game elements, and their anticipated player experiences.

Game Idea Booklets [7] help to brainstorm different topics concerning a game idea (e.g., title, idea, goal, course of the game, motivation, rules, characters, opponents, obstacles, or controller).

Game idea video prototypes (e.g., concept sketching with stop-motion-videos or brickfilms) explain and demonstrate the game idea concept without big effort. There are tool/apps, like the Stop Motion Studio[5], that enable easy and fast production of such videos.

The participants are encouraged to familiarize themselves with the approaches beforehand, in order to choose selected ones during the Game Idea Jam they would like to work with. Additionally, a lot of other creative materials will be provided to the participants for inspiration (e.g., sensors, balls, bats, or wigs).

Workshop Procedure

This is a one-day workshop with two key components: 1) game jam break-out sessions and 2) a video production sessions. The Game Ideas Jam will start with an introduction round, i.e., each participant explains briefly the motivation to participate in the workshop. The workshop organizers will give a short

[4] http://www.gamesjam.nl/

[5] http://www.stopmotionpro.com

introduction to the workshop topic on creative game ideas for sport and exertion games combatting physical inactivity. Afterwards, the participants form different groups based on interest and expertise and start with the first game jam break-out session. In this session, game ideas should be brainstormed by actively moving around, i.e., engaging in physical activity.

After the coffee break, the second break-out session will take place until lunch and another one after lunch. In these two sessions, one game idea should be selected and elaborated into a concept. Due to time constraints, the final game will not be implemented but developed in the form of a conceptual video demonstrating the player experience. In the next session following the coffee break the video will be finished. The last activity is a group discussion where the participants are encouraged to share their experiences, which can be continued at the informal dinner afterwards. The produced videos will be exhibited during the poster and demo session at the conference if possible.

Participation

We encourage game researchers and practitioners with and without game development skill to participate in the Game Idea Jam. Workshop candidates are asked to send a motivation statement (e.g., how they will benefit from the participation), a short list of skills and expertise that helps to evaluate potential matches for good collaborative teams and a brief bio/portfolio URL that helps other participants to identify potential partners, via email to christiane.moser@sbg.ac.at. This application should be no more than three pages in total in ACM Extended Abstract format[6].

[6] http://www.sigchi.org/publications/chipubform

References

[1] Blair, S.N. Physical inactivity: the biggest public health problem of the 21st century. *British Journal of Sports Medicine*, 43(1) (2009), 1-2.

[2] Chatham, A., Schouten, B., Toprak, C., Mueller, F., Deen, M., Bernhaupt, R., Khot, R. and Pijnappel, S. Game jam. *In CHI '13 Extended Abstracts on Human Factors in Computing Systems* (2013), 3175-3178, ACM.

[3] Deen, M., Cercos, R., Chatman, A., Naseem, A., Bernhaupt, R., Fowler, A., Schouten, B. and Mueller, F. 2014. Game jam: [4 research]. In *CHI '14 Extended Abstracts on Human Factors in Computing Systems* (2014), 25-28.

[4] Fowler, A., Khosmood, F, and Arya, A. The evolution and significance of the Global Game Jam, In Proc. *FDG2013*, (2013).

[5] Lucero, A. and Arrasvuori, J. The PLEX Cards and its techniques as sources of inspiration when designing for playfulness. *International Journal of Arts and Technology*, 6(1), (2013), 22-43.

[6] Malaka, R. How Computer Games Can Improve Your Health and Fitness. *Games for Training, Education, Health and Sports*. Springer, (2014), 1-7.

[7] Moser, C. Child-Centered Game Development (CCGD): Developing Games with Children at School. *Personal and Ubiquitous Computing*, 17(8), (2013), 1647-1661.

[8] Moser, C. Children Ideation Workshop. In *Proc. ACE 2013*. Springer, (2013), 592-599.

[9] Moser, C., Chisik, Y. and Tscheligi, M. Around the World in 8 Workshops: Investigating Anticipated Player Experiences of Children. In *Proc. CHI PLAY '14*, ACM, (2014).

[10] Mueller, F., Gibbs, M.R., Vetere, F. and Edge, D. Supporting the creative game design process with exertion cards. In *Proc. CHI 2014*, ACM Press (2014), 2211-2220.

EyePlay: Applications for Gaze in Games

Jayson Turner
Lancaster University
Lancaster
United Kingdom
j.turner@lancaster.ac.uk

Eduardo Velloso
Lancaster University
Lancaster
United Kingdom
e.velloso@lancaster.ac.uk

Hans Gellersen
Lancaster University
Lancaster
United Kingdom
hwg@comp.lancs.ac.uk

Veronica Sundstedt
Blekinge Institute of Technology
Karlskrona
Sweden
veronica.sundstedt@bth.se

CHI-PLAY'14, October 19–21, 2014, Toronto, ON, Canada.
ACM 978-1-4503-3014-5/14/10.
http://dx.doi.org/10.1145/2658537.2659016

Abstract
What new challenges does the combination of games and eye-tracking present? The *EyePlay* workshop brings together researchers and industry specialists from the fields of eye-tracking and games to address this question. Eye-tracking been investigated extensively in a variety of domains in human-computer Interaction, but little attention has been given to its application for gaming. As eye-tracking technology is now an affordable commodity, its appeal as a sensing technology for games is set to become the driving force for novel methods of player-computer interaction and games evaluation. This workshop presents a forum for eye-based gaming research, with a focus on identifying the opportunities that eye-tracking brings to games design and research, on plotting the landscape of the work in this area, and on formalising a research agenda for EyePlay as a field. Possible topics are, but not limited to, novel interaction techniques and game mechanics, usability and evaluation, accessibility, learning, and serious games contexts.

Author Keywords
Gaze Interaction; Eye-tracking; Games;

ACM Classification Keywords
H.5.2 [Information Interfaces and Presentation]: User Interfaces–input devices and strategies.

Introduction

Within the world of games, novel sensing technologies such as motion and depth sensing have brought new gaming peripherals, mechanics, and experiences into the hands of designers and players. Now, eye-tracking hardware is on the cusp of becoming a commodity and has started to pique the interest of independent games developers. *Son of Nor*[1], a Kickstarter funded game due for release this year, will support Tobii's 'EyeX' consumer orientated eye-tracker[2]. As adoption grows, the demand for new experiences and practical applications will follow. This brings with it the opportunity for focused research that pushes the field into unexplored territory.

Eye-tracking research has given rise to new interaction techniques, user experiences (UX), and usability insights in the field of human-computer interaction (HCI) both in desktop [14] and pervasive environments [12]. Eye-based player-computer interaction (PCI), however, remains relatively unexplored. The focus of this workshop is to explore the use of eye-tracking as an input modality for gaming, and its use as a games research tool. We aim to bring together eye-tracking and games specialists to identify possible avenues of research that arise at the intersection of these two fields.

The fundamental question we ask is *What new challenges does the combination of games and eye-tracking present?* Given a future where eye-tracking is robust and pervasive, what new compelling experiences could be designed? what are the benefits and drawbacks of eye-based games design? and what can we learn about players from their eyes to improve and develop experiences?

[1]http://sonofnor.com
[2]http://www.tobii.com/en/eye-experience

Previous work has explored different mechanics for eye-based games [11]. The eyes naturally indicate users' point-of-regard. This can be explored both by simplifying or adding complexity to the gaming experience. On one hand, for example, in the arcade classic *Breakout*, players must control a paddle to hit a ball. By assigning the control of the paddle to the gaze point, just by following the ball with the eyes, the paddle automatically hits the ball [3]. On the other hand, by designing mechanics that lure the player's gaze point away, we can include new additional obstacles and interface mastery challenges for players. Other control mechanisms have enabled multimodal [1] and eyes-only [10] navigation in virtual environments.

Games can also benefit from the natural behaviour of the eyes to increase immersion and to monitor attention. For example, by tracking players' point-of-regard, 3D game engines can render a matching depth-of-field blur, creating an effect similar to real life perception [4]. Moreover, by using gaze to estimate where attention is directed, games can adapt their storyline [9], use appropriate cues to reengage inattentive players [2], or predict player behaviour [8].

Eye-tracking can be used as research tool to inform game design. The analysis of players eye behaviour has revealed distinct gaze patterns in players of varying skill and gender, resulting in new considerations for future design in serious games [6]. Similarly, common areas-of-interest in *Guitar Hero* were used to develop an accessible version of the game, controlled by the eyes alone [13]. These types of analyses have also been applied to games for learning [7] and to encourage games designers to consider gaze as a usability measure to inform future design [5].

The work presented here has motivated this workshop, and given the growth of the eye-tracking community and its broad range of applications, we believe there is great potential for beneficial and exciting research in this space. We welcome position papers from PhD Students, academics, and industry with an interest in the use of eye-tracking within games. The scope of submissions is intentionally broad to allow exploration of the many possible facets of this new field. We provide an outline below to instigate interesting directions for submissions:

- Eye-tracking as input for games for PC, consoles and mobiles (interaction and experiences)
- Application and evaluation of existing eye-based interaction techniques in a games context
- Multi-modal/Multi-sensor input (Gaze + Manual input, physiological input, GPS, etc.)
- Eye-tracking as an evaluation and research tool (e.g., Methods, Case studies)
- Gaze in serious games for learning, simulation, and health

Goals

This workshop is designed to create a community of academic and industry experts around the use of eye-tracking in games. We structure the day to allow participants to share their contributions and viewpoints on how game design, development and research can benefit from eye-tracking and use these to create a research agenda for the topic. We will use the following research questions as a starting point:

- **What new challenges does the combination of games and eye-tracking present?** How could this new modality enrich existing games? How can eye-based games design be approached from the ground up?
- **How can existing eye-tracking research be applied in a games context?** What has been shown for input and usability evaluation? What were the lessons learned, and what are the implications when findings are applied to games?
- **What are the big questions?** In which direction should we be heading to reach a vision of eye-enriched gaming?

Plan

Pre-Workshop

We will distribute the call for papers through mailing lists, social media, special interest groups and through the workshop's website. We will invite 2-4 page position papers from industry and academia, which will be reviewed along with the authors' short bio by our organisation committee. We will select participants with well-argued views and contributions to the field.

Workshop Plan

The workshop will be divided into three activities:

1. **Paper presentations.** Participants will have a 10-minute slot to present their position papers and answer questions from the audience in two 90-minute sessions, with an interval in between.
2. **Brainstorming.** A session involving all workshop participants, to identify open research questions and

challenges to build a research agenda for the use of the eyes in games development and research. Throughout the activity, the organisers will document participants' ideas using a mind-map or similar tool.

3. **Breakout activity.** In groups, participants will develop a design that addresses a challenge from those identified in the previous session. We will bring 10 Tobii EyeX eye-trackers for them to experiment their ideas.

We will conclude the day with the presentations of the group designs.

Outcome

The results of the workshop, including the position papers, slides, photos, mind-maps and the group designs will be published on the workshop's website. We plan to turn the research agenda created in the workshop into a magazine article and invite accepted submissions to revise and extend their papers for a special issue on eye-tracking in games in a journal or magazine to be discussed during the workshop.

References

[1] Castellina, E., and Corno, F. Multimodal gaze interaction in 3d virtual environments. In *Proc. COGAIN '08* (2008).

[2] Da Silva, M. P., Courboulay, V., and Prigent, A. Gameplay experience based on a gaze tracking system. In *Proc. COGAIN '07* (2007).

[3] Dorr, M., Böhme, M., Martinetz, T., and Barth, E. Gaze beats mouse: a case study. In *Proc. COGAIN '07* (2007).

[4] Hillaire, S., Lecuyer, A., Cozot, R., and Casiez, G. Using an eye-tracking system to improve camera motions and depth-of-field blur effects in virtual environments. In *Proc. VR '08* (2008).

[5] Johansen, S. A., Noergaard, M., and Rau, J. Can eye tracking boost usability evaluation of computer games. In *Proc. CHI '08* (2008).

[6] Kickmeier-Rust, M., Hillemann, E., and Albert, D. Tracking the ufo?s paths: Using eye-tracking for the evaluation of serious games. In *Virtual and Mixed Reality - New Trends*, Lecture Notes in Computer Science. 2011.

[7] Muir, M., and Conati, C. An analysis of attention to student ? adaptive hints in an educational game. In *Intelligent Tutoring Systems*, Lecture Notes in Computer Science. 2012.

[8] Munoz, J., Yannakakis, G. N., Mulvey, F., Hansen, D. W., Gutierrez, G., and Sanchis, A. Towards gaze-controlled platform games. In *Proc. CIG '11* (2011).

[9] Starker, I., and Bolt, R. A. A gaze-responsive self-disclosing display. In *Proc. CHI '90* (1990).

[10] Stellmach, S., and Dachselt, R. Designing gaze-based user interfaces for steering in virtual environments. In *Proc. ETRA '12* (2012).

[11] Sundstedt, V. Gazing at games: An introduction to eye tracking control. *Synthesis Lectures on Computer Graphics and Animation* (2012).

[12] Turner, J., Bulling, A., Alexander, J., and Gellersen, H. Cross-device gaze-supported point-to-point content transfer. In *Proc. ETRA '14* (2014).

[13] Vickers, S., Istance, H., and Smalley, M. Eyeguitar: Making rhythm based music video games accessible using only eye movements. In *Proc. ACE '10* (2010).

[14] Ware, C., and Mikaelian, H. H. An evaluation of an eye tracker as a device for computer input. In *Proc. CHI '87* (1987).

Making the Best of Imperfect Data: Reflections on an Ideal World

Mike Ambinder
Valve Corporation

Abstract
As we gather data to inform game design choices, we often run into situations where the information we gather is acquired through biased methodologies or incomplete in some fashion or not necessarily suited to answer the specific question at hand. This talk will speculate on how we could attempt to solve some of these common issues as well as look to the future of what might be possible in Games User Research.

By drawing on relevant findings from psychology, examples drawn from real world experience, advances in technology, and a healthy dose of optimism, this talk will attempt to envision a world where our processes are less biased, our data is more complete, and we are able to address a much broader range of investigations than is currently possible.

Categories and Subject Descriptors
K.8.0 Computing Milieux,PERSONAL COMPUTING, General: Games

Keywords
Game Design; Games User Research; Psychology; Technology

Short Bio
Mike Ambinder is an experimental psychologist at Valve who has worked on Alien Swarm, Counter-Strike: Global Offensive, DOTA 2, Left 4 Dead, Left 4 Dead 2, Portal 2, and Team Fortress 2. He has a PhD in Experimental Psychology (with an emphasis on visual cognition) from the University of Illinois, and a BA in Computer Science and Psychology from Yale University. His current work at Valve focuses on the application of knowledge and methodologies from psychology to game design.

CHI PLAY'14, October 19–21, 2014, Toronto, ON, Canada.
ACM 978-1-4503-3014-5/14/10
http://dx.doi.org/10.1145/2658537.2674094

DIY Game Console Development

Trevor M. Tomesh
Department of
Computer Science
University of Regina
Regina, SK S4S 0A2 CAN
tomesh2t@cs.uregina.ca

Daryl H. Hepting
Department of
Computer Science
University of Regina
Regina, SK S4S 0A2 CAN
hepting@cs.uregina.ca

CHI PLAY'14, October 1921, 2014, Toronto, ON, Canada.
ACM 978-1-4503-3014-5/14/10
http://dx.doi.org/10.1145/2658537.2662411

Abstract

Video games have become a driving force for innovation in many aspects of the entertainment industry and beyond [1, 2]. Since gaming may also be in a position to drive the emerging "maker movement", we consider the "DIY game industry".

In this half-day course, attendees will be introduced to DIY Game Console construction and programming by building their own game console, based on a simple 12 LED and 4 button design, and then programming their console to play very simple, yet entertaining, games. Attendees will also be exposed to the tradeoffs in design between capabilities in gameplay and complexity of hardware and software.

Author Keywords

DIY; game console; hardware; software

ACM Classification Keywords

K.8.0 [Personal Computing]: Games; B.7.1 [Hardware]: Microprocessors and microcomputers; H.5.m [Information interfaces and presentation (e.g., HCI)]: Miscellaneous; K.3.0 [Computers and Education]: General

Duration
This course will be a half-day in length, although supplemental instruction will be online for attendees who may require it.

Features

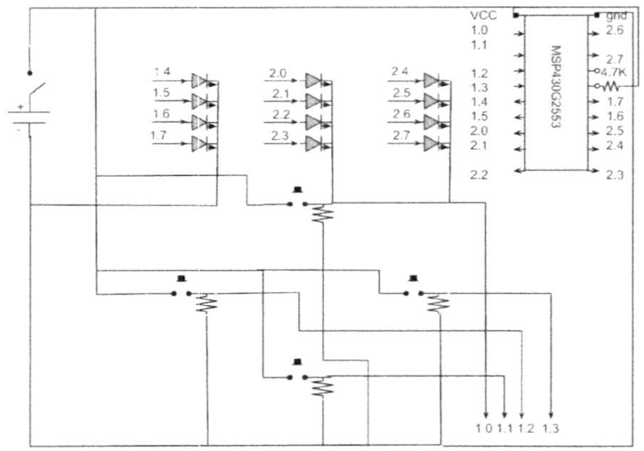

Figure 1: Schematic diagram for the game console to be built during the course.

The educational goals and major course elements are as follows:

- Construction of a simple, yet fully functional, hand-held gaming system through the application of basic electronics and breadboarding. The game console will be based on the schematic diagram illustrated in Figure 2.
- Application of essential video game design theory [3] in the context of the DIY game console to program (on the microcontroller of the console) simple, yet entertaining, games.

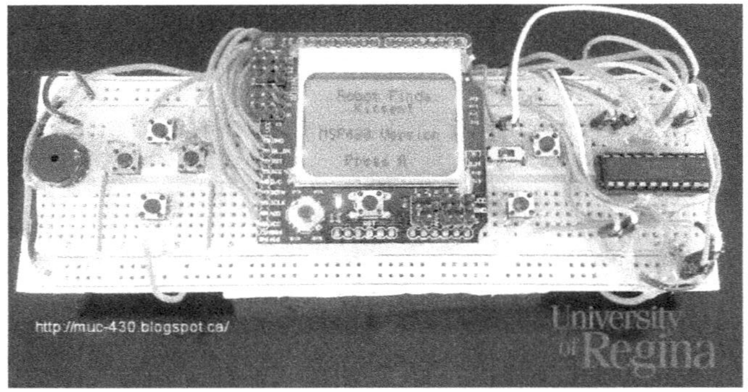

Figure 2: Advanced version of console with LCD

Audience
This course is appropriate for audience members of any discipline with an interest in games programming and hardware development – because there is a construction component, audience size may be limited depending upon funding allotted.

Prerequisites
While no particular background is assumed or required it would be beneficial for participants to have a basic understanding of programming.

Presentation
This course will be presented in an informal "lab" format whereby participants will be given a basic introduction to elementary game design principles, basic electronics (and bread boarding), and micro-controller programming. Attendees will then be provided materials and led through the construction and programming of their own hand-held gaming systems.

Instructor Background

Trevor M. Tomesh

Mr. Trevor Tomesh is a PhD student in computer science at the University of Regina. He holds a B.Sc. in Physics (minor in mathematics) from the University of Wisconsin - River Falls and spent two years doing graduate research at the University of Worcester (England) in educational game design and development. He has lectured and given tutorials at a number of conferences and symposiums including the 2012 Blender (3D Creation Software) conference and the Irish Symposium for Games Based Learning. He has also worked as a sessional lecturer at the University of Worcester and as a lab instructor (teaching assistant) at the University of Regina.

Daryl H. Hepting

Daryl Hepting is an Associate Professor in the Department of Computer Science at the University of Regina where he teaches about multimedia and interaction design, amongst other subjects. He is a member of ACM SIGCHI, SIGGRAPH, and SIGCAS, is becoming involved with the local makerspace (Crash Bang Labs), and building and programming LEGO robots as a means of outreach about Computer Science. He has a long-held interest in open source software and the democratization of technology.

Resources

A website about the course will be created under the http://www.cs.uregina.ca address that will feature further details about the course and the instructors.

References

[1] Crandall, R. W., and Sidak, J. G. Video games: Serious business for america's economy. Tech. rep., Entertainment Software Association, 2006.

[2] Evans, D. S., Hagiu, A., and Schmalensee, R. *Invisible Engines: How Software Platforms Drive Innovation and Transform Industries*. The MIT Press, 2006.

[3] Koster, R. *A Theory of Fun for Game Design*, 2 ed. O'Reilly, 2014.

Beyond Gamification: Designing Behavior Change Games

Dustin DiTommaso
Mad*Pow
Portsmouth, NH, USA
dustin@madpow.net

Ciara Taylor
Mad*Pow
Portsmouth, NH, USA
ctaylor@madpow.net

CHI PLAY'14, October 19–21, 2014, Toronto, ON, Canada.
ACM 978-1-4503-3014-5/14/10.
http://dx.doi.org/10.1145/2658537.2662410

Abstract
Participants in this hands-on workshop will learn the mechanics of clinically tested behavior change interventions, as well as techniques game designers use to motivate, engage and reward players through a game's lifecycle. A practical, step-by-step methodology will be introduced and built upon throughout this 4 hour course, resulting in a scalable framework and process for designing playful and practical behavior change games.

Author Keywords
Gamification, behavior change, game design, gameplay, games, gamified, interaction design, methods, motivation

ACM Classification Keywords
K.8.0 Games - Games

Engines of Play: How Player Motivation Changes Over Time

Jason VandenBerghe
Ubisoft Entertainment S. A.
Montreal, Canada

Abstract

The talk is a first (probably doomed and certainly biased) attempt by the speaker to fuse his work-to-date on the 5 Domains of Play (a gamer-translation of the Big 5 psychological model) with Scott Rigby & co.'s PENS model (a gamer-translation of Self-Determination Theory).

While trying to form this Player Motivational Voltron, we may touch briefly on how a few other existing models might also be compatible this horrid abomination, but the focus of this talk will be squarely on PENS and the 5 Domains. The goal is to describe a map of player motivations that not only talks about player typologies and satisfactions, but that can also describe how player motivations change as they move from first-contact, engagement, and on into nostalgia. It will probably never work. But the attempt should at least be entertaining to watch.

Categories and Subject Descriptors:
K.8.0 [**Personal Computing**]: General – *Games*; J.4 [Social and Behavioral Sciences]: – *Psychology*

CHI PLAY'14, October 19–22, 2014, Toronto, ON, Canada.
ACM 978-1-4503-3014-5/14/10.
http://dx.doi.org/10.1145/2658537.2677953

Keywords
Game Design; Psychology; Personality

Short Bio

Jason VandenBerghe has been making games for nearly 2 decades. He is currently a Creative Director at Ubisoft (working most recently on Far Cry 3 and on Ghost Recon: Future Soldier). He has been a programmer, producer, designer, and director. His work on gamer motivation and the Big 5 has been pretty well-received, which is a great relief. Jason has worked on bad games, good games, hard-to-make games, and, er, less hard-to-make games, and intends to keep on doing this kind of thing for as long as he can get away with it.

Author Index

www.ingramcontent.com/pod-product-compliance
Ingram Content Group UK Ltd.
Pitfield, Milton Keynes, MK11 3LW, UK
UKHW051414290926
15471UKWH00009B/1597

9 781450 333795